13

KORTE
1499

LITERATURE

The Human Experience

EIGHTH EDITION

LITERATURE
The Human Experience

RICHARD ABCARIAN
AND
MARVIN KLOTZ

California State University, Northridge, Emeriti

BEDFORD/ST. MARTIN'S
Boston ◆ New York

For Bedford/St. Martin's

Executive Editor: Stephen A. Scipione
Developmental Editor: Maura Shea
Editorial Assistant: Emily Goodall
Senior Production Editor: Michael Weber
Senior Production Supervisor: Joe Ford
Marketing Manager: Richard Cadman
Art Director: Lucy Krikorian
Copy Editor: Jamie Nan Thaman
Cover Design: Dick Hannus of Hannus Design Associates
Cover Art: Eyeglasses, Susan Leopold
Composition: Stratford Publishing Services
Printing and Binding: R. R. Donnelley & Sons Company

President: Charles H. Christensen
Editorial Director: Joan E. Feinberg
Editor in Chief: Nancy Perry
Director of Marketing: Karen R. Melton
Director of Editing, Design, and Production: Marcia Cohen
Managing Editor: Erica T. Appel

Library of Congress Control Number: 2001090422

Manufactured in the United States of America.

7 6 5 4 3 2
f e d c b a

For information, write: Bedford/St. Martin's, 75 Arlington Street,
Boston, MA 02116   (617-399-4000)

ISBN: 0-312-39326-1

Again, for Joan and Debra. And for David, Dan, Jennifer and Steve, Robin and Tom, Sara, Peter and Vivianne, Rick and Marie, and all their children that are and may be.

Preface

And wisdom is a butterfly
And not a gloomy bird of prey.
— William Butler Yeats

Since the inception of the first edition of *Literature: The Human Experience*
in the early 1970s, we have been governed by the belief that the principal
task of an introductory anthology of literature is to engage the reader's interest and to make the experience of literature immediate and exciting. Thus,
we have selected works not primarily because they illustrate critical definitions or lend themselves to a particular approach but because they are exciting to read and lend us insight into the great themes of humanity. Our further
goal is to enhance students' response to literature by inviting them to participate in a conversation about literary works and by providing them with
opportunities to talk back to the works through writing.

LITERATURE THAT EMPHASIZES
THE HUMAN EXPERIENCE

In our own teaching, we have found that the most effective literary works
speak to students' own experience. By reading, thinking about, and writing
about such works, and by comparing and contrasting them with other works
that speak to the same experience, students reach a level of understanding
that goes far beyond the works themselves. They gain insight into the ways in
which literature makes meaning of life. To further the connection with life
experiences, we have arranged the selections in this anthology under five
universal themes: Innocence and Experience, Conformity and Rebellion,
Culture and Identity, Love and Hate, and the Presence of Death. A short introductory essay embodying some general observations about each theme is
followed by a series of questions that ask students to consider their own attitudes — highlighting the relationship between the reader and the selections.

Within each thematic section, the stories, poems, plays, and essays are
grouped separately so it is easy for an instructor to emphasize the preferred
genre. Within each genre, selections are arranged chronologically according
to the author's birth date. (We also include a date for each individual work.
Most of these indicate the work's first appearance in a published book, but
the dates enclosed in parentheses indicate the date of either the work's composition or its appearance in a publication other than a book. We have
not attempted to date traditional ballads.) This organization, along with our

inclusion of Biographical Notes on the Authors as an appendix, provides students with a context for further understanding these works through the course of cultural and literary history.

SUPPORT FOR CAREFUL READING AND THOUGHTFUL WRITING

Two introductory chapters on reading and writing equip students with the tools they need to take part in a written or spoken conversation about literature. In these chapters, we discuss the important elements of each genre and provide guidelines for writing commonly assigned essays. A Glossary of Literary Terms and a Glossary of Critical Approaches give students additional frameworks for critical reading and thinking.

In our experience, even accomplished readers are sometimes unsure of how to begin a conversation about literature. Throughout the thematic sections, questions prompt students to consider individual works in terms of style, language, and literary elements, and to make connections to other works and to the broader themes.

NEW TO THIS EDITION

In addition to the many new selections, what sets the eighth edition of *Literature: The Human Experience* apart from prior editions is how it attempts to help students think and write more deeply about literature.

New Selections That Reflect Students' Experience For the eighth edition, we have added eighty new selections. They include fifteen new stories, ranging from Charlotte Perkin Gilman's "The Yellow Wallpaper" to Jamaica Kincaid's "Girl"; forty-nine new poems, including works by Robert Frost, Robert Pinsky, Judith Ortiz Cofer, and Deborah Pope; three new plays, including August Wilson's *Fences;* and thirteen new essays, ranging from Maya Angelou's "Graduation in Stamps" to Bernard Cooper's "A Clack of Tiny Sparks." We have included more stories and essays than ever before — genres that students find more accessible and that reflect more deeply on their own experience.

New Opportunities for Exploring the Connections between Literature and Other Disciplines Each of the five thematic sections includes new "Looking Deeper" casebooks that prompt students to consider the differing ways in which literature and other humanities make meaning of the human experience. For instance, Looking Deeper: From History to Literature presents historical documents that provide cultural contexts for Martin Luther King Jr.'s classic essay "Letter from Birmingham Jail." Other Looking Deeper casebooks ask students to explore literature's connection with music, art, film, and classical mythology.

Introductory Quotations Prompt More Thoughtful Responses to Each Theme
Each thematic section now opens with brief reflections from notable writers and thinkers, offering students opportunities to clarify their own thinking about a universal theme and to venture their own responses to it before encountering the literary selections that follow.

Deeper Coverage of the Research Paper   For the first time, we have included an annotated literary research paper by a student, along with up-to-date information on documenting online and other electronic sources.

INSTRUCTOR'S MANUAL AND WEB SITE

In the *Editors' Notes for Teaching LITERATURE: THE HUMAN EXPERIENCE,* we offer teaching ideas for each selection in the anthology as well as additional thematic connections and writing topics. Our revised companion Web site at *<www.bedfordstmartins.com/experience_literature>* provides further resources for students and instructors, including:

- *VirtuaLit Interactive Poetry Tutorial:* VirtuaLit guides students through a series of interactive exercises that gets them to actively engage in closely reading a poem — both its elements and its cultural and critical contexts.
- *LitQuiz:* Our new database of interactive quizzes tests reading comprehension for many of the stories, poems, plays, and essays in the book. LitQuiz can be used by students for self-study or by instructors to monitor students' reading and comprehension.
- *LitLinks:* Clear, concise annotations and links to more than 500 professionally maintained sites help students browse with direction, whether they are looking for a favorite text, additional biographical information about an author, a critical article, or conversation with other students and scholars.

COMPACT EDITION

The previous edition of this book — *Literature: Reading and Writing the Human Experience,* Seventh Edition — is available in a compact edition containing 37 stories, 144 poems, 8 plays, and 16 essays. The compact edition retains all of the longer seventh edition's editorial features for those who want a smaller, less expensive anthology.

ACKNOWLEDGMENTS

We wish to thank Krissa Lagos, whose precocious writing skills provided us with a superb research paper and whose sangfroid and sense of irony made her a pleasure to work with. As well, we thank David Klotz for suggestions based on his comprehensive knowledge of modern song lyrics and the music that animates them. We also wish to thank Anita Zubère, who helped untangle some knotty lines of poetry; Roy Merrens for explaining some of the arcane features of the urban London landscape; and Bainbridge Scott, whose knowledge of music made our task easier.

Experienced and wise people at Bedford/St. Martin's have guided this book along the way. We thank President Charles Christensen and Editorial Director Joan Feinberg for nurturing this eighth edition. As well, we are grateful to Sandy Schechter for procuring permissions and to Erica Appel, Michael Weber, and Sarah Ludwig for shepherding the book through production. We thank Donna Dennison and Zenobia Rivetna for overseeing the design of an engaging new cover and Richard Cadman for providing expert marketing advice. Editors Steve Scipione and Maura Shea and their assistant Emily Goodall displayed astounding intelligence, tact, and energy as we worked together on this revision. Their instincts, their comprehensive understanding of books such as this, their research skills, and, especially, their generous aid at every phase of this project — all served to alter what could have been a chore into a pleasant, even memorable, experience.

We would also like to thank the professors who generously took time to share their ideas about the previous edition of this anthology. They include Earl V. Bryant, University of New Orleans; Stanley Corkin, University of Cincinnati; George A. Crispin, Rowan University; Frances Secco Davidson, Mercer County Community College; MaryBeth DeMeo, Alvemia College; Judith Dorn, St. Cloud State University; Ralph Edsell, Southwestern College; James R. Grimord, University of Hartford; Randy Hendricks, State University of West Georgia; Maude Jennings, Ball State University; Don S. Lawson, Lander University; Marci Lingo, Bakersfield College; Patrick McMahon, Tallahassee Community College; Zach Miller, Brookhaven College; John Pekins, Tallahassee Community College; Marguerite Quintelli-Neary, Winthrop University; Lolly Smith, Everett Community College; Ann Tippett, Monroe Community College; Emily B. Todd, Westfield State College; William Tomory, Southwestern Michigan University; David Upchurch, Ball State University; and Dennis Williams, College of Charleston.

Richard Abcarian
Marvin Klotz

Contents

Innocence and Experience   76

Conformity and Rebellion 330

Culture and Identity 662

The Presence of Death 1276

Alternate Contents

arranged by genre and alphabetically by the author's last name

DRAMA

LITERATURE

The Human Experience

Introduction

Responding to Literature

There is no Frigate like a Book
To take us Lands away
Nor any Coursers like a Page
Of prancing poetry —

This Traverse may the poorest take
Without oppress of Toll —
How frugal is the Chariot
That bears the Human soul.
— Emily Dickinson (c. 1873)

WHY WE READ LITERATURE

Perhaps even the thought of reading *literature* creates a weighty and intimidating burden. But you have been reading and responding to literature all of your life. The cartoons you watched as a child; the movies, TV dramas, and sitcoms you enjoyed during middle and high school (and may still enjoy) — all have marked your life. Inevitably, you responded to those popular genres; you distinguished good from evil, right from wrong. The writers conveyed cultural ideas about the nature of love, of duty, of heroism — sometimes broadly, sometimes with subtlety. But as you matured, your taste surely changed. Certainly you would not now be moved by the same literature that entranced you when you were a child. Just as certainly, you probably still enjoy a rousing thriller, a convoluted tale of international espionage, those romantic comedies that take up so much screen time. And some of these "popular" stories reveal the complexity and the artfulness that animate our "serious" literary tradition. And some "popular" authors — John LeCarre, Dorothy Sayers, P. D. James, and others — who write spy novels and detective fiction are routinely read in college courses that celebrate literature. Their exciting and suspenseful novels are often made into films, but so, too, are the classic works of Shakespeare, Jane Austen, Charles Dickens, Henry James, William Faulkner, and Ernest Hemingway.

"Serious" literature, no less than "popular" literature, embodies thrilling adventure. Serious literature is replete with monsters (consider the old English epic *Beowulf*), ghosts (at the outset of Shakespeare's *Hamlet* and the middle of *Macbeth*), witches, supernatural spirits, magical transformations, unspeakably brutal wars, terrible murders, and bloody vengeance. When we speak of serious literature, we do not mean to denigrate the movies you enjoy, the TV dramas you watch, or the books you read for pleasure. By all means, keep enjoying them! When teachers speak of serious literature, they refer to a literary canon. And here things get a bit murky. *Canon* is derived from the Latin word meaning "measuring line or rule," and is used ecclesiastically to signify "sacred writings admitted to the catalog according to the rule." Early theologians decided which books were the authentic word of God — and which were not. But, alas, they did not always agree. The *literary canon* is quite different. Although it attempts to establish the body of literature that humans need to study and master, the literary canon changes frequently in response to political and social changes. Further, a literary canon is bound to reflect the cultural tradition that produces it. The literary canon of China will differ markedly from the literary canon of the United States. And both will change with the eruptions of history and the demands of fashion.

For example, although American literary history is replete with women writers, they were often undervalued by the literary canon's guardians. But a century of political struggle that led, first, to enfranchising women as voters and, later, to a feminist movement that demanded equality for women and their works has forever changed the canon. Writers like Kate Chopin and Charlotte Perkins Gilman are now routinely included in university courses, and women writers are broadly represented in this anthology. Further, the political struggles of Native American, African American, Latin American, and Asian American citizens have drawn considerable attention to a large and diverse body of writing that was unjustly overlooked by Eurocentric critics. Skillful literary artists from these groups are also represented here.

You might reasonably ask, what difference does broadening the literary canon make? It makes a tremendous difference. You learn a great deal about the society you live in from your reading — what it values, what it condemns, how it expects you to behave, what constitutes success both economically and morally, what it sees as the very nature of good and evil. If your reading is limited to, say, Eurocentric works and you are embedded in a non-European social group, you will not discover yourself or your peers in the books you read. Thus, schools and anthologies that project a narrow literary canon present a world foreign to your experience. The resulting sense of anomie — a rootless lack of purpose, identity, and values — can be terribly damaging to its victim. At the same time, ignorance of your neighbors' lifestyles can also seriously impair your life by denying you insight into cultural differences. All of us can avoid the baleful consequences of racism, hypernationalism, and human ignorance by embracing a wide and inclusive literary canon. Reading will make wise, humane, and just citizens of us all.

READING ACTIVELY

Read attentively! Don't read passively! Don't let the author con you. Keep a pencil in your hand, and interact with the page. Mark words you don't recognize, and look them up in the dictionary (you might want to do this when you've finished the piece). When you feel a protest rising in your throat, mark your feeling in the margin. When you find a line that tickles you, mark that also. If you feel the author has generated an insight, state it in the margin. We might sum up this advice by urging you to read *interactively* — to engage in a conversation with the author or even with the story's characters.

READING AND THINKING CRITICALLY

In a well-ordered universe, you would enjoy all your reading — and your delight would derive from your complete understanding of what you read. But if you have already reached this happy condition, you would have no need of a course such as this. You would know how literature "worked." You would recognize its historical sources, all the allusions, all the verbal wit, all the moral energy. You would be an authoritative judge of the success or failure of each piece you read. Alas, none of us will ever reach that exalted plane. We all keep on learning and acquiring new tools that allow us to pry the lids off new containers of wit and wisdom. When we ask you to read critically, we ask that you bring that complex set of experiences that define you as a human being to bear on the work you encounter. Primarily, you need to bring sensitivity to language as well as a sense of the cultural imperatives among which you live.

When you become a critical reader, you learn to address your biases, enlarge your universe, and test your comfortable convictions. Thus, when you adopt a critical position toward a piece of literature, you need to test and question that position. To read a work critically, ask, What perspective does the author have that led him or her to write this work? What social, cultural, or historical conditions influenced the production of the work of literature? What other ways might the author have presented the ideas or subjects of the work? Are the author's values different from your own? How do your views and experiences affect whether you like or dislike the work?

As you begin writing about a work, developing a working thesis, test the evidence you use. Does any evidence in the story point to conclusions other than the ones you draw? Review the work and your notes on it to be certain you have not overlooked or misinterpreted details that might contradict your thesis. Are the reasons for your interpretation good ones? Scrutinize your argument to determine whether your readers will find your thesis persuasive and your supporting evidence convincing.

For example, read Peter Meinke's "Advice to My Son" (p. 171). On a first look at the poem's imagery, it might seem to readers familiar with Christian practice that the bread and wine mentioned in the last three lines allude to Holy Communion. But review the entire poem for evidence of this interpretation. The speaker's paradoxical advice on how best to live in a dangerous world counsels a combination of prudence ("plant squash and spinach, turnips and tomatoes") and intense pleasure ("the peony and the rose," "marry a pretty girl"). It concludes with an admonition to "serve bread with your wine." The body of the poem strongly suggests that "bread" represents a prudent attention to the mundane requirements of living, while "wine" represents physical pleasure. Temper your pursuit of pleasure by serving bread when wine is served; but enjoy life passionately by always serving wine. Carefully scrutinizing your evidence and reasons in this way — and setting aside arguments not supported by the work — will strengthen your thesis and make it more convincing.

READING FICTION

Like other literary genres, fiction creates imaginary worlds. Unlike other sorts of literature, however, novels and short stories do so primarily by telling stories written in *prose* (ordinary, unrhymed language), about realistic characters, set in physical environments, and with sustained attention to descriptive detail.

Works of fiction *narrate,* or tell, stories. Of course, narrative is not specific to fiction or to any other literary genre: telling stories pervades almost every aspect of our daily lives. We learn very early on how to recognize and tell stories, and we rely heavily on narrative to organize and make sense of our experience. For example, when we study history, we mostly study stories of various events. Likewise, an astronomer's account of the universe's origins may take the shape of a narrative. Even in our sleep, we tell ourselves stories in the form of dreams. It is impossible to imagine our lives without these narratives; in fact, every culture uses them to order and make sense of lived experience. Narrative fiction is not meant to recount actual events, of course, though it may refer to real events or real persons. Rather than relate actual experiences, fiction uses narrative to shape imaginary ones.

Works of fiction, however, cannot be reduced to a listing of their narrative events any more than paintings can be replaced by diagrams. Such summaries diminish the realism of a work, a realism produced by the careful description of characters, settings, and actions. By inventing, developing, and amassing descriptive details, works of fiction create the illusion of full, authentic, and realistic reports of human experience. Although not all works of fiction strive to imitate reality in this way, many do. This imitation of reality makes it easy for readers to suspend disbelief, or to enter the imaginary world of the novel or short story.

The Methods of Fiction

In order to examine the methods of fiction — tone, setting, plot, theme, characterization, point of view, and irony — let us explore in detail one story, James Joyce's "Araby" (p. 100).

Tone   One of the things most readers first respond to in a short story is its *tone*. Because it is like a mood, tone is difficult to talk about. It can be defined as an author's implicit attitude toward the characters, places, and events in the story and toward the reader of the work. Tone depends for its substance on delicate emotional responses to language and situation. Notice how a distinct tone is established in the language of the opening lines of "Araby":

> North Richmond Street, being blind, was a quiet street except at the hour when the Christian Brothers' School set the boys free. An uninhabited house of two storeys stood at the blind end, detached from its neighbours in a square ground. The other houses of the street, conscious of decent lives within them, gazed at one another with brown imperturbable faces.

Is this scene cheerful? Vital and active? Should we expect this story to celebrate the joys of growing up in Dublin? Negative responses to these questions arise from the tone of the opening description. Notice, for example, that the dead-end street is "blind"; that the school is said to "set the boys free," which makes it sound like a prison; that the uninhabited house is "detached from its neighbours"; and that the other houses, personified, gaze at one another with "brown imperturbable faces" — *brown* being a nondescript color and *imperturbable* reinforcing the still, lifeless, somber quality of the passage as a whole.

Plot   Through the series of events that make up a story's *plot*, an author presents us with a carefully created fictional world. In "Araby," the plot, or the arrangement of a connected sequence of narrative events, can be simply stated. A young boy who lives in a drab but respectable neighborhood develops a crush on his playmate's sister. She asks him if he intends to go to a charity fair that she cannot attend. He resolves to go and purchase a gift for her. He is tormented by the late and drunken arrival of his uncle, who has promised him the money he needs. When the boy finally arrives at the bazaar, he is disappointed by the difference between his expectation and the actuality of the almost deserted fair. He perceives some minor events, overhears some minor conversation, and the climax occurs when he confronts the darkened fair and the banal expression of sexual attraction between two gentlemen and a young woman. This sequence of events prompts the boy to see himself "as a creature driven and derided by vanity."

Characterization   One of the obvious differences between short stories and novels is that story writers develop characters rapidly and limit the number of developed characters. Many stories have only one fleshed out, or *round*, character; the other characters are frequently two-dimensional, or *flat*. Rarely does a short story have more than three developed characters.

One feature that distinguishes "Araby" is its *characterization*, or the process by which the characters are rendered to make them seem real to the reader. Characterization, however, cannot easily be separated from the other elements of fiction; that is, it depends heavily on tone, plot, theme, setting, and so on. It is part of the boy's character, for example, that he lives in a brown imperturbable house on North Richmond Street, that he does the things he does (which constitute the plot of the story), and that he learns about what he does (which is the theme). Much of this characterization in "Araby" emerges from Joyce's rich *style,* or the way he uses language and images. Consider how the boy's character is revealed in the following paragraph:

> Her image accompanied me even in places the most hostile to romance. On Saturday evenings when my aunt went marketing I had to go to carry some of the parcels. We walked through the flaring streets, jostled by drunken men and bargaining women, amid the curses of labourers, the shrill litanies of shop-boys who stood on guard by the barrels of pigs' cheeks, the nasal chanting of street-singers, who sang a *come-all-you* about O'Donovan Rossa, or a ballad about the troubles in our native land. These noises converged in a single sensation of life for me: I imagined that I bore my chalice safely through a throng of foes. Her name sprang to my lips at moments in strange prayers and praises which I myself did not understand. My eyes were often full of tears (I could not tell why) and at times a flood from my heart seemed to pour itself out into my bosom. I thought little of the future. I did not know whether I would ever speak to her or not or, if I spoke to her, how I could tell her of my confused adoration. But my body was like a harp and her words and gestures were like fingers running upon the wires.

In this passage, character is revealed through *diction,* or choice of words. By using the words *litanies, prayers,* and *adoration,* the narrator draws heavily from the distinctive vocabulary of the Roman Catholic Church. (The reference to the harp also reinforces the religious tone of the passage.) *Chalice* and *throng of foes* are related to this tradition as well; a chalice is a cup for the consecrated wine of the Eucharist, and throngs of foes often confronted the Christian martyrs whose deeds are immortalized in religious literature. At the same time, however, these last two phrases call up the world of chivalric romance, which is alluded to in the first line of the paragraph. The narrator's diction casts his awakening sexuality in the mold of high romance on the one hand and Christian devotion on the other. This sense of holy chivalry (reinforced by the earlier reference to the priest who owned a chivalric novel) stands in sharp contrast to the humdrum experience of carrying groceries home from the market.

Setting Unlike novels, short stories usually work themselves out in a restricted geographical *setting* — in a single place and within a short period of time. Any consideration of setting should include the historical time when a story takes place, the social situation set in the story, as well as the physical location of the events. In "Araby," the dreary details of Dublin are significantly described in the story's very first lines.

Point of View   A character's or narrator's diction raises important questions about who is narrating the story. What is the narrator like? Is he reliable or unreliable? How can we judge? These questions help us distinguish another element of fiction, *point of view.* "Araby" is a first-person narrative; that is, the story is told from the perspective of a narrator who speaks in the first person (*I, we, my, our*).

Third-person point of view — in which the narrator does not appear as a character in the story — is the most common perspective used to tell stories. Using third-person point of view, a narrator tells a story from the outside, referring to the characters as *she, he,* and *they.* A narrator who knows everything, can tell us what the characters are thinking, and can move around in space and time at will is an *omniscient narrator.* Alternatively, a narrator who chooses to focus on the thoughts, feelings, and actions of a single character is called a *limited omniscient narrator.* Generally, the brevity of the short story makes the first-person or limited omniscient narrations the most frequently used points of view for these works, while the lengthy and comparatively complex narrative of novels is more suited to the omniscient point of view.

A less frequently employed point of view is that of the second person, in which the author addresses the action to a character identified as *you.* For example, "You ask the clerk for change; he gives you four quarters. You go outside and wait for the bus." (For an example of a story using second-person narration, see Pam Houston's "How to Talk to a Hunter," p. 1077.)

Irony   Authors' decisions about point of view create powerful narrative effects. Throughout "Araby," we sense a gap between the boy's sensibility and that of the more mature narrator, who refers at various times to his "innumerable follies" and "foolish blood." That is, we see the events of "Araby" from the boy's perspective, even though the language is that of an adult. The gap between the boy's knowledge and the narrator's creates *irony.*

There may be more than one level of irony at work in a story. When the narrator calls himself "a creature driven and derided by vanity," whose eyes "burned with anguish and anger," this overstatement is known as *verbal irony.* Some critics have maintained that the romanticized language of the story's conclusion itself invites an ironical reading, which is to say that we readers may know something about the narrator that he does not know himself — that he idealizes disenchantment as fervently as the boy idealized romance and religion. In short, Joyce may be using *dramatic irony,* encouraging the reader to see things about the first-person narrator that he does not see about himself. Both kinds of irony hinge on differing levels of knowledge and the author's skillful manipulation of narrative perspective.

Theme   *Theme* is an underlying idea, a statement that a work makes about its subject. This tiny stretch of experience out of the boy's life introduces him to an awareness of the differences between imagination and reality, between his romantic infatuation and the vulgar reality all about him. The theme of "Araby" emerges from the drab setting and mundane events of the story as a general statement about an intensely idealized and childish love, the shattering recognition of the false sentimentality that occasions it, and the enveloping vulgarity of adult life. By detailing a few events from one boy's life, the story illuminates the painful loss of innocence we all endure. In this case, the *protagonist,* or main character, experiences what Joyce called an *epiphany,* or sudden flash of recognition, that signals the awareness of a set of moral complexities in a world that once seemed uncomplicated and predictable.

We often speak of tone, setting, plot, theme, characterization, and point of view as separate aspects of a story in order to break down a complex narrative into more manageable parts. But this analytic process of identifying various elements is something we have done to the story: the story (if it is a good one) is an integrated whole. The more closely we examine the separate elements, the clearer it becomes that each is integrally related to the others.

In "Araby," Joyce employs the methods of fiction to create a world based on 1895 Dublin and Irish middle-class society. The success or failure of the story depends on Joyce's ability to render that world convincingly and our willingness to enter it imaginatively. We must not refuse to engage that world because the characters do not act as we would have them act or because the events never actually happened. Novelist Henry James urged that readers allow the author to have his or her *donnée,* or "given." When we grant this, the act of reading fiction provides us with much more pleasure and emotional insight.

Exploring Fiction

Here are some questions to ask when you face the task of reading or writing about fiction. Your answers to these questions will help you brainstorm and develop the ideas that form your response to a story.

1. What is the tone of the story? Read the first several paragraphs to see how the tone is established. Does the tone change with the events in the story or remain fixed? How does the tone contribute to the effect of the story?

2. What is the plot of the story? Does the sequence of events that make up the plot emerge logically from the nature of the characters and circumstances? Or does the plot rely on coincidence and arbitrary events?

3. Who are the principal characters in the story? (There are rarely more than three in a short story; the other characters are often portrayed sketchily, sometimes even as stereotypes.) What functions do the minor characters serve? Do any characters change during the course of the story? How, and why?

4. What is the setting of the story? Does it play an important role, or is it simply the place and time where things happen? How would some other setting affect the story?

5. From what point of view is the narrator telling the story? If a first-person narrator who participates in the action is telling the story, what significant changes would occur if the narrator were omniscient? Keep in mind that first-person narrators do not know what other characters think but that omniscient third-person narrators know everything about the lives of the characters.

6. What is the theme of the story? All the elements of fiction — tone, setting, plot, characterization, point of view, irony, imagery — have been marshaled to project a theme, the moral proposition the author wishes to advance. Does the title reinforce or point to the theme? Can you locate any particular places in the story where the theme is addressed?

7. Do you find ambiguities in the story? That is, can you interpret some element of the story in more than one way? Does that ambiguity result in confusion, or does it add to the complexity of the story?

8. Does the story seem to support or conflict with your own political and moral positions?

9. When was the story written? Draw on your knowledge of history and contemporary events as you read the story. Does the story clarify, enhance, or contradict your understanding of history?

READING POETRY

Reading poetry is unlike the other reading you do. To appreciate the sounds and meaning of a poem, it is best to start by reading it aloud. Some poems are straightforward, requiring little analysis; others are more dense and complex. Try reading the poem "When I Heard the Learn'd Astronomer" (1865) by Walt Whitman out loud.

> When I heard the learn'd astronomer,
> When the proofs, the figures, were ranged in columns before me,
> When I was shown the charts and diagrams, to add, divide, and measure
>   them,
> When I sitting heard the astronomer where he lectured with much
>   applause in the lecture-room,
> How soon unaccountable I became tired and sick,
> Till rising and gliding out I wander'd off by myself,
> In the mystical moist night-air, and from time to time,
> Look'd up in perfect silence at the stars.

Whitman's distinction between mind (intellectual knowledge) and heart (emotion and feelings) is an old but a useful one. Compelled to analyze, dissect, categorize, and classify, the poem's narrator finally yearns for the simple pleasure of unanalytical enjoyment — to look up "in perfect silence at the stars." You may very well enjoy a poem without recognizing its patterns of imagery or the intricate way its author weaves together the past and the present. But understanding the elements of poetry will allow you to use analysis to enhance your emotional response to a poem — and thereby deepen the pleasure a poem can give you.

Poems have to be read with great intensity but without any sense of urgency. Reading with a relaxed but complete mindfulness, try to slow down, pay attention, and allow the language of the poem to work.

Word Choice

Once you have listened to the poem, what should you pay attention to next? Start with the words that make up the poem. *Where* a poem takes the reader is inseparable from *how* it takes the reader. Poets pay especially close attention to *diction,* or their choice of words; every word in a poem counts. In your everyday reading, you encounter unfamiliar words and phrases, and figure out their meanings from the contexts in which they occur. Reading poetry requires even more scrupulous attention to unusual words and phrases.

Critics often describe poetry as "heightened language," meaning that the poet strives for precision and richness in the words he or she uses. For the poet, "precision" and "richness" are not contradictory. Words have dictionary, or *denotative,* meanings as well as associative, or *connotative,* meanings; they also have histories and relationships with other words. The English language is rich in synonyms — words whose denotative meanings are roughly the same but whose connotations vary widely (*excite, stimulate, titillate, inflame; poor, impoverished, indigent, destitute*). Many words are identical in sound and often in spelling but differ in meaning (*forepaws, four paws; lie* ["recline"], *lie* ["fib"]). The meanings of words have changed over time, and the poet may deliberately select a word whose older meaning adds a dimension to the poem.

Henry Reed's "Naming of Parts" (p. 772) develops a contrast between the instructions a group of soldiers are receiving on how to operate a rifle (in order to cause death) and the lovely world of nature (representing life and beauty). In the fourth stanza, bees are described as "assaulting and fumbling the flowers." "Fumbling," with its meaning of awkwardness and nervous uncertainty, may at first strike us as a puzzling word. Yet anyone who has watched a bee pollinating a flower will find the word denotatively effective. In addition, *fumbling* describes the actions of human beings caught up in sexual passion — a connotation appropriate to the poet's purposes, since pollination is a kind of sexual process. Furthermore, the meanings of *fumbling* contrast powerfully with the cold, mechanical precision of the death-dealing instruments the recruits are learning to use. The next line of the poem exhibits yet another resource of words: "They call it easing the

Spring." The line is an almost-exact repetition of a phrase used two lines earlier except *Spring* is now capitalized. While *Spring* retains its first meaning as part of the bolt action of the rifle, the capitalization makes it the season of the year when flowers are pollinated and the world of nature is reborn. With a typographical change, Reed is able to evoke in a single word the contrast (the old steel of a rifle and the fecund beauty of nature) that gives the poem its structure and meaning.

Figurative Language

Figurative language is the general term we use to describe the many devices of language that allow us to speak nonliterally in order to achieve some special effect. Figurative language makes a comparison between the thing being written about and something else that allows the reader to better picture or understand it. When Robert Burns compares his love to a red rose in his poem "A Red, Red Rose" (p. 1106), and Keats, in "On First Looking into Chapman's Homer" (p. 150), speaks of reading as travel "in the realms of gold," they abandon literal language because the emotional energy of their thoughts can be expressed more effectively in figurative language.

Figurative language allows us — and the poet — to use *imagery* to transcend both the confinement of the literal and the vagueness of the abstract. The world is revealed to us through our senses — sight, sound, taste, touch, and smell. Through imagery, the poet creates a recognizable world by drawing on this fund of common experiences. Bad poetry is often bad because the imagery is stale ("golden sunset," "the smiling sun," "the rolling sea") or so skimpy that the poem dissolves into vague and meaningless abstraction.

The difference between good and bad poetry often turns on the skill with which imagery (or other figurative language) is used. When Robert Frost in his poem "Birches" (p. 159) compares life to "a pathless wood" (l. 44), the image strikes us as natural and appropriate (life sometimes feels like a path or road, and we find it easy to accept the author's use of a wood or forest as a metaphor for a state of moral bewilderment).

Consider these familiar old sayings: "The grass is always greener on the other side of the fence"; "A bird in the hand is worth two in the bush"; "The early bird catches the worm." Although these sayings make literal sense (the grass you see from a distance looks greener than the grass under your feet), their meaning to a native speaker of English is clearly not literal. When we use them, we are making general and highly abstract observations about human attitudes and behavior. Yet these generalizations and abstractions are embodied in concrete imagery. Try to explain what any of these expressions mean and you will quickly discover that you are using many more words and much vaguer language than the expression itself. This is precisely what happens when you try to paraphrase or put into your own words the language of a poem. Like poetry, these sayings rely on the figurative use of language.

Because poetry is an intense and heightened use of language, it relies on more frequent and original use of figurative language than does ordinary speech. One of the most common figurative devices, *metaphor,* in which one thing is compared to something else, occurs frequently in everyday language. "School is a rat race," or "That issue is a minefield for the mayor," we say, and the meaning is vividly clear. When W. H. Auden, commenting on the death of William Butler Yeats, says, "Let the Irish vessel lie/Emptied of his poetry," he pays a complex tribute to the great Irish poet with a metaphor that compels readers to confront not only the loss of a man but also the loss of his poetic voice.

Simile is closely related to metaphor. But where metaphor says that one thing *is* another, simile says that one thing *is like* another, as in Burns's "O My Luve's like a red, red rose" and Frost's "life is too much like a pathless wood." The distinction between simile and metaphor, while easy enough to make technically, is often difficult to distinguish in terms of effect. Frost establishes a comparison between life and a pathless wood and keeps the two even more fully separated by adding the qualifier "too much." Burns's simile maintains the same separation and, in addition, because it occurs in the opening line of the poem, eliminates any possible confusion the reader might experience if the line were "O My Luve is a red, red rose." You can test the difference in effect by changing a metaphor into a simile or a simile into a metaphor to see if the meaning is in any way altered.

Personification is another device of figurative language that attributes human qualities to things or ideas. Personification can make an abstract thing more understandable in terms of human form, emotion, or action. For example, when John Donne, in his poem "Death, Be Not Proud" (p. 1384), exclaims "Death, thou shalt die," he transforms the abstraction death into a human adversary.

Allusion to other literary works, persons, places, or events enables poets to call up associations and contexts that complicate and enrich their poems. Whether these allusions are obvious or subtle, they draw on knowledge shared by the poet and the reader. In T. S. Eliot's dense and difficult "The Love Song of J. Alfred Prufrock" (p. 766), the speaker says at one point "I have seen my head (grown slightly bald) brought in upon a platter." A reader familiar with the New Testament might recognize this allusion to the story of John the Baptist's decapitation and better understand Prufrock's sense of spiritual desolation. The association Eliot makes brings an added, intensified layer of meaning to the work. Similarly, a reader familiar with the theories of Sigmund Freud will recognize the allusion and the relevance embodied in the title of Frank O'Connor's story "My Oedipus Complex" (p. 109).

A *symbol,* in its broadest sense, is anything that stands for something else. In this sense, most words are symbolic: the word *tree* stands for an object in the real world. When we speak of a symbol in a literary work, however, we mean something more precise. In poetry, a symbol is an object or event that suggests more than itself. It is one of the most common and powerful devices available to the poet, for it allows him or her to convey economically and simply a wide range of meanings.

It is useful to distinguish between two kinds of symbols: *public symbols* and *contextual symbols*. Public symbols are those objects or events that history has invested with rich meanings and associations — for example, national flags or religious objects such as a cross. Yeats uses such a symbol in his poem "Sailing to Byzantium" (p. 1390), drawing on the celebrated and enduring art of the ancient Byzantine empire as a symbol of timelessness.

In contrast to public symbols, contextual symbols are objects or events that are symbolic by virtue of the poet's handling of them in a particular work — that is, by virtue of the context. Consider, for example, the opening lines of Robert Frost's "After Apple-Picking" (p. 1392):

My long two-pointed ladder's sticking through a tree
Toward heaven still,
And there's a barrel that I didn't fill
Beside it, and there may be two or three
Apples I didn't pick upon some bough.

The apple tree is a literal tree, but it also symbolizes the speaker's life, with a wide range of possible meanings (Do the few unpicked apples symbolize the dreams that even the fullest life cannot satisfy?). Contextual symbols tend to present more interpretive difficulties than public symbols do because recognizing them depends on a sensitivity to everything else in the poem.

The Music of Poetry

To appreciate the *music* of poetry, which most poets consider at least as important as its sense, we can use a variety of terms to describe its sound patterns. Of these, *rhyme* — the repetition of the final stressed vowel sound and any sounds following — is the best known: *brow, now; debate, relate;* and so on. *Alliteration,* or the repetition of a consonant sound, usually at the beginning of words in close proximity, is also common: "*b*esiege thy *b*row." Alliteration is frequently used to underscore key words and ideas.

Rhythm, created by the relationship between stressed and unstressed syllables, is another way poets can convey meaning. The pattern formed when the lines of a poem follow a recurrent or similar rhythm is the poem's *meter.* The smallest repeated unit in this pattern is called a *foot.* Looking, for example, at the first line of one of Shakespeare's sonnets, we see that the foot consists of an *iamb* — an unstressed syllable followed by a stressed one:

When forty winters shall besiege thy brow.

Because the line consists of five iambs, or sets of unstressed syllables followed by stressed ones, it is called *iambic pentameter.* (If the line had four iambic feet, it would be in iambic tetrameter; if six, iambic hexameter; and so on.)

Other metrical feet include the *trochee, anapest, dactyl,* and *spondee* (all of which are defined in the "Glossary of Literary Terms"); but such terms are the tools of literary study and not its object. Perhaps the most important thing to remember about meter is that it should not be mistaken for the actual rhythm of the poem. Instead, it is best thought of as a kind of ideal rhythm that the poem can play against. Just as genre suggests certain characteristics, meter suggests certain patterns that invite expectations that may or may not be satisfied. Much of the poet's art consists of crafting variations of sound and rhythm to create specific effects.

Some of these effects are illustrated nicely in the following passage from Alexander Pope's "An Essay on Criticism," in which the definitions of bad and good verse are ingeniously supported by the music of the lines.

> These[1] equal syllables alone require,
> Though oft the ear the open vowels tire;
> While expletives their feeble aid do join;
> And ten low words oft creep in one dull line;
> While they ring round the same unvaried chimes,
> With sure returns of still expected rhymes;
> Where 'er you find "the cooling western breeze,"
> In the next line, it "whispers through the trees";
> If crystal streams "with pleasing murmurs creep,"
> The reader's threatened (not in vain) with "sleep";
> Then, at the last and only couplet fraught
> With some unmeaning thing they call a thought,
> A needless Alexandrine[2] ends the song
> That, like a wounded snake, drags its slow length along.
>
> · · · · ·
>
> True ease in writing comes from art, not chance,
> As those move easiest who have learned to dance.
> 'Tis not enough no harshness gives offense,
> The sound must seem an echo to the sense:
> Soft is the strain when Zephyr gently blows,
> And the smooth stream in smoother numbers flows;
> But when loud surges lash the sounding shore,
> The hoarse, rough verse should like the torrent roar:
> When Ajax[3] strives some rock's vast weight to throw,
> The line too labors, and the words move slow;
> Not so, when swift Camilla[4] scours the plain,
> Flies o'er the unbending corn, and skims along the main.

When the speaker condemns the use of ten monosyllables, the line contains ten monosyllables: "And ten low words oft creep in one dull line." When he

[1] Bad poets.
[2] Twelve-syllable line.
[3] A Greek warrior celebrated for his strength.
[4] A swift-footed queen in Virgil's *Aeneid.*

speaks of the wind, the line is rich in hissing sounds that imitate that wind. When he speaks of Ajax striving, clusters of consonants and stressed syllables combine to slow the line; when he speaks of Camilla's swiftness, the final consonants and initial sounds form liaisons that can be pronounced swiftly.

Consider also the following opening lines of Wilfred Owen's poem "Dulce et Decorum Est" (p. 1406) (from "Dulce et decorum est pro patria mori" — it is sweet and fitting to die for one's country — a quotation from the Roman writer Horace). The lines describe a company of battle-weary World War I soldiers trudging toward their camp and rest:

> Bent double, like old beggars under sacks,
> Knock-kneed, coughing like hags, we cursed through sludge.

These lines are dominated by harsh, explosive, and alliterating consonant sounds (*b, d, c, g*) that manage to reinforce the ungainly and indecorous images in these lines. In particular, the first two syllables of each line are heavily stressed, which serves to slow the reading. While the poem ultimately develops a prevailing meter, the irregular rhythms of these opening lines imitate a weary, stumbling march.

Analysis of this sort can illuminate and enrich our understanding of poetry, but it does not exhaust the significance of a poem. As Dylan Thomas once remarked,

> You can tear a poem apart to see what makes it technically tick and say to yourself when the works are laid out before you — the vowels, the consonants, the rhymes, and rhythms — "Yes, this is it. This is why the poem moves me so. It is because of the craftsmanship." But you're back where you began. The best craftsmanship always leaves holes and gaps in the works of the poem so that something that is not in the poem can creep, crawl, flash, or thunder in.

A truly fine poem not only repays attention to its formal features but also points beyond its technique to something more sensuous and less domesticated.

Exploring Poetry
Here are some questions to ask when you face the task of reading and writing about poetry.

1. Who is the speaker? What does the poem reveal about the speaker's character? In some poems the speaker may be nothing more than a voice meditating on a theme, while in others the speaker takes on a specific personality. For example, the speaker in Shelley's "Ozymandias" (p. 1384) is a voice meditating on the transitoriness of all things; except for the views expressed in the poem, we know nothing about the speaker's character. The same might be said of the speaker in Hopkins's "Spring and Fall" (p. 155), but with this important exception: we know that he is older than Margaret and therefore has a wisdom she does not.

2. Is the speaker addressing a particular person? If so, who is that person, and why is the speaker interested in him or her? Many poems, like "Ozymandias," are addressed to no one in particular and therefore to anyone, any reader. Others, such as Donne's "A Valediction: Forbidding Mourning" (p. 1102), while addressed to a specific person, reveal nothing about that person because the focus of the poem is on the speaker's feelings and attitudes. In a dramatic monologue (see "Glossary of Literary Terms"), the speaker usually addresses a silent auditor. The identity of the auditor will be important to the poem.

3. Does the poem have a setting? Is the poem occasioned by a particular event? The answer to these questions will often be no for lyric poems, such as Frost's "Fire and Ice" (p. 1110). It will always be yes if the poem is a dramatic monologue or a poem that tells or implies a story, such as Tennyson's "Ulysses" (p. 434) and Lowell's "Patterns" (p. 761).

4. Is the theme of the poem stated directly or indirectly? Some poems, such as Owen's "Dulce et Decorum Est" (p. 1406), use language in a fairly straightforward and literal way and state the theme, often in the final lines. Others may conclude with a statement of the theme that is more difficult to apprehend because it is made with figurative language and symbols. This difference will be readily apparent if you compare the final lines of the Owen poem mentioned above with, say, the final stanzas of Stevens's "Sunday Morning" (p. 442).

5. From what perspective (or point of view) is the speaker describing specific events? Is the speaker recounting events of the past or events that are occurring in the present? If past events are being recalled, what present meaning do they have for the speaker? These questions are particularly appropriate to the works in the section "Innocence and Experience," many of which contrast an early innocence with adult experience.

6. Does a close examination of the figurative language (see p. 13 and "Glossary of Literary Terms") of the poem reveal any patterns? Yeats's "Sailing to Byzantium" (p. 1390) may begin to open up to you once you recognize the pattern of bird imagery. Likewise, Thomas's attitude toward his childhood in "Fern Hill" (p. 165) will be clearer if you detect the pattern of biblical imagery that associates childhood with Adam and Eve before the Fall.

7. What is the structure of the poem? Since narrative poems — those that tell stories — reveal a high degree of selectivity, it is useful to ask why the poet has focused on particular details and left out others. Analyzing the structure of a nonnarrative or lyric poem can be more difficult because it does not contain an obvious series of chronologically related events. The structure of Thomas's "Fern Hill," for example, is based in part on a description of perhaps a day and a half in the speaker's life as a child. But more significant in terms of its structure is the speaker's realization that the immortality he felt as a child was merely a stage in the inexorable movement of life toward death. The structure of the poem, therefore, will be revealed through an analysis of patterns of images (biblical, color, day and night, dark and light) that embody the theme. To take another example, Marvell's "To His Coy Mistress" (p. 1104) is divided into three verse paragraphs, the opening words of each ("Had we . . . ," "But . . . ," "Now therefore . . . ") suggesting a logically constructed argument.

8. What do sound and meter (see "Glossary of Literary Terms") contribute to the poem? Alexander Pope said that in good poetry, "the sound must seem an echo to the sense" — a statement that is sometimes easier to agree with than to demonstrate. For sample analyses of the music of poetry, see the section on music (p. 15).

9. What was your response to the poem on first reading? Did your response change after study of the poem or class discussions about it?

READING DRAMA

Drama is fundamentally different from other literary forms. Unlike fiction, for example, most plays are designed to be performed in public and not read in private. The public nature of drama is reflected in the words we use to discuss it. The word *drama* itself is derived from the Greek word for "action, deed, or performance," and *theater* derives from the Greek word for "sight or contemplation." By their nature, plays are more spectacular than poems or works of fiction. Directors and their staffs pay great attention to costumes, set design, lights, and stage movement; the reader, who doesn't experience these elements, must imagine the action on the basis of words alone. Dramatists use words as starting points for, rather than realizations of, their artistic visions.

Although plays typically lack narration and description — they are designed to show, not tell — they can be considered in terms of setting, plot, theme, characterization, and irony. Indeed, these notions are even more important in drama than in fiction, where narrative style and point of view carry great weight, or in poetry, where diction and imagery are central.

As much as possible, the way to read a play is to imagine that you are its director. In this role you must visualize yourself creating the set and the lighting. You will envision people dressed so that their clothes give support to their words. You will think about timing — how long between events and speeches — and blocking — how the characters move as they interact on stage. Perhaps the best way to confront the literature of the stage, to respond most fully to what is there, is to attempt to produce some scenes either in class or after class. If possible, attend the rehearsals of plays in production on campus. Nothing will provide better insight into the complexities of the theater than attending a rehearsal where the problems are encountered and solved.

As you read any of the opening speeches of any of the plays in this anthology, imagine yourself the director and make decisions. How should the lines be spoken (quietly, angrily, haltingly)? What should the characters do as they speak (remain stationary, look in some direction, traverse the stage)? How should the stage be lit (partially, brightly, in some color that contributes to the mood of the dialogue and action)? What should the characters who are not speaking do? What possibilities exist for conveying appropriate signals solely through gesture and facial expression — signals not contained in the words you read?

Stages and Staging

Although staging is more important to spectators than to readers, some knowledge of staging history can enrich your reading of a play. For example, it helps to know that in the Greek theater of Dionysius in Athens (below), there was no scene shifting. In *Antigonê* (p. 467), which was staged in an open-air amphitheater seating about 14,000 people, actors entered from the *skene,* or a fixed stage house, which might have had painted panels to suggest a scene. Consequently, the Palace of Creon is the fixed backdrop for all of *Antigonê.* Important events, especially violent ones, occur offstage, and the audience learns of these events from a messenger, who comes onstage to describe them. This convention was partly a matter of taste, but the conditions of the Greek stage also prevented Sophocles from moving the action to another scene. Later dramatists, writing for a more flexible stage and a more intimate theater, exploited the dramatic possibilities of such violence.

The Dionysius Theatre in Athens

Interior of the Swan Theatre, London, 1596

The vast outdoor theater imposed restrictions on acting style. Facial expressions played no role in the actor's craft; in fact, the actors wore large masks, which were probably equipped with some sort of megaphone to amplify speech. As a result, it was difficult to modulate speech to create subtle effects, and the speeches were probably delivered in formal, declamatory style. In addition to these limitations, the Athenian government made available only three principal actors, all male, as the cast (excluding the *chorus,* a group of citizens that commented on the action and characters) for each play. Consequently, there were never more than three players onstage at once, and the roles were designed so that each actor could take several parts, each signified by a different mask.

Shakespeare's stage was altogether different from Sophocles'. Although both theaters were open-air, the enclosure around the Elizabethan stage was much smaller than the Greek amphitheater, and the theater's capacity was limited to between 2,000 and 3,000 spectators. As in classical drama, men played all the roles, but they no longer wore masks. The stage protruded into the audience, allowing for more intimacy and a greater range of speech, gesture, and expression. Even so, and despite Hamlet's advice to the troupe "to hold as 't were, the mirror up to nature," Shakespearean tragedy did not lend itself to a modern realistic style. Those great speeches are written in verse; they are frequently meant to augment the meager set design with verbal imagery; and they are much denser in texture, image, and import than is ordinary speech. Most of the important action was played out on the uncurtained main platform, jutting into the audience and surrounded on three

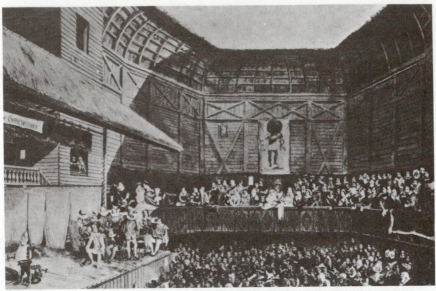

Hypothetical reconstruction of the interior of the Globe Theatre in the days of Shakespeare

sides by spectators. The swiftly moving scenes followed each other without interruption, doubtless using different areas of the stage to signify different locations. There was some sort of terrace or balcony one story above the main stage, and there was an area at the back of the main protruding stage that could be curtained off when not in use. Although Shakespeare's plays are usually divided into five separate acts in printed versions, they were played straight through, without intermission, much like a modern motion picture. These characteristics distinguish the Shakespearean stage from the familiar realism of most contemporary theater.

Much current theater uses a *box stage* — essentially a box with one wall removed so that the audience can see into the playing area. The box stage lends itself to realistic settings. It can easily be furnished to look like a room; or, if outdoor scenes are required, painted backdrops and angled sets provide perspective. Shortly after the introduction of the box stage, the possibilities for scenic design produced great set designers and increasingly sophisticated stage machinery. These new possibilities, in turn, freed the dramatist from the physical limitations imposed by earlier stages.

By the late nineteenth century, the versatility of the box stage enabled playwrights such as Henrik Ibsen to write detailed stage settings for the various locations in which the drama unfolds. Further, the furnishing of the stage in Ibsen's plays sometimes functions symbolically to visually reinforce the claustrophobic quality of the bourgeois life depicted in his plays. Later dramatists have relied on realistic settings to convey meaning and to serve symbolic functions. The modern production may take place in a theater that

A seventeenth-century French box stage

is simply a large empty room (with provisions for technical flexibility in the matter of lighting) that can be rearranged to suit the requirements of specific productions. This ideal of a "theater space" that can be freely manipulated has become increasingly attractive since it frees the dramatist and the performance from limitations built into permanent stage design.

The Elements of Drama

Characters Plays usually consist of narratives with plots, settings, themes, characters, and irony, and most plays have no narrators as such. In Greek drama, the chorus functions as a kind of narrator (Tom, in Tennessee Williams's *The Glass Menagerie* [p. 243], is something of a modern-day chorus). In Shakespearean drama, the *soliloquy,* in which an actor speaks thoughts aloud, allows the audience to hear what a character is thinking. But in most plays, the story unfolds before your eyes without the intervention of an authorial voice or point of view.

Without a narrator to tell us what a character is thinking, we usually infer a character's thoughts by his or her actions and demeanor, and by *dialogue,* or the words a character speaks to others. *Characterization,* in plays as in fiction, is a process by which the author establishes the personality of a character, revealed through what the particular character does and says, and by what other characters say. The main character, the hero or *protagonist,* is the center of our attention. He or she is often opposed by another major character, the *antagonist,* whose opposition creates the central conflict of the drama. The protagonist and the antagonist, as well as other characters of major significance in the drama, have a vital interest in the outcome of the action, and grow and develop as the action progresses and are therefore described as *rounded* characters. Those characters who are peripheral to the action, who often supply the kind of exposition a third-person narrator does in fiction, are minor, or *flat,* characters.

Dramatic Irony   *Dramatic irony* allows the audience to know more than the characters do about their own circumstances by letting the audience hear more than the characters hear. Shakespeare's *Othello* (p. 1144) provides an excellent illustration of the uses of dramatic irony. At the end of Act II, Cassio, who has lost his position as Othello's lieutenant, asks Iago for advice on how to regain favor. Iago, who, unknown to Cassio, had engineered Cassio's disgrace, advises him to ask Desdemona, Othello's adored wife, to intervene. Actually this is good advice; ordinarily the tactic would succeed, so much does Othello love his wife and wish to please her. But Iago explains, in a soliloquy to the audience, that he is laying groundwork for the ruin of all the objects of his envy and hatred — Cassio, Desdemona, and Othello:

> . . . for while this honest fool
> Plies Desdemona to repair his fortunes,
> And she for him pleads strongly to the Moor,
> I'll pour this pestilence into his ear
> That she repeals him for her body's lust;
> And, by how much she strives to do him good,
> She shall undo her credit with the Moor.
> So will I turn her virtue into pitch,
> And out of her goodness make the net
> That shall enmesh them all.

Of course Desdemona, Cassio, and Othello are ignorant of Iago's enmity. Worse, all of them consider Iago a loyal friend. But the audience knows Iago's design, and that knowledge provides the chilling dramatic irony of Act III, scene 3.

When Cassio asks for Desdemona's help, she immediately consents, declaring, "I'll intermingle every thing he does / With Cassio's suit." At this, the audience, knowing what it does, grows a little uneasy. As Iago and Othello come onstage, Cassio, understandably ill at ease, leaves at the approach of the commander who has stripped him of his rank, thus providing Iago with a magnificent tactical advantage. And as Cassio leaves, Iago utters an exclamation and four simple words:

> Ha! I like not that.

These words do not mean much either to Othello or to Desdemona. But they are for the audience the intensely anticipated first drop of poison. Othello hasn't heard clearly:

What dost thou say?

Maybe it will all pass, and Iago's clever design will fail. But what a hiss of held breath the audience expels when Iago replies:

Nothing, my lord: or if — I know not what.

And Othello is hooked:

Was not that Cassio parted from my wife?

The bait taken, Iago begins to play his line:

Cassio, my lord? No, sure, I cannot think it,
That he would steal away so guilty-like,
Seeing you coming.

And from this point on in the scene, Iago cleverly and cautiously leads Othello. He assumes the role of Cassio's great friend — reluctant to say anything that might cast suspicion on him. But he is also the "friend" of Othello and cannot keep silent in his suspicions. So "honest" Iago, apparently full of sympathy and kindness, skillfully brings the trusting Othello to emotional chaos. And every word they exchange is doubly meaningful to the audience, which perceives Othello led on the descent into a horrible jealousy by his "friend." The scene ends with Othello visibly shaken and convinced of Desdemona's faithlessness and Cassio's disloyalty:

Damn her, lewd minx! O, damn her!
Come, go with me apart; I will withdraw.
To furnish me with some swift means of death
For the fair devil. Now art thou my lieutenant.

To which Iago replies:

I am your own for ever.

All the emotional tautness in the audience results from irony, from knowing what the victims do not know. But dramatic irony is the special tool of the dramatist, well suited to produce an electric tension in a live audience that watches and overhears the action onstage.

Plot and Conflict   Plays often portray oppositions between characters or groups or even between two aspects of a character's personality. This opposition often takes the form of a *conflict* that drives the plot. Sometimes a single conflict has many dimensions. In *Antigonê* (p. 467), for example — when the young, female protagonist challenges the aging king's refusal to allow customary burial rights to her brother — the conflict between Creon and Antigonê can be viewed as a conflict between man and woman, age and youth, the state and the family, the living and the dead, and mortals and gods.

Understanding the methods of drama can help us analyze a play and its various effects. But such analysis only gestures at the emotional experience produced by successful drama. More than other forms of literature, plays give physical expression to the social and psychological conflicts that define us individually and collectively. As in *Antigonê,* a play may torment its audience by imposing on a courageous character a duty that will end in tragic death. Or, as in Susan Glaspell's *Trifles* (p. 1236), a play may mock prevalent attitudes and compel an audience to reexamine its values. By giving expression to human impulses and conflicts, plays enact our most persistent concerns with the greatest possible intensity.

A traditional and still useful way of looking at the plot of a play is to see it in five parts: exposition, rising action, climax, falling action, and denouement. *Exposition* provides the audience with information about background matters important to the play. The first part of the plot also includes *rising action,* as the plot progresses toward complexity and conflict, which reaches a crisis, or *climax,* of some sort. This is the turning point of the play, when the protagonist must act decisively or make a critical choice from which there is no turning back. This in turn leads to the *falling action,* as the protagonist confronts the inexorable consequences of his or her act or decision. The play ends with the *denouement* (French for "untying or unraveling"), with the conflict resolved or the mystery solved. Although this template cannot be applied to every play, it comes close enough in describing the structure of many plays to make it a useful tool for analyzing much drama.

Exploring Drama

Here are some more specific questions to ask when you are faced with the task of reading or writing about drama. Write out your answers to check your understanding of a play or to begin collecting ideas for an essay assignment.

1. How does the play begin? Is the exposition presented dramatically as characters interact, novelistically through long speeches that convey a lot of information, or through some device such as a messenger who delivers long letters or lengthy reports?

2. How does the information conveyed in exposition (which may occur at various moments throughout the play) establish the basis for dramatic irony?

Does the audience know more than the characters do? How does that irony create tension in the audience?

3. Who are the principal characters, and how are the distinctive qualities of each dramatically conveyed? How do they change as the play proceeds? Are they sympathetic? What function do the minor characters serve? (An essay that thoughtfully assesses the role of minor characters can often succeed better than an attempt to analyze major figures who may be too complex to deal with in 1,000 words.)

4. Where is the play set? Why does it matter that it is set there? Does the setting play a significant role in the drama, or is it merely a place, any place?

5. What is the central conflict in the play — between characters, between groups, or even between two parts of a character's personality? How is it resolved? Is the resolution satisfying?

6. To appreciate the play fully, do you need to know the historical circumstances out of which the play emerged, or something of the life of the author? If so, how does the information enhance your understanding?

7. Since plays are usually written to be performed rather than read, what visual and auditory elements of the play are significant to your response? If you are reading a text, place yourself in the position of the director and the actors to respond to this aspect of drama.

8. What is the play's theme? How does the dramatic action embody that theme?

9. Has the play been made into a film? In the adaptation, what has been added and what has been deleted? How does this production compare with your reading of the play?

READING ESSAYS

Essays differ from fiction in that they generally do not create imaginary worlds inhabited by fictional characters. We know, for example, through media accounts and the testimony of his friends, that Martin Luther King Jr. was indeed jailed in Birmingham, Alabama, where he wrote his famous argument for social justice, "Letter from Birmingham Jail" (p. 634). And, although we cannot independently verify that George Orwell actually shot an elephant (p. 993), his work exhibits the formal nonfictional qualities of the essay rather than the imagined world of the short story.

Writers turn to the essay form when they wish to confront their readers directly with an idea, a problem (often with a proposed solution), an illuminating experience, an important definition, or some flaw (or virtue) in the social system. Usually, the essay is relatively short, and almost always embodies the writer's personal viewpoint. And although the essay may share many elements with other literary forms, it generally speaks with the voice of a real person about the real world. The term *essay* derives from the French verb *essayer* — "try, attempt." That verb, in turn, derives from the Latin verb *exigere* — "weigh out, examine."

While the French term calls attention to the personal perspective that characterizes the essay, the Latin verb suggests another dimension. The essay not only examines personal experiences but also explores and clarifies ideas by arguing for or against a position. Thus, Jessica Mitford's "The American Way of Death" (p. 1485) suggests that the essay will be analytical, perhaps even argumentative.

As you read an essay, you need to ask yourself, What is the central argument or idea? Sometimes the answer is obvious. "The American Way of Death" attacks extravagant funerals promoted by the undertaker industry. The essay, if successful, will change — or, perhaps, reinforce — the reader's attitudes toward death rituals.

Some essays address the inner lives of their readers. John Donne's "Meditation XVII" (p. 1480), for example, does not attack or justify anything. Rather, it reminds us to be aware of our mortality and thereby to alter our interactions with or perceptions of the people around us.

Types of Essays

In first-year composition, you may have read and written narrative, descriptive, expository, and argumentative essays. While reviewing the characteristics of each of these types, keep in mind that in the real world, authors of essays are more interested in effectiveness than in purity of form, and frequently combine features of different formal types.

Narrative Essays   Narrative essays recount a sequence of related events and are often autobiographical. But those events are chosen because they suggest or illustrate some truth or insight. In "Shooting an Elephant" (p. 993), for example, George Orwell narrates an episode from his life that led him to an important insight about imperialism. In "Graduation in Stamps" (p. 1000), Maya Angelou learns for the first time what it means to be black in a white world. In these narrative essays, the writers discover in their own experiences the evidence for generalizations about themselves and their societies.

Descriptive Essays   Descriptive essays depict sensory observations in words. They evoke in the reader's imagination the sights and sounds, perhaps even the smells, that transport him or her to such places as Joan Didion's Death Valley or George Orwell's Burma. Sometimes, the writer is satisfied simply to create a lifelike evocation of some engaging object or landscape, but Didion uses her description as a vehicle for expressing ideas about morality. The descriptive essay, like the narrative essay, often addresses complex issues that trouble our lives, but it does so by appealing primarily to sensory awareness — sight, sound, touch, taste, smell — rather than to intellect. The power of description is so great that narrative and expository essays often use lengthy descriptive passages to communicate forcefully.

Expository Essays   Expository essays attempt to explain and elucidate, to organize and provide information. Often they embody an extended definition of a complex conception such as love or patriotism; other times, they describe a process — how to do something. This book's coverage of essays, for example, is clearly not narrative because it doesn't depend for its form on a chronological sequence of meaningful events. It is not descriptive in the pure sense of that type because it does not depend on conveying sensory impressions. It is, in fact, expository. It acquaints its readers with the techniques and types of essays and provides some tips to help students read essays both analytically and pleasurably. This discussion uses a number of rhetorical strategies that you may recognize from other writing courses. We *classify* essays by type; we *compare and contrast* them; we use *definition;* we give *examples* to make a point; we imply that there is a *cause-and-effect* relationship between what readers bring to an essay and the pleasure they derive from it. Similarly, the essayists represented in this book use a variety of such rhetorical strategies to achieve their aims.

Argumentative Essays   Although Orwell's "Shooting an Elephant" can be categorized as a narrative essay, we might reasonably assert that it is also argumentative because it is designed to convince readers that imperialism is as destructive to the oppressors as to the oppressed. The argumentative essay wishes to persuade its readers. Thus, it usually deals with controversial ideas, marshals arguments and evidence to support a view, and anticipates and answers opposing arguments. Martin Luther King Jr. accomplishes all these ends in his "Letter from Birmingham Jail" (p. 634). So does Jonathan Swift in "A Modest Proposal" (p. 615), with an approach complicated by his reliance on irony and satire.

Analyzing the Essay

The Thesis   The best way to begin analyzing an essay is to ask, what is the point of this piece of writing; what is the author trying to show, attack, defend, or prove? If you can answer that question satisfactorily and succinctly, then the analysis of the essay's elements (i.e., its rhetorical strategies, its structure, style, tone, and language) becomes easier. Randall Robinson's "Can a Black Family Be a Legal Nuisance?" (p. 659) is a very short essay, so powerfully simple that its painfully clear thesis does not have to be stated at all. On the other hand, a much more complex and ambitious essay, such as Virginia Woolf's "What If Shakespeare Had Had a Sister?" (p. 980), does not yield up its thesis quite so easily. We might say that Woolf's examination of the historical record leads her to argue that women did not write during the Elizabethan period because literary talent could not flourish in a social system that made women the ill-educated property of men. This formulation of the essay's thesis, as you will see when you read the essay, leaves a good deal out — notably the exhortation to action with which Woolf concludes the piece.

Structure and Detail   Read carefully the first and last paragraphs of a number of essays. Note the writers' strategy for engaging you at the outset with an irresistible proposition:

> In Moulmein, in Lower Burma, I was hated by large numbers of people — the only time in my life that I have been important enough for this to happen to me.

> If I speak in tongues of men and of angels, but have not love, I am a noisy gong or a clanging cymbal.

> I was saved from sin when I was going on thirteen.

These opening sentences are startling, hooking readers so that they will eagerly read on to find out what it was that made the writer so hated in Burma, why love is so important, how Langston Hughes was saved from sin. You will find that the opening lines of most well-wrought essays instantly capture your attention.

Endings, too, are critical. And if you examine the concluding lines of any of the essays in this collection, you will find forceful assertions that sharply focus the matter that precedes them. Essayists, unsurprisingly, systematically use gripping beginnings and forceful endings.

What comes between those beginnings and endings are often abstract issues — the nature of love, the inevitability of death, the evils of imperialism. Though such abstractions do significantly influence our lives, as subject matter for reading they seem impersonal and distant. Reading about great ideas becomes a sort of academic task, relegated to some intellectual sphere, separate from the pain and passion of our own humanity. The accomplished essay writer, however, entices us to confront such issues by converting abstract ideas into concrete and illustrative detail.

For example, George Orwell points out early in "Shooting an Elephant" that the "anti-European feeling was very bitter" in British-controlled Burma. But he immediately moves from the abstraction of "anti-European feeling" to "if a European woman went through the bazaars alone somebody would probably spit betel juice over her dress" and "when a nimble Burman tripped me up on the football field and the referee (another Burman) looked the other way, the crowd yelled with hideous laughter." The tiny bits of hateful experience, because they are physical and concrete, powerfully reinforce the abstract assertion about "anti-European feeling" that lies at the center of

Orwell's essay, and the narrative account of the speaker's behavior in front of the mob culminates in an illuminating insight: "I perceived in this moment that when the white man turns tyrant it is his own freedom that he destroys." The large generality emerges from deeply felt personal experience.

Style and Tone   The word *style* refers to all the writing skills that contribute to the effect of any piece of literature. And *tone* — the attitude conveyed by the language a writer chooses — is a particularly significant aspect of writing style. As an illustration of the effect of tone, consider these opening lines of two essays — Martin Luther King Jr.'s "Letter from Birmingham Jail" and Langston Hughes's "Salvation":

> While confined here in the Birmingham city jail, I came across your recent statement calling my present activities "unwise and untimely." Seldom do I pause to answer criticism of my work and ideas. If I sought to answer all the criticisms that cross my desk, my secretaries would have little time for anything other than such correspondence in the course of the day, and I would have no time for constructive work. But since I feel that you are men of genuine good will and that your criticisms are sincerely set forth, I want to try to answer your statement in what I hope will be patient and reasonable terms.

> I was saved from sin when I was going on thirteen. But not really saved. It happened like this. There was a big revival at my Auntie Reed's church. Every night for weeks there had been much preaching, singing, praying, and shouting, and some very hardened sinners had been brought to Christ, and the membership of the church had grown by leaps and bounds. Then just before the revival ended, they held a special meeting for children, "to bring the young lambs to the fold."

Both first-person accounts use provocative openings, immediately hooking the reader. King's tone, however, is formal; his grave rhythm ("Seldom do I pause") and diction ("If I sought to answer") recall a certain kind of well-known oratory. Consider his mature and studied word choices: *confined, statement, correspondence, constructive, sincerely, patient, reasonable.*

Hughes's tone, in his first-person account, is personal and informal. He uses colloquial diction ("It happened like this"; "leaps and bounds") and a sardonic wit ("some very hardened sinners had been brought to Christ"). Although a reminiscing adult describes the event, the writer creates the voice of a child by using simple grammar and a child's vocabulary.

The tone a writer creates contributes substantially to the message he or she conveys. Jonathan Swift might have written a sound, academic essay about the economic diseases of Ireland and how to cure them — but his invention of the speaker of "A Modest Proposal," who ironically and sardonically proposes the establishment of a human-baby meat-exporting industry, jars the readers in ways no scholarly essay could. The outraged tone of Jessica Mitford's "The American Way of Death" comically reinforces her attack on greedy undertakers. The high seriousness of Donne's tone in "Meditation

XVII" perfectly suits his contemplation of the relationship among the living, the dying, and the dead.

Style is a more difficult quality to define than tone. Dictionaries define style as both "a manner of expression in language" and "excellence in expression." Certainly it is easier to distinguish between various *manners* of expression than it is to describe just what constitutes *excellence* in expression. For example, the manners of expression of John Donne in "Meditation XVII" and of Jessica Mitford in "The American Way of Death" clearly differ. The first muses about death in a style characterized by formality and complex extended images. The second uses the breezy style of a muckraking journalist, replete with contemptuous asides and sardonic exclamations.

Nonetheless, we can describe the excellence of each style. Donne, an Anglican priest, meditates on the community of all living humans and the promise of eternal life in the face of physical death. He creates a remarkable image when he argues that "all mankind is of one author." Not so remarkable, you might argue; God is often called the "author of mankind." But Donne insists on the figurative quality of God as author and the intimate relationship among all people when he adds that all humankind "is one volume." Then he extends this metaphor by arguing that "when one man dies, one chapter is not torn out of the book, but translated into a better language." The daring image is further extended. "God," Donne tells us, "employs several translators; some pieces are translated by age, some by sickness, some by war, some by justice." By alluding to the actual making of a book by the bookbinder, Donne elaborates on the central image and reestablishes the idea of community: "God's hand is in every translation, and his hand shall bind up all our scattered leaves again for that library where every book shall lie open to one another." Surely, this magnificent figurative characterization of death (regardless of your personal beliefs) exhibits stylistic excellence.

Jessica Mitford's attack on the American funeral industry begins

> O Death, where is thy sting? O grave, where is thy victory? Where, indeed. Many a badly stung survivor, faced with the aftermath of some relative's funeral, has ruefully concluded that the victory has been won hands down by a funeral establishment — in disastrously unequal battle.

This essay opens with a quote from Paul's Letter to the Corinthians — certainly a sober and exalted allusion. But immediately, the tone turns sardonic with the question "Where, indeed?" And the writer compounds the sarcasm by extending the biblical metaphor that compares death to a painful bee sting to the equally painful experience of the "stung" survivor who has been conned into enormous expenditure by a funeral establishment. Her breezy style juxtaposes the ancient biblical promise of a spiritual victory over death with the crass modern reality: the only victor, nowadays, is the greedy funeral director. The perception is "rueful," and the victory "has been won hands down" in an encounter characterized as a "disastrously unequal battle." Mitford's language, playing off the high seriousness of the biblical quotation, stylistically advances her purpose by introducing a note of mockery. Certainly her argument gains force from the pervasive sardonic tone that characterizes her style.

These writers exhibit distinctive manners of expression and distinctive varieties of excellence — in short, distinctive styles.

Your principal concern, when reading an essay, must always be to discover the essay's central thesis. What does the writer wish you to understand about his or her experience, the world, or yourself? Once you have understood the essay's thesis, you can enhance your understanding by examining the means the author used to convey it and, perhaps, recognize techniques that will enhance the quality of your own writing. To that end, you ought to examine the essay's structure and the rhetorical strategies that shape it. How does it begin and end? What type is it — narrative, descriptive, expository, argumentative? How do rhetorical strategies — definition, cause and effect, classification, exemplification, comparison and contrast — function to serve the author's purposes? Then analyze the sources of the essay's effectiveness by closely analyzing the language of the essay. Watch writers energize abstract ideas with details and moving experience; consider the uses of figurative language — the metaphors and similes that create both physical and emotional landscapes in the prose; respond to the tone of voice and the stylistic choices that create it. When you have done all this successfully, when you have discovered not only *what* the author has said but also *how* the author moved you to his or her point of view — then you will have understood the essay.

Exploring Essays
Here are some questions to ask when you face the task of reading and writing about essays.

1. What is the author's thesis (or unifying idea)? What evidence or arguments does the author advance to support the thesis? Is the thesis convincing? If not, why not? Does the author rely on any basic but unstated assumptions?

2. What is the author's tone? Select for analysis a passage you consider illustrative of the author's tone. Does the author maintain that tone consistently throughout the essay?

3. How would you characterize the author's style? For example, are the syntax, length of sentences, and diction elevated and formal or familiar and informal?

4. What rhetorical strategies does the author use? For example, can you identify the effective use of narration, description, classification, comparison and contrast, analogy, cause and effect, or definition? Note that one of these rhetorical strategies may constitute the unifying idea of the essay or the means of structuring it. Jessica Mitford's "The American Way of Death" is an essay organized as a definition that effectively uses comparison and contrast and analogy as supporting rhetorical strategies.

5. What are the major divisions in the essay, and how are they set off? Are the transitions between the divisions effective and easy to follow?

6. Analyze the author's opening paragraph. Is it effective in gaining the reader's attention? Does it clearly state the essay's thesis? If it does not, at what point do the author's thesis and purpose become clear?

Writing about Literature

If reading literature offers a way to listen to the outrageously alive voices of the past, writing about literature affords the opportunity to respond to these voices. Sometimes your responses are just a jumble of vague impressions. Classroom discussion can help to clarify your thoughts, but the best ideas do not usually come together until you sit down and write. The act of composition often generates a line of thinking. Writing about literature is an invitation to organize your impressions and to check those impressions against the work that prompted them. When you accept this invitation, you undertake a process that helps make sense of the literary work and helps you understand your reactions to it.

RESPONDING TO YOUR READING

As you know from your own experience, complete essays do not pop into a writer's head immediately after he or she reads a work of literature. The process starts with an impression here, a fragment there, or a question about something that catches your attention.

Imagine this scenario. Your teacher asks you to write an essay about one of the works you've read, and you don't have a clue about where to start. Consider the following very short poem, "The Span of Life" (1936), by Robert Frost:

> The old dog barks backward without getting up.
> I can remember when he was a pup.

Take five minutes to write a response to the poem. Don't worry about style or grammatical correctness — just start writing anything that comes to mind.

You may be able to write very little at first. What is there to say? The poem — plain and clear — seems to need no explanation; its words are familiar, and the dog image unambiguous. How could someone write even a short essay about this piece? Is this a joke?

But looking at it again closely, we may come to a few more observations. First, the title seems awfully grand for this tiny poem. Somehow, these two lines and sixteen words are to make a poetic statement about the nature of life itself. Perhaps we had better look at the lines and words carefully. As a first step, let's scan the poem:

Th̆e óld dóg bárks báckwărd wĭthŏut gétting úp.

Í căn remémber whĕn hĕ wăs ă púp.

Speak the poem aloud. Note that the first half of line 1 seems to move slowly, while line 2 seems to prance. That series of four stressed syllables in line 1 "slows" the line. Further, it seems that the words are hard to say quickly — perhaps because the last letter of each stressed syllable has to be finished before you can speak the first letter of the following word: "old *dog barks backward* without." The *meter* and the sound patterns that describe the dog, old and tired as he is, contribute to the lethargy described in line 1. But is this poem about a mere dog's life or, perhaps, life in general?

In the second line, the lilting *anapestic meter* dances across the page. (An *anapest* is a metrical foot consisting of two unaccented syllables followed by an accented syllable. See *Meter* in the "Glossary of Literary Terms.") The final *n* of "can" slides easily into the initial *r* of "remember"; the easy movements between words and in the sound sequences that follow all contribute to the quickness of the line. (Don't take our word for it; say the words aloud!) Thus, the joyful playfulness of a puppy, suggested by the bounding anapestic meter, is reinforced by the sound patterns embodied in the words chosen to evoke the old dog's youth. Since the title of the poem invites the reader to generalize, we could assume that human life spans, like the old dog's, move from the energetic exuberance of youth to the fatigued immobility of advanced age.

Now the title makes sense — and the *poetic* quality of the sixteen-word *couplet* (two consecutive rhyming lines) emerges from the rhythm and the sounds that reinforce the meaning of the words.

Reread your five-minute exploratory writing. Did you note any of these matters? Did you wonder about the poem's title? Do you have an alternative reading to suggest? After this discussion, could you now write a short essay on Frost's poem? These first jottings do not require that you bring any special knowledge to this poem, just that you attend to what's there on the page — a puzzling title, an unusual variation of metrical patterns, and the sounds that embody the poem.

Writing about literature challenges you to teach yourself. Every element in a literary work has been deliberately put there by the author — the description of the setting, the events that form the plot, the dialogue, the imagery. Readers experience a mysterious intellectual and emotional event as a result of the writer's purposeful manipulation of language. When you write about what you've read, you confront not only your response to a work but the elements within the work that cause your response.

Think about a short story or novel that you have read or a movie you have seen recently. Did you like or dislike the story? Try to list the reasons for your general reaction and evaluation: the characters were interesting or dull and lifeless; the ending satisfied expectations or, perhaps, was surprising; the story was easy to understand; it offered new insights about people, or places, or a different society; you couldn't wait to see what would happen next (or found the story so boring that you had trouble finishing it). Your personal impressions, as you jot them down, represent your response to the work.

When you write about literature, you begin with your response to the work. Then you need to consider the writer's purpose. This is not easy; in fact, some critics argue that the reader can never fully recover the writer's purpose. But you can explore the text, try to discover how the plot, setting, characterizations — the very words (sometimes symbolic) — all conspire to generate the theme, and, finally, work on your feelings so that you have some response.

To write about literature is, in one way or another, an attempt to discover and describe how the writer's art created the reader's response. In other words, whatever your assignment, the fundamental task is to answer two questions: How do I respond to this piece? How has the author brought about my response?

Keeping a Journal

Your instructor may require you to keep a journal — a day-by-day account of your reactions to and reflections on your reading. Even if a journal is not required, you might want to keep one for a variety of reasons. From a purely practical perspective, writing in a journal regularly is excellent practice at conquering the blank page and generating ideas. You need not construct grammatical sentences, write cohesive paragraphs, develop your ideas, or even make sense. In a journal you are free to comment on only one aspect of a work or on a personal recollection that something in the work triggered. You are recording your reactions, ideas, feelings, questions. If you are conscientious about keeping your journal, you may come to find writing in it a pleasant activity.

A journal's helpfulness extends beyond its use as a place for reflection. When the time comes to write a full-length essay for your class, the journal can provide many possible topics. Use your journal to express in writing the pleasure (or pain) of each reading assignment. Jot down hard words (which you should then, of course, look up in your dictionary). Note your reactions to characters — that some are nasty, others too saintly, some realistically rendered, still others unbelievable. Some of your journal entries may be confessions of confusion, posing open-ended questions about a reading.

You may want to write about the personal feelings and recollections triggered by a work. Dylan Thomas's "Fern Hill" might remind you of feelings you experienced during a particular period of your childhood. Exploring your own childhood feelings and comparing them with those expressed in Thomas's poem could lead to a fascinating essay — for example, about how poets give memorable and vivid expression to experiences we've all had. Or you might jot down, after reading Kate Chopin's "The Storm," your disapproval of the story's central event — marital infidelity. You might then reread the story to discover whether it seems to disapprove of infidelity or whether you have imposed on it your own moral values. Thinking critically about such reactions might generate an essay that examines the conflict between your own moral values and those embodied in a particular work.

Finally, remember that — unless your instructor has specific guidelines for journal keeping — your journal will be the one place where you can write as much or as little as you please, as often or infrequently as you wish, with care and deliberation or careless speed. Its only purpose is to serve your needs. But if you write fairly regularly, you will probably be surprised not only at how much easier the act of writing becomes but also at how many ideas suddenly pop into your head in the act of writing. Henry Adams was surely right when he observed, "The habit of expression leads to the search for something to express."

Exploring and Planning

Asking Good Questions   Often the best ideas for paper topics begin as questions or as responses that can be turned into questions. In reading James Joyce's "Araby," for example, you may notice that the narrator makes a big deal out of carrying the groceries home. This observation can be converted into a question: Why the big deal about carrying the groceries home? Or, to focus the question a bit, Why and how does the boy idealize these everyday situations? Note that these questions do not lead to a single irrefutable answer. When you write responses to literature, your goal is to pose a good question, answer it clearly, and support the answer with evidence from the work.

While it is important to clear up basic questions — for example, what a word or phrase means, or who did what, or how the characters are related to one another — successful papers usually take up questions that are less easily settled. For example, you would probably not want to ask whether or not Creon made mistakes of judgment in *Antigonê* or whether the tragedy could have been avoided if he had acted otherwise. Questions such as these do not lend themselves to sustained discussion. Questions of personal taste are not immediately useful for the same reason; if you say you like a particular work, there is little anyone can say to the contrary. Sometimes such assertions can be usefully converted, especially if you begin to ask why you like or dislike a work. In general, however, you should strive to explore open-ended interpretative and thematic questions rather than rehash the facts or declare personal preferences.

Establishing a Working Thesis   Early in the writing process, as you gather ideas about what to write, you should formulate a tentative *working thesis* that states your topic and the point or comment you wish to make about the topic. Although your working thesis will probably change as you collect information, articulating it will help you focus your thoughts and further research. Make your working thesis as specific as possible to limit your topic and keep the scope of the essay manageable. Consider the audience appeal of your working thesis, as well.

A *thesis* states the main point you'll make in your final essay. In your opening paragraph, a clear thesis statement should both indicate the position you intend to take and prepare your reader for what follows. The thesis statement should be accompanied by some indication of the *scope* of your argument — the several issues you intend to explore.

For example, generating ideas for an essay about *Antigonê,* you may be struck by the peculiar line uttered by Creon after Antigonê defies him: "Who is the man here, / She or I, if this crime goes unpunished?" This line prompts the question, How does Creon understand manhood? At first these lines suggest that Creon cannot separate his ideas about manhood from his ideas about justice. This preliminary answer is the beginning of a working thesis. The next step is to reexamine *Antigonê* and ask whether any other details in the work support the claim and, if not, whether the thesis needs refining to accommodate those details.

Gathering Information   Once you have chosen your topic and articulated a working thesis, you need to consider what additional information you will need to explore the issue. This may mean identifying examples from the text of the literary work you are analyzing to support your thesis or gathering information from other sources. The library is likely to be the principal source of additional information, though online research is becoming increasingly more reliable.

If you use an electronic source, it is often a simple matter to print online information. If you use print sources in a library, you will need to make a photocopy or take notes. In any case, be sure to indicate on your printout or your note cards the exact publication and location information for all your sources so that you can properly document your sources in the final essay. If you are using even just one source, you will need to provide information crediting that source in your list of works cited. For more information about crediting sources and creating a Works Cited page, see p. 73.

Organizing Information   In an ideal world, you would know what you want to write about before you begin your research and thus could prepare a succinct thesis followed by a structured outline in which arguments I, II, and III would be supported by points A, B, and C. In the real world, writers research a preliminary topic and then impose order on the information they have amassed. Think about how best to group or organize your points so that they will be persuasive to your readers.

One general approach to organizing an essay is to complete this statement: "The purpose of this essay is X. To demonstrate X, I will argue A, B, and C," substituting your thesis and the arguments that support it for X, A, B, and C. In an essay on *Othello,* for example, you might write, "The purpose of this essay is to argue that Othello's fall is a logical consequence of his situation and his character. To demonstrate this thesis, I will examine his age and race, his military life, and his inexperience with European women."

Once you've nailed down the thesis and scope of the essay, you can, in your draft, add layers to support your claim:

> Many writers have argued that the rapid fall of
> the noble Moor Othello is unbelievable. But consider
> his situation. He is a black man in a white country; he
> is much older than his beautiful wife. As a military
> man, he self-consciously lacks social grace. And his
> inexperience with European women contributes to the
> emotional insecurity that finally destroys him.

Where you cite other writers' arguments — as in the first sentence — you must offer documentation for your sources.

The next several paragraphs would follow the organization set up by the opening. First might be a paragraph on his race and age and the attitudes toward him established in Act I, followed by a paragraph on Othello's self-conscious unfamiliarity with the behavior of European women. The next paragraph might argue that he sees himself as unappealing to women from his adopted city. Each of these assertions should be supported with dialogue from the play. A conclusion would follow: Othello was never quite as noble as some have suggested and, under the circumstances, was doomed from the start.

DRAFTING THE ESSAY

It is important to start writing even if you are unsure about the exact shape or direction of your argument since frequently your ideas develop and become more focused as you proceed. In working through a draft, you may become more interested in Creon's ideas about manhood, for example, especially his sense that masculinity is something that can be won (by Antigonê) or lost (by himself) depending on the outcome of the conflict. As you write your first draft and your thoughts evolve, you may wish to try a new thesis, perhaps that Creon's decisions have more to do with gender than with the ideals of good governance he proclaims in his first speech. Here again do not feel that all the details must be worked out before you begin writing. The main thing is to get started and to be flexible. The first draft does not have to be perfect.

Refining Your Opening   Once the draft is done and you have a clear idea of your thesis and the passages in the work that best support it, you can begin to shape and refine the essay. In doing so, pay special attention to the introductory paragraph, which should introduce the topic and lead directly to a

clear, arguable thesis. While there is no sure-fire formula for a first paragraph, some strategies are better than others. Avoid the following types of
opening sentences:

```
    Ever since the dawn of time, people have been
    interested in the principles of good governance.


    Gender is an important issue for many people.
```

This kind of throat-clearing generalization is common and even helpful at
the draft stage, but it gets the essay off to a slow start. If the working thesis is
that Creon's decisions have more to do with ideas about gender than with his
stated principles of governance, a direct approach is more effective:

```
    Creon's first speech in Antigonê articulates the
    principles by which he intends to govern Thebes. These
    principles, including his view that private friend-
    ships should not be set above the public welfare, seem
    reasonable, especially in light of the bloody civil war
    that immediately preceded his ascension to the throne.
    As the drama unfolds, however, Creon's decisions seem to
    reflect considerations quite different from those
    articulated in his opening speech. In particular, his
    actions seem motivated more by his attitudes about
    gender, especially his fear that Antigonê will unman
    him, than by his concern for the welfare of Thebes.
```

Note that this opening paragraph introduces the topic and moves directly
toward an explicit and arguable claim. By doing so, it lets the reader — and
the writer — know where the essay is going. That is, once a clear thesis is in
place, both writer and reader can use it as a kind of road map for the rest of
the essay.

Supporting Your Thesis   The body of the essay will be devoted to supporting the thesis. The best way to establish a claim is to cite and analyze carefully selected passages from the text that relate directly to it. The following
paragraph focuses on lines that support our sample claim directly:

```
    At several points in the play, Creon calls
    attention to the fact that Antigonê is a woman. To him,
```

```
this fact compounds the seriousness of her crime, for
he sees their conflict as a battle in the war between
the sexes:
            We keep the laws then, and the lawmakers,
            And no woman shall seduce us. If we must lose,
            Let's lose to a man, at least! Is a woman
            stronger than we? (3.46-48)
As these lines indicate, Creon sees the situation in
terms of winning and losing, and he is especially averse
to the idea of losing to a woman.
```

The first part of the paragraph tells the reader what to look for in the cited lines, and the subsequent analysis underscores their relevance to the overall argument clearly and convincingly.

If you offer a claim, support it with an analysis of the relevant passages, and consider different interpretations of those passages, you have completed the main task in much writing about literature. Concluding paragraphs can move toward closure by reviewing the claim and its significance, which you should be careful not to overstate. In the essay on *Antigonê,* for example, it would not be effective to conclude by claiming that gender is the sole source of contention between the main characters or by making sweeping statements about Athenian society. Your readers will find your claims more convincing if you do not exaggerate their importance.

REVISING THE ESSAY

After you've completed your draft, it is time to look at the essay more critically, paying special attention to revision. Revision involves taking a fresh look at your essay's thesis and support, as well as its organization and language. Reading your essay aloud, or asking someone else to read it, will help you catch many problems. Revision is most effective if begun well before the paper is due. Start writing early so that you have time to review your decisions, ask for feedback from others, and revise accordingly. Because you cannot always anticipate audience reaction, a preliminary reading of your writing by a friend, a teaching assistant, a tutor, or an instructor can highlight the areas that need attention or additional revision.

The basic guidelines for good style are not mysterious; in fact, you use them every day in conversation. In conversation and in writing, we all rely heavily on cooperation to make sense of exchanges, and a polished practical style makes cooperation easier. Writers develop such a style by acknowledging that readers expect the same things that listeners expect in conversation: clarity, relevance, and proportion. If you listen to someone who is not clear, who cannot stay on the topic, or who offers too much or too little information, you will quickly lose interest in the conversation. Writers, too, need to be clear, stay on the topic, and give information appropriately. In fact, this attention to audience and appropriateness may be even more important in writing than in conversation because writing does not permit the nonverbal communication and immediate feedback that are part of conversation. As writers, we have to anticipate the absent reader's response; in effect, we have to imagine both halves of a virtual conversation.

Begin by evaluating your essay's thesis: Is it clear? Vagueness or tentativeness here may mean problems later in the essay, so make sure your thesis is crystal clear. Second, is the evidence you present relevant to each major point? While it is tempting and sometimes productive to go off on tangents while drafting a paper, in the final essay if the evidence doesn't fit the claim, tinker with the claim, or go back to the early exploratory writing you did and to your sources to look for better evidence. Are there any points that need to be clarified? Check all your quotations, paraphrases, and summaries for their citations and for accuracy.

Next, can you tighten the organization of your draft? Are your claims and evidence unified? Put yourself in your reader's place, and clarify ambiguities. Each detail or piece of evidence in a paragraph should relate back to the claim it supports in the topic sentence of that paragraph. At the same time, avoid oversupporting some points with too much discussion or detail.

Finally, ask yourself if the general proportions of your essay are suitable. A five-page paper should not use three of those pages to introduce the topic or recount a work's plot. If the essay is too short, the trouble might be an unarguable thesis or insufficient evidence. If it is running too long, eliminate or compress the parts that do not bear directly on the main claim, or limit the claim to something more manageable.

Editing Your Draft

After you have evaluated and revised your draft and determined the format for your paper, you are ready to edit it carefully, paying close attention to each sentence and paragraph. These guidelines will help you focus on some common trouble spots.

Selecting Strong Verbs   Careful selection of lively, active verbs will make your writing more interesting to your audience. Consider the main verb in the following sentence:

```
Three conflicts, all of which play crucial roles in the

plot, are evident in Antigonê.
```

The core assertion of this sentence is that "Three conflicts . . . are evident." Notice that nothing actually happens in this sentence. To stir things up, borrow the verb *play* from another part of the sentence:

> Three conflicts play crucial roles in the plot of
>
> <u>Antigonê</u>.

The revision is better, but the sentence can be made even more concise using *drive:*

> Three conflicts drive the plot of <u>Antigonê</u>.

The revised sentence more clearly gets to the point, an effect that is rarely lost on an audience. It also permits a more direct move to the topic — namely, the conflicts. Finally, in an economical seven words rather than a verbose fifteen, it neither belabors nor omits anything of importance in the first sentence.

   Writing that relies too heavily on *be* verbs often produces wordiness and unnecessary abstraction:

> There <u>was</u> opposition to the law among the citizens of
>
> Thebes.

Deleting the *be* verb (*was*) and converting the abstract noun *opposition* into a verb make the sentence more active:

> The citizens of Thebes <u>opposed</u> the law.

This clearer sentence lets the verb do the major work. Of course, a good verb does not always present itself as an abstract noun in an early draft. Sometimes you'll need to consult a thesaurus or a dictionary to find just the right word.

   Search your draft for weak verbs and insignificant words and for sentences that begin *There is, There are, It is.* Often, a few words later, a *that, which,* or *who* will appear. Overuse of *There is* and *There are* produces sentences where the action is buried. Edit these sentences by deleting the weak verb constructions and replacing them with strong, precise verbs. For example, change "*There is* a destiny *that* controls the fate of Sam" to "Destiny controls Sam's fate."

   Finally, check your draft for passive constructions (the ball *was thrown*), and replace them when possible with active verbs. Passive sentences are often wordy and dull the action of a sentence. For example, change "The essay was read by the class" to "The class read the essay."

Eliminating Unnecessary Modifiers   When choosing or revising a verb, you are also choosing the sentence elements that necessarily accompany it. These other sentence elements are called *complements* because they complete the meaning of the verb. In the following sentences the complements are underlined:

```
Creon governed Thebes.
```

```
The boy idealized his situation.
```

Creon cannot just govern; he has to govern something. Likewise, *his situation* completes the meaning of the verb *idealized*. Almost everything else added to these sentences will be *modifiers* — additional elements that will modify, rather than complete, the meaning of the sentences. A writer can add any number of modifiers to a sentence:

```
Creon governed Thebes with an iron hand, selfishly, and
without due regard for the traditional claims of kinship
and religion.
```

From a grammatical standpoint, these modifiers are optional; without them the sentence still expresses a complete thought. Unnecessary modifiers can make your writing heavy and murky:

```
Basically, the Greeks invented a rather innovative and
distinctive form of government known as democracy.
```

Eliminating the modifiers and making a few other snips results in the following:

```
The Greeks invented democracy.
```

The clearer sentence does not lose much in the way of content. Of course, being able to eliminate modifiers does not mean that you should; sometimes modifiers are the most significant parts of a sentence. You can always use modifiers for nuance or emphasis, but you must ruthlessly trim unnecessary modifiers from wordy, unclear sentences.

Making Connections   Make sure your sentences and paragraphs are firmly linked by using explicit transitional phrases such as *however, although, likewise, for example, therefore,* and so on. Note in this sample opening paragraph how the underlined transitional phrases indicate the relationships between the sentences:

```
In his first speech in Antigonê, Creon articu-
lates the principles by which he intends to govern
Thebes. These principles, including his view that pri-
vate friendships should not be set above the public
```

> welfare, strike the reader as reasonable, especially in
> light of the bloody civil war that immediately preceded
> his ascension to the throne. As the drama unfolds,
> <u>however</u>, the basis for Creon's decisions seem to reflect
> considerations quite different from those articulated
> in his opening speech. <u>In particular</u>, his actions seem
> motivated more by his attitudes about gender, especially
> his fear that Antigonê will unman him, than by his
> concern for the welfare of Thebes.

The appearance of *however* halfway through the paragraph signals the contrast between Creon's principles and his attitudes toward gender. The transitional phrase *in particular* in the next sentence signals that we are narrowing the preceding point and focusing our discussion. Experienced readers look for such transitional phrases that suggest an interpretive path through an argument.

Note also that the second sentence of the paragraph repeats a key word from the first one (*principles*). This repetition helps keep the spotlight on Creon's ideals, an important notion in the paragraph. By repeating key terms, sometimes with slight variation, you can illuminate the main idea of a paragraph clearly and intensively.

After checking for explicit connections within paragraphs, make sure that the progression of ideas from one paragraph to another is clear. Here again, transitional phrases are useful. A simple transition such as *nevertheless, furthermore,* or *on the other hand* is often adequate. Sometimes the entire opening sentence of a paragraph may provide the transition, including keywords, pronouns, or other references to the previous paragraph.

Proofreading Your Draft

Print out, type, or neatly write in ink the final copy of your essay for submission to your instructor, taking care to follow any special instructions about format that you have been given. Don't rush; be meticulous. When you have finished, proofread the final copy carefully, looking for spelling or punctuation errors, omitted words, disagreement between subjects and verbs or between pronouns and antecedents, and typographical errors that will detract from the essay you have worked hard to write.

For additional advice on checking your use of sources and documenting in your final essay, see "Some Matters of Form and Documentation" (p. 71). Finally, use "A Checklist for Writing about Literature" (p. 75) to help with a quick review of your final draft.

SOME COMMON WRITING ASSIGNMENTS

A writing assignment for a literature course may require any of a variety of kinds of writing. You might be called on to compare and contrast literary works, to analyze the language of a work, to discuss the interaction of a work's parts, to discuss a work's theme, or to articulate your own responses to the work. Sometimes an instructor may ask simply that you write an essay on one of the pieces you have read. This type of assignment requires you to create your own boundaries — to find a specific focus that both suits the piece you choose and is manageable within a paper of the assigned length. However, in many literature courses, assigned essays tend to fall into one of three modes — explication, analysis, and comparison and contrast — or some combination of these. Familiarity with these three kinds of writing about literature will help you not only with full-length essay assignments but also with exams and other in-class writing.

Explication

In an explication essay, you examine a work in much detail. Line by line, stanza by stanza, scene by scene, you explain each part as fully as you can and show how the author's techniques produce your response. An explication is essentially a demonstration of your thorough understanding of a work.

Here is a sample essay that explicates a relatively difficult poem, Dylan Thomas's "Do Not Go Gentle into That Good Night" (p. 1412).

> Dylan Thomas's villanelle "Do Not Go Gentle into That Good Night" is addressed to his aged father. The poem is remarkable in a number of ways, most notably in that contrary to most common poetic treatments of the inevitability of death, which argue for serenity or celebrate the peace that death provides, this poem urges resistance and rage in the face of death. It justifies that unusual attitude by describing the rage and resistance to death of four kinds of men, who each can summon up the image of a complete and satisfying life that is denied to him by death.
>
> The first tercet of the intricately rhymed villa- nelle opens with an arresting line. The adjective <u>gentle</u> appears where we would expect the adverb <u>gently</u>. The

strange diction suggests that <u>gentle</u> may describe both
the going (i.e., gently dying) and the person (i.e.,
gentleman) who confronts death. Further, the speaker
characterizes "night," here clearly a figure for death,
as "good." Yet in the next line, the speaker urges that
the aged should violently resist death, characterized as
the "close of day" and "the dying of the light." In
effect, the first three lines argue that however good
death may be, the aged should refuse to die gently,
should passionately rave and rage against death.

In the second tercet, the speaker turns to a
description of the way the first of four types of men
confronts death (which is figuratively defined throughout the poem as "that good night" and "the dying of the
light"). These are the "wise men," the scholars, the
philosophers, those who understand the inevitability of
death, men who "know dark is right." But they do not
acquiesce in death "because their words had forked no
lightning," because their published wisdom failed to
bring them to that sense of completeness and fulfillment
that can accept death. Therefore, wise as they are, they
reject the theoretical "rightness" of death and refuse
to "go gentle."

The second sort of men--"good men," the moralists,
the social reformers, those who attempt to better the
world through action as the wise men attempt to better
it through "words"--also rage against death. Their deeds
are, after all, "frail." With sea imagery, the speaker
suggests that these men might have accomplished fine and
fertile things--their deeds "might have danced in a
green bay." But with the "last wave" gone, they see only
the frailty, the impermanence of their acts, and so

they, too, rage against the death that deprives them of the opportunity to leave a meaningful legacy.

The "wild men," the poets who "sang" the loveliness and vitality of nature, also learn as they approach death that the sensuous joys of human existence wane. As the life-giving sun moves toward dusk, as death approaches, their singing turns to grieving, and they refuse to surrender gently, to leave willingly the warmth, pleasure, and beauty that life can give.

Finally, with a pun suggestive of death, the "grave men," those who go through life with such high serious-ness as never to experience gaiety and pleasure, see all the joyous possibilities that they were blind to in life. And they, too, rage against the dying of a light that they had never properly seen before.

The speaker then calls on his aged father to join these men raging against death. Only in this final stanza do we discover that the entire poem is addressed to the speaker's father and that, despite the general-ized statements about old age and the focus on types of men, the poem is a personal lyric. The edge of death becomes a "sad height," the summit of wisdom and experi-ence old age attains includes the sad knowledge of life's failure to satisfy the vision we all pursue. The depth and complexity of the speaker's sadness is startlingly given in the second line when he calls on his father to both curse and bless him. These opposites richly suggest several related possibilities: "Curse me for not living up to your expectations. Curse me for remaining alive as you die. Bless me with forgive-ness for my failings. Bless me for teaching you to rage against death." And the curses and blessings are

> contained in the "fierce tears"--fierce because you will
> burn and rave and rage against death. As the poem closes
> by bringing together the two powerful refrains, the
> speaker himself seems to rage because his father's death
> will cut off a relationship that is incomplete.

This explication deals with the entire poem by coming to grips with each element in it.

You can learn a great deal about the technique of drama by selecting a short, self-contained scene and writing a careful description of it. The length of plays will probably require that you focus on a single segment — a scene, for example — rather than the entire play. This method of explication will force you to confront every speech and stage direction and to come to some conclusion regarding its function. Why is the set furnished as it is? Why does a character speak the words he or she does or remain silent? What do we learn of characters from the interchanges among them? Assume that everything that occurs in the play, whether on the printed page or on the stage, is put there for a purpose. Seek to discover the purpose, and you will, at the same time, discover the peculiar nature of drama.

Fiction, too, can be treated effectively in a formal explication. As with drama, it will be necessary to limit the text: you will not be able to explicate a 10-page story in a 1,000-word essay. Choose a key passage — a half page that reflects the form and content of the overall story, if possible. Often the first half page of a story, where the author, like the playwright, must supply information to the reader, will make a fine text for an explication. Although the explication will deal principally with only an excerpt, feel free to range across the story and show how the introductory material foreshadows what is to come. Or, perhaps, you can explicate the climax of the story — the half page that most pointedly establishes the story's theme — and subject it to a close line-by-line reading that illuminates the whole story.

Analysis

Breaking a literary work down into its elements is only the first step in literary analysis. When you are assigned an analysis essay, you are expected to focus on one of the elements that contributes to the complex compound of a work. This process requires you to extricate the element you plan to explore from the other elements that you can identify, to study this element — not only in isolation but also in relation to the other elements and the work as a whole — and, using the insights you have gained from your special perspective, to make an informed statement about it.

This process may sound complicated, but if you approach it methodically, each stage follows naturally from the stage that precedes it. If, for example, you are to write an analysis essay on characterization in *Othello*, you would begin by thinking about each character in the play. You would then select the character whose development you would like to explore and reread carefully those speeches that help to establish his or her substance. Exploring a character's development in this way involves a good deal of explication: in order to identify the "building blocks" that Shakespeare uses to create a three-dimensional role, you must comb very carefully through that character's speeches and actions. You must also be sensitive to the ways in which other characters respond to these speeches and actions. When you have completed this investigation, you will probably have a good understanding of why you intuitively responded to the character as you did when you first read the play. You will also probably be prepared to make a statement about the character's development: "From a realistic perspective, it is hard to believe that a man of Othello's position could be so gullible; however, Shakespeare develops the role with such craft that we accept the Moor as flesh and blood." At this point, you have moved from the broad *subject* of "characterization in *Othello*" to a *thesis,* a statement that you must prove. As you formulate your thesis, think of it as a position that you intend to *argue* for with a reader you need to persuade. This approach is useful in any essay that requires a thesis, where you move beyond simple explication and commit yourself to a stand. Note that our sample thesis is *argumentative* on two counts; "characterization in *Othello*" is not remotely argumentative. Further, you have more than enough material to write a well-documented essay of 1,000 words supporting your proposition; you cannot write a well-documented 1,000-word essay on the general subject of characterization in *Othello* without being superficial.

You may be one among the many writers who find it difficult to find a starting point. For example, you have been assigned an analysis essay on a very broad subject, such as imagery in love poetry. A few poems come to mind, but you don't know where to begin. You read these poems and underline all the images that you can find. You look at these images over and over, finding no relation among them. You read some more poems, again underlining the images, but you still do not have even the germ of a thesis.

The technique of *freewriting* might help to overcome your block. You have read and reread the poems you intend to write about. Now, put the assignment temporarily out of your mind, and start writing about one or two of the poems without organizing your ideas, without trying to reach a point. Write down what you like about a poem, what you dislike about it, what sort of person the speaker is, which images seemed striking to you — anything at all about the work. If you do this for perhaps ten minutes, you will probably discover that you are voicing opinions. Pick one that interests you or seems the most promising to explore.

The basic form of the analysis assignment has a few variations. Your instructor might narrow the subject in a specific assignment: analyze the development of Othello's character in Act I. This sort of assignment limits the amount of text that you will have to study, but the process from this point on is no different from the process that you would employ to address a broader subject. Sometimes instructors will supply you with a thesis, and you will have to work backward from the thesis to find supporting material. Again, careful analysis of the text is required. The problem you will have to address when writing an analytical essay remains the same regardless of the literary genre you are asked to discuss. You must find an arguable thesis that deals with the sources of your response to the work.

Suppose your instructor has made the following assignment: write an analysis of Harlan Ellison's story " 'Repent, Harlequin!' Said the Ticktock-man," in which you discuss the theme of the story in terms of the characters and the setting. Now consider the following opening (taken from a student paper):

> " 'Repent, Harlequin!' Said the Ticktockman" is a story depicting a society in which time governs one's life. The setting is the United States, the time approximately A.D. 2400 somewhere in the heart of the country. Business deals, work shifts, and school lessons are started and finished with exacting precision. Tardiness is intolerable as this would hinder the system. In a society of order, precision, and punctuality, there is no room for likes, dislikes, scruples, or morals. Thus, personalities in people no longer exist. As these "personless" people know no good or bad, they very happily follow in the course of activities that their society has dictated.

At the outset, can you locate a thesis statement? The only sentences that would seem to qualify are the last three in the paragraph. But notice that, although those sentences are not unreasonable responses to the story, they do not establish a thesis that is *responsive to the assignment*. Because the assignment calls for a discussion of theme in terms of character and setting, a thesis statement should argue how character and setting embody the theme. Here is another opening paragraph on the same assignment (also taken from a student paper):

> Harlan Ellison's " 'Repent, Harlequin!' Said the Ticktockman" opens with a quotation from Thoreau's essay "Civil Disobedience," which establishes the story's

theme. Thoreau's observations about three varieties of
men--those who serve the state as machines, those who
serve it with their heads, and those who serve it with
their consciences--are dramatized in Ellison's story,
which takes place about 400 years in the future in a
setting characterized by machinelike order. The interaction among the three characters, each of whom represents one of Thoreau's types, results in a telling
restatement of his observation that "heroes, patriots,
martyrs, reformers in the great sense, and men . . .
necessarily resist [the state] and . . . are commonly
treated as enemies by it."

Compare these two opening paragraphs sentence by sentence for their re-
sponsiveness to the assignment. The first sentence of the first opening does
not refer to the theme of the story (or to its setting or characterization). In the
second sentence, the discussion of the setting ignores the most important
aspect — that the story is set in a machine- and time-dominated future. The
last three sentences deal obliquely with character, but they are imprecise
and do not establish a thesis. The second opening, on the other hand, immediately states the theme of the story. It goes on to emphasize the relevant
aspects of the futuristic setting and then refers to the three characters that
animate the story in terms of their reactions to the setting. The last sentence
addresses the assignment directly and also serves as a thesis statement for
the paper. It states the proposition that will be developed and supported
in the rest of the paper. The reader of the second opening will expect the
next paragraph of the paper to discuss the setting of the story and subsequent
paragraphs to discuss the response to the setting of the three principal
characters.

   The middles of essays are largely determined by their opening paragraphs.
However long the middle of any essay may be, each of its paragraphs ought
to be responsive to some explicit statement made at the beginning of the
essay. Note that it is practically impossible to predict what the paragraph following the first opening will address. Here is the first half of that next paragraph as the first student wrote it:

   The Harlequin is a man in the society with no
sense of time. His having a personality enables him to
have a sense of moral values and a mind of his own. The

Harlequin thinks that it is obscene and wrong to let
time totally govern the lives of people. So he sets out
to disrupt the time schedule with ridiculous antics such
as showering people with jelly beans to try to break up
the military fashion in which they are used to doing
things.

The paragraph then goes on to discuss the Ticktockman, the capture and brainwashing of the Harlequin, and the resulting lateness of the Ticktockman.

Note that nothing in the opening of this student's paper prepared readers for the introduction of the Harlequin. In fact, the opening concluded rather inaccurately that the people within the story "happily follow in the course of activities that their society has dictated." Hence, the description of the Harlequin in the second paragraph is wholly unexpected. Further, because the student has not dealt with the theme of the story (as the assignment asked), the comments about the Harlequin's antics remain disconnected from any clear purpose. They are essentially devoted to what teachers constantly warn against: a mere plot summary. The student has obviously begun to write before she has analyzed the story sufficiently to understand its theme. With further thought, the student would have perceived that the central thematic issue is resistance to an oppressive state — the issue stated in the epigraph from Thoreau. On the other hand, because the second opening makes that thematic point clearly, we can expect it to be followed by a discussion of the environment (that is, the setting) in which the action occurs. Here is such a paragraph taken from the second student's paper:

Ellison creates a society that reflects one possible future development of the modern American passion
for productivity and efficiency. The setting is in
perfect keeping with the time-conscious people who
inhabit the city. It is pictured as a neat, colorless,
and mechanized city. No mention is made of nature:
grass, flowers, trees, and birds do not appear. The
buildings are in a "Mondrian arrangement," stark and
geometrical. The cold steel sidewalks, slowstrips, and
expresstrips move with precision. Like a chorus line,
people move in unison to board the movers without a

```
wasted motion. Doors close silently and lock themselves
automatically. An ideal efficiency so dominates the
social system that any "wasted time" is deducted from
the life of an inefficient citizen.
```

Once the setting has been established, the writer turns to the characters, linking those characters to thematic considerations, beginning with a short transitional paragraph that shapes the remainder of the middle of the essay:

```
     Into this smoothly functioning but coldly mech-
anized society, Ellison introduces three characters:
Pretty Alice, one of Thoreau's machinelike creatures;
the Ticktockman, one of those who "serve the state
chiefly with their heads, and, as they rarely make any
moral distinctions, they are as likely to serve the
devil without intending it, as God"; and Everett C.
Marm, the Harlequin, whose conscience forces him to
resist the oppressive state.
```

Following a logical organization, the essay then includes a paragraph devoted to each of the three characters:

```
     Pretty Alice is, probably, very pretty. (Everett
didn't fall in love with her brains.) In the brief
section in which we meet her, we find her hopelessly
ordinary in her attitudes. She is upset that Marm finds
it necessary to go about "annoying people." She finds
him ridiculous and wishes only that he would stay home,
as other people do. Clearly, she has no understanding of
what Everett is struggling against. Though her anger
finally leads her to betray him, Everett himself can't
believe that she has done so. His own loyal and under-
standing nature colors his view of her so thoroughly
that he cannot imagine the treachery that must have been
```

so simple and satisfying for Pretty Alice, whose only
desire is to be like everybody else.

The Ticktockman is more complex. He sees himself as
a servant of the state, and he performs his duties with
resolution and competence. He skillfully supports a
System he has never questioned. The System exists; it
must be good. His conscience is simply not involved in
the performance of his duty. He is one of those who
follows orders and expects others to follow orders. As a
result, the behavior of the Harlequin is more than just
an irritant or a rebellion against authority. It is
unnerving. The Ticktockman wishes to understand that
behavior, and with Everett's time-card in his hand, he
muses that he has the name of "what he is . . . not who
he is. . . . Before I can exercise proper revocation, I
have to know who this what is." And when he confronts
Everett, he does not just liquidate him. He insists that
Everett repent. He tries to convince Everett that the
System is sound, and when he cannot win the argument,
he dutifully reconditions Everett, since he is, after
all, more interested in justifying the System than in
destroying its enemies. It is easy to see this man
as a competent servant of the devil who thinks he is
serving God.

But only Everett C. Marm truly serves the state
because his conscience requires him to resist. He is
certainly not physically heroic. His very name suggests
weak conformity. Though he loves his Pretty Alice, he
cannot resign from the rebellious campaign on which his
conscience insists. So without violence, and mainly
with the weapon of laughter, he attacks the mechanical
precision of the System and succeeds in breaking it down

    simply by making people late. He is himself, as Pretty

    Alice points out, always late, and the delays that his

    antics produce seriously threaten the well-being of the

    smooth but mindless System he hates. He is captured and

    refuses, even then, to submit, and so his personality is

    destroyed by the authorities that fear him. The

    Ticktockman is too strong for him.

An appropriate ending emerges naturally from this student's treatment of the assignment. Having established that the story presents characters who deal in different ways with the oppressive quality of life in a time- and machine-obsessed society, the student concludes with a comment on the author's criticisms of such a society:

    Harlequin is defeated, but Ellison, finally, leaves

    us with an optimistic note. The idea of rebellion

    against the System will linger in the minds of others.

    There will be more Harlequins and more disruption of

    this System. Many rebels will be defeated, but any

    System that suppresses individualism will give birth to

    resistance. And Harlequin's defeat is by no means total.

    The story ends with the Ticktockman himself arriving for

    work three minutes late.

Comparison and Contrast

An essay in comparison and contrast shows how two works are similar to and different from one another. It almost always starts with a recognition of similarities, often of subject matter. Most comparison-and-contrast assignments involve two works of the same genre. While it is possible to compare *any* two works, the best comparison-and-contrast essays emerge from the analysis of two works similar enough to illuminate each other. Two works about love, or death, or conformity, or innocence, or identity give you something to begin with. Both Dickinson's "Apparently with no surprise" (p. 1389) and Frost's "Design" (p. 1395) are about death, and they both use remarkably similar events as the occasion for their poems. Starting with these similarities, you would soon find yourself noting the contrasts (in tone, for example, and theme) between nineteenth-century and twentieth-century views of the nature of God.

Before you begin writing a comparison-and-contrast essay, it is especially important to have clearly in mind the points of comparison and contrast you wish to discuss and the order in which you can most effectively discuss them. You will need to give careful thought to the best way to organize your paper, jotting down the plan your comparison will follow. As a general rule, it is best to avoid dividing the essay into separate discussions of each work. That method tends to produce two separate, loosely joined analysis essays. The successful comparison-and-contrast essay treats some point of similarity or contrast between the two works, then moves on to succeeding points, and ends with an evaluation of the comparative merits of the works.

Like any essay that goes beyond simple explication, a comparison-and-contrast essay requires a strong thesis statement. However, a comparison-and-contrast thesis is generally not difficult to formulate: you must identify the works under consideration and state clearly your reasons for making the comparison.

Here is a student paper that compares and contrasts Dylan Thomas's "Do Not Go Gentle into That Good Night" with the poetic response it triggered from a poet with different views:

Dylan Thomas's "Do Not Go Gentle into That Good Night" and Catherine Davis's "After a Time" demand comparison: Davis's poem was written in deliberate response to Thomas's. Davis assumes the reader's familiarity with "Do Not Go Gentle . . . ," which she uses to articulate her contrasting ideas. "After a Time," although it is a literary work in its own right, might even be thought of as serious parody--perhaps the greatest compliment one writer can pay another.

"Do Not Go Gentle into That Good Night" was written by a young man of thirty-eight who addresses it to his old and ailing father. Perhaps because Thomas had very little of his own self-destructive life left as he was composing this piece, he seems to have more insight into the subject of death than most people of his age. He advocates raging and fighting against it, not giving in and accepting it.

"After a Time" was written by Davis at about the same age and is addressed to no one in particular. Davis has a different philosophy about death. She "answers" Thomas's poem and presents her differing views using the same poetic form--a villanelle. Evidently, she felt it necessary to present a contrasting point of view eight years after Thomas's death.

While "Do Not Go Gentle . . ." protests and rages against death, Davis's poem suggests a quiet resignation and acquiescence. She seems to feel that raging against death is useless and profitless. She argues that we will eventually become tame, anyway, after the raging is done.

Thomas talks about different types of men and why they rage against death. "Wise men" desire immortality. They rage against death occurring before they've made their mark on history. "Good men" lament the frailty of their deeds. Given more time, they might have accomplished great things. "Wild men" regret their constant hedonistic pursuits. With more time they could prove their worth. "Grave men" are quite the opposite and regret they never took time for the pleasures in life. Now it is too late. They rage against death because they are not ready for it.

His father's death is painful to Thomas because he sees himself lying in that bed; his father's dying reminds him of his own inevitable death. The passion of the last stanza, in which the poet asks his father to bless and curse him, suggests that he has doubts about his relationship with his father. He may feel that he has not been a good enough son. He put off doing things with and for his father because he always felt there would be time later. Now time has run out and he feels cheated.

Catherine Davis advocates a calm submission, a peaceful acquiescence. She feels raging is useless and says that those of us who rage will finally "go tame / When what we have we can no longer use." When she says "One more thing lost is one thing less to lose," the reader can come to terms with the loss of different aspects of the mind and body, such as strength, eyesight, hearing, and intellect. Once one of these is lost, it's one thing less to worry about losing. After a time, everything will be lost, and we'll accept that, too, because we'll be ready for it.

Thomas's imagery is vivid and powerful. His various men not only rage and rave, they <u>burn</u>. Their words "forked no lightning," their deeds might have "danced in a green bay," they "sang the sun in flight," and they see that "blind eyes could blaze like meteors." Davis's images are quiet and generally abstract, without much sensory suggestiveness, as in "things lost," a "reassuring ruse," and "all losses are the same." Her most powerful image--"And we go stripped at last the way we came"--makes its point with none of the excitement of Thomas's rage. And yet, I prefer the quiet intelligence of Davis to the high energy of Thomas.

"And we go stripped at last the way we came" can give strange comfort and solace to those of us who always envied those in high places. People are not

```
all created equal at birth, not by a long shot. But
we will all be equal when we die. All wealth, power,
and trappings will be left behind and we will all
ultimately be equal. So why rage? It won't do us
any good.
```

THE RESEARCH PAPER

Research papers depend on secondary sources (the primary source is, of course, the work, the historical event, or the literary theory you are studying). Research assignments send you to the library, to the Web, or to any source of information that bears on your project. Whether you are researching to discover the varied responses to a work, to gain some insight into the author's life and times, or to identify relevant critical principles, you will synthesize what you have read *about* the work into a well-organized paper and provide *proper documentation*. But a research paper is not a mindless recitation of what your secondary sources have said. Nor does it require you to suspend your own critical judgment. By the time you settle into writing your paper, you will have learned some things you didn't know before. You have earned — and ought to exercise — the right to make some judgments. An assigned research topic will probably ask you to come to some conclusions. If you choose your own topic, you must discover in your research support for a clear, focused thesis before you begin to write.

Here is a sample student research paper that illustrates the technique. The marginal notes call attention to some of the details that make this a successful effort. In general, notice that the author has done research, but the paper is not weighed down with it. The opening paragraph provides a historical context for the subject of the paper, Kate Chopin's short story "The Storm" (p. 1016). The writer has a point of view about the story, or thesis, stated in the second paragraph. While that thesis is developed throughout, the writer makes interesting observations on such matters as the relationship of other Chopin works to the story, the names of characters, local color, and a notable change in American moral attitudes. Note how the writer concludes with two paragraphs that resolve the issues raised in the opening two paragraphs.

The sample paper embodies the Modern Language Association's (MLA) standard documentation and footnote form. The section that follows the research paper provides further samples that will help you manage formal matters and documentation. It concludes with a checklist that you might want to consult both before you begin writing your paper and before you submit your final draft.

An Annotated Student Research Paper

Writer's name
and page
number.

Krissa Lagos

Use MLA
standard style or
follow
instructor's
criteria.

Professor Richard Abcarian

English 255

Center title.

Sex and Sensibility

in Kate Chopin's "The Storm"

Kate Chopin's openly erotic depictions of

marital infidelity in her literary works separate her

First paragraph
establishes
context.

from all other American female writers of her time.

The adulterous affair of a strong independent woman

depicted in her novel The Awakening (1899) created a

public scandal. And, though she "never flouted

convention as strongly as did her fictitious heroine,

she did exhibit an individuality and strength

Documents an
Internet source
with no page
number (see
Works Cited).

remarkable for upper-middle-class women of the time"

(Moon). Her honest and direct portrayal of the

sexuality of her female characters was rejected until

well into the 1900s, when the minds of readers caught

Documents a
book in Works
Cited and gives
page number.

up to her advanced thinking (Skaggs 5). Works such

as "The Storm"--once shunned (especially by the

male community) because of their focus on sexual

exploration--are now celebrated as serious liter-

ature. In fact, when Chopin wrote "The Storm" in 1898,

she knew that no magazine would ever publish such an

uninhibited and uncritical account of an adulterous

encounter, and so never attempted to have it published

(Toth 206).

Lagos 2

In "The Storm," Chopin utilizes the irony
characteristic of her writing to give the story a
light, easy feel. She also uses diction and imagery to
draw the reader into the emotions of her characters.
She ignores the usual implications of unfaithfulness
to a spouse, and instead focuses on the pleasure
inspired by the instant gratification of physical
desire.

States the elements of the paper's thesis.

"The Storm" is in fact a sequel to another short
story, "At the 'Cadian Ball." In the first tale, which
takes place in Louisiana, a favorite setting for
Chopin,[1] a farmer named Bobinôt is captivated with
spirited, Spanish-blooded Calixta. Calixta, however,
has her eyes on a handsome local planter, Alcée
Laballière, who is charmed by her attractive features
and openly sexual attitude. At the end of the night,
however, Clarisse, a woman who is Alcée's social equal
(and also happens to be his cousin), suddenly appears
and agrees to marry him. Calixta, deserted by Alcée,
is "deemed lucky to get anyone, even stodgy Bobinôt"
(Ewell 77).

Provides important context for the story's events.

By setting "The Storm" in Louisiana, Chopin is
able to take advantage of the unstable, muggy weather
of the region to help build up to the story's climax.
The events of the tale occur because of the weather:
the storm strands Bobinôt and his son Bibi at a store
while wife and mother Calixta is at home, and Alcée is
driven into Bobinôt and Calixta's house by the
approaching rain. More subtle events, nearly all of
which carry sensual undercurrents, are also inspired
by the weather conditions.

Discusses the significance of setting.

Uses concrete examples to bolster assertions.

For instance, when Calixta is first mentioned she is sewing, and Chopin immediately introduces an indirect sexual undertone to her movements: "[. . .] she felt very warm and often stopped to mop her face on which the perspiration gathered in beads. She unfastened her white sacque at the throat" (Chopin, "The Storm" 1016). Except for what follows, there would be no reason at all to interpret this minor event. However, when Alcée arrives, the loosened collar eventually leads to more than one would imagine possible. First, Calixta is driven into his arms by the lightning crashing all around the house. Alcée attempts to ease her fears while at the same time fighting the desire for her that has been reawakened by contact with her body. Her unbuttoned collar is part of what defeats his battle against his desires:

> He pushed her hair back from her face that
> was warm and steaming. Her lips were as red
> and moist as pomegranate seed. Her white
> neck and a glimpse of her full firm bosom
> disturbed him powerfully. As she glanced
> up at him the fear in her liquid blue eyes
> had given place to a drowsy gleam that
> unconsciously betrayed a sensuous desire.
> (Chopin, "The Storm" 1018)

Obviously the sole reason for Calixta and Alcée succumbing to their passions is not that she unbuttoned her shirt collar. However, the accumulation of this and other details--their shared climax with the storm, the correspondence between them lying

Bracketed ellipses indicate omission in a direct quote.

Identifies the specific work from the Works Cited list when there is more than one work by the same author.

Shows how Chopin uses details to advance the plot.

contented afterward while the storm departs softly--
make this story a powerful work of art. Chopin crafts
her sentences to enhance her narrative's power.

The French Louisiana setting of "The Storm" is
typical of many of her writings (Ewell 52). The
detailed local color is reflected by the French names
of the characters. Calixta, Bobinôt, and Bibi speak
the 'Cadian dialect of Louisiana, which in Calixta's
case occasionally includes a small smattering of
French (Ewell 77). Alcée, in contrast, speaks
impeccable English, reflective of his better education. Chopin inserts a significant detail at the
beginning of the story when Bobinôt purchases
"a can of shrimps, of which Calixta was very fond"
(Chopin, "The Storm" 1016). The small gesture reveals
Bobinôt's affectionate appreciation of his wife.

In "The Storm," Chopin conveys the theme of
autonomy, something familiar to her female characters, especially in "The Story of an Hour."[2] Both
Calixta and Clarisse are happiest in "The Storm" when
they are separated from their husbands and free to do
as they wish.

> As for Clarisse, she was charmed upon
> receiving her husband's letter. She and the
> babies were doing well. The society was
> agreeable; many of her old friends seemed to
> restore the pleasant liberty of her maiden
> days. Devoted as she was to her husband,
> their intimate conjugal life was something
> which she was more than willing to forego
> for a while. (Chopin, "The Storm" 1020)

Discusses
Chopin's view
of the rights of
women.

Therefore Clarisse, though far from the actual storm, benefits from its effects. She feels unfettered, pleased at being given space for the first time since she has been married to Alcée. For Calixta, the short time she spends with Alcée during the storm is enough to make her lift "her pretty chin in the air" and laugh with delight (Chopin "The Storm" 1019).

Earlier story is used to establish Alcée's character.

In "At the 'Cadian Ball," the two couples are paired together at the end of the night due to Alcée's notion of honor and propriety (Ewell 77). As Chopin explains in "The Storm," he never intended to marry Calixta, but he did want more from her than what he took in the story's prequel at the ball: "If she was not an immaculate dove in those days, she was still inviolate; a passionate creature whose very defense-lessness had made her defense, against which his honor forbade him to prevail" (Chopin, "The Storm" 1018). When the ball ended only Calixta was left unsatisfied, but by the time "The Storm" takes place, only Bobinôt is still utterly content.

The fact that Calixta is now married somehow frees Alcée from his previous restraints, and he is able to satisfy his craving for her at last. As a result, Alcée is also more content with his wife away, which leads him to write the letter to her urging her to prolong her stay in Biloxi. Bobinôt is the most easily pleased of all. He reaches home cringing at what his wife will say to him and Bibi when she notices how dirty they are. Luckily for the father and son, she is still glowing from her brief interlude with Alcée, and "they laughed

much and so loud that anyone might have heard them
as far away as Laballière's" (Chopin, "The Storm"
1019).

Chopin's irony shines through "The Storm" in
many parts of the story. One of these moments occurs
when she addresses the issue of natural right while
Calixta and Alcée are making love: "Her firm, elastic
flesh that was knowing for the first time its birthright, was like a creamy lily that the sun invites to
contribute its breath and perfume to the undying life
of the world" (Chopin, "The Storm" 1018). Chopin goes
further than condoning the affair between Calixta and
Alcée by describing it as something completely
natural, an event that was meant to occur.

What would have been most shocking to audiences
in the nineteenth century was the fact that when the
storm ended, there were no repercussions. Alcée
"turned and smiled" at Calixta "with a beaming
face" and rode away. Calixta showed "nothing but
satisfaction" when her husband and son returned home,
Bobinôt and Bibi "began to relax and enjoy themselves" when they saw that Calixta was in good
spirits, and Clarisse stayed in Biloxi, enjoying
herself. For such severe sins to be committed and go
unpunished was unheard of in Chopin's time, and "even
today some readers find that conclusion unforgivable"
(Skaggs 62).

Asserts the
proven thesis
stated in the
second
paragraph.

In truth, this very conclusion elevates "The
Storm" to the high level it resides on. Through
adultery, deception, and self-indulgence, the
characters achieve happiness, a surprise ending that

Chopin adopted from Maupassant.[3] This ironic twist makes the story a unique departure from the norm, even today, and "The Storm" ends on a comic note, the reader left as contented as the story's characters.

Lagos 8

Notes

[1]Chopin set many of her stories in the Cane River
country of Louisiana; her husband, Oscar, was raised
in Louisiana, and they lived there together for twelve
years (Toth 92).

[2]In Chopin's "The Story of an Hour," the main
character discovers that she prizes individual
freedom over all else--even the life and love of her
husband.

[3]Guy de Maupassant (1850-1893) was a French
writer whose short stories often featured surprise
endings.

Lagos 9

Works Cited

Abcarian, Richard, and Marvin Klotz, eds. <u>Literature:</u>
   <u>The Human Experience</u>. 8th ed. Boston: Bedford,
   2002.

Chopin, Kate. "At the 'Cadian Ball." <u>The Complete</u>
   <u>Works of Kate Chopin</u>. Ed. Per Seyersted. Baton
   Rouge: Louisiana State UP, 1969. 219-227.

---. "The Storm." Abcarian and Klotz 1016-1020.

Ewell, Barbara C. <u>Kate Chopin</u>. New York: Ungar, 1986.

Moon, Jennifer. "ClassicNote on Kate Chopin."
   <u>ClassicNotes by GradeSaver</u>. 30 Mar. 2000
   <http://www.classicnote.com/ClassicNotes
   /Authors/about_kate_chopin.html>.

Skaggs, Peggy. <u>Kate Chopin</u>. New York: Twayne, 1985.

Toth, Emily. <u>Unveiling Kate Chopin</u>. Jackson: UP of
   Mississippi, 1999.

SOME MATTERS OF FORM AND DOCUMENTATION

After you have worked hard to draft, revise, and edit an essay, check to be sure you have documented your sources accurately and fairly. A consistent, well-documented essay allows readers to focus on your argument rather than on your document.

Titles

When included in the body of your essay, the first word and all main words of titles are capitalized. Ordinarily (unless they are the first or last word), articles (*a, an,* and *the*), prepositions (*in, on, of, with, about,* and so on), conjunctions (*and, but, or,* and so on), and the *to* in an infinitive ("A Good Man Is Hard to Find") are not capitalized.

The titles of short stories, poems, articles, essays, songs, episodes of television programs, and parts of larger collections are enclosed in quotation marks.

The titles of plays, books, movies, periodicals, operas, television series, recordings, paintings, Web sites, and newspapers are italicized or underlined. If you are not writing with a word processor that produces italic type that is easily distinguishable from nonitalic type, use underlining.

The title you give your own essay is neither placed in quotation marks nor underlined. However, the title of a literary work used as a part of your title would be either placed in quotation marks or italicized, depending on the type of work it is.

Quotations

Quotation marks indicate that you are transcribing someone else's words; those words must, therefore, be *exactly* as they appear in your source.

As a general rule, quotations of not more than four lines of prose or two lines of poetry are placed between quotation marks and incorporated in your own text:

> Near the end of "Young Goodman Brown," the narrator asks, "Had Goodman Brown fallen asleep in the forest and only dreamed a wild dream of a witch-meeting?" (16).

If you are quoting two lines of verse in your text, indicate the division between lines with a slash. Leave a space before and after the slash:

> Prufrock hears the dilettantish talk in a room where "the women come and go / Talking of Michelangelo."

Longer quotations are indented ten spaces from the left margin and are double-spaced. They are not enclosed in quotation marks, since the indention signals a quotation.

Brackets and Ellipses   If you insert anything into a quotation — even a word — the inserted material must be placed within brackets. If you wish to omit some material from a passage in quotation marks, the omission must be indicated with ellipsis points — three equally spaced periods. The latest edition of the Modern Language Association's (MLA) handbook (1999) recommends placing brackets around ellipsis points you insert to distinguish them from spaced periods used in your source. (You may wish to check with your instructor before following this new guideline.) When an ellipsis occurs between complete sentences or at the end of a sentence, a fourth period, indicating the end of the sentence, should be inserted.

Here is an example of a full quotation from an original source:

> As one critic puts it, "Richard Wright, like Dostoevsky before him, sends his hero underground to discover the truth about the upper world, a world that has forced him to confess to a crime he has not committed."

Here is the quotation with insertion and omissions:

> As one critic puts it, "Richard Wright [. . .] sends his hero [Fred Daniels] underground to discover the truth about the upper world [. . .]."

Use a full line of spaced periods within brackets to indicate the omission of a line or more of poetry:

> For I have known them all already, known them all--
> Have known the evenings, mornings, afternoons,
> I have measured out my life with coffee spoons;
> [. . . . .]
> And I have known the eyes already, known them all--
> The eyes that fix you in a formulated phrase.

Quotation Marks and Other Punctuation   Periods and commas are placed *inside* quotation marks:

> In "The Lesson," the narrator describes Miss Moore as someone "who always looked like she was going to church, though she never did."

Other punctuation marks such as colons or semicolons go outside the concluding quotation marks unless they are part of the material being quoted.

```
Bartleby repeatedly insists that he "would prefer not

to"; eventually these words become haunting.
```

For poetry quotations, provide the line number or numbers in parentheses
immediately following the quotation:

```
With ironic detachment, Prufrock declares that he is "no

prophet" (83).
```

Documentation

You must acknowledge sources for the ideas you paraphrase or summarize
and material you quote. Such acknowledgments are extremely important,
for even an unintentional failure to give formal credit to others for their
words or ideas can leave you open to an accusation of *plagiarism* — that is,
the presentation of someone else's ideas as your own.

In the body of your essay, use parenthetical citations to document those
works that you quote, paraphrase, or summarize. A list of your sources
should be the last page of your essay, the Works Cited page. If you use other
kinds of sources not listed here, consult the *MLA Handbook for Writers of
Research Papers,* fifth edition (1999), or online at <www.mla.org>.

This whimsical paragraph demonstrates the use of parenthetical citations.

```
     Leslie Fiedler's view of the relationship between

Jim and Huck (669-70) uses a method often discussed by

other critics (Abcarian and Klotz 6-10). Cooper's 1971

study (180) raises similar issues, although such methods

are not useful when dealing with such a line as "North

Richmond Street, being blind, was a quiet street except

at the hour when the Christian Brothers' School set the

boys free" (Joyce, "Araby" 100). But when Joyce refers

to the weather (Dubliners 224), the issue becomes

clouded.
```

The first citation gives only the page reference, which is all that is necessary because the author's name is given in the text and only one work by that
author appears in the list of works cited. The second citation gives the
editors' names and thus identifies the work being cited. It then indicates the

appropriate pages. The third citation, because the author's name is mentioned in the text, gives only a page reference. The fourth citation must provide the author's name *and* the work cited, because two works by the same author appear in the list of works cited. The last citation, because it refers to an author with two works in the list of works cited, gives the name of the work and the page where the reference can be found.

In short, your parenthetical acknowledgment should contain (1) the *minimum* information required to lead the reader to the appropriate work in the list of works cited and (2) the location within the work to which you refer. Citations give credit whenever it is due and enable your reader to go directly to your sources as quickly and easily as possible.

Works Cited

Abcarian, Richard, and Marvin Klotz, eds. Literature:

The Human Experience. 8th ed. Boston: Bedford,

2002.

Cooper, Wendy. Hair, Sex, Society, Symbolism. New York:

Stein, 1971.

Fiedler, Leslie. "Come Back to the Raft Ag'in, Huck

Honey." Partisan Review 15 (1948): 664-71.

Joyce, James. "Araby." Abcarian and Klotz 100-04.

---. Dubliners. Eds. Robert Scholes and A. Walton Litz.

New York: Penguin, 1976.

The first of these citations is for this book. Note that the first editor's name is presented surname first, but the second is presented with the surname last. The second entry illustrates the form for citing a book with one author. The third gives the form for an article published in a periodical (note that the title of the article is in quotes and the title of the journal is underlined). The fourth entry shows how to cite a work included in an anthology. The fifth citation, because it is by the same author as the fourth, begins with three hyphens in place of the author's name.

Documenting Internet Sources The *MLA Handbook for Writers of Research Papers,* fifth edition (1999), one of the standard guides in the field, notes that the Internet as a research source is so new that "few standards currently govern the presentation of electronic publications." The form suggested below will probably serve for most citations to online books, articles, online databases, and other kinds of sites. Keep in mind, however, that if it does not, you will have to decide for yourself the best way to include additional information.

1. Author's name
2. Title of the work in quotation marks
3. Name of the periodical (underlined)
4. Volume or issue number (if any)
5. Date of publication
6. Page number(s)
7. Network address (enclosed in <angle brackets>)

> Moon, Jennifer. "ClassicNote on Kate Chopin."
> <u>ClassicNotes by GradeSaver</u>. 30 March 2000
> <http://www.classicnote.com/ClassicNotes
> /Authors/about_kate_chopin.html>.

A CHECKLIST FOR WRITING ABOUT LITERATURE

1. Is my essay clearly responsive to the assignment?

2. Does my essay put forward a clearly defined thesis at the outset?

3. Does each paragraph have an identifiable topic sentence?

4. Have I marshaled my paragraphs logically and provided appropriate transitions?

5. Do I support my assertions with evidence?

6. Have I used direct quotations appropriately, and have I transcribed them accurately?

7. Do I document the sources of other people's ideas and the direct quotations I use? Is the documentation in appropriate form?

8. Have I written syntactically correct sentences (no run-ons and no fragments except by design)?

9. Have I eliminated as many passive constructions and forms of the verb *to be* as possible?

10. Have I avoided long sequences (say, three or more) of prepositional phrases?

11. Can I feel good about this essay? Does it embody serious thinking in attractive form (free of typos and other errors)? Can I put my name on the essay with pride?

Innocence and Experience

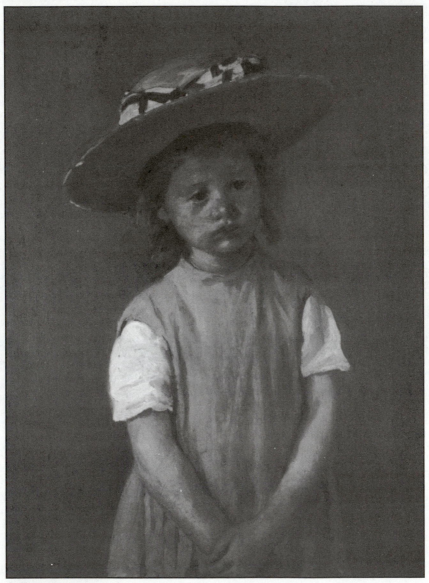

Child in a Straw Hat, 1886, by Mary Cassatt.

We come newborn to every milestone of life's journey, and often act
like novices at each, no matter what our age.

— LA ROCHEFOUCAULD

. . . if anything is a suprise then there is not much difference between
older or younger because the only thing that does make anybody
older is that they cannot be surprised.

— GERTRUDE STEIN

In the eyes of youth we see a flame, but in the eyes
of the aged we see light.

— VICTOR HUGO

Children's talent to endure stems from their ignorance of alternatives.

— MAYA ANGELOU

The trouble with using experience as a guide is that the final exam often
comes first and then the lesson.

— UNKNOWN

One of the definitions of the loss of innocence is perhaps the fragmenting
of that united self — a split that is different, and emblematic, not only for
each sex, but also for each era.

— MOLLY HASKELL

Youth, have no pity; leave no farthing here. For age
to invest in compromise and fear.

— EDNA ST. VINCENT MILLAY

Humans strive to give order and meaning to their lives, to reduce the mystery and unpredictability that constantly threaten them. Life is infinitely more complex and surprising than we imagine, and the categories we establish to give it order and meaning are, for the most part, "momentary stays against confusion." At any time, the equilibrium of our lives, the comfortable image of ourselves and the world around us, may be disrupted by something new, forcing us into painful reevaluation. These disruptions create pain, anxiety, and terror but also wisdom and awareness.

The works in this section deal generally with the movement of a central character from moral simplicities and certainties into a more complex and problematic world. Though these works frequently deal with awareness, even wisdom, their central figures rarely act decisively. The main character or protagonist is more often a passive figure who learns the difference between the ideal world he or she imagines and the injurious real world. If the protagonist survives the ordeal, he or she often becomes a better human — better able to wrest some satisfaction from a bleak and threatening world. Many of the works here deal with the passage from childhood to adulthood, a time of simplicities and certainties that give way to the complexities and uncertainties of adult life.

Almost universally, innocence is associated with childhood and youth, as experience is with age. We teach the young about an ideal world, without explaining that it has not yet been and may never be achieved. As innocents, children are terribly vulnerable to falsehood, to intrusive sexuality, and to the machinations of the wicked, who often triumph.

But the terms *innocence* and *experience* range widely in meaning, and that range is reflected here. Innocence may be defined almost biologically, as illustrated by the sexual innocence of the young boy in Frank O'Connor's "My Oedipus Complex." Innocence may be social — the innocence of Brown in Nathaniel Hawthorne's "Young Goodman Brown." Or innocence may be seen as the child's ignorance of his or her own mortality, as in Gerard Manley Hopkins's "Spring and Fall" and Dylan Thomas's "Fern Hill." In such works as Nathaniel Hawthorne's "Young Goodman Brown" and Robert Browning's "My Last Duchess," one discovers the tragic consequences of an innocence that is blind.

The contrast between what we thought in our youth and what we have come to know, painfully, as adults stands as an emblem of the passage from innocence to experience. Yet all of us remain, to one degree or another, innocent throughout life, since we never — except with death — stop learning from experience. Looked at in this way, experience is the ceaseless assault life makes on our innocence, moving us to a greater wisdom about ourselves and the world around us.

LOOKING AHEAD:
Questions for Thinking and Writing

As you read the selections in this section, consider the following questions. You may want to write out your thoughts informally in a journal or notebook as a way of preparing to respond to the selections, or you may wish to make one of these questions the basis for a formal essay.

1. Innocence is often associated with childhood, and responsibility with adulthood. Were you happier or more contented as a preteen than you are now? Why? Which particular aspects of your childhood do you remember with pleasure? Which with pain? Do you look forward to the future with pleasurable anticipation or with dread? Why?

2. Do you know any adults who seem to be innocents? On what do you base your judgment? Do you know any preteens who seem to be particularly "adult" in their behavior (beyond politeness and good manners — they may, for example, have to cope with severe family difficulties)? On what do you base your judgment?

3. Most of you have spent your lives under the authority of others, such as parents, teachers, and employers. How do you deal with authorities you resent? Do you look forward to exercising authority over others (your own children, your own students, employees under your supervision)? How will your experiences affect your behavior as an authority figure?

4. How does the growth from innocence to experience affect one's sexual behavior? Social behavior? Political behavior?

Innocence and Experience

Fiction

Nathaniel Hawthorne (1804–1864)

Young Goodman Brown 1846

Young Goodman[1] Brown came forth at sunset into the street at Salem village;
but put his head back, after crossing the threshold, to exchange a parting
kiss with his young wife. And Faith, as the wife was aptly named, thrust her own
pretty head into the street, letting the wind play with the pink ribbons of her cap
while she called to Goodman Brown.

"Dearest heart," whispered she, softly and rather sadly, when her lips were
close to his ear, "prithee put off your journey until sunrise and sleep in your own
bed to-night. A lone woman is troubled with such dreams and such thoughts
that she's afeared of herself sometimes. Pray tarry with me this night, dear husband, of all nights in the year."

"My love and my Faith," replied young Goodman Brown, "of all nights in
the year, this one night must I tarry away from thee. My journey, as thou callest
it, forth and back again, must needs be done 'twixt now and sunrise. What,
my sweet, pretty wife, dost thou doubt me already, and we but three months
married?"

"Then God bless you!" said Faith, with the pink ribbons; "and may you find all
well when you come back."

"Amen!" cried Goodman Brown. "Say thy prayers, dear Faith, and go to bed 5
at dusk, and no harm will come to thee."

So they parted; and the young man pursued his way until, being about to turn
the corner by the meeting-house, he looked back and saw the head of Faith still
peeping after him with a melancholy air, in spite of her pink ribbons.

"Poor little Faith!" thought he, for his heart smote him. "What a wretch am I
to leave her on such an errand! She talks of dreams, too. Methought as she
spoke there was trouble in her face, as if a dream had warned her what work is

---

[1] Equivalent to *Mr.*, a title given to a man below the rank of gentleman.

to be done to-night. But no, no; 'twould kill her to think it. Well, she's a blessed angel on earth; and after this one night I'll cling to her skirts and follow her to heaven."

With this excellent resolve for the future, Goodman Brown felt himself justified in making more haste on his present evil purpose. He had taken a dreary road, darkened by all the gloomiest trees of the forest, which barely stood aside to let the narrow path creep through, and closed immediately behind. It was all as lonely as could be; and there is this peculiarity in such a solitude, that the traveller knows not who may be concealed by the innumerable trunks and the thick boughs overhead; so that with lonely footsteps he may yet be passing through an unseen multitude.

"There may be a devilish Indian behind every tree," said Goodman Brown to himself; and he glanced fearfully behind him as he added, "What if the devil himself should be at my very elbow!"

His head being turned back, he passed a crook of the road, and, looking for- 10 ward again, beheld the figure of a man, in grave and decent attire, seated at the foot of an old tree. He arose at Goodman Brown's approach and walked onward side by side with him.

"You are late, Goodman Brown," said he. "The clock of the Old South[2] was striking as I came through Boston, and that is full fifteen minutes agone."

"Faith kept me back a while," replied the young man, with a tremor in his voice, caused by the sudden appearance of his companion, though not wholly unexpected.

It was now deep dusk in the forest, and deepest in that part of it where these two were journeying. As nearly as could be discerned, the second traveller was about fifty years old, apparently in the same rank of life as Goodman Brown, and bearing a considerable resemblance to him, though perhaps more in expression than features. Still they might have been taken for father and son. And yet, though the elder person was as simply clad as the younger, and as simple in manner too, he had an indescribable air of one who knew the world, and who would not have felt abashed at the governor's dinner table or in King William's[3] court, were it possible that his affairs should call him thither. But the only thing about him that could be fixed upon as remarkable was his staff, which bore the likeness of a great black snake, so curiously wrought that it might almost be seen to twist and wriggle itself like a living serpent. This, of course, must have been an ocular deception, assisted by the uncertain light.

"Come, Goodman Brown," cried his fellow-traveller, "this is a dull pace for the beginning of a journey. Take my staff, if you are so soon weary."

"Friend," said the other, exchanging his slow pace for a full stop, "having kept 15 covenant by meeting thee here, it is my purpose now to return whence I came. I have scruples touching the matter thou wot'st of."

"Sayest thou so?" replied he of the serpent, smiling apart. "Let us walk on,

[2] A church in Boston.
[3] Ruler of England from 1689 to 1702.

nevertheless, reasoning as we go; and if I convince thee not thou shalt turn back. We are but a little way in the forest yet."

"Too far! too far!" exclaimed the goodman, unconsciously resuming his walk. "My father never went into the woods on such an errand, nor his father before him. We have been a race of honest men and good Christians since the days of the martyrs;[4] and shall I be the first of the name of Brown that ever took this path and kept — "

"Such company, thou wouldst say," observed the elder person, interpreting his pause. "Well said, Goodman Brown! I have been as well acquainted with your family as with ever a one among the Puritans; and that's no trifle to say. I helped your grandfather, the constable, when he lashed the Quaker woman so smartly through the streets of Salem; and it was I that brought your father a pitch-pine knot, kindled at my own hearth, to set fire to an Indian village, in King Philip's war.[5] They were my good friends, both; and many a pleasant walk have we had along this path, and returned merrily after midnight. I would fain be friends with you for their sake."

"If it be as thou sayest," replied Goodman Brown, "I marvel they never spoke of these matters; or, verily, I marvel not, seeing that the least rumor of the sort would have driven them from New England. We are a people of prayer, and good works to boot, and abide no such wickedness."

"Wickedness or not," said the traveller, with the twisted staff, "I have a very general acquaintance here in New England. The deacons of many a church have drunk the communion wine with me; the selectmen of divers towns make me their chairman; and a majority of the Great and General Court[6] are firm supporters of my interest. The governor and I, too — But these are state secrets." 20

"Can this be so?" cried Goodman Brown, with a stare of amazement at his undisturbed companion. "Howbeit, I have nothing to do with the governor and council; they have their own ways, and are no rule for a simple husbandman[7] like me. But, were I to go on with thee, how should I meet the eye of that good old man, our minister, at Salem village? Oh, his voice would make me tremble both Sabbath day and lecture day."

Thus far the elder traveller had listened with due gravity; but now burst into a fit of irrepressible mirth, shaking himself so violently that his snake-like staff actually seemed to wriggle in sympathy.

"Ha! ha! ha!" shouted he again and again; then composing himself, "Well, go on, Goodman Brown, go on; but, prithee, don't kill me with laughing."

"Well, then, to end the matter at once," said Goodman Brown, considerably nettled, "there is my wife, Faith. It would break her dear little heart; and I'd rather break my own."

---

[4] A reference to the persecution of Protestants in England (1553–1558) by the Catholic monarch Mary Tudor.
[5] War waged (1675–1676) against the colonists of New England by the Indian chief Metacomset, also known as "King Philip."
[6] The Puritan legislature.
[7] An ordinary person.

"Nay, if that be the case," answered the other, "e'en go thy ways, Goodman 25
Brown. I would not for twenty old women like the one hobbling before us that
Faith should come to any harm."

As he spoke he pointed his staff at a female figure on the path, in whom
Goodman Brown recognized a very pious and exemplary dame, who had taught
him his catechism in youth, and was still his moral and spiritual adviser, jointly
with the minister and Deacon Gookin.

"A marvel, truly, that Goody⁸ Cloyse should be so far in the wilderness at
nightfall," said he. "But with your leave, friend, I shall take a cut through the
woods until we have left this Christian woman behind. Being a stranger to you,
she might ask whom I was consorting with and whither I was going."

"Be it so," said his fellow-traveller. "Betake you to the woods, and let me keep
the path."

Accordingly the young man turned aside, but took care to watch his companion, who advanced softly along the road until he had come within a staff's length
of the old dame. She, meanwhile, was making the best of her way, with singular
speed for so aged a woman, and mumbling some indistinct words — a prayer,
doubtless — as she went. The traveller put forth his staff and touched her withered neck with what seemed the serpent's tail.

"The devil!" screamed the pious old lady. 30

"Then Goody Cloyse knows her old friend?" observed the traveller, con-
fronting her and leaning on his writhing stick.

"Ah, forsooth, and is it your worship indeed?" cried the good dame. "Yea,
truly is it, and in the very image of my old gossip, Goodman Brown, the grandfather of the silly fellow that now is. But — would your worship believe it? — my
broomstick hath strangely disappeared, stolen, as I suspect, by that unhanged
witch, Goody Cory, and that, too, when I was all anointed with the juice of smal-
lage and cinquefoil and wolf's bane"⁹ —

"Mingled with fine wheat and the fat of a new-born babe," said the shape of
old Goodman Brown.

"Ah, your worship knows the recipe," cried the old lady, cackling aloud. "So,
as I was saying, being all ready for the meeting, and no horse to ride on, I made
up my mind to foot it; for they tell me there is a nice young man to be taken into
communion to-night. But now your good worship will lend me your arm, and
we shall be there in a twinkling."

"That can hardly be," answered her friend. "I may not spare you my arm, 35
Goody Cloyse; but here is my staff, if you will."

So saying, he threw it down at her feet, where, perhaps, it assumed life, being
one of the rods which its owner had formerly lent to the Egyptian magi.¹⁰ Of
this fact, however, Goodman Brown could not take cognizance. He had cast
up his eyes in astonishment, and, looking down again, beheld neither Goody

⁸ A polite title for a wife of humble rank.
⁹ All these plants were associated with magic and witchcraft.
¹⁰ Allusion to the biblical magicians who turned their rods into serpents (Exodus 7:11–12).

Cloyse nor the serpentine staff, but his fellow-traveller alone, who waited for him as calmly as if nothing had happened.

"That old woman taught me my catechism," said the young man; and there was a world of meaning in this simple comment.

They continued to walk onward, while the elder traveller exhorted his companion to make good speed and persevere in the path, discoursing so aptly that his arguments seemed rather to spring up in the bosom of his auditor than to be suggested by himself. As they went, he plucked a branch of maple to serve for a walking stick, and began to strip it of the twigs and little boughs, which were wet with evening dew. The moment his fingers touched them they became strangely withered and dried up as with a week's sunshine. Thus the pair proceeded, at a good free pace, until suddenly, in a gloomy hollow of the road, Goodman Brown sat himself down on the stump of a tree and refused to go any farther.

"Friend," said he, stubbornly, "my mind is made up. Not another step will I budge on this errand. What if a wretched old woman do choose to go to the devil when I thought she was going to heaven: is that any reason why I should quit my dear Faith and go after her?"

"You will think better of this by and by," said his acquaintance, composedly. 40 "Sit here and rest yourself a while; and when you feel like moving again, there is my staff to help you along."

Without more words, he threw his companion the maple stick, and was as speedily out of sight as if he had vanished into the deepening gloom. The young man sat a few moments by the roadside, applauding himself greatly, and thinking with how clear a conscience he should meet the minister in his morning walk, nor shrink from the eye of good old Deacon Gookin. And what calm sleep would be his that very night, which was to have been spent so wickedly, but so purely and sweetly now, in the arms of Faith! Amidst these pleasant and praiseworthy meditations, Goodman Brown heard the tramp of horses along the road, and deemed it advisable to conceal himself within the verge of the forest, conscious of the guilty purpose that had brought him thither, though now so happily turned from it.

On came the hoof tramps and the voices of the riders, two grave old voices, conversing soberly as they drew near. These mingled sounds appeared to pass along the road, within a few yards of the young man's hiding-place; but, owing doubtless to the depth of the gloom at that particular spot, neither the travellers nor their steeds were visible. Though their figures brushed the small boughs by the wayside, it could not be seen that they intercepted, even for a moment, the faint gleam from the strip of bright sky athwart which they must have passed. Goodman Brown alternately crouched and stood on tiptoe, pulling aside the branches and thrusting forth his head as far as he durst without discerning so much as a shadow. It vexed him the more, because he could have sworn, were such a thing possible, that he recognized the voices of the minister and Deacon Gookin, jogging along quietly, as they were wont to do, when bound to some ordination or ecclesiastical council. While yet within hearing, one of the riders stopped to pluck a switch.

"Of the two, reverend sir," said the voice like the deacon's, "I had rather miss an ordination dinner than to-night's meeting. They tell me that some of our community are to be here from Falmouth[11] and beyond, and others from Connecticut and Rhode Island, besides several of the Indian powwows,[12] who, after their fashion, know almost as much deviltry as the best of us. Moreover, there is a goodly young woman to be taken into communion."

"Mighty well, Deacon Gookin!" replied the solemn old tones of the minister. "Spur up, or we shall be late. Nothing can be done, you know, until I get on the ground."

The hoofs clattered again; and the voices, talking so strangely in the empty 45 air, passed on through the forest, where no church had ever been gathered, nor solitary Christian prayed. Whither, then, could these holy men be journeying so deep into the heathen wilderness? Young Goodman Brown caught hold of a tree for support, being ready to sink down on the ground, faint and overburdened with the heavy sickness of his heart. He looked up to the sky, doubting whether there really was a heaven above him. Yet there was the blue arch, and the stars brightening in it.

"With heaven above and Faith below, I will yet stand firm against the devil!" cried Goodman Brown.

While he still gazed upward into the deep arch of the firmament and had lifted his hands to pray, a cloud, though no wind was stirring, hurried across the zenith and hid the brightening stars. The blue sky was still visible, except directly overhead, where this black mass of cloud was sweeping swiftly northward. Aloft in the air, as if from the depths of the cloud, came a confused and doubtful sound of voices. Once the listener fancied that he could distinguish the accents of towns-people of his own, men and women, both pious and ungodly, many of whom he had met at the communion table, and had seen others rioting at the tavern. The next moment, so indistinct were the sounds, he doubted whether he had heard aught but the murmur of the old forest, whispering without a wind. Then came a stronger swell of those familiar tones, heard daily in the sunshine at Salem village, but never until now from a cloud of night. There was one voice, of a young woman, uttering lamentations, yet with an uncertain sorrow, and entreating for some favor, which, perhaps, it would grieve her to obtain; and all the unseen multitude, both saints and sinners, seemed to encourage her onward.

"Faith!" shouted Goodman Brown, in a voice of agony and desperation; and the echoes of the forest mocked him, crying, "Faith! Faith!" as if bewildered wretches were seeking her all through the wilderness.

The cry of grief, rage, and terror was yet piercing the night, when the unhappy

---

[11] A town near Salem, Massachusetts.
[12] Medicine men.

husband held his breath for a response. There was a scream, drowned immediately in a louder murmur of voices, fading into far-off laughter, as the dark cloud swept away, leaving the clear and silent sky above Goodman Brown. But something fluttered lightly down through the air and caught on the branch of a tree. The young man seized it, and beheld a pink ribbon.

"My Faith is gone!" cried he, after one stupefied moment. "There is no good 50 on earth; and sin is but a name. Come, devil; for to thee is this world given."

And, maddened with despair, so that he laughed loud and long, did Goodman Brown grasp his staff and set forth again, at such a rate that he seemed to fly along the forest path rather than to walk or run. The road grew wilder and drearier and more faintly traced, and vanished at length, leaving him in the heart of the dark wilderness, still rushing onward with the instinct that guides mortal man to evil. The whole forest was peopled with frightful sounds — the creaking of the trees, the howling of wild beasts, and the yell of Indians; while sometimes the wind tolled like a distant church bell, and sometimes gave a broad roar around the traveller, as if all Nature were laughing him to scorn. But he was himself the chief horror of the scene, and shrank not from its other horrors.

"Ha! ha! ha!" roared Goodman Brown when the wind laughed at him. "Let us hear which will laugh loudest. Think not to frighten me with your deviltry. Come witch, come wizard, come Indian powwow, come devil himself, and here comes Goodman Brown. You may as well fear him as he fears you."

In truth, all through the haunted forest there could be nothing more frightful than the figure of Goodman Brown. On he flew among the black pines, brandishing his staff with frenzied gestures, now giving vent to an inspiration of horrid blasphemy, and now shouting forth such laughter as set all the echoes of the forest laughing like demons around him. The fiend in his own shape is less hideous than when he rages in the breast of man. Thus sped the demoniac on his course, until, quivering among the trees, he saw a red light before him, as when the felled trunks and branches of a clearing have been set on fire, and throw up their lurid blaze against the sky, at the hour of midnight. He paused, in a lull of the tempest that had driven him onward, and heard the swell of what seemed a hymn, rolling solemnly from a distance with the weight of many voices. He knew the tune; it was a familiar one in the choir of the village meeting-house. The verse died heavily away, and was lengthened by a chorus, not of human voices, but of all the sounds of the benighted wilderness pealing in awful harmony together. Goodman Brown cried out, and his cry was lost to his own ear by its unison with the cry of the desert.

In the interval of silence he stole forward until the light glared full upon his eyes. At one extremity of an open space, hemmed in by the dark wall of the forest, arose a rock, bearing some rude, natural resemblance either to an altar or a pulpit, and surrounded by four blazing pines, their tops aflame, their stems untouched, like candles at an evening meeting. The mass of foliage that had overgrown the summit of the rock was all on fire, blazing high into the night and fitfully illuminating the whole field. Each pendent twig and leafy festoon was in a blaze. As the red light arose and fell, a numerous congregation alternately shone forth, then disappeared in shadow, and again grew, as it were, out of the darkness, peopling the heart of the solitary woods at once.

"A grave and dark-clad company," quoth Goodman Brown. 55

In truth they were such. Among them, quivering to and fro between gloom and splendor, appeared faces that would be seen next day at the council board of the province, and others which, Sabbath after Sabbath, looked devoutly heavenward, and benignantly over the crowded pews, from the holiest pulpits in the land. Some affirm that the lady of the governor was there. At least there were high dames well known to her, and wives of honored husbands, and widows, a great multitude, and ancient maidens, all of excellent repute, and fair young girls, who trembled lest their mothers should espy them. Either the sudden gleams of light flashing over the obscure field bedazzled Goodman Brown, or he recognized a score of the church members of Salem village famous for their especial sanctity. Good old Deacon Gookin had arrived, and waited at the skirts of that venerable saint, his revered pastor. But, irreverently consorting with these grave, reputable, and pious people, these elders of the church, these chaste dames and dewy virgins, there were men of dissolute lives and women of spotted fame, wretches given over to all mean and filthy vice, and suspected even of horrid crimes. It was strange to see that the good shrank not from the wicked, nor were the sinners abashed by the saints. Scattered also among their pale-faced enemies were the Indian priests, or powwows, who had often scared their native forest with more hideous incantations than any known to English witchcraft.

"But where is Faith?" thought Goodman Brown; and, as hope came into his heart, he trembled.

Another verse of the hymn arose, a slow and mournful strain, such as the pious love, but joined to words which expressed all that our nature can conceive of sin, and darkly hinted at far more. Unfathomable to mere mortals is the lore of fiends. Verse after verse was sung; and still the chorus of the desert swelled between like the deepest tone of a mighty organ; and with the final peal of that dreadful anthem there came a sound, as if the roaring wind, the rushing streams, the howling beasts, and every other voice of the unconcerted wilderness were mingling and according with the voice of guilty man in homage to the prince of all. The four blazing pines threw up a loftier flame, and obscurely discovered shapes and visages of horror on the smoke wreaths above the impious assembly. At the same moment the fire on the rock shot redly forth and formed a glowing arch above its base, where now appeared a figure. With reverence be it spoken, the figure bore no slight similitude, both in garb and manner, to some grave divine of the New England churches.

"Bring forth the converts!" cried a voice that echoed through the field and rolled into the forest.

At the word, Goodman Brown stepped forth from the shadow of the trees 60 and approached the congregation, with whom he felt a loathful brotherhood by the sympathy of all that was wicked in his heart. He could have well-nigh sworn that the shape of his own dead father beckoned him to advance, looking downward from a smoke wreath, while a woman, with dim features of despair, threw out her hand to warn him back. Was it his mother? But he had no power to retreat one step, nor to resist, even in thought, when the minister and good old Deacon Gookin seized his arms and led him to the blazing rock. Thither came also the slender form of a veiled female, led between Goody Cloyse, that pious teacher of the catechism, and Martha Carrier,[13] who had received the devil's promise to be queen of hell. A rampant hag was she. And there stood the proselytes beneath the canopy of fire.

"Welcome, my children," said the dark figure, "to the communion of your race. Ye have found thus young your nature and your destiny. My children, look behind you!"

They turned; and flashing forth, as it were, in a sheet of flame, the fiend worshippers were seen; the smile of welcome gleamed darkly on every visage.

"There," resumed the sable form, "are all whom ye have reverenced from youth. Ye deemed them holier than yourselves, and shrank from your own sin, contrasting it with their lives of righteousness and prayerful aspirations heavenward. Yet here are they all in my worshipping assembly. This night it shall be granted you to know their secret deeds: how hoary-bearded elders of the church have whispered wanton words to the young maids of their households; how many a woman, eager for widows' weeds, has given her husband a drink at bedtime and let him sleep his last sleep in her bosom; how beardless youths have made haste to inherit their fathers' wealth; and how fair damsels — blush not, sweet ones — have dug little graves in the garden, and bidden me, the sole guest, to an infant's funeral. By the sympathy of your human hearts for sin ye shall scent out all the places — whether in church, bed-chamber, street, field, or forest — where crime has been committed, and shall exult to behold the whole earth one stain of guilt, one mighty blood spot. Far more than this. It shall be yours to penetrate, in every bosom, the deep mystery of sin, the fountain of all wicked arts, and which inexhaustibly supplies more evil impulses than human power — than my power at its utmost — can make manifest in deeds. And now, my children, look upon each other."

They did so; and, by the blaze of the hell-kindled torches, the wretched man beheld his Faith, and the wife her husband, trembling before that unhallowed altar.

"Lo, there ye stand, my children," said the figure, in a deep and solemn tone, 65 almost sad with its despairing awfulness, as if his once angelic nature could yet mourn for our miserable race. "Depending upon one another's hearts, ye had still hoped that virtue were not all a dream. Now are ye undeceived. Evil is the nature of mankind. Evil must be your only happiness. Welcome again, my children, to the communion of your race."

"Welcome," repeated the fiend worshippers, in one cry of despair and triumph.

---

[13] One of the women hanged in Salem in 1697 for witchcraft.

And there they stood, the only pair, as it seemed, who were yet hesitating on the verge of wickedness in this dark world. A basin was hollowed, naturally, in the rock. Did it contain water, reddened by the lurid light? or was it blood? or, perchance, a liquid flame? Herein did the shape of evil dip his hand and prepare to lay the mark of baptism upon their foreheads, that they might be partakers of the mystery of sin, more conscious of the secret guilt of others, both in deed and thought, than they could now be of their own. The husband cast one look at his pale wife, and Faith at him. What polluted wretches would the next glance show them to each other, shuddering alike at what they disclosed and what they saw!

"Faith! Faith!" cried the husband, "look up to heaven, and resist the wicked one."

Whether Faith obeyed he knew not. Hardly had he spoken when he found himself amid calm night and solitude, listening to a roar of the wind which died heavily away through the forest. He staggered against the rock, and felt it chill and damp; while a hanging twig, that had been all on fire, besprinkled his cheek with the coldest dew.

The next morning young Goodman Brown came slowly into the street of 70 Salem village, staring around him like a bewildered man. The good old minister was taking a walk along the graveyard to get an appetite for breakfast and meditate his sermon, and bestowed a blessing, as he passed, on Goodman Brown. He shrank from the venerable saint as if to avoid an anathema. Old Deacon Gookin was at domestic worship, and the holy words of his prayer were heard through the open window. "What God doth the wizard pray to?" quoth Goodman Brown. Goody Cloyse, that excellent old Christian, stood in the early sunshine at her own lattice, catechizing a little girl who had brought her a pint of morning's milk. Goodman Brown snatched away the child as from the grasp of the fiend himself. Turning the corner by the meeting-house, he spied the head of Faith, with the pink ribbons, gazing anxiously forth, and bursting into such joy at sight of him that she skipped along the street and almost kissed her husband before the whole village. But Goodman Brown looked sternly and sadly into her face, and passed on without a greeting.

Had Goodman Brown fallen asleep in the forest and only dreamed a wild dream of a witch-meeting?

Be it so if you will; but, alas! it was a dream of evil omen for young Goodman Brown. A stern, a sad, a darkly meditative, a distrustful, if not a desperate man did he become from the night of that fearful dream. On the Sabbath day, when the congregation were singing a holy psalm, he could not listen because an anthem of sin rushed loudly upon his ear and drowned all the blessed strain. When the minister spoke from the pulpit with power and fervid eloquence, and, with his hand on the open Bible, of the sacred truths of our religion, and of saint-like lives and triumphant deaths, and of future bliss or misery unutterable, then did Goodman Brown turn pale, dreading lest the roof should thunder down upon the gray blasphemer and his hearers. Often, awakening suddenly at midnight, he shrank from the bosom of Faith; and at morning or eventide, when the family knelt down at prayer, he scowled and muttered to himself, and gazed sternly at his wife, and turned away. And when he had lived long, and was borne to his grave a hoary corpse, followed by Faith, an aged woman, and children and grandchildren, a goodly procession, besides neighbors not a few, they carved no hopeful verse upon his tombstone, for his dying hour was gloom.

For Analysis

1. At the end of the story, the narrator asks, "Had Goodman Brown fallen asleep in the forest and only dreamed a wild dream of a witch-meeting?" Why, instead of answering the question, does he say, "Be it so if you will"?

2. Examine the seemingly supernatural events Brown experiences as he penetrates ever deeper into the forest. Can the reader determine whether those events are really taking place? If not, what purpose does the ambiguity serve?

3. What attitude does this story express toward the church of Puritan New England?

4. What purpose do Faith's pink ribbons serve?

5. What is the "guilty purpose" (para. 41) that has drawn Brown to the forest?

On Style

1. How would you characterize the **setting** of this story?

2. What elements of the story can be described as **allegorical** or **symbolic**?

Making Connections

1. Both this story and Melville's "Bartleby the Scrivener" (p. 334) deal with protagonists who withdraw from life. What similarities and differences do you find in the reasons for their withdrawal, the ways in which they withdraw, and the consequences of their withdrawal?

2. Both Hawthorne's "Young Goodman Brown" and Ellison's "'Repent, Harlequin!' Said the Ticktockman" (p. 399) rely on fantasy. What advantages does the use of fantasy give the authors?

Writing Topics

1. Write an essay in which you argue for or against the proposition that the "truth" Brown discovers during the night in the forest justifies his gloom and withdrawal.

2. Write out a paraphrase of Satan's sermon.

Stephen Crane (1871–1900)

The Bride Comes to Yellow Sky 1898

I

The great Pullman was whirling onward with such dignity of motion that a glance from the window seemed simply to prove that the plains of Texas were pouring eastward. Vast flats of green grass, dull-hued space of mesquit and cactus, little groups of frame houses, woods of light and tender trees, all were sweeping into the east, sweeping over the horizon, a precipice.

A newly married pair had boarded this coach at San Antonio. The man's face was reddened from many days in the wind and sun, and a direct result of his new black clothes was that his brick-colored hands were constantly performing in a most conscious fashion. From time to time he looked down respectfully at his attire. He sat with a hand on each knee, like a man waiting in a barber's shop. The glances he devoted to other passengers were furtive and shy.

The bride was not pretty, nor was she very young. She wore a dress of blue cashmere, with small reservations of velvet here and there, and with steel buttons abounding. She continually twisted her head to regard her puff sleeves, very stiff, straight, and high. They embarrassed her. It was quite apparent that she had cooked, and that she expected to cook, dutifully. The blushes caused by the careless scrutiny of some passengers as she had entered the car were strange to see upon this plain, under-class countenance, which was drawn in placid, almost emotionless lines.

They were evidently very happy. "Ever been in a parlour-car before?" he asked, smiling with delight.

"No," she answered; "I never was. It's fine, ain't it?"

"Great! And then after a while we'll go forward to the diner, and get a big layout. Finest meal in the world. Charge a dollar."

"Oh, do they?" cried the bride. "Charge a dollar? Why, that's too much — for us — ain't it, Jack?"

"Not this trip, anyhow," he answered bravely. "We're going to go the whole thing."

Later he explained to her about the trains. "You see, it's a thousand miles from one end of Texas to the other; and this train runs right across it, and never stops but four times." He had the pride of an owner. He pointed out to her the dazzling fittings of the coach; and in truth her eyes opened wider as she contemplated the sea-green figured velvet, the shining brass, silver, and glass, the wood that gleamed as darkly brilliant as the surface of a pool of oil. At one end a

5

91

bronze figure sturdily held a support for a separated chamber, and at convenient places on the ceiling were frescos in olive and silver.

To the minds of the pair, their surroundings reflected the glory of their marriage that morning in San Antonio; this was the environment of their new estate; and the man's face in particular beamed with an elation that made him appear ridiculous to the negro porter. This individual at times surveyed them from afar with an amused and superior grin. On other occasions he bullied them with skill in ways that did not make it exactly plain to them that they were being bullied. He subtly used all the manners of the most unconquerable kind of snobbery. He oppressed them; but of this oppression they had small knowledge, and they speedily forgot that infrequently a number of travellers covered them with stares of derisive enjoyment. Historically there was supposed to be something infinitely humorous in their situation.

"We are due in Yellow Sky at 3:42," he said, looking tenderly into her eyes.

"Oh, are we?" she said, as if she had not been aware of it. To evince surprise at her husband's statement was part of her wifely amiability. She took from a pocket a little silver watch; and as she held it before her, and stared at it with a frown of attention, the new husband's face shone.

"I bought it in San Anton' from a friend of mine," he told her gleefully.

"It's seventeen minutes past twelve," she said, looking up at him with a kind of shy and clumsy coquetry. A passenger, noting this play, grew excessively sardonic, and winked at himself in one of the numerous mirrors.

At last they went to the dining-car. Two rows of negro waiters, in glowing white suits, surveyed their entrance with the interest, and also the equanimity, of men who had been forewarned. The pair fell to the lot of a waiter who happened to feel pleasure in steering them through their meal. He viewed them with the manner of a fatherly pilot, his countenance radiant with benevolence. The patronage, entwined with the ordinary deference, was not plain to them. And yet, as they returned to their coach, they showed in their faces a sense of escape.

To the left, miles down a long purple slope, was a little ribbon of mist where moved the keening Rio Grande. The train was approaching it at an angle, and the apex was Yellow Sky. Presently it was apparent that, as the distance from Yellow Sky grew shorter, the husband became commensurately restless. His brick-red hands were more insistent in their prominence. Occasionally he was even rather absent-minded and far-away when the bride leaned forward and addressed him.

As a matter of truth, Jack Potter was beginning to find the shadow of a deed weigh upon him like a leaden slab. He, the town marshal of Yellow Sky, a man known, liked, and feared in his corner, a prominent person, had gone to San Antonio to meet a girl he believed he loved, and there, after the usual prayers, had actually induced her to marry him, without consulting Yellow Sky for any part of the transaction. He was now bringing his bride before an innocent and unsuspecting community.

Of course people in Yellow Sky married as it pleased them, in accordance with a general custom; but such was Potter's thought of his duty to his friends, or of their idea of his duty, or of an unspoken form which does not control men in these matters, that he felt he was heinous. He had committed an extraordinary crime. Face to face with this girl in San Antonio, and spurred by his sharp impulse, he had gone headlong over all the social hedges. At San Antonio he was like a man hidden in the dark. A knife to sever any friendly duty, any form, was easy to his hand in that remote city. But the hour of Yellow Sky — the hour of daylight — was approaching.

He knew full well that his marriage was an important thing to his town. It could only be exceeded by the burning of the new hotel. His friends could not forgive him. Frequently he had reflected on the advisability of telling them by telegraph, but a new cowardice had been upon him. He feared to do it. And now the train was hurrying him toward a scene of amazement, glee, and reproach. He glanced out of the window at the line of haze swinging slowly in toward the train.

Yellow Sky had a kind of brass band, which played painfully, to the delight of 20 the populace. He laughed without heart as he thought of it. If the citizens could dream of his prospective arrival with his bride, they would parade the band at the station and escort them, amid cheers and laughing congratulations, to his adobe home.

He resolved that he would use all the devices of speed and plainscraft in making the journey from the station to his house. Once within that safe citadel, he could issue some sort of vocal bulletin, and then not go among the citizens until they had time to wear off a little of their enthusiasm.

The bride looked anxiously at him. "What's worrying you, Jack?"

He laughed again. "I'm not worrying, girl; I'm only thinking of Yellow Sky."

She flushed in comprehension.

A sense of mutual guilt invaded their minds and developed a finer tender- 25 ness. They looked at each other with eyes softly aglow. But Potter often laughed the same nervous laugh; the flush upon the bride's face seemed quite permanent.

The traitor to the feelings of Yellow Sky narrowly watched the speeding landscape. "We're nearly there," he said.

Presently the porter came and announced the proximity of Potter's home. He held a brush in his hand, and, with all his airy superiority gone, he brushed Potter's new clothes as the latter slowly turned this way and that way. Potter fumbled out a coin and gave it to the porter, as he had seen others do. It was a heavy and muscle-bound business, as that of a man shoeing his first horse.

The porter took their bag, and as the train began to slow they moved forward to the hooded platform of the car. Presently the two engines and their string of coaches rushed into the station of Yellow Sky.

"They have to take water here," said Potter, from a constricted throat and in mournful cadence, as one announcing death. Before the train stopped his eye had swept the length of the platform, and he was glad and astonished to see there was none upon it but the station-agent, who, with a slightly hurried and anxious air, was walking toward the water-tanks. When the train had halted, the porter alighted first, and placed in position a little temporary step.

"Come on, girl," said Potter, hoarsely. As he helped her down they each 30 laughed on a false note. He took the bag from the negro, and bade his wife cling to his arm. As they slunk rapidly away, his hang-dog glance perceived that they were unloading the two trunks, and also that the station-agent, far ahead near the baggage-car, had turned and was running toward him, making gestures. He laughed, and groaned as he laughed, when he noted the first effect of his marital bliss upon Yellow Sky. He gripped his wife's arm firmly to his side, and they fled. Behind them the porter stood, chuckling fatuously.

II

The California express on the Southern Railway was due at Yellow Sky in twenty-one minutes. There were six men at the bar of the Weary Gentleman saloon. One was a drummer[1] who talked a great deal and rapidly; three were Texans who did not care to talk at that time; and two were Mexican sheep-herders, who did not talk as a general practice in the Weary Gentleman saloon. The barkeeper's dog lay on the board walk that crossed in front of the door. His head was on his paws, and he glanced drowsily here and there with the constant vigilance of a dog that is kicked on occasion. Across the sandy street were some vivid green grass-plots, so wonderful in appearance, amid the sands that burned near them in a blazing sun, that they caused a doubt in the mind. They exactly resembled the grass mats used to represent lawns on the stage. At the cooler end of the railway station, a man without a coat sat in a tilted chair and smoked his pipe. The fresh-cut bank of the Rio Grande circled near the town, and there could be seen beyond it a great plum-coloured plain of mesquit.

Save for the busy drummer and his companions in the saloon, Yellow Sky was dozing. The new-comer leaned gracefully upon the bar, and recited many tales with the confidence of a bard who has come upon a new field.

" — and at the moment that the old man fell downstairs with the bureau in his arms, the old woman was coming up with two scuttles of coal, and of course — "

The drummer's tale was interrupted by a young man who suddenly appeared in the open door. He cried: "Scratchy Wilson's drunk, and has turned loose with both hands." The two Mexicans at once set down their glasses and faded out of the rear entrance of the saloon.

The drummer, innocent and jocular, answered: "All right, old man. S'pose he has? Come in and have a drink, anyhow."

But the information had made such an obvious cleft in every skull in the room that the drummer was obliged to see its importance. All had become instantly solemn. "Say," said he, mystified, "what is this?" His three companions made the introductory gesture of eloquent speech; but the young man at the door fore-stalled them.

"It means, my friend," he answered, as he came into the saloon, "that for the next two hours this town won't be a health resort."

The barkeeper went to the door, and locked and barred it; reaching out of the

---

[1] A traveling salesman.

window, he pulled in heavy wooden shutters, and barred them. Immediately a solemn, chapel-like gloom was upon the place. The drummer was looking from one to another.

"But, say," he cried, "what is this, anyhow? You don't mean there is going to be a gun-fight?"

"Don't know whether there'll be a fight or not," answered one man, grimly; 40 "but there'll be some shootin' — some good shootin'."

The young man who had warned them waved his hand. "Oh, there'll be a fight fast enough, if any one wants it. Anybody can get a fight out there in the street. There's a fight just waiting."

The drummer seemed to be swayed between the interest of a foreigner and a perception of personal danger.

"What did you say his name was?" he asked.

"Scratchy Wilson," they answered in chorus.

"And will he kill anybody? What are you going to do? Does this happen of- 45 ten? Does he rampage around like this once a week or so? Can he break in that door?"

"No; he can't break down that door," replied the barkeeper. "He's tried it three times. But when he comes you'd better lay down on the floor, stranger. He's dead sure to shoot at it, and a bullet may come through."

Thereafter the drummer kept a strict eye upon the door. The time had not yet called for him to hug the floor, but, as a minor precaution, he sidled near the wall. "Will he kill anybody?" he said again.

The men laughed low and scornfully at the question.

"He's out to shoot, and he's out for trouble. Don't see any good in experi- mentin' with him."

"But what do you do in a case like this? What do you do?" 50

A man responded: "Why, he and Jack Potter — "

"But," in chorus the other men interrupted, "Jack Potter's in San Anton'."

"Well, who is he? What's he got to do with it?"

"Oh, he's the town marshal. He goes out and fights Scratchy when he gets on one of these tears."

"Wow!" said the drummer, mopping his brow. "Nice job he's got." 55

The voices had toned away to mere whisperings. The drummer wished to ask further questions, which were born of an increasing anxiety and bewilderment; but when he attempted them, the men merely looked at him in irritation and motioned him to remain silent. A tense waiting hush was upon them. In the deep shadows of the room their eyes shone as they listened for sounds from the street. One man made three gestures at the barkeeper; and the latter, moving like a ghost, handed him a glass and a bottle. The man poured a full glass of whisky, and set down the bottle noiselessly. He gulped the whisky in a swallow, and turned again toward the door in immovable silence. The drummer saw that the barkeeper, without a sound, had taken a Winchester from beneath the bar. Later he saw this individual beckoning to him, so he tiptoed across the room.

"You better come with me back of the bar."

"No thanks," said the drummer, perspiring; "I'd rather be where I can make a break for the back door."

Whereupon the man of bottles made a kindly but peremptory gesture. The drummer obeyed it, and, finding himself seated on a box with his head below the level of the bar, balm was laid upon his soul at sight of various zinc and copper fittings that bore a resemblance to armour-plate. The barkeeper took a seat comfortably upon an adjacent box.

"You see," he whispered, "this here Scratchy Wilson is a wonder with a gun — 60
a perfect wonder; and when he goes on the war-trail, we hunt our holes — naturally. He's about the last one of the old gang that used to hang out along the river here. He's a terror when he's drunk. When he's sober he's all right — kind of simple — wouldn't hurt a fly — nicest fellow in town. But when he's drunk — whoo!"

There were periods of stillness. "I wish Jack Potter was back from San Anton'," said the barkeeper. "He shot Wilson up once — in the leg — and he would sail in and pull out the kinks in this thing."

Presently they heard from a distance the sound of a shot, followed by three wild yowls. It instantly removed a bond from the men in the darkened saloon. There was a shuffling of feet. They looked at each other. "Here he comes," they said.

III

A man in a maroon-coloured flannel shirt, which had been purchased for purposes of decoration, and made principally by some Jewish women on the East Side of New York, rounded a corner and walked into the middle of the main street of Yellow Sky. In either hand the man held a long, heavy, blue-black revolver. Often he yelled, and these cries rang through a semblance of a deserted village, shrilly flying over the roofs in a volume that seemed to have no relation to the ordinary vocal strength of a man. It was as if the surrounding stillness formed the arch of a tomb over him. These cries of ferocious challenge rang against walls of silence. And his boots had red tops with gilded imprints, of the kind beloved in winter by little sledding boys on the hillsides of New England.

The man's face flamed in a rage begot of whisky. His eyes, rolling, and yet keen for ambush, hunted the still doorways and windows. He walked with the creeping movement of the midnight cat. As it occurred to him, he roared menacing information. The long revolvers in his hands were as easy as straws; they were moved with an electric swiftness. The little fingers of each hand played sometimes in a musician's way. Plain from the low collar of the shirt, the cords of his neck straightened and sank, straightened and sank, as passion moved him. The only sounds were his terrible invitations. The calm adobes preserved their demeanor at the passing of this small thing in the middle of the street.

There was no offer of fight — no offer of fight. The man called to the sky. 65
There were no attractions. He bellowed and fumed and swayed his revolvers here and everywhere.

The dog of the barkeeper of the Weary Gentleman saloon had not appreciated the advance of events. He yet lay dozing in front of his master's door. At
sight of the dog, the man paused and raised his revolver humorously. At sight of
the man, the dog sprang up and walked diagonally away, with a sullen head, and
growling. The man yelled, and the dog broke into a gallop. As it was about to
enter an alley, there was a loud noise, a whistling, and something spat the
ground directly before it. The dog screamed, and, wheeling in terror, galloped
headlong in a new direction. Again there was a noise, a whistling, and sand was
kicked viciously before it. Fear-stricken, the dog turned and flurried like an animal in a pen. The man stood laughing, his weapons at his hips.

Ultimately the man was attracted by the closed door of the Weary Gentleman
saloon. He went to it and, hammering with a revolver, demanded drink.

The door remaining imperturbable, he picked a bit of paper from the walk,
and nailed it to the framework with a knife. He then turned his back contemptuously upon this popular resort and, walking to the opposite side of the street
and spinning there on his heel quickly and lithely, fired at the bit of paper. He
missed it by a half-inch. He swore at himself, and went away. Later he comfortably fusilladed the windows of his most intimate friend. The man was playing
with this town; it was a toy for him.

But still there was no offer of fight. The name of Jack Potter, his ancient
antagonist, entered his mind, and he concluded that it would be a glad thing if
he should go to Potter's house and by bombardment induce him to come out
and fight. He moved in the direction of his desire, chanting Apache scalp-music.

When he arrived at it, Potter's house presented the same still front as had the 70
other adobes. Taking up a strategic position, the man howled a challenge. But this
house regarded him as might a great stone god. It gave no sign. After a decent
wait, the man howled further challenges, mingling with them wonderful epithets.

Presently there came the spectacle of a man churning himself into deepest
rage over the immobility of a house. He fumed at it as the winter wind attacks a
prairie cabin in the North. To the distance there should have gone the sound of
a tumult like the fighting of two hundred Mexicans. As necessity bade him, he
paused for breath or to reload his revolvers.

IV

Potter and his bride walked sheepishly and with speed. Sometimes they laughed
together shamefacedly and low.

"Next corner, dear," he said finally.

They put forth the efforts of a pair walking bowed against a strong wind. Potter was about to raise a finger to point the first appearance of the new home
when, as they circled the corner, they came face to face with a man in a maroon-
coloured shirt, who was feverishly pushing cartridges into a large revolver. Upon
the instant the man dropped his revolver to the ground and, like lightning,
whipped another from its holster. The second weapon was aimed at the bridegroom's chest.

There was a silence. Potter's mouth seemed to be merely a grave for his 75
tongue. He exhibited an instinct to at once loosen his arm from the woman's
grip, and he dropped the bag to the sand. As for the bride, her face had gone as
yellow as old cloth. She was a slave to hideous rites, gazing at the apparitional
snake.

The two men faced each other at a distance of three paces. He of the revolver
smiled with a new and quiet ferocity.

"Tried to sneak up on me," he said. "Tried to sneak up on me!" His eyes grew
more baleful. As Potter made a slight movement, the man thrust his revolver
venomously forward. "No, don't you do it, Jack Potter. Don't you move a finger
toward a gun just yet. Don't you move an eyelash. The time has come for me to
settle with you, and I'm goin' to do it my own way, and loaf along with no inter-
ferin'. So if you don't want a gun bent on you, just mind what I tell you."

Potter looked at his enemy. "I ain't got a gun on me, Scratchy," he said. "Honest, I ain't." He was stiffening and steadying, but yet somewhere at the back of
his mind a vision of the Pullman floated: the sea-green figured velvet, the shining brass, silver, and glass, the wood that gleamed as darkly brilliant as the surface of a pool of oil — all the glory of marriage, the environment of the new
estate. "You know I fight when it comes to fighting, Scratchy Wilson; but I ain't
got a gun on me. You'll have to do all the shootin' yourself."

His enemy's face went livid. He stepped forward, and lashed his weapon to
and fro before Potter's chest. "Don't you tell me you ain't got no gun on you, you
whelp. Don't tell me no lie like that. There ain't a man in Texas ever seen you
without no gun. Don't take me for no kid." His eyes blazed with light, and his
throat worked like a pump.

"I ain't takin' you for no kid," answered Potter. His heels had not moved an 80
inch backward. "I'm takin' you for a damn fool. I tell you I ain't got a gun, and I
ain't. If you're goin' to shoot me up, you better begin now; you'll never get a
chance like this again."

So much enforced reasoning had told on Wilson's rage; he was calmer. "If you
ain't got a gun, why ain't you got a gun?" he sneered. "Been to Sunday-school?"

"I ain't got a gun because I've just come from San Anton' with my wife. I'm
married," said Potter. "And if I'd thought there was going to be any galoots like
you prowling around when I brought my wife home, I'd had a gun, and don't
you forget it."

"Married!" said Scratchy, not at all comprehending.

"Yes, married. I'm married," said Potter, distinctly.

"Married?" said Scratchy. Seemingly for the first time, he saw the drooping, 85
drowning woman at the other man's side. "No!" he said. He was like a creature
allowed a glimpse of another world. He moved a pace backward, and his arm,
with the revolver, dropped to his side. "Is this the lady?" he asked.

"Yes; this is the lady," answered Potter.

There was another period of silence.

"Well," said Wilson at last, slowly, "I s'pose it's all off now."

"It's all off if you say so, Scratchy. You know I didn't make the trouble." Potter lifted his valise.

"Well, I 'low it's off, Jack," said Wilson. He was looking at the ground. "Married!" He was not a student of chivalry; it was merely that in the presence of this foreign condition he was a simple child of the earlier plains. He picked up his starboard revolver, and, placing both weapons in their holsters, he went away. His feet made funnel-shaped tracks in the heavy sand.

For Analysis

1. Explain how the opening paragraph establishes the **tone** and **theme** of the story.

2. Scratchy is described in the final paragraph as "a simple child of the earlier plains." What does this mean? Was Potter ever a simple child of the earlier plains?

3. Early in the story we read that "Jack Potter was beginning to find the shadow of a deed weigh upon him like a leaden slab. He, the town marshal of Yellow Sky, a man known, liked, and feared in his corner, a prominent person, had gone to San Antonio to meet a girl he believed he loved, and there, after the usual prayers, had actually induced her to marry him, without consulting Yellow Sky for any part of the transaction. He was now bringing his bride before an innocent and unsuspecting community" (para. 17). Jack Potter, like any adult, has the right to marry. How do you account for his feelings as described in this passage?

4. A "drummer" is a traveling salesman. What effect does his presence have on the myth of the West?

5. Characterize Scratchy's behavior. How does it relate to the myth of the West preserved in films and Western novels? Why is Scratchy disconsolate at the end?

On Style

1. Analyze Crane's **metaphors** and **images**. What functions do they serve?

2. What is the narrator's attitude toward the story he is telling?

Making Connections

1. Contrast this story, which seems to be about the end of a tradition, with Alice Walker's "Everyday Use" (p. 717), which seems to be about preserving a tradition.

2. In what ways is Scratchy's innocence similar to or different from the innocence of Hulga in O'Connor's "Good Country People" (p. 118) and of the young waiter in Hemingway's "A Clean, Well-Lighted Place" (p. 105)?

Writing Topics

1. Write a brief paragraph speculating on how the description of Scratchy's shirt at the beginning of Part III, especially the detail that it was made "by some Jewish women on the East Side of New York" (para. 63), relates to the theme of the story.

2. Describe the source of your own views about the "old West," and explain how Crane makes use of such stereotypes to achieve comic effects.

James Joyce   (1882–1941)

Araby   1914

North Richmond Street, being blind, was a quiet street except at the hour when the Christian Brothers' School set the boys free. An uninhabited house of two storeys stood at the blind end, detached from its neighbours in a square ground. The other houses of the street, conscious of decent lives within them, gazed at one another with brown imperturbable faces.

The former tenant of our house, a priest, had died in the back drawing-room. Air, musty from having been long enclosed, hung in all the rooms, and the waste room behind the kitchen was littered with old useless papers. Among these I found a few paper-covered books, the pages of which were curled and damp: *The Abbot,* by Walter Scott, *The Devout Communicant* and *The Memoirs of Vidocq.* I liked the last best because its leaves were yellow. The wild garden behind the house contained a central apple-tree and a few straggling bushes under one of which I found the late tenant's rusty bicycle pump. He had been a very charitable priest; in his will he had left all his money to institutions and the furniture of his house to his sister.

When the short days of winter came dusk fell before we had well eaten our dinners. When we met in the street the houses had grown sombre. The space of sky above us was the colour of ever-changing violet and towards it the lamps of the street lifted their feeble lanterns. The cold air stung us and we played till our bodies glowed. Our shouts echoed in the silent street. The career of our play brought us through the dark muddy lanes behind the houses where we ran the gauntlet of the rough tribes from the cottages, to the back doors of the dark dripping gardens where odours arose from the ashpits, to the dark odorous stables where a coachman smoothed and combed the horse or shook music from the buckled harness. When we returned to the street light from the kitchen windows had filled the areas. If my uncle was seen turning the corner we hid in the shadow until we had seen him safely housed. Or if Mangan's sister came out on the doorstep to call her brother in to his tea we watched her from our shadow peer up and down the street. We waited to see whether she would remain or go in and, if she remained, we left our shadow and walked up to Mangan's steps resignedly. She was waiting for us, her figure defined by the light from the half-opened door. Her brother always teased her before he obeyed and I stood by the railings looking at her. Her dress swung as she moved her body and the soft rope of her hair tossed from side to side.

Every morning I lay on the floor in the front parlour watching her door. The blind was pulled down to within an inch of the sash so that I could not be seen. When she came out on the doorstep my heart leaped. I ran to the hall, seized my books and followed her. I kept her brown figure always in my eye and, when we came near the point at which our ways diverged, I quickened my pace and passed her. This happened morning after morning. I had never spoken to her, except for a few casual words, and yet her name was like a summons to all my foolish blood.

Her image accompanied me even in places the most hostile to romance. On Saturday evenings when my aunt went marketing I had to go to carry some of the parcels. We walked through the flaring streets, jostled by drunken men and bargaining women, amid the curses of labourers, the shrill litanies of shop-boys who stood on guard by the barrels of pigs' cheeks, the nasal chanting of street-singers, who sang a *come-all-you*[1] about O'Donovan Rossa, or a ballad about the troubles in our native land. These noises converged in a single sensation of life for me: I imagined that I bore my chalice safely through a throng of foes. Her name sprang to my lips at moments in strange prayers and praises which I myself did not understand. My eyes were often full of tears (I could not tell why) and at times a flood from my heart seemed to pour itself out into my bosom. I thought little of the future. I did not know whether I would ever speak to her or not or, if I spoke to her, how I could tell her of my confused adoration. But my body was like a harp and her words and gestures were like fingers running upon the wires.

One evening I went into the back drawing-room in which the priest had died. It was a dark rainy evening and there was no sound in the house. Through one of the broken panes I heard the rain impinge upon the earth, the fine incessant needles of water playing in the sodden beds. Some distant lamp or lighted window gleamed below me. I was thankful that I could see so little. All my senses seemed to desire to veil themselves and, feeling that I was about to slip from them, I pressed the palms of my hands together until they trembled, murmuring: *"O love! O love!"* many times.

At last she spoke to me. When she addressed the first words to me I was so confused that I did not know what to answer. She asked me was I going to *Araby.* I forgot whether I answered yes or no. It would be a splendid bazaar, she said she would love to go.

"And why can't you?" I asked.

While she spoke she turned a silver bracelet round and round her wrist. She could not go, she said, because there would be a retreat that week in her convent. Her brother and two other boys were fighting for their caps and I was alone at the railings. She held one of the spikes, bowing her head towards me. The light from the lamp opposite our door caught the white curve of her neck, lit up her hair that rested there and, falling, lit up the hand upon the railing. It fell over one side of her dress and caught the white border of a petticoat, just visible as she stood at ease.

"It's well for you," she said.

[1] A street ballad beginning with these words. This one is about Jeremiah Donovan, a nineteenth-century Irish nationalist popularly known as O'Donovan Rossa.

"If I go," I said, "I will bring you something."

What innumerable follies laid waste my waking and sleeping thoughts after that evening! I wished to annihilate the tedious intervening days. I chafed against the work of school. At night in my bedroom and by day in the classroom her image came between me and the page I strove to read. The syllables of the word *Araby* were called to me through the silence in which my soul luxuriated and cast an Eastern enchantment over me. I asked for leave to go to the bazaar on Saturday night. My aunt was surprised and hoped it was not some Freemason affair. I answered few questions in class. I watched my master's face pass from amiability to sternness; he hoped I was not beginning to idle. I could not call my wandering thoughts together. I had hardly any patience with the serious work of life which, now that it stood between me and my desire, seemed to me child's play, ugly monotonous child's play.

On Saturday morning I reminded my uncle that I wished to go to the bazaar in the evening. He was fussing at the hallstand, looking for the hat-brush, and answered me curtly:

"Yes, boy, I know."

As he was in the hall I could not go into the front parlour and lie at the window. I left the house in bad humour and walked slowly towards the school. The air was pitilessly raw and already my heart misgave me. 15

When I came home to dinner my uncle had not yet been home. Still it was early. I sat staring at the clock for some time and, when its ticking began to irritate me, I left the room. I mounted the staircase and gained the upper part of the house. The high cold empty gloomy rooms liberated me and I went from room to room singing. From the front window I saw my companions playing below in the street. Their cries reached me weakened and indistinct and, leaning my forehead against the cool glass, I looked over at the dark house where she lived. I may have stood there for an hour, seeing nothing but the brown-clad figure cast by my imagination, touched discreetly by the lamplight at the curved neck, at the hand upon the railings and at the border below the dress.

When I came downstairs again I found Mrs. Mercer sitting at the fire. She was an old garrulous woman, a pawnbroker's widow, who collected used stamps for some pious purpose. I had to endure the gossip of the tea-table. The meal was prolonged beyond an hour and still my uncle did not come. Mrs. Mercer stood up to go: she was sorry she couldn't wait any longer, but it was after eight o'clock and she did not like to be out late, as the night air was bad for her. When she had gone I began to walk up and down the room, clenching my fists. My aunt said:

"I'm afraid you may put off your bazaar for this night of Our Lord."

At nine o'clock I heard my uncle's latchkey in the hall door. I heard him talking to himself and heard the hallstand rocking when it had received the weight of his overcoat. I could interpret these signs. When he was midway through his dinner I asked him to give me the money to go to the bazaar. He had forgotten.

"The people are in bed and after their first sleep now," he said.   20

I did not smile. My aunt said to him energetically:

"Can't you give him the money and let him go? You've kept him late enough as it is."

My uncle said he was very sorry he had forgotten. He said he believed in the old saying: "All work and no play makes Jack a dull boy." He asked me where I was going and, when I had told him a second time he asked me did I know *The Arab's Farewell to His Steed*. When I left the kitchen he was about to recite the opening lines of the piece to my aunt.

I held a florin tightly in my hand as I strode down Buckingham Street towards the station. The sight of the streets thronged with buyers and glaring with gas recalled to me the purpose of my journey. I took my seat in a third-class carriage of a deserted train. After an intolerable delay the train moved out of the station slowly. It crept onward among ruinous houses and over the twinkling river. At Westland Row Station a crowd of people pressed to the carriage doors; but the porters moved them back, saying that it was a special train for the bazaar. I remained alone in the bare carriage. In a few minutes the train drew up beside an improvised wooden platform. I passed out on to the road and saw by the lighted dial of a clock that it was ten minutes to ten. In front of me was a large building which displayed the magical name.

I could not find any sixpenny entrance and, fearing that the bazaar would be   25 closed, I passed in quickly through a turnstile, handing a shilling to a weary-looking man. I found myself in a big hall girdled at half its height by a gallery. Nearly all the stalls were closed and the greater part of the hall was in darkness. I recognised a silence like that which pervades a church after a service. I walked into the centre of the bazaar timidly. A few people were gathered about the stalls which were still open. Before a curtain, over which the words *Café Chantant* were written in coloured lamps, two men were counting money on a salver. I listened to the fall of the coins.

Remembering with difficulty why I had come I went over to one of the stalls and examined porcelain vases and flowered tea-sets. At the door of the stall a young lady was talking and laughing with two young gentlemen. I remarked their English accents and listened vaguely to their conversation.

"O, I never said such a thing!"

"O, but you did!"

"O, but I didn't!"

"Didn't she say that?"   30

"Yes. I heard her."

"O, there's a . . . fib!"

Observing me the young lady came over and asked me did I wish to buy anything. The tone of her voice was not encouraging; she seemed to have spoken to me out of a sense of duty. I looked humbly at the great jars that stood like Eastern guards at either side of the dark entrance to the stall and murmured:

"No, thank you."

The young lady changed the position of one of the vases and went back to the 35 two young men. They began to talk of the same subject. Once or twice the young lady glanced at me over her shoulder.

I lingered before her stall, though I knew my stay was useless, to make my interest in her wares seem the more real. Then I turned away slowly and walked down the middle of the bazaar. I allowed the two pennies to fall against the six-pence in my pocket. I heard a voice call from one end of the gallery that the light was out. The upper part of the hall was now completely dark.

Gazing up into the darkness I saw myself as a creature driven and derided by vanity; and my eyes burned with anguish and anger.

For Analysis

1. Reread the opening paragraph. How does it set the tone for the story?

2. What do we learn about the narrator from his comment (para. 2) that he liked *The Memoirs of Vidocq* best "because its leaves were yellow"?

3. What does Mangan's sister represent to the narrator?

4. Why does the dialogue the narrator overhears at the bazaar trigger the climax of the story and the insight described in the final paragraph?

On Style

1. What does the **tone** of this story, particularly its lack of humor, tell us about the kind of significance the adult narrator attaches to this childhood experience?

2. Carefully examine the language of paragraph 5. What stylistic devices allow the narrator to transform a simple shopping trip into a chivalric romance?

Making Connections

1. Compare the use of the first-person **point of view** in this story with the first-person point of view in O'Connor's "My Oedipus Complex" (p. 109).

2. Describe an experience that led you to realize that you were not acting out of the selfless motives you had thought you were.

Writing Topics

1. Write a page describing a romantic infatuation you experienced when you were younger that blinded you to the reality of the person you adored.

2. Analyze the imagery of light and vision in this story.

Ernest Hemingway   (1899–1961)

A Clean, Well-Lighted Place   1933

It was late and everyone had left the café except an old man who sat in the shadow the leaves of the tree made against the electric light. In the day time the street was dusty, but at night the dew settled the dust and the old man liked to sit late because he was deaf and now at night it was quiet and he felt the difference. The two waiters inside the café knew that the old man was a little drunk, and while he was a good client they knew that if he became too drunk he would leave without paying, so they kept watch on him.

"Last week he tried to commit suicide," one waiter said.

"Why?"

"He was in despair."

"What about?"

"Nothing."   5

"How do you know it was nothing?"

"He has plenty of money."

They sat together at a table that was close against the wall near the door of the café and looked at the terrace where the tables were all empty except where the old man sat in the shadow of the leaves of the tree that moved slightly in the wind. A girl and a soldier went by in the street. The street light shone on the brass number on his collar. The girl wore no head covering and hurried beside him.

"The guard will pick him up," one waiter said.   10

"What does it matter if he gets what he's after?"

"He had better get off the street now. The guard will get him. They went by five minutes ago."

The old man sitting in the shadow rapped on his saucer with his glass. The younger waiter went over to him.

"What do you want?"

The old man looked at him. "Another brandy," he said.   15

"You'll be drunk," the waiter said. The old man looked at him. The waiter went away.

"He'll stay all night," he said to his colleague. "I'm sleepy now. I never get into bed before three o'clock. He should have killed himself last week."

The waiter took the brandy bottle and another saucer from the counter inside the café and marched out to the old man's table. He put down the saucer and poured the glass full of brandy.

"You should have killed yourself last week," he said to the deaf man. The old man motioned with his finger. "A little more," he said. The waiter poured on into the glass so that the brandy slopped over and ran down the stem into the top saucer of the pile. "Thank you," the old man said. The waiter took the bottle back inside the café. He sat down at the table with his colleague again.

"He's drunk now," he said.   20

"He's drunk every night."

"What did he want to kill himself for?"

"How should I know."

"How did he do it?"

"He hung himself with a rope."   25

"Who cut him down?"

"His niece."

"Why did they do it?"

"Fear for his soul."

"How much money has he got?"   30

"He's got plenty."

"He must be eighty years old."

"Anyway I should say he was eighty."

"I wish he would go home. I never get to bed before three o'clock. What kind of hour is that to go to bed?"

"He stays up because he likes it."   35

"He's lonely. I'm not lonely. I have a wife waiting in bed for me."

"He had a wife once too."

"A wife would be no good to him now."

"You can't tell. He might be better with a wife."

"His niece looks after him. You said she cut him down."   40

"I know."

"I wouldn't want to be that old. An old man is a nasty thing."

"Not always. This old man is clean. He drinks without spilling. Even now, drunk. Look at him."

"I don't want to look at him. I wish he would go home. He has no regard for those who must work."

The old man looked from his glass across the square, then over at the waiters.   45

"Another brandy," he said, pointing to his glass. The waiter who was in a hurry came over.

"Finished," he said, speaking with that omission of syntax stupid people employ when talking to drunken people or foreigners. "No more tonight. Close now."

"Another," said the old man.

"No. Finished." The waiter wiped the edge of the table with a towel and shook his head.

The old man stood up, slowly counted the saucers, took a leather coin purse   50
from his pocket and paid for the drinks, leaving half a peseta tip.

The waiter watched him go down the street, a very old man walking unsteadily but with dignity.

"Why didn't you let him stay and drink?" the unhurried waiter asked. They were putting up the shutters. "It is not half-past two."

"I want to go home to bed."

"What is an hour?"

"More to me than to him." 55

"An hour is the same."

"You talk like an old man yourself. He can buy a bottle and drink at home."

"It's not the same."

"No, it is not," agreed the waiter with a wife. He did not wish to be unjust. He was only in a hurry.

"And you? You have no fear of going home before your usual hour?" 60

"Are you trying to insult me?"

"No, hombre, only to make a joke."

"No," the waiter who was in a hurry said, rising from pulling down the metal shutters. "I have confidence. I am all confidence."

"You have youth, confidence, and a job," the older waiter said. "You have everything."

"And what do you lack?" 65

"Everything but work."

"You have everything I have."

"No. I have never had confidence and I am not young."

"Come on. Stop talking nonsense and lock up."

"I am of those who like to stay late at the café," the older waiter said. "With 70 all those who do not want to go to bed. With all those who need a light for the night."

"I want to go home and into bed."

"We are of two different kinds," the older waiter said. He was now dressed to go home. "It is not only a question of youth and confidence although those things are very beautiful. Each night I am reluctant to close up because there may be some one who needs the café."

"Hombre, there are bodegas open all night long."

"You do not understand. This is a clean and pleasant café. It is well lighted. The light is very good and also, now, there are shadows of the leaves."

"Good night," said the younger waiter. 75

"Good night," the other said. Turning off the electric light he continued the conversation with himself. It is the light of course but it is necessary that the place be clean and pleasant. You do not want music. Certainly you do not want music. Nor can you stand before a bar with dignity although that is all that is provided for these hours. What did he fear? It was not fear or dread. It was a nothing that he knew too well. It was all a nothing and a man was nothing too. It was only that and light was all it needed and a certain cleanness and order. Some lived in it and never felt it but he knew it was nada y pues nada y pues nada.[1] Our nada who art in nada, nada be thy name thy kingdom nada thy will be nada in nada as it is in nada. Give us this nada our daily nada and nada us our nada as we nada our nadas and nada us not into nada but deliver us from nada; pues

---

[1] Nothing, and then nothing, and then nothing.

nada. Hail nothing full of nothing, nothing is with thee. He smiled and stood before a bar with a shining steam pressure coffee machine.

"What's yours?" asked the barman.

"Nada."

"Otro loco más,"[2] said the barman and turned away.

"A little cup," said the waiter.   80

The barman poured it for him.

"The light is very bright and pleasant but the bar is unpolished," the waiter said.

The barman looked at him but did not answer. It was too late at night for conversation.

"You want another copita?" the barman asked.

"No, thank you," said the waiter and went out. He disliked bars and bodegas. 85
A clean, well-lighted café was a very different thing. Now, without thinking further, he would go home to his room. He would lie in the bed and finally, with daylight, he would go to sleep. After all, he said to himself, it is probably only insomnia. Many must have it.

For Analysis

1. How does the first dialogue between the two waiters establish the differences between them?

2. What bearing do the waiters' two different views toward the old man have on the **theme** of the story? Is the difference in age between them relevant to the theme? Explain.

3. How does the setting contribute to the story's theme?

4. Explain the meaning of the story's title.

5. What arguments could be made that this is a religious story?

On Style

Hemingway relies heavily on **dialogue** in this story. How effective is this use of dialogue?

Making Connections

1. What thematic similarities do you find among this story, Hawthorne's "Young Goodman Brown" (p. 80), and Melville's "Bartleby the Scrivener" (p. 334)?

2. Compare and contrast the meaning of *nada* in this story and Hulga's belief in "nothing" in O'Connor's "Good Country People" (p. 118).

Writing Topic

Write an essay on the connection between the **parody** of the Lord's Prayer (para. 76) and the title of the story.

---

[2] Another crazy one.

Frank O'Connor (1903–1966)

My Oedipus Complex 1950

F ather was in the army all through the war — the first war, I mean — so, up
to the age of five, I never saw much of him, and what I saw did not worry
me. Sometimes I woke and there was a big figure in khaki peering down at me
in the candlelight. Sometimes in the early morning I heard the slamming of
the front door and the clatter of nailed boots down the cobbles of the lane.
These were Father's entrances and exits. Like Santa Claus he came and went
mysteriously.

In fact, I rather liked his visits, though it was an uncomfortable squeeze between Mother and him when I got into the big bed in the early morning. He
smoked, which gave him a pleasant musty smell, and shaved, an operation of
astounding interest. Each time he left a trail of souvenirs — model tanks and
Gurkha knives with handles made of bullet cases, and German helmets and cap
badges and button-sticks, and all sorts of military equipment — carefully stowed
away in a long box on top of the wardrobe, in case they ever came in handy.
There was a bit of the magpie about Father; he expected everything to come in
handy. When his back was turned, Mother let me get a chair and rummage
through his treasures. She didn't seem to think so highly of them as he did.

The war was the most peaceful period of my life. The window of my attic faced
southeast. My mother had curtained it, but that had small effect. I always woke
with the first light and, with all the responsibilities of the previous day melted,
feeling myself rather like the sun, ready to illumine and rejoice. Life never
seemed so simple and clear and full of possibilities as then. I put my feet out
from under the clothes — I called them Mrs. Left and Mrs. Right — and invented dramatic situations for them in which they discussed the problems of the
day. At least Mrs. Right did; she was very demonstrative, but I hadn't the same
control of Mrs. Left, so she mostly contented herself with nodding agreement.

They discussed what Mother and I should do during the day, what Santa
Claus should give a fellow for Christmas, and what steps should be taken to
brighten the home. There was that little matter of the baby, for instance.
Mother and I could never agree about that. Ours was the only house in the terrace without a new baby, and Mother said we couldn't afford one till Father
came back from the war because they cost seventeen and six. That showed how
simple she was. The Geneys up the road had a baby, and everyone knew they
couldn't afford seventeen and six. It was probably a cheap baby, and Mother
wanted something really good, but I felt she was too exclusive. The Geneys'
baby would have done us fine.

Having settled my plans for the day, I got up, put a chair under the attic win- 5
dow, and lifted the frame high enough to stick out my head. The window overlooked the front gardens of the terrace behind ours, and beyond these it looked
over a deep valley to the tall, red-brick houses terraced up the opposite hillside,
which were all still in shadow, while those at our side of the valley were all lit up,
though with long strange shadows that made them seem unfamiliar, rigid and
painted.

After that I went into Mother's room and climbed into the big bed. She woke
and I began to tell her of my schemes. By this time, though I never seem to have
noticed it, I was petrified in my nightshirt, and I thawed as I talked until, the last
frost melted, I fell asleep beside her and woke again only when I heard her
below in the kitchen, making the breakfast.

After breakfast we went into town; heard Mass at St. Augustine's and said a
prayer for Father, and did the shopping. If the afternoon was fine we either
went for a walk in the country or a visit to Mother's great friend in the convent,
Mother St. Dominic. Mother had them all praying for Father, and every night,
going to bed, I asked God to send him back safe from the war to us. Little,
indeed, did I know what I was praying for!

One morning, I got into the big bed, and there, sure enough, was Father in
his usual Santa Claus manner, but later, instead of uniform, he put on his best
blue suit, and Mother was as pleased as anything. I saw nothing to be pleased
about, because, out of uniform, Father was altogether less interesting, but she
only beamed, and explained that our prayers had been answered, and off we
went to Mass to thank God for having brought Father safely home.

The irony of it! That very day when he came in to dinner he took off his boots
and put on his slippers, donned the dirty old cap he wore about the house to
save him from colds, crossed his legs, and began to talk gravely to Mother, who
looked anxious. Naturally, I disliked her looking anxious, because it destroyed
her good looks, so I interrupted him.

"Just a moment, Larry!" she said gently. 10

This was only what she said when we had boring visitors, so I attached no
importance to it and went on talking.

"Do be quiet, Larry!" she said impatiently. "Don't you hear me talking to
Daddy?"

This was the first time I had heard those ominous words, "talking to Daddy,"
and I couldn't help feeling that if this was how God answered prayers, he
couldn't listen to them very attentively.

"Why are you talking to Daddy?" I asked with as great a show of indifference
as I could muster.

"Because Daddy and I have business to discuss. Now, don't interrupt again!" 15

In the afternoon, at Mother's request, Father took me for a walk. This time
we went into town instead of out to the country, and I thought at first, in my
usual optimistic way, that it might be an improvement. It was nothing of the
sort. Father and I had quite different notions of a walk in town. He had no
proper interest in trams, ships, and horses, and the only thing that seemed to

divert him was talking to fellows as old as himself. When I wanted to stop he simply went on, dragging me behind him by the hand; when he wanted to stop I had no alternative but to do the same. I noticed that it seemed to be a sign that he wanted to stop for a long time whenever he leaned against a wall. The second time I saw him do it I got wild. He seemed to be settling himself forever. I pulled him by the coat and trousers, but, unlike Mother who, if you were too persistent, got into a wax and said: "Larry, if you don't behave yourself, I'll give you a good slap," Father had an extraordinary capacity for amiable inattention. I sized him up and wondered would I cry, but he seemed to be too remote to be annoyed even by that. Really, it was like going for a walk with a mountain! He either ignored the wrenching and pummeling entirely, or else glanced down with a grin of amusement from his peak. I had never met anyone so absorbed in himself as he seemed.

At teatime, "talking to Daddy" began again, complicated this time by the fact that he had an evening paper, and every few minutes he put it down and told Mother something new out of it. I felt this was foul play. Man for man, I was prepared to compete with him any time for Mother's attention, but when he had it all made up for him by other people it left me no chance. Several times I tried to change the subject without success.

"You must be quiet while Daddy is reading, Larry," Mother said impatiently.

It was clear that she either genuinely liked talking to Father better than talking to me, or else that he had some terrible hold on her which made her afraid to admit the truth.

"Mummy," I said that night when she was tucking me up, "do you think if I 20 prayed hard God would send Daddy back to the war?"

She seemed to think about that for a moment.

"No, dear," she said with a smile. "I don't think he would."

"Why wouldn't he, Mummy?"

"Because there isn't a war any longer, dear."

"But, Mummy, couldn't God make another war, if he liked?"   25

"He wouldn't like to, dear. It's not God who makes wars, but bad people."

"Oh!" I said.

I was disappointed about that. I began to think that God wasn't quite what he was cracked up to be.

Next morning I woke at my usual hour, feeling like a bottle of champagne. I put out my feet and invented a long conversation in which Mrs. Right talked of the trouble she had with her own father till she put him in the Home. I didn't quite know what the Home was but it sounded the right place for Father. Then I got my chair and stuck my head out of the attic window. Dawn was just breaking, with a guilty air that made me feel I had caught it in the act. My head bursting with stories and schemes, I stumbled in next door, and in the half-darkness scrambled into the big bed. There was no room at Mother's side so I had to get between her and Father. For the time being I had forgotten about him, and for several minutes I sat bolt upright, racking my brains to know what I could do with him. He was taking up more than his fair share of the bed, and I couldn't get comfortable, so I gave him several kicks that made him grunt and stretch. He made room all right, though. Mother waked and felt for me. I settled back comfortably in the warmth of the bed with my thumb in my mouth.

"Mummy!" I hummed, loudly and contentedly.   30

"Ssh! dear," she whispered. "Don't wake Daddy!"

This was a new development, which threatened to be even more serious than "talking to Daddy." Life without my early-morning conferences was unthinkable.

"Why?" I asked severely.

"Because poor Daddy is tired."

This seemed to me a quite inadequate reason, and I was sickened by the sen- 35 timentality of her "poor Daddy." I never liked that sort of gush; it always struck me as insincere.

"Oh!" I said lightly. Then in my most winning tone: "Do you know where I want to go with you today, Mummy?"

"No, dear," she sighed.

"I want to go down the Glen and fish for thornybacks with my new net, and then I want to go out to the Fox and Hounds, and — "

"Don't-wake-Daddy!" she hissed angrily, clapping her hand across my mouth.

But it was too late. He was awake, or nearly so. He grunted and reached for 40 the matches. Then he stared incredulously at his watch.

"Like a cup of tea, dear?" asked Mother in a meek, hushed voice I had never heard her use before. It sounded almost as though she were afraid.

"Tea?" he exclaimed indignantly. "Do you know what the time is?"

"And after that I want to go up the Rathcooney Road," I said loudly, afraid I'd forget something in all those interruptions.

"Go to sleep at once, Larry!" she said sharply.

I began to snivel. I couldn't concentrate, the way that pair went on, and smoth- 45 ering my early-morning schemes was like burying a family from the cradle.

Father said nothing, but lit his pipe and sucked it, looking out into the shadows without minding Mother or me. I knew he was mad. Every time I made a remark Mother hushed me irritably. I was mortified. I felt it wasn't fair; there was even something sinister in it. Every time I had pointed out to her the waste of making two beds when we could both sleep in one, she had told me it was healthier like that, and now here was this man, this stranger, sleeping with her without the least regard for her health!

He got up early and made tea, but though he brought Mother a cup he brought none for me.

"Mummy," I shouted, "I want a cup of tea, too."

"Yes, dear," she said patiently. "You can drink from Mummy's saucer."

That settled it. Either Father or I would have to leave the house. I didn't want 50 to drink from Mother's saucer; I wanted to be treated as an equal in my own home, so, just to spite her, I drank it all and left none for her. She took that quietly, too.

But that night when she was putting me to bed she said gently: "Larry, I want you to promise me something."

"What is it?" I asked.

"Not to come in and disturb poor Daddy in the morning. Promise?"

"Poor Daddy" again! I was becoming suspicious of everything involving that quite impossible man.

"Why?" I asked.

"Because poor Daddy is worried and tired and he doesn't sleep well."

"Why doesn't he, Mummy?"

"Well, you know, don't you, that while he was at the war Mummy got the pennies from the Post Office?"

"From Miss MacCarthy?"

"That's right. But now, you see, Miss MacCarthy hasn't any more pennies, so Daddy must go out and find us some. You know what would happen if he couldn't?"

"No," I said, "tell us."

"Well, I think we might have to go out and beg for them like the poor old woman on Fridays. We wouldn't like that, would we?"

"No," I agreed. "We wouldn't."

"So you'll promise not to come in and wake him?"

"Promise."

Mind you, I meant that. I knew pennies were a serious matter, and I was all against having to go out and beg like the old woman on Fridays. Mother laid out all my toys in a complete ring round the bed so that, whatever way I got out, I was bound to fall over one of them.

When I woke I remembered my promise all right. I got up and sat on the floor and played — for hours, it seemed to me. Then I got my chair and looked out the attic window for more hours. I wished it was time for Father to wake; I wished someone would make me a cup of tea. I didn't feel in the least like the sun; instead, I was bored and so very, very cold! I simply longed for the warmth and depth of the big featherbed.

At last I could stand it no longer. I went into the next room. As there was still no room at Mother's side I climbed over her and she woke with a start.

"Larry," she whispered, gripping my arm very tightly, "what did you promise?"

"But I did, Mummy," I wailed, caught in the very act. "I was quiet for ever so long."

"Oh, dear, and you're perished!" she said sadly, feeling me all over. "Now, if I let you stay will you promise not to talk?"

"But I want to talk, Mummy," I wailed.

"That has nothing to do with it," she said with a firmness that was new to me. "Daddy wants to sleep. Now, do you understand that?"

I understood it only too well. I wanted to talk, he wanted to sleep — whose house was it, anyway?

"Mummy," I said with equal firmness, "I think it would be healthier for 75
Daddy to sleep in his own bed."

That seemed to stagger her, because she said nothing for a while.

"Now, once for all," she went on, "you're to be perfectly quiet or go back to
your own bed. Which is it to be?"

The injustice of it got me down. I had convicted her out of her own mouth of
inconsistency and unreasonableness, and she hadn't even attempted to reply.
Full of spite, I gave Father a kick, which she didn't notice but which made him
grunt and open his eyes in alarm.

"What time is it?" he asked in a panic-stricken voice, not looking at Mother
but the door, as if he saw someone there.

"It's early yet," she replied soothingly. "It's only the child. Go to sleep 80
again. . . . Now, Larry," she added, getting out of bed, "you've wakened Daddy
and you must go back."

This time, for all her quiet air, I knew she meant it, and knew that my principal rights and privileges were as good as lost unless I asserted them at once. As
she lifted me, I gave a screech, enough to wake the dead, not to mind Father.
He groaned.

"That damn child! Doesn't he ever sleep?"

"It's only a habit, dear," she said quietly, though I could see she was vexed.

"Well, it's time he got out of it," shouted Father, beginning to heave in the
bed. He suddenly gathered all the bedclothes about him, turned to the wall, and
then looked back over his shoulder with nothing showing, only two small, spiteful, dark eyes. The man looked very wicked.

To open the bedroom door, Mother had to let me down, and I broke free and 85
dashed for the farthest corner, screeching. Father sat bolt upright in bed.

"Shut up, you little puppy!" he said in a choking voice.

I was so astonished that I stopped screeching. Never, never had anyone spoken to me in that tone before. I looked at him incredulously and saw his face
convulsed with rage. It was only then that I fully realized how God had codded
me, listening to my prayers for the safe return of this monster.

"Shut up, you!" I bawled, beside myself.

"What's that you said?" shouted Father, making a wild leap out of bed.

"Mick, Mick!" cried Mother. "Don't you see the child isn't used to you?" 90

"I see he's better fed than taught," snarled Father, waving his arms wildly.
"He wants his bottom smacked."

All his previous shouting was as nothing to these obscene words referring to
my person. They really made my blood boil.

"Smack your own!" I screamed hysterically. "Smack your own! Shut up!
Shut up!"

At this he lost his patience and let fly at me. He did it with the lack of conviction you'd expect of a man under Mother's horrified eyes, and it ended up
as a mere tap, but the sheer indignity of being struck at all by a stranger, a
total stranger who had cajoled his way back from the war into our big bed as a
result of my innocent intercession, made me completely dotty. I shrieked and

shrieked, and danced in my bare feet, and Father, looking awkward and hairy in nothing but a short grey army shirt, glared down at me like a mountain out for murder. I think it must have been then that I realized he was jealous too. And there stood Mother in her nightdress, looking as if her heart was broken between us. I hoped she felt as she looked. It seemed to me that she deserved it all.

From that morning out my life was a hell. Father and I were enemies, open 95 and avowed. We conducted a series of skirmishes against one another, he trying to steal my time with Mother and I his. When she was sitting on my bed, telling me a story, he took to looking for some pair of old boots which he alleged he had left behind him at the beginning of the war. While he talked to Mother I played loudly with my toys to show my total lack of concern. He created a terrible scene one evening when he came in from work and found me at his box, playing with his regimental badges, Gurkha knives and button-sticks. Mother got up and took the box from me.

"You mustn't play with Daddy's toys unless he lets you, Larry," she said severely. "Daddy doesn't play with yours."

For some reason Father looked at her as if she had struck him and then turned away with a scowl.

"Those are not toys," he growled, taking down the box again to see had I lifted anything. "Some of those curios are very rare and valuable."

But as time went on I saw more and more how he managed to alienate Mother and me. What made it worse was that I couldn't grasp his method or see what attraction he had for Mother. In every possible way he was less winning than I. He had a common accent and made noises at his tea. I thought for a while that it might be the newspapers she was interested in, so I made up bits of news of my own to read to her. Then I thought it might be the smoking, which I personally thought attractive, and took his pipes and went round the house dribbling into them till he caught me. I even made noises at my tea, but Mother only told me I was disgusting. It all seemed to hinge round that unhealthy habit of sleeping together, so I made a point of dropping into their bedroom and nosing round, talking to myself, so that they wouldn't know I was watching them, but they were never up to anything that I could see. In the end it beat me. It seemed to depend on being grown-up and giving people rings, and I realized I'd have to wait.

But at the same time I wanted him to see that I was only waiting, not giving 100 up the fight. One evening when he was being particularly obnoxious, chattering away well above my head, I let him have it.

"Mummy," I said, "do you know what I'm going to do when I grow up?"

"No, dear," she replied. "What?"

"I'm going to marry you," I said quietly.

Father gave a great guffaw out of him, but he didn't take me in. I knew it must only be pretense. And Mother, in spite of everything, was pleased. I felt she was probably relieved to know that one day Father's hold on her would be broken.

"Won't that be nice?" she said with a smile.   105

"It'll be very nice," I said confidentially. "Because we're going to have lots and lots of babies."

"That's right, dear," she said placidly. "I think we'll have one soon, and then you'll have plenty of company."

I was no end pleased about that because it showed that in spite of the way she gave in to Father she still considered my wishes. Besides, it would put the Geneys in their place.

It didn't turn out like that, though. To begin with, she was very preoccu-pied — I supposed about where she would get the seventeen and six — and though Father took to staying out late in the evenings it did me no particular good. She stopped taking me for walks, became as touchy as blazes, and smacked me for nothing at all. Sometimes I wished I'd never mentioned the confounded baby — I seemed to have a genius for bringing calamity on myself.

And calamity it was! Sonny arrived in the most appalling hullabaloo — even   110
that much he couldn't do without a fuss — and from the first moment I disliked him. He was a difficult child — so far as I was concerned he was always dif-ficult — and demanded far too much attention. Mother was simply silly about him, and couldn't see when he was only showing off. As company he was worse than useless. He slept all day, and I had to go round the house on tiptoe to avoid waking him. It wasn't any longer a question of not waking Father. The slogan now was "Don't-wake-Sonny!" I couldn't understand why the child wouldn't sleep at the proper time, so whenever Mother's back was turned I woke him. Sometimes to keep him awake I pinched him as well. Mother caught me at it one day and gave me a most unmerciful flaking.

One evening, when Father was coming from work, I was playing trains in the front garden. I let on not to notice him; instead, I pretended to be talking to myself, and said in a loud voice: "If another bloody baby comes into this house, I'm going out."

Father stopped dead and looked at me over his shoulder.

"What's that you said?" he asked sternly.

"I was only talking to myself," I replied, trying to conceal my panic. "It's private."

He turned and went in without a word. Mind you, I intended it as a solemn   115
warning, but its effect was quite different. Father started being quite nice to me. I could understand that, of course. Mother was quite sickening about Sonny. Even at mealtimes she'd get up and gawk at him in the cradle with an idi-otic smile, and tell Father to do the same. He was always polite about it, but he looked so puzzled you could see he didn't know what she was talking about. He complained of the way Sonny cried at night, but she only got cross and said that Sonny never cried except when there was something up with him — which was a flaming lie, because Sonny never had anything up with him, and only cried for attention. It was really painful to see how simple-minded she was. Father wasn't attractive, but he had a fine intelligence. He saw through Sonny, and now he knew that I saw through him as well.

One night I woke with a start. There was someone beside me in the bed. For one wild moment I felt sure it must be Mother, having come to her senses and left Father for good, but then I heard Sonny in convulsions in the next room, and Mother saying: "There! There! There!" and I knew it wasn't she. It was Father. He was lying beside me, wide awake, breathing hard and apparently as mad as hell.

After a while it came to me what he was mad about. It was his turn now. After turning me out of the big bed, he had been turned out himself. Mother had no consideration now for anyone but that poisonous pup, Sonny. I couldn't help feeling sorry for Father. I had been through it all myself, and even at that age I was magnanimous. I began to stroke him down and say: "There! There!" He wasn't exactly responsive.

"Aren't you asleep either?" he snarled.

"Ah, come on and put your arm around us, can't you?" I said, and he did, in a sort of way. Gingerly, I suppose, is how you'd describe it. He was very bony but better than nothing.

At Christmas he went out of his way to buy me a really nice model railway.   120

For Analysis

1. Is the story narrated from the **point of view** of a young child or an adult? Explain.

2. What does the title allude to?

3. Examine the phrases that refer to or evoke the narrator's father in the opening paragraph. How are they appropriate to the story the narrator is about to tell?

On Style

How does the author create the comic **tone** of this story?

Making Connections

1. Compare the use of the first-person narrator in this story, in Bambara's "The Lesson" (p. 134), and in Cisneros's "The House on Mango Street" (p. 141).

2. Compare and contrast the way the family is portrayed in this story with the portrayal of the family in Joyce's "Araby" (p. 100).

Writing Topics

1. Analyze the use of **irony** as a comic device in this story.

2. Write an essay explaining which character you find the most sympathetic and why.

Flannery O'Connor (1925–1964)

Good Country People 1955

Besides the neutral expression that she wore when she was alone, Mrs. Freeman had two others, forward and reverse, that she used for all her human dealings. Her forward expression was steady and driving like the advance of a heavy truck. Her eyes never swerved to left or right but turned as the story turned as if they followed a yellow line down the center of it. She seldom used the other expression because it was not often necessary for her to retract a statement, but when she did, her face came to a complete stop, there was an almost imperceptible movement of her black eyes, during which they seemed to be receding, and then the observer would see that Mrs. Freeman, though she might stand there as real as several grain sacks thrown on top of each other, was no longer there in spirit. As for getting anything across to her when this was the case, Mrs. Hopewell had given it up. She might talk her head off. Mrs. Freeman could never be brought to admit herself wrong on any point. She would stand there and if she could be brought to say anything, it was something like, "Well, I wouldn't of said it was and I wouldn't of said it wasn't," or letting her gaze range over the top kitchen shelf where there was an assortment of dusty bottles, she might remark, "I see you ain't ate many of them figs you put up last summer."

They carried on their most important business in the kitchen at breakfast. Every morning Mrs. Hopewell got up at seven o'clock and lit her gas heater and Joy's. Joy was her daughter, a large blonde girl who had an artificial leg. Mrs. Hopewell thought of her as a child though she was thirty-two years old and highly educated. Joy would get up while her mother was eating and lumber into the bathroom and slam the door, and before long, Mrs. Freeman would arrive at the back door. Joy would hear her mother call, "Come on in," and then they would talk for a while in low voices that were indistinguishable in the bathroom. By the time Joy came in, they had usually finished the weather report and were on one or the other of Mrs. Freeman's daughters, Glynese or Carramae. Joy called them Glycerin and Caramel. Glynese, a redhead, was eighteen and had many admirers; Carramae, a blonde, was only fifteen but already married and pregnant. She could not keep anything on her stomach. Every morning Mrs. Freeman told Mrs. Hopewell how many times she had vomited since the last report.

Mrs. Hopewell liked to tell people that Glynese and Carramae were two of the finest girls she knew and that Mrs. Freeman was a *lady* and that she was never ashamed to take her anywhere or introduce her to anybody they might meet. Then she would tell how she had happened to hire the Freemans in the first place and how they were a godsend to her and how she had had them four years. The reason for her keeping them so long was that they were not trash. They were good country people. She had telephoned the man whose name they had given as a reference and he had told her that Mr. Freeman was a good farmer but that his wife was the nosiest woman ever to walk the earth. "She's got to be into everything," the man said. "If she don't get there before the dust settles, you can bet she's dead, that's all. She'll want to know all your business. I can stand him real good," he had said, "but me nor my wife neither could have stood that woman one more minute on this place." That had put Mrs. Hopewell off for a few days.

She had hired them in the end because there were no other applicants but she had made up her mind beforehand exactly how she would handle the woman. Since she was the type who had to be into everything, then, Mrs. Hopewell had decided, she would not only let her be into everything, she would *see* to it that she was into everything — she would give her the responsibility of everything, she would put her in charge. Mrs. Hopewell had no bad qualities of her own but she was able to use other people's in such a constructive way that she never felt the lack. She had hired the Freemans and she had kept them four years.

Nothing is perfect. This was one of Mrs. Hopewell's favorite sayings. Another 5 was: that is life! And still another, the most important, was: well, other people have their opinions too. She would make these statements, usually at the table, in a tone of gentle insistence as if no one held them but her, and the large hulking Joy, whose constant outrage had obliterated every expression from her face, would stare just a little to the side of her, her eyes icy blue, with the look of someone who has achieved blindness by an act of will and means to keep it.

When Mrs. Hopewell said to Mrs. Freeman that life was like that, Mrs. Freeman would say, "I always said so myself." Nothing had been arrived at by anyone that had not first been arrived at by her. She was quicker than Mr. Freeman. When Mrs. Hopewell said to her after they had been on the place a while, "You know, you're the wheel behind the wheel," and winked, Mrs. Freeman had said, "I know it. I've always been quick. It's some that are quicker than others."

"Everybody is different," Mrs. Hopewell said.

"Yes, most people is," Mrs. Freeman said.

"It takes all kinds to make the world."

"I always said it did myself." 10

The girl was used to this kind of dialogue for breakfast and more of it for dinner; sometimes they had it for supper too. When they had no guest they ate in the kitchen because that was easier. Mrs. Freeman always managed to arrive at some point during the meal and to watch them finish it. She would stand in the doorway if it were summer but in the winter she would stand with one elbow on top of the refrigerator and look down on them, or she would stand by the gas heater, lifting the back of her skirt slightly. Occasionally she would stand against the wall and roll her head from side to side. At no time was she in any hurry to leave. All this was very trying on Mrs. Hopewell but she was a woman of great patience. She realized that nothing is perfect and that in the Freemans she had good country people and that if, in this day and age, you get good country people, you had better hang onto them.

She had had plenty of experience with trash. Before the Freemans she had averaged one tenant family a year. The wives of these farmers were not the kind you would want to be around you for very long. Mrs. Hopewell, who had divorced her husband long ago, needed someone to walk over the fields with her; and when Joy had to be impressed for these services, her remarks were usually so ugly and her face so glum that Mrs. Hopewell would say, "If you can't come pleasantly, I don't want you at all," to which the girl, standing square and rigid-shouldered with her neck thrust slightly forward, would reply, "If you want me, here I am — LIKE I AM."

Mrs. Hopewell excused this attitude because of the leg (which had been shot off in a hunting accident when Joy was ten). It was hard for Mrs. Hopewell to realize that her child was thirty-two now and that for more than twenty years she had had only one leg. She thought of her still as a child because it tore her heart to think instead of the poor stout girl in her thirties who had never danced a step or had any *normal* good times. Her name was really Joy but as soon as she was twenty-one and away from home, she had had it legally changed. Mrs. Hopewell was certain that she had thought and thought until she had hit upon the ugliest name in any language. Then she had gone and had the beautiful name, Joy, changed without telling her mother until after she had done it. Her legal name was Hulga.

When Mrs. Hopewell thought the name, Hulga, she thought of the broad blank hull of a battleship. She would not use it. She continued to call her Joy to which the girl responded but in a purely mechanical way.

Hulga had learned to tolerate Mrs. Freeman, who saved her from taking 15 walks with her mother. Even Glynese and Carramae were useful when they occupied attention that might otherwise have been directed at her. At first she had thought she could not stand Mrs. Freeman for she had found that it was not possible to be rude to her. Mrs. Freeman would take on strange resentments and for days together she would be sullen but the source of her displeasure was always obscure; a direct attack, a positive leer, blatant ugliness to her face — these never touched her. And without warning one day, she began calling her Hulga.

She did not call her that in front of Mrs. Hopewell who would have been incensed but when she and the girl happened to be out of the house together, she would say something and add the name Hulga to the end of it, and the big spectacled Joy-Hulga would scowl and redden as if her privacy had been intruded upon. She considered the name her personal affair. She had arrived at it first purely on the basis of its ugly sound and then the full genius of its fitness had struck her. She had a vision of the name working like the ugly sweating Vulcan who stayed in the furnace and to whom, presumably, the goddess had to come when called. She saw it as the name of her highest creative act. One of her major triumphs was that her mother had not been able to turn her dust into Joy, but the greater one was that she had been able to turn it herself into Hulga. However, Mrs. Freeman's relish for using the name only irritated her. It was as if Mrs. Freeman's beady steel-pointed eyes had penetrated far enough behind her face to reach some secret fact. Something about her seemed to fascinate Mrs. Freeman and then one day Hulga realized that it was the artificial leg. Mrs. Freeman had a special fondness for the details of secret infections, hidden deformities, assaults upon children. Of diseases, she preferred the lingering or incurable. Hulga had heard Mrs. Hopewell give her the details of the hunting accident, how the leg had been literally blasted off, how she had never lost consciousness. Mrs. Freeman could listen to it any time as if it had happened an hour ago.

When Hulga stumped into the kitchen in the morning (she could walk without making the awful noise but she made it — Mrs. Hopewell was certain — because it was ugly-sounding), she glanced at them and did not speak. Mrs. Hopewell would be in her red kimono with her hair tied around her head in rags. She would be sitting at the table, finishing her breakfast and Mrs. Freeman would be hanging by her elbow outward from the refrigerator, looking down at the table. Hulga always put her eggs on the stove to boil and then stood over them with her arms folded, and Mrs. Hopewell would look at her — a kind of indirect gaze divided between her and Mrs. Freeman — and would think that if she would only keep herself up a little, she wouldn't be so bad looking. There was nothing wrong with her face that a pleasant expression wouldn't help. Mrs. Hopewell said that people who looked on the bright side of things would be beautiful even if they were not.

Whenever she looked at Joy this way, she could not help but feel that it would have been better if the child had not taken the Ph.D. It had certainly not brought her out any and now that she had it, there was no more excuse for her to go to school again. Mrs. Hopewell thought it was nice for girls to go to school to have a good time but Joy had "gone through." Anyhow, she would not have been strong enough to go again. The doctors had told Mrs. Hopewell that with the best of care, Joy might see forty-five. She had a weak heart. Joy had made it plain that if it had not been for this condition, she would be far from these red hills and good country people. She would be in a university lecturing to people who knew what she was talking about. And Mrs. Hopewell could very well picture her there, looking like a scarecrow and lecturing to more of the same. Here she went about all day in a six-year-old skirt and a yellow sweat shirt with a faded cowboy on a horse embossed on it. She thought this was funny; Mrs. Hopewell thought it was idiotic and showed simply that she was still a child. She was brilliant but she didn't have a grain of sense. It seemed to Mrs. Hopewell that every year she grew less like other people and more like herself — bloated, rude, and squint-eyed. And she said such strange things! To her own mother she had said — without warning, without excuse, standing up in the middle of a meal with her face purple and her mouth half full — "Woman! do you ever look inside? Do you ever look inside and see what you are *not*? God!" she had cried sinking down again and staring at her plate, "Malebranche was right: we are not our own light. We are not our own light!" Mrs. Hopewell had no idea to this day what brought that on. She had only made the remark, hoping Joy would take it in, that a smile never hurt anyone.

The girl had taken the Ph.D. in philosophy and this left Mrs. Hopewell at a complete loss. You could say, "My daughter is a nurse," or "My daughter is a school teacher," or even, "My daughter is a chemical engineer." You could not say, "My daughter is a philosopher." That was something that had ended with the Greeks and Romans. All day Joy sat on her deck in a deep chair, reading. Sometimes she went for walks but she didn't like dogs or cats or birds or flowers or nature or nice young men. She looked at nice young men as if she could smell their stupidity.

One day Mrs. Hopewell had picked up one of the books the girl had just put 20 down and opening it at random, she read, "Science, on the other hand, has to assert its soberness and seriousness afresh and declare that it is concerned solely with what-is. Nothing — how can it be for science anything but a horror and a phantasm? If science is right, then one thing stands firm: science wishes to know nothing of nothing. Such is after all the strictly scientific approach to Nothing. We know it by wishing to know nothing of Nothing." These words had been underlined with a blue pencil and they worked on Mrs. Hopewell like some evil incantation in gibberish. She shut the book quickly and went out of the room as if she were having a chill.

This morning when the girl came in, Mrs. Freeman was on Carramae. "She thrown up four times after supper," she said, "and was up twict in the night after three o'clock. Yesterday she didn't do nothing but ramble in the bureau drawer. All she did. Stand up there and see what she could run up on."

"She's got to eat," Mrs. Hopewell muttered, sipping her coffee, while she watched Joy's back at the stove. She was wondering what the child had said to the Bible salesman. She could not imagine what kind of a conversation she could possibly have had with him.

He was a tall gaunt hatless youth who had called yesterday to sell them a Bible. He had appeared at the door, carrying a large black suitcase that weighted him so heavily on one side that he had to brace himself against the door facing. He seemed on the point of collapse but he said in a cheerful voice, "Good morning, Mrs. Cedars!" and set the suitcase down on the mat. He was not a bad-looking young man though he had on a bright blue suit and yellow socks that were not pulled up far enough. He had prominent face bones and a streak of sticky-looking brown hair falling across his forehead.

"I'm Mrs. Hopewell," she said.

"Oh!" he said, pretending to look puzzled but with his eyes sparkling, "I saw it 25 said 'The Cedars,' on the mailbox so I thought you was Mrs. Cedars!" and he burst out in a pleasant laugh. He picked up the satchel and under cover of a pant, he fell forward into her hall. It was rather as if the suitcase had moved first, jerking him after it. "Mrs. Hopewell!" he said and grabbed her hand. "I hope you are well!" and he laughed again and then all at once his face sobered completely. He paused and gave her a straight earnest look and said, "Lady, I've come to speak of serious things."

"Well, come in," she muttered, none too pleased because her dinner was almost ready. He came into the parlor and sat down on the edge of a straight chair and put the suitcase between his feet and glanced around the room as if he were sizing her up by it. Her silver gleamed on the two sideboards; she decided he had never been in a room as elegant as this.

"Mrs. Hopewell," he began, using her name in a way that sounded almost intimate, "I know you believe in Christian service."

"Well yes," she murmured.

"I know," he said and paused, looking very wise with his head cocked on one side, "that you're a good woman. Friends have told me."

Mrs. Hopewell never liked to be taken for a fool. "What are you selling?" she 30 asked.

"Bibles," the young man said and his eye raced around the room before he added, "I see you have no family Bible in your parlor, I see that is the one lack you got!"

Mrs. Hopewell could not say, "My daughter is an atheist and won't let me keep the Bible in the parlor." She said, stiffening slightly, "I keep my Bible by my bedside." This was not the truth. It was in the attic somewhere.

"Lady," he said, "the word of God ought to be in the parlor."

"Well, I think that's a matter of taste," she began. "I think . . ."

"Lady," he said, "for a Christian, the word of God ought to be in every room 35 in the house besides in his heart. I know you're a Christian because I can see it in every line of your face."

She stood up and said, "Well, young man, I don't want to buy a Bible and I smell my dinner burning."

He didn't get up. He began to twist his hands and looking down at them, he said softly, "Well lady, I'll tell you the truth — not many people want to buy one nowadays and besides, I know I'm real simple. I don't know how to say a thing but to say it. I'm just a country boy." He glanced up into her unfriendly face. "People like you don't like to fool with country people like me!"

"Why!" she cried, "good country people are the salt of the earth! Besides, we all have different ways of doing, it takes all kinds to make the world go 'round. That's life!"

"You said a mouthful," he said.

"Why, I think there aren't enough good country people in the world!" she 40 said, stirred. "I think that's what's wrong with it!"

His face had brightened. "I didn't inraduce myself," he said. "I'm Manley Pointer from out in the country around Willohobie, not even from a place, just from near a place."

"You wait a minute," she said. "I have to see about my dinner." She went out to the kitchen and found Joy standing near the door where she had been listening.

"Get rid of the salt of the earth," she said, "and let's eat."

Mrs. Hopewell gave her a pained look and turned the heat down under the vegetables. "*I* can't be rude to anybody," she murmured and went back into the parlor.

He had opened the suitcase and was sitting with a Bible on each knee.   45

"You might as well put those up," she told him. "I don't want one."

"I appreciate your honesty," he said. "You don't see any more real honest people unless you go way out in the country."

"I know," she said, "real genuine folks!" Through the crack in the door she heard a groan.

"I guess a lot of boys come telling you they're working their way through college," he said, "but I'm not going to tell you that. Somehow," he said, "I don't want to go to college. I want to devote my life to Chrustian service. See," he said, lowering his voice, "I got this heart condition. I may not live long. When you know it's something wrong with you and you may not live long, well then, lady . . ." He paused, with his mouth open, and stared at her.

He and Joy had the same condition! She knew that her eyes were filling with   50
tears but she collected herself quickly and murmured, "Won't you stay for dinner? We'd love to have you!" and was sorry the instant she heard herself say it.

"Yes mam," he said in an abashed voice. "I would sher love to do that!"

Joy had given him one look on being introduced to him and then throughout the meal had not glanced at him again. He had addressed several remarks to her, which she pretended not to hear. Mrs. Hopewell could not understand deliberate rudeness, although she lived with it, and she felt she had always to overflow with hospitality to make up for Joy's lack of courtesy. She urged him to talk about himself and he did. He said he was the seventh child of twelve and that his father had been crushed under a tree when he himself was eight years old. He had been crushed very badly, in fact, almost cut in two and was practically not recognizable. His mother had got along the best she could by hard working and she had always seen that her children went to Sunday School and that they read the Bible every evening. He was now nineteen years old and he had been selling Bibles for four months. In that time he had sold seventy-seven Bibles and had the promise of two more sales. He wanted to become a missionary because he thought that was the way you could do most for people. "He who losest his life shall find it," he said simply and he was so sincere, so genuine and earnest that Mrs. Hopewell would not for the world have smiled. He prevented his peas from sliding onto the table by blocking them with a piece of bread which he later cleaned his plate with. She could see Joy observing sidewise how he handled his knife and fork and she saw too that every few minutes, the boy would dart a keen appraising glance at the girl as if he were trying to attract her attention.

After dinner Joy cleared the dishes off the table and disappeared and Mrs. Hopewell was left to talk with him. He told her again about his childhood and his father's accident and about various things that had happened to him. Every five minutes or so she would stifle a yawn. He sat for two hours until finally she told him she must go because she had an appointment in town. He packed his Bibles and thanked her and prepared to leave, but in the doorway he stopped and wrung her hand and said that not on any of his trips had he met a lady as nice as her and he asked if he could come again. She had said she would always be happy to see him.

Joy had been standing in the road, apparently looking at something in the distance, when he came down the steps toward her, bent to the side with his heavy valise. He stopped where she was standing and confronted her directly. Mrs. Hopewell could not hear what he said but she trembled to think what Joy would say to him. She could see that after a minute Joy said something and that then the boy began to speak again, making an excited gesture with his free hand. After a minute Joy said something else at which the boy began to speak once more. Then to her amazement, Mrs. Hopewell saw the two of them walk off together, toward the gate. Joy had walked all the way to the gate with him and Mrs. Hopewell could not imagine what they had said to each other, and she had not yet dared to ask.

Mrs. Freeman was insisting upon her attention. She had moved from the re- 55 frigerator to the heater so that Mrs. Hopewell had to turn and face her in order to seem to be listening. "Glynese gone out with Harvey Hill again last night," she said. "She had this sty."

"Hill," Mrs. Hopewell said absently, "is that the one who works in the garage?"

"Nome, he's the one that goes to chiropracter school," Mrs. Freeman said. "She had this sty. Been had it two days. So she says when he brought her in the other night he says, 'Lemme get rid of that sty for you,' and she says, 'How?' and he says, 'You just lay yourself down acrost the seat of that car and I'll show you.' So she done it and he popped her neck. Kept on a-popping it several times until she made him quit. This morning," Mrs. Freeman said, "she ain't got no sty. She ain't got no traces of a sty."

"I never heard of that before," Mrs. Hopewell said.

"He ast her to marry him before the Ordinary," Mrs. Freeman went on, "and she told him she wasn't going to be married in no *office*."

"Well, Glynese is a fine girl," Mrs. Hopewell said. "Glynese and Carramae are 60 both fine girls."

"Carramae said when her and Lyman was married Lyman said it sure felt sacred to him. She said he said he wouldn't take five hundred dollars for being married by a preacher."

"How much would he take?" the girl asked from the stove.

"He said he wouldn't take five hundred dollars," Mrs. Freeman repeated.

"Well we all have work to do," Mrs. Hopewell said.

"Lyman said it just felt more sacred to him," Mrs. Freeman said. "The doctor 65 wants Carramae to eat prunes. Says instead of medicine. Says them cramps is coming from pressure. You know where I think it is?"

"She'll be better in a few weeks," Mrs. Hopewell said.

"In the tube," Mrs. Freeman said. "Else she wouldn't be as sick as she is."

Hulga had cracked her two eggs into a saucer and was bringing them to the table along with a cup of coffee that she had filled too full. She sat down carefully and began to eat, meaning to keep Mrs. Freeman there by questions if for any reason she showed an inclination to leave. She could perceive her mother's eye on her. The first roundabout question would be about the Bible salesman and she did not wish to bring it on. "How did he pop her neck?" she asked.

Mrs. Freeman went into a description of how he had popped her neck. She said he owned a '55 Mercury but that Glynese said she would rather marry a man with only a '36 Plymouth who would be married by a preacher. The girl asked what if he had a '32 Plymouth and Mrs. Freeman said what Glynese had said was a '36 Plymouth.

Mrs. Hopewell said there were not many girls with Glynese's common sense. 70 She said what she admired in those girls was their common sense. She said that reminded her that they had a nice visitor yesterday, a young man selling Bibles. "Lord," she said, "he bored me to death but he was so sincere and genuine I couldn't be rude to him. He was just good country people, you know," she said, " — just the salt of the earth."

"I seen him walk up," Mrs. Freeman said, "and then later — I seen him walk off," and Hulga could feel the slight shift in her voice, the slight insinuation, that he had not walked off alone, had he? Her face remained expressionless but the color rose into her neck and she seemed to swallow it down with the next spoonful of egg. Mrs. Freeman was looking at her as if they had a secret together.

"Well, it takes all kinds of people to make the world go 'round," Mrs. Hopewell said. "It's very good we aren't all alike."

"Some people are more alike than others," Mrs. Freeman said.

Hulga got up and stumped, with about twice the noise that was necessary, into her room and locked the door. She was to meet the Bible salesman at ten o'clock at the gate. She had thought about it half the night. She had started thinking of it as a great joke and then she had begun to see profound implications in it. She had lain in bed imagining dialogues for them that were insane on the surface but that reached below to depths that no Bible salesman would be aware of. Their conversation yesterday had been of this kind.

He had stopped in front of her and had simply stood there. His face was bony 75 and sweaty and bright, with a little pointed nose in the center of it, and his look was different from what it had been at the dinner table. He was gazing at her with open curiosity, with fascination, like a child watching a new fantastic animal at the zoo, and he was breathing as if he had run a great distance to reach her. His gaze seemed somehow familiar but she could not think where she had been regarded with it before. For almost a minute he didn't say anything. Then on what seemed an insuck of breath, he whispered, "You ever ate a chicken that was two days old?"

The girl looked at him stonily. He might have just put this question up for consideration at the meeting of a philosophical association. "Yes," she presently replied as if she had considered it from all angles.

"It must have been mighty small!" he said triumphantly and shook all over with little nervous giggles, getting very red in the face, and subsiding finally into his gaze of complete admiration, while the girl's expression remained exactly the same.

"How old are you?" he asked softly.

She waited some time before she answered. Then in a flat voice she said, "Seventeen."

His smiles came in succession like waves breaking on the surface of a little 80 lake. "I see you got a wooden leg," he said. "I think you're real brave. I think you're real sweet."

The girl stood blank and solid and silent.

"Walk to the gate with me," he said. "You're a brave sweet little thing and I liked you the minute I seen you walk in the door."

Hulga began to move forward.

"What's your name?" he asked, smiling down on the top of her head.

"Hulga," she said. 85

"Hulga," he murmured, "Hulga. Hulga. I never heard of anybody name Hulga before. You're shy, aren't you, Hulga?" he asked.

She nodded, watching his large red hand on the handle of the giant valise.

"I like girls that wear glasses," he said. "I think a lot. I'm not like these people that a serious thought don't ever enter their heads. It's because I may die."

"I may die too," she said suddenly and looked up at him. His eyes were very small and brown, glittering feverishly.

"Listen," he said, "don't you think some people was meant to meet on ac- 90 count of what all they got in common and all? Like they both think serious thoughts and all?" He shifted the valise to his other hand so that the hand nearest her was free. He caught hold of her elbow and shook it a little. "I don't work on Saturday," he said. "I like to walk in the woods and see what Mother Nature is wearing. O'er the hills and far away. Pic-nics and things. Couldn't we go on a pic-nic tomorrow? Say yes, Hulga," he said and gave her a dying look as if he felt his insides about to drop out of him. He had even seemed to sway slightly toward her.

During the night she had imagined that she seduced him. She imagined that the two of them walked on the place until they came to the storage barn beyond the two back fields and there, she imagined, that things came to such a pass that she very easily seduced him and that then, of course, she had to reckon with his remorse. True genius can get an idea across even to an inferior mind. She imagined that she took his remorse in hand and changed it into a deeper understanding of life. She took all his shame away and turned it into something useful.

She set off for the gate at exactly ten o'clock, escaping without drawing Mrs. Hopewell's attention. She didn't take anything to eat, forgetting that food is usually taken on a picnic. She wore a pair of slacks and a dirty white shirt, and as an afterthought, she had put some Vapex on the collar of it since she did not own any perfume. When she reached the gate no one was there.

She looked up and down the empty highway and had the furious feeling that she had been tricked, that he had only meant to make her walk to the gate after the idea of him. Then suddenly he stood up, very tall, from behind a bush on the opposite embankment. Smiling, he lifted his hat which was new and wide-brimmed. He had not worn it yesterday and she wondered if he had bought it for the occasion. It was toast-colored with a red and white band around it and was slightly too large for him. He stepped from behind the bush still carrying the black valise. He had on the same suit and the same yellow socks sucked down in his shoes from walking. He crossed the highway and said, "I knew you'd come!"

The girl wondered acidly how he had known this. She pointed to the valise and asked, "Why did you bring your Bibles?"

He took her elbow, smiling down on her as if he could not stop. "You can 95 never tell when you'll need the word of God, Hulga," he said. She had a moment in which she doubted that this was actually happening and then they began to climb the embankment. They went down into the pasture toward the woods. The boy walked lightly by her side, bouncing on his toes. The valise did not seem to be heavy today; he even swung it. They crossed half the pasture without saying anything and then, putting his hand easily on the small of her back, he asked softly, "Where does your wooden leg join on?"

She turned an ugly red and glared at him and for an instant the boy looked abashed. "I didn't mean you no harm," he said. "I only meant you're so brave and all. I guess God takes care of you."

"No," she said, looking forward and walking fast, "I don't even believe in God."

At this he stopped and whistled. "No!" he exclaimed as if he were too astonished to say anything else.

She walked on and in a second he was bouncing at her side, fanning with his hat. "That's very unusual for a girl," he remarked, watching her out of the corner of his eye. When they reached the edge of the wood, he put his hand on her back again and drew her against him without a word and kissed her heavily.

The kiss, which had more pressure than feeling behind it, produced that extra 100 surge of adrenalin in the girl that enables one to carry a packed trunk out of a burning house, but in her, the power went at once to the brain. Even before he released her, her mind, clear and detached and ironic anyway, was regarding him from a great distance, with amusement but with pity. She had never been kissed before and she was pleased to discover that it was an unexceptional experience and all a matter of the mind's control. Some people might enjoy drain water if they were told it was vodka. When the boy, looking expectant but uncertain, pushed her gently away, she turned and walked on, saying nothing as if such business, for her, were common enough.

He came along panting at her side, trying to help her when he saw a root that she might trip over. He caught and held back the long swaying blades of thorn vine until she had passed beyond them. She led the way and he came breathing heavily behind her. Then they came out on a sunlit hillside, sloping softly into another one a little smaller. Beyond, they could see the rusted top of the old barn where the extra hay was stored.

The hill was sprinkled with small pink weeds. "Then you ain't saved?" he asked suddenly, stopping.

The girl smiled. It was the first time she had smiled at him at all. "In my economy," she said, "I'm saved and you are damned but I told you I didn't believe in God."

Nothing seemed to destroy the boy's look of admiration. He gazed at her now as if the fantastic animal at the zoo had put its paw through the bars and given him a loving poke. She thought he looked as if he wanted to kiss her again and she walked on before he had the chance.

"Ain't there somewheres we can sit down sometime?" he murmured, his   105
voice softening toward the end of the sentence.

"In that barn," she said.

They made for it rapidly as if it might slide away like a train. It was a large two-story barn, cool and dark inside. The boy pointed up the ladder that led into the loft and said, "It's too bad we can't go up there."

"Why can't we?" she asked.

"Yer leg," he said reverently.

The girl gave him a contemptuous look and putting both hands on the lad-   110
der, she climbed it while he stood below, apparently awestruck. She pulled herself expertly through the opening and then looked down at him and said, "Well, come on if you're coming," and he began to climb the ladder, awkwardly bringing the suitcase with him.

"We won't need the Bible," she observed.

"You never can tell," he said, panting. After he had got into the loft, he was a few seconds catching his breath. She had sat down in a pile of straw. A wide sheath of sunlight, filled with dust particles, slanted over her. She lay back against a bale, her face turned away, looking out the front opening of the barn where hay was thrown from a wagon into the loft. The two pink-speckled hillsides lay back against a dark ridge of woods. The sky was cloudless and cold blue. The boy dropped down by her side and put one arm under her and the other over her and began methodically kissing her face, making little noises like a fish. He did not remove his hat but it was pushed far enough back not to interfere. When her glasses got in his way, he took them off of her and slipped them into his pocket.

The girl at first did not return any of the kisses but presently she began to and after she had put several on his cheek, she reached his lips and remained there, kissing him again and again as if she were trying to draw all the breath out of him. His breath was clear and sweet like a child's and the kisses were sticky like a child's. He mumbled about loving her and about knowing when he first seen her that he loved her, but the mumbling was like the sleepy fretting of a child being put to sleep by his mother. Her mind, throughout this, never stopped or lost itself for a second to her feelings. "You ain't said you love me none," he whispered finally, pulling back from her. "You got to say that."

She looked away from him off into the hollow sky and then down at a black ridge and then down farther into what appeared to be two green swelling lakes.

She didn't realize he had taken her glasses but this landscape could not seem exceptional to her for she seldom paid any close attention to her surroundings.

"You got to say it," he repeated. "You got to say you love me." 115

She was always careful how she committed herself. "In a sense," she began, "if you use the word loosely, you might say that. But it's not a word I use. I don't have illusions. I'm one of those people who see *through* to nothing."

The boy was frowning. "You got to say it. I said it and you got to say it," he said.

The girl looked at him almost tenderly. "You poor baby," she murmured. "It's just as well you don't understand," and she pulled him by the neck, face-down, against her. "We are all damned," she said, "but some of us have taken off our blindfolds and see that there's nothing to see. It's a kind of salvation."

The boy's astonished eyes looked blankly through the ends of her hair. "Okay," he almost whined, "but do you love me or don'tcher?"

"Yes," she said and added, "in a sense. But I must tell you something. There 120 mustn't be anything dishonest between us." She lifted his head and looked him in the eye. "I am thirty years old," she said. "I have a number of degrees."

The boy's look was irritated but dogged. "I don't care," he said. "I don't care a thing about what all you done. I just want to know if you love me or don'tcher?" and he caught her to him and wildly planted her face with kisses until she said, "Yes, yes."

"Okay then," he said, letting her go. "Prove it."

She smiled, looking dreamily out on the shifty landscape. She had seduced him without even making up her mind to try. "How?" she asked, feeling that he should be delayed a little.

He leaned over and put his lips to her ear. "Show me where your wooden leg joins on," he whispered.

The girl uttered a sharp little cry and her face instantly drained of color. The 125 obscenity of the suggestion was not what shocked her. As a child she had some-times been subject to feelings of shame but education had removed the last traces of that as a good surgeon scrapes for cancer; she would no more have felt it over what he was asking than she would have believed in his Bible. But she was as sensitive about the artificial leg as a peacock about his tail. No one ever touched it but her. She took care of it as someone else would his soul, in private and almost with her own eyes turned away. "No," she said.

"I known it," he muttered, sitting up. "You're just playing me for a sucker."

"Oh no no!" she cried. "It joins on at the knee. Only at the knee. Why do you want to see it?"

The boy gave her a long penetrating look. "Because," he said, "it's what makes you different. You ain't like nobody else."

She sat staring at him. There was nothing about her face or her round freezing-blue eyes to indicate that this had moved her; but she felt as if her heart had stopped and left her mind to pump her blood. She decided that for the first time in her life she was face to face with real innocence. This boy, with an instinct that came from beyond wisdom, had touched the truth about her.

When after a minute, she said in a hoarse high voice, "All right," it was like surrendering to him completely. It was like losing her own life and finding it again, miraculously, in his.

Very gently he began to roll the slack leg up. The artificial limb, in a white 130 sock and brown flat shoe, was bound in a heavy material like canvas and ended in an ugly jointure where it was attached to the stump. The boy's face and his voice were entirely reverent as he uncovered it and said, "Now show me how to take it off and on."

She took it off for him and put it back on again and then he took it off himself, handling it as tenderly as if it were a real one. "See!" he said with a delighted child's face. "Now I can do it myself!"

"Put it back on," she said. She was thinking that she would run away with him and that every night he would take the leg off and every morning put it back on again. "Put it back on," she said.

"Not yet," he murmured, setting it on its foot out of her reach. "Leave it off for a while. You got me instead."

She gave a little cry of alarm but he pushed her down and began to kiss her again. Without the leg she felt entirely dependent on him. Her brain seemed to have stopped thinking altogether and to be about some other function that it was not very good at. Different expressions raced back and forth over her face. Every now and then the boy, his eyes like two steel spikes, would glance behind him where the leg stood. Finally she pushed him off and said, "Put it back on me now."

"Wait," he said. He leaned the other way and pulled the valise toward him 135 and opened it. It had a pale blue spotted lining and there were only two Bibles in it. He took one of these out and opened the cover of it. It was hollow and contained a pocket flask of whiskey, a pack of cards, and a small blue box with printing on it. He laid these out in front of her one at a time in an evenly spaced row, like one presenting offerings at the shrine of a goddess. He put the blue box in her hand. THIS PRODUCT TO BE USED ONLY FOR THE PREVENTION OF DISEASE, she read, and dropped it. The boy was unscrewing the top of the flask. He stopped and pointed, with a smile, to the deck of cards. It was not an ordinary deck but one with an obscene picture on the back of each card. "Take a swig," he said, offering her the bottle first. He held it in front of her, but like one mesmerized, she did not move.

Her voice when she spoke had an almost pleading sound. "Aren't you," she murmured, "aren't you just good country people?"

The boy cocked his head. He looked as if he were just beginning to understand that she might be trying to insult him. "Yeah," he said, curling his lip slightly, "but it ain't held me back none. I'm as good as you any day in the week."

"Give me my leg," she said.

He pushed it farther away with his foot. "Come on now, let's begin to have us a good time," he said coaxingly. "We ain't got to know one another good yet."

"Give me my leg!" she screamed and tried to lunge for it but he pushed her 140 down easily.

"What's the matter with you all of a sudden?" he asked, frowning as he screwed the top on the flask and put it quickly inside the Bible. "You just a while ago said you didn't believe in nothing. I thought you was some girl!"

Her face was almost purple. "You're a Christian!" she hissed. "You're a fine Christian! You're just like them all — say one thing and do another. You're a perfect Christian, you're . . ."

The boy's mouth was set angrily. "I hope you don't think," he said in a lofty indignant tone, "that I believe in that crap! I may sell Bibles but I know which end is up and I wasn't born yesterday and I know where I'm going!"

"Give me my leg!" she screeched. He jumped up so quickly that she barely saw him sweep the cards and the blue box back into the Bible and throw the Bible into the valise. She saw him grab the leg and then she saw it for an instant slanted forlornly across the inside of the suitcase with a Bible at either side of its opposite ends. He slammed the lid shut and snatched up the valise and swung it down the hole and then stepped through himself.

When all of him had passed but his head, he turned and regarded her with a look that no longer had any admiration in it. "I've gotten a lot of interesting things," he said. "One time I got a woman's glass eye this way. And you needn't to think you'll catch me because Pointer ain't really my name. I use a different name at every house I call at and don't stay nowhere long. And I'll tell you another thing, Hulga," he said, using the name as if he didn't think much of it, "you ain't so smart. I been believing in nothing ever since I was born!" and then the toast-colored hat disappeared down the hole and the girl was left, sitting on the straw in the dusty sunlight. When she turned her churning face toward the opening, she saw his blue figure struggling successfully over the green speckled lake.

Mrs. Hopewell and Mrs. Freeman, who were in the back pasture, digging up onions, saw him emerge a little later from the woods and head across the meadow toward the highway. "Why, that looks like that nice dull young man that tried to sell me a Bible yesterday," Mrs. Hopewell said, squinting. "He must have been selling them to the Negroes back in there. He was so simple," she said, "but I guess the world would be better off if we were all that simple."

Mrs. Freeman's gaze drove forward and just touched him before he disappeared under the hill. Then she returned her attention to the evil-smelling onion shoot she was lifting from the ground. "Some can't be that simple," she said. "I know I never could."

For Analysis

1. Why does Joy feel that changing her name to Hulga is "her highest creative act" (para. 16)?

2. How appropriate are the names of each of the characters?

3. In what ways do Mrs. Freeman's descriptions of her daughters Glynese and Carramae contribute to the **theme** of the story?

4. Does Mrs. Hopewell's character in any way help to explain her daughter's character? Explain.

5. Briefly describe the central conflict in this story and the manner in which it is resolved.

6. Is the title **ironic**? Explain.

7. Does the story have any admirable characters or heroes in the conventional sense? Explain.

8. Why does Hulga agree to meet with Manley Pointer? Does her experience with him confirm her cynical philosophy of "nothing"? Explain.

9. What is Manley Pointer's motive for humiliating Hulga?

On Style
Analyze the use of **irony** in this story.

Making Connections
1. Compare and contrast the meaning of Hulga's belief in "nothing" in this story with "nada" in Hemingway's "A Clean, Well-Lighted Place" (p. 105).

2. Compare the causes or the consequences of Hulga's disillusionment with that of Young Goodman Brown in Hawthorne's "Young Goodman Brown" (p. 80).

Writing Topics
1. The story opens with a description of Mrs. Hopewell and Mrs. Freeman and ends with a dialogue between the two women. Write an essay showing how these two scenes appropriately frame the story of Hulga and Manley Pointer.

2. Discuss the function of the character of Mrs. Freeman in the story.

Toni Cade Bambara   (1939–1995)

The Lesson   1972

Back in the days when everyone was old and stupid or young and foolish and me and Sugar were the only ones just right, this lady moved on our block with nappy hair and proper speech and no makeup. And quite naturally we laughed at her, laughed the way we did at the junk man who went about his business like he was some big-time president and his sorry-ass horse his secretary. And we kinda hated her too, hated the way we did the winos who cluttered up our parks and pissed on our handball walls and stank up our hallways and stairs so you couldn't halfway play hide-and-seek without a goddamn gas mask. Miss Moore was her name. The only woman on the block with no first name. And she was black as hell, cept for her feet, which were fish-white and spooky. And she was always planning these boring-ass things for us to do, us being my cousin, mostly, who lived on the block cause we all moved North the same time and to the same apartment then spread out gradual to breathe. And our parents would yank our heads into some kinda shape and crisp up our clothes so we'd be presentable for travel with Miss Moore, who always looked like she was going to church, though she never did. Which is just one of the things the grownups talked about when they talked behind her back like a dog. But when she came calling with some sachet she'd sewed up or some gingerbread she'd made or some book, why then they'd all be too embarrassed to turn her down and we'd get handed over all spruced up. She'd been to college and said it was only right that she should take responsibility for the young ones' education, and she not even related by marriage or blood. So they'd go for it. Specially Aunt Gretchen. She was the main gofer in the family. You got some old dumb shit foolishness you want somebody to go for, you send for Aunt Gretchen. She been screwed into the go-along for so long, it's a blood-deep natural thing with her. Which is how she got saddled with me and Sugar and Junior in the first place while our mothers were in a la-de-da apartment up the block having a good ole time.

So this one day Miss Moore rounds us all up at the mailbox and it's puredee hot and she's knockin herself out about arithmetic. And school suppose to let up in summer I heard, but she don't never let up. And the starch in my pinafore scratching the shit outta me and I'm really hating this nappy-head bitch and her goddamn college degree. I'd much rather go to the pool or to the show where it's cool. So me and Sugar leaning on the mailbox being surly, which is a Miss Moore word. And Flyboy checking out what everybody brought for lunch. And Fat Butt already wasting his peanut-butter-and-jelly sandwich like the pig he is. And Junebug punchin on Q.T.'s arm for potato chips. And Rosie Giraffe shifting from one hip to the other waiting for somebody to step on her foot or ask her if she from Georgia so she can kick ass, preferably Mercedes'. And Miss Moore asking us do we know what money is, like we a bunch of retards. I mean real money, she say, like it's only poker chips or monopoly papers we lay on the grocer. So right away I'm tired of this and say so. And would much rather snatch Sugar and go to the Sunset and terrorize the West Indian kids and take their hair ribbons and their money too. And Miss Moore files that remark away for next week's lesson on brotherhood, I can tell. And finally I say we oughta get to the subway cause it's cooler and besides we might meet some cute boys. Sugar done swiped her mama's lipstick, so we ready.

So we heading down the street and she's boring us silly about what things cost and what our parents make and how much goes for rent and how money ain't divided up right in this country. And then she gets to the part about we all poor and live in the slums, which I don't feature. And I'm ready to speak on that, but she steps out in the street and hails two cabs just like that. Then she hustles half the crew in with her and hands me a five-dollar bill and tells me to calculate 10 percent tip for the driver. And we're off. Me and Sugar and Junebug and Flyboy hangin out the window and hollering to everybody, putting lipstick on each other cause Flyboy a faggot anyway, and making farts with our sweaty armpits. But I'm mostly trying to figure how to spend this money. But they all fascinated with the meter ticking and Junebug starts laying bets as to how much it'll read when Flyboy can't hold his breath no more. Then Sugar lays bets as to how much it'll be when we get there. So I'm stuck. Don't nobody want to go for my plan, which is to jump out at the next light and run off to the first bar-b-que we can find. Then the driver tells us to get the hell out cause we there already. And the meter reads eighty-five cents. And I'm stalling to figure out the tip and Sugar say give him a dime. And I decide he don't need it bad as I do, so later for him. But then he tries to take off with Junebug foot still in the door so we talk about his mama something ferocious. Then we check out that we on Fifth Avenue and everybody dressed up in stockings. One lady in a fur coat, hot as it is. White folks crazy.

"This is the place," Miss Moore say, presenting it to us in the voice she uses at the museum. "Let's look in the windows before we go in."

"Can we steal?" Sugar asks very serious like she's getting the ground rules 5 squared away before she plays. "I beg your pardon," say Miss Moore, and we fall out. So she leads us around the windows of the toy store and me and Sugar screamin, "This is mine, that's mine, I gotta have that, that was made for me, I was born for that," till Big Butt drowns us out.

"Hey, I'm goin to buy that there."

"That there? You don't even know what it is, stupid."

"I do so," he say punchin on Rosie Giraffe. "It's a microscope."

"Whatcha gonna do with a microscope, fool?"

"Look at things." 10

"Like what, Ronald?" ask Miss Moore. And Big Butt ain't got the first notion. So here go Miss Moore gabbing about the thousands of bacteria in a drop of water and the somethinorother in a speck of blood and the million and one living things in the air around us is invisible to the naked eye. And what she say that for? Junebug go to town on that "naked" and we rolling. Then Miss Moore ask what it cost. So we all jam into the window smudgin it up and the price tag say $300. So then she ask how long'd take for Big Butt and Junebug to save up their allowances. "Too long," I say. "Yeh," adds Sugar, "outgrown it by that time." And Miss Moore say no, you never outgrow learning instruments. "Why, even medical students and interns and," blah, blah, blah. And we ready to choke Big Butt for bringing it up in the first damn place.

"This here costs four hundred eighty dollars," say Rosie Giraffe. So we pile up all over her to see what she pointin out. My eyes tell me it's a chunk of glass cracked with something heavy, and different-color inks dripped into the splits, then the whole thing put into a oven or something. But for $480 it don't make sense.

"That's a paperweight made of semi-precious stones fused together under tremendous pressure," she explains slowly, with her hands doing the mining and all the factory work.

"So what's a paperweight?" asks Rosie Giraffe.

"To weigh paper with, dumbbell," say Flyboy, the wise man from the East.   15

"Not exactly," say Miss Moore, which is what she say when you warm or way off too. "It's to weigh paper down so it won't scatter and make your desk untidy." So right away me and Sugar curtsy to each other and then to Mercedes who is more the tidy type.

"We don't keep paper on top of the desk in my class," say Junebug, figuring Miss Moore crazy or lyin one.

"At home, then," she say. "Don't you have a calendar and pencil case and a blotter and a letter-opener on your desk at home where you do your homework?" And she know damn well what our homes look like cause she nosys around in them every chance she gets.

"I don't even have a desk," say Junebug. "Do we?"

"No. And I don't get no homework neither," says Big Butt.   20

"And I don't even have a home," say Flyboy like he do at school to keep the white folks off his back and sorry for him. Send this poor kid to camp posters, is his specialty.

"I do," says Mercedes. "I have a box of stationery on my desk and a picture of my cat. My godmother bought the stationery and the desk. There's a big rose on each sheet and the envelopes smell like roses."

"Who wants to know about your smelly-ass stationery," say Rosie Giraffe fore I can get my two cents in.

"It's important to have a work area all your own so that . . ."

"Will you look at this sailboat, please," say Flyboy, cuttin her off and pointin   25 to the thing like it was his. So once again we tumble all over each other to gaze at this magnificent thing in the toy store which is just big enough to maybe sail two kittens across the pond if you strap them to the posts tight. We all start reciting the price tag like we in assembly. "Handcrafted sailboat of fiberglass at one thousand one hundred ninety-five dollars."

"Unbelievable," I hear myself say and am really stunned. I read it again for myself just in case the group recitation put me in a trance. Same thing. For some reason this pisses me off. We look at Miss Moore and she lookin at us, waiting for I dunno what.

"Who'd pay all that when you can buy a sailboat set for a quarter at Pop's, a tube of glue for a dime, and a ball of string for eight cents? It must have a motor and a whole lot else besides," I say. "My sailboat cost me about fifty cents."

"But will it take water?" say Mercedes with her smart ass.

"Took mine to Alley Pond Park once," say Flyboy. "String broke. Lost it. Pity."

"Sailed mine in Central Park and it keeled over and sank. Had to ask my 30 father for another dollar."

"And you got the strap," laugh Big Butt. "The jerk didn't even have a string on it. My old man wailed on his behind."

Little Q.T. was staring hard at the sailboat and you could see he wanted it bad. But he too little and somebody'd just take it from him. So what the hell. "This boat for kids, Miss Moore?"

"Parents silly to buy something like that just to get all broke up," say Rosie Giraffe.

"That much money it should last forever," I figure.

"My father'd buy it for me if I wanted it." 35

"Your father, my ass," say Rosie Giraffe getting a chance to finally push Mercedes.

"Must be rich people shop here," say Q.T.

"You are a very bright boy," say Flyboy. "What was your first clue?" And he rap him on the head with the back of his knuckles, since Q.T. the only one he could get away with. Though Q.T. liable to come up behind you years later and get his licks in when you half expect it.

"What I want to know is," I says to Miss Moore though I never talk to her, I wouldn't give the bitch that satisfaction, "is how much a real boat costs? I figure a thousand'd get you a yacht any day."

"Why don't you check that out," she says, "and report back to the group?" 40 Which really pains my ass. If you gonna mess up a perfectly good swim day least you could do is have some answers. "Let's go in," she say like she got something up her sleeve. Only she don't lead the way. So me and Sugar turn the corner to where the entrance is, but when we get there I kinda hang back. Not that I'm scared, what's there to be afraid of, just a toy store. But I feel funny, shame. But what I got to be shamed about? Got as much right to go in as anybody. But somehow I can't seem to get hold of the door, so I step away for Sugar to lead. But she hangs back too. And I look at her and she looks at me and this is ridiculous. I mean, damn, I have never ever been shy about doing nothing or going nowhere. But then Mercedes steps up and then Rosie Giraffe and Big Butt crowd in behind and shove, and next thing we all stuffed into the doorway with only Mercedes squeezing past us, smoothing out her jumper and walking right down the aisle. Then the rest of us tumble in like a glued-together jigsaw done all wrong. And people lookin at us. And it's like the time me and Sugar crashed into the Catholic church on a dare. But once we got in there and everything so hushed and holy and the candles and the bowin and the handkerchiefs on all the drooping heads, I just couldn't go through with the plan. Which was for me to run up to the altar and do a tap dance while Sugar played the nose flute and messed around in the holy water. And Sugar kept givin me the elbow. Then later teased me so bad I tied her up in the shower and turned it on and locked her in. And she'd be there till this day if Aunt Gretchen hadn't finally figured I was lyin about the boarder takin a shower.

Same thing in the store. We all walkin on tiptoe and hardly touchin the games and puzzles and things. And I watched Miss Moore who is steady watchin us like she waitin for a sign. Like Mama Drewery watches the sky and sniffs the air and takes note of just how much slant is in the bird formation. Then me and Sugar bump smack into each other, so busy gazing at the toys, 'specially the sailboat. But we don't laugh and go into our fat-lady bump-stomach routine. We just stare at that price tag. Then Sugar run a finger over the whole boat. And I'm jealous and want to hit her. Maybe not her, but I sure want to punch somebody in the mouth.

"Watcha bring us here for, Miss Moore?"

"You sound angry, Sylvia. Are you mad about something?" Givin me one of them grins like she tellin a grown-up joke that never turns out to be funny. And she's lookin very closely at me like maybe she planning to do my portrait from memory. I'm mad, but I won't give her that satisfaction. So I slouch around the store bein very bored and say, "Let's go."

Me and Sugar at the back of the train watchin the tracks whizzin by large then small then gettin gobbled up in the dark. I'm thinkin about this tricky toy I saw in the store. A clown that somersaults on a bar then does chin-ups just cause you yank lightly at his leg. Cost $35. I could see me askin my mother for a $35 birth-day clown. "You wanna who that costs what?" she'd say, cocking her head to the side to get a better view of the hole in my head. Thirty-five dollars could buy new bunk beds for Junior and Gretchen's boy. Thirty-five dollars and the whole household could go visit Granddaddy Nelson in the country. Thirty-five dollars would pay for the rent and the piano bill too. Who are these people that spend that much for performing clowns and $1000 for toy sailboats? What kinda work they do and how they live and how come we ain't in on it? Where we are is who we are, Miss Moore always pointin out. But it don't necessarily have to be that way, she always adds then waits for somebody to say that poor people have to wake up and demand their share of the pie and don't none of us know what kind of pie she talking about in the first damn place. But she ain't so smart cause I still got her four dollars from the taxi and she sure ain't gettin it. Messin up my day with this shit. Sugar nudges me in my pocket and winks.

Miss Moore lines us up in front of the mailbox where we started from, seem 45 like years ago, and I got a headache for thinkin so hard. And we lean all over each other so we can hold up under the draggy-ass lecture she always finishes us off with at the end before we thank her for borin us to tears. But she just looks at us like she readin tea leaves. Finally she say, "Well, what did you think of F. A. O. Schwarz?"

Rosie Giraffe mumbles, "White folks crazy."

"I'd like to go there again when I get my birthday money," says Mercedes, and we shove her out the pack so she has to lean on the mailbox by herself.

"I'd like a shower. Tiring day," say Flyboy.

Then Sugar surprises me by sayin, "You know, Miss Moore, I don't think all of us here put together eat in a year what that sailboat costs." And Miss Moore lights up like somebody goosed her. "And?" she say, urging Sugar on. Only I'm standin on her foot so she don't continue.

"Imagine for a minute what kind of society it is in which some people can 50 spend on a toy what it would cost to feed a family of six or seven. What do you think?"

"I think," say Sugar pushing me off her feet like she never done before, cause I whip her ass in a minute, "that this is not much of a democracy if you ask me. Equal chance to pursue happiness means an equal crack at the dough, don't it?" Miss Moore is besides herself and I am disgusted with Sugar's treachery. So I stand on her foot one more time to see if she'll shove me. She shuts up, and Miss Moore looks at me, sorrowfully I'm thinkin. And somethin weird is goin on, I can feel it in my chest.

"Anybody else learn anything today?" lookin dead at me. I walk away and Sugar has to run to catch up and don't even seem to notice when I shrug her arm off my shoulder.

"Well, we got four dollars anyway," she says.

"Uh hunh."

"We could go to Hascombs and get half a chocolate layer and then go to the 55 Sunset and still have plenty money for potato chips and ice cream sodas."

"Un hunh."

"Race you to Hascombs," she say.

We start down the block and she gets ahead which is O.K. by me cause I'm going to the West End and then over to the Drive to think this day through. She can run if she want to and even run faster. But ain't nobody gonna beat me at nuthin.

For Analysis

1. What are Sylvia's outstanding traits? How are they reflected in her language and in her description of her neighborhood?

2. How is Sylvia's character revealed through her relationship with Sugar?

3. Describe the lesson Miss Moore tries to teach the children by taking them to visit F. A. O. Schwarz.

4. How is Sylvia's assessment of Miss Moore at the beginning of the story borne out by the ending?

5. What evidence is there that Sylvia has been changed by the experience?

On Style

Analyze Bambara's use of language to create the sense of a young, bright narrator rambling aimlessly when in fact the story is carefully structured.

Making Connections

1. Compare and contrast the use of the **first-person narrator** in this story, in O'Connor's "My Oedipus Complex" (p. 109), and in Cisneros's "The House on Mango Street" (p. 141).

2. This story and Richard Wright's "The Man Who Was Almost a Man" (p. 376) deal with a child whose sense of justice is offended. What differences and similarities do you find in the source of the distress and the way the distress is resolved?

Writing Topics

1. Write an essay arguing for or against the proposition that the story ends optimistically.

2. In your opinion, is Sylvia a reliable or unreliable narrator?

Sandra Cisneros   (b. 1954)

The House on Mango Street   1983

We didn't always live on Mango Street. Before that we lived on Loomis on the third floor, and before that we lived on Keeler. Before Keeler it was Paulina, and before that I can't remember. But what I remember most is moving a lot. Each time it seemed there'd be one more of us. By the time we got to Mango Street we were six — Mama, Papa, Carlos, Kiki, my sister Nenny and me.

The house on Mango Street is ours and we don't have to pay rent to anybody or share the yard with the people downstairs or be careful not to make too much noise and there isn't a landlord banging on the ceiling with a broom. But even so, it's not the house we'd thought we'd get.

We had to leave the flat on Loomis quick. The water pipes broke and the landlord wouldn't fix them because the house was too old. We had to leave fast. We were using the washroom next door and carrying water over in empty milk gallons. That's why Mama and Papa looked for a house, and that's why we moved into the house on Mango Street, far away, on the other side of town.

They always told us that one day we would move into a house, a real house that would be ours for always so we wouldn't have to move each year. And our house would have running water and pipes that worked. And inside it would have real stairs, not hallway stairs, but stairs inside like the houses on T.V. And we'd have a basement and at least three washrooms so when we took a bath we didn't have to tell everybody. Our house would be white with trees around it, a great big yard and grass growing without a fence. This was the house Papa talked about when he held a lottery ticket and this was the house Mama dreamed up in the stories she told us before we went to bed.

But the house on Mango Street is not the way they told it at all. It's small and red with tight little steps in front and windows so small you'd think they were holding their breath. Bricks are crumbling in places, and the front door is so swollen you have to push hard to get in. There is no front yard, only four little elms the city planted by the curb. Out back is a small garage for the car we don't own yet and a small yard that looks smaller between the two buildings on either side. There are stairs in our house, but they're ordinary hallway stairs, and the house has only one washroom, very small. Everybody has to share a bedroom — Mama and Papa, Carlos and Kiki, me and Nenny.

Once when we were living on Loomis, a nun from my school passed by and saw me playing out front. The laundromat downstairs had been boarded up because it had been robbed two days before and the owner had painted on the wood YES WE'RE OPEN so as not to lose business.

Where do you live? she asked.

There, I said pointing up to the third floor.

You live *there?*

There. I had to look to where she pointed — the third floor, the paint peeling, 10
wooden bars Papa had nailed on the windows so we wouldn't fall out. You live
there? The way she said it made me feel like nothing. *There.* I lived *there.* I
nodded.

I knew then I had to have a house. A real house. One I could point to. But this
isn't it. The house on Mango Street isn't it. For the time being, Mama said.
Temporary, said Papa. But I know how those things go.

For Analysis

1. Why did the family have to leave the flat on Loomis Street so fast?

2. What does the Loomis house represent to the speaker?

3. What is the significance of the nun's comment on the speaker's house (para. 9)?

4. Describe the speaker's feelings about the move to Mango Street.

5. Would you describe the narrator's family as healthy and happy? Explain.

6. How would you characterize the **tone** of the final paragraph?

On Style

1. What effect does Cisneros achieve by using the present tense in paragraphs 2
and 5?

2. How might this story differ if it were told by an **omniscient** rather than a **first-
person narrator**?

Making Connections

1. Compare the symbolism of the house in this story with that of the quilt in Alice
Walker's "Everyday Use" (p. 717) as symbols.

2. Compare the significance for the narrator of the house on Mango Street to the significance for the speaker of the farm in Dylan Thomas's "Fern Hill" (p. 165).

Writing Topics

1. Write a personal essay that is organized, like Cisneros's story, around some place
or object (home, neighborhood, toy) or person (parent, sibling, friend, teacher) that
symbolized important emotions and meanings for your life.

2. Describe the effects of moving to different homes during your childhood.

3. The narrator yearns for what she calls "a real house. One I could point to." Write
an essay describing your own experience of living in what you did not consider a
"real house."

Poetry

William Blake   (1757–1827)

The Chimney Sweeper 1789

When my mother died I was very young,
And my Father sold me while yet my tongue
Could scarcely cry " 'weep! 'weep! 'weep! 'weep!"
So your chimneys I sweep, and in soot I sleep.

There's little Tom Dacre, who cried when his head,
That curled like a lamb's back, was shaved: so I said,
"Hush, Tom! never mind it, for when your head's bare
You know that the soot cannot spoil your white hair."

And so he was quiet and that very night
As Tom was a-sleeping, he had such a sight!   10
That thousands of sweepers, Dick, Joe, Ned, and Jack,
Were all of them locked up in coffins of black.

And by came an Angel who had a bright key,
And he opened the coffins and set them all free;
Then down a green plain leaping, laughing, they run,
And wash in a river, and shine in the Sun.

Then naked and white, all their bags left behind,
They rise upon clouds and sport in the wind;
And the Angel told Tom, if he'd be a good boy,
He'd have God for his father, and never want joy.   20

And so Tom awoke; and we rose in the dark,
And got with our bags and our brushes to work.
Though the morning was cold, Tom was happy and warm;
So if all do their duty they need not fear harm.

The Tyger 1794

Tyger! Tyger! burning bright
In the forests of the night,
What immortal hand or eye
Could frame thy fearful symmetry?

In what distant deeps or skies
Burnt the fire of thine eyes?
On what wings dare he aspire?
What the hand dare seize the fire?

And what shoulder, & what art,
Could twist the sinews of thy heart?   10
And when thy heart began to beat,
What dread hand? & what dread feet?

What the hammer? what the chain?
In what furnace was thy brain?
What the anvil? what dread grasp
Dare its deadly terrors clasp?

When the stars threw down their spears,
And water'd heaven with their tears,
Did he smile his work to see?
Did he who made the Lamb make thee?   20

Tyger! Tyger! burning bright
In the forests of the night,
What immortal hand or eye
Dare frame thy fearful symmetry?

The Garden of Love 1793

I went to the Garden of Love,
And saw what I never had seen:
A Chapel was built in the midst,
Where I used to play on the green.

And the gates of this Chapel were shut,
And "Thou shalt not" writ over the door;

So I turn'd to the Garden of Love,
That so many sweet flowers bore,

And I saw it was filled with graves,
And tomb-stones where flowers should be: 10
And Priests in black gowns were walking their rounds,
And binding with briars my joys & desires.

For Analysis

1. What meanings does the word *love* have in this poem?
2. What is Blake's judgment on established religion?
3. Explain the meaning of *Chapel* (l. 3) and of *briars* (l. 12).

Writing Topic

Read the definition of **irony** in "Glossary of Literary Terms." Write an essay in which you distinguish between the types of irony used in "The Chimney Sweeper" and "The Garden of Love."

London 1794

I wander through each chartered[1] street,
Near where the chartered Thames does flow
And mark in every face I meet
Marks of weakness, marks of woe.

In every cry of every man,
In every infant's cry of fear,
In every voice; in every ban,
The mind-forged manacles I hear:

How the chimney-sweeper's cry
Every blackening church appalls,   10
And the hapless soldier's sigh
Runs in blood down palace-walls.

But most, through midnight streets I hear
How the youthful harlot's curse
Blasts the new-born infant's tear,
And blights with plagues the marriage-hearse.

London
  [1] Preempted by the state and leased out under royal patent.

William Wordsworth   (1770–1850)

Lines[1] 1798

*Composed a Few Miles above Tintern Abbey
on Revisiting the Banks of the Wye
during a Tour. July 13, 1798*

Five years have passed;[2] five summers, with the length
Of five long winters! and again I hear
These waters, rolling from their mountain-springs
With a soft inland murmur. Once again
Do I behold these steep and lofty cliffs,
That on a wild secluded scene impress
Thoughts of more deep seclusion; and connect
The landscape with the quiet of the sky.
The day is come when I again repose
Here, under this dark sycamore, and view   10
These plots of cottage ground, these orchard tufts,
Which at this season, with their unripe fruits,
Are clad in one green hue, and lose themselves
'Mid groves and copses. Once again I see
These hedgerows, hardly hedgerows, little lines
Of sportive wood run wild; these pastoral farms,
Green to the very door; and wreaths of smoke
Sent up, in silence, from among the trees!
With some uncertain notice, as might seem
Of vagrant dwellers in the houseless woods,   20
Or of some Hermit's cave, where by his fire
The Hermit sits alone.

     These beauteous forms,
Through a long absence, have not been to me
As is a landscape to a blind man's eye;
But oft, in lonely rooms, and 'mid the din
Of towns and cities, I have owed to them
In hours of weariness, sensations sweet,
Felt in the blood, and felt along the heart;

[1] Wordsworth wrote this poem during a four- or five-day walking tour through the Wye valley with his sister Dorothy.
[2] The poet had visited the region on a solitary walking tour in August 1793 when he was twenty-three years old.

And passing even into my purer mind,
With tranquil restoration — feelings too   30
Of unremembered pleasure; such, perhaps,
As have no slight or trivial influence
On that best portion of a good man's life,
His little, nameless, unremembered, acts
Of kindness and of love. Nor less, I trust,
To them I may have owed another gift,
Of aspect more sublime; that blessed mood,
In which the burthen of the mystery,
In which the heavy and the weary weight
Of all this unintelligible world,   40
Is lightened — that serene and blessed mood,
In which the affections gently lead us on —
Until, the breath of this corporeal frame
And even the motion of our human blood
Almost suspended, we are laid asleep
In body, and become a living soul;
While with an eye made quiet by the power
Of harmony, and the deep power of joy,
We see into the life of things.

                    If this
Be but a vain belief, yet, oh! how oft —   50
In darkness and amid the many shapes
Of joyless daylight; when the fretful stir
Unprofitable, and the fever of the world,
Have hung upon the beatings of my heart —
How oft, in spirit, have I turned to thee,
O sylvan Wye! thou wanderer through the woods,
How often has my spirit turned to thee!

    And now, with gleams of half-extinguished thought
With many recognitions dim and faint,
And somewhat of a sad perplexity,   60
The picture of the mind revives again;
While here I stand, not only with the sense
Of present pleasure, but with pleasing thoughts
That in this moment there is life and food
For future years. And so I dare to hope,
Though changed, no doubt, from what I was when first
I came among these hills; when like a roe
I bounded o'er the mountains, by the sides
Of the deep rivers, and the lonely streams,

Wherever nature led — more like a man   70
Flying from something that he dreads than one
Who sought the thing he loved. For nature then
(The coarser pleasures of my boyish days,
And their glad animal movements all gone by)
To me was all in all. — I cannot paint
What then I was. The sounding cataract
Haunted me like a passion; the tall rock,
The mountain, and the deep and gloomy wood,
Their colors and their forms, were then to me
An appetite; a feeling and a love,   80
That had no need of a remoter charm,
By thought supplied, nor any interest
Unborrowed from the eye. — That time is past,
And all its aching joys are now no more,
And all its dizzy raptures. Not for this
Faint[3] I, nor mourn nor murmur; other gifts
Have followed; for such loss, I would believe,
Abundant recompense. For I have learned
To look on nature, not as in the hour
Of thoughtless youth; but hearing oftentimes   90
The still, sad music of humanity,
Nor harsh nor grating, though of ample power
To chasten and subdue. And I have felt
A presence that disturbs me with the joy
Of elevated thoughts; a sense sublime
Of something far more deeply interfused,
Whose dwelling is the light of setting suns,
And the round ocean and the living air,
And the blue sky, and in the mind of man:
A motion and a spirit, that impels   100
All thinking things, all objects of all thought,
And rolls through all things. Therefore am I still
A lover of the meadows and the woods,
And mountains; and of all that we behold
From this green earth; of all the mighty world
Of eye, and ear — both what they half create,
And what perceive; well pleased to recognize
In nature and the language of the sense
The anchor of my purest thoughts, the nurse,
The guide, the guardian of my heart, and soul   110
Of all my moral being.

[3] Lose heart.

Nor perchance,
If I were not thus taught, should I the more
Suffer my genial spirits to decay:
For thou art with me here upon the banks
Of this fair river; thou my dearest Friend,[4]
My dear, dear Friend; and in thy voice I catch
The language of my former heart, and read
My former pleasures in the shooting lights
Of thy wild eyes. Oh! yet a little while
May I behold in thee what I was once,   120
My dear, dear Sister! and this prayer I make,
Knowing that Nature never did betray
The heart that loved her; 'tis her privilege,
Through all the years of this our life, to lead
From joy to joy: for she can so inform
The mind that is within us, so impress
With quietness and beauty, and so feed
With lofty thoughts, that neither evil tongues,
Rash judgments, nor the sneers of selfish men,
Nor greetings where no kindness is, nor all   130
The dreary intercourse of daily life,
Shall e'er prevail against us, or disturb
Our cheerful faith, that all which we behold
Is full of blessings. Therefore let the moon
Shine on thee in thy solitary walk;
And let the misty mountain winds be free
To blow against thee: and, in after years,
When these wild ecstasies shall be matured
Into a sober pleasure; when thy mind
Shall be a mansion for all lovely forms,   140
Thy memory be as a dwelling place
For all sweet sounds and harmonies; oh! then,
If solitude, or fear, or pain, or grief
Should be thy portion, with what healing thoughts
Of tender joy wilt thou remember me,
And these my exhortations! Nor, perchance —
If I should be where I no more can hear
Thy voice, nor catch from thy wild eyes these gleams
Of past existence[5] — wilt thou then forget
That on the banks of this delightful stream   150
We stood together; and that I, so long

---

[4] The poet addresses his sister Dorothy.
[5] I.e., the poet's past experience. Note lines 116–19.

A worshiper of Nature, hither came
Unwearied in that service; rather say
With warmer love — oh! with far deeper zeal
Of holier love. Nor wilt thou then forget,
That after many wanderings, many years
Of absence, these steep woods and lofty cliffs,
And this green pastoral landscape, were to me
More dear, both for themselves and for thy sake!

For Analysis

1. In this poem the poet distinguishes between two important periods in his life: the first is described in lines 65–83, and the second is described in lines 83–111. How does he characterize these two periods?

2. The poem describes a visit to a familiar scene of the poet's youth and includes a meditation on the changes that have occurred. Are the changes in the poet, the scene itself, or both?

Writing Topic

Discuss the ways in which the poet contrasts the city and the countryside.

John Keats   (1795–1821)

On First Looking into Chapman's Homer [1]   1816

Much have I travelled in the realms of gold,
And many goodly states and kingdoms seen:
Round many western islands have I been
Which bards in fealty to Apollo[2] hold.
Oft of one wide expanse had I been told
That deep-browed Homer ruled as his demesne;°   realm
Yet did I never breathe its pure serene°   clear air
Till I heard Chapman speak out loud and bold:
Then felt I like some watcher of the skies
When a new planet swims into his ken;   10

On First Looking into Chapman's Homer
   [1] George Chapman published translations of *The Iliad* (1611) and *The Odyssey* (1616).
   [2] The god of poetry.

Or like stout Cortez[3] when with eagle eyes
He stared at the Pacific — and all his men
Looked at each other with a wild surmise —
   Silent, upon a peak in Darien.

Robert Browning   (1812–1889)

My Last Duchess 1842

FERRARA

That's my last Duchess painted on the wall,
Looking as if she were alive. I call
That piece a wonder, now: Frà Pandolf's[1] hands
Worked busily a day, and there she stands.
Will't please you sit and look at her? I said
"Frà Pandolf" by design, for never read
Strangers like you that pictured countenance,
The depth and passion of its earnest glance,
But to myself they turned (since none puts by
The curtain I have drawn for you, but I)   10
And seemed as they would ask me, if they durst,
How such a glance came there; so, not the first
Are you to turn and ask thus. Sir, 'twas not
Her husband's presence only, called that spot
Of joy into the Duchess' cheek: perhaps
Frà Pandolf chanced to say "Her mantle laps
Over my lady's wrist too much," or "Paint
Must never hope to reproduce the faint
Half-flush that dies along her throat": such stuff
Was courtesy, she thought, and cause enough   20
For calling up that spot of joy. She had
A heart — how shall I say? — too soon made glad,
Too easily impressed; she liked whate'er
She looked on, and her looks went everywhere.

On First Looking into Chapman's Homer
  [3] Keats mistakenly attributes the discovery of the Pacific Ocean by Europeans to Hernando Cortez (1485–1547), the Spanish conqueror of Mexico. Vasco Nuñez de Balboa (1475–1519) first saw the Pacific from a mountain located in eastern Panama.

My Last Duchess
  [1] Frà Pandolf and Claus of Innsbruck (who is mentioned in the last line) are fictitious artists.

Sir, 'twas all one! My favor at her breast,
The dropping of the daylight in the West,
The bough of cherries some officious fool
Broke in the orchard for her, the white mule
She rode with round the terrace — all and each
Would draw from her alike the approving speech,   30
Or blush, at least. She thanked men — good! but thanked
Somehow — I know not how — as if she ranked
My gift of a nine-hundred-years-old name
With anybody's gift. Who'd stoop to blame
This sort of trifling? Even had you skill
In speech — which I have not — to make your will
Quite clear to such an one, and say, "Just this
Or that in you disgusts me; here you miss,
Or there exceed the mark" — and if she let
Herself be lessoned° so, nor plainly set   taught   40
Her wits to yours, forsooth, and made excuse,
— E'en then would be some stooping; and I choose
Never to stoop. Oh sir, she smiled, no doubt,
Whene'er I passed her; but who passed without
Much the same smile? This grew; I gave commands;
Then all smiles stopped together. There she stands
As if alive. Will't please you rise? We'll meet
The company below, then. I repeat,
The Count your master's known munificence°   generosity
Is ample warrant that no just pretense   50
Of mine for dowry will be disallowed;
Though his fair daughter's self, as I avowed
At starting, is my object. Nay, we'll go
Together down, sir. Notice Neptune, though,
Taming a sea-horse, thought a rarity,
Which Claus of Innsbruck cast in bronze for me!

For Analysis

1. To whom is the duke speaking, and what is the occasion?

2. What does a comparison between the duke's feelings about his artwork and his feelings about his last duchess reveal about his character?

3. What became of the duke's last duchess?

On Style

Does this poem rely on **irony**? Explain.

Writing Topic

Write an essay in which you argue that the reader either is or is not meant to sympathize with the duke's characterization of his wife.

Emily Dickinson   (1830–1886)

I felt a Funeral, in my Brain   1861

I felt a Funeral, in my Brain,
And Mourners to and fro
Kept treading — treading — till it seemed
That Sense was breaking through —

And when they all were seated,
A Service, like a Drum —
Kept beating — beating — till I thought
My Mind was going numb —

And then I heard them lift a Box
And creak across my Soul   10
With those same Boots of Lead, again,
Then Space — began to toll,

As all the Heavens were a Bell,
And Being, but an Ear,
And I, and Silence, some strange Race
Wrecked, solitary, here —

And then a Plank in Reason, broke,
And I dropped down, and down —
And hit a World, at every plunge,
And Finished knowing — then —   20

Thomas Hardy   (1840–1928)

Hap   1898

If but some vengeful god would call to me
From up the sky, and laugh: "Thou suffering thing,
Know that thy sorrow is my ecstasy,
That thy love's loss is my hate's profiting!"

Then would I bear it, clench myself, and die,
Steeled by the sense of ire unmerited;

Half-eased in that a Powerfuller than I
Had willed and meted me the tears I shed.

But not so. How arrives it joy lies slain,
And why unblooms the best hope ever sown?   10
— Crass Casualty° obstructs the sun and rain,   chance
And dicing Time for gladness casts a moan. . . .
These purblind Doomsters[1] had as readily strown
Blisses about my pilgrimage as pain.

The Ruined Maid   1902

"O 'Melia, my dear, this does everything crown!
Who could have supposed I should meet you in Town?
And whence such fair garments, such prosperi-ty?"
"O didn't you know I'd been ruined?" said she.

"You left us in tatters, without shoes or socks,
Tired of digging potatoes, and spudding up docks;°   digging herbs
And now you've gay bracelets and bright feathers three!"
"Yes: that's how we dress when we're ruined," said she.

"At home in the barton° you said 'thee' and 'thou,'   farmyard
And 'thik oon,' and 'theäs oon,' and 't'other'; but now   10
Your talking quite fits 'ee for high compa-ny!"
"Some polish is gained with one's ruin," said she.

"Your hands were like paws then, your face blue and bleak
But now I'm bewitched by your delicate cheek,
And your little gloves fit as on any la-dy!"
"We never do work when we're ruined," said she.

"You used to call home-life a hag-ridden dream,
And you'd sigh, and you'd sock; but at present you seem
To know not of megrims° or melancho-ly!"   sick headaches
"True. One's pretty lively when ruined," said she.   20

"I wish I had feathers, a fine sweeping gown,
And a delicate face, and could strut about Town!"
"My dear — a raw country girl, such as you be,
Cannot quite expect that. You ain't ruined," said she.

Hap
[1] Those who decide one's fate.

Gerard Manley Hopkins (1844–1889)

Spring and Fall 1880

To a Young Child

Márgarét, áre you gríeving
Over Goldengrove unleaving?°   losing leaves
Leáves, líke the things of man, you
With your fresh thoughts care for, can you?
Áh! ás the heart grows older
It will come to such sights colder
By and by, nor spare a sigh
Though worlds of wanwood leafmeal[1] lie;
And yet you wíll weep and know why.
Now no matter, child, the name: 10
Sórrow's spríngs áre the same.
Nor mouth had, no nor mind, expressed
What heart heard of, ghost° guessed: soul
It ís the blight man was born for,
It is Margaret you mourn for.

For Analysis
1. In this poem Margaret grieves over the passing of spring and the coming of fall. What does the coming of fall symbolize?

2. Why, when Margaret grows older, will she not sigh over the coming of fall?

3. What are "Sórrow's spríngs" (l. 11)?

A. E. Housman (1859–1936)

When I Was One-and-Twenty 1896

When I was one-and-twenty
    I heard a wise man say,
"Give crowns and pounds and guineas
    But not your heart away;

Spring and Fall
  [1] Pale woods littered with mouldering leaves.

Give pearls away and rubies
     But keep your fancy free."
But I was one-and-twenty,
     No use to talk to me.

When I was one-and-twenty
     I heard him say again,   10
"The heart out of the bosom
     Was never given in vain;
'Tis paid with sighs a plenty
     And sold for endless rue."
And I am two-and-twenty,
     And oh, 'tis true, 'tis true.

Terence, This Is
Stupid Stuff[1] 1896

"Terence, this is stupid stuff:
You eat your victuals fast enough;
There can't be much amiss, 'tis clear,
To see the rate you drink your beer.
But oh, good Lord, the verse you make,
It gives a chap the bellyache.
The cow, the old cow, she is dead;
It sleeps well, the hornéd head:
We poor lads, 'tis our turn now
To hear such tunes as killed the cow.   10
Pretty friendship 'tis to rhyme
Your friends to death before their time
Moping melancholy mad:
Come, pipe a tune to dance to, lad."

Why, if 'tis dancing you would be,
There's brisker pipes than poetry.
Say, for what were hopyards meant,
Or why was Burton built on Trent?[2]
Oh many a peer of England brews
Livelier liquor than the Muse,   20

Terence, This Is Stupid Stuff
     [1] Housman originally titled the volume in which this poem appeared *The Poems of Terence Hearsay*. Terence was a Roman satiric playwright.
     [2] The river Trent provides water for the town's brewing industry.

And malt does more than Milton can
To justify God's ways to man.[3]
Ale, man, ale's the stuff to drink
For fellows whom it hurts to think:
Look into the pewter pot
To see the world as the world's not.
And faith, 'tis pleasant till 'tis past:
The mischief is that 'twill not last.
Oh I have been to Ludlow fair
And left my necktie God knows where,   30
And carried halfway home, or near,
Pints and quarts of Ludlow beer:
Then the world seemed none so bad,
And I myself a sterling lad;
And down in lovely muck I've lain,
Happy till I woke again.
Then I saw the morning sky:
Heigho, the tale was all a lie;
The world, it was the old world yet,
I was I, my things were wet,   40
And nothing now remained to do
But begin the game anew.

    Therefore, since the world has still
Much good, but much less good than ill,
And while the sun and moon endure
Luck's a chance, but trouble's sure,
I'd face it as a wise man would,
And train for ill and not for good.
'Tis true the stuff I bring for sale
Is not so brisk a brew as ale: 50
Out of a stem that scored the hand
I wrung it in a weary land.
But take it: if the smack is sour,
The better for the embittered hour;
It should do good to heart and head
When your soul is in my soul's stead;
And I will friend you, if I may,
In the dark and cloudy day.

    There was a king reigned in the East:
There, when kings will sit to feast,   60
They get their fill before they think

---

[3] In the invocation to *Paradise Lost,* Milton declares that his epic will "justify the ways of God to men."

With poisoned meat and poisoned drink.
He gathered all that springs to birth
From the many-venomed earth;
First a little, thence to more,
He sampled all her killing store;
And easy, smiling, seasoned sound,
Sate the king when healths went round.
They put arsenic in his meat
And stared aghast to watch him eat;
They poured strychnine in his cup
And shook to see him drink it up:
They shook, they stared as white's their shirt:
Them it was their poison hurt.
— I tell the tale that I heard told.
Mithridates, he died old.[4]

70

For Analysis

1. What does the speaker of the first fourteen lines object to in Terence's poetry?

2. What is Terence's response to the criticism of his verse? What function of true poetry is implied by his comparison of bad poetry with liquor?

Writing Topic

How does the story of Mithridates (ll. 59–76) illustrate the theme of the poem?

William Butler Yeats   (1865–1939)

Leda and the Swan[1] 1928

A sudden blow: the great wings beating still
Above the staggering girl, her thighs caressed
By the dark webs, her nape caught in his bill,
He holds her helpless breast upon his breast.

Terence, This Is Stupid Stuff
   [4] Mithridates, the King of Pontus (in Asia Minor), reputedly immunized himself against poisons by administering to himself gradually increasing doses.

Leda and the Swan
   [1] In Greek myth, Zeus, in the form of a swan, rapes Leda. As a consequence, Helen and Clytemnestra are born. Each sister marries the king of a city-state; Helen marries Menelaus and Clytemnestra marries Agamemnon. Helen, the most beautiful woman on earth, elopes with Paris, a prince of Troy, an act that precipitates the Trojan War in which Agamemnon commands the combined Greek armies. The war ends with the destruction of Troy. Agamemnon, when he returns to his home, is murdered by his unfaithful wife.

How can those terrified vague fingers push
The feathered glory from her loosening thighs?
And how can body, laid in that white rush,
But feel the strange heart beating where it lies?

A shudder in the loins engenders there
The broken wall, the burning roof and tower   10
And Agamemnon dead.
                              Being so caught up,
So mastered by the brute blood of the air,
Did she put on his knowledge with his power
Before the indifferent beak could let her drop?

The Spur   1938

You think it horrible that lust and rage
Should dance attention upon my old age;
They were not such a plague when I was young;
What else have I to spur me into song?

Robert Frost   (1874–1963)

Birches   1916

When I see birches bend to left and right
Across the lines of straighter darker trees,
I like to think some boy's been swinging them.
But swinging doesn't bend them down to stay
As ice-storms do. Often you must have seen them
Loaded with ice a sunny winter morning
After a rain. They click upon themselves
As the breeze rises, and turn many-colored
As the stir cracks and crazes their enamel.
Soon the sun's warmth makes them shed crystal shells   10
Shattering and avalanching on the snow-crust —
Such heaps of broken glass to sweep away
You'd think the inner dome of heaven had fallen.
They are dragged to the withered bracken by the load,
And they seem not to break; though once they are bowed

So low for long, they never right themselves:
You may see their trunks arching in the woods
Years afterwards, trailing their leaves on the ground
Like girls on hands and knees that throw their hair
Before them over their heads to dry in the sun.   20
But I was going to say when Truth broke in
With all her matter-of-fact about the ice-storm
I should prefer to have some boy bend them
As he went out and in to fetch the cows —
Some boy too far from town to learn baseball,
Whose only play was what he found himself,
Summer or winter, and could play alone.
One by one he subdued his father's trees
By riding them down over and over again
Until he took the stiffness out of them,   30
And not one but hung limp, not one was left
For him to conquer. He learned all there was
To learn about not launching out too soon
And so not carrying the tree away
Clear to the ground. He always kept his poise
To the top branches, climbing carefully
With the same pains you use to fill a cup
Up to the brim, and even above the brim.
Then he flung outward, feet first, with a swish,
Kicking his way down through the air to the ground.   40
So was I once myself a swinger of birches.
And so I dream of going back to be.
It's when I'm weary of considerations,
And life is too much like a pathless wood
Where your face burns and tickles with the cobwebs
Broken across it, and one eye is weeping
From a twig's having lashed across it open.
I'd like to get away from earth awhile
And then come back to it and begin over.
May no fate willfully misunderstand me   50
And half grant what I wish and snatch me away
Not to return. Earth's the right place for love:
I don't know where it's likely to go better.
I'd like to go by climbing a birch tree,
And climb black branches up a snow-white trunk
Toward heaven, till the tree could bear no more,
But dipped its top and set me down again.
That would be good both going and coming back.
One could do worse than be a swinger of birches.

The Road Not Taken (1915)

Two roads diverged in a yellow wood,
And sorry I could not travel both
And be one traveler, long I stood
And looked down one as far as I could
To where it bent in the undergrowth;

Then took the other, as just as fair,
And having perhaps the better claim,
Because it was grassy and wanted wear;
Though as for that the passing there
Had worn them really about the same,   10

And both that morning equally lay
In leaves no step had trodden black.
Oh, I kept the first for another day!
Yet knowing how way leads on to way,
I doubted if I should ever come back.

I shall be telling this with a sigh
Somewhere ages and ages hence:
Two roads diverged in a wood, and I —
I took the one less traveled by,
And that has made all the difference.   20

Robert Graves   (1895–1985)

The Naked and the Nude   1957

For me, the naked and the nude
(By lexicographers construed
As synonyms that should express
The same dificiency of dress
Or shelter) stand as wide apart
As love from lies, or truth from art.

Lovers without reproach will gaze
On bodies naked and ablaze;
The hippocratic eye will see
In nakedness, anatomy;   10
And naked shines the Goddess when
She mounts her lion among men.

The nude are bold, the nude are sly
To hold each treasonable eye.
While draping by a showman's trick
Their dishabille in rhetoric,
They grin a mock-religious grin
Of scorn at those of naked skin.

The naked, therefore, who compete
Against the nude may know defeat;   20
Yet when they both together tread
The briary pastures of the dead,
By Gorgons with long whips pursued,
How naked go the sometime nude!

For Analysis

1. What distinction does the speaker draw between the naked and the nude? Which does he prefer?

2. Identify the Latinate vocabulary in the first stanza. Suggest why the poet chose such scholarly words.

3. In the second stanza, what is the "hippocratic eye" (l. 9)?

4. In stanza 3, what words reveal the speaker's feelings about the nude?

Writing Topic

In a paragraph, discuss the reversal and wordplay that animate the last stanza.

Stevie Smith   (1902–1971)

To Carry the Child   1966

To carry the child into adult life
Is good? I say it is not,
To carry the child into adult life
Is to be handicapped.

The child in adult life is defenceless
And if he is grown-up, knows it,
And the grown-up looks at the childish part
And despises it.

The child, too, despises the clever grown-up,
The man-of-the-world, the frozen,   10
For the child has the tears alive on his cheek
And the man has none of them.

As the child has colours, and the man sees no
Colours or anything,
Being easy only in things of the mind,
The child is easy in feeling.

Easy in feeling, easily excessive
And in excess powerful,
For instance, if you do not speak to the child
He will make trouble.   20

You would say a man had the upper hand
Of the child, if a child survive,
But I say the child has fingers of strength
To strangle the man alive.

Oh! it is not happy, it is never happy,
To carry the child into adulthood,
Let the children lie down before full growth
And die in their infanthood
And be guilty of no man's blood.

But oh the poor child, the poor child, what can he do,   30
Trapped in a grown-up carapace,
But peer outside of his prison room
With the eye of an anarchist?

Not Waving but Drowning   1957

Nobody heard him, the dead man,
But still he lay moaning:
I was much further out than you thought
And not waving but drowning.

Poor chap, he always loved larking
And now he's dead
It must have been too cold for him his heart gave way,
They said.

Oh, no no no, it was too cold always
(Still the dead one lay moaning)   10
I was much too far out all my life
And not waving but drowning.

For Analysis

1. Explain the **paradox** in the first and last stanzas, where the speaker describes someone dead as moaning. Who do you suppose the *you* of line 3 is? The *they* of line 8?

2. Explain the meaning of line 7. Can it be interpreted in more than one way? Explain.

3. Explain the meanings of *drowning*.

4. The only thing we learn about the dead man is that "he always loved larking" (l. 5). Why is this detail significant? What kind of man do you think he was?

5. Does the speaker know more about the dead man than the man's friends do? Explain.

Writing Topics

1. Write an essay describing how you or someone you know suffered the experience of "not waving but drowning."

2. Write an essay describing how you came to the realization that someone close to you was not the person you thought he or she was.

Countee Cullen   (1903–1946)

Incident   1925

Once riding in old Baltimore,
    Heart-filled, head-filled with glee,
I saw a Baltimorean
    Keep looking straight at me.

Now I was eight and very small,
    And he was no whit bigger,
And so I smiled, but he poked out
    His tongue and called me, "Nigger."

I saw the whole of Baltimore
    From May until December: 10
Of all the things that happened there
    That's all that I remember.

Dylan Thomas   (1914–1953)

Fern Hill 1946

Now as I was young and easy under the apple boughs
About the lilting house and happy as the grass was green,
    The night above the dingle° starry,   small wooded valley
        Time let me hail and climb
    Golden in the heydays of his eyes,
And honored among wagons I was prince of the apple towns
And once below a time I lordly had the trees and leaves
        Trail with daisies and barley
    Down the rivers of the windfall light.

And as I was green and carefree, famous among the barns   10
About the happy yard and singing as the farm was home,
    In the sun that is young once only,
        Time let me play and be
    Golden in the mercy of his means,
And green and golden I was huntsman and herdsman, the calves
Sang to my horn, the foxes on the hills barked clear and cold,
        And the sabbath rang slowly
    In the pebbles of the holy streams.

All the sun long it was running, it was lovely, the hay
Fields high as the house, the tunes from the chimneys, it was air   20
    And playing, lovely and watery
        And fire green as grass.
    And nightly under the simple stars
As I rode to sleep the owls were bearing the farm away,
All the moon long I heard, blessed among stables, the nightjars[1]
    Flying with the ricks, and the horses
        Flashing into the dark.

[1] Nightjars are harsh-sounding nocturnal birds.

And then to awake, and the farm, like a wanderer white
With the dew, come back, the cock on his shoulder: it was all
    Shining, it was Adam and maiden,   30
        The sky gathered again
And the sun grew round that very day.
So it must have been after the birth of the simple light
In the first, spinning place, the spellbound horses walking warm
    Out of the whinnying green stable
        On to the fields of praise.

And honored among foxes and pheasants by the gay house
Under the new made clouds and happy as the heart was long,
    In the sun born over and over,
        I ran my heedless ways,   40
    My wishes raced through the house high hay
And nothing I cared, at my sky blue trades, that time allows
In all his tuneful turning so few and such morning songs
    Before the children green and golden
        Follow him out of grace.

Nothing I cared, in the lamb white days, that time would take me
Up to the swallow thronged loft by the shadow of my hand,
    In the moon that is always rising,
        Nor that riding to sleep
    I should hear him fly with the high fields   50
And wake to the farm forever fled from the childless land.
Oh as I was young and easy in the mercy of his means,
        Time held me green and dying
    Though I sang in my chains like the sea.

For Analysis

1. What emotional impact does the color imagery in the poem provide?

2. Trace the behavior of "time" in the poem.

3. Fairy tales often begin with the words "once upon a time." Why does Thomas alter that formula in line 7?

4. Explain the **paradox** in line 53.

Writing Topics

1. Lines 17–18, 30, and 45–46 incorporate religious language and biblical allusion. How do those allusions clarify the poet's vision of his childhood?

2. Compare this poem with either Hopkins's "Spring and Fall" (p. 155) or Housman's "When I Was One-and-Twenty" (p. 155).

Lawrence Ferlinghetti   (b. 1919)

Constantly Risking Absurdity   1958

Constantly risking absurdity
>   and death
>   whenever he performs
>   above the heads
>   of his audience
>   the poet like an acrobat
>   climbs on rime
>   to a high wire of his own making
> and balancing on eyebeams
>   above a sea of faces   10
>   paces his way
>   to the other side of day
> performing entrechats[1]
>   and sleight-of-foot tricks
> and other high theatrics
>   and all without mistaking
>   any thing
>   for what it may not be

>   For he's the super realist
>   who must perforce perceive   20
>   taut truth
>   before the taking of each stance or step
>   in his supposed advance
>   toward that still higher perch
> where Beauty stands and waits
>   with gravity
>   to start her death-defying leap

And he
>   a little charleychaplin[2] man
>   who may or may not catch   30
>   her fair eternal form
>   spreadeagled in the empty air
>   of existence

[1] In ballet, a leap straight upward in which the dancer repeatedly crosses her legs or strikes her heels together.

[2] Charles Spencer Chaplin (1889–1977) was cinema's most celebrated comedian of the silent film era. His trademark was the mustachioed Little Tramp, whose pathos and comedy were accompanied by extraordinary acrobatic skills.

167

Philip Larkin   (1922–1985)

This Be the Verse   1974

They fuck you up, your mum and dad.
   They may not mean to, but they do.
They fill you with the faults they had
   And add some extra, just for you.

But they were fucked up in their turn
   By fools in old-style hats and coats,
Who half the time were soppy-stern
   And half at one another's throats.

Man hands on misery to man.
   It deepens like a coastal shelf.   10
Get out as early as you can,
   And don't have any kids yourself.

A Study of Reading Habits   1960

When getting my nose in a book
Cured most things short of school,
It was worth ruining my eyes
To know I could still keep cool,
And deal out the old right hook
To dirty dogs twice my size.

Later, with inch-thick specs,
Evil was just my lark:
Me and my cloak and fangs
Had ripping times in the dark.   10
The women I clubbed with sex!
I broke them up like meringues.

Don't read much now: the dude
Who lets the girl down before
The hero arrives, the chap
Who's yellow and keeps the store,

168

Seem far too familiar. Get stewed:
Books are a load of crap.

For Analysis

1. What sort of books did the speaker read (stanza 1) as a schoolchild?

2. How might reading cure "most things short of school" (l. 2)?

3. Describe the change in the speaker's reading habits revealed in the second stanza.

4. Explain why the speaker asserts that he doesn't read much now (l. 13). What experiences led him to the conclusion that "Books are a load of crap" (l. 18)?

Writing Topic

Describe the poem's metrical pattern and its rhyme scheme. See *Ballad* in the "Glossary of Literary Terms" (p. 1580), read some ballads in this book, and argue for or against the proposition that this poem is a modern ballad.

Anthony Hecht   (b. 1923)

"More Light! More Light!"[1]   1961

For Heinrich Blücher and Hannah Arendt[2]

Composed in the Tower[3] before his execution
These moving verses, and being brought at that time
Painfully to the stake, submitted, declaring thus:
"I implore my God to witness that I have made no crime."

Nor was he forsaken of courage, but the death was horrible,
The sack of gunpowder failing to ignite.
His legs were blistered sticks on which the black sap
Bubbled and burst as he howled for the Kindly Light.

And that was but one, and by no means one of the worst;
Permitted at least his pitiful dignity;   10

"More Light! More Light"

[1] These were the last words of the German poet Johann Wolfgang von Goethe (1749–1832).

[2] Husband and wife who emigrated to the United States from Germany in 1940. Hannah Arendt wrote extensively on political totalitarianism.

[3] The Tower of London was used as a prison for eminent political prisoners. What follows is an account of a priest's execution for the crime of heresy. The punishment was death by fire, and often a sack of gunpowder was placed at the condemned's neck to shorten the agony.

And such as were by made prayers in the name of Christ,
That shall judge all men, for his soul's tranquillity.

We move now to outside a German wood
Three men are there commanded to dig a hole
In which the two Jews are ordered to lie down
And be buried by the third, who is a Pole.

Not light from the shrine at Weimar[4] beyond the hill
Nor light from heaven appeared. But he did refuse.
A Lüger[5] settled back deeply in its glove.
He was ordered to change places with the Jews.   20

Much casual death had drained away their souls.
The thick dirt mounted toward the quivering chin.
When only the head was exposed the order came
To dig him out again and to get back in.

No light, no light in the blue Polish eye.
When he finished a riding boot packed down the earth.
The Lüger hovered lightly in its glove.
He was shot in the belly and in three hours bled to death.

No prayers or incense rose up in those hours
Which grew to be years, and every day came mute   30
Ghosts from the ovens, sifting through crisp air,
And settled upon his eyes in a black soot.

For Analysis

1. What relationship does the event (which occurred in sixteenth-century England) recounted in the first three stanzas of the poem bear to the event recounted in the last five stanzas?

2. What **irony** do you find in the title of the poem and the use of the word *light* in lines 8, 17, 18, and 25? How would you define *light* in each case? Can you imagine yourself in the place of the three prisoners in line 14? What would you do?

---

[4] Goethe spent most of his life in Weimar, and his humanistic achievements are honored there in the Goethe National Museum. The event recounted here occurred at Buchenwald, a German concentration camp north of Weimar.
[5] A German automatic pistol.

Peter Meinke (b. 1932)

Advice to My Son 1965

— *for Tim*

The trick is, to live your days
as if each one may be your last
(for they go fast, and young men lose their lives
in strange and unimaginable ways)
but at the same time, plan long range
(for they go slow: if you survive
the shattered windshield and the bursting shell
you will arrive
at our approximation here below
of heaven or hell).   10

To be specific, between the peony and the rose
plant squash and spinach, turnips and tomatoes;
beauty is nectar
and nectar, in a desert, saves —
but the stomach craves stronger sustenance
than the honied vine.
Therefore, marry a pretty girl
after seeing her mother;
speak truth to one man,
work with another;   20
and always serve bread with your wine.

But, son,
always serve wine.

For Analysis
1. Explain how the advice of lines 17–21 is logically related to the preceding lines.
2. What do the final two lines tell the reader about the speaker?

Writing Topic
The advice of the first stanza seems contradictory. In what ways does the second stanza attempt to resolve the contradiction or explain "the trick" (l. 1)? What do the various plants and the bread and wine symbolize?

Robert Mezey   (b. 1935)

My Mother 1970

My mother writes from Trenton,
a comedian to the bone
but underneath, serious
and all heart. "Honey," she says,
"be a mensch[1] and Mary too,
it's no good to worry, you
are doing the best you can
your Dad and everyone
thinks you turned out very well
as long as you pay your bills   10
nobody can say a word
you can tell them to drop dead
so save a dollar it can't
hurt—remember Frank you went
to highschool with? he still lives
with his wife's mother, his wife
works while he writes his books and
did he ever sell a one
the four kids run around naked
36 and he's never had,   20
you'll forgive my expression
even a pot to piss in
or a window to throw it,
such a smart boy he couldn't
read the footprints on the wall
honey you think you know all
the answers you don't, please try
to put some money away
believe me it wouldn't hurt
artist shmartist life's too short   30
for that kind of, forgive me,
horseshit, I know what you want
better than you, all that counts
is to make a good living
and the best of everything,
as Sholem Aleichem said
he was a great writer did
you ever read his books dear,

[1] Man, in the sense of "human being."

172

you should make what he makes a year
anyway he says some place   40
Poverty is no disgrace
but it's no honor either
that's what I say,
                    love,
                        Mother"

June Jordan   (b. 1936)

Memo: 1980

When I hear some woman say she
has finally decided you can spend time with
other women, I wonder what she means: Her
mother? My mother?
I've always despised my woman friends. Even
if they introduced me to a man I found
attractive I have never let them become
what you could call my intimates. Why
should I? Men are the ones with the money and
the big way with waiters and the passkey   10
to excitement in strange places of real
danger and the power to make things happen
like babies or war and all these great ideas
about mass magazines for members of the weaker sex
who need permission
to eat potatoes or a doctor's opinion on orgasm after death
or the latest word on what the female
executive should do, after hours, wearing
what. They must be morons: women!
Don't you think?   20
I guess you could say
I'm stuck in my ways
as
That Cosmopolitan Girl.

For Analysis

1. Explain the title.

2. What do the first three lines mean? Why would a woman feel she *can't* spend time with other women?

3. Does this poem accurately describe the power relations in our society? Explain.

4. Describe the **tone** of this poem.

Writing Topic

Examine a few issues of *Cosmopolitan* magazine, and write an essay imagining how it inspired this poem.

Affonso Romano DeSant'Anna   (b. 1937)

Letter to the Dead   2000

Friends, nothing has changed
in essence.

Wages don't cover expenses,
wars persist without end,
and there are new and terrible viruses,
beyond the advances of medicine.
From time to time, a neighbor
falls dead over questions of love.
There are interesting films, it is true,
and, as always, voluptuous women   10
seducing us with their mouths and legs,
but in matters of love
we haven't invented a single position that's new.

Some astronauts stay in space
six months or more, testing
equipment and solitude.
In each Olympics new records are predicted
and in the countries social advances and setbacks.
But not a single bird has changed its song
with the times.   20

We put on the same Greek tragedies,
reread "Don Quixote," and spring
arrives on time each year.

Some habits, rivers, and forests are lost.
Nobody sits in front of his house anymore
or takes in the breezes of afternoon,

but we have amazing computers
that keep us from thinking.

On the disappearance of the dinosaurs
and the formation of galaxies   30
we have no new knowledge.
Clothes come and go with the fashions.
Strong governments fall, others rise,
countries are divided,
and the ants and the bees continue
faithful to their work.

Nothing has changed in essence.

We sing congratulations at parties,
argue football on street corners,
die in senseless disasters,   40
and from time to time
one of us looks at the star-filled sky
with the same amazement we had
when we looked at caves.
And each generation, full of itself,
continues to think
that it lives at the summit of history.

(Translated from the Portuguese, by Mark Strand)

Bruce Bennett   (b. 1940)

The True Story of
Snow White   1989

Almost before the princess had grown cold
Upon the floor beside the bitten fruit,
The Queen gave orders to her men to shoot
The dwarfs, and thereby clinched her iron hold
Upon the state. Her mirror learned to lie,
And no one dared speak ill of her for fear
She might through her devices overhear.
So, in this manner, many years passed by,

And now today not even children weep
When someone whispers how, for her beauty's sake,   10
A child was harried once into a grove
And doomed, because her heart was full of love,
To lie forever in unlovely sleep
Which not a prince on earth has power to break.

For Analysis

1. Describe the allusion at the center of this poem, and explain how it contributes to the poem's force.

2. Note that the poem is a sonnet. How might that choice of form contribute an ironic element that reinforces the poem's grim message?

3. Why would the mirror "learn to lie" (l. 5)? What "devices" (l. 7) might frighten the Queen's subjects?

Writing Topic

Compare and contrast this sonnet (see the "Glossary of Literary Terms" on p. 1580) with two others from the text, and characterize each. How do they differ, and how do they resemble each other? Are they personal lyrics, political statements, or psychological insights?

Deborah Pope   (b. ?)

Bad Child   1999

He says he wishes I was not
even living, he says he wishes
I would go away,
swinging his small fists at me,
his shirt with spilled milk
still dripping, his arms
two jerking propellers
of fury and shame.
I am wiping at milk on the couch,
the dashed basin it is making,   10
saying milk of all things,
the smell, the stain, how
can you be so clumsy, careless,

running through my spiral
of tirade toward everything
so shabby, used, nobody cares,
no one looks after things
in this house and can't you
even say you're sorry?
He skulks in the hall,   20
making sure I can hear
how he hates me.
I clamp shut not to yell
I hate you back, rigid
with fatigue, the unspilled
angers of the house.
It is not good to tell children
you hate them, but they go on
yelling and yelling it,
somewhere their father   30
saying wearily that's enough.
It is no good to go
my own children running,
arms stretched,
their elongated, arrowing shadows
wincing my heart,
a step before they do.

The Last Lesson 1999

Ignorance is all
that makes choice
possible.
To live
however blindly
is to choose.
Thus must it
always be
we learn
what we love   10
by what we lose.

Molly Peacock   (b. 1947)

Our Room   1984

I tell the children in school sometimes
why I hate alcoholics: my father was one.
"Alcohol" and "disease" I use, and shun
the word "drunk" or even "drinking," since one time
the kids burst out laughing when I told them.
I felt as though they were laughing at me.
I waited for them, wounded, remembering how I imagined they'd howl at me
when I was in grade 5. Acting drunk
is a guaranteed screamer, especially   10
for boys. I'm quiet when I sort the junk
of my childhood for them, quiet so we
will all be quiet, and they can ask what
questions they have to and tell about what
happened to them, too. The classroom becomes
oddly lonely when we talk about our homes.

For Analysis
1. The implication of line 6 is that the children were laughing not at the speaker but at something else. What might that have been?

2. Describe the speaker's attitude toward her classmates.

3. Explain the title.

Writing Topic
Have you ever experienced shame about your family? Describe what caused the shame, your feelings at the time, and your present feelings about it.

Katherine McAlpine   (b. 1948)

Plus C'est la Même Chose[1] 1994

Lines Written upon Chaperoning the
Seventh Grade Dance

When did these little girls turn into women?
Lip-glossed and groomed, alarmingly possessed
of polish, poise and, in some cases, breasts,
they're clustered at one corner of the gym in
elaborate indifference to the boys,
who, at the other end, convene with cables,
adjusting speakers, tuners and turntables
to make the optimum amount of noise.
If nobody plans to dance, what's this dance for?
Finally the boys all gather in formation,   10
tentatively begin a group migration
across the fearsome distance of the floor—
and then retreat, noticing no one's there.
The girls have gone, en masse, to fix their hair.

For Analysis

1. What is the **tone** of this sonnet? Point to specific elements to support your response.

2. Explain the title.

3. Explain the appropriateness of "elaborate indifference" (l. 5), "gather in formation" (l. 10), and "migration" (l. 11).

Writing Topic

Write an essay in which you use one of the following as a thesis statement: (1) the poem embodies a traditional, sexist view of gender differences, or (2) the poem describes, without making a judgment, the culturally determined differences between males and females. If you disagree with both of these statements, formulate your own.

---

[1] The title comes from the French expression *plus ça change, plus c'est la même chose*, which means "the more things change, the more they remain the same."

Katharyn Howd Machan   (b. 1952)

Hazel Tells LaVerne 1976

last night
im cleanin out my
howard johnsons ladies room
when all of a sudden
up pops this frog
musta come from the sewer
swimmin aroun an tryin ta
climb up the sida the bowl
so i goes ta flushm down
but sohelpmegod he starts talkin   10
bout a golden ball
an how i can be a princess
me a princess
well my mouth drops
all the way to the floor
an he says
kiss me just kiss me
once on the nose
well i screams
ya little green pervert   20
an i hitsm with my mop
an has ta flush
the toilet down three times
me
a princess

For Analysis

1. How would you describe Hazel?

2. What does Hazel's language tell us about her?

3. Would the use of punctuation change the poem in any way?

Writing Topic

Write an analysis of this poem's humor.

180

Sandra Cisneros   (b. 1954)

My Wicked Wicked Ways   1987

This is my father.
See? He is young.
He looks like Errol Flynn.[1]
He is wearing a hat
that tips over one eye,
a suit that fits him good,
and baggy pants.

He is also wearing
those awful shoes,
the two-toned ones   10
my mother hates.

Here is my mother.
She is not crying.
She cannot look into the lens
because the sun is bright.
The woman,
the one my father knows,
is not here.
She does not come till later.

My mother will get very mad.   20
Her face will turn red
and she will throw one shoe.
My father will say nothing.
After a while everyone
will forget it.
Years and years will pass.
My mother will stop mentioning it.

This is me she is carrying.
I am a baby.
She does not know   30
I will turn out bad.

[1] Errol Flynn (1909–1959) was a handsome leading man in many Hollywood movies during the
1930s and 1940s.

181

For Analysis
1. Why does the speaker tell us that her mother "is not crying" (l. 13)?
2. What will the speaker's mother "get very mad" about (l. 20)?
3. What is the connection between the last four lines and the rest of the poem?

Writing Topic
Discuss the meaning of the final line of the poem. What does the speaker mean by *bad?*

Jill Bialosky   (b. 1957)

The End of Desire   1997

When I was a child
I used to love to stare at lovers —
at couples kissing, a man looking
longingly into a woman's eyes,
a woman adoring back
and marvel over the possibilities of love.
Usually I was with my sister,
standing in a grocery line,
or outside a theater.
She would tug at my sleeve,   10
roll her eyes and banish me with her words:
"Stop staring! What's wrong with you!"
I *did* feel that something was wrong
that I could be so content absorbing
the wave of her hair, the scent of perfume,
his strong fingers cupped around her shoulder.
It was the long, uninterrupted gaze I most preferred.
At the movies, I would draw into myself
as I watched on the big screen lovers kiss
and felt a stab of pain in the center of my stomach   20
travel through my body like a drug —
and for that brief time it was as though
I was the lover, the receiver of such rapt attention.
When the lights came on I carried the kiss
with me all through the rest of the late afternoon,
through the long walk home underneath the autumn arbors,
through the dull and tedious routine of dinner,

until I was alone in my bedroom and could replay
the scene in my mind without interruption.
I knew that as long as I was allowed to look,   30
to linger, to stare,
to become one with that spell that was so other,
to know and then to have
that one day, my desire would end.

For Analysis

1. Suggest how the poet, as a child, learned "the possibilities of love" (l. 6).
2. Why does the speaker stare at lovers?
3. What role do motion pictures play in her fantasies?
4. Explain the last five lines. How would her fantasies result in "the end of desire"?

Writing Topic

Describe, from your own experience, the interaction between fantasy and "real life."

Nick Flynn   (b. 1960)

Cartoon Physics   2000

Children under, say, *ten* shouldn't know
that the universe is ever-expanding,
inexorably pushing into the vacuum, galaxies

swallowed by galaxies, whole

solar systems collapsing, all of it
acted out in silence. At ten we are still learning

the rules of cartoon animation,

that if a man draws a door on a rock
only he can pass through it.
Anyone else who tries   10

will crash into the rock. Ten year olds
should stick with burning houses, car wrecks,
ships going down — earthbound, tangible
disasters, arenas

where they can be heroes. You can run
back into a burning house, sinking ships

have lifeboats, the trucks will come
with their ladders, if you jump

you will be saved. A child

places her hand on the roof of a schoolbus,   20
& drives across a city of sand. She knows

the exact spot where it will skid, at which point
the bridge will give, who will swim to safety
& who will be pulled under by sharks. She will learn

that if a man runs off the edge of a cliff
he will not fall

until he notices his mistake.

Major Jackson   (b. 1968)

Euphoria   2000

Late winter, sky darkening after school
& groceries bought from Shop-Mart,
My mother leaves me parked on Diamond
To guard her Benz, her keys half turned
So I can listen to the Quiet Storm
While she smokes a few white pebbles
At the house crumbling across the street.

I clamber to the steering wheel,
Undo my school tie, just as Luther Vandross
Starts in on that one-word tune "Creepin'."   10
The dashboard's panel of neon glows,
And a girl my age, maybe sixteen or so,
In a black miniskirt, her hair crimped
With glitter, squats down to pane glass,

And asks, *A date, baby? For five?*
Outside, street light washes the avenue
A cheap orange: garbage swirling
A vacant lot; a crew of boys slap-boxing
On the corner, throwing back large swills
Of malt; even the sidewalk teeming with addicts,   20
Their eyes spread thin as egg whites.

She crams the crushed bill down
Her stockings, cradles & slides her palm
In rhythm to my hips' thrashing,
In rhythm to Luther's voice, which flutters
Around that word I now mistake for "Weep"
As sirens blast the neighborhood &
My own incomprehensible joy to silence.

Out of the house my mother steps,
As though returned from the ride of her life,   30
Studies pavement cracks for half-empty vials,
Then looks back at bricked-over windows
As though what else mattered —
A family, a dinner, a car, nothing
But this happiness so hard to come by.

For Analysis

1. What does *euphoria* mean? How do the mother and son attain it?
2. Of what social class are the boy and his mother? How do you know?
3. Why is the boy's joy "incomprehensible" (l. 28)?
4. Do you find the last stanza hopeful? Explain.

Making Connections

James Baldwin's story "Sonny's Blues" (p. 674), like this poem, deals with drug addiction. What similarities do you find between them in their handling of this subject? What differences?

Writing Topic

In an imaginative essay, describe the coming year in the life of this family.

Drama

Sophocles   (496?–406 B.C.)

Oedipus Rex[1]   ca. 429 B.C.

PERSONS REPRESENTED

Oedipus	**Messenger**
A Priest	**Shepherd of Laïos**
Creon	**Second Messenger**
Teiresias	**Chorus of Theban Elders**
Iocastê	

Scene

Before the palace of Oedipus, King of Thebes. A central door and two lateral doors open onto a platform which runs the length of the facade. On the platform, right and left, are altars; and three steps lead down into the "orchestra," or chorus-ground. At the beginning of the action these steps are crowded by suppliants who have brought branches and chaplets of olive leaves and who lie in various attitudes of despair. Oedipus enters.

Prologue

Oedipus.   My children, generations of the living
  In the line of Kadmos,[2] nursed at his ancient hearth:
  Why have you strewn yourselves before these altars
  In supplication, with your boughs and garlands?
  The breath of incense rises from the city
  With a sound of prayer and lamentation.

---

[1] An English version by Dudley Fitts and Robert Fitzgerald.   [2] The legendary founder of Thebes.

Children,
I would not have you speak through messengers,
And therefore I have come myself to hear you —
I, Oedipus, who bear the famous name.
[*To a Priest.*] You, there, since you are eldest in the company,   10
Speak for them all, tell me what preys upon you,
Whether you come in dread, or crave some blessing:
Tell me, and never doubt that I will help you
In every way I can; I should be heartless
Were I not moved to find you suppliant here.

Priest.   Great Oedipus, O powerful King of Thebes!
You see how all the ages of our people
Cling to your altar steps: here are boys
Who can barely stand alone, and here are priests
By weight of age, as I am a priest of God,   20
And young men chosen from those yet unmarried;
As for the others, all that multitude,
They wait with olive chaplets in the squares,
At the two shrines of Pallas,[3] and where Apollo[4]
Speaks in the glowing embers.

                    Your own eyes
Must tell you: Thebes is in her extremity
And can not lift her head from the surge of death.
A rust consumes the buds and fruits of the earth;
The herds are sick; children die unborn,
And labor is vain. The god of plague and pyre   30
Raids like detestable lightning through the city,
And all the house of Kadmos is laid waste,
All emptied, and all darkened: Death alone
Battens upon the misery of Thebes.

You are not one of the immortal gods, we know;
Yet we have come to you to make our prayer
As to the man of all men best in adversity
And wisest in the ways of God. You saved us
From the Sphinx,[5] that flinty singer, and the tribute
We paid to her so long; yet you were never   40
Better informed than we, nor could we teach you:
It was some god breathed in you to set us free.
Therefore, O mighty King, we turn to you:

---

[3] Athena, goddess of wisdom.   [4] God of sunlight, medicine, and prophecy.   [5] A winged monster, with a woman's head and breasts and a lion's body, that destroyed those who failed to answer her riddle: "What walks on four feet in the morning, two at noon, and three in the evening?" When the young Oedipus correctly answered, "Man" ("three" alluding to a cane in old age), the Sphinx killed herself, and the plague ended.

Find us our safety, find us a remedy,
Whether by counsel of the gods or men.
A king of wisdom tested in the past
Can act in a time of troubles, and act well.
Noblest of men, restore
Life to your city! Think how all men call you
Liberator for your triumph long ago;   50
Ah, when your years of kingship are remembered,
Let them not say *We rose, but later fell* —
Keep the State from going down in the storm!
Once, years ago, with happy augury,
You brought us fortune; be the same again!
No man questions your power to rule the land:
But rule over men, not over a dead city!
Ships are only hulls, citadels are nothing,
When no life moves in the empty passageways.

Oedipus.   Poor children! You may be sure I know   60
All that you longed for in your coming here.
I know that you are deathly sick; and yet,
Sick as you are, not one is as sick as I.
Each of you suffers in himself alone
His anguish, not another's; but my spirit
Groans for the city, for myself, for you.

I was not sleeping, you are not waking me.
No, I have been in tears for a long while
And in my restless thought walked many ways.
In all my search, I found one helpful course,   70
And that I have taken: I have sent Creon,
Son of Menoikeus, brother of the Queen,
To Delphi, Apollo's place of revelation,
To learn there, if he can,
What act or pledge of mine may save the city.
I have counted the days, and now, this very day,
I am troubled, for he has overstayed his time.
What is he doing? He has been gone too long.
Yet whenever he comes back, I should do ill
To scant whatever hint the god may give.   80

Priest.   It is a timely promise. At this instant
They tell me Creon is here.

Oedipus.   O Lord Apollo!
May his news be fair as his face is radiant!

Priest.   It could not be otherwise: he is crowned with bay,
The chaplet is thick with berries.

Oedipus. We shall soon know;
He is near enough to hear us now.

[*Enter Creon.*]

O Prince:
Brother: son of Menoikeus:
What answer do you bring us from the god?
Creon. It is favorable. I can tell you, great afflictions
Will turn out well, if they are taken well. 90
Oedipus. What was the oracle? These vague words
Leave me still hanging between hope and fear.
Creon. Is it your pleasure to hear me with all these
Gathered around us? I am prepared to speak,
But should we not go in?
Oedipus. Let them all hear it.
It is for them I suffer, more than for myself.
Creon. Then I will tell you what I heard at Delphi.

In plain words
The god commands us to expel from the land of Thebes
An old defilement that it seems we shelter. 100
It is a deathly thing, beyond expiation.
We must not let it feed upon us longer.
Oedipus. What defilement? How shall we rid ourselves of it?
Creon. By exile or death, blood for blood. It was
Murder that brought the plague-wind on the city.
Oedipus. Murder of whom? Surely the god has named him?
Creon. My lord: long ago Laïos was our king,
Before you came to govern us.
Oedipus. I know;
I learned of him from others; I never saw him.
Creon. He was murdered; and Apollo commands us now 110
To take revenge upon whoever killed him.
Oedipus. Upon whom? Where are they? Where shall we find a clue
To solve that crime, after so many years?
Creon. Here in this land, he said.
If we make enquiry,
We may touch things that otherwise escape us.
Oedipus. Tell me: Was Laïos murdered in his house,
Or in the fields, or in some foreign country?
Creon. He said he planned to make a pilgrimage.
He did not come home again.
Oedipus. And was there no one,

No witness, no companion, to tell what happened?   120
Creon. They were all killed but one, and he got away
So frightened that he could remember one thing only.
Oedipus. What was that one thing? One may be the key
To everything, if we resolve to use it.
Creon. He said that a band of highwaymen attacked them,
Outnumbered them, and overwhelmed the King.
Oedipus. Strange, that a highwayman should be so daring —
Unless some faction here bribed him to do it.
Creon. We thought of that. But after Laïos' death
New troubles arose and we had no avenger.   130
Oedipus. What troubles could prevent your hunting down the killers?
Creon. The riddling Sphinx's song
Made us deaf to all mysteries but her own.
Oedipus. Then once more I must bring what is dark to light.
It is most fitting that Apollo shows,
As you do, this compunction for the dead.
You shall see how I stand by you, as I should,
To avenge the city and the city's god,
And not as though it were for some distant friend,
But for my own sake, to be rid of evil.   140
Whoever killed King Laïos might — who knows? —
Decide at any moment to kill me as well.
By avenging the murdered king I protect myself.
Come, then, my children: leave the altar steps,
Lift up your olive boughs!
                    One of you go
And summon the people of Kadmos to gather here.
I will do all that I can; you may tell them that.

[*Exit a page.*]

So, with the help of God,
We shall be saved — or else indeed we are lost.
Priest. Let us rise, children. It was for this we came,   150
And now the King has promised it himself.
Phoibos[6] has sent us an oracle; may he descend
Himself to save us and drive out the plague.

[*Exeunt Oedipus and Creon into the palace by the central door. The Priest and the suppliants disperse R and L. After a short pause the Chorus enters the orchestra.*]

   [6] Phoebus Apollo, god of the sun.

Párodos[7]

Chorus.   What is God singing in his profound   [*Strophe 1*]
　　Delphi of gold and shadow?
　　What oracle for Thebes, the sunwhipped city?
　　Fear unjoints me, the roots of my heart tremble.
　　Now I remember, O Healer, your power, and wonder;
　　Will you send doom like a sudden cloud, or weave it
　　Like nightfall of the past?
　　Speak, speak to us, issue of holy sound:
　　Dearest to our expectancy: be tender!

　　Let me pray to Athenê, the immortal daughter of Zeus,   [*Antistrophe 1*]
　　And to Artemis her sister
　　Who keeps her famous throne in the market ring,
　　And to Apollo, bowman at the far butts of heaven —

　　O gods, descend! Like three streams leap against
　　The fires of our grief, the fires of darkness;
　　Be swift to bring us rest!

　　As in the old time from the brilliant house
　　Of air you stepped to save us, come again!

　　Now our afflictions have no end,   [*Strophe 2*]
　　Now all our stricken host lies down   20
　　And no man fights off death with his mind;

　　The noble plowland bears no grain,
　　And groaning mothers can not bear —

　　See, how our lives like birds take wing,
　　Like sparks that fly when a fire soars,
　　To the shore of the god of evening.

　　The plague burns on, it is pitiless,   [*Antistrophe 2*]
　　Though pallid children laden with death
　　Lie unwept in the stony ways,

---

[7] The *Párodos* is the ode sung by the Chorus as it entered the theater and moved down the aisles to the playing area. The *strophe*, in Greek tragedy, is the unit of verse the Chorus chanted as it moved to the left in a dance rhythm. The Chorus sang the *antistrophe* as it moved to the right, and the *epode* while standing still.

And old gray women by every path   30
Flock to the strand about the altars
There to strike their breasts and cry
Worship of Phoibos in wailing prayers:
Be kind, God's golden child!

There are no swords in this attack by fire,   *[Strophe 3]*
No shields, but we are ringed with cries.
Send the besieger plunging from our homes
Into the vast sea-room of the Atlantic
Or into the waves that foam eastward of Thrace —
For the day ravages what the night spares —   40

Destroy our enemy, lord of the thunder!
Let him be riven by lightning from heaven!

Phoibos Apollo, stretch the sun's bowstring,   *[Antistrophe 3]*
That golden cord, until it sing for us,
Flashing arrows in heaven!
                    Artemis, Huntress
Race with flaring lights upon our mountains!

O scarlet god, O golden-banded brow,
O Theban Bacchos in a storm of Maenads,[8]

[*Enter Oedipus, C.*]

Whirl upon Death, that all the Undying hate!
Come with blinding cressets, come in joy!   50

Scene I

Oedipus.   Is this your prayer? It may be answered. Come,
Listen to me, act as the crisis demands,
And you shall have relief from all these evils.
Until now I was a stranger to this tale,
As I had been a stranger to the crime.
Could I track down the murderer without a clue?
But now, friends,

---

[8] Bacchos is the god of wine and revelry, hence scarlet-faced. The Maenads were Bacchos' female attendants.

As one who became a citizen after the murder,
I make this proclamation to all Thebans:
If any man knows by whose hand Laïos, son of Labdakos,   10
Met his death, I direct that man to tell me everything,
No matter what he fears for having so long withheld it.
Let it stand as promised that no further trouble
Will come to him, but he may leave the land in safety.

Moreover: If anyone knows the murderer to be foreign,
Let him not keep silent: he shall have his reward from me.
However, if he does conceal it, if any man
Fearing for his friend or for himself disobeys this edict,
Hear what I propose to do:

I solemnly forbid the people of this country,   20
Where power and throne are mine, ever to receive that man
Or speak to him, no matter who he is, or let him
Join in sacrifice, lustration, or in prayer.
I decree that he be driven from every house,
Being, as he is, corruption itself to us: the Delphic
Voice of Zeus has pronounced this revelation.
Thus I associate myself with the oracle
And take the side of the murdered king.

As for the criminal, I pray to God —
Whether it be a lurking thief, or one of a number —   30
I pray that that man's life be consumed in evil and wretchedness.
And as for me, this curse applies no less
If it should turn out that the culprit is my guest here,
Sharing my hearth.
                    You have heard the penalty.
I lay it on you now to attend to this
For my sake, for Apollo's, for the sick
Sterile city that heaven has abandoned.
Suppose the oracle had given you no command:
Should this defilement go uncleansed for ever?
You should have found the murderer: your king,   40
A noble king, had been destroyed!
                    Now I,
Having the power that he held before me,
Having his bed, begetting children there
Upon his wife, as he would have, had he lived —
Their son would have been my children's brother,
If Laïos had had luck in fatherhood!
(But surely ill luck rushed upon his reign) —

I say I take the son's part, just as though
I were his son, to press the fight for him
And see it won! I'll find the hand that brought   50
Death to Labdakos' and Polydoros' child,
Heir of Kadmos' and Agenor's line.
And as for those who fail me,
May the gods deny them the fruit of the earth,
Fruit of the womb, and may they rot utterly!
Let them be wretched as we are wretched, and worse!

For you, for loyal Thebans, and for all
Who find my actions right, I pray the favor
Of justice, and of all the immortal gods.
Choragos.[9]   Since I am under oath, my lord, I swear   60
I did not do the murder. I can not name
The murderer. Might not the oracle
That has ordained the search tell where to find him?
Oedipus.   An honest question. But no man in the world
Can make the gods do more than the gods will.
Choragos.   There is one last expedient —
Oedipus.   Tell me what it is.
Though it seem slight, you must not hold it back.
Choragos.   A lord clairvoyant to the lord Apollo,
As we all know, is the skilled Teiresias.
One might learn much about this from him, Oedipus.   70
Oedipus.   I am not wasting time:
Creon spoke of this, and I have sent for him —
Twice, in fact; it is strange that he is not here.
Choragos.   The other matter — that old report — seems useless.
Oedipus.   Tell me. I am interested in all reports.
Choragos.   The King was said to have been killed by highwaymen.
Oedipus.   I know. But we have no witnesses to that.
Choragos.   If the killer can feel a particle of dread,
Your curse will bring him out of hiding!
Oedipus.   No.
The man who dared that act will fear no curse.   80

[*Enter the blind seer Teiresias, led by a page.*]

Choragos.   But there is one man who may detect the criminal.
This is Teiresias, this is the holy prophet
In whom, alone of all men, truth was born.
Oedipus.   Teiresias: seer: student of mysteries,

---

[9] Choragos is the leader of the Chorus.

Of all that's taught and all that no man tells,
Secrets of Heaven and secrets of the earth:
Blind though you are, you know the city lies
Sick with plague; and from this plague, my lord,
We find that you alone can guard or save us.

Possibly you did not hear the messengers? 90
Apollo, when we sent to him,
Sent us back word that this great pestilence
Would lift, but only if we established clearly
The identity of those who murdered Laïos.
They must be killed or exiled.
                              Can you use
Birdflight or any art of divination
To purify yourself, and Thebes, and me
From this contagion? We are in your hands.
There is no fairer duty
Than that of helping others in distress. 100
Teiresias.   How dreadful knowledge of the truth can be
  When there's no help in truth! I knew this well,
  But did not act on it: else I should not have come.
Oedipus.   What is troubling you? Why are your eyes so cold?
Teiresias.   Let me go home. Bear your own fate, and I'll
  Bear mine. It is better so: trust what I say.
Oedipus.   What you say is ungracious and unhelpful
  To your native country. Do not refuse to speak.
Teiresias.   When it comes to speech, your own is neither temperate
  Nor opportune. I wish to be more prudent. 110
Oedipus.   In God's name, we all beg you —
Teiresias.   You are all ignorant.
  No; I will never tell you what I know.
  Now it is my misery; then, it would be yours.
Oedipus.   What! You do know something, and will not tell us?
  You would betray us all and wreck the State?
Teiresias.   I do not intend to torture myself, or you.
  Why persist in asking? You will not persuade me.
Oedipus.   What a wicked old man you are! You'd try a stone's
  Patience! Out with it! Have you no feeling at all?
Teiresias.   You call me unfeeling. If you could only see 120
  The nature of your own feelings . . .
Oedipus.   Why,
  Who would not feel as I do? Who could endure
  Your arrogance toward the city?
Teiresias.   What does it matter!
  Whether I speak or not, it is bound to come.

Oedipus.   Then, if "it" is bound to come, you are bound to tell me.
Teiresias.   No, I will not go on. Rage as you please.
Oedipus.   Rage? Why not!
                    And I'll tell you what I think:
  You planned it, you had it done, you all but
  Killed him with your own hands: if you had eyes,
  I'd say the crime was yours, and yours alone.   130
Teiresias.   So? I charge you, then,
  Abide by the proclamation you have made:
  From this day forth
  Never speak again to these men or to me;
  You yourself are the pollution of this country.
Oedipus.   You dare say that! Can you possibly think you have
  Some way of going free, after such insolence?
Teiresias.   I have gone free. It is the truth sustains me.
Oedipus.   Who taught you shamelessness? It was not your craft.
Teiresias.   You did. You made me speak. I did not want to.   140
Oedipus.   Speak what? Let me hear it again more clearly.
Teiresias.   Was it not clear before? Are you tempting me?
Oedipus.   I did not understand it. Say it again.
Teiresias.   I say that you are the murderer whom you seek.
Oedipus.   Now twice you have spat out infamy! You'll pay for it!
Teiresias.   Would you care for more? Do you wish to be really angry?
Oedipus.   Say what you will. Whatever you say is worthless.
Teiresias.   I say you live in hideous shame with those
  Most dear to you. You can not see the evil.
Oedipus.   It seems you can go on mouthing like this for ever.   150
Teiresias.   I can, if there is power in truth.
Oedipus.   There is:
  But not for you, not for you,
  You sightless, witless, senseless, mad old man!
Teiresias.   You are the madman. There is no one here
  Who will not curse you soon, as you curse me.
Oedipus.   You child of endless night! You can not hurt me
  Or any other man who sees the sun.
Teiresias.   True: it is not from me your fate will come.
  That lies within Apollo's competence,
  As it is his concern.
Oedipus.   Tell me: 160
  Are you speaking for Creon or for yourself?
Teiresias.   Creon is no threat. You weave your own doom.
Oedipus.   Wealth, power, craft of statesmanship!
  Kingly position, everywhere admired!
  What savage envy is stored up against these,
  If Creon, whom I trusted, Creon my friend,

For this great office which the city once
Put in my hands unsought — if for this power
Creon desires in secret to destroy me!

He has brought this decrepit fortune-teller, this   170
Collector of dirty pennies, this prophet fraud —
Why, he is no more clairvoyant than I am!
                                        Tell us:
Has your mystic mummery ever approached the truth?
When that hellcat the Sphinx was performing here,
What help were you to these people?
Her magic was not for the first man who came along:
It demanded a real exorcist. Your birds —
What good were they? or the gods, for the matter of that?
But I came by,
Oedipus, the simple man, who knows nothing —   180
I thought it out for myself, no birds helped me!
And this is the man you think you can destroy,
That you may be close to Creon when he's king!
Well, you and your friend Creon, it seems to me,
Will suffer most. If you were not an old man,
You would have paid already for your plot.
Choragos.   We can not see that his words or yours
   Have been spoken except in anger, Oedipus,
   And of anger we have no need. How can God's will
   Be accomplished best? That is what most concerns us.   190
Teiresias.   You are a king. But where argument's concerned
   I am your man, as much a king as you.
   I am not your servant, but Apollo's.
   I have no need of Creon to speak for me.

   Listen to me. You mock my blindness, do you?
   But I say that you, with both your eyes, are blind:
   You can not see the wretchedness of your life,
   Nor in whose house you live, no, nor with whom.
   Who are your father and mother? Can you tell me?
   You do not even know the blind wrongs   200
   That you have done them, on earth and in the world below.
   But the double lash of your parents' curse will whip you
   Out of this land some day, with only night
   Upon your precious eyes.
   Your cries then — where will they not be heard?
   What fastness of Kithairon[10] will not echo them?

---

[10] A mountain range near Thebes where the infant Oedipus was left to die.

And that bridal-descant of yours — you'll know it then,
The song they sang when you came here to Thebes
And found your misguided berthing.
All this, and more, that you can not guess at now,   210
Will bring you to yourself among your children.

Be angry, then. Curse Creon. Curse my words.
I tell you, no man that walks upon the earth
Shall be rooted out more horribly than you.
Oedipus.   Am I to bear this from him? — Damnation
Take you! Out of this place! Out of my sight!
Teiresias.   I would not have come at all if you had not asked me.
Oedipus.   Could I have told that you'd talk nonsense, that
You'd come here to make a fool of yourself, and of me?
Teiresias.   A fool? Your parents thought me sane enough.   220
Oedipus.   My parents again! — Wait: who were my parents?
Teiresias.   This day will give you a father, and break your heart.
Oedipus.   Your infantile riddles! Your damned abracadabra!
Teiresias.   You were a great man once at solving riddles.
Oedipus.   Mock me with that if you like; you will find it true.
Teiresias.   It was true enough. It brought about your ruin.
Oedipus.   But if it saved this town?
Teiresias [*to the page*].   Boy, give me your hand.
Oedipus.   Yes, boy; lead him away.

                         While you are here
We can do nothing. Go; leave us in peace.   230
Teiresias.   I will go when I have said what I have to say.
How can you hurt me? And I tell you again:
The man you have been looking for all this time,
The damned man, the murderer of Laïos,
That man is in Thebes. To your mind he is foreignborn,
But it will soon be shown that he is a Theban,
A revelation that will fail to please.

                         A blind man,
Who has his eyes now; a penniless man, who is rich now;
And he will go tapping the strange earth with his staff;
To the children with whom he lives now he will be   240
Brother and father — the very same; to her
Who bore him, son and husband — the very same
Who came to his father's bed, wet with his father's blood.
Enough. Go think that over.
If later you find error in what I have said,
You may say that I have no skill in prophecy.

[*Exit Teiresias, led by his page. Oedipus goes into the palace.*]

Ode I

Chorus.   The Delphic stone of prophecies   [*Strophe 1*]
  Remembers ancient regicide
  And a still bloody hand.
  That killer's hour of flight has come.
  He must be stronger than riderless
  Coursers of untiring wind,
  For the son of Zeus[11] armed with his father's thunder
  Leaps in lightning after him;
  And the Furies follow him, the sad Furies.[12]

  Holy Parnassos' peak of snow   [*Antistrophe 1*]
  Flashes and blinds that secret man,
  That all shall hunt him down:
  Though he may roam the forest shade
  Like a bull gone wild from pasture
  To rage through glooms of stone.
  Doom comes down on him; flight will not avail him;
  For the world's heart calls him desolate,
  And the immortal Furies follow, for ever follow.

  But now a wilder thing is heard   [*Strophe 2*]
  From the old man skilled at hearing Fate in the wingbeat of a bird.   20
  Bewildered as a blown bird, my soul hovers and can not find
  Foothold in this debate, or any reason or rest of mind.
  But no man ever brought — none can bring
  Proof of strife between Thebes' royal house,
  Labdakos' line, and the son of Polybus;[13]
  And never until now has any man brought word
  Of Laïos' dark death staining Oedipus the King.

  Divine Zeus and Apollo hold   [*Antistrophe 2*]
  Perfect intelligence alone of all tales ever told;
  And well though this diviner works, he works in his own night;   30
  No man can judge that rough unknown or trust in second sight,
  For wisdom changes hands among the wise.
  Shall I believe my great lord criminal
  At a raging word that a blind old man let fall?
  I saw him, when the carrion woman faced him of old,
  Prove his heroic mind! These evil words are lies.

---

[11] I.e., Apollo (see note 4).   [12] The goddesses of divine vengeance.   [13] Labdakos was an early king of Thebes and an ancestor of Oedipus. Oedipus is mistakenly referred to as the son of Polybus.

Scene II

Creon.   Men of Thebes:
I am told that heavy accusations
Have been brought against me by King Oedipus.

I am not the kind of man to bear this tamely.

If in these present difficulties
He holds me accountable for any harm to him
Through anything I have said or done — why, then,
I do not value life in this dishonor.
It is not as though this rumor touched upon
Some private indiscretion. The matter is grave.   10
The fact is that I am being called disloyal
To the State, to my fellow citizens, to my friends.
Choragos.   He may have spoken in anger, not from his mind.
Creon.   But did you not hear him say I was the one
Who seduced the old prophet into lying?
Choragos.   The thing was said; I do not know how seriously.
Creon.   But you were watching him! Were his eyes steady?
Did he look like a man in his right mind?
Choragos.   I do not know.
I can not judge the behavior of great men.
But here is the King himself.

[*Enter Oedipus.*]

Oedipus.   So you dared come back.   20
Why? How brazen of you to come to my house,
You murderer!
                    Do you think I do not know
That you plotted to kill me, plotted to steal my throne?
Tell me, in God's name: am I coward, a fool,
That you should dream you could accomplish this?
A fool who could not see your slippery game?
A coward, not to fight back when I saw it?
You are the fool, Creon, are you not? hoping
Without support or friends to get a throne?
Thrones may be won or bought: you could do neither.   30
Creon.   Now listen to me. You have talked; let me talk, too.
You can not judge unless you know the facts.
Oedipus.   You speak well: there is one fact; but I find it hard
To learn from the deadliest enemy I have.

Creon. That above all I must dispute with you.

Oedipus. That above all I will not hear you deny.

Creon. If you think there is anything good in being stubborn
Against all reason, then I say you are wrong.

Oedipus. If you think a man can sin against his own kind
And not be punished for it, I say you are mad.   40

Creon. I agree. But tell me: what have I done to you?

Oedipus. You advised me to send for that wizard, did you not?

Creon. I did. I should do it again.

Oedipus.   Very well. Now tell me:
How long has it been since Laïos —

Creon.   What of Laïos?

Oedipus. Since he vanished in that onset by the road?

Creon. It was long ago, a long time.

Oedipus.   And this prophet,
Was he practicing here then?

Creon.   He was; and with honor, as now.

Oedipus. Did he speak of me at that time?

Creon.   He never did;
At least, not when I was present.

Oedipus.   But . . . the enquiry?
I suppose you held one?

Creon.   We did, but we learned nothing.   50

Oedipus. Why did the prophet not speak against me then?

Creon. I do not know; and I am the kind of man
Who holds his tongue when he has no facts to go on.

Oedipus. There's one fact that you know, and you could tell it.

Creon. What fact is that? If I know it, you shall have it.

Oedipus. If he were not involved with you, he could not say
That it was I who murdered Laïos.

Creon. If he says that, you are the one that knows it! —
But now it is my turn to question you.

Oedipus. Put your questions. I am no murderer.   60

Creon. First then: You married my sister?

Oedipus.   I married your sister.

Creon. And you rule the kingdom equally with her?

Oedipus. Everything that she wants she has from me.

Creon. And I am the third, equal to both of you?

Oedipus. That is why I call you a bad friend.

Creon. No. Reason it out, as I have done.
Think of this first. Would any sane man prefer
Power, with all a king's anxieties,
To that same power and the grace of sleep?
Certainly not I.   70
I have never longed for the king's power — only his rights.

Would any wise man differ from me in this?
As matters stand, I have my way in everything
With your consent, and no responsibilities.
If I were king, I should be a slave to policy.

How could I desire a scepter more
Than what is now mine — untroubled influence?
No, I have not gone mad; I need no honors,
Except those with the perquisites I have now.
I am welcome everywhere; every man salutes me,   80
And those who want your favor seek my ear,
Since I know how to manage what they ask.
Should I exchange this ease for that anxiety?
Besides, no sober mind is treasonable.
I hate anarchy
And never would deal with any man who likes it.

Test what I have said. Go to the priestess
At Delphi, ask if I quoted her correctly.
And as for this other thing: if I am found
Guilty of treason with Teiresias,   90
Then sentence me to death! You have my word
It is a sentence I should cast my vote for —
But not without evidence!
                         You do wrong
When you take good men for bad, bad men for good.
A true friend thrown aside — why, life itself
Is not more precious!
                    In time you will know this well:
For time, and time alone, will show the just man,
Though scoundrels are discovered in a day.
Choragos.   This is well said, and a prudent man would ponder it.
Judgments too quickly formed are dangerous.   100
Oedipus.   But is he not quick in his duplicity?
And shall I not be quick to parry him?
Would you have me stand still, hold my peace, and let
This man win everything, through my inaction?
Creon.   And you want — what is it, then? To banish me?
Oedipus.   No, not exile. It is your death I want,
So that all the world may see what treason means.
Creon.   You will persist, then? You will not believe me?
Oedipus.   How can I believe you?
Creon.   Then you are a fool.
Oedipus.   To save myself?

Creon.   In justice, think of me.   110
Oedipus.   You are evil incarnate.
Creon.   But suppose that you are wrong?
Oedipus.   Still I must rule.
Creon.   But not if you rule badly.
Oedipus.   O city, city!
Creon.   It is my city, too!
Choragos.   Now, my lords, be still. I see the Queen,
    Iocastê, coming from her palace chambers;
    And it is time she came, for the sake of you both.
    This dreadful quarrel can be resolved through her.

[*Enter Iocastê.*]

Iocastê.   Poor foolish men, what wicked din is this?
    With Thebes sick to death, is it not shameful
    That you should rake some private quarrel up?   120
    [*To Oedipus.*] Come into the house.
                            — And you, Creon, go now:
    Let us have no more of this tumult over nothing.
Creon.   Nothing? No, sister: what your husband plans for me
    Is one of two great evils: exile or death.
Oedipus.   He is right.
                        Why, woman I have caught him squarely
    Plotting against my life.
Creon.   No! Let me die
    Accurst if ever I have wished you harm!
Iocastê.   Ah, believe it, Oedipus!
    In the name of the gods, respect this oath of his
    For my sake, for the sake of these people here!   130

Choragos.   Open your mind to her my lord. Be ruled by her,   [*Strophe 1*]
    I beg you!
Oedipus.   What would you have me do?
Choragos.   Respect Creon's word. He has never spoken like a fool,
    And now he has sworn an oath.
Oedipus.   You know what you ask?
Choragos.   I do.
Oedipus.   Speak on, then.
Choragos.   A friend so sworn should not be baited so,
    In blind malice, and without final proof.
Oedipus.   You are aware, I hope, that what you say
    Means death for me, or exile at the least.

Choragos.   No, I swear by Helios,[14] first in Heaven!   [*Strophe 2*]
  May I die friendless and accurst,   140
  The worst of deaths, if ever I meant that!
    It is the withering fields
      That hurt my sick heart:
    Must we bear all these ills,
      And now your bad blood as well?
Oedipus.   Then let him go. And let me die, if I must,
  Or be driven by him in shame from the land of Thebes.
  It is your unhappiness, and not his talk,
  That touches me.
               As for him —
  Wherever he is, I will hate him as long as I live.   150
Creon.   Ugly in yielding, as you were ugly in rage!
  Natures like yours chiefly torment themselves.
Oedipus.   Can you not go? Can you not leave me?
Creon.   I can.
  You do not know me; but the city knows me,
  And in its eyes I am just, if not in yours.

[*Exit Creon.*]

Choragos.   Lady Iocastê, did you not ask the King to go   [*Antistrophe 1*]
  to his chambers?
Iocastê.   First tell me what has happened.
Choragos.   There was suspicion without evidence; yet it rankled
  As even false charges will.
Iocastê.   On both sides?
Choragos.   On both.
Iocastê.   But what was said?
Choragos.   Oh let it rest, let it be done with!   160
  Have we not suffered enough?
Oedipus.   You see to what your decency has brought you:
  You have made difficulties where my heart saw none.

Choragos.   Oedipus, it is not once only I have told you —   [*Antistrophe 2*]
  You must know I should count myself unwise
  To the point of madness, should I now forsake you —
    You, under whose hand,
      In the storm of another time,
    Our dear land sailed out free.
      But now stand fast at the helm!   170

---

[14] The sun god.

Iocastê.   In God's name, Oedipus, inform your wife as well:
  Why are you so set in this hard anger?
Oedipus.   I will tell you, for none of these men deserves
  My confidence as you do. It is Creon's work,
  His treachery, his plotting against me.
Iocastê.   Go on, if you can make this clear to me.
Oedipus.   He charges me with the murder of Laïos.
Iocastê.   Has he some knowledge? Or does he speak from hearsay?
Oedipus.   He would not commit himself to such a charge,
  But he has brought in that damnable soothsayer   180
  To tell his story.
Iocastê.   Set your mind at rest.
  If it is a question of soothsayers, I tell you
  That you will find no man whose craft gives knowledge
  Of the unknowable.

                     Here is my proof:

  An oracle was reported to Laïos once
  (I will not say from Phoibos himself, but from
  His appointed ministers, at any rate)
  That his doom would be death at the hands of his own son —
  His son, born of his flesh and of mine!

  Now, you remember the story: Laïos was killed   190
  By marauding strangers where three highways meet;
  But his child had not been three days in this world
  Before the King had pierced the baby's ankles
  And left him to die on a lonely mountainside.

  Thus, Apollo never caused that child
  To kill his father, and it was not Laïos' fate
  To die at the hands of his son, as he had feared.
  This is what prophets and prophecies are worth!
  Have no dread of them.
                      It is God himself
  Who can show us what he wills, in his own way.   200
Oedipus.   How strange a shadowy memory crossed my mind,
  Just now while you were speaking; it chilled my heart.
Iocastê.   What do you mean? What memory do you speak of?
Oedipus.   If I understand you, Laïos was killed
  At a place where three roads meet.
Iocastê.   So it was said;
  We have no later story.
Oedipus.   Where did it happen?

Iocastê.   Phokis, it is called: at a place where the Theban Way
Divides into the roads towards Delphi and Daulia.
Oedipus.   When?
Iocastê.   We had the news not long before you came
And proved the right to your succession here.   210
Oedipus.   Ah, what net has God been weaving for me?
Iocastê.   Oedipus! Why does this trouble you?
Oedipus.   Do not ask me yet.
First, tell me how Laïos looked, and tell me
How old he was.
Iocastê.   He was tall, his hair just touched
With white; his form was not unlike your own.
Oedipus.   I think that I myself may be accurst
By my own ignorant edict.
Iocastê.   You speak strangely.
It makes me tremble to look at you, my King.
Oedipus.   I am not sure that the blind man can not see.
But I should know better if you were to tell me —   220
Iocastê.   Anything — though I dread to hear you ask it.
Oedipus.   Was the King lightly escorted, or did he ride
With a large company, as a ruler should?
Iocastê.   There were five men with him in all: one was a herald;
And a single chariot, which he was driving.
Oedipus.   Alas, that makes it plain enough!
                                                  But who —
Who told you how it happened?
Iocastê.   A household servant,
The only one to escape.
Oedipus.   And is he still
A servant of ours?
Iocastê.   No; for when he came back at last
And found you enthroned in the place of the dead king,   230
He came to me, touched my hand with his, and begged
That I would send him away to the frontier district
Where only the shepherds go —
As far away from the city as I could send him.
I granted his prayer; for although the man was a slave,
He had earned more than this favor at my hands.
Oedipus.   Can he be called back quickly?
Iocastê.   Easily.
But why?
Oedipus.   I have taken too much upon myself
Without enquiry; therefore I wish to consult him.

Iocastê.   Then he shall come.

                            But am I not one also   240
To whom you might confide these fears of yours?
Oedipus.   That is your right; it will not be denied you,
Now least of all; for I have reached a pitch
Of wild foreboding. Is there anyone
To whom I should sooner speak?
Polybus of Corinth is my father.
My mother is a Dorian: Meropê.
I grew up chief among the men of Corinth
Until a strange thing happened —
Not worth my passion, it may be, but strange.   250

At a feast, a drunken man maundering in his cups
Cries out that I am not my father's son!

I contained myself that night, though I felt anger
And a sinking heart. The next day I visited
My father and mother, and questioned them. They stormed,
Calling it all the slanderous rant of a fool;
And this relieved me. Yet the suspicion
Remained always aching in my mind;
I knew there was talk; I could not rest;
And finally, saying nothing to my parents,   260
I went to the shrine at Delphi.
The god dismissed my question without reply;
He spoke of other things.

                           Some were clear,
Full of wretchedness, dreadful, unbearable:
As, that I should lie with my own mother, breed
Children from whom all men would turn their eyes;
And that I should be my father's murderer.

I heard all this, and fled. And from that day
Corinth to me was only in the stars
Descending in that quarter of the sky,   270
As I wandered farther and farther on my way
To a land where I should never see the evil
Sung by the oracle. And I came to this country
Where, so you say, King Laïos was killed.

I will tell you all that happened there, my lady.

There were three highways
Coming together at a place I passed;
And there a herald came towards me, and a chariot
Drawn by horses, with a man such as you describe
Seated in it. The groom leading the horses   280
Forced me off the road at his lord's command;
But as this charioteer lurched over towards me
I struck him in my rage. The old man saw me
And brought his double goad down upon my head
As I came abreast.

              He was paid back, and more!
Swinging my club in this right hand I knocked him
Out of his car, and he rolled on the ground.

                        I killed him.

I killed them all.
Now if that stranger and Laïos were — kin,
Where is a man more miserable than I?   290
More hated by the gods? Citizen and alien alike
Must never shelter me or speak to me —
I must be shunned by all.

              And I myself
Pronounced this malediction upon myself!

Think of it: I have touched you with these hands,
These hands that killed your husband. What defilement!

Am I all evil, then? It must be so,
Since I must flee from Thebes, yet never again
See my own countrymen, my own country,
For fear of joining my mother in marriage   300
And killing Polybus, my father.

                  Ah,
If I was created so, born to this fate,
Who could deny the savagery of God?

O holy majesty of heavenly powers!
May I never see that day! Never!
Rather let me vanish from the race of men
Than know the abomination destined me!

Choragos.   We too, my lord, have felt dismay at this.
But there is hope: you have yet to hear the shepherd.

Oedipus.   Indeed, I fear no other hope is left me.   310

Iocastê.   What do you hope from him when he comes?

Oedipus. This much:
  If his account of the murder tallies with yours,
  Then I am cleared.
Iocastê. What was it that I said
  Of such importance?
Oedipus. Why, "marauders," you said,
  Killed the King, according to this man's story.
  If he maintains that still, if there were several,
  Clearly the guilt is not mine: I was alone.
  But if he says one man, singlehanded, did it,
  Then the evidence all points to me.
Iocastê. You may be sure that he said there were several;   320
  And can he call back that story now? He can not.
  The whole city heard it as plainly as I.
  But suppose he alters some detail of it:
  He can not ever show that Laïos' death
  Fulfilled the oracle: For Apollo said
  My child was doomed to kill him; and my child —
  Poor baby! — it was my child that died first.

  No. From now on, where oracles are concerned,
  I would not waste a second thought on any.
Oedipus. You may be right.
                            But come: let someone go   330
  For the shepherd at once. This matter must be settled.
Iocastê. I will send for him.
  I would not wish to cross you in anything.
  And surely not in this. — Let us go in.

[*Exeunt into the palace.*]

Ode II

Chorus. Let me be reverent in the ways of right,   [*Strophe 1*]
  Lowly the paths I journey on;
  Let all my words and actions keep
  The laws of the pure universe
  From highest Heaven handed down.
  For Heaven is their bright nurse,
  Those generations of the realms of light;

Ah, never of mortal kind were they begot,
Nor are they slaves of memory, lost in sleep:
Their Father is greater than Time, and ages not.   10

The tyrant is a child of Pride   [*Antistrophe 1*]
Who drinks from his great sickening cup
Recklessness and vanity,
Until from his high crest headlong
He plummets to the dust of hope.
That strong man is not strong.
But let no fair ambition be denied;
May God protect the wrestler for the State
In government, in comely policy,
Who will fear God, and on His ordinance wait.   20

Haughtiness and the high hand of disdain   [*Strophe 2*]
Tempt and outrage God's holy law;
And any mortal who dares hold
No immortal Power in awe
Will be caught up in a net of pain:
The price for which his levity is sold.
Let each man take due earnings, then,
And keep his hands from holy things,
And from blasphemy stand apart —
Else the crackling blast of heaven   30
Blows on his head, and on his desperate heart;
Though fools will honor impious men,
In their cities no tragic poet sings.

Shall we lose faith in Delphi's obscurities,   [*Antistrophe 2*]
We who have heard the world's core
Discredited, and the sacred wood
Of Zeus at Elis praised no more?
The deeds and the strange prophecies
Must make a pattern yet to be understood.
Zeus, if indeed you are lord of all,   40
Throned in light over night and day,
Mirror this in your endless mind:
Our masters call the oracle
Words on the wind, and the Delphic vision blind!
Their hearts no longer know Apollo,
And reverence for the gods has died away.

Scene III

[*Enter Iocastê.*]

Iocastê.   Princes of Thebes, it has occurred to me
To visit the altars of the gods, bearing
These branches as a suppliant, and this incense.
Our King is not himself: his noble soul
Is overwrought with fantasies of dread,
Else he would consider
The new prophecies in the light of the old.
He will listen to any voice that speaks disaster,
And my advice goes for nothing.

[*She approaches the altar, R.*]

                        To you, then, Apollo,
Lycean lord, since you are nearest, I turn in prayer.   10
Receive these offerings, and grant us deliverance
From defilement. Our hearts are heavy with fear
When we see our leader distracted, as helpless sailors
Are terrified by the confusion of their helmsman.

[*Enter Messenger.*]

Messenger.   Friends, no doubt you can direct me:
Where shall I find the house of Oedipus,
Or, better still, where is the King himself?
Choragos.   It is this very place, stranger; he is inside.
This is his wife and mother of his children.
Messenger.   I wish her happiness in a happy house,   20
Blest in all the fulfillment of her marriage.
Iocastê.   I wish as much for you: your courtesy
Deserves a like good fortune. But now, tell me:
Why have you come? What have you to say to us?
Messenger.   Good news, my lady, for your house and your husband.
Iocastê.   What news? Who sent you here?
Messenger.   I am from Corinth.
The news I bring ought to mean joy for you,
Though it may be you will find some grief in it.
Iocastê.   What is it? How can it touch us in both ways?
Messenger.   The people of Corinth, they say,   30
Intend to call Oedipus to be their king.
Iocastê.   But old Polybus — is he not reigning still?

Messenger.   No. Death holds him in his sepulchre.

Iocastê.   What are you saying? Polybus is dead?

Messenger.   If I am not telling the truth, may I die myself.

Iocastê [*to a maidservant*].   Go in, go quickly; tell this to your master.
O riddlers of God's will, where are you now!
This was the man whom Oedipus, long ago,
Feared so, fled so, in dread of destroying him —
But it was another fate by which he died.   40

[*Enter Oedipus, C.*]

Oedipus.   Dearest Iocastê, why have you sent for me?

Iocastê.   Listen to what this man says, and then tell me
What has become of the solemn prophecies.

Oedipus.   Who is this man? What is his news for me?

Iocastê.   He has come from Corinth to announce your father's death!

Oedipus.   Is it true, stranger? Tell me in your own words.

Messenger.   I can not say it more clearly: the King is dead.

Oedipus.   Was it by treason? Or by an attack of illness?

Messenger.   A little thing brings old men to their rest.

Oedipus.   It was sickness, then?

Messenger.   Yes, and his many years.   50

Oedipus.   Ah!
Why should a man respect the Pythian hearth,[15] or
Give heed to the birds that jangle above his head?
They prophesied that I should kill Polybus,
Kill my own father; but he is dead and buried,
And I am here — I never touched him, never,
Unless he died of grief for my departure,
And thus, in a sense, through me. No. Polybus
Has packed the oracles off with him underground.
They are empty words.

Iocastê.   Had I not told you so?   60

Oedipus.   You had; it was my faint heart that betrayed me.

Iocastê.   From now on never think of those things again.

Oedipus.   And yet — must I not fear my mother's bed?

Iocastê.   Why should anyone in this world be afraid,
Since Fate rules us and nothing can be foreseen?
A man should live only for the present day.

Have no more fear of sleeping with your mother:
How many men, in dreams, have lain with their mothers!
No reasonable man is troubled by such things.

---

[15] Delphi, where Apollo spoke through an oracle.

Oedipus. That is true; only —   70
    If only my mother were not still alive!
    But she is alive. I can not help my dread.
Iocastê. Yet this news of your father's death is wonderful.
Oedipus. Wonderful. But I fear the living woman.
Messenger. Tell me, who is this woman that you fear?
Oedipus. It is Meropê, man; the wife of King Polybus.
Messenger. Meropê? Why should you be afraid of her?
Oedipus. An oracle of the gods, a dreadful saying.
Messenger. Can you tell me about it or are you sworn to silence?
Oedipus. I can tell you, and I will.   80
    Apollo said through his prophet that I was the man
    Who should marry his own mother, shed his father's blood
    With his own hands. And so, for all these years
    I have kept clear of Corinth, and no harm has come —
    Though it would have been sweet to see my parents again.
Messenger. And is this the fear that drove you out of Corinth?
Oedipus. Would you have me kill my father?
Messenger.   As for that
    You must be reassured by the news I gave you.
Oedipus. If you could reassure me, I would reward you.
Messenger. I had that in mind, I will confess: I thought   90
    I could count on you when you returned to Corinth.
Oedipus. No: I will never go near my parents again.
Messenger. Ah, son, you still do not know what you are doing —
Oedipus. What do you mean? In the name of God tell me!
Messenger. — If these are your reasons for not going home.
Oedipus. I tell you, I fear the oracle may come true.
Messenger. And guilt may come upon you through your parents?
Oedipus. That is the dread that is always in my heart.
Messenger. Can you not see that all your fears are groundless?
Oedipus. How can you say that? They are my parents, surely?   100
Messenger. Polybus was not your father.
Oedipus.   Not my father?
Messenger. No more your father than the man speaking to you.
Oedipus. But you are nothing to me!
Messenger.   Neither was he.
Oedipus. Then why did he call me son?
Messenger.   I will tell you:
    Long ago he had you from my hands, as a gift.
Oedipus. Then how could he love me so, if I was not his?
Messenger. He had no children, and his heart turned to you.
Oedipus. What of you? Did you buy me? Did you find me by chance?
Messenger. I came upon you in the crooked pass of Kithairon.
Oedipus. And what were you doing there?

Messenger.   Tending my flocks.   110
Oedipus.   A wandering shepherd?
Messenger.   But your savior, son, that day.
Oedipus.   From what did you save me?
Messenger.   Your ankles should tell you that.
Oedipus.   Ah, stranger, why do you speak of that childhood pain?
Messenger.   I cut the bonds that tied your ankles together.
Oedipus.   I have had the mark as long as I can remember.
Messenger.   That was why you were given the name you bear.[16]
Oedipus.   God! Was it my father or my mother who did it?
Tell me!
Messenger.   I do not know. The man who gave you to me
Can tell you better than I.   120
Oedipus.   It was not you that found me, but another?
Messenger.   It was another shepherd gave you to me.
Oedipus.   Who was he? Can you tell me who he was?
Messenger.   I think he was said to be one of Laïos' people.
Oedipus.   You mean the Laïos who was king here years ago?
Messenger.   Yes; King Laïos; and the man was one of his herdsmen.
Oedipus.   Is he still alive? Can I see him?
Messenger.   These men here
Know best about such things.
Oedipus.   Does anyone here
Know this shepherd that he is talking about?
Have you seen him in the fields, or in the town?   130
If you have, tell me. It is time things were made plain.
Choragos.   I think the man he means is that same shepherd
You have already asked to see. Iocastê perhaps
Could tell you something.
Oedipus.   Do you know anything
About him, Lady? Is he the man we have summoned?
Is that the man this shepherd means?
Iocastê.   Why think of him?
Forget this herdsman. Forget it all.
This talk is a waste of time.
Oedipus.   How can you say that?
When the clues to my true birth are in my hands?
Iocastê.   For God's love, let us have no more questioning!   140
Is your life nothing to you?
My own is pain enough for me to bear.
Oedipus.   You need not worry. Suppose my mother a slave,
And born of slaves: no baseness can touch you.
Iocastê.   Listen to me, I beg you: do not do this thing!

---

[16] *Oedipus* literally means "swollen-foot."

Oedipus.   I will not listen; the truth must be made known.
Iocastê.   Everything that I say is for your own good!
Oedipus.   My own good
   Snaps my patience, then; I want none of it.
Iocastê.   You are fatally wrong! May you never learn who you are!
Oedipus.   Go, one of you, and bring the shepherd here.   150
   Let us leave this woman to brag of her royal name.
Iocastê.   Ah, miserable!
   That is the only word I have for you now.
   That is the only word I can ever have.

[*Exit into the palace.*]

Choragos.   Why has she left us, Oedipus? Why has she gone
   In such a passion of sorrow? I fear this silence:
   Something dreadful may come of it.
Oedipus.   Let it come!
   However base my birth, I must know about it.
   The Queen, like a woman, is perhaps ashamed
   To think of my low origin. But I   160
   Am a child of Luck; I can not be dishonored.
   Luck is my mother; the passing months, my brothers,
   Have seen me rich and poor.
                                        If this is so,
   How could I wish that I were someone else?
   How could I not be glad to know my birth?

Ode III

Chorus.   If ever the coming time were known   [*Strophe*]
   To my heart's pondering,
   Kithairon, now by Heaven I see the torches
   At the festival of the next full moon,
   And see the dance, and hear the choir sing
   A grace to your gentle shade:
   Mountain where Oedipus was found,
   O mountain guard of a noble race!
   May the god who heals us lend his aid,
   And let that glory come to pass   10
   For our king's cradling-ground.

   Of the nymphs that flower beyond the years,   [*Antistrophe*]
   Who bore you, royal child,

To Pan of the hills or the timberline Apollo,
Cold in delight where the upland clears,
Or Hermês for whom Kyllenê's heights are piled?[17]
Or flushed as evening cloud,
Great Dionysos, roamer of mountains,
He — was it he who found you there,
And caught you up in his own proud   20
Arms from the sweet god-ravisher
Who laughed by the Muses' fountains?

Scene IV

Oedipus.   Sirs: though I do not know the man,
  I think I see him coming, this shepherd we want:
  He is old, like our friend here, and the men
  Bringing him seem to be servants of my house.
  But you can tell, if you have ever seen him.

[*Enter Shepherd escorted by servants.*]

Choragos.   I know him, he was Laïos' man. You can trust him.
Oedipus.   Tell me first, you from Corinth: is this the shepherd
  We were discussing?
Messenger.   This is the very man.
Oedipus [*to Shepherd*].   Come here. No, look at me. You must answer
  Everything I ask. You belonged to Laïos?   10
Shepherd.   Yes: born his slave, brought up in his house.
Oedipus.   Tell me what kind of work did you do for him?
Shepherd.   I was a shepherd of his, most of my life.
Oedipus.   Where mainly did you go for pasturage?
Shepherd.   Sometimes Kithairon, sometimes the hills near-by.
Oedipus.   Do you remember ever seeing this man out there?
Shepherd.   What would he be doing there? This man?
Oedipus.   This man standing here. Have you ever seen him before?
Shepherd.   No. At least, not to my recollection.
Messenger.   And that is not strange, my lord. But I'll refresh   20
  His memory: he must remember when we two
  Spent three whole seasons together, March to September,
  On Kithairon or thereabouts. He had two flocks;

[17] Hermês, the herald of the Olympian gods, was born on the mountain of Kyllenê.

I had one. Each autumn I'd drive mine home
And he would go back with his to Laïos' sheepfold. —
Is this not true, just as I have described it?

Shepherd.   True, yes; but it was all so long ago.

Messenger.   Well, then: do you remember, back in those days
That you gave me a baby boy to bring up as my own?

Shepherd.   What if I did? What are you trying to say?   30

Messenger.   King Oedipus was once that little child.

Shepherd.   Damn you, hold your tongue!

Oedipus.   No more of that!
It is your tongue needs watching, not this man's.

Shepherd.   My King, my Master, what is it I have done wrong?

Oedipus.   You have not answered his question about the boy.

Shepherd.   He does not know . . . He is only making trouble . . .

Oedipus.   Come, speak plainly, or it will go hard with you.

Shepherd.   In God's name, do not torture an old man!

Oedipus.   Come here, one of you; bind his arms behind him.

Shepherd.   Unhappy king! What more do you wish to learn?   40

Oedipus.   Did you give this man the child he speaks of?

Shepherd.   I did.
And I would to God I had died that very day.

Oedipus.   You will die now unless you speak the truth.

Shepherd.   Yet if I speak the truth, I am worse than dead.

Oedipus.   Very well; since you insist on delaying —

Shepherd.   No! I have told you already that I gave him the boy.

Oedipus.   Where did you get him? From your house? From somewhere else?

Shepherd.   Not from mine, no. A man gave him to me.

Oedipus.   Is that man here? Do you know whose slave he was?

Shepherd.   For God's love, my King, do not ask me any more!   50

Oedipus.   You are a dead man if I have to ask you again.

Shepherd.   Then . . . Then the child was from the palace of Laïos.

Oedipus.   A slave child? or a child of his own line?

Shepherd.   Ah, I am on the brink of dreadful speech!

Oedipus.   And I of dreadful hearing. Yet I must hear.

Shepherd.   If you must be told, then . . .
                                                   They said it was Laïos' child,
But it is your wife who can tell you about that.

Oedipus.   My wife! — Did she give it to you?

Shepherd.   My lord, she did.

Oedipus.   Do you know why?

Shepherd.   I was told to get rid of it.

Oedipus.   An unspeakable mother!

Shepherd.   There had been prophecies . . .   60

Oedipus.   Tell me.

Shepherd.   It was said that the boy would kill his own father.
Oedipus.   Then why did you give him over to this old man?
Shepherd.   I pitied the baby, my King,
   And I thought that this man would take him far away
   To his own country.
                He saved him — but for what a fate!
   For if you are what this man says you are,
   No man living is more wretched than Oedipus.
Oedipus.   Ah God!
   It was true!
         All the prophecies!
                — Now,
   O Light, may I look on you for the last time!   70
   I, Oedipus,
   Oedipus, damned in his birth, in his marriage damned,
   Damned in the blood he shed with his own hand!

[*He rushes into the palace.*]

Ode IV

Chorus.   Alas for the seed of men.   [*Strophe 1*]

   What measure shall I give these generations
   That breathe on the void and are void
   And exist and do not exist?

   Who bears more weight of joy
   Than mass of sunlight shifting in images,
   Or who shall make his thought stay on
   That down time drifts away?

   Your splendor is all fallen.

   O naked brow of wrath and tears,   10
   O change of Oedipus!
   I who saw your days call no man blest —
   Your great days like ghosts gone.

   That mind was a strong bow.   [*Antistrophe 1*]

   Deep, how deep you drew it then, hard archer,

At a dim fearful range,
And brought dear glory down!

You overcame the stranger —
The virgin with her hooking lion claws —
And though death sang, stood like a tower   20
To make pale Thebes take heart.

Fortress against our sorrow!

Divine king, giver of laws,
Majestic Oedipus!
No prince in Thebes had ever such renown,
No prince won such grace of power.

And now of all men ever known   [*Strophe 2*]
Most pitiful is this man's story:
His fortunes are most changed, his state
Fallen to a low slave's   30
Ground under bitter fate.

O Oedipus, most royal one!
The great door that expelled you to the light
Gave at night — ah, gave night to your glory:
As to the father, to the fathering son.

All understood too late.

How could that queen whom Laïos won,
The garden that he harrowed at his height,
Be silent when that act was done?

But all eyes fail before time's eye,   [*Antistrophe 2*]
All actions come to justice there
Though never willed, though far down the deep past,
Your bed, your dread sirings,
Are brought to book at last.

Child by Laïos doomed to die,
Then doomed to lose that fortunate little death,
Would God you never took breath in this air
That with my wailing lips I take to cry:

For I weep the world's outcast.

I was blind, and now I can tell why: 50
Asleep, for you had given ease of breath
To Thebes, while the false years went by.

Exodos

[*Enter, from the palace, Second Messenger.*]

Second Messenger.   Elders of Thebes, most honored in this land,
What horrors are yours to see and hear, what weight
Of sorrow to be endured, if, true to your birth,
You venerate the line of Labdakos!
I think neither Istros nor Phasis, those great rivers,
Could purify this place of the corruption
It shelters now, or soon must bring to light —
Evil not done unconsciously, but willed.

The greatest griefs are those we cause ourselves.
Choragos.   Surely, friend, we have grief enough already; 10
What new sorrow do you mean?
Second Messenger.   The Queen is dead.
Choragos.   Iocastê? Dead? But at whose hand?
Second Messenger.   Her own.
The full horror of what happened you can not know,
For you did not see it; but I, who did, will tell you
As clearly as I can how she met her death.

When she had left us,
In passionate silence, passing through the court,
She ran to her apartment in the house,
Her hair clutched by the fingers of both hands.

She closed the doors behind her; then, by that bed 20
Where long ago the fatal son was conceived —
The son who should bring about his father's death —
We heard her call upon Laïos, dead so many years,
And heard her wail for the double fruit of her marriage,
A husband by her husband, children by her child.

Exactly how she died I do not know:
For Oedipus burst in moaning and would not let us
Keep vigil to the end: it was by him

As he stormed about the room that our eyes were caught.
From one to another of us he went, begging a sword,   30
Cursing the wife who was not his wife, the mother
Whose womb had carried his own children and himself.
I do not know: it was none of us aided him,
But surely one of the gods was in control!
For with a dreadful cry
He hurled his weight, as though wrenched out of himself,
At the twin doors: the bolts gave, and he rushed in.
And there we saw her hanging, her body swaying
From the cruel cord she had noosed about her neck.
A great sob broke from him, heartbreaking to hear,   40
As he loosed the rope and lowered her to the ground.

I would blot out from my mind what happened next!
For the King ripped from her gown the golden brooches
That were her ornament, and raised them, and plunged them down
Straight into his own eyeballs, crying, "No more,
No more shall you look on the misery about me,
The horrors of my own doing! Too long have you known
The faces of those whom I should never have seen,
Too long been blind to those for whom I was searching!
From this hour, go in darkness!" And as he spoke,   50
He struck at his eyes — not once, but many times;
And the blood spattered his beard,
Bursting from his ruined sockets like red hail.

So from the unhappiness of two this evil has sprung,
A curse on the man and woman alike. The old
Happiness of the house of Labdakos
Was happiness enough: where is it today?
It is all wailing and ruin, disgrace, death — all
The misery of mankind that has a name —
And it is wholly and for ever theirs.   60
Choragos.   Is he in agony still? Is there no rest for him?
Second Messenger.   He is calling for someone to lead him to the gates
So that all the children of Kadmos may look upon
His father's murderer, his mother's — no,
I can not say it!
            And then he will leave Thebes,
Self-exiled, in order that the curse
Which he himself pronounced may depart from the house.
He is weak, and there is none to lead him,
So terrible is his suffering.
            But you will see:

Look, the doors are opening; in a moment   70
You will see a thing that would crush a heart of stone.

[*The central door is opened; Oedipus, blinded, is led in.*]

Choragos.   Dreadful indeed for men to see.
  Never have my own eyes
  Looked on a sight so full of fear.

  Oedipus!
  What madness came upon you, what daemon
  Leaped on your life with heavier
  Punishment than a mortal man can bear?
  No: I can not even
  Look at you, poor ruined one.   80
  And I would speak, question, ponder,
  If I were able. No.
  You make me shudder.
Oedipus.   God. God.
  Is there a sorrow greater?
  Where shall I find harbor in this world?
  My voice is hurled far on a dark wind.
  What has God done to me?
Choragos.   Too terrible to think of, or to see.

Oedipus.   O cloud of night,   [*Strophe 1*]
  Never to be turned away: night coming on,
  I can not tell how: night like a shroud!

  My fair winds brought me here.
                           Oh God. Again
  The pain of the spikes where I had sight,
  The flooding pain
  Of memory, never to be gouged out.
Choragos.   This is not strange.
  You suffer it all twice over, remorse in pain,
  Pain in remorse.

Oedipus.   Ah dear friend   [*Antistrophe 1*]
  Are you faithful even yet, you alone?
  Are you still standing near me, will you stay here,
  Patient, to care for the blind?
                           The blind man!
  Yet even blind I know who it is attends me,

By the voice's tone —
Though my new darkness hide the comforter.
Choragos.   Oh fearful act!
What god was it drove you to rake black
Night across your eyes?
Oedipus.   Apollo. Apollo. Dear   [*Strophe 2*]
Children, the god was Apollo.
He brought my sick, sick fate upon me.
But the blinding hand was my own!
How could I bear to see
When all my sight was horror everywhere?
Choragos.   Everywhere; that is true.
Oedipus.   And now what is left?
Images? Love? A greeting even,
Sweet to the senses? Is there anything?
Ah no, friends: lead me away.   120
Lead me away from Thebes.
                                   Lead the great wreck
And hell of Oedipus, whom the gods hate.
Choragos.   Your fate is clear, you are not blind to that.
Would God you had never found it out!

Oedipus.   Death take the man who unbound   [*Antistrophe 2*]
My feet on that hillside
And delivered me from death to life! What life?
If only I had died,
This weight of monstrous doom
Could not have dragged me and my darlings down.   130
Choragos.   I would have wished the same.
Oedipus.   Oh never to have come here
With my father's blood upon me! Never
To have been the man they call his mother's husband!
Oh accurst! Oh child of evil,
To have entered that wretched bed —
                                   the selfsame one!
More primal than sin itself, this fell to me.
Choragos.   I do not know how I can answer you.
You were better dead than alive and blind.
Oedipus.   Do not counsel me any more. This punishment   140
That I have laid upon myself is just.
If I had eyes,
I do not know how I could bear the sight
Of my father, when I came to the house of Death,
Or my mother: for I have sinned against them both

So vilely that I could not make my peace
By strangling my own life.
                                    Or do you think my children,
Born as they were born, would be sweet to my eyes?
Ah never, never! Nor this town with its high walls,
Nor the holy images of the gods.
                                    For I,   150
Thrice miserable! — Oedipus, noblest of all the line
Of Kadmos, have condemned myself to enjoy
These things no more, by my own malediction
Expelling that man whom the gods declared
To be a defilement in the house of Laïos.
After exposing the rankness of my own guilt,
How could I look men frankly in the eyes?
No, I swear it,
If I could have stifled my hearing at its source,
I would have done it and made all this body   160
A tight cell of misery, blank to light and sound:
So I should have been safe in a dark agony
Beyond all recollection.
                                    Ah Kithairon!
Why did you shelter me? When I was cast upon you,
Why did I not die? Then I should never
Have shown the world my execrable birth.

Ah Polybus! Corinth, city that I believed
The ancient seat of my ancestors: how fair
I seemed, your child! And all the while this evil
Was cancerous within me!
                                    For I am sick   170
In my daily life, sick in my origin.

O three roads, dark ravine, woodland and way
Where three roads met: you, drinking my father's blood,
My own blood, spilled by my own hand: can you remember
The unspeakable things I did there, and the things
I went on from there to do?
                                    O marriage, marriage!
The act that engendered me, and again the act
Performed by the son in the same bed —
                                    Ah, the net
Of incest, mingling fathers, brothers, sons,
With brides, wives, mothers; the last evil   180
That can be known by men: no tongue can say
How evil!

No. For the love of God, conceal me
Somewhere far from Thebes; or kill me; or hurl me
Into the sea, away from men's eyes for ever.
Come, lead me. You need not fear to touch me.
Of all men, I alone can bear this guilt.

[*Enter Creon.*]

Choragos.   We are not the ones to decide; but Creon here
  May fitly judge of what you ask. He only
  Is left to protect the city in your place.
Oedipus.   Alas, how can I speak to him? What right have I   190
  To beg his courtesy whom I have deeply wronged?
Creon.   I have not come to mock you, Oedipus,
  Or to reproach you, either.
  [*To attendants.*]   — You, standing there:
  If you have lost all respect for man's dignity,
  At least respect the flame of Lord Helios:
  Do not allow this pollution to show itself
  Openly here, an affront to the earth
  And Heaven's rain and the light of day. No, take him
  Into the house as quickly as you can.
  For it is proper   200
  That only the close kindred see his grief.
Oedipus.   I pray you in God's name, since your courtesy
  Ignores my dark expectation, visiting
  With mercy this man of all men most execrable:
  Give me what I ask — for your good, not mine.
Creon.   And what is it that you would have me do?
Oedipus.   Drive me out of this country as quickly as may be
  To a place where no human voice can ever greet me.
Creon.   I should have done that before now — only,
  God's will had not been wholly revealed to me.   210
Oedipus.   But his command is plain: the parricide
  Must be destroyed. I am that evil man.
Creon.   That is the sense of it, yes; but as things are,
  We had best discover clearly what is to be done.
Oedipus.   You would learn more about a man like me?
Creon.   You are ready now to listen to the god.
Oedipus.   I will listen. But it is to you
  That I must turn for help. I beg you, hear me.

  The woman in there —
  Give her whatever funeral you think proper: 220
  She is your sister.

— But let me go, Creon!
Let me purge my father's Thebes of the pollution
Of my living here, and go out to the wild hills,
To Kithairon, that has won such fame with me,
The tomb my mother and father appointed for me,
And let me die there, as they willed I should.
And yet I know
Death will not ever come to me through sickness
Or in any natural way: I have been preserved
For some unthinkable fate. But let that be.   230
As for my sons, you need not care for them.
They are men, they will find some way to live.
But my poor daughters, who have shared my table,
Who never before have been parted from their father —
Take care of them, Creon; do this for me.
And will you let me touch them with my hands
A last time, and let us weep together?
Be kind, my lord,
Great prince, be kind!
     Could I but touch them,
They would be mine again, as when I had my eyes.   240

[*Enter Antigone and Ismene, attended.*]

Ah, God!
Is it my dearest children I hear weeping?
Has Creon pitied me and sent my daughters?
Creon. Yes, Oedipus: I knew that they were dear to you
In the old days, and know you must love them still.
Oedipus. May God bless you for this — and be a friendlier
Guardian to you than he has been to me!

Children, where are you?
Come quickly to my hands: they are your brother's —
Hands that have brought your father's once clear eyes   250
To this way of seeing —
     Ah dearest ones,
I had neither sight nor knowledge then, your father
By the woman who was the source of his own life!
And I weep for you — having no strength to see you — ,
I weep for you when I think of the bitterness
That men will visit upon you all your lives.
What homes, what festivals can you attend
Without being forced to depart again in tears?

And when you come to marriageable age,
Where is the man, my daughters, who would dare   260
Risk the bane that lies on all my children?
Is there any evil wanting? Your father killed
His father; sowed the womb of her who bore him;
Engendered you at the fount of his own existence!
That is what they will say of you.

                        Then whom
Can you ever marry? There are no bridegrooms for you,
And your lives must wither away in sterile dreaming.
O Creon, son of Menoikeus!
You are the only father my daughters have,
Since we, their parents, are both of us gone for ever.   270
They are your own blood: you will not let them
Fall into beggary and loneliness;
You will keep them from the miseries that are mine!
Take pity on them; see, they are only children,
Friendless except for you. Promise me this,
Great Prince, and give me your hand in token of it.

[*Creon clasps his right hand.*]

Children:
I could say much, if you could understand me,
But as it is, I have only this prayer for you:
Live where you can, be as happy as you can —   280
Happier, please God, than God has made your father!
Creon.   Enough. You have wept enough. Now go within.
Oedipus.   I must; but it is hard.
Creon.   Time eases all things.
Oedipus.   But you must promise —
Creon.   Say what you desire.
Oedipus.   Send me from Thebes!
Creon.   God grant that I may!
Oedipus.   But since God hates me . . .
Creon.   No, he will grant your wish.
Oedipus.   You promise?
Creon.   I can not speak beyond my knowledge.
Oedipus.   Then lead me in.
Creon.   Come now, and leave your children.
Oedipus.   No! Do not take them from me!
Creon.   Think no longer
That you are in command here, but rather think   290
How, when you were, you served your own destruction.

[*Exeunt into the house all but the Chorus; the Choragos chants directly to the audience.*]

Choragos. Men of Thebes: look upon Oedipus.

This is the king who solved the famous riddle
And towered up, most powerful of men.
No mortal eyes but looked on him with envy,
Yet in the end ruin swept over him.
Let every man in mankind's frailty
Consider his last day; and let none
Presume on his good fortune until he find
Life, at his death, a memory without pain.   300

For Analysis

1. How does the Prologue establish the mood and theme of the play? What aspects of Oedipus's character are revealed there?

2. Sophocles' audience knew the Oedipus story as others, for instance, know the story of the Buddha, of the crucifixion of Jesus, or of Allah. What literary devices does Sophocles use nonetheless to create suspense and interest in the outcome of the action?

3. What is the nature of the conflict in the play? Who or what is the antagonist who opposes Oedipus, the protagonist?

4. A classic **tragedy** tells the story of a noble and heroic protagonist who is brought down by arrogance and pride. What evidence do you find that Oedipus suffers from these frailties?

5. Teiresias is one of many figures in legend and literature whose wisdom and spirituality is somehow connected with blindness. Speculate on what the connection might be based on.

6. What function does the Exodos serve?

On Style

1. Discuss the role of the chorus in the dramatic development and creation of suspense in the play.

2. The play embodies a pattern of figurative and literal **allusions** to darkness and light, to blindness and vision. How does that figurative language function, and what relationship does it bear to Oedipus's self-inflicted punishment?

3. Analyze the use of **dramatic irony** in this play.

Making Connections

1. Compare Oedipus and Shakespeare's Othello (p. 1144) as classic tragic protagonists.

2. Examine Creon's role in both this play and Sophocles' *Antigonê* (p. 467), and describe how his character changes.

3. Although Oedipus is a king, a man of great power and high station, and Willy Loman, in Arthur Miller's *Death of a Salesman* (p. 790), is an ordinary man and a seeming failure, what connection might be made between the two protagonists?

4. Sigmund Freud, the father of psychoanalytic theory, was fascinated by the Oedipus story. How would you define Freud's conception of the Oedipus complex? You might look at Frank O'Connor's "My Oedipus Complex" (p. 109) for some hints.

Writing Topics

1. In the Exodos, Oedipus declares that Apollo "brought my sick, sick fate upon me. / But the blinding hand was my own!" (ll. 112–13) and "This punishment / That I have laid upon myself is just" (ll. 140–41); later he declares, ". . . the parricide / Must be destroyed. I am that evil man" (ll. 211–12). How can Oedipus's acceptance of responsibility for his fate be reconciled with the fact that his fate was divinely ordained? Consider a similar paradox in Christian theology, which holds that God is all-knowing and has foreknowledge and yet humans exercise free will and thus are responsible for their acts.

2. Analyze Scene IV, the shortest of the four scenes, as the climax of the play, bringing together all the threads of the drama.

3. Find out who Electra was in ancient Greek dramatic literature. What did she do, and why? What is the Electra complex?

LOOKING DEEPER:
From Myth to Tragedy

Sophocles' *Oedipus* (sometimes *Rex,* sometimes *Tyrannus,* depending on the translator) is the most celebrated of the relatively few ancient Greek tragedies that have survived. Its role in literary history makes it a particularly interesting candidate for in-depth study. We gather here a few texts, ancient and modern, designed to excite further investigation and to introduce you to certain nagging problems in literary theory and interpretation.

In preparation for this in-depth look, first read the definition of *Tragedy* in the "Glossary of Literary Terms" (p. 1590); then read the short biography of Sophocles in "Biographical Notes on the Authors" (p. 1568).

The Oedipus story was well known to Sophocles' audience — in fact, it was well known even before Homer told it in *The Odyssey* some 300 years before the dramatist created his play. (A compilation of the Oedipus folklore is included here for your consideration.) Hence, the outcome of the drama did not surprise its audience, and suggestions that the play is a detective story are certainly misleading. Oedipus, as detective, finally understands the twisted sequence of events that bring him down — but the audience knows from the outset that Oedipus is the cause of the plague afflicting Thebes. The ancient Greek audience would be similar to a modern Western audience watching a play based on the life of Jesus, or of Moses leading his people out of Egypt. That audience knows that Jesus will be crucified, that the Red Sea will part, even if the characters within the drama do not. *Dramatic irony* occurs when the audience knows things a character does not and, consequently, hears things differently. Remarkably little has been written about how dramatic irony might have affected the sensibilities of the contemporary audience as it watched the inexorable degradation of this noble man.

Sophocles' *Oedipus Rex* raises a serious question. In *The Poetics,* which we excerpt here, Aristotle, as literary theorist, asserts that a tragic hero falls because of some flaw *(hamartia)* in his character. Generations of commentators such as D. W. Lucas, whose essay we include here, have been struggling to identify just what flaw brought Oedipus down. Would any action on his part serve to avert the fate that the oracles had proclaimed? Strangely, one of the most pervasive suggestions has been that Oedipus is guilty of *hubris* — overweening pride — for attempting to avert the will of the gods who had predicted that he would murder his father and marry his mother.

In *The Poetics* (ca. 340 B.C.), Aristotle rather casually reveals the assumptions embedded in the politics of his time. He asserts that the protagonist of a tragedy must be a noble man — and the tragedy will be his fall from his noble position. Note that Western literary history mirrors this political perspective — Shakespeare's tragedies (like those of other European writers prior to the nineteenth century) feature kings, princes, and military heroes. Not until the political upheavals that culminated in the French Revolution did writers represent common men and women as proper subjects of tragedy. Although Arthur Miller might conceivably have written something like *Oedipus Rex,* it would be utterly inconceivable for Sophocles to have written something like *Death of a Salesman.*

This opportunity to look deeper includes Robert Graves's version of the Oedipus myth that forms a foundation for Sophocles' tragedy; brief excerpts from Aristotle's *The Poetics;* an excerpt from a modern scholar on the Oedipus drama; and Arthur Miller's modern definition of the nature of tragedy.

Robert Graves   (1895–1985)
from **The Greek Myths**   1955

Oedipus

Laius, son of Labdacus, married Iocaste, and ruled over Thebes. Grieved by his prolonged childlessness, he secretly consulted the Delphic Oracle, which informed him that this seeming misfortune was a blessing, because any child born to Iocaste would become his murderer. He therefore put Iocaste away, though without offering any reason for his decision, which caused her such vexation that, having made him drunk, she inveigled him into her arms again as soon as night fell. When, nine months later, Iocaste was brought to bed of a son, Laius snatched him from the nurse's arms, pierced his feet with a nail and, binding them together, exposed him on Mount Cithaeron.

b. Yet the Fates had ruled that this boy should reach a green old age. A Corinthian shepherd found him, named him Oedipus because his feet were deformed by the nail-wound, and brought him to Corinth, where King Polybus was reigning at the time.[1]

c. According to another version of the story, Laius did not expose Oedipus on the mountain, but locked him in a chest, which was lowered into the sea from a ship. This chest drifted ashore at Sicyon, where Periboea, Polybus's queen, happened to be on the beach, supervising her royal laundry-women. She picked up Oedipus, retired to a thicket and pretended to have been overcome by the pangs of labour. Since the laundry-women were too busy to notice what she was about, she deceived them all into thinking that he had only just been born. But Periboea told the truth to Polybus who, also being childless, was pleased to rear Oedipus as his own son.

[1] Apollodorus: iii. 5. 7.

One day, taunted by a Corinthian youth with not in the least resembling his supposed parents, Oedipus went to ask the Delphic Oracle what future lay in store for him. "Away from the shrine, wretch!" the Pythoness cried in disgust. "You will kill your father and marry your mother!"

d. Since Oedipus loved Polybus and Periboea, and shrank from bringing disaster upon them, he at once decided against returning to Corinth. But in the narrow defile between Delphi and Daulis he happened to meet Laius, who ordered him roughly to step off the road and make way for his betters; Laius, it should be explained, was in a chariot and Oedipus on foot. Oedipus retorted that he acknowledged no betters except the gods and his own parents.

"So much the worse for you!" cried Laius, and ordered his charioteer Polyphontes to drive on.

One of the wheels bruised Oedipus's foot and, transported by rage, he killed Polyphontes with his spear. Then, flinging Laius on the road entangled in the reins, and whipping up the team, he made them drag him to death. It was left to the king of Plataeae to bury both corpses.[2]

e. Laius had been on his way to ask the Oracle how he might rid Thebes of the Sphinx. This monster was a daughter of Typhon and Echidne or, some say, of the dog Orthrus and the Chimaera, and had flown to Thebes from the uttermost part of Ethiopia. She was easily recognized by her woman's head, lion's body, serpent's tail, and eagle's wings.[3] Hera had recently sent the Sphinx to punish Thebes for Laius's abduction of the boy Chrysippus from Pisa and, settling on Mount Phicium, close to the city, she now asked every Theban wayfarer a riddle taught her by the Three Muses: "What being, with only one voice, has sometimes two feet, sometimes three, sometimes four, and is weakest when it has the most?" Those who could not solve the riddle she throttled and devoured on the spot, among which unfortunates was Iocaste's nephew Haemon, whom the Sphinx made *haimon,* or "bloody," indeed.

Oedipus, approaching Thebes fresh from the murder of Laius, guessed the answer. "Man," he replied, "because he crawls on all fours as an infant, stands firmly on his two feet in his youth, and leans upon a staff in his old age." The mortified Sphinx leaped from Mount Phicium and dashed herself to pieces in the valley below. At this the grateful Thebans acclaimed Oedipus king, and he married Iocaste, unaware that she was his mother.

f. Plague then descended upon Thebes, and the Delphic Oracle, when consulted once more, replied: "Expel the murderer of Laius!" Oedipus, not knowing whom he had met in the defile, pronounced a curse on Laius's murderer and sentenced him to exile.

g. Blind Teiresias, the most renowned seer in Greece at this time, now demanded an audience with Oedipus. Some say that Athene, who had blinded him for having inadvertently seen her bathing, was moved by his mother's plea

---

[2] Hyginus: *Fabula* 66; Scholiast on Euripides's *Phoenician Women* 13 and 26; Apollodorus: *loc. cit.*; Pausanias: x. 5. 2.

[3] Apollodorus: iii. 5. 8; Hesiod: *Theogony* 326; Sophocles: *Oedipus the Tyrant* 391; Scholiast on Aristophanes's *Frogs* 1287.

and, taking the serpent Erichthonius from her aegis, gave the order: "Cleanse Teiresias's ears with your tongue that he may understand the language of prophetic birds."

h. Others say that once, on Mount Cyllene, Teiresias had seen two serpents in the act of coupling. When both attacked him, he struck at them with his staff, killing the female. Immediately he was turned into a woman, and became a celebrated harlot; but seven years later he happened to see the same sight again at the same spot, and this time regained his manhood by killing the male serpent. Still others say that when Aphrodite and the three Charites, Pasithea, Cale, and Euphrosyne, disputed as to which of the four was most beautiful, Teiresias awarded Cale the prize; whereupon Aphrodite turned him into an old woman. But Cale took him with her to Crete and presented him with a lovely head of hair. Some days later Hera began reproaching Zeus for his numerous infidelities. He defended them by arguing that, at any rate, when he did share her couch, she had the more enjoyable time by far. "Women, of course, derive infinitely greater pleasure from the sexual act than men," he blustered.

"What nonsense!" cried Hera. "The exact contrary is the case, and well you know it."

Teiresias, summoned to settle the dispute from his personal experience, answered:

> If the parts of love-pleasure be counted as ten,
> Thrice three go to women, one only to men.

Hera was so exasperated by Zeus's triumphant grin that she blinded Teiresias; but Zeus compensated him with inward sight, and a life extended to seven generations.[4]

i. Teiresias now appeared at Oedipus's court, leaning on the cornel-wood staff given him by Athene, and revealed to Oedipus the will of the gods: that the plague would cease only if a Sown Man died for the sake of the city. Iocaste's father Menoeceus, one of those who had risen out of the earth when Cadmus sowed the serpent's teeth, at once leaped from the walls, and all Thebes praised his civic devotion.

Teiresias then announced further: "Menoeceus did well, and the plague will now cease. Yet the gods had another of the Sown Men in mind, one of the third generation: for he has killed his father and married his mother. Know, Queen Iocaste, that it is your husband Oedipus!"

j. At first, none would believe Teiresias, but his words were soon confirmed by a letter from Periboea at Corinth. She wrote that the sudden death of King Polybus now allowed her to reveal the circumstances of Oedipus's adoption; and this she did in damning detail. Iocaste then hanged herself for shame and grief, while Oedipus blinded himself with a pin taken from her garments.[5]

[4] Apollodorus: iii. 6. 7; Hyginus: *Fabula* 75; Ovid: *Metamorphoses* iii. 320; Pindar: *Nemean Odes* i. 91; Tzetzes: *On Lycophron* 682; Sosostratus, quoted by Eustathius: p. 1665.
[5] Apollodorus: iii. 5. 8; Sophocles: *Oedipus the Tyrant* 447, 713, 731, 774, 1285, etc.

k. Some say that, although tormented by the Erinnyes, who accused him of having brought about his mother's death, Oedipus continued to reign over Thebes for awhile, until he fell gloriously in battle.[6] According to others, however, Iocaste's brother Creon expelled him, but not before he had cursed Eteocles and Polyneices — who were at once his sons and his brothers — when they insolently sent him the inferior portion of the sacrificial beast, namely haunch instead of royal shoulder. They therefore watched dry-eyed as he left the city which he had delivered from the Sphinx's power. After wandering for many years through country after country, guided by his faithful daughter Antigone, Oedipus finally came to Colonus in Attica, where the Erinnyes, who have a grove there, hounded him to death, and Theseus buried his body in the precinct of the Solemn Ones at Athens, lamenting by Antigone's side.[7]

Questions for Looking Deeper

1. What elements of the story of Laius and Oedipus reported by Graves are absent from Sophocles' play?

2. How does the playwright convey the story of Laius at the time of Oedipus's birth?

3. As a matter of historical interest, can you identify other stories in which a woman conceives by tricking a man, or making him drunk? You might begin by looking at Genesis 19:30–38.

4. Graves reports one version of Oedipus's escape from death that involved his being set afloat in a chest. Can you think of other ancient stories that use the same device? Begin by looking at Exodus 2:1–10.

---

[6] Homer: *Odyssey* xi. 270 and *Iliad* xxiii. 679.
[7] Sophocles: *Oedipus at Colonus* 166 and scholiast on 1375; Euripides: *Phoenician Women, Proem;* Apollodorus: iii. 5. 9; Hyginus: *Fabula* 67; Pausanias: i. 20. 7.

Aristotle   (384–322 B.C.)
from **The Poetics**   ca. 340 B.C.

Let us now discuss tragedy, bringing together the definition of its essence that has emerged from what we have already said. Tragedy is, then, an imitation of a noble and complete action, having the proper magnitude;[1] it employs language that has been artistically enhanced by each of the kinds of linguistic adornment, applied separately in the various parts of the play; it is presented in dramatic,

---

[1] There is no word in the Greek text for "proper," but I have followed the practice of several other translators who add a modifier to the term "magnitude" where it is logically warranted. The term "representation" has also been added to the final clause of this sentence because of Aristotle's insistence that the pleasure of tragedy is achieved *through imitation* (Ch. 14, ll. 18–19). See L. Golden, "Catharsis," *TAPA* 93 (1962): 58. [Tr.]

not narrative form, and achieves, through the representation of pitiable and fearful incidents, the catharsis of such pitiable and fearful incidents. I mean by "language that has been artistically enhanced," that which is accompanied by rhythm and harmony and song; and by the phrase "each of the kinds of linguistic adornment, applied separately in the various parts of the play," I mean that some parts are accomplished by meter alone and others, in turn, through song. . . .

Now I mean by the plot the arrangement of the incidents, and by character that element in accordance with which we say that agents are of a certain type; and by thought I mean that which is found in whatever things men say when they prove a point or, it may be, express a general truth. It is necessary, therefore, that tragedy as a whole have six parts in accordance with which, as a genre, it achieves its particular quality. These parts are plot, character, diction, thought, spectacle, and melody. . . . Plots are divided into the simple and the complex, for the actions of which the plots are imitations are naturally of this character. An action that is, as has been defined, continuous and unified I call simple when its change of fortune arises without reversal and recognition, and complex when its change of fortune arises through recognition or reversal or both. Now these aspects of the plot must develop directly from the construction of the plot itself, so that they occur from prior events either out of necessity or according to the laws of probability. For it makes quite a difference whether they occur *because* of those events or merely *after* them.

Reversal is the change of fortune in the action of the play to the opposite state of affairs, just as has been said; and this change, we argue, should be in accordance with probability and necessity. Thus, in the *Oedipus* the messenger comes to cheer Oedipus and to remove his fears in regard to his mother; but by showing him who he actually is he accomplishes the very opposite effect. . . .

Recognition, as the same indicates, is a change from ignorance to knowledge, bringing about either a state of friendship or one of hostility on the part of those who have been marked out for good fortune or bad. The most effective recognition is one that occurs together with reversal, for example, as in the *Oedipus*. . . . For such a recognition and reversal will evoke pity or fear, and we have defined tragedy as an imitation of actions of this type; and furthermore, happiness and misery will appear in circumstances of this type. . . .

Now then, these are two parts of the plot, reversal and recognition, and there 5 is also a third part, suffering. Of these, reversal and recognition have been discussed; the incident of suffering results from destructive or painful action such as death on the stage, scenes of very great pain, the infliction of wounds, and the like. . . .

Since the plots of the best tragedies must be complex, not simple, and the plot of a tragedy must be an imitation of pitiable and fearful incidents (for this is the specific nature of the imitation under discussion), it is clear, first of all, that unqualifiedly good human beings must not appear to fall from good fortune to bad; for that is neither pitiable nor fearful; it is, rather, repellent. Nor must an extremely evil man appear to move from bad fortune to good fortune for that is

the most untragic situation of all because it has none of the necessary requirements of tragedy; it both violates our human sympathy and contains nothing of
the pitiable or fearful in it. Furthermore, a villainous man should not appear to
fall from good fortune to bad. For, although such a plot would be in accordance
with our human sympathy, it would not contain the necessary elements of pity
and fear; for pity is aroused by someone who undeservedly falls into misfortune,
and fear is evoked by our recognizing that it is someone like ourselves who
encounters this misfortune (pity, as I say, arising for the former reason, fear for
the latter). Therefore the emotional effect of the situation just mentioned will
be neither pitiable nor fearful. What is left, after our considerations, is someone
in between these extremes. This would be a person who is neither perfect in
virtue and justice, nor one who falls into misfortune through vice and depravity;
but rather, one who succumbs through some miscalculation. He must also be a
person who enjoys great reputation and good fortune, such as Oedipus,
Thyestes, and other illustrious men from similar families. It is necessary, furthermore, for the well-constructed plot to have a single rather than a double
construction, as some urge, and to illustrate a change of fortune not from bad
fortune to good but, rather, the very opposite, from good fortune to bad, and for
this to take place not because of depravity but through some great miscalculation on the part of the type of person we have described (or a better rather than
a worse one). . . .

Pity and fear can arise from the spectacle and also from the very structure of
the plot, which is the superior way and shows the better poet. The poet should
construct the plot so that even if the action is not performed before spectators,
one who merely hears the incidents that have occurred both shudders and feels
pity from the way they turn out. That is what anyone who hears the plot of the
Oedipus would experience. The achievement of this effect through the spectacle does not have much to do with poetic art and really belongs to the business
of producing the play. Those who use the spectacle to create not the fearful but
only the monstrous have no share in the creation of tragedy; for we should not
seek every pleasure from tragedy but only the one proper to it.

Since the poet should provide pleasure from pity and fear through imitation,
it is apparent that this function must be worked into the incidents. Let us try to
understand what type of occurrences appear to be terrifying and pitiable. It is,
indeed, necessary that any such action occur either between those who are
friends or enemies to each other, or between those who have no relationship,
whatsoever, to each other. If an enemy takes such an action against an enemy,
there is nothing pitiable in the performance of the act or in the intention to perform it, except the suffering itself. Nor would there be anything pitiable if neither party had any relationship with the other. But whenever the tragic
incidents occur in situations involving strong ties of affection — for example, if
a brother kills or intends to kill a brother or a son a father or a mother a son or a
son a mother or commits some equally terrible act — there will be something
pitiable. These situations, then, are the ones to be sought. Now, it is not possible
for a poet to alter completely the traditional stories. I mean, for example, the

given fact that Clytemnestra dies at the hands of Orestes, and Eriphyle at the hands of Alcmaeon; but it is necessary for the poet to be inventive and skillful in adapting the stories that have been handed down. Let us define more clearly what we mean by the skillful adaptation of a story. It is possible for the action to occur, as our early poets handled it, with the characters knowing and understanding what they are doing, as indeed Euripides makes Medea kill her children. It is also possible to have the deed done with those who accomplish the terrible deed in ignorance of the identity of their victim, only later recognizing the relationship as in Sophocles' *Oedipus*. . . .

In character, as in the construction of the incidents, we must always seek for either the necessary or the probable, so that a given type of person says or does certain kinds of things, and one event follows another according to necessity or probability. Thus, it is apparent that the resolutions of the plots should also occur through the plot itself and not by means of the deus ex machina, as in the *Medea*, and also in regard to the events surrounding the department of the fleet in the *Iliad*. The deus ex machina must be reserved for the events that lie outside the plot, either those that happened before it that are not capable of being known by men, or those that occur after that need to be announced and spoken of beforehand. For we grant to the gods the power of seeing all things. There should, then, be nothing improbable in the action; but if this is impossible, it should be outside the plot as, for example, in Sophocles' *Oedipus*.

Because tragedy is an imitation of the nobler sort of men it is necessary for 10 poets to imitate good portrait painters. For even though they reproduce the specific characteristics of their subjects and represent them faithfully, they also paint them better than they are. Thus, also, the poet imitating men who are prone to anger or who are indifferent or who are disposed in other such ways in regard to character makes them good as well, even though they have such characteristics, just as Agathon[2] and Homer portray Achilles.

Questions for Looking Deeper

1. How does Aristotle define the dramatic representations we call *tragedy*?

2. He asserts that a tragedy must have six parts: plot, character, diction, thought, spectacle, and melody. Plot and character are relatively easy to define; what does he mean by the other four elements?

3. What are *reversal* and *recognition*?

4. *Pity* and *fear* play an important part in this discussion of tragedy. What produces pity and fear? What doesn't?

5. What is *hamartia*?

6. Can you justify Aristotle's assertion that "tragedy is an imitation of the nobler sort of men"? Or do you agree with Arthur Miller's view that "the common man is as apt a subject for tragedy [. . .] as kings were"? Explain.

---

[2] Tragic poet (ca. 450 B.C.–ca. 399 B.C.) mentioned by Aristophanes and Plato.

D. W. Lucas   (1905–1985)
The Drama of Oedipus   1950

There was once a collision in a fog between a liner and an aircraft carrier in the Mediterranean; one of the carrier's aircraft exercising above the fog, and powerless to intervene, could see the converging mastheads of the two vessels and the disaster in which their courses must end. That is a type of situation to which the term "dramatic" is applied; it is by no means the only kind of drama, but it is a recognizable category, and no plot could be better raw material for such a drama of "the convergence of the twain" than that supplied by the myth of Oedipus.

Oedipus was famous for his cleverness, yet this cleverness serves only to enmesh him in a net of illusion. He starts, through no fault of his own, from a false premise; he does not know who he is, that is his *hamartia*. Tiresias tells him of his guilt, and he jumps, not indeed unreasonably from the evidence in his possession, to the conclusion that Creon and Tiresias are conspiring against him. Jocasta intervenes to stop the quarrel between her husband and her brother, but in attempting to show the absurdity of the charge that he had murdered Laius she gives him a clue to his guilt. The final discovery depends on putting together the evidence of two parties each of whom knows only half the truth. The Theban Herdsman knows that the child he was ordered to expose was Jocasta's and that Laius was killed by Oedipus; he does not know that Oedipus was the child. The Corinthian Herdsman knows that Oedipus is the baby that he received from the Theban Herdsman. When the two are brought together, the pieces of the puzzle fit. Nothing could exceed the brilliance and dexterity with which Sophocles handles his material so as to extract the last ounce of drama from it.

Some readers may find these claims highly irritating, for it is possible to look at the play in another way. The actual story is puerile, the antecedents of the play are full of impossibilities, and the play itself contains not a few things which will not bear looking into; Oedipus's ignorance about his predecessor, his failure to respond to the plainest hints in spite of early doubts about his parentage, and the extreme irritability of Tiresias which leads to such momentous indiscretion, all these can be made the subject of easy wit, which would be justified if Oedipus was intended to be a Sherlock Holmes. The answer is that when the play is acting we do not think of looking into these things, and Sophocles never troubled himself to provide answers to questions which were not going to enter the mind of his audience. The simple and poetic fancy which contrives the folktale is puerile when judged from a certain angle; Sophocles, if less simple, is still moving in the world of poetry, and his plays can only be seen or read by those who are prepared to enter that world leaving all irrelevant cleverness behind.

The question of the guilt of Oedipus has been much discussed; here we are troubled by fundamental differences between primitive and sophisticated thought. Though things were moving fast when the *Oedipus* was written, men were finding great difficulty in escaping from the notion that certain acts brought with them a physical contamination as definite as the infection conveyed by contact with a leper. To this sort of guilt intention is irrelevant, though the Greeks at all times distinguished between acts done willingly and under compulsion. The incestuous parricide is a pariah; it is futile to try to analyse the horror felt by Oedipus and the Chorus at the discovery, but it is clear that they did not feel the purity of his intentions to be relevant. In the *Oedipus Coloneus* written many years later Oedipus does feel this, but he still thinks that his touch conveys contamination. It is not, however, allowable to infer anything about the ideas implicit in an earlier play from the views expressed later in the poet's life.

Questions for Looking Deeper

1. Do you agree with Lucas's assertion: "he [Oedipus] does not know who he is, that is his *hamartia*"? Explain. Would Aristotle agree?

2. Oedipus strove to do the right thing — to avoid the horror that the oracles decreed. Why is he (in Lucas's view), nonetheless, guilty?

Arthur Miller (b. 1915)
Tragedy and the Common Man 1949

In this age few tragedies are written. It has often been held that the lack is due to a paucity of heroes among us, or else that modern man has had the blood drawn out of his organs of belief by the skepticism of science, and the heroic attack on life cannot feed on an attitude of reserve and circumspection. For one reason or another, we are often held to be below tragedy — or tragedy above us. The inevitable conclusion is, of course, that the tragic mode is archaic, fit only for the very highly placed, the kings or the kingly, and where this admission is not made in so many words it is most often implied.

I believe that the common man is as apt a subject for tragedy in its highest sense as kings were. On the face of it this ought to be obvious in the light of modern psychiatry, which bases its analysis upon classic formulations, such as the Oedipus and Orestes complexes, for instance, which were enacted by royal beings, but which apply to everyone in similar emotional situations.

More simply, when the question of tragedy in art is not at issue, we never hesitate to attribute to the well-placed and the exalted the very same mental processes as the lowly. And finally, if the exaltation of tragic action were truly a property of the high-bred character alone, it is inconceivable that the mass of mankind should cherish tragedy above all other forms, let alone be capable of understanding it.

As a general rule, to which there may be exceptions unknown to me, I think the tragic feeling is evoked in us when we are in the presence of a character who is ready to lay down his life, if need be, to secure one thing — his sense of personal dignity. From Orestes to Hamlet, Medea to Macbeth, the underlying struggle is that of the individual attempting to gain his "rightful" position in his society.

Sometimes he is one who has been displaced from it, sometimes one who seeks to attain it for the first time, but the fateful wound from which the inevitable events spiral is the wound of indignity, and its dominant force is indignation. Tragedy, then, is the consequence of a man's total compulsion to evaluate himself justly.

In the sense of having been initiated by the hero himself, the tale always reveals what has been called his "tragic flaw," a failing that is not peculiar to grand or elevated characters. Nor is it necessarily a weakness. The flaw, or crack in the character, is really nothing — and need be nothing — but his inherent unwillingness to remain passive in the face of what he conceives to be a challenge to his dignity, his image of his rightful status. Only the passive, only those who accept their lot without active retaliation, are "flawless." Most of us are in that category.

But there are among us today, as there always have been, those who act against the scheme of things that degrades them, and in the process of action, everything we have accepted out of fear or insensitivity or ignorance is shaken before us and examined and from this total onslaught by an individual against the seemingly stable cosmos surrounding us — from this total examination of the "unchangeable" environment — comes the terror and the fear that is classically associated with tragedy.

More important, from this total questioning of what has been previously unquestioned, we learn. And such a process is not beyond the common man. In revolutions around the world, these past thirty years, he has demonstrated again and again this inner dynamic of all tragedy.

Insistence upon the rank of the tragic hero, or the so-called nobility of his character, is really but a clinging to the outward forms of tragedy. If rank or nobility of character was indispensable, then it would follow that the problems of those with rank were the particular problems of tragedy. But surely the right of one monarch to capture the domain from another no longer raises our passions, nor are our concepts of justice what they were to the mind of an Elizabethan king.

The quality in such plays that does shake us, however, derives from the underlying fear of being displaced, the disaster inherent in being torn away from our chosen image of what and who we are in this world. Among us today this fear is as strong, and perhaps stronger, than it ever was. In fact, it is the common man who knows this fear best.

Now, if it is true that tragedy is the consequence of a man's total compulsion to evaluate himself justly, his destruction in the attempt posits a wrong or an evil in his environment. And this is precisely the morality of tragedy and its lesson. The discovery of the moral law, which is what the enlightenment of tragedy consists of, is not the discovery of some abstract or metaphysical quantity.

The tragic right is a condition of life, a condition in which the human personality is able to flower and realize itself. The wrong is the condition which suppresses man, perverts the flowing out of his love and creative instinct. Tragedy enlightens — and it must, in that it points the heroic finger at the enemy of man's freedom. The thrust for freedom is the quality in tragedy which exalts. The revolutionary questioning of the stable environment is what terrifies. In no way is the common man debarred from such thoughts or such actions.

Seen in this light, our lack of tragedy may be partially accounted for by the turn which modern literature has taken toward the purely psychiatric view of life, or the purely sociological. If all our miseries, our indignities, are born and bred within our minds, then all action, let alone heroic action, is obviously impossible.

And if society alone is responsible for the cramping of our lives, then the protagonist must need be so pure and faultless as to force us to deny his validity as a character. From neither of these views can tragedy derive, simply because neither represents a balanced concept of life. Above all else, tragedy requires the finest appreciation by the writer of cause and effect.

No tragedy can therefore come about when its author fears to question 15 absolutely everything, when he regards any institution, habit or custom as being either everlasting, immutable or inevitable. In the tragic view the need of man to wholly realize himself is the only fixed star, and whatever it is that hedges his nature and lowers it is ripe for attack and examination. Which is not to say that tragedy must preach revolution.

The Greeks could probe the very heavenly origin of their ways and return to confirm the rightness of laws. And Job could face God in anger, demanding his right, and end in submission. But for a moment everything is in suspension, nothing is accepted, and in this stretching and tearing apart of the cosmos, in the very action of so doing, the character gains "size," the tragic stature which is spuriously attached to the royal or the high born in our minds. The commonest of men may take on that stature to the extent of his willingness to throw all he has into the contest, the battle to secure his rightful place in his world.

There is a misconception of tragedy with which I have been struck in review after review, and in many conversations with writers and readers alike. It is the idea that tragedy is of necessity allied to pessimism. Even the dictionary says nothing more about the word than that it means a story with a sad or unhappy ending. This impression is so firmly fixed that I almost hesitate to claim that in truth tragedy implies more optimism in its author than does comedy, and that its final result ought to be the reinforcement of the onlooker's brightest opinions of the human animal.

For, if it is true to say that in essence the tragic hero is intent upon claiming his whole due as a personality, and if this struggle must be total and without reservation, then it automatically demonstrates the indestructible will of man to achieve his humanity.

The possibility of victory must be there in tragedy. Where pathos rules, where pathos is finally derived, a character has fought a battle he could not possibly have won. The pathetic is achieved when the protagonist is, by virtue of his witlessness, his insensitivity, or the very air he gives off, incapable of grappling with a much superior force.

Pathos truly is the mode for the pessimist. But tragedy requires a nicer 20 balance between what is possible and what is impossible. And it is curious, although edifying, that the plays we revere, century after century, are the tragedies. In them, and in them alone, lies the belief — optimistic, if you will — in the perfectibility of man.

It is time, I think, that we who are without kings, took up this bright thread of our history and followed it to the only place it can possibly lead our time — the heart and spirit of the average man.

Questions for Looking Deeper

1. In what fundamental way does Miller's view of tragedy differ from Aristotle's?

2. Historically, what political changes underlie Miller's view?

3. Ancient comedies depicted ordinary people on the stage — why were they appropriate subjects for comedies but not for tragedies?

Tennessee Williams (1911–1983)

The Glass Menagerie 1945

nobody, not even the rain, has such small hands
— E. E. Cummings

LIST OF CHARACTERS

Amanda Wingfield, the mother. A little woman of great but confused vitality clinging frantically to another time and place. Her characterization must be carefully created, not copied from type. She is not paranoiac, but her life is paranoia. There is much to admire in Amanda, and as much to love and pity as there is to laugh at. Certainly she has endurance and a kind of heroism, and though her foolishness makes her unwittingly cruel at times, there is tenderness in her slight person.

Laura Wingfield, her daughter. Amanda, having failed to establish contact with reality, continues to live vitally in her illusions, but Laura's situation is even graver. A childhood illness has left her crippled, one leg slightly shorter than the other, and held in a brace. This defect need not be more than suggested on the stage. Stemming from this, Laura's separation increases till she is like a piece of her own glass collection, too exquisitely fragile to move from the shelf.

Tom Wingfield, her son. And the narrator of the play. A poet with a job in a warehouse. His nature is not remorseless, but to escape from a trap he has to act without pity.

Jim O'Connor, the gentleman caller. A nice, ordinary, young man.

Scene.   An alley in St. Louis.
Part I.   Preparation for a Gentleman Caller.
Part II.   The Gentleman Calls.
Time.   Now and the Past.

Scene 1

The Wingfield apartment is in the rear of the building, one of those vast hivelike conglomerations of cellular living-units that flower as warty growths in over-crowded urban centers of lower middle-class population and are symptomatic of the impulse of this largest and fundamentally enslaved section of American society to avoid fluidity and differentiation and to exist and function as one interfused mass of automatism.

The apartment faces an alley and is entered by a fire-escape, a structure whose name is a touch of accidental poetic truth, for all of these huge buildings are always burning with the slow and implacable fires of human desperation. The fire-escape is included in the set — that is, the landing of it and steps descending from it.

The scene is memory and is therefore nonrealistic. Memory takes a lot of poetic license. It omits some details; others are exaggerated, according to the emotional value of the articles it touches, for memory is seated predominantly in the heart. The interior is therefore rather dim and poetic.

At the rise of the curtain, the audience is faced with the dark, grim rear wall of the Wingfield tenement. This building, which runs parallel to the footlights, is flanked on both sides by dark, narrow alleys which run into murky canyons of tangled clotheslines, garbage cans, and the sinister latticework of neighboring fire-escapes. It is up and down these side alleys that exterior entrances and exits are made, during the play. At the end of Tom's opening commentary, the dark tenement wall slowly reveals (by means of a transparency) the interior of the ground floor Wingfield apartment.

Downstage is the living room, which also serves as a sleeping room for Laura, the sofa unfolding to make her bed. Upstage, center, and divided by a wide arch or second proscenium with transparent faded portieres (or second curtain), is the dining room. In an old-fashioned what-not in the living room are seen scores of transparent glass animals. A blown-up photograph of the father hangs on the wall of the living room, facing the audience, to the left of the archway. It is the face of a very handsome young man in a doughboy's First World War cap. He is gallantly smiling, ineluctably smiling, as if to say, "I will be smiling forever."

The audience hears and sees the opening scene in the dining room through both the transparent fourth wall of the building and the transparent gauze portieres of the dining-room arch. It is during this revealing scene that the fourth wall slowly ascends, out of sight. This transparent exterior wall is not brought down again until the very end of the play, during Tom's final speech.

The narrator is an undisguised convention of the play. He takes whatever license with dramatic convention as is convenient to his purposes.

Tom enters dressed as a merchant sailor from alley, stage left, and strolls across the front of the stage to the fire-escape. There he stops and lights a cigarette. He addresses the audience.

Tom.   Yes, I have tricks in my pocket, I have things up my sleeve. But I am the opposite of a stage magician. He gives you illusion that has the appearance of truth. I give you truth in the pleasant disguise of illusion. To begin with, I turn back time. I reverse it to that quaint period, the thirties, when the huge middle class of America was matriculating in a school for the blind.

Their eyes had failed them, or they had failed their eyes, and so they were having their fingers pressed forcibly down on the fiery Braille alphabet of a dissolving economy. In Spain there was revolution. Here there was only shouting and confusion. In Spain there was Guernica.[1] Here there were disturbances of labor, sometimes pretty violent, in otherwise peaceful cities such as Chicago, Cleveland, Saint Louis. . . . This is the social background of the play.

(*Music.*)

The play is memory. Being a memory play, it is dimly lighted, it is sentimental, it is not realistic. In memory everything seems to happen to music. That explains the fiddle in the wings. I am the narrator of the play, and also a character in it. The other characters are my mother, Amanda, my sister, Laura, and a gentleman caller who appears in the final scenes. He is the most realistic character in the play, being an emissary from a world of reality that we were somehow set apart from. But since I have a poet's weakness for symbols, I am using this character also as a symbol; he is the long delayed but always expected something that we live for. There is a fifth character in the play who doesn't appear except in this larger-than-life photograph over the mantel. This is our father who left us a long time ago. He was a telephone man who fell in love with long distances; he gave up his job with the telephone company and skipped the light fantastic out of town. . . . The last we heard of him was a picture post-card from Mazatlán, on the Pacific coast of Mexico, containing a message of two words — "Hello — Good-bye!" and no address. I think the rest of the play will explain itself. . . .

Amanda's voice becomes audible through the portieres.

(*Legend on screen: "Où sont les neiges."*[2])
  He divides the portieres and enters the upstage area.
  Amanda and Laura are seated at a drop-leaf table. Eating is indicated by gestures without food or utensils. Amanda faces the audience.
  Tom and Laura are seated in profile.
  The interior has lit up softly and through the scrim we see Amanda and Laura seated at the table in the upstage area.

Amanda (*calling*). Tom?
Tom. Yes, Mother.

---

[1] A town in northern Spain without military significance that was destroyed in 1937 by German bombers supporting Francisco Franco's fascists during the Spanish Civil War.
[2] From a famous medieval ballad by François Villon (1431–?). The complete line generates a wistful nostalgia by asking, "Where are the snows of yesteryear?"

Amanda. We can't say grace until you come to the table!

Tom. Coming, Mother. (*He bows slightly and withdraws, reappearing a few moments later in his place at the table.*)

Amanda (*to her son*). Honey, don't *push* with your *fingers*. If you have to push with something, the thing to push with is a crust of bread. And chew — chew! Animals have sections in their stomachs which enable them to digest food without mastication, but human beings are supposed to chew their food before they swallow it down. Eat food leisurely, son, and really enjoy it. A well-cooked meal has lots of delicate flavors that have to be held in the mouth for appreciation. So chew your food and give your salivary glands a chance to function!

Tom deliberately lays his imaginary fork down and pushes his chair back from the table.

Tom. I haven't enjoyed one bite of this dinner because of your constant directions on how to eat it. It's you that makes me rush through meals with your hawklike attention to every bite I take. Sickening — spoils my appetite — all this discussion of animals' secretion — salivary glands — mastication!

Amanda (*lightly*). Temperament like a Metropolitan star! (*He rises and crosses downstage.*) You're not excused from the table.

Tom. I am getting a cigarette.

Amanda. You smoke too much.

Laura rises.

Laura. I'll bring in the blanc mange.

He remains standing with his cigarette by the portieres during the following.

Amanda (*rising*). No, sister, no, sister — you be the lady this time and I'll be the darky.

Laura. I'm already up.

Amanda. Resume your seat, little sister — I want you to stay fresh and pretty — for gentlemen callers!

Laura. I'm not expecting any gentlemen callers.

Amanda (*crossing out to kitchenette. Airily*). Sometimes they come when they are least expected! Why, I remember one Sunday afternoon in Blue Mountain — (*Enters kitchenette.*)

Tom. I know what's coming!

Laura. Yes. But let her tell it.

Tom. Again?

Laura. She loves to tell it.

Amanda returns with bowl of dessert.

Amanda. One Sunday afternoon in Blue Mountain — your mother received — *seventeen!* — gentlemen callers! Why, sometimes there weren't chairs enough to accommodate them all. We had to send the nigger over to bring in folding chairs from the parish house.

Tom (*remaining at portieres*). How did you entertain those gentlemen callers?

Amanda. I understood the art of conversation!

Tom. I bet you could talk.

Amanda. Girls in those days *knew* how to talk, I can tell you.

Tom. Yes?

(*Image: Amanda as a girl on a porch greeting callers.*)

Amanda. They knew how to entertain their gentlemen callers. It wasn't enough for a girl to be possessed of a pretty face and a graceful figure — although I wasn't slighted in either respect. She also needed to have a nimble wit and a tongue to meet all occasions.

Tom. What did you talk about?

Amanda. Things of importance going on in the world! Never anything coarse or common or vulgar. (*She addresses Tom as though he were seated in the vacant chair at the table though he remains by portieres. He plays this scene as though he held the book.*) My callers were gentlemen — all! Among my callers were some of the most prominent young planters of the Mississippi Delta — planters and sons of planters!

Tom motions for music and a spot of light on Amanda.
Her eyes lift, her face glows, her voice becomes rich and elegiac.
(*Screen legend: "Où sont les neiges."*)

There was young Champ Laughlin who later became vice-president of the Delta Planters Bank. Hadley Stevenson who was drowned in Moon Lake and left his widow one hundred and fifty thousand in Government bonds. There were the Cutrere brothers, Wesley and Bates. Bates was one of my bright particular beaux! He got in a quarrel with that wild Wainright boy. They shot it out on the floor of Moon Lake Casino. Bates was shot through the stomach. Died in the ambulance on his way to Memphis. His widow was also well-provided for, came into eight or ten thousand acres, that's all. She married him on the rebound — never loved her — carried my picture on him the night he died! And there was that boy that every girl in the Delta had set her cap for! That beautiful, brilliant young Fitzhugh boy from Green County!

Tom. What did he leave his widow?

Amanda. He never married! Gracious, you talk as though all of my old admirers had turned up their toes to the daisies!

Tom. Isn't this the first you mentioned that still survives?

Amanda. That Fitzhugh boy went North and made a fortune — came to be known as the Wolf of Wall Street! He had the Midas touch, whatever he touched turned to gold! And I could have been Mrs. Duncan J. Fitzhugh, mind you! But — I picked your *father!*

Laura *(rising).*   Mother, let me clear the table.

Amanda.   No dear, you go in front and study your typewriter chart. Or practice your shorthand a little. Stay fresh and pretty! — It's almost time for our gentlemen callers to start arriving. *(She flounces girlishly toward the kitchenette.)* How many do you suppose we're going to entertain this afternoon?

Tom throws down the paper and jumps up with a groan.

Laura *(alone in the dining room).*   I don't believe we're going to receive any, Mother.

Amanda *(reappearing, airily).*   What? No one — not one? You must be joking! *(Laura nervously echoes her laugh. She slips in a fugitive manner through the half-open portieres and draws them gently behind her. A shaft of very clear light is thrown on her face against the faded tapestry of the curtains.) (Music: "The Glass Menagerie" under faintly.) (Lightly.)* Not one gentleman caller? It can't be true! There must be a flood, there must have been a tornado!

Laura.   It isn't a flood, it's not a tornado, Mother. I'm just not popular like you were in Blue Mountain. . . . *(Tom utters another groan. Laura glances at him with a faint, apologetic smile. Her voice catching a little.)* Mother's afraid I'm going to be an old maid.

(The scene dims out with "Glass Menagerie" music.)

Scene 2

"Laura, Haven't You Ever Liked Some Boy?"

On the dark stage the screen is lighted with the image of blue roses.
    Gradually Laura's figure becomes apparent and the screen goes out.
    The music subsides.
    Laura is seated in the delicate ivory chair at the small clawfoot table.
    She wears a dress of soft violet material for a kimono — her hair tied back from her forehead with a ribbon.
    She is washing and polishing her collection of glass.
    Amanda appears on the fire-escape steps. At the sound of her ascent, Laura catches her breath, thrusts the bowl of ornaments away, and seats herself stiffly

before the diagram of the typewriter keyboard as though it held her spellbound. Something has happened to Amanda. It is written in her face as she climbs to the landing: a look that is grim and hopeless and a little absurd.

She has on one of those cheap or imitation velvety-looking cloth coats with imitation fur collar. Her hat is five or six years old, one of those dreadful cloche hats that were worn in the late twenties, and she is clasping an enormous black patent-leather pocketbook with nickel clasp and initials. This is her full-dress outfit, the one she usually wears to the D.A.R.[3]

Before entering she looks through the door.

She purses her lips, opens her eyes wide, rolls them upward, and shakes her head.

Then she slowly lets herself in the door. Seeing her mother's expression Laura touches her lips with a nervous gesture.

Laura.   Hello, Mother, I was — (*She makes a nervous gesture toward the chart on the wall. Amanda leans against the shut door and stares at Laura with a martyred look.*)

Amanda.   Deception? Deception? (*She slowly removes her hat and gloves, continuing the swift suffering stare. She lets the hat and gloves fall on the floor — a bit of acting.*)

Laura (*shakily*).   How was the D.A.R. meeting? (*Amanda slowly opens her purse and removes a dainty white handkerchief, which she shakes out delicately and delicately touches to her lips and nostrils.*) Didn't you go to the D.A.R. meeting, Mother?

Amanda (*faintly, almost inaudibly*).   — No. — No. (*Then more forcibly.*) I did not have the strength — to go to the D.A.R. In fact, I did not have the courage! I wanted to find a hole in the ground and hide myself in it forever! (*She crosses slowly to the wall and removes the diagram of the typewriter keyboard. She holds it in front of her for a second, staring at it sweetly and sorrowfully — then bites her lips and tears it in two pieces.*)

Laura (*faintly*).   Why did you do that, Mother? (*Amanda repeats the same procedure with the chart of the Gregg Alphabet.*[4]) Why are you —

Amanda.   Why? Why? How old are you, Laura?

Laura.   Mother, you know my age.

Amanda.   I thought that you were an adult; it seems that I was mistaken. (*She crosses slowly to the sofa and sinks down and stares at Laura.*)

Laura.   Please don't stare at me, Mother.

Amanda closes her eyes and lowers her head. Count ten.

---

[3] Daughters of the American Revolution — a society of women who can trace their ancestry to American patriots who fought in the Revolutionary War.

[4] Shorthand symbols created by John Robert Gregg, designed to allow secretaries to take dictation rapidly.

Amanda. What are we going to do, what is going to become of us, what is the future?

Count ten.

Laura. Has something happened, Mother? *(Amanda draws a long breath and takes out the handkerchief again. Dabbing process.)* Mother, has — something happened?

Amanda. I'll be all right in a minute. I'm just bewildered — *(count five)* — by life. . . .

Laura. Mother, I wish that you would tell me what's happened.

Amanda. As you know, I was supposed to be inducted into my office at the D.A.R. this afternoon. *(Image: A swarm of typewriters.)* But I stopped off at Rubicam's Business College to speak to your teachers about your having a cold and ask them what progress they thought you were making down there.

Laura. Oh. . . .

Amanda. I went to the typing instructor and introduced myself as your mother. She didn't know who you were. Wingfield, she said. We don't have any such student enrolled at the school! I assured her she did, that you had been going to classes since early in January. "I wonder," she said, "if you could be talking about that terribly shy little girl who dropped out of school after only a few days' attendance?" "No," I said, "Laura, my daughter, has been going to school every day for the past six weeks!" "Excuse me," she said. She took the attendance book out and there was your name, unmistakably printed, and all the dates you were absent until they decided that you had dropped out of school. I still said, "No, there must have been some mistake! There must have been some mix-up in the records!" And she said, "No — I remember her perfectly now. Her hand shook so that she couldn't hit the right keys! The first time we gave a speed-test, she broke down completely — was sick at the stomach and almost had to be carried into the washroom! After that morning she never showed up any more. We phoned the house but never got any answer" — while I was working at Famous and Barr, I suppose, demonstrating those — Oh! I felt so weak I could barely keep on my feet. I had to sit down while they got me a glass of water! Fifty dollars' tuition, all of our plans — my hopes and ambitions for you — just gone up the spout, just gone up the spout like that. *(Laura draws a long breath and gets awkwardly to her feet. She crosses to the Victrola, and winds it up.)* What are you doing?

Laura. Oh! *(She releases the handle and returns to her seat.)*

Amanda. Laura, where have you been going when you've gone out pretending that you were going to business college?

Laura. I've just been going out walking.

Amanda. That's not true.

Laura.   It is. I just went walking.

Amanda.   Walking? Walking? In winter? Deliberately courting pneumonia in that light coat? Where did you walk to, Laura?

Laura.   It was the lesser of two evils, Mother. (*Image: Winter scene in park.*) I couldn't go back up. I — threw up — on the floor!

Amanda.   From half past seven till after five every day you mean to tell me you walked around in the park, because you wanted to make me think that you were still going to Rubicam's Business College?

Laura.   It wasn't as bad as it sounds. I went inside places to get warmed up.

Amanda.   Inside where?

Laura.   I went in the art museum and the bird-houses at the Zoo. I visited the penguins every day! Sometimes I did without lunch and went to the movies. Lately I've been spending most of my afternoons in the Jewel-box, that big glass house where they raise the tropical flowers.

Amanda.   You did all this to deceive me, just for the deception? (*Laura looks down.*) Why?

Laura.   Mother, when you're disappointed, you get that awful suffering look on your face, like the picture of Jesus' mother in the museum!

Amanda.   Hush!

Laura.   I couldn't face it.

Pause. A whisper of strings.
(Legend: "The Crust of Humility.")

Amanda (*hopelessly fingering the huge pocketbook*).   So what are we going to do the rest of our lives? Stay home and watch the parades go by? Amuse ourselves with the glass menagerie, darling? Eternally play those worn-out phonograph records your father left as a painful reminder of him? We won't have a business career — we've given that up because it gave us nervous indigestion! (*Laughs wearily.*) What is there left but dependency all our lives? I know so well what becomes of unmarried women who aren't prepared to occupy a position. I've seen such pitiful cases in the South — barely tolerated spinsters living upon the grudging patronage of sister's husband or brother's wife! — stuck away in some little mousetrap of a room — encouraged by one in-law to visit another — little birdlike women without any nest — eating the crust of humility all their life! Is that the future that we've mapped out for ourselves? I swear it's the only alternative I can think of! It isn't a very pleasant alternative, is it? Of course — some girls *do marry.* (*Laura twists her hands nervously.*) Haven't you ever liked some boy?

Laura.   Yes. I liked one once. (*Rises.*) I came across his picture a while ago.

Amanda (*with some interest*).   He gave you his picture?

Laura.   No, it's in the year-book.

Amanda (*disappointed*).   Oh — a high-school boy.

(Screen image: Jim as a high-school hero bearing a silver cup.)

Laura.   Yes. His name was Jim. *(Laura lifts the heavy annual from the claw-foot table.)* Here he is in *The Pirates of Penzance*.
Amanda *(absently)*.   The what?
Laura.   The operetta the senior class put on. He had a wonderful voice and we sat across the aisle from each other Mondays, Wednesdays, and Fridays in the Aud. Here he is with the silver cup for debating! See his grin?
Amanda *(absently)*.   He must have had a jolly disposition.
Laura.   He used to call me — Blue Roses.

(Image: Blue roses.)

Amanda.   Why did he call you such a name as that?
Laura.   When I had that attack of pleurosis — he asked me what was the matter when I came back. I said pleurosis — he thought that I said Blue Roses! So that's what he always called me after that. Whenever he saw me, he'd holler, "Hello, Blue Roses!" I didn't care for the girl that he went out with. Emily Meisenbach. Emily was the best-dressed girl at Soldan. She never struck me, though, as being sincere. . . . It says in the Personal Section — they're engaged. That's — six years ago! They must be married by now.
Amanda.   Girls that aren't cut out for business careers usually wind up married to some nice man. *(Gets up with a spark of revival.)* Sister, that's what you'll do!

Laura utters a startled, doubtful laugh. She reaches quickly for a piece of glass.

Laura.   But, Mother —
Amanda.   Yes? *(Crossing to photograph.)*
Laura *(in a tone of frightened apology)*.   I'm — crippled!

(Image: Screen.)

Amanda.   Nonsense! Laura, I've told you never, never to use that word. Why, you're not crippled, you just have a little defect — hardly noticeable, even! When people have some slight disadvantage like that, they cultivate other things to make up for it — develop charm — and vivacity — and — *charm!* That's all you have to do! *(She turns again to the photograph.)* One thing your father had *plenty of* — was *charm!*

Tom motions to the fiddle in the wings.
    (The scene fades out with music.)

Scene 3

(Legend on the screen: "After the Fiasco — ")
Tom speaks from the fire-escape landing.

Tom.   After the fiasco at Rubicam's Business College, the idea of getting a gentleman caller for Laura began to play a more important part in Mother's calculations. It became an obsession. Like some archetype of the universal unconscious, the image of the gentleman caller haunted our small apartment. . . . *(Image: Young man at door with flowers.)* An evening at home rarely passed without some allusion to this image, this specter, this hope. . . . Even when he wasn't mentioned, his presence hung in Mother's preoccupied look and in my sister's frightened, apologetic manner — hung like a sentence passed upon the Wingfields! Mother was a woman of action as well as words. She began to take logical steps in the planned direction. Late that winter and in the early spring — realizing that extra money would be needed to properly feather the nest and plume the bird — she conducted a vigorous campaign on the telephone, roping in subscribers to one of those magazines for matrons called *The Home-maker's Companion,* the type of journal that features the serialized sublimations of ladies of letters who think in terms of delicate cuplike breasts, slim, tapering waists, rich, creamy thighs, eyes like wood-smoke in autumn, fingers that soothe and caress like strains of music, bodies as powerful as Etruscan sculpture.

(Screen image: Glamour *magazine cover.)*
Amanda enters with phone on long extension cord. She is spotted in the dim stage.

Amanda.   Ida Scott? This is Amanda Wingfield! We *missed* you at the D.A.R. last Monday! I said to myself: She's probably suffering with that sinus condition! How is that sinus condition? Horrors! Heaven have mercy! — You're a Christian martyr, yes, that's what you are, a Christian martyr! Well, I just now happened to notice that your subscription to the *Companion's* about to expire! Yes, it expires with the next issue, honey! — just when that wonderful new serial by Bessie Mae Hopper is getting off to such an exciting start. Oh, honey, it's something that you can't miss! You remember how *Gone with the Wind* took everybody by storm? You simply couldn't go out if you hadn't read it. All everybody *talked* was Scarlett O'Hara. Well, this is a book that critics already compare to *Gone with the Wind.* It's the *Gone with the Wind* of the post–World War generation! — What? — Burning? — Oh, honey, don't let them burn, go take a look in the oven and I'll hold the wire! Heavens — I think she's hung up!

(Dim out.)
  (Legend on screen: "You think I'm in love with Continental Shoemakers?")
  Before the stage is lighted, the violent voices of Tom and Amanda are heard. They are quarreling behind the portieres. In front of them stands Laura with clenched hands and panicky expression.
  A clear pool of light on her figure throughout this scene.

Tom. What in Christ's name am I —
Amanda *(shrilly).* Don't you use that —
Tom. Supposed to do!
Amanda. Expression! Not in my —
Tom. Ohhh!
Amanda. Presence! Have you gone out of your senses?
Tom. I have, that's true, *driven* out!
Amanda. What is the matter with you, you — big — big — IDIOT!
Tom. Look — I've got *no thing,* no single thing —
Amanda. Lower your voice!
Tom. In my life here that I can call my own! Everything is —
Amanda. Stop that shouting!
Tom. Yesterday you confiscated my books! You had the nerve to —
Amanda. I took that horrible novel back to the library — yes! That hideous book by that insane Mr. Lawrence.[5] *(Tom laughs wildly.)* I cannot control the output of diseased minds or people who cater to them — *(Tom laughs still more wildly.)* BUT I WON'T ALLOW SUCH FILTH BROUGHT INTO MY HOUSE! No, no, no, no, no!
Tom. House, house! Who pays rent on it, who makes a slave of himself to —
Amanda *(fairly screeching).* Don't you DARE to —
Tom. No, no, *I* mustn't say things! *I've* got to just —
Amanda. Let me tell you —
Tom. I don't want to hear any more! *(He tears the portieres open. The upstage area is lit with a turgid smoky red glow.)*

Amanda's hair is in metal curlers and she wears a very old bathrobe, much too large for her slight figure, a relic of the faithless Mr. Wingfield.
  An upright typewriter and a wild disarray of manuscripts are on the drop-leaf table. The quarrel was probably precipitated by Amanda's interruption of his creative labor. A chair lying overthrown on the floor.
  Their gesticulating shadows are cast on the ceiling by the fiery glow.

Amanda. You *will* hear more, you —
Tom. No, I won't hear more, I'm going out!

---

[5] D. H. Lawrence (1885–1930), a controversial English novelist who startled readers with the frank sexuality depicted in his work.

Amanda.   You come right back in —

Tom.   Out, out, out! Because I'm —

Amanda.   Come back here, Tom Wingfield! I'm not through talking to you!

Tom.   Oh, go —

Laura (*desperately*).   Tom!

Amanda.   You're going to listen, and no more insolence from you! I'm at the end of my patience! (*He comes back toward her.*)

Tom.   What do you think I'm at? Aren't I supposed to have any patience to reach the end of, Mother? I know, I know. It seems unimportant to you, what I'm *doing* — what I *want* to do — having a little *difference* between them! You don't think that —

Amanda.   I think you've been doing things that you're ashamed of. That's why you act like this. I don't believe that you go every night to the movies. Nobody goes to the movies night after night. Nobody in their right minds goes to the movies as often as you pretend to. People don't go to the movies at nearly midnight, and movies don't let out at two A.M. Come in stumbling. Muttering to yourself like a maniac! You get three hours' sleep and then go to work. Oh, I can picture the way you're doing down there. Moping, doping, because you're in no condition.

Tom (*wildly*).   No, I'm in no condition!

Amanda.   What right have you got to jeopardize your job? Jeopardize the security of us all? How do you think we'd manage if you were —

Tom.   Listen! You think I'm crazy *about* the *warehouse!* (*He bends fiercely toward her slight figure.*) You think I'm in love with the Continental Shoe-makers? You think I want to spend fifty-five *years* down there in that — *celotex interior!* with — *fluorescent* — *tubes!* Look! I'd rather somebody picked up a crowbar and battered out my brains — than go back mornings! I *go!* Every time you come in yelling that God damn *"Rise and Shine!"* *"Rise and Shine!"* I say to myself "How *lucky dead* people are!" But I get up. I *go!* For sixty-five dollars a month I give up all that I dream of doing and being *ever!* And you say self — *self's* all I ever think of. Why, listen, if self is what I thought of, Mother, I'd be where he is — ! (*Pointing to father's picture.*) As far as the system of transportation reaches! (*He starts past her. She grabs his arm.*) Don't grab at me, Mother!

Amanda.   Where are you going?

Tom.   I'm going to the *movies!*

Amanda.   I don't believe that lie!

Tom (*crouching toward her, overtowering her tiny figure. She backs away, gasping*).   I'm going to opium dens! Yes, opium dens, dens of vice and criminals' hang-outs, Mother. I've joined the Hogan gang, I'm a hired assassin, I carry a tommy-gun in a violin case! I run a string of cat-houses in the Valley! They call me Killer, Killer Wingfield, I'm leading a double-life, a simple, honest warehouse worker by day, by night a dynamic *czar* of the *underworld*, *Mother*. I go to gambling casinos, I spin away fortunes on the roulette table! I wear a patch over one eye and a false mustache, sometimes I put on green whiskers. On those occasions they call me — *El Diablo!*[6] Oh, I could tell you things to make you sleepless! My enemies plan to dynamite this place. They're going to blow us all sky-high some night! I'll be glad, very happy, and so will you! You'll go up, up on a broomstick, over Blue Mountain with seventeen gentlemen callers! You ugly — babbling old — *witch*.... (*He goes through a series of violent, clumsy movements, seizing his overcoat, lunging to the door, pulling it fiercely open. The women watch him, aghast. His arm catches in the sleeve of the coat as he struggles to pull it on. For a moment he is pinioned by the bulky garment. With an outraged groan he tears the coat off again, splitting the shoulders of it, and hurls it across the room. It strikes against the shelf of Laura's glass collection, there is a tinkle of shattering glass. Laura cries out as if wounded.*)

(*Music legend: "The Glass Menagerie."*)

Laura (*shrilly*).   My glass! — menagerie.... (*She covers her face and turns away.*)

But Amanda is still stunned and stupefied by the "ugly witch" so that she barely notices this occurrence. Now she recovers her speech.

Amanda (*in an awful voice*).   I won't speak to you — until you apologize! (*She crosses through portieres and draws them together behind her. Tom is left with Laura. Laura clings weakly to the mantel with her face averted. Tom stares at her stupidly for a moment. Then he crosses to shelf. Drops awkwardly to his knees to collect the fallen glass, glancing at Laura as if he would speak but couldn't.*)

"The Glass Menagerie" music steals in as the scene dims out.

Scene 4

The interior is dark. Faint light in the alley.

A deep-voiced bell in a church is tolling the hour of five as the scene commences.

Tom appears at the top of the alley. After each solemn boom of the bell in the tower, he shakes a little noise-maker or rattle as if to express the tiny spasm of man in contrast to the sustained power and dignity of the Almighty. This and the unsteadiness of his advance make it evident that he has been drinking.

---

[6] The devil.

As he climbs the few steps to the fire-escape landing light steals up inside. Laura appears in night-dress, observing Tom's empty bed in the front room.

Tom fishes in his pockets for the door-key, removing a motley assortment of articles in the search, including a perfect shower of movie-ticket stubs and an empty bottle. At last he finds the key, but just as he is about to insert it, it slips from his fingers. He strikes a match and crouches below the door.

Tom *(bitterly).* One crack — and it falls through!

Laura opens the door.

Laura. Tom! Tom, what are you doing?
Tom. Looking for a door-key.
Laura. Where have you been all this time?
Tom. I have been to the movies.
Laura. All this time at the movies?
Tom. There was a very long program. There was a Garbo picture and a Mickey Mouse and a travelogue and a newsreel and a preview of coming attractions. And there was an organ solo and a collection for the milk-fund — simultaneously — which ended up in a terrible fight between a fat lady and an usher!
Laura *(innocently).* Did you have to stay through everything?
Tom. Of course! And, oh, I forgot! There was a big stage show! The headliner on this stage show was Malvolio the Magician. He performed wonderful tricks, many of them, such as pouring water back and forth between pitchers. First it turned to wine and then it turned to beer and then it turned to whiskey. I know it was whiskey it finally turned into because he needed somebody to come up out of the audience to help him, and I came up — both shows! It was Kentucky Straight Bourbon. A very generous fellow, he gave souvenirs. *(He pulls from his back pocket a shimmering rainbow-colored scarf.)* He gave me this. This is his magic scarf. You can have it, Laura. You wave it over a canary cage and you get a bowl of gold-fish. You wave it over the gold-fish bowl and they fly away canaries. . . . But the wonderfullest trick of all was the coffin trick. We nailed him into a coffin and he got out of the coffin without removing one nail. *(He has come inside.)* There is a trick that would come in handy for me — get me out of this 2 by 4 situation! *(Flops onto bed and starts removing shoes.)*
Laura. Tom — Shhh!
Tom. What you shushing me for?
Laura. You'll wake up Mother.
Tom. Goody, goody! Pay 'er back for all those "Rise an' Shines." *(Lies down, groaning.)* You know it don't take much intelligence to get yourself into a nailed-up coffin, Laura. But who in hell ever got himself out of one without removing one nail?

As if in answer, the father's grinning photograph lights up.

(Scene dims out.)

Immediately following: The church bell is heard striking six. At the sixth stroke the alarm clock goes off in Amanda's room, and after a few moments we hear her calling: "Rise and Shine! Rise and Shine! Laura, go tell your brother to rise and shine!"

Tom *(sitting up slowly).*   I'll rise — but I won't shine.

The light increases.

Amanda.   Laura, tell your brother his coffee is ready.

Laura slips into front room.

Laura.   Tom! it's nearly seven. Don't make Mother nervous. *(He stares at her stupidly. Beseechingly.)* Tom, speak to Mother this morning. Make up with her, apologize, speak to her!

Tom.   She won't to me. It's her that started not speaking.

Laura.   If you just say you're sorry she'll start speaking.

Tom.   Her not speaking — is that such a tragedy?

Laura.   Please — please!

Amanda *(calling from kitchenette).*   Laura, are you going to do what I asked you to do, or do I have to get dressed and go out myself?

Laura.   Going, going — soon as I get on my coat! *(She pulls on a shapeless felt hat with nervous, jerky movement, pleadingly glancing at Tom. Rushes awkwardly for coat. The coat is one of Amanda's, inaccurately made-over, the sleeves too short for Laura.)* Butter and what else?

Amanda *(entering upstage).*   Just butter. Tell them to charge it.

Laura.   Mother, they make such faces when I do that.

Amanda.   Sticks and stones may break my bones, but the expression on Mr. Garfinkel's face won't harm us! Tell your brother his coffee is getting cold.

Laura *(at door).*   Do what I asked you, will you, will you, Tom?

He looks sullenly away.

Amanda.   Laura, go now or just don't go at all!

Laura *(rushing out).*   Going — going! *(A second later she cries out. Tom springs up and crosses to the door. Amanda rushes anxiously in. Tom opens the door.)*

Tom.   Laura?

Laura.   I'm all right. I slipped, but I'm all right.

Amanda *(peering anxiously after her).*   If anyone breaks a leg on those fire-escape steps, the landlord ought to be sued for every cent he possesses! *(She shuts door. Remembers she isn't speaking and returns to other room.)*

As Tom enters listlessly for his coffee, she turns her back to him and stands rigidly facing the window on the gloomy gray vault of the areaway. Its light on her face with its aged but childish features is cruelly sharp, satirical as a Daumier[7] print.

(Music under: "Ave Maria.")

Tom glances sheepishly but sullenly at her averted figure and slumps at the table. The coffee is scalding hot; he sips it and gasps and spits it back in the cup. At his gasp, Amanda catches her breath and half turns. Then catches herself and turns back to window.

Tom blows on his coffee, glancing sidewise at his mother. She clears her throat. Tom clears his. He starts to rise. Sinks back down again, scratches his head, clears his throat again. Amanda coughs. Tom raises his cup in both hands to blow on it, his eyes staring over the rim of it at his mother for several moments. Then he slowly sets the cup down and awkwardly and hesitantly rises from the chair.

Tom *(hoarsely).* Mother. I — I apologize. Mother. *(Amanda draws a quick, shuddering breath. Her face works grotesquely. She breaks into childlike tears.)* I'm sorry for what I said, for everything that I said, I didn't mean it.

Amanda *(sobbingly).* My devotion has made me a witch and so I make myself hateful to my children!

Tom. No, you *don't.*

Amanda. I worry so much, don't sleep, it makes me nervous!

Tom *(gently).* I understand that.

Amanda. I've had to put up a solitary battle all these years. But you're my right-hand bower! Don't fall down, don't fail!

Tom *(gently).* I try, Mother.

Amanda *(with great enthusiasm).* Try and you will SUCCEED! *(The notion makes her breathless.)* Why, you — you're just *full* of natural endowments! Both of my children — they're *unusual* children! Don't you think I know it? I'm so — *proud!* Happy and — feel I've — so much to be thankful for but — Promise me one thing, son!

Tom. What, Mother?

Amanda. Promise, son, you'll — never be a drunkard!

Tom *(turns to her grinning).* I will never be a drunkard, Mother.

Amanda. That's what frightened me so, that you'd be drinking! Eat a bowl of Purina!

Tom. Just coffee, Mother.

Amanda. Shredded wheat biscuit?

Tom. No. No, Mother, just coffee.

Amanda. You can't put in a day's work on an empty stomach. You've got

---

[7] Honoré Daumier (1808–1879), French painter and satirical caricaturist of French middle-class society.

ten minutes — don't gulp! Drinking too-hot liquids makes cancer of the stomach. . . . Put cream in.

Tom.   No, thank you.

Amanda.   To cool it.

Tom.   No! No, thank you, I want it black.

Amanda.   I know, but it's not good for you. We have to do all that we can to build ourselves up. In these trying times we live in, all that we have to cling to is — each other. . . . That's why it's so important to — Tom, I — I sent out your sister so I could discuss something with you. If you hadn't spoken I would have spoken to you. *(Sits down.)*

Tom *(gently)*.   What is it, Mother, that you want to discuss?

Amanda.   Laura!

Tom puts his cup down slowly.

(Legend on screen: "Laura.")
(Music: "The Glass Menagerie.")

Tom.   — Oh. — Laura . . .

Amanda *(touching his sleeve)*.   You know how Laura is. So quiet but — still water runs deep! She notices things and I think she — broods about them. *(Tom looks up.)* A few days ago I came in and she was crying.

Tom.   What about?

Amanda.   You.

Tom.   Me?

Amanda.   She has an idea that you're not happy here.

Tom.   What gave her that idea?

Amanda.   What gives her any idea? However, you do act strangely. I — I'm not criticizing, understand *that!* I know your ambitions do not lie in the warehouse, that like everybody in the whole wide world — you've had to — make sacrifices, but — Tom — Tom — life's not easy, it calls for — Spartan endurance! There's so many things in my heart that I cannot describe to you! I've never told you but I — *loved* your father. . . .

Tom *(gently)*.   I know that, Mother.

Amanda.   And you — when I see you taking after his ways! Staying out late — and — well, you *had* been drinking the night you were in that — terrifying condition! Laura says that you hate the apartment and that you go out nights to get away from it! Is that true, Tom?

Tom.   No. You say there's so much in your heart that you can't describe to me. That's true of me, too. There's so much in my heart that I can't describe to *you!* So let's respect each other's —

Amanda.   But, why — *why*, Tom — are you always so *restless?* Where do you go to, nights?

Tom.   I — go to the movies.

Amanda.   Why do you go to the movies so much, Tom?

Tom. I go to the movies because — I like adventure. Adventure is something I don't have much of at work, so I go to the movies.

Amanda. But, Tom, you go to the movies *entirely too much!*

Tom. I like a lot of adventure.

Amanda looks baffled, then hurt. As the familiar inquisition resumes he becomes hard and impatient again. Amanda slips back into her querulous attitude toward him.

(Image on screen: Sailing vessel with Jolly Roger.)

Amanda. Most young men find adventure in their careers.

Tom. Then most young men are not employed in a warehouse.

Amanda. The world is full of young men employed in warehouses and offices and factories.

Tom. Do all of them find adventure in their careers?

Amanda. They do or they do without it! Not everybody has a craze for adventure.

Tom. Man is by instinct a lover, a hunter, a fighter, and none of those instincts are given much play at the warehouse!

Amanda. Man is by instinct! Don't quote instinct to me! Instinct is something that people have got away from! It belongs to animals! Christian adults don't want it!

Tom. What do Christian adults want, then, Mother?

Amanda. Superior things! Things of the mind and the spirit! Only animals have to satisfy instincts! Surely your aims are somewhat higher than theirs! Than monkeys — pigs —

Tom. I reckon they're not.

Amanda. You're joking. However, that isn't what I wanted to discuss.

Tom *(rising).* I haven't much time.

Amanda *(pushing his shoulders).* Sit down.

Tom. You want me to punch in red[8] at the warehouse, Mother?

Amanda. You have five minutes. I want to talk about Laura.

(Legend: "Plans and Provisions.")

Tom. All right! What about Laura?

Amanda. We have to be making plans and provisions for her. She's older than you, two years, and nothing has happened. She just drifts along doing nothing. It frightens me terribly how she just drifts along.

Tom. I guess she's the type that people call home girls.

Amanda. There's no such type, and if there is, it's a pity! That is unless the home is hers, with a husband!

---

[8] Be late for work.

Tom. What?

Amanda. Oh, I can see the handwriting on the wall as plain as I see the nose in front of my face! It's terrifying! More and more you remind me of your father! He was out all hours without explanation — Then *left! Good-bye!* And me with the bag to hold. I saw that letter you got from the Merchant Marine. I know what you're dreaming of. I'm not standing here blindfolded. Very well, then. Then *do* it! But not till there's somebody to take your place.

Tom. What do you mean?

Amanda. I mean that as soon as Laura has got somebody to take care of her, married, a home of her own, independent — why, then you'll be free to go wherever you please, on land, on sea, whichever way the wind blows! But until that time you've got to look out for your sister. I don't say me because I'm old and don't matter! I say for your sister because she's young and dependent. I put her in business college — a dismal failure! Frightened her so it made her sick to her stomach. I took her over to the Young People's League at the church. Another fiasco. She spoke to nobody, nobody spoke to her. Now all she does is fool with those pieces of glass and play those worn-out records. What kind of a life is that for a girl to lead!

Tom. What can I do about it?

Amanda. Overcome selfishness! Self, self, self is all that you ever think of! (*Tom springs up and crosses to get his coat. It is ugly and bulky. He pulls on a cap with earmuffs.*) Where is your muffler? Put your wool muffler on! (*He snatches it angrily from the closet and tosses it around his neck and pulls both ends tight.*) Tom! I haven't said what I had in mind to ask you.

Tom. I'm too late to —

Amanda (*catching his arms — very importunately. Then shyly.*) Down at the warehouse, aren't there some — nice young men?

Tom. No!

Amanda. There *must* be — *some.*

Tom. Mother —

Gesture.

Amanda. Find out one that's clean-living — doesn't drink and — ask him out for sister!

Tom. What?

Amanda. For *sister!* To *meet!* Get *acquainted!*

Tom (*stamping to door*). Oh, my *go-osh!*

Amanda. Will you? (*He opens door. Imploringly.*) Will you? (*He starts down.*) Will you? *Will* you, dear?

Tom (*calling back*). YES!

Amanda closes the door hesitantly and with a troubled but faintly hopeful expression.

(*Screen image:* Glamour *magazine cover.*)
Spot Amanda at phone.

Amanda.   Ella Cartwright? This is Amanda Wingfield! How are you, honey?
How is that kidney condition? (*Count five.*) *Horrors!* (*Count five.*) You're a
Christian martyr, yes, honey, that's what you are, a Christian martyr! Well, I
just happened to notice in my little red book that your subscription to the
Companion has just run out! I knew that you wouldn't want to miss out on the
wonderful serial starting in this new issue. It's by Bessie Mae Hopper, the first
thing she's written since *Honeymoon for Three*. Wasn't that a strange and
interesting story? Well, this one is even lovelier, I believe. It has a sophisticated society background. It's all about the horsey set on Long Island!

(*Fade out.*)

Scene 5

(*Legend on screen:* "Annunciation.") *Fade with music.*
    *It is early dusk of a spring evening. Supper has just been finished in the
Wingfield apartment. Amanda and Laura in light colored dresses are removing
dishes from the table, in the upstage area, which is shadowy, their movements
formalized almost as a dance or ritual, their moving forms as pale and silent as
moths.*
    *Tom, in white shirt and trousers, rises from the table and crosses toward the
fire-escape.*

Amanda (*as he passes her*).   Son, will you do me a favor?
Tom.   What?
Amanda.   Comb your hair! You look so pretty when your hair is combed! (*Tom
    slouches on sofa with evening paper. Enormous caption "Franco Triumphs."*[9])
    There is only one respect in which I would like you to emulate your father.
Tom.   What respect is that?
Amanda.   The care he always took of his appearance. He never allowed him-
    self to look untidy. (*He throws down the paper and crosses to fire-escape.*)
    Where are you going?
Tom.   I'm going out to smoke.
Amanda.   You smoke too much. A pack a day at fifteen cents a pack. How
    much would that amount to in a month? Thirty times fifteen is how much,

---

[9] General Francisco Franco led fascist Spanish rebels, aided by Nazi Germany, in a civil war
against Loyalists to the Spanish throne, aided by the Soviet Union. Franco's forces triumphed in
1939.

Tom? Figure it out and you will be astounded at what you could save. Enough to give you a night-school course in accounting at Washington U! Just think what a wonderful thing that would be for you, son!

Tom is unmoved by the thought.

Tom. I'd rather smoke. (*He steps out on landing, letting the screen door slam.*)
Amanda (*sharply*). I know! That's the tragedy of it. . . . (*Alone, she turns to look at her husband's picture.*)

(*Dance music: "All the World Is Waiting for the Sunrise!"*)

Tom (*to the audience*). Across the alley from us was the Paradise Dance Hall. On evenings in spring the windows and doors were open and the music came outdoors. Sometimes the lights were turned out except for a large glass sphere that hung from the ceiling. It would turn slowly about and filter the dusk with delicate rainbow colors. Then the orchestra played a waltz or a tango, something that had a slow and sensuous rhythm. Couples would come outside, to the relative privacy of the alley. You could see them kissing behind ash-pits and telephone poles. This was the compensation for lives that passed like mine, without any change or adventure. Adventure and change were imminent in this year. They were waiting around the corner for all these kids. Suspended in the mist over the Berchtesgaden,[10] caught in the folds of Chamberlain's[11] umbrella — In Spain there was Guernica! But here there was only hot swing music and liquor, dance halls, bars, and movies, and sex that hung in the gloom like a chandelier and flooded the world with brief, deceptive rainbows. . . . All the world was waiting for bombardments!

Amanda turns from the picture and comes outside.

Amanda (*sighing*). A fire-escape landing's a poor excuse for a porch. (*She spreads a newspaper on a step and sits down, gracefully and demurely as if she were settling into a swing on a Mississippi veranda.*) What are you looking at?
Tom. The moon.
Amanda. Is there a moon this evening?
Tom. It's rising over Garfinkel's Delicatessen.
Amanda. So it is! A little silver slipper of a moon. Have you made a wish on it yet?
Tom. Um-hum.
Amanda. What did you wish for?
Tom. That's a secret.

---

[10] The location of Hitler's mountain resort in Bavaria.
[11] Neville Chamberlain (1869–1940), famous for carrying an umbrella, and infamous for appeasing Hitler in an attempt to avoid war.

Amanda.   A secret, huh? Well, I won't tell mine either. I will be just as mysterious as you.

Tom.   I bet I can guess what yours is.

Amanda.   Is my head so transparent?

Tom.   You're not a sphinx.

Amanda.   No, I don't have secrets. I'll tell you what I wished for on the moon.
Success and happiness for my precious children! I wish for that whenever
there's a moon, and when there isn't a moon, I wish for it, too.

Tom.   I thought perhaps you wished for a gentleman caller.

Amanda.   Why do you say that?

Tom.   Don't you remember asking me to fetch one?

Amanda.   I remember suggesting that it would be nice for your sister if you
brought home some nice young man from the warehouse. I think I've made
that suggestion more than once.

Tom.   Yes, you have made it repeatedly.

Amanda.   Well?

Tom.   We are going to have one.

Amanda.   *What?*

Tom.   A gentleman caller!

(The Annunciation is celebrated with music.)
   Amanda rises.
   (Image on screen: Caller with bouquet.)

Amanda.   You mean you have asked some nice young man to come over?

Tom.   Yep. I've asked him to dinner.

Amanda.   You really did?

Tom.   I did!

Amanda.   You did, and did he — *accept?*

Tom.   He did!

Amanda.   Well, well — well, well! That's — lovely!

Tom.   I thought that you would be pleased.

Amanda.   It's definite, then?

Tom.   Very definite.

Amanda.   Soon?

Tom.   Very soon.

Amanda.   For heaven's sake, stop putting on and tell me some things, will
you?

Tom.   What things do you want me to tell you?

Amanda.   Naturally I would like to know when he's *coming!*

Tom.   He's coming tomorrow.

Amanda.   *Tomorrow?*

Tom.   Yep. Tomorrow.

Amanda.   But, Tom!

Tom.   Yes, Mother?

Amanda. Tomorrow gives me no time!

Tom. Time for what?

Amanda. Preparations! Why didn't you phone me at once, as soon as you asked him, the minute that he accepted? Then, don't you see, I could have been getting ready!

Tom. You don't have to make any fuss.

Amanda. Oh, Tom, Tom, Tom, of course I have to make a fuss! I want things nice, not sloppy! Not thrown together. I'll certainly have to do some fast thinking, won't I?

Tom. I don't see why you have to think at all.

Amanda. You just don't know. We can't have a gentleman caller in a pig-sty! All my wedding silver has to be polished, the monogrammed table linen ought to be laundered! The windows have to be washed and fresh curtains put up. And how about clothes? We have to *wear* something, don't we?

Tom. Mother, this boy is no one to make a fuss over!

Amanda. Do you realize he's the first young man we've introduced to your sister? It's terrible, dreadful, disgraceful that poor little sister has never received a single gentleman caller! Tom, come inside! *(She opens the screen door.)*

Tom. What for?

Amanda. I want to ask you some things.

Tom. If you're going to make such a fuss, I'll call it off, I'll tell him not to come.

Amanda. You certainly won't do anything of the kind. Nothing offends people worse than broken engagements. It simply means I'll have to work like a Turk! We won't be brilliant, but we'll pass inspection. Come on inside. *(Tom follows, groaning.)* Sit down.

Tom. Any particular place you would like me to sit?

Amanda. Thank heavens I've got that new sofa! I'm also making payments on a floor lamp I'll have sent out! And put the chintz covers on, they'll brighten things up! Of course I'd hoped to have these walls re-papered. . . . What is the young man's name?

Tom. His name is O'Connor.

Amanda. That, of course, means fish — tomorrow is Friday! I'll have that salmon loaf — with Durkee's dressing! What does he do? He works at the warehouse?

Tom. Of course! How else would I —

Amanda. Tom, he — doesn't drink?

Tom. Why do you ask me that?

Amanda. Your father *did!*

Tom. Don't get started on that!

Amanda. He *does* drink, then?

Tom. Not that I know of!

Amanda. Make sure, be certain! The last thing I want for my daughter's a boy who drinks!

Tom.   Aren't you being a little premature? Mr. O'Connor has not yet appeared on the scene!

Amanda.   But will tomorrow. To meet your sister, and what do I know about his character? Nothing! Old maids are better off than wives of drunkards!

Tom.   Oh, my God!

Amanda.   Be still!

Tom (*leaning forward to whisper*).   Lots of fellows meet girls whom they don't marry!

Amanda.   Oh, talk sensibly, Tom — and don't be sarcastic! (*She has gotten a hairbrush.*)

Tom.   What are you doing?

Amanda.   I'm brushing that cow-lick down! What is this young man's position at the warehouse?

Tom (*submitting grimly to the brush and the interrogation*).   This young man's position is that of a shipping clerk, Mother.

Amanda.   Sounds to me like a fairly responsible job, the sort of a job *you* would be in if you just had more *get-up*. What is his salary? Have you got any idea?

Tom.   I would judge it to be approximately eighty-five dollars a month.

Amanda.   Well — not princely, but —

Tom.   Twenty more than I make.

Amanda.   Yes, how well I know! But for a family man, eighty-five dollars a month is not much more than you can just get by on. . . .

Tom.   Yes, but Mr. O'Connor is not a family man.

Amanda.   He might be, mightn't he? Some time in the future?

Tom.   I see. Plans and provisions.

Amanda.   You are the only young man that I know of who ignores the fact that the future becomes the present, the present the past, and the past turns into everlasting regret if you don't plan for it!

Tom.   I will think that over and see what I can make of it.

Amanda.   Don't be supercilious with your mother! Tell me some more about this — what do you call him?

Tom.   James D. O'Connor. The D. is for Delaney.

Amanda.   Irish on *both* sides! *Gracious!* And doesn't drink?

Tom.   Shall I call him up and ask him right this minute?

Amanda.   The only way to find out about those things is to make discreet inquiries at the proper moment. When I was a girl in Blue Mountain and it was suspected that a young man drank, the girl whose attentions he had been receiving, if any girl *was*, would sometimes speak to the minister of his church, or rather her father would if her father was living, and sort of feel him out on the young man's character. That is the way such things are discreetly handled to keep a young woman from making a tragic mistake!

Tom.   Then how did you happen to make a tragic mistake?

Amanda.   That innocent look of your father's had everyone fooled! He *smiled* — the world was *enchanted!* No girl can do worse than put herself at the mercy of a handsome appearance! I hope that Mr. O'Connor is not too good-looking.

Tom. No, he's not too good-looking. He's covered with freckles and hasn't too much of a nose.

Amanda. He's not right-down homely, though?

Tom. Not right-down homely. Just medium homely, I'd say.

Amanda. Character's what to look for in a man.

Tom. That's what I've always said, Mother.

Amanda. You've never said anything of the kind and I suspect you would never give it a thought.

Tom. Don't be suspicious of me.

Amanda. At least I hope he's the type that's up and coming.

Tom. I think he really goes in for self-improvement.

Amanda. What reason have you to think so?

Tom. He goes to night school.

Amanda (*beaming*). Splendid! What does he do, I mean study?

Tom. Radio engineering and public speaking!

Amanda. Then he has visions of being advanced in the world! Any young man who studies public speaking is aiming to have an executive job some day! And radio engineering? A thing for the future! Both of these facts are very illuminating. Those are the sort of things that a mother should know concerning any young man who comes to call on her daughter. Seriously or — not.

Tom. One little warning. He doesn't know about Laura. I didn't let on that we had dark ulterior motives. I just said, why don't you come have dinner with us? He said okay and that was the whole conversation.

Amanda. I bet it was! You're eloquent as an oyster. However, he'll know about Laura when he gets here. When he sees how lovely and sweet and pretty she is, he'll thank his lucky stars he was asked to dinner.

Tom. Mother, you mustn't expect too much of Laura.

Amanda. What do you mean?

Tom. Laura seems all those things to you and me because she's ours and we love her. We don't even notice she's crippled any more.

Amanda. Don't say crippled! You know that I never allow that word to be used!

Tom. But face facts, Mother. She is and — that's not all —

Amanda. What do you mean "not all"?

Tom. Laura is very different from other girls.

Amanda. I think the difference is all to her advantage.

Tom. Not quite all — in the eyes of others — strangers — she's terribly shy and lives in a world of her own and those things make her seem a little peculiar to people outside the house.

Amanda. Don't say peculiar.

Tom. Face the facts. She is.

(*The dance-hall music changes to a tango that has a minor and somewhat ominous tone.*)

Amanda.   In what way is she peculiar — may I ask?

Tom *(gently).*   She lives in a world of her own — a world of — little glass ornaments, Mother. . . . *(Gets up. Amanda remains holding brush, looking at him,
troubled.)* She plays old phonograph records and — that's about all — *(He
glances at himself in the mirror and crosses to door.)*

Amanda *(sharply).*   Where are you going?

Tom.   I'm going to the movies. *(Out screen door.)*

Amanda.   Not to the movies, every night to the movies! *(Follows quickly to
screen door.)* I don't believe you always go to the movies! *(He is gone. Amanda
looks worriedly after him for a moment. Then vitality and optimism return
and she turns from the door. Crossing to portieres.)* Laura! Laura! *(Laura
answers from kitchenette.)*

Laura.   Yes, Mother.

Amanda.   Let those dishes go and come in front! *(Laura appears with dish
towel. Gaily.)* Laura, come here and make a wish on the moon!

Laura *(entering).*   Moon — moon?

Amanda.   A little silver slipper of a moon. Look over your left shoulder,
Laura, and make a wish! *(Laura looks faintly puzzled as if called out of sleep.
Amanda seizes her shoulders and turns her at angle by the door.)* Now! Now,
darling, *wish!*

Laura.   What shall I wish for, Mother?

Amanda *(her voice trembling and her eyes suddenly filling with tears).*   Happiness! Good Fortune!

The violin rises and the stage dims out.

Scene 6

(Image: High-school hero.)

Tom.   And so the following evening I brought Jim home to dinner. I had
known Jim slightly in high school. In high school Jim was a hero. He had
tremendous Irish good nature and vitality with the scrubbed and polished
look of white chinaware. He seemed to move in a continual spotlight. He was
a star in basketball, captain of the debating club, president of the senior class
and the glee club and he sang the male lead in the annual light operas. He
was always running or bounding, never just walking. He seemed always at the
point of defeating the law of gravity. He was shooting with such velocity
through his adolescence that you would logically expect him to arrive at nothing short of the White House by the time he was thirty. But Jim apparently
ran into more interference after his graduation from Soldan. His speed had

definitely slowed. Six years after he left high school he was holding a job that wasn't much better than mine.

(Image: Clerk.)

He was the only one at the warehouse with whom I was on friendly terms. I was valuable to him as someone who could remember his former glory, who had seen him win basketball games and the silver cup in debating. He knew of my secret practice of retiring to a cabinet of the washroom to work on poems when business was slack in the warehouse. He called me Shakespeare. And while the other boys in the warehouse regarded me with suspicious hostility, Jim took a humorous attitude toward me. Gradually his attitude affected the others, their hostility wore off, and they also began to smile at me as people smile at an oddly fashioned dog who trots across their paths at some distance.

I knew that Jim and Laura had known each other at Soldan, and I had heard Laura speak admiringly of his voice. I didn't know if Jim remembered her or not. In high school Laura had been as unobtrusive as Jim had been astonishing. If he did remember Laura, it was not as my sister, for when I asked him to dinner, he grinned and said, "You know, Shakespeare, I never thought of you as having folks!"

He was about to discover that I did. . . .

(Light upstage.)
(Legend on screen: "The Accent of a Coming Foot.")
Friday evening. It is about five o'clock of a late spring evening which comes "scattering poems in the sky."
A delicate lemony light is in the Wingfield apartment.
Amanda has worked like a Turk in preparation for the gentleman caller. The results are astonishing. The new floor lamp with its rose-silk shade is in place, a colored paper lantern conceals the broken light fixture in the ceiling, new billowing white curtains are at the windows, chintz covers are on chairs and sofa, a pair of new sofa pillows make their initial appearance.
Open boxes and tissue paper are scattered on the floor.
Laura stands in the middle with lifted arms while Amanda crouches before her, adjusting the hem of the new dress, devout and ritualistic. The dress is colored and designed by memory. The arrangement of Laura's hair is changed; it is softer and more becoming. A fragile, unearthly prettiness has come out in Laura: she is like a piece of translucent glass touched by light, given a momentary radiance, not actual, not lasting.

Amanda *(impatiently).* Why are you trembling?
Laura. Mother, you've made me so nervous!
Amanda. How have I made you nervous?
Laura. By all this fuss! You make it seem so important!

Amanda. I don't understand you, Laura. You couldn't be satisfied with just sitting home, and yet whenever I try to arrange something for you, you seem to resist it. (*She gets up.*) Now take a look at yourself. No, wait! Wait just a moment — I have an idea!

Laura. What is it now?

Amanda produces two powder puffs which she wraps in handkerchiefs and stuffs in Laura's bosom.

Laura. Mother, what are you doing?

Amanda. They call them "Gay Deceivers"!

Laura. I won't wear them!

Amanda. You will!

Laura. Why should I?

Amanda. Because, to be painfully honest, your chest is flat.

Laura. You make it seem like we were setting a trap.

Amanda. All pretty girls are a trap, a pretty trap, and men expect them to be. (*Legend: "A Pretty Trap."*) Now look at yourself, young lady. This is the prettiest you will ever be! I've got to fix myself now! You're going to be surprised by your mother's appearance! (*She crosses through portieres, humming gaily.*)

Laura moves slowly to the long mirror and stares solemnly at herself.
   A wind blows the white curtains inward in a slow, graceful motion and with a faint, sorrowful sighing.

Amanda (*off stage*). It isn't dark enough yet. (*She turns slowly before the mirror with a troubled look.*)

(*Legend on screen: "This Is My Sister: Celebrate Her with Strings!" Music.*)

Amanda (*laughing, off*). I'm going to show you something. I'm going to make a spectacular appearance!

Laura. What is it, Mother?

Amanda. Possess your soul in patience — you will see! Something I've resurrected from that old trunk! Styles haven't changed so terribly much after all. . . . (*She parts the portieres.*) Now just look at your mother! (*She wears a girlish frock of yellowed voile with a blue silk sash. She carries a bunch of jonquils — the legend of her youth is nearly revived. Feverishly.*) This is the dress in which I led the cotillion. Won the cakewalk twice at Sunset Hill, wore one spring to the Governor's ball in Jackson! See how I sashayed around the ballroom, Laura? (*She raises her skirt and does a mincing step around the room.*) I wore it on Sundays for my gentlemen callers! I had it on the day I met your father — I had malaria fever all that spring. The change of climate from East Tennessee to the Delta — weakened resistance — I had a little temperature all the time — not enough to be serious — just enough to make me restless and giddy! Invitations poured in — parties all over the Delta! — "Stay in bed," said Mother, "you have fever!" — but I just wouldn't. — I took quinine but kept on going, going! — Evenings, dances! — Afternoons, long, long rides! Picnics — lovely! — So lovely, that country in May. — All lacy with dogwood, literally flooded with jonquils! — That was the spring I had the craze for jonquils. Jonquils became an absolute obsession. Mother said, "Honey, there's no more room for jonquils." And still I kept bringing in more jonquils. Whenever, wherever I saw them, I'd say, "Stop! Stop! I see jonquils!" I made the young men help me gather the jonquils! It was a joke, Amanda and her jonquils! Finally there were no more vases to hold them, every available space was filled with jonquils. No vases to hold them? All right, I'll hold them myself! And then I — (*She stops in front of the picture.*) (*Music.*) met your father! Malaria fever and jonquils and then — this — boy. . . . (*She switches on the rose-colored lamp.*) I hope they get here before it starts to rain. (*She crosses upstage and places the jonquils in bowl on table.*) I gave your brother a little extra change so he and Mr. O'Connor could take the service car home.

Laura (*with altered look*).   What did you say his name was?
Amanda.   O'Connor.
Laura.   What is his first name?
Amanda.   I don't remember. Oh, yes, I do. It was — Jim!

Laura sways slightly and catches hold of a chair.
  (*Legend on screen: "Not Jim!"*)

Laura (*faintly*)   Not — Jim!
Amanda.   Yes, that was it, it was Jim! I've never known a Jim that wasn't nice!

(*Music: Ominous.*)

Laura.   Are you sure his name is Jim O'Connor?
Amanda.   Yes. Why?
Laura.   Is he the one that Tom used to know in high school?
Amanda.   He didn't say so. I think he just got to know him at the warehouse.
Laura.   There was a Jim O'Connor we both knew in high school — (*Then, with effort.*) If that is the one that Tom is bringing to dinner — you'll have to excuse me, I won't come to the table.
Amanda.   What sort of nonsense is this?
Laura.   You asked me once if I'd ever liked a boy. Don't you remember I showed you this boy's picture?
Amanda.   You mean the boy you showed me in the year-book?
Laura.   Yes, that boy.
Amanda.   Laura, Laura, were you in love with that boy?

Laura. I don't know, Mother. All I know is I couldn't sit at the table if it was him!

Amanda. It won't be him! It isn't the least bit likely. But whether it is or not, you will come to the table. You will not be excused.

Laura. I'll have to be, Mother.

Amanda. I don't intend to humor your silliness, Laura. I've had too much from you and your brother, both! So just sit down and compose yourself till they come. Tom has forgotten his key so you'll have to let them in, when they arrive.

Laura (*panicky*). Oh, Mother — *you* answer the door!

Amanda (*lightly*). I'll be in the kitchen — busy!

Laura. Oh, Mother, please answer the door, don't make me do it!

Amanda (*crossing into kitchenette*). I've got to fix the dressing for the salmon. Fuss, fuss — silliness! — over a gentleman caller!

Door swings shut. Laura is left alone.
  (*Legend: "Terror!"*)
  She utters a low moan and turns off the lamp — sits stiffly on the edge of the sofa, knotting her fingers together.
  (*Legend on screen: "The Opening of a Door!"*)
  Tom and Jim appear on the fire-escape steps and climb to landing. Hearing their approach, Laura rises with a panicky gesture. She retreats to the portieres. The doorbell. Laura catches her breath and touches her throat. Low drums.

Amanda (*calling*). Laura, sweetheart! The door!

Laura stares at it without moving.

Jim. I think we just beat the rain.

Tom. Uh-huh. (*He rings again, nervously. Jim whistles and fishes for a cigarette.*)

Amanda (*very, very gaily*). Laura, that is your brother and Mr. O'Connor! Will you let them in, darling?

Laura crosses toward kitchenette door.

Laura (*breathlessly*). Mother — you go to the door!

Amanda steps out of kitchenette and stares furiously at Laura. She points imperiously at the door.

Laura. Please, please!

Amanda (*in a fierce whisper*). What is the matter with you, you silly thing?

Laura (*desperately*). Please, you answer it, *please!*

Amanda. I told you I wasn't going to humor you, Laura. Why have you chosen this moment to lose your mind?

Laura. Please, please, please, you go!

Amanda. You'll have to go to the door because I can't!

Laura (*despairingly*). I can't either!

Amanda. Why?

Laura. I'm *sick!*

Amanda. I'm sick, too — of your nonsense! Why can't you and your brother be normal people? Fantastic whims and behavior! (*Tom gives a long ring.*) Preposterous goings on! Can you give me one reason — (*Calls out lyrically.*) — why should you be afraid to open a door? Now you answer it, Laura!

Laura. Oh, oh, oh . . . (*She returns through the portieres. Darts to the Victrola and winds it frantically and turns it on.*)

Amanda. Laura Wingfield, you march right to that door!

Laura. Yes — yes, Mother!

A faraway, scratchy rendition of "Dardanella" softens the air and gives her strength to move through it. She slips to the door and draws it cautiously open. Tom enters with the caller, Jim O'Connor.

Tom. Laura, this is Jim. Jim, this is my sister, Laura.

Jim (*stepping inside*). I didn't know that Shakespeare had a sister!

Laura (*retreating stiff and trembling from the door*). How — how do you do?

Jim (*heartily extending his hand*). Okay!

Laura touches it hesitantly with hers.

Jim. Your hand's *cold*, Laura!

Laura. Yes, well — I've been playing the Victrola . . .

Jim. Must have been playing classical music on it! You ought to play a little hot swing music to warm you up!

Laura. Excuse me — I haven't finished playing the Victrola . . .

She turns awkwardly and hurries into the front room. She pauses a second by the Victrola. Then catches her breath and darts through the portieres like a frightened deer.

Jim (*grinning*). What was the matter?

Tom. Oh — with Laura? Laura is — terribly shy.

Jim. Shy, huh? It's unusual to meet a shy girl nowadays. I don't believe you ever mentioned you had a sister.

Tom. Well, now you know. I have one. Here is the *Post Dispatch*. You want a piece of it?

Jim. Uh-huh.

Tom. What piece? The comics?

Jim.   Sports! *(Glances at it.)* Ole Dizzy Dean is on his bad behavior.

Tom *(disinterest).*   Yeah? *(Lights cigarette and crosses back to fire-escape door.)*

Jim.   Where are *you* going?

Tom.   I'm going out on the terrace.

Jim *(goes after him).*   You know, Shakespeare — I'm going to sell you a bill of goods!

Tom.   What goods?

Jim.   A course I'm taking.

Tom.   Huh?

Jim.   In public speaking! You and me, we're not the warehouse type.

Tom.   Thanks — that's good news. But what has public speaking got to do with it?

Jim.   It fits you for — executive positions!

Tom.   Awww.

Jim.   I tell you it's done a helluva lot for me.

(Image: Executive at desk.)

Tom.   In what respect?

Jim.   In every! Ask yourself what is the difference between you an' me and men in the office down front? Brains? — No! — Ability? — No! Then what? Just one little thing —

Tom.   What is that one little thing?

Jim.   Primarily it amounts to — social poise! Being able to square up to people and hold your own on any social level!

Amanda *(off stage).*   Tom?

Tom.   Yes, Mother?

Amanda.   Is that you and Mr. O'Connor?

Tom.   Yes, Mother.

Amanda.   Well, you just make yourselves comfortable in there.

Tom.   Yes, Mother.

Amanda.   Ask Mr. O'Connor if he would like to wash his hands.

Jim.   Aw — no — no — thank you — I took care of that at the warehouse. Tom —

Tom.   Yes?

Jim.   Mr. Mendoza was speaking to me about you.

Tom.   Favorably?

Jim.   What do you think?

Tom.   Well —

Jim.   You're going to be out of a job if you don't wake up.

Tom.   I am waking up —

Jim.   You show no signs.

Tom.   The signs are interior.

(Image on screen: The sailing vessel with Jolly Roger again.)

Tom. I'm planning to change. (*He leans over the rail speaking with quiet exhilaration. The incandescent marquees and signs of the first-run movie houses light his face from across the alley. He looks like a voyager.*) I'm right at the point of committing myself to a future that doesn't include the warehouse and Mr. Mendoza or even a night-school course in public speaking.

Jim. What are you gassing about?

Tom. I'm tired of the movies.

Jim. Movies!

Tom. Yes, movies! Look at them — (*A wave toward the marvels of Grand Avenue.*) All of those glamorous people — having adventures — hogging it all, gobbling the whole thing up! You know what happens? People go to the *movies* instead of *moving!* Hollywood characters are supposed to have all the adventures for everybody in America, while everybody in America sits in a dark room and watches them have them! Yes, until there's a war. That's when adventure becomes available to the masses! *Everyone's* dish, not only Gable's! Then the people in the dark room come out of the dark room to have some adventures themselves — Goody, goody — It's our turn now, to go to the South Sea Island — to make a safari — to be exotic, far-off — But I'm not patient. I don't want to wait till then. I'm tired of the *movies* and I am *about* to *move!*

Jim (*incredulously*). Move?

Tom. Yes.

Jim. When?

Tom. Soon!

Jim. Where? Where?

(*Theme three: Music seems to answer the question, while Tom thinks it over. He searches among his pockets.*)

Tom. I'm starting to boil inside. I know I seem dreamy, but inside — well, I'm boiling! Whenever I pick up a shoe, I shudder a little thinking how short life is and what I am doing! — Whatever that means. I know it doesn't mean shoes — except as something to wear on a traveler's feet! (*Finds paper.*) Look —

Jim. What?

Tom. I'm a member.

Jim (*reading*). The Union of Merchant Seamen.

Tom. I paid my dues this month, instead of the light bill.

Jim. You will regret it when they turn the lights off.

Tom. I won't be here.

Jim. How about your mother?

Tom. I'm like my father. The bastard son of a bastard! See how he grins? And he's been absent going on sixteen years!

Jim. You're just talking, you drip. How does your mother feel about it?

Tom. Shhh — Here comes Mother! Mother is not acquainted with my plans!

Amanda (*enters portieres*). Where are you all?

Tom.   On the terrace, Mother.

They start inside. She advances to them. Tom is distinctly shocked at her appearance. Even Jim blinks a little. He is making his first contact with girlish Southern vivacity and in spite of the night-school course in public speaking is somewhat thrown off the beam by the unexpected outlay of social charm.

Certain responses are attempted by Jim but are swept aside by Amanda's gay laughter and chatter. Tom is embarrassed but after the first shock Jim reacts very warmly. Grins and chuckles, is altogether won over.

(Image: Amanda as a girl.)

Amanda (*coyly smiling, shaking her girlish ringlets*).   Well, well, well, so this is Mr. O'Connor. Introductions entirely unnecessary. I've heard so much about you from my boy. I finally said to him, Tom — good gracious! — why don't you bring this paragon to supper? I'd like to meet this nice young man at the warehouse! — Instead of just hearing him sing your praises so much! I don't know why my son is so stand-offish — that's not Southern behavior! Let's sit down and — I think we could stand a little more air in here! Tom, leave the door open. I felt a nice fresh breeze a moment ago. Where has it gone? Mmm, so warm already! And not quite summer, even. We're going to burn up when summer really gets started. However, we're having — we're having a very light supper. I think light things are better fo' this time of year. The same as light clothes are. Light clothes an' light food are what warm weather calls fo'. You know our blood gets so thick during th' winter — it takes a while fo' us to *adjust* ou'selves! — when the season changes. . . . It's come so quick this year. I wasn't prepared. All of a sudden — heavens! Already summer! — I ran to the trunk an' pulled out this light dress — Terribly old! Historical almost! But feels so good — so good an' co-ol, y'know. . . .

Tom.   Mother —

Amanda.   Yes, honey?

Tom.   How about — supper?

Amanda.   Honey, you go ask Sister if supper is ready! You know that Sister is in full charge of supper! Tell her you hungry boys are waiting for it. (*To Jim.*) Have you met Laura?

Jim.   She —

Amanda.   Let you in? Oh, good, you've met already! It's rare for a girl as sweet an' pretty as Laura to be domestic! But Laura is, thank heavens, not only pretty but also very domestic. I'm not at all. I never was a bit. I never could make a thing but angel-food cake. Well, in the South we had so many servants. Gone, gone, gone. All vestiges of gracious living! Gone completely! I wasn't prepared for what the future brought me. All of my gentlemen callers were sons of planters and so of course I assumed that I would be married to one and raise my family on a large piece of land with plenty of servants. But man proposes — and woman accepts the proposal! — To vary that old, old saying a little bit — I married no planter! I married a man who worked for the telephone company! — that gallantly smiling gentleman over there! *(Points to the picture.)* A telephone man who — fell in love with long distance! — Now he travels and I don't even know where! — But what am I going on for about my — tribulations! Tell me yours — I hope you don't have any! Tom?

Tom *(returning).*   Yes, Mother?

Amanda.   Is supper nearly ready?

Tom.   It looks to me like supper is on the table.

Amanda.   Let me look — *(She rises prettily and looks through portieres.)* Oh, lovely — But where is Sister?

Tom.   Laura is not feeling well and she says that she thinks she'd better not come to the table.

Amanda.   What? — Nonsense! — Laura? Oh, Laura!

Laura *(off stage, faintly).*   Yes, Mother.

Amanda.   You really must come to the table. We won't be seated until you come to the table! Come in, Mr. O'Connor. You sit over there and I'll — Laura? Laura Wingfield! You're keeping us waiting, honey! We can't say grace until you come to the table!

The back door is pushed weakly open and Laura comes in. She is obviously quite faint, her lips trembling, her eyes wide and staring. She moves unsteadily toward the table.

(Legend: "Terror!")

Outside a summer storm is coming abruptly. The white curtains billow inward at the windows and there is a sorrowful murmur and deep blue dusk.

Laura suddenly stumbles — She catches at a chair with a faint moan.

Tom.   Laura!

Amanda.   Laura! *(There is a clap of thunder.)* *(Legend: "Ah!")* *(Despairingly.)* Why, Laura, you *are* sick, darling! Tom, help your sister into the living room, dear! Sit in the living room, Laura — rest on the sofa. Well! *(To the gentleman caller.)* Standing over the hot stove made her ill! — I told her that it was just too warm this evening, but — *(Tom comes back in. Laura is on the sofa.)* Is Laura all right now?

Tom.   Yes.

Amanda.   What *is* that? Rain? A nice cool rain has come up! *(She gives the gentleman caller a frightened look.)* I think we may — have grace — now . . . *(Tom looks at her stupidly.)* Tom, honey — you say grace!

Tom.   Oh . . . "For these and all thy mercies — " *(They bow their heads, Amanda stealing a nervous glance at Jim. In the living room Laura, stretched on the sofa, clenches her hand to her lips, to hold back a shuddering sob.)* God's Holy Name be praised —

(The scene dims out.)

Scene 7

A Souvenir

Half an hour later. Dinner is just being finished in the upstage area, which is concealed by the drawn portieres.

As the curtain rises Laura is still huddled upon the sofa, her feet drawn under her, her head resting on a pale blue pillow, her eyes wide and mysteriously watchful. The new floor lamp with its shade of rose-colored silk gives a soft, becoming light to her face, bringing out the fragile, unearthly prettiness which usually escapes attention. There is a steady murmur of rain, but it is slackening and stops soon after the scene begins; the air outside becomes pale and luminous as the moon breaks out.

A moment after the curtain rises, the lights in both rooms flicker and go out.

Jim. Hey, there, Mr. Light Bulb!

Amanda laughs nervously.
    (Legend: "Suspension of a Public Service.")

Amanda. Where was Moses when the lights went out? Ha-ha. Do you know the answer to that one, Mr. O'Connor?

Jim. No, Ma'am, what's the answer?

Amanda. In the dark! (*Jim laughs appreciatively.*) Everybody sit still. I'll light the candles. Isn't it lucky we have them on the table? Where's a match? Which of you gentlemen can provide a match?

Jim. Here.

Amanda. Thank you, sir.

Jim. Not at all, Ma'am!

Amanda. I guess the fuse has burnt out. Mr. O'Connor, can you tell a burnt-out fuse? I know I can't and Tom is a total loss when it comes to mechanics. (*Sound: Getting up: Voices recede a little to kitchenette.*) Oh, be careful you don't bump into something. We don't want our gentleman caller to break his neck. Now wouldn't that be a fine howdy-do?

Jim. Ha-ha! Where is the fuse-box?

Amanda. Right here next to the stove. Can you see anything?

Jim. Just a minute.

Amanda. Isn't electricity a mysterious thing? Wasn't it Benjamin Franklin who tied a key to a kite? We live in such a mysterious universe, don't we? Some people say that science clears up all the mysteries for us. In my opinion it only creates more! Have you found it yet?

Jim. No, Ma'am. All these fuses look okay to me.

Amanda. Tom!

Tom. Yes, Mother?

Amanda. That light bill I gave you several days ago. The one I told you we got the notices about?

Tom. Oh. — Yeah.

(Legend: "Ha!")

Amanda. You didn't neglect to pay it by any chance?

Tom. Why, I —

Amanda. Didn't! I might have known it!

Jim. Shakespeare probably wrote a poem on that light bill, Mrs. Wingfield.

Amanda. I might have known better than to trust him with it! There's such a high price for negligence in this world!

Jim. Maybe the poem will win a ten-dollar prize.

Amanda. We'll just have to spend the remainder of the evening in the nineteenth century, before Mr. Edison made the Mazda lamp!

Jim. Candlelight is my favorite kind of light.

Amanda. That shows you're romantic! But that's no excuse for Tom. Well, we got through dinner. Very considerate of them to let us get through dinner before they plunged us into everlasting darkness, wasn't it, Mr. O'Connor?

Jim. Ha-ha!

Amanda. Tom, as a penalty for your carelessness you can help me with the dishes.

Jim. Let me give you a hand.

Amanda. Indeed you will not!

Jim. I ought to be good for something.

Amanda. Good for something? *(Her tone is rhapsodic.)* You? Why, Mr. O'Connor, nobody, *nobody's* given me this much entertainment in years — as you have!

Jim. Aw, now, Mrs. Wingfield!

Amanda. I'm not exaggerating, not one bit! But Sister is all by her lonesome. You go keep her company in the parlor! I'll give you this lovely old candelabrum that used to be on the altar at the church of the Heavenly Rest. It was melted a little out of shape when the church burnt down. Lightning struck it one spring. Gypsy Jones was holding a revival at the time and he intimated that the church was destroyed because the Episcopalians gave card parties.

Jim. Ha-ha.

Amanda. And how about coaxing Sister to drink a little wine? I think it would be good for her! Can you carry both at once?

Jim. Sure. I'm Superman!

Amanda. Now, Thomas, get into this apron!

The door of the kitchenette swings closed on Amanda's gay laughter; the flickering light approaches the portieres.

Laura sits up nervously as he enters. Her speech at first is low and breathless from the almost intolerable strain of being alone with a stranger.

(Legend: "I Don't Suppose You Remember Me at All!")

In her first speeches in this scene, before Jim's warmth overcomes her paralyzing shyness, Laura's voice is thin and breathless as though she has run up a steep flight of stairs.

Jim's attitude is gently humorous. In playing this scene it should be stressed that while the incident is apparently unimportant, it is to Laura the climax of her secret life.

Jim.   Hello, there, Laura.

Laura *(faintly)*.   Hello. *(She clears her throat.)*

Jim.   How are you feeling now? Better?

Laura.   Yes. Yes, thank you.

Jim.   This is for you. A little dandelion wine. *(He extends it toward her with extravagant gallantry.)*

Laura.   Thank you.

Jim.   Drink it — but don't get drunk! *(He laughs heartily. Laura takes the glass uncertainly; laughs shyly.)* Where shall I set the candles?

Laura.   Oh — oh, anywhere . . .

Jim.   How about here on the floor? Any objections?

Laura.   No.

Jim.   I'll spread a newspaper under to catch the drippings. I like to sit on the floor. Mind if I do?

Laura.   Oh, no.

Jim.   Give me a pillow?

Laura.   What?

Jim.   A pillow!

Laura.   Oh . . . *(Hands him one quickly.)*

Jim.   How about you? Don't you like to sit on the floor?

Laura.   Oh — yes.

Jim.   Why don't you, then?

Laura.   I — will.

Jim.   Take a pillow! *(Laura does. Sits on the other side of the candelabrum. Jim crosses his legs and smiles engagingly at her.)* I can't hardly see you sitting way over there.

Laura.   I can — see you.

Jim.   I know, but that's not fair, I'm in the limelight. *(Laura moves her pillow closer.)* Good! Now I can see you! Comfortable?

Laura.   Yes.

Jim.   So am I. Comfortable as a cow. Will you have some gum?

Laura.   No, thank you.

Jim.   I think that I will indulge, with your permission. *(Musingly unwraps it and holds it up.)* Think of the fortune made by the guy that invented the first piece of chewing gum. Amazing, huh? The Wrigley Building is one of the sights of Chicago. — I saw it summer before last when I went up to the Century of Progress. Did you take in the Century of Progress?

Laura. No, I didn't.

Jim. Well, it was quite a wonderful exposition. What impressed me most was the Hall of Science. Gives you an idea of what the future will be in America, even more wonderful than the present time is! *(Pause. Smiling at her.)* Your brother tells me you're shy. Is that right, Laura?

Laura. I — don't know.

Jim. I judge you to be an old-fashioned type of girl. Well, I think that's a pretty good type to be. Hope you don't think I'm being too personal — do you?

Laura *(hastily, out of embarrassment).* I believe I *will* take a piece of gum, if you — don't mind. *(Clearing her throat.)* Mr. O'Connor, have you — kept up with your singing?

Jim. Singing? Me?

Laura. Yes. I remember what a beautiful voice you had.

Jim. When did you hear me sing?

(Voice off stage in the pause.)

Voice *(off stage).* O blow, ye winds, heigh-ho,
A-roving I will go!
I'm off to my love
With a boxing glove —
Ten thousand miles away!

Jim. You say you've heard me sing?

Laura. Oh, yes! Yes, very often . . . I — don't suppose you remember me — at all?

Jim *(smiling doubtfully).* You know I have an idea I've seen you before. I had that idea soon as you opened the door. It seemed almost like I was about to remember your name. But the name that I started to call you — wasn't a name! And so I stopped myself before I said it.

Laura. Wasn't it — Blue Roses?

Jim *(springs up, grinning).* Blue Roses! My gosh, yes — Blue Roses! That's what I had on my tongue when you opened the door! Isn't it funny what tricks your memory plays? I didn't connect you with the high school somehow or other. But that's where it was; it was high school. I didn't even know you were Shakespeare's sister! Gosh, I'm sorry.

Laura. I didn't expect you to. You — barely knew me!

Jim. But we did have a speaking acquaintance, huh?

Laura. Yes, we — spoke to each other.

Jim. When did you recognize me?

Laura. Oh, right away!

Jim. Soon as I came in the door?

Laura. When I heard your name I thought it was probably you. I knew that Tom used to know you a little in high school. So when you came in the door — Well, then I was — sure.

Jim. Why didn't you *say* something, then?

Laura (*breathlessly*). I didn't know what to say, I was — too surprised!

Jim. For goodness' sakes! You know, this sure is funny!

Laura. Yes! Yes, isn't it, though . . .

Jim. Didn't we have a class in something together?

Laura. Yes, we did.

Jim. What class was that?

Laura. It was — singing — Chorus!

Jim. Aw!

Laura. I sat across the aisle from you in the Aud.

Jim. Aw.

Laura. Mondays, Wednesdays, and Fridays.

Jim. Now I remember — you always came in late.

Laura. Yes, it was so hard for me, getting upstairs. I had that brace on my leg — it clumped so loud!

Jim. I never heard any clumping.

Laura (*wincing in the recollection*). To me it sounded like — thunder!

Jim. Well, well, well. I never even noticed.

Laura. And everybody was seated before I came in. I had to walk in front of all those people. My seat was in the back row. I had to go clumping all the way up the aisle with everyone watching!

Jim. You shouldn't have been self-conscious.

Laura. I know, but I was. It was always such a relief when the singing started.

Jim. Aw, yes, I've placed you now! I used to call you Blue Roses. How was it that I got started calling you that?

Laura. I was out of school a little while with pleurosis. When I came back you asked me what was the matter. I said I had pleurosis — you thought I said Blue Roses. That's what you always called me after that!

Jim. I hope you didn't mind.

Laura. Oh, no — I liked it. You see, I wasn't acquainted with many — people. . . .

Jim. As I remember you sort of stuck by yourself.

Laura. I — I — never had much luck at — making friends.

Jim. I don't see why you wouldn't.

Laura. Well, I — started out badly.

Jim. You mean being —

Laura. Yes, it sort of — stood between me —

Jim. You shouldn't have let it!

Laura. I know, but it did, and —

Jim. You were shy with people!

Laura. I tried not to be but never could —

Jim.   Overcome it?

Laura.   No, I — I never could!

Jim.   I guess being shy is something you have to work out of kind of gradually.

Laura (*sorrowfully*).   Yes — I guess it —

Jim.   Takes time!

Laura.   Yes —

Jim.   People are not so dreadful when you know them. That's what you have to remember! And everybody has problems, not just you, but practically everybody has got some problems. You think of yourself as having the only problems, as being the only one who is disappointed. But just look around you and you will see lots of people as disappointed as you are. For instance, I hoped when I was going to high school that I would be further along at this time, six years later, than I am now — You remember that wonderful write-up I had in *The Torch*?

Laura.   Yes! (*She rises and crosses to table.*)

Jim.   It said I was bound to succeed in anything I went into! (*Laura returns with the annual.*) Holy Jeez! *The Torch!* (*He accepts it reverently. They smile across it with mutual wonder. Laura crouches beside him and they begin to turn through it. Laura's shyness is dissolving in his warmth.*)

Laura.   Here you are in *Pirates of Penzance*!

Jim (*wistfully*).   I sang the baritone lead in that operetta.

Laura (*rapidly*).   So — *beautifully!*

Jim (*protesting*).   Aw —

Laura.   Yes, yes — beautifully — beautifully!

Jim.   You heard me?

Laura.   All three times!

Jim.   No!

Laura.   Yes!

Jim.   All three performances?

Laura (*looking down*).   Yes.

Jim.   Why?

Laura.   I — wanted to ask you to — autograph my program.

Jim.   Why didn't you ask me to?

Laura.   You were always surrounded by your own friends so much that I never had a chance to.

Jim.   You should have just —

Laura.   Well, I — thought you might think I was —

Jim.   Thought I might think you was — what?

Laura.   Oh —

Jim (*with reflective relish*).   I was beleaguered by females in those days.

Laura.   You were terribly popular!

Jim.   Yeah —

Laura.   You had such a — friendly way —

Jim.   I was spoiled in high school.

Laura.   Everybody — liked you!

Jim. Including you?

Laura. I — yes, I — I did, too — (*She gently closes the book in her lap.*)

Jim. Well, well, well! — Give me that program, Laura. (*She hands it to him. He signs it with a flourish.*) There you are — better late than never!

Laura. Oh, I — what a — surprise!

Jim. My signature isn't worth very much right now. But some day — maybe — it will increase in value! Being disappointed is one thing and being discouraged is something else. I am disappointed but I'm not discouraged. I'm twenty-three years old. How old are you?

Laura. I'll be twenty-four in June.

Jim. That's not old age.

Laura. No, but —

Jim. You finished high school?

Laura (*with difficulty*). I didn't go back.

Jim. You mean you dropped out?

Laura. I made bad grades in my final examinations. (*She rises and replaces the book and the program. Her voice strained.*) How is — Emily Meisenbach getting along?

Jim. Oh, that kraut-head!

Laura. Why do you call her that?

Jim. That's what she was.

Laura. You're not still — going with her?

Jim. I never see her.

Laura. It said in the Personal Section that you were — engaged!

Jim. I know, but I wasn't impressed by that — propaganda!

Laura. It wasn't — the truth?

Jim. Only in Emily's optimistic opinion!

Laura. Oh —

(*Legend: "What Have You Done since High School?"*)

Jim lights a cigarette and leans indolently back on his elbows smiling at Laura with a warmth and charm which light her inwardly with altar candles. She remains by the table and turns in her hands a piece of glass to cover her tumult.

Jim (*after several reflective puffs on a cigarette*). What have you done since high school? (*She seems not to hear him.*) Huh? (*Laura looks up.*) I said what have you done since high school, Laura?

Laura. Nothing much.

Jim. You must have been doing something these six long years.

Laura. Yes.

Jim. Well, then, such as what?

Laura. I took a business course at business college —

Jim. How did that work out?

Laura. Well, not very — well — I had to drop out, it gave me — indigestion —

Jim laughs gently.

Jim. What are you doing now?

Laura. I don't do anything — much. Oh, please don't think I sit around doing nothing! My glass collection takes up a good deal of my time. Glass is something you have to take good care of.

Jim. What did you say — about glass?

Laura. Collection I said — I have one — (*She clears her throat and turns away again, acutely shy.*)

Jim (*abruptly*). You know what I judge to be the trouble with you? Inferiority complex! Know what that is? That's what they call it when someone low-rates himself! I understand it because I had it, too. Although my case was not so aggravated as yours seems to be. I had it until I took up public speaking, developed my voice, and learned that I had an aptitude for science. Before that time I never thought of myself as being outstanding in any way whatsoever! Now I've never made a regular study of it, but I have a friend who says I can analyze people better than doctors that make a profession of it. I don't claim that to be necessarily true, but I can sure guess a person's psychology, Laura! (*Takes out his gum.*) Excuse me, Laura. I always take it out when the flavor is gone. I'll use this scrap of paper to wrap it in. I know how it is to get it stuck on a shoe. Yep — that's what I judge to be your principal trouble. A lack of confidence in yourself as a person. You don't have the proper amount of faith in yourself. I'm basing that fact on a number of your remarks and also on certain observations I've made. For instance that clumping you thought was so awful in high school. You say that you even dreaded to walk into class. You see what you did? You dropped out of school, you gave up an education because of a clump, which as far as I know was practically nonexistent! A little physical defect is what you have. Hardly noticeable even! Magnified thousands of times by imagination! You know what my strong advice to you is? Think of yourself as *superior* in some way!

Laura. In what way would I think?

Jim. Why, man alive, Laura! Just look about you a little. What do you see? A world full of common people! All of 'em born and all of 'em going to die! Which of them has one-tenth of your good points! Or mine! Or anyone else's, as far as that goes — Gosh! Everybody excels in some one thing. Some in many! (*Unconsciously glances at himself in the mirror.*) All you've got to do is discover in *what!* Take me, for instance. (*He adjusts his tie at the mirror.*) My interest happened to lie in electrodynamics. I'm taking a course in radio engineering at night school, Laura, on top of a fairly responsible job at the warehouse. I'm taking that course and studying public speaking.

Laura. Ohhhh.

Jim. Because I believe in the future of television! (*Turning back to her.*) I wish to be ready to go up right along with it. Therefore I'm planning to get in on the ground floor. In fact, I've already made the right connections and all that remains is for the industry itself to get under way! Full steam — (*His eyes are* *starry.*) Knowledge — Zzzzzp! *Money* — Zzzzzzp! — *Power!* That's the cycle democracy is built on! (*His attitude is convincingly dynamic. Laura stares at him, even her shyness eclipsed in her absolute wonder. He suddenly grins.*) I guess you think I think a lot of myself!

Laura. No — o-o-o, I —

Jim. Now how about you? Isn't there something you take more interest in than anything else?

Laura. Well, I do — as I said — have my — glass collection —

A peal of girlish laughter from the kitchen.

Jim. I'm not right sure I know what you're talking about. What kind of glass is it?

Laura. Little articles of it, they're ornaments mostly! Most of them are little animals made out of glass, the tiniest little animals in the world. Mother calls them a glass menagerie! Here's an example of one, if you'd like to see it! This one is one of the oldest. It's nearly thirteen. (*He stretches out his hand.*) (*Music: "The Glass Menagerie."*) Oh, be careful — if you breathe, it breaks!

Jim. I'd better not take it. I'm pretty clumsy with things.

Laura. Go on, I trust you with him! (*Places it in his palm.*) There now — you're holding him gently! Hold him over the light, he loves the light! You see how the light shines through him?

Jim. It sure does shine!

Laura. I shouldn't be partial, but he is my favorite one.

Jim. What kind of thing is this one supposed to be?

Laura. Haven't you noticed the single horn on his forehead?

Jim. A unicorn, huh?

Laura. Mmm-hmmm!

Jim. Unicorns, aren't they extinct in the modern world?

Laura. I know!

Jim. Poor little fellow, he must feel sort of lonesome.

Laura (*smiling*). Well, if he does he doesn't complain about it. He stays on a shelf with some horses that don't have horns and all of them seem to get along nicely together.

Jim. How do you know?

Laura (*lightly*). I haven't heard any arguments among them!

Jim (*grinning*). No arguments, huh? Well, that's a pretty good sign! Where shall I set him?

Laura. Put him on the table. They all like a change of scenery once in a while!

Jim (*stretching*). Well, well, well, well — Look how big my shadow is when I stretch!

Laura. Oh, oh, yes — it stretches across the ceiling!

Jim (*crossing to door*). I think it's stopped raining. (*Opens fire-escape door.*) Where does the music come from?

Laura. From the Paradise Dance Hall across the alley.

Jim. How about cutting the rug a little, Miss Wingfield?

Laura. Oh, I —

Jim. Or is your program filled up? Let me have a look at it. (*Grasps imaginary card.*) Why, every dance is taken! I'll have to scratch some out. (*Waltz music: "La Golondrina."*) Ahhh, a waltz! (*He executes some sweeping turns by himself then holds his arms toward Laura.*)

Laura (*breathlessly*). I — can't dance!

Jim. There you go, that inferiority stuff!

Laura. I've never danced in my life!

Jim. Come on, try!

Laura. Oh, but I'd step on you!

Jim. I'm not made out of glass.

Laura. How — how — how do we start?

Jim. Just leave it to me. You hold your arms out a little.

Laura. Like this?

Jim. A little bit higher. Right. Now don't tighten up, that's the main thing about it — relax.

Laura (*laughing breathlessly*). It's hard not to.

Jim. Okay.

Laura. I'm afraid you can't budge me.

Jim. What do you bet I can't? (*He swings her into motion.*)

Laura. Goodness, yes, you can!

Jim. Let yourself go, now, Laura, just let yourself go.

Laura. I'm —

Jim. Come on!

Laura. Trying.

Jim. Not so stiff — Easy does it!

Laura. I know but I'm —

Jim. Loosen th' backbone! There now, that's a lot better.

Laura. Am I?

Jim. Lots, lots better! (*He moves her about the room in a clumsy waltz.*)

Laura. Oh, my!

Jim. Ha-ha!

Laura. Goodness, yes you can!

Jim. Ha-ha-ha! (*They suddenly bump into the table. Jim stops.*) What did we hit on?

Laura. Table.

Jim. Did something fall off it? I think —

Laura. Yes.

Jim. I hope it wasn't the little glass horse with the horn!

Laura. Yes.

Jim. Aw, aw, aw. Is it broken?

Laura. Now it is just like all the other horses.

Jim. It's lost its —

Laura. Horn! It doesn't matter. Maybe it's a blessing in disguise.

Jim.   You'll never forgive me. I bet that that was your favorite piece of glass.

Laura.   I don't have favorites much. It's no tragedy, Freckles. Glass breaks so easily. No matter how careful you are. The traffic jars the shelves and things fall off them.

Jim.   Still I'm awfully sorry that I was the cause.

Laura (*smiling*).   I'll just imagine he had an operation. The horn was removed to make him feel less — freakish! (*They both laugh.*) Now he will feel more at home with the other horses, the ones that don't have horns . . .

Jim.   Ha-ha, that's very funny! (*Suddenly serious.*) I'm glad to see that you have a sense of humor. You know — you're — well — very different! Surprisingly different from anyone else I know! (*His voice becomes soft and hesitant with a genuine feeling.*) Do you mind me telling you that? (*Laura is abashed beyond speech.*) You make me feel sort of — I don't know how to put it! I'm usually pretty good at expressing things, but — This is something that I don't know how to say! (*Laura touches her throat and clears it — turns the broken unicorn in her hands.*) (*Even softer.*) Has anyone ever told you that you were pretty?

Pause: Music.

> (*Laura looks up slowly, with wonder, and shakes her head.*) Well, you are! In a very different way from anyone else. And all the nicer because of the difference, too. (*His voice becomes low and husky. Laura turns away, nearly faint with the novelty of her emotions.*) I wish that you were my sister. I'd teach you to have some confidence in yourself. The different people are not like other people, but being different is nothing to be ashamed of. Because other people are not such wonderful people. They're one hundred times one thousand. You're one times one! They walk all over the earth. You just stay here. They're common as — weeds, but — you — well, you're — *Blue Roses!*

(*Image on screen: Blue Roses.*)
(*Music changes.*)

Laura.   But blue is wrong for — roses . . .

Jim.   It's right for you — You're — pretty!

Laura.   In what respect am I pretty?

Jim.   In all respects — believe me! Your eyes — your hair — are pretty! Your hands are pretty! (*He catches hold of her hand.*) You think I'm making this up because I'm invited to dinner and have to be nice. Oh, I could do that! I could put on an act for you, Laura, and say lots of things without being very sincere. But this time I am. I'm talking to you sincerely. I happened to notice you had this inferiority complex that keeps you from feeling comfortable with people. Somebody needs to build your confidence up and make you proud instead of shy and turning away and — blushing — Somebody ought to — ought to — kiss you, Laura! (*His hand slips slowly up her arm to her shoulder.*) (*Music* *swells tumultuously.) (He suddenly turns her about and kisses her on the lips. When he releases her Laura sinks on the sofa with a bright, dazed look. Jim backs away and fishes in his pocket for a cigarette.) (Legend on screen: "Souvenir.")* Stumble-john! *(He lights the cigarette, avoiding her look. There is a peal of girlish laughter from Amanda in the kitchen. Laura slowly raises and opens her hand. It still contains the little broken glass animal. She looks at it with a tender, bewildered expression.)* Stumble-john! I shouldn't have done that — That was way off the beam. You don't smoke, do you? *(She looks up, smiling, not hearing the question. He sits beside her a little gingerly. She looks at him speechlessly — waiting. He coughs decorously and moves a little farther aside as he considers the situation and senses her feelings, dimly, with perturbation. Gently.)* Would you — care for a — mint? *(She doesn't seem to hear him but her look grows brighter even.)* Peppermint — Life Saver? My pocket's a regular drug store — wherever I go . . . *(He pops a mint in his mouth. Then gulps and decides to make a clean breast of it. He speaks slowly and gingerly.)* Laura, you know, if I had a sister like you, I'd do the same thing as Tom. I'd bring out fellows — introduce her to them. The right type of boys of a type to — appreciate her. Only — well — he made a mistake about me. Maybe I've got no call to be saying this. That may not have been the idea in having me over. But what if it was? There's nothing wrong about that. The only trouble is that in my case — I'm not in a situation to — do the right thing. I can't take down your number and say I'll phone. I can't call up next week and — ask for a date. I thought I had better explain the situation in case you misunderstood it and — hurt your feelings. . . . *(Pause. Slowly, very slowly, Laura's look changes, her eyes returning slowly from his to the ornament in her palm.)*

Amanda utters another gay laugh in the kitchen.

Laura *(faintly).*   You — won't — call again?

Jim.   No, Laura, I can't. *(He rises from the sofa.)* As I was just explaining, I've — got strings on me, Laura, I've — been going steady! I go out all the time with a girl named Betty. She's a home-girl like you, and Catholic, and Irish, and in a great many ways we — get along fine. I met her last summer on a moonlight boat trip up the river to Alton, on the *Majestic*. Well — right away from the start it was — love! *(Legend: Love!) (Laura sways slightly forward and grips the arm of the sofa. He fails to notice, now enrapt in his own comfortable being.)* Being in love has made a new man of me! *(Leaning stiffly forward, clutching the arm of the sofa, Laura struggles visibly with her storm. But Jim is oblivious, she is a long way off.)* The power of love is really pretty tremendous! Love is something that — changes the whole world, Laura! *(The storm abates a little and Laura leans back. He notices her again.)* It happened that Betty's aunt took sick, she got a wire and had to go to Centralia. So Tom — when he asked me to dinner — I naturally just accepted the invitation, not knowing that you — that he — that I — *(He stops awkwardly.)* Huh —

I'm a stumble-john! (*He flops back on the sofa. The holy candles in the altar of Laura's face have been snuffed out! There is a look of almost infinite desolation. Jim glances at her uneasily.*) I wish that you would — say something. (*She bites her lip which was trembling and then bravely smiles. She opens her hand again on the broken glass ornament. Then she gently takes his hand and raises it level with her own. She carefully places the unicorn in the palm of his hand, then pushes his fingers closed upon it.*) What are you — doing that for? You want me to have him? — Laura? (*She nods.*) What for?

Laura. A — souvenir . . .

She rises unsteadily and crouches beside the Victrola to wind it up.
(*Legend on screen: "Things Have a Way of Turning Out So Badly."*)
(*Or image: "Gentleman caller waving good-bye! — Gaily."*)
At this moment Amanda rushes brightly back in the front room. She bears a pitcher of fruit punch in an old-fashioned cut-glass pitcher and a plate of macaroons. The plate has a gold border and poppies painted on it.

Amanda. Well, well, well! Isn't the air delightful after the shower? I've made you children a little liquid refreshment. (*Turns gaily to the gentleman caller.*) Jim, do you know that song about lemonade?
"Lemonade, lemonade
Made in the shade and stirred with a spade —
Good enough for any old maid!"

Jim (*uneasily*). Ha-ha! No — I never heard it.

Amanda. Why, Laura! You look so serious!

Jim. We were having a serious conversation.

Amanda. Good! Now you're better acquainted!

Jim (*uncertainly*). Ha-ha! Yes.

Amanda. You modern young people are much more serious-minded than my generation. I was so gay as a girl!

Jim. You haven't changed, Mrs. Wingfield.

Amanda. Tonight I'm rejuvenated! The gaiety of the occasion, Mr. O'Connor! (*She tosses her head with a peal of laughter. Spills lemonade.*) Oooo! I'm baptizing myself!

Jim. Here — let me —

Amanda (*setting the pitcher down*). There now. I discovered we had some maraschino cherries. I dumped them in, juice and all!

Jim. You shouldn't have gone to that trouble, Mrs. Wingfield.

Amanda. Trouble, trouble? Why it was loads of fun! Didn't you hear me cutting up in the kitchen? I bet your ears were burning! I told Tom how outdone with him I was for keeping you to himself so long a time! He should have brought you over much, much sooner! Well, now that you've found your way, I want you to be a very frequent caller! Not just occasional but all the time. Oh, we're going to have a lot of gay times together! I see them coming! Mmm, just breathe that air! So fresh, and the moon's so pretty! I'll skip back out — I know where my place is when young folks are having a — serious conversation!

Jim. Oh, don't go out, Mrs. Wingfield. The fact of the matter is I've got to be going.

Amanda. Going, now? You're joking! Why, it's only the shank of the evening, Mr. O'Connor!

Jim. Well, you know how it is.

Amanda. You mean you're a young workingman and have to keep working-men's hours. We'll let you off early tonight. But only on the condition that next time you stay later. What's the best night for you? Isn't Saturday night the best night for you workingmen?

Jim. I have a couple of time-clocks to punch, Mrs. Wingfield. One at morning, another one at night!

Amanda. My, but you *are* ambitious! You work at night, too?

Jim. No, Ma'am, not work but — Betty! (*He crosses deliberately to pick up his hat. The band at the Paradise Dance Hall goes into a tender waltz.*)

Amanda. Betty? Betty? Who's — Betty! (*There is an ominous cracking sound in the sky.*)

Jim. Oh, just a girl. The girl I go steady with! (*He smiles charmingly. The sky falls.*)

(*Legend: "The Sky Falls."*)

Amanda (*a long-drawn exhalation*). Ohhhh . . . Is it a serious romance, Mr. O'Connor?

Jim. We're going to be married the second Sunday in June.

Amanda. Ohhhh — how nice! Tom didn't mention that you were engaged to be married.

Jim. The cat's not out of the bag at the warehouse yet. You know how they are. They call you Romeo and stuff like that. (*He stops at the oval mirror to put on his hat. He carefully shapes the brim and the crown to give a discreetly dash-ing effect.*) It's been a wonderful evening, Mrs. Wingfield. I guess this is what they mean by Southern hospitality.

Amanda. It really wasn't anything at all.

Jim. I hope it don't seem like I'm rushing off. But I promised Betty I'd pick her up at the Wabash depot, an' by the time I get my jalopy down there her train'll be in. Some women are pretty upset if you keep 'em waiting.

Amanda. Yes, I know — The tyranny of women! (*Extends her hand.*) Good-bye, Mr. O'Connor. I wish you luck — and happiness — and success! All three of them, and so does Laura — Don't you, Laura?

Laura. Yes!

Jim (*taking her hand*). Good-bye, Laura. I'm certainly going to treasure that souvenir. And don't you forget the good advice I gave you. (*Raises his voice to a cheery shout.*) So long, Shakespeare! Thanks again, ladies — Good night!

He grins and ducks jauntily out.

Still bravely grimacing, Amanda closes the door on the gentleman caller. Then she turns back to the room with a puzzled expression. She and Laura don't dare to face each other. Laura crouches beside the Victrola to wind it.

Amanda *(faintly).*   Things have a way of turning out so badly. I don't believe that I would play the Victrola. Well, well — well — Our gentleman caller was engaged to be married! Tom!

Tom *(from back).*   Yes, Mother?

Amanda.   Come in here a minute. I want to tell you something awfully funny.

Tom *(enters with macaroon and a glass of the lemonade).*   Has the gentleman caller gotten away already?

Amanda.   The gentleman caller has made an early departure. What a wonderful joke you played on us!

Tom.   How do you mean?

Amanda.   You didn't mention that he was engaged to be married.

Tom.   Jim? Engaged?

Amanda.   That's what he just informed us.

Tom.   I'll be jiggered! I didn't know about that.

Amanda.   That seems very peculiar.

Tom.   What's peculiar about it?

Amanda.   Didn't you call him your best friend down at the warehouse?

Tom.   He is, but how did I know?

Amanda.   It seems extremely peculiar that you wouldn't know your best friend was going to be married!

Tom.   The warehouse is where I work, not where I know things about people!

Amanda.   You don't know things anywhere! You live in a dream; you manufacture illusions! *(He crosses to door.)* Where are you going?

Tom.   I'm going to the movies.

Amanda.   That's right, now that you've had us make such fools of ourselves. The effort, the preparations, all the expense! The new floor lamp, the rug, the clothes for Laura! All for what? To entertain some other girl's fiancé! Go to the movies, go! Don't think about us, a mother deserted, an unmarried sister who's crippled and has no job! Don't let anything interfere with your selfish pleasure! Just go, go, go — to the movies!

Tom.   All right, I will! The more you shout about my selfishness to me the quicker I'll go, and I won't go to the movies!

Amanda.   Go, then! Then go to the moon — you selfish dreamer!

Tom smashes his glass on the floor. He plunges out on the fire-escape, slamming the door. Laura screams — cut by door.

Dance-hall music up. Tom goes to the rail and grips it desperately, lifting his face in the chill white moonlight penetrating the narrow abyss of the alley.

(Legend on screen: "And So Good-Bye . . .")

Tom's closing speech is timed with the interior pantomime. The interior scene is played as though viewed through sound-proof glass. Amanda appears to be making a comforting speech to Laura who is huddled upon the sofa. Now that we cannot hear the mother's speech, her silliness is gone and she has dignity and tragic beauty. Laura's dark hair hides her face until at the end of the speech she lifts it to smile at her mother. Amanda's gestures are slow and graceful, almost dancelike, as she comforts the daughter. At the end of her speech she glances a moment at the father's picture — then withdraws through the portieres. At close of Tom's speech, Laura blows out the candles, ending the play.

Tom.   I didn't go to the moon, I went much further — for time is the longest distance between two places — Not long after that I was fired for writing a poem on the lid of a shoe-box. I left Saint Louis. I descended the steps of this fire-escape for a last time and followed, from then on, in my father's footsteps, attempting to find in motion what was lost in space — I traveled around a great deal. The cities swept about me like dead leaves, leaves that were brightly colored but torn away from the branches. I would have stopped, but I was pursued by something. It always came upon me unawares, taking me altogether by surprise. Perhaps it was a familiar bit of music. Perhaps it was only a piece of transparent glass — Perhaps I am walking along a street at night, in some strange city, before I have found companions. I pass the lighted window of a shop where perfume is sold. The window is filled with pieces of colored glass, tiny transparent bottles in delicate colors, like bits of a shattered rainbow. Then all at once my sister touches my shoulder. I turn around and look into her eyes. . . . Oh, Laura, Laura, I tried to leave you behind me, but I am more faithful than I intended to be! I reach for a cigarette, I cross the street, I run into the movies or a bar, I buy a drink, I speak to the nearest stranger — anything that can blow your candles out! *(Laura bends over the candles)* — for nowadays the world is lit by lightning! Blow out your candles, Laura — and so good-bye . . .

She blows the candles out.
(The scene dissolves.)

For Analysis

1. Who is the central character in the play? Explain.

2. What does the glass menagerie symbolize? Specifically, what does the unicorn symbolize? Why does Laura give the unicorn, after its horn has broken off, to Jim?

3. In his address at the start of the play, Tom tells the audience that Jim "is the most realistic character in the play . . . an emissary from a world of reality that we were somehow set apart from." What is the world of reality Jim represents? Is Tom paying him a compliment?

4. In his opening address, Tom sketches in "the social background of the play." How does this background help us to understand the Wingfield family?

5. Although she has refused to accept the characterization from Tom, in her final words Amanda refers to Laura as crippled. Why?

6. Is Tom's escape as complete as his father's seems to have been? Explain.

7. Explain why you do or do not find effective the device of projecting images and titles on a screen above the stage.

On Style

1. How does the fact that the play is presented as Tom's memory shape its structure and meaning?

2. Are the nonrealistic staging techniques effective and appropriate to the **theme** of the play?

Making Connections

1. In what ways is Tom's function in this play similar to the function of the chorus in Sophocles' *Antigonê* (p. 467)? In what ways is it different?

2. Compare and contrast the use of nonrealistic devices in this play and in Arthur Miller's *Death of a Salesman* (p. 790). Do you find one or the other of the plays more successful in employing these devices?

Writing Topics

1. Are we meant to admire Amanda for holding her family together under very difficult circumstances or to condemn her for her destructive illusions? With your answer in mind, explain the statement in the final stage direction: "Now that we cannot hear the mother's speech, her silliness is gone and she has dignity and tragic beauty."

2. Examine the nonrealistic, unconventional techniques Williams uses, such as the screen projections, and write an analysis of how they contribute to the overall effect of the work.

Essays

Langston Hughes   (1902–1967)

Salvation   1940

I was saved from sin when I was going on thirteen. But not really saved. It happened like this. There was a big revival at my Auntie Reed's church. Every night for weeks there had been much preaching, singing, praying, and shouting, and some very hardened sinners had been brought to Christ, and the membership of the church had grown by leaps and bounds. Then just before the revival ended, they held a special meeting for children, "to bring the young lambs to the fold." My aunt spoke of it for days ahead. That night I was escorted to the front row and placed on the mourners' bench with all the other young sinners, who had not yet been brought to Jesus.

My aunt told me that when you were saved you saw a light, and something happened to you inside! And Jesus came into your life! And God was with you from then on! She said you could see and hear and feel Jesus in your soul. I believed her. I had heard a great many old people say the same thing and it seemed to me they ought to know. So I sat there calmly in the hot, crowded church, waiting for Jesus to come to me.

The preacher preached a wonderful rhythmical sermon, all moans and shouts and lonely cries and dire pictures of hell, and then he sang a song about the ninety and nine safe in the fold, but one little lamb was left out in the cold. Then he said: "Won't you come? Won't you come to Jesus? Young lambs, won't you come?" And he held out his arms to all us young sinners there on the mourners' bench. And the little girls cried. And some of them jumped up and went to Jesus right away. But most of us just sat there.

A great many old people came and knelt around us and prayed, old women with jet-black faces and braided hair, old men with work-gnarled hands. And the church sang a song about the lower lights are burning, some poor sinners to be saved. And the whole building rocked with prayer and song.

Still I kept waiting to *see* Jesus.

5

Finally all the young people had gone to the altar and were saved, but one boy and me. He was a rounder's son named Westley. Westley and I were surrounded by sisters and deacons praying. It was very hot in the church, and getting late now. Finally Westley said to me in a whisper: "God damn! I'm tired o' sitting here. Let's get up and be saved." So he got up and was saved.

Then I was left all alone on the mourners' bench. My aunt came and knelt at my knees and cried, while prayers and song swirled all around me in the little church. The whole congregation prayed for me alone, in a mighty wail of moans and voices. And I kept waiting serenely for Jesus, waiting, waiting — but he didn't come. I wanted to see him, but nothing happened to me. Nothing! I wanted something to happen to me, but nothing happened.

I heard the songs and the minister saying: "Why don't you come? My dear child, why don't you come to Jesus? Jesus is waiting for you. He wants you. Why don't you come? Sister Reed, what is this child's name?"

"Langston," my aunt sobbed.

"Langston, why don't you come? Why don't you come and be saved? Oh,   10 Lamb of God! Why don't you come?"

Now it was really getting late. I began to be ashamed of myself, holding everything up so long. I began to wonder what God thought about Westley, who certainly hadn't seen Jesus either, but who was now sitting proudly on the platform, swinging his knickerbockered legs and grinning down at me, surrounded by deacons and old women on their knees praying. God had not struck Westley dead for taking his name in vain or for lying in the temple. So I decided that maybe to save further trouble, I'd better lie, too, and say that Jesus had come, and get up and be saved.

So I got up.

Suddenly the whole room broke into a sea of shouting, as they saw me rise. Waves of rejoicing swept the place. Women leaped in the air. My aunt threw her arms around me. The minister took me by the hand and led me to the platform.

When things quieted down, in a hushed silence, punctuated by a few ecstatic "Amens," all the new young lambs were blessed in the name of God. Then joyous singing filled the room.

That night, for the last time in my life but one — for I was a big boy twelve   15 years old — I cried. I cried, in bed alone, and couldn't stop. I buried my head under the quilts, but my aunt heard me. She woke up and told my uncle I was crying because the Holy Ghost had come into my life, and because I had seen Jesus. But I was really crying because I couldn't bear to tell her that I had lied, that I had deceived everybody in the church, that I hadn't seen Jesus, and that now I didn't believe there was a Jesus any more, since he didn't come to help me.

For Analysis

1. Is the tone of this essay comic or serious or both? Explain.
2. What role does Westley (para. 6) play in the narrative?

3. Can the word *salvation* as Hughes uses it be construed in more than one way? Explain.

4. Is this a story about the loss of religious faith? Explain.

On Style
Discuss how the **point of view** of a narrator who looks back on a childhood experience helps define the meaning of the experience.

Making Connections
1. Compare and contrast Hughes's loss of innocence with that of the narrator in O'Connor's "My Oedipus Complex" (p. 109) and Sylvia in Bambara's "The Lesson" (p. 134).

2. Compare and contrast the narrator's attitude toward adult authority in this story with Sylvia's in Bambara's "The Lesson" (p. 134).

Writing Topic
Describe an experience where public pressure forced you to express an opinion or belief that you didn't really hold, or to act in a way you otherwise would not have.

Joan Didion   (b. 1934)

On Morality   1965

As it happens I am in Death Valley, in a room at the Enterprise Motel and Trailer Park, and it is July, and it is hot. In fact it is 119°. I cannot seem to make the air conditioner work, but there is a small refrigerator, and I can wrap ice cubes in a towel and hold them against the small of my back. With the help of the ice cubes I have been trying to think, because *The American Scholar*[1] asked me to, in some abstract way about "morality," a word I distrust more every day, but my mind veers inflexibly toward the particular.

Here are some particulars. At midnight last night, on the road in from Las Vegas to Death Valley Junction, a car hit a shoulder and turned over. The driver, very young and apparently drunk, was killed instantly. His girl was found alive but bleeding internally, deep in shock. I talked this afternoon to the nurse who had driven the girl to the nearest doctor, 185 miles across the floor of the Valley and three ranges of lethal mountain road. The nurse explained that her husband, a talc miner, had stayed on the highway with the boy's body until the coroner could get over the mountains from Bishop, at dawn today. "You can't just leave a body on the highway," she said. "It's immoral."

It was one instance in which I did not distrust the word, because she meant something quite specific. She meant that if a body is left alone for even a few minutes on the desert, the coyotes close in and eat the flesh. Whether or not a corpse is torn apart by coyotes may seem only a sentimental consideration, but of course it is more: one of the promises we make to one another is that we will try to retrieve our casualties, try not to abandon our dead to the coyotes. If we have been taught to keep our promises — if, in the simplest terms, our upbringing is good enough — we stay with the body, or have bad dreams.

I am talking, of course, about the kind of social code that is sometimes called, usually pejoratively, "wagon-train morality." In fact that is precisely what it is. For better or worse, we are what we learned as children: my own childhood was illuminated by graphic litanies of the grief awaiting those who failed in their loyalties to each other. The Donner-Reed Party,[2] starving in the Sierra snows, all the ephemera of civilization gone save that one vestigial taboo, the provision that no one should eat his own blood kin. The Jayhawkers, who quarreled and separated not far from where I am tonight. Some of them died in the

---

[1] A general-interest journal published by the Phi Beta Kappa Society.

[2] A group of eighty-seven people who tried to cross the mountains into California during the stormy winter of 1846. The forty-seven who survived the ordeal ate the flesh of those who died.

Funerals[3] and some of them died down near Badwater and most of the rest of them died in the Panamints. A woman who got through gave the Valley its name. Some might say that the Jayhawkers were killed by the desert summer, and the Donner Party by the mountain winter, by circumstances beyond control; we were taught instead that they had somewhere abdicated their responsibilities, somehow breached their primary loyalties, or they would not have found themselves helpless in the mountain winter or the desert summer, would not have given way to acrimony, would not have deserted one another, would not have *failed.* In brief, we heard such stories as cautionary tales, and they still suggest the only kind of "morality" that seems to me to have any but the most potentially mendacious meaning.

You are quite possibly impatient with me by now; I am talking, you want to 5 say, about a "morality" so primitive that it scarcely deserves the name, a code that has as its point only survival, not the attainment of the ideal good. Exactly. Particularly out here tonight, in this country so ominous and terrible that to live in it is to live with antimatter, it is difficult to believe that "the good" is a knowable quantity. Let me tell you what it is like out here tonight. Stories travel at night on the desert. Someone gets in his pickup and drives a couple of hundred miles for a beer, and he carries news of what is happening, back wherever he came from. Then he drives another hundred miles for another beer, and passes along stories from the last place as well as from the one before; it is a network kept alive by people whose instincts tell them that if they do not keep moving at night on the desert they will lose all reason. Here is a story that is going around the desert tonight: over across the Nevada line, sheriff's deputies are diving in some underground pools, trying to retrieve a couple of bodies known to be in the hole. The widow of one of the drowned boys is over there; she is eighteen, and pregnant, and is said not to leave the hole. The divers go down and come up, and she just stands there and stares into the water. They have been diving for ten days but have found no bottom to the caves, no bodies and no trace of them, only the black 90° water going down and down and down, and a single translucent fish, not classified. The story tonight is that one of the divers has been hauled up incoherent, out of his head, shouting — until they got him out of there so that the widow could not hear — about water that got hotter instead of cooler as he went down, about light flickering through the water, about magma, about underground nuclear testing.

That is the tone stories take out here, and there are quite a few of them tonight. And it is more than the stories alone. Across the road at the Faith Community Church a couple of dozen old people, come here to live in trailers and die in the sun, are holding a prayer sing. I cannot hear them and do not want to. What I can hear are occasional coyotes and a constant chorus of "Baby the Rain Must Fall" from the jukebox in the Snake Room next door, and if I were also to

---

[3] The Funerals and the Panamints are mountain ranges close to Death Valley.

hear those dying voices, those Midwestern voices drawn to this lunar country for some unimaginable atavistic rites, *rock of ages cleft for me,* I think I would lose my own reason. Every now and then I imagine I hear a rattlesnake, but my husband says that it is a faucet, a paper rustling, the wind. Then he stands by a window, and plays a flashlight over the dry wash outside.

What does it mean? It means nothing manageable. There is some sinister hysteria in the air out here tonight, some hint of the monstrous perversion to which any human idea can come. "I followed my own conscience." "I did what I thought was right." How many madmen have said it and meant it? How many murderers? Klaus Fuchs said it, and the men who committed the Mountain Meadows Massacre said it, and Alfred Rosenberg[4] said it. And, as we are rotely and rather presumptuously reminded by those who would say it now, Jesus said it. Maybe we have all said it, and maybe we have been wrong. Except on that most primitive level — our loyalties to those we love — what could be more arrogant than to claim the primacy of personal conscience? ("Tell me," a rabbi asked Daniel Bell when he said, as a child, that he did not believe in God. "Do you think God cares?") At least some of the time, the world appears to me as a painting by Hieronymus Bosch;[5] were I to follow my conscience then, it would lead me out onto the desert with Marion Faye, out to where he stood in *The Deer Park*[6] looking east to Los Alamos and praying, as if for rain, that it would happen: "*. . . let it come and clear the rot and the stench and the stink, let it come for all of everywhere, just so it comes and the world stands clear in the white dead dawn.*"

Of course you will say that I do not have the right, even if I had the power, to inflict that unreasonable conscience upon you; nor do I want you to inflict your conscience, however reasonable, however enlightened, upon me. ("We must be aware of the dangers which lie in our most generous wishes," Lionel Trilling[7] once wrote. "Some paradox of our nature leads us, when once we have made our fellow men the objects of our enlightened interest, to go on to make them the objects of our pity, then of our wisdom, ultimately of our coercion.") That the ethic of conscience is intrinsically insidious seems scarcely a revelatory point, but it is one raised with increasing infrequency; even those who do raise it tend to *segue* with troubling readiness into the quite contradictory position that

---

[4] Klaus Fuchs fled Germany to the United States, where he worked on the development of the atomic bomb during World War II. He moved to Great Britain to assume an important position at the British atomic energy center. He was convicted and imprisoned for providing atomic energy secrets to the Soviet Union. The Mountain Meadows Massacre occurred in September 1857 in Utah. A group of 130 to 140 emigrants heading for California were attacked by Indians incited and joined by Mormons angry at the treatment they had received during their earlier trek across the continent. All but seventeen children were massacred. Alfred Rosenberg was a Nazi leader often called "The Grand Inquisitor of the Third Reich." He was hanged for war crimes in 1946.

[5] Hieronymus Bosch (1450?–1516), a Dutch painter of fantastic and hellish images.

[6] A novel by Norman Mailer.

[7] Lionel Trilling (1905–1975), an eminent critic of literature and modern culture.

the ethic of conscience is dangerous when it is "wrong," and admirable when it is "right."

You see I want to be quite obstinate about insisting that we have no way of knowing — beyond that fundamental loyalty to the social code — what is "right" and what is "wrong," what is "good" and what "evil." I dwell so upon this because the most disturbing aspect of "morality" seems to me to be the frequency with which the word now appears; in the press, on television, in the most perfunctory kinds of conversation. Questions of straightforward power (or survival) politics, questions of quite indifferent public policy, questions of almost anything: they are all assigned these factitious moral burdens. There is something facile going on, some self-indulgence at work. Of course we would all like to "believe" in something, like to assuage our private guilts in public causes, like to lose our tiresome selves; like, perhaps, to transform the white flag of defeat at home into the brave white banner of battle away from home. And of course it is all right to do that; that is how, immemorially, things have gotten done. But I think it is all right only so long as we do not delude ourselves about what we are doing, and why. It is all right only so long as we remember that all the *ad hoc* committees, all the picket lines, all the brave signatures in *The New York Times*, all the tools of agitprop straight across the spectrum, do not confer upon anyone any *ipso facto* virtue. It is all right only so long as we recognize that the end may or may not be expedient, may or may not be a good idea, but in any case has nothing to do with "morality." Because when we start deceiving ourselves into thinking not that we want something or need something, not that it is a pragmatic necessity for us to have it, but that it is a *moral imperative* that we have it, then is when we join the fashionable madmen, and then is when the thin whine of hysteria is heard in the land, and then is when we are in bad trouble. And I suspect we are already there.

For Analysis

1. What instances of "wagon-train" or "primitive" morality does Didion cite? How would you characterize that morality? Why is Didion comfortable with that sort of morality?

2. Why is Didion pleased that the music from a jukebox drowns out the singing of the prayer meeting near the motel (para. 6)? How does her identification of the musical pieces contribute to the argument of this essay?

3. What is the point of her including the speech from *The Deer Park* (para. 7)?

4. What names and, by implication, events does Didion use to illustrate some possibilities of abstract morality?

5. What role does the quotation from Lionel Trilling (para. 8) play in the essay?

On Style

As Didion states in the first paragraph, this essay examines an abstraction — morality. Comment on the author's use of concrete illustrations to illuminate abstract ideas.

Making Connections

1. Didion says that "we are what we learned as children" (para. 4). Are your own moral values reflections of what you learned as a child, or did those values change as you grew older? Explain.

2. Compare and contrast Didion's views on morality with King's in "Letter from Birmingham Jail" (p. 634).

Writing Topics

1. Focusing on the next-to-last sentence of this piece, write an essay in which you distinguish between *needs, wants,* and *pragmatic necessities* on the one hand, and *moral imperatives* on the other. Give examples of each, and suggest the relationship each bears to some meaning of the word *morality.* Conclude with your own judgment on the usefulness or necessity of moral imperatives.

2. Write an essay describing a personal experience that required you to make a choice among alternatives that were not clearly "right" or "wrong." Explain how you resolved the dilemma.

Lars Eighner   (b. 1948)

On Dumpster Diving[1] 1993

Long before I began Dumpster diving I was impressed with Dumpsters, enough so that I wrote the Merriam-Webster research service to discover what I could about the word *Dumpster.* I learned from them that it is a proprietary word belonging to the Dempster Dumpster company. Since then I have dutifully capitalized the word, although it was lowercased in almost all the citations Merriam-Webster photocopied for me. Dempster's word is too apt. I have never heard these things called anything but Dumpsters. I do not know anyone who knows the generic name for these objects. From time to time I have heard a wino or hobo give some corrupted credit to the original and call them Dipsy Dumpsters.

I began Dumpster diving about a year before I became homeless.

I prefer the word *scavenging* and use the word *scrounging* when I mean to be obscure. I have heard people, evidently meaning to be polite, use the word *foraging*, but I prefer to reserve that word for gathering nuts and berries and such, which I do also according to the season and the opportunity. *Dumpster diving* seems to me to be a little too cute and, in my case, inaccurate because I lack the athletic ability to lower myself into the Dumpsters as the true divers do, much to their increased profit.

I like the frankness of the word *scavenging*, which I can hardly think of without picturing a big black snail on an aquarium wall. I live from the refuse of others. I am a scavenger. I think it a sound and honorable niche, although if I could I would naturally prefer to live the comfortable consumer life, perhaps — and only perhaps — as a slightly less wasteful consumer, owing to what I have learned as a scavenger.

While Lizbeth[2] and I were still living in the shack on Avenue B as my savings 5 ran out, I put almost all my sporadic income into rent. The necessities of daily life I began to extract from Dumpsters. Yes, we ate from them. Except for jeans, all my clothes came from Dumpsters. Boom boxes, candles, bedding, toilet paper, a virgin male love doll, medicine, books, a typewriter, dishes, furnishings, and change, sometimes amounting to many dollars — I acquired many things from the Dumpsters.

---

[1] This chapter was composed while the author was homeless. The present tense has been preserved [Eighner's note].

[2] The author's dog, apparently a Labrador mix.

I have learned much as a scavenger. I mean to put some of what I have learned down here, beginning with the practical art of Dumpster diving and proceeding to the abstract.

What is safe to eat?

After all, the finding of objects is becoming something of an urban art. Even respectable employed people will sometimes find something tempting sticking out of a Dumpster or standing beside one. Quite a number of people, not all of them of the bohemian type, are willing to brag that they found this or that piece in the trash. But eating from Dumpsters is what separates the dilettanti from the professionals. Eating safely from the Dumpsters involves three principles: using the senses and common sense to evaluate the condition of the found materials, knowing the Dumpsters of a given area and checking them regularly, and seeking always to answer the question "Why was this discarded?"

Perhaps everyone who has a kitchen and a regular supply of groceries has, at one time or another, made a sandwich and eaten half of it before discovering mold on the bread or got a mouthful of milk before realizing the milk had turned. Nothing of the sort is likely to happen to a Dumpster diver because he is constantly reminded that most food is discarded for a reason. Yet a lot of perfectly good food can be found in Dumpsters.

Canned goods, for example, turn up fairly often in the Dumpsters I frequent. 10 All except the most phobic people would be willing to eat from a can, even if it came from a Dumpster. Canned goods are among the safest of foods to be found in Dumpsters but are not utterly foolproof.

Although very rare with modern canning methods, botulism is a possibility. Most other forms of food poisoning seldom do lasting harm to a healthy person, but botulism is almost certainly fatal and often the first symptom is death. Except for carbonated beverages, all canned goods should contain a slight vacuum and suck air when first punctured. Bulging, rusty, and dented cans and cans that spew when punctured should be avoided, especially when the contents are not very acidic or syrupy.

Heat can break down the botulin, but this requires much more cooking than most people do to canned goods. To the extent that botulism occurs at all, of course, it can occur in cans on pantry shelves as well as in cans from Dumpsters. Need I say that home-canned goods are simply too risky to be recommended.

From time to time one of my companions, aware of the source of my provisions, will ask, "Do you think these crackers are really safe to eat?" For some reason it is most often the crackers they ask about.

This question has always made me angry. Of course I would not offer my companion anything I had doubts about. But more than that, I wonder why he cannot evaluate the condition of the crackers for himself. I have no special knowledge and I have been wrong before. Since he knows where the food comes from, it seems to me he ought to assume some of the responsibility for deciding what he will put in his mouth. For myself I have few qualms about dry foods such as crackers, cookies, cereal, chips, and pasta if they are free of visible contaminates and still dry and crisp. Most often such things are found in the original packaging, which is not so much a positive sign as it is the absence of a negative one.

Raw fruits and vegetables with intact skins seem perfectly safe to me, exclud- 15 ing of course the obviously rotten. Many are discarded for minor imperfections that can be pared away. Leafy vegetables, grapes, cauliflower, broccoli, and similar things may be contaminated by liquids and may be impractical to wash.

Candy, especially hard candy, is usually safe if it has not drawn ants. Chocolate is often discarded only because it has become discolored as the cocoa butter de-emulsified. Candying, after all, is one method of food preservation because pathogens do not like very sugary substances.

All of these foods might be found in any Dumpster and can be evaluated with some confidence largely on the basis of appearance. Beyond these are foods that cannot be correctly evaluated without additional information.

I began scavenging by pulling pizzas out of the Dumpster behind a pizza delivery shop. In general, prepared food requires caution, but in this case I knew when the shop closed and went to the Dumpster as soon as the last of the help left.

Such shops often get prank orders; both the orders and the products made to fill them are called *bogus*. Because help seldom stays long at these places, pizzas are often made with the wrong topping, refused on delivery for being cold, or baked incorrectly. The products to be discarded are boxed up because inventory is kept by counting boxes: A boxed pizza can be written off; an unboxed pizza does not exist.

I never placed a bogus order to increase the supply of pizzas and I believe no 20 one else was scavenging in this Dumpster. But the people in the shop became suspicious and began to retain their garbage in the shop overnight. While it lasted I had a steady supply of fresh, sometimes warm pizza. Because I knew the Dumpster I knew the source of the pizza, and because I visited the Dumpster regularly I knew what was fresh and what was yesterday's.

The area I frequent is inhabited by many affluent college students. I am not here by chance; the Dumpsters in this area are very rich. Students throw out many good things, including food. In particular they tend to throw everything out when they move at the end of a semester, before and after breaks, and around midterm, when many of them despair of college. So I find it advantageous to keep an eye on the academic calendar.

Students throw food away around breaks because they do not know whether it has spoiled or will spoil before they return. A typical discard is a half jar of peanut butter. In fact, nonorganic peanut butter does not require refrigeration and is unlikely to spoil in any reasonable time. The student does not know that, and since it is Daddy's money, the student decides not to take a chance. Opened containers require caution and some attention to the question "Why was this discarded?" But in the case of discards from student apartments, the answer may be that the item was thrown out through carelessness, ignorance, or wastefulness. This can sometimes be deduced when the item is found with many others, including some that are obviously perfectly good.

Some students, and others, approach defrosting a freezer by chucking out the whole lot. Not only do the circumstances of such a find tell the story, but also the mass of frozen goods stays cold for a long time and items may be found still frozen or freshly thawed.

Yogurt, cheese, and sour cream are items that are often thrown out while they are still good. Occasionally I find a cheese with a spot of mold, which of course I pare off, and because it is obvious why such a cheese was discarded, I treat it with less suspicion than an apparently perfect cheese found in similar circumstances. Yogurt is often discarded, still sealed, only because the expiration date on the carton had passed. This is one of my favorite finds because yogurt will keep for several days, even in warm weather.

Students throw out canned goods and staples at the end of semesters and 25 when they give up college at midterm. Drugs, pornography, spirits, and the like are often discarded when parents are expected — Dad's Day, for example. And spirits also turn up after big party weekends, presumably discarded by the newly reformed. Wine and spirits, of course, keep perfectly well even once opened, but the same cannot be said of beer.

My test for carbonated soft drinks is whether they still fizz vigorously. Many juices or other beverages are too acidic or too syrupy to cause much concern, provided they are not visibly contaminated. I have discovered nasty molds in vegetable juices, even when the product was found under its original seal; I recommend that such products be decanted slowly into a clear glass. Liquids always require some care. One hot day I found a large jug of Pat O'Brien's Hurricane mix. The jug had been opened but was still ice cold. I drank three large glasses before it became apparent to me that someone had added the rum to the mix, and not a little rum. I never tasted the rum, and by the time I began to feel the effects I had already ingested a very large quantity of the beverage. Some divers would have considered this a boon, but being suddenly intoxicated in a public place in the early afternoon is not my idea of a good time.

I have heard of people maliciously contaminating discarded food and even handouts, but mostly I have heard of this from people with vivid imaginations who have had no experience with the Dumpsters themselves. Just before the pizza shop stopped discarding its garbage at night, jalapeños began showing up on most of the thrown-out pizzas. If indeed this was meant to discourage me, it was a wasted effort because I am a native Texan.

For myself, I avoid game, poultry, pork, and egg-based foods, whether I find them raw or cooked. I seldom have the means to cook what I find, but when I do I avail myself of plentiful supplies of beef, which is often in very good condition. I suppose fish becomes disagreeable before it becomes dangerous. Lizbeth is happy to have any such thing that is past its prime and, in fact, does not recognize fish as food until it is quite strong.

Home leftovers, as opposed to surpluses from restaurants, are very often bad. Evidently, especially among students, there is a common type of personality that carefully wraps up even the smallest leftover and shoves it into the back of the refrigerator for six months or so before discarding it. Characteristic of this type are the reused jars and margarine tubs to which the remains are committed. I avoid ethnic foods I am unfamiliar with. If I do not know what it is supposed to look like when it is good, I cannot be certain I will be able to tell if it is bad.

No matter how careful I am I still get dysentery at least once a month, oftener 30 in warm weather. I do not want to paint too romantic a picture. Dumpster diving has serious drawbacks as a way of life.

I learned to scavenge gradually, on my own. Since then I have initiated several companions into the trade. I have learned that there is a predictable series of stages a person goes through in learning to scavenge.

At first the new scavenger is filled with disgust and self-loathing. He is ashamed of being seen and may lurk around, trying to duck behind things, or he may try to dive at night. (In fact, most people instinctively look away from a scavenger. By skulking around, the novice calls attention to himself and arouses suspicion. Diving at night is ineffective and needlessly messy.)

Every grain of rice seems to be a maggot. Everything seems to stink. He can wipe the egg yolk off the found can, but he cannot erase from his mind the stigma of eating garbage.

That stage passes with experience. The scavenger finds a pair of running shoes that fit and look and smell brand-new. He finds a pocket calculator in perfect working order. He finds pristine ice cream, still frozen, more than he can eat or keep. He begins to understand: People throw away perfectly good stuff, a lot of perfectly good stuff.

At this stage, Dumpster shyness begins to dissipate. The diver, after all, has 35 the last laugh. He is finding all manner of good things that are his for the taking. Those who disparage his profession are the fools, not he.

He may begin to hang on to some perfectly good things for which he has neither a use nor a market. Then he begins to take note of the things that are not perfectly good but are nearly so. He mates a Walkman with broken earphones and one that is missing a battery cover. He picks up things that he can repair.

At this stage he may become lost and never recover. Dumpsters are full of things of some potential value to someone and also of things that never have much intrinsic value but are interesting. All the Dumpster divers I have known come to the point of trying to acquire everything they touch. Why not take it, they reason, since it is all free? This is, of course, hopeless. Most divers come to realize that they must restrict themselves to items of relatively immediate utility. But in some cases the diver simply cannot control himself. I have met several of these pack-rat types. Their ideas of the values of various pieces of junk verge on the psychotic. Every bit of glass may be a diamond, they think, and all that glitters, gold.

I tend to gain weight when I am scavenging. Partly this is because I always find far more pizza and doughnuts than water-packed tuna, nonfat yogurt, and fresh vegetables. Also I have not developed much faith in the reliability of

Dumpsters as a food source, although it has been proven to me many times. I tend to eat as if I have no idea where my next meal is coming from. But mostly I just hate to see food go to waste and so I eat much more than I should. Something like this drives the obsession to collect junk.

As for collecting objects, I usually restrict myself to collecting one kind of small object at a time, such as pocket calculators, sunglasses, or campaign buttons. To live on the street I must anticipate my needs to a certain extent: I must pick up and save warm bedding I find in August because it will not be found in Dumpsters in November. As I have no access to health care, I often hoard essential drugs, such as antibiotics and antihistamines. (This course can be recommended only to those with some grounding in pharmacology. Antibiotics, for example, even when indicated are worse than useless if taken in insufficient amounts.) But even if I had a home with extensive storage space, I could not save everything that might be valuable in some contingency.

I have proprietary feelings about my Dumpsters. As I have mentioned, it is 40 no accident that I scavenge from ones where good finds are common. But my limited experience with Dumpsters in other areas suggests to me that even in poorer areas, Dumpsters, if attended with sufficient diligence, can be made to yield a livelihood. The rich students discard perfectly good kiwifruit; poorer people discard perfectly good apples. Slacks and polo shirts are found in the one place; jeans and T-shirts in the other. The population of competitors rather than the affluence of the dumpers most affects the feasibility of survival by scavenging. The large number of competitors is what puts me off the idea of trying to scavenge in places like Los Angeles.

Curiously, I do not mind my direct competition, other scavengers, so much as I hate the can scroungers.

People scrounge cans because they have to have a little cash. I have tried scrounging cans with an able-bodied companion. Afoot a can scrounger simply cannot make more than a few dollars a day. One can extract the necessities of life from the Dumpsters directly with far less effort than would be required to accumulate the equivalent value in cans. (These observations may not hold in places with container redemption laws.)

Can scroungers, then, are people who must have small amounts of cash. These are drug addicts and winos, mostly the latter because the amounts of cash are so small. Spirits and drugs do, like all other commodities, turn up in Dumpsters and the scavenger will from time to time have a half bottle of a rather good wine with his dinner. But the wino cannot survive on these occasional finds; he must have his daily dose to stave off the DTs. All the cans he can carry will buy about three bottles of Wild Irish Rose.

I do not begrudge them the cans, but can scroungers tend to tear up the Dumpsters, mixing the contents and littering the area. They become so specialized that they can see only cans. They earn my contempt by passing up change, canned goods, and readily hockable items.

There are precious few courtesies among scavengers. But it is common prac- 45 tice to set aside surplus items: pairs of shoes, clothing, canned goods, and such.

A true scavenger hates to see good stuff go to waste, and what he cannot use he leaves in good condition in plain sight.

Can scroungers lay waste to everything in their path and will stir one of a pair of good shoes to the bottom of a Dumpster, to be lost or ruined in the muck. Can scroungers will even go through individual garbage cans, something I have never seen a scavenger do.

Individual garbage cans are set out on the public easement only on garbage days. On other days going through them requires trespassing close to a dwelling. Going through individual garbage cans without scattering litter is almost impossible. Litter is likely to reduce the public's tolerance of scavenging. Individual cans are simply not as productive as Dumpsters; people in houses and duplexes do not move so often and for some reason do not tend to discard as much useful material. Moreover, the time required to go through one garbage can that serves one household is not much less than the time required to go through a Dumpster that contains the refuse of twenty apartments.

But my strongest reservation about going through individual garbage cans is that this seems to me a very personal kind of invasion to which I would object if I were a householder. Although many things in Dumpsters are obviously meant never to come to light, a Dumpster is somehow less personal.

I avoid trying to draw conclusions about the people who dump in the Dumpsters I frequent. I think it would be unethical to do so, although I know many people will find the idea of scavenger ethics too funny for words.

Dumpsters contain bank statements, correspondence, and other documents, 50 just as anyone might expect. But there are also less obvious sources of information. Pill bottles, for example. The labels bear the name of the patient, the name of the doctor, and the name of the drug. AIDS drugs and antipsychotic medicines, to name but two groups, are specific and are seldom prescribed for any other disorders. The plastic compacts for birth-control pills usually have complete label information.

Despite all this sensitive information, I have had only one apartment resident object to my going through the Dumpster. In that case it turned out the resident was a university athlete who was taking bets and who was afraid I would turn up his wager slips.

Occasionally a find tells a story. I once found a small paper bag containing some unused condoms, several partial tubes of flavored sexual lubricants, a partially used compact of birth-control pills, and the torn pieces of a picture of a young man. Clearly she was through with him and planning to give up sex altogether.

Dumpster things are often sad — abandoned teddy bears, shredded wedding books, despaired-of sales kits. I find many pets lying in state in Dumpsters. Although I hope to get off the streets so Lizbeth can have a long and comfortable old age, I know this hope is not very realistic. So I suppose when her time comes she too will go into a Dumpster. I will have no better place for her. And after all, it is fitting, since for most of her life her livelihood has come from the

Dumpster. When she finds something I think is safe that has been spilled from a Dumpster, I let her have it. She already knows the route around the best ones. I like to think that if she survives me she will have a chance of evading the dog catcher and of finding her sustenance on the route.

Silly vanities also come to rest in the Dumpsters. I am a rather accomplished needleworker. I get a lot of material from the Dumpsters. Evidently sorority girls, hoping to impress someone, perhaps themselves, with their mastery of a womanly art, buy a lot of embroider-by-number kits, work a few stitches horribly, and eventually discard the whole mess. I pull out their stitches, turn the canvas over, and work an original design. Do not think I refrain from chuckling as I make gifts from these kits.

I find diaries and journals. I have often thought of compiling a book of literary   55 found objects. And perhaps I will one day. But what I find is hopelessly commonplace and bad without being, even unconsciously, camp. College students also discard their papers. I am horrified to discover the kind of paper that now merits an A in an undergraduate course. I am grateful, however, for the number of good books and magazines the students throw out.

In the area I know best I have never discovered vermin in the Dumpsters, but there are two kinds of kitty surprise. One is alley cats whom I meet as they leap, claws first, out of Dumpsters. This is especially thrilling when I have Lizbeth in tow. The other kind of kitty surprise is a plastic garbage bag filled with some ponderous, amorphous mass. This always proves to be used cat litter.

City bees harvest doughnut glaze and this makes the Dumpster at the doughnut shop more interesting. My faith in the instinctive wisdom of animals is always shaken whenever I see Lizbeth attempt to catch a bee in her mouth, which she does whenever bees are present. Evidently some birds find Dumpsters profitable, for birdie surprise is almost as common as kitty surprise of the first kind. In hunting season all kinds of small game turn up in Dumpsters, some of it, sadly, not entirely dead. Curiously, summer and winter, maggots are uncommon.

The worst of the living and near-living hazards of the Dumpsters are the fire ants. The food they claim is not much of a loss, but they are vicious and aggressive. It is very easy to brush against some surface of the Dumpster and pick up half a dozen or more fire ants, usually in some sensitive area such as the underarm. One advantage of bringing Lizbeth along as I make Dumpster rounds is that, for obvious reasons, she is very alert to ground-based fire ants. When Lizbeth recognizes a fire-ant infestation around our feet, she does the Dance of the Zillion Fire Ants. I have learned not to ignore this warning from Lizbeth, whether I perceive the tiny ants or not, but to remove ourselves at Lizbeth's first pas de bourrée.[3] All the more so because the ants are the worst in the summer months when I wear flip-flops if I have them. (Perhaps someone will misunderstand this. Lizbeth does the Dance of the Zillion Fire Ants when she recognizes more fire ants than she cares to eat, not when she is being bitten. Since I have

---

[3] A ballet dance step.

learned to react promptly, she does not get bitten at all. It is the isolated patrol of fire ants that falls in Lizbeth's range that deserves pity. She finds them quite tasty.)

By far the best way to go through a Dumpster is to lower yourself into it. Most of the good stuff tends to settle at the bottom because it is usually weightier than the rubbish. My more athletic companions have often demonstrated to me that they can extract much good material from a Dumpster I have already been over.

To those psychologically or physically unprepared to enter a Dumpster, I rec- 60 ommend a stout stick, preferably with some barb or hook at one end. The hook can be used to grab plastic garbage bags. When I find canned goods or other objects loose at the bottom of a Dumpster, I lower a bag into it, roll the desired object into the bag, and then hoist the bag out — a procedure more easily described than executed. Much Dumpster diving is a matter of experience for which nothing will do except practice.

Dumpster diving is outdoor work, often surprisingly pleasant. It is not entirely predictable; things of interest turn up every day and some days there are finds of great value. I am always very pleased when I can turn up exactly the thing I most wanted to find. Yet in spite of the element of chance, scavenging more than most other pursuits tends to yield returns in some proportion to the effort and intelligence brought to bear. It is very sweet to turn up a few dollars in change from a Dumpster that has just been gone over by a wino.

The land is now covered with cities. The cities are full of Dumpsters. If a member of the canine race is ever able to know what it is doing, then Lizbeth knows that when we go around to the Dumpsters, we are hunting. I think of scavenging as a modern form of self-reliance. In any event, after having survived nearly ten years of government service, where everything is geared to the lowest common denominator, I find it refreshing to have work that rewards initiative and effort. Certainly I would be happy to have a sinecure again, but I am no longer heartbroken that I left one.

I find from the experience of scavenging two rather deep lessons. The first is to take what you can use and let the rest go by. I have come to think that there is no value in the abstract. A thing I cannot use or make useful, perhaps by trading, has no value however rare or fine it may be. I mean useful in a broad sense — some art I would find useful and some otherwise.

I was shocked to realize that some things are not worth acquiring, but now I think it is so. Some material things are white elephants that eat up the possessor's substance. The second lesson is the transience of material being. This has not quite converted me to a dualist, but it has made some headway in that direction. I do not suppose that ideas are immortal, but certainly mental things are longer lived than other material things.

Once I was the sort of person who invests objects with sentimental value. 65 Now I no longer have those objects, but I have the sentiments yet.

Many times in our travels I have lost everything but the clothes I was wearing and Lizbeth. The things I find in Dumpsters, the love letters and rag dolls of so many lives, remind me of this lesson. Now I hardly pick up a thing without envisioning the time I will cast it aside. This I think is a healthy state of mind. Almost everything I have now has already been cast out at least once, proving that what I own is valueless to someone.

Anyway, I find my desire to grab for the gaudy bauble has been largely sated. I think this is an attitude I share with the very wealthy — we both know there is plenty more where what we have came from. Between us are the rat-race millions who nightly scavenge the cable channels looking for they know not what.

I am sorry for them.

For Analysis

1. What purpose does the opening paragraph serve?

2. What kind of reader is the author writing for?

3. Do Eighner's comments about students ring true?

4. What, in your opinion, are the writer's outstanding personality traits?

5. What is your reaction to the conclusion of the essay, particularly the final sentence?

On Style

1. How would you characterize the **tone** of this essay?

2. In paragraph 6, Eighner explains that his essay will begin with the practical and move to the abstract. Is this an effective organizational principle? Explain.

Making Connections

Describe how Eighner's essay altered your views about homelessness and Dumpster diving.

Writing Topics

1. Use the following comment from a review in the *New Yorker* magazine as the basis for an analysis of the tone and style of Eighner's essay: "Part of the fascination of reading Eighner comes from the cleavage between his stately, slightly fussbudget diction and the indignity of his circumstances."

2. Discuss Eighner's essay in terms of Henry David Thoreau's assertion in *Walden* that "a man is rich in proportion to the number of things which he can afford to let alone."

Bernard Cooper   (b. 1951)

A Clack of Tiny Sparks: Remembrances of a Gay Boyhood   1991

Theresa Sanchez sat behind me in ninth-grade algebra. When Mr. Hubbley faced the blackboard, I'd turn around to see what she was reading; each week a new book was wedged inside her copy of *Today's Equations*. The deception worked; from Mr. Hubbley's point of view, Theresa was engrossed in the value of X, but I knew otherwise. One week she perused *The Wisdom of the Orient*, and I could tell from Theresa's contemplative expression that the book contained exotic thoughts, guidelines handed down from high. Another week it was a paperback novel whose title, *Let Me Live My Life*, appeared in bold print atop every page, and whose cover, a gauzy photograph of a woman biting a strand of pearls, head thrown back in an attitude of ecstasy, confirmed my suspicion that Theresa Sanchez was mature beyond her years. She was the tallest girl in school. Her bouffant hairdo, streaked with blond, was higher than the flaccid bouffants of other girls. Her smooth skin, plucked eyebrows, and painted fingernails suggested hours of pampering, a worldly and sensual vanity that placed her within the domain of adults. Smiling dimly, steeped in daydreams, Theresa moved through the crowded halls with a languid, self-satisfied indifference to those around her. "You are merely children," her posture seemed to say. "I can't be bothered." The week Theresa hid *101 Ways to Cook Hamburger* behind her algebra book, I could stand it no longer and, after the bell rang, ventured a question.

"Because I'm having a dinner party," said Theresa. "Just a couple of intimate friends."

No fourteen-year-old I knew had ever given a dinner party, let alone used the word "intimate" in conversation. "Don't you have a mother?" I asked.

Theresa sighed a weary sigh, suffered my strange inquiry. "Don't be so naive," she said. "Everyone has a mother." She waved her hand to indicate the brick school buildings outside the window. "A higher education should have taught you that." Theresa draped an angora sweater over her shoulders, scooped her books from the graffiti-covered desk, and just as she was about to walk away, she turned and asked me, "Are you a fag?"

There wasn't the slightest hint of rancor or condescension in her voice. The   5 tone was direct, casual. Still I was stunned, giving a sidelong glance to make sure no one had heard. "No," I said. Blurted really, with too much defensiveness,

314

too much transparent fear in my response. Octaves lower than usual, I tried a "Why?"

Theresa shrugged. "Oh, I don't know. I have lots of friends who are fags. You remind me of them." Seeing me bristle, Theresa added, "It was just a guess." I watched her erect, angora back as she sauntered out the classroom door.

She had made an incisive and timely guess. Only days before, I'd invited Grady Rogers to my house after school to go swimming. The instant Grady shot from the pool, shaking water from his orange hair, freckled shoulders shining, my attraction to members of my own sex became a matter I could no longer suppress or rationalize. Sturdy and boisterous and gap-toothed, Grady was an inveterate backslapper, a formidable arm wrestler, a wizard at basketball. Grady was a boy at home in his body.

My body was a marvel I hadn't gotten used to; my arms and legs would some-times act of their own accord, knocking over a glass at dinner or flinching at an oncoming pitch. I was never singled out as a sissy, but I could have been just as easily as Bobby Keagan, a gentle, intelligent, and introverted boy reviled by my classmates. And although I had always been aware of a tacit rapport with Bobby, a suspicion that I might find with him a rich friendship, I stayed away. Instead, I emulated Grady in the belief that being seen with him, being like him, would somehow vanquish my self-doubt, would make me normal by association.

Apart from his athletic prowess, Grady had been gifted with all the trappings of what I imagined to be a charmed life: a fastidious, aproned mother who radi-ated calm, maternal concern; a ruddy, stoic father with a knack for home re-pairs. Even the Rogerses' small suburban house in Hollywood, with its spindly Colonial furniture and chintz curtains, was a testament to normalcy.

Grady and his family bore little resemblance to my clan of Eastern European 10 Jews, a dark and vociferous people who ate with abandon — matzo and halvah and gefilte fish; foods the goyim couldn't pronounce — who cajoled one an-other during endless games of canasta, making the simplest remark about the weather into a lengthy philosophical discourse on the sun and the seasons and the passage of time. My mother was a chain-smoker, a dervish in a frowsy house-dress. She showed her love in the most peculiar and obsessive ways, like spend-ing hours extracting every seed from a watermelon before she served it in perfectly bite-sized, geometric pieces. Preoccupied and perpetually frantic, my mother succumbed to bouts of absentmindedness so profound she'd forget what she was saying midsentence, smile and blush and walk away. A divorce attorney, my father wore roomy, iridescent suits, and the intricacies, the deceits inherent in his profession, had the effect of making him forever tense and vigi-lant. He was "all wound up," as my mother put it. But when he relaxed, his laughter was explosive, his disposition prankish: "Walk this way," a waitress would say, leading us to our table, and my father would mimic the way she walked, arms akimbo, hips liquid, while my mother and I were wracked with laughter. Buoyant or brooding, my parents' moods were unpredictable, and in a household fraught with extravagant emotion it was odd and awful to keep my longing secret.

One day I made the mistake of asking my mother what a "fag" was. I knew exactly what Theresa had meant but hoped against hope it was not what I thought; maybe "fag" was some French word, a harmless term like "naive." My mother turned from the stove, flew at me, and grabbed me by the shoulders. "Did someone call you that?" she cried.

"Not me," I said. "Bobby Keagan."

"Oh," she said, loosening her grip. She was visibly relieved. And didn't answer. The answer was unthinkable.

For weeks after, I shook with the reverberations from that afternoon in the kitchen with my mother, pained by the memory of her shocked expression and, most of all, her silence. My longing was wrong in the eyes of my mother, whose hazel eyes were the eyes of the world, and if that longing continued unchecked, the unwieldy shape of my fate would be cast, and I'd be subjected to a lifetime of scorn.

During the remainder of the semester, I became the scientist of my own 15 desire, plotting ways to change my yearning for boys into a yearning for girls. I had enough evidence to believe that any habit, regardless of how compulsive, how deeply ingrained, could be broken once and for all: The plastic cigarette my mother purchased at the Thrifty pharmacy — one end was red to approximate an ember, the other tan like a filtered tip — was designed to wean her from the real thing. To change a behavior required self-analysis, cold resolve, and the substitution of one thing for another: plastic, say, for tobacco. Could I also find a substitute for Grady? What I needed to do, I figured, was kiss a girl and learn to like it.

This conclusion was affirmed one Sunday morning when my father, seeing me wrinkle my nose at the pink slabs of lox he layered on a bagel, tried to convince me of its salty appeal. "You should try some," he said. "You don't know what you're missing."

"It's loaded with protein," added my mother, slapping a platter of sliced onions onto the dinette table. She hovered above us, cinching her housedress, eyes wet from onion fumes, the mock cigarette dangling from her lips.

My father sat there chomping with gusto, emitting a couple of hearty grunts to dramatize his satisfaction. And still I was not convinced. After a loud and labored swallow, he told me I may not be fond of lox today, but sooner or later I'd learn to like it. One's tastes, he assured me, are destined to change.

"Live," shouted my mother over the rumble of the Mixmaster. "Expand your horizons. Try new things." And the room grew fragrant with the batter of a spice cake.

The opportunity to put their advice into practice, and try out my plan to adapt 20 to girls, came the following week when Debbie Coburn, a member of Mr. Hubbley's algebra class, invited me to a party. She cornered me in the hall, furtive as a spy, telling me her parents would be gone for the evening and slipping into my palm a wrinkled sheet of notebook paper. On it were her address and telephone number, the lavender ink in a tidy cursive. "Wear cologne," she advised, wary eyes darting back and forth. "It's a make-out party. Anything can happen."

The Santa Ana wind blew relentlessly the night of Debbie's party, careening down the slopes of the Hollywood hills, shaking the road signs and stoplights in its path. As I walked down Beachwood Avenue, trees thrashed, surrendered their leaves, and carob pods bombarded the pavement. The sky was a deep but luminous blue, the air hot, abrasive, electric. I had to squint in order to check the number of the Coburns' apartment, a three-story building with glitter embedded in its stucco walls. Above the honeycombed balconies was a sign that read BEACHWOOD TERRACE in lavender script resembling Debbie's.

From down the hall, I could hear the plaintive strains of Little Anthony's "I Think I'm Going Out of My Head." Debbie answered the door bedecked in an Empire dress, the bodice blue and orange polka dots, the rest a sheath of black and white stripes. "Op art," proclaimed Debbie. She turned in a circle, then proudly announced that she'd rolled her hair in orange juice cans. She patted the huge unmoving curls and dragged me inside. Reflections from the swimming pool in the courtyard, its surface ruffled by wind, shuddered over the ceiling and walls. A dozen of my classmates were seated on the sofa or huddled together in corners, their whispers full of excited imminence, their bodies barely discernible in the dim light. Drapes flanking the sliding glass doors bowed out with every gust of wind, and it seemed that the room might lurch from its foundations and sail with its cargo of silhouettes into the hot October night.

Grady was the last to arrive. He tossed a six-pack of beer into Debbie's arms, barreled toward me, and slapped my back. His hair was slicked back with Vitalis, lacquered furrows left by the comb. The wind hadn't shifted a single hair. "Ya ready?" he asked, flashing the gap between his front teeth and leering into the darkened room. "You bet," I lied.

Once the beers had been passed around, Debbie provoked everyone's attention by flicking on the overhead light. "Okay," she called. "Find a partner." This was the blunt command of a hostess determined to have her guests aroused in an orderly fashion. Everyone blinked, shuffled about, and grabbed a member of the opposite sex. Sheila Garabedian landed beside me — entirely at random, though I wanted to believe she was driven by passion — her timid smile giving way to plain fear as the light went out. Nothing for a moment but the heave of the wind and the distant banter of dogs. I caught a whiff of Sheila's perfume, tangy and sweet as Hawaiian Punch. I probed her face with my own, grazing the small scallop of an ear, a velvety temple, and though Sheila's trembling made me want to stop, I persisted with my mission until I found her lips, tightly sealed as a private letter. I held my mouth over hers and gathered her shoulders closer, resigned to the possibility that, no matter how long we stood there, Sheila would be too scared to kiss me back. Still, she exhaled through her nose, and I listened to the squeak of every breath as though it were a sigh of inordinate pleasure. Diving within myself, I monitored my heartbeat and respiration, trying to will stimulation into being, and all the while an image intruded, an image of Grady erupting from our pool, rivulets of water sliding down his chest. "Change," shouted Debbie, switching on the light. Sheila thanked me, pulled away, and continued her routine of gracious terror with every boy throughout the evening. It didn't matter whom I held — Margaret Sims, Betty Vernon, Elizabeth Lee — my experiment was a failure; I continued to picture Grady's wet chest, and Debbie would bellow "change" with such fervor, it could have been my own voice, my own incessant reprimand.

Our hostess commandeered the light switch for nearly half an hour. When- 25 ever the light came on, I watched Grady pivot his head toward the newest prospect, his eyebrows arched in expectation, his neck blooming with hickeys, his hair, at last, in disarray. All that shuffling across the carpet charged every-one's arms and lips with static, and eventually, between low moans and soft osculations, I could hear the clack of tiny sparks and see them flare here and there in the dark like meager, short-lived stars.

I saw Theresa, sultry and aloof as ever, read three more books — *North American Reptiles, Bonjour Tristesse,* and *MGM: A Pictorial History,* — before she vanished early in December. Rumors of her fate abounded. Debbie Coburn swore that Theresa had been "knocked up" by an older man, a traffic cop, she thought, or a grocer. Nearly quivering with relish, Debbie told me and Grady about the home for unwed mothers in the San Fernando Valley, a compound teeming with pregnant girls who had nothing to do but touch their stomachs and contemplate their mistake. Even Bobby Keagan, who took Theresa's place behind me in algebra, had a theory regarding her disappearance colored by his own wish for escape; he imagined that Theresa, disillusioned with society, booked passage to a tropical island, there to live out the rest of her days without restrictions or ridicule. "No wonder she flunked out of school," I overheard Mr. Hubbley tell a fellow teacher one afternoon. "Her head was always in a book."

Along with Theresa went my secret, or at least the dread that she might divulge it, and I felt, for a while, exempt from suspicion. I was, however, to run across Theresa one last time. It happened during a period of torrential rain that, according to reports on the six o'clock news, washed houses from the hillsides and flooded the downtown streets. The halls of Joseph Le Conte Junior High were festooned with Christmas decorations: crepe-paper garlands, wreaths studded with plastic berries, and one requisite Star of David twirling above the attendance desk. In Arts and Crafts, our teacher, Gerald (he was the only teacher who allowed us — *required* us — to call him by his first name), handed out blocks of balsa wood and instructed us to carve them into bugs. We would paint eyes and antennae with tempera and hang them on a Christmas tree he'd made the previous night. "Voila," he crooned, unveiling his creation from a burlap sack. Before us sat a tortured scrub, a wardrobe-worth of wire hangers that were bent like branches and soldered together. Gerald credited his inspiration to a Charles Addams cartoon he's seen in which Morticia, grimly preparing for the holidays, hangs vampire bats on a withered pine. "All that red and green," said Gerald. "So predictable. So *boring.*"

As I chiseled a beetle and listened to rain pummel the earth, Gerald handed me an envelope and asked me to take it to Mr. Kendrick, the drama teacher. I would have thought nothing of his request if I hadn't seen Theresa on my way down the hall. She was cleaning out her locker, blithely dropping the sum of its contents — pens and textbooks and mimeographs — into a trash can. "Have a nice life," she sang as I passed. I mustered the courage to ask her what had happened. We stood alone in the silent hall, the reflections of wreaths and garlands submerged in brown linoleum.

"I transferred to another school. They don't have grades or bells, and you get to study whatever you want." Theresa was quick to sense my incredulity. "Honest," she said. "The school is progressive." She gazed into a glass cabinet that held the trophies of track meets and intramural spelling bees. "God," she sighed, "this place is so . . . barbaric." I was still trying to decide whether or not to believe her story when she asked me where I was headed. "Dear," she said, her exclamation pooling in the silence, "that's no ordinary note, if you catch my drift." The envelope was blank and white; I looked up at Theresa, baffled. "Don't be so naive," she muttered, tossing an empty bottle of nail polish into the trash can. It struck bottom with a resolute thud. "Well," she said, closing her locker and breathing deeply, "bon voyage." Theresa swept through the double doors and in seconds her figure was obscured by rain.

As I walked toward Mr. Kendrick's room, I could feel Theresa's insinuation 30 burrow in. I stood for a moment and watched Mr. Kendrick through the pane in the door. He paced intently in front of the class, handsome in his shirt and tie, reading from a thick book. Chalked on the blackboard behind him was THE ODYSSEY BY HOMER. I have no recollection of how Mr. Kendrick reacted to the note, whether he accepted it with pleasure or embarrassment, slipped it into his desk drawer or the pocket of his shirt. I have scavenged that day in retrospect, trying to see Mr. Kendrick's expression, wondering if he acknowledged me in any way as his liaison. All I recall is the sight of his mime through a pane of glass, a lone man mouthing an epic, his gestures ardent in empty air.

Had I delivered a declaration of love? I was haunted by the need to know. In fantasy, a kettle shot steam, the glue released its grip, and I read the letter with impunity. But how would such a letter begin? Did the common endearments apply? This was a message between two men, a message for which I had no precedent, and when I tried to envision the contents, apart from a hasty, impassioned scrawl, my imagination faltered.

Once or twice I witnessed Gerald and Mr. Kendrick walk together into the faculty lounge or say hello at the water fountain, but there was nothing especially clandestine or flirtatious in their manner. Besides, no matter how acute my scrutiny, I wasn't sure, short of a kiss, exactly what to look for — what semaphore of gesture, what encoded word. I suspected there were signs, covert signs that would give them away, just as I'd unwittingly given myself away to Theresa.

In the school library, a *Webster's* unabridged dictionary lay on a wooden podium, and I padded toward it with apprehension; along with clues to the bond between my teachers, I risked discovering information that might incriminate me as well. I had decided to consult the dictionary during lunch period, when most of the students would be on the playground. I clutched my notebook, moving in such a way as to appear both studious and nonchalant, actually believing that, unless I took precautions, someone would see me and guess what I was up to. The closer I came to the podium, the more obvious, I thought, was my endeavor; I felt like the model of The Visible Man in our science class, my heart's undulations, my overwrought nerves legible through transparent skin. A couple of kids riffled through the card catalogue. The librarian, a skinny woman whose perpetual whisper and rubber-soled shoes caused her to drift through the room like a phantom, didn't seem to register my presence. Though I'd looked up dozens of words before, the pages felt strange beneath my fingers. *Homer* was the first word I saw. *Hominid. Homogenize.* I feigned interest and skirted other words before I found the word I was after. Under the heading HO•MO•SEX•U•AL was the terse definition: *adj. Pertaining to, characteristic of, or exhibiting homosexuality. —n. A homosexual person.* I read the definition again and again, hoping the words would yield more than they could. I shut the dictionary, swallowed hard, and, none the wiser, hurried away.

As for Gerald and Mr. Kendrick, I never discovered evidence to prove or dispute Theresa's claim. By the following summer, however, I had overheard from my peers a confounding amount about homosexuals: They wore green on Thursday, couldn't whistle, hypnotized boys with a piercing glance. To this lore, Grady added a surefire test to ferret them out.

"A test?" I said.

"You ask a guy to look at his fingernails, and if he looks at them like this" — Grady closed his fingers into a fist and examined his nails with manly detachment — "then he's okay. But if he does this" — he held out his hands at arm's length, splayed his fingers, and coyly cocked his head — "you'd better watch out." Once he'd completed his demonstration, Grady peeled off his shirt and plunged into our pool. I dove in after. It was early June, the sky immense, glassy, placid. My father was cooking spareribs on the barbecue, an artist with a basting brush. His apron bore the caricature of a frazzled French chef. Mother curled on a chaise lounge, plumes of smoke wafting from her nostrils. In a stupor of contentment she took another drag, closed her eyes, and arched her face toward the sun.

Grady dog-paddled through the deep end, spouting a fountain of chlorinated water. Despite shame and confusion, my longing for him hadn't diminished; it continued to thrive without air and light, like a luminous fish in the dregs of the sea. In the name of play, I swam up behind him, encircled his shoulders, astonished by his taut flesh. The two of us flailed, pretended to drown. Beneath the heavy press of water, Grady's orange hair wavered, a flame that couldn't be doused.

35

. . .

I've lived with a man for seven years. Some nights, when I'm half-asleep and the room is suffused with blue light, I reach out to touch the expanse of his back, and it seems as if my fingers sink into his skin, and I feel the pleasure a diver feels the instant he enters a body of water.

I have few regrets. But one is that I hadn't said to Theresa, "Of course I'm a fag." Maybe I'd have met her friends. Or become friends with her. Imagine the meals we might have concocted: hamburger Stroganoff, Swedish meatballs in a sweet translucent sauce, steaming slabs of Salisbury steak.

For Analysis

1. How would you characterize Theresa Sanchez? Do you think she is unintelligent? Explain.

2. What do you make of Mr. Hubbley's remark about her: "No wonder she flunked out of school. . . . Her head was always in a book"?

3. Contrast the responses of Theresa and the narrator's mother to the possibility that he might be gay.

4. Discuss the force of the mother's advice regarding lox: "Live. . . . Expand your horizons. Try new things."

5. How does the fourteen-year-old narrator feel about his own sexuality?

6. Discuss the impact of the final paragraph.

On Style

1. Although this essay addresses some large abstractions — adolescents at school, awakening sexual awareness — it embodies numerous concrete details to animate the abstractions. Choose a paragraph or short section of the piece, and note the details that humanize the abstractions. Consider, for example, how the narrator describes Theresa's hair, Debbie's hair and clothing, the music at the party, and the ethnicity of his family.

Making Connections

1. Does the narrator's experience correspond in any way to your own experience as a fourteen-year-old? Explain.

2. Langston Hughes in "Salvation" (p. 296) and Judith Ortiz Cofer in "American History" (p. 322) also reveal painful memories. Which of the three reminiscences strikes you as most intense? Explain.

Writing Topics

1. Write a reminiscence of your childhood that focuses on a particularly pleasurable or painful experience.

2. Compare and contrast the speaker's sexual awareness with the religious awareness in Langston Hughes's "Salvation."

3. Create a character sketch of a friend or acquaintance from your early adolescence (someone like Theresa, perhaps, or Grady); be sure to animate your description with concrete details.

Judith Ortiz Cofer   (b. 1952)

American History   1993

I once read in a *Ripley's Believe It or Not* column that Paterson, New Jersey, is the place where the Straight and Narrow (streets) intersect. The Puerto Rican tenement known as El Building was one block up from Straight. It was, in fact, the corner of Straight and Market; not "at" the corner, but *the* corner. At almost any hour of the day, El Building was like a monstrous jukebox, blasting out *salsas* from open windows as the residents, mostly new immigrants just up from the island, tried to drown out whatever they were currently enduring with loud music. But the day President Kennedy was shot, there was a profound silence in El Building, even the abusive tongues of viragoes, the cursing of the unemployed, and the screeching of small children had been somehow muted. President Kennedy was a saint to these people. In fact, soon his photograph would be hung along-side the Sacred Heart and over the spiritist altars that many women kept in their apartments. He would become part of the hierarchy of martyrs they prayed to for favors that only one who had died for a cause would understand.

On the day that President Kennedy was shot, my ninth grade class had been out in the fenced playground of Public School Number 13. We had been given "free" exercise time and had been ordered by our P.E. teacher, Mr. DePalma, to "keep moving." That meant that the girls should jump rope and the boys toss basketballs through a hoop at the far end of the yard. He in the meantime would "keep an eye" on us from just inside the building.

It was a cold gray day in Paterson. The kind that warns of early snow. I was miserable, since I had forgotten my gloves and my knuckles were turning red and raw from the jump rope. I was also taking a lot of abuse from the black girls for not turning the rope hard and fast enough for them.

"Hey, Skinny Bones, pump it, girl. Ain't you got no energy today?" Gail, the biggest of the black girls who had the other end of the rope yelled, "Didn't you eat your rice and beans and pork chops for breakfast today?"

The other girls picked up the "pork chop" and made it into a refrain: "pork 5 chop, pork chop, did you eat your pork chop?" They entered the double ropes in pairs and exited without tripping or missing a beat. I felt a burning on my cheeks, and then my glasses fogged up so that I could not manage to coordinate the jump rope with Gail. The chill was doing to me what it always did, entering my bones, making me cry, humiliating me. I hated the city, especially in winter. I hated Public School Number 13. I hated my skinny flat-chested body, and I envied the black girls who could jump rope so fast that their legs became a blur. They always seemed to be warm while I froze.

There was only one source of beauty and light for me that school year. The only thing I had anticipated at the start of the semester. That was seeing Eugene. In August, Eugene and his family had moved into the only house on the block that had a yard and trees. I could see his place from my window in El Building. In fact, if I sat on the fire escape I was literally suspended above Eugene's backyard. It was my favorite spot to read my library books in the summer. Until that August the house had been occupied by an old Jewish couple. Over the years I had become part of their family, without their knowing it, of course. I had a view of their kitchen and their backyard, and though I could not hear what they said, I knew when they were arguing, when one of them was sick, and many other things. I knew all this by watching them at mealtimes. I could see their kitchen table, the sink and the stove. During good times, he sat at the table and read his newspapers while she fixed the meals. If they argued, he would leave and the old woman would sit and stare at nothing for a long time. When one of them was sick, the other would come and get things from the kitchen and carry them out on a tray. The old man had died in June. The last week of school I had not seen him at the table at all. Then one day I saw that there was a crowd in the kitchen. The old woman had finally emerged from the house on the arm of a stocky middle-aged woman whom I had seen there a few times before, maybe her daughter. Then a man had carried out suitcases. The house had stood empty for weeks. I had had to resist the temptation to climb down into the yard and water the flowers the old lady had taken such good care of.

By the time Eugene's family moved in, the yard was a tangled mass of weeds. The father had spent several days mowing, and when he finished, I didn't see the red, yellow, and purple clusters that meant flowers to me from where I sat. I didn't see this family sit down at the kitchen table together. It was just the mother, a red-headed tall woman who wore a white uniform — a nurse's, I guessed it was; the father was gone before I got up in the morning and was never there at dinner time. I only saw him on weekends when they sometimes sat on lawn chairs under the oak tree, each hidden behind a section of the newspaper; and there was Eugene. He was tall and blond, and he wore glasses. I liked him right away because he sat at the kitchen table and read books for hours. That summer, before we had even spoken one word to each other, I kept him company on my fire escape.

Once school started I looked for him in all my classes, but P.S. 13 was a huge, overpopulated place and it took me days and many discreet questions to discover that Eugene was in honors classes for all his subjects; classes that were not open to me because English was not my first language, though I was a straight A student. After much maneuvering I managed "to run into him" in the hallway where his locker was — on the other side of the building from mine — and in study hall at the library, where he first seemed to notice me but did not speak; and finally, on the way home after school one day when I decided to approach him directly, though my stomach was doing somersaults.

I was ready for rejection, snobbery, the worst. But when I came up to him, practically panting in my nervousness, and blurted out: "You're Eugene. Right?" He smiled, pushed his glasses up on his nose, and nodded. I saw then that he was blushing deeply. Eugene liked me, but he was shy. I did most of the talking that day. He nodded and smiled a lot. In the weeks that followed, we walked home together. He would linger at the corner of El Building for a few minutes then walk down to his two-story house. It was not until Eugene moved into that house that I noticed that El Building blocked most of the sun and that the only spot that got a little sunlight during the day was the tiny square of earth the old woman had planted with flowers.

I did not tell Eugene that I could see inside his kitchen from my bedroom. I 10 felt dishonest, but I liked my secret sharing of his evenings, especially now that I knew what he was reading, since we chose our books together at the school library.

One day my mother came into my room as I was sitting on the windowsill staring out. In her abrupt way she said: "Elena, you are acting 'moony.' " *Enamorada* was what she really said — that is, like a girl stupidly infatuated. Since I had turned fourteen and started menstruating my mother had been more vigilant than ever. She acted as if I was going to go crazy or explode or something if she didn't watch me and nag me all the time about being a señorita now. She kept talking about virtue, morality, and other subjects that did not interest me in the least. My mother was unhappy in Paterson, but my father had a good job at the blue jeans factory in Passaic, and soon, he kept assuring us, we would be moving to our own house there. Every Sunday we drove out to the suburbs of Paterson, Clifton, and Passaic, out to where people mowed grass on Sundays in the summer and where children made snowmen in the winter from pure white snow, not like the gray slush of Paterson, which seemed to fall from the sky in that hue. I had learned to listen to my parents' dreams, which were spoken in Spanish, as fairy tales, like the stories about life in the island paradise of Puerto Rico before I was born. I had been to the Island once as a little girl, to grandmother's funeral, and all I remembered was wailing women in black, my mother becoming hysterical and being given a pill that made her sleep two days, and me feeling lost in a crowd of strangers all claiming to be my aunts, uncles, and cousins. I had actually been glad to return to the city. We had not been back there since then, though my parents talked constantly about buying a house on the beach someday, retiring on the island — that was a common topic among the residents of El Building. As for me, I was going to go to college and become a teacher.

But after meeting Eugene I began to think of the present more than of the future. What I wanted now was to enter that house I had watched for so many years. I wanted to see the other rooms where the old people had lived and where the boy I liked spent his time. Most of all, I wanted to sit at the kitchen table with Eugene like two adults, like the old man and his wife had done, maybe drink some coffee and talk about books. I had started reading *Gone with the Wind*. I was enthralled by it, with the daring and the passion of the beautiful girl living in a mansion, and with her devoted parents and the slaves who did everything for them. I didn't believe such a world had ever really existed, and I wanted to ask Eugene some questions, since he and his parents, he had told me, had come up from Georgia, the same place where the novel was set. His father worked for a company that had transferred him to Paterson. His mother was very unhappy, Eugene said, in his beautiful voice that rose and fell over words in a strange, lilting way. The kids at school called him the Hick and made fun of the way he talked. I knew I was his only friend so far, and I liked that, though I felt sad for him sometimes. Skinny Bones and the Hick, was what they called us at school when we were seen together.

The day Mr. DePalma came out into the cold and asked us to line up in front of him was the day that President Kennedy was shot. Mr. DePalma, a short, muscular man with slicked-down black hair, was the science teacher, P.E. coach, and disciplinarian at P.S. 13. He was the teacher to whose homeroom you got assigned if you were a troublemaker, and the man called out to break up play-ground fights, and to escort violently angry teenagers to the office. And Mr. DePalma was the man who called your parents in for "a conference."

That day, he stood in front of two rows of mostly black and Puerto Rican kids, brittle from their efforts to "keep moving" on a November day that was turning bitter cold. Mr. DePalma, to our complete shock, was crying. Not just silent adult tears, but really sobbing. There were a few titters from the back of the line where I stood, shivering.

"Listen," Mr. DePalma raised his arms over his head as if he were about to 15 conduct an orchestra. His voice broke, and he covered his face with his hands. His barrel chest was heaving. Someone giggled behind me.

"Listen," he repeated, "something awful has happened." A strange gurgling came from his throat, and he turned around and spit on the cement behind him.

"Gross," someone said, and there was a lot of laughter.

"The president is dead, you idiots. I should have known that wouldn't mean anything to a bunch of losers like you kids. Go home." He was shrieking now. No one moved for a minute or two, but then a big girl let out a "yeah!" and ran to get her books piled up with the others against the brick wall of the school build-ing. The others followed in a mad scramble to get to their things before some-body caught on. It was still an hour to the dismissal bell.

A little scared, I headed for El Building. There was an eerie feeling on the streets. I looked into Mario's drugstore, a favorite hangout for the high school crowd, but there were only a couple of old Jewish men at the soda bar, talking with the short order cook in tones that sounded almost angry, but they were keeping their voices low. Even the traffic on one of the busiest intersections in Paterson — Straight Street and Park Avenue — seemed to be moving slower. There were no horns blasting that day. At El Building, the usual little group of unemployed men were not hanging out on the front stoop, making it difficult for women to enter the front door. No music spilled out from open doors in the hallway. When I walked into our apartment, I found my mother sitting in front of the grainy picture of the television set.

She looked up at me with a tear-streaked face and just said: "Dios mío," turn- 20
ing back to the set as if it were pulling at her eyes. I went into my room.

Though I wanted to feel the right thing about President Kennedy's death, I
could not fight the feeling of elation that stirred in my chest. Today was the day
I was to visit Eugene in his house. He had asked me to come over after school to
study for an American history test with him. We had also planned to walk to the
public library together. I looked down into his yard. The oak tree was bare of
leaves, and the ground looked gray with ice. The light through the large kitchen
window of his house told me that El Building blocked the sun to such an extent
that they had to turn lights on in the middle of the day. I felt ashamed about it.
But the white kitchen table with the lamp hanging just above it looked cozy and
inviting. I would soon sit there, across from Eugene, and I would tell him about
my perch just above his house. Maybe I would.

In the next thirty minutes I changed clothes, put on a little pink lipstick, and
got my books together. Then I went in to tell my mother that I was going to a
friend's house to study. I did not expect her reaction.

"You are going out *today?*" The way she said "today" sounded as if a storm
warning had been issued. It was said in utter disbelief. Before I could answer,
she came toward me and held my elbows as I clutched my books.

"*Hija,* the president has been killed. We must show respect. He was a great
man. Come to church with me tonight."

She tried to embrace me, but my books were in the way. My first impulse was 25
to comfort her, she seemed so distraught, but I had to meet Eugene in fifteen
minutes.

"I have a test to study for, Mama. I will be home by eight."

"You are forgetting who you are, *Niña.* I have seen you staring down at that
boy's house. You are heading for humiliation and pain." My mother said this in
Spanish and in a resigned tone that surprised me, as if she had no intention of
stopping me from "heading for humiliation and pain." I started for the door. She
sat in front of the TV, holding a white handkerchief to her face.

I walked out to the street and around the chain-link fence that separated El
Building from Eugene's house. The yard was neatly edged around the little walk
that led to the door. It always amazed me how Paterson, the inner core of the
city, had no apparent logic to its architecture. Small, neat, single residences like
this one could be found right next to huge, dilapidated apartment buildings
like El Building. My guess was that the little houses had been there first, then
the immigrants had come in droves, and the monstrosities had been raised for
them — the Italians, the Irish, the Jews, and now us, the Puerto Ricans, and the
blacks. The door was painted a deep green: *verde,* the color of hope. I had heard
my mother say it: *Verde-Esperanza.*

I knocked softly. A few suspenseful moments later the door opened just a
crack. The red, swollen face of a woman appeared. She had a halo of red hair
floating over a delicate ivory face — the face of a doll — with freckles on the
nose. Her smudged eye makeup made her look unreal to me, like a mannequin
seen through a warped store window.

"What do you want?" Her voice was tiny and sweet-sounding, like a little 30 girl's, but her tone was not friendly.

"I'm Eugene's friend. He asked me over. To study." I thrust out my books, a silly gesture that embarrassed me almost immediately.

"You live there?" She pointed up to El Building, which looked particularly ugly, like a gray prison with its many dirty windows and rusty fire escapes. The woman had stepped halfway out, and I could see that she wore a white nurse's uniform with "St. Joseph's Hospital" on the name tag.

"Yes. I do."

She looked intently at me for a couple of heartbeats, then said as if to herself, "I don't know how you people do it." Then directly to me: "Listen. Honey. Eugene doesn't want to study with you. He is a smart boy. Doesn't need help. You understand me. I am truly sorry if he told you you could come over. He cannot study with you. It's nothing personal. You understand? We won't be in this place much longer, no need for him to get close to people — it'll just make it harder for him later. Run back home now."

I couldn't move. I just stood there in shock at hearing these things said to me 35 in such a honey-drenched voice. I had never heard an accent like hers except for Eugene's softer version. It was as if she were singing me a little song.

"What's wrong? Didn't you hear what I said?" She seemed very angry, and I finally snapped out of my trance. I turned away from the green door and heard her close it gently.

Our apartment was empty when I got home. My mother was in someone else's kitchen, seeking the solace she needed. Father would come in from his late shift at midnight. I would hear them talking softly in the kitchen for hours that night. They would not discuss their dreams for the future, or life in Puerto Rico, as they often did; that night they would talk sadly about the young widow and her two children, as if they were family. For the next few days, we would observe *luto* in our apartment; that is, we would practice restraint and silence — no loud music or laughter. Some of the women of El Building would wear black for weeks.

That night, I lay in my bed, trying to feel the right thing for our dead president. But the tears that came up from a deep source inside me were strictly for me. When my mother came to the door, I pretended to be sleeping. Sometime during the night, I saw from my bed the streetlight come on. It had a pink halo around it. I went to my window and pressed my face to the cool glass. Looking up at the light I could see the white snow falling like a lace veil over its face. I did not look down to see it turning gray as it touched the ground below.

For Analysis

1. Suggest a reason for the narrator's spying on the neighbors.

2. Why does Elena's mother warn her that "you are forgetting who you are" and that "you are heading for humiliation and pain" (para. 27)?

3. What does Eugene's mother reveal when she comments: "I don't know how you people do it" (para. 34)? Why does she refuse to let Elena study with Eugene?

4. The author contrasts two tragedies. Which was the more meaningful? Why?

5. Discuss the implications of the essay's title.

On Style

1. How would you characterize the tone of this essay? Is it bitter? Belligerent? Argumentative? Accepting? Explain.

2. The narrator reveals that both mothers are "unhappy." How do those emotional states contribute to the essay's structure?

Making Connections

Compare this essay with Robinson's essay "Can a Black Family Be a Legal Nuisance?" (p. 659). In what ways are they similar? How do they differ?

Writing Topics

1. Explain which event — Kennedy's death or Eugene's mother's remarks — more significantly shapes the narrator's view of American history.

2. Compare and contrast Cofer's experience with Angelou's experience related in "Graduation in Stamps" (p. 1000).

LOOKING BACK:
Further Questions for Thinking and Writing

1. What support do the works in this section provide for Thomas Gray's well-known observation that "where ignorance is bliss, / 'Tis folly to be wise"? **Writing Topic:** Use Gray's observation as the basis for an analysis of Flannery O'Connor's "Good Country People" or Toni Cade Bambara's "The Lesson."

2. In poems such as William Blake's "The Garden of Love," William Wordsworth's "Lines Composed a Few Miles above Tintern Abbey," Robert Frost's "Birches," and Stevie Smith's "To Carry the Child," growing up is seen as a growing away from a kind of truth and reality; in other poems, such as Gerard Manley Hopkins's "Spring and Fall" and Dylan Thomas's "Fern Hill," growing up is seen as growing into truth and reality. Do these two groups of poems embody contradictory and mutually exclusive conceptions of childhood? Explain. **Writing Topic:** Select one poem from each of these two groups, and contrast the conception of childhood embodied in each.

3. An eighteenth-century novelist wrote: "Oh Innocence, how glorious and happy a portion art thou to the breast that possesses thee! Thou fearest neither the eyes nor the tongues of men. Truth, the most powerful of all things, is thy strongest friend; and the brighter the light is in which thou art displayed, the more it discovers thy transcendent beauties." Which works in this section support this assessment of innocence? Which works contradict it? How would you characterize the relationship between "truth" and "innocence" in the fiction, drama, and the essays presented here? **Writing Topic:** Use this observation as the basis for an analysis of Nathaniel Hawthorne's "Young Goodman Brown" (p. 80) or Toni Cade Bambara's "The Lesson " (p. 134).

4. A certain arrogance is associated with the innocence of both Hulga in Flannery O'Connor's "Good Country People" and Brown in Nathaniel Hawthorne's "Young Goodman Brown." On what is their arrogance based, and how is it modified? **Writing Topic:** Contrast the nature and the consequences of the central characters' arrogance in these works.

5. James Joyce's "Araby" and Frank O'Connor's "My Oedipus Complex" deal with some aspect of sexuality as a force that moves the protagonist from innocence toward experience. How does the recognition of sexuality function in each of the stories? **Writing Topic:** Discuss the relationship between sexuality and innocence in these stories.

6. Which poems in this section depend largely on irony for their force? Can you suggest why irony is a useful device in literature that portrays innocence and experience? **Writing Topic:** Write an analysis of the function of irony in Blake's "The Garden of Love" and Hardy's "The Ruined Maid."

7. Some authors treat the passage from innocence to experience as comedy, while others treat it more seriously, even as tragedy. Do you find one or the other treatment more satisfying? Explain. **Writing Topic:** Select one short story, and show how the author achieves either a comic or a serious tone.

Conformity and Rebellion

The Fall from Terrestrial Paradise, from the Sistine Chapel, 1509–10, by Michelangelo.

What is a rebel? A man who says no but whose refusal does not imply a renunciation. He is also a man who says yes as soon as he begins to think for himself.

— ALBERT CAMUS

Most human beings today waste some twenty-five to thirty years of their lives before they break through the actual and conventional lives which surround them.

— ISADORA DUNCAN

In order for the artist to have a world to express he must first be situated in this world, oppressed or oppressing, resigned or rebellious, a man among men.

— SIMONE DE BEAUVOIR

Risk! Risk anything! Care no more for the opinions of others, for those voices. Do the hardest thing on earth for you. Act for yourself. Face the truth.

— KATHERINE MANSFIELD

Human history begins with a man's act of disobedience which is at the very same time the beginning of his freedom and development of his reason.

— ERICH FROMM

. . . we must stop equating sanity with conformity, eccentricity with craziness, and normalcy with numbers. We must get in touch with our own liberating ludicrousness and practice being harmlessly deviant.

— SARAH J. MCCARTHY

The works in this section, "Conformity and Rebellion," feature a clash between two well-articulated positions in which a rebel, on principle, confronts and struggles with established authority. Central in these works are powerful external forces — the state, the church, tradition — which sometimes can be obeyed only at the expense of conscience and humanity. At the most general level, these works confront a dilemma older than the one Antigonê encountered in Thebes: the very organizations men and women establish to protect and nurture the individual often demand — on pain of economic ruin, social ostracism, even spiritual or physical death — that individuals violate their most deeply cherished beliefs. In these works, some individuals refuse such a demand and translate their awareness of a hostile social order into action against it. In *Antigonê,* the issue is drawn with utter clarity: Antigonê must obey either the state (Creon) or the gods. In *A Doll's House,* Nora realizes that dehumanization is too high a price to pay for domestic tranquillity. On a different note, in Melville's "Bartleby the Scrivener" and Richard Wright's "The Man Who Was Almost a Man," the crises arise out of the protagonists' passive refusal to conform to the expectations of society.

Many of the works in this section, particularly the poems, do not treat the theme of conformity and rebellion quite so explicitly and dramatically. Some, like Emily Dickinson's "She rose to His Requirement," reveal the painful injustice of certain traditional values; others, like W. H. Auden's "The Unknown Citizen," tell us that the price exacted for total conformity to the industrial superstate is spiritual death. In "Easter 1916," William Butler Yeats meditates on the awesome meaning of the lives and deaths of political revolutionaries, and in "Harlem," Langston Hughes warns that an inflexible and constricting social order will generate explosion.

While in many of the works the individual is caught up in a crisis that forces him or her into rebellion, in other works the focus may be on the individual's failure to move from awareness into action. For example, the portrait of Auden's unknown citizen affirms the necessity for rebellion by rendering so effectively the hollow life of mindless conformity.

Although diverse in treatment and technique, all the works in this section are about individuals struggling with complex sets of external forces that regulate and define their lives. As social beings, these individuals may recognize that they must be controlled for some larger good; yet they are aware that established social power is often abusive. The institution at its best can act as a conserving force, keeping in check the individual's disruptive impulse to abandon and destroy, without cause, old ways and ideas. At its worst, the power of social institutions is self-serving. It is up to the individual to judge whether power is being abused. Because the power of the individual is often negligible beside that of abusive social forces, it is not surprising that many artists find a fundamental human dignity in the resistance of the individual to organized society. One of humanity's ancient and profound recognitions, after all, is that the impulse of a Creon is always to make unknown citizens of us all.

LOOKING AHEAD:
Questions for Thinking and Writing

Before you begin reading the selections in "Conformity and Rebellion," consider the following questions. Write out your thoughts informally in a reading journal, if you are keeping one, as a way of preparing to respond to the selections. Or you may wish to make your response to one of these questions the basis for a formal essay.

1. How would you define *conformity*? What forms of rebellion are possible for a person in your situation? Do you perceive yourself as a conformist? A rebel? Some combination of the two? Explain.

2. How would you define *sanity*? Based on your own definition, do you know an insane person? What form does that insanity take? Do you agree or disagree with Emily Dickinson's assertion that "Much Madness is divinest Sense"? Explain.

3. Discuss this proposition: Governments routinely engage in behavior that would cause an individual to be imprisoned or institutionalized.

4. Freewrite an extended response to each of the following questions: Is war sane? Should one obey an "unjust" law? Should one be guided absolutely by religious principles?

Fiction

Herman Melville   (1819–1891)

Bartleby the Scrivener   1853

A Story of Wall Street

I am a rather elderly man. The nature of my avocations, for the last thirty years, has brought me into more than ordinary contact with what would seem an interesting and somewhat singular set of men, of whom, as yet, nothing, that I know of, has ever been written — I mean, the law-copyists, or scriveners. I have known very many of them, professionally and privately, and, if I pleased, could relate divers histories, at which good-natured gentlemen might smile, and sentimental souls might weep. But I waive the biographies of all other scriveners, for a few passages in the life of Bartleby, who was a scrivener, the strangest I ever saw, or heard of. While, of other law-copyists, I might write the complete life, of Bartleby nothing of that sort can be done. I believe that no materials exist for a full and satisfactory biography of this man. It is an irreparable loss to literature. Bartleby was one of those beings of whom nothing is ascertainable, except from the original sources, and, in his case, those are very small. What my own astonished eyes saw of Bartleby, *that* is all I know of him, except, indeed, one vague report, which will appear in the sequel.

Ere introducing the scrivener, as he first appeared to me, it is fit I make some mention of myself, my employees, my business, my chambers, and general surroundings; because some such description is indispensable to an adequate understanding of the chief character about to be presented. Imprimis: I am a man who, from his youth upwards, has been filled with a profound conviction that the easiest way of life is the best. Hence, though I belong to a profession proverbially energetic and nervous, even to turbulence, at times, yet nothing of that sort have I ever suffered to invade my peace. I am one of those unambitious lawyers who never addresses a jury, or in any way draws down public applause; but, in the cool tranquillity of a snug retreat, do a snug business among rich men's bonds, and mortgages, and title-deeds. All who know me, consider me an eminently *safe* man. The late John Jacob Astor,[1] a personage little given to poetic enthusiasm, had no hesitation in pronouncing my first grand point to be prudence; my next, method. I do not speak it in vanity, but simply record the fact, that I was not unemployed in my profession by the late John Jacob Astor; a name which, I admit, I love to repeat; for it hath a rounded and orbicular sound to it, and rings like unto bullion. I will freely add, that I was not insensible to the late John Jacob Astor's good opinion.

Some time prior to the period at which this little history begins, my avocations had been largely increased. The good old office, now extinct in the State of New York, of a Master in Chancery,[2] had been conferred upon me. It was not a very arduous office, but very pleasantly remunerative. I seldom lose my temper; much more seldom indulge in dangerous indignation at wrongs and outrages; but, I must be permitted to be rash here, and declare that I consider the sudden and violent abrogation of the office of Master in Chancery, by the new Constitution, as a — premature act; inasmuch as I had counted upon a lifelease of the profits, whereas I only received those of a few short years. But this is by the way.

My chambers were up stairs, at No. ——— Wall Street. At one end, they looked upon the white wall of the interior of a spacious sky-light shaft, penetrating the building from top to bottom.

This view might have been considered rather tame than otherwise, deficient 5 in what landscape painters call "life." But, if so, the view from the other end of my chambers offered, at least, a contrast, if nothing more. In that direction, my windows commanded an unobstructed view of a lofty brick wall, black by age and everlasting shade; which wall required no spyglass to bring out its lurking beauties, but, for the benefit of all near-sighted spectators, was pushed up to within ten feet of my window panes. Owing to the great height of the surrounding buildings, and my chambers being on the second floor, the interval between this wall and mine not a little resembled a huge square cistern.

At the period just preceding the advent of Bartleby, I had two persons as copyists in my employment, and a promising lad as an office-boy. First, Turkey; second, Nippers; third, Ginger Nut. These may seem names, the like of which are not usually found in the Directory. In truth, they were nicknames, mutually conferred upon each other by my three clerks, and were deemed expressive of their respective persons or characters. Turkey was a short, pursy Englishman, of about my own age — that is, somewhere not far from sixty. In the morning, one might say, his face was of a fine florid hue, but after twelve o'clock, meridian — his dinner hour — it blazed like a grate full of Christmas coals; and continued blazing — but, as it were, with a gradual wane — till six o'clock P.M., or thereabouts; after which, I saw no more of the proprietor of the face, which, gaining its meridian with the sun, seemed to set with it, to rise, culminate, and decline the following day, with the like regularity and undiminished glory. There are many singular coincidences I have known in the course of

[1] A poor immigrant who rose to become one of the great business tycoons of the nineteenth century.
[2] Courts of Chancery often adjudicated business disputes.

my life, not the least among which was the fact, that, exactly when Turkey displayed his fullest beams from his red and radiant countenance, just then, too, at that critical moment, began the daily period when I considered his business capacities as seriously disturbed for the remainder of the twenty-four hours. Not that he was absolutely idle, or averse to business, then; far from it. The difficulty was, he was apt to be altogether too energetic. There was a strange, inflamed, flurried, flighty recklessness of activity about him. He would be incautious in dipping his pen into his inkstand. All his blots upon my documents were dropped there after twelve o'clock meridian. Indeed, not only would he be reckless, and sadly given to making blots in the afternoon, but, some days, he went further, and was rather noisy. At such times, too, his face flamed with augmented blazonry, as if cannel coal had been heaped on anthracite. He made an unpleasant racket with his chair; spilled his sand-box; in mending his pens, impatiently split them all to pieces, and threw them on the floor in a sudden passion; stood up, and leaned over his table, boxing his papers about in a most indecorous manner, very sad to behold in an elderly man like him. Nevertheless, as he was in many ways a most valuable person to me, and all the time before twelve o'clock meridian, was the quickest, steadiest creature, too, accomplishing a great deal of work in a style not easily to be matched — for these reasons, I was willing to overlook his eccentricities, though, indeed, occasionally, I remonstrated with him. I did this very gently, however, because, though the civilest, nay, the blandest and most reverential of men in the morning, yet, in the afternoon, he was disposed, upon provocation, to be slightly rash with his tongue — in fact, insolent. Now, valuing his morning services as I did, and resolved not to lose them — yet, at the same time, made uncomfortable by his inflamed ways after twelve o'clock — and being a man of peace, unwilling by my admonitions to call forth unseemly retorts from him, I took upon me, one Saturday noon (he was always worse on Saturdays) to hint to him, very kindly, that, perhaps, now that he was growing old, it might be well to abridge his labors; in short, he need not come to my chambers after twelve o'clock, but, dinner over, had best go home to his lodgings, and rest himself till tea-time. But no; he insisted upon his afternoon devotions. His countenance became intolerably fervid, as he oratorically assured me — gesticulating with a long ruler at the other end of the room — that if his services in the morning were useful, how indispensable, then, in the afternoon?

"With submission, sir," said Turkey, on this occasion, "I consider myself your right-hand man. In the morning I but marshal and deploy my columns; but in the afternoon I put myself at their head, and gallantly charge the foe, thus" — and he made a violent thrust with the ruler.

"But the blots, Turkey," intimated I.

"True; but, with submission, sir, behold these hairs! I am getting old. Surely, sir, a blot or two of a warm afternoon is not to be severely urged against gray hairs. Old age — even if it blot the page — is honorable. With submission, sir, we *both* are getting old."

This appeal to my fellow-feeling was hardly to be resisted. At all events, I saw 10
that go he would not. So, I made up my mind to let him stay, resolving, nevertheless, to see to it that, during the afternoon, he had to do with my less important papers.

Nippers, the second on my list, was a whiskered, sallow, and, upon the whole,
rather piratical-looking young man, of about five and twenty. I always deemed
him the victim of two evil powers — ambition and indigestion. The ambition
was evinced by a certain impatience of the duties of a mere copyist, an unwarrantable usurpation of strictly professional affairs, such as the original drawing
up of legal documents. The indigestion seemed betokened in an occasional
nervous testiness and grinning irritability, causing the teeth to audibly grind
together over mistakes committed in copying; unnecessary maledictions,
hissed, rather than spoken, in the heat of business; and especially by a continual
discontent with the height of the table where he worked. Though of a very
ingenious, mechanical turn, Nippers could never get this table to suit him. He
put chips under it, blocks of various sorts, bits of pasteboard, and at last went so
far as to attempt an exquisite adjustment, by final pieces of folded blotting-
paper. But no invention would answer. If, for the sake of easing his back, he
brought the table-lid at a sharp angle well up towards his chin, and wrote there
like a man using the steep roof of a Dutch house for his desk, then he declared
that it stopped the circulation in his arms. If now he lowered the table to his
waistbands, and stooped over it in writing, then there was a sore aching in his
back. In short, the truth of the matter was, Nippers knew not what he wanted.
Or, if he wanted anything, it was to be rid of a scrivener's table altogether.
Among the manifestations of his diseased ambition was a fondness he had for
receiving visits from certain ambiguous-looking fellows in seedy coats, whom he
called his clients. Indeed, I was aware that not only was he, at times, considerable of a ward-politician, but he occasionally did a little business at the Justices'
courts, and was not unknown on the steps of the Tombs.[3] I have good reason to
believe, however, that one individual who called upon him at my chambers, and
who, with a grand air, he insisted was his client, was no other than a dun, and the
alleged title-deed, a bill. But, with all his failings, and the annoyances he caused
me, Nippers, like his compatriot Turkey, was a very useful man to me; wrote a
neat, swift hand; and, when he chose, was not deficient in a gentlemanly sort of
deportment. Added to this, he always dressed in a gentlemanly sort of way; and
so, incidentally, reflected credit upon my chambers. Whereas, with respect to
Turkey, I had much ado to keep him from being a reproach to me. His clothes
were apt to look oily, and smell of eating houses. He wore his pantaloons very
loose and baggy in summer. His coats were execrable, his hat not to be handled.
But while the hat was a thing of indifference to me, inasmuch as his natural
civility and deference, as a dependent Englishman, always led him to doff it the
moment he entered the room, yet his coat was another matter. Concerning his

[3] A prison in New York City.

coats, I reasoned with him; but with no effect. The truth was, I suppose, that a man with so small an income could not afford to sport such a lustrous face and a lustrous coat at one and the same time. As Nippers once observed, Turkey's money went chiefly for red ink. One winter day, I presented Turkey with a highly respectable-looking coat of my own — a padded gray coat, of a most comfortable warmth, and which buttoned straight up from the knee to the neck. I thought Turkey would appreciate the favor, and abate his rashness and obstreperousness of afternoons. But no; I verily believe that buttoning himself up in so downy and blanket-like a coat had a pernicious effect upon him — upon the same principle that too much oats are bad for horses. In fact, precisely as a rash, restive horse is said to feel his oats, so Turkey felt his coat. It made him insolent. He was a man whom prosperity harmed.

Though, concerning the self-indulgent habits of Turkey, I had my own private surmises, yet, touching Nippers, I was well persuaded that, whatever might be his faults in other respects, he was, at least, a temperate young man. But, indeed, nature herself seemed to have been his vintner, and, at his birth, charged him so thoroughly with an irritable, brandy-like disposition, that all subsequent potations were needless. When I consider how, amid the stillness of my chambers, Nippers would sometimes impatiently rise from his seat, and stooping over his table, spread his arms wide apart, seize the whole desk, and move it, and jerk it, with a grim, grinding motion on the floor, as if the table were a perverse voluntary agent and vexing him, I plainly perceive that, for Nippers, brandy-and-water were altogether superfluous.

It was fortunate for me that, owing to its peculiar cause — indigestion — the irritability and consequent nervousness of Nippers were mainly observable in the morning, while in the afternoon he was comparatively mild. So that, Turkey's paroxysms only coming on about twelve o'clock, I never had to do with their eccentricities at one time. Their fits relieved each other, like guards. When Nippers's was on, Turkey's was off; and *vice versa*. This was a good natural arrangement, under the circumstances.

Ginger Nut, the third on my list, was a lad, some twelve years old. His father was a car-man, ambitious of seeing his son on the bench instead of a cart, before he died. So he sent him to my office, as student at law, errand-boy, cleaner and sweeper, at the rate of one dollar a week. He had a little desk to himself; but he did not use it much. Upon inspection, the drawer exhibited a great array of shells of various sorts of nuts. Indeed, to this quick-witted youth, the whole noble science of the law was contained in a nutshell. Not the least among the employments of Ginger Nut, as well as one which he discharged with the most alacrity, was his duty as cake and apple purveyor for Turkey and Nippers. Copying law-papers being proverbially a dry, husky sort of business, my two scriveners were fain to moisten their mouths very often with Spitzenbergs,[4] to be had at the numerous stalls nigh the Custom House and Post Office. Also, they sent Ginger Nut very frequently for that peculiar cake — small, flat, round, and very

_____
[4] A variety of apple.

spicy — after which he had been named by them. Of a cold morning, when business was but dull, Turkey would gobble up scores of these cakes, as if they were mere wafers — indeed, they sell them at the rate of six or eight for a penny — the scrape of his pen blending with the crunching of the crisp particles in his mouth. Rashest of all the fiery afternoon blunders and flurried rashnesses of Turkey, was his once moistening a ginger-cake between his lips, and clapping it on to a mortgage, for a seal. I came within an ace of dismissing him then. But he mollified me by making an oriental bow, and saying —

"With submission, sir, it was generous of me to find you in stationery on my 15 own account."

Now my original business — that of a conveyancer and title hunter, and drawer-up of recondite documents of all sorts — was considerably increased by receiving the master's office. There was now great work for scriveners. Not only must I push the clerks already with me, but I must have additional help.

In answer to my advertisement, a motionless young man one morning stood upon my office threshold, the door being open, for it was summer. I can see that figure now — pallidly neat, pitiably respectable, incurably forlorn! It was Bartleby.

After a few words touching his qualifications, I engaged him, glad to have among my corps of copyists a man of so singularly sedate an aspect, which I thought might operate beneficially upon the flighty temper of Turkey, and the fiery one of Nippers.

I should have stated before that ground-glass folding-doors divided my premises into two parts, one of which was occupied by my scriveners, the other by myself. According to my humor, I threw open these doors, or closed them. I resolved to assign Bartleby a corner by the folding-doors, but on my side of them, so as to have this quiet man within easy call, in case any trifling thing was to be done. I placed his desk close up to a small side-window in that part of the room, a window which originally had afforded a lateral view of certain grimy backyards and bricks, but which, owing to subsequent erections, commanded at present no view at all, though it gave some light. Within three feet of the panes was a wall, and the light came down from far above, between two lofty buildings, as from a very small opening in a dome. Still further to a satisfactory arrangement, I procured a high green folding screen, which might entirely isolate Bartleby from my sight, though not remove him from my voice. And thus, in a manner, privacy and society were conjoined.

At first, Bartleby did an extraordinary quantity of writing. As if long famishing 20 for something to copy, he seemed to gorge himself on my documents. There was no pause for digestion. He ran a day and night line, copying by sun-light and by candle-light. I should have been quite delighted with his application, had he been cheerfully industrious. But he wrote on silently, palely, mechanically.

It is, of course, an indispensable part of a scrivener's business to verify the accuracy of his copy, word by word. Where there are two or more scriveners in an office, they assist each other in this examination, one reading from the copy, the other holding the original. It is a very dull, wearisome, and lethargic affair. I

can readily imagine that, to some sanguine temperaments, it would be altogether intolerable. For example, I cannot credit that the mettlesome poet,
Byron, would have contentedly sat down with Bartleby to examine a law document of, say five hundred pages, closely written in a crimpy hand.

Now and then, in the haste of business, it had been my habit to assist in comparing some brief document myself, calling Turkey or Nippers for this purpose.
One object I had, in placing Bartleby so handy to me behind the screen, was to
avail myself of his services on such trivial occasions. It was on the third day, I
think, of his being with me, and before any necessity had arisen for having his
own writing examined, that, being much hurried to complete a small affair I had
in hand, I abruptly called to Bartleby. In my haste and natural expectancy of
instant compliance, I sat with my head bent over the original on my desk, and
my right hand sideways, and somewhat nervously extended with the copy, so
that, immediately upon emerging from his retreat, Bartleby might snatch it and
proceed to business without the least delay.

In this very attitude did I sit when I called to him, rapidly stating what it was I
wanted him to do — namely, to examine a small paper with me. Imagine my
surprise, nay, my consternation, when, without moving from his privacy,
Bartleby, in a singularly mild, firm voice, replied, "I would prefer not to."

I sat awhile in perfect silence, rallying my stunned faculties. Immediately it
occurred to me that my ears had deceived me, or Bartleby had entirely misunderstood my meaning. I repeated my request in the clearest tone I could assume;
but in quite as clear a one came the previous reply, "I would prefer not to."

"Prefer not to," echoed I, rising in high excitement, and crossing the room 25
with a stride. "What do you mean? Are you moon-struck? I want you to help me
compare this sheet here — take it," and I thrust it towards him.

"I would prefer not to," said he.

I looked at him steadfastly. His face was leanly composed; his gray eye dimly
calm. Not a wrinkle of agitation rippled him. Had there been the least uneasiness, anger, impatience, or impertinence in his manner; in other words, had
there been any thing ordinarily human about him, doubtless I should have violently dismissed him from the premises. But as it was, I should have as soon
thought of turning my pale plaster-of-paris bust of Cicero out of doors. I stood
gazing at him awhile, as he went on with his own writing, and then reseated
myself at my desk. This is very strange, thought I. What had one best do? But
my business hurried me. I concluded to forget the matter for the present,
reserving it for my future leisure. So calling Nippers from the other room, the
paper was speedily examined.

A few days after this, Bartleby concluded four lengthy documents, being
quadruplicates of a week's testimony taken before me in my High Court of
Chancery. It became necessary to examine them. It was an important suit, and
great accuracy was imperative. Having all things arranged, I called Turkey, Nippers, and Ginger Nut from the next room, meaning to place the four copies in
the hands of my four clerks, while I should read from the original. Accordingly,

Turkey, Nippers, and Ginger Nut had taken their seats in a row, each with his document in his hand, when I called to Bartleby to join this interesting group.

"Bartleby! quick, I am waiting."

I heard a slow scrape of his chair legs on the uncarpeted floor, and soon he appeared standing at the entrance of his hermitage.

"What is wanted?" said he, mildly.

"The copies, the copies," said I, hurriedly. "We are going to examine them. There — " and I held towards him the fourth quadruplicate.

"I would prefer not to," he said, and gently disappeared behind the screen.

For a few moments I was turned into a pillar of salt, standing at the head of my seated column of clerks. Recovering myself, I advanced towards the screen, and demanded the reason for such extraordinary conduct.

"*Why* do you refuse?"

"I would prefer not to."

With any other man I should have flown outright into a dreadful passion, scorned all further words, and thrust him ignominiously from my presence. But there was something about Bartleby that not only strangely disarmed me, but in a wonderful manner, touched and disconcerted me. I began to reason with him.

"These are your own copies we are about to examine. It is labor saving to you, because one examination will answer for your four papers. It is common usage. Every copyist is bound to help examine his copy. Is it not so? Will you not speak? Answer!"

"I prefer not to," he replied in a flutelike tone. It seemed to me that, while I had been addressing him, he carefully revolved every statement that I made; fully comprehended the meaning; could not gainsay the irresistible conclusion; but, at the same time, some paramount consideration prevailed with him to reply as he did.

"You are decided, then, not to comply with my request — a request made according to common usage and common sense?"

He briefly gave me to understand, that on that point my judgment was sound. Yes: his decision was irreversible.

It is not seldom the case that, when a man is browbeaten in some unprecedented and violently unreasonable way, he begins to stagger in his own plainest faith. He begins, as it were, vaguely to surmise that, wonderful as it may be, all the justice and all the reason is on the other side. Accordingly, if any disinterested persons are present, he turns to them for some reinforcement of his own faltering mind.

"Turkey," said I, "what do you think of this? Am I not right?"

"With submission, sir," said Turkey, in his blandest tone, "I think that you are."

"Nippers," said I, "what do *you* think of it?"

"I think I should kick him out of the office."

(The reader, of nice perceptions, will here perceive that, it being morning, Turkey's answer is couched in polite and tranquil terms, but Nippers replies in

ill-tempered ones. Or, to repeat a previous sentence, Nippers's ugly mood was
on duty, and Turkey's off.)

"Ginger Nut," said I, willing to enlist the smallest suffrage in my behalf, "what
do *you* think of it?"

"I think, sir, he's a little *luny*," replied Ginger Nut, with a grin.

"You hear what they say," said I, turning towards the screen, "come forth and 50
do your duty."

But he vouchsafed no reply. I pondered a moment in sore perplexity. But
once more business hurried me. I determined again to postpone the consideration of this dilemma to my future leisure. With a little trouble we made out to
examine the papers without Bartleby, though at every page or two Turkey deferentially dropped his opinion, that this proceeding was quite out of the common;
while Nippers, twitching in his chair with a dyspeptic nervousness, ground out,
between his set teeth, occasional hissing maledictions against the stubborn oaf
behind the screen. And for his (Nippers's) part, this was the first and the last
time he would do another man's business without pay.

Meanwhile Bartleby sat in his hermitage, oblivious to everything but his own
peculiar business there.

Some days passed, the scrivener being employed upon another lengthy work.
His late remarkable conduct led me to regard his ways narrowly. I observed that
he never went to dinner; indeed, that he never went anywhere. As yet I had
never, of my personal knowledge, known him to be outside of my office. He was
a perpetual sentry in the corner. At about eleven o'clock though, in the morning,
I noticed that Ginger Nut would advance toward the opening in Bartleby's
screen, as if silently beckoned thither by a gesture invisible to me where I sat.
The boy would then leave the office, jingling a few pence, and reappear with a
handful of ginger-nuts, which he delivered in the hermitage, receiving two of
the cakes for his trouble.

He lives, then, on ginger-nuts, thought I; never eats a dinner, properly speaking; he must be a vegetarian, then; but no; he never eats even vegetables; he eats
nothing but ginger-nuts. My mind then ran on in reveries concerning the probable effects upon the human constitution of living entirely on ginger-nuts.
Ginger-nuts are so called, because they contain ginger as one of their peculiar
constituents, and the final flavoring one. Now, what was ginger? A hot, spicy
thing. Was Bartleby hot and spicy? Not at all. Ginger, then, had no effect upon
Bartleby. Probably he preferred it should have none.

Nothing so aggravates an earnest person as a passive resistance. If the indi- 55
vidual so resisted be of a not inhumane temper, and the resisting one perfectly
harmless in his passivity, then, in the better moods of the former, he will
endeavor charitably to construe to his imagination what proves impossible to be
solved by his judgment. Even so, for the most part, I regarded Bartleby and his
ways. Poor fellow! thought I, he means no mischief; it is plain he intends no
insolence; his aspect sufficiently evinces that his eccentricities are involuntary.
He is useful to me. I can get along with him. If I turn him away, the chances are
he will fall in with some less-indulgent employer, and then he will be rudely

treated, and perhaps driven forth miserably to starve. Yes. Here I can cheaply purchase a delicious self-approval. To befriend Bartleby; to humor him in his strange willfulness, will cost me little or nothing, while I lay up in my soul what will eventually prove a sweet morsel for my conscience. But this mood was not invariable with me. The passiveness of Bartleby sometimes irritated me. I felt strangely goaded on to encounter him in new opposition — to elicit some angry spark from him answerable to my own. But, indeed, I might as well have essayed to strike fire with my knuckles against a bit of Windsor soap. But one afternoon the evil impulse in me mastered me, and the following little scene ensued:

"Bartleby," said I, "when those papers are all copied, I will compare them with you."

"I would prefer not to."

"How? Surely you do not mean to persist in that mulish vagary?"

No answer.

I threw open the folding-doors near by, and, turning upon Turkey and Nip- 60
pers, exclaimed:

"Bartleby a second time says, he won't examine his papers. What do you think of it, Turkey?"

It was afternoon, be it remembered. Turkey sat glowing like a brass boiler; his bald head steaming; his hands reeling among his blotted papers.

"Think of it?" roared Turkey; "I think I'll just step behind his screen, and black his eyes for him!"

So saying, Turkey rose to his feet and threw his arms into a pugilistic position. He was hurrying away to make good his promise, when I detained him, alarmed at the effect of incautiously rousing Turkey's combativeness after dinner.

"Sit down, Turkey," said I, "and hear what Nippers has to say. What do you 65
think of it, Nippers? Would I not be justified in immediately dismissing Bartleby?"

"Excuse me, that is for you to decide, sir. I think his conduct quite unusual, and, indeed, unjust, as regards Turkey and myself. But it may only be a passing whim."

"Ah," exclaimed I, "you have strangely changed your mind, then — you speak very gently of him now."

"All beer," cried Turkey; "gentleness is effects of beer — Nippers and I dined together to-day. You see how gentle *I* am, sir. Shall I go and black his eyes?"

"You refer to Bartleby, I suppose. No, not to-day, Turkey," I replied; "pray, put up your fists."

I closed the doors, and again advanced towards Bartleby. I felt additional 70
incentives tempting me to my fate. I burned to be rebelled against again. I remembered that Bartleby never left the office.

"Bartleby," said I, "Ginger Nut is away; just step around to the post office, won't you? (it was but a three minutes' walk), and see if there is anything for me."

"I would prefer not to."

"You *will* not?"

"I *prefer* not."

I staggered to my desk, and sat there in a deep study. My blind inveteracy 75
returned. Was there any other thing in which I could procure myself to be ignominiously repulsed by this lean, penniless wight? — my hired clerk? What
added thing is there, perfectly reasonable, that he will be sure to refuse to do?

"Bartleby!"

No answer.

"Bartleby," in a louder tone.

No answer.

"Bartleby," I roared.

Like a very ghost, agreeably to the laws of magical invocation, at the third 80
summons, he appeared at the entrance of his hermitage.

"Go to the next room, and tell Nippers to come to me."

"I prefer not to," he respectfully and slowly said and mildly disappeared.

"Very good, Bartleby," said I, in a quiet sort of serenely-severe, self-possessed
tone, intimating the unalterable purpose of some terrible retribution very close
at hand. At the moment I half intended something of the kind. But upon the
whole, as it was drawing towards my dinner-hour, I thought it best to put on my
hat and walk home for the day, suffering much from perplexity and distress of
mind.

Shall I acknowledge it? The conclusion of this whole business was, that it
soon became a fixed fact of my chambers, that a pale young scrivener, by the
name of Bartleby, had a desk there; that he copied for me at the usual rate of
four cents a folio (one hundred words); but he was permanently exempt from
examining the work done by him, that duty being transferred to Turkey and
Nippers, out of compliment, doubtless, to their superior acuteness; moreover,
said Bartleby was never, on any account, to be dispatched on the most trivial
errand of any sort; and that even if entreated to take upon him such a matter, it
was generally understood that he would "prefer not to" — in other words, he
would refuse point blank.

As days passed on, I became considerably reconciled to Bartleby. His steadi- 85
ness, his freedom from all dissipation, his incessant industry (except when he
chose to throw himself into a standing revery behind his screen), his great stillness, his unalterableness of demeanor under all circumstances, made him a
valuable acquisition. One prime thing was this — *he was always there* — first in
the morning, continually through the day, and the last at night. I had a singular
confidence in his honesty. I felt my most precious papers perfectly safe in his
hands. Sometimes, to be sure, I could not, for the very soul of me, avoid falling
into sudden spasmodic passions with him. For it was exceeding difficult to bear
in mind all the time those strange peculiarities, privileges, and unheard of
exemptions, forming the tacit stipulations on Bartleby's part under which he
remained in my office. Now and then, in the eagerness of dispatching pressing
business, I would inadvertently summon Bartleby, in a short, rapid tone, to put
his finger, say, on the incipient tie of a bit of red tape with which I was about

compressing some papers. Of course, from behind the screen the usual answer, "I prefer not to," was sure to come; and then, how could a human creature, with the common infirmities of our nature, refrain from bitterly exclaiming upon such perverseness — such unreasonableness? However, every added repulse of this sort which I received only tended to lessen the probability of my repeating the inadvertence.

Here it must be said, that according to the custom of most legal gentlemen occupying chambers in densely-populated law buildings, there were several keys to my door. One was kept by a woman residing in the attic, which person weekly scrubbed and daily swept and dusted my apartments. Another was kept by Turkey for convenience sake. The third I sometimes carried in my own pocket. The fourth I knew not who had.

Now, one Sunday morning I happened to go to Trinity Church, to hear a celebrated preacher, and finding myself rather early on the ground I thought I would walk round to my chambers for a while. Luckily I had my key with me; but upon applying it to the lock, I found it resisted by something inserted from the inside. Quite surprised, I called out; when to my consternation a key was turned from within; and thrusting his lean visage at me, and holding the door ajar, the apparition of Bartleby appeared, in his shirt sleeves, and otherwise in a strangely tattered *déshabillé,* saying quietly that he was sorry, but he was deeply engaged just then, and — preferred not admitting me at present. In a brief word or two, he moreover added, that perhaps I had better walk around the block two or three times, and by that time he would probably have concluded his affairs.

Now, the utterly unsurmised appearance of Bartleby, tenanting my law-chambers of a Sunday morning, with his cadaverously gentlemanly *nonchalance,* yet withal firm and self-possessed, had such a strange effect upon me, that incontinently I slunk away from my own door, and did as desired. But not without sundry twinges of impotent rebellion against the mild effrontery of this unaccountable scrivener. Indeed, it was his wonderful mildness chiefly, which not only disarmed me, but unmanned me as it were. For I consider that one, for the time, is somehow unmanned when he tranquilly permits his hired clerk to dictate to him, and order him away from his own premises. Furthermore, I was full of uneasiness as to what Bartleby could possibly be doing in my office in his shirt sleeves, and in an otherwise dismantled condition of a Sunday morning. Was anything amiss going on? Nay, that was out of the question. It was not to be thought of for a moment that Bartleby was an immoral person. But what could he be doing there? — copying? Nay again, whatever might be his eccentricities, Bartleby was an eminently decorous person. He would be the last man to sit down to his desk in any state approaching to nudity. Besides, it was Sunday; and there was something about Bartleby that forbade the supposition that he would by any secular occupation violate the proprieties of the day.

Nevertheless, my mind was not pacified; and full of a restless curiosity, at last I returned to the door. Without hindrance I inserted my key, opened it, and entered. Bartleby was not to be seen. I looked round anxiously, peeped behind his screen; but it was very plain that he was gone. Upon more closely examining the place, I surmised that for an indefinite period Bartleby must have eaten, dressed, and slept in my office, and that, too, without plate, mirror, or bed. The cushioned seat of a rickety old sofa in one corner bore the faint impress of a lean, reclining form. Rolled away under his desk, I found a blanket; under the empty grate, a blacking box and brush; on a chair, a tin basin, with soap and a ragged towel; in a newspaper a few crumbs of ginger-nuts and a morsel of cheese. Yes, thought I, it is evident enough that Bartleby has been making his home here, keeping bachelor's hall all by himself. Immediately then the thought came sweeping across me, what miserable friendlessness and loneliness are here revealed! His poverty is great; but his solitude, how horrible! Think of it. Of a Sunday, Wall Street is deserted as Petra;[5] and every night of every day it is an emptiness. This building, too, which of week-days hums with industry and life, at nightfall echoes with sheer vacancy, and all through Sunday is forlorn. And here Bartleby makes his home; sole spectator of a solitude which he has seen all populous — a sort of innocent and transformed Marius brooding among the ruins of Carthage![6]

For the first time in my life a feeling of over-powering stinging melancholy 90 seized me. Before, I had never experienced aught but a not unpleasing sadness. The bond of a common humanity now drew me irresistibly to gloom. A fraternal melancholy! For both I and Bartleby were sons of Adam. I remembered the bright silks and sparkling faces I had seen that day, in gala trim, swan-like sailing down the Mississippi of Broadway; and I contrasted them with the pallid copy-ist, and thought to myself, Ah, happiness courts the light, so we deem the world is gay; but misery hides aloof, so we deem that misery there is none. These sad fancyings — chimeras, doubtless, of a sick and silly brain — led on to other and more special thoughts, concerning the eccentricities of Bartleby. Presentiments of strange discoveries hovered round me. The scrivener's pale form appeared to me laid out, among uncaring strangers, in its shivering winding sheet.

Suddenly I was attracted by Bartleby's closed desk, the key in open sight left in the lock.

I mean no mischief, seek the gratification of no heartless curiosity, thought I; besides, the desk is mine, and its contents, too, so I will make bold to look within. Everything was methodically arranged, the papers smoothly placed. The pigeon holes were deep, and removing the files of documents, I groped into their recesses. Presently I felt something there, and dragged it out. It was an old bandanna handkerchief, heavy and knotted. I opened it, and saw it was a sav-ing's bank.

I now recalled all the quiet mysteries which I had noted in the man. I remem-bered that he never spoke but to answer; that, though at intervals he had consid-erable time to himself, yet I had never seen him reading — no, not even a

---

[5] A city in Palestine found by explorers in 1812. It had been deserted and lost for centuries.
[6] Gaius Marius (155–86 B.C.), a plebeian general who was forced to flee from Rome. Nineteenth-century democratic literature sometimes pictured him old and alone among the ruins of Carthage.

newspaper; that for long periods he would stand looking out, at his pale window behind the screen, upon the dead brick wall; I was quite sure he never visited any refectory or eating house; while his pale face clearly indicated that he never drank beer like Turkey; or tea and coffee even, like other men; that he never went anywhere in particular that I could learn; never went out for a walk, unless, indeed, that was the case at present; that he had declined telling who he was, or whence he came, or whether he had any relatives in the world; that though so thin and pale, he never complained of ill health. And more than all, I remembered a certain unconscious air of pallid — how shall I call it? — of pallid haughtiness, say, or rather an austere reserve about him, which had positively awed me into my tame compliance with his eccentricities, when I had feared to ask him to do the slightest incidental thing for me, even though I might know, from his long-continued motionlessness, that behind his screen he must be standing in one of those dead-wall reveries of his.

Revolving all these things, and coupling them with the recently discovered fact, that he made my office his constant abiding place and home, and not forgetful of his morbid moodiness; revolving all these things, a prudential feeling began to steal over me. My first emotions had been those of pure melancholy and sincerest pity; but just in proportion as the forlornness of Bartleby grew and grew to my imagination, did that same melancholy merge into fear, that pity into repulsion. So true it is, and so terrible, too, that up to a certain point the thought or sight of misery enlists our best affections; but, in certain special cases, beyond that point it does not. They err who would assert that invariably this is owing to the inherent selfishness of the human heart. It rather proceeds from a certain hopelessness of remedying excessive and organic ill. To a sensitive being, pity is not seldom pain. And when at last it is perceived that such pity cannot lead to effectual succor, common sense bids the soul be rid of it. What I saw that morning persuaded me that the scrivener was the victim of innate and incurable disorder. I might give alms to his body; but his body did not pain him; it was his soul that suffered, and his soul I could not reach.

I did not accomplish the purpose of going to Trinity Church that morning. 95 Somehow, the things I had seen disqualified me for the time from churchgoing. I walked homeward, thinking what I would do with Bartleby. Finally, I resolved upon this — I would put certain calm questions to him the next morning, touching his history, etc., and if he declined to answer them openly and unreservedly (and I supposed he would prefer not), then to give him a twenty dollar bill over and above whatever I might owe him, and tell him his services were no longer required; but that if in any other way I could assist him, I would be happy to do so, especially if he desired to return to his native place, wherever that might be, I would willingly help to defray the expenses. Moreover, if, after reaching home, he found himself at any time in want of aid, a letter from him would be sure of a reply.

The next morning came.

"Bartleby," said I, gently calling to him behind his screen.

No reply.

"Bartleby," said I, in a still gentler tone, "come here; I am not going to ask you to do anything you would prefer not to do — I simply wish to speak to you."

Upon this he noiselessly slid into view.   100

"Will you tell me, Bartleby, where you were born?"

"I would prefer not to."

"Will you tell me *anything* about yourself?"

"I would prefer not to."

"But what reasonable objection can you have to speak to me? I feel friendly 105
towards you."

He did not look at me while I spoke, but kept his glance fixed upon my bust of Cicero, which, as I then sat, was directly behind me, some six inches above my head.

"What is your answer, Bartleby," said I, after waiting a considerable time for a reply, during which his countenance remained immovable, only there was the faintest conceivable tremor of the white attenuated mouth.

"At present I prefer to give no answer," he said, and retired into his hermitage.

It was rather weak in me I confess, but his manner, on this occasion, nettled me. Not only did there seem to lurk in it a certain calm disdain, but his perverseness seemed ungrateful, considering the undeniable good usage and indulgence he had received from me.

Again I sat ruminating what I should do. Mortified as I was at his behavior, 110
and resolved as I had been to dismiss him when I entered my office, nevertheless I strangely felt something superstitious knocking at my heart, and forbidding me to carry out my purpose, and denouncing me for a villain if I dared to breathe one bitter word against this forlornest of mankind. At last, familiarly drawing my chair behind his screen, I sat down and said: "Bartleby, never mind, then, about revealing your history; but let me entreat you, as a friend, to comply as far as may be with the usages of this office. Say now, you will help to examine papers to-morrow or next day: in short, say now, that in a day or two you will begin to be a little reasonable — say so, Bartleby."

"At present I would prefer not to be a little reasonable," was his mildly cadaverous reply.

Just then the folding-doors opened, and Nippers approached. He seemed suffering from an unusually bad night's rest, induced by severer indigestion than common. He overheard those final words of Bartleby.

"*Prefer not*, eh?" gritted Nippers — "I'd *prefer* him, if I were you, sir," addressing me — "I'd *prefer* him; I'd give him preferences, the stubborn mule! What is it, sir, pray, that he *prefers* not to do now?"

Bartleby moved not a limb.

"Mr. Nippers," said I, "I'd prefer that you would withdraw for the present."   115

Somehow, of late, I had got into the way of involuntarily using this word "prefer" upon all sorts of not exactly suitable occasions. And I trembled to think that my contact with the scrivener had already and seriously affected me in a mental way. And what further and deeper aberration might it not yet produce? This apprehension had not been without efficacy in determining me to summary measures.

As Nippers, looking very sour and sulky, was departing, Turkey blandly and deferentially approached.

"With submission, sir," said he, "yesterday I was thinking about Bartleby here, and I think that if he would but prefer to take a quart of good ale every day, it would do much towards mending him, and enabling him to assist in examining his papers."

"So you have got the word, too," said I, slightly excited.

"With submission, what word, sir," asked Turkey, respectfully crowding him- 120
self into the contracted space behind the screen, and by so doing, making me jostle the scrivener. "What word, sir?"

"I would prefer to be left alone here," said Bartleby, as if offended at being mobbed in his privacy.

"*That's* the word, Turkey," said I — "*that's* it."

"Oh, *prefer?* oh yes — queer word. I never use it myself. But, sir, as I was saying, if he would but prefer — "

"Turkey," interrupted I, "you will please withdraw."

"Oh certainly, sir, if you prefer that I should." 125

As he opened the folding-door to retire, Nippers at his desk caught a glimpse of me, and asked whether I would prefer to have a certain paper copied on blue paper or white. He did not in the least roguishly accent the word prefer. It was plain that it involuntarily rolled from his tongue. I thought to myself, surely I must get rid of a demented man, who already has in some degree turned the tongues, if not the heads of myself and clerks. But I thought it prudent not to break the dismission at once.

The next day I noticed that Bartleby did nothing but stand at his window in his dead-wall revery. Upon asking him why he did not write, he said that he had decided upon doing no more writing.

"Why, how now? What next?" exclaimed I, "do no more writing?"

"No more."

"And what is the reason?" 130

"Do you not see the reason for yourself?" he indifferently replied.

I looked steadfastly at him, and perceived that his eyes looked dull and glazed. Instantly it occurred to me, that his unexampled diligence in copying by his dim window for the first few weeks of his stay with me might have temporarily impaired his vision.

I was touched. I said something in condolence with him. I hinted that of course he did wisely in abstaining from writing for a while; and urged him to embrace that opportunity of taking wholesome exercise in the open air. This, however, he did not do. A few days after this, my other clerks being absent, and being in a great hurry to dispatch certain letters by the mail, I thought that, having nothing else earthly to do, Bartleby would surely be less inflexible than usual, and carry these letters to the post office. But he blankly declined. So, much to my inconvenience, I went myself.

Still added days went by. Whether Bartleby's eyes improved or not, I could not say. To all appearance, I thought they did. But when I asked him if they did, he vouchsafed no answer. At all events, he would do no copying. At last, in reply to my urgings, he informed me that he had permanently given up copying.

"What!" exclaimed I; "suppose your eyes should get entirely well — better   135 than ever before — would you not copy then?"

"I have given up copying," he answered, and slid aside.

He remained as ever, a fixture in my chamber. Nay — if that were possible — he became still more of a fixture than before. What was to be done? He would do nothing in the office; why should he stay there? In plain fact, he had now become a millstone to me, not only useless as a necklace, but afflictive to bear. Yet I was sorry for him. I speak less than truth when I say that, on his own account, he occasioned me uneasiness. If he would but have named a single relative or friend, I would instantly have written, and urged their taking the poor fellow away to some convenient retreat. But he seemed alone, absolutely alone in the universe. A bit of wreck in the mid-Atlantic. At length, necessities connected with my business tyrannized over all other considerations. Decently as I could, I told Bartleby that in six days time he must unconditionally leave the office. I warned him to take measures, in the interval, for procuring some other abode. I offered to assist him in this endeavor, if he himself would but take the first step towards a removal. "And when you finally quit me, Bartleby," added I, "I shall see that you go not away entirely unprovided. Six days from this hour, remember."

At the expiration of that period, I peeped behind the screen, and lo! Bartleby was there.

I buttoned up my coat, balanced myself; advanced slowly towards him, touched his shoulder, and said, "The time has come; you must quit this place; I am sorry for you; here is money; but you must go."

"I would prefer not," he replied, with his back still towards me.   140

"You *must*."

He remained silent.

Now I had an unbounded confidence in this man's common honesty. He had frequently restored to me sixpences and shillings carelessly dropped upon the floor, for I am apt to be very reckless in such shirt-button affairs. The proceeding, then, which followed will not be deemed extraordinary.

"Bartleby," said I, "I owe you twelve dollars on account; here are thirty-two, the odd twenty are yours — Will you take it?" and I handed the bills towards him.

But he made no motion.   145

"I will leave them here, then," putting them under a weight on the table. Then taking my hat and cane and going to the door, I tranquilly turned and added — "After you have removed your things from these offices, Bartleby, you will of course lock the door — since every one is now gone for the day but you — and if you please, slip your key underneath the mat, so that I may have it in the morning. I shall not see you again; so good-by to you. If, hereafter, in your new place of abode, I can be of any service to you, do not fail to advise me by letter. Good-by, Bartleby, and fare you well."

But he answered not a word; like the last column of some ruined temple, he remained standing mute and solitary in the middle of the otherwise deserted room.

As I walked home in a pensive mood, my vanity got the better of my pity. I could not but highly plume myself on my masterly management in getting rid of Bartleby. Masterly I call it, and such it must appear to any dispassionate thinker. The beauty of my procedure seemed to consist in its perfect quietness. There was no vulgar bullying, no bravado of any sort, no choleric hectoring, and striding to and fro across the apartment, jerking out vehement commands for Bartleby to bundle himself off with his beggarly traps. Nothing of the kind. Without loudly bidding Bartleby depart — as an inferior genius might have done — I *assumed* the ground that depart he must; and upon that assumption built all I had to say. The more I thought over my procedure, the more I was charmed with it. Nevertheless, next morning, upon awakening, I had my doubts — I had somehow slept off the fumes of vanity. One of the coolest and wisest hours a man has, is just after he awakes in the morning. My procedure seemed as sagacious as ever — but only in theory. How it would prove in practice — there was the rub. It was truly a beautiful thought to have assumed Bartleby's departure; but, after all, that assumption was simply my own, and none of Bartleby's. The great point was, not whether I had assumed that he would quit me, but whether he would prefer to do so. He was more a man of preferences than assumptions.

After breakfast, I walked down town, arguing the probabilities *pro* and *con*. One moment I thought it would prove a miserable failure, and Bartleby would be found all alive at my office as usual; the next moment it seemed certain that I should find his chair empty. And so I kept veering about. At the corner of Broadway and Canal Street, I saw quite an excited group of people standing in earnest conversation.

"I'll take odds he doesn't," said a voice as I passed.   150

"Doesn't go? — done!" said I; "put up your money."

I was instinctively putting my hand in my pocket to produce my own, when I remembered that this was an election day. The words I had overheard bore no reference to Bartleby, but to the success or non-success of some candidate for the mayoralty. In my intent frame of mind, I had, as it were, imagined that all Broadway shared in my excitement, and were debating the same question with me. I passed on, very thankful that the uproar of the street screened my momentary absent-mindedness.

As I had intended, I was earlier than usual at my office door. I stood listening for a moment. All was still. He must be gone. I tried the knob. The door was locked. Yes, my procedure had worked to a charm; he indeed must be vanished. Yet a certain melancholy mixed with this: I was almost sorry for my brilliant success. I was fumbling under the door mat for the key, which Bartleby was to have left there for me, when accidentally my knee knocked against a panel, producing a summoning sound, and in response a voice came to me from within — "Not yet; I am occupied."

It was Bartleby.

I was thunderstruck. For an instant I stood like the man who, pipe in mouth, 155
was killed one cloudless afternoon long ago in Virginia, by summer lightning; at
his own warm open window he was killed, and remained leaning out there upon
the dreamy afternoon, till some one touched him, when he fell.

"Not gone!" I murmured at last. But again obeying that wondrous ascendancy
which the inscrutable scrivener had over me, and from which ascendancy, for all
my chafing, I could not completely escape, I slowly went down stairs and out
into the street, and while walking round the block, considered what I should
next do in this unheard-of perplexity. Turn the man out by an actual thrusting I
could not; to drive him away by calling him hard names would not do; calling in
the police was an unpleasant idea; and yet, permit him to enjoy his cadaverous
triumph over me — this, too, I could not think of. What was to be done? or, if
nothing could be done, was there anything further that I could *assume* in the
matter? Yes, as before I had prospectively assumed that Bartleby would depart,
so now I might retrospectively assume that departed he was. In the legitimate
carrying out of this assumption, I might enter my office in a great hurry, and
pretending not to see Bartleby at all, walk straight against him as if he were air.
Such a proceeding would in a singular degree have the appearance of a home-
thrust. It was hardly possible that Bartleby could withstand such an application
of the doctrine of assumption. But upon second thoughts the success of the plan
seemed rather dubious. I resolved to argue the matter over with him again.

"Bartleby," said I, entering the office, with a quietly severe expression, "I am
seriously displeased. I am pained, Bartleby. I had thought better of you. I had
imagined you of such a gentlemanly organization, that in any delicate dilemma a
slight hint would suffice — in short, an assumption. But it appears I am
deceived. Why," I added, unaffectedly starting, "you have not even touched that
money yet," pointing to it, just where I had left it the evening previous.

He answered nothing.

"Will you, or will you not, quit me?" I now demanded in a sudden passion,
advancing close to him.

"I would prefer *not* to quit you," he replied, gently emphasizing the *not*. 160

"What earthly right have you to stay here? Do you pay any rent? Do you pay
my taxes? Or is this property yours?"

He answered nothing.

"Are you ready to go on and write now? Are your eyes recovered? Could you
copy a small paper for me this morning? or help examine a few lines? or step
round to the post office? In a word, will you do anything at all, to give a coloring
to your refusal to depart the premises?"

He silently retired into his hermitage.

I was now in such a state of nervous resentment that I thought it but prudent 165
to check myself at present from further demonstrations. Bartleby and I were
alone. I remembered the tragedy of the unfortunate Adams and the still more
unfortunate Colt in the solitary office of the latter; and how poor Colt, being
dreadfully incensed by Adams, and imprudently permitting himself to get
wildly excited, was at unawares hurried into his fatal act — an act which certainly

no man could possibly deplore more than the actor himself.[7] Often it had occurred to me in my ponderings upon the subject that had that altercation taken place in the public street, or at a private residence, it would not have terminated as it did. It was the circumstance of being alone in a solitary office, up stairs, of a building entirely unhallowed by humanizing domestic associations — an uncarpeted office, doubtless, of a dusty, haggard sort of appearance — this it must have been, which greatly helped to enhance the irritable desperation of the hapless Colt.

But when this old Adam of resentment rose in me and tempted me concerning Bartleby, I grappled him and threw him. How? Why, simply by recalling the divine injunction: "A new commandment give I unto you, that ye love one another." Yes, this it was that saved me. Aside from higher considerations, charity often operates as a vastly wise and prudent principle — a great safeguard to its possessor. Men have committed murder for jealousy's sake, and anger's sake, and hatred's sake, and selfishness' sake, and spiritual pride's sake; but no man, that ever I heard of, ever committed a diabolical murder for sweet charity's sake. Mere self-interest, then, if no better motive can be enlisted, should, especially with high-tempered men, prompt all beings to charity and philanthropy. At any rate, upon the occasion in question, I strove to drown my exasperated feelings towards the scrivener by benevolently construing his conduct. Poor fellow, poor fellow! thought I, he don't mean anything; and besides, he has seen hard times, and ought to be indulged.

I endeavored, also, immediately to occupy myself, and at the same time to comfort my despondency. I tried to fancy, that in the course of the morning, at such time as might prove agreeable to him, Bartleby, of his own free accord, would emerge from his hermitage and take up some decided line of march in the direction of the door. But no. Half-past twelve o'clock came; Turkey began to glow in the face, overturn his inkstand, and become generally obstreperous; Nippers abated down into quietude and courtesy; Ginger Nut munched his noon apple; and Bartleby remained standing at his window in one of his profoundest dead-wall reveries. Will it be credited? Ought I to acknowledge it? That afternoon I left the office without saying one further word to him.

Some days now passed, during which, at leisure intervals I looked a little into "Edwards on the Will," and "Priestley on Necessity."[8] Under the circumstances, those books induced a salutary feeling. Gradually I slid into the persuasion that these troubles of mine, touching the scrivener, had been all predestinated from eternity, and Bartleby was billeted upon me for some mysterious purpose of an all-wise Providence, which it was not for a mere mortal like me to fathom. Yes, Bartleby, stay there behind your screen, thought I; I shall persecute you no more; you are harmless and noiseless as any of these old chairs; in short, I never feel so private as when I know you are here. At last I see it, I feel it; I penetrate

---

[7] A sensational homicide case in which Colt murdered Adams in a fit of passion.

[8] Jonathan Edwards (1703–1758), American theologian, and Joseph Priestley (1733–1804), English clergyman and chemist, both held that a person's life was predetermined.

to the predestinated purpose of my life. I am content. Others may have loftier parts to enact; but my mission in this world, Bartleby, is to furnish you with office-room for such period as you may see fit to remain.

I believe that this wise and blessed frame of mind would have continued with me, had it not been for the unsolicited and uncharitable remarks obtruded upon me by my professional friends who visited the rooms. But thus it often is, that the constant friction of illiberal minds wears out at last the best resolves of the more generous. Though to be sure, when I reflected upon it, it was not strange that people entering my office should be struck by the peculiar aspect of the unaccountable Bartleby, and so be tempted to throw out some sinister observations concerning him. Sometimes an attorney, having business with me, and calling at my office, and finding no one but the scrivener there, would undertake to obtain some sort of precise information from him touching my whereabouts; but without heeding his idle talk, Bartleby would remain standing immovable in the middle of the room. So after contemplating him in that position for a time, the attorney would depart, no wiser than he came.

Also, when a reference was going on, and the room full of lawyers and wit-   170
nesses, and business driving fast, some deeply-occupied legal gentleman present, seeing Bartleby wholly unemployed, would request him to run round to his (the legal gentleman's) office and fetch some papers for him. Thereupon, Bartleby would tranquilly decline, and yet remain idle as before. Then the lawyer would give a great stare, and turn to me. And what could I say? At last I was made aware that all through the circle of my professional acquaintance, a whisper of wonder was running round, having reference to the strange creature I kept at my office. This worried me very much. And as the idea came upon me of his possibly turning out a long-lived man, and keep occupying my chambers, and denying my authority; and perplexing my visitors; and scandalizing my professional reputation; and casting a general gloom over the premises; keeping soul and body together to the last upon his savings (for doubtless he spent but half a dime a day), and in the end perhaps outlive me, and claim possession of my office by right of his perpetual occupancy: as all these dark anticipations crowded upon me more and more, and my friends continually intruded their relentless remarks upon the apparition in my room; a great change was wrought in me. I resolved to gather all my faculties together, and forever rid me of this intolerable incubus.

Ere revolving any complicated project, however, adapted to this end, I first simply suggested to Bartleby the propriety of his permanent departure. In a calm and serious tone, I commended the idea to his careful and mature consideration. But, having taken three days to meditate upon it, he apprised me, that his original determination remained the same; in short, that he still preferred to abide with me.

What shall I do? I now said to myself, buttoning up my coat to the last button. What shall I do? what ought I to do? what does conscience say I *should* do with this man, or, rather, ghost. Rid myself of him, I must; go, he shall. But how? You will not thrust him, the poor, pale, passive mortal — you will not thrust such a helpless creature out of your door? you will not dishonor yourself by such cruelty? No, I will not, I cannot do that. Rather would I let him live and die here, and then mason up his remains in the wall. What, then, will you do? For all your coaxing, he will not budge. Bribes he leaves under your own paper-weight on your table; in short, it is quite plain that he prefers to cling to you.

Then something severe, something unusual must be done. What! surely you will not have him collared by a constable, and commit his innocent pallor to the common jail? And upon what ground could you procure such a thing to be done? — a vagrant, is he? What! he a vagrant, a wanderer, who refuses to budge? It is because he will *not* be a vagrant, then, that you seek to count him *as* a vagrant. That is too absurd. No visible means of support: there I have him. Wrong again: for indubitably he *does* support himself, and that is the only unanswerable proof that any man can show of his possessing the means so to do. No more, then. Since he will not quit me, I must quit him. I will change my offices; I will move elsewhere, and give him fair notice, that if I find him in my new premises I will then proceed against him as a common trespasser.

Acting accordingly, next day I thus addressed him: "I find these chambers too far from the City Hall; the air is unwholesome. In a word, I propose to remove my offices next week, and shall no longer require your services. I tell you this now, in order that you may seek another place."

He made no reply, and nothing more was said.   175

On the appointed day I engaged carts and men, proceeded to my chambers, and, having but little furniture, everything was removed in a few hours. Throughout, the scrivener remained standing behind the screen, which I directed to be removed the last thing. It was withdrawn; and, being folded up like a huge folio, left him the motionless occupant of a naked room. I stood in the entry watching him a moment, while something from within me upbraided me.

I re-entered, with my hand in my pocket — and — and my heart in my mouth.

"Good-by, Bartleby; I am going — good-by, and God some way bless you; and take that," slipping something in his hand. But it dropped upon the floor, and then — strange to say — I tore myself from him whom I had so longed to be rid of.

Established in my new quarters, for a day or two I kept the door locked, and started at every footfall in the passages. When I returned to my rooms, after any little absence, I would pause at the threshold for an instant, and attentively listen, ere applying my key. But these fears were needless. Bartleby never came nigh me.

I thought all was going well, when a perturbed-looking stranger visited   180 me, inquiring whether I was the person who had recently occupied rooms at No. ——— Wall Street.

Full of forebodings, I replied that I was.

"Then, sir," said the stranger, who proved a lawyer, "you are responsible for the man you left there. He refuses to do any copying; he refuses to do anything; he says he prefers not to; and he refuses to quit the premises."

"I am very sorry, sir," said I, with assumed tranquillity, but an inward tremor, "but, really, the man you allude to is nothing to me — he is no relation or apprentice of mine, that you should hold me responsible for him."

"In mercy's name, who is he?"

"I certainly cannot inform you. I know nothing about him. Formerly I em- 185 ployed him as a copyist; but he has done nothing for me now for some time past."

"I shall settle him, then — good morning, sir."

Several days passed, and I heard nothing more; and, though I often felt a charitable prompting to call at the place and see poor Bartleby, yet a certain squeamishness, of I know not what, withheld me.

All is over with him, by this time, thought I, at last, when, through another week, no further intelligence reached me. But, coming to my room the day after, I found several persons waiting at my door in a high state of nervous excitement.

"That's the man — here he comes," cried the foremost one, whom I recognized as the lawyer who had previously called upon me alone.

"You must take him away, sir, at once," cried a portly person among them, ad- 190 vancing upon me, and whom I knew to be the landlord of No. ———— Wall Street. "These gentlemen, my tenants, cannot stand it any longer; Mr. B————," pointing to the lawyer, "has turned him out of his room, and he now persists in haunting the building generally, sitting upon the banisters of the stairs by day, and sleeping in the entry by night. Everybody is concerned; clients are leaving the offices; some fears are entertained of a mob; something you must do, and that without delay."

Aghast at this torrent, I fell back before it, and would fain have locked myself in my new quarters. In vain I persisted that Bartleby was nothing to me — no more than to any one else. In vain — I was the last person known to have anything to do with him, and they held me to the terrible account. Fearful, then, of being exposed in the papers (as one person present obscurely threatened), I considered the matter, and, at length, said, that if the lawyer would give me a confidential interview with the scrivener, in his (the lawyer's) own room, I would, that afternoon, strive my best to rid them of the nuisance they complained of.

Going up stairs to my old haunt, there was Bartleby silently sitting upon the banister at the landing.

"What are you doing here, Bartleby?" said I.

"Sitting upon the banister," he mildly replied.

I motioned him into the lawyer's room, who then left us. 195

"Bartleby," said I, "are you aware that you are the cause of great tribulation to me, by persisting in occupying the entry after being dismissed from the office?"

No answer.

"Now one of two things must take place. Either you must do something, or something must be done to you. Now what sort of business would you like to engage in? Would you like to re-engage in copying for some one?"

"No; I would prefer not to make any change."

"Would you like a clerkship in a dry-goods store?" 200

"There is too much confinement about that. No, I would not like a clerkship; but I am not particular."

"Too much confinement," I cried, "why, you keep yourself confined all the time!"

"I would prefer not to take a clerkship," he rejoined, as if to settle that little item at once.

"How would a bar-tender's business suit you? There is no trying of the eyesight in that."

"I would not like it at all; though, as I said before, I am not particular." 205

His unwonted wordiness inspirited me. I returned to the charge.

"Well, then, would you like to travel through the country collecting bills for the merchants? That would improve your health."

"No, I would prefer to be doing something else."

"How, then, would going as a companion to Europe, to entertain some young gentleman with your conversation — how would that suit you?"

"Not at all. It does not strike me that there is anything definite about that. I 210 like to be stationary. But I am not particular."

"Stationary you shall be, then," I cried, now losing all patience, and, for the first time in all my exasperating connection with him, fairly flying into a passion. "If you do not go away from these premises before night, I shall feel bound — indeed, I *am* bound — to — to — to quit the premises myself!" I rather absurdly concluded, knowing not with what possible threat to try to frighten his immobility into compliance. Despairing of all further efforts, I was precipitately leaving him, when a final thought occurred to me — one which had not been wholly unindulged before.

"Bartleby," said I, in the kindest tone I could assume under such exciting circumstances, "will you go home with me now — not to my office, but my dwelling — and remain there till we can conclude upon some convenient arrangement for you at our leisure? Come, let us start now, right away."

"No: at present I would prefer not to make any change at all."

I answered nothing; but, effectually dodging every one by the suddenness and rapidity of my flight, rushed from the building, ran up Wall Street towards Broadway, and, jumping into the first omnibus, was soon removed from pursuit. As soon as tranquillity returned, I distinctly perceived that I had now done all that I possibly could, both in respect to the demands of the landlord and his tenants, and with regard to my own desire and sense of duty, to benefit Bartleby, and shield him from rude persecution. I now strove to be entirely care-free and quiescent; and my conscience justified me in the attempt; though, indeed, it was not so successful as I could have wished. So fearful was I of being again hunted out by the incensed landlord and his exasperated tenants, that, surrendering my business to Nippers, for a few days, I drove about the upper part of the town and through the suburbs, in my rockaway; crossed over to Jersey City and Hoboken, and paid fugitive visits to Manhattanville and Astoria. In fact, I almost lived in my rockaway for the time.

When again I entered my office, lo, a note from the landlord lay upon the 215
desk. I opened it with trembling hands. It informed me that the writer had sent
to the police, and had Bartleby removed to the Tombs as a vagrant. Moreover,
since I knew more about him than any one else, he wished me to appear at that
place, and make a suitable statement of the facts. These tidings had a conflicting
effect upon me. At first I was indignant; but, at last, almost approved. The landlord's energetic, summary disposition, had led him to adopt a procedure which I
do not think I would have decided upon myself; and yet, as a last resort, under
such peculiar circumstances, it seemed the only plan.

As I afterwards learned, the poor scrivener, when told that he must be conducted to the Tombs, offered not the slightest obstacle, but, in his pale, unmoving way, silently acquiesced.

Some of the compassionate and curious by-standers joined the party; and
headed by one of the constables arm in arm with Bartleby, the silent procession
filed its way through all the noise, and heat, and joy of the roaring thoroughfares
at noon.

The same day I received the note, I went to the Tombs, or, to speak more
properly, the Halls of Justice. Seeking the right officer, I stated the purpose
of my call, and was informed that the individual I described was, indeed,
within. I then assured the functionary that Bartleby was a perfectly honest man,
and greatly to be compassionated, however unaccountably eccentric. I narrated
all I knew, and closed by suggesting the idea of letting him remain in as indulgent confinement as possible, till something less harsh might be done —
though, indeed, I hardly knew what. At all events, if nothing else could be
decided upon, the alms-house must receive him. I then begged to have an interview.

Being under no disgraceful charge, and quite serene and harmless in all his
ways, they had permitted him freely to wander about the prison, and, especially,
in the inclosed grass-platted yards thereof. And so I found him there, standing
all alone in the quietest of the yards, his face towards a high wall, while all
around, from the narrow slits of the jail windows, I thought I saw peering out
upon him the eyes of murderers and thieves.

"Bartleby!"   220

"I know you," he said, without looking round — "and I want nothing to say to
you."

"It was not I that brought you here, Bartleby," said I, keenly pained at his
implied suspicion. "And to you, this should not be so vile a place. Nothing
reproachful attaches to you by being here. And see, it is not so sad a place as one
might think. Look, there is the sky, and here is the grass."

"I know where I am," he replied, but would say nothing more, and so I left
him.

As I entered the corridor again, a broad meat-like man, in an apron, accosted
me, and, jerking his thumb over his shoulder, said — "Is that your friend?"

"Yes."   225

"Does he want to starve? If he does, let him live on the prison fare, that's all."

"Who are you?" asked I, not knowing what to make of such an unofficially speaking person in such a place.

"I am the grub-man. Such gentlemen as have friends here, hire me to provide them with something good to eat."

"Is this so?" said I, turning to the turnkey.

He said it was.   230

"Well, then," said I, slipping some silver into the grub-man's hands (for so they called him), "I want you to give particular attention to my friend there; let him have the best dinner you can get. And you must be as polite to him as possible."

"Introduce me, will you?" said the grub-man, looking at me with an expression which seemed to say he was all impatience for an opportunity to give a specimen of his breeding.

Thinking it would prove of benefit to the scrivener, I acquiesced; and, asking the grub-man his name, went up with him to Bartleby.

"Bartleby, this is a friend; you will find him very useful to you."

"Your sarvant, sir, your sarvant," said the grub-man, making a low salutation 235 behind his apron. "Hope you find it pleasant here, sir; nice grounds — cool apartments — hope you'll stay with us some time — try to make it agreeable. What will you have for dinner to-day?"

"I prefer not to dine to-day," said Bartleby, turning away. "It would disagree with me; I am unused to dinners." So saying, he slowly moved to the other side of the inclosure, and took up a position fronting the deadwall.

"How's this?" said the grub-man, addressing me with a stare of astonishment. "He's odd, ain't he?"

"I think he is a little deranged," said I, sadly.

"Deranged? deranged is it? Well, now, upon my word, I thought that friend of yourn was a gentleman forger; they are always pale and genteel-like, them forgers. I can't help pity 'em — can't help it, sir. Did you know Monroe Edwards?" he added, touchingly, and paused. Then, laying his hand piteously on my shoulder, sighed, "he died of consumption at Sing-Sing.[9] So you weren't acquainted with Monroe?"

"No, I was never socially acquainted with any forgers. But I cannot stop 240 longer. Look to my friend yonder. You will not lose by it. I will see you again."

Some few days after this, I again obtained admission to the Tombs, and went through the corridors in quest of Bartleby; but without finding him.

"I saw him coming from his cell not long ago," said a turnkey, "may be he's gone to loiter in the yards."

So I went in that direction.

"Are you looking for the silent man?" said another turnkey, passing me. "Yonder he lies — sleeping in the yard there. 'Tis not twenty minutes since I saw him lie down."

The yard was entirely quiet. It was not accessible to the common prisoners. 245

[9] The state prison near Ossining, New York.

The surrounding walls of amazing thickness, kept off all sounds behind them. The Egyptian character of the masonry weighed upon me with its gloom. But a soft imprisoned turf grew under foot. The heart of the eternal pyramids, it seemed, wherein, by some strange magic, through the clefts, grass-seed, dropped by birds, had sprung.

Strangely huddled at the base of the wall, his knees drawn up, and lying on his side, his head touching the cold stones, I saw the wasted Bartleby. But nothing stirred. I paused; then went close up to him; stooped over, and saw that his dim eyes were open; otherwise he seemed profoundly sleeping. Something prompted me to touch him. I felt his hand, when a tingling shiver ran up my arm and down my spine to my feet.

The round face of the grub-man peered upon me now. "His dinner is ready. Won't he dine to-day, either? Or does he live without dining?"

"Lives without dining," said I, and closed the eyes.

"Eh! — He's asleep, ain't he?"

"With kings and counselors," murmured I.   250

There would seem little need for proceeding further in this history. Imagination will readily supply the meagre recital of poor Bartleby's interment. But, ere parting with the reader, let me say, that if this little narrative has sufficiently interested him, to awaken curiosity as to who Bartleby was, and what manner of life he led prior to the present narrator's making his acquaintance, I can only reply, that in such curiosity I fully share, but am wholly unable to gratify it. Yet here I hardly know whether I should divulge one little item of rumor, which came to my ear a few months after the scrivener's decease. Upon what basis it rested, I could never ascertain; and hence, how true it is I cannot now tell. But, inasmuch as this vague report has not been without a certain suggestive interest to me, however said, it may prove the same with some others; and so I will briefly mention it. The report was this: that Bartleby had been a subordinate clerk in the Dead Letter[10] Office at Washington, from which he had been suddenly removed by a change in the administration. When I think over this rumor, hardly can I express the emotions which seize me. Dead letters! does it not sound like dead men? Conceive a man by nature and misfortune prone to a pallid hopelessness, can any business seem more fitted to heighten it than that of continually handling these dead letters, and assorting them for the flames? For by the cart-load they are annually burned. Some times from out the folded paper the pale clerk takes a ring — the finger it was meant for, perhaps, moulders in the grave; a bank-note sent in swiftest charity — he whom it would relieve, nor eats nor hungers any more; pardon for those who died despairing; hope for those who died unhoping; good tidings for those who died stifled by unrelieved calamities. On errands of life, these letters speed to death.

Ah, Bartleby! Ah, humanity!

---

[10] A letter that is undeliverable because it lacks a correct address and unreturned to the sender.

For Analysis

1. List a half dozen adjectives that describe the narrator. Would the narrator agree that these adjectives are accurate?

2. What is it about Bartleby that so intrigues and fascinates the narrator? Why does the narrator continue to feel a moral obligation to an employee who refuses to work and curtly rejects kind offers of help?

3. What thematic function do Turkey and Nippers serve?

4. As the narrator congratulates himself on the cleverness of his scheme to dismiss Bartleby, he becomes fascinated with his "assumptions" about how Bartleby will behave. Examine the passage (paras. 149–56), and show how it advances the narrator's growing awareness of what Bartleby represents.

5. Readers differ as to whether this is the story of Bartleby or the lawyer-narrator. What is your view?

6. Would it be fair to describe Bartleby as a rebel without a cause, as a young man who refuses to participate in a comfortable and well-ordered business world but fails to offer any alternative way of life? Write a paragraph or two explaining why or why not.

On Style

1. Identify the humor in this somber story, and discuss its sources.

2. Suppose that Melville had given us some biographical information that would help explain Bartleby's character—say, a hideous childhood of abuse and neglect. Would that make this a better story? Explain.

Making Connections

What comparisons and contrasts can be drawn between Bartleby's form of rebellion and the rebellion of those who leave Omelas in Le Guin's "The Ones Who Walk Away from Omelas" (p. 393)?

Writing Topics

1. About midway through the story (paras. 87–94), the narrator discovers that Bartleby has been living in the law offices and is profoundly moved when his eyes fall on the scrivener's worldly possessions. Reread those paragraphs, and write an analysis showing how they describe the narrator's growing awareness of who Bartleby is.

2. With his final utterance, "Ah, Bartleby! Ah, humanity!" the narrator apparently penetrates the mystery of the silent scrivener. The comment suggests that the narrator sees Bartleby as a representative of humanity. In what sense might the narrator have come to see Bartleby in this light?

3. Why does Melville allow the narrator (and the reader) to discover so little about Bartleby and the causes of his behavior? All we learn of Bartleby's past is related in the next-to-last paragraph. What clues does this paragraph give us to the narrator's fascination with Bartleby?

Franz Kafka   (1883–1924)

A Hunger Artist   1924

Translated by Edwin and Willa Muir

During these last decades the interest in professional fasting has markedly diminished. It used to pay very well to stage such great performances under one's own management, but today that is quite impossible. We live in a different world now. At one time the whole town took a lively interest in the hunger artist; from day to day of his fast the excitement mounted; everybody wanted to see him at least once a day; there were people who bought season tickets for the last few days and sat from morning till night in front of his small barred cage; even in the nighttime there were visiting hours, when the whole effect was heightened by torch flares; on fine days the cage was set out in the open air, and then it was the children's special treat to see the hunger artist; for their elders he was often just a joke that happened to be in fashion, but the children stood open-mouthed, holding each other's hands for greater security, marveling at him as he sat there pallid in black tights, with his ribs sticking out so prominently, not even on a seat but down among straw on the ground, sometimes giving a courteous nod, answering questions with a constrained smile, or perhaps stretching an arm through the bars so that one might feel how thin it was, and then again withdrawing deep into himself, paying no attention to anyone or anything, not even to the all-important striking of the clock that was the only piece of furniture in his cage, but merely staring into vacancy with half shut eyes, now and then taking a sip from a tiny glass of water to moisten his lips.

Besides casual onlookers there were also relays of permanent watchers selected by the public, usually butchers, strangely enough, and it was their task to watch the hunger artist day and night, three of them at a time, in case he should have some secret recourse to nourishment. This was nothing but a formality, instituted to reassure the masses, for the initiates knew well enough that during his fast the artist would never in any circumstances, not even under forcible compulsion, swallow the smallest morsel of food; the honor of his profession forbade it. Not every watcher, of course, was capable of understanding this; there were often groups of night watchers who were very lax in carrying out their duties and deliberately huddled together in a retired corner to play cards with great absorption, obviously intending to give the hunger artist the chance of a little refreshment, which they supposed he could draw from some private hoard. Nothing annoyed the artist more than such watchers; they made him miserable; they made his fast seem unendurable; sometimes he mastered his feebleness sufficiently to sing during their watch for as long as he could keep going, to show them how unjust their suspicions were. But that was of little use; they only wondered at his cleverness in being able to fill his mouth even while singing. Much more to his taste were the watchers who sat close up to the bars, who were not content with the dim night lighting of the hall but focused him in the full glare of the electric pocket torch given them by the impresario. The harsh light did not trouble him at all, in any case he could never sleep properly, and he could always drowse a little, whatever the light, at any hour, even when the hall was thronged with noisy onlookers. He was quite happy at the prospect of spending a sleepless night with such watchers; he was ready to exchange jokes with them, to tell them stories out of his nomadic life, anything at all to keep them awake and demonstrate to them again that he had no eatables in his cage and that he was fasting as not one of them could fast. But his happiest moment was when the morning came and an enormous breakfast was brought them, at his expense, on which they flung themselves with the keen appetite of healthy men after a weary night of wakefulness. Of course there were people who argued that this breakfast was an unfair attempt to bribe the watchers, but that was going rather too far, and when they were invited to take on a night's vigil without a breakfast, merely for the sake of the cause, they made themselves scarce, although they stuck stubbornly to their suspicions.

Such suspicions, anyhow, were a necessary accompaniment to the profession of fasting. No one could possibly watch the hunger artist continuously, day and night, and so no one could produce first-hand evidence that the fast had really been rigorous and continuous; only the artist himself could know that, he was therefore bound to be the sole completely satisfied spectator of his own fast. Yet for other reasons he was never satisfied; it was not perhaps mere fasting that had brought him to such skeleton thinness that many people had regretfully to keep away from his exhibitions, because the sight of him was too much for them, perhaps it was dissatisfaction with himself that had worn him down. For he alone knew, what no other initiate knew, how easy it was to fast. It was the easiest thing in the world. He made no secret of this, yet people did not believe him, at the best they set him down as modest; most of them, however, thought he was out for publicity or else was some kind of cheat who found it easy to fast because he had discovered a way of making it easy, and then had the impudence to admit the fact, more or less. He had to put up with all that, and in the course of time had got used to it, but his inner dissatisfaction always rankled, and never yet, after any term of fasting — this must be granted to his credit — had he left the cage of his own free will. The longest period of fasting was fixed by his impresario at forty days, beyond that term he was not allowed to go, not even in great cities, and there was good reason for it, too. Experience had proved that for about forty days the interest of the public could be stimulated by a steadily increasing pressure of advertisement, but after that the town began to lose interest, sympathetic support began notably to fall off; there were of course local variations as between one town and another or one country and another, but as a general rule forty days marked the limit. So on the fortieth day the flower bedecked cage was opened, enthusiastic spectators filled the hall, a military band played, two doctors entered the cage to measure the results of the fast, which were announced through a megaphone, and finally two young ladies appeared, blissful at having been selected for the honor, to help the hunger artist down the few steps leading to a small table on which was spread a carefully chosen invalid repast. And at this very moment the artist always turned stubborn. True, he would entrust his bony arms to the outstretched helping hands of the ladies bending over him, but stand up he would not. Why stop fasting at this particular moment, after forty days of it? He had held out for a long time, an illimitably long time; why stop now, when he was in his best fasting form, or rather, not yet quite in his best fasting form? Why should he be cheated of the fame he would get for fasting longer, for being not only the record hunger artist of all time, which presumably he was already, but for beating his own record by a performance beyond human imagination, since he felt that there were no limits to his capacity for fasting? His public pretended to admire him so much, why should it have so little patience with him; if he could endure fasting longer, why shouldn't the public endure it? Besides, he was tired, he was comfortable sitting in the straw, and now he was supposed to lift himself to his full height and go down to a meal the very thought of which gave him a nausea that only the presence of the ladies kept him from betraying, and even that with an effort. And he looked up into the eyes of the ladies who were apparently so friendly and in reality so cruel, and shook his head, which felt too heavy on its strengthless neck. But then there happened yet again what always happened. The impresario came forward, without a word — for the band made speech impossible — lifted his arms in the air above the artist, as if inviting Heaven to look down upon its creature here in the straw, this suffering martyr, which indeed he was, although in quite another sense; grasped him round the emaciated waist, with exaggerated caution, so that the frail condition he was in might be appreciated; and committed him to the care of the blenching ladies, not without secretly giving him a shaking so that his legs and body tottered and swayed. The artist now submitted completely; his head lolled on his breast as if it had landed there by chance; his body was hollowed out; his legs in a spasm of self-preservation clung close to each other at the knees, yet scraped on the ground as if it were not really solid ground, as if they were only trying to find solid ground; and the whole weight of his body, a feather-weight after all, relapsed onto one of the ladies, who, looking round for help and panting a little — this post of honor was not at all what she had expected it to be — first stretched her neck as far as she could to keep her face at least free from contact with the artist, when finding this impossible, and her more fortunate companion not coming to her aid but merely holding extended on her own trembling hand the little bunch of knucklebones that was the artist's, to the great delight of the spectators burst into tears and had to be replaced by an attendant who had long been stationed in readiness. Then came the food, a little of which the impresario managed to get between the artist's lips, while he sat in a kind of half-fainting trance, to the accompaniment of cheerful patter designed to distract the public's attention from the artist's condition; after that a toast was drunk to the public, supposedly prompted by a whisper from the artist in the impresario's ear; the band confirmed it with a mighty flourish, the spectators melted away, and no one had any cause to be dissatisfied with the proceedings, no one except the hunger artist himself, he only, as always.

So he lived for many years, with small regular intervals of recuperation, in visible glory, honored by the world, yet in spite of that troubled in spirit, and all the more troubled because no one would take his trouble seriously. What comfort could he possibly need? What more could he possibly wish for? And if some good-natured person, feeling sorry for him, tried to console him by pointing out that his melancholy was probably caused by fasting; it could happen, especially when he had been fasting for some time, that he reacted with an outburst of fury and to the general alarm began to shake the bars of his cage like a wild animal. Yet the impresario had a way of punishing these outbreaks which he rather enjoyed putting into operation. He would apologize publicly for the artist's behavior, which was only to be excused, he admitted, because of the irritability caused by fasting; a condition hardly to be understood by well-fed people; then by natural transition he went on to mention the artist's equally incomprehensible boast that he could fast for much longer than he was doing; he praised the high ambition, the good will, the great self-denial undoubtedly implicit in such a statement; and then quite simply countered it by bringing out photographs, which were also on sale to the public, showing the artist on the fortieth day of a fast lying in bed almost dead from exhaustion. This perversion of the truth, familiar to the artist though it was, always unnerved him afresh and proved too much for him. What was a consequence of the premature ending of his fast was here presented as the cause of it! To fight against this lack of understanding, against a whole world of nonunderstanding, was impossible. Time and again in good faith he stood by the bars listening to the impresario, but as soon as the photographs appeared he always let go and sank with a groan back on to his straw, and the reassured public could once more come close and gaze at him.

A few years later when the witnesses of such scenes called them to mind, they 5 often failed to understand themselves at all. For meanwhile the aforementioned change in public interest had set in; it seemed to happen almost overnight; there may have been profound causes for it, but who was going to bother about that; at any rate the pampered hunger artist suddenly found himself deserted one fine day by the amusement seekers, who were streaming past him to other more favored attractions. For the last time the impresario hurried him over half Europe to discover whether the old interest might still survive here and there; all in vain; everywhere, as if by secret agreement, a positive revulsion from professional fasting was in evidence. Of course it could not really have sprung up so suddenly as all that, and many premonitory symptoms which had not been sufficiently remarked or suppressed during the rush and glitter of success now came retrospectively to mind, but it was now too late to take any countermeasures. Fasting would surely come into fashion again at some future date, yet that was no comfort for those living in the present. What, then, was the hunger artist to do? He had been applauded by thousands in his time and could hardly come down to showing himself in a street booth at village fairs, and as for adopting another profession, he was not only too old for that but too frantically devoted to fasting. So he took leave of the impresario, his partner in an unparalleled career, and hired himself to a large circus; in order to spare his own feelings he avoided reading the conditions of his contract.

A large circus with its enormous traffic in replacing and recruiting men, animals, and apparatus can always find a use for people at any time, even for a hunger artist, provided of course that he does not ask too much, and in this particular case anyhow it was not only the artist who was taken on but his famous and long-known name as well, indeed considering the peculiar nature of his performance, which was not impaired by advancing age, it could not be objected that there was an artist past his prime, no longer at the height of his professional skill, seeking a refuge in some quiet corner of a circus; on the contrary, the hunger artist averred that he could fast as well as ever, which was entirely credible; he even alleged that if he were allowed to fast as he liked, and this was at once promised him without more ado, he could astound the world by establishing a record never yet achieved, a statement which certainly provoked a smile among the other professionals, since it left out of account the change in public opinion, which the hunger artist in his zeal conveniently forgot.

He had not, however, actually lost his sense of the real situation and took it as a matter of course that he and his cage should be stationed, not in the middle of the ring as a main attraction, but outside, near the animal cages, on a site that was after all easily accessible. Large and gaily painted placards made a frame for the cage and announced what was to be seen inside it. When the public came thronging out in the intervals to see the animals, they could hardly avoid passing the hunger artist's cage and stopping there for a moment; perhaps they might even have stayed longer had not those pressing behind them in the narrow gangway, who did not understand why they should be held up on their way toward the excitements of the menagerie, made it impossible for anyone to stand gazing quietly for any length of time. And that was the reason why the hunger artist, who had of course been looking forward to these visiting hours as the main achievement of his life, began instead to shrink from them. At first he could hardly wait for the intervals; it was exhilarating to watch the crowds come streaming his way, until only too soon — not even the most obstinate self-deception, clung to almost consciously, could hold out against the fact — the conviction was borne in upon him that these people, most of them, to judge from their actions, again and again, without exception, were all on their way to the menagerie. And the first sight of them from the distance remained the best. For when they reached his cage he was at once deafened by the storm of shouting and abuse that arose from the two contending factions, which renewed themselves continuously, of those who wanted to stop and stare at him — he soon began to dislike them more than the others — not out of real interest but only out of obstinate self-assertiveness, and those who wanted to go straight on to the animals. When the first great rush was past, the stragglers came along, and these, whom nothing could have prevented from stopping to look at him as long as they had breath, raced past with long strides, hardly even glancing at him, in their haste to get to the menagerie in time. And all too rarely did it happen that he had a stroke of luck, when some father of a family fetched up before him with his children, pointed a finger at the hunger artist, and explained at length what the phenomenon meant, telling stories of earlier years when he himself had watched similar but much more thrilling performances, and the children, still rather uncomprehending, since neither inside nor outside school had they been sufficiently prepared for this lesson — what did they care about fasting? — yet showed by the brightness of their intent eyes that new and better times might be coming. Perhaps, said the hunger artist to himself many a time, things would be a little better if his cage were set not quite so near the menagerie. That made it too easy for people to make their choice, to say nothing of what he suffered from the stench of the menagerie, the animals' restlessness by night, the carrying past of raw lumps of flesh for the beasts of prey, the roaring at feeding times, which depressed him continually. But he did not dare to lodge a complaint with the management; after all, he had the animals to thank for the troops of people who passed his cage, among whom there might always be one here and there to take an interest in him, and who could tell where they might seclude him if he called attention to his existence and thereby to the fact that, strictly speaking, he was only an impediment on the way to the menagerie.

A small impediment, to be sure, one that grew steadily less. People grew familiar with the strange idea that they could be expected, in times like these, to take an interest in a hunger artist, and with this familiarity the verdict went out against him. He might fast as much as he could, and he did so; but nothing could save him now, people passed him by. Just try to explain to anyone the art of fasting! Anyone who has no feeling for it cannot be made to understand it. The fine placards grew dirty and illegible, they were torn down; the little notice board telling the number of fast days achieved, which at first was changed carefully every day, had long stayed at the same figure, for after the first few weeks even this small task seemed pointless to the staff; and so the artist simply fasted on and on, as he had once dreamed of doing, and it was no trouble to him, just as he had always foretold, but no one counted the days, no one, not even the artist himself, knew what records he was already breaking, and his heart grew heavy. And when once in a time some leisurely passerby stopped, made merry over the old figure on the board, and spoke of swindling, that was in its way the stupidest lie ever invented by indifference and inborn malice, since it was not the hunger artist who was cheating; he was working honestly, but the world was cheating him of his reward.

Many more days went by, however, and that too came to an end. An overseer's eye fell on the cage one day and asked the attendants why this perfectly good cage should be left standing there unused with dirty straw inside it; nobody knew, until one man, helped out by the notice board, remembered about the hunger artist. They poked into the straw with sticks and found him in it. "Are you still fasting?" asked the overseer. "When on earth do you mean to stop?" "Forgive me, everybody," whispered the hunger artist; only the overseer, who had his ear to the bars, understood him. "Of course," said the overseer, and tapped his forehead with a finger to let the attendants know what state the man was in, "we forgive you." "I always wanted you to admire my fasting," said the hunger artist. "We do admire it," said the overseer, affably. "But you shouldn't admire it," said the hunger artist. "Well, then we don't admire it," said the overseer, "but why shouldn't we admire it?" "Because I have to fast, I can't help it," said the hunger artist. "What a fellow you are," said the overseer, "and why can't you help it?" "Because," said the hunger artist, lifting his head a little and speaking, with his lips pursed, as if for a kiss, right into the overseer's ear, so that no syllable might be lost, "because I couldn't find the food I liked. If I had found it, believe me, I should have made no fuss and stuffed myself like you or anyone else." These were his last words, but in his dimming eyes remained the firm though no longer proud persuasion that he was still continuing to fast.

"Well, clear this out now!" said the overseer, and they buried the hunger 10 artist, straw and all. Into the cage they put a young panther. Even the most insensitive felt it refreshing to see this wild creature leaping around the cage that had so long been dreary. The panther was all right. The food he liked was brought him without hesitation by the attendants; he seemed not even to miss his freedom; his noble body, furnished almost to the bursting point with all that it needed, seemed to carry freedom around with it too; somewhere in his jaws it seemed to lurk; and the joy of life streamed with such ardent passion from his throat that for the onlookers it was not easy to stand the shock of it. But they braced themselves, crowded round the cage, and did not want ever to move away.

For Analysis

1. Many readers interpret this story as a parable of the artist in the modern world, while others see it as a religious parable. What evidence do you find in the story to support either reading?

2. Suggest reasons for Kafka's selection of an expert in fasting (rather than a priest or a singer, for example) as the central figure in the story.

3. Describe the hunger artist's relationship with his audience.

4. Since his greatest achievements involve inwardness and withdrawal, why does the hunger artist, nevertheless, seem to need an audience?

On Style

1. How does Kafka manage to achieve such a bizarre, dreamlike effect with dry and factual prose?

2. Note that the story is told from the point of view of an **omniscient** narrator. How might its impact differ if it were told from the point of view of the hunger artist or of his agent/manager?

Making Connections

1. Compare this story with Hawthorne's "Young Goodman Brown" (p. 80) and Melville's "Bartleby the Scrivener" (p. 334). What similarities do the central figures in the three stories share? What differences do you find? How does the alienation of each of the central figures contribute to each story's theme?

2. Describe feelings of isolation and alienation that you have personally experienced. What caused those feelings? How did you cope with them? How, finally, do you differ from the hunger artist?

Writing Topics

1. Should the hunger artist be admired for his passionate and single-minded devotion to his art or condemned for his withdrawal from humanity and his sickness of will? Why? Your response should discuss the significance of the panther put in the cage after the artist's death.

2. In an essay, compare the hunger artist with Melville's Bartleby. Consider the origins, rationale, consequences, and significance of their behavior.

James Thurber   (1894–1961)

The Greatest Man in the World   1935

Looking back on it now, from the vantage point of 1950, one can only marvel that it hadn't happened long before it did. The United States of America had been, ever since Kitty Hawk, blindly constructing the elaborate petard by which, sooner or later, it must be hoist. It was inevitable that some day there would come roaring out of the skies a national hero of insufficient intelligence, background, and character successfully to endure the mounting orgies of glory prepared for aviators who stayed up a long time or flew a great distance. Both Lindbergh and Byrd, fortunately for national decorum and international amity, had been gentlemen; so had our other famous aviators. They wore their laurels gracefully, withstood the awful weather of publicity, married excellent women, usually of fine family, and quietly retired to private life and the enjoyment of their varying fortunes. No untoward incidents, on a worldwide scale, marred the perfection of their conduct on the perilous heights of fame. The exception to the rule was, however, bound to occur and it did, in July, 1937, when Jack ("Pal") Smurch, erstwhile mechanics' helper in a small garage in Westfield, Iowa, flew a second-hand, single-motored Bresthaven Dragon-Fly III monoplane all the way around the world, without stopping.

Never before in the history of aviation had such a flight as Smurch's ever been dreamed of. No one had even taken seriously the weird floating auxiliary gas tanks, invention of the mad New Hampshire professor of astronomy, Dr. Charles Lewis Gresham, upon which Smurch placed full reliance. When the garage worker, a slightly built, surly, unprepossessing young man of twenty-two, appeared at Roosevelt Field in early July, 1937, slowly chewing a great quid of scrap tobacco, and announced "Nobody ain't seen no flyin' yet," the newspapers touched briefly and satirically upon his projected twenty-five-thousand-mile flight. Aeronautical and automotive experts dismissed the idea curtly, implying that it was a hoax, a publicity stunt. The rusty, battered, second-hand plane wouldn't go. The Gresham auxiliary tanks wouldn't work. It was simply a cheap joke.

Smurch, however, after calling on a girl in Brooklyn who worked in the flap-folding department of a large paper-box factory, a girl whom he later described as his "sweet patootie," climbed nonchalantly into his ridiculous plane at dawn of the memorable seventh of July, 1937, spat a curve of tobacco juice into the still air, and took off, carrying with him only a gallon of bootleg gin and six pounds of salami.

370

When the garage boy thundered out over the ocean the papers were forced to record, in all seriousness, that a mad, unknown young man — his name was variously misspelled — had actually set out upon a preposterous attempt to span the world in a rickety, one-engined contraption, trusting to the long-distance refueling device of a crazy schoolmaster. When, nine days later, without having stopped once, the tiny plane appeared above San Francisco Bay, headed for New York, spluttering and choking, to be sure, but still magnificently and miraculously aloft, the headlines, which long since had crowded everything else off the front page — even the shooting of the Governor of Illinois by the Vileti gang — swelled to unprecedented size, and the news stories began to run to twenty-five and thirty columns. It was noticeable, however, that the accounts of the epoch-making flight touched rather lightly upon the aviator himself. This was not because facts about the hero as a man were too meagre, but because they were too complete.

Reporters, who had been rushed out to Iowa when Smurch's plane was first 5 sighted over the little French coast town of Serly-le-Mar, to dig up the story of the great man's life, had promptly discovered that the story of his life could not be printed. His mother, a sullen short-order cook in a shack restaurant on the edge of a tourists' camping ground near Westfield, met all enquiries as to her son with an angry, "Ah, the hell with him; I hope he drowns." His father appeared to be in jail somewhere for stealing spotlights and laprobes from tourists' automobiles; his younger brother, a weak-minded lad, had but recently escaped from the Preston, Iowa, Reformatory and was already wanted in several Western towns for the theft of money-order blanks from post offices. These alarming discoveries were still piling up at the very time that Pal Smurch, the greatest hero of the twentieth century, blear-eyed, dead for sleep, half-starved, was piloting his crazy junk-heap high above the region in which the lamentable story of his private life was being unearthed, headed for New York under greater glory than any man of his time had ever known.

The necessity for printing some account in the papers of the young man's career and personality had led to a remarkable predicament. It was of course impossible to reveal the facts, for a tremendous popular feeling in favor of the young hero had sprung up, like a grass fire, when he was halfway across Europe on his flight around the globe. He was, therefore, described as a modest chap, taciturn, blond, popular with his friends, popular with girls. The only available snapshot of Smurch, taken at the wheel of a phony automobile in a cheap photo studio at an amusement park, was touched up so that the little vulgarian looked quite handsome. His twisted leer was smoothed into a pleasant smile. The truth was, in this way, kept from the youth's ecstatic compatriots; they did not dream that the Smurch family was despised and feared by its neighbors in the obscure Iowa town, nor that the hero himself, because of numerous unsavory exploits, had come to be regarded in Westfield as a nuisance and a menace. He had, the reporters discovered, once knifed the principal of his high school — not mortally, to be sure, but he had knifed him; and on another occasion, surprised in the act of stealing an altar-cloth from a church, he had bashed the sacristan over the head with a pot of Easter lilies; for each of these offences he had served a sentence in the reformatory.

Inwardly, the authorities, both in New York and in Washington, prayed that an understanding Providence might, however awful such a thing seemed, bring disaster to the rusty, battered plane and its illustrious pilot, whose unheard-of flight had aroused the civilized world to hosannas of hysterical praise. The authorities were convinced that the character of the renowned aviator was such that the limelight of adulation was bound to reveal him to all the world, as a congenital hooligan mentally and morally unequipped to cope with his own prodigious fame. "I trust," said the Secretary of State, at one of many secret Cabinet meetings called to consider the national dilemma, "I trust that his mother's prayer will be answered," by which he referred to Mrs. Emma Smurch's wish that her son might be drowned. It was, however, too late for that — Smurch had leaped the Atlantic and then the Pacific as if they were millponds. At three minutes after two o'clock in the afternoon of 17 July, 1937, the garage boy brought his idiotic plane into Roosevelt Field for a perfect three-point landing.

It had, of course, been out of the question to arrange a modest little reception for the greatest flier in the history of the world. He was received at Roosevelt Field with such elaborate and pretentious ceremonies as rocked the world. Fortunately, however, the worn and spent hero promptly swooned, had to be removed bodily from his plane, and was spirited from the field without having opened his mouth once. Thus he did not jeopardize the dignity of this first reception, a reception illumined by the presence of the Secretaries of War and the Navy, Mayor Michael J. Moriarity of New York, the Premier of Canada, Governors Fanniman, Groves, McFeely, and Critchfield, and a brilliant array of European diplomats. Smurch did not, in fact, come to in time to take part in the gigantic hullabaloo arranged at City Hall for the next day. He was rushed to a secluded nursing home and confined to bed. It was nine days before he was able to get up, or to be more exact, before he was permitted to get up. Meanwhile the greatest minds in the country, in solemn assembly, had arranged a secret conference of city, state and government officials, which Smurch was to attend for the purpose of being instructed in the ethics and behavior of heroism.

On the day that the little mechanic was finally allowed to get up and dress and, for the first time in two weeks, took a great chew of tobacco, he was permitted to receive the newspapermen — this by way of testing him out. Smurch did not wait for questions. "Youse guys," he said — and the *Times* man winced — "youse guys can tell the cock-eyed world dat I put it over on Lindbergh, see? Yes — an' made an ass o' them two frogs." The "two frogs" was a reference to a pair of gallant French fliers who, in attempting a flight only halfway round the world, had, two weeks before, unhappily been lost at sea. The *Times* man was bold enough, at this point, to sketch out for Smurch the accepted formula for interviews in cases of this kind; he explained that there should be no arrogant statements belittling the achievements of other heroes, particularly heroes of foreign nations. "Ah, the hell with that," said Smurch. "I did it, see? I did it, an' I'm talkin' about it." And he did talk about it.

None of this extraordinary interview was, of course, printed. On the contrary, 10
the newspapers, already under the disciplined direction of a secret directorate
created for the occasion and composed of statesmen and editors, gave out to a
panting and restless world that "Jacky," as he had been arbitrarily nicknamed,
would consent to say only that he was very happy and that anyone could have
done what he did. "My achievement has been, I fear, slightly exaggerated," the
Times man's article had him protest, with a modest smile. These newspaper stories were kept from the hero, a restriction which did not serve to abate the rising
malevolence of his temper. The situation was, indeed, extremely grave, for Pal
Smurch was, as he kept insisting, "rarin' to go." He could not much longer be
kept from a nation clamorous to lionize him. It was the most desperate crisis the
United States of America had faced since the sinking of the *Lusitania*.

On the afternoon of the twenty-seventh of July, Smurch was spirited away to a
conference-room in which were gathered mayors, governors, government officials, behaviorist psychologists, and editors. He gave them each a limp, moist
paw and a brief unlovely grin. "Hah ya?" he said. When Smurch was seated, the
Mayor of New York arose and, with obvious pessimism, attempted to explain
what he must say and how he must act when presented to the world, ending his
talk with a high tribute to the hero's courage and integrity. The Mayor was followed by Governor Fanniman of New York, who, after a touching declaration of
faith, introduced Cameron Spottiswood, Second Secretary of the American
Embassy in Paris, the gentleman selected to coach Smurch in the amenities of
public ceremonies. Sitting in a chair, with a soiled yellow tie in his hand and his
shirt open at the throat, unshaved, smoking a rolled cigarette, Jack Smurch listened with a leer on his lips. "I get ya, I get ya," he cut in nastily. "Ya want me to
ack like a softy, huh? Ya want me to ack like that — baby-faced Lindbergh, huh?
Well, nuts to that, see?" Everyone took in his breath sharply; it was a sigh and a
hiss. "Mr. Lindbergh," began a United States Senator, purple with rage, "and
Mr. Byrd — " Smurch, who was paring his nails with a jackknife, cut in again.
"Byrd!" he exclaimed. "Aw fa God's sake, dat big — " Somebody shut off his
blasphemies with a sharp word. A newcomer had entered the room. Everyone
stood up, except Smurch, who, still busy with his nails, did not even glance up.
"Mr. Smurch," said someone sternly, "the President of the United States!"
It had been thought that the presence of the Chief Executive might have a
chastening effect upon the young hero, and the former had been, thanks to
the remarkable co-operation of the press, secretly brought to the obscure
conference-room.

A great, painful silence fell. Smurch looked up, waved a hand at the President. "How ya comin'?" he asked, and began rolling a fresh cigarette. The
silence deepened. Someone coughed in a strained way. "Geez, it's hot, ain't it?"
said Smurch. He loosened two more shirt buttons, revealing a hairy chest and
the tattooed word "Sadie" enclosed in a stenciled heart. The great and important men in the room, faced by the most serious crisis in recent American history, exchanged worried frowns. Nobody seemed to know how to proceed.
"Come awn, come awn," said Smurch. "Let's get the hell out of here! When do I

start cuttin' in on de parties, huh? And what's they goin' to be *in* it?" He rubbed a thumb and a forefinger together meaningly. "Money!" exclaimed a state senator, shocked, pale. "Yeh, money," said Pal, flipping his cigarette out of a window, "an' big money." He began rolling a fresh cigarette. "Big money," he repeated, frowning over the rice paper. He tilted back in his chair, and leered at each gentleman, separately, the leer of an animal that knows its power, the leer of a leopard loose in a bird-and-dog shop. "Aw, fa God's sake, let's get some place where it's cooler," he said. "I been cooped up plenty for three weeks!"

Smurch stood up and walked over to an open window, where he stood staring down into the street, nine floors below. The faint shouting of newsboys floated up to him. He made out his name. "Hot dog!" he cried, grinning, ecstatic. He leaned out over the sill. "You tell 'em, babies!" he shouted down. "Hot diggity dog!" In the tense little knot of men standing behind him, a quick, mad impulse flared up. An unspoken word of appeal, of command, seemed to ring through the room. Yet it was deadly silent. Charles K. L. Brand, secretary to the Mayor of New York City, happened to be standing nearest Smurch; he looked inquiringly at the President of the United States. The President, pale, grim, nodded shortly. Brand, a tall, powerfully built man, once a tackle at Rutgers, stepped forward, seized the greatest man in the world by his left shoulder and the seat of his pants, and pushed him out of the window.

"My God, he's fallen out the window!" cried a quick-witted editor.

"Get me out of here!" cried the President. Several men sprang to his side and 15 he was hurriedly escorted out of a door toward a side-entrance to the building. The editor of the Associated Press took charge, being used to such things. Crisply he ordered certain men to leave, others to stay; quickly he outlined a story which all the papers were to agree on, sent two men to the street to handle that end of the tragedy, commanded a Senator to sob and two Congressmen to go to pieces nervously. In a word, he skillfully set the stage for the gigantic task that was to follow, the task of breaking to a grief-stricken world the sad story of the untimely, accidental death of its most illustrious and spectacular figure.

The funeral was, as you know, the most elaborate, the finest, the solemnest, and the saddest ever held in the United States of America. The monument in Arlington Cemetery, with its clean white shaft of marble and the simple device of a tiny plane carved on its base, is a place for pilgrims, in deep reverence, to visit. The nations of the world paid lofty tributes to little Jacky Smurch, America's greatest hero. At a given hour there were two minutes of silence throughout the nation. Even the inhabitants of the small, bewildered town of Westfield, Iowa, observed this touching ceremony; agents of the Department of Justice saw to that. One of them was especially assigned to stand grimly in the doorway of a little shack restaurant on the edge of the tourists' camping ground just outside the town. There, under his stern scrutiny, Mrs. Emma Smurch bowed her head above two hamburger steaks sizzling on her grill — bowed her head and turned away, so that the Secret Service man could not see the twisted, strangely familiar, leer on her lips.

For Analysis

1. In what respects is Smurch a typical American hero? In what respects is he not?

2. Could it be argued that Jack Smurch is a distinctively modern hero? How does he compare to heroes of earlier eras?

3. What connotations does the name Smurch evoke?

4. Why does the government feel compelled to get rid of Smurch?

On Style

How does the contrast between the formal, rather elevated narrative **style** and the subject of the story, Jack ("Pal") Smurch, help create the comic **tone**?

Making Connections

1. Compare Smurch and Jack Potter in Crane's "The Bride Comes to Yellow Sky" (p. 91) as heroes.

2. Compare Everett C. Marm in Ellison's "'Repent, Harlequin!' Said the Ticktock-man" (p. 399) and Pal Smurch as heroes. Which do you find more admirable and heroic? In what ways are the names they bear appropriate?

Writing Topics

1. Use Thurber's story as the basis for a discussion of the nature and responsibilities of heroes in America.

2. Write an essay arguing for or against the assertion that in contrast to the America Thurber writes about in this story, a Pal Smurch today would not represent a public and official problem.

Richard Wright (1908–1960)

The Man Who
Was Almost a Man 1940

Dave struck out across the fields looking homeward through paling light. Whut's the use talking wid em niggers in the field? Anyhow, his mother was putting supper on the table. Them niggers can't understan nothing. One of these days he was going to get a gun and practice shooting, then they couldn't talk to him as though he were a little boy. He slowed, looking at the ground. Shucks, Ah ain scareda them even ef they are biggern me! Aw, Ah know whut Ahma do. Ahm going by ol Joe's sto n git that Sears Roebuck catlog n look at them guns. Mebbe Ma will lemme buy one when she gits mah pay from ol man Hawkins. Ahma beg her t gimme some money. Ahm ol ernough to hava gun. Ahm seventeen. Almost a man. He strode, feeling his long loose-jointed limbs. Shucks, a man oughta hava little gun aftah he done worked hard all day.

He came in sight of Joe's store. A yellow lantern glowed on the front porch. He mounted steps and went through the screen door, hearing it bang behind him. There was a strong smell of coal oil and mackerel fish. He felt very confident until he saw fat Joe walk in through the rear door, then his courage began to ooze.

"Howdy, Dave! Wutcha want?"

"How yuh, Mistah Joe? Aw, Ah don wanna buy nothing. Ah jus wanted t see ef yuhd lemme look at that catlog erwhile."

"Sure! You wanna see it here?" 5

"Nawsuh. Ah wans t take it home wid me. Ah'll bring it back termorrow when Ah come in from the fiels."

"You plannin on buying something?"

"Yessuh."

"Your ma lettin you have your own money now?"

"Shucks. Mistah Joe, Ahm gittin t be a man like anybody else!" 10

Joe laughed and wiped his greasy white face with a red bandanna.

"Whut you plannin on buyin?"

Dave looked at the floor, scratched his head, scratched his thigh, and smiled. Then he looked up shyly.

"Ah'll tell yuh, Mistah Joe, ef yuh promise yuh won't tell."

"I promise." 15

"Waal, Ahma buy a gun."

"A gun? Whut you want with a gun?"

"Ah wanna keep it."

"You ain't nothing but a boy. You don't need a gun."

376

"Aw, lemme have the catlog, Mistah Joe. Ah'll bring it back."   20

Joe walked through the rear door. Dave was elated. He looked around at barrels of sugar and flour. He heard Joe coming back. He craned his neck to see if he were bringing the book. Yeah, he's got it. Gawddog, he's got it!

"Here, but be sure you bring it back. It's the only one I got."

"Sho, Mistah Joe."

"Say, if you wanna buy a gun, why don't you buy one from me? I gotta gun to sell."

"Will it shoot?"   25

"Sure it'll shoot."

"Whut kind is it?"

"Oh, it's kinda old . . . a left-handed Wheeler. A pistol. A big one."

"Is it got bullets in it?"

"It's loaded."   30

"Kin Ah see it?"

"Where's your money?"

"What you wan fer it?"

"I'll let you have it for two dollars."

"Just two dollahs! Shucks, Ah could buy tha when Ah git mah pay."   35

"I'll have it here when you want it."

"Awright, suh. Ah be in fer it."

He went through the door, hearing it slam again behind him. Ahma git some money from Ma n buy me a gun! Only two dollahs! He tucked the thick catalogue under his arm and hurried.

"Where yuh been, boy?" His mother held a steaming dish of blackeyed peas.

"Aw, Ma, Ah just stopped down the road t talk wid the boys."   40

"Yuh know bettah t keep suppah waitin."

He sat down, resting the catalogue on the edge of the table.

"Yuh git up from there and git to the well n wash yoself! Ah ain feedin no hogs in mah house!"

She grabbed his shoulder and pushed him. He stumbled out of the room, then came back to get the catalogue.

"Whut this?"   45

"Aw, Ma, it's jusa catlog."

"Who yuh git it from?"

"From Joe, down at the sto."

"Waal, thas good. We kin use it in the outhouse."

"Naw, Ma." He grabbed for it. "Gimme ma catlog, Ma."   50

She held onto it and glared at him.

"Quit hollerin at me! Whut's wrong wid yuh? Yuh crazy?"

"But, Ma, please. It ain mine! It's Joe's! He tol me t bring it back tim termorrow."

She gave up the book. He stumbled down the back steps, hugging the thick book under his arm. When he had splashed water on his face and hands, he groped back to the kitchen and fumbled in a corner for the towel. He bumped into a chair; it clattered to the floor. The catalogue sprawled at his feet. When he had dried his eyes he snatched up the book and held it again under his arm. His mother stood watching him.

"Now, ef yuh gonna act a fool over that ol book, Ah'll take it n burn it up." 55

"Naw, Ma, please."

"Waal, set down n be still!"

He sat down and drew the oil lamp close. He thumbed page after page, unaware of the food his mother set on the table. His father came in. Then his small brother.

"Whutcha got there, Dave?" his father asked.

"Jusa catlog," he answered, not looking up. 60

"Yeah, here they is!" His eyes glowed at blue-and-black revolvers. He glanced up, feeling sudden guilt. His father was watching him. He eased the book under the table and rested it on his knees. After the blessing was asked, he ate. He scooped up peas and swallowed fat meat without chewing. Buttermilk helped to wash it down. He did not want to mention money before his father. He would do much better by cornering his mother when she was alone! He looked at his father uneasily out of the edge of his eye.

"Boy, how come yuh don quit foolin wid tha book n eat yo suppah?"

"Yessuh."

"How you n ol man Hawkins gitten erlong?"

"Suh?" 65

"Can't yuh hear! Why don yuh lissen? Ah ast yu how wuz yuh n ol man Hawkins gittin erlong?"

"Oh, swell, Pa. Ah plows mo lan than anybody over there."

"Waal, yuh oughta keep yo mind on whut yuh doin."

"Yessuh."

He poured his plate full of molasses and sopped it up slowly with a chunk of 70 cornbread. When his father and brother had left the kitchen, he still sat and looked again at the guns in the catalogue, longing to muster courage enough to present his case to his mother. Lawd, ef Ah only had tha pretty one! He could almost feel the slickness of the weapon with his fingers. If he had a gun like that he would polish it and keep it shining so it would never rust. N Ah'd keep it loaded, by Gawd!

"Ma?" His voice was hesitant.

"Hunh?"

"Ol man Hawkins give yuh mah money yit?"

"Yeah, but ain no usa yuh thinking bout throwin nona it erway. Ahm keepin tha money sos yuh kin have cloes t go to school this winter."

He rose and went to her side with the open catalogue in his palms. She was 75 washing dishes, her head bent low over a pan. Shyly he raised the book. When he spoke, his voice was husky, faint.

"Ma, Gawd knows Ah wans one of these."

"One of whut?" she asked, not raising her eyes.

"One of these," he said again, not daring even to point. She glanced up at the page, then at him with wide eyes.

"Nigger, is yuh gone plumb crazy?"

"Aw, Ma — "   80

"Git outta here! Don yuh talk t me bout no gun! Yuh a fool!"

"Ma, Ah kin buy one fer two dollahs."

"Not ef Ah knows it, yuh ain!"

"But yuh promised me one — "

"Ah don care whut Ah promised! Yuh ain nothing but a boy yit!"   85

"Ma, ef yuh lemme buy one Ah'll *never* ast yuh fer nothing no mo."

"Ah tol yuh t git outta here! Yuh ain gonna toucha penny of tha money fer no gun! Thas how come Ah has Mistah Hawkins t pay yo wages to me, cause Ah knows yuh ain got no sense."

"But, Ma, we needa gun. Pa ain got no gun. We needa gun in the house. Yuh kin never tell whut might happen."

"Now don yuh try to maka fool outta me, boy! Ef we did hava gun, yuh wouldn't have it!"

He laid the catalogue down and slipped his arm around her waist.   90

"Aw, Ma, Ah done worked hard alla summer n ain ast yuh fer nothing, is Ah, now?"

"Thas whut yuh spose t do!"

"But Ma, Ah wans a gun. Yuh kin lemme have two dollahs outta mah money. Please, Ma. I kin give it to Pa . . . Please Ma! Ah loves yuh, Ma."

When she spoke her voice came soft and low.

"Whut yu wan wida gun, Dave? Yuh don need no gun. Yuh'll git in trouble. N   95
ef yo pa just thought Ah let yuh have money t buy a gun he'd hava fit."

"Ah'll hide it, Ma. It ain but two dollahs."

"Lawd, chil, whut's wrong wid yuh?"

"Ain nothin wrong, Ma. Ahm almos a man now. Ah wans a gun."

"Who gonna sell yuh a gun?"

"Ol Joe at the sto."   100

"N it don cos but two dollahs?"

"Thas all, Ma. Jus two dollahs. Please, Ma."

She was stacking the plates away; her hands moved slowly, reflectively. Dave kept an anxious silence. Finally, she turned to him.

"Ah'll let yuh git tha gun ef yuh promise me one thing."

"Whut's tha, Ma?"   105

"Yuh bring it straight back t me, yuh hear? It be fer Pa."

"Yessum! Lemme go now, Ma."

She stooped, turned slightly to one side, raised the hem of her dress, rolled down the top of her stocking, and came up with a slender wad of bills.

"Here," she said. "Lawd knows yuh don need no gun. But yer pa does. Yuh bring it right back t me, yuh hear? Ahma put it up. Now ef yuh don, Ahma have yuh pa lick yuh so hard yuh won fergit it."

"Yessum." 110
He took the money, ran down the steps, and across the yard.
"Dave! Yuuuuuh Daaaaave!"
He heard, but he was not going to stop now. "Naw, Lawd!"

The first movement he made the following morning was to reach under his pillow for the gun. In the gray light of dawn he held it loosely, feeling a sense of power. Could kill a man with a gun like this. Kill anybody, black or white. And if he were holding his gun in his hand, nobody could run over him; they would have to respect him. It was a big gun, with a long barrel and a heavy handle. He raised and lowered it in his hand, marveling at its weight.

He had not come straight home with it as his mother had asked; instead he 115 had stayed out in the fields, holding the weapon in his hand, aiming it now and then at some imaginary foe. But he had not fired it; he had been afraid that his father might hear. Also he was not sure he knew how to fire it.

To avoid surrendering the pistol he had not come into the house until he knew that they were all asleep. When his mother had tiptoed to his bedside late that night and demanded the gun, he had first played possum; then he had told her that the gun was hidden outdoors, that he would bring it to her in the morning. Now he lay turning it slowly in his hands. He broke it, took out the cartridges, felt them, and then put them back.

He slid out of bed, got a long strip of old flannel from a trunk, wrapped the gun in it, and tied it to his naked thigh while it was still loaded. He did not go in to breakfast. Even though it was not yet daylight, he started for Jim Hawkins' plantation. Just as the sun was rising he reached the barns where the mules and plows were kept.

"Hey! That you, Dave?"
He turned. Jim Hawkins stood eying him suspiciously.
"What're yuh doing here so early?" 120
"Ah didn't know Ah wuz gittin up so early, Mistah Hawkins. Ah wuz fixin t hitch up ol Jenny n take her t the fiels."
"Good. Since you're so early, how about plowing that stretch down by the woods?"
"Suits me, Mistah Hawkins."
"O.K. Go to it!"
He hitched Jenny to a plow and started across the fields. Hot dog! This was 125 just what he wanted. If he could get down by the woods, he could shoot his gun and nobody would hear. He walked behind the plow, hearing the traces creaking, feeling the gun tied tight to his thigh.

When he reached the woods, he plowed two whole rows before he decided to take out the gun. Finally, he stopped, looked in all directions, then he untied the gun and held it in his hand. He turned to the mule and smiled.

"Know whut this is, Jenny? Naw, yuh wouldn know! Yuhs jusa ol mule! Anyhow, this is a gun, n it kin shoot, by Gawd!"

He held the gun at arm's length. Whut t hell, Ahma shoot this thing! He looked at Jenny again.

"Lissen here, Jenny! When Ah pull this ol trigger, Ah don wan yuh t run n acka fool now!"

Jenny stood with head down, her short ears pricked straight. Dave walked off 130 about twenty feet, held the gun far out from him at arm's length, and turned his head. Hell, he told himself, Ah ain afraid. The gun felt loose in his fingers; he waved it wildly for a moment. Then he shut his eyes and tightened his forefinger. Bloom! A report half deafened him and he thought his right hand was torn from his arm. He heard Jenny whinnying and galloping over the field, and he found himself on his knees, squeezing his fingers hard between his legs. His hand was numb; he jammed it into his mouth, trying to warm it, trying to stop the pain. The gun lay at his feet. He did not quite know what had happened. He stood up and stared at the gun as though it were a living thing. He gritted his teeth and kicked the gun. Yuh almos broke mah arm! He turned to look for Jenny; she was far over the fields, tossing her head and kicking wildly.

"Hol on there, ol mule!"

When he caught up with her she stood trembling, walling her big white eyes at him. The plow was far away; the traces had broken. Then Dave stopped short, looking, not believing. Jenny was bleeding. Her left side was red and wet with blood. He went closer. Lawd, have mercy! Wondah did Ah shoot this mule? He grabbed for Jenny's mane. She flinched, snorted, whirled, tossing her head.

"Hol on now! Hol on."

Then he saw the hole in Jenny's side, right between the ribs. It was round, wet, red. A crimson stream streaked down the front leg, flowing fast. Good Gawd! Ah wuzn't shootin at tha mule. He felt panic. He knew he had to stop that blood, or Jenny would bleed to death. He had never seen so much blood in all his life. He chased the mule for a half mile, trying to catch her. Finally she stopped, breathing hard, stumpy tail half arched. He caught her mane and led her back to where the plough and gun lay. Then he stooped and grabbed handfuls of damp black earth and tried to plug the bullet hole, Jenny shuddered, whinnied, and broke from him.

"Hol on! Hol on now!"   135

He tried to plug it again, but blood came anyhow. His fingers were hot and sticky. He rubbed dirt into his palms, trying to dry them. Then again he attempted to plug the bullet hole, but Jenny shied away, kicking her heels high. He stood helpless. He had to do something. He ran at Jenny; she dodged him. He watched a red stream of blood flow down Jenny's leg and form a bright pool at her feet.

"Jenny . . . Jenny," he called weakly.

His lips trembled. She's bleeding t death! He looked in the direction of home, wanting to go back, wanting to get help. But he saw the pistol lying in the damp black clay. He had a queer feeling that if he only did something, this would not be; Jenny would not be there bleeding to death.

When he went to her this time, she did not move. She stood with sleepy, dreamy eyes; and when he touched her she gave a low-pitched whinny and knelt to the ground, her front knees slopping in blood.

"Jenny . . . Jenny . . . " he whispered.   140

For a long time she held her neck erect; then her head sank, slowly. Her ribs swelled with a mighty heave and she went over.

Dave's stomach felt empty, very empty. He picked up the gun and held it gingerly between his thumb and fore-finger. He buried it at the foot of a tree. He took a stick and tried to cover the pool of blood with dirt — but what was the use? There was Jenny lying with her mouth open and her eyes walled and glassy. He could not tell Jim Hawkins he had shot his mule. But he had to tell something. Yeah, Ah'll tell em Jenny started gittin wil n fell on the joint of the plow. . . . But that would hardly happen to a mule. He walked across the field slowly, head down.

It was sunset. Two of Jim Hawkins' men were over near the edge of the woods digging a hole in which to bury Jenny. Dave was surrounded by a knot of people, all of whom were looking down at the dead mule.

"I don't see how in the world it happened," said Jim Hawkins for the tenth time.

The crowd parted and Dave's mother, father, and small brother pushed into   145
the center.

"Where Dave?" his mother called.

"There he is," said Jim Hawkins.

His mother grabbed him.

"Whut happened, Dave? Whut yuh done?"

"Nothin."   150

"C mon, boy, talk," his father said.

Dave took a deep breath and told the story he knew nobody believed.

"Waal," he drawled. "Ah brung ol Jenny down here sos Ah could do mah plowin. Ah plowed bout two rows, just like yuh see." He stopped and pointed at the long rows of upturned earth. "Then somethin musta been wrong wid ol Jenny. She wouldn ack right a-tall. She started snortin n kickin her heels. Ah tried t hol her, but she pulled erway, rearin n going in. Then when the point of the plow was stickin up in the air, she swung erroun n twisted herself back on it . . . She stuck herself n started t bleed. N fo Ah could do anything, she wuz dead."

"Did you ever hear of anything like that in all your life?" asked Jim Hawkins.

There were white and black standing in the crowd. They murmured. Dave's   155
mother came close to him and looked hard into his face. "Tell the truth, Dave," she said.

"Looks like a bullet hole to me," said one man.

"Dave, whut yuh do wid the gun?" his mother asked.

The crowd surged in, looking at him. He jammed his hands into his pockets, shook his head slowly from left to right, and backed away. His eyes were wide and painful.

"Did he hava gun?" asked Jim Hawkins.

"By Gawd, Ah tol yuh tha wuz a gun wound," said a man, slapping his thigh.   160
His father caught his shoulders and shook him till his teeth rattled.

"Tell whut happened, yuh rascal! Tell whut . . . "

Dave looked at Jenny's stiff legs and began to cry.

"Whut yuh do wid the gun?" his mother asked.

"Whut wuz he doin wida gun?" his father asked.

"Come on and tell the truth," said Hawkins. "Ain't nobody going to hurt   165
you . . . "

His mother crowded close to him.

"Did yuh shoot tha mule, Dave?"

Dave cried, seeing blurred white and black faces.

"Ahh ddinn gggo tt sshooot hher . . . Ah sssswear ffo Gawd Ah ddin. . . . Ah
wuz a-tryin t sssee ef the old gggun would sshoot — "

"Where yuh git the gun from?" his father asked.   170

"Ah got it from Joe, at the sto."

"Where yuh git the money?"

"Ma give it t me."

"He kept worryin me, Bob. Ah had t. Ah tol im t bring the gun right back t
me . . . It was fer yuh, the gun."

"But how yuh happen to shoot that mule?" asked Jim Hawkins.   175

"Ah wuzn shootin at the mule, Mistah Hawkins. The gun jumped when Ah
pulled the trigger . . . N fo Ah knowed anythin Jenny was there a-bleedin."

Somebody in the crowd laughed. Jim Hawkins walked close to Dave and
looked into his face.

"Well, looks like you have bought you a mule, Dave."

"Ah swear fo Gawd, Ah didn go t kill the mule, Mistah Hawkins!"

"But you killed her!"   180

All the crowd was laughing now. They stood on tiptoe and poked heads over
one another's shoulders.

"Well, boy, looks like yuh done bought a dead mule! Hahaha!"

"Ain tha ershame."

"Hohohohoho."

Dave stood, head down, twisting his feet in the dirt.   185

"Well, you needn't worry about it, Bob," said Jim Hawkins to Dave's father.
"Just let the boy keep on working and pay me two dollars a month."

"What yuh wan fer yo mule, Mistah Hawkins?"

Jim Hawkins screwed up his eyes.

"Fifty dollars."

"Whut yuh do wid tha gun?" Dave's father demanded.   190

Dave said nothing.

"Yuh wan me t take a tree n beat yuh till yuh talk!"

"Nawsuh!"

"Whut yuh do wid it?"

"Ah throwed it erway."   195

"Where?"

"Ah . . . ah throwed it in the creek."

"Waal, c mon home. N firs thing in the mawnin git to tha creek n fin tha gun."

"Yessuh."

"Whut yuh pay fer it?"   200

"Two dollahs."

"Take tha gun n git yo money back n carry it t Mistah Hawkins, yuh hear? N don fergit Ahma lam you black bottom good fer this! Now march yosef on home, suh!"

Dave turned and walked slowly. He heard people laughing. Dave glared, his eyes welling with tears. Hot anger bubbled in him. Then he swallowed and stumbled on.

That night Dave did not sleep. He was glad that he had gotten out of killing the mule so easily, but he was hurt. Something hot seemed to turn over inside him each time he remembered how they had laughed. He tossed on his bed, feeling his hard pillow. N Pa says he's gonna beat me . . . He remembered other beatings, and his back quivered. Naw, naw, Ah sho don wan im t beat me tha way no mo. Dam em all! Nobody ever gave him anything. All he did was work. They treat me like a mule, n then they beat me. He gritted his teeth. N Ma had t toll on me.

Well, if he had to, he would take old man Hawkins that two dollars. But that   205 meant selling the gun. And he wanted to keep that gun. Fifty dollars for a dead mule.

He turned over, thinking how he fired the gun. He had an itch to fire it again. Ef other men kin shoota gun, by Gawd, Ah kin! He was still, listening. Mebbe they all sleepin now. The house was still. He heard the soft breathing of his brother. Yes, now! He would go down and get that gun and see if he could fire it! He eased out of bed and slipped into overalls.

The moon was bright. He ran almost all the way to the edge of the woods. He stumbled over the ground, looking for the spot where he had buried the gun. Yeah, here it is. Like a hungry dog scratching for a bone, he pawed it up. He puffed his black cheeks and blew dirt from the trigger and barrel. He broke it and found four cartridges unshot. He looked around; the fields were filled with silence and moonlight. He clutched the gun stiff and hard in his fingers. But, as soon as he wanted to pull the trigger, he shut his eyes and turned his head. Naw, Ah can't shoot wid mah eyes closed n mah head turned. With effort he held his eyes open; then he squeezed. *Blooooom!* He was stiff, not breathing. The gun was still in his hands. Dammit, he'd done it! He fired again. *Blooooom!* He smiled. *Blooooom! Blooooom! Click, click.* There! It was empty. If anybody could shoot a gun, he could. He put the gun into his hip pocket and started across the fields.

When he reached the top of a ridge he stood straight and proud in the moon-light, looking at Jim Hawkins' big white house, feeling the gun sagging in his pocket. Lawd, ef Ah had just one mo bullet Ah'd taka shot at tha house. Ah'd like t scare ol man Hawkins jusa little . . . Jusa enough t let im know Dave Saunders is a man.

To his left the road curved, running to the tracks of the Illinois Central. He jerked his head, listening. From far off came a faint *hoooof-hoooof; hoooof-hoooof; hoooof-hoooof* . . . He stood rigid. Two dollahs a mont. Les see now . . . Tha mean it'll take bout two years. Shucks! Ah'll be dam!

He started down the road, toward the tracks. Yeah, here she comes! He stood   210
beside the track and held himself stiffly. Here she comes, erroun the ben . . . C mon, yuh slow poke! C mon! He had his hand on his gun; something quivered in his stomach. Then the train thundered past, the gray and brown box cars rumbling and clinking. He gripped the gun tightly; then he jerked his hand out of his pocket. Ah betcha Bill wouldn't do it! Ah betcha . . . The cars slid past, steel grinding upon steel. Ahm ridin yuh ternight, so hep me Gawd! He was hot all over. He hesitated just a moment; then he grabbed, pulled atop of a car, and lay flat. He felt his pocket; the gun was still there. Ahead the long rails glinting in the moonlight, stretching away, away to somewhere, somewhere where he could be a man . . .

For Analysis

1. Explain the paradox of the title.

2. Why does Dave equate owning a gun with manhood?

3. Describe Dave's relationship with his father.

4. Can we judge whether the fifty dollars Hawkins asks for his mule is reasonable? Explain.

5. Wright's story is set in the rural South and ends with Dave riding the rails to "somewhere where he could be a man." Why must Dave leave to be a man? Where historically has that place been for southern blacks? What are Dave's prospects of winning his manhood?

On Style

Why does Wright use the third-person **point of view** in this story, even though the focus is on Dave's thoughts and feelings? How would the story differ if Dave were the narrator?

Making Connections

1. In what ways does McKay's poem "If We Must Die" (p. 446) cast light on the meaning of Dave's actions?

2. Contrast Dave's family with the Younger family in Hansberry's play *A Raisin in the Sun* (p. 867).

Writing Topics

1. Discuss Dave's relationship with his mother and father and the kind of family life they have.

2. Write a descriptive essay about an event or the acquisition of some thing that you regarded as marking your entry into adulthood.

Shirley Jackson (1919–1965)

The Lottery 1948

The morning of June 27th was clear and sunny, with the fresh warmth of a full-summer day; the flowers were blossoming profusely and the grass was richly green. The people of the village began to gather in the square, between the post office and the bank, around ten o'clock; in some towns there were so many people that the lottery took two days and had to be started on June 26th, but in this village, where there were only about three hundred people, the whole lottery took less than two hours, so it could begin at ten o'clock in the morning and still be through in time to allow the villagers to get home for noon dinner.

The children assembled first, of course. School was recently over for the summer, and the feeling of liberty sat uneasily on most of them; they tended to gather together quietly for a while before they broke into boisterous play, and their talk was still of the classroom and the teacher, of books and reprimands. Bobby Martin had already stuffed his pockets full of stones, and the other boys soon followed his example, selecting the smoothest and roundest stones; Bobby and Harry Jones and Dickie Delacroix — the villagers pronounced his name "Dellacroy" — eventually made a great pile of stones in one corner of the square and guarded it against the raids of the other boys. The girls stood aside, talking among themselves, looking over their shoulders at the boys, and the very small children rolled in the dust or clung to the hands of their older brothers or sisters.

Soon the men began to gather, surveying their own children, speaking of planting and rain, tractors and taxes. They stood together, away from the pile of stones in the corner, and their jokes were quiet and they smiled rather than laughed. The women, wearing faded house dresses and sweaters, came shortly after their menfolk. They greeted one another and exchanged bits of gossip as they went to join their husbands. Soon the women, standing by their husbands, began to call to their children, and the children came reluctantly, having to be called four or five times. Bobby Martin ducked under his mother's grasping hand and ran, laughingly, back to the pile of stones. His father spoke up sharply, and Bobby came quickly and took his place, between his father and his oldest brother.

The lottery was conducted — as were the square dances, the teenage club, the Halloween program — by Mr. Summers, who had time and energy to devote to civic activities. He was a round-faced, jovial man and he ran the coal business, and people were sorry for him, because he had no children and his wife was a scold. When he arrived in the square, carrying the black wooden box, there was a murmur of conversation among the villagers, and he waved and called "Little late today, folks." The postmaster, Mr. Graves, followed him, carrying a three-legged stool, and the stool was put in the center of the square and Mr. Summers set the black box down on it. The villagers kept their distance, leaving a space between themselves and the stool, and when Mr. Summers said, "Some of you fellows want to give me a hand?" there was a hesitation before two men, Mr. Martin and his oldest son, Baxter, came forward to hold the box steady on the stool while Mr. Summers stirred up the papers inside it.

The original paraphernalia for the lottery had been lost long ago, and the   5 black box now resting on the stool had been put into use even before Old Man Warner, the oldest man in town, was born. Mr. Summers spoke frequently to the villagers about making a new box, but no one liked to upset even as much tradition as was represented by the black box. There was a story that the present box had been made with some pieces of the box that had preceded it, the one that had been constructed when the first people settled down to make a village here. Every year, after the lottery, Mr. Summers began talking about a new box, but every year the subject was allowed to fade off without anything's being done. The black box grew shabbier each year; by now it was no longer completely black but splintered badly along one side to show the original wood color, and in some places faded and stained.

Mr. Martin and his oldest son, Baxter, held the black box securely on the stool until Mr. Summers had stirred the papers thoroughly with his hand. Because so much of the ritual had been forgotten or discarded, Mr. Summers had been successful in having slips of paper substituted for the chips of wood that had been used for generations. Chips of wood, Mr. Summers had argued, had been all very well when the village was tiny, but now that the population was more than three hundred and likely to keep on growing, it was necessary to use something that would fit more easily into the black box. The night before the lottery, Mr. Summers and Mr. Graves made up the slips of paper and put them in the box, and it was then taken to the safe of Mr. Summers' coal company and locked up until Mr. Summers was ready to take it to the square the next morning. The rest of the year, the box was put away, sometimes one place, sometimes another; it had spent one year in Mr. Graves' barn and another year underfoot in the post office, and sometimes it was set on a shelf in the Martin grocery and left there.

There was a great deal of fussing to be done before Mr. Summers declared the lottery open. There were the lists to make up — of heads of families, heads of households in each family, members of each household in each family. There was the proper swearing-in of Mr. Summers by the postmaster, as the official of the lottery; at one time, some people remembered, there had been a recital of some sort, performed by the official of the lottery, a perfunctory, tuneless chant that had been rattled off duly each year; some people believed that the official of the lottery used to stand just so when he said or sang it, others believed that he was supposed to walk among the people, but years and years ago this part of the ritual had been allowed to lapse. There had been, also, a ritual salute, which the official of the lottery had had to use in addressing each person who came up to draw from the box, but this also had changed with time, until now it was felt necessary only for the official to speak to each person approaching. Mr. Summers was very good at all this; in his clean white shirt and blue jeans, with one hand resting carelessly on the black box, he seemed very proper and important as he talked interminably to Mr. Graves and the Martins.

Just as Mr. Summers finally left off talking and turned to the assembled villagers, Mrs. Hutchinson came hurriedly along the path to the square, her sweater thrown over her shoulders, and slid into place in the back of the crowd. "Clean forgot what day it was," she said to Mrs. Delacroix, who stood next to her, and they both laughed softly. "Thought my old man was out back stacking wood," Mrs. Hutchinson went on, "and then I looked out the window and the kids were gone, and then I remembered it was the twenty-seventh and came a-running." She dried her hands on her apron, and Mrs. Delacroix said, "You're in time, though. They're still talking away up there."

Mrs. Hutchinson craned her neck to see through the crowd and found her husband and children standing near the front. She tapped Mrs. Delacroix on the arm as a farewell and began to make her way through the crowd. The people separated good-humoredly to let her through; two or three people said, in voices just loud enough to be heard across the crowd, "Here comes your Missus, Hutchinson," and "Bill, she made it after all." Mrs. Hutchinson reached her husband, and Mr. Summers, who had been waiting, said cheerfully, "Thought we were going to have to get on without you, Tessie." Mrs. Hutchinson said, grinning, "Wouldn't have me leave m'dishes in the sink, now, would you, Joe?" and soft laughter ran through the crowd as the people stirred back into position after Mrs. Hutchinson's arrival.

"Well, now," Mr. Summers said soberly, "guess we better get started, get this 10 over with, so's we can go back to work. Anybody ain't here?"

"Dunbar," several people said. "Dunbar, Dunbar."

Mr. Summers consulted his list. "Clyde Dunbar," he said. "That's right. He's broke his leg, hasn't he? Who's drawing for him?"

"Me, I guess," a woman said, and Mr. Summers turned to look at her. "Wife draws for her husband," Mr. Summers said. "Don't you have a grown boy to do it for you, Janey?" Although Mr. Summers and everyone else in the village knew the answer perfectly well, it was the business of the official of the lottery to ask such questions formally. Mr. Summers waited with an expression of polite interest while Mrs. Dunbar answered.

"Horace's not but sixteen yet," Mrs. Dunbar said regretfully. "Guess I gotta fill in for the old man this year."

"Right," Mr. Summers said. He made a note on the list he was holding. Then 15 he asked, "Watson boy drawing this year?"

A tall boy in the crowd raised his hand. "Here," he said. "I'm drawing for m'mother and me." He blinked his eyes nervously and ducked his head as several voices in the crowd said things like "Good fellow, Jack," and "Glad to see your mother's got a man to do it."

"Well," Mr. Summers said, "guess that's everyone. Old Man Warner make it?"

"Here," a voice said, and Mr. Summers nodded.

. . .

A sudden hush fell on the crowd as Mr. Summers cleared his throat and looked at the list. "All ready?" he called. "Now, I'll read the names — heads of families first — and the men come up and take a paper out of the box. Keep the paper folded in your hand without looking at it until everyone has had a turn. Everything clear?"

The people had done it so many times that they only half listened to the direc- 20 tions; most of them were quiet, wetting their lips, not looking around. Then Mr. Summers raised one hand high and said, "Adams." A man disengaged himself from the crowd and came forward. "Hi, Steve," Mr. Summers said, and Mr. Adams said, "Hi, Joe." They grinned at one another humorlessly and nervously. Then Mr. Adams reached into the black box and took out a folded paper. He held it firmly by one corner as he turned and went hastily back to his place in the crowd, where he stood a little apart from his family, not looking down at his hand.

"Allen." Mr. Summers said. "Anderson. . . . Betham."

"Seems like there's no time at all between lotteries any more," Mrs. Delacroix said to Mrs. Graves in the back row. "Seems like we got through the last one only last week."

"Time sure goes fast," Mrs. Graves said.

"Clark. . . . Delacroix."

"There goes my old man," Mrs. Delacroix said. She held her breath while her 25 husband went forward.

"Dunbar," Mr. Summers said, and Mrs. Dunbar went steadily to the box while one of the women said, "Go on, Janey," and another said, "There she goes."

"We're next," Mrs. Graves said. She watched while Mr. Graves came around from the side of the box, greeted Mr. Summers gravely, and selected a slip of paper from the box. By now, all through the crowd there were men holding the small folded papers in their large hands, turning them over and over nervously. Mrs. Dunbar and her two sons stood together, Mrs. Dunbar holding the slip of paper.

"Harburt. . . . Hutchinson."

"Get up there, Bill," Mrs. Hutchinson said, and the people near her laughed.

"Jones." 30

"They do say," Mr. Adams said to Old Man Warner, who stood next to him, "that over in the north village they're talking of giving up the lottery."

Old Man Warner snorted. "Pack of crazy fools," he said. "Listening to the young folks, nothing's good enough for *them*. Next thing you know, they'll be wanting to go back to living in caves, nobody work any more, live *that* way for a while. Used to be a saying about 'Lottery in June, corn be heavy soon.' First thing you know, we'd all be eating stewed chickweed and acorns. There's *always* been a lottery," he added petulantly. "Bad enough to see young Joe Summers up there joking with everybody."

"Some places have already quit lotteries," Mrs. Adams said.

"Nothing but trouble in *that*," Old Man Warner said stoutly. "Pack of young fools."

"Martin." And Bobby Martin watched his father go forward. "Overdyke. . . . 35
Percy."

"I wish they'd hurry," Mrs. Dunbar said to her older son. "I wish they'd hurry."

"They're almost through," her son said.

"You get ready to run tell Dad," Mrs. Dunbar said.

Mr. Summers called his own name and then stepped forward precisely and
selected a slip from the box. Then he called, "Warner."

"Seventy-seventh year I been in the lottery," Old Man Warner said as he went 40
through the crowd. "Seventy-seventh time."

"Watson." The tall boy came awkwardly through the crowd. Someone said,
"Don't be nervous, Jack," and Mr. Summers said, "Take your time, son."

"Zanini."

After that, there was a long pause, a breathless pause, until Mr. Summers,
holding his slip of paper in the air, said, "All right fellows." For a minute, no one
moved, and then all the slips of paper were opened. Suddenly, all the women
began to speak at once, saying, "Who is it," "Who's got it?," "Is it the Dunbars?,"
"Is it the Watsons?" Then the voices began to say, "It's Hutchinson. It's Bill,"
"Bill Hutchinson's got it."

"Go tell your father," Mrs. Dunbar said to her older son.

People began to look around to see the Hutchinsons. Bill Hutchinson was 45
standing quiet, staring down at the paper in his hand. Suddenly, Tessie Hutchinson shouted to Mr. Summers, "You didn't give him time enough to take any
paper he wanted. I saw you. It wasn't fair!"

"Be a good sport, Tessie," Mrs. Delacroix called, and Mrs. Graves said, "All of
us took the same chance."

"Shut up, Tessie," Bill Hutchinson said.

"Well, everyone," Mr. Summers said, "That was done pretty fast, and now
we've got to be hurrying a little more to get it done in time." He consulted his
next list. "Bill," he said, "you draw for the Hutchinson family. You got any other
households in the Hutchinsons?"

"There's Don and Eva," Mrs. Hutchinson yelled. "Make *them* take their
chance!"

"Daughters draw with their husbands' families, Tessie," Mr. Summers said 50
gently. "You know that as well as anyone else."

"It wasn't *fair*," Tessie said.

"I guess not, Joe," Bill Hutchinson said regretfully. "My daughter draws with
her husband's family, that's only fair. And I've got no other family except the kids."

"Then, as far as drawing for families is concerned, it's you," Mr. Summers said
in explanation, "and as far as drawing for households is concerned, that's you,
too. Right?"

"Right," Bill Hutchinson said.

"How many kids, Bill?" Mr. Summers asked formally. 55

"Three," Bill Hutchinson said. "There's Bill, Jr., and Nancy, and little Dave.
And Tessie and me."

"All right then," Mr. Summers said. "Harry, you got their tickets back?"

Mr. Graves nodded and held up the slips of paper. "Put them in the box, then," Mr. Summers directed. "Take Bill's and put it in."

"I think we ought to start over," Mrs. Hutchinson said, as quietly as she could. "I tell you it wasn't *fair*. You didn't give him time enough to choose. *Everybody* saw that."

Mr. Graves had selected the five slips and put them in the box, and he 60 dropped all the papers but those onto the ground, where the breeze caught them and lifted them off.

"Listen, everybody," Mrs. Hutchinson was saying to the people around her.

"Ready, Bill?" Mr. Summers asked, and Bill Hutchinson, with one quick glance around at his wife and children, nodded.

"Remember," Mr. Summers said, "take the slips and keep them folded until each person has taken one. Harry, you help little Dave." Mr. Graves took the hand of the little boy, who came willingly with him up to the box. "Take a paper out of the box, Davy," Mr. Summers said. Davy put his hand into the box and laughed. "Take just *one* paper," Mr. Summers said. "Harry, you hold it for him." Mr. Graves took the child's hand and removed the folded paper from the tight fist and held it while little Dave stood next to him and looked up at him wonderingly.

"Nancy next," Mr. Summers said. Nancy was twelve, and her school friends breathed heavily as she went forward, switching her skirt, and took a slip daintily from the box. "Bill, Jr.," Mr. Summers said, and Billy, his face red and his feet over-large, nearly knocked the box over as he got a paper out. "Tessie," Mr. Summers said. She hesitated for a minute, looking around defiantly, and then set her lips and went up to the box. She snatched a paper out and held it behind her.

"Bill," Mr. Summers said, and Bill Hutchinson reached into the box and felt 65 around, bringing his hand out at last with the slip of paper in it.

The crowd was quiet. A girl whispered, "I hope it's not Nancy," and the sound of the whisper reached the edges of the crowd.

"It's not the way it used to be," Old Man Warner said clearly. "People ain't the way they used to be."

"All right," Mr. Summers said. "Open the papers. Harry, you open little Dave's."

Mr. Graves opened the slip of paper and there was a general sigh through the crowd as he held it up and everyone could see that it was blank. Nancy and Bill, Jr., opened theirs at the same time, and both beamed and laughed, turning around to the crowd and holding their slips of paper above their heads.

"Tessie," Mr. Summers said. There was a pause, and then Mr. Summers looked 70 at Bill Hutchinson, and Bill unfolded his paper and showed it. It was blank.

"It's Tessie," Mr. Summers said, and his voice was hushed. "Show us her paper, Bill."

Bill Hutchinson went over to his wife and forced the slip of paper out of her hand. It had a black spot on it, the black spot Mr. Summers had made the night before with the heavy pencil in the coal-company office. Bill Hutchinson held it up, and there was a stir in the crowd.

"All right, folks," Mr. Summers said. "Let's finish quickly."

Although the villagers had forgotten the ritual and lost the original black box, they still remembered to use stones. The pile of stones the boys had made earlier was ready; there were stones on the ground with the blowing scraps of paper that had come out of the box. Mrs. Delacroix selected a stone so large she had to pick it up with both hands and turned to Mrs. Dunbar. "Come on," she said. "Hurry up."

Mrs. Dunbar had small stones in both hands, and she said, gasping for breath, 75 "I can't run at all. You'll have to go ahead and I'll catch up with you."

The children had stones already, and someone gave little Davy Hutchinson a few pebbles.

Tessie Hutchinson was in the center of a cleared space by now, and she held her hands out desperately as the villagers moved in on her. "It isn't fair," she said. A stone hit her on the side of the head.

Old Man Warner was saying, "Come on, come on, everyone." Steve Adams was in the front of the crowd of villagers, with Mrs. Graves beside him.

"It isn't fair, it isn't right," Mrs. Hutchinson screamed, and then they were upon her.

For Analysis

1. What evidence in the story suggests that the lottery is a ritualistic ceremony?

2. What beliefs underlie the old saying "Lottery in June, corn be heavy soon" (para. 32)?

3. Might the story be a comment on religious orthodoxy? Explain.

On Style

Does the straightforward narrative **style** describing the holiday atmosphere diminish or intensify the horror of the story's conclusion? Explain.

Making Connections

1. Can you identify ritualistic acts you perform without examining the reasons for or the consequences of your behavior? What motivates you to act in such cases?

2. Compare this story with Head's "Looking for a Rain God" (p. 1356) and Silko's "The Man to Send Rain Clouds" (p. 1374). What similarities do you find? What differences?

3. Do you voluntarily make sacrifices — to celebrate Lent or Passover, for example, or to ensure good fortune? What tacit set of beliefs controls the occasion for and the nature of such personal sacrifices?

Writing Topics

1. Explain the purpose of the lottery, and identify contemporary rituals that seem to exhibit similar purposes.

2. Magic and religion differ because magicians can compel change whereas priests can only ask for change. Comment on this distinction. Can you identify magical elements in religion?

Ursula K. Le Guin   (b. 1929)

The Ones Who Walk Away from Omelas 1974

With a clamor of bells that set the swallows soaring, the Festival of Summer came to the city Omelas, bright-towered by the sea. The rigging of the boats in harbor sparkled with flags. In the streets between houses with red roofs and painted walls, between old moss-grown gardens and under avenues of trees, past great parks and public buildings, processions moved. Some were decorous: old people in long stiff robes of mauve and grey, grave master work-men, quiet, merry women carrying their babies and chatting as they walked. In other streets the music beat faster, a shimmering of gong and tambourine, and the people went dancing, the procession was a dance. Children dodged in and out, their high calls rising like the swallows' crossing flights over the music and the singing. All the processions wound towards the north side of the city, where on the great water-meadow called the Green Fields boys and girls, naked in the bright air, with mud-stained feet and ankles and long, lithe arms, exer-cised their restive horses before the race. The horses wore no gear at all but a halter without bit. Their manes were braided with streamers of silver, gold, and green. They flared their nostrils and pranced and boasted to one another; they were vastly excited, the horse being the only animal who has adopted our cere-monies as his own. Far off to the north and west the mountains stood up half encircling Omelas on her bay. The air of morning was so clear that the snow still crowning the Eighteen Peaks burned with white-gold fire across the miles of sunlit air, under the dark blue of the sky. There was just enough wind to make the banners that marked the racecourse snap and flutter now and then. In the silence of the broad green meadows one could hear the music winding through the city streets, farther and nearer and ever approaching, a cheerful faint sweet-ness of the air that from time to time trembled and gathered together and broke out into the great joyous clanging of the bells.

Joyous! How is one to tell about joy? How describe the citizens of Omelas?

They were not simple folk, you see, though they were happy. But we do not say the words of cheer much any more. All smiles have become archaic. Given a description such as this one tends to make certain assumptions. Given a descrip-tion such as this one tends to look next for the King, mounted on a splendid stal-lion and surrounded by his noble knights, or perhaps in a golden litter borne by great-muscled slaves. But there was no king. They did not use swords, or keep slaves. They were not barbarians. I do not know the rules and laws of their soci-ety, but I suspect that they were singularly few. As they did without monarchy and slavery, so they also got on without the stock exchange, the advertisement, the secret police, and the bomb. Yet I repeat that these were not simple folk, not dulcet shepherds, noble savages, bland utopians. They were not less complex than us. The trouble is that we have a bad habit, encouraged by pedants and sophisticates, of considering happiness as something rather stupid. Only pain is intellectual, only evil interesting. This is the treason of the artist: a refusal to admit the banality of evil and the terrible boredom of pain. If you can't lick 'em, join 'em. If it hurts, repeat it. But to praise despair is to condemn delight, to embrace violence is to lose hold of everything else. We have almost lost hold; we can no longer describe a happy man, nor make any celebration of joy. How can I tell you about the people of Omelas? They were not naïve and happy children — though their children were, in fact, happy. They were mature, intelligent, passionate adults whose lives were not wretched. O miracle! but I wish I could describe it better. I wish I could convince you. Omelas sounds in my words like a city in a fairy tale, long ago and far away, once upon a time. Perhaps it would be best if you imagined it as your own fancy bids, assuming it will rise to the occasion, for certainly I cannot suit you all. For instance, how about technology? I think that there would be no cars or helicopters in and above the streets; this follows from the fact that the people of Omelas are happy people. Happiness is based on a just discrimination of what is necessary, what is neither necessary nor destructive, and what is destructive. In the middle category, however — that of the unnecessary but undestructive, that of comfort, luxury, exuberance, etc. — they could perfectly well have central heating, subway trains, washing machines, and all kinds of marvelous devices not yet invented here, floating light-sources, fuelless power, a cure for the common cold. Or they could have none of that: it doesn't matter. As you like it. I incline to think that people from towns up and down the coast have been coming in to Omelas during the last days before the Festival on very fast little trains and double-decker trams, and that the train station of Omelas is actually the handsomest building in town, though plainer than the magnificent Farmers' Market. But even granted trains, I fear that Omelas so far strikes some of you as goody-goody. Smiles, bells, parades, horses, bleh. If so, please add an orgy. If an orgy would help, don't hesitate. Let us not, however, have temples from which issue beautiful nude priests and priestesses already half in ecstasy and ready to copulate with any man or woman, lover or stranger, who desires union with the deep godhead of the blood, although that was my first idea. But really it would be better not to have any temples in Omelas — at least, not manned temples. Religion yes, clergy no. Surely the beautiful nudes can just wander about, offering themselves like divine soufflés to the hunger of the needy and the rapture of the flesh. Let them join the processions. Let tambourines be struck above the copulations, and the glory of desire be proclaimed upon the gongs, and (a not unimportant point) let the offspring of these delightful rituals be beloved and looked after by all. One thing I know there is none of in Omelas is guilt. But what else should there be? I thought at first there were no drugs, but that is puritanical. For those who like it, the faint insistent sweetness of *drooz* may perfume the ways of the city, *drooz* which first brings a great lightness and brilliance to the mind and limbs, and then after some hours a dreamy languor, and wonderful visions at last of the very arcana and inmost secrets of the Universe, as well as exciting the pleasure of sex beyond all belief; and it is not habit-forming. For more modest tastes I think there ought to be beer. What else, what else belongs in the joyous city? The sense of victory, surely, the celebration of courage. But as we did without clergy, let us do without soldiers. The joy built upon successful slaughter is not the right kind of joy; it will not do; it is fearful and it is trivial. A boundless and generous contentment, a magnanimous triumph felt not against some outer enemy but in communion with the finest and fairest in the souls of all men everywhere and the splendor of the world's summer: this is what swells the hearts of the people of Omelas, and the victory they celebrate is that of life. I really don't think many of them need to take *drooz*.

Most of the processions have reached the Green Fields by now. A marvelous smell of cooking goes forth from the red and blue tents of the provisioners. The faces of small children are amiably sticky; in the benign grey beard of a man a couple of crumbs of rich pastry are entangled. The youths and girls have mounted their horses and are beginning to group around the starting line of the course. An old woman, small, fat, and laughing, is passing out flowers from a basket, and tall young men wear her flowers in their shining hair. A child of nine or ten sits at the edge of the crowd, alone, playing on a wooden flute. People pause to listen, and they smile, but they do not speak to him, for he never ceases playing and never sees them, his dark eyes wholly rapt in the sweet, thin magic of the tune.

5

He finishes, and slowly lowers his hands holding the wooden flute.

As if that little private silence were the signal, all at once a trumpet sounds from the pavilion near the starting line: imperious, melancholy, piercing. The horses rear on their slender legs, and some of them neigh in answer. Sober-faced, the young riders stroke the horses' necks and soothe them, whispering, "Quiet, quiet, there my beauty, my hope. . . ." They begin to form in rank along the starting line. The crowds along the racecourse are like a field of grass and flowers in the wind. The Festival of Summer has begun.

Do you believe? Do you accept the festival, the city, the joy? No? Then let me describe one more thing.

In a basement under one of the beautiful public buildings of Omelas, or perhaps in the cellar of one of its spacious private homes, there is a room. It has one locked door, and no window. A little light seeps in dustily between cracks in the boards, secondhand from a cobwebbed window somewhere across the cellar. In one corner of the little room a couple of mops, with stiff, clotted, foul-smelling heads, stand near a rusty bucket. The floor is dirt, a little damp to the touch, as cellar dirt usually is. The room is about three paces long and two wide: a mere broom closet or disused tool room. In the room a child is sitting. It could be a boy or a girl. It looks about six, but actually is nearly ten. It is feeble-minded. Perhaps it was born defective, or perhaps it has become imbecile through fear, malnutrition, and neglect. It picks its nose and occasionally fumbles vaguely with its toes or genitals, as it sits hunched in the corner farthest from the bucket and the two mops. It is afraid of the mops. It finds them horrible. It shuts its eyes, but it knows the mops are still standing there; and the door is locked; and nobody will come. The door is always locked; and nobody ever comes, except that sometimes — the child has no understanding of time or interval — sometimes the door rattles terribly and opens, and a person, or several people, are there. One of them may come in and kick the child to make it stand up. The others never come close, but peer in at it with frightened, disgusted eyes. The food bowl and the water jug are hastily filled, the door is locked, the eyes disappear. The people at the door never say anything, but the child, who has not always lived in the tool room, and can remember sunlight and its mother's voice, sometimes speaks. "I will be good," it says. "Please let me out. I will be good!" They never answer. The child used to scream for help at night, and cry a good deal, but now it only makes a kind of whining, "eh-haa, eh-haa," and it speaks less and less often. It is so thin there are no calves to its legs; its belly protrudes; it lives on a half-bowl of corn meal and grease a day. It is naked. Its buttocks and thighs are a mass of festered sores, as it sits in its own excrement continually.

They all know it is there, all the people of Omelas. Some of them have come to see it, others are content merely to know it is there. They all know that it has to be there. Some of them understand why, and some do not, but all understand that their happiness, the beauty of their city, the tenderness of their friendships, the health of their children, the wisdom of their scholars, the skill of their makers, even the abundance of their harvest and the kindly weathers of their skies, depend wholly on this child's abominable misery.

This is usually explained to children when they are between eight and twelve, 10 whenever they seem capable of understanding; and most of those who come to see the child are young people, though often enough an adult comes, or comes back, to see the child. No matter how well the matter has been explained to them, these young spectators are always shocked and sickened at the sight. They feel disgust, which they had thought themselves superior to. They feel anger, outrage, impotence, despite all the explanations. They would like to do something for the child. But there is nothing they can do. If the child were brought up into the sunlight out of that vile place, if it were cleaned and fed and comforted, that would be a good thing, indeed; but if it were done, in that day and hour all the prosperity and beauty and delight of Omelas would wither and be destroyed. Those are the terms. To exchange all the goodness and grace of every life in Omelas for that single, small improvement: to throw away the happiness of thousands for the chance of the happiness of one: that would be to let guilt within the walls indeed.

The terms are strict and absolute; there may not even be a kind word spoken to the child.

Often the young people go home in tears, or in a tearless rage, when they have seen the child and faced this terrible paradox. They may brood over it for weeks or years. But as time goes on they begin to realize that even if the child could be released, it would not get much good of its freedom: a little vague pleasure of warmth and food, no doubt, but little more. It is too degraded and imbecile to know any real joy. It has been afraid too long ever to be free of fear. Its habits are too uncouth for it to respond to humane treatment. Indeed, after so long it would probably be wretched without walls about it to protect it, and darkness for its eyes, and its own excrement to sit in. Their tears at the bitter injustice dry when they begin to perceive the terrible justice of reality, and to accept it. Yet it is their tears and anger, the trying of their generosity and the acceptance of their helplessness, which are perhaps the true source of the splendor of their lives. Theirs is no vapid, irresponsible happiness. They know that they, like the child, are not free. They know compassion. It is the existence of the child, and their knowledge of its existence, that makes possible the nobility of their architecture, the poignancy of their music, the profundity of their science. It is because of the child that they are so gentle with children. They know that if the wretched one were not there snivelling in the dark, the other one, the flute-player, could make no joyful music as the young riders line up in their beauty for the race in the sunlight of the first morning of summer.

Now do you believe in them? Are they not more credible? But there is one more thing to tell, and this is quite incredible.

At times one of the adolescent girls or boys who go to see the child does not go home to weep or rage, does not, in fact, go home at all. Sometimes also a man or woman much older falls silent for a day or two, and then leaves home. These people go out into the street, and walk down the street alone. They keep walking, and walk straight out of the city of Omelas, through the beautiful gates. They keep walking across the farmlands of Omelas. Each one goes alone, youth or girl, man or woman. Night falls; the traveler must pass down village streets, between the houses with yellow-lit windows, and on out into the darkness of the fields. Each alone, they go west or north, towards the mountains. They go on. They leave Omelas, they walk ahead into the darkness, and they do not come back. The place they go towards is a place even less imaginable to most of us than the city of happiness. I cannot describe it at all. It is possible that it does not exist. But they seem to know where they are going, the ones who walk away from Omelas.

For Analysis

1. Who is the narrator? What are her feelings about Omelas, particularly about the misery of the child on which the happiness of the city depends?

2. Does the narrator sympathize with those who walk away? Or with those who remain? Or is she ambivalent?

3. Is Omelas described in sufficient detail, or are there other things about the city you wish the author had included?

4. Look up the dictionary definition of *utopia*. Does Omelas fit that definition?

5. How would you describe the **conflict** in this story? Is there a **protagonist** and **antagonist**? Who are they?

On Style

Characterize the **tone** of this story. What details can you locate in the story that contribute to the author's tone?

Making Connections

1. This story, Hawthorne's "Young Goodman Brown" (p. 80), and Ellison's "'Repent, Harlequin!' Said the Ticktockman" (p. 399) all rely on fantasy. What advantages does the use of fantasy give the authors?

2. Do you find this story a compelling comment on human society, or is it too remote from reality to be believable?

3. Compare the statement this story makes about the human spirit with that made in Ellison's "'Repent, Harlequin!' Said the Ticktockman." Do the ones who walk away from Omelas share any of the attributes of the Harlequin?

Writing Topics

1. The narrator comments: "The trouble is that we have a bad habit, encouraged by pedants and sophisticates, of considering happiness as something rather stupid. Only pain is intellectual, only evil interesting. This is the treason of the artist: a refusal to admit the banality of evil and the terrible boredom of pain" (para. 3). Write an essay examining this statement. Are the narrator's claims persuasive?

2. Is Le Guin's story, first published in 1975, still relevant? Why or why not?

Harlan Ellison   (b. 1934)

"Repent, Harlequin!" Said the Ticktockman   1965

There are always those who ask, what is it all about? For those who need to ask, for those who need points sharply made, who need to know "where it's at," this:

> The mass of men serve the state thus, not as men mainly, but as machines, with their bodies. They are the standing army, and the militia, jailors, constables, posse comitatus, etc. In most cases there is no free exercise whatever of the judgment or of the moral sense; but they put themselves on a level with wood and earth and stones; and wooden men can perhaps be manufactured that will serve the purpose as well. Such command no more respect than men of straw or a lump of dirt. They have the same sort of worth only as horses and dogs. Yet such as these even are commonly esteemed good citizens. Others — as most legislators, politicians, lawyers, ministers, and officeholders — serve the state chiefly with their heads; and, as they rarely make any moral distinctions, they are as likely to serve the Devil, without intending it, as God. A very few, as heroes, patriots, martyrs, reformers in the great sense, and men, serve the state with their consciences also, and so necessarily resist it for the most part; and they are commonly treated as enemies by it.
>
> Henry David Thoreau
> **CIVIL DISOBEDIENCE**

That is the heart of it. Now begin in the middle, and later learn the beginning; the end will take care of itself.

But because it was the very world it was, the very world they had allowed it to *become,* for months his activities did not come to the alarmed attention of The Ones Who Kept The Machine Functioning Smoothly, the ones who poured the very best butter over the cams and mainsprings of the culture. Not until it had become obvious that somehow, someway, he had become a notoriety, a celebrity, perhaps even a hero for (what Officialdom inescapably tagged) "an emotionally disturbed segment of the populace," did they turn it over to the Ticktockman and his legal machinery. But by then, because it was the very world it was, and they had no way to predict he would happen — possibly a strain of disease long-defunct, now, suddenly, reborn in a system where immunity had been forgotten, had lapsed — he had been allowed to become too real. Now he had form and substance.

He had become a *personality,* something they had filtered out of the system many decades before. But there it was, and there *he* was, a very definitely imposing personality. In certain circles — middle-class circles — it was thought disgusting. Vulgar ostentation. Anarchistic. Shameful. In others, there was only sniggering: those strata where thought is subjugated to form and ritual, niceties, proprieties. But down below, ah, down below, where the people always needed their saints and sinners, their bread and circuses, their heroes and villains, he was considered a Bolivar; a Napoleon; a Robin Hood; a Dick Bong (Ace of Aces); a Jesus; a Jomo Kenyatta.

And at the top — where, like socially attuned Shipwreck Kellys, every tremor 5 and vibration threatening to dislodge the wealthy, powerful and titled from their flagpoles — he was considered a menace; a heretic; a rebel; a disgrace; a peril. He was known down the line, to the very heart-meat core, but the important reactions were high above and far below. At the very top, at the very bottom.

So his file was turned over, along with his time-card and his cardioplate, to the office of the Ticktockman.

The Ticktockman: very much over six feet tall, often silent, a soft purring man when things went timewise. The Ticktockman.

Even in the cubicles of the hierarchy, where fear was generated, seldom suffered, he was called the Ticktockman. But no one called him that to his mask.

You don't call a man a hated name, not when that man, behind his mask, is capable of revoking the minutes, the hours, the days and nights, the years of your life. He was called the Master Timekeeper to his mask. It was safer that way.

"That is *what* he is," said the Ticktockman with genuine softness, "but not 10 *who* he is. This time-card I'm holding in my left hand has a name on it, but it is the name of *what* he is, not *who* he is. The cardioplate here in my right hand is also named, but not *whom* named, merely *what* named. Before I can exercise proper revocation, I have to know *who* this *what* is."

To his staff, all the ferrets, all the loggers, all the finks, all the commex, even the mineez, he said, "Who is this Harlequin?"

He was not purring smoothly. Timewise, it was jangle.

However, it *was* the longest speech they had ever heard him utter at one time, the staff, the ferrets, the loggers, the finks, the commex, but not the mineez, who usually weren't around to know, in any case. But even they scurried to find out.

Who is the Harlequin?

High above the third level of the city, he crouched on the humming 15 aluminum-frame platform of the air-boat (foof! air-boat, indeed! swizzleskid is what it was, with a tow-rack jerry-rigged) and he stared down at the neat Mondrian arrangement of the buildings.

Somewhere nearby, he could hear the metronomic left-right-left of the 2:47 PM shift, entering the Timkin roller-bearing plant in their sneakers. A minute later, precisely, he heard the softer right-left-right of the 5:00 AM formation, going home.

An elfin grin spread across his tanned features, and his dimples appeared for a moment. Then, scratching at his thatch of auburn hair, he shrugged within his motley, as though girding himself for what came next, and threw the joystick forward, and bent into the wind as the air-boat dropped. He skimmed over a slidewalk, purposely dropping a few feet to crease the tassels of the ladies of fashion, and — inserting thumbs in large ears — he stuck out his tongue, rolled his eyes and went wugga-wugga-wugga. It was a minor diversion. One pedestrian skittered and tumbled, sending parcels everywhichway, another wet herself, a third keeled slantwise and the walk was stopped automatically by the servitors till she could be resuscitated. It was a minor diversion.

Then he swirled away on a vagrant breeze, and was gone. Hi-ho.

As he rounded the cornice of the Time-Motion Study Building, he saw the shift, just boarding the slidewalk. With practiced motion and an absolute conservation of movement, they sidestepped up onto the slow-strip and (in a chorus line reminiscent of a Busby Berkeley film of the antediluvian 1930s) advanced across the strips ostrich-walking till they were lined up on the expresstrip.

Once more, in anticipation, the elfin grin spread, and there was a tooth miss- 20
ing back there on the left side. He dipped, skimmed, and swooped over them; and then, scrunching about on the air-boat, he released the holding pins that fastened shut the ends of the home-made pouring troughs that kept his cargo from dumping prematurely. And as he pulled the trough-pins, the air-boat slid over the factory workers and one hundred and fifty thousand dollars' worth of jelly beans cascaded down on the expresstrip.

Jelly beans! Millions and billions of purples and yellows and greens and licorice and grape and raspberry and mint and round and smooth and crunchy outside and soft-mealy inside and sugary and bouncing jouncing tumbling clittering clattering skittering fell on the heads and shoulders and hardhats and carapaces of the Timkin workers, tinkling on the slidewalk and bouncing away and rolling about underfoot and filling the sky on their way down with all the colors of joy and childhood and holidays, coming down in a steady rain, a solid wash, a torrent of color and sweetness out of the sky from above, and entering a universe of sanity and metronomic order with quite-mad coocoo newness. Jelly beans!

The shift workers howled and laughed and were pelted, and broke ranks, and the jelly beans managed to work their way into the mechanism of the slidewalks after which there was a hideous scraping as the sound of a million fingernails rasped down a quarter of a million blackboards, followed by a coughing and a sputtering, and then the slidewalks all stopped and everyone was dumped thisawayandthataway in a jackstraw tumble, still laughing and popping little jelly bean eggs of childish color into their mouths. It was a holiday, and a jollity, an absolute insanity, a giggle. But . . .

The shift was delayed seven minutes.

They did not get home for seven minutes.

The master schedule was thrown off by seven minutes.   25

Quotas were delayed by inoperative slidewalks for seven minutes.

He had tapped the first domino in the line, and one after another, like chik chik chik, the others had fallen.

The System had been seven minutes' worth of disrupted. It was a tiny matter, one hardly worthy of note, but in a society where the single driving force was order and unity and equality and promptness and clocklike precision and attention to the clock, reverence of the gods of the passage of time, it was a disaster of major importance.

So he was ordered to appear before the Ticktockman. It was broadcast across every channel of the communications web. He was ordered to be *there* at 7:00 dammit on time. And they waited, and they waited, but he didn't show up till almost ten-thirty, at which time he merely sang a little song about moonlight in a place no one had ever heard of, called Vermont, and vanished again. But they had all been waiting since seven, and it wrecked *hell* with their schedules. So the question remained: Who is the Harlequin?

But the *unasked* question (more important of the two) was: how did we get   30 *into* this position, where a laughing, irresponsible japer of jabberwocky and jive could disrupt our entire economic and cultural life with a hundred and fifty thousand dollars' worth of jelly beans . . .

Jelly for God's sake *beans!* This is madness! Where did he get the money to buy a hundred and fifty thousand dollars' worth of jelly beans? (They knew it would have cost that much, because they had a team of Situation Analysts pulled off another assignment, and rushed to the slidewalk scene to sweep up and count the candies, and produce findings, which disrupted *their* schedules and threw their entire branch at least a day behind.) Jelly beans! Jelly . . . *beans?* Now wait a second — a second accounted for — no one has manufactured jelly beans for over a hundred years. Where did he get jelly beans?

That's another good question. More than likely it will never be answered to your complete satisfaction. But then, how many questions ever are?

The middle you know. Here is the beginning. How it starts:

A DESK PAD. DAY FOR DAY, AND TURN EACH DAY. 9:00 — OPEN THE MAIL. 9:45 — APPOINTMENT WITH PLANNING COMMISSION BOARD. 10:30 — DISCUSS INSTALLATION PROGRESS CHARTS WITH J.L. 11:45 — PRAY FOR RAIN. 12:00 — LUNCH. *AND SO IT GOES.*

"I'm sorry, Miss Grant, but the time for interviews was set at 2:30, and it's almost five   35 now. I'm sorry you're late, but those are the rules. You'll have to wait till next year to submit application for this college again." *And so it goes.*

The 10:10 local stops at Cresthaven, Galesville, Tonawanda Junction, Selby and Farnhurst, but not at Indiana City, Lucasville and Colton, except on Sunday. The 10:35 express stops at Galesville, Selby and Indiana City, except on Sundays & Holidays, at which time it stops at . . . *and so it goes.*

"I couldn't wait, Fred. I had to be at Pierre Cartain's by 3:00, and you said you'd meet me under the clock in the terminal at 2:45, and you weren't there, so I had to go on. You're always late, Fred. If you'd been there, we could have sewed it up together, but as it was, well, I took the order alone . . ." *And so it goes.*

Dear Mr. and Mrs. Atterley: In reference to your son Gerold's constant tardiness, I am afraid we will have to suspend him from school unless some more reliable method can be instituted guaranteeing he will arrive at his classes on time. Granted he is an exemplary student, and his marks are high, his constant flouting of the schedules of this school makes it impractical to maintain him in a system where the other children seem capable of getting where they are supposed to be on time *and so it goes.*

YOU CANNOT VOTE UNLESS YOU APPEAR AT 8:45 AM.

"I don't care if the script is *good,* I need it Thursday!"   40

CHECK-OUT TIME IS 2:00 PM.

"You got here late. The job's taken. Sorry."

YOUR SALARY HAS BEEN DOCKED FOR TWENTY MINUTES TIME LOST.

"God, what time is it, I've gotta run!"

And so it goes. And so it goes. And so it goes. And so it goes goes goes goes   45
goes tick tock tick tock tick tock and one day we no longer let time serve us, we serve time and we are slaves of the schedule, worshippers of the sun's passing, bound into a life predicated on restrictions because the system will not function if we don't keep the schedule tight.

Until it becomes more than a minor inconvenience to be late. It becomes a sin. Then a crime. Then a crime punishable by this:

EFFECTIVE 15 JULY 2389 12:00:00 midnight, the office of the Master Timekeeper will require all citizens to submit their time-cards and cardioplates for processing. In accordance with Statute 555-7-SGH-999 governing the revocation of time per capita, all cardioplates will be keyed to the individual holder and —

What they had done was devise a method of curtailing the amount of life a person could have. If he was ten minutes late, he lost ten minutes of his life. An hour was proportionately worth more revocation. If someone was consistently tardy, he might find himself, on a Sunday night, receiving a communiqué from the Master Timekeeper that his time had run out, and he would be "turned off" at high noon on Monday, please straighten your affairs, sir, madame or bisex.

And so, by this simple scientific expedient (utilizing a scientific process held dearly secret by the Ticktockman's office) the System was maintained. It was the only expedient thing to do. It was, after all, patriotic. The schedules had to be met. After all, there *was* a war on!

But, wasn't there always? 50

"Now that is really disgusting," the Harlequin said, when Pretty Alice showed him the wanted poster. "Disgusting and *highly* improbable. After all, this isn't the Day of the Desperado. A *wanted* poster!"

"You know," Pretty Alice noted, "you speak with a great deal of inflection."

"I'm sorry," said the Harlequin, humbly.

"No need to be sorry. You're always saying 'I'm sorry.' You have such massive guilt, Everett, it's really very sad."

"I'm sorry," he said again, then pursed his lips so the dimples appeared 55 momentarily. He hadn't wanted to say that at all. "I have to go out again. I have to *do* something."

Pretty Alice slammed her coffee-bulb down on the counter. "Oh for God's *sake,* Everett, can't you stay home just *one* night! Must you always be out in that ghastly clown suit, running around an*noy*ing people?"

"I'm — " He stopped, and clapped the jester's hat onto his auburn thatch with a tiny tinkling of bells. He rose, rinsed out his coffee-bulb at the spray, and put it into the dryer for a moment. "I have to go."

She didn't answer. The faxbox was purring, and she pulled a sheet out, read it, threw it toward him on the counter. "It's about you. Of course. You're ridiculous."

He read it quickly. It said the Ticktockman was trying to locate him. He didn't care, he was going out to be late again. At the door, dredging for an exit line, he hurled back petulantly, "Well, *you* speak with inflection, *too!*"

Pretty Alice rolled her pretty eyes heavenward. "You're ridiculous." 60

The Harlequin stalked out, slamming the door, which sighed shut softly, and locked itself.

There was a gentle knock, and Pretty Alice got up with an exhalation of exasperated breath, and opened the door. He stood there. "I'll be back about ten-thirty, okay?"

She pulled a rueful face. "Why do you tell me that? Why? You *know* you'll be late! You *know* it! You're *always* late, so why do you tell me these dumb things?" She closed the door.

On the other side, the Harlequin nodded to himself. *She's right. She's always right. I'll be late. I'm always late. Why* do *I tell her these dumb things?*

He shrugged again, and went off to be late once more.

He had fired off the firecracker rockets that said: I will attend the 115th 65 annual International Medical Association Invocation at 8:00 PM precisely. I do hope you will all be able to join me.

The words had burned in the sky, and of course the authorities were there, lying in wait for him. They assumed, naturally, that he would be late. He arrived twenty minutes early, while they were setting up the spiderwebs to trap and hold him. Blowing a large bullhorn, he frightened and unnerved them so, their own moisturized encirclement webs sucked closed, and they were hauled up, kicking and shrieking, high above the amphitheater's floor. The Harlequin laughed and laughed, and apologized profusely. The physicians, gathered in solemn conclave, roared with laughter, and accepted the Harlequin's apologies with exaggerated bowing and posturing, and a merry time was had by all, who thought the Harlequin was a regular foofaraw in fancy pants; all, that is, but the authorities, who had been sent out by the office of the Ticktockman; they hung there like so much dockside cargo, hauled up above the floor of the amphitheater in a most unseemly fashion.

(In another part of the same city where the Harlequin carried on his "activities," totally unrelated in every way to what concerns us here, save that it illustrates the Ticktockman's power and import, a man named Marshall Delahanty received his turn-off notice from the Ticktockman's office. His wife received the notification from the gray-suited minee who delivered it, with the traditional "look of sorrow" plastered hideously across his face. She knew what it was, even without unsealing it. It was a billet-doux of immediate recognition to everyone these days. She gasped, and held it as though it were a glass slide tinged with botulism, and prayed it was not for her. Let it be for Marsh, she thought, brutally, realistically, or one of the kids, but not for me, please dear God, not for me. And then she opened it, and it *was* for Marsh, and she was at one and the same time horrified and relieved. The next trooper in the line had caught the bullet. "Marshall," she screamed, "Marshall! Termination, Marshall! OhmiGod, Marshall, whattl we do, whattl we do, Marshall omigodmarshall . . ." and in their home that night was the sound of tearing paper and fear, and the stink of madness went up the flue and there was nothing, absolutely nothing they could do about it.

(But Marshall Delahanty tried to run. And early the next day, when turn-off time came, he was deep in the Canadian forest two hundred miles away, and the office of the Ticktockman blanked his cardioplate, and Marshall Delahanty keeled over, running, and his heart stopped, and the blood dried up on its way to his brain, and he was dead that's all. One light went out on the sector map in the office of the Master Timekeeper, while notification was entered for fax reproduction, and Georgette Delahanty's name was entered on the dole roles till she could remarry. Which is the end of the footnote, and all the point that need be made, except don't laugh, because that is what would happen to the Harlequin if ever the Ticktockman found out his real name. It isn't funny.)

The shopping level of the city was thronged with the Thursday-colors of the buyers. Women in canary yellow chitons and men in pseudo-Tyrolean outfits that were jade and leather and fit very tightly, save for the balloon pants.

When the Harlequin appeared on the still-being-constructed shell of the new 70 Efficiency Shopping Center, his bullhorn to his elfishly-laughing lips, everyone pointed and stared, and he berated them:

"Why let them order you about? Why let them tell you to hurry and scurry like ants or maggots? Take your time! Saunter a while! Enjoy the sunshine, enjoy the breeze, let life carry you at your own pace! Don't be slaves of time, it's a helluva way to die, slowly, by degrees . . . down with the Ticktockman!"

Who's the nut? most of the shoppers wanted to know. Who's the nut oh wow I'm gonna be late I gotta run . . .

And the construction gang on the Shopping Center received an urgent order from the office of the Master Timekeeper that the dangerous criminal known as the Harlequin was atop their spire, and their aid was urgently needed in apprehending him. The work crew said no, they would lose time on their construction schedule, but the Ticktockman managed to pull the proper threads of governmental webbing, and they were told to cease work and catch that nitwit up there on the spire; up there with the bullhorn. So a dozen and more burly workers began climbing into their construction platforms, releasing the a-grav plates, and rising toward the Harlequin.

After the debacle (in which, through the Harlequin's attention to personal safety, no one was seriously injured), the workers tried to reassemble, and assault him again, but it was too late. He had vanished. It had attracted quite a crowd, however, and the shopping cycle was thrown off by hours, simply hours. The purchasing needs of the system were therefore falling behind, and so measures were taken to accelerate the cycle for the rest of the day, but it got bogged down and speeded up and they sold too many float-valves and not nearly enough wegglers, which meant that the popli ratio was off, which made it necessary to rush cases and cases of spoiling Smash-O to stores that usually needed a case only every three or four hours. The shipments were bollixed, the transshipments were misrouted, and in the end, even the swizzleskid industries felt it.

"Don't come back till you have him!" the Ticktockman said, very quietly, very 75 sincerely, extremely dangerously.

They used dogs. They used probes. They used cardioplate crossoffs. They used teepers. They used bribery. They used stiktytes. They used intimidation. They used torment. They used torture. They used finks. They used cops. They used search&seizure. They used fallaron. They used betterment incentive. They used fingerprints. They used the Bertillon system. They used cunning. They used guile. They used treachery. They used Raoul Mitgong, but he didn't help much. They used applied physics. They used techniques of criminology.

And what the hell: they caught him.

After all, his name was Everett C. Marm, and he wasn't much to begin with, except a man who had no sense of time.

"Repent, Harlequin!" said the Ticktockman.

"Get stuffed!" the Harlequin replied, sneering.   80

"You've been late a total of sixty-three years, five months, three weeks, two days, twelve hours, forty-one minutes, fifty-nine seconds, point oh three six one one one microseconds. You've used up everything you can, and more. I'm going to turn you off."

"Scare someone else. I'd rather be dead than live in a dumb world with a bogeyman like you."

"It's my job."

"You're full of it. You're a tyrant. You have no right to order people around and kill them if they show up late."

"You can't adjust. You can't fit in."   85

"Unstrap me, and I'll fit my fist into your mouth."

"You're a nonconformist."

"That didn't used to be a felony."

"It is now. Live in the world around you."

"I hate it. It's a terrible world."   90

"Not everyone thinks so. Most people enjoy order."

"I don't, and most of the people I know don't."

"That's not true. How do you think we caught you?"

"I'm not interested."

"A girl named Pretty Alice told us who you were."   95

"That's a lie."

"It's true. You unnerve her. She wants to belong; she wants to conform; I'm going to turn you off."

"Then do it already, and stop arguing with me."

"I'm not going to turn you off."

"You're an idiot!"   100

"Repent, Harlequin!" said the Ticktockman.

"Get stuffed."

So they sent him to Coventry. And in Coventry they worked him over. It was just like what they did to Winston Smith in NINETEEN EIGHTY-FOUR, which was a book none of them knew about, but the techniques are really quite ancient, and so they did it to Everett C. Marm; and one day, quite a long time later, the Harlequin appeared on the communications web, appearing elfin and dimpled and bright-eyed, and not at all brainwashed, and he said he had been wrong, that it was a good, a very good thing indeed, to belong, to be right on time hip-ho and away we go, and everyone stared up at him on the public screens that covered an entire city block, and they said to themselves, well, you see, he was just a nut after all, and if that's the way the system is run, then let's do it that way, because it doesn't pay to fight city hall, or in this case, the Ticktock-man. So Everett C. Marm was destroyed, which was a loss, because of what Thoreau said earlier, but you can't make an omelet without breaking a few eggs, and in every revolution a few die who shouldn't, but they have to, because that's the way it happens, and if you make only a little change, then it seems to be worthwhile. Or, to make the point lucidly:

. . .

"Uh, excuse me, sir, I, uh, don't know how to uh, to uh, tell you this, but you were three minutes late. The schedule is a little, uh, bit off."

He grinned sheepishly.   105

"That's ridiculous!" murmured the Ticktockman behind his mask. "Check your watch." And then he went into his office, going *mrmee, mrmee, mrmee, mrmee.*

For Analysis

1. What are the connotations of the names Harlequin and Everett C. Marm? Is the contrast between the names similar to that between, say, Superman and Clark Kent?

2. What is it about his society that drives Everett C. Marm to rebel?

3. What is Pretty Alice's role in the story?

4. Explain the final section of the story (paras. 104–6). Has the Ticktockman triumphed?

On Style

1. Why does Ellison not present the events in **chronological order**?

2. How would you characterize the prose **style** of this story? What effect is the author trying to achieve? Is he successful?

Making Connections

1. Compare the statement this story makes about the human spirit with that made in Le Guin's "The Ones Who Walk Away from Omelas" (p. 393). Does Everett C. Marm share any of the attributes of the ones who walk away from Omelas?

2. As heroes, compare Everett C. Marm with Pal Smurch in James Thurber's "The Greatest Man in the World" (p. 370). Which do you find more admirable and heroic?

Writing Topics

1. Carefully read the passage taken from Thoreau's "Civil Disobedience" (para. 1). Write an essay explaining why you do or do not agree (in whole or in part) with Thoreau's view of "the state" and with his classification of citizens as those who serve the state with their "bodies," those who serve it with their "heads," and those who serve it with their "consciences." Where would you place Everett C. Marm?

2. Characterize Pretty Alice. Why does she turn Everett in?

James Alan McPherson   (b. 1943)

A Loaf of Bread   1979

It was one of those obscene situations, pedestrian to most people, but invested with meaning for a few poor folk whose lives are usually spent outside the imaginations of their fellow citizens. A grocer named Harold Green was caught red-handed selling to one group of people the very same goods he sold at lower prices at similar outlets in better neighborhoods. He had been doing this for many years, and at first he could not understand the outrage heaped upon him. He acted only from habit, he insisted, and had nothing personal against the people whom he served. They were his neighbors. Many of them he had carried on the cuff during hard times. Yet, through some mysterious access to a television station, the poor folk were now empowered to make grand denunciations of the grocer. Green's children now saw their father's business being picketed on the Monday evening news.

No one could question the fact that the grocer had been overcharging the people. On the news even the reporter grimaced distastefully while reading the statistics. His expression said, "It is my job to report the news, but sometimes even I must disassociate myself from it to protect my honor." This, at least, was the impression the grocer's children seemed to bring away from the television. Their father's name had not been mentioned, but there was a close-up of his store with angry black people and a few outraged whites marching in groups of three in front of it. There was also a close-up of his name. After seeing this, they were in no mood to watch cartoons. At the dinner table, disturbed by his children's silence, Harold Green felt compelled to say, "I am not a dishonest man." Then he felt ashamed. The children, a boy and his older sister, immediately left the table, leaving Green alone with his wife. "Ruth, I am not dishonest," he repeated to her.

Ruth Green did not say anything. She knew, and her husband did not, that the outraged people had also picketed the school attended by their children. They had threatened to return each day until Green lowered his prices. When they called her at home to report this, she had promised she would talk with him. Since she could not tell him this, she waited for an opening. She looked at her husband across the table.

"I did not make the world," Green began, recognizing at once the seriousness in her stare. "My father came to this country with nothing but his shirt. He was exploited for as long as he couldn't help himself. He did not protest or picket. He put himself in a position to play by the rules he had learned." He waited for his wife to answer, and when she did not, he tried again. "I did not make this world," he repeated. "I only make my way in it. Such people as these, they do

409

not know enough to not be exploited. If not me, there would be a Greek, a Chinaman, maybe an Arab or a smart one of their own kind. Believe me, I deal with them. There is something in their style that lacks the patience to run a concern such as mine. If I closed down, take my word on it, someone else would do what has to be done."

But Ruth Green was not thinking of his leaving. Her mind was on other matters. Her children had cried when they came home early from school. She had no special feeling for the people who picketed, but she did not like to see her children cry. She had kissed them generously, then sworn them to silence. "One day this week," she told her husband, "you will give free, for eight hours, anything your customers come in to buy. There will be no publicity, except what they spread by word of mouth. No matter what they say to you, no matter what they take, you will remain silent." She stared deeply into him for what she knew was there. "If you refuse, you have seen the last of your children and myself."

Her husband grunted. Then he leaned toward her. "I will not knuckle under," he said. "I will *not* give!"

"We shall see," his wife told him.

The black pickets, for the most part, had at first been frightened by the audacity of their undertaking. They were peasants whose minds had long before become resigned to their fate as victims. None of them, before now, had thought to challenge this. But now, when they watched themselves on television, they hardly recognized the faces they saw beneath the hoisted banners and placards. Instead of reflecting the meekness they all felt, the faces looked angry. The close-ups looked especially intimidating. Several of the first pickets, maids who worked in the suburbs, reported that their employers, seeing the activity on the afternoon news, had begun treating them with new respect. One woman, midway through the weather report, called around the neighborhood to disclose that her employer had that very day given her a new china plate for her meals. The paper plates, on which all previous meals had been served, had been thrown into the wastebasket. One recipient of this call, a middle-aged woman known for her bashfulness and humility, rejoined that her husband, a sheet-metal worker, had only a few hours before been called "Mister" by his supervisor, a white man with a passionate hatred of color. She added the tale of a neighbor down the street, a widow woman named Murphy, who had at first been reluctant to join the picket; this woman now was insisting it should be made a daily event. Such talk as this circulated among the people who had been instrumental in raising the issue. As news of their victory leaked into the ears of others who had not participated, they received all through the night calls from strangers requesting verification, offering advice, and vowing support. Such strangers listened and then volunteered stories about indignities inflicted on them by city officials, policemen, other grocers. In this way, over a period of hours, the community became even more incensed and restless than it had been at the time of the initial picket.

Soon the man who had set events in motion found himself a hero. His name was Nelson Reed, and all his adult life he had been employed as an assembly-line worker. He was a steady husband, the father of three children, and a deacon in the Baptist church. All his life he had trusted in God and gotten along. But now something in him capitulated to the reality that came suddenly into focus. "I was wrong," he told people who called him. "The onliest thing that matters in this world is *money*. And when was the last time you seen a picture of Jesus on a dollar bill?" This line, which he repeated over and over, caused a few callers to laugh nervously, but not without some affirmation that this was indeed the way things were. Many said they had known it all along. Others argued that although it was certainly true, it was one thing to live without money and quite another to live without faith. But still most callers laughed and said, "You right. You *know* I know you right. Ain't it the truth, though?" Only a few people, among them Nelson Reed's wife, said nothing and looked very sad.

Why they looked sad, however, they would not communicate. And anyone 10 observing their troubled faces would have to trust his own intuition. It is known that Reed's wife, Betty, measured all events against the fullness of her own experience. She was skeptical of everything. Brought to the church after a number of years of living openly with a jazz musician, she had embraced religion when she married Nelson Reed. But though she no longer believed completely in the world, she nonetheless had not fully embraced God. There was something in the nature of Christ's swift rise that had always bothered her, and something in the blood and vengeance of the Old Testament that was mellowing and refreshing. But she had never communicated these thoughts to anyone, especially her husband. Instead, she smiled vacantly while others professed leaps of faith, remained silent when friends spoke fiercely of their convictions. The presence of this vacuum in her contributed to her personal mystery; people said she was beautiful, although she was not outwardly so. Perhaps it was because she wished to protect this inner beauty that she did not smile now, and looked extremely sad, listening to her husband on the telephone.

Nelson Reed had no reason to be sad. He seemed to grow more energized and talkative as the days passed. He was invited by an alderman, on the Tuesday after the initial picket, to tell his story on a local television talk show. He sweated heavily under the hot white lights and attempted to be philosophical. "I notice," the host said to him, "that you are not angry at this exploitative treatment. What, Mr. Reed, is the source of your calm?" The assembly-line worker looked unabashedly into the camera and said, "I have always believed in *Justice* with a capital *J*. I was raised up from a baby believin' that God ain't gonna let nobody go *too* far. See, in *my* mind God is in charge of *all* the capital letters in the alphabet of this world. It say in the Scripture He is Alpha and Omega, the first and the last. He is just about the *onliest* capitalizer they is." Both Reed and the alderman laughed. "Now, when *men* start to capitalize, they gets *greedy*. They put a little *j* in *joy* and a littler one in *justice*. They raise up a big *G* in *Greed* and a big *E* in *Evil*. Well, soon as they commence to put a little *g* in *god,* you can expect some kind of reaction. The Savior will just raise up the *H* in *Hell* and go on from there. And that's just what I'm doin', giving these sharpies *HELL* with a big *H*." The talk show host laughed along with Nelson Reed and the alderman. After the taping they drank coffee in the back room of the studio and talked about the sad shape of the world.

Three days before he was to comply with his wife's request, Green, the grocer, saw this talk show on television while at home. The words of Nelson Reed sent a chill through him. Though Reed had attempted to be philosophical, Green did not perceive the statement in this light. Instead, he saw a vindictive-looking black man seated between an ambitious alderman and a smug talk-show host. He saw them chatting comfortably about the nature of evil. The cameraman had shot mostly close-ups, and Green could see the set in Nelson Reed's jaw. The color of Reed's face was maddening. When his children came into the den, the grocer was in a sweat. Before he could think, he had shouted at them and struck the button turning off the set. The two children rushed from the room screaming. Ruth Green ran in from the kitchen. She knew why he was upset because she had received a call about the show, but she said nothing and pretended ignorance. Her children's school had been picketed that day, as it had the day before. But both children were still forbidden to speak of this to their father.

"Where do they get so much power?" Green said to his wife. "Two days ago nobody would have cared. Now everywhere, even in my home, I am condemned as a rascal. And what do I own? An airline? A multinational? Half of South America? *No!* I own three stores, one of which happens to be in a certain neighborhood inhabited by people who cost me money to run it." He sighed and sat upright on the sofa, his chubby legs spread wide. "A cabdriver has a meter that clicks as he goes along. I pay extra for insurance, iron bars, pilfering by customers and employees. Nothing clicks. But when I add a little overhead to my prices, suddenly everything clicks. But for someone else. When was there last such a world?" He pressed the palms of both hands to his temples, suggesting a bombardment of brain-stinging sounds.

This gesture evoked no response from Ruth Green. She remained standing by the door, looking steadily at him. She said, "To protect yourself, I would not stock any more fresh cuts of meat in the store until after the giveaway on Saturday. Also, I would not tell it to the employees until after the first customer of the day has begun to check out. But I would urge you to hire several security guards to close the door promptly at seven-thirty, as is usual." She wanted to say much more than this, but did not. Instead she watched him. He was looking at the blank gray television screen, his palms still pressed against his ears. "In case you need to hear again," she continued in a weighty tone of voice, "I said two days ago, and I say again now, that if you fail to do this you will not see your children again for many years."

He twisted his head and looked up at her. "What is the color of these 15 people?" he asked.

"Black," his wife said.

"And what is the name of my children?"

"Green."

The grocer smiled. "There is your answer," he told his wife. "Green is the only color I am interested in."

His wife did not smile. "Insufficient," she said.   20

"The world is mad!" he moaned. "But it is a point of sanity with me to not bend. I will not bend." He crossed his legs and pressed one hand firmly atop his knee. *"I will not bend,"* he said.

"We will see," his wife said.

Nelson Reed, after the television interview, became the acknowledged leader of the disgruntled neighbors. At first a number of them met in the kitchen at his house; then, as space was lacking for curious newcomers, a mass meeting was held on Thursday in an abandoned theater. His wife and three children sat in the front row. Behind them sat the widow Murphy, Lloyd Dukes, Tyrone Brown, Les Jones — those who had joined him on the first picket line. Behind these sat people who bought occasionally at the store, people who lived on the fringes of the neighborhood, people from other neighborhoods come to investigate the problem, and the merely curious. The middle rows were occupied by a few people from the suburbs, those who had seen the talk show and whose outrage at the grocer proved much more powerful than their fear of black people. In the rear of the theater crowded aging, old-style leftists, somber students, cynical young black men with angry grudges to explain with inarticulate gestures. Leaning against the walls, huddled near the doors at the rear, tape-recorder-bearing social scientists looked as detached and serene as bookies at the track. Here and there, in this diverse crowd, a politician stationed himself, pumping hands vigorously and pressing his palms gently against the shoulders of elderly people. Other visitors passed out leaflets, buttons, glossy color prints of men who promoted causes, the familiar and obscure. There was a hubbub of voices, a blend of the strident and the playful, the outraged and the reverent, lending an undercurrent of ominous energy to the assembly.

Nelson Reed spoke from a platform on the stage, standing before a yellowed, shredded screen that had once reflected the images of matinee idols. "I don't mind sayin' that I have always been a sucker," he told the crowd. "All my life I have been a sucker for the words of Jesus. Being a natural-born fool, I just ain't never had the *sense* to learn no better. Even right today, while the whole world is sayin' wrong is right and up is down, I'm so dumb I'm *still* steady believin' what is wrote in the Good Book. . . ."

From the audience, especially the front rows, came a chorus singing,   25 "Preach!"

"I have no doubt," he continued in a low baritone, "that it's true what is writ in the Good Book: 'The last shall be first and the first shall be last.' I don't know about y'all, but I have *always* been the last. I never wanted to be the first, but sometimes it look like the world get so bad that them that's holdin' onto the tree of life is the onliest ones left when God commence to blowin' dead leafs off the branches."

"Now you preaching," someone called.

In the rear of the theater a white student shouted an awkward "Amen."

Nelson Reed began walking across the stage to occupy the major part of his nervous energy. But to those in the audience, who now hung on his every word, it looked as though he strutted. "All my life," he said, "I have claimed to be a man without earnin' the right to call myself that. You know, the *average* man ain't really a man. The average man is a *bootlicker.* In fact, the *average* man would *run away* if he found hisself standing alone facin' down a adversary. I have done that *too many a time* in my life! But *not no more.* Better to be *once* was than *never* was a man. I will tell you tonight, there is somethin' *wrong* in being average. *I intend to stand up!* Now, if your average man that ain't really a man stand up, two things gonna happen: *one,* he gon bust through all the weights that been place on his head, and, *two,* he gon feel a lot of pain. But that same hurt is what make things fall in place. That, and gettin' your hands on one of these slick four-flushers tight enough so's you can squeeze him and say, *'No more!'* You do that, you g'on hurt some, but *you won't be average no more....*"

"No *more!*" a few people in the front rows repeated.   30

"I say *no more!*" Nelson Reed shouted.

"No more! No more! No more!" The chant rustled through the crowd like the rhythm of an autumn wind against a shedding tree.

Then people laughed and chattered in celebration.

As for the grocer, from the evening of the television interview he had begun to make plans. Unknown to his wife, he cloistered himself several times with his brother-in-law, an insurance salesman, and plotted a course. He had no intention of tossing steaks to the crowd. "And why should I, Tommy?" he asked his wife's brother, a lean, bald-headed man named Thomas. "I don't cheat anyone. I have never cheated anyone. The businesses I run are always on the up-and-up. So why should I pay?"

"Quite so," the brother-in-law said, chewing an unlit cigarillo. "The world has   35
gone crazy. Next they will say that people in my business are responsible for prolonging life. I have found that people who refuse to believe in death refuse also to believe in the harshness of life. I sell well by saying that death is a long happiness. I show people the realities of life and compare this to a funeral with dignity, *and* the promise of a bundle for every loved one salted away. When they look around hard at life, they usually buy."

"So?" asked Green. Thomas was a college graduate with a penchant for philosophy.

"So," Thomas answered. "You must fight to show these people the reality of both your situation and theirs. How would it be if you visited one of their meetings and chalked out, on a blackboard, the dollars and cents of your operation? Explain your overhead, your security fees, all the additional expenses. If you treat them with respect, they might understand."

MCPHERSON/A LOAF OF BREAD • 415

Green frowned. "That I would never do," he said. "It would be admission of a certain guilt."

The brother-in-law smiled, but only with one corner of his mouth. "Then you have something to feel guilty about?" he asked.

The grocer frowned at him. "*Nothing!*" he said with great emphasis.   40

"So?" Thomas said.

This first meeting between the grocer and his brother-in-law took place on Thursday, in a crowded barroom.

At the second meeting, in a luncheonette, it was agreed that the grocer should speak privately with the leader of the group, Nelson Reed. The meeting at which this was agreed took place on Friday afternoon. After accepting this advice from Thomas, the grocer resigned himself to explain to Reed, in as finite detail as possible, the economic structure of his operation. He vowed to suppress no information. He would explain everything: inventories, markups, sale items, inflation, balance sheets, specialty items, overhead, and that mysterious item called profit. This last item, promising to be the most difficult to explain, Green and his brother-in-law debated over for several hours. They agreed first of all that a man should not work for free, then they agreed that it was unethical to ruthlessly exploit. From these parameters, they staked out an area between fifteen and forty percent, and agreed that someplace between these two borders lay an amount of return that could be called fair. This was easy, but then Thomas introduced the factor of circumstance. He questioned whether the fact that one serviced a risky area justified the earning of profits, closer to the forty-percent edge of the scale. Green was unsure. Thomas smiled. "Here is a case that will point out an analogy," he said, licking a cigarillo. "I read in the papers that a family wants to sell an electric stove. I call the home and the man says fifty dollars. I ask to come out and inspect the merchandise. When I arrive I see they are poor, have already bought a new stove that is connected, and are selling the old one for fifty dollars because they want it out of the place. The electric stove is in good condition, worth much more than fifty. But because I see what I see I offer forty-five."

Green, for some reason, wrote down this figure on the back of the sales slip for the coffee they were drinking.

The brother-in-law smiled. He chewed his cigarillo. "The man agrees to take   45 forty-five dollars, saying he has had no other calls. I look at the stove again and see a spot of rust. I say I will give him forty dollars. He agrees to this, on condition that I myself haul it away. I say I will haul it away if he comes down to thirty. You, of course, see where I am going."

The grocer nodded. "The circumstances of his situation, his need to get rid of the stove quickly, placed him in a position where he has little room to bargain?"

"Yes," Thomas answered. "So? Is it ethical, Harry?"

Harold Green frowned. He had never liked his brother-in-law, and now he thought the insurance agent was being crafty. "But," he answered, "this man does not *have* to sell! It is his choice whether to wait for other calls. It is not the fault of the buyer that the seller is in a hurry. It is the right of the buyer to get what he wants at the lowest price possible. That is the rule. That has *always* been the rule. And the reverse of it applies to the seller as well."

"Yes," Thomas said, sipping coffee from the Styrofoam cup. "But suppose that in addition to his hurry to sell, the owner was also of a weak soul. There are, after all, many such people." He smiled. "Suppose he placed no value on the money?"

"Then," Green answered, "your example is academic. Here we are not talking 50 about real life. One man lives by the code, one man does not. Who is there free enough to make a judgment?" He laughed. "Now you see," he told his brother-in-law. "Much more than a few dollars are at stake. If this one buyer is to be condemned, then so are most people in the history of the world. An examination of history provides the only answer to your question. This code will be here tomorrow, long after the ones who do not honor it are not."

They argued fiercely late into the afternoon, the brother-in-law leaning heavily on his readings. When they parted, a little before five o'clock, nothing had been resolved.

Neither was much resolved during the meeting between Green and Nelson Reed. Reached at home by the grocer in the early evening, the leader of the group spoke coldly at first, but consented finally to meet his adversary at a nearby drugstore for coffee and a talk. They met at the lunch counter, shook hands awkwardly, and sat for a few minutes discussing the weather. Then the grocer pulled two gray ledgers from his briefcase. "You have for years come into my place," he told the man. "In my memory I have always treated you well. Now our relationship has come to this." He slid the books along the counter until they touched Nelson Reed's arm.

Reed opened the top book and flipped the thick green pages with his thumb. He did not examine the figures. "All I know," he said, "is over at your place a can of soup cost me fifty-five cents, and two miles away at your other store for white folks you chargin' thirty-nine cents." He said this with the calm authority of an outraged soul. A quality of condescension tinged with pity crept into his gaze.

The grocer drummed his fingers on the counter top. He twisted his head and looked away, toward shelves containing cosmetics, laxatives, toothpaste. His eyes lingered on a poster of a woman's apple-red lips and milk-white teeth. The rest of the face was missing.

"Ain't no use to hide," Nelson Reed said, as to a child. "*I* know you wrong, *you* 55 know you wrong, and before I finish, *everybody in this city* g'on know you wrong. God don't *like* ugly." He closed his eyes and gripped the cup of coffee. Then he swung his head suddenly and faced the grocer again. "Man, why you want to *do* people that way?" he asked. "We human, same as you."

"Before *God!*" Green exclaimed, looking squarely into the face of Nelson Reed. "Before *God!*" he said again. "*I am not an evil man!*" These last words sounded more like a moan as he tightened the muscles in his throat to lower the sound of his voice. He tossed his left shoulder as if adjusting the sleeve of his coat, or as if throwing off some unwanted weight. Then he peered along the counter top. No one was watching. At the end of the counter the waitress was scrubbing the coffee urn. "Look at these figures, please," he said to Reed.

The man did not drop his gaze. His eyes remained fixed on the grocer's face.

"All right," Green said. "Don't look. I'll tell you what is in these books, believe me if you want. I work twelve hours a day, one day off per week, running my business in three stores. I am not a wealthy person. In one place, in the area you call white, I get by barely by smiling lustily at old ladies, stocking gourmet stuff on the chance I will build a reputation as a quality store. The two clerks there cheat me; there is nothing I can do. In this business you must be friendly with everybody. The second place is on the other side of town, in a neighborhood as poor as this one. I get out there seldom. The profits are not worth the gas. I use the loss there as a write-off against some other properties," he paused. "Do you understand write-off?" he asked Nelson Reed.

"Naw," the man said.

Harold Green laughed. "What does it matter?" he said in a tone of voice 60 intended for himself alone. "In this area I will admit I make a profit, but it is not so much as you think. But I do not make a profit here because the people are black. I make a profit because a profit is here to be made. I invest more here in window bars, theft losses, insurance, spoilage; I deserve to make more here than at the other places." He looked, almost imploringly, at the man seated next to him. "You don't accept this as the right of a man in business?"

Reed grunted. "Did the bear shit in the woods?" he said.

Again Green laughed. He gulped his coffee awkwardly, as if eager to go. Yet his motions slowed once he had set his coffee cup down on the blue plastic saucer. "Place yourself in *my* situation," he said, his voice high and tentative. "If *you* were running my store in this neighborhood, what would be *your* position? Say on a profit scale of fifteen to forty percent, at what point in between would you draw the line?"

Nelson Reed thought. He sipped his coffee and seemed to chew the liquid. "Fifteen to forty?" he repeated.

"Yes."

"I'm a churchgoin' man," he said. "Closer to fifteen than to forty." 65

"How close?"

Nelson Reed thought. "In church you tithe ten percent."

"In restaurants you tip fifteen," the grocer said quickly.

"All right," Reed said. "Over fifteen."

"How much over?" 70

Nelson Reed thought.

"Twenty, thirty, thirty-five?" Green chanted, leaning closer to Reed.

Still the man thought.

"Forty? Maybe even forty-five or fifty?" the grocer breathed in Reed's ear. "In the supermarkets, you know, they have more subtle ways of accomplishing such feats."

Reed slapped his coffee cup with the back of his right hand. The brown liquid 75
swirled across the counter top, wetting the books. *"Damn this!"* he shouted.

Startled, Green rose from his stool.

Nelson Reed was trembling. "I ain't *you*," he said in a deep baritone. "I ain't
the *supermarket* neither. All I is is a poor man that works *too* hard to see his pay
slip through his fingers like rainwater. All I know is you done *cheat* me, you done
cheat everybody in the neighborhood, and we organized now to get some of it
back!" Then he stood and faced the grocer. "My daddy sharecropped down in
Mississippi and bought in the company store. He owed them twenty-three years
when he died. I paid off five of them years and then run away to up here. Now,
I'm a deacon in the Baptist church. I raised my kids the way my daddy raise me
and don't bother nobody. Now come to find out, after all my runnin', they done
lift that *same company store* up out of Mississippi and slip it down on us here!
Well, my daddy was a *fighter*, and if he hadn't owed all them years he would of
raise him some hell. Me, I'm steady my daddy's child, plus I got seniority in my
union. I'm a free man. Buddy, don't you know *I'm gonna raise me some hell!*"

Harold Green reached for a paper napkin to sop the coffee soaking into his
books.

Nelson Reed threw a dollar on top of the books and walked away.

"I *will not* do it!" Harold Green said to his wife that same evening. They were 80
in the bathroom of their home. Bending over the face bowl, she was washing
her hair with a towel draped around her neck. The grocer stood by the door,
looking in at her. "I will not bankrupt myself tomorrow," he said.

"I've been thinking about it, too," Ruth Green said, shaking her wet hair.
"You'll do it, Harry."

"Why should I?" he asked. "You won't leave. You know it was a bluff. I've
waited this long for you to calm down. Tomorrow is Saturday. This week has
been a hard one. Tonight let's be realistic."

"Of course you'll do it," Ruth Green said. She said it the way she would say
"Have some toast." She said. "You'll do it because you want to see your children
grow up."

"And for what other reason?" he asked.

She pulled the towel tighter around her neck. "Because you are at heart a 85
moral man."

He grinned painfully. "If I am, why should I have to prove it to *them?*"

"Not them," Ruth Green said, freezing her movements and looking in the
mirror. "Certainly not them. By no means them. They have absolutely nothing
to do with this."

"Who, then?" he asked, moving from the door into the room. "Who else
should I prove something to?"

His wife was crying. But her entire face was wet. The tears moved secretly
down her face.

"Who else?" Harold Green asked. 90

It was almost eleven P.M. and the children were in bed. They had also cried when they came home from school. Ruth Green said, "For yourself, Harry. For the love that lives inside your heart."

All night the grocer thought about this.

Nelson Reed also slept little that Friday night. When he returned home from the drugstore, he reported to his wife as much of the conversation as he could remember. At first he had joked about the exchange between himself and the grocer, but as more details returned to his conscious mind he grew solemn and then bitter. "He ask me to put myself in *his* place," Reed told his wife. "Can you imagine that kind of gumption? I never cheated nobody in my life. All my life I have lived on Bible principles. I am a deacon in the church. I have worked all my life for other folks and I don't even own the house I live in." He paced up and down the kitchen, his big arms flapping loosely at his sides. Betty Reed sat at the table, watching. "This here's a low-down, ass-kicking world," he said. "I swear to God it is! All my life I have lived on principle and I ain't got a dime in the bank. Betty," he turned suddenly toward her, "don't you think I'm a fool?"

"Mr. Reed," she said. "Let's go on to bed."

But he would not go to bed. Instead, he took the fifth of bourbon from the 95 cabinet under the sink and poured himself a shot. His wife refused to join him. Reed drained the glass of whiskey, and then another, while he resumed pacing the kitchen floor. He slapped his hands against his sides. "*I* think I'm a fool," he said. "Ain't got a dime in the bank, ain't got a pot to *pee* in or a wall to pitch it over, and that there *cheat* ask me to put myself inside *his* shoes. Hell, I can't even *afford* the kind of shoes he wears." He stopped pacing and looked at his wife.

"Mr. Reed," she whispered, "tomorrow ain't a work day. Let's go to bed."

Nelson Reed laughed, the bitterness in his voice rattling his wife. "The *hell* I will!" he said.

He strode to the yellow telephone on the wall beside the sink and began to dial. The first call was to Lloyd Dukes, a neighbor two blocks away and a lieutenant in the organization. Dukes was not at home. The second call was to McElroy's Bar on the corner of Sixty-fifth and Carroll, where Stanley Harper, another of the lieutenants, worked as a bartender. It was Harper who spread the word, among those men at the bar, that the organization would picket the grocer's store the following morning. And all through the night, in the bedroom of their house, Betty Reed was awakened by telephone calls coming from Lester Jones, Nat Lucas, Mrs. Tyrone Brown, the widow-woman named Murphy, all coordinating the time when they would march in a group against the store owned by Harold Green. Betty Reed's heart beat loudly beneath the covers as she listened to the bitterness and rage in her husband's voice. On several occasions, hearing him declare himself a fool, she pressed the pillow against her eyes and cried.

The grocer opened later than usual this Saturday morning, but still it was early enough to make him one of the first walkers in the neighborhood. He parked his car one block from the store and strolled to work. There were no birds singing. The sky in this area was not blue. It was smog-smutted and gray, seeming on the verge of a light rain. The street, as always, was littered with cans, papers, bits of broken glass. As always the garbage cans overflowed. The morning breeze plastered a sheet of newspaper playfully around the sides of a rusted garbage can. For some reason, using his right foot, he loosened the paper and stood watching it slide into the street and down the block. The movement made him feel good. He whistled while unlocking the bars shielding the windows and door of his store. When he had unlocked the main door he stepped in quickly and threw a switch to the right of the jamb, before the shrill sound of the alarm could shatter his mood. Then he switched on the lights. Everything was as it had been the night before. He had already telephoned his two employees and given them the day off. He busied himself doing the usual things — hauling milk and vegetables from the cooler, putting cash in the till — not thinking about the silence of his wife, or the look in her eyes, only an hour before when he left home. He had determined, at some point while driving through the city, that today it would be business as usual. But he expected very few customers.

The first customer of the day was Mrs. Nelson Reed. She came in around 100 nine-thirty A.M. and wandered about the store. He watched her from the checkout counter. She seemed uncertain of what she wanted to buy. She kept glancing at him down the center aisle. His suspicions aroused, he said finally, "Yes, may I help you, Mrs. Reed?" His words caused her to jerk, as if some devious thought had been perceived going through her mind. She reached over quickly and lifted a loaf of whole wheat bread from the rack and walked with it to the counter. She looked at him and smiled. The smile was a broad, shy one, that rare kind of smile one sees on virgin girls when they first confess love to themselves. Betty Reed was a woman of about forty-five. For some reason he could not comprehend, this gesture touched him. When she pulled a dollar from her purse and laid it on the counter, an impulse, from no place he could locate with his mind, seized control of his tongue. "Free," he told Betty Reed. She paused, then pushed the dollar toward him with a firm and determined thrust of her arm. "Free," he heard himself saying strongly, his right palm spread and meeting her thrust with absolute force. She clutched the loaf of bread and walked out of his store.

The next customer, a little girl, arriving well after ten-thirty A.M., selected a candy bar from the rack beside the counter. "Free," Green said cheerfully. The little girl left the candy on the counter and ran out of the store.

At eleven-fifteen A.M. a wino came in looking desperate enough to sell his soul. The grocer watched him only for an instant. Then he went to the wine counter and selected a half-gallon of medium-grade red wine. He shoved the jug into the belly of the wino, the man's sour breath bathing his face. "Free," the grocer said. "But you must not drink it in here."

He felt good about the entire world, watching the wino through the window gulping the wine and looking guiltily around.

At eleven twenty-five A.M. the pickets arrived.

Two dozen people, men and women, young and old, crowded the pavement   105
in front of his store. Their signs, placards, and voices denounced him as a para-
site. The grocer laughed inside himself. He felt lighthearted and wild, like a
man drugged. He rushed to the meat counter and pulled a long roll of brown
wrapping paper from the rack, tearing it neatly with a quick shift of his body
resembling a dance step practiced fervently in his youth. He laid the paper on
the chopping block and with the black-inked, felt-tipped marker scrawled, in
giant letters, the word FREE. This he took to the window and pasted in place
with many strands of Scotch tape. He was laughing wildly. "Free!" he shouted
from behind the brown paper. "Free! Free! Free! Free! Free! Free!" He rushed
to the door, pushed his head out, and screamed to the confused crowd, *"Free!"*
Then he ran back to the counter and stood behind it, like a soldier at attention.

They came in slowly.

Nelson Reed entered first, working his right foot across the dirty tile as if
tracking a squiggling worm. The others followed: Lloyd Dukes dragging a plac-
ard, Mr. and Mrs. Tyrone Brown, Stanley Harper walking with his fists
clenched, Lester Jones with three of his children, Nat Lucas looking sheepish
and detached, a clutch of winos, several bashful nuns, ironic-smiling teenagers
and a few students. Bringing up the rear was a bearded social scientist holding a
tape recorder to his chest. "Free!" the grocer screamed. He threw up his arms
in a gesture that embraced, or dismissed, the entire store. *"All free!"* he
shouted. He was grinning with the grace of a madman.   •

The winos began grabbing first. They stripped the shelf of wine in a matter of
seconds. Then they fled, dropping bottles on the tile in their wake. The others,
stepping quickly through this liquid, soon congealed it into a sticky, bloodlike
consistency. The young men went for the cigarettes and luncheon meats and
beer. One of them had the prescience to grab a sack from the counter, while the
others loaded their arms swiftly, hugging cartons and packages of cold cuts like
long-lost friends. The students joined them, less for greed than for the thrill of
the experience. The two nuns backed toward the door. As for the older people,
men and women, they stood at first as if stuck to the wine-smeared floor. Then
Stanley Harper, the bartender, shouted, "The man said *free,* y'all heard him."
He paused. "Didn't you say *free* now?" he called to the grocer.

"I said free," Harold Green answered, his temples pounding.

A cheer went up. The older people began grabbing, as if the secret lusts of a   110
lifetime had suddenly seized command of their arms and eyes. They grabbed
toilet tissue, cold cuts, pickles, sardines, boxes of raisins, boxes of starch, cans of
soup, tins of tuna fish and salmon, bottles of spices, cans of boned chicken, slippery cans of olive oil. Here a man, Lester Jones, burdened himself with several
heads of lettuce, while his wife, in another aisle, shouted for him to drop those
small items and concentrate on the gourmet section. She herself took imported
sardines, wheat crackers, bottles of candied pickles, herring, anchovies,
imported olives, French wafers, an ancient, half-rusted can of paté, stocked, by
mistake, from the inventory of another store. Others packed their arms with
detergents, hams, chocolate-coated cereal, whole chickens with hanging asses,

wedges of bologna and salami like squashed footballs, chunks of cheeses, yellow and white, shriveled onions, and green peppers. Mrs. Tyrone Brown hung a curve of pepperoni around her neck and seemed to take on instant dignity, much like a person of noble birth in possession now of a long sought-after gem. Another woman, the widow Murphy, stuffed tomatoes into her bosom, holding a half-chewed lemon in her mouth. The more enterprising fought desperately over the three rusted shopping carts, and the victors wheeled these along the narrow aisles, sweeping into them bulk items — beer in six-packs, sacks of sugar, flour, glass bottles of syrup, toilet cleanser, sugar cookies, prune, apple and tomato juices — while others endeavored to snatch the carts from them. There were several fistfights and much cursing. The grocer, standing behind the counter, hummed and rang his cash register like a madman.

Nelson Reed, the first into the store, followed the nuns out, empty-handed.

In less than half an hour the others had stripped the store and vanished in many directions up and down the block. But still more people came, those late in hearing the news. And when they saw the shelves were bare, they cursed soberly and chased those few stragglers still bearing away goods. Soon only the grocer and the social scientist remained, the latter stationed at the door with his tape recorder sucking in leftover sounds. Then he, too, slipped away up the block.

By twelve-ten P.M. the grocer was leaning against the counter, trying to make his mind slow down. Not a man given to drink during work hours, he nonetheless took a swallow from a bottle of wine, a dusty bottle from beneath the wine shelf, somehow overlooked by the winos. Somewhat recovered, he was preparing to remember what he should do next when he glanced toward a figure at the door. Nelson Reed was standing there, watching him.

"All gone," Harold Green said. "My friend, Mr. Reed, there is no more." Still the man stood in the doorway, peering into the store.

The grocer waved his arms about the empty room. Not a display case had a 115 single item standing. "All gone," he said again, as if addressing a stupid child. "There is nothing left to get. You, my friend, have come back too late for a second load. I am cleaned out."

Nelson Reed stepped into the store and strode toward the counter. He moved through wine-stained flour, lettuce leaves, red, green, and blue labels, bits and pieces of broken glass. He walked toward the counter.

"All day," the grocer laughed, not quite hysterically now, "all day long I have not made a single cent of profit. The entire day was a loss. This store, like the others, is *bleeding* me." He waved his arms about the room in a magnificent gesture of uncaring loss. "Now do you understand?" he said. "Now will you put yourself in my shoes? I have nothing here. Come, now, Mr. Reed, would it not be so bad a thing to walk in my shoes?"

"Mr. Green," Nelson Reed said coldly. "My wife bought a loaf of bread in here this mornin'. She forgot to pay you. I, myself, have come here to pay you your money."

"Oh," the grocer said.

"I think it was brown bread. Don't that cost more than white?" 120

The two men looked away from each other, but not at anything in the store.

"In my store, yes," Harold Green said. He rang the register with the most casual movement of his finger. The register read fifty-five cents.

Nelson Reed held out a dollar.

"And two cents tax," the grocer said.

The man held out the dollar. 125

"After all," Harold Green said. "We are all, after all, Mr. Reed, in debt to the government."

He rang the register again. It read fifty-seven cents.

Nelson Reed held out a dollar.

For Analysis

1. Is Harold Green an exploiter of the poor and ignorant or, as his wife declares, a "moral" man?

2. Is Nelson Reed an opportunist or a man genuinely seeking to combat racism and exploitation?

3. What does Green's conversation with his brother-in-law, particularly the part that includes the analogy about the family selling a stove (paras. 43–51), contribute to the theme of the story?

4. What does Green mean when he tells Reed, during their meeting in the drugstore, ". . . I do not make a profit here because the people are black. I make a profit because a profit is here to be made" (para. 60)?

5. Does the scene in which the neighbors empty the store vindicate Green's position?

6. Explain the significance of the title.

On Style

Why is the third-person narrative **point of view** right for this story? How would the story be changed if it were told from the first-person point of view by Harold Green? By Nelson Reed?

Making Connections

Contrast the treatment of racial injustice in this story with that in Toni Cade Bambara's "The Lesson" (p. 134).

Writing Topics

1. Write an essay focusing on the conflict between Harold Green and Nelson Reed as a mirror of the larger struggle in American society for racial justice and equality.

2. Argue for or against the proposition that this story has a single hero — Harold Green or Nelson Reed — whose position and actions are vindicated in the end.

Amy Tan   (b. 1952)

Two Kinds   1989

My mother believed you could be anything you wanted to be in America. You could open a restaurant. You could work for the government and get good retirement. You could buy a house with almost no money down. You could become rich. You could become instantly famous.

"Of course you can be prodigy, too," my mother told me when I was nine. "You can be best anything. What does Auntie Lindo know? Her daughter, she is only best tricky."

America was where all my mother's hopes lay. She had come here in 1949 after losing everything in China: her mother and father, her family home, her first husband, and two daughters, twin baby girls. But she never looked back with regret. There were so many ways for things to get better.

We didn't immediately pick the right kind of prodigy. At first my mother thought I could be a Chinese Shirley Temple. We'd watch Shirley's old movies on TV as though they were training films. My mother would poke my arm and say, "*Ni kan*" — You watch. And I would see Shirley tapping her feet, or singing a sailor song, or pursing her lips into a very round O while saying, "Oh my goodness."

"*Ni kan,*" said my mother as Shirley's eyes flooded with tears. "You already 5 know how. Don't need talent for crying!"

Soon after my mother got this idea about Shirley Temple, she took me to a beauty training school in the Mission district and put me in the hands of a student who could barely hold the scissors without shaking. Instead of getting big fat curls, I emerged with an uneven mass of crinkly black fuzz. My mother dragged me off to the bathroom and tried to wet down my hair.

"You look like Negro Chinese," she lamented, as if I had done this on purpose.

The instructor of the beauty training school had to lop off these soggy clumps to make my hair even again. "Peter Pan is very popular these days," the instructor assured my mother. I now had hair the length of a boy's, with straight-across bangs that hung at a slant two inches above my eyebrows. I liked the haircut and it made me actually look forward to my future fame.

In fact, in the beginning, I was just as excited as my mother, maybe even more so. I pictured this prodigy part of me as many different images, trying each one on for size. I was a dainty ballerina girl standing by the curtains, waiting to hear the right music that would send me floating on my tiptoes. I was like the Christ child lifted out of the straw manger, crying with holy indignity. I was Cinderella stepping from her pumpkin carriage with sparkly cartoon music filling the air.

In all of my imaginings, I was filled with a sense that I would soon become 10 *perfect*. My mother and father would adore me. I would be beyond reproach. I would never feel the need to sulk for anything.

But sometimes the prodigy in me became impatient. "If you don't hurry up and get me out of here, I'm disappearing for good," it warned. "And then you'll always be nothing."

Every night after dinner, my mother and I would sit at the Formica kitchen table. She would present new tests, taking her examples from stories of amazing children she had read in *Ripley's Believe It or Not*, or *Good Housekeeping*, *Reader's Digest*, and a dozen other magazines she kept in a pile in our bathroom. My mother got these magazines from people whose houses she cleaned. And since she cleaned many houses each week, we had a great assortment. She would look through them all, searching for stories about remarkable children.

The first night she brought out a story about a three-year-old boy who knew the capitals of all the states and even of most of the European countries. A teacher was quoted as saying the little boy could also pronounce the names of the foreign cities correctly.

"What's the capital of Finland?" my mother asked me, looking at the magazine story.

All I knew was the capital of California, because Sacramento was the name of 15 the street we lived on in Chinatown. "Nairobi!" I guessed, saying the most foreign word I could think of. She checked to see if that was possibly one way to pronounce "Helsinki" before showing me the answer.

The tests got harder — multiplying numbers in my head, finding the queen of hearts in a deck of cards, trying to stand on my head without using my hands, predicting the daily temperatures in Los Angeles, New York, and London.

One night I had to look at a page from the Bible for three minutes and then report everything I could remember. "Now Jehoshaphat had riches and honor in abundance and . . . that's all I remember, Ma," I said.

And after seeing my mother's disappointed face once again, something inside of me began to die. I hated the tests, the raised hopes and failed expectations. Before going to bed that night, I looked in the mirror above the bathroom sink and when I saw only my face staring back — and that it would always be this ordinary face — I began to cry. Such a sad, ugly girl! I made high-pitched noises like a crazed animal, trying to scratch out the face in the mirror.

And then I saw what seemed to be the prodigy side of me — because I had never seen that face before. I looked at my reflection, blinking so I could see more clearly. The girl staring back at me was angry, powerful. This girl and I were the same. I had new thoughts, willful thoughts, or rather thoughts filled with lots of won'ts. I won't let her change me, I promised myself. I won't be what I'm not.

So now on nights when my mother presented her tests, I performed listlessly, 20 my head propped on one arm. I pretended to be bored. And I was. I got so bored I started counting the bellows of the foghorns out on the bay while my mother drilled me in other areas. The sound was comforting and reminded me of the cow jumping over the moon. And the next day, I played a game with myself, seeing if my mother would give up on me before eight bellows. After a while I usually counted only one, maybe two bellows at most. At last she was beginning to give up hope.

Two or three months had gone by without any mention of my being a prodigy again. And then one day my mother was watching *The Ed Sullivan Show* on TV. The TV was old and the sound kept shorting out. Every time my mother got halfway up from the sofa to adjust the set, the sound would come back on and Ed would be talking. As soon as she sat down, Ed would go silent again. She got up, the TV broke into loud piano music. She sat down. Silence. Up and down, back and forth, quiet and loud. It was like a stiff embraceless dance between her and the TV set. Finally she stood by the set with her hand on the sound dial.

She seemed entranced by the music, a little frenzied piano piece with this mesmerizing quality, sort of quick passages and then teasing lilting ones before it returned to the quick playful parts.

"*Ni kan,*" my mother said, calling me over with hurried hand gestures, "Look here."

I could see why my mother was fascinated by the music. It was being pounded out by a little Chinese girl, about nine years old, with a Peter Pan haircut. The girl had the sauciness of a Shirley Temple. She was proudly modest like a proper Chinese child. And she also did a fancy sweep of a curtsy, so that the fluffy skirt of her white dress cascaded slowly to the floor like the petals of a large carnation.

In spite of these warning signs, I wasn't worried. Our family had no piano and 25 we couldn't afford to buy one, let alone reams of sheet music and piano lessons. So I could be generous in my comments when my mother bad-mouthed the little girl on TV.

"Play note right, but doesn't sound good! No singing sound," complained my mother.

"What are you picking on her for?" I said carelessly. "She's pretty good. Maybe she's not the best, but she's trying hard." I knew almost immediately I would be sorry I said that.

"Just like you," she said. "Not the best. Because you not trying." She gave a little huff as she let go of the sound dial and sat down on the sofa.

The little Chinese girl sat down also to play an encore of "Anitra's Dance" by Grieg.[1] I remember the song, because later on I had to learn how to play it.

Three days after watching *The Ed Sullivan Show,* my mother told me what my 30 schedule would be for piano lessons and piano practice. She had talked to Mr. Chong, who lived on the first floor of our apartment building. Mr. Chong was a retired piano teacher, and my mother had traded housecleaning services for

---

[1] From Edvard Grieg's (1843–1907) incidental music composed for Henrik Ibsen's play *Peer Gynt.*

weekly lessons and a piano for me to practice on every day, two hours a day, from four until six.

When my mother told me this, I felt as though I had been sent to hell. I whined and then kicked my foot a little when I couldn't stand it anymore.

"Why don't you like me the way I am? I'm *not* a genius! I can't play the piano. And even if I could, I wouldn't go on TV if you paid me a million dollars!" I cried.

My mother slapped me. "Who ask you be genius?" she shouted. "Only ask you be your best. For you sake. You think I want you be genius? Hnnh! What for! Who ask you!"

"So ungrateful," I heard her mutter in Chinese. "If she had as much talent as she has temper, she would be famous now."

Mr. Chong, whom I secretly nicknamed Old Chong, was very strange, always 35 tapping his fingers to the silent music of an invisible orchestra. He looked ancient in my eyes. He had lost most of the hair on top of his head and he wore thick glasses and had eyes that always looked tired and sleepy. But he must have been younger than I thought, since he lived with his mother and was not yet married.

I met Old Lady Chong once and that was enough. She had this peculiar smell like a baby that had done something in its pants. And her fingers felt like a dead person's, like an old peach I once found in the back of the refrigerator; the skin just slid off the meat when I picked it up.

I soon found out why Old Chong had retired from teaching piano. He was deaf. "Like Beethoven!" he shouted to me. "We're both listening only in our head!" And he would start to conduct his frantic silent sonatas.

Our lessons went like this. He would open the book and point to different things, explaining their purpose: "Key! Treble! Bass! No sharps or flats! So this is C major! Listen now and play after me!"

And then he would play the C scale a few times, a simple chord, and then, as if inspired by an old unreachable itch, he would gradually add more notes and running trills and a pounding bass until the music was really something quite grand.

I would play after him, the simple scale, the simple chord, and then I just 40 played some nonsense that sounded like a cat running up and down on top of garbage cans. Old Chong smiled and applauded and then said, "Very good! But now you must learn to keep time!"

So that's how I discovered that Old Chong's eyes were too slow to keep up with the wrong notes I was playing. He went through the motions in half-time. To help me keep rhythm, he stood behind me, pushing down on my right shoulder for every beat. He balanced pennies on top of my wrists so I would keep them still as I slowly played scales and arpeggios. He had me curve my hand around an apple and keep that shape when playing chords. He marched stiffly to show me how to make each finger dance up and down, staccato like an obedient little soldier.

He taught me all these things, and that was how I also learned I could be lazy and get away with mistakes, lots of mistakes. If I hit the wrong notes because I hadn't practiced enough, I never corrected myself. I just kept playing in rhythm. And Old Chong kept conducting his own private reverie.

So maybe I never really gave myself a fair chance. I did pick up the basics pretty quickly, and I might have become a good pianist at that young age. But I was so determined not to try, not to be anybody different that I learned to play only the most ear-splitting preludes, the most discordant hymns.

Over the next year, I practiced like this, dutifully in my own way. And then one day I heard my mother and her friend Lindo Jong both talking in a loud bragging tone of voice so others could hear. It was after church, and I was leaning against the brick wall wearing a dress with stiff white petticoats. Auntie Lindo's daughter, Waverly, who was about my age, was standing farther down the wall about five feet away. We had grown up together and shared all the closeness of two sisters squabbling over crayons and dolls. In other words, for the most part, we hated each other. I thought she was snotty. Waverly Jong had gained a certain amount of fame as "Chinatown's Littlest Chinese Chess Champion."

"She bring home too many trophy," lamented Auntie Lindo that Sunday. "All 45 day she play chess. All day I have no time do nothing but dust off her winnings." She threw a scolding look at Waverly, who pretended not to see her.

"You lucky you don't have this problem," said Auntie Lindo with a sigh to my mother.

And my mother squared her shoulders and bragged: "Our problem worser than yours. If we ask Jing-mei wash dish, she hear nothing but music. It's like you can't stop this natural talent."

And right then I was determined to put a stop to her foolish pride.

A few weeks later, Old Chong and my mother conspired to have me play in a talent show which would be held in the church hall. By then, my parents had saved up enough to buy me a secondhand piano, a black Wurlitzer spinet with a scarred bench. It was the showpiece of our living room.

For the talent show, I was to play a piece called "Pleading Child" from 50 Schumann's *Scenes from Childhood*. It was a simple, moody piece that sounded more difficult than it was. I was supposed to memorize the whole thing, playing the repeat parts twice to make the piece sound longer. But I dawdled over it, playing a few bars and then cheating, looking up to see what notes followed. I never really listened to what I was playing. I daydreamed about being somewhere else, about being someone else.

The part I liked to practice best was the fancy curtsy: right foot out, touch the rose on the carpet with a pointed foot, sweep to the side, left leg bends, look up, and smile.

My parents invited all the couples from the Joy Luck Club to witness my debut. Auntie Lindo and Uncle Tin were there. Waverly and her two older brothers had also come. The first two rows were filled with children both younger and older than I was. The littlest ones got to go first. They recited simple nursery rhymes, squawked out tunes on miniature violins, twirled Hula Hoops, pranced in pink ballet tutus, and when they bowed or curtsied, the audience would sigh in unison, "Awww," and then clap enthusiastically.

When my turn came, I was very confident. I remember my childish excitement. It was as if I knew, without a doubt, that the prodigy side of me really did exist. I had no fear whatsoever, no nervousness. I remember thinking to myself, This is it! This is it! I looked out over the audience, at my mother's blank face, my father's yawn, Auntie Lindo's stiff-lipped smile, Waverly's sulky expression. I had on a white dress, layered with sheets of lace, and a pink bow in my Peter Pan haircut. As I sat down, I envisioned people jumping to their feet and Ed Sullivan rushing up to introduce me to everyone on TV.

And I started to play. It was so beautiful. I was so caught up in how lovely I looked that at first I didn't worry how I would sound. So it was a surprise to me when I hit the first wrong note and I realized something didn't sound quite right. And then I hit another and another followed that. A chill started at the top of my head and began to trickle down. Yet I couldn't stop playing, as though my hands were bewitched. I kept thinking my fingers would adjust themselves back, like a train switching to the right track. I played this strange jumble through two repeats, the sour notes staying with me all the way to the end.

When I stood up, I discovered my legs were shaking. Maybe I had just been 55 nervous and the audience, like Old Chong, had seen me go through the right motions and had not heard anything wrong at all. I swept my right foot out, went down on my knee, looked up and smiled. The room was quiet, except for Old Chong, who was beaming and shouting, "Bravo! Bravo! Well done!" But then I saw my mother's face, her stricken face. The audience clapped weakly, and as I walked back to my chair, with my whole face quivering as I tried not to cry, I heard a little boy whisper loudly to his mother, "That was awful," and the mother whispered, "Well, she certainly tried."

And now I realized how many people were in the audience, the whole world, it seemed. I was aware of eyes burning into my back. I felt the shame of my mother and father as they sat stiffly throughout the rest of the show.

We could have escaped during intermission. Pride and some strange sense of honor must have anchored my parents to their chairs. And so we watched it all: The eighteen-year-old boy with a fake moustache who did a magic show and juggled flaming hoops while riding a unicycle. The breasted girl with white makeup who sang an aria from *Madama Butterfly* and got an honorable mention. And the eleven-year-old boy who won first prize playing a tricky violin song that sounded like a busy bee.

After the show, the Hsus, the Jongs, and the St. Clairs from the Joy Luck Club came up to my mother and father.

"Lots of talented kids," Auntie Lindo said vaguely, smiling broadly.

"That was somethin' else," my father said, and I wondered if he was referring 60 to me in a humorous way, or whether he even remembered what I had done.

Waverly looked at me and shrugged her shoulders. "You aren't a genius like me," she said matter-of-factly. And if I hadn't felt so bad, I would have pulled her braids and punched her stomach.

But my mother's expression was what devastated me: a quiet, blank look that said she had lost everything. I felt the same way, and it seemed as if everybody were now coming up, like gawkers at the scene of an accident, to see what parts were actually missing. When we got on the bus to go home, my father was humming the busy-bee tune and my mother was silent. I kept thinking she wanted to wait until we got home before shouting at me. But when my father unlocked the door to our apartment, my mother walked in and then went to the back, into the bedroom. No accusations. No blame. And in a way, I felt disappointed. I had been waiting for her to start shouting, so I could shout back and cry and blame her for all my misery.

I assumed my talent-show fiasco meant I never had to play the piano again. But two days later, after school, my mother came out of the kitchen and saw me watching TV.

"Four clock," she reminded me as if it were any other day. I was stunned, as though she were asking me to go through the talent-show torture again. I wedged myself more tightly in front of the TV.

"Turn off TV," she called from the kitchen five minutes later.   65

I didn't budge. And then I decided. I didn't have to do what my mother said anymore. I wasn't her slave. This wasn't China. I had listened to her before, and look what happened. She was the stupid one.

She came out of the kitchen and stood in the arched entryway of the living room. "Four clock," she said once again, louder.

"I'm not going to play anymore," I said nonchalantly. "Why should I? I'm not a genius."

She stood in front of the TV. I saw her chest was heaving up and down in an angry way.

"No!" I said, and I now felt stronger, as if my true self had finally emerged. So   70
this was what had been inside me all along.

"No! I won't!" I screamed.

She yanked me by the arm, pulled me off the floor, snapped off the TV. She was frighteningly strong, half pulling, half carrying me toward the piano as I kicked the throw rugs under my feet. She lifted me up and onto the hard bench. I was sobbing by now, looking at her bitterly. Her chest was heaving even more and her mouth was open, smiling crazily as if she were pleased that I was crying.

"You want me to be someone that I'm not!" I sobbed. "I'll never be the kind of daughter you want me to be!"

"Only two kinds of daughters," she shouted in Chinese. "Those who are obedient and those who follow their own mind! Only one kind of daughter can live in this house. Obedient daughter!"

"Then I wish I weren't your daughter. I wish you weren't my mother," I   75
shouted. As I said these things I got scared. It felt like worms and toads and slimy things crawling out of my chest, but it also felt good, as if this awful side of me had surfaced, at last.

"Too late change this," said my mother shrilly.

And I could sense her anger rising to its breaking point. I wanted to see it spill over. And that's when I remembered the babies she had lost in China, the ones we never talked about. "Then I wish I'd never been born!" I shouted. "I wish I were dead! Like them."

It was as if I had said the magic words. Alakazam! — and her face went blank, her mouth closed, her arms went slack, and she backed out of the room, stunned, as if she were blowing away like a small brown leaf, thin, brittle, lifeless.

It was not the only disappointment my mother felt in me. In the years that followed, I failed her so many times, each time asserting my own will, my right to fall short of expectations. I didn't get straight As. I didn't become class president. I didn't get into Stanford. I dropped out of college.

For unlike my mother, I did not believe I could be anything I wanted to be. I 80 could only be me.

And for all those years, we never talked about the disaster at the recital or my terrible accusations afterward at the piano bench. All that remained unchecked, like a betrayal that was now unspeakable. So I never found a way to ask her why she had hoped for something so large that failure was inevitable.

And even worse, I never asked her about what frightened me the most: Why had she given up hope?

For after our struggle at the piano, she never mentioned my playing again. The lessons stopped. The lid to the piano was closed, shutting out the dust, my misery, and her dreams.

So she surprised me. A few years ago, she offered to give me the piano, for my thirtieth birthday. I had not played in all those years. I saw the offer as a sign of forgiveness, a tremendous burden removed.

"Are you sure?" I asked shyly. "I mean, won't you and Dad miss it?" 85

"No, this your piano," she said firmly. "Always your piano. You only one can play."

"Well, I probably can't play anymore," I said. "It's been years."

"You pick up fast," said my mother, as if she knew this was certain. "You have natural talent. You could been genius if you want to."

"No I couldn't."

"You just not trying," said my mother. And she was neither angry nor sad. She 90 said it as if to announce a fact that could never be disproved. "Take it," she said.

But I didn't at first. It was enough that she had offered it to me. And after that, every time I saw it in my parents' living room, standing in front of the bay windows, it made me feel proud, as if it were a shiny trophy that I had won back.

Last week I sent a tuner over to my parents' apartment and had the piano reconditioned, for purely sentimental reasons. My mother had died a few months before and I had been getting things in order for my father, a little bit at a time. I put the jewelry in special silk pouches. The sweaters she had knitted in yellow, pink, bright orange — all the colors I hated — I put those in moth-proof boxes. I found some old Chinese silk dresses, the kind with little slits up the sides. I rubbed the old silk against my skin, then wrapped them in tissue and decided to take them home with me.

After I had the piano tuned, I opened the lid and touched the keys. It sounded even richer than I remembered. Really, it was a very good piano. Inside the bench were the same exercise notes with handwritten scales, the same secondhand music books with their covers held together with yellow tape.

I opened up the Schumann book to the dark little piece I had played at the recital. It was on the left-hand page, "Pleading Child." It looked more difficult than I remembered. I played a few bars, surprised at how easily the notes came back to me.

And for the first time, or so it seemed, I noticed the piece on the right-hand side. It was called "Perfectly Contented." I tried to play this one as well. It had a lighter melody but the same flowing rhythm and turned out to be quite easy. "Pleading Child" was shorter but slower; "Perfectly Contented" was longer, but faster. And after I played them both a few times, I realized they were two halves of the same song. 95

For Analysis

1. Do you think the conflict between the mother and daughter is unique to this family? To Asian American families? To any group of families? Why or why not?

2. What does the mother want for her daughter?

3. What does the daughter want for herself?

4. What is the significance of the story's last paragraph?

On Style

1. What effect does the mother's broken English and occasional Chinese expressions create in the dialogue of the story?

2. The mother proclaims that there are two kinds of daughters; the daughter, in the final paragraph, discovers the truth of that proclamation. Discuss the relationship between the story's title and its structure.

Making Connections

1. Does this story reflect some aspects of your own interaction with your parents? Explain.

2. Several of the stories in "Conformity and Rebellion" are driven by tensions between parents and children. Compare "Two Kinds" with stories from elsewhere in this anthology: Faulkner's "A Rose for Emily" (p. 666), Achebe's "Marriage Is a Private Affair" (p. 699), Mukherjee's "Orbiting" (p. 704), and Walker's "Everyday Use" (p. 717). Each of these stories deals with a different culture. What similarities do you find among them? What substantive differences?

Writing Topics

1. Describe the similarities or the differences between the mother's attempt to influence her daughter's life and your own family's attempt to influence yours.

2. Compare and contrast the representation of family pressure revealed in "Two Kinds" and in Mukherjee's "Orbiting."

3. Defend or attack this proposition: Children should be allowed to choose their own paths.

William Wordsworth (1770–1850)

The World Is Too Much with Us 1807

The world is too much with us; late and soon,
Getting and spending, we lay waste our powers;
Little we see in Nature that is ours;
We have given our hearts away, a sordid boon!
This Sea that bares her bosom to the moon,
The winds that will be howling at all hours,
And are up-gathered now like sleeping flowers,
For this, for everything, we are out of tune;
It moves us not. — Great God! I'd rather be
A Pagan suckled in a creed outworn;   10
So might I, standing on this pleasant lea,
Have glimpses that would make me less forlorn;
Have sight of Proteus rising from the sea;
Or hear old Triton blow his wreathèd horn.[1]

For Analysis

1. What does "world" mean in line 1?

2. What does Wordsworth complain of in the first four lines?

3. In lines 4–8 Wordsworth tells us what we have lost; in the concluding lines he suggests a remedy. What is that remedy? What do Proteus and Triton symbolize?

Writing Topic

In what ways does Wordsworth's use of images both define what we have lost and suggest a remedy for this loss?

---

[1] Proteus and Triton are both figures from Greek mythology. Proteus had the power to assume different forms; Triton was often represented blowing on a conch shell.

Alfred, Lord Tennyson   (1809–1892)

Ulysses[1] 1833

It little profits that an idle king,
By this still hearth, among these barren crags,
Matched with an agéd wife, I mete and dole
Unequal laws unto a savage race,
That hoard, and sleep, and feed, and know not me.

   I cannot rest from travel; I will drink
Life to the lees. All times I have enjoyed
Greatly, have suffered greatly, both with those
That loved me, and alone; on shore, and when
Through scudding drifts the rainy Hyades[2]   10
Vexed the dim sea. I am become a name;
For always roaming with a hungry heart
Much have I seen and known — cities of men
And manners, climates, councils, governments,
Myself not least, but honored of them all —
And drunk delight of battle with my peers,
Far on the ringing plains of windy Troy.
I am a part of all that I have met;
Yet all experience is an arch wherethrough
Gleams that untraveled world whose margin fades   20
Forever and forever when I move.
How dull it is to pause, to make an end,
To rust unburnished, not to shine in use!
As though to breathe were life. Life piled on life
Were all too little, and of one to me
Little remains; but every hour is saved
From that eternal silence, something more,
A bringer of new things; and vile it were
For some three suns to store and hoard myself,
And this gray spirit yearning in desire   30
To follow knowledge like a sinking star,
Beyond the utmost bound of human thought.

---

[1] Ulysses, according to Greek legend, was the king of Ithaca and a hero of the Trojan War. Tennyson represents him as eager to resume the life of travel and adventure.
[2] A group of stars in the constellation Taurus. According to Greek mythology, the rising of these stars with the sun foretold rain.

This is my son, mine own Telemachus,
To whom I leave the scepter and the isle —
Well-loved of me, discerning to fulfill
This labor, by slow prudence to make mild
A rugged people, and through soft degrees
Subdue them to the useful and the good.
Most blameless is he, centered in the sphere
Of common duties, decent not to fail   40
In offices of tenderness, and pay
Meet° adoration to my household gods,   proper
When I am gone. He works his work, I mine.

    There lies the port; the vessel puffs her sail;
There gloom the dark, broad seas. My mariners,
Souls that have toiled, and wrought, and thought with me —
That ever with a frolic welcome took
The thunder and the sunshine, and opposed
Free hearts, free foreheads — you and I are old;
Old age hath yet his honor and his toil.   50
Death closes all; but something ere the end,
Some work of noble note, may yet be done,
Not unbecoming men that strove with Gods.
The lights begin to twinkle from the rocks;
The long day wanes; the slow moon climbs; the deep
Moans round with many voices. Come, my friends,
'Tis not too late to seek a newer world.
Push off, and sitting well in order smite
The sounding furrows; for my purpose holds
To sail beyond the sunset, and the baths   60
Of all the western stars, until I die.
It may be that the gulfs will wash us down;
It may be we shall touch the Happy Isles,[3]
And see the great Achilles, whom we knew.
Though much is taken, much abides; and though
We are not now that strength which in old days
Moved earth and heaven, that which we are, we are —
One equal temper of heroic hearts,
Made weak by time and fate, but strong in will
To strive, to seek, to find, and not to yield.   70

---

[3] The Islands of the Blessed (also Elysium), thought to be in the far western oceans, where those favored by the gods, such as Achilles, enjoyed life after death.

For Analysis

1. Is Ulysses' desire to abdicate his duties as king irresponsible?

2. Contrast Ulysses with his son Telemachus as the latter is described in lines 33–43. Is Telemachus admirable?

3. At the conclusion of the poem, Ulysses is determined not to yield. Yield to what?

Emily Dickinson   (1830–1886)

Much Madness is divinest Sense — 1862

Much Madness is divinest Sense —
To a discerning Eye —
Much Sense — the starkest Madness —
'Tis the Majority
In this, as All, prevail —
Assent — and you are sane —
Demur — you're straightway dangerous —
And handled with a Chain —

She rose to His Requirement ca. 1863

She rose to His Requirement — dropt
The Playthings of Her Life
To take the honorable Work
Of Woman, and of Wife —

If ought° She missed in Her new Day,   anything
Of Amplitude, or Awe —
Or first Prospective — Or the Gold
In using, wear away,

It lay unmentioned — as the Sea
Develope Pearl, and Weed,   10
But only to Himself — be known
The Fathoms they abide —

For Analysis

1. What are the "Playthings" referred to in line 2?

2. Why does the poet refer to both "Woman" and "Wife" in line 4, since a wife is also a woman?

3. Look up the words *amplitude, awe,* and *prospective* in your dictionary, and consider how these words help you to understand the woman's losses.

4. What does "It" in the third stanza refer to?

5. Why is the sea image at the end of the poem appropriate? What does the contrast between "Pearl" and "Weed" suggest?

6. The last word of the poem, "abide," has several meanings. Which of them are relevant to the meaning of the poem?

Making Connections

Compare and contrast the attitudes toward marriage in this poem with those in Achebe's "Marriage Is a Private Affair" (p. 699) and Sexton's "The Farmer's Wife" (p. 1122).

Writing Topic

Write an essay describing a woman you know who gave up an important part of herself to be a wife.

William Butler Yeats   (1865–1939)

Easter 1916 [1]   1916

I have met them at close of day
Coming with vivid faces
From counter or desk among grey
Eighteenth-century houses.
I have passed with a nod of the head
Or polite meaningless words,
Or have lingered awhile and said
Polite meaningless words,
And thought before I had done
Of a mocking tale or a gibe   10
To please a companion
Around the fire at the club,

[1] On Easter Sunday of 1916, a group of Irish nationalists seized key points in Ireland, including the Dublin Post Office, from which they proclaimed an independent Irish Republic. At first, most Irishmen were indifferent to the nationalists' futile and heroic gesture, but as the rebellion was crushed and the leaders executed, they became heroes in their countrymen's eyes. Some of those leaders are alluded to in the second stanza and are named in lines 75 and 76.

Being certain that they and I
But lived where motley is worn:
All changed, changed utterly:
A terrible beauty is born.

That woman's days were spent
In ignorant good-will,
Her nights in argument
Until her voice grew shrill.   20
What voice more sweet than hers
When, young and beautiful,
She rode to harriers?²
This man had kept a school
And rode our wingéd horse;³
This other his helper and friend
Was coming into his force;
He might have won fame in the end,
So sensitive his nature seemed,
So daring and sweet his thought.   30
This other man I had dreamed
A drunken, vainglorious lout.
He had done most bitter wrong
To some who are near my heart,
Yet I number him in the song;
He, too, has resigned his part
In the casual comedy;
He, too, has been changed in his turn,
Transformed utterly:
A terrible beauty is born.   40

Hearts with one purpose alone
Through summer and winter seem
Enchanted to a stone
To trouble the living stream.
The horse that comes from the road,
The rider, the birds that range
From cloud to tumbling cloud,
Minute by minute they change;
A shadow of cloud on the stream

---

² In the aristocratic sport of hare hunting, a "pack of harriers" refers to the hounds as well as the persons following the chase.
³ In Greek mythology, a winged horse is associated with poetic inspiration.

Changes minute by minute; 50
A horse-hoof slides on the brim,
And a horse plashes within it;
The long-legged moor-hens dive,
And hens to moor-cocks call;
Minute by minute they live:
The stone's in the midst of all.

Too long a sacrifice
Can make a stone of the heart.
O when may it suffice?
That is Heaven's part, our part 60
To murmur name upon name,
As a mother names her child
When sleep at last has come
On limbs that had run wild.
What is it but nightfall?
No, no, not night but death;
Was it needless death after all?
For England may keep faith
For all that is done and said.
We know their dream; enough 70
To know they dreamed and are dead;
And what if excess of love
Bewildered them till they died?
I write it out in a verse —
MacDonagh and MacBride
And Connolly and Pearse
Now and in time to be,
Wherever green is worn,
Are changed, changed utterly:
A terrible beauty is born. 80

For Analysis

1. What is "changed utterly," and in what sense can beauty be "terrible" (ll. 15–16)?

2. What does "they" in line 55 refer to? What does the "stone" in lines 43 and 56 symbolize? What is Yeats contrasting?

3. How does the poet answer the question he asks in line 67?

Writing Topic

In the first stanza, the attitude of the poet toward the people he is describing is indifferent, even contemptuous. How is that attitude modified in the rest of the poem?

The Second Coming[1] 1921

Turning and turning in the widening gyre°   spiral
The falcon cannot hear the falconer;
Things fall apart; the center cannot hold;
Mere anarchy is loosed upon the world,
The blood-dimmed tide is loosed, and everywhere
The ceremony of innocence is drowned;
The best lack all conviction, while the worst
Are full of passionate intensity.

Surely some revelation is at hand;
Surely the Second Coming is at hand;   10
The Second Coming! Hardly are those words out
When a vast image out of *Spiritus Mundi*[2]
Troubles my sight: somewhere in sands of the desert
A shape with lion body and the head of a man,
A gaze blank and pitiless as the sun,
Is moving its slow thighs, while all about it
Reel shadows of the indignant desert birds.
The darkness drops again; but now I know
That twenty centuries of stony sleep
Were vexed to nightmare by a rocking cradle,   20
And what rough beast, its hour come round at last,
Slouches towards Bethlehem to be born?

The Great Day 1939

Hurrah for revolution and more cannon-shot!
A beggar upon horseback lashes a beggar on foot.
Hurrah for revolution and cannon come again!
The beggars have changed places, but the lash goes on.

The Second Coming
   [1] The New Testament (Matthew 24:29–44) describes the Second Coming of Christ as following a period of tribulation to judge the living and the dead and to inaugurate the millennium. Yeats, who believed in historical cycles, foresees the end of civil warfare in his native Ireland and the beginning of a new millennium.
   [2] The Soul or Spirit of the Universe, which Yeats believed constituted a fund of racial images and memories.

Edwin Arlington Robinson   (1869–1935)

Miniver Cheevy   1910

Miniver Cheevy, child of scorn,
    Grew lean while he assailed the seasons;
He wept that he was ever born,
    And he had reasons.

Miniver loved the days of old
    When swords were bright and steeds were prancing;
The vision of a warrior bold
    Would set him dancing.

Miniver sighed for what was not,
    And dreamed, and rested from his labors;   10
He dreamed of Thebes and Camelot,
    And Priam's neighbors.[1]

Miniver mourned the ripe renown
    That made so many a name so fragrant,
He mourned Romance, now on the town,
    And Art, a vagrant.

Miniver loved the Medici,[2]
    Albeit he had never seen one;
He would have sinned incessantly
    Could he have been one.   20

Miniver cursed the commonplace
    And eyed a khaki suit with loathing;
He missed the medieval grace
    Of iron clothing.

Miniver scorned the gold he sought,
    But sore annoyed was he without it;
Miniver thought, and thought, and thought,
    And thought about it.

---

[1] Thebes was an ancient Greek city, famous in history and legend; Camelot was the site of the legendary King Arthur's court; Priam was king of Troy during the Trojan War.
[2] A family of bankers and statesmen, notorious for their cruelty, who ruled Florence for nearly two centuries during the Italian Renaissance.

Miniver Cheevy, born too late,
    Scratched his head and kept on thinking;   30
Miniver coughed, and called it fate,
    And kept on drinking.

Robert Frost   (1874–1963)

A Semi-Revolution   1942

I advocate a semi-revolution.
The trouble with a total revolution
(Ask any reputable Rosicrucian)[1]
Is that it brings the same class up on top.
Executives of skillful execution
Will therefore plan to go half-way and stop.
Yes, revolutions are the only salves,
But they're one thing that should be done by halves.

Wallace Stevens   (1879–1955)

Sunday Morning   1923

I

Complacencies of the peignoir, and late
Coffee and oranges in a sunny chair,
And the green freedom of a cockatoo
Upon a rug mingle to dissipate
The holy hush of ancient sacrifice.
She dreams a little, and she feels the dark
Encroachment of that old catastrophe,
As a calm darkens among water-lights.
The pungent oranges and bright, green wings

A Semi-Revolution
   [1] Rosicrucians are members of a society professing mystic religious principles and a belief in occult knowledge and powers. William Butler Yeats was a member of this group (see his poem "The Great Day" on p. 440).

Seem things in some procession of the dead,   10
Winding across wide water, without sound.
The day is like wide water, without sound,
Stilled for the passing of her dreaming feet
Over the seas, to silent Palestine,
Dominion of the blood and sepulchre.

II

Why should she give her bounty to the dead?
What is divinity if it can come
Only in silent shadows and in dreams?
Shall she not find in comforts of the sun,
In pungent fruit and bright, green wings, or else   20
In any balm or beauty of the earth,
Things to be cherished like the thought of heaven?
Divinity must live within herself:
Passions of rain, or moods in falling snow;
Grievings in loneliness, or unsubdued
Elations when the forest blooms; gusty
Emotions on wet roads on autumn nights;
All pleasures and all pains, remembering
The bough of summer and the winter branch.
These are the measures destined for her soul.   30

III

Jove in the clouds had his inhuman birth.[1]
No mother suckled him, no sweet land gave
Large-mannered motions to his mythy mind
He moved among us, as a muttering king,
Magnificent, would move among his hinds,°   farm servants
Until our blood, commingling, virginal,
With heaven, brought such requital to desire
The very hinds discerned it, in a star.
Shall our blood fail? Or shall it come to be
The blood of paradise? And shall the earth   40
Seem all of paradise that we shall know?
The sky will be much friendlier then than now,
A part of labor and a part of pain,
And next in glory to enduring love,
Not this dividing and indifferent blue.

---

[1] Jove is Jupiter, the principal god of the Romans, who, unlike Jesus, had an "inhuman birth."

IV

She says, "I am content when wakened birds,
Before they fly, test the reality
Of misty fields, by their sweet questionings;
But when the birds are gone, and their warm fields
Return no more, where, then, is paradise?"   50
There is not any haunt of prophecy,
Nor any old chimera[2] of the grave,
Neither the golden underground, nor isle
Melodious, where spirits gat them home,
Nor visionary south, nor cloudy palm
Remote on heaven's hill, that has endured
As April's green endures; or will endure
Like her remembrance of awakened birds,
Or her desire for June and evening, tipped
By the consummation of the swallow's wings.   60

V

She says, "But in contentment I still feel
The need of some imperishable bliss."
Death is the mother of beauty; hence from her,
Alone, shall come fulfilment to our dreams
And our desires. Although she strews the leaves
Of sure obliteration on our paths,
The path sick sorrow took, the many paths
Where triumph rang its brassy phrase, or love
Whispered a little out of tenderness,
She makes the willow shiver in the sun   70
For maidens who were wont to sit and gaze
Upon the grass, relinquished to their feet.
She causes boys to pile new plums and pears
On disregarded plate. The maidens taste
And stray impassioned in the littering leaves.

VI

Is there no change of death in paradise?
Does ripe fruit never fall? Or do the boughs
Hang always heavy in that perfect sky,
Unchanging, yet so like our perishing earth,
With rivers like our own that seek for seas   80

---

[2] A monster with a lion's head, a goat's body, and a serpent's tail. Here an emblem for the belief in other worlds described in the following lines.

They never find, the same receding shores
That never touch with inarticulate pang?
Why set the pear upon those river-banks
Or spice the shores with odors of the plum?
Alas, that they should wear our colors there,
The silken weavings of our afternoons,
And pick the strings of our insipid lutes!
Death is the mother of beauty, mystical,
Within whose burning bosom we devise
Our earthly mothers waiting, sleeplessly.   90

VII

Supple and turbulent, a ring of men
Shall chant in orgy on a summer morn
Their boisterous devotion to the sun,
Not as a god, but as a god might be,
Naked among them, like a savage source.
Their chant shall be a chant of paradise,
Out of their blood, returning to the sky;
And in their chant shall enter, voice by voice,
The windy lake wherein their lord delights,
The trees, like serafin,[3] and echoing hills,   100
That choir among themselves long afterward.
They shall know well the heavenly fellowship
Of men that perish and of summer morn.
And whence they came and whither they shall go
The dew upon their feet shall manifest.

VIII

She hears, upon that water without sound,
A voice that cries, "The tomb in Palestine
Is not the porch of spirits lingering.
It is the grave of Jesus, where he lay."
We live in an old chaos of the sun,   110
Or old dependency of day and night,
Or island solitude, unsponsored, free,
Of that wide water, inescapable.
Deer walk upon our mountains, and the quail
Whistle about us their spontaneous cries;
Sweet berries ripen in the wilderness;
And, in the isolation of the sky,

---

[3] The plural form of *seraph,* an angel.

At evening, casual flocks of pigeons make
Ambiguous undulations as they sink,
Downward to darkness, on extended wings.   120

For Analysis

1. In the opening stanza, the woman's enjoyment of a late Sunday morning breakfast in a relaxed and sensuous atmosphere is troubled by thoughts of what Sunday morning *should* mean to her. What are the thoughts that disturb her complacency?

2. What does the speaker mean when he says, "Death is the mother of beauty" (ll. 63 and 88)?

3. In stanza VI, what is the speaker's attitude toward the conventional conception of paradise?

4. Stanza VII presents the speaker's vision of an alternative religion. How does it differ from the paradise of stanza VI?

5. In what ways does the cry of the voice in the final stanza (ll. 107–109) state the woman's dilemma? How do the lines about the pigeons at the end of the poem sum up the speaker's belief?

Writing Topic

This poem is, in a sense, a commentary by the speaker on the woman's desire for truth and certainty more enduring than the physical world can provide. Is the speaker sympathetic to her quest?

Claude McKay   (1890–1948)

If We Must Die   1922

If we must die, let it not be like hogs
Hunted and penned in an inglorious spot,
While round us bark the mad and hungry dogs,
Making their mock at our accurséd lot.
If we must die, O let us nobly die,
So that our precious blood may not be shed
In vain; then even the monsters we defy
Shall be constrained to honor us though dead!
O kinsmen! we must meet the common foe!
Though far outnumbered let us show us brave,   10
And for their thousand blows deal one deathblow!
What though before us lies the open grave?
Like men we'll face the murderous, cowardly pack,
Pressed to the wall, dying, but fighting back!

Bertolt Brecht   (1898–1956)

War Has Been Given
a Bad Name[1]   1957

I am told that the best people have begun saying
How, from a moral point of view, the Second World War
Fell below the standard of the First. The Wehrmacht[2]
Allegedly deplores the methods by which the SS[3] effected
The extermination of certain peoples. The Ruhr industrialists[4]
Are said to regret the bloody manhunts
Which filled their mines and factories with slave workers. The intellectuals
So I heard, condemn industry's demand for slave workers
Likewise their unfair treatment. Even the bishops
Dissociate themselves from this way of waging war; in short the feeling   10
Prevails in every quarter that the Nazis did the Fatherland
A lamentably bad turn, and that war
While in itself natural and necessary, has, thanks to the
Unduly uninhibited and positively inhuman
Way in which it was conducted on this occasion, been
Discredited for some time to come.

For Analysis

1. Characterize the **tone** of this poem, including the title. How does the **diction** contribute to this tone?

2. What is Brecht's attitude toward the "Wehrmacht" (l. 3), the "Ruhr industrialists" (l. 5), the "intellectuals" (l. 7), and the "bishops" (l. 9)? What do these groups have in common?

3. What is the effect of the phrases "I am told" (l. 1) and "So I heard" (l. 8)?

Writing Topic

Compare and contrast the handling of the antiwar **theme** in this poem with Wilfred Owen's "Dulce et Decorum Est" (p. 1406).

---

[1] Translated by John Willett.
[2] The German armed forces.
[3] Abbreviated form of the *Schutzstaffel*, the elite guard of the Nazi army.
[4] One of Germany's most important industrial regions.

Oscar Williams   (1900–1964)

A Total Revolution   1952

(An Answer for Robert Frost)

I advocate a total revolution.
The trouble with a semi-revolution,
It's likely to be slow as evolution.
Who wants to spend the ages in collusion
With Compromise, Complacence and Confusion?
As for the same class coming up on top
That's wholecloth from the propaganda shop;
The old saw says there's loads of room on top,
That's where the poor should really plan to stop.
And speaking of those people called the "haves,"   10
Who own the whole cow and must have the calves
(And plant the wounds so they can sell the salves)
They won't be stopped by doing things by halves.

Langston Hughes   (1902–1967)

Harlem   1951

What happens to a dream deferred?

　　Does it dry up
　　like a raisin in the sun?
　　Or fester like a sore —
　　And then run?
　　Does it stink like rotten meat?
　　Or crust and sugar over —
　　like a syrupy sweet?

　　Maybe it just sags
　　like a heavy load.   10

　　Or does it explode?

W. H. Auden   (1907–1973)

The Unknown Citizen   1940

(To JS/07/M/378
This Marble Monument
Is Erected by the State)

He was found by the Bureau of Statistics to be
One against whom there was no official complaint,
And all the reports on his conduct agree
That, in the modern sense of an old-fashioned word, he was a saint,
For in everything he did he served the Greater Community.
Except for the War till the day he retired
He worked in a factory and never got fired,
But satisfied his employers, Fudge Motors Inc.
Yet he wasn't a scab or odd in his views,
For his Union reports that he paid his dues,   10
(Our report on his Union shows it was sound)
And our Social Psychology workers found
That he was popular with his mates and liked a drink.
The Press are convinced that he bought a paper every day
And that his reactions to advertisements were normal in every way.
Policies taken out in his name prove that he was fully insured,
And his Health-card shows he was once in hospital but left it cured.
Both Producers Research and High-Grade Living declare
He was fully sensible to the advantages of the Installment Plan
And had everything necessary to the Modern Man,   20
A phonograph, radio, a car and a frigidaire.
Our researchers into Public Opinion are content
That he held the proper opinions for the time of year;
When there was peace, he was for peace; when there was war, he went.
He was married and added five children to the population,
Which our Eugenist says was the right number for a parent of his generation,
And our teachers report that he never interfered with their education.
Was he free? Was he happy? The question is absurd:
Had anything been wrong, we should certainly have heard.

Helen Sorrells (b. 1908)

From a Correct Address in a Suburb of a Major City 1971

She wears her middle age like a cowled
gown, sleeved in it, folded high
at the breast,

charming, proper at cocktails
but the inner one raging
and how to hide her,

how to keep her leashed, contain
the heat of her, the soaring cry
never yet loosed,

demanding a chance before the years devour her,   10
before the marrow of her fine long legs
congeals and she

settles forever for this street, this house,
her face set to the world
sweet, sweet

above the shocked, astonished
hunger.

Muriel Rukeyser (1913–1980)

Myth 1973

Long afterward, Oedipus, old and blinded, walked the
roads.[1]   He smelled a familiar smell.   It was
the Sphinx.   Oedipus said, "I want to ask one question.

Myth
[1] Oedipus became King of Thebes when he solved the riddle of the Sphinx quoted in the poem.
He blinded himself when he discovered that he had killed his father and married his own mother.

Why didn't I recognize my mother?"   "You gave the
wrong answer," said the Sphinx.   "But that was what
made everything possible," said Oedipus.   "No," she said.
"When I asked, What walks on four legs in the morning,
two at noon, and three in the evening, you answered,
Man.   You didn't say anything about woman."
"When you say Man," said Oedipus, "you include women   10
too. Everyone knows that."   She said, "That's what
you think."

Dudley Randall   (b. 1914)

Ballad of Birmingham 1969

*(On the Bombing of a Church in
Birmingham, Alabama, 1963)*[1]

"Mother dear, may I go downtown
Instead of out to play,
And march the streets of Birmingham
In a Freedom March today?"

"No, baby, no, you may not go,
For the dogs are fierce and wild,
And clubs and hoses, guns and jails
Aren't good for a little child."

"But, mother, I won't be alone.
Other children will go with me,
And march the streets of Birmingham   10
To make our country free."

"No, baby, no, you may not go,
For I fear those guns will fire.
But you may go to church instead
And sing in the children's choir."

Ballad of Birmingham
   [1] This poem commemorates the murder of four young African American girls when a bomb was
thrown into the Sixteenth Street Baptist Church in 1963, one of the early and most traumatic events
in the modern civil rights movement.

She has combed and brushed her night-dark hair,
And bathed rose petal sweet.
And drawn white gloves on her small brown hands,
And white shoes on her feet.   20

The mother smiled to know her child
Was in the sacred place,
But that smile was the last smile
To come upon her face.

For when she heard the explosion,
Her eyes grew wet and wild.
She raced through the streets of Birmingham
Calling for her child.

She clawed through bits of glass and brick,
Then lifted out a shoe.   30
"Oh, here's the shoe my baby wore,
But, baby, where are you?"

Richard Wilbur   (b. 1921)

Museum Piece   1948

The good grey guardians of art
Patrol the halls on spongy shoes,
Impartially protective, though
Perhaps suspicious of Toulouse.[1]

Here dozes one against the wall,
Disposed upon a funeral chair.
A Degas[2] dancer pirouettes
Upon the parting of his hair.

See how she spins! The grace is there,
But strain as well is plain to see.   10

Museum Piece
  [1] Henri de Toulouse-Lautrec (1864–1901), a French artist, celebrated for his paintings of the dancers, actresses, and prostitutes of Parisian nightlife.
  [2] Edgar Degas (1834–1917), a French impressionist who often painted ballet dancers.

Degas loved the two together:
Beauty joined to energy.

Edgar Degas purchased once
A fine El Greco,[3] which he kept
Against the wall beside his bed
To hang his pants on while he slept.

For Analysis

1. Who are the guardians mentioned in the first stanza? Why are they described as "grey"?

2. Explain the **image** of the second stanza.

3. How does the anecdote of the final stanza embody the **theme** of the poem?

Writing Topic

Write an essay in which you compare and contrast this poem with W. H. Auden's "Musée des Beaux Arts" (p. 1397) as attempts to define the relationship between art and life.

Denise Levertov   (1923–1997)

Protesters   1992

Living on the rim
of the raging cauldron, disasters

witnessed but
not suffered in the flesh.

The choice: to speak
or not to speak.
We spoke.

Those of whom we spoke
had not that choice.

Museum Piece
   [3] El Greco is the sobriquet of Doménikos Theotokópoulos (1541–1614), a Greek-born Spanish painter.

At every epicenter, beneath
roar and tumult,   10

enforced:
their silence.

Writing Topic

Write an essay about a decision you made to speak out even though you were not
personally involved in (or threatened by) the event or issue you were protesting.

Philip Levine   (b. 1928)

A Theory of Prosody   1988

When Nellie, my old pussy
cat, was still in her prime,
she would sit behind me
as I wrote, and when the line
got too long she'd reach
one sudden black foreleg down
and paw at the moving hand,
the offensive one. The first
time she drew blood I learned
it was poetic to end   10
a line anywhere to keep her
quiet. After all, many mornings she'd gotten to the chair
long before I was even up.
Those nights I couldn't sleep
she'd come and sit in my lap
to calm me. So I figured
I owed her the short cat line.
She's dead now almost nine years,
and before that there was one   20
during which she faked attention
and I faked obedience.
Isn't that what it's about —
pretending there's an alert cat
who leaves nothing to chance.

Jenny Joseph   (b. 1932)

Warning   1992

When I am an old woman I shall wear purple
With a red hat which doesn't go, and doesn't suit me.
And I shall spend my pension on brandy and summer gloves
And satin sandals, and say we've no money for butter.
I shall sit down on the pavement when I'm tired
And gobble up samples in shops and press alarm bells
And run my stick along the public railings
And make up for the sobriety of my youth.
I shall go out in my slippers in the rain
And pick the flowers in other people's gardens   10
And learn to spit.

You can wear terrible shirts and grow more fat
And eat three pounds of sausages at a go
Or only bread and pickle for a week
And hoard pens and pencils and beermats and things in boxes.

But now we must have clothes that keep us dry
And pay our rent and not swear in the street
And set a good example for the children.
We must have friends to dinner and read the papers.

But maybe I ought to practice a little now?   20
So people who know me are not too shocked and surprised
When suddenly I am old, and start to wear purple.

Marge Piercy   (b. 1936)

The market economy   1973

Suppose some peddler offered
you can have a color TV
but your baby will be
born with a crooked spine;

you can have polyvinyl cups
and wash and wear
suits but it will cost
you your left lung
rotted with cancer; suppose
somebody offered you   10
a frozen precooked dinner
every night for ten years
but at the end
your colon dies
and then you do,
slowly and with much pain.
You get a house in the suburbs
but you work in a new plastics
factory and die at fifty-one
when your kidneys turn off.   20
But where else will you
work? where else can
you rent but Smog City?
The only houses for sale
are under the yellow sky.
You've been out of work for
a year and they're hiring
at the plastics factory.
Don't read the fine
print, there isn't any.   30

For Analysis

1. Characterize the **tone** of this poem.

2. Would this still be a poem if it were printed as a paragraph? Compare this poem with Carolyn Forché's "The Colonel" (p. 466), which is written as a paragraph. Which do you find more "poetic"? Explain.

3. What is meant by the last two lines of the poem?

Writing Topic

One theory of literature says that fiction allows us to vicariously experience moral dilemmas and test our own reactions. Discuss this poem and Ursula K. Le Guin's story "The Ones Who Walk Away from Omelas" (p. 393) from this perspective. How would you answer the poet's questions? Would you walk away from Omelas?

The truth according to Ludd[1] 1992

The pleasure of kicking the vacuum cleaner
is irrational, yes, for it has no nerves
but is it more rational to kick the dog
when the cappuccino maker blows its lid?

Who is to blame when the washing machine
turns into a gusher? When the answering
machine drones your message from under water?
When the electrical system on your car

goes at midnight in January up on Killer
Mountain or in the fast lane on the expressway   10
at five fifteen? Machines flash us their idiot
plastic grins but we know that inside

something that turns the crank can go on strike.
Demons live in electricity as eels in water
lurking, equally happy to drink our blood
or simply curdle the milk and fry our hair.

When the computer prints for the sixteenth straight
time Bad Command or Can't Find That File
you know it is laughing silently inside,
like the car whose secret motto is Born to Cough.   20

We imagine they are extensions to our bodies,
sleek, perfect. Our egos preen in them.
Machines do not love us as we love them.
They have the contempt the whore does for johns.

For Analysis

1. What statement does the opening stanza make about rationality?

2. Is this just a clever, comic poem or is the poet making a serious point? Explain.

3. What does the final stanza say about our relation to machines?

---

[1] Luddites were members of bands of workers in early nineteenth-century England who destroyed the new industrial machinery that was depriving workers of jobs. The name, of uncertain origin, has come to denote anyone opposed to new technologies.

Alicia Suskin Ostriker (b. 1937)

Poem Beginning with a Line by Fitzgerald/Hemingway 1998

The very rich are different from us, they
Have more money, fewer scruples.[1] The very

Attractive have more lovers, the very sensitive
Go mad more easily, and the very brave

Distress a coward like myself, so listen
Scott, listen Ernest, and you also can

Listen, Walt Whitman. I understand the large
Language of rhetoricians, but not the large

Hearts of the heroes.[2] I am reading up.
I want someone to tell me what solvent saves   10

Their cardiac chambers from sediment, what is
The shovel that cuts the sluice

Straight from the obvious mottoes such as *Love
Your neighbor as yourself,*[3] or *I am human, therefore*

Nothing human is alien,[4] to the physical arm
In the immaculate ambassadorial shirtsleeves[5]

— We are in Budapest, '44 — that waves
Off the muddy Gestapo in the railroad yard

---

[1] In a famous conversation recorded by Ernest Hemingway in his memoir *A Moveable Feast*, Hemingway's fellow-novelist F. Scott Fitzgerald remarked, "The very rich are different from us," and Hemingway responded, "Yes, Scott, they have more money."

[2] See Walt Whitman, "Song of Myself," sec. 33, "I understand the large hearts of heroes."

[3] See the New Testament, Mark 12:31.

[4] A line from *The Self-Tormentor,* a play by the Roman dramatist Terence (186?–159? B.C.).

[5] Raoul Wallenberg (1912–1947), a Swedish diplomat who became legendary through his activities in rescuing Hungarian Jews during World War II. He is "The handsome Swede" of line 42.

With an imperious, an impatient flourish,
And is handing Swedish passports to anonymous   20

Yellow-starred arms[6] reaching from the very boxcars
That are packed and ready to glide with a shrill

Whistle and grate on steel, out of the town,
Like God's biceps and triceps gesturing

Across the void to Adam:[7] Live. In Cracow
A drinking, wenching German businessman[8]

Bribes and cajoles, laughs and negotiates
Over the workers, spends several times a fortune,

Saves a few thousand Jews, including one
He wins at a card game, and sets to work   30

In his kitchenware factory. A summer twilight
Soaks a plateau in southern France, the mountains

Mildly visible, and beyond them Switzerland,
As the policeman climbs from the khaki bus

To Le Chambon square, where the tall pastor[9]
Refuses to give names of refugees;

Meanwhile young men slip through the plotted streets,
Fan out to the farms — it is '42 —

So that the houses empty and the cool woods fill
With Jews and their false papers, so that the morning   40

---

[6] The Nazis required that Jews identify themselves by wearing a visible Star of David on their clothing.

[7] An allusion to the famous Michelangelo fresco on the ceiling of the Vatican's Sistine Chapel depicting the creation of life.

[8] Oskar Schindler (1908–1974) was a German businessman who saved many Jews from the Nazi death camps by employing them in his factory in Poland. His exploits described in this passage are the subject of Thomas Keneally's book *Schindler's List* and Steven Spielberg's film of the same name.

[9] André Trocmé (1908–1973), Protestant minister of Le Chambon, Switzerland, built a rescue network to shelter Jews from the Nazis during World War II.

Search finds no soul to arrest. It happens
Over and over, but how? The handsome Swede[10]

Was rich, was bored, one might have said. The pastor
Had his habit of hugging and kissing, and was good

At organizing peasants, intellectuals
And bible students. The profiteer intended

To amass wealth. He did, lived steep, and ended
Penniless, though the day the war ended,

The day they heard, over the whistling wireless,
the distant voice of Churchill[11] barking victory   50

As the Russians advanced, his *Schindlerjuden*[12]
Still in the plant, still safe, as he moved to flee,

Made him a small present. Jerets provided
His mouth's gold bridgework, Licht[13] melted it down,

Engraved the circle of the ring with what
One reads in Talmud:[14] *Who saves a single life,*

It is as if he saved the universe; and Schindler
The German took it, he wears it in his grave;

I am reading up on this. I did not know
Life had undone so many deaths.[15] *Now go*   60

And do likewise,[16] snaps every repercussion
Of my embarrassed heart, which is like a child

---

[10] See note 5.

[11] Sir Winston Churchill (1874–1965), British prime minister during World War II.

[12] Literally "Schindler's Jews," the group name adopted by the Jews Schindler saved from the Nazi death camps (see note 8).

[13] Jerets and Licht are the names of two of "Schindler's Jews."

[14] The Talmud is the ancient collection of Jewish law and tradition.

[15] The line echoes a line from T. S. Eliot's landmark *The Waste Land* (1922), a long poem on the decay and spiritual aridity of modern Western civilization. At the conclusion of section 1, titled "The Burial of the Dead," the speaker watches as crowds flow robot-like over London Bridge, and exclaims: "I had not thought death had undone so many."

[16] In the biblical parable of the good Samaritan (Luke 10:30–37), Jesus tells the story of the Samaritan who, in contrast to the priest and the Levite who "passed by on the other side," tended to a traveler beaten and robbed by thieves. Jesus' admonition to follow the example of the good Samaritan illustrates the Christian response to the question: "Who is my neighbor?"

Alone in a classroom full of strangers, thinking
She would like to run away. Let me repeat,

Though I do not forget ovens or guns,
Their names: Raoul Wallenberg, Oskar Schindler,

André Trocmé. Europe was full of others
As empty space is full of burning suns;

Not equally massive or luminous,
Creating heat, nevertheless, and light,   70

Creating what we may plausibly write
Up as the sky, a that without which nothing;

We cannot guess how many, only that they
Were subject to arrest each bloody day

And managed. Maybe it's like the muse, incalculable,
What you can pray in private for. Or a man

You distantly adore, who may someday love you
In the very cave of loneliness. We are afraid —

Yet as no pregnant woman knows beforehand
If she will go through labor strong, undrugged,   80

Unscreaming, and no shivering soldier knows
During pre-combat terror who will retreat,

Who stand and fight, so we cannot predict
Who among us will risk the fat that clings

Sweetly to our own bones —
None sweeter, Whitman promises — [17]

Our life, to save doomed lives, and none of us
Can know before the very day arrives.

---

[17] See Walt Whitman, "Song of Myself," line 20: "I find no sweeter fat than clings to my own bones."

For Analysis

1. Why does the poet begin with the exchange between Fitzgerald and Hemingway?

2. How does the speaker characterize herself?

3. Explain the phrase "the large / Language of rhetoricians" (ll.7–8).

4. Formulate the questions the speaker is trying to answer in this poem.

For Writing

1. Examine the metaphor of the "cardiac chambers" and the "shovel that cuts the sluice" (ll. 11–12), the allusion to Michelangelo's fresco (ll. 24–25), and the simile of the "pregnant woman" (ll. 79–80). How effective are they?

2. Use this poem as a starting point for an essay on the meaning of heroism.

3. If you have personally risked some danger in acting on your beliefs, describe the experience.

Steve Kowit   (b. 1938)

Lurid Confessions   1990

One fine morning they move in for the pinch
& snap on the cuffs — just like that.
Turns out they've known all about you for years,
have a file the length of a paddy-wagon
with everything — tapes, prints, film . . .
the whole shmear. Don't ask me how but
they've managed to plug a mike into one of your molars
and know every felonious move & transgression
back to the very beginning, with ektachromes[1]
of your least indiscretion & peccadillo.   10
Needless to say, you are thrilled,
tho sitting there in the docket
you bogart[2] it, tough as an old tooth —
your jaw set, your sleeves rolled
& three days of stubble. . . . Only,
when they play it back it looks different:
a life common & loathsome as gum stuck to a chair.
Tedious hours of you picking your nose,
scratching, eating, clipping your toenails . . .

---

[1] A type of camera film.
[2] A reference to film star Humphrey Bogart (1899–1957), famous for his portrayals of tough guys.

Alone, you look stupid; in public, your rapier   20
wit is slimy & limp as an old bandaid.
They have thousands of pictures of people around you
stifling yawns. As for sex — a bit
of pathetic groping among the unlovely & luckless:
a dance with everyone making steamy love in the dark
& you alone in a corner eating a pretzel.
You leap to your feet protesting
that's not how it was, they have it all wrong.
But nobody hears you. The bailiff
is snoring, the judge is cleaning his teeth,   30
the jurors are all wearing glasses with eyes painted open.
The flies have folded their wings and stopped buzzing.
In the end, after huge doses of coffee,
the jury is polled. One after another
they manage to rise to their feet
like narcoleptics in August, sealing your fate:
Innocent . . . innocent . . . innocent. . . . Right down the line.
You are carried out screaming.

For Analysis

1. Who are "they" in the poem? Why doesn't the poet identify them more clearly?

2. Speculate on the charges the speaker is being tried on.

3. Why does the speaker describe himself as "thrilled" (l. 11)?

4. Why, in the end, does the speaker become unhinged when he is found innocent?

5. Would you characterize the **tone** of this poem as serious or comic or both? Explain.

Stephen Dunn   (b. 1939)

Bourgeois   1998

What we would never let ourselves become,
tra la. Especially a petit.[1] Wasn't the edge the
only place to be? Or of the working class,
which would rise someday. Startling that it

Bourgeois
   [1] *Petit bourgeois,* person who belongs to the lower middle class, often applied disparagingly to
suggest a preoccupation with material goods and respectability.

rose, without rancor, happily in fact, toward
the bourgeoisie. Startling, too: capitalism's
elasticity, that fat boy with quick feet, subtly
accommodating, and not quite there when
we swung. In a few long years we'd be his
wary friend. We'd own mutual funds. Our   10
property was our property, and fences were
good. Parents now, we offered "Be carefuls"
as often as we once cried, "Fascist pigs." Oh
not petit, but grand! So what if we still believed in the efficacies of art, and still spoke
about souls? So what if we resisted the God-
fearing and the Republicans and a few of
their little, dispiriting rules? Each year we felt
less and less dislocated at the mall. We used
our remotes without irony and for entire eve-   20
nings hardly moved.

Robert Pinsky (b. 1940)

An Old Man 1990

After Cavafy[1]

Back in a corner, alone in the clatter and babble
An old man sits with his head bent over a table
And his newspaper in front of him, in the café.

Sour with old age, he ponders a dreary truth —
How little he enjoyed the years when he had youth,
Good looks and strength and clever things to say.

He knows he's quite old now: he feels it, he sees it,
And yet the time when he was young seems — was it?
Yesterday. How quickly, how quickly it slipped away.

An Old Man
   [1] Constantine P. Cavafy (1863–1933), a Greek poet.

Now he sees how Discretion has betrayed him,   10
And how stupidly he let the liar persuade him
With phrases: *Tomorrow. There's plenty of time. Some day.*

He recalls the pull of impulses he suppressed,
The joy he sacrificed. Every chance he lost
Ridicules his brainless prudence a different way.

But all these thoughts and memories have made
The old man dizzy. He falls asleep, his head
Resting on the table in the noisy café.

For Analysis

1. What is the effect of having the old man sitting at a table in a café? What difference would it make if he were sitting on a park bench or in a hotel room?

2. Why is "Discretion" (l. 10) capitalized?

3. How do you interpret the final stanza?

Nikki Giovanni   (b. 1943)

Dreams   1968

i used to dream militant
dreams of taking
over america to show
these white folks how it should be
done
i used to dream radical dreams
of blowing everyone away with my perceptive powers
of correct analysis
i even used to think i'd be the one
to stop the riot and negotiate the peace   10
then i awoke and dug
that if i dreamed natural
dreams of being a natural
woman doing what a woman
does when she's natural
i would have a revolution

Carolyn Forché   (b. 1950)

The Colonel   1981

What you have heard is true. I was in his house. His wife carried a tray of coffee
and sugar. His daughter filed her nails, his son went out for the night. There
were daily papers, pet dogs, a pistol on the cushion beside him. The moon
swung bare on its black cord over the house. On the television was a cop show.
It was in English. Broken bottles were embedded in the walls round the house
to scoop the kneecaps from a man's legs or cut his hands to lace. On the windows there were gratings like those in liquor stores. We had dinner, rack of
lamb, good wine, a gold bell was on the table for calling the maid. The maid
brought green mangoes, salt, a type of bread. I was asked how I enjoyed the
country. There was a brief commercial in Spanish. His wife took everything 10
away. There was some talk then of how difficult it had become to govern. The
parrot said hello on the terrace. The colonel told it to shut up, and pushed himself from the table. My friend said to me with his eyes: say nothing. The colonel
returned with a sack used to bring groceries home. He spilled many human ears
on the table. They were like dried peach halves. There is no other way to say
this. He took one of them in his hands, shook it in our faces, dropped it into a
water glass. It came alive there. I am tired of fooling around he said. As for the
rights of anyone, tell your people they can go fuck themselves. He swept the
ears to the floor with his arm and held the last of his wine in the air. Something
for your poetry, no? he said. Some of the ears on the floor caught this scrap of 20
his voice. Some of the ears on the floor were pressed to the ground.

For Analysis

1. What is the occasion of this poem? Where is it set? How would you characterize
the colonel's family?

2. In line 11 the speaker recounts, "There was some talk then of how difficult it had
become to govern." Can you suggest why it had become difficult to govern? How
does the colonel respond to these difficulties?

3. What does the last sentence suggest?

4. This piece is printed as if it were prose. Does it have any of the formal characteristics of a poem?

Drama

Sophocles   (496?–406 B.C.)

Antigonê [1]   ca. 441 B.C.

CHARACTERS

Antigonê	Teiresias
Ismenê	A Sentry
Eurydicê	A Messenger
Creon	Chorus
Haimon	

Scene   *Before the Palace of Creon, King of Thebes. A central double door, and two lateral doors. A platform extends the length of the façade, and from this platform three steps lead down into the "orchestra," or chorus-ground.*

Time   *Dawn of the day after the repulse of the Argive army from the assault on Thebes.*

Prologue

(Antigonê and Ismenê enter from the central door of the Palace.)

Antigonê.   Ismenê, dear sister,
You would think that we had already suffered enough
For the curse on Oedipus:[2]

---

[1] An English version by Dudley Fitts and Robert Fitzgerald.   [2] Oedipus, a former king of Thebes, unwittingly killed his father and married his own mother, Iocastê. By her he had four children, the sisters Antigonê and Ismenê and the brothers Polyneicês and Eteoclês. When Oedipus realized what he had done, he blinded himself and left Thebes. Eteoclês drove Polyneicês out of Thebes after a quarrel, but Polyneicês returned with an army and laid siege to Thebes. In the ensuing struggle, the brothers killed each other. Creon became king and, as a punishment, decreed that Polyneicês be denied the rites of burial.

I cannot imagine any grief
That you and I have not gone through. And now —
Have they told you of the new decree of our King Creon?

Ismenê.   I have heard nothing: I know
That two sisters lost two brothers, a double death
In a single hour; and I know that the Argive army
Fled in the night; but beyond this, nothing.   10

Antigonê.   I thought so. And that is why I wanted you
To come out here with me. There is something we must do.

Ismenê.   Why do you speak so strangely?

Antigonê.   Listen, Ismenê:
Creon buried our brother Eteoclês
With military honors, gave him a soldier's funeral,
And it was right that he should; but Polyneicês,
Who fought as bravely and died as miserably, —
They say that Creon has sworn
No one shall bury him, no one mourn for him,   20
But his body must lie in the fields, a sweet treasure
For carrion birds to find as they search for food.
That is what they say, and our good Creon is coming here
To announce it publicly; and the penalty —
Stoning to death in the public square!
                             There it is,
And now you can prove what you are:
A true sister, or a traitor to your family.

Ismenê.   Antigonê, you are mad! What could I possibly do?

Antigonê.   You must decide whether you will help me or not.

Ismenê.   I do not understand you. Help you in what?   30

Antigonê.   Ismenê, I am going to bury him. Will you come?

Ismenê.   Bury him! You have just said the new law forbids it.

Antigonê.   He is my brother. And he is your brother, too.

Ismenê.   But think of the danger! Think what Creon will do!

Antigonê.   Creon is not strong enough to stand in my way.

Ismenê.   Ah sister!
Oedipus died, everyone hating him
For what his own search brought to light, his eyes
Ripped out by his own hand; and Iocastê died,
His mother and wife at once: she twisted the cords   40
That strangled her life; and our two brothers died,
Each killed by the other's sword. And we are left:
But oh, Antigonê,
Think how much more terrible than these
Our own death would be if we should go against Creon
And do what he has forbidden! We are only women,
We cannot fight with men, Antigonê!

The law is strong, we must give in to the law
In this thing, and in worse. I beg the Dead
To forgive me, but I am helpless: I must yield   50
To those in authority. And I think it is dangerous business
To be always meddling.

Antigonê.   If that is what you think,
I should not want you, even if you asked to come.
You have made your choice, you can be what you want to be.
But I will bury him; and if I must die,
I say that this crime is holy: I shall lie down
With him in death, and I shall be as dear
To him as he to me.

It is the dead,
Not the living, who make the longest demands:
We die for ever . . .

You may do as you like,   60
Since apparently the laws of the gods mean nothing to you.

Ismenê.   They mean a great deal to me; but I have no strength
To break laws that were made for the public good.

Antigonê.   That must be your excuse, I suppose. But as for me,
I will bury the brother I love.

Ismenê.   Antigonê,
I am so afraid for you!

Antigonê.   You need not be:
You have yourself to consider, after all.

Ismenê.   But no one must hear of this, you must tell no one!
I will keep it a secret, I promise!

Antigonê.   Oh tell it! Tell everyone!
Think how they'll hate you when it all comes out   70
If they learn that you knew about it all the time!

Ismenê.   So fiery! You should be cold with fear.

Antigonê.   Perhaps. But I am doing only what I must.

Ismenê.   But can you do it? I say that you cannot.

Antigonê.   Very well: when my strength gives out, I shall do no more.

Ismenê.   Impossible things should not be tried at all.

Antigonê.   Go away, Ismenê:
I shall be hating you soon, and the dead will too,
For your words are hateful. Leave me my foolish plan:
I am not afraid of the danger; if it means death,   80
It will not be the worst of deaths — death without honor.

Ismenê.   Go then, if you feel you must.
You are unwise,
But a loyal friend indeed to those who love you.

(Exit into the Palace. Antigonê goes off, L. Enter the Chorus.)

Párodos³

Chorus. Now the long blade of the sun, lying   (*Strophe 1*)
   Level east to west, touches with glory
   Thebes of the Seven Gates. Open, unlidded
   Eye of golden day! O marching light
   Across the eddy and rush of Dircê's stream,⁴
   Striking the white shields of the enemy
   Thrown headlong backward from the blaze of morning!
Choragos.⁵ Polyneicês their commander
   Roused them with windy phrases,
   He the wild eagle screaming   10
   Insults above our land,
   His wings their shields of snow,
   His crest their marshalled helms.

Chorus. Against our seven gates in a yawning ring   (*Antistrophe 1*)
   The famished spears came onward in the night;
   But before his jaws were sated with our blood,
   Or pinefire took the garland of our towers,
   He was thrown back; and as he turned, great Thebes —
   No tender victim for his noisy power —
   Rose like a dragon behind him, shouting war.   20
Choragos. For God hates utterly
   The bray of bragging tongues;
   And when he beheld their smiling,
   Their swagger of golden helms,
   The frown of his thunder blasted
   Their first man from our walls.

Chorus. We heard his shout of triumph high in the air   (*Strophe 2*)
   Turn to a scream; far out in a flaming arc
   He fell with his windy torch, and the earth struck him.
   And others storming in fury no less than his   30
   Found shock of death in the dusty joy of battle.
Choragos. Seven captains at seven gates
   Yielded their clanging arms to the god
   That bends the battle-line and breaks it.
   These two only, brothers in blood,
   Face to face in matchless rage,

---

³ The Párodos is the ode sung by the Chorus as it entered the theater and moved down the aisles to the playing area. The *strophe*, in Greek tragedy, is the unit of verse the Chorus chanted as it moved to the left in a dance rhythm. The Chorus sang the *antistrophe* as it moved to the right, and the *epode* while standing still.   ⁴ A stream near Thebes.   ⁵ Choragos is the leader of the Chorus.

Mirroring each the other's death,
Clashed in long combat.

Chorus. But now in the beautiful morning of victory   (*Antistrophe 2*)
 Let Thebes of the many chariots sing for joy!   40
 With hearts for dancing we'll take leave of war:
 Our temples shall be sweet with hymns of praise,
 And the long night shall echo with our chorus.

Scene 1

Choragos. But now at last our new King is coming:
 Creon of Thebes, Menoikeus' son.
 In this auspicious dawn of his reign
 What are the new complexities
 That shifting Fate has woven for him?
 What is his counsel? Why has he summoned
 The old men to hear him?

(*Enter Creon from the Palace, C. He addresses the Chorus from the top step.*)

Creon. Gentlemen: I have the honor to inform you that our Ship of State, which recent storms have threatened to destroy, has come safely to harbor at last, guided by the merciful wisdom of Heaven. I have summoned you here 10 this morning because I know that I can depend upon you: your devotion to King Laïos was absolute; you never hesitated in your duty to our late ruler Oedipus; and when Oedipus died, your loyalty was transferred to his children. Unfortunately, as you know, his two sons, the princes Eteoclês and Polyneicês, have killed each other in battle; and I, as the next in blood, have succeeded to the full power of the throne.

   I am aware, of course, that no Ruler can expect complete loyalty from his subjects until he has been tested in office. Nevertheless, I say to you at the very outset that I have nothing but contempt for the kind of Governor who is afraid, for whatever reason, to follow the course that he knows is best for the 20 State; and as for the man who sets private friendship above the public welfare, — I have no use for him, either. I call God to witness that if I saw my country headed for ruin, I should not be afraid to speak out plainly; and I need hardly remind you that I would never have any dealings with an enemy of the people. No one values friendship more highly than I; but we must remember that friends made at the risk of wrecking our Ship are not real friends at all.

   These are my principles, at any rate, and that is why I have made the following decision concerning the sons of Oedipus: Eteoclês, who died as a man

should die, fighting for his country, is to be buried with full military honors, 30
with all the ceremony that is usual when the greatest heroes die; but his
brother Polyneicês, who broke his exile to come back with fire and sword
against his native city and the shrines of his fathers' gods, whose one idea
was to spill the blood of his blood and sell his own people into slavery —
Polyneicês, I say, is to have no burial: no man is to touch him or say the least
prayer for him; he shall lie on the plain, unburied; and the birds and the scavenging dogs can do with him whatever they like.

    This is my command, and you can see the wisdom behind it. As long as I
am King, no traitor is going to be honored with the loyal man. But whoever
shows by word and deed that he is on the side of the State, — he shall have 40
my respect while he is living and my reverence when he is dead.

Choragos.   If that is your will, Creon, son of Menoikeus,
   You have the right to enforce it: we are yours.
Creon.   That is my will. Take care that you do your part.
Choragos.   We are old men: let the younger ones carry it out.
Creon.   I do not mean that: the sentries have been appointed.
Choragos.   Then what is it that you would have us do?
Creon.   You will give no support to whoever breaks this law.
Choragos.   Only a crazy man is in love with death!
Creon.   And death it is; yet money talks, and the wisest   50
   Have sometimes been known to count a few coins too many.

(Enter Sentry from L.)

Sentry.   I'll not say that I'm out of breath from running, King, because every
   time I stopped to think about what I have to tell you, I felt like going back.
   And all the time a voice kept saying, "You fool, don't you know you're walking
   straight into trouble?"; and then another voice: "Yes, but if you let somebody
   else get the news to Creon first, it will be even worse than that for you!" But
   good sense won out, at least I hope it was good sense, and here I am with a
   story that makes no sense at all; but I'll tell it anyhow, because, as they say,
   what's going to happen's going to happen, and —
Creon.   Come to the point. What have you to say?   60
Sentry.   I did not do it. I did not see who did it. You must not punish me for
   what someone else has done.
Creon.   A comprehensive defense! More effective, perhaps,
   If I knew its purpose. Come: what is it?
Sentry.   A dreadful thing . . . I don't know how to put it —
Creon.   Out with it!
Sentry.   Well, then;
   The dead man —
                 Polyneicês —

(Pause. The Sentry is overcome, fumbles for words. Creon waits impassively.)

out there —
someone, —
New dust on the slimy flesh!

(Pause. No sign from Creon.)

Someone has given it burial that way, and
Gone . . .   70

(Long pause. Creon finally speaks with deadly control.)

Creon.   And the man who dared do this?
Sentry.   I swear I
Do not know! You must believe me!
                                                     Listen:
The ground was dry, not a sign of digging, no,
Not a wheeltrack in the dust, no trace of anyone.
It was when they relieved us this morning: and one of them,
The corporal, pointed to it.
                                    There it was,
The strangest —
                       Look:
The body, just mounded over with light dust: you see?
Not buried really, but as if they'd covered it
Just enough for the ghost's peace. And no sign   80
Of dogs or any wild animal that had been there.

And then what a scene there was! Every man of us
Accusing the other: we all proved the other man did it,
We all had proof that we could not have done it.
We were ready to take hot iron in our hands,
Walk through fire, swear by all the gods,
It was not I!
I do not know who it was, but it was not I!

*(Creon's rage has been mounting steadily, but the Sentry is too intent upon his
story to notice it.)*

And then, when this came to nothing, someone said
A thing that silenced us and made us stare   90
Down at the ground: you had to be told the news,
And one of us had to do it! We threw the dice,
And the bad luck fell to me. So here I am,
No happier to be here than you are to have me:
Nobody likes the man who brings bad news.

Choragos.   I have been wondering, King: can it be that the gods have done
   this?
Creon (*furiously*).   Stop!
   Must you doddering wrecks
   Go out of your heads entirely? "The gods!"   100
   Intolerable!
   The gods favor this corpse? Why? How had he served them?
   Tried to loot their temples, burn their images,
   Yes, and the whole State, and its laws with it!
   Is it your senile opinion that the gods love to honor bad men?
   A pious thought! —
                              No, from the very beginning
   There have been those who have whispered together,
   Stiff-necked anarchists, putting their heads together,
   Scheming against me in alleys. These are the men,
   And they have bribed my own guard to do this thing.   110
   (*Sententiously.*) Money!
   There's nothing in the world so demoralizing as money.
   Down go your cities,
   Homes gone, men gone, honest hearts corrupted,
   Crookedness of all kinds, and all for money!
   (*To Sentry.*)   But you — !
   I swear by God and by the throne of God,
   The man who has done this thing shall pay for it!
   Find that man, bring him here to me, or your death
   Will be the least of your problems: I'll string you up
   Alive, and there will be certain ways to make you   120
   Discover your employer before you die;
   And the process may teach you a lesson you seem to have missed:
   The dearest profit is sometimes all too dear:
   That depends on the source. Do you understand me?
   A fortune won is often misfortune.
Sentry.   King, may I speak?
Creon.   Your very voice distresses me.
Sentry.   Are you sure that it is my voice, and not your conscience?
Creon.   By God, he wants to analyze me now!
Sentry.   It is not what I say, but what has been done, that hurts you.
Creon.   You talk too much.
Sentry.   Maybe; but I've done nothing.   130
Creon.   Sold your soul for some silver: that's all you've done.
Sentry.   How dreadful it is when the right judge judges wrong!
Creon.   Your figures of speech
   May entertain you now; but unless you bring me the man,
   You will get little profit from them in the end.

(Exit Creon into the Palace.)

Sentry.   "Bring me the man" — !
   I'd like nothing better than bringing him the man!
   But bring him or not, you have seen the last of me here.
   At any rate, I am safe!

(Exit Sentry.)

Ode I

Chorus.   Numberless are the world's wonders, but none   *(Strophe 1)*
   More wonderful than man; the stormgray sea
   Yields to his prows, the huge crests bear him high;
   Earth, holy and inexhaustible, is graven
   With shining furrows where his plows have gone
   Year after year, the timeless labor of stallions.

   The lightboned birds and beasts that cling to cover,   *(Antistrophe 1)*
   The lithe fish lighting their reaches of dim water,
   All are taken, tamed in the net of his mind;
   The lion on the hill, the wild horse windy-maned,   10
   Resign to him; and his blunt yoke has broken
   The sultry shoulders of the mountain bull.

   Words also, and thought as rapid as air,   *(Strophe 2)*
   He fashions to his good use; statecraft is his,
   And his the skill that deflects the arrows of snow,
   The spears of winter rain: from every wind
   He has made himself secure — from all but one:
   In the late wind of death he cannot stand.

   O clear intelligence, force beyond all measure!   *(Antistrophe 2)*
   O fate of man, working both good and evil!   20
   When the laws are kept, how proudly his city stands!
   When the laws are broken, what of his city then?
   Never may the anarchic man find rest at my hearth,
   Never be it said that my thoughts are his thoughts.

Scene 2

(Re-enter Sentry leading Antigonê.)

Choragos.   What does this mean? Surely this captive woman
   Is the Princess, Antigonê. Why should she be taken?
Sentry.   Here is the one who did it! We caught her
   In the very act of burying him. — Where is Creon?
Choragos.   Just coming from the house.

(Enter Creon, C.)

Creon.   What has happened?
   Why have you come back so soon?
Sentry *(expansively)*.   O King,
   A man should never be too sure of anything:
   I would have sworn
   That you'd not see me here again: your anger
   Frightened me so, and the things you threatened me with;   10
   But how could I tell then
   That I'd be able to solve the case so soon?
   No dice-throwing this time: I was only too glad to come!

   Here is this woman. She is the guilty one:
   We found her trying to bury him.
   Take her, then; question her; judge her as you will.
   I am through with the whole thing now, and glad of it.
Creon.   But this is Antigonê! Why have you brought her here?
Sentry.   She was burying him, I tell you!
Creon *(severely)*.   Is this the truth?
Sentry.   I saw her with my own eyes. Can I say more?   20
Creon.   The details: come, tell me quickly!
Sentry.   It was like this:
   After those terrible threats of yours, King,
   We went back and brushed the dust away from the body.
   The flesh was soft by now, and stinking,
   So we sat on a hill to windward and kept guard.
   No napping this time! We kept each other awake.
   But nothing happened until the white round sun
   Whirled in the center of the round sky over us:
   Then, suddenly,
   A storm of dust roared up from the earth, and the sky   30
   Went out, the plain vanished with all its trees
   In the stinging dark. We closed our eyes and endured it.

The whirlwind lasted a long time, but it passed;
And then we looked, and there was Antigonê!
I have seen
A mother bird come back to a stripped nest, heard
Her crying bitterly a broken note or two
For the young ones stolen. Just so, when this girl
Found the bare corpse, and all her love's work wasted,
She wept, and cried on heaven to damn the hands   40
That had done this thing.
                  And then she brought more dust
And sprinkled wine three times for her brother's ghost.
We ran and took her at once. She was not afraid,
Not even when we charged her with what she had done.
She denied nothing.
            And this was a comfort to me,
And some uneasiness: for it is a good thing
To escape from death, but it is no great pleasure
To bring death to a friend.
                Yet I always say
There is nothing so comfortable as your own safe skin!
Creon (*slowly, dangerously*).   And you, Antigonê,   50
You with your head hanging, — do you confess this thing?
Antigonê.   I do. I deny nothing.
Creon (*to Sentry*).   You may go.

(*Exit Sentry.*)

(*To Antigonê.*) Tell me, tell me briefly:
Had you heard my proclamation touching this matter?
Antigonê.   It was public. Could I help hearing it?
Creon.   And yet you dared defy the law.
Antigonê.   I dared.
It was not God's proclamation. That final Justice
That rules the world below makes no such laws.

Your edict, King, was strong,
But all your strength is weakness itself against   60
The immortal unrecorded laws of God.
They are not merely now: they were, and shall be,
Operative for ever, beyond man utterly.

I knew I must die, even without your decree:
I am only mortal. And if I must die
Now, before it is my time to die,
Surely this is no hardship: can anyone

Living, as I live, with evil all about me,
Think Death less than a friend? This death of mine
Is of no importance; but if I had left my brother   70
Lying in death unburied, I should have suffered.
Now I do not.
                              You smile at me. Ah Creon,
Think me a fool, if you like; but it may well be
That a fool convicts me of folly.
Choragos.   Like father, like daughter: both headstrong, deaf to reason!
She has never learned to yield.
Creon.   She has much to learn.
The inflexible heart breaks first, the toughest iron
Cracks first, and the wildest horses bend their necks
At the pull of the smallest curb.
                              Pride? In a slave?
This girl is guilty of a double insolence,   80
Breaking the given laws and boasting of it.
Who is the man here,
She or I, if this crime goes unpunished?
Sister's child, or more than sister's child,
Or closer yet in blood — she and her sister
Win bitter death for this!
(To servants.)   Go, some of you,
Arrest Ismenê. I accuse her equally.
Bring her: you will find her sniffling in the house there.

Her mind's a traitor: crimes kept in the dark
Cry for light, and the guardian brain shudders;   90
But how much worse than this
Is brazen boasting of barefaced anarchy!
Antigonê.   Creon, what more do you want than my death?
Creon.   Nothing.
That gives me everything.
Antigonê.   Then I beg you: kill me.
This talking is a great weariness: your words
Are distasteful to me, and I am sure that mine
Seem so to you. And yet they should not seem so:
I should have praise and honor for what I have done.
All these men here would praise me
Were their lips not frozen shut with fear of you.   100
(Bitterly.) Ah the good fortune of kings,
Licensed to say and do whatever they please!
Creon.   You are alone here in that opinion.
Antigonê.   No, they are with me. But they keep their tongues in leash.
Creon.   Maybe. But you are guilty, and they are not.

Antigonê.   There is no guilt in reverence for the dead.
Creon.   But Eteoclês — was he not your brother too?
Antigonê.   My brother too.
Creon.   And you insult his memory?
Antigonê (*softly*).   The dead man would not say that I insult it.
Creon.   He would: for you honor a traitor as much as him.   110
Antigonê.   His own brother, traitor or not, and equal in blood.
Creon.   He made war on his country. Eteoclês defended it.
Antigonê.   Nevertheless, there are honors due all the dead.
Creon.   But not the same for the wicked as for the just.
Antigonê.   Ah Creon, Creon,
   Which of us can say what the gods hold wicked?
Creon.   An enemy is an enemy, even dead.
Antigonê.   It is my nature to join in love, not hate.
Creon (*finally losing patience*).   Go join them, then; if you must have your
   love,
   Find it in hell!   120
Choragos.   But see, Ismenê comes:

(*Enter Ismenê, guarded.*)

   Those tears are sisterly, the cloud
   That shadows her eyes rains down gentle sorrow.
Creon.   You too, Ismenê,
   Snake in my ordered house, sucking my blood
   Stealthily — and all the time I never knew
   That these two sisters were aiming at my throne!
                                                                        Ismenê,
   Do you confess your share in this crime, or deny it?
   Answer me.
Ismenê.   Yes, if she will let me say so. I am guilty.   130
Antigonê (*coldly*).   No, Ismenê. You have no right to say so.
   You would not help me, and I will not have you help me.
Ismenê.   But now I know what you meant; and I am here
   To join you, to take my share of punishment.
Antigonê.   The dead man and the gods who rule the dead
   Know whose act this was. Words are not friends.
Ismenê.   Do you refuse me, Antigonê? I want to die with you:
   I too have a duty that I must discharge to the dead.
Antigonê.   You shall not lessen my death by sharing it.
Ismenê.   What do I care for life when you are dead?   140
Antigonê.   Ask Creon. You're always hanging on his opinions.
Ismenê.   You are laughing at me. Why, Antigonê?
Antigonê.   It's a joyless laughter, Ismenê.
Ismenê.   But can I do nothing?

Antigonê.   Yes. Save yourself. I shall not envy you.
There are those who will praise you; I shall have honor, too.
Ismenê.   But we are equally guilty!
Antigonê.   No more, Ismenê.
You are alive, but I belong to Death.
Creon *(to the Chorus).*   Gentlemen, I beg you to observe these girls:
One has just now lost her mind; the other,
It seems, has never had a mind at all.   150
Ismenê.   Grief teaches the steadiest minds to waver, King.
Creon.   Yours certainly did, when you assumed guilt with the guilty!
Ismenê.   But how could I go on living without her?
Creon.   You are.
She is already dead.
Ismenê.   But your own son's bride!
Creon.   There are places enough for him to push his plow.
I want no wicked women for my sons!
Ismenê.   O dearest Haimon, how your father wrongs you!
Creon.   I've had enough of your childish talk of marriage!
Choragos.   Do you really intend to steal this girl from your son?
Creon.   No; Death will do that for me.
Choragos.   Then she must die?   160
Creon *(ironically).*   You dazzle me.
                                        — But enough of this talk!
(To Guards.) You there, take them away and guard them well:
For they are but women, and even brave men run
When they see Death coming.

(Exeunt Ismenê, Antigonê, and Guards.)

Ode II

Chorus.   Fortunate is the man who has never tasted   *(Strophe 1)*
     God's vengeance!
Where once the anger of heaven has struck, that house is shaken
For ever: damnation rises behind each child
Like a wave cresting out of the black northeast,
When the long darkness under sea roars up
And bursts drumming death upon the windwhipped sand.

I have seen this gathering sorrow from time long past   *(Antistrophe 1)*
Loom upon Oedipus' children: generation from generation
Takes the compulsive rage of the enemy god.   10
So lately this last flower of Oedipus' line

Drank the sunlight! but now a passionate word
And a handful of dust have closed up all its beauty.

    What mortal arrogance   *(Strophe 2)*
    Transcends the wrath of Zeus?
Sleep cannot lull him, nor the effortless long months
Of the timeless gods: but he is young for ever,
And his house is the shining day of high Olympos.
    And that is and shall be,
    And all the past, is his.   20
No pride on earth is free of the curse of heaven.

    The straying dreams of men   *(Antistrophe 2)*
    May bring them ghosts of joy:
But as they drowse, the waking embers burn them;
Or they walk with fixed eyes, as blind men walk.
But the ancient wisdom speaks for our own time:
    Fate works most for woe
    With Folly's fairest show.
Man's little pleasure is the spring of sorrow.

Scene 3

Choragos.   But here is Haimon, King, the last of all your sons.
    Is it grief for Antigonê that brings him here,
    And bitterness at being robbed of his bride?

(Enter Haimon.)

Creon.   We shall soon see, and no need of diviners.
                                      — Son,
    You have heard my final judgment on that girl:
    Have you come here hating me, or have you come
    With deference and with love, whatever I do?
Haimon.   I am your son, father. You are my guide.
    You make things clear for me, and I obey you.
    No marriage means more to me than your continuing wisdom.   10
Creon.   Good. That is the way to behave: subordinate
    Everything else, my son, to your father's will.
    This is what a man prays for, that he may get
    Sons attentive and dutiful in his house,
    Each one hating his father's enemies,

Honoring his father's friends. But if his sons
Fail him, if they turn out unprofitably,
What has he fathered but trouble for himself
And amusement for the malicious?
                                        So you are right
Not to lose your head over this woman.   20
Your pleasure with her would soon grow cold, Haimon,
And then you'd have a hellcat in bed and elsewhere.
Let her find her husband in Hell!
Of all the people in this city, only she
Has had contempt for my law and broken it.

Do you want me to show myself weak before the people?
Or to break my sworn word? No, and I will not.
The woman dies.
I suppose she'll plead "family ties." Well, let her.
If I permit my own family to rebel,   30
How shall I earn the world's obedience?
Show me the man who keeps his house in hand,
He's fit for public authority.
                                        I'll have no dealings
With law-breakers, critics of the government:
Whoever is chosen to govern should be obeyed —
Must be obeyed, in all things, great and small,
Just and unjust! O Haimon,
The man who knows how to obey, and that man only,
Knows how to give commands when the time comes.
You can depend on him, no matter how fast   40
The spears come: he's a good soldier, he'll stick it out.
Anarchy, anarchy! Show me a greater evil!
This is why cities tumble and the great houses rain down,
This is what scatters armies!

No, no: good lives are made so by discipline.
We keep the laws then, and the lawmakers,
And no woman shall seduce us. If we must lose,
Let's lose to a man, at least! Is a woman stronger than we?
Choragos.   Unless time has rusted my wits,
What you say, King, is said with point and dignity.   50
Haimon (*boyishly earnest*).   Father:
Reason is God's crowning gift to man, and you are right
To warn me against losing mine. I cannot say —
I hope that I shall never want to say! — that you
Have reasoned badly. Yet there are other men

Who can reason, too; and their opinions might be helpful.
You are not in a position to know everything
That people say or do, or what they feel:
Your temper terrifies them — everyone
Will tell you only what you like to hear.   60
But I, at any rate, can listen; and I have heard them
Muttering and whispering in the dark about this girl.
They say no woman has ever, so unreasonably,
Died so shameful a death for a generous act:
"She covered her brother's body. Is this indecent?
She kept him from dogs and vultures. Is this a crime?
Death? — She should have all the honor that we can give her!"

This is the way they talk out there in the city.

You must believe me:
Nothing is closer to me than your happiness.   70
What could be closer? Must not any son
Value his father's fortune as his father does his?
I beg you, do not be unchangeable:
Do not believe that you alone can be right.
The man who thinks that,
The man who maintains that only he has the power
To reason correctly, the gift to speak, the soul —
A man like that, when you know him, turns out empty.
It is not reason never to yield to reason!

In flood time you can see how some trees bend   80
And because they bend, even their twigs are safe,
While stubborn trees are torn up, roots and all.
And the same thing happens in sailing:
Make your sheet fast, never slacken — and over you go,
Head over heels and under: and there's your voyage.
Forget you are angry! Let yourself be moved!
I know I am young; but please let me say this:
The ideal condition
Would be, I admit, that men should be right by instinct;
But since we are all too likely to go astray,   90
The reasonable thing is to learn from those who can teach.
Choragos.   You will do well to listen to him, King,
If what he says is sensible. And you, Haimon,
Must listen to your father. — Both speak well.
Creon.   You consider it right for a man of my years and experience
To go to school to a boy?

Haimon.   It is not right
If I am wrong. But if I am young, and right,
What does my age matter?
Creon.   You think it right to stand up for an anarchist?
Haimon.   Not at all. I pay no respect to criminals.   100
Creon.   Then she is not a criminal?
Haimon.   The City would deny it, to a man.
Creon.   And the City proposes to teach me how to rule?
Haimon.   Ah. Who is it that's talking like a boy now?
Creon.   My voice is the one voice giving orders in this City!
Haimon.   It is no City if it takes orders from one voice.
Creon.   The State is the King!
Haimon.   Yes, if the State is a desert.

(Pause.)

Creon.   This boy, it seems, has sold out to a woman.
Haimon.   If you are a woman: my concern is only for you.
Creon.   So? Your "concern"! In a public brawl with your father!   110
Haimon.   How about you, in a public brawl with justice?
Creon.   With justice, when all that I do is within my rights?
Haimon.   You have no right to trample on God's right.
Creon *(completely out of control).*   Fool, adolescent fool! Taken in by a
woman!
Haimon.   You'll never see me taken in by anything vile.
Creon.   Every word you say is for her!
Haimon *(quietly, darkly).*   And for you.
And for me. And for the gods under the earth.
Creon.   You'll never marry her while she lives.
Haimon.   Then she must die. — But her death will cause another.
Creon.   Another?   120
Have you lost your senses? Is this an open threat?
Haimon.   There is no threat in speaking to emptiness.
Creon.   I swear you'll regret this superior tone of yours!
You are the empty one!
Haimon.   If you were not my father,
I'd say you were perverse.
Creon.   You girlstruck fool, don't play at words with me!
Haimon.   I am sorry. You prefer silence.
Creon.   Now, by God — !
I swear, by all the gods in heaven above us,
You'll watch it, I swear you shall!
(To the servants.)   Bring her out!
Bring the woman out! Let her die before his eyes!   130
Here, this instant, with her bridegroom beside her!

Haimon.   Not here, no; she will not die here, King.
  And you will never see my face again.
  Go on raving as long as you've a friend to endure you.

(Exit Haimon.)

Choragos.   Gone, gone.
  Creon, a young man in a rage is dangerous!
Creon.   Let him do, or dream to do, more than a man can.
  He shall not save these girls from death.
Choragos.   These girls?
  You have sentenced them both?
Creon.   No, you are right.
  I will not kill the one whose hands are clean.   140
Choragos.   But Antigonê?
Creon *(somberly).*   I will carry her far away
  Out there in the wilderness, and lock her
  Living in a vault of stone. She shall have food,
  As the custom is, to absolve the State of her death.
  And there let her pray to the gods of hell:
  They are her only gods:
  Perhaps they will show her an escape from death,
  Or she may learn,
                though late,
  That piety shown the dead is pity in vain.   150

(Exit Creon.)

Ode III

Chorus.   Love, unconquerable   *(Strophe)*
  Waster of rich men, keeper
  Of warm lights and all-night vigil
  In the soft face of a girl:
  Sea-wanderer, forest-visitor!
  Even the pure Immortals cannot escape you,
  And mortal man, in his one day's dusk,
  Trembles before your glory.

  Surely you swerve upon ruin   *(Antistrophe)*
  The just man's consenting heart,   10
  As here you have made bright anger

Strike between father and son —
And none had conquered but Love!
A girl's glance working the will of heaven:
Pleasure to her alone who mocks us,
Merciless Aphroditê.[6]

Scene 4

Choragos (*as Antigonê enters guarded*).   But I can no longer stand in awe of
  this,
Nor, seeing what I see, keep back my tears.
Here is Antigonê, passing to that chamber
Where all find sleep at last.

Antigonê.   Look upon me, friends, and pity me   (*Strophe 1*)
Turning back at the night's edge to say
Good-by to the sun that shines for me no longer;
Now sleepy Death
Summons me down to Acheron,[7] that cold shore:
There is no bridesong there, nor any music.   10
Chorus.   Yet not unpraised, not without a kind of honor,
You walk at last into the underworld;
Untouched by sickness, broken by no sword.
What woman has ever found your way to death?
Antigonê.   How often I have heard the story of Niobê,[8]   (*Antistrophe 1*)
Tantalos' wretched daughter, how the stone
Clung fast about her, ivy-close: and they say
The rain falls endlessly
And sifting soft snow; her tears are never done.
I feel the loneliness of her death in mine.   20
Chorus.   But she was born of heaven, and you
Are woman, woman-born. If her death is yours,
A mortal woman's, is this not for you
Glory in our world and in the world beyond?

Antigonê.   You laugh at me. Ah, friends, friends,   (*Strophe 2*)
Can you not wait until I am dead? O Thebes,
O men many-charioted, in love with Fortune,

---

[6] Aphroditê is the goddess of love.   [7] A river of Hades.   [8] Niobê married an ancestor of Oedipus named Amphion. Her fourteen children were killed by Apollo and Artemis after Niobê boasted to their mother, Leto, that her children were superior to them. She wept incessantly and was finally transformed into a rock on Mt. Sipylos, whose streams are her tears.

Dear springs of Dircê, sacred Theban grove,
Be witnesses for me, denied all pity,
Unjustly judged! and think a word of love 30
For her whose path turns
Under dark earth, where there are no more tears.

Chorus.   You have passed beyond human daring and come at last
Into a place of stone where Justice sits.
I cannot tell
What shape of your father's guilt appears in this.

Antigonê.   You have touched it at last: that bridal bed   *(Antistrophe 2)*
Unspeakable, horror of son and mother mingling:
Their crime, infection of all our family!
O Oedipus, father and brother! 40
Your marriage strikes from the grave to murder mine.
I have been a stranger here in my own land:
All my life
The blasphemy of my birth has followed me.

Chorus.   Reverence is a virtue, but strength
Lives in established law: that must prevail.
You have made your choice,
Your death is the doing of your conscious hand.

Antigonê.   Then let me go, since all your words are bitter,   *(Epode)*
And the very light of the sun is cold to me. 50
Lead me to my vigil, where I must have
Neither love nor lamentation; no song, but silence.

(Creon interrupts impatiently.)

Creon.   If dirges and planned lamentations could put off death,
Men would be singing for ever.
(To the servants.)   Take her, go!
You know your orders: take her to the vault
And leave her alone there. And if she lives or dies,
That's her affair, not ours: our hands are clean.

Antigonê.   O tomb, vaulted bride-bed in eternal rock,
Soon I shall be with my own again
Where Persephonê[9] welcomes the thin ghosts underground: 60
And I shall see my father again, and you, mother,
And dearest Polyneicês —
                    dearest indeed
To me, since it was my hand

[9] Queen of Hades.

That washed him clean and poured the ritual wine:
And my reward is death before my time!

And yet, as men's hearts know, I have done no wrong,
I have not sinned before God. Or if I have,
I shall know the truth in death. But if the guilt
Lies upon Creon who judged me, then, I pray,
May his punishment equal my own.

Choragos.   O passionate heart,   70
Unyielding, tormented still by the same winds!

Creon.   Her guards shall have good cause to regret their delaying.

Antigonê.   Ah! That voice is like the voice of death!

Creon.   I can give you no reason to think you are mistaken.

Antigonê.   Thebes, and you my fathers' gods,
And rulers of Thebes, you see me now, the last
Unhappy daughter of a line of kings,
Your kings, led away to death. You will remember
What things I suffer, and at what men's hands,
Because I would not transgress the laws of heaven.   80
(To the guards, simply.) Come: let us wait no longer.

(Exit Antigonê, L., guarded.)

Ode IV

Chorus.   All Danaê's[10] beauty was locked away   *(Strophe 1)*
In a brazen cell where the sunlight could not come:
A small room, still as any grave, enclosed her.
Yet she was a princess too,
And Zeus in a rain of gold poured love upon her.
O child, child,
No power in wealth or war
Or tough sea-blackened ships
Can prevail against untiring Destiny!

And Dryas' son[11] also, that furious king,   *(Antistrophe 1)*
Bore the god's prisoning anger for his pride:
Sealed up by Dionysos in deaf stone,
His madness died among echoes.

---

[10] Though Danaê, a beautiful princess of Argos, was confined by her father, Zeus visited her in the form of a shower of gold, and she gave birth to Perseus as a result.   [11] Lycurgus, King of Thrace, who was driven mad by Dionysos, the god of wine.

So at the last he learned what dreadful power
His tongue had mocked:
For he had profaned the revels,
And fired the wrath of the nine
Implacable Sisters[12] that love the sound of the flute.

And old men tell a half-remembered tale   *(Strophe 2)*
Of horror where a dark ledge splits the sea   20
And a double surf beats on the gray shores:
How a king's new woman,[13] sick
With hatred for the queen he had imprisoned,
Ripped out his two sons' eyes with her bloody hands
While grinning Arês[14] watched the shuttle plunge
Four times: four blind wounds crying for revenge,

Crying, tears and blood mingled. — Piteously born,   *(Antistrophe 2)*
Those sons whose mother was of heavenly birth!
Her father was the god of the North Wind
And she was cradled by gales,   30
She raced with young colts on the glittering hills
And walked untrammeled in the open light:
But in her marriage deathless Fate found means
To build a tomb like yours for all her joy.

Scene 5

(Enter blind Teiresias, led by a boy. The opening speeches of Teiresias should be in singsong contrast to the realistic lines of Creon.)

Teiresias.   This is the way the blind man comes, Princes, Princes,
  Lock-step, two heads lit by the eyes of one.
Creon.   What new thing have you to tell us, old Teiresias?
Teiresias.   I have much to tell you: listen to the prophet, Creon.
Creon.   I am not aware that I have ever failed to listen.
Teiresias.   Then you have done wisely, King, and ruled well.
Creon.   I admit my debt to you. But what have you to say?
Teiresias.   This, Creon: you stand once more on the edge of fate.
Creon.   What do you mean? Your words are a kind of dread.

---

[12] The Muses.   [13] The ode alludes to a story indicating the uselessness of high birth against implacable fate. The king's new woman is Eidothea, the second wife of King Phineus. Though Cleopatra, his first wife, was the daughter of Boreas, the north wind, and Phineus himself was descended from kings, Eidothea, out of hatred for Cleopatra, blinded her two sons.   [14] The god of war.

Teiresias.   Listen, Creon: 10
     I was sitting in my chair of augury, at the place
     Where the birds gather about me. They were all a-chatter,
     As is their habit, when suddenly I heard
     A strange note in their jangling, a scream, a
     Whirring fury; I knew that they were fighting,
     Tearing each other, dying
     In a whirlwind of wings clashing. And I was afraid.
     I began the rites of burnt-offering at the altar,
     But Hephaistos[15] failed me: instead of bright flame,
     There was only the sputtering slime of the fat thigh-flesh   20
     Melting: the entrails dissolved in gray smoke;
     The bare bone burst from the welter. And no blaze!

     This was a sign from heaven. My boy described it,
     Seeing for me as I see for others.

     I tell you, Creon, you yourself have brought
     This new calamity upon us. Our hearths and altars
     Are stained with the corruption of dogs and carrion birds
     That glut themselves on the corpse of Oedipus' son.
     The gods are deaf when we pray to them, their fire
     Recoils from our offering, their birds of omen   30
     Have no cry of comfort, for they are gorged
     With the thick blood of the dead.
                             O my son,
     These are no trifles! Think: all men make mistakes,
     But a good man yields when he knows his course is wrong,
     And repairs the evil. The only crime is pride.

     Give in to the dead man, then: do not fight with a corpse —
     What glory is it to kill a man who is dead?
     Think, I beg you:
     It is for your own good that I speak as I do.
     You should be able to yield for your own good.   40
Creon.   It seems that prophets have made me their especial province.
     All my life long
     I have been a kind of butt for the dull arrows
     Of doddering fortune-tellers!
                        No, Teiresias:
     If your birds — if the great eagles of God himself
     Should carry him stinking bit by bit to heaven,
     I would not yield. I am not afraid of pollution:

---

[15] The god of fire.

No man can defile the gods.
Do what you will,
Go into business, make money, speculate
In India gold or that synthetic gold from Sardis,   50
Get rich otherwise than by my consent to bury him.
Teiresias, it is a sorry thing when a wise man
Sells his wisdom, lets out his words for hire!

Teiresias.   Ah Creon! Is there no man left in the world —
Creon.   To do what? — Come, let's have the aphorism!
Teiresias.   No man who knows that wisdom outweighs any wealth?
Creon.   As surely as bribes are baser than any baseness.
Teiresias.   You are sick, Creon! You are deathly sick!
Creon.   As you say: it is not my place to challenge a prophet.
Teiresias.   Yet you have said my prophecy is for sale.   60
Creon.   The generation of prophets has always loved gold.
Teiresias.   The generation of kings has always loved brass.
Creon.   You forget yourself! You are speaking to your King.
Teiresias.   I know it. You are a king because of me.
Creon.   You have a certain skill; but you have sold out.
Teiresias.   King, you will drive me to words that —
Creon.   Say them, say them!
Only remember: I will not pay you for them.
Teiresias.   No, you will find them too costly.
Creon.   No doubt. Speak:
Whatever you say, you will not change my will.
Teiresias.   Then take this, and take it to heart!   70
The time is not far off when you shall pay back
Corpse for corpse, flesh of your own flesh.
You have thrust the child of this world into living night,
You have kept from the gods below the child that is theirs:
The one in a grave before her death, the other,
Dead, denied the grave. This is your crime:
And the Furies and the dark gods of Hell
Are swift with terrible punishment for you.

Do you want to buy me now, Creon?
Not many days,
And your house will be full of men and women weeping,   80
And curses will be hurled at you from far
Cities grieving for sons unburied, left to rot
Before the walls of Thebes.
These are my arrows, Creon: they are all for you.

(To boy.) But come, child: lead me home.
Let him waste his fine anger upon younger men.

Maybe he will learn at last
To control a wiser tongue in a better head.

(Exit Teiresias.)

Choragos.   The old man has gone, King, but his words
Remain to plague us. I am old, too,   90
But I cannot remember that he was ever false.
Creon.   That is true. . . . It troubles me.
Oh it is hard to give in! but it is worse
To risk everything for stubborn pride.
Choragos.   Creon: take my advice.
Creon.   What shall I do?
Choragos.   Go quickly: free Antigonê from her vault
And build a tomb for the body of Polyneicês.
Creon.   You would have me do this?
Choragos.   Creon, yes!
And it must be done at once: God moves
Swiftly to cancel the folly of stubborn men.   100
Creon.   It is hard to deny the heart! But I
Will do it: I will not fight with destiny.
Choragos.   You must go yourself, you cannot leave it to others.
Creon.   I will go.
                       — Bring axes, servants:
Come with me to the tomb. I buried her, I
Will set her free.
                       Oh quickly!
My mind misgives —
The laws of the gods are mighty, and a man must serve them
To the last days of his life!

(Exit Creon.)

Paean[16]

Choragos.   God of many names   *(Strophe 1)*
Chorus.   O Iacchos[17]
                              son

---

[16] A hymn.   [17] Iacchos is a name for Dionysos. His mother was Sémelê, daughter of Kadmos, the founder of Thebes. His father was Zeus. The Maenads were priestesses of Dionysos who cry "evohé evohé."

of Kadmeian Sémelê
> O born of the Thunder!

Guardian of the West
> Regent

of Eleusis's plain
> O Prince of maenad Thebes

and the Dragon Field by rippling Ismenos:[18]

Choragos. God of many names   *(Antistrophe 1)*
Chorus.   the flame of torches
flares on our hills
> the nymphs of Iacchos

dance at the spring of Castalia:[19]
from the vine-close mountain
> come ah come in ivy:

Evohé evohé! sings through the streets of Thebes   10

Choragos. God of many names   *(Strophe 2)*
Chorus.   Iacchos of Thebes
heavenly Child
> of Sémelê bride of the Thunderer!

The shadow of plague is upon us:
> come

with clement feet
> oh come from Parnasos

down the long slopes
> across the lamenting water

Choragos. Iô Fire! Chorister of the throbbing stars!   *(Antistrophe 2)*
O purest among the voices of the night!
Thou son of God, blaze for us!
Chorus. Come with choric rapture of circling Maenads
Who cry *Iô Iacche!*
> *God of many names!*   20

---

[18] A river of Thebes, sacred to Apollo. Dragon Field refers to the legend that the ancestors of Thebes sprang from the dragon's teeth sown by Kadmos.   [19] A spring on Mt. Parnasos.

Exodos

(Enter Messenger, L.)

Messenger.   Men of the line of Kadmos, you who live
  Near Amphion's[20] citadel:
                    I cannot say
  Of any condition of human life "This is fixed,
  This is clearly good, or bad." Fate raises up,
  And Fate casts down the happy and unhappy alike:
  No man can foretell his Fate.
                    Take the case of Creon:
  Creon was happy once, as I count happiness:
  Victorious in battle, sole governor of the land,
  Fortunate father of children nobly born.
  And now it has all gone from him! Who can say   10
  That a man is still alive when his life's joy fails?
  He is a walking dead man. Grant him rich,
  Let him live like a king in his great house:
  If his pleasure is gone, I would not give
  So much as the shadow of smoke for all he owns.
Choragos.   Your words hint at sorrow: what is your news for us?
Messenger.   They are dead. The living are guilty of their death.
Choragos.   Who is guilty? Who is dead? Speak!
Messenger.   Haimon.
  Haimon is dead; and the hand that killed him
  Is his own hand.   20
Choragos.   His father's? or his own?
Messenger.   His own, driven mad by the murder his father had done.
Choragos.   Teiresias, Teiresias, how clearly you saw it all!
Messenger.   This is my news: you must draw what conclusions you can from it.
Choragos.   But look: Eurydicê, our Queen:
  Has she overheard us?

(Enter Eurydicê from the Palace, C.)

Eurydicê.   I have heard something, friends:
  As I was unlocking the gate of Pallas'[21] shrine,
  For I needed her help today, I heard a voice
  Telling of some new sorrow. And I fainted   30
  There at the temple with all my maidens about me.

---

[20] A child of Zeus and Antiope. He is noted for building the walls of Thebes by charming the stones into place with a lyre.   [21] Pallas Athene, goddess of wisdom.

But speak again: whatever it is, I can bear it:
Grief and I are no strangers.
Messenger.   Dearest lady,
I will tell you plainly all that I have seen.
I shall not try to comfort you: what is the use,
Since comfort could lie only in what is not true?
The truth is always best.
                              I went with Creon
To the outer plain where Polyneicês was lying,
No friend to pity him, his body shredded by dogs.
We made our prayers in that place to Hecatê[22]   40
And Pluto,[23] that they would be merciful. And we bathed
The corpse with holy water, and we brought
Fresh-broken branches to burn what was left of it,
And upon the urn we heaped up a towering barrow
Of the earth of his own land.
                              When we were done, we ran
To the vault where Antigonê lay on her couch of stone.
One of the servants had gone ahead,
And while he was yet far off he heard a voice
Grieving within the chamber, and he came back
And told Creon. And as the King went closer,   50
The air was full of wailing, the words lost,
And he begged us to make all haste. "Am I a prophet?"
He said, weeping, "And must I walk this road,
The saddest of all that I have gone before?
My son's voice calls me on. Oh quickly, quickly!
Look through the crevice there, and tell me
If it is Haimon, or some deception of the gods!"

We obeyed; and in the cavern's farthest corner
We saw her lying:
She had made a noose of her fine linen veil   60
And hanged herself. Haimon lay beside her,
His arms about her waist, lamenting her,
His love lost under ground, crying out
That his father had stolen her away from him.

When Creon saw him the tears rushed to his eyes
And he called to him: "What have you done, child? Speak to me.
What are you thinking that makes your eyes so strange?
O my son, my son, I come to you on my knees!"

---

[22] Hecatê is often identified with Persephone, a goddess of Hades; generally Hecatê is a goddess of sorcery and witchcraft.   [23] King of Hades and brother of Zeus and Poseidon.

But Haimon spat in his face. He said not a word,
Staring —
           And suddenly drew his sword   70
And lunged. Creon shrank back, the blade missed; and the boy,
Desperate against himself, drove it half its length
Into his own side, and fell. And as he died
He gathered Antigonê close in his arms again,
Choking, his blood bright red on her white cheek.
And now he lies dead with the dead, and she is his
At last, his bride in the houses of the dead.

(Exit Eurydicê into the Palace.)

Choragos.   She has left us without a word. What can this mean?
Messenger.   It troubles me, too; yet she knows what is best,
  Her grief is too great for public lamentation,   80
  And doubtless she has gone to her chamber to weep
  For her dead son, leading her maidens in his dirge.
Choragos.   It may be so: but I fear this deep silence.

(Pause.)

Messenger.   I will see what she is doing. I will go in.

(Exit Messenger into the Palace.)
(Enter Creon with attendants, bearing Haimon's body.)

Choragos.   But here is the King himself: oh look at him,
  Bearing his own damnation in his arms.
Creon.   Nothing you say can touch me any more.
  My own blind heart has brought me
  From darkness to final darkness. Here you see
  The father murdering, the murdered son —   90
  And all my civic wisdom!
  Haimon my son, so young to die,
  I was the fool, not you; and you died for me.
Choragos.   That is the truth; but you were late in learning it.
Creon.   This truth is hard to bear. Surely a god
  Has crushed me beneath the hugest weight of heaven,
  And driven me headlong a barbaric way
  To trample out the thing I held most dear.

  The pains that men will take to come to pain!

(Enter Messenger from the Palace.)

Messenger.   The burden you carry in your hands is heavy,   100
  But it is not all: you will find more in your house.
Creon.   What burden worse than this shall I find there?
Messenger.   The Queen is dead.
Creon.   O port of death, deaf world,
  Is there no pity for me? And you, Angel of evil,
  I was dead, and your words are death again.
  Is it true, boy? Can it be true?
  Is my wife dead? Has death bred death?
Messenger.   You can see for yourself.

(The doors are opened, and the body of Eurydicê is disclosed within.)

Creon.   Oh pity!   110
  All true, all true, and more than I can bear!
  O my wife, my son!
Messenger.   She stood before the altar, and her heart
  Welcomed the knife her own hand guided,
  And a great cry burst from her lips for Megareus[24] dead,
  And for Haimon dead, her sons; and her last breath
  Was a curse for their father, the murderer of her sons,
  And she fell, and the dark flowed in through her closing eyes.
Creon.   O God, I am sick with fear.
  Are there no swords here? Has no one a blow for me?   120
Messenger.   Her curse is upon you for the deaths of both.
Creon.   It is right that it should be. I alone am guilty.
  I know it, and I say it. Lead me in,
  Quickly, friends.
  I have neither life nor substance. Lead me in.
Choragos.   You are right, if there can be right in so much wrong.
  The briefest way is best in a world of sorrow.
Creon.   Let it come,
  Let death come quickly, and be kind to me.
  I would not ever see the sun again.   130
Choragos.   All that will come when it will; but we, meanwhile,
  Have much to do. Leave the future to itself.
Creon.   All my heart was in that prayer!
Choragos.   Then do not pray any more: the sky is deaf.
Creon.   Lead me away. I have been rash and foolish.
  I have killed my son and my wife.
  I look for comfort; my comfort lies here dead.
  Whatever my hands have touched has come to nothing.
  Fate has brought all my pride to a thought of dust.

[24] Son of Creon who was killed in the attack on Thebes.

(As Creon is being led into the house, the Choragos advances and speaks directly to the audience.)

Choragos.   There is no happiness where there is no wisdom;   140
No wisdom but in submission to the gods.
Big words are always punished,
And proud men in old age learn to be wise.

For Analysis

1. Critics have divided over the question of whether Antigonê or Creon is the **protagonist** of the play. How does the answer to this question affect one's interpretation of the play?

2. Show how the Prologue establishes the **mood** and **theme** of the play. What does it reveal about the characters of the two sisters?

3. What evidence is there that Creon would treat Antigonê differently if she were a man?

4. Does the character of Antigonê change in the course of the play?

5. Does the action of the play prepare us for Creon's sudden realization that he has been wrong?

6. Is there any justification for Antigonê's cold refusal to allow Ismenê to share her martyrdom?

7. Speculate on why Sophocles never brings Haimon and Antigonê together.

On Style

1. How does the chorus contribute to the dramatic development and tension of the play?

2. Analyze the use of **dramatic irony** in the play.

Making Connections

What arguments used by Martin Luther King Jr. in "Letter from Birmingham Jail" (p. 634) echo Antigonê's arguments and actions?

Writing Topics

1. In a brief paragraph, summarize the **theme** of this play.

2. Write a one-page essay using this play and Susan Glaspell's *Trifles* (p. 1236) as the basis for defining poetic drama on the one hand and realistic drama on the other.

Henrik Ibsen (1828–1906)

A Doll's House[1] 1879

CHARACTERS

Torvald Helmer, a lawyer
Nora, his wife
Dr. Rank
Mrs. Linde
Krogstad

The Helmers' three small
 children
Anne, the children's nurse
A Maid
A Porter

Act I

Scene *A room furnished comfortably and tastefully, but not extravagantly. At the back, a door to the right leads to the entrance hall, another to the left leads to Helmer's study. Between the doors stands a piano. In the middle of the left-hand wall is a door, and beyond it a window. Near the window are a round table, armchairs and a small sofa. In the right-hand wall, at the farther end, another door; and on the same side, nearer the footlights, a stove, two easy chairs and a rocking-chair; between the stove and the door, a small table. Engravings on the walls; a cabinet with china and other small objects; a small book-case with well-bound books. The floors are carpeted, and a fire burns in the stove. It is winter.*

A bell rings in the hall; shortly afterwards the door is heard to open. Enter Nora, humming a tune and in high spirits. She is in out-door dress and carries a number of parcels; these she lays on the table to the right. She leaves the outer door open after her, and through it is seen a Porter who is carrying a Christmas tree and a basket, which he gives to the Maid who has opened the door.

Nora. Hide the Christmas tree carefully, Helen. Be sure the children do not see it till this evening, when it is dressed. *(To the Porter, taking out her purse.)* How much?
Porter. Sixpence.
Nora. There is a shilling. No, keep the change. *(The Porter thanks her, and goes out. Nora shuts the door. She is laughing to herself, as she takes off her hat and coat. She takes a packet of macaroons from her pocket and eats one or two; then goes cautiously to her husband's door and listens.)* Yes, he is in.

(Still humming, she goes to the table on the right.)

[1] Translated by R. Farquharson Sharp.

Helmer *(calls out from his room).*   Is that my little lark twittering out there?

Nora *(busy opening some of the parcels).*   Yes, it is!

Helmer.   Is it my little squirrel bustling about?

Nora.   Yes!

Helmer.   When did my squirrel come home?

Nora.   Just now. *(Puts the bag of macaroons into her pocket and wipes her mouth.)* Come in here, Torvald, and see what I have bought.

Helmer.   Don't disturb me. *(A little later, he opens the door and looks into the room, pen in hand.)* Bought, did you say? All these things? Has my little spendthrift been wasting money again?

Nora.   Yes, but, Torvald, this year we really can let ourselves go a little. This is the first Christmas that we have not needed to economise.

Helmer.   Still, you know, we can't spend money recklessly.

Nora.   Yes, Torvald, we may be a wee bit more reckless now, mayn't we? Just a tiny wee bit! You are going to have a big salary and earn lots and lots of money.

Helmer.   Yes, after the New Year; but then it will be a whole quarter before the salary is due.

Nora.   Pooh! we can borrow till then.

Helmer.   Nora! *(Goes up to her and takes her playfully by the ear.)* The same little featherhead! Suppose, now, that I borrowed fifty pounds to-day, and you spent it all in the Christmas week, and then on New Year's Eve a slate fell on my head and killed me, and ——

Nora *(putting her hands over his mouth).*   Oh! don't say such horrid things.

Helmer.   Still, suppose that happened, — what then?

Nora.   If that were to happen, I don't suppose I should care whether I owed money or not.

Helmer.   Yes, but what about the people who had lent it?

Nora.   They? Who would bother about them? I should not know who they were.

Helmer.   That is like a woman! But seriously, Nora, you know what I think about that. No debt, no borrowing. There can be no freedom or beauty about a home life that depends on borrowing and debt. We two have kept bravely on the straight road so far, and we will go on the same way for the short time longer that there need be any struggle.

Nora *(moving towards the stove).*   As you please, Torvald.

Helmer *(following her).*   Come, come, my little skylark must not droop her wings. What is this! Is my little squirrel out of temper? *(Taking out his purse.)* Nora, what do you think I have got here?

Nora *(turning round quickly).*   Money!

Helmer.   There you are. *(Gives her some money.)* Do you think I don't know what a lot is wanted for house-keeping at Christmas-time?

Nora *(counting).*   Ten shillings — a pound — two pounds! Thank you, thank you, Torvald; that will keep me going for a long time.

Helmer.   Indeed it must.

Nora. Yes, yes, it will. But come here and let me show you what I have bought. And all so cheap! Look, here is a new suit for Ivar, and a sword; and a horse and a trumpet for Bob; and a doll and dolly's bedstead for Emmy, — they are very plain, but anyway she will soon break them in pieces. And here are dress-lengths and handkerchiefs for the maids; old Anne ought really to have something better.

Helmer. And what is in this parcel?

Nora *(crying out).* No, no! you mustn't see that till this evening.

Helmer. Very well. But now tell me something reasonable that you would particularly like to have.

Nora. No, I really can't think of anything — unless, Torvald ——

Helmer. Well?

Nora *(playing with his coat buttons, and without raising her eyes to his).* If you really want to give me something, you might — you might ——

Helmer. Well, out with it!

Nora *(speaking quickly).* You might give me money, Torvald. Only just as much as you can afford; and then one of these days I will buy something with it.

Helmer. But, Nora ——

Nora. Oh, do! dear Torvald; please, please do! Then I will wrap it up in beautiful gilt paper and hang it on the Christmas tree. Wouldn't that be fun?

Helmer. What are little people called that are always wasting money?

Nora. Spendthrifts — I know. Let us do as you suggest, Torvald, and then I shall have time to think what I am most in want of. That is a very sensible plan, isn't it?

Helmer *(smiling).* Indeed it is — that is to say, if you were really to save out of the money I give you, and then really buy something for yourself. But if you spend it all on the housekeeping and any number of unnecessary things, then I merely have to pay up again.

Nora. Oh but, Torvald ——

Helmer. You can't deny it, my dear little Nora. *(Puts his arm round her waist.)* It's a sweet little spendthrift, but she uses up a deal of money. One would hardly believe how expensive such little persons are!

Nora. It's a shame to say that. I do really save all I can.

Helmer *(laughing).* That's very true, — all you can. But you can't save anything!

Nora *(smiling quietly and happily).* You haven't any idea how many expenses we skylarks and squirrels have, Torvald.

Helmer. You are an odd little soul. Very like your father. You always find some new way of wheedling money out of me, and, as soon as you have got it, it seems to melt in your hands. You never know where it has gone. Still, one must take you as you are. It is in the blood; for indeed it is true that you can inherit these things, Nora.

Nora. Ah, I wish I had inherited many of papa's qualities.

Helmer. And I would not wish you to be anything but just what you are, my sweet little skylark. But, do you know, it strikes me that you are looking rather — what shall I say — rather uneasy to-day?

Nora. Do I?

Helmer. You do, really. Look straight at me.

Nora *(looks at him)*. Well?

Helmer *(wagging his finger at her)*. Hasn't Miss Sweet-Tooth been breaking rules in town to-day?

Nora. No; what makes you think that?

Helmer. Hasn't she paid a visit to the confectioner's?

Nora. No, I assure you, Torvald ——

Helmer. Not been nibbling sweets?

Nora. No, certainly not.

Helmer. Not even taken a bite at a macaroon or two?

Nora. No, Torvald, I assure you really ——

Helmer. There, there, of course I was only joking.

Nora *(going to the table on the right)*. I should not think of going against your wishes.

Helmer. No, I am sure of that! Besides, you gave me your word —— *(Going up to her.)* Keep your little Christmas secrets to yourself, my darling. They will all be revealed to-night when the Christmas tree is lit, no doubt.

Nora. Did you remember to invite Doctor Rank?

Helmer. No. But there is no need; as a matter of course he will come to dinner with us. However, I will ask him, when he comes in this morning. I have ordered some good wine. Nora, you can't think how I am looking forward to this evening.

Nora. So am I! And how the children will enjoy themselves, Torvald!

Helmer. It is splendid to feel that one has a perfectly safe appointment, and a big enough income. It's delightful to think of, isn't it?

Nora. It's wonderful!

Helmer. Do you remember last Christmas? For a full three weeks beforehand you shut yourself up every evening till long after midnight, making ornaments for the Christmas tree and all the other fine things that were to be a surprise to us. It was the dullest three weeks I ever spent!

Nora. I didn't find it dull.

Helmer *(smiling)*. But there was precious little result, Nora.

Nora. Oh, you shouldn't tease me about that again. How could I help the cat's going in and tearing everything to pieces?

Helmer. Of course you couldn't, poor little girl. You had the best of intentions to please us all, and that's the main thing. But it is a good thing that our hard times are over.

Nora. Yes, it is really wonderful.

Helmer. This time I needn't sit here and be dull all alone, and you needn't ruin your dear eyes and your pretty little hands ——

Nora (*clapping her hands*).   No, Torvald, I needn't any longer, need I! It's wonderfully lovely to hear you say so! (*Taking his arm.*) Now I will tell you how I have been thinking we ought to arrange things, Torvald. As soon as Christmas is over —— (*A bell rings in the hall.*) There's the bell. (*She tidies the room a little.*) There's someone at the door. What a nuisance!

Helmer.   If it is a caller, remember I am not at home.

Maid (*in the doorway*).   A lady to see you, ma'am, — a stranger.

Nora.   Ask her to come in.

Maid (*to Helmer*).   The doctor came at the same time, sir.

Helmer.   Did he go straight into my room?

Maid.   Yes, sir.

(*Helmer goes into his room. The Maid ushers in Mrs. Linde, who is in traveling dress, and shuts the door.*)

Mrs. Linde (*in a dejected and timid voice*).   How do you do, Nora?

Nora (*doubtfully*).   How do you do ——

Mrs. Linde.   You don't recognise me, I suppose.

Nora.   No, I don't know — yes, to be sure, I seem to —— (*Suddenly.*) Yes! Christine! Is it really you?

Mrs. Linde.   Yes, it is I.

Nora.   Christine! To think of my not recognising you! And yet how could I —— (*In a gentle voice.*) How you have altered, Christine!

Mrs. Linde.   Yes, I have indeed. In nine, ten long years ——

Nora.   Is it so long since we met? I suppose it is. The last eight years have been a happy time for me, I can tell you. And so now you have come into the town, and have taken this long journey in winter — that was plucky of you.

Mrs. Linde.   I arrived by steamer this morning.

Nora.   To have some fun at Christmas-time, of course. How delightful! We will have such fun together! But take off your things. You are not cold, I hope. (*Helps her.*) Now we will sit down by the stove, and be cosy. No, take this arm-chair; I will sit here in the rocking-chair. (*Takes her hands.*) Now you look like your old self again; it was only the first moment —— You are a little paler, Christine, and perhaps a little thinner.

Mrs. Linde.   And much, much older, Nora.

Nora.   Perhaps a little older; very, very little; certainly not much. (*Stops suddenly and speaks seriously.*) What a thoughtless creature I am, chattering away like this. My poor, dear Christine, do forgive me.

Mrs. Linde.   What do you mean, Nora?

Nora (*gently*).   Poor Christine, you are a widow.

Mrs. Linde.   Yes; it is three years ago now.

Nora.   Yes, I knew; I saw it in the papers. I assure you, Christine, I meant ever so often to write to you at the time, but I always put it off and something always prevented me.

Mrs. Linde. I quite understand, dear.

Nora. It was very bad of me, Christine. Poor thing, how you must have suffered. And he left you nothing?

Mrs. Linde. No.

Nora. And no children?

Mrs. Linde. No.

Nora. Nothing at all, then?

Mrs. Linde. Not even any sorrow or grief to live upon.

Nora (*looking incredulously at her*). But, Christine, is that possible?

Mrs. Linde (*smiles sadly and strokes her hair*). It sometimes happens, Nora.

Nora. So you are quite alone. How dreadfully sad that must be. I have three lovely children. You can't see them just now, for they are out with their nurse. But now you must tell me all about it.

Mrs. Linde. No, no; I want to hear you.

Nora. No, you must begin. I mustn't be selfish to-day, to-day I must only think of your affairs. But there is one thing I must tell you. Do you know we have just had a great piece of good luck?

Mrs. Linde. No, what is it?

Nora. Just fancy, my husband has been made manager of the Bank!

Mrs. Linde. Your husband? What good luck!

Nora. Yes, tremendous! A barrister's profession is such an uncertain thing, especially if he won't undertake unsavoury cases; and naturally Torvald has never been willing to do that, and I quite agree with him. You may imagine how pleased we are! He is to take up his work in the Bank at the New Year, and then he will have a big salary and lots of commissions. For the future we can live quite differently — we can do just as we like. I feel so relieved and so happy, Christine! It will be splendid to have heaps of money and not need to have any anxiety, won't it?

Mrs. Linde. Yes, anyhow I think it would be delightful to have what one needs.

Nora. No, not only what one needs, but heaps and heaps of money.

Mrs. Linde (*smiling*). Nora, Nora, haven't you learnt sense yet? In our schooldays you were a great spendthrift.

Nora (*laughing*). Yes, that is what Torvald says now. (*Wags her finger at her.*) But "Nora, Nora" is not so silly as you think. We have not been in a position for me to waste money. We have both had to work.

Mrs. Linde. You too?

Nora. Yes; odds and ends, needlework, crochet-work, embroidery, and that kind of thing. (*Dropping her voice.*) And other things as well. You know Torvald left his office when we were married? There was no prospect of promotion there, and he had to try and earn more than before. But during the first year he overworked himself dreadfully. You see, he had to make money every way he could, and he worked early and late; but he couldn't stand it, and fell dreadfully ill, and the doctors said it was necessary for him to go south.

Mrs. Linde. You spent a whole year in Italy, didn't you?

Nora. Yes. It was no easy matter to get away, I can tell you. It was just after Ivar was born; but naturally we had to go. It was a wonderfully beautiful journey, and it saved Torvald's life. But it cost a tremendous lot of money, Christine.

Mrs. Linde. So I should think.

Nora. It cost about two hundred and fifty pounds. That's a lot, isn't it?

Mrs. Linde. Yes, and in emergencies like that it is lucky to have the money.

Nora. I ought to tell you that we had it from papa.

Mrs. Linde. Oh, I see. It was just about that time that he died, wasn't it?

Nora. Yes; and, just think of it, I couldn't go and nurse him. I was expecting little Ivar's birth every day and I had my poor sick Torvald to look after. My dear, kind father — I never saw him again, Christine. That was the saddest time I have known since our marriage.

Mrs. Linde. And your husband came back quite well?

Nora. As sound as a bell!

Mrs. Linde. But — the doctor?

Nora. What doctor?

Mrs. Linde. I thought your maid said the gentleman who arrived here just as I did was the doctor?

Nora. Yes, that was Doctor Rank, but he doesn't come here professionally. He is our greatest friend, and comes in at least once every day. No, Torvald has not had an hour's illness since then, and our children are strong and healthy and so am I. (*Jumps up and claps her hands.*) Christine! Christine! it's good to be alive and happy! —— But how horrid of me; I am talking of nothing but my own affairs. (*Sits on a stool near her, and rests her arms on her knees.*) You mustn't be angry with me. Tell me, is it really true that you did not love your husband? Why did you marry him?

Mrs. Linde. My mother was alive then, and was bedridden and helpless, and I had to provide for my two younger brothers; so I did not think I was justified in refusing his offer.

Nora. No, perhaps you were quite right. He was rich at that time, then?

Mrs. Linde. I believe he was quite well off. But his business was a precarious one; and, when he died, it all went to pieces and there was nothing left.

Nora. And then? ——

Mrs. Linde. Well, I had to turn my hand to anything I could find — first a small shop, then a small school, and so on. The last three years have seemed like one long working-day, with no rest. Now it is at an end, Nora. My poor mother needs me no more, for she is gone; and the boys do not need me either; they have got situations and can shift for themselves.

Nora. What a relief you must feel it ——

Mrs. Linde. No, indeed; I only feel my life unspeakably empty. No one to live for any more. (*Gets up restlessly.*) That was why I could not stand the life in my little backwater any longer. I hope it may be easier here to find something which will busy me and occupy my thoughts. If only I could have the good luck to get some regular work — office work of some kind ——

Nora. But, Christine, that is so frightfully tiring, and you look tired out now. You had far better go away to some watering-place.

Mrs. Linde *(walking to the window).* I have no father to give me money for a journey, Nora.

Nora *(rising).* Oh, don't be angry with me.

Mrs. Linde *(going up to her).* It is you that must not be angry with me, dear. The worst of a position like mine is that it makes one so bitter. No one to work for, and yet obliged to be always on the look-out for chances. One must live, and so one becomes selfish. When you told me of the happy turn your fortunes have taken — you will hardly believe it — I was delighted not so much on your account as on my own.

Nora. How do you mean? — Oh, I understand. You mean that perhaps Torvald could get you something to do.

Mrs. Linde. Yes, that was what I was thinking of.

Nora. He must, Christine. Just leave it to me; I will broach the subject very cleverly — I will think of something that will please him very much. It will make me so happy to be of some use to you.

Mrs. Linde. How kind you are, Nora, to be so anxious to help me! It is doubly kind in you, for you know so little of the burdens and troubles of life.

Nora. I —— ? I know so little of them?

Mrs. Linde *(smiling).* My dear! Small household cares and that sort of thing! — You are a child, Nora.

Nora *(tosses her head and crosses the stage).* You ought not to be so superior.

Mrs. Linde. No?

Nora. You are just like the others. They all think that I am incapable of anything really serious ——

Mrs. Linde. Come, come ——

Nora. — that I have gone through nothing in this world of cares.

Mrs. Linde. But, my dear Nora, you have just told me all your troubles.

Nora. Pooh! — those were trifles. *(Lowering her voice.)* I have not told you the important thing.

Mrs. Linde. The important thing? What do you mean?

Nora. You look down upon me altogether, Christine — but you ought not to. You are proud, aren't you, of having worked so hard and so long for your mother?

Mrs. Linde. Indeed, I don't look down on any one. But it is true that I am both proud and glad to think that I was privileged to make the end of my mother's life almost free from care.

Nora. And you are proud to think of what you have done for your brothers.

Mrs. Linde. I think I have the right to be.

Nora. I think so, too. But now, listen to this; I too have something to be proud and glad of.

Mrs. Linde. I have no doubt you have. But what do you refer to?

Nora. Speak low. Suppose Torvald were to hear! He mustn't on any account — no one in the world must know, Christine, except you.

Mrs. Linde. But what is it?

Nora. Come here. (*Pulls her down on the sofa beside her.*) Now I will show you that I too have something to be proud and glad of. It was I who saved Torvald's life.

Mrs. Linde. "Saved"? How?

Nora. I told you about our trip to Italy. Torvald would never have recovered if he had not gone there ——

Mrs. Linde. Yes, but your father gave you the necessary funds.

Nora (*smiling*). Yes, that is what Torvald and all the others think, but ——

Mrs. Linde. But ——

Nora. Papa didn't give us a shilling. It was I who procured the money.

Mrs. Linde. You? All that large sum?

Nora. Two hundred and fifty pounds. What do you think of that?

Mrs. Linde. But, Nora, how could you possibly do it? Did you win a prize in the Lottery?

Nora (*contemptuously*). In the Lottery? There would have been no credit in that.

Mrs. Linde. But where did you get it from, then?

Nora (*humming and smiling with an air of mystery*). Hm, hm! Aha!

Mrs. Linde. Because you couldn't have borrowed it.

Nora. Couldn't I? Why not?

Mrs. Linde. No, a wife cannot borrow without her husband's consent.

Nora (*tossing her head*). Oh, if it is a wife who has any head for business — a wife who has the wit to be a little bit clever ——

Mrs. Linde. I don't understand it at all, Nora.

Nora. There is no need you should. I never said I had borrowed the money. I may have got it some other way. (*Lies back on the sofa.*) Perhaps I got it from some other admirer. When anyone is as attractive as I am ——

Mrs. Linde. You are a mad creature.

Nora. Now, you know you're full of curiosity, Christine.

Mrs. Linde. Listen to me, Nora dear. Haven't you been a little bit imprudent?

Nora (*sits up straight*). Is it imprudent to save your husband's life?

Mrs. Linde. It seems to me imprudent, without his knowledge, to ——

Nora. But it was absolutely necessary that he should not know! My goodness, can't you understand that? It was necessary he should have no idea what a dangerous condition he was in. It was to me that the doctors came and said that his life was in danger, and that the only thing to save him was to live in the south. Do you suppose I didn't try, first of all, to get what I wanted as if it were for myself? I told him how much I should love to travel abroad like other young wives; I tried tears and entreaties with him; I told him that he ought to remember the condition I was in, and that he ought to be kind and indulgent to me; I even hinted that he might raise a loan. That nearly made him angry, Christine. He said I was thoughtless, and that it was his duty as my husband not to indulge me in my whims and caprices — as I believe he called them.

Very well I thought, you must be saved — and that was how I came to devise a way out of the difficulty ——

Mrs. Linde. And did your husband never get to know from your father that the money had not come from him?

Nora. No, never. Papa died just at that time. I had meant to let him into the secret and beg him never to reveal it. But he was so ill then — alas, there never was any need to tell him.

Mrs. Linde. And since then have you never told your secret to your husband?

Nora. Good Heavens, no! How could you think so? A man who has such strong opinions about these things! And besides, how painful and humiliating it would be for Torvald, with his manly independence, to know that he owed me anything! It would upset our mutual relations altogether; our beautiful happy home would no longer be what it is now.

Mrs. Linde. Do you mean never to tell him about it?

Nora (*meditatively, and with a half smile*). Yes — some day, perhaps, after many years, when I am no longer as nice-looking as I am now. Don't laugh at me! I mean, of course, when Torvald is no longer as devoted to me as he is now; when my dancing and dressing-up and reciting have palled on him; then it may be a good thing to have something in reserve —— (*Breaking off.*) What nonsense! That time will never come. Now, what do you think of my great secret, Christine? Do you still think I am of no use? I can tell you, too, that this affair has caused me a lot of worry. It has been by no means easy for me to meet my engagements punctually. I may tell you that there is something that is called, in business, quarterly interest, and another thing called payment in instalments, and it is always so dreadfully difficult to manage them. I have had to save a little here and there, where I could, you understand. I have not been able to put aside much from my housekeeping money, for Torvald must have a good table. I couldn't let my children be shabbily dressed; I have felt obliged to use up all he gave me for them, the sweet little darlings!

Mrs. Linde. So it has all had to come out of your own necessaries of life, poor Nora?

Nora. Of course. Besides, I was the one responsible for it. Whenever Torvald has given me money for new dresses and such things, I have never spent more than half of it; I have always bought the simplest and cheapest things. Thank Heaven, any clothes look well on me, and so Torvald has never noticed it. But it was often very hard on me, Christine — because it is delightful to be really well dressed, isn't it?

Mrs. Linde. Quite so.

Nora. Well, then I have found other ways of earning money. Last winter I was lucky enough to get a lot of copying to do; so I locked myself up and sat writing every evening until quite late at night. Many a time I was desperately tired; but all the same it was a tremendous pleasure to sit there working and earning money. It was like being a man.

Mrs. Linde. How much have you been able to pay off in that way?

Nora. I can't tell you exactly. You see, it is very difficult to keep an account of a business matter of that kind. I only know that I have paid every penny that I could scrape together. Many a time I was at my wits' end. (*Smiles.*) Then I used to sit here and imagine that a rich old gentleman had fallen in love with me ——

Mrs. Linde. What! Who was it?

Nora. Be quiet! — that he had died; and that when his will was opened it contained, written in big letters, the instruction: "The lovely Mrs. Nora Helmer is to have all I possess paid over to her at once in cash."

Mrs. Linde. But, my dear Nora — who could the man be?

Nora. Good gracious, can't you understand? There was no old gentleman at all; it was only something that I used to sit here and imagine, when I couldn't think of any way of procuring money. But it's all the same now; the tiresome old person can stay where he is, as far as I am concerned; I don't care about him or his will either, for I am free from care now. (*Jumps up.*) My goodness, it's delightful to think of, Christine! Free from care! To be able to be free from care, quite free from care; to be able to play and romp with the children; to be able to keep the house beautifully and have everything just as Torvald likes it! And, think of it, soon the spring will come and the big blue sky! Perhaps we shall be able to take a little trip — perhaps I shall see the sea again! Oh, it's a wonderful thing to be alive and be happy. (*A bell is heard in the hall.*)

Mrs. Linde (*rising*). There is the bell; perhaps I had better go.

Nora. No, don't go; no one will come in here; it is sure to be for Torvald.

Servant (*at the hall door*). Excuse me, ma'am — there is a gentleman to see the master, and as the doctor is with him ——

Nora. Who is it?

Krogstad (*at the door*). It is I, Mrs. Helmer. (*Mrs. Linde starts, trembles, and turns to the window.*)

Nora (*takes a step towards him, and speaks in a strained, low voice*). You? What is it? What do you want to see my husband about?

Krogstad. Bank business — in a way. I have a small post in the Bank, and I hear your husband is to be our chief now ——

Nora. Then it is ——

Krogstad. Nothing but dry business matters, Mrs. Helmer; absolutely nothing else.

Nora. Be so good as to go into the study, then. (*She bows indifferently to him and shuts the door into the hall; then comes back and makes up the fire in the stove.*)

Mrs. Linde. Nora — who was that man?

Nora. A lawyer, of the name of Krogstad.

Mrs. Linde. Then it really was he.

Nora. Do you know the man?

Mrs. Linde. I used to — many years ago. At one time he was a solicitor's clerk in our town.

Nora. Yes, he was.

Mrs. Linde. He is greatly altered.

Nora. He made a very unhappy marriage.

Mrs. Linde. He is a widower now, isn't he?

Nora. With several children. There now, it is burning up.

(Shuts the door of the stove and moves the rocking-chair aside.)

Mrs. Linde. They say he carries on various kinds of business.

Nora. Really! Perhaps he does; I don't know anything about it. But don't let us think of business; it is so tiresome.

Doctor Rank *(comes out of Helmer's study. Before he shuts the door he calls to him).* No, my dear fellow, I won't disturb you; I would rather go into your wife for a little while. *(Shuts the door and sees Mrs. Linde.)* I beg your pardon; I am afraid I am disturbing you too.

Nora. No, not at all. *(Introducing him.)* Doctor Rank, Mrs. Linde.

Rank. I have often heard Mrs. Linde's name mentioned here. I think I passed you on the stairs when I arrived, Mrs. Linde?

Mrs. Linde. Yes, I go up very slowly; I can't manage stairs well.

Rank. Ah! some slight internal weakness?

Mrs. Linde. No, the fact is I have been overworking myself.

Rank. Nothing more than that? Then I suppose you have come to town to amuse yourself with our entertainments?

Mrs. Linde. I have come to look for work.

Rank. Is that a good cure for overwork?

Mrs. Linde. One must live, Doctor Rank.

Rank. Yes, the general opinion seems to be that it is necessary.

Nora. Look here, Doctor Rank — you know you want to live.

Rank. Certainly. However wretched I may feel, I want to prolong the agony as long as possible. All my patients are like that. And so are those who are morally diseased; one of them, and a bad case too, is at this very moment with Helmer ——

Mrs. Linde *(sadly).* Ah!

Nora. Whom do you mean?

Rank. A lawyer of the name of Krogstad, a fellow you don't know at all. He suffers from a diseased moral character, Mrs. Helmer; but even he began talking of its being highly important that he should live.

Nora. Did he? What did he want to speak to Torvald about?

Rank. I have no idea; I only heard that it was something about the Bank.

Nora. I didn't know this — what's his name — Krogstad had anything to do with the Bank.

Rank. Yes, he has some sort of appointment there. *(To Mrs. Linde.)* I don't know whether you find also in your part of the world that there are certain people who go zealously snuffing about to smell out moral corruption, and, as soon as they have found some, put the person concerned into some lucrative position where they can keep their eye on him. Healthy natures are left out in the cold.

Mrs. Linde. Still I think the sick are those who most need taking care of.

Rank (*shrugging his shoulders*). Yes, there you are. That is the sentiment that is turning Society into a sickhouse.

(*Nora, who has been absorbed in her thoughts, breaks out into smothered laughter and claps her hands.*)

Rank. Why do you laugh at that? Have you any notion what Society really is?

Nora. What do I care about tiresome Society? I am laughing at something quite different, something extremely amusing. Tell me, Doctor Rank, are all the people who are employed in the Bank dependent on Torvald now?

Rank. Is that what you find so extremely amusing?

Nora (*smiling and humming*). That's my affair! (*Walking about the room.*) It's perfectly glorious to think that we have — that Torvald has so much power over so many people. (*Takes the packet from her pocket.*) Doctor Rank, what do you say to a macaroon?

Rank. What, macaroons? I thought they were forbidden here.

Nora. Yes, but these are some Christine gave me.

Mrs. Linde. What! I? —

Nora. Oh, well, don't be alarmed! You couldn't know that Torvald had forbidden them. I must tell you that he is afraid they will spoil my teeth. But, bah! — once in a way —— That's so, isn't it, Doctor Rank? By your leave? (*Puts a macaroon into his mouth.*) You must have one too, Christine. And I shall have one, just a little one — or at most two. (*Walking about.*) I am tremendously happy. There is just one thing in the world now that I should dearly love to do.

Rank. Well, what is that?

Nora. It's something I should dearly love to say, if Torvald could hear me.

Rank. Well, why can't you say it?

Nora. No, I daren't; it's so shocking.

Mrs. Linde. Shocking?

Rank. Well, I should not advise you to say it. Still, with us you might. What is it you would so much like to say if Torvald could hear you?

Nora. I should just love to say — Well, I'm damned!

Rank. Are you mad?

Mrs. Linde. Nora, dear —— !

Rank. Say it, here he is!

Nora (*hiding the packet*). Hush! Hush! Hush!

(*Helmer comes out of his room, with his coat over his arm and his hat in his hand.*)

Nora. Well, Torvald dear, have you got rid of him?

Helmer. Yes, he has just gone.

Nora. Let me introduce you — this is Christine, who has come to town.

Helmer. Christine —— ? Excuse me, but I don't know ——

Nora. Mrs. Linde, dear; Christine Linde.

Helmer. Of course. A school friend of my wife's, I presume?

Mrs. Linde. Yes, we have known each other since then.

Nora. And just think, she has taken a long journey in order to see you.

Helmer. What do you mean?

Mrs. Linde. No, really, I ——

Nora. Christine is tremendously clever at book-keeping, and she is frightfully anxious to work under some clever man, so as to perfect herself ——

Helmer. Very sensible, Mrs. Linde.

Nora. And when she heard you had been appointed manager of the Bank — the news was telegraphed, you know — she travelled here as quick as she could, Torvald, I am sure you will be able to do something for Christine, for my sake, won't you?

Helmer. Well, it is not altogether impossible. I presume you are a widow, Mrs. Linde?

Mrs. Linde. Yes.

Helmer. And have had some experience of book-keeping?

Mrs. Linde. Yes, a fair amount.

Helmer. Ah! well, it's very likely I may be able to find something for you ——

Nora (*clapping her hands*). What did I tell you? What did I tell you?

Helmer. You have just come at a fortunate moment, Mrs. Linde.

Mrs. Linde. How am I to thank you?

Helmer. There is no need. (*Puts on his coat.*) But to-day you must excuse me ——

Rank. Wait a minute; I will come with you.

(*Brings his fur coat from the hall and warms it at the fire.*)

Nora. Don't be long away, Torvald dear.

Helmer. About an hour, not more.

Nora. Are you going too, Christine?

Mrs. Linde (*putting on her cloak*). Yes, I must go and look for a room.

Helmer. Oh, well then, we can walk down the street together.

Nora (*helping her*). What a pity it is we are so short of space here; I am afraid it is impossible for us ——

Mrs. Linde. Please don't think of it! Good-bye, Nora dear, and many thanks.

Nora. Good-bye for the present. Of course you will come back this evening. And you too, Dr. Rank. What do you say? If you are well enough? Oh, you must be! Wrap yourself up well.

(They go to the door all talking together. Children's voices are heard on the staircase.)

Nora.   There they are. There they are! *(She runs to open the door. The Nurse comes in with the children.)* Come in! Come in! *(Stoops and kisses them.)* Oh, you sweet blessings! Look at them, Christine! Aren't they darlings?

Rank.   Don't let us stand here in the draught.

Helmer.   Come along, Mrs. Linde; the place will only be bearable for a mother now!

(Rank, Helmer and Mrs. Linde go downstairs. The Nurse comes forward with the children; Nora shuts the hall door.)

Nora.   How fresh and well you look! Such red cheeks! — like apples and roses. *(The children all talk at once while she speaks to them.)* Have you had great fun? That's splendid! What, you pulled both Emmy and Bob along on the sledge? — both at once? — that *was* good. You are a clever boy, Ivar. Let me take her for a little, Anne. My sweet little baby doll! *(Takes the baby from the Maid and dances it up and down.)* Yes, yes, mother will dance with Bob too. What! Have you been snowballing? I wish I had been there too! No, no, I will take their things off, Anne; please let me do it, it is such fun. Go in now, you look half frozen. There is some hot coffee for you on the stove.

(The Nurse goes into the room on the left. Nora takes off the children's things and throws them about, while they all talk to her at once.)

Nora.   Really! Did a big dog run after you? But it didn't bite you? No, dogs don't bite nice little dolly children. You mustn't look at the parcels, Ivar. What are they? Ah, I daresay you would like to know. No, no — it's something nasty! Come, let us have a game! What shall we play at? Hide and Seek? Yes, we'll play Hide and Seek. Bob shall hide first. Must I hide? Very well, I'll hide first.

(She and the children laugh and shout, and romp in and out of the room; at last Nora hides under the table, the children rush in and look for her, but do not see her; they hear her smothered laughter, run to the table, lift up the cloth and find her. Shouts of laughter. She crawls forward and pretends to frighten them. Fresh laughter. Meanwhile there has been a knock at the hall door, but none of them has noticed it. The door is half opened, and Krogstad appears. He waits a little; the game goes on.)

Krogstad.   Excuse me, Mrs. Helmer.

Nora *(with a stifled cry, turns round and gets up on to her knees).*   Ah! what do you want?

Krogstad. Excuse me, the outer door was ajar; I suppose someone forgot to shut it.

Nora *(rising).* My husband is out, Mr. Krogstad.

Krogstad. I know that.

Nora. What do you want here, then?

Krogstad. A word with you.

Nora. With me? — *(to the children, gently.)* Go in to nurse. What? No, the strange man won't do mother any harm. When he has gone we will have another game. *(She takes the children into the room on the left, and shuts the door after them.)* You want to speak to me?

Krogstad. Yes, I do.

Nora. To-day? It is not the first of the month yet.

Krogstad. No, it is Christmas Eve, and it will depend on yourself what sort of a Christmas you will spend.

Nora. What do you want? To-day it is absolutely impossible for me ——

Krogstad. We won't talk about that till later on. This is something different. I presume you can give me a moment?

Nora. Yes — yes, I can — although ——

Krogstad. Good. I was in Olsen's Restaurant and saw your husband going down the street ——

Nora. Yes?

Krogstad. With a lady.

Nora. What then?

Krogstad. May I make so bold as to ask if it was a Mrs. Linde?

Nora. It was.

Krogstad. Just arrived in town?

Nora. Yes, to-day.

Krogstad. She is a great friend of yours, isn't she?

Nora. She is. But I don't see ——

Krogstad. I knew her too, once upon a time.

Nora. I am aware of that.

Krogstad. Are you? So you know all about it; I thought as much. Then I can ask you, without beating about the bush — is Mrs. Linde to have an appointment in the Bank?

Nora. What right have you to question me, Mr. Krogstad? — You, one of my husband's subordinates! But since you ask, you shall know. Yes, Mrs. Linde *is* to have an appointment. And it was I who pleaded her cause, Mr. Krogstad, let me tell you that.

Krogstad. I was right in what I thought, then.

Nora *(walking up and down the stage).* Sometimes one has a tiny little bit of influence, I should hope. Because one is a woman, it does not necessarily follow that —— . When anyone is in a subordinate position, Mr. Krogstad, they should really be careful to avoid offending anyone who — who ——

Krogstad. Who has influence?

Nora. Exactly.

Krogstad *(changing his tone).*   Mrs. Helmer, you will be so good as to use your influence on my behalf.

Nora.   What? What do you mean?

Krogstad.   You will be so kind as to see that I am allowed to keep my subordinate position in the Bank.

Nora.   What do you mean by that? Who proposes to take your post away from you?

Krogstad.   Oh, there is no necessity to keep up the pretence of ignorance. I can quite understand that your friend is not very anxious to expose herself to the chance of rubbing shoulders with me; and I quite understand, too, whom I have to thank for being turned off.

Nora.   But I assure you ——

Krogstad.   Very likely; but, to come to the point, the time has come when I should advise you to use your influence to prevent that.

Nora.   But, Mr. Krogstad, I *have* no influence.

Krogstad.   Haven't you? I thought you said yourself just now ——

Nora.   Naturally I did not mean you to put that construction on it. I! What should make you think I have any influence of that kind with my husband?

Krogstad.   Oh, I have known your husband from our student days. I don't suppose he is any more unassailable than other husbands.

Nora.   If you speak slightingly of my husband, I shall turn you out of the house.

Krogstad.   You are bold, Mrs. Helmer.

Nora.   I am not afraid of you any longer. As soon as the New Year comes, I shall in a very short time be free of the whole thing.

Krogstad *(controlling himself).*   Listen to me, Mrs. Helmer. If necessary, I am prepared to fight for my small post in the Bank as if I were fighting for my life.

Nora.   So it seems.

Krogstad.   It is not only for the sake of the money; indeed, that weighs least with me in the matter. There is another reason — well, I may as well tell you. My position is this. I daresay you know, like everybody else, that once, many years ago, I was guilty of an indiscretion.

Nora.   I think I have heard something of the kind.

Krogstad.   The matter never came into court; but every way seemed to be closed to me after that. So I took to the business that you know of. I had to do something; and, honestly, I don't think I've been one of the worst. But now I must cut myself free from all that. My sons are growing up; for their sake I must try and win back as much respect as I can in the town. This post in the Bank was like the first step up for me — and now your husband is going to kick me downstairs again into the mud.

Nora.   But you must believe me, Mr. Krogstad; it is not in my power to help you at all.

Krogstad.   Then it is because you haven't the will; but I have means to compel you.

Nora.   You don't mean that you will tell my husband that I owe you money?

Krogstad. Hm! — suppose I were to tell him?

Nora. It would be perfectly infamous of you. *(Sobbing.)* To think of his learning my secret, which has been my joy and pride, in such an ugly, clumsy way — that he should learn it from you! And it would put me in a horribly disagreeable position ——

Krogstad. Only disagreeable?

Nora *(impetuously).* Well, do it, then! — and it will be the worse for you. My husband will see for himself what a blackguard you are, and you certainly won't keep your post then.

Krogstad. I asked you if it was only a disagreeable scene at home that you were afraid of?

Nora. If my husband does get to know of it, of course he will at once pay you what is still owing, and we shall have nothing more to do with you.

Krogstad *(coming a step nearer).* Listen to me, Mrs. Helmer. Either you have a very bad memory or you know very little of business. I shall be obliged to remind you of a few details.

Nora. What do you mean?

Krogstad. When your husband was ill, you came to me to borrow two hundred and fifty pounds.

Nora. I didn't know anyone else to go to.

Krogstad. I promised to get you that amount ——

Nora. Yes, and you did so.

Krogstad. I promised to get you that amount, on certain conditions. Your mind was so taken up with your husband's illness, and you were so anxious to get the money for your journey, that you seem to have paid no attention to the conditions of our bargain. Therefore it will not be amiss if I remind you of them. Now, I promised to get the money on the security of a bond which I signed.

Nora. Yes, and which I signed.

Krogstad. Good. But below your signature there were a few lines constituting your father a surety for the money; those lines your father should have signed.

Nora. Should? He did sign them.

Krogstad. I had left the date blank; that is to say your father should himself have inserted the date on which he signed the paper. Do you remember that?

Nora. Yes, I think I remember ——

Krogstad. Then I gave you the bond to send by post to your father. Is that not so?

Nora. Yes.

Krogstad. And you naturally did so at once, because five or six days afterwards you brought me the bond with your father's signature. And then I gave you the money.

Nora. Well, haven't I been paying it off regularly?

Krogstad. Fairly so, yes. But — to come back to the matter in hand — that must have been a very trying time for you, Mrs. Helmer?

Nora. It was, indeed.

Krogstad. Your father was very ill, wasn't he?

Nora. He was very near his end.

Krogstad. And died soon afterwards?

Nora. Yes.

Krogstad. Tell me, Mrs. Helmer, can you by any chance remember what day your father died? — on what day of the month, I mean.

Nora. Papa died on the 29th of September.

Krogstad. That is correct; I have ascertained it for myself. And, as that is so, there is a discrepancy (*taking a paper from his pocket*) which I cannot account for.

Nora. What discrepancy? I don't know ——

Krogstad. The discrepancy consists, Mrs. Helmer, in the fact that your father signed this bond three days after his death.

Nora. What do you mean? I don't understand ——

Krogstad. Your father died on the 29th of September. But, look here; your father has dated his signature the 2nd of October. It is a discrepancy, isn't it? (*Nora is silent.*) Can you explain it to me? (*Nora is still silent.*) It is a remarkable thing, too, that the words "2nd of October," as well as the year, are not written in your father's handwriting but in one that I think I know. Well, of course it can be explained; your father may have forgotten to date his signature, and someone else may have dated it haphazard before they knew of his death. There is no harm in that. It all depends on the signature of the name; and *that* is genuine, I suppose, Mrs. Helmer? It was your father himself who signed his name here?

Nora (*after a short pause, throws her head up and looks defiantly at him*). No, it was not. It was I that wrote papa's name.

Krogstad. Are you aware that is a dangerous confession?

Nora. In what way? You shall have your money soon.

Krogstad. Let me ask you a question; why did you not send the paper to your father?

Nora. It was impossible; papa was so ill. If I had asked him for his signature, I should have had to tell him what the money was to be used for; and when he was so ill himself I couldn't tell him that my husband's life was in danger — it was impossible.

Krogstad. It would have been better for you if you had given up your trip abroad.

Nora. No, that was impossible. That trip was to save my husband's life; I couldn't give that up.

Krogstad. But did it never occur to you that you were committing a fraud on me?

Nora. I couldn't take that into account; I didn't trouble myself about you at all. I couldn't bear you, because you put so many heartless difficulties in my way, although you knew what a dangerous condition my husband was in.

Krogstad. Mrs. Helmer, you evidently do not realise clearly what it is that you have been guilty of. But I can assure you that my one false step, which lost me all my reputation, was nothing more or nothing worse than what you have done.

Nora. You? Do you ask me to believe that you were brave enough to run a risk to save your wife's life?

Krogstad. The law cares nothing about motives.

Nora. Then it must be a very foolish law.

Krogstad. Foolish or not, it is the law by which you will be judged, if I produce this paper in court.

Nora. I don't believe it. Is a daughter not to be allowed to spare her dying father anxiety and care? Is a wife not to be allowed to save her husband's life? I don't know much about law; but I am certain that there must be laws permitting such things as that. Have you no knowledge of such laws — you who are a lawyer? You must be a very poor lawyer, Mr. Krogstad.

Krogstad. Maybe. But matters of business — such business as you and I have had together — do you think I don't understand that? Very well. Do as you please. But let me tell you this — if I lose my position a second time, you shall lose yours with me.

(He bows, and goes out through the hall.)

Nora *(appears buried in thought for a short time, then tosses her head).* Nonsense! Trying to frighten me like that — I am not so silly as he thinks. *(Begins to busy herself putting the children's things in order.)* And yet —— ? No, it's impossible! I did it for love's sake.

The Children *(in the doorway on the left).* Mother, the stranger man has gone out through the gate.

Nora. Yes, dears, I know. But don't tell anyone about the stranger man. Do you hear? Not even papa.

Children. No, mother; but will you come and play again?

Nora. No, no, — not now.

Children. But, mother, you promised us.

Nora. Yes, but I can't now. Run away in; I have such a lot to do. Run away in, my sweet little darlings. *(She gets them into the room by degrees and shuts the door on them; then sits down on the sofa, takes up a piece of needlework and sews a few stitches, but soon stops.)* No! *(Throws down the work, gets up, goes to the hall door and calls out.)* Helen! bring the tree in. *(Goes to the table on the left, opens a drawer, and stops again.)* No, no! it is quite impossible!

Maid *(coming in with the tree).* Where shall I put it, ma'am?

Nora. Here, in the middle of the floor.

Maid. Shall I get you anything else?

Nora. No, thank you. I have all I want.

(Exit Maid.)

Nora *(begins dressing the tree).*   A candle here — and flowers here ——— . The horrible man! It's all nonsense — there's nothing wrong. The tree shall be splendid! I will do everything I can think of to please you, Torvald! — I will sing for you, dance for you — *(Helmer comes in with some papers under his arm.)* Oh! are you back already?

Helmer.   Yes. Has anyone been here?

Nora.   Here? No.

Helmer.   That is strange. I saw Krogstad going out of the gate.

Nora.   Did you? Oh yes, I forgot, Krogstad was here for a moment.

Helmer.   Nora, I can see from your manner that he has been here begging you to say a good word for him.

Nora.   Yes.

Helmer.   And you were to appear to do it of your own accord; you were to conceal from me the fact of his having been here; didn't he beg that of you too?

Nora.   Yes, Torvald, but ——

Helmer.   Nora, Nora, and you would be a party to that sort of thing? To have any talk with a man like that, and give him any sort of promise? And to tell me a lie into the bargain?

Nora.   A lie —— ?

Helmer.   Didn't you tell me no one had been here? *(Shakes his finger at her.)* My little song-bird must never do that again. A song-bird must have a clean beak to chirp with — no false notes! *(Puts his arm round her waist.)* That is so, isn't it? Yes, I am sure it is. *(Lets her go.)* We will say no more about it. *(Sits down by the stove.)* How warm and snug it is here!

(Turns over his papers.)

Nora *(after a short pause, during which she busies herself with the Christmas tree).*   Torvald!

Helmer.   Yes.

Nora.   I am looking forward tremendously to the fancy dress ball at the Stenborgs' the day after to-morrow.

Helmer.   And I am tremendously curious to see what you are going to surprise me with.

Nora.   It was very silly of me to want to do that.

Helmer.   What do you mean?

Nora.   I can't hit upon anything that will do; everything I think of seems so silly and insignificant.

Helmer.   Does my little Nora acknowledge that at last?

Nora *(standing behind his chair with her arms on the back of it).*   Are you very busy, Torvald?

Helmer.   Well ——

Nora.   What are all those papers?

Helmer. Bank business.

Nora. Already?

Helmer. I have got authority from the retiring manager to undertake the necessary changes in the staff and in the rearrangement of the work; and I must make use of the Christmas week for that, so as to have everything in order for the new year.

Nora. Then that was why this poor Krogstad ——

Helmer. Hm!

Nora *(leans against the back of his chair and strokes his hair).* If you hadn't been so busy I should have asked you a tremendously big favour, Torvald.

Helmer. What is that? Tell me.

Nora. There is no one has such good taste as you. And I do so want to look nice at the fancy-dress ball. Torvald, couldn't you take me in hand and decide what I shall go as, and what sort of a dress I shall wear?

Helmer. Aha! so my obstinate little woman is obliged to get someone to come to her rescue?

Nora. Yes, Torvald, I can't get along a bit without your help.

Helmer. Very well, I will think it over, we shall manage to hit upon something.

Nora. That *is* nice of you. *(Goes to the Christmas tree. A short pause.)* How pretty the red flowers look ——. But, tell me, was it really something very bad that this Krogstad was guilty of?

Helmer. He forged someone's name. Have you any idea what that means?

Nora. Isn't it possible that he was driven to do it by necessity?

Helmer. Yes; or, as in so many cases, by imprudence. I am not so heartless as to condemn a man altogether because of a single false step of that kind.

Nora. No you wouldn't, would you, Torvald?

Helmer. Many a man has been able to retrieve his character, if he has openly confessed his fault and taken his punishment.

Nora. Punishment —— ?

Helmer. But Krogstad did nothing of that sort; he got himself out of it by a cunning trick, and that is why he has gone under altogether.

Nora. But do you think it would —— ?

Helmer. Just think how a guilty man like that has to lie and play the hypocrite with everyone, how he has to wear a mask in the presence of those near and dear to him, even before his own wife and children. And about the children — that is the most terrible part of it all, Nora.

Nora. How?

Helmer. Because such an atmosphere of lies infects and poisons the whole life of a home. Each breath the children take in such a house is full of the germs of evil.

Nora *(coming nearer him).* Are you sure of that?

Helmer. My dear, I have often seen it in the course of my life as a lawyer. Almost everyone who has gone to the bad early in life has had a deceitful mother.

Nora. Why do you only say — mother?

Helmer. It seems most commonly to be the mother's influence, though natu- rally a bad father's would have the same result. Every lawyer is familiar with the fact. This Krogstad, now, has been persistently poisoning his own children with lies and dissimulation; that is why I say he has lost all moral character. (*Holds out his hands to her.*) That is why my sweet little Nora must promise me not to plead his cause. Give me your hand on it. Come, come, what is this? Give me your hand. There now, that's settled. I assure you it would be quite impossible for me to work with him; I literally feel physically ill when I am in the company of such people.

Nora (*takes her hand out of his and goes to the opposite side of the Christmas tree*). How hot it is in here; and I have such a lot to do.

Helmer (*getting up and putting his papers in order*). Yes, and I must try and read through some of these before dinner; and I must think about your cos- tume, too. And it is just possible I may have something ready in gold paper to hang up on the tree. (*Puts his hand on her head.*) My precious little singing- bird!

(*He goes into his room and shuts the door after him.*)

Nora (*after a pause, whispers*). No, no — it isn't true. It's impossible; it must be impossible.

(*The Nurse opens the door on the left.*)

Nurse. The little ones are begging so hard to be allowed to come in to mamma.

Nora. No, no, no! Don't let them come in to me! You stay with them, Anne.

Nurse. Very well, ma'am.

(*Shuts the door.*)

Nora (*pale with terror*). Deprave my little children? Poison my home? (*A short pause. Then she tosses her head.*) It's not true. It can't possibly be true.

Act II

The Same Scene *The Christmas tree is in the corner by the piano, stripped of its ornaments and with burnt-down candle-ends on its dishevelled branches. Nora's cloak and hat are lying on the sofa. She is alone in the room, walking about uneasily. She stops by the sofa and takes up her cloak.*

Nora (*drops the cloak*). Someone is coming now! (*Goes to the door and listens.*) No — it is no one. Of course, no one will come to-day, Christmas Day — nor tomorrow either. But, perhaps — (*Opens the door and looks out*). No, nothing in the letter-box; it is quite empty. (*Comes forward.*) What rubbish! of course he can't be in earnest about it. Such a thing couldn't happen; it is impossible — I have three little children.

(*Enter the Nurse from the room on the left, carrying a big cardboard box.*)

Nurse. At last I have found the box with the fancy dress.
Nora. Thanks; put it on the table.
Nurse (*doing so*). But it is very much in want of mending.
Nora. I should like to tear it into a hundred thousand pieces.
Nurse. What an idea! It can easily be put in order — just a little patience.
Nora. Yes, I will go and get Mrs. Linde to come and help me with it.
Nurse. What, out again? In this horrible weather? You will catch cold, ma'am, and make yourself ill.
Nora. Well, worse than that might happen. How are the children?
Nurse. The poor little souls are playing with their Christmas presents, but ——
Nora. Do they ask much for me?
Nurse. You see, they are so accustomed to have their mamma with them.
Nora. Yes, but, nurse, I shall not be able to be so much with them now as I was before.
Nurse. Oh well, young children easily get accustomed to anything.
Nora. Do you think so? Do you think they would forget their mother if she went away altogether?
Nurse. Good heavens! — went away altogether?
Nora. Nurse, I want you to tell me something I have often wondered about — how could you have the heart to put your own child out among strangers?
Nurse. I was obliged to, if I wanted to be little Nora's nurse.
Nora. Yes, but how could you be willing to do it?
Nurse. What, when I was going to get such a good place by it? A poor girl who has got into trouble should be glad to. Besides, that wicked man didn't do a single thing for me.
Nora. But I suppose your daughter has quite forgotten you.
Nurse. No, indeed she hasn't. She wrote to me when she was confirmed, and when she was married.
Nora (*putting her arms round her neck*). Dear old Anne, you were a good mother to me when I was little.
Nurse. Little Nora, poor dear, had no other mother but me.
Nora. And if my little ones had no other mother, I am sure you would ——
What nonsense I am talking! (*Opens the box.*) Go in to them. Now I must —— . You will see to-morrow how charming I shall look.
Nurse. I am sure there will be no one at the ball so charming as you, ma'am.

(*Goes into the room on the left.*)

Nora *(begins to unpack the box, but soon pushes it away from her).* If only I dared go out. If only no one would come. If only I could be sure nothing would happen here in the meantime. Stuff and nonsense! No one will come. Only I mustn't think about it. I will brush my muff. What lovely, lovely gloves! Out of my thoughts, out of my thoughts! One, two, three, four, five, six —— *(Screams.)* Ah! there is someone coming ——

(Makes a movement towards the door, but stands irresolute. Enter Mrs. Linde from the hall, where she has taken off her cloak and hat.)

Nora. Oh, it's you, Christine. There is no one else out there, is there? How good of you to come!

Mrs. Linde. I heard you were up asking for me.

Nora. Yes, I was passing by. As a matter of fact, it is something you could help me with. Let us sit down here on the sofa. Look here. To-morrow evening there is to be a fancy-dress ball at the Stenborgs', who live above us; and Torvald wants me to go as a Neapolitan fisher-girl, and dance the Tarantella that I learnt at Capri.

Mrs. Linde. I see; you are going to keep up the character.

Nora. Yes, Torvald wants me to. Look, here is the dress; Torvald had it made for me there, but now it is all so torn, and I haven't any idea ——

Mrs. Linde. We will easily put that right. It is only some of the trimming come unsewn here and there. Needle and thread? Now then, that's all we want.

Nora. It *is* nice of you.

Mrs. Linde *(sewing).* So you are going to be dressed up to-morrow, Nora. I will tell you what — I shall come in for a moment and see you in your fine feathers. But I have completely forgotten to thank you for a delightful evening yesterday.

Nora *(gets up, and crosses the stage).* Well I don't think yesterday was as pleasant as usual. You ought to have come to town a little earlier, Christine. Certainly Torvald does understand how to make a house dainty and attractive.

Mrs. Linde. And so do you, it seems to me; you are not your father's daughter for nothing. But tell me, is Doctor Rank always as depressed as he was yesterday?

Nora. No; yesterday it was very noticeable. I must tell you that he suffers from a very dangerous disease. He has consumption of the spine, poor creature. His father was a horrible man who committed all sorts of excesses; and that is why his son was sickly from childhood, do you understand?

Mrs. Linde *(dropping her sewing).* But, my dearest Nora, how do you know anything about such things?

Nora *(walking about).* Pooh! When you have three children, you get visits now and then from — from married women, who know something of medical matters, and they talk about one thing and another.

Mrs. Linde (*goes on sewing. A short silence*).   Does Doctor Rank come here every day?

Nora.   Every day regularly. He is Torvald's most intimate friend, and a great friend of mine too. He is just like one of the family.

Mrs. Linde.   But tell me this — is he perfectly sincere? I mean, isn't he the kind of man that is very anxious to make himself agreeable?

Nora.   Not in the least. What makes you think that?

Mrs. Linde.   When you introduced him to me yesterday, he declared he had often heard my name mentioned in this house; but afterwards I noticed that your husband hadn't the slightest idea who I was. So how could Doctor Rank —— ?

Nora.   That is quite right, Christine. Torvald is so absurdly fond of me that he wants me absolutely to himself, as he says. At first he used to seem almost jealous if I mentioned any of the dear folk at home, so naturally I gave up doing so. But I often talk about such things with Doctor Rank, because he likes hearing about them.

Mrs. Linde.   Listen to me, Nora. You are still very like a child in many things, and I am older than you in many ways and have a little more experience. Let me tell you this — you ought to make an end of it with Doctor Rank.

Nora.   What ought I to make an end of?

Mrs. Linde.   Of two things, I think. Yesterday you talked some nonsense about a rich admirer who was to leave you money ——

Nora.   An admirer who doesn't exist, unfortunately! But what then?

Mrs. Linde.   Is Doctor Rank a man of means?

Nora.   Yes, he is.

Mrs. Linde.   And has no one to provide for?

Nora.   No, no one; but ——

Mrs. Linde.   And comes here every day?

Nora.   Yes, I told you so.

Mrs. Linde.   But how can this well-bred man be so tactless?

Nora.   I don't understand you at all.

Mrs. Linde.   Don't prevaricate, Nora. Do you suppose I don't guess who lent you the two hundred and fifty pounds?

Nora.   Are you out of your senses? How can you think of such a thing! A friend of ours, who comes here every day! Do you realise what a horribly painful position that would be?

Mrs. Linde.   Then it really isn't he?

Nora.   No, certainly not. It would never have entered into my head for a moment. Besides, he had no money to lend then; he came into his money afterwards.

Mrs. Linde.   Well, I think that was lucky for you, my dear Nora.

Nora.   No, it would never have come into my head to ask Doctor Rank. Although I am quite sure that if I had asked him ——

Mrs. Linde.   But of course you won't.

Nora. Of course not. I have no reason to think it could possibly be necessary. But I am quite sure that if I told Doctor Rank ——

Mrs. Linde. Behind your husband's back?

Nora. I must make an end of it with the other one, and that will be behind his back too. I *must* make an end of it with him.

Mrs. Linde. Yes, that is what I told you yesterday, but ——

Nora (*walking up and down*). A man can put a thing like that straight much easier than a woman ——

Mrs. Linde. One's husband, yes.

Nora. Nonsense! (*Standing still.*) When you pay off a debt you get your bond back, don't you?

Mrs. Linde. Yes, as a matter of course.

Nora. And can tear it into a hundred thousand pieces, and burn it up — the nasty dirty paper!

Mrs. Linde (*looks hard at her, lays down her sewing and gets up slowly*). Nora, you are concealing something from me.

Nora. Do I look as if I were?

Mrs. Linde. Something has happened to you since yesterday morning. Nora, what is it?

Nora (*going nearer to her*). Christine! (*Listens.*) Hush! there's Torvald come home. Do you mind going in to the children for the present? Torvald can't bear to see dressmaking going on. Let Anne help you.

Mrs. Linde (*gathering some of the things together*). Certainly — but I am not going away from here till we have had it out with one another.

(*She goes into the room on the left, as Helmer comes in from the hall.*)

Nora (*going up to Helmer*). I have wanted you so much, Torvald dear.

Helmer. Was that the dressmaker?

Nora. No, it was Christine; she is helping me to put my dress in order. You will see I shall look quite smart.

Helmer. Wasn't that a happy thought of mine, now?

Nora. Splendid! But don't you think it is nice of me, too, to do as you wish?

Helmer. Nice? — because you do as your husband wishes? Well, well, you little rogue, I am sure you did not mean it in that way. But I am not going to disturb you; you will want to be trying on your dress, I expect.

Nora. I suppose you are going to work.

Helmer. Yes. (*Shows her a bundle of papers.*) Look at that. I have just been into the bank.

(*Turns to go into his room.*)

Nora. Torvald.

Helmer. Yes.

Nora. If your little squirrel were to ask you for something very, very prettily —— ?

Helmer. What then?

Nora. Would you do it?

Helmer. I should like to hear what it is, first.

Nora. Your squirrel would run about and do all her tricks if you would be nice, and do what she wants.

Helmer. Speak plainly.

Nora. Your skylark would chirp about in every room, with her song rising and falling ——

Helmer. Well, my skylark does that anyhow.

Nora. I would play the fairy and dance for you in the moonlight, Torvald.

Helmer. Nora — you surely don't mean that request you made of me this morning?

Nora (*going near him*). Yes, Torvald, I beg you so earnestly ——

Helmer. Have you really the courage to open up that question again?

Nora. Yes, dear, you *must* do as I ask; you *must* let Krogstad keep his post in the Bank.

Helmer. My dear Nora, it is his post that I have arranged Mrs. Linde shall have.

Nora. Yes, you have been awfully kind about that; but you could just as well dismiss some other clerk instead of Krogstad.

Helmer. This simply incredible obstinacy! Because you chose to give him a thoughtless promise that you would speak for him, I am expected to ——

Nora. That isn't the reason, Torvald. It is for your own sake. This fellow writes in the most scurrilous newspapers; you have told me so yourself. He can do you an unspeakable amount of harm. I am frightened to death of him ——

Helmer. Ah, I understand; it is recollections of the past that scare you.

Nora. What do you mean?

Helmer. Naturally you are thinking of your father.

Nora. Yes — yes, of course. Just recall to your mind what these malicious creatures wrote in the papers about papa, and how horribly they slandered him. I believe they would have procured his dismissal if the Department had not sent you over to inquire into it, and if you had not been so kindly disposed and helpful to him.

Helmer. My little Nora, there is an important difference between your father and me. Your father's reputation as a public official was not above suspicion. Mine is, and I hope it will continue to be so, as long as I hold my office.

Nora. You never can tell what mischief these men may contrive. We ought to be so well off, so snug and happy here in our peaceful home, and have no cares — you and I and the children, Torvald! That is why I beg of you so earnestly ——

Helmer. And it is just by interceding for him that you make it impossible for me to keep him. It is already known at the Bank that I mean to dismiss

Krogstad. Is it to get about now that the new manager has changed his mind at his wife's bidding ——

Nora. And what if it did?

Helmer. Of course! — if only this obstinate little person can get her way! Do you suppose I am going to make myself ridiculous before my whole staff, to let people think that I am a man to be swayed by all sorts of outside influence? I should very soon feel the consequences of it, I can tell you! And besides, there is one thing that makes it quite impossible for me to have Krogstad in the Bank as long as I am manager.

Nora. Whatever is that?

Helmer. His moral failings I might perhaps have overlooked, if necessary ——

Nora. Yes, you could — couldn't you?

Helmer. And I hear he is a good worker, too. But I knew him when we were boys. It was one of those rash friendships that so often prove an incubus in after life. I may as well tell you plainly, we were once on very intimate terms with one another. But this tactless fellow lays no restraint on himself when other people are present. On the contrary, he thinks it gives him the right to adopt a familiar tone with me, and every minute it is "I say, Helmer, old fellow!" and that sort of thing. I assure you it is extremely painful for me. He would make my position in the Bank intolerable.

Nora. Torvald, I don't believe you mean that.

Helmer. Don't you? Why not?

Nora. Because it is such a narrow-minded way of looking at things.

Helmer. What are you saying? Narrow-minded? Do you think I am narrow-minded?

Nora. No, just the opposite, dear — and it is exactly for that reason.

Helmer. It's the same thing. You say my point of view is narrow-minded, so I must be so too. Narrow-minded! Very well — I must put an end to this. (*Goes to the hall-door and calls.*) Helen!

Nora. What are you going to do?

Helmer (*looking among his papers*). Settle it. (*Enter Maid.*) Look here; take this letter and go downstairs with it at once. Find a messenger and tell him to deliver it, and be quick. The address is on it, and here is the money.

Maid. Very well, sir. (*Exit with the letter.*)

Helmer (*putting his papers together*). Now then, little Miss Obstinate.

Nora (*breathlessly*). Torvald — what was that letter?

Helmer. Krogstad's dismissal.

Nora. Call her back, Torvald! There is still time. Oh Torvald, call her back! Do it for my sake — for your own sake — for the children's sake! Do you hear me, Torvald? Call her back! You don't know what that letter can bring upon us.

Helmer. It's too late.

Nora. Yes, it's too late.

Helmer. My dear Nora, I can forgive the anxiety you are in, although really it is an insult to me. It is, indeed. Isn't it an insult to think that I should be afraid of a starving quill-driver's vengeance? But I forgive you nevertheless, because it is such eloquent witness to your great love for me. *(Takes her in his arms.)* And that is as it should be, my darling Nora. Come what will, you may be sure I shall have both courage and strength if they be needed. You will see I am man enough to take everything upon myself.

Nora *(in a horror-stricken voice).*   What do you mean by that?

Helmer.   Everything, I say ——

Nora *(recovering herself).*   You will never have to do that.

Helmer.   That's right. Well, we will share it, Nora, as man and wife should. That is how it shall be. *(Caressing her.)* Are you content now? There! there! — not these frightened dove's eyes! The whole thing is only the wildest fancy! — Now, you must go and play through the Tarantella and practise with your tambourine. I shall go into the inner office and shut the door, and I shall hear nothing; you can make as much noise as you please. *(Turns back at the door.)* And when Rank comes, tell him where he will find me.

(Nods to her, takes his papers and goes into his room, and shuts the door after him.)

Nora   *(bewildered with anxiety, stands as if rooted to the spot, and whispers).* He was capable of doing it. He will do it. He will do it in spite of everything. — No, not that! Never, never! Anything rather than that! Oh, for some help, some way out of it! *(The door-bell rings.)* Doctor Rank! Anything rather than that — anything, whatever it is!

(She puts her hands over her face, pulls herself together, goes to the door and opens it. Rank is standing without, hanging up his coat. During the following dialogue it begins to grow dark.)

Nora.   Good-day, Doctor Rank. I knew your ring. But you mustn't go into Torvald now; I think he is busy with something.

Rank.   And you?

Nora *(brings him in and shuts the door after him).*   Oh, you know very well I always have time for you.

Rank.   Thank you. I shall make use of as much of it as I can.

Nora.   What do you mean by that? As much of it as you can?

Rank.   Well, does that alarm you?

Nora.   It was such a strange way of putting it. Is anything likely to happen?

Rank.   Nothing but what I have long been prepared for. But certainly didn't expect it to happen so soon.

Nora *(gripping him by the arm).*   What have you found out? Doctor Rank, you must tell me.

Rank *(sitting down by the stove).*   It is all up with me. And it can't be helped.

Nora *(with a sigh of relief).*   Is it about yourself?

Rank. Who else? It is no use lying to one's self. I am the most wretched of all my patients, Mrs. Helmer. Lately I have been taking stock of my internal economy. Bankrupt! Probably within a month I shall lie rotting in the church-yard.

Nora. What an ugly thing to say!

Rank. The thing itself is cursedly ugly, and the worst of it is that I shall have to face so much more that is ugly before that. I shall only make one more examination of myself; when I have done that, I shall know pretty certainly when it will be that the horrors of dissolution will begin. There is something I want to tell you. Helmer's refined nature gives him an unconquerable disgust at everything that is ugly; I won't have him in my sick-room.

Nora. Oh, but, Doctor Rank ——

Rank. I won't have him there. Not on any account. I bar my door to him. As soon as I am quite certain that the worst has come, I shall send you my card with a black cross on it, and then you will know that the loathsome end has begun.

Nora. You are quite absurd to-day. And I wanted you so much to be in a really good humour.

Rank. With death stalking beside me? — To have to pay this penalty for another man's sin! Is there any justice in that? And in every single family, in one way or another, some such inexorable retribution is being exacted ——

Nora (*putting her hands over her ears*). Rubbish! Do talk of something cheer-ful.

Rank. Oh, it's a mere laughing matter, the whole thing. My poor innocent spine has to suffer for my father's youthful amusements.

Nora (*sitting at the table on the left*). I suppose you mean that he was too partial to asparagus and pâté de foie gras, don't you.

Rank. Yes, and to truffles.

Nora. Truffles, yes. And oysters too, I suppose?

Rank. Oysters, of course, that goes without saying.

Nora. And heaps of port and champagne. It is sad that all these nice things should take their revenge on our bones.

Rank. Especially that they should revenge themselves on the unlucky bones of those who have not had the satisfaction of enjoying them.

Nora. Yes, that's the saddest part of it all.

Rank (*with a searching look at her*). Hm! ——

Nora (*after a short pause*). Why did you smile?

Rank. No, it was you that laughed.

Nora. No, it was you that smiled, Doctor Rank!

Rank (*rising*). You are a greater rascal than I thought.

Nora. I am in a silly mood to-day.

Rank. So it seems.

Nora (*putting her hands on his shoulders*). Dear, dear Doctor Rank, death mustn't take you away from Torvald and me.

Rank. It is a loss you would easily recover from. Those who are gone are soon forgotten.

Nora (*looking at him anxiously*). Do you believe that?

Rank. People form new ties, and then ——

Nora. Who will form new ties?

Rank. Both you and Helmer, when I am gone. You yourself are already on the high road to it, I think. What did that Mrs. Linde want here last night?

Nora. Oho! — you don't mean to say you are jealous of poor Christine?

Rank. Yes, I am. She will be my successor in this house. When I am done for, this woman will —

Nora. Hush! don't speak so loud. She is in that room.

Rank. To-day again. There, you see.

Nora. She has only come to sew my dress for me. Bless my soul, how unreasonable you are! (*Sits down on the sofa.*) Be nice now, Doctor Rank, and tomorrow you will see how beautifully I shall dance, and you can imagine I am doing it all for you — and for Torvald too, of course. (*Takes various things out of the box.*) Doctor Rank, come and sit down here, and I will show you something.

Rank (*sitting down*). What is it?

Nora. Just look at those!

Rank. Silk stockings.

Nora. Flesh-coloured. Aren't they lovely? It is so dark here now, but tomorrow — . No, no, no! you must only look at the feet. Oh well, you may have leave to look at the legs too.

Rank. Hm! —

Nora. Why are you looking so critical? Don't you think they will fit me?

Rank. I have no means of forming an opinion about that.

Nora (*looks at him for a moment*). For shame! (*Hits him lightly on the ear with the stockings.*) That's to punish you. (*Folds them up again.*)

Rank. And what other nice things am I to be allowed to see?

Nora. Not a single thing more, for being so naughty. (*She looks among the things, humming to herself.*)

Rank (*after a short silence*). When I am sitting here, talking to you as intimately as this, I cannot imagine for a moment what would have become of me if I had never come into this house.

Nora (*smiling*). I believe you do feel thoroughly at home with us.

Rank (*in a lower voice, looking straight in front of him*). And to be obliged to leave it all ——

Nora. Nonsense, you are not going to leave it.

Rank (*as before*). And not be able to leave behind one the slightest token of one's gratitude, scarcely even a fleeting regret — nothing but an empty place which the first comer can fill as well as any other.

Nora. And if I asked you now for a — ? No!

Rank. For what?

Nora. For a big proof of your friendship ——

Rank. Yes, yes!

Nora. I mean a tremendously big favour ——

Rank. Would you really make me so happy for once?

Nora. Ah, but you don't know what it is yet.

Rank. No — but tell me.

Nora. I really can't, Doctor Rank. It is something out of all reason; it means advice, and help, and a favour ——

Rank. The bigger a thing it is the better. I can't conceive what it is you mean. Do tell me. Haven't I your confidence?

Nora. More than anyone else. I know you are my truest and best friend, and so I will tell you what it is. Well, Doctor Rank, it is something you must help me to prevent. You know how devotedly, how inexpressibly deeply Torvald loves me; he would never for a moment hesitate to give his life for me.

Rank (*leaning towards her*). Nora — do you think he is the only one —— ?

Nora (*with a slight start*). The only one — ?

Rank. The only one who would gladly give his life for your sake.

Nora (*sadly*). Is that it?

Rank. I was determined you should know it before I went away, and there will never be a better opportunity than this. Now you know it, Nora. And now you know, too, that you can trust me as you would trust no one else.

Nora (*rises, deliberately and quietly*). Let me pass.

Rank (*makes room for her to pass him, but sits still*). Nora!

Nora (*at the hall door*). Helen, bring in the lamp. (*Goes over to the stove.*) Dear Doctor Rank, that was really horrid of you.

Rank. To have loved you as much as anyone else does? Was that horrid?

Nora. No, but to go and tell me so. There was really no need ——

Rank. What do you mean? Did you know — ? (*Maid enters with lamp, puts it down on the table, and goes out.*) Nora — Mrs. Helmer — tell me, had you any idea of this?

Nora. Oh, how do I know whether I had or whether I hadn't? I really can't tell you — To think you could be so clumsy, Doctor Rank! We were getting on so nicely.

Rank. Well, at all events you know now that you can command me, body and soul. So won't you speak out?

Nora (*looking at him*). After what happened?

Rank. I beg you to let me know what it is.

Nora. I can't tell you anything now.

Rank. Yes, yes. You mustn't punish me in that way. Let me have permission to do for you whatever a man may do.

Nora. You can do nothing for me now. Besides, I really don't need any help at all. You will find that the whole thing is merely fancy on my part. It really is so — of course it is! (*Sits down in the rocking-chair, and looks at him with a smile.*) You are a nice sort of man, Doctor Rank! — don't you feel ashamed of yourself, now the lamp has come?

Rank. Not a bit. But perhaps I had better go — forever?

Nora. No, indeed, you shall not. Of course you must come here just as before. You know very well Torvald can't do without you.

Rank. Yes, but you?

Nora. Oh, I am always tremendously pleased when you come.

Rank. It is just that, that put me on the wrong track. You are a riddle to me. I have often thought that you would almost as soon be in my company as in Helmer's.

Nora. Yes — you see there are some people one loves best, and others whom one would almost always rather have as companions.

Rank. Yes, there is something in that.

Nora. When I was at home, of course I loved papa best. But I always thought it tremendous fun if I could steal down into the maids' room, because they never moralised at all, and talked to each other about such entertaining things.

Rank. I see — it is *their* place I have taken.

Nora (*jumping up and going to him*). Oh, dear, nice Doctor Rank, I never meant that at all. But surely you can understand that being with Torvald is a little like being with papa ——

(*Enter Maid from the hall.*)

Maid. If you please, ma'am. (*Whispers and hands her a card.*)

Nora (*glancing at the card*). Oh! (*Puts it in her pocket.*)

Rank. Is there anything wrong?

Nora. No, no, not in the least. It is only something — it is my new dress ——

Rank. What? Your dress is lying there.

Nora. Oh, yes, that one; but this is another. I ordered it. Torvald mustn't know about it ——

Rank. Oho! Then that was the great secret.

Nora. Of course. Just go in to him; he is sitting in the inner room. Keep him as long as ——

Rank. Make your mind easy; I won't let him escape. (*Goes into Helmer's room.*)

Nora (*to the Maid*). And he is standing waiting in the kitchen?

Maid. Yes; he came up the back stairs.

Nora. But didn't you tell him no one was in?

Maid. Yes, but it was no good.

Nora. He won't go away?

Maid. No; he says he won't until he has seen you, ma'am.

Nora. Well, let him come in — but quietly. Helen, you mustn't say anything about it to anyone. It is a surprise for my husband.

Maid. Yes ma'am, I quite understand. (*Exit.*)

Nora. This dreadful thing is going to happen! It will happen in spite of me! No, no, no, it can't happen — it shan't happen!

(She bolts the door of Helmer's room. The Maid opens the hall door for Krogstad and shuts it after him. He is wearing a fur coat, high boots and a fur cap.)

Nora *(advancing towards him).* Speak low — my husband is at home.

Krogstad. No matter about that.

Nora. What do you want of me?

Krogstad. An explanation of something.

Nora. Make haste then. What is it?

Krogstad. You know, I suppose, that I have got my dismissal.

Nora. I couldn't prevent it, Mr. Krogstad. I fought as hard as I could on your side, but it was no good.

Krogstad. Does your husband love you so little, then? He knows what I can expose you to, and yet he ventures ——

Nora. How can you suppose that he has any knowledge of the sort?

Krogstad. I didn't suppose so at all. It would not be the least like our dear Torvald Helmer to show so much courage —

Nora. Mr. Krogstad, a little respect for my husband, please.

Krogstad. Certainly — all the respect he deserves. But since you have kept the matter so carefully to yourself, I make bold to suppose that you have a little clearer idea, than you had yesterday, of what it actually is that you have done?

Nora. More than you could ever teach me.

Krogstad. Yes, such a bad lawyer as I am.

Nora. What is it you want of me?

Krogstad. Only to see how you were, Mrs. Helmer. I have been thinking about you all day long. A mere cashier, a quill-driver, a — well, a man like me — even he has a little of what is called feeling, you know.

Nora. Show it, then; think of my little children.

Krogstad. Have you and your husband thought of mine? But never mind about that. I only wanted to tell you that you need not take this matter too seriously. In the first place there will be no accusation made on my part.

Nora. No, of course not; I was sure of that.

Krogstad. The whole thing can be arranged amicably; there is no reason why anyone should know anything about it. It will remain a secret between us three.

Nora. My husband must never get to know anything about it.

Krogstad. How will you be able to prevent it? Am I to understand that you can pay the balance that is owing?

Nora. No, not just at present.

Krogstad. Or perhaps that you have some expedient for raising the money soon?

Nora. No expedient that I mean to make use of.

Krogstad. Well, in any case, it would have been of no use to you now. If you stood there with ever so much money in your hand, I would never part with your bond.

Nora. Tell me what purpose you mean to put it to.

Krogstad. I shall only preserve it — keep it in my possession. No one who is not concerned in the matter shall have the slightest hint of it. So that if the thought of it has driven you to any desperate resolution ——

Nora. It has.

Krogstad. If you had it in your mind to run away from your home ——

Nora. I had.

Krogstad. Or even something worse ——

Nora. How could you know that?

Krogstad. Give up the idea.

Nora. How did you know I had thought of *that?*

Krogstad. Most of us think of that at first. I did, too — but I hadn't the courage.

Nora (*faintly*). No more had I.

Krogstad (*in a tone of relief*). No, that's it, isn't it — you hadn't the courage either?

Nora. No, I haven't — I haven't.

Krogstad. Besides, it would have been a great piece of folly. Once the first storm at home is over — . I have a letter for your husband in my pocket.

Nora. Telling him everything?

Krogstad. In as lenient a manner as I possibly could.

Nora (*quickly*). He mustn't get the letter. Tear it up. I will find some means of getting money.

Krogstad. Excuse me, Mrs. Helmer, but I think I told you just now ——

Nora. I am not speaking of what I owe you. Tell me what sum you are asking my husband for, and I will get the money.

Krogstad. I am not asking your husband for a penny.

Nora. What do you want, then?

Krogstad. I will tell you. I want to rehabilitate myself, Mrs. Helmer; I want to get on; and in that your husband must help me. For the last year and a half I have not had a hand in anything dishonourable, and all that time I have been struggling in most restricted circumstances. I was content to work my way up step by step. Now I am turned out, and I am not going to be satisfied with merely being taken into favour again. I want to get on, I tell you. I want to get into the Bank again, in a higher position. Your husband must make a place for me ——

Nora. That he will never do!

Krogstad. He will; I know him; he dare not protest. And as soon as I am in there again with him, then you will see! Within a year I shall be the manager's right hand. It will be Nils Krogstad and not Torvald Helmer who manages the Bank.

Nora. That's a thing you will never see!

Krogstad. Do you mean that you will —— ?

Nora. I have courage enough for it now.

Krogstad. Oh, you can't frighten me. A fine, spoilt lady like you ——

Nora. You will see, you will see.

Krogstad. Under the ice, perhaps? Down into the cold, coal-black water? And then, in the spring, to float up to the surface, all horrible and unrecognisable, with your hair fallen out ——

Nora. You can't frighten me.

Krogstad. Nor you me. People don't do such things, Mrs. Helmer. Besides, what use would it be? I should have him completely in my power all the same.

Nora. Afterwards? When I am no longer ——

Krogstad. Have you forgotten that it is I who have the keeping of your reputation? (*Nora stands speechlessly looking at him.*) Well, now, I have warned you. Do not do anything foolish. When Helmer has had my letter, I shall expect a message from him. And be sure you remember that it is your husband himself who has forced me into such ways as this again. I will never forgive him for that. Good-bye, Mrs. Helmer. (*Exit through the hall.*)

Nora (*goes to the hall door, opens it slightly and listens*). He is going. He is not putting the letter in the box. Oh no, no! that's impossible! (*Opens the door by degrees.*) He is going. He is standing outside. He is not going downstairs. Is he hesitating? Can he ——

(*A letter drops into the box; then Krogstad's footsteps are heard, till they die away as he goes downstairs. Nora utters a stifled cry and runs across the room to the table by the sofa. A short pause.*)

Nora. In the letter-box. (*Steals across to the hall door.*) There it lies —— Torvald, Torvald, there is no hope for us now!

(*Mrs. Linde comes in from the room on the left carrying the dress.*)

Mrs. Linde. There, I can't see anything more to mend now. Would you like to try it on —— ?

Nora (*in a hoarse whisper*). Christine, come here.

Mrs. Linde (*throwing the dress down on the sofa*). What is the matter with you? You look so agitated!

Nora. Come here. Do you see that letter? There look —— you can see it through the glass in the letter-box.

Mrs. Linde. Yes, I see it.

Nora. That letter is from Krogstad.

Mrs. Linde. Nora —— it was Krogstad who lent you the money!

Nora. Yes, and now Torvald will know all about it.

Mrs. Linde. Believe me, Nora, that's the best thing for both of you.

Nora. You don't know all. I forged a name.

Mrs. Linde. Good heavens —— !

Nora. I only want to say this to you, Christine —— you must be my witness.

Mrs. Linde. Your witness? What do you mean? What am I to —— ?

Nora. If I should go out of my mind —— and it might easily happen ——

Mrs. Linde. Nora!

Nora. Or if anything else should happen to me — anything, for instance, that might prevent my being here —

Mrs. Linde. Nora! Nora! you are quite out of your mind.

Nora. And if it should happen that there were someone who wanted to take all the responsibility, all the blame, you understand ——

Mrs. Linde. Yes, yes — but how can you suppose — ?

Nora. Then you must be my witness, that it is not true, Christine. I am not out of my mind at all; I am in my right senses now, and I tell you no one else has known anything about it; I, and I alone, did the whole thing. Remember that.

Mrs. Linde. I will, indeed. But I don't understand all this.

Nora. How should you understand it? A wonderful thing is going to happen.

Mrs. Linde. A wonderful thing?

Nora. Yes, a wonderful thing! — But it is so terrible, Christine; it *mustn't* happen, not for all the world.

Mrs. Linde. I will go at once and see Krogstad.

Nora. Don't go to him; he will do you some harm.

Mrs. Linde. There was a time when he would gladly do anything for my sake.

Nora. He?

Mrs. Linde. Where does he live?

Nora. How should I know — ? Yes *(feeling in her pocket)* here is his card. But the letter, the letter —— !

Helmer *(calls from his room, knocking at the door).* Nora!

Nora *(cries out anxiously).* Oh, what's that? What do you want?

Helmer. Don't be so frightened. We are not coming in; you have locked the door. Are you trying on your dress?

Nora. Yes, that's it. I look so nice, Torvald.

Mrs. Linde *(who has read the card).* I see he lives at the corner here.

Nora. Yes, but it's no use. It is hopeless. The letter is lying there in the box.

Mrs. Linde. And your husband keeps the key?

Nora. Yes, always.

Mrs. Linde. Krogstad must ask for his letter back unread, he must find some pretence ——

Nora. But it is just at this time that Torvald generally ——

Mrs. Linde. You must delay him. Go in to him in the meantime. I will come back as soon as I can.

(She goes out hurriedly through the hall door.)

Nora *(goes to Helmer's door, opens it and peeps in).* Torvald!

Helmer *(from the inner room).* Well? May I venture at last to come into my own room again? Come along, Rank, now you will see — *(Halting in the doorway.)* But what is this?

Nora. What is what, dear?

Helmer. Rank led me to expect a splendid transformation.

Rank (*in the doorway*).   I understood so, but evidently I was mistaken.

Nora.   Yes, nobody is to have the chance of admiring me in my dress until to-morrow.

Helmer.   But, my dear Nora, you look so worn out. Have you been practising too much?

Nora.   No, I have not practised at all.

Helmer.   But you will need to —

Nora.   Yes, indeed I shall, Torvald. But I can't get on a bit without you to help me; I have absolutely forgotten the whole thing.

Helmer.   Oh, we will soon work it up again.

Nora.   Yes, help me, Torvald. Promise that you will! I am so nervous about it — all the people — . You must give yourself up to me entirely this evening. Not the tiniest bit of business — you mustn't even take a pen in your hand. Will you promise, Torvald dear?

Helmer.   I promise. This evening I will be wholly and absolutely at your service, you helpless little mortal. Ah, by the way, first of all I will just ——

(*Goes towards the hall door.*)

Nora.   What are you going to do there?

Helmer.   Only see if any letters have come.

Nora.   No, no! don't do that, Torvald!

Helmer.   Why not?

Nora.   Torvald, please don't. There is nothing there.

Helmer.   Well, let me look. (*Turns to go to the letter-box. Nora at the piano, plays the first bars of the Tarantella. Helmer stops in the doorway.*) Aha!

Nora.   I can't dance to-morrow if I don't practise with you.

Helmer (*going up to her*).   Are you really so afraid of it, dear?

Nora.   Yes, so dreadfully afraid of it. Let me practise at once; there is time now, before we go to dinner. Sit down and play for me, Torvald dear; criticise me, and correct me as you play.

Helmer.   With great pleasure, if you wish me to.

(*Sits down at the piano.*)

Nora (*takes out of the box a tambourine and a long variegated shawl. She hastily drapes the shawl round her. Then she springs to the front of the stage and calls out*).   Now play for me! I am going to dance!

(*Helmer plays and Nora dances. Rank stands by the piano behind Helmer and looks on.*)

Helmer (*as he plays*).   Slower, slower!

Nora.   I can't do it any other way.

Helmer.   Not so violently, Nora!

Nora. This is the way.

Helmer (*stops playing*). No, no — that is not a bit right.

Nora (*laughing and swinging the tambourine*). Didn't I tell you so?

Rank. Let me play for her.

Helmer (*getting up*). Yes, do. I can correct her better then.

(*Rank sits down at the piano and plays. Nora dances more and more wildly. Helmer has taken up a position beside the stove, and during her dance gives her frequent instructions. She does not seem to hear him; her hair comes down and falls over her shoulders; she pays no attention to it, but goes on dancing. Enter Mrs. Linde.*)

Mrs. Linde (*standing as if spell-bound in the doorway*). Oh! ——

Nora (*as she dances*). Such fun, Christine!

Helmer. My dear darling Nora, you are dancing as if your life depended on it.

Nora. So it does.

Helmer. Stop, Rank; this is sheer madness. Stop, I tell you! (*Rank stops playing, and Nora suddenly stands still. Helmer goes up to her.*) I could never have believed it. You have forgotten everything I taught you.

Nora (*throwing away the tambourine*). There, you see.

Helmer. You will want a lot of coaching.

Nora. Yes, you see how much I need it. You must coach me up to the last minute. Promise me that, Torvald!

Helmer. You can depend on me.

Nora. You must not think of anything but me, either to-day or to-morrow; you mustn't open a single letter — not even open the letter-box ——

Helmer. Ah, you are still afraid of that fellow ——

Nora. Yes, indeed I am.

Helmer. Nora, I can tell from your looks that there is a letter from him lying there.

Nora. I don't know; I think there is; but you must not read anything of that kind now. Nothing horrid must come between us till this is all over.

Rank (*whispers to Helmer*). You mustn't contradict her.

Helmer (*taking her in his arms*). The child shall have her way. But to-morrow night, after you have danced ——

Nora. Then you will be free.

(*The Maid appears in the doorway to the right.*)

Maid. Dinner is served, ma'am.

Nora. We will have champagne, Helen.

Maid. Very good, ma'am. (*Exit.*)

Helmer. Hullo! — are we going to have a banquet?

Nora. Yes, a champagne banquet till the small hours. (*Calls out.*) And a few macaroons, Helen — lots, just for once!

Helmer.   Come, come, don't be so wild and nervous. Be my own little skylark, as you used.

Nora.   Yes, dear, I will. But go in now and you too, Doctor Rank. Christine, you must help me to do up my hair.

Rank (*whispers to Helmer as they go out*).   I suppose there is nothing — she is not expecting anything?

Helmer.   Far from it, my dear fellow; it is simply nothing more than this child- ish nervousness I was telling you of.

(*They go into the right-hand room.*)

Nora.   Well!

Mrs. Linde.   Gone out of town.

Nora.   I could tell from your face.

Mrs. Linde.   He is coming home to-morrow evening. I wrote a note for him.

Nora.   You should have let it alone; you must prevent nothing. After all, it is splendid to be waiting for a wonderful thing to happen.

Mrs. Linde.   What is it that you are waiting for?

Nora.   Oh, you wouldn't understand. Go in to them, I will come in a moment. (*Mrs. Linde goes into the dining-room. Nora stands still for a little while, as if to compose herself. Then she looks at her watch.*) Five o'clock. Seven hours till midnight. Then the Tarantella will be over. Twenty-four and seven? Thirty-one hours to live.

Helmer (*from the doorway on the right*).   Where's my little skylark?

Nora (*going to him with her arms outstretched*). Here she is!

Act III

The Same Scene   *The table has been placed in the middle of the stage, with chairs round it. A lamp is burning on the table. The door into the hall stands open. Dance music is heard in the room above. Mrs. Linde is sitting at the table idly turning over the leaves of a book; she tries to read, but does not seem able to collect her thoughts. Every now and then she listens intently for a sound at the outer door.*

Mrs. Linde (*looking at her watch*).   Not yet — and the time is nearly up. If only he does not — . (*Listens again.*) Ah, there he is. (*Goes into the hall and opens the outer door carefully. Light footsteps are heard on the stairs. She whispers.*) Come in. There is no one here.

Krogstad (*in the doorway*).   I found a note from you at home. What does this mean?

Mrs. Linde.   It is absolutely necessary that I should have a talk with you.

Krogstad.   Really? And is it absolutely necessary that it should be here?

Mrs. Linde.   It is impossible where I live; there is no private entrance to my rooms. Come in; we are quite alone. The maid is asleep, and the Helmers are at the dance upstairs.

Krogstad *(coming into the room).*   Are the Helmers really at a dance to-night?

Mrs. Linde.   Yes, why not?

Krogstad.   Certainly — why not?

Mrs. Linde.   Now, Nils, let us have a talk.

Krogstad.   Can we two have anything to talk about?

Mrs. Linde.   We have a great deal to talk about.

Krogstad.   I shouldn't have thought so.

Mrs. Linde.   No, you have never properly understood me.

Krogstad.   Was there anything else to understand except what was obvious to all the world — a heartless woman jilts a man when a more lucrative chance turns up?

Mrs. Linde.   Do you believe I am as absolutely heartless as all that? And do you believe that I did it with a light heart?

Krogstad.   Didn't you?

Mrs. Linde.   Nils, did you really think that?

Krogstad.   If it were as you say, why did you write to me as you did at the time?

Mrs. Linde.   I could do nothing else. As I had to break with you, it was my duty also to put an end to all that you felt for me.

Krogstad *(wringing his hands).*   So that was it. And all this — only for the sake of money!

Mrs. Linde.   You must not forget that I had a helpless mother and two little brothers. We couldn't wait for you, Nils; your prospects seemed hopeless then.

Krogstad.   That may be so, but you had no right to throw me over for anyone else's sake.

Mrs. Linde.   Indeed I don't know. Many a time did I ask myself if I had the right to do it.

Krogstad *(more gently).*   When I lost you, it was as if all the solid ground went from under my feet. Look at me now — I am a shipwrecked man clinging to a bit of wreckage.

Mrs. Linde.   But help may be near.

Krogstad.   It *was* near; but then you came and stood in my way.

Mrs. Linde.   Unintentionally, Nils. It was only to-day that I learnt it was your place I was going to take in the Bank.

Krogstad.   I believe you, if you say so. But now that you know it, are you not going to give it up to me?

Mrs. Linde.   No, because that would not benefit you in the least.

Krogstad.   Oh, benefit, benefit — I would have done it whether or no.

Mrs. Linde.   I have learnt to act prudently. Life, and hard, bitter necessity have taught me that.

Krogstad.   And life has taught me not to believe in fine speeches.

Mrs. Linde.   Then life has taught you something very reasonable. But deeds you must believe in?

Krogstad.   What do you mean by that?

Mrs. Linde.   You said you were like a shipwrecked man clinging to some wreckage.

Krogstad.   I had good reason to say so.

Mrs. Linde.   Well, I am like a shipwrecked woman clinging to some wreckage — no one to mourn for, no one to care for.

Krogstad.   It was your own choice.

Mrs. Linde.   There was no other choice — then.

Krogstad.   Well, what now?

Mrs. Linde.   Nils, how would it be if we two shipwrecked people could join forces?

Krogstad.   What are you saying?

Mrs. Linde.   Two on the same piece of wreckage would stand a better chance than each on their own.

Krogstad.   Christine!

Mrs. Linde.   What do you suppose brought me to town?

Krogstad.   Do you mean that you gave me a thought?

Mrs. Linde.   I could not endure life without work. All my life, as long as I can remember, I have worked, and it has been my greatest and only pleasure. But now I am quite alone in the world — my life is so dreadfully empty and I feel so forsaken. There is not the least pleasure in working for one's self. Nils, give me someone and something to work for.

Krogstad.   I don't trust that. It is nothing but a woman's overstrained sense of generosity that prompts you to make such an offer of yourself.

Mrs. Linde.   Have you ever noticed anything of the sort in me?

Krogstad.   Could you really do it? Tell me — do you know all about my past life?

Mrs. Linde.   Yes.

Krogstad.   And do you know what they think of me here?

Mrs. Linde.   You seemed to me to imply that with me you might have been quite another man.

Krogstad.   I am certain of it.

Mrs. Linde.   Is it too late now?

Krogstad.   Christine, are you saying this deliberately? Yes, I am sure you are. I see it in your face. Have you really the courage then — ?

Mrs. Linde.   I want to be a mother to someone, and your children need a mother. We two need each other. Nils, I have faith in your real character — I can dare anything together with you.

Krogstad (*grasps her hands*).   Thanks, thanks, Christine! Now I shall find a way to clear myself in the eyes of the world. Ah, but I forgot ——

Mrs. Linde (*listening*).   Hush! The Tarantella! Go, go!

Krogstad.   Why? What is it?

Mrs. Linde. Do you hear them up there? When that is over, we may expect them back.

Krogstad. Yes, yes — I will go. But it is all no use. Of course you are not aware what steps I have taken in the matter of the Helmers.

Mrs. Linde. Yes, I know all about that.

Krogstad. And in spite of that have you the courage to — ?

Mrs. Linde. I understand very well to what lengths a man like you might be driven by despair.

Krogstad. If I could only undo what I have done!

Mrs. Linde. You cannot. Your letter is lying in the letter-box now.

Krogstad. Are you sure of that?

Mrs. Linde. Quite sure, but ——

Krogstad *(with a searching look at her).* Is that what it all means? — that you want to save your friend at my cost? Tell me frankly. Is that it?

Mrs. Linde. Nils, a woman who has once sold herself for another's sake, doesn't do it a second time.

Krogstad. I will ask for my letter back.

Mrs. Linde. No, no.

Krogstad. Yes, of course I will. I will wait here till Helmer comes; I will tell him he must give me my letter back — that it only concerns my dismissal — that he is not to read it ——

Mrs. Linde. No, Nils, you must not recall your letter.

Krogstad. But, tell me, wasn't it for that very purpose that you asked me to meet you here?

Mrs. Linde. In my first moment of fright, it was. But twenty-four hours have elapsed since then, and in that time I have witnessed incredible things in this house. Helmer must know all about it. This unhappy secret must be disclosed; they must have a complete understanding between them, which is impossible with all this concealment and falsehood going on.

Krogstad. Very well, if you will take the responsibility. But there is one thing I can do in any case, and I shall do it at once.

Mrs. Linde *(listening).* You must be quick and go! The dance is over; we are not safe a moment longer.

Krogstad. I will wait for you below.

Mrs. Linde. Yes, do. You must see me back to my door.

Krogstad. I have never had such an amazing piece of good fortune in my life.

(Goes out through the outer door. The door between the room and the hall remains open.)

Mrs. Linde *(tidying up the room and laying her hat and cloak ready).* What a difference! what a difference! Someone to work for and live for — a home to bring comfort into. That I will do, indeed. I wish they would be quick and come — *(Listens.)* Ah, there they are now. I must put on my things.

(Takes up her hat and cloak. Helmer's and Nora's voices are heard outside; a key is turned, and Helmer brings Nora almost by force into the hall. She is in an Italian costume with a large black shawl round her; he is in evening dress and a black domino[2] *which is flying open.)*

Nora *(hanging back in the doorway, and struggling with him).*   No, no, no! — don't take me in. I want to go upstairs again; I don't want to leave so early.

Helmer.   But, my dearest Nora ——

Nora.   Please, Torvald dear — please, *please* — only an hour more.

Helmer.   Not a single minute, my sweet Nora. You know that was our agreement. Come along into the room; you are catching cold standing there.

(He brings her gently into the room, in spite of her resistance.)

Mrs. Linde.   Good evening.

Nora.   Christine!

Helmer.   You here, so late, Mrs. Linde?

Mrs. Linde.   Yes, you must excuse me; I was so anxious to see Nora in her dress.

Nora.   Have you been sitting here waiting for me?

Mrs. Linde.   Yes, unfortunately I came too late, you had already gone upstairs; and I thought I couldn't go away again without having seen you.

Helmer *(taking off Nora's shawl).*   Yes, take a good look at her. I think she is worth looking at. Isn't she charming, Mrs. Linde?

Mrs. Linde.   Yes, indeed she is.

Helmer.   Doesn't she look remarkably pretty? Everyone thought so at the dance. But she is terribly self-willed, this sweet little person. What are we to do with her? You will hardly believe that I had almost to bring her away by force.

Nora.   Torvald, you will repent not having let me stay, even if it were only for half an hour.

Helmer.   Listen to her, Mrs. Linde! She had danced her Tarantella, and it had been a tremendous success, as it deserved — although possibly the performance was a trifle too realistic — a little more so, I mean, than was strictly compatible with the limitations of art. But never mind about that! The chief thing is, she had made a success — she had made a tremendous success. Do you think I was going to let her remain there after that, and spoil the effect? No indeed! I took my charming little Capri maiden — my capricious little Capri maiden, I should say — on my arm; took one quick turn round the room; a curtsey on either side, and, as they say in novels, the beautiful apparition disappeared. An exit ought always to be effective, Mrs. Linde; but that is what I cannot make Nora understand. Pooh! this room is hot. *(Throws his*

[2] A long loose hooded cloak.

domino on a chair and opens the door of his room.) Hullo! it's dark in here. Oh, of course — excuse me —— .

(*He goes in and lights some candles.*)

Nora (*in a hurried and breathless whisper*).   Well?

Mrs. Linde (*in a low voice*).   I have had a talk with him.

Nora.   Yes, and ——

Mrs. Linde.   Nora, you must tell your husband all about it.

Nora (*in an expressionless voice*).   I knew it.

Mrs. Linde.   You have nothing to be afraid of as far as Krogstad is concerned; but you must tell him.

Nora.   I won't tell him.

Mrs. Linde.   Then the letter will.

Nora.   Thank you, Christine. Now I know what I must do. Hush —— !

Helmer (*coming in again*).   Well, Mrs. Linde, have you admired her?

Mrs. Linde.   Yes, and now I will say good-night.

Helmer.   What, already? Is this yours, this knitting?

Mrs. Linde (*taking it*).   Yes, thank you, I have very nearly forgotten it.

Helmer.   So you knit?

Mrs. Linde.   Of course.

Helmer.   Do you know, you ought to embroider.

Mrs. Linde.   Really? Why?

Helmer.   Yes, it's far more becoming. Let me show you. You hold the embroidery thus in your left hand, and use the needle with the right — like this — with a long, easy sweep. Do you see?

Mrs. Linde.   Yes, perhaps ——

Helmer.   But in the case of knitting — that can never be anything but ungraceful; look here — the arms close together, the knitting-needles going up and down — it has a sort of Chinese effect — . That was really excellent champagne they gave us.

Mrs. Linde.   Well, — good-night, Nora, and don't be self-willed any more.

Helmer.   That's right, Mrs. Linde.

Mrs. Linde.   Good-night, Mr. Helmer.

Helmer (*accompanying her to the door*).   Good-night, good-night. I hope you will get home all right. I should be very happy to — but you haven't any great distance to go. Good-night, good-night. (*She goes out; he shuts the door after her, and comes in again.*) Ah! — at last we have got rid of her. She is a frightful bore, that woman.

Nora.   Aren't you very tired, Torvald?

Helmer.   No, not in the least.

Nora.   Nor sleepy?

Helmer.   Not a bit. On the contrary, I feel extraordinarily lively. And you? — you really look both tired and sleepy.

Nora.   Yes, I am very tired. I want to go to sleep at once.

Helmer. There, you see it was quite right of me not to let you stay there any longer.

Nora. Everything you do is quite right, Torvald.

Helmer (*kissing her on the forehead*). Now my little skylark is speaking reasonably. Did you notice what good spirits Rank was in this evening?

Nora. Really? Was he? I didn't speak to him at all.

Helmer. And I very little, but I have not for a long time seen him in such good form. (*Looks for a while at her and then goes nearer to her.*) It is delightful to be at home by ourselves again, to be all alone with you — you fascinating, charming little darling!

Nora. Don't look at me like that, Torvald.

Helmer. Why shouldn't I look at my dearest treasure? — at all the beauty that is mine, all my very own?

Nora (*going to the other side of the table*). You mustn't say things like that to me to-night.

Helmer (*following her*). You have still got the Tarantella in your blood, I see. And it makes you more captivating than ever. Listen — the guests are beginning to go now. (*In a lower voice.*) Nora — soon the whole house will be quiet.

Nora. Yes, I hope so.

Helmer. Yes, my own darling Nora. Do you know, when I am out at a party with you like this, why I speak so little to you, keep away from you, and only send a stolen glance in your direction now and then? — do you know why I do that? It is because I make believe to myself that we are secretly in love, and you are my secretly promised bride, and that no one suspects there is anything between us.

Nora. Yes, yes — I know very well your thoughts are with me all the time.

Helmer. And when we are leaving, and I am putting the shawl over your beautiful young shoulders — on your lovely neck — then I imagine that you are my young bride and that we have just come from the wedding, and I am bringing you for the first time into our home — to be alone with you for the first time — quite alone with my shy little darling! All this evening I have longed for nothing but you. When I watched the seductive figures of the Tarantella, my blood was on fire; I could endure it no longer, and that was why I brought you down so early ——

Nora. Go away, Torvald! You must let me go. I won't ——

Helmer. What's that? You're joking, my little Nora! You won't — you won't? Am I not your husband — ?

(*A knock is heard at the outer door.*)

Nora (*starting*). Did you hear —— ?

Helmer (*going into the hall*). Who is it?

Rank (*outside*). It is I. May I come in for a moment?

Helmer (*in a fretful whisper*). Oh, what does he want now? (*Aloud.*) Wait a minute? (*Unlocks the door.*) Come, that's kind of you not to pass by our door.

Rank. I thought I heard your voice, and felt as if I should like to look in. *(With a swift glance round.)* Ah, yes! — these dear familiar rooms. You are very happy and cosy in here, you two.

Helmer. It seems to me that you looked after yourself pretty well upstairs too.

Rank. Excellently. Why shouldn't I? Why shouldn't one enjoy everything in this world? — at any rate as much as one can, and as long as one can. The wine was capital ——

Helmer. Especially the champagne.

Rank. So you noticed that too? It is almost incredible how much I managed to put away!

Nora. Torvald drank a great deal of champagne tonight, too.

Rank. Did he?

Nora. Yes, and he is always in such good spirits afterwards.

Rank. Well, why should one not enjoy a merry evening after a well-spent day?

Helmer. Well spent? I am afraid I can't take credit for that.

Rank *(clapping him on the back).* But I can, you know!

Nora. Doctor Rank, you must have been occupied with some scientific investigation to-day.

Rank. Exactly.

Helmer. Just listen — little Nora talking about scientific investigations!

Nora. And may I congratulate you on the result?

Rank. Indeed you may.

Nora. Was it favourable, then?

Rank. The best possible, for both doctor and patient — certainty.

Nora *(quickly and searchingly).* Certainty?

Rank. Absolute certainty. So wasn't I entitled to make a merry evening of it after that?

Nora. Yes, you certainly were, Doctor Rank.

Helmer. I think so too, so long as you don't have to pay for it in the morning.

Rank. Oh well, one can't have anything in this life without paying for it.

Nora. Doctor Rank — are you fond of fancy-dress balls?

Rank. Yes, if there is a fine lot of pretty costumes.

Nora. Tell me — what shall we two wear at the next?

Helmer. Little featherbrain! — are you thinking of the next already?

Rank. We two? Yes, I can tell you. You shall go as a good fairy ——

Helmer. Yes, but what do you suggest as an appropriate costume for that?

Rank. Let your wife go dressed just as she is in everyday life.

Helmer. That was really very prettily turned. But can't you tell us what you will be?

Rank. Yes, my dear friend, I have quite made up my mind about that.

Helmer. Well?

Rank. At the next fancy dress ball I shall be invisible.

Helmer. That's a good joke!

Rank. There is a big black hat — have you never heard of hats that make you invisible? If you put one on, no one can see you.

Helmer (*suppressing a smile*).   Yes, you are quite right.

Rank.   But I am clean forgetting what I came for. Helmer, give me a cigar —
one of the dark Havanas.

Helmer.   With the greatest pleasure.

(*Offers him his case.*)

Rank (*takes a cigar and cuts off the end*).   Thanks.

Nora (*striking a match*).   Let me give you a light.

Rank.   Thank you. (*She holds the match for him to light his cigar.*) And now
good-bye!

Helmer.   Good-bye, good-bye, dear old man!

Nora.   Sleep well, Doctor Rank.

Rank.   Thank you for that wish.

Nora.   Wish me the same.

Rank.   You? Well, if you want me to — sleep well! And thanks for the light.

(*He nods to them both and goes out.*)

Helmer (*in a subdued voice*).   He has drunk more than he ought.

Nora (*absently*).   Maybe. (*Helmer takes a bunch of keys out of his pocket and
goes into the hall.*) Torvald! what are you going to do there?

Helmer.   Empty the letter-box; it is quite full; there will be no room to put the
newspaper in to-morrow morning.

Nora.   Are you going to work to-night?

Helmer.   You know quite well I'm not. What is this? Some one has been at the
lock.

Nora.   At the lock — ?

Helmer.   Yes, someone has. What can it mean? I should never have thought
the maid — . Here is a broken hairpin. Nora, it is one of yours.

Nora (*quickly*).   Then it must have been the children —

Helmer.   Then you must get them out of those ways. There, at last I have got
it open. (*Takes out the contents of the letter-box, and calls to the kitchen.*)
Helen! — Helen, put out the light over the front door. (*Goes back into the
room and shuts the door into the hall. He holds out his hand full of letters.*)
Look at that — look what a heap of them there are. (*Turning them over.*)
What on earth is that?

Nora (*at the window*).   The letter — No! Torvald, no!

Helmer.   Two cards — of Rank's.

Nora.   Of Doctor Rank's?

Helmer (*looking at them*).   Doctor Rank. They were on the top. He must have
put them in when he went out.

Nora.   Is there anything written on them?

Helmer.   There is a black cross over the name. Look there — what an uncomfortable idea! It looks as if he were announcing his own death.

Nora.   It is just what he is doing.

Helmer.   What? Do you know anything about it? Has he said anything to you?

Nora.   Yes. He told me that when the cards came it would be his leave-taking from us. He means to shut himself up and die.

Helmer.   My poor old friend. Certainly I knew we should not have him very long with us. But so soon! And so he hides himself away like a wounded animal.

Nora.   If it has to happen, it is best it should be without a word — don't you think so, Torvald?

Helmer (*walking up and down*).   He had so grown into our lives. I can't think of him as having gone out of them. He, with his sufferings and his loneliness, was like a cloudy background to our sunlit happiness. Well, perhaps it is best so. For him, anyway. (*Standing still.*) And perhaps for us too, Nora. We two are thrown quite upon each other now. (*Puts his arms round her.*) My darling wife, I don't feel as if I could hold you tight enough. Do you know, Nora, I have often wished that you might be threatened by some great danger, so that I might risk my life's blood, and everything, for your sake.

Nora (*disengages herself, and says firmly and decidedly*).   Now you must read your letters, Torvald.

Helmer.   No, no; not to-night. I want to be with you, my darling wife.

Nora.   With the thought of your friend's death ——

Helmer.   You are right, it has affected us both. Something ugly has come between us — the thought of the horrors of death. We must try and rid our minds of that. Until then — we will each go to our own room.

Nora (*hanging on his neck*).   Good-night, Torvald — Good-night!

Helmer (*kissing her on the forehead*).   Good-night, my little singing-bird. Sleep sound, Nora. Now I will read my letters through.

(*He takes his letters and goes into his room, shutting the door after him.*)

Nora (*gropes distractedly about, seizes Helmer's domino, throws it round her, while she says in quick, hoarse, spasmodic whispers*).   Never to see him again. Never! Never! (*Puts her shawl over her head.*) Never to see my children again either — never again. Never! Never! — Ah! the icy, black water — the unfathomable depths — If only it were over! He has got it now — now he is reading it. Good-bye, Torvald and my children!

(*She is about to rush out through the hall, when Helmer opens his door hurriedly and stands with an open letter in his hand.*)

Helmer.   Nora!

Nora.   Ah! ——

Helmer.   What is this? Do you know what is in this letter?

Nora.   Yes, I know. Let me go! Let me get out!

Helmer (*holding her back*).   Where are you going?

Nora *(trying to get free).* You shan't save me, Torvald!

Helmer *(reeling).* True? Is this true, what I read here? Horrible! No, no — it is impossible that it can be true.

Nora. It is true. I have loved you above everything else in the world.

Helmer. Oh, don't let us have any silly excuses.

Nora *(taking a step towards him).* Torvald ——!

Helmer. Miserable creature — what have you done?

Nora. Let me go. You shall not suffer for my sake. You shall not take it upon yourself.

Helmer. No tragedy airs, please. *(Locks the hall door.)* Here you shall stay and give me an explanation. Do you understand what you have done? Answer me? Do you understand what you have done?

Nora *(looks steadily at him and says with a growing look of coldness in her face).* Yes, now I am beginning to understand thoroughly.

Helmer *(walking about the room).* What a horrible awakening! All these eight years — she who was my joy and pride — a hypocrite, a liar — worse, worse — a criminal! The unutterable ugliness of it all! For shame! For shame! *(Nora is silent and looks steadily at him. He stops in front of her.)* I ought to have suspected that something of the sort would happen. I ought to have foreseen it. All your father's want of principle — be silent! — all your father's want of principle has come out in you. No religion, no morality, no sense of duty — . How I am punished for having winked at what he did! I did it for your sake, and this is how you repay me.

Nora. Yes, that's just it.

Helmer. Now you have destroyed all my happiness. You have ruined all my future. It is horrible to think of! I am in the power of an unscrupulous man; he can do what he likes with me, ask anything he likes of me, give me any orders he pleases — I dare not refuse. And I must sink to such miserable depths because of a thoughtless woman!

Nora. When I am out of the way, you will be free.

Helmer. No fine speeches, please. Your father had always plenty of those ready, too. What good would it be to me if you were out of the way, as you say? Not the slightest. He can make the affair known everywhere; and if he does, I may be falsely suspected of having been a party to your criminal action. Very likely people will think I was behind it all — that it was I who prompted you! And I have to thank you for all this — you whom I have cherished during the whole of our married life. Do you understand now what it is you have done for me?

Nora *(coldly and quietly).* Yes.

Helmer. It is so incredible that I can't take it in. But we must come to some understanding. Take off that shawl. Take it off, I tell you. I must try and appease him some way or another. The matter must be hushed up at any cost. And as for you and me, it must appear as if everything between us were just as before — but naturally only in the eyes of the world. You will still remain in my house, that is a matter of course. But I shall not allow you to bring up the children; I dare not trust them to you. To think that I should be obliged to say so to one whom I have loved so dearly, and whom I still ——— . No, that is all over. From this moment happiness is not the question; all that concerns us is to save the remains, the fragments, the appearance ———

(A ring is heard at the front-door bell.)

Helmer (with a start). What is that? So late! Can the worst ——— ? Can he ——— ? Hide yourself, Nora. Say you are ill.

(Nora stands motionless. Helmer goes and unlocks the hall door.)

Maid (half-dressed, comes to the door). A letter for the mistress.
Helmer. Give it to me. (Takes the letter, and shuts the door.) Yes, it is from him. You shall not have it; I will read it myself.
Nora. Yes, read it.
Helmer (standing by the lamp). I scarcely have the courage to do it. It may mean ruin for both of us. No, I must know. (Tears open the letter, runs his eye over a few lines, looks at a paper enclosed and gives a shout of joy.) Nora! (She looks at him questioningly.) Nora! — No, I must read it once again ——— . Yes, it is true! I am saved! Nora, I am saved!
Nora. And I?
Helmer. You too, of course; we are both saved, both you and I. Look, he sends you your bond back. He says he regrets and repents — that a happy change in his life — never mind what he says! We are saved, Nora! No one can do anything to you. Oh, Nora, Nora! — no, first I must destroy these hateful things. Let me see ——— . (Takes a look at the bond.) No, no, I won't look at it. The whole thing shall be nothing but a bad dream to me. (Tears up the bond and both letters, throws them all into the stove, and watches them burn.) There — now it doesn't exist any longer. He says that since Christmas Eve you ——— . These must have been three dreadful days for you, Nora.
Nora. I have fought a hard fight these three days.
Helmer. And suffered agonies, and seen no way out but ——— . No, we won't call any of the horrors to mind. We will only shout with joy, and keep saying, "It's all over! It's all over!" Listen to me, Nora. You don't seem to realise that it is all over. What is this? — such a cold, set face! My poor little Nora, I quite understand; you don't feel as if you could believe that I have forgiven you. But it is true, Nora, I swear it; I have forgiven you everything. I know that what you did, you did out of love for me.
Nora. That is true.
Helmer. You have loved me as a wife ought to love her husband. Only you had not sufficient knowledge to judge of the means you used. But do you suppose you are any the less dear to me, because you don't understand how to act on your own responsibility? No, no; only lean on me; I will advise you and

direct you. I should not be a man if this womanly helplessness did not just give you a double attractiveness in my eyes. You must not think any more about the hard things I said in my first moment of consternation, when I thought everything was going to overwhelm me. I have forgiven you, Nora; I swear to you I have forgiven you.

(She goes out through the door to the right.)

Helmer.   No, don't go ——— . *(Looks in.)* What are you doing in there?

Nora *(from within).*   Taking off my fancy dress.

Helmer *(standing at the open door).*   Yes, do. Try and calm yourself, and make your mind easy again, my frightened little singing-bird. Be at rest, and feel secure; I have broad wings to shelter you under. *(Walks up and down by the door.)* How warm and cosy our home is, Nora. Here is shelter for you; here I will protect you like a hunted dove that I have saved from a hawk's claws. I will bring peace to your poor beating heart. It will come, little by little, Nora, believe me. Tomorrow morning you will look upon it all quite differently; soon everything will be just as it was before. Very soon you won't need me to assure you that I have forgiven you; you will yourself feel the certainty that I have done so. Can you suppose I should ever think of such a thing as repudiating you, or even reproaching you? You have no idea what a true man's heart is like, Nora. There is something so indescribably sweet and satisfying, to a man, in the knowledge that he has forgiven his wife — forgiven her freely, and with all his heart. It seems as if that had made her, as it were, doubly his own; he has given her a new life, so to speak; and she has in a way become both wife and child to him. So you shall be for me after this, my little scared, helpless darling. Have no anxiety about anything, Nora; only be frank and open with me, and I will serve as will and conscience both to you ——— . What is this? Not gone to bed? Have you changed your things?

Nora *(in everyday dress).*   Yes, Torvald, I have changed my things now.

Helmer.   But what for? — so late as this.

Nora.   I shall not sleep to-night.

Helmer.   But, my dear Nora ———

Nora *(looking at her watch).*   It is not so very late. Sit down here, Torvald. You and I have much to say to one another.

(She sits down at one side of the table.)

Helmer.   Nora — what is this? — this cold, set face?

Nora.   Sit down. It will take some time; I have a lot to talk over with you.

Helmer *(sits down at the opposite side of the table).*   You alarm me, Nora! — and I don't understand you.

Nora.   No, that is just it. You don't understand me, and I have never understood you either — before to-night. No, you mustn't interrupt me. You must simply listen to what I say. Torvald, this is a settling of accounts.

Helmer.   What do you mean by that?

Nora *(after a short silence).*   Isn't there one thing that strikes you as strange in our sitting here like this?

Helmer.   What is that?

Nora.   We have been married now eight years. Does it not occur to you that this is the first time we two, you and I, husband and wife, have had a serious conversation?

Helmer.   What do you mean by serious?

Nora.   In all these eight years — longer than that — from the very beginning of our acquaintance, we have never exchanged a word on any serious subject.

Helmer.   Was it likely that I would be continually and for ever telling you about worries that you could not help me to bear?

Nora.   I am not speaking about business matters. I say that we have never sat down in earnest together to try and get at the bottom of anything.

Helmer.   But, dearest Nora, would it have been any good to you?

Nora.   That is just it; you have never understood me. I have been greatly wronged, Torvald — first by papa and then by you.

Helmer.   What! By us two — by us two, who have loved you better than anyone else in the world?

Nora *(shaking her head).*   You have never loved me. You have only thought it pleasant to be in love with me.

Helmer.   Nora, what do I hear you saying?

Nora.   It is perfectly true, Torvald. When I was at home with papa, he told me his opinion about everything, and so I had the same opinions; and if I differed from him I concealed the fact, because he would not have liked it. He called me his doll-child, and he played with me just as I used to play with my dolls. And when I came to live with you ——

Helmer.   What sort of an expression is that to use about our marriage?

Nora *(undisturbed).*   I mean that I was simply transferred from papa's hands into yours. You arranged everything according to your own taste, and so I got the same tastes as you — or else I pretended to, I am really not quite sure which — I think sometimes the one and sometimes the other. When I look back on it, it seems to me as if I had been living here like a poor woman — just from hand to mouth. I have existed merely to perform tricks for you, Torvald. But you would have it so. You and papa have committed a great sin against me. It is your fault that I have made nothing of my life.

Helmer.   How unreasonable and how ungrateful you are, Nora! Have you not been happy here?

Nora.   No, I have never been happy. I thought I was, but it has never really been so.

Helmer.   Not — not happy!

Nora.   No, only merry. And you have always been so kind to me. But our home has been nothing but a playroom. I have been your doll-wife, just as at home I was papa's doll-child; and here the children have been my dolls. I thought it great fun when you played with me, just as they thought it great fun when I played with them. That is what our marriage has been, Torvald.

Helmer. There is some truth in what you say — exaggerated and strained as your view of it is. But for the future it shall be different. Playtime shall be over, and lesson-time shall begin.

Nora. Whose lessons? Mine, or the children's?

Helmer. Both your and the children's, my darling Nora.

Nora. Alas, Torvald, you are not the man to educate me into being a proper wife for you.

Helmer. And you can say that!

Nora. And I — how am I fitted to bring up the children?

Helmer. Nora!

Nora. Didn't you say so yourself a little while ago — that you dare not trust me to bring them up?

Helmer. In a moment of anger! Why do you pay any heed to that?

Nora. Indeed, you were perfectly right. I am not fit for the task. There is another task I must undertake first. I must try and educate myself — you are not the man to help me in that. I must do that for myself. And that is why I am going to leave you now.

Helmer (*springing up*). What do you say?

Nora. I must stand quite alone, if I am to understand myself and everything about me. It is for that reason that I cannot remain with you any longer.

Helmer. Nora! Nora!

Nora. I am going away from here now, at once. I am sure Christine will take me in for the night ——

Helmer. You are out of your mind! I won't allow it! I forbid you!

Nora. It is no use forbidding me anything any longer. I will take with me what belongs to myself. I will take nothing from you, either now or later.

Helmer. What sort of madness is this!

Nora. To-morrow I shall go home — I mean, to my old home. It will be easiest for me to find something to do there.

Helmer. You blind, foolish woman!

Nora. I must try and get some sense, Torvald.

Helmer. To desert your home, your husband and your children! And you don't consider what people will say!

Nora. I cannot consider that at all. I only know that it is necessary for me.

Helmer. It's shocking. This is how you would neglect your most sacred duties.

Nora. What do you consider my most sacred duties?

Helmer. Do I need to tell you that? Are they not your duties to your husband and your children?

Nora. I have other duties just as sacred.

Helmer. That you have not. What duties could those be?

Nora. Duties to myself.

Helmer.   Before all else, you are a wife and a mother.

Nora.   I don't believe that any longer. I believe that before all else I am a reasonable human being, just as you are — or, at all events, that I must try and become one. I know quite well, Torvald, that most people would think you right, and that views of that kind are to be found in books; but I can no longer content myself with what most people say, or with what is found in books. I must think over things for myself and get to understand them.

Helmer.   Can you not understand your place in your own home? Have you not a reliable guide in such matters as that? — have you no religion?

Nora.   I am afraid, Torvald, I do not exactly know what religion is.

Helmer.   What are you saying?

Nora.   I know nothing but what the clergyman said, when I went to be confirmed. He told us that religion was this, and that, and the other. When I am away from all this, and am alone, I will look into that matter too. I will see if what the clergyman said is true, or at all events if it is true for me.

Helmer.   This is unheard of in a girl of your age! But if religion cannot lead you aright, let me try and awaken your conscience. I suppose you have some moral sense? Or — answer me — am I to think you have none?

Nora.   I assure you, Torvald, that is not an easy question to answer. I really don't know. The thing perplexes me altogether. I only know that you and I look at it in quite another light. I am learning, too, that the law is quite another thing from what I supposed; but I find it impossible to convince myself that the law is right. According to it a woman has no right to spare her old dying father, or to save her husband's life. I can't believe that.

Helmer.   You talk like a child. You don't understand the conditions of the world in which you live.

Nora.   No, I don't. But now I am going to try. I am going to see if I can make out who is right, the world or I.

Helmer.   You are ill, Nora; you are delirious; I almost think you are out of your mind.

Nora.   I have never felt my mind so clear and certain as to-night.

Helmer.   And is it with a clear and certain mind that you forsake your husband and your children?

Nora.   Yes, it is.

Helmer.   Then there is only one possible explanation.

Nora.   What is that?

Helmer.   You do not love me any more.

Nora.   No, that is just it.

Helmer.   Nora! — and you can say that?

Nora.   It gives me great pain, Torvald, for you have always been so kind to me, but I cannot help it. I do not love you any more.

Helmer (*regaining his composure*).   Is that a clear and certain conviction too?

Nora.   Yes, absolutely clear and certain. That is the reason why I will not stay here any longer.

Helmer. And can you tell me what I have done to forfeit your love?

Nora. Yes, indeed I can. It was to-night, when the wonderful thing did not happen; then I saw you were not the man I had thought you.

Helmer. Explain yourself better — I don't understand you.

Nora. I have waited so patiently for eight years; for, goodness knows, I knew very well that wonderful things don't happen every day. Then this horrible misfortune came upon me; and then I felt quite certain that the wonderful thing was going to happen at last. When Krogstad's letter was lying out there, never for a moment did I imagine that you would consent to accept this man's conditions. I was so absolutely certain that you would say to him: Publish the thing to the whole world. And when that was done ——

Helmer. Yes, what then? — when I had exposed my wife to shame and disgrace?

Nora. When that was done, I was so absolutely certain, you would come forward and take everything upon yourself, and say: I am the guilty one.

Helmer. Nora —— !

Nora. You mean that I would never have accepted such a sacrifice on your part? No, of course not. But what would my assurances have been worth against yours? That was the wonderful thing which I hoped for and feared; and it was to prevent that, that I wanted to kill myself.

Helmer. I would gladly work night and day for you, Nora — bear sorrow and want for your sake. But no man would sacrifice his honour for the one he loves.

Nora. It is a thing hundreds of thousands of women have done.

Helmer. Oh, you think and talk like a heedless child.

Nora. Maybe. But you neither think nor talk like the man I could bind myself to. As soon as your fear was over — and it was not fear for what threatened me, but for what might happen to you — when the whole thing was past, as far as you were concerned it was exactly as if nothing at all had happened. Exactly as before, I was your little skylark, your doll, which you would in future treat with doubly gentle care, because it was so brittle and fragile. (*Getting up.*) Torvald — it was then it dawned upon me that for eight years I had been living here with a strange man, and had borne him three children ——. Oh, I can't bear to think of it! I could tear myself into little bits!

Helmer (*sadly*). I see, I see. An abyss has opened between us — there is no denying it. But, Nora, would it not be possible to fill it up?

Nora. As I am now, I am no wife for you.

Helmer. I have it in me to become a different man.

Nora. Perhaps — if your doll is taken away from you.

Helmer. But to part! — to part from you! No, no, Nora, I can't understand that idea.

Nora (*going out to the right*). That makes it all the more certain that it must be done.

(She comes back with her cloak and hat and a small bag which she puts on a chair by the table.)

Helmer.   Nora, Nora, not now! Wait till to-morrow.

Nora *(putting on her cloak).*   I cannot spend the night in a strange man's room.

Helmer.   But can't we live here like brother and sister —— ?

Nora *(putting on her hat).*   You know very well that would not last long. *(Puts the shawl round her.)* Good-bye, Torvald. I won't see the little ones. I know they are in better hands than mine. As I am now, I can be of no use to them.

Helmer.   But some day, Nora — some day?

Nora.   How can I tell? I have no idea what is going to become of me.

Helmer.   But you are my wife, whatever becomes of you.

Nora.   Listen, Torvald. I have heard that when a wife deserts her husband's house, as I am doing now, he is legally freed from all obligations towards her. In any case I set you free from all your obligations. You are not to feel yourself bound in the slightest way, any more than I shall. There must be perfect freedom on both sides. See here is your ring back. Give me mine.

Helmer.   That too?

Nora.   That too.

Helmer.   Here it is.

Nora.   That's right. Now it is all over. I have put the keys here. The maids know all about everything in the house — better than I do. To-morrow, after I have left her, Christine will come here and pack up my own things that I brought with me from home. I will have them sent after me.

Helmer.   All over! All over! — Nora, shall you never think of me again?

Nora.   I know I shall often think of you and the children and this house.

Helmer.   May I write to you, Nora?

Nora.   No — never. You must not do that.

Helmer.   But at least let me send you ——

Nora.   Nothing — nothing ——

Helmer.   Let me help you if you are in want.

Nora.   No. I can receive nothing from a stranger.

Helmer.   Nora — can I never be anything more than a stranger to you?

Nora *(taking her bag).*   Ah, Torvald, the most wonderful thing of all would have to happen.

Helmer.   Tell me what that would be!

Nora.   Both you and I would have to be so changed that —— . Oh, Torvald, I don't believe any longer in wonderful things happening.

Helmer.   But I will believe in it. Tell me? So changed that —— ?

Nora.   That our life together would be a real wedlock. Good-bye.

(She goes out through the hall.)

Helmer *(sinks down on a chair at the door and buries his face in his hands).* Nora! Nora! *(Looks round, and rises.)* Empty. She is gone. *(A hope flashes across his mind.)* The most wonderful thing of all —— ?

(The sound of a door shutting is heard from below.)

For Analysis

1. What evidence can you find to support the interpretation that this play is not only about the Helmers' marriage but also about the institution of marriage itself?

2. What does the first meeting between Nora and Mrs. Linde tell us about Nora's character?

3. On a number of occasions, Nora recalls her father. What relevance do these recollections have to the development of the **theme**?

4. Is Krogstad presented as a conventional villain, or are we meant to sympathize with him? Explain.

5. What function does Dr. Rank serve in the play?

6. Examine the stage directions at the beginning of each act. In what ways do they contribute to and reflect the developing action?

7. Acts I and II contain early dialogues between Nora and Torvald. What changes in Nora does a comparison between the two dialogues reveal?

8. At what point in the action, in your opinion, does Nora begin to understand the truth of her situation and to take responsibility for her life?

9. Summarize the various arguments Torvald uses in his attempt to persuade Nora not to leave.

10. Is the feminist theme of the play weakened by Ibsen's failure to suggest how Nora could conceivably make it on her own in such a patriarchal society? Explain.

On Style

1. Analyze and evaluate Ibsen's use of **exposition** in Act I.

2. In the first two acts, Ibsen uses the impending party and the tarantella Nora is to perform to create suspense and dramatic tension. Discuss the way in which he achieves these effects.

Making Connections

1. Compare the attitudes toward women revealed in this play with those in Susan Glaspell's *Trifles* (p. 1236) and Lorraine Hansberry's *A Raisin in the Sun* (p. 867)?

2. Compare Nora and Antigonê in Sophocles' *Antigonê* (p. 467) as rebels against the constrictions of a patriarchal society. As part of this comparison, examine the similarities and differences between the arguments used by Creon and those used by Torvald to dissuade Antigonê and Nora from their respective courses of action.

Writing Topics

1. Does the fact that Nora abandons her children undermine her otherwise heroic decision to walk out on a hollow marriage? For an 1880 German production,

Ibsen — in response to public demand — provided an alternate ending in which Nora, after struggling with her conscience, decides that she cannot abandon her children. Do you think this is a better ending than the original one?

2. How does the subplot involving the relationship between Mrs. Linde and Krogstad add force to the main plot of *A Doll's House*?

3. Have you ever defied social pressure because the cost of conforming was too high? Describe the source of the pressure, the issues at stake, and the consequences of your refusal. Since then, have you had second thoughts about your actions?

4. Write a brief description of a marriage you are familiar with that endured only out of inertia, economic pressure, or fear.

August Wilson (b. 1945)

Fences 1987

CHARACTERS

Troy Maxson
Jim Bono, Troy's friend
Rose, Troy's wife
Lyons, Troy's oldest son by previous
  marriage

Gabriel, Troy's brother
Cory, Troy and Rose's son
Raynell, Troy's daughter

Setting: The setting is the yard which fronts the only entrance to the Maxson household, an ancient two-story brick house set back off a small alley in a big-city neighborhood. The entrance to the house is gained by two or three steps leading to a wooden porch badly in need of paint.

A relatively recent addition to the house and running its full width, the porch lacks congruence. It is a sturdy porch with a flat roof. One or two chairs of dubious value sit at one end where the kitchen window opens onto the porch. An old-fashioned icebox stands silent guard at the opposite end.

The yard is a small dirt yard, partially fenced, except for the last scene, with a wooden sawhorse, a pile of lumber, and other fence-building equipment set off to the side. Opposite is a tree from which hangs a ball made of rags. A baseball bat leans against the tree. Two oil drums serve as garbage receptacles and sit near the house at right to complete the setting.

The Play: Near the turn of the century, the destitute of Europe sprang on the city with tenacious claws and an honest and solid dream. The city devoured them. They swelled its belly until it burst into a thousand furnaces and sewing machines, a thousand butcher shops and bakers' ovens, a thousand churches and hospitals and funeral parlors and money-lenders. The city grew. It nourished itself and offered each man a partnership limited only by his talent, his guile, and his willingness and capacity for hard work. For the immigrants of Europe, a dream dared and won true.

The descendants of African slaves were offered no such welcome or participation. They came from places called the Carolinas and the Virginias, Georgia, Alabama, Mississippi, and Tennessee. They came strong, eager, searching. The city rejected them and they fled and settled along the riverbanks and under bridges in shallow, ramshackle houses made of sticks and tarpaper. They collected rags and wood. They sold the use of their muscles and their bodies. They cleaned houses and washed clothes, they shined shoes, and in quiet desperation and vengeful pride, they stole, and lived in pursuit of their own dream. That they could breathe free, finally, and stand to meet life with the force of dignity and whatever eloquence the heart could call upon.

By 1957, the hard-won victories of the European immigrants had solidified the industrial might of America. War had been confronted and won with new energies that used loyalty and patriotism as its fuel. Life was rich, full, and flourishing. The Milwaukee Braves won the World Series, and the hot winds of change that would make the sixties a turbulent, racing, dangerous, and provocative decade had not yet begun to blow full.

Act I

Scene I: It is 1957. Troy and Bono enter the yard, engaged in conversation. Troy is fifty-three years old, a large man with thick, heavy hands; it is this largeness that he strives to fill out and make an accommodation with. Together with his blackness, his largeness informs his sensibilities and the choices he has made in his life.

Of the two men, Bono is obviously the follower. His commitment to their friendship of thirty-odd years is rooted in his admiration of Troy's honesty, capacity for hard work, and his strength, which Bono seeks to emulate.

It is Friday night, payday, and the one night of the week the two men engage in a ritual of talk and drink. Troy is usually the most talkative and at times he can be crude and almost vulgar, though he is capable of rising to profound heights of expression. The men carry lunch buckets and wear or carry burlap aprons and are dressed in clothes suitable to their jobs as garbage collectors.

Bono.   Troy, you ought to stop that lying!
Troy.   I ain't lying! The nigger had a watermelon this big. *(He indicates with his hands.)* Talking about . . . "What watermelon, Mr. Rand?" I liked to fell out! "What watermelon, Mr. Rand?" . . . And it sitting there big as life.
Bono.   What did Mr. Rand say?
Troy.   Ain't said nothing. Figure if the nigger too dumb to know he carrying a watermelon, he wasn't gonna get much sense out of him. Trying to hide that great big old watermelon under his coat. Afraid to let the white man see him carry it home.
Bono.   I'm like you . . . I ain't got no time for them kind of people.
Troy.   Now what he look like getting mad cause he see the man from the union talking to Mr. Rand?
Bono.   He come to me talking about . . . "Maxson gonna get us fired." I told him to get away from me with that. He walked away from me calling you a troublemaker. What Mr. Rand say?

Troy. Ain't said nothing. He told me to go down the Commissioner's office next Friday. They called me down there to see them.

Bono. Well, as long as you got your complaint filed, they can't fire you. That's what one of them white fellows tell me.

Troy. I ain't worried about them firing me. They gonna fire me cause I asked a question? That's all I did. I went to Mr. Rand and asked him, "Why? Why you got the white mens driving and the colored lifting?" Told him "what's the matter, don't I count? You think only white fellows got sense enough to drive a truck. That ain't no paper job! Hell, anybody can drive a truck. How come you got all whites driving and the colored lifting?" He told me "take it to the union." Well, hell, that's what I done! Now they wanna come up with this pack of lies.

Bono. I told Brownie if the man come and ask him any questions . . . just tell the truth! It ain't nothing but something they done trumped up on you cause you filed a complaint on them.

Troy. Brownie don't understand nothing. All I want them to do is change the job description. Give everybody a chance to drive the truck. Brownie can't see that. He ain't got that much sense.

Bono. How you figure he be making out with that gal be up at Taylors' all the time . . . that Alberta gal?

Troy. Same as you and me. Getting just as much as we is. Which is to say nothing.

Bono. It is, huh? I figure you doing a little better than me . . . and I ain't saying what I'm doing.

Troy. Aw, nigger, look here . . . I know you. If you had got anywhere near that gal, twenty minutes later you be looking to tell somebody. And the first one you gonna tell . . . that you gonna want to brag to . . . is gonna be me.

Bono. I ain't saying that. I see where you be eyeing her.

Troy. I eye all the women. I don't miss nothing. Don't never let nobody tell you Troy Maxson don't eye the women.

Bono. You been doing more than eyeing her. You done bought her a drink or two.

Troy. Hell yeah, I bought her a drink! What that mean? I bought you one, too. What that mean cause I buy her a drink? I'm just being polite.

Bono. It's all right to buy her one drink. That's what you call being polite. But when you wanna be buying two or three . . . that's what you call eyeing her.

Troy. Look here, as long as you known me . . . you ever known me to chase after women?

Bono. Hell yeah! Long as I done known you. You forgetting I knew you when.

Troy. Naw, I'm talking about since I been married to Rose?

Bono. Oh, not since you been married to Rose. Now, that's the truth, there. I can say that.

Troy. All right then! Case closed.

Bono. I see you be walking up around Alberta's house. You supposed to be at Taylors' and you be walking up around there.

Troy.   What you watching where I'm walking for? I ain't watching after you.

Bono.   I seen you walking around there more than once.

Troy.   Hell, you liable to see me walking anywhere! That don't mean nothing cause you see me walking around there.

Bono.   Where she come from anyway? She just kinda showed up one day.

Troy.   Tallahassee. You can look at her and tell she one of them Florida gals. They got some big healthy women down there. Grow them right up out the ground. Got a little bit of Indian in her. Most of them niggers down in Florida got some Indian in them.

Bono.   I don't know about that Indian part. But she damn sure big and healthy. Woman wear some big stockings. Got them great big old legs and hips as wide as the Mississippi River.

Troy.   Legs don't mean nothing. You don't do nothing but push them out of the way. But them hips cushion the ride!

Bono.   Troy, you ain't got no sense.

Troy.   It's the truth! Like you riding on Goodyears!

Rose enters from the house. She is ten years younger than Troy, her devotion to him stems from her recognition of the possibilities of her life without him: a succession of abusive men and their babies, a life of partying and running the streets, the Church, or aloneness with its attendant pain and frustration. She recognizes Troy's spirit as a fine and illuminating one and she either ignores or forgives his faults, only some of which she recognizes. Though she doesn't drink, her presence is an integral part of the Friday night rituals. She alternates between the porch and the kitchen, where supper preparations are under way.

Rose.   What you all out here getting into?

Troy.   What you worried about what we getting into for? This is men talk, woman.

Rose.   What I care what you all talking about? Bono, you gonna stay for supper?

Bono.   No, I thank you, Rose. But Lucille say she cooking up a pot of pigfeet.

Troy.   Pigfeet! Hell, I'm going home with you! Might even stay the night if you got some pigfeet. You got something in there to top them pigfeet, Rose?

Rose.   I'm cooking up some chicken. I got some chicken and collard greens.

Troy.   Well, go on back in the house and let me and Bono finish what we was talking about. This is men talk. I got some talk for you later. You know what kind of talk I mean. You go on and powder it up.

Rose.   Troy Maxson, don't you start that now!

Troy *(puts his arm around her).*   Aw, woman . . . come here. Look here, Bono . . . when I met this woman . . . I got out that place, say, "Hitch up my pony, saddle up my mare . . . there's a woman out there for me somewhere. I looked here. Looked there. Saw Rose and latched on to her." I latched on to her and told her — I'm gonna tell you the truth — I told her, "Baby, I don't wanna marry, I just wanna be your man." Rose told me . . . tell him what you told me, Rose.

Rose.   I told him if he wasn't the marrying kind, then move out the way so the marrying kind could find me.

Troy.   That's what she told me. "Nigger, you in my way. You blocking the view! Move out the way so I can find me a husband." I thought it over two or three days. Come back —

Rose.   Ain't no two or three days nothing. You was back the same night.

Troy.   Come back, told her . . . "Okay, baby . . . but I'm gonna buy me a banty rooster and put him out there in the backyard . . . and when he see a stranger come, he'll flap his wings and crow . . ." Look here, Bono, I could watch the front door by myself . . . it was that back door I was worried about.

Rose.   Troy, you ought not talk like that. Troy ain't doing nothing but telling a lie.

Troy.   Only thing is . . . when we first got married . . . forget the rooster . . . we ain't had no yard!

Bono.   I hear you tell it. Me and Lucille was staying down there on Logan Street. Had two rooms with the outhouse in the back. I ain't mind the out-house none. But when that goddamn wind blow through there in the winter . . . that's what I'm talking about! To this day I wonder why in the hell I ever stayed down there for six long years. But see, I didn't know I could do no better. I thought only white folks had inside toilets and things.

Rose.   There's a lot of people don't know they can do no better than they doing now. That's just something you got to learn. A lot of folks still shop at Bella's.

Troy.   Ain't nothing wrong with shopping at Bella's. She got fresh food.

Rose.   I ain't said nothing about if she got fresh food. I'm talking about what she charge. She charge ten cents more than the A&P.

Troy.   The A&P ain't never done nothing for me. I spends my money where I'm treated right. I go down to Bella, say, "I need a loaf of bread, I'll pay you Friday." She give it to me. What sense that make when I got money to go and spend it somewhere else and ignore the person who done right by me? That ain't in the Bible.

Rose.   We ain't talking about what's in the Bible. What sense it make to shop there when she overcharge?

Troy.   You shop where you want to. I'll do my shopping where the people been good to me.

Rose.   Well, I don't think it's right for her to overcharge. That's all I was saying.

Bono.   Look here . . . I got to get on. Lucille going be raising all kind of hell.

Troy.   Where you going, nigger? We ain't finished this pint. Come here, finish this pint.

Bono.   Well, hell, I am . . . if you ever turn the bottle loose.

Troy (*hands him the bottle*).   The only thing I say about the A&P is I'm glad Cory got that job down there. Help him take care of his school clothes and things. Gabe done moved out and things getting tight around here. He got that job. . . . He can start to look out for himself.

Rose.   Cory done went and got recruited by a college football team.

Troy.   I told that boy about that football stuff. The white man ain't gonna let him get nowhere with that football. I told him when he first come to me with it. Now you come telling me he done went and got more tied up in it. He ought to go and get recruited in how to fix cars or something where he can make a living.

Rose. He ain't talking about making no living playing football. It's just something the boys in school do. They gonna send a recruiter by to talk to you. He'll tell you he ain't talking about making no living playing football. It's a honor to be recruited.

Troy. It ain't gonna get him nowhere. Bono'll tell you that.

Bono. If he be like you in the sports . . . he's gonna be all right. Ain't but two men ever played baseball as good as you. That's Babe Ruth and Josh Gibson.[1] Them's the only two men ever hit more home runs than you.

Troy. What it ever get me? Ain't got a pot to piss in or a window to throw it out of.

Rose. Times have changed since you was playing baseball, Troy. That was before the war. Times have changed a lot since then.

Troy. How in hell they done changed?

Rose. They got lots of colored boys playing ball now. Baseball and football.

Bono. You right about that, Rose. Times have changed, Troy. You just come along too early.

Troy. There ought not never have been no time called too early! Now you take that fellow . . . what's that fellow they had playing right field for the Yankees back then? You know who I'm talking about, Bono. Used to play right field for the Yankees.

Rose. Selkirk?

Troy. Selkirk! That's it! Man batting .269, understand? .269. What kind of sense that make? I was hitting .432 with thirty-seven home runs! Man batting .269 and playing right field for the Yankees! I saw Josh Gibson's daughter yesterday. She walking around with raggedy shoes on her feet. Now I bet you Selkirk's daughter ain't walking around with raggedy shoes on her feet! I bet you that!

Rose. They got a lot of colored baseball players now. Jackie Robinson[2] was the first. Folks had to wait for Jackie Robinson.

Troy. I done seen a hundred niggers play baseball better than Jackie Robinson. Hell, I know some teams Jackie Robinson couldn't even make! What you talking about Jackie Robinson. Jackie Robinson wasn't nobody. I'm talking about if you could play ball then they ought to have let you play. Don't care what color you were. Come telling me I come along too early. If you could play . . . then they ought to have let you play.

Troy takes a long drink from the bottle.

---

[1] Babe Ruth (1895–1948) was a legendary white American baseball player. Josh Gibson (1911–1947) was a baseball star in the Negro National League.

[2] In 1947, Jackie Robinson (1919–1972) became the first African American baseball player to join the major leagues.

Rose. You gonna drink yourself to death. You don't need to be drinking like that.

Troy. Death ain't nothing. I done seen him. Done wrassled with him. You can't tell me nothing about death. Death ain't nothing but a fastball on the outside corner. And you know what I'll do to that! Lookee here, Bono . . . am I lying? You get one of them fastballs, about waist high, over the outside corner of the plate where you can get the meat of the bat on it . . . and good god! You can kiss it goodbye. Now, am I lying?

Bono. Naw, you telling the truth there. I seen you do it.

Troy. If I'm lying . . . that 450 feet worth of lying! (*Pause.*) That's all death is to me. A fastball on the outside corner.

Rose. I don't know why you want to get on talking about death.

Troy. Ain't nothing wrong with talking about death. That's part of life. Everybody gonna die. You gonna die, I'm gonna die. Bono's gonna die. Hell, we all gonna die.

Rose. But you ain't got to talk about it. I don't like to talk about it.

Troy. You the one brought it up. Me and Bono was talking about baseball . . . you tell me I'm gonna drink myself to death. Ain't that right, Bono? You know I don't drink this but one night out of the week. That's Friday night. I'm gonna drink just enough to where I can handle it. Then I cuts it loose. I leave it alone. So don't you worry about me drinking myself to death. 'Cause I ain't worried about Death. I done seen him. I done wrestled with him.

Look here, Bono . . . I looked up one day and Death was marching straight at me. Like Soldiers on Parade! The Army of Death was marching straight at me. The middle of July, 1941. It got real cold just like it be winter. It seem like Death himself reached out and touched me on the shoulder. He touch me just like I touch you. I got cold as ice and Death standing there grinning at me.

Rose. Troy, why don't you hush that talk.

Troy. I say . . . What you want, Mr. Death? You be wanting me? You done brought your army to be getting me? I looked him dead in the eye. I wasn't fearing nothing. I was ready to tangle. Just like I'm ready to tangle now. The Bible say be ever vigilant. That's why I don't get but so drunk. I got to keep watch.

Rose. Troy was right down there in Mercy Hospital. You remember he had pneumonia? Laying there with a fever talking plumb out of his head.

Troy. Death standing there staring at me . . . carrying that sickle in his hand. Finally he say, "You want bound over for another year?" See, just like that . . . "You want bound over for another year?" I told him, "Bound over hell! Let's settle this now!"

It seem like he kinda fell back when I said that, and all the cold went out of me. I reached down and grabbed that sickle and threw it just as far as I could throw it . . . and me and him commenced to wrestling.

We wrestled for three days and three nights. I can't say where I found the strength from. Every time it seemed like he was gonna get the best of me, I'd reach way down deep inside myself and find the strength to do him one better.

Rose.   Every time Troy tell that story he find different ways to tell it. Different things to make up about it.

Troy.   I ain't making up nothing. I'm telling you the facts of what happened. I wrestled with Death for three days and three nights and I'm standing here to tell you about it. *(Pause.)* All right. At the end of the third night we done weakened each other to where we can't hardly move. Death stood up, throwed on his robe . . . had him a white robe with a hood on it. He throwed on that robe and went off to look for his sickle. Say, "I'll be back." Just like that. "I'll be back." I told him, say, "Yeah, but . . . you gonna have to find me!" I wasn't no fool. I wan't going looking for him. Death ain't nothing to play with. And I know he's gonna get me. I know I got to join his army . . . his camp followers. But as long as I keep my strength and see him coming . . . as long as I keep up my vigilance . . . he's gonna have to fight to get me. I ain't going easy.

Bono.   Well, look here, since you got to keep up your vigilance . . . let me have the bottle.

Troy.   Aw hell, I shouldn't have told you that part. I should have left out that part.

Rose.   Troy be talking that stuff and half the time don't even know what he be talking about.

Troy.   Bono know me better than that.

Bono.   That's right. I know you. I know you got some Uncle Remus[3] in your blood. You got more stories than the devil got sinners.

Troy.   Aw hell, I done seen him too! Done talked with the devil.

Rose.   Troy, don't nobody wanna be hearing all that stuff.

Lyons enters the yard from the street. Thirty-four years old, Troy's son by a previous marriage, he sports a neatly trimmed goatee, sport coat, white shirt, tieless and buttoned at the collar. Though he fancies himself a musician, he is more caught up in the rituals and "idea" of being a musician than in the actual practice of the music. He has come to borrow money from Troy, and while he knows he will be successful, he is uncertain as to what extent his lifestyle will be held up to scrutiny and ridicule.

Lyons.   Hey, Pop.

Troy.   What you come "Hey, Popping" me for?

Lyons.   How you doing, Rose? *(He kisses her.)* Mr. Bono. How you doing?

Bono.   Hey, Lyons . . . how you been?

Troy.   He must have been doing all right. I ain't seen him around here last week.

---

[3] The narrator in Joel Chandler Harris's 1880 collection of traditional African American tales and verses.

Rose.   Troy, leave your boy alone. He come by to see you and you wanna start all that nonsense.

Troy.   I ain't bothering Lyons. *(Offers him the bottle.)* Here . . . get you a drink. We got an understanding. I know why he come by to see me and he know I know.

Lyons.   Come on, Pop . . . I just stopped by to say hi . . . see how you was doing.

Troy.   You ain't stopped by yesterday.

Rose.   You gonna stay for supper, Lyons? I got some chicken cooking in the oven.

Lyons.   No, Rose . . . thanks. I was just in the neighborhood and thought I'd stop by for a minute.

Troy.   You was in the neighborhood all right, nigger. You telling the truth there. You was in the neighborhood cause it's my payday.

Lyons.   Well, hell, since you mentioned it . . . let me have ten dollars.

Troy.   I'll be damned! I'll die and go to hell and play blackjack with the devil before I give you ten dollars.

Bono.   That's what I wanna know about . . . that devil you done seen.

Lyons.   What . . . Pop done seen the devil? You too much, Pops.

Troy.   Yeah, I done seen him. Talked to him too!

Rose.   You ain't seen no devil. I done told you that man ain't had nothing to do with the devil. Anything you can't understand, you want to call it the devil.

Troy.   Look here, Bono . . . I went down to see Hertzberger about some furniture. Got three rooms for two-ninety-eight. That what it say on the radio. "Three rooms . . . two-ninety-eight." Even made up a little song about it. Go down there . . . man tell me I can't get no credit. I'm working every day and can't get no credit. What to do? I got an empty house with some raggedy furniture in it. Cory ain't got no bed. He's sleeping on a pile of rags on the floor. Working every day and can't get no credit. Come back here — Rose'll tell you — madder than hell. Sit down . . . try to figure what I'm gonna do. Come a knock on the door. Ain't been living here but three days. Who know I'm here? Open the door . . . devil standing there bigger than life. White fellow . . . got on good clothes and everything. Standing there with a clipboard in his hand. I ain't had to say nothing. First words come out of his mouth was . . . "I understand you need some furniture and can't get no credit." I liked to fell over. He say, "I'll give you all the credit you want, but you got to pay the interest on it." I told him, "Give me three rooms worth and charge whatever you want." Next day a truck pulled up here and two men unloaded them three rooms. Man what drove the truck give me a book. Say send ten dollars, first of every month to the address in the book and everything will be all right. Say if I miss a payment the devil was coming back and it'll be hell to pay. That was fifteen years ago. To this day . . . the first of the month I send my ten dollars, Rose'll tell you.

Rose.   Troy lying.

Troy.   I ain't never seen that man since. Now you tell me who else that could have been but the devil? I ain't sold my soul or nothing like that, you understand. Naw, I wouldn't have truck with the devil about nothing like that. I got my furniture and pays my ten dollars the first of the month just like clockwork.

Bono. How long you say you been paying this ten dollars a month?

Troy. Fifteen years!

Bono. Hell, ain't you finished paying for it yet? How much the man done charged you?

Troy. Ah hell, I done paid for it. I done paid for it ten times over! The fact is I'm scared to stop paying it.

Rose. Troy lying. We got that furniture from Mr. Glickman. He ain't paying no ten dollars a month to nobody.

Troy. Aw hell, woman. Bono know I ain't that big a fool.

Lyons. I was just getting ready to say . . . I know where there's a bridge for sale.

Troy. Look here, I'll tell you this . . . it don't matter to me if he was the devil. It don't matter if the devil give credit. Somebody has got to give it.

Rose. It ought to matter. You going around talking about having truck with the devil . . . God's the one you gonna have to answer to. He's the one gonna be at the Judgment.

Lyons. Yeah, well, look here, Pop . . . let me have that ten dollars. I'll give it back to you. Bonnie got a job working at the hospital.

Troy. What I tell you, Bono? The only time I see this nigger is when he wants something. That's the only time I see him.

Lyons. Come on, Pop, Mr. Bono don't want to hear all that. Let me have the ten dollars. I told you Bonnie working.

Troy. What that mean to me? "Bonnie working." I don't care if she working. Go ask her for the ten dollars if she working. Talking about "Bonnie working." Why ain't you working?

Lyons. Aw, Pop, you know I can't find no decent job. Where am I gonna get a job at? You know I can't get no job.

Troy. I told you I know some people down there. I can get you on the rubbish if you want to work. I told you that the last time you came by here asking me for something.

Lyons. Naw, Pop . . . thanks. That ain't for me. I don't wanna be carrying nobody's rubbish. I don't wanna be punching nobody's time clock.

Troy. What's the matter, you too good to carry people's rubbish? Where you think that ten dollars you talking about come from? I'm just supposed to haul people's rubbish and give my money to you cause you too lazy to work. You too lazy to work and wanna know why you ain't got what I got.

Rose. What hospital Bonnie working at? Mercy?

Lyons. She's down at Passavant working in the laundry.

Troy. I ain't got nothing as it is. I give you that ten dollars and I got to eat beans the rest of the week. Naw . . . you ain't getting no ten dollars here.

Lyons. You ain't got to be eating no beans. I don't know why you wanna say that.

Troy. I ain't got no extra money. Gabe done moved over to Miss Pearl's paying her the rent and things done got tight around here. I can't afford to be giving you every payday.

Lyons. I ain't asked you to give me nothing. I asked you to loan me ten dollars. I know you got ten dollars.

Troy. Yeah, I got it. You know why I got it? Cause I don't throw my money away out there in the streets. You living the fast life . . . wanna be a musician . . . running around in them clubs and things . . . then, you learn to take care of yourself. You ain't gonna find me going and asking nobody for nothing. I done spent too many years without.

Lyons. You and me is two different people, Pop.

Troy. I done learned my mistake and learned to do what's right by it. You still trying to get something for nothing. Life don't owe you nothing. You owe it to yourself. Ask Bono. He'll tell you I'm right.

Lyons. You got your way of dealing with the world . . . I got mine. The only thing that matters to me is music.

Troy. Yeah, I can see that! It don't matter how you gonna eat . . . where your next dollar is coming from. You telling the truth there.

Lyons. I know I got to eat. But I got to live too. I need something that gonna help me to get out of the bed in the morning. Make me feel like I belong in the world. I don't bother nobody. I just stay with my music cause that's the only way I can find to live in the world. Otherwise there ain't no telling what I might do. Now I don't come criticizing you and how you live. I just come by to ask you for ten dollars. I don't wanna hear all that about how I live.

Troy. Boy, your mamma did a hell of a job raising you.

Lyons. You can't change me, Pop. I'm thirty-four years old. If you wanted to change me, you should have been there when I was growing up. I come by to see you . . . ask for ten dollars and you want to talk about how I was raised. You don't know nothing about how I was raised.

Rose. Let the boy have ten dollars, Troy.

Troy (to Lyons). What the hell you looking at me for? I ain't got no ten dollars. You know what I do with my money. (To Rose.) Give him ten dollars if you want him to have it.

Rose. I will. Just as soon as you turn it loose.

Troy (handing Rose the money). There it is. Seventy-six dollars and forty-two cents. You see this, Bono? Now, I ain't gonna get but six of that back.

Rose. You ought to stop telling that lie. Here, Lyons. (She hands him the money.)

Lyons. Thanks, Rose. Look . . . I got to run . . . I'll see you later.

Troy. Wait a minute. You gonna say, "thanks, Rose" and ain't gonna look to see where she got that ten dollars from? See how they do me, Bono?

Lyons. I know she got it from you, Pop. Thanks. I'll give it back to you.

Troy. There he go telling another lie. Time I see that ten dollars . . . he'll be owing me thirty more.

Lyons. See you, Mr. Bono.

Bono. Take care, Lyons!
Lyons. Thanks, Pop. I'll see you again.

Lyons exits the yard.

Troy. I don't know why he don't go and get him a decent job and take care of that woman he got.
Bono. He'll be all right, Troy. The boy is still young.
Troy. The *boy* is thirty-four years old.
Rose. Let's not get off into all that.
Bono. Look here . . . I got to be going. I got to be getting on. Lucille gonna be waiting.
Troy (*puts his arm around Rose*). See this woman, Bono? I love this woman. I love this woman so much it hurts. I love her so much . . . I done run out of ways of loving her. So I got to go back to basics. Don't you come by my house Monday morning talking about time to go to work . . . 'cause I'm still gonna be stroking!
Rose. Troy! Stop it now!
Bono. I ain't paying him no mind, Rose. That ain't nothing but gin-talk. Go on, Troy. I'll see you Monday.
Troy. Don't you come by my house, nigger! I done told you what I'm gonna be doing.

The lights go down to black.

Scene II: The lights come up on Rose hanging up clothes. She hums and sings softly to herself. It is the following morning.

Rose (*sings*). Jesus, be a fence all around me every day
Jesus, I want you to protect me as I travel on my way.
Jesus, be a fence all around me every day.

Troy enters from the house.

Jesus, I want you to protect me
As I travel on my way.
(*To Troy.*) 'Morning. You ready for breakfast? I can fix it soon as I finish hanging up these clothes.
Troy. I got the coffee on. That'll be all right. I'll just drink some of that this morning.
Rose. That 651 hit yesterday. That's the second time this month. Miss Pearl hit for a dollar . . . seem like those that need the least always get lucky. Poor folks can't get nothing.

Troy. Them numbers don't know nobody. I don't know why you fool with them. You and Lyons both.

Rose. It's something to do.

Troy. You ain't doing nothing but throwing your money away.

Rose. Troy, you know I don't play foolishly. I just play a nickel here and a nickel there.

Troy. That's two nickels you done thrown away.

Rose. Now I hit sometimes . . . that makes up for it. It always comes in handy when I do hit. I don't hear you complaining then.

Troy. I ain't complaining now. I just say it's foolish. Trying to guess out of six hundred ways which way the number gonna come. If I had all the money niggers, these Negroes, throw away on numbers for one week — just one week — I'd be a rich man.

Rose. Well, you wishing and calling it foolish ain't gonna stop folks from playing numbers. That's one thing for sure. Besides . . . some good things come from playing numbers. Look where Pope done bought him that restaurant off of numbers.

Troy. I can't stand niggers like that. Man ain't had two dimes to rub together. He walking around with his shoes all run over bumming money for cigarettes. All right. Got lucky there and hit the numbers . . .

Rose. Troy, I know all about it.

Troy. Had good sense, I'll say that for him. He ain't throwed his money away. I seen niggers hit the numbers and go through two thousand dollars in four days. Man bought him that restaurant down there . . . fixed it up real nice . . . and then didn't want nobody to come in it! A Negro go in there and can't get no kind of service. I seen a white fellow come in there and order a bowl of stew. Pope picked all the meat out the pot for him. Man ain't had nothing but a bowl of meat! Negro come behind him and ain't got nothing but the potatoes and carrots. Talking about what numbers do for people, you picked a wrong example. Ain't done nothing but make a worser fool out of him than he was before.

Rose. Troy, you ought to stop worrying about what happened at work yesterday.

Troy. I ain't worried. Just told me to be down there at the Commissioner's office on Friday. Everybody think they gonna fire me. I ain't worried about them firing me. You ain't got to worry about that. *(Pause.)* Where's Cory? Cory in the house? *(Calls.)* Cory?

Rose. He gone out.

Troy. Out, huh? He gone out 'cause he know I want him to help me with this fence. I know how he is. That boy scared of work.

Gabriel enters. He comes halfway down the alley and, hearing Troy's voice, stops.

Troy *(continues).* He ain't done a lick of work in his life.

Rose. He had to go to football practice. Coach wanted them to get in a little extra practice before the season start.

Troy. I got his practice . . . running out of here before he get his chores done.

Rose. Troy, what is wrong with you this morning? Don't nothing set right with you. Go on back in there and go to bed . . . get up on the other side.

Troy. Why something got to be wrong with me? I ain't said nothing wrong with me.

Rose. You got something to say about everything. First it's the numbers . . . then it's the way the man runs his restaurant . . . then you done got on Cory. What's it gonna be next? Take a look up there and see if the weather suits you . . . or is it gonna be how you gonna put up the fence with the clothes hanging in the yard.

Troy. You hit the nail on the head then.

Rose. I know you like I know the back of my hand. Go on in there and get you some coffee . . . see if that straighten you up. 'Cause you ain't right this morning.

Troy starts into the house and sees Gabriel. Gabriel starts singing. Troy's brother, he is seven years younger than Troy. Injured in World War II, he has a metal plate in his head. He carries an old trumpet tied around his waist and believes with every fiber of his being that he is the Archangel Gabriel.[4] He carries a chipped basket with an assortment of discarded fruits and vegetables he has picked up in the strip district and which he attempts to sell.

Gabriel (*singing*). Yes, ma'am, I got plums
    You ask me how I sell them
    Oh ten cents apiece
    Three for a quarter
    Come and buy now
    'Cause I'm here today
    And tomorrow I'll be gone

Gabriel enters.

    Hey, Rose!

Rose. How you doing, Gabe?

Gabriel. There's Troy . . . Hey, Troy!

Troy. Hey, Gabe.

Exit into kitchen.

Rose (*to Gabriel*). What you got there?

Gabriel. You know what I got, Rose. I got fruits and vegetables.

---

[4] One of the seven archangels who carries God's messages.

Rose (*looking in basket*).   Where's all these plums you talking about?

Gabriel.   I ain't got no plums today, Rose. I was just singing that. Have some tomorrow. Put me in a big order for plums. Have enough plums tomorrow for St. Peter [5] and everybody.

Troy reenters from kitchen, crosses to steps.

(*To Rose.*) Troy's mad at me.

Troy.   I ain't mad at you. What I got to be mad at you about? You ain't done nothing to me.

Gabriel.   I just moved over to Miss Pearl's to keep out from in your way. I ain't mean no harm by it.

Troy.   Who said anything about that? I ain't said anything about that.

Gabriel.   You ain't mad at me, is you?

Troy.   Naw . . . I ain't mad at you, Gabe. If I was mad at you I'd tell you about it.

Gabriel.   Got me two rooms. In the basement. Got my own door too. Wanna see my key? (*He holds up a key.*) That's my own key! Ain't nobody else got a key like that. That's my key! My two rooms!

Troy.   Well, that's good, Gabe. You got your own key . . . that's good.

Rose.   You hungry, Gabe? I was just fixing to cook Troy his breakfast.

Gabriel.   I'll take some biscuits. You got some biscuits? Did you know when I was in heaven . . . every morning me and St. Peter would sit down by the gate and eat some big fat biscuits? Oh, yeah! We had us a good time. We'd sit there and eat us them biscuits and then St. Peter would go off to sleep and tell me to wake him up when it's time to open the gates for the judgment.

Rose.   Well, come on . . . I'll make up a batch of biscuits.

Rose exits into the house.

Gabriel.   Troy . . . St. Peter got your name in the book. I seen it. It say . . . Troy Maxson. I say . . . I know him! He got the same name like what I got. That's my brother!

Troy.   How many times you gonna tell me that, Gabe?

Gabriel.   Ain't got my name in the book. Don't have to have my name. I done died and went to heaven. He got your name though. One morning St. Peter was looking at his book . . . marking it up for the judgment . . . and he let me see your name. Got it in there under M. Got Rose's name . . . I ain't seen it like I seen yours . . . but I know it's in there. He got a great big book. Got everybody's name what was ever been born. That's what he told me. But I seen your name. Seen it with my own eyes.

Troy.   Go on in the house there. Rose going to fix you something to eat.

Gabriel.   Oh, I ain't hungry. I done had breakfast with Aunt Jemimah. She

---

[5] One of Jesus' disciples.

come by and cooked me up a whole mess of flapjacks. Remember how we used to eat them flapjacks?

Troy.   Go on in the house and get you something to eat now.

Gabriel.   I got to go sell my plums. I done sold some tomatoes. Got me two quarters. Wanna see? *(He shows Troy his quarters.)* I'm gonna save them and buy me a new horn so St. Peter can hear me when it's time to open the gates. *(Gabriel stops suddenly. Listens.)* Hear that? That's the hellhounds. I got to chase them out of here. Go on get out of here! Get out! *(Gabriel exits singing.)*

Better get ready for the judgment
Better get ready for the judgment
My Lord is coming down

Rose enters from the house.

Troy.   He gone off somewhere.

Gabriel *(offstage)*.   Better get ready for the judgment
Better get ready for the judgment morning
Better get ready for the judgment
My God is coming down

Rose.   He ain't eating right. Miss Pearl say she can't get him to eat nothing.

Troy.   What you want me to do about it, Rose? I done did everything I can for the man. I can't make him get well. Man got half his head blown away . . . what you expect?

Rose.   Seem like something ought to be done to help him.

Troy.   Man don't bother nobody. He just mixed up from that metal plate he got in his head. Ain't no sense for him to go back into the hospital.

Rose.   Least he be eating right. They can help him take care of himself.

Troy.   Don't nobody wanna be locked up, Rose. What you wanna lock him up for? Man go over there and fight the war . . . messin' around with them Japs, get half his head blown off . . . and they give him a lousy three thousand dollars. And I had to swoop down on that.

Rose.   Is you fixing to go into that again?

Troy.   That's the only way I got a roof over my head . . . cause of that metal plate.

Rose.   Ain't no sense you blaming yourself for nothing. Gabe wasn't in no condition to manage that money. You done what was right by him. Can't nobody say you ain't done what was right by him. Look how long you took care of him . . . till he wanted to have his own place and move over there with Miss Pearl.

Troy.   That ain't what I'm saying, woman! I'm just stating the facts. If my brother didn't have that metal plate in his head . . . I wouldn't have a pot to piss in or a window to throw it out of. And I'm fifty-three years old. Now see if you can understand that!

Troy gets up from the porch and starts to exit the yard.

Rose.   Where you going off to? You been running out of here every Saturday for weeks. I thought you was gonna work on this fence?

Troy.   I'm gonna walk down to Taylors'. Listen to the ball game. I'll be back in a bit. I'll work on it when I get back.

He exits the yard. The lights go to black.

Scene III: The lights come up on the yard. It is four hours later. Rose is taking down the clothes from the line. Cory enters carrying his football equipment.

Rose.   Your daddy like to had a fit with you running out of here this morning without doing your chores.

Cory.   I told you I had to go to practice.

Rose.   He say you were supposed to help him with this fence.

Cory.   He been saying that the last four or five Saturdays, and then he don't never do nothing but go down to Taylors'. Did you tell him about the recruiter?

Rose.   Yeah, I told him.

Cory.   What he say?

Rose.   He ain't said nothing too much. You get in there and get started on your chores before he gets back. Go on and scrub down them steps before he gets back here hollering and carrying on.

Cory.   I'm hungry. What you got to eat, Mama?

Rose.   Go on and get started on your chores. I got some meat loaf in there. Go on and make you a sandwich . . . and don't leave no mess in there.

Cory exits into the house. Rose continues to take down the clothes. Troy enters the yard and sneaks up and grabs her from behind.

Troy! Go on, now. You liked to scared me to death. What was the score of the game? Lucille had me on the phone and I couldn't keep up with it.

Troy.   What I care about the game? Come here, woman. *(He tries to kiss her.)*

Rose.   I thought you went down Taylors' to listen to the game. Go on, Troy! You supposed to be putting up this fence.

Troy *(attempting to kiss her again).*   I'll put it up when I finish with what is at hand.

Rose.   Go on, Troy. I ain't studying you.

Troy *(chasing after her).*   I'm studying you . . . fixing to do my homework!

Rose.   Troy, you better leave me alone.

Troy.   Where's Cory? That boy brought his butt home yet?

Rose.   He's in the house doing his chores.

Troy *(calling).*   Cory! Get your butt out here, boy!

Rose exits into the house with the laundry. Troy goes over to the pile of wood, picks up a board, and starts sawing. Cory enters from the house.

Troy.   You just now coming in here from leaving this morning?
Cory.   Yeah, I had to go to football practice.
Troy.   Yeah, what?
Cory.   Yessir.
Troy.   I ain't but two seconds off you noway. The garbage sitting in there over-flowing . . . you ain't done none of your chores . . . and you come in here talking about "Yeah."
Cory.   I was just getting ready to do my chores now, Pop . . .
Troy.   Your first chore is to help me with this fence on Saturday. Everything else come after that. Now get that saw and cut them boards.

Cory takes the saw and begins cutting the boards. Troy continues working. There is a long pause.

Cory.   Hey, Pop . . . why don't you buy a TV?
Troy.   What I want with a TV? What I want one of them for?
Cory.   Everybody got one. Earl, Ba Bra . . . Jesse!
Troy.   I ain't asked you who had one. I say what I want with one?
Cory.   So you can watch it. They got lots of things on TV. Baseball games and everything. We could watch the World Series.
Troy.   Yeah . . . and how much this TV cost?
Cory.   I don't know. They got them on sale for around two hundred dollars.
Troy.   Two hundred dollars, huh?
Cory.   That ain't that much, Pop.
Troy.   Naw, it's just two hundred dollars. See that roof you got over your head at night? Let me tell you something about that roof. It's been over ten years since that roof was last tarred. See now . . . the snow come this winter and sit up there on that roof like it is . . . and it's gonna seep inside. It's just gonna be a little bit . . . ain't gonna hardly notice it. Then the next thing you know, it's gonna be leaking all over the house. Then the wood rot from all that water and you gonna need a whole new roof. Now, how much you think it cost to get that roof tarred?
Cory.   I don't know.
Troy.   Two hundred and sixty-four dollars . . . cash money. While you thinking about a TV, I got to be thinking about the roof . . . and whatever else go wrong around here. Now if you had two hundred dollars, what would you do . . . fix the roof or buy a TV?
Cory.   I'd buy a TV. Then when the roof started to leak . . . when it needed fixing . . . I'd fix it.

Troy. Where you gonna get the money from? You done spent it for a TV. You gonna sit up and watch the water run all over your brand new TV.

Cory. Aw, Pop. You got money. I know you do.

Troy. Where I got it at, huh?

Cory. You got it in the bank.

Troy. You wanna see my bankbook? You wanna see that seventy-three dollars and twenty-two cents I got sitting up in there.

Cory. You ain't got to pay for it all at one time. You can put a down payment on it and carry it on home with you.

Troy. Not me. I ain't gonna owe nobody nothing if I can help it. Miss a payment and they come and snatch it right out your house. Then what you got? Now, soon as I get two hundred dollars clear, then I'll buy a TV. Right now, as soon as I get two hundred and sixty-four dollars, I'm gonna have this roof tarred.

Cory. Aw . . . Pop!

Troy. You go on and get you two hundred dollars and buy one if ya want it. I got better things to do with my money.

Cory. I can't get no two hundred dollars. I ain't never seen two hundred dollars.

Troy. I'll tell you what . . . you get you a hundred dollars and I'll put the other hundred with it.

Cory. All right, I'm gonna show you.

Troy. You gonna show me how you can cut them boards right now.

Cory begins to cut the boards. There is a long pause.

Cory. The Pirates won today. That makes five in a row.

Troy. I ain't thinking about the Pirates. Got an all-white team. Got that boy . . . that Puerto Rican boy . . . Clemente. Don't even half-play him. That boy could be something if they give him a chance. Play him one day and sit him on the bench the next.

Cory. He gets a lot of chances to play.

Troy. I'm talking about playing regular. Playing every day so you can get your timing. That's what I'm talking about.

Cory. They got some white guys on the team that don't play every day. You can't play everybody at the same time.

Troy. If they got a white fellow sitting on the bench . . . you can bet your last dollar he can't play! The colored guy got to be twice as good before he get on the team. That's why I don't want you to get all tied up in them sports. Man on the team and what it get him? They got colored on the team and don't use them. Same as not having them. All them teams the same.

Cory. The Braves got Hank Aaron and Wes Covington. Hank Aaron hit two home runs today. That makes forty-three.

Troy. Hank Aaron ain't nobody. That's what you supposed to do. That's how you supposed to play the game. Ain't nothing to it. It's just a matter of timing . . . getting the right follow-through. Hell, I can hit forty-three home runs right now!

Cory. Not off no major-league pitching, you couldn't.

Troy. We had better pitching in the Negro leagues. I hit seven home runs off of Satchel Paige.[6] You can't get no better than that!

Cory. Sandy Koufax. He's leading the league in strikeouts.

Troy. I ain't thinking of no Sandy Koufax.

Cory. You got Warren Spahn and Lew Burdette. I bet you couldn't hit no home runs off of Warren Spahn.

Troy. I'm through with it now. You go on and cut them boards. *(Pause.)* Your mama tell me you done got recruited by a college football team? Is that right?

Cory. Yeah. Coach Zellman say the recruiter gonna be coming by to talk to you. Get you to sign the permission papers.

Troy. I thought you supposed to be working down there at the A&P. Ain't you suppose to be working down there after school?

Cory. Mr. Stawicki say he gonna hold my job for me until after the football season. Say starting next week I can work weekends.

Troy. I thought we had an understanding about this football stuff? You suppose to keep up with your chores and hold that job down at the A&P. Ain't been around here all day on a Saturday. Ain't none of your chores done . . . and now you telling me you done quit your job.

Cory. I'm gonna be working weekends.

Troy. You damn right you are! And ain't no need for nobody coming around here to talk to me about signing nothing.

Cory. Hey, Pop . . . you can't do that. He's coming all the way from North Carolina.

Troy. I don't care where he coming from. The white man ain't gonna let you get nowhere with that football noway. You go on and get your book-learning so you can work yourself up in that A&P or learn how to fix cars or build houses or something, get you a trade. That way you have something can't nobody take away from you. You go on and learn how to put your hands to some good use. Besides hauling people's garbage.

Cory. I get good grades, Pop. That's why the recruiter wants to talk with you. You got to keep up your grades to get recruited. This way I'll be going to college. I'll get a chance . . .

Troy. First you gonna get your butt down there to the A&P and get your job back.

Cory. Mr. Stawicki done already hired somebody else 'cause I told him I was playing football.

Troy. You a bigger fool than I thought . . . to let somebody take away your job so you can play some football. Where you gonna get your money to take out

---

[6] Leroy Robert "Satchel" Paige (1906–1982) was a legendary pitcher in the Negro leagues.

your girlfriend and whatnot? What kind of foolishness is that to let somebody take away your job?

Cory.   I'm still gonna be working weekends.

Troy.   Naw . . . naw. You getting your butt out of here and finding you another job.

Cory.   Come on, Pop! I got to practice. I can't work after school and play football too. The team needs me. That's what Coach Zellman say . . .

Troy.   I don't care what nobody else say. I'm the boss . . . you understand? I'm the boss around here. I do the only saying what counts.

Cory.   Come on, Pop!

Troy.   I asked you . . . did you understand?

Cory.   Yeah . . .

Troy.   What?!

Cory.   Yessir.

Troy.   You go on down there to that A&P and see if you can get your job back. If you can't do both . . . then you quit the football team. You've got to take the crookeds with the straights.

Cory.   Yessir. *(Pause.)* Can I ask you a question?

Troy.   What the hell you wanna ask me? Mr. Stawicki the one you got the questions for.

Cory.   How come you ain't never liked me?

Troy.   Liked you? Who the hell say I got to like you? What law is there say I got to like you? Wanna stand up in my face and ask a damn fool-ass question like that. Talking about liking somebody. Come here, boy, when I talk to you.

Cory comes over to where Troy is working. He stands slouched over and Troy shoves him on his shoulder.

Straighten up, goddammit! I asked you a question . . . what law is there say I got to like you?

Cory.   None.

Troy.   Well, all right then! Don't you eat every day? *(Pause.)* Answer me when I talk to you! Don't you eat every day?

Cory.   Yeah.

Troy.   Nigger, as long as you in my house, you put that sir on the end of it when you talk to me!

Cory.   Yes . . . sir.

Troy.   You eat every day.

Cory.   Yessir!

Troy.   Got a roof over your head.

Cory.   Yessir!

Troy.   Got clothes on your back.

Cory.   Yessir.

Troy.   Why you think that is?

Cory.   Cause of you.

Troy.   Ah, hell I know it's 'cause of me . . . but why do you think that is?

Cory *(hesitant).*   Cause you like me.

Troy.   Like you? I go out of here every morning . . . bust my butt . . . putting up with them crackers[7] every day . . . cause I like you? You about the biggest fool I ever saw. *(Pause.)* It's my job. It's my responsibility! You understand that? A man got to take care of his family. You live in my house . . . sleep you behind on my bedclothes . . . fill you belly up with my food . . . cause you my son. You my flesh and blood. Not 'cause I like you! Cause it's my duty to take care of you. I owe a responsibility to you! Let's get this straight right here . . . before it go along any further . . . I ain't got to like you. Mr. Rand don't give me my money come payday cause he likes me. He gives me cause he owe me. I done give you everything I had to give you. I gave you your life! Me and your mama worked that out between us. And liking your black ass wasn't part of the bargain. Don't you try and go through life worrying about if somebody like you or not. You best be making sure they doing right by you. You understand what I'm saying, boy?

Cory.   Yessir.

Troy.   Then get the hell out of my face, and get on down to that A&P.

Rose has been standing behind the screen door for much of the scene. She enters as Cory exits.

Rose.   Why don't you let the boy go ahead and play football, Troy? Ain't no harm in that. He's just trying to be like you with the sports.

Troy.   I don't want him to be like me! I want him to move as far away from my life as he can get. You the only decent thing that ever happened to me. I wish him that. But I don't wish him a thing else from my life. I decided seventeen years ago that boy wasn't getting involved in no sports. Not after what they did to me in the sports.

Rose.   Troy, why don't you admit you was too old to play in the major leagues? For once . . . why don't you admit that?

Troy.   What do you mean too old? Don't come telling me I was too old. I just wasn't the right color. Hell, I'm fifty-three years old and can do better than Selkirk's .269 right now!

Rose.   How's was you gonna play ball when you were over forty? Sometimes I can't get no sense out of you.

Troy.   I got good sense, woman. I got sense enough not to let my boy get hurt over playing no sports. You been mothering that boy too much. Worried about if people like him.

Rose.   Everything that boy do . . . he do for you. He wants you to say "Good job, son." That's all.

Troy.   Rose, I ain't got time for that. He's alive. He's healthy. He's got to make

---

[7] A derisive term used by African Americans to describe poor whites.

his own way. I made mine. Ain't nobody gonna hold his hand when he get out there in that world.

Rose. Times have changed from when you was young, Troy. People change. The world's changing around you and you can't even see it.

Troy (*slow, methodical*). Woman . . . I do the best I can do. I come in here every Friday. I carry a sack of potatoes and a bucket of lard. You all line up at the door with your hands out. I give you the lint from my pockets. I give you my sweat and my blood. I ain't got no tears. I done spent them. We go upstairs in that room at night . . . and I fall down on you and try to blast a hole into forever. I get up Monday morning . . . find my lunch on the table. I go out. Make my way. Find my strength to carry me through to the next Friday. (*Pause.*) That's all I got, Rose. That's all I got to give. I can't give nothing else.

Troy exits into the house. The lights go down to black.

Scene IV: It is Friday. Two weeks later. Cory starts out of the house with his football equipment. The phone rings.

Cory (*calling*). I got it! (*He answers the phone and stands in the screen door talking.*) Hello? Hey, Jesse. Naw . . . I was just getting ready to leave now.

Rose (*calling*). Cory!

Cory. I told you, man, them spikes is all tore up. You can use them if you want, but they ain't no good. Earl got some spikes.

Rose (*calling*). Cory!

Cory (*calling to Rose*). Mam? I'm talking to Jesse. (*Into phone.*) When she say that? (*Pause.*) Aw, you lying, man. I'm gonna tell her you said that.

Rose (*calling*). Cory, don't you go nowhere!

Cory. I got to go to the game, Ma! (*Into the phone.*) Yeah, hey, look, I'll talk to you later. Yeah, I'll meet you over Earl's house. Later. Bye, Ma.

Cory exits the house and starts out the yard.

Rose. Cory, where you going off to? You got that stuff all pulled out and thrown all over your room.

Cory (*in the yard*). I was looking for my spikes. Jesse wanted to borrow my spikes.

Rose. Get up there and get that cleaned up before your daddy get back in here.

Cory. I got to go to the game! I'll clean it up *when I get back.*

Cory exits.

Rose. That's all he need to do is see that room all messed up.

Rose exits into the house. Troy and Bono enter the yard. Troy is dressed in clothes other than his work clothes.

Bono. He told him the same thing he told you. Take it to the union.

Troy. Brownie ain't got that much sense. Man wasn't thinking about nothing. He wait until I confront them on it . . . then he wanna come crying seniority. (*Calls.*) Hey, Rose!

Bono. I wish I could have seen Mr. Rand's face when he told you.

Troy. He couldn't get it out of his mouth! Liked to bit his tongue! When they called me down there to the Commissioner's office . . . he thought they was gonna fire me. Like everybody else.

Bono. I didn't think they was gonna fire you. I thought they was gonna put you on the warning paper.

Troy. Hey, Rose! (*To Bono.*) Yeah, Mr. Rand like to bit his tongue.

Troy breaks the seal on the bottle, takes a drink, and hands it to Bono.

Bono. I see you run right down to Taylors' and told that Alberta gal.

Troy (*calling*). Hey, Rose! (*To Bono.*) I told everybody. Hey, Rose! I went down there to cash my check.

Rose (*entering from the house*). Hush all that hollering, man! I know you out here. What they say down there at the Commissioner's office?

Troy. You supposed to come when I call you, woman. Bono'll tell you that. (*To Bono.*) Don't Lucille come when you call her?

Rose. Man, hush your mouth. I ain't no dog . . . talk about "come when you call me."

Troy (*puts his arm around Rose*). You hear this Bono? I had me an old dog used to get uppity like that. You say, "C'mere, Blue!" . . . and he just lay there and look at you. End up getting a stick and chasing him away trying to make him come.

Rose. I ain't studying you and your dog. I remember you used to sing that old song.

Troy (*he sings*). Hear it ring! Hear it ring!
I had a dog his name was Blue.

Rose. Don't nobody wanna hear you sing that old song.

Troy (*sings*). You know Blue was mighty true.

Rose. Used to have Cory running around here singing that song.

Bono. Hell, I remember that song myself.

Troy (*sings*). You know Blue was a good old dog.
Blue treed a possum in a hollow log.
That was my daddy's song. My daddy made up that song.

Rose. I don't care who made it up. Don't nobody wanna hear you sing it.

Troy (*makes a song like calling a dog*). Come here, woman.

Rose. You come in here carrying on, I reckon they ain't fired you. What they say down there at the Commissioner's office?

Troy. Look here, Rose . . . Mr. Rand called me into his office today when I got back from talking to them people down there . . . it come from up top . . . he called me in and told me they was making me a driver.

Rose. Troy, you kidding!

Troy. No I ain't. Ask Bono.

Rose. Well, that's great, Troy. Now you don't have to hassle them people no more.

Lyons enters from the street.

Troy. Aw hell, I wasn't looking to see you today. I thought you was in jail. Got it all over the front page of the *Courier* about them raiding Sefus' place . . . where you be hanging out with all them thugs.

Lyons. Hey, Pop . . . that ain't got nothing to do with me. I don't go down there gambling. I go down there to sit in with the band. I ain't got nothing to do with the gambling part. They got some good music down there.

Troy. They got some rogues . . . is what they got.

Lyons. How you been, Mr. Bono? Hi, Rose.

Bono. I see where you playing down at the Crawford Grill tonight.

Rose. How come you ain't brought Bonnie like I told you. You should have brought Bonnie with you, she ain't been over in a month of Sundays.

Lyons. I was just in the neighborhood . . . thought I'd stop by.

Troy. Here he come . . .

Bono. Your daddy got a promotion on the rubbish. He's gonna be the first colored driver. Ain't got to do nothing but sit up there and read the paper like them white fellows.

Lyons. Hey, Pop . . . if you knew how to read you'd be all right.

Bono. Naw . . . naw . . . you mean if the nigger knew how to *drive* he'd be all right. Been fighting with them people about driving and ain't even got a license. Mr. Rand know you ain't got no driver's license?

Troy. Driving ain't nothing. All you do is point the truck where you want it to go. Driving ain't nothing.

Bono. Do Mr. Rand know you ain't got no driver's license? That's what I'm talking about. I ain't asked if driving was easy. I asked if Mr. Rand know you ain't got no driver's license.

Troy. He ain't got to know. The man ain't got to know my business. Time he find out, I have two or three driver's licenses.

Lyons (*going into his pocket*). Say, look here, Pop . . .

Troy. I knew it was coming. Didn't I tell you, Bono? I know what kind of "Look here, Pop" that was. The nigger fixing to ask me for some money. It's Friday night. It's my payday. All them rogues down there on the avenue . . . the ones that ain't in jail . . . and Lyons is hopping in his shoes to get down there with them.

Lyons. See, Pop . . . if you give somebody else a chance to talk sometime, you'd see that I was fixing to pay you back your ten dollars like I told you. Here . . . I told you I'd pay you when Bonnie got paid.

Troy. Naw . . . you go ahead and keep that ten dollars. Put it in the bank. The next time you feel like you wanna come by here and ask me for something . . . you go on down there and get that.

Lyons.   Here's your ten dollars, Pop. I told you I don't want you to give me nothing. I just wanted to borrow ten dollars.

Troy.   Naw . . . you go on and keep that for the next time you want to ask me.

Lyons.   Come on, Pop . . . here go your ten dollars.

Rose.   Why don't you go on and let the boy pay you back, Troy?

Lyons.   Here you go, Rose. If you don't take it I'm gonna have to hear about it for the next six months. (*He hands her the money.*)

Rose.   You can hand yours over here too, Troy.

Troy.   You see this, Bono. You see how they do me.

Bono.   Yeah, Lucille do me the same way.

Gabriel is heard singing offstage. He enters.

Gabriel.   Better get ready for the Judgment! Better get ready for . . . Hey! . . . Hey! . . . There's Troy's boy!

Lyons.   How are you doing, Uncle Gabe?

Gabriel.   Lyons . . . The King of the jungle! Rose . . . hey, Rose. Got a flower for you. (*He takes a rose from his pocket.*) Picked it myself. That's the same rose like you is!

Rose.   That's right nice of you, Gabe.

Lyons.   What you been doing, Uncle Gabe?

Gabriel.   Oh, I been chasing hellhounds and waiting on the time to tell St. Peter to open the gates.

Lyons.   You been chasing hellhounds, huh? Well . . . you doing the right thing, Uncle Gabe. Somebody got to chase them.

Gabriel.   Oh, yeah . . . I know it. The devil's strong. The devil ain't no pushover. Hellhounds snipping at everybody's heels. But I got my trumpet waiting on the judgment time.

Lyons.   Waiting on the Battle of Armageddon, huh?

Gabriel.   Ain't gonna be too much of a battle when God get to waving that Judgment sword. But the people's gonna have a hell of a time trying to get into heaven if them gates ain't open.

Lyons (*putting his arm around Gabriel*).   You hear this, Pop. Uncle Gabe, you all right!

Gabriel (*laughing with Lyons*).   Lyons! King of the jungle.

Rose.   You gonna stay for supper, Gabe. Want me to fix you a plate?

Gabriel.   I'll take a sandwich, Rose. Don't want no plate. Just wanna eat with my hands. I'll take a sandwich.

Rose.   How about you, Lyons? You staying? Got some short ribs cooking.

Lyons.   Naw, I won't eat nothing till after we finished playing. (*Pause.*) You ought to come down and listen to me play, Pop.

Troy.   I don't like that Chinese music. All that noise.

Rose.   Go on in the house and wash up, Gabe . . . I'll fix you a sandwich.

Gabriel (*to Lyons, as he exits*).   Troy's mad at me.

Lyons.   What you mad at Uncle Gabe for, Pop.

Rose.   He thinks Troy's mad at him cause he moved over to Miss Pearl's.

Troy.   I ain't mad at the man. He can live where he want to live at.

Lyons.   What he move over there for? Miss Pearl don't like nobody.

Rose.   She don't mind him none. She treats him real nice. She just don't allow all that singing.

Troy.   She don't mind that rent he be paying . . . that's what she don't mind.

Rose.   Troy, I ain't going through that with you no more. He's over there cause he want to have his own place. He can come and go as he please.

Troy.   Hell, he could come and go as he please here. I wasn't stopping him. I ain't put no rules on him.

Rose.   It ain't the same thing, Troy. And you know it.

Gabriel comes to the door.

Now, that's the last I wanna hear about that. I don't wanna hear nothing else about Gabe and Miss Pearl. And next week . . .

Gabriel.   I'm ready for my sandwich, Rose.

Rose.   And next week . . . when that recruiter come from that school . . . I want you to sign that paper and go on and let Cory play football. Then that'll be the last I have to hear about that.

Troy *(to Rose as she exits into the house).*   I ain't thinking about Cory nothing.

Lyons.   What . . . Cory got recruited? What school he going to?

Troy.   That boy walking around here smelling his piss . . . thinking he's grown. Thinking he's gonna do what he want, irrespective of what I say. Look here, Bono . . . I left the Commissioner's office and went down to the A&P . . . that boy ain't working down there. He lying to me. Telling me he got his job back . . . telling me he working weekends . . . telling me he working after school . . . Mr. Stawicki tell me he ain't working down there at all!

Lyons.   Cory just growing up. He's just busting at the seams trying to fill out your shoes.

Troy.   I don't care what he's doing. When he get to the point where he wanna disobey me . . . then it's time for him to move on. Bono'll tell you that. I bet he ain't never disobeyed his daddy without paying the consequences.

Bono.   I ain't never had a chance. My daddy came on through . . . but I ain't never knew him to see him . . . or what he had on his mind or where he went. Just moving on through. Searching out the New Land. That's what the old folks used to call it. See a fellow moving around from place to place . . . woman to woman . . . called it searching out the New Land. I can't say if he ever found it. I come along, didn't want no kids. Didn't know if I was gonna be in one place long enough to fix on them right as their daddy. I figured I was going searching too. As it turned out I been hooked up with Lucille near about as long as your daddy been with Rose. Going on sixteen years.

Troy.   Sometimes I wish I hadn't known my daddy. He ain't cared nothing about no kids. A kid to him wasn't nothing. All he wanted was for you to learn how to walk so he could start you to working. When it come time for eating . . . he ate first. If there was anything left over, that's what you got. Man would sit down and eat two chickens and give you the wing.

Lyons.   You ought to stop that, Pop. Everybody feed their kids. No matter how hard times is . . . everybody care about their kids. Make sure they have something to eat.

Troy.   The only thing my daddy cared about was getting them bales of cotton in to Mr. Lubin. That's the only thing that mattered to him. Sometimes I used to wonder why he was living. Wonder why the devil hadn't come and got him. "Get them bales of cotton in to Mr. Lubin" and find out he owe him money . . .

Lyons.   He should have just went on and left when he saw he couldn't get nowhere. That's what I would have done.

Troy.   How he gonna leave with eleven kids? And where he gonna go? He ain't knew how to do nothing but farm. No, he was trapped and I think he knew it. But I'll say this for him . . . he felt a responsibility toward us. Maybe he ain't treated us the way I felt he should have . . . but without that responsibility he could have walked off and left us . . . made his own way.

Bono.   A lot of them did. Back in those days what you talking about . . . they walk out their front door and just take on down one road or another and keep on walking.

Lyons.   There you go! That's what I'm talking about.

Bono.   Just keep on walking till you come to something else. Ain't you never heard of nobody having the walking blues? Well, that's what you call it when you just take off like that.

Troy.   My daddy ain't had them walking blues! What you talking about? He stayed right there with his family. But he was just as evil as he could be. My mama couldn't stand him. Couldn't stand that evilness. She run off when I was about eight. She sneaked off one night after he had gone to sleep. Told me she was coming back for me. I ain't never seen her no more. All his women run off and left him. He wasn't good for nobody.

When my turn come to head out, I was fourteen and got to sniffing around Joe Canewell's daughter. Had us an old mule we called Greyboy. My daddy sent me out to do some plowing and I tied up Greyboy and went to fooling around with Joe Canewell's daughter. We done found us a nice little spot, got real cozy with each other. She about thirteen and we done figured we was grown anyway . . . so we down there enjoying ourselves . . . ain't thinking about nothing. We didn't know Greyboy had got loose and wandered back to the house and my daddy was looking for me. We down there by the creek enjoying ourselves when my daddy come up on us. Surprised us. He had them leather straps off the mule and commenced to whupping me like there was no tomorrow. I jumped up, mad and embarrassed. I was scared of my daddy. When he commenced to whupping on me . . . quite naturally I run to get out of the way. *(Pause.)*

Now I thought he was mad cause I ain't done my work. But I see where he was chasing me off so he could have the gal for himself. When I see what the matter of it was, I lost all fear of my daddy. Right there is where I become a man . . . at fourteen years of age. *(Pause.)*

Now it was my turn to run him off. I picked up them same reins that he had used on me. I picked up them reins and commenced to whupping on him. The gal jumped up and run off . . . and when my daddy turned to face me, I could see why the devil had never come to get him . . . cause he was the devil himself. I don't know what happened. When I woke up, I was laying right there by the creek, and Blue . . . this old dog we had . . . was licking my face. I thought I was blind. I couldn't see nothing. Both my eyes were swollen shut. I layed there and cried. I didn't know what I was gonna do. The only thing I knew was the time had come for me to leave my daddy's house. And right there the world suddenly got big. And it was a long time before I could cut it down to where I could handle it.

Part of that cutting down was when I got to the place where I could feel him kicking in my blood and knew that the only thing that separated us was the matter of a few years.

Gabriel enters from the house with a sandwich.

Lyons.   What you got there, Uncle Gabe?

Gabriel.   Got me a ham sandwich. Rose gave me a ham sandwich.

Troy.   I don't know what happened to him. I done lost touch with everybody except Gabriel. But I hope he's dead. I hope he found some peace.

Lyons.   That's a heavy story, Pop. I didn't know you left home when you was fourteen.

Troy.   And didn't know nothing. The only part of the world I knew was the forty-two acres of Mr. Lubin's land. That's all I knew about life.

Lyons.   Fourteen's kinda young to be out on your own. *(Phone rings.)* I don't even think I was ready to be out on my own at fourteen. I don't know what I would have done.

Troy.   I got up from the creek and walked on down to Mobile. I was through with farming. Figured I could do better in the city. So I walked the two hundred miles to Mobile.

Lyons.   Wait a minute . . . you ain't walked no two hundred miles, Pop. Ain't nobody gonna walk no two hundred miles. You talking about some walking there.

Bono.   That's the only way you got anywhere back in them days.

Lyons.   Shhh. Damn if I wouldn't have hitched a ride with somebody!

Troy.   Who you gonna hitch it with? They ain't had no cars and things like they got now. We talking about 1918.

Rose *(entering).*   What you all out here getting into?

Troy *(to Rose).*   I'm telling Lyons how good he got it. He don't know nothing about this I'm talking.

Rose.   Lyons, that was Bonnie on the phone. She say you supposed to pick her up.

Lyons.   Yeah, okay, Rose.

Troy.   I walked on down to Mobile and hitched up with some of them fellows that was heading this way. Got up here and found out . . . not only couldn't you get a job . . . you couldn't find no place to live. I thought I was in freedom. Shhh. Colored folks living down there on the riverbanks in whatever kind of shelter they could find for themselves. Right down there under the Brady Street Bridge. Living in shacks made of sticks and tarpaper. Messed around there and went from bad to worse. Started stealing. First it was food. Then I figured, hell, if I steal money I can buy me some food. Buy me some shoes too! One thing led to another. Met your mama. I was young and anxious to be a man. Met your mama and had you. What I do that for? Now I got to worry about feeding you and her. Got to steal three times as much. Went out one day looking for somebody to rob . . . that's what I was, a robber. I'll tell you the truth. I'm ashamed of it today. But it's the truth. Went to rob this fellow . . . pulled out my knife . . . and he pulled out a gun. Shot me in the chest. It felt just like somebody had taken a hot branding iron and laid it on me. When he shot me I jumped at him with my knife. They told me I killed him and they put me in the penitentiary and locked me up for fifteen years. That's where I met Bono. That's where I learned how to play baseball. Got out that place and your mama had taken you and went on to make life without me. Fifteen years was a long time for her to wait. But that fifteen years cured me of that robbing stuff. Rose'll tell you. She asked me when I met her if I had gotten all that foolishness out of my system. And I told her, "Baby, it's you and baseball all what count with me." You hear me, Bono? I meant it too. She say "Which one comes first?" I told her, "Baby, ain't no doubt it's baseball . . . but you stick and get old with me and we'll both outlive this baseball." Am I right, Rose? And it's true.

Rose.   Man, hush your mouth. You ain't said no such thing. Talking about, "Baby, you know you'll always be number one with me." That's what you was talking.

Troy.   You hear that, Bono. That's why I love her.

Bono.   Rose'll keep you straight. You get off the track, she'll straighten you up.

Rose.   Lyons, you better get on up and get Bonnie. She waiting on you.

Lyons (*gets up to go*).   Hey, Pop, why don't you come on down to the Grill and hear me play?

Troy.   I ain't going down there. I'm too old to be sitting around in them clubs.

Bono.   You got to be good to play down at the Grill.

Lyons.   Come on, Pop . . .

Troy.   I got to get up in the morning.

Lyons.   You ain't got to stay long.

Troy.   Naw, I'm gonna get my supper and go on to bed.

Lyons.   Well, I got to go. I'll see you again.

Troy.   Don't you come around my house on my payday.

Rose.   Pick up the phone and let somebody know you coming. And bring Bonnie with you. You know I'm always glad to see her.

Lyons. Yeah, I'll do that, Rose. You take care now. See you, Pop. See you, Mr. Bono. See you, Uncle Gabe.

Gabriel. Lyons! King of the jungle!

Lyons exits.

Troy. Is supper ready, woman? Me and you got some business to take care of. I'm gonna tear it up too.

Rose. Troy, I done told you now!

Troy (*puts his arm around Bono*). Aw hell, woman . . . this is Bono. Bono like family. I done known this nigger since . . . how long I done know you?

Bono. It's been a long time.

Troy. I done known this nigger since Skippy was a pup. Me and him done been through some times.

Bono. You sure right about that.

Troy. Hell, I done know him longer than I known you. And we still standing shoulder to shoulder. Hey, look here, Bono . . . a man can't ask for no more than that. (*Drinks to him.*) I love you, nigger.

Bono. Hell, I love you too . . . but I got to get home see my woman. You got yours in hand. I got to go get mine.

Bono starts to exit as Cory enters the yard, dressed in his football uniform. He gives Troy a hard, uncompromising look.

Cory. What you do that for, Pop?

He throws his helmet down in the direction of Troy.

Rose. What's the matter? Cory . . . what's the matter?

Cory. Papa done went up to the school and told Coach Zellman I can't play football no more. Wouldn't even let me play the game. Told him to tell the recruiter not to come.

Rose. Troy . . .

Troy. What you Troying me for. Yeah, I did it. And the boy know why I did it.

Cory. Why you wanna do that to me? That was the one chance I had.

Rose. Ain't nothing wrong with Cory playing football, Troy.

Troy. The boy lied to me. I told the nigger if he wanna play football . . . to keep up his chores and hold down that job at the A&P. That was the conditions. Stopped down there to see Mr. Stawicki . . .

Cory. I can't work after school during the football season, Pop! I tried to tell you that Mr. Stawicki's holding my job for me. You don't never want to listen to nobody. And then you wanna go and do this to me!

Troy. I ain't done nothing to you. You done it to yourself.

Cory. Just cause you didn't have a chance! You just scared I'm gonna be better than you, that's all.

Troy. Come here.
Rose. Troy . . .

Cory reluctantly crosses over to Troy.

Troy. All right! See. You done made a mistake.
Cory. I didn't even do nothing!
Troy. I'm gonna tell you what your mistake was. See . . . you swung at the ball and didn't hit it. That's strike one. See, you in the batter's box now. You swung and you missed. That's strike one. Don't you strike out!

Lights fade to black.

Act II

Scene I: The following morning. Cory is at the tree hitting the ball with the bat. He tries to mimic Troy, but his swing is awkward, less sure. Rose enters from the house.

Rose. Cory, I want you to help me with this cupboard.
Cory. I ain't quitting the team. I don't care what Poppa say.
Rose. I'll talk to him when he gets back. He had to go see about your Uncle Gabe. The police done arrested him. Say he was disturbing the peace. He'll be back directly. Come on in here and help me clean out the top of this cupboard.

Cory exits into the house. Rose sees Troy and Bono coming down the alley.

Troy . . . what they say down there?
Troy. Ain't said nothing. I give them fifty dollars and they let him go. I'll talk to you about it. Where's Cory?
Rose. He's in there helping me clean out these cupboards.
Troy. Tell him to get his butt out here.

Troy and Bono go over to the pile of wood. Bono picks up the saw and begins sawing.

Troy *(to Bono).* All they want is the money. That makes six or seven times I done went down there and got him. See me coming they stick out their hands.
Bono. Yeah. I know what you mean. That's all they care about . . . that money. They don't care about what's right. *(Pause.)* Nigger, why you got to go and get some hard wood? You ain't doing nothing but building a little old fence. Get you some soft pine wood. That's all you need.
Troy. I know what I'm doing. This is outside wood. You put pine wood inside

the house. Pine wood is inside wood. This here is outside wood. Now you tell me where the fence is gonna be?

Bono. You don't need this wood. You can put it up with pine wood and it'll stand as long as you gonna be here looking at it.

Troy. How you know how long I'm gonna be here, nigger? Hell, I might just live forever. Live longer than old man Horsely.

Bono. That's what Magee used to say.

Troy. Magee's a damn fool. Now you tell me who you ever heard of gonna pull their own teeth with a pair of rusty pliers.

Bono. The old folks . . . my granddaddy used to pull his teeth with pliers. They ain't had no dentists for the colored folks back then.

Troy. Get clean pliers! You understand? Clean pliers! Sterilize them! Besides we ain't living back then. All Magee had to do was walk over to Doc Goldblum's.

Bono. I see where you and that Tallahassee gal . . . that Alberta . . . I see where you all done got tight.

Troy. What you mean "got tight"?

Bono. I see where you be laughing and joking with her all the time.

Troy. I laughs and jokes with all of them, Bono. You know me.

Bono. That ain't the kind of laughing and joking I'm talking about.

Cory enters from the house.

Cory. How you doing, Mr. Bono?

Troy. Cory? Get that saw from Bono and cut some wood. He talking about the wood's too hard to cut. Stand back there, Jim, and let that young boy show you how it's done.

Bono. He's sure welcome to it.

Cory takes the saw and begins to cut the wood.

Whew-e-e! Look at that. Big old strong boy. Look like Joe Louis.[8] Hell, must be getting old the way I'm watching that boy whip through that wood.

Cory. I don't see why Mama want a fence around the yard noways.

Troy. Damn if I know either. What the hell she keeping out with it? She ain't got nothing nobody want.

Bono. Some people build fences to keep people out . . . and other people build fences to keep people in. Rose wants to hold on to you all. She loves you.

Troy. Hell, nigger, I don't need nobody to tell me my wife loves me, Cory . . . go on in the house and see if you can find that other saw.

Cory. Where's it at?

Troy. I said find it! Look for it till you find it!

Cory exits into the house.

What's that supposed to mean? Wanna keep us in?

---

[8] Joe Louis (1914–1981) was an African American boxer who held the heavyweight title from 1937 to 1949.

Bono. Troy . . . I done known you seem like damn near my whole life. You and Rose both. I done know both of you all for a long time. I remember when you met Rose. When you was hitting them baseball out the park. A lot of them old gals was after you then. You had the pick of the litter. When you picked Rose, I was happy for you. That was the first time I knew you had any sense. I said . . . My man Troy knows what he's doing . . . I'm gonna follow this nigger . . . he might take me somewhere. I been following you too. I done learned a whole heap of things about life watching you. I done learned how to tell where the shit lies. How to tell it from the alfalfa. You done learned me a lot of things. You showed me how to not make the same mistakes . . . to take life as it comes along and keep putting one foot in front of the other. *(Pause.)* Rose a good woman, Troy.

Troy. Hell, nigger, I know she a good woman. I been married to her for eighteen years. What you got on your mind, Bono?

Bono. I just say she a good woman. Just like I say anything. I ain't got to have nothing on my mind.

Troy. You just gonna say she a good woman and leave it hanging out there like that? Why you telling me she a good woman?

Bono. She loves you, Troy. Rose loves you.

Troy. You saying I don't measure up. That's what you trying to say. I don't measure up cause I'm seeing this other gal. I know what you trying to say.

Bono. I know what Rose means to you, Troy. I'm just trying to say I don't want to see you mess up.

Troy. Yeah, I appreciate that, Bono. If you was messing around on Lucille I'd be telling you the same thing.

Bono. Well, that's all I got to say. I just say that because I love you both.

Troy. Hell, you know me . . . I wasn't out there looking for nothing. You can't find a better woman than Rose. I know that. But seems like this woman just stuck onto me where I can't shake her loose. I done wrestled with it, tried to throw her off me . . . but she just stuck on tighter. Now she's stuck on for good.

Bono. You's in control . . . that's what you tell me all the time. You responsible for what you do.

Troy. I ain't ducking the responsibility of it. As long as it sets right in my heart . . . then I'm okay. Cause that's all I listen to. It'll tell me right from wrong every time. And I ain't talking about doing Rose no bad turn. I love Rose. She done carried me a long ways and I love and respect her for that.

Bono. I know you do. That's why I don't want to see you hurt her. But what you gonna do when she find out? What you got then? If you try and juggle both of them . . . sooner or later you gonna drop one of them. That's common sense.

Troy. Yeah, I hear what you saying, Bono. I been trying to figure a way to work it out.

Bono. Work it out right, Troy. I don't want to be getting all up between you and Rose's business . . . but work it so it come out right.

Troy. Ah hell, I get all up between you and Lucille's business. When you gonna get that woman that refrigerator she been wanting? Don't tell me you ain't got no money now. I know who your banker is. Mellon don't need that money bad as Lucille want that refrigerator. I'll tell you that.

Bono. Tell you what I'll do . . . when you finish building this fence for Rose . . . I'll buy Lucille that refrigerator.

Troy. You done stuck your foot in your mouth now!

Troy grabs up a board and begins to saw. Bono starts to walk out the yard.

Hey, nigger . . . where you going?

Bono. I'm going home. I know you don't expect me to help you now. I'm protecting my money. I wanna see you put that fence up by yourself. That's what I want to see. You'll be here another six months without me.

Troy. Nigger, you ain't right.

Bono. When it comes to my money . . . I'm right as fireworks on the Fourth of July.

Troy. All right, we gonna see now. You better get out your bankbook.

Bono exits, and Troy continues to work. Rose enters from the house.

Rose. What they say down there? What's happening with Gabe?

Troy. I went down there and got him out. Cost me fifty dollars. Say he was disturbing the peace. Judge set up a hearing for him in three weeks. Say to show cause why he shouldn't be recommitted.

Rose. What was he doing that cause them to arrest him?

Troy. Some kids was teasing him and he run them off home. Say he was howling and carrying on. Some folks seen him and called the police. That's all it was.

Rose. Well, what's you say? What'd you tell the judge?

Troy. Told him I'd look after him. It didn't make no sense to recommit the man. He stuck out his big greasy palm and told me to give him fifty dollars and take him on home.

Rose. Where's he at now? Where'd he go off to?

Troy. He's gone on about his business. He don't need nobody to hold his hand.

Rose. Well, I don't know. Seem like that would be the best place for him if they did put him into the hospital. I know what you're gonna say. But that's what I think would be best.

Troy. The man done had his life ruined fighting for what? And they wanna take and lock him up. Let him be free. He don't bother nobody.

Rose. Well, everybody got their own way of looking at it I guess. Come on and get your lunch. I got a bowl of lima beans and some cornbread in the oven. Come on get something to eat. Ain't no sense you fretting over Gabe.

Rose turns to go into the house.

Troy. Rose . . . got something to tell you.

Rose. Well, come on . . . wait till I get this food on the table.

Troy. Rose!

She stops and turns around.

I don't know how to say this. *(Pause.)* I can't explain it none. It just sort of grows on you till it gets out of hand. It starts out like a little bush . . . and the next thing you know it's a whole forest.

Rose. Troy . . . what is you talking about?

Troy. I'm talking, woman, let me talk. I'm trying to find a way to tell you . . . I'm gonna be a daddy. I'm gonna be somebody's daddy.

Rose. Troy . . . you're not telling me this? You're gonna be . . . what?

Troy. Rose . . . now . . . see . . .

Rose. You telling me you gonna be somebody's daddy? You telling your *wife* this?

Gabriel enters from the street. He carries a rose in his hand.

Gabriel. Hey, Troy! Hey, Rose!

Rose. I have to wait eighteen years to hear something like this.

Gabriel. Hey, Rose . . . I got a flower for you. *(He hands it to her.)* That's a rose. Same rose like you is.

Rose. Thanks, Gabe.

Gabriel. Troy, you ain't mad at me is you? Them bad mens come and put me away. You ain't mad at me is you?

Troy. Naw, Gabe, I ain't mad at you.

Rose. Eighteen years and you wanna come with this.

Gabriel *(takes a quarter out of his pocket).* See what I got? Got a brand new quarter.

Troy. Rose . . . it's just . . .

Rose. Ain't nothing you can say, Troy. Ain't no way of explaining that.

Gabriel. Fellow that give me this quarter had a whole mess of them. I'm gonna keep this quarter till it stop shining.

Rose. Gabe, go on in the house there. I got some watermelon in the frigidaire. Go on and get you a piece.

Gabriel. Say, Rose . . . you know I was chasing hellhounds and them bad mens come and get me and take me away. Troy helped me. He come down there and told them they better let me go before he beat them up. Yeah, he did!

Rose. You go on and get you a piece of watermelon, Gabe. Them bad mens is gone now.

Gabriel. Okay, Rose . . . gonna get me some watermelon. The kind with the stripes on it.

Gabriel exits into the house.

Rose. Why, Troy? Why? After all these years to come dragging this in to me now. It don't make no sense at your age. I could have expected this ten or fifteen years ago, but not now.

Troy. Age ain't got nothing to do with it, Rose.

Rose. I done tried to be everything a wife should be. Everything a wife could be. Been married eighteen years and I got to live to see the day you tell me you been seeing another woman and done fathered a child by her. And you know I ain't never wanted no half nothing in my family. My whole family is half. Everybody got different fathers and mothers . . . my two sisters and my brother. Can't hardly tell who's who. Can't never sit down and talk about Papa and Mama. It's your papa and your mama and my papa and my mama . . .

Troy. Rose . . . stop it now.

Rose. I ain't never wanted that for none of my children. And now you wanna drag your behind in here and tell me something like this.

Troy. You ought to know. It's time for you to know.

Rose. Well, I don't want to know, goddamn it!

Troy. I can't just make it go away. It's done now. I can't wish the circumstance of the thing away.

Rose. And you don't want to either. Maybe you want to wish me and my boy away. Maybe that's what you want? Well, you can't wish us away. I've got eighteen years of my life invested in you. You ought to have stayed upstairs in my bed where you belong.

Troy. Rose . . . now listen to me . . . we can get a handle on this thing. We can talk this out . . . come to an understanding.

Rose. All of a sudden it's "we." Where was "we" at when you was down there rolling around with some godforsaken woman? "We" should have come to an understanding before you started making a damn fool of yourself. You're a day late and a dollar short when it comes to an understanding with me.

Troy. It's just . . . She gives me a different idea . . . a different understanding about myself. I can step out of this house and get away from the pressures and problems . . . be a different man. I ain't got to wonder how I'm gonna pay the bills or get the roof fixed. I can just be a part of myself that I ain't never been.

Rose. What I want to know . . . is do you plan to continue seeing her. That's all you can say to me.

Troy. I can sit up in her house and laugh. Do you understand what I'm saying. I can laugh out loud . . . and it feels good. It reaches all the way down to the bottom of my shoes. (*Pause.*) Rose, I can't give that up.

Rose. Maybe you ought to go on and stay down there with her . . . if she's a better woman than me.

Troy. It ain't about nobody being a better woman or nothing. Rose, you ain't the blame. A man couldn't ask for no woman to be a better wife than you've been. I'm responsible for it. I done locked myself into a pattern trying to take care of you all that I forgot about myself.

Rose. What the hell was I there for? That was my job, not somebody else's.

Troy. Rose, I done tried all my life to live decent . . . to live a clean . . .

hard . . . useful life. I tried to be a good husband to you. In every way I knew how. Maybe I come into the world backwards, I don't know. But . . . you born with two strikes on you before you come to the plate. You got to guard it closely . . . always looking for the curve ball on the inside corner. You can't afford to let none get past you. You can't afford a call strike. If you going down . . . you going down swinging. Everything lined up against you. What you gonna do. I fooled them, Rose. I bunted. When I found you and Cory and a halfway decent job . . . I was safe. Couldn't nothing touch me. I wasn't gonna strike out no more. I wasn't going back to the penitentiary. I wasn't gonna lay in the street with a bottle of wine. I was safe. I had me a family. A job. I wasn't gonna get that last strike. I was on first looking for one of them boys to knock me in. To get me home.

Rose.   You should have stayed in my bed, Troy.

Troy.   Then when I saw that gal . . . she firmed up my backbone. And I got to thinking that if I tried . . . I just might be able to steal second. Do you understand after eighteen years I wanted to steal second.

Rose.   You should have held me tight. You should have grabbed me and held on.

Troy.   I stood on first base for eighteen years and I thought . . . well, goddamn it . . . go on for it!

Rose.   We're not talking about baseball! We're talking about you going off to lay in bed with another woman . . . and then bring it home to me. That's what we're talking about. We ain't talking about no baseball.

Troy.   Rose, you're not listening to me. I'm trying the best I can to explain it to you. It's not easy for me to admit that I been standing in the same place for eighteen years.

Rose.   I been standing with you! I been right here with you, Troy. I got a life too. I gave eighteen years of my life to stand in the same spot with you. Don't you think I ever wanted other things? Don't you think I had dreams and hopes? What about my life? What about me? Don't you think it ever crossed my mind to want to know other men? That I wanted to lay up somewhere and forget about my responsibilities? That I wanted someone to make me laugh so I could feel good? You not the only one who's got wants and needs. But I held on to you, Troy. I took all my feelings, my wants and needs, my dreams . . . and I buried them inside you. I planted a seed and watched and prayed over it. I planted myself inside you and waited to bloom. And it didn't take me no eighteen years to find out the soil was hard and rocky and it wasn't never gonna bloom.

But I held on to you, Troy. I held you tighter. You was my husband. I owed you everything I had. Every part of me I could find to give you. And upstairs in that room . . . with the darkness falling in on me . . . I gave everything I had to try and erase the doubt that you wasn't the finest man in the world. And wherever you was going . . . I wanted to be there with you. Cause you was my husband. Cause that's the only way I was gonna survive as your wife. You always talking about what you give . . . and what you don't have to give. But you take too. You take . . . and don't even know nobody's giving!

Rose turns to exit into the house; Troy grabs her arm.

Troy. You say I take and don't give!
Rose. Troy! You're hurting me!
Troy. You say I take and don't give.
Rose. Troy . . . you're hurting my arm! Let go!
Troy. I done give you everything I got. Don't you tell that lie on me.
Rose. Troy!
Troy. Don't you tell that lie on me!

Cory enters from the house.

Cory. Mama!
Rose. Troy. You're hurting me.
Troy. Don't you tell me about no taking and giving.

Cory comes up behind Troy and grabs him. Troy, surprised, is thrown off balance just as Cory throws a glancing blow that catches him on the chest and knocks him down. Troy is stunned, as is Cory.

Rose. Troy. Troy. No!

Troy gets to his feet and starts at Cory.

Troy . . . no. Please! Troy!

Rose pulls on Troy to hold him back. Troy stops himself.

Troy *(to Cory).* All right. That's strike two. You stay away from around me, boy. Don't you strike out. You living with a full count. Don't you strike out.

Troy exits out the yard as the lights go down.

Scene II: It is six months later, early afternoon. Troy enters from the house and starts to exit the yard. Rose enters from the house.

Rose. Troy, I want to talk to you.
Troy. All of a sudden, after all this time, you want to talk to me, huh? You ain't wanted to talk to me for months. You ain't wanted to talk to me last night. You ain't wanted no part of me then. What you wanna talk to me about now?
Rose. Tomorrow's Friday.
Troy. I know what day tomorrow is. You think I don't know tomorrow's Friday? My whole life I ain't done nothing but look to see Friday coming and you got to tell me it's Friday.

Rose. I want to know if you're coming home.

Troy. I always come home, Rose. You know that. There ain't never been a night I ain't come home.

Rose. That ain't what I mean . . . and you know it. I want to know if you're coming straight home after work.

Troy. I figure I'd cash my check . . . hang out at Taylors' with the boys . . . maybe play a game of checkers . . .

Rose. Troy, I can't live like this. I won't live like this. You livin' on borrowed time with me. It's been going on six months now you ain't been coming home.

Troy. I be here every night. Every night of the year. That's 365 days.

Rose. I want you to come home tomorrow after work.

Troy. Rose . . . I don't mess up my pay. You know that now. I take my pay and I give it to you. I don't have no money but what you give me back. I just want to have a little time to myself . . . a little time to enjoy life.

Rose. What about me? When's my time to enjoy life?

Troy. I don't know what to tell you, Rose. I'm doing the best I can.

Rose. You ain't been home from work but time enough to change your clothes and run out . . . and you wanna call that the best you can do?

Troy. I'm going over to the hospital to see Alberta. She went into the hospital this afternoon. Look like she might have the baby early. I won't be gone long.

Rose. Well, you ought to know. They went over to Miss Pearl's and got Gabe today. She said you told them to go ahead and lock him up.

Troy. I ain't said no such thing. Whoever told you that is telling a lie. Pearl ain't doing nothing but telling a big fat lie.

Rose. She ain't had to tell me. I read it on the papers.

Troy. I ain't told them nothing of the kind.

Rose. I saw it right there on the papers.

Troy. What it say, huh?

Rose. It said you told them to take him.

Troy. Then they screwed that up, just the way they screw up everything. I ain't worried about what they got on the paper.

Rose. Say the government send part of his check to the hospital and the other part to you.

Troy. I ain't got nothing to do with that if that's the way it works. I ain't made up the rules about how it work.

Rose. You did Gabe just like you did Cory. You wouldn't sign the paper for Cory . . . but you signed for Gabe. You signed that paper.

The telephone is heard ringing inside the house.

Troy. I told you I ain't signed nothing, woman! The only thing I signed was the release form. Hell, I can't read, I don't know what they had on that paper! I ain't signed nothing about sending Gabe away.

Rose. I said send him to the hospital . . . you said let him be free . . . now you done went down there and signed him to the hospital for half his money. You went back on yourself, Troy. You gonna have to answer for that.

Troy. See now . . . you been over there talking to Miss Pearl. She done got mad cause she ain't getting Gabe's rent money. That's all it is. She's liable to say anything.

Rose. Troy, I seen where you signed the paper.

Troy. You ain't seen nothing I signed. What she doing got papers on my brother anyway? Miss Pearl telling a big fat lie. And I'm gonna tell her about it too! You ain't seen nothing I signed. Say . . . you ain't seen nothing I signed.

Rose exits into the house to answer the telephone. Presently she returns.

Rose. Troy . . . that was the hospital. Alberta had the baby.

Troy. What she have? What is it?

Rose. It's a girl.

Troy. I better get on down to the hospital to see her.

Rose. Troy . . .

Troy. Rose . . . I got to go see her now. That's only right . . . what's the matter . . . the baby's all right, ain't it?

Rose. Alberta died having the baby.

Troy. Died . . . you say she's dead? Alberta's dead?

Rose. They said they done all they could. They couldn't do nothing for her.

Troy. The baby? How's the baby?

Rose. They say it's healthy. I wonder who's gonna bury her.

Troy. She had family, Rose. She wasn't living in the world by herself.

Rose. I know she wasn't living in the world by herself.

Troy. Next thing you gonna want to know if she had any insurance.

Rose. Troy, you ain't got to talk like that.

Troy. That's the first thing that jumped out your mouth. "Who's gonna bury her?" Like I'm fixing to take on that task for myself.

Rose. I am your wife. Don't push me away.

Troy. I ain't pushing nobody away. Just give me some space. That's all. Just give me some room to breathe.

Rose exits into the house. Troy walks about the yard.

Troy (*with a quiet rage that threatens to consume him*). All right . . . Mr. Death. See now . . . I'm gonna tell you what I'm gonna do. I'm gonna take and build me a fence around this yard. See? I'm gonna build me a fence around what belongs to me. And then I want you to stay on the other side. See? You stay over there until you're ready for me. Then you come on. Bring your army. Bring your sickle. Bring your wrestling clothes. I ain't gonna fall down on my vigilance this time. You ain't gonna sneak up on me no more. When you ready for me . . . when the top of your list say Troy Maxson . . . that's when you come around here. You come up and knock on the front door. Ain't nobody else got nothing to do with this. This is between you and me. Man to man. You stay on the other side of that fence until you ready for me. Then you come up and knock on the front door. Anytime you want. I'll be ready for you.

The lights go down to black.

Scene III: The lights come up on the porch. It is late evening three days later. Rose sits listening to the ball game waiting for Troy. The final out of the game is made and Rose switches off the radio. Troy enters the yard carrying an infant wrapped in blankets. He stands back from the house and calls.

　　Rose enters and stands on the porch. There is a long, awkward silence, the weight of which grows heavier with each passing second.

Troy.   Rose . . . I'm standing here with my daughter in my arms. She ain't but a wee bittie little old thing. She don't know nothing about grownups' business. She innocent . . . and she ain't got no mama.
Rose.   What you telling me for, Troy?

She turns and exits into the house.

Troy.   Well . . . I guess we'll just sit out here on the porch. (*He sits down on the porch. There is an awkward indelicateness about the way he handles the baby. His largeness engulfs and seems to swallow it. He speaks loud enough for Rose to hear.*) A man's got to do what's right for him. I ain't sorry for nothing I done. It felt right in my heart. (*To the baby.*) What you smiling at? Your daddy's a big man. Got these great big old hands. But sometimes he's scared. And right now your daddy's scared cause we sitting out here and ain't got no home. Oh, I been homeless before. I ain't had no little baby with me. But I been homeless. You just be out on the road by your lonesome and you see one of them trains coming and you just kinda go like this . . . (*He sings as a lullaby.*)

> Please, Mr. Engineer let a man ride the line
> Please, Mr. Engineer let a man ride the line
> I ain't got no ticket please let me ride the blinds

(*Rose enters from the house. Troy hearing her steps behind him, stands and faces her.*)

She's my daughter, Rose. My own flesh and blood. I can't deny her no more than I can deny them boys. (*Pause.*) You and them boys is my family. You and them and this child is all I got in the world. So I guess what I'm saying is . . . I'd appreciate it if you'd help me take care of her.

Rose. Okay, Troy . . . you're right. I'll take care of your baby for you . . . cause . . . like you say . . . she's innocent . . . and you can't visit the sins of the father upon the child. A motherless child has got a hard time. (*She takes the baby from him.*) From right now . . . this child got a mother. But you a womanless man.

Rose turns and exits into the house with the baby. Lights go down to black.

Scene IV: It is two months later. Lyons enters from the street. He knocks on the door and calls.

Lyons. Hey, Rose! (*Pause.*) Rose!

Rose (*from inside the house*).   Stop that yelling. You gonna wake up Raynell. I just got her to sleep.

Lyons. I just stopped by to pay Papa this twenty dollars I owe him. Where's Papa at?

Rose. He should be here in a minute. I'm getting ready to go down to the church. Sit down and wait on him.

Lyons. I got to go pick up Bonnie over her mother's house.

Rose. Well, sit it down there on the table. He'll get it.

Lyons (*enters the house and sets the money on the table*).   Tell Papa I said thanks. I'll see you again.

Rose. All right, Lyons. We'll see you.

Lyons starts to exit as Cory enters.

Cory. Hey, Lyons.

Lyons. What's happening, Cory. Say man, I'm sorry I missed your graduation. You know I had a gig and couldn't get away. Otherwise, I would have been there, man. So what you doing?

Cory. I'm trying to find a job.

Lyons. Yeah I know how that go, man. It's rough out here. Jobs are scarce.

Cory. Yeah, I know.

Lyons. Look here, I got to run. Talk to Papa . . . he know some people. He'll be able to help get you a job. Talk to him . . . see what he say.

Cory. Yeah . . . all right, Lyons.

Lyons. You take care. I'll talk to you soon. We'll find some time to talk.

Lyons exits the yard. Cory wanders over to the tree, picks up the bat, and assumes a batting stance. He studies an imaginary pitcher and swings. Dissatisfied with the result, he tries again. Troy enters. They eye each other for a beat. Cory puts the bat down and exits the yard. Troy starts into the house as Rose exits with Raynell. She is carrying a cake.

Troy. I'm coming in and everybody's going out.

Rose. I'm taking this cake down to the church for the bake sale. Lyons was by to see you. He stopped by to pay you your twenty dollars. It's laying in there on the table.

Troy (*going into his pocket*). Well . . . here go this money.

Rose. Put it in there on the table, Troy. I'll get it.

Troy. What time you coming back?

Rose. Ain't no use in you studying me. It don't matter what time I come back.

Troy. I just asked you a question, woman. What's the matter . . . can't I ask you a question?

Rose. Troy, I don't want to go into it. Your dinner's in there on the stove. All you got to do is heat it up. And don't you be eating the rest of them cakes in there. I'm coming back for them. We having a bake sale at the church tomorrow.

Rose exits the yard. Troy sits down on the steps, takes a pint bottle from his pocket, opens it, and drinks. He begins to sing.

Troy. Hear it ring! Hear it ring!
Had an old dog his name was Blue
You know Blue was mighty true
You know Blue as a good old dog
Blue trees a possum in a hollow log
You know from that he was a good old dog

Bono enters the yard.

Bono. Hey, Troy.

Troy. Hey, what's happening, Bono?

Bono. I just thought I'd stop by to see you.

Troy. What you stop by and see me for? You ain't stopped by in a month of Sundays. Hell, I must owe you money or something.

Bono. Since you got your promotion I can't keep up with you. Used to see you every day. Now I don't even know what route you working.

Troy. They keep switching me around. Got me out in Greentree now . . . hauling white folks' garbage.

Bono. Greentree, huh? You lucky, at least you ain't got to be lifting them barrels. Damn if they ain't getting heavier. I'm gonna put in my two years and call it quits.

Troy. I'm thinking about retiring myself.

Bono. You got it easy. You can *drive* for another five years.

Troy. It ain't the same, Bono. It ain't like working the back of the truck. Ain't got nobody to talk to . . . feel like you working by yourself. Naw, I'm thinking about retiring. How's Lucille?

Bono. She all right. Her arthritis get to acting up on her sometime. Saw Rose on my way in. She going down to the church, huh?

Troy. Yeah, she took up going down there. All them preachers looking for somebody to fatten their pockets. *(Pause.)* Got some gin here.

Bono. Naw, thanks. I just stopped by to say hello.

Troy. Hell, nigger . . . you can take a drink. I ain't never known you to say no to a drink. You ain't got to work tomorrow.

Bono. I just stopped by. I'm fixing to go over to Skinner's. We got us a domino game going over his house every Friday.

Troy. Nigger, you can't play no dominoes. I used to whup you four games out of five.

Bono. Well, that learned me. I'm getting better.

Troy. Yeah? Well, that's all right.

Bono. Look here . . . I got to be getting on. Stop by sometime, huh?

Troy. Yeah, I'll do that, Bono. Lucille told Rose you bought her a new refrigerator.

Bono. Yeah, Rose told Lucille you had finally built your fence . . . so I figured we'd call it even.

Troy. I knew you would.

Bono. Yeah . . . okay. I'll be talking to you.

Troy. Yeah, take care, Bono. Good to see you. I'm gonna stop over.

Bono. Yeah. Okay, Troy.

Bono exits. Troy drinks from the bottle.

Troy. Old Blue died and I dig his grave
Let him down with a golden chain
Every night when I hear old Blue bark
I know Blue treed a possum in Noah's Ark.
Hear it ring! Hear it ring!

Cory enters the yard. They eye each other for a beat. Troy is sitting in the middle of the steps. Cory walks over.

Cory. I got to get by.

Troy. Say what? What's you say?

Cory. You in my way. I got to get by.

Troy. You got to get by where? This is my house. Bought and paid for. In full. Took me fifteen years. And if you wanna go in my house and I'm sitting on the steps . . . you say excuse me. Like your mama taught you.

Cory. Come on, Pop . . . I got to get by.

Cory starts to maneuver his way past Troy. Troy grabs his leg and shoves him back.

Troy.   You just gonna walk over top of me?

Cory.   I live here too!

Troy (*advancing toward him*).   You just gonna walk over top of me in my own house?

Cory.   I ain't scared of you.

Troy.   I ain't asked if you was scared of me. I asked you if you was fixing to walk over top of me in my own house? That's the question. You ain't gonna say excuse me? You just gonna walk over top of me?

Cory.   If you wanna put it like that.

Troy.   How else am I gonna put it?

Cory.   I was walking by you to go into the house cause you sitting on the steps drunk, singing to yourself. You can put it like that.

Troy.   Without saying excuse me???

Cory doesn't respond.

I asked you a question. Without saying excuse me???

Cory.   I ain't got to say excuse me to you. You don't count around here no more.

Troy.   Oh, I see . . . I don't count around here no more. You ain't got to say excuse me to your daddy. All of a sudden you done got so grown that your daddy don't count around here no more . . . Around here in his own house and yard that he done paid for with the sweat of his brow. You done got so grown to where you gonna take over. You gonna take over my house. Is that right? You gonna wear my pants. You gonna go in there and stretch out on my bed. You ain't got to say excuse me cause I don't count around here no more. Is that right?

Cory.   That's right. You always talking this dumb stuff. Now, why don't you just get out my way.

Troy.   I guess you got someplace to sleep and something to put in your belly. You got that, huh? You got that? That's what you need. You got that, huh?

Cory.   You don't know what I got. You ain't got to worry about what I got.

Troy.   You right! You one hundred percent right! I done spent the last seventeen years worrying about what you got. Now it's your turn, see? I'll tell you what to do. You grown . . . we done established that. You a man. Now, let's see you act like one. Turn your behind around and walk out this yard. And when you get out there in the alley . . . you can forget about this house. See? 'Cause this is my house. You go on and be a man and get your own house. You can forget about this. 'Cause this is mine. You go on and get yours 'cause I'm through with doing for you.

Cory.   You talking about what you did for me . . . what'd you ever give me?

Troy.   Them feet and bones! That pumping heart, nigger! I give you more than anybody else is ever gonna give you.

Cory.   You ain't never gave me nothing! You ain't never done nothing but hold me back. Afraid I was gonna be better than you. All you ever did was try and make me scared of you. I used to tremble every time you called my name. Every time I heard your footsteps in the house. Wondering all the time . . . what's Papa gonna say if I do this? . . . What's he gonna say if I do that? . . . What's Papa gonna say if I turn on the radio? And Mama, too . . . she tries . . . but she's scared of you.

Troy. You leave your mama out of this. She ain't got nothing to do with this.

Cory. I don't know how she stand you . . . after what you did to her.

Troy. I told you to leave your mama out of this!

He advances toward Cory.

Cory. What you gonna do . . . give me a whupping? You can't whup me no more. You're too old. You just an old man.

Troy *(shoves him on his shoulder)*. Nigger! That's what you are. You just another nigger on the street to me!

Cory. You crazy! You know that?

Troy. Go on now! You got the devil in you. Get on away from me!

Cory. You just a crazy old man . . . talking about I got the devil in me.

Troy. Yeah, I'm crazy! If you don't get on the other side of that yard . . . I'm gonna show you how crazy I am! Go on . . . get the hell out of my yard.

Cory. It ain't your yard. You took Uncle Gabe's money he got from the army to buy this house and then you put him out.

Troy *(Troy advances on Cory)*. Get your black ass out of my yard!

Troy's advance backs Cory up against the tree. Cory grabs up the bat.

Cory. I ain't going nowhere! Come on . . . put me out! I ain't scared of you.

Troy. That's my bat!

Cory. Come on!

Troy. Put my bat down!

Cory. Come on, put me out.

Cory swings at Troy, who backs across the yard.

What's the matter? You so bad . . . put me out!

Troy advances toward Cory.

Cory *(backing up)*. Come on! Come on!

Troy. You're gonna have to use it! You wanna draw that bat back on me . . . you're gonna have to use it.

Cory. Come on! . . . Come on!

Cory swings the bat at Troy a second time. He misses. Troy continues to advance toward him.

Troy. You're gonna have to kill me! You wanna draw that bat back on me. You're gonna have to kill me.

Cory, backed up against the tree, can go no farther. Troy taunts him. He sticks out his head and offers him a target.

Come on! Come on!

Cory is unable to swing the bat. Troy grabs it.

Troy. Then I'll show you.

Cory and Troy struggle over the bat. The struggle is fierce and fully engaged. Troy ultimately is the stronger and takes the bat from Cory and stands over him ready to swing. He stops himself.

Go on and get away from around my house.

Cory, stung by his defeat, picks himself up, walks slowly out of the yard and up the alley.

Cory. Tell Mama I'll be back for my things.
Troy. They'll be on the other side of that fence.

Cory exits.

Troy. I can't taste nothing. Helluljah! I can't taste nothing no more. (*Troy assumes a batting posture and begins to taunt Death, the fastball on the outside corner.*) Come on! It's between you and me now! Come on! Anytime you want! Come on! I be ready for you . . . but I ain't gonna be easy.

The lights go down on the scene.

Scene V: The time is 1965. The lights come up in the yard. It is the morning of Troy's funeral. A funeral plaque with a light hangs beside the door. There is a small garden plot off to the side. There is noise and activity in the house as Rose, Lyons, and Bono have gathered. The door opens and Raynell, seven years old, enters dressed in a flannel nightgown. She crosses to the garden and pokes around with a stick. Rose calls from the house.

Rose. Raynell!
Raynell. Mam?
Rose. What you doing out there?
Raynell. Nothing.

Rose comes to the door.

Rose. Girl, get in here and get dressed. What you doing?
Raynell. Seeing if my garden growed.
Rose. I told you it ain't gonna grow overnight. You got to wait.
Raynell. It don't look like it never gonna grow. Dag!
Rose. I told you a watched pot never boils. Get in here and get dressed.
Raynell. This ain't even no pot, Mama.
Rose. You just have to give it a chance. It'll grow. Now you come on and do what I told you. We got to be getting ready. This ain't no morning to be playing around. You hear me?
Raynell. Yes, mam.

Rose exits into the house. Raynell continues to poke at her garden with a stick. Cory enters. He is dressed in a Marine corporal's uniform, and carries a duffel bag. His posture is that of a military man, and his speech has a clipped sternness.

Cory *(to Raynell).* Hi. *(Pause.)* I bet your name is Raynell.
Raynell. Uh huh.
Cory. Is your mama home?

Raynell runs up on the porch and calls through the screen door.

Raynell. Mama . . . there's some man out here. Mama?

Rose comes to the door.

Rose. Cory? Lord have mercy! Look here, you all!

Rose and Cory embrace in a tearful reunion as Bono and Lyons enter from the house dressed in funeral clothes.

Bono. Aw, looka here . . .
Rose. Done got all grown up!
Cory. Don't cry, Mama. What you crying about?
Rose. I'm just so glad you made it.
Cory. Hey Lyons. How you doing, Mr. Bono.

Lyons goes to embrace Cory.

Lyons. Look at you, man. Look at you. Don't he look good, Rose. Got them Corporal stripes.
Rose. What took you so long?
Cory. You know how the Marines are, Mama. They got to get all their paperwork straight before they let you do anything.

Rose. Well, I'm sure glad you made it. They let Lyons come. Your Uncle Gabe's still in the hospital. They don't know if they gonna let him out or not. I just talked to them a little while ago.

Lyons. A Corporal in the United States Marines.

Bono. Your daddy knew you had it in you. He used to tell me all the time.

Lyons. Don't he look good, Mr. Bono?

Bono. Yeah, he remind me of Troy when I first met him. *(Pause.)* Say, Rose, Lucille's down at the church with the choir. I'm gonna go down and get the pallbearers lined up. I'll be back to get you all.

Rose. Thanks, Jim.

Cory. See you, Mr. Bono.

Lyons *(with his arm around Raynell).* Cory . . . look at Raynell. Ain't she precious? She gonna break a whole lot of hearts.

Rose. Raynell, come and say hello to your brother. This is your brother, Cory. You remember Cory.

Raynell. No, Mam.

Cory. She don't remember me, Mama.

Rose. Well, we talk about you. She heard us talk about you. *(To Raynell.)* This is your brother, Cory. Come on and say hello.

Raynell. Hi.

Cory. Hi. So you're Raynell. Mama told me a lot about you.

Rose. You all come on into the house and let me fix you some breakfast. Keep up your strength.

Cory. I ain't hungry, Mama.

Lyons. You can fix me something, Rose. I'll be in there in a minute.

Rose. Cory, you sure you don't want nothing. I know they ain't feeding you right.

Cory. No, Mama . . . thanks. I don't feel like eating. I'll get something later.

Rose. Raynell . . . get on upstairs and get that dress on like I told you.

Rose and Raynell exit into the house.

Lyons. So . . . I hear you thinking about getting married.

Cory. Yeah, I done found the right one, Lyons. It's about time.

Lyons. Me and Bonnie been split up about four years now. About the time Papa retired. I guess she just got tired of all them changes I was putting her through. *(Pause.)* I always knew you was gonna make something out yourself. Your head was always in the right direction. So . . . you gonna stay in . . . make it a career . . . put in your twenty years?

Cory. I don't know. I got six already, I think that's enough.

Lyons. Stick with Uncle Sam and retire early. Ain't nothing out here. I guess Rose told you what happened with me. They got me down the workhouse. I thought I was being slick cashing other people's checks.

Cory. How much time you doing?

Lyons.   They give me three years. I got that beat now. I ain't got but nine more months. It ain't so bad. You learn to deal with it like anything else. You got to take the crookeds with the straights. That's what Papa used to say. He used to say that when he struck out. I seen him strike out three times in a row . . . and the next time up he hit the ball over the grandstand. Right out there in Homestead Field. He wasn't satisfied hitting in the seats . . . he want to hit it over everything! After the game he had two hundred people standing around waiting to shake his hand. You got to take the crookeds with the straights. Yeah, Papa was something else.

Cory.   You still playing?

Lyons.   Cory . . . you know I'm gonna do that. There's some fellows down there we got us a band . . . we gonna try and stay together when we get out . . . but, yeah, I'm still playing. It still helps me to get out of bed in the morning. As long as it do that I'm gonna be right there playing and trying to make some sense out of it.

Rose *(calling).*   Lyons, I got these eggs in the pan.

Lyons.   Let me go on and get these eggs, man. Get ready to go bury Papa. *(Pause.)* How you doing? You doing all right?

Cory nods. Lyons touches him on the shoulder and they share a moment of silent grief. Lyons exits into the house. Cory wanders about the yard. Raynell enters.

Raynell.   Hi.

Cory.   Hi.

Raynell.   Did you used to sleep in my room?

Cory.   Yeah . . . that used to be my room.

Raynell.   That's what Papa call it. "Cory's room." It got your football in the closet.

Rose comes to the door.

Rose.   Raynell, get in there and get them good shoes on.

Raynell.   Mama, can't I wear these. Them other one hurt my feet.

Rose.   Well, they just gonna have to hurt your feet for a while. You ain't said they hurt your feet when you went down to the store and got them.

Raynell.   They didn't hurt then. My feet done got bigger.

Rose.   Don't you give me no backtalk now. You get in there and get them shoes on.

Raynell exits into the house.

Ain't too much changed. He still got that piece of rag tied to that tree. He was out here swinging that bat. I was just ready to go back in the house. He swung that bat and then he just fell over. Seem like he swung it and stood there with this grin on his face . . . and then he just fell over. They carried him on down to the hospital, but I knew there wasn't no need . . . why don't you come on in the house?

Cory. Mama . . . I got something to tell you. I don't know how to tell you this . . . but I've got to tell you . . . I'm not going to Papa's funeral.

Rose. Boy, hush your mouth. That's your daddy you talking about. I don't want hear that kind of talk this morning. I done raised you to come to this? You standing there all healthy and grown talking about you ain't going to your daddy's funeral?

Cory. Mama . . . listen . . .

Rose. I don't want to hear it, Cory. You just get that thought out of your head.

Cory. I can't drag Papa with me everywhere I go. I've got to say no to him. One time in my life I've got to say no.

Rose. Don't nobody have to listen to nothing like that. I know you and your daddy ain't seen eye to eye, but I ain't got to listen to that kind of talk this morning. Whatever was between you and your daddy . . . the time has come to put it aside. Just take it and set it over there on the shelf and forget about it. Disrespecting your daddy ain't gonna make you a man, Cory. You got to find a way to come to that on your own. Not going to your daddy's funeral ain't gonna make you a man.

Cory. The whole time I was growing up . . . living in his house . . . Papa was like a shadow that followed you everywhere. It weighed on you and sunk into your flesh. It would wrap around you and lay there until you couldn't tell which one was you anymore. That shadow digging in your flesh. Trying to crawl in. Trying to live through you. Everywhere I looked, Troy Maxson was staring back at me . . . hiding under the bed . . . in the closet. I'm just saying I've got to find a way to get rid of that shadow, Mama.

Rose. You just like him. You got him in you good.

Cory. Don't tell me that, Mama.

Rose. You Troy Maxson all over again.

Cory. I don't want to be Troy Maxson. I want to be me.

Rose. You can't be nobody but who you are, Cory. That shadow wasn't nothing but you growing into yourself. You either got to grow into it or cut it down to fit you. But that's all you got to make life with. That's all you got to measure yourself against that world out there. Your daddy wanted you to be everything he wasn't . . . and at the same time he tried to make you into everything he was. I don't know if he was right or wrong . . . but I do know he meant to do more good than he meant to do harm. He wasn't always right. Sometimes when he touched he bruised. And sometimes when he took me in his arms he cut.

When I first met your daddy I thought . . . Here is a man I can lay down with and make a baby. That's the first thing I thought when I seen him. I was thirty years old and had done seen my share of men. But when he walked up to me and said "I can dance a waltz that'll make you dizzy," I thought, Rose

Lee, here is a man that you can open yourself up to and be filled to bursting. Here is a man that can fill all them empty spaces you been tipping around the edges of. One of them empty spaces was being somebody's mother.

I married your daddy and settled down to cooking his supper and keeping clean sheets on the bed. When your daddy walked through the house he was so big he filled it up. That was my first mistake. Not to make him leave some room for me. For my part in the matter. But at that time I wanted that. I wanted a house that I could sing in. And that's what your daddy gave me. I didn't know to keep up his strength I had to give up little pieces of mine. I did that. I took on his life as mine and mixed up the pieces so that you couldn't hardly tell which was which anymore. It was my choice. It was my life and I didn't have to live it like that. But that's what life offered me in the way of being a woman and I took it. I grabbed hold of it with both hands.

By the time Raynell came into the house, me and your daddy had done lost touch with one another. I didn't want to make my blessing off of nobody's misfortune . . . but I took on to Raynell like she was all them babies I had wanted and never had. (*The phone rings.*) Like I'd been blessed to relive a part of my life. And if the Lord see fit to keep up my strength . . . I'm gonna do her just like your daddy did you . . . I'm gonna give her the best of what's in me.

Raynell (*entering, still with her old shoes*).   Mama . . . Reverend Tollivier on the phone.

Rose exits into the house.

Raynell.   Hi.
Cory.   Hi.
Raynell.   You in the Army or the Marines?
Cory.   Marines.
Raynell.   Papa said it was the Army. Did you know Blue?
Cory.   Blue? Who's Blue?
Raynell.   Papa's dog what he sing about all the time.
Cory (*singing*).   Hear it ring! Hear it ring!
   I had a dog his name was Blue
   You know Blue was mighty true
   You know Blue was a good old dog
   Blue treed a possum in a hollow log
   You know from that he was a good old dog.
   Hear it ring! Hear it ring!

Raynell joins in singing.

Cory and Raynell.   Blue treed a possum out on a limb
   Blue looked at me and I looked at him
   Grabbed that possum and put him in a sack

Blue stayed there till I came back
Old Blue's feets was big and round
Never allowed a possum to touch the ground.

Old Blue died and I dug his grave
I dug his grave with a silver spade
Let him down with a golden chain
And every night I call his name
Go on Blue, you good dog you
Go on Blue, you good dog you

Raynell.   Blue laid down and died like a man
Blue laid down and died . . .

Both.   Blue laid down and died like a man
Now he's treeing possums in the Promised Land
I'm gonna tell you this to let you know
Blue's gone where the good dogs go
When I hear old Blue bark
When I hear old Blue bark
Blue treed a possum in Noah's Ark
Blue treed a possum in Noah's Ark.

Rose comes to the screen door.

Rose.   Cory, we gonna be ready to go in a minute.

Cory *(to Raynell).*   You go on in the house and change them shoes like Mama
told you so we can go to Papa's funeral.

Raynell.   Okay, I'll be back.

*Raynell exits into the house. Cory gets up and crosses over to the tree. Rose
stands in the screen door watching him. Gabriel enters from the alley.*

Gabriel *(calling).*   Hey, Rose!

Rose.   Gabe?

Gabriel.   I'm here, Rose. Hey Rose, I'm here!

Rose enters from the house.

Rose.   Lord . . . Look here, Lyons!

Lyons.   See, told you, Rose . . . I told you they'd let him come.

Cory.   How you doing, Uncle Gabe?

Lyons.   How you doing, Uncle Gabe?

Gabriel.   Hey, Rose. It's time. It's time to tell St. Peter to open the gates. Troy,
you ready? You ready, Troy. I'm gonna tell St. Peter to open the gates. You get
ready now.

(Gabriel, with great fanfare, braces himself to blow. The trumpet is without a mouthpiece. He puts the end of it into his mouth and blows with great force, like a man who has been waiting some twenty-odd years for this single moment. No sound comes out of the trumpet. He braces himself and blows again with the same result. A third time he blows. There is a weight of impossible description that falls away and leaves him bare and exposed to a frightful realization. It is a trauma that a sane and normal mind would be unable to withstand. He begins to dance. A slow, strange dance, eerie and life-giving. A dance of atavistic signature and ritual. Lyons attempts to embrace him. Gabriel pushes Lyons away. He begins to howl in what is an attempt at song, or perhaps a song turning back into itself in an attempt at speech. He finishes his dance and the gates of heaven stand open as wide as God's closet.)

That's the way that go!

For Analysis

1. What is the relevance of the anecdote about the watermelon and Mr. Rand that begins the play?

2. What does Gabriel's character contribute to the play? Why is he given such prominence at the end?

3. How are we meant to judge Troy's infidelity? Is Rose's reaction to it credible? Explain.

4. Are Troy's criticisms of his sons justified? Explain.

5. What are Troy's conversations about death meant to tell us about his character?

6. In Act I, Scene IV, Troy describes his early years. How does this narration help us to understand his character?

7. Besides language, what elements of the play evoke African American life and culture?

On Style

1. Identify some of the **symbols** Wilson employs in the play.

2. Explain how Troy's baseball game **metaphor** helps define his character and the **theme** of the play.

3. *Fences* does not have one single, dominant **plot** but a number of related plots. Identify those plots and examine how Wilson weaves them into a coherent whole.

Making Connections

1. Troy Maxson and Willy Loman, in Arthur Miller's *Death of a Salesman* (p. 790), both struggle with the difficulties of holding a family together. In what ways are their struggles similar? In what ways are they different?

2. Compare the function of Gabriel with that of Isaac, Mendel's idiot son, in Bernard Malamud's story "Idiots First" (p. 1348).

3. This play and Alice Walker's story "Everyday Use" (p. 717) focus on a conflict between generations. Discuss the similarities and differences in the treatment of that conflict.

4. In important ways, the lives of the Maxson family and the Younger family in Lorraine Hansberry's *A Raisin in the Sun* (p. 867) are shaped by racism. Compare and contrast the impact of racism on the two families.

Writing Topics

1. Write an essay analyzing Troy's character, including what you identify as his strengths and weaknesses. Does he emerge in your eyes as a hero?

2. Analyze the conflicts between generations in the play. What do they contribute to the **theme** of the play? Are the conflicts resolved?

3. How does the first scene define the major characters and establish the major **themes** of the play?

4. Analyze the literal and symbolic meanings of "fences" in the play.

5. Write a funeral elegy for Troy from the perspective of one of the other characters in the play.

Jonathan Swift   (1667–1745)

A Modest Proposal   1729

It is a melancholy object to those who walk through this great town[1] or travel in the country, when they see the streets, the roads, and cabin doors, crowded with beggars of the female sex, followed by three, four, or six children, all in rags and importuning every passenger for an alms. These mothers, instead of being able to work for their honest livelihood, are forced to employ all their time in strolling to beg sustenance for their helpless infants, who, as they grow up, either turn thieves for want of work, or leave their dear native country to fight for the Pretender in Spain, or sell themselves to the Barbados.[2]

I think it is agreed by all parties that this prodigious number of children in the arms, or on the backs, or at the heels of their mothers, and frequently of their fathers, is in the present deplorable state of the kingdom a very great additional grievance; and therefore whoever could find out a fair, cheap, and easy method of making these children sound, useful members of the commonwealth would deserve so well of the public as to have his statue set up for a preserver of the nation.

But my intention is very far from being confined to provide only for the children of professed beggars; it is of a much greater extent, and shall take in the whole number of infants at a certain age who are born of parents in effect as little able to support them as those who demand our charity in the streets.

As to my own part, having turned my thoughts for many years upon this important subject, and maturely weighed the several schemes of other projectors,[3] I have always found them grossly mistaken in their computation. It is true, a

---

[1] Dublin.

[2] Many Irish men joined the army of the exiled James Stuart (1688–1766), who laid claim to the British throne. Others exchanged their labor for passage to the British colony of Barbados, in the Caribbean.

[3] People with projects.

615

child just dropped from its dam may be supported by her milk for a solar year, with little other nourishment; at most not above the value of two shillings,[4] which the mother may certainly get, or the value in scraps, by her lawful occupation of begging; and it is exactly at one year that I propose to provide for them in such a manner as instead of being a charge upon their parents or the parish, or wanting food and raiment for the rest of their lives, they shall on the contrary contribute to the feeding, and partly to the clothing, of many thousands.

There is likewise another great advantage in my scheme, that it will prevent 5 those voluntary abortions, and that horrid practice of women murdering their bastard children, alas, too frequent among us, sacrificing the poor innocent babes, I doubt, more to avoid the expense than the shame, which would move tears and pity in the most savage and inhuman breast.

The number of souls in this kingdom being usually reckoned one million and a half, of these I calculate there may be about two hundred thousand couples whose wives are breeders; from which number I subtract thirty thousand couples who are able to maintain their own children, although I apprehend there cannot be so many under the present distress of the kingdom; but this being granted, there will remain an hundred and seventy thousand breeders. I again subtract fifty thousand for those women who miscarry, or whose children die by accident or disease within the year. There only remain an hundred and twenty thousand children of poor parents annually born. The question therefore is, how this number shall be reared and provided for, which, as I have already said, under the present situation of affairs, is utterly impossible by all the methods hitherto proposed. For we can neither employ them in handicraft or agriculture; we neither build houses (I mean in the country) nor cultivate land. They can very seldom pick up a livelihood by stealing till they arrive at six years old except where they are of towardly parts;[5] although I confess they learn the rudiments much earlier, during which time they can however be looked upon only as probationers, as I have been informed by a principal gentleman in the country of Cavan, who protested to me that he never knew above one or two instances under the age of six, even in a part of the kingdom so renowned for the quickest proficiency in that art.

I am assured by our merchants that a boy or a girl before twelve years old is no salable commodity; and even when they come to this age they will not yield above three pounds, or three pounds and half a crown at most on the Exchange;[6] which cannot turn to account either to the parents or the kingdom, the charge of nutriment and rags having been at least four times that value.

I shall now therefore humbly propose my own thoughts, which I hope will not be liable to the least objection.

I have been assured by a very knowing American of my acquaintance in London, that a young healthy child well nursed is at a year old a most delicious,

[4] A shilling was worth about twenty-five cents.
[5] Able and eager to learn.
[6] A pound was twenty shillings; a crown, five shillings.

nourishing, and wholesome food, whether stewed, roasted, baked, or boiled; and I make no doubt that it will equally serve in a fricassee or a ragout.

I do therefore humbly offer it to public consideration that of the hundred and 10 twenty thousand children, already computed, twenty thousand may be reserved for breed, whereof only one fourth part to be males, which is more than we allow to sheep, black cattle, or swine; and my reason is that these children are seldom the fruits of marriage, a circumstance not much regarded by our savages, therefore one male will be sufficient to serve four females. That the remaining hundred thousand may at a year old be offered in sale to the persons of quality and fortune through the kingdom, always advising the mother to let them suck plentifully in the last month, so as to render them plump and fat for a good table. A child will make two dishes at an entertainment for friends; and when the family dines alone, the fore or hind quarter will make a reasonable dish, and seasoned with a little pepper or salt will be very good boiled on the fourth day, especially in winter.

I have reckoned upon a medium that a child just born will weigh twelve pounds, and in a solar year if tolerably nursed increaseth to twenty-eight pounds.

I grant this food will be somewhat dear, and therefore very proper for landlords, who, as they have already devoured most of the parents, seem to have the best title to the children.

Infant's flesh will be in season throughout the year, but more plentiful in March, and a little before and after. For we are told by a grave author, an eminent French physician,[7] that fish being a prolific diet, there are more children born in Roman Catholic countries about nine months after Lent than at any other season; therefore, reckoning a year after Lent, the markets will be more glutted than usual, because the number of popish infants is at least three to one in this kingdom; and therefore it will have one other collateral advantage, by lessening the number of Papists among us.

I have already computed the charge of nursing a beggar's child (in which list I reckon all cottagers, laborers, and four-fifths of the farmers) to be about two shillings per annum, rags included; and I believe no gentleman would repine to give ten shillings for the carcass of a good fat child, which, as I have said, will make four dishes of excellent nutritive meat, when he hath only some particular friend or his own family to dine with him. Thus the squire will learn to be a good landlord, and grow popular among the tenants; the mother will have eight shillings net profit, and be fit for work till she produces another child.

Those who are more thrifty (as I must confess the times require) may flay the 15 carcass; the skin of which artificially[8] dressed will make admirable gloves for ladies, and summer boots for fine gentlemen.

As to our city of Dublin, shambles[9] may be appointed for this purpose in the most convenient parts of it, and butchers we may be assured will not be want-

---

[7] François Rabelais, sixteenth-century French comic writer.
[8] Skillfully.
[9] Slaughterhouses.

ing; although I rather recommend buying the children alive, and dressing them hot from the knife as we do roasting pigs.

A very worthy person, a true lover of his country, and whose virtues I highly esteem, was lately pleased in discoursing on this matter to offer a refinement upon my scheme. He said that many gentlemen of his kingdom, having of late destroyed their deer, he conceived that the want of venison might be well supplied by the bodies of young lads and maidens, not exceeding fourteen years of age nor under twelve, so great a number of both sexes in every country being now ready to starve for want of work or service; and these to be disposed of by their parents, if alive, or otherwise by their nearest relations. But with due deference to so excellent a friend and so deserving a patriot, I cannot be altogether in his sentiments; for as to the males, my American acquaintance assured me from frequent experience that their flesh was generally tough and lean, like that of our schoolboys, by continual exercise, and their taste disagreeable; and to fatten them would not answer the charge. Then as to the females; it would, I think with humble submission, be a loss to the public, because they soon would become breeders themselves; and besides, it is not improbable that some scrupulous people might be apt to censure such a practice (although indeed very unjustly) as a little bordering upon cruelty; which, I confess, hath always been with me the strongest objection against any project, how well soever intended.

But in order to justify my friend, he confessed that this expedient was put into his head by the famous Psalmanazar,[10] a native of the island Formosa, who came from thence to London above twenty years ago, and in conversation told my friend that in his country when any young person happened to be put to death, the executioner sold the carcass to persons of quality as a prime dainty; and that in his time the body of a plump girl of fifteen, who was crucified for an attempt to poison the emperor, was sold to his Imperial Majesty's prime minister of state, and other great mandarins of the court, in joints from the gibbet, at four hundred crowns. Neither indeed can I deny that if the same use were made of several plump young girls in this town, who without one single groat[11] to their fortunes cannot stir abroad without a chair,[12] and appear at the playhouse and assemblies in foreign fineries which they never will pay for, the kingdom would not be the worse.

Some persons of a desponding spirit are in great concern about the vast number of poor people who are aged, diseased, or maimed, and I have been desired to employ my thoughts what course may be taken to ease the nation of so grievous an encumberance. But I am not in the least pain upon the matter, because it is very well known that they are every day dying and rotting by cold and famine, and filth and vermin, as fast as can be reasonably expected. And as to the

---

[10] George Psalmanazar was a Frenchman who passed himself off as a native of Formosa (the former name for Taiwan).

[11] A coin worth about four cents.

[12] A sedan chair, an enclosed chair carried by poles on the front and back.

younger laborers, they are now in almost as hopeful a condition. They cannot get work, and consequently pine away for want of nourishment to a degree that if any time they are accidently hired to common labor, they have not the strength to perform it; and thus the country and themselves are happily delivered from the evils to come.

I have too long digressed, and therefore I shall return to my subject. I think 20 the advantages by the proposal which I have made are obvious and many, as well as of the highest importance.

For first, I have already observed, it would greatly lessen the number of Papists, with whom we are yearly overrun, being the principal breeders of the nation as well as our most dangerous enemies; and who stay at home on purpose to deliver the kingdom to the Pretender, hoping to take their advantage by the absence of so many good Protestants, who have chose rather to leave their country than to stay at home and pay tithes against their conscience to an Episcopal curate.

Secondly, the poorer tenants will have something valuable of their own, which by law may be made liable to distress,[13] and help to pay their landlord's rent, their corn and cattle being already seized and money a thing unknown.

Thirdly, whereas the maintenance of a hundred thousand children, from two years old and upwards, cannot be computed at less than ten shillings a piece per annum, the nation's stock will be thereby increased fifty thousand pounds per annum, besides the profit of a new dish introduced to the tables of all gentlemen of fortune in the kingdom who have any refinement in taste. And all the money will circulate among ourselves, the goods being entirely of our own growth and manufacture.

Fourthly, the constant breeders, besides the gain of eight shillings sterling per annum by the sale of their children, will be rid of the charge of maintaining them after the first year.

Fifthly, this food would likewise bring great custom to taverns, where the 25 vintners will certainly be so prudent as to procure the best receipts[14] for dressing it to perfection, and consequently have their houses frequented by all the fine gentlemen, who justly value themselves upon their knowledge in good eating; and a skillful cook, who understands how to oblige his guests, will contrive to make it as expensive as they please.

Sixthly, this would be a great inducement to marriage, which all wise nations have either encouraged by rewards or enforced by laws and penalties. It would increase the care and tenderness of mothers towards their children, when they were sure of a settlement for life to the poor babes, provided in some sort by the public, to their annual profit instead of expense. We should see an honest emulation among the married women, which of them could bring the fattest child to the market. Men would become as fond of their wives during the time of their pregnancy as they are now of their mares in foal, their cows in calf, or sows

---

[13] Seizure for payment of debts.
[14] Recipes.

when they are ready to farrow; nor offer to beat or kick them (as is too frequent a practice) for fear of a miscarriage.

Many other advantages might be enumerated. For instance, the addition of some thousand carcasses in our exportation of barreled beef, the propagation of swine's flesh, and improvements in the art of making good bacon, so much wanted among us by the great destruction of pigs, too frequent at our tables, which are no way comparable in taste or magnificence to a well-grown, fat, year-ling child, which roasted whole will make a considerable figure at a lord mayor's feast or any other public entertainment. But this and many others I omit, being studious of brevity.

Supposing that one thousand families in this city would be constant cus-tomers for infants' flesh, besides others who might have it at merry meetings, particularly weddings and christenings, I compute that Dublin would take off annually about twenty thousand carcasses, and the rest of the kingdom (where probably they will be sold somewhat cheaper) the remaining eighty thousand.

I can think of no one objection that will possibly be raised against this pro-posal unless it should be urged that the number of people will be thereby much lessened in the kingdom. This I freely own, and it was indeed one princi-pal design in offering it to the world. I desire the reader will observe, that I cal-culate my remedy for this one individual kingdom of Ireland and for no other that ever was, is, or I think ever can be upon earth. Therefore let no man talk to me of other expedients: of taxing our absentees at five shillings a pound: of using neither clothes nor household furniture except what is of our own growth and manufacture: of utterly rejecting the materials and instruments that pro-mote foreign luxury: of curing the expensiveness of pride, vanity, idleness, and gaming in our women: of introducing a vein of parsimony, prudence, and tem-perance: of learning to love our country, in the want of which we differ even from Laplanders and the inhabitants of Topinamboo:[15] of quitting our animosi-ties and factions, nor acting any longer like the Jews, who were murdering one another at the very moment their city was taken:[16] of being a little cautious not to sell our country and conscience for nothing: of teaching landlords to have at least one degree of mercy toward their tenants: lastly, of putting a spirit of hon-esty, industry, and skill into our shopkeepers; who, if a resolution could now be taken to buy only our native goods, would immediately unite to cheat and exact upon us in the price, the measure, and the goodness, nor could ever yet be brought to make one fair proposal of just dealing, though often and earnestly invited to it.

Therefore, I repeat, let no man talk to me of these and the like expedients, till he hath at least some glimpse of hope that there will be some hearty and sincere attempt to put them in practice.

---

[15] A district in Brazil, inhabited in Swift's day by primitive tribes.
[16] While the Roman emperor Titus laid siege to Jerusalem in A.D. 70, bloody fighting erupted among factions within the city.

But as to myself, having been wearied out for many years of offering vain, idle, visionary thoughts, and at length utterly despairing of success, I fortunately fell upon this proposal, which, as it is wholly new, so it hath something solid and real, of no expense and little trouble, full in our own power, and whereby we can incur no danger in disobliging England. For this kind of commodity will not bear exportation, the flesh being of too tender a consistence to admit a long continuance in salt, although perhaps I could name a country[17] which would be glad to eat up our whole nation without it.

After all, I am not so violently bent upon my own opinion as to reject any offer proposed by wise men, which shall be found equally innocent, cheap, easy, and effectual. But before something of that kind shall be advanced in contradiction to my scheme, and offering a better, I desire the author or authors will be pleased maturely to consider two points. First, as things now stand, how they will be able to find food and raiment for an hundred thousand useless mouths and backs. And secondly, there being a round million of creatures in human figure throughout this kingdom, whose sole subsistence put into a common stock would leave them in debt two millions of pounds sterling, adding those who are beggars by profession to the bulk of farmers, cottagers, and laborers, with their wives and children who are beggars in effect; I desire those politicians who dislike my overture, and may perhaps be so bold to attempt to answer, that they will first ask the parents of these mortals whether they would not at this day think it a great happiness to have been sold for food at a year old in this manner I prescribe, and thereby have avoided such a perpetual scene of misfortunes as they have since gone through by the oppression of landlords, the impossibility of paying rent without money or trade, the want of common sustenance, with neither house nor clothes to cover them from the inclemencies of the weather, and the most inevitable prospect of entailing the like or greater miseries upon their breed forever.

I profess, in the sincerity of my heart, that I have not the least personal interest in endeavoring to promote this necessary work, having no other motive than the public good of my country, by advancing our trade, providing for infants, relieving the poor, and giving some pleasure to the rich. I have no children by which I can propose to get a single penny; the youngest being nine years old, and my wife past childbearing.

For Analysis

1. What kind of person is the speaker? What does his tone of voice reveal about who he is? Is his voice direct and transparent, or does it seem deliberately created to achieve a specific effect?

2. In what sense is the proposal "modest"?

3. Where are the major divisions of the essay? What function does each serve?

[17] England.

4. What function does paragraph 29 serve?

5. Explain what Swift means when he says in paragraph 20, "I have too long digressed."

6. Whom is Swift addressing in this essay?

On Style
Characterize the **tone** of the essay, paying particular attention to the speaker's diction. How does the tone contribute to the effectiveness of the piece?

Making Connections
Some other works in this anthology that use **satire** include: E. E. Cummings, "the Cambridge ladies who live in furnished souls" (p. 771); W. H. Auden, "The Unknown Citizen" (p. 449); Richard Wilbur, "Museum Piece" (p. 452); Harlan Ellison, "'Repent, Harlequin!' Said the Ticktockman" (p. 399); and Pam Houston, "How to Talk to a Hunter" (p. 1077). Compare and contrast the use of satire in one of these works with Swift's use of satire.

Writing Topics
1. Some background information on Swift's life and familiarity with his other works would make it clear that in this essay he is being satiric. Without that background — that is, on the basis of this essay alone — how would you conclude that Swift is writing satire?

2. In a single, brief paragraph, paraphrase the major arguments Swift uses to support his plan.

Thomas Jefferson   (1743–1826)

The Declaration of Independence[1]   1776

When in the course of human Events, it becomes necessary for one People to dissolve the Political Bands which have connected them with another, and to assume among the Powers of the Earth, the separate and equal Station to which the Laws of Nature and of Nature's God entitle them, a decent Respect to the Opinions of Mankind requires that they should declare the causes which impel them to the Separation.

We hold these Truths to be self-evident, that all Men are created equal, that they are endowed by their Creator with certain unalienable Rights, that among these are Life, Liberty, and the Pursuit of Happiness — That to secure these Rights, Governments are instituted among Men, deriving their just Powers from the Consent of the Governed, that whenever any Form of Government becomes destructive of these Ends, it is the Right of the People to alter or to abolish it, and to institute new Government, laying its Foundation on such Principles, and organizing its Powers in such Form, as to them shall seem most likely to effect their Safety and Happiness. Prudence, indeed, will dictate that Governments long established should not be changed for light and transient Causes; and accordingly all Experience hath shewn, that Mankind are more disposed to suffer, while Evils are sufferable, than to right themselves by abolishing the Forms to which they are accustomed. But when a long Train of Abuses and Usurpations, pursuing invariably the same Object, evinces a Design to reduce them under absolute Despotism, it is their Right, it is their Duty, to throw off such Government, and to provide new Guards for their future Security. Such has been the patient Sufferance of these Colonies; and such is now the Necessity which constrains them to alter their former Systems of Government. The History of the present King of Great-Britain is a History of repeated Injuries and Usurpations, all having in direct Object the Establishment of an absolute Tyranny over these States. To prove this, let Facts be submitted to a candid World.

He has refused his Assent to Laws, the most wholesome and necessary for the public Good.

He has forbidden his Governors to pass Laws of immediate and pressing Importance, unless suspended in their Operation till his Assent should be obtained; and when so suspended, he has utterly neglected to attend to them.

He has refused to pass other Laws for the Accommodation of large Districts 5 of People, unless those People would relinquish the Right of Representation in the Legislature, a Right inestimable to them, and formidable to Tyrants only.

[1] For earlier versions of this text see Writing Topic 2 (p. 626).

He has called together Legislative Bodies at Places unusual, uncomfortable, and distant from the Depository of their public Records, for the sole Purpose of fatiguing them into Compliance with his Measures.

He has dissolved Representative Houses repeatedly, for opposing with manly Firmness his Invasions on the Rights of the People.

He has refused for a long Time, after such Dissolutions, to cause others to be elected; whereby the Legislative Powers, incapable of Annihilation, have returned to the People at large for their exercise; the State remaining in the mean time exposed to all the Dangers of Invasion from without, and Convulsions within.

He has endeavoured to prevent the Population of these States; for that Purpose obstructing the Laws for Naturalization of Foreigners; refusing to pass others to encourage their Migrations hither, and raising the Conditions of new Appropriations of Lands.

He has obstructed the Administration of Justice, by refusing his Assent to 10
Laws for establishing Judiciary Powers.

He has made Judges dependent on his Will alone, for the Tenure of their Offices, and the Amount and Payment of their Salaries.

He has erected a Multitude of new Offices, and sent hither Swarms of Officers to harrass our People, and eat out their Substance.

He has kept among us, in Times of Peace, Standing Armies, without the consent of our Legislatures.

He has affected to render the Military independent of and superior to the Civil Power.

He has combined with others to subject us to a Jurisdiction foreign to our 15
Constitution, and unacknowledged by our Laws; giving his Assent to their Acts of pretended Legislation:

For quartering large Bodies of Armed Troops among us:

For protecting them, by a mock Trial, from Punishment for any Murders which they should commit on the Inhabitants of these States:

For cutting off our Trade with all Parts of the World:

For imposing Taxes on us without our Consent:

For depriving us, in many Cases, of the Benefits of Trial by Jury: 20

For transporting us beyond Seas to be tried for pretended Offences:

For abolishing the free System of English Laws in a neighboring Province, establishing therein an arbitrary Government, and enlarging its Boundaries, so as to render it at once an Example and fit Instrument for introducing the same absolute Rule into these Colonies:

For taking away our Charters, abolishing our most valuable Laws, and altering fundamentally the Forms of our Governments:

For suspending our own Legislatures, and declaring themselves invested with Power to legislate for us in all Cases whatsoever.

He has abdicated Government here, by declaring us out of his Protection and 25
waging War against us.

He has plundered our Seas, ravaged our Coasts, burnt our Towns, and destroyed the Lives of our People.

He is, at this Time, transporting large Armies of foreign Mercenaries to compleat the Works of Death, Desolation, and Tyranny, already begun with circumstances of Cruelty and Perfidy, scarcely paralleled in the most barbarous Ages, and totally unworthy the Head of a civilized Nation.

He has constrained our fellow Citizens taken Captive on the high Seas to bear Arms against their Country, to become the Executioners of their Friends and Brethren, or to fall themselves by their Hands.

He has excited domestic Insurrections amongst us, and has endeavoured to bring on the Inhabitants of our Frontiers, the merciless Indian Savages, whose known Rule of Warfare, is an undistinguished Destruction, of all Ages, Sexes and Conditions.

In every stage of these Oppressions we have Petitioned for Redress in the 30 most humble Terms: Our repeated Petitions have been answered only by repeated Injury. A Prince, whose Character is thus marked by every act which may define a Tyrant, is unfit to be the Ruler of a free People.

Nor have we been wanting in Attentions to our British Brethren. We have warned them from Time to Time of Attempts by their Legislature to extend an unwarrantable Jurisdiction over us. We have reminded them of the Circumstances of our Emigration and Settlement here. We have appealed to their native Justice and Magnanimity, and we have conjured them by the Ties of our common Kindred to disavow these Usurpations, which, would inevitably interrupt our Connections and Correspondence. They too have been deaf to the Voice of Justice and of Consanguinity. We must, therefore, acquiesce in the Necessity, which denounces our Separation, and hold them, as we hold the rest of Mankind, Enemies in War, in Peace, Friends.

We, therefore, the Representatives of the UNITED STATES OF AMERICA, in General Congress, Assembled, appealing to the Supreme Judge of the World for the Rectitude of our Intentions, do, in the Name, and by Authority of the good People of these Colonies, solemnly Publish and Declare, That these United Colonies are, and of Right ought to be, Free and Independent States; that they are absolved from all Allegiance to the British Crown, and that all political Connection between them and the State of Great-Britain, is and ought to be totally dissolved; and that as Free and Independent States, they have full Power to levy War, conclude Peace, contract Alliances, establish Commerce, and to do all other Acts and Things which Independent States may of right do. And for the support of this Declaration, with a firm Reliance on the Protection of divine Providence, we mutually pledge to each other our Lives, our Fortunes, and our sacred Honor.

Signed by Order *and in* Behalf *of the* Congress,
JOHN HANCOCK, President.

Attest.
CHARLES THOMSON, Secretary.

For Analysis

1. In what sense can it be said that the "Truths" enumerated in the second paragraph are "self-evident"?

2. Whose "Opinions" is the Declaration addressing?

3. Are we to understand the famous phrase "all Men are created equal" as excluding women? Any other groups? What kind of historical information would be necessary to answer these questions fully?

4. Historian Howard Zinn, in his *A People's History of the United States* (1980), argues that "the Declaration functioned to mobilize certain groups of Americans, ignoring others. Surely, inspirational language to create a secure consensus is still used in our time to cover up serious conflicts of interest in that consensus, and to cover up, also, the omissions of large parts of the human race." Identify some modern examples of language used "to cover up serious conflicts of interest."

Writing Topics

1. Research and write up your findings on one of the grievances enumerated against the king of England.

2. Write a research paper on any historical issue relating to the Declaration that you would like to know more about. The text of the Declaration and its earlier drafts can be found on the Internet at *<http://odur.let.rug.nl/~usa/D/1776-1800/independence /doi.htm>*. Each of the underlined links will connect you to background material related to the specific phrase. The site also provides links to other relevant sites.

Emma Goldman (1869–1940)

Defense[1] 1916

Your Honor: My presence before you this afternoon proves conclusively that there is no free speech in the city or county of New York. I hope that there is free speech in your court.

I have delivered the lecture which caused my arrest in at least fifty cities throughout the country, always in the presence of detectives. I have never been arrested. I delivered the same address in New York City seven times, prior to my arrest, always in the presence of detectives, because in my case, Your Honor, "the police never cease out of the land." Yet for some reason unknown to me I have never been molested until February 11th, nor would I have been then, if free speech were a living factor, and not a dead letter to be celebrated only on the 4th of July.

Your Honor, I am charged with the crime of having given information to men and women as to how to prevent conception. For the last three weeks, every night before packed houses, a stirring social indictment is being played at the Candler Theatre. I refer to "Justice" by John Galsworthy.[2] The council for the Defense in summing up the charge against the defendant says among other things: "Your Honor: back of the commission of every crime, is life, palpitating life."

Now what is the palpitating life back of my crime? I will tell you, Your Honor. According to the bulletin of the Department of Health, 30,000,000 people in America are underfed. They are always in a state of semi-starvation. Not only because their average income is too small to sustain them properly — the bulletin states that eight hundred dollars a year is the minimum income necessary for every family — but because there are too many members in each family to be sustained on a meagre income. Hence 30,000,000 people in this land go through life underfed and overworked.

Your Honor: what kind of children do you suppose these parents can bring 5 into the world? I will tell you: children so poor and anemic that they take their leave from this, our kind world, before their first year of life. In that way, 300,000 babies, according to the baby welfare association, are sacrificed in the

[1] Emma Goldman was arrested while lecturing in New York on February 11, 1916. She was charged with violating Section 1142 of the New York Penal Code, which made it a misdemeanor to "sell, lend, or give away" or to advertise, loan, or distribute "any recipe, drug, or medicine for the prevention of conception." Tried and convicted on April 20, she was offered the choice between a hundred-dollar fine or fifteen days in jail. As a matter of principle, she chose jail.

[2] John Galsworthy (1867–1933), English novelist and playwright, whose play *Justice* (1909) deals with crime and disproportionate punishment.

United States each year. This, Your Honor, is the palpitating life which has confronted me for many years, and which is back of the commission of my crime. I have been part of the great social struggle of this country for twenty-six years, as nurse, as lecturer, as publisher. During this time I have gone up and down the land in the large industrial centres, in the mining region, in the slums of our large cities. I have seen conditions appalling and heart-rending, which no creative genius could adequately describe. I do not intend to take up the time of the court to go into many of these cases, but I must mention a few.

A woman, married to a consumptive husband has eight children, six are in the tuberculosis hospital. She is on the way with the ninth child.

A woman whose husband earns $12 per week has six children, on the way with the seventh child.

A woman with twelve children living in three squalid rooms, dies in confinement with the 13th child, the oldest, now the mainstay of the 12 orphans, is 14 years of age.

These are but very few of the victims of our economic grinding mill, which sets a premium upon poverty, and our puritanic law which maintains a conspiracy of silence.

Your Honor: if giving one's life for the purpose of awakening race conscious- 10
ness in the masses, a consciousness which will impel them to bring quality and not quantity into society, if that be a crime, I am glad to be such a criminal. But I assure you I am in good company. I have as my illustrious colleagues the greatest men and women of our time; scientists, political economists, artists, men of letters in Europe and America. And what is even more important, I have the working class, and women in every walk of life, to back me. No isolated individuals here and there, but thousands of them.

After all, the question of birth control is largely a workingman's question, above all a workingwoman's question. She it is who risks her health, her youth, her very life in giving out of herself the units of the race. She it is who ought to have the means and the knowledge to say how many children she shall give, and to what purpose she shall give them, and under what conditions she shall bring forth life.

Statesmen, politicians, men of the cloth, men, who own the wealth of the world, need a large race, no matter how poor in quality. Who else would do their work, and fight their wars? But the people who toil and drudge and create, and receive a mere pittance in return, what reason have they to bring hapless children into the world? They are beginning to realize their debt to the children already in existence, and in order to make good their obligations, they absolutely refuse to go on like cattle breeding more and more.

That which constitutes my crime, Your Honor, is therefore, enabling the mass of humanity to give to the world fewer and better children — birth control, which in the last two years has grown to such gigantic dimensions that no amount of laws can possibly stop the ever-increasing tide.

And this is true, not only because of what I may or may not say, or of how many propagandists may or may not be sent to jail; there is a much profounder reason for the tremendous growth and importance of birth control. That reason is conditioned in the great modern social conflict, or rather social war, I should say. A war not for military conquest or material supremacy, a war of the oppressed and disinherited of the earth against their enemies, capitalism and the state, a war for a seat at the table of life, a war for well-being, for beauty, for liberty. Above all, this war is for a free motherhood and a joyous playful, glorious childhood.

Birth control, Your Honor, is only one of the ways which leads to the victory 15 in that war, and I am glad and proud to be able to indicate that way.

For Analysis
1. What are the strengths and weaknesses of Goldman's argument? Reflect on your own feelings about birth control. How persuasive is she?

2. Do you think Goldman is right to characterize birth control as "largely a working-man's question, above all a workingwoman's question" (para. 11)?

3. Are Goldman's arguments equally relevant to the issue of abortion? Explain.

On Style
Goldman invokes many cases and examples to support her argument. How do these examples strengthen her argument?

Making Connections
What similarities do you find between Martin Luther King Jr.'s arguments to support civil disobedience (p. 634) and those Emma Goldman makes in her "Defense"? Which essay do you find more persuasive?

Writing Topic
In criminal trials that concern larger political and social issues, defendants will sometimes forgo a narrow legal defense and attempt instead to use the trial as a forum for expounding their views to the public. Analyze Goldman's defense in terms of the audiences she is trying to reach.

James Thurber   (1894–1961)

The Little Girl and the Wolf 1940

One afternoon a big wolf waited in a dark forest for a little girl to come along carrying a basket of food to her grandmother. Finally a little girl did come along and she was carrying a basket of food. "Are you carrying that basket to your grandmother?" asked the wolf. The little girl said yes, she was. So the wolf asked her where her grandmother lived and the little girl told him and he disappeared into the wood.

When the little girl opened the door of her grandmother's house she saw that there was somebody in bed with a nightcap and nightgown on. She had approached no nearer than twenty-five feet from the bed when she saw that it was not her grandmother but the wolf, for even in a nightcap a wolf does not look any more like your grandmother than the Metro-Goldwyn lion looks like Calvin Coolidge. So the little girl took an automatic out of her basket and shot the wolf dead.

Moral: It is not so easy to fool little girls nowadays as it used to be.

The Very Proper Gander 1940

Not so very long ago there was a very fine gander. He was strong and smooth and beautiful and he spent most of his time singing to his wife and children. One day somebody who saw him strutting up and down in his yard and singing remarked, "There is a very proper gander." An old hen overheard this and told her husband about it that night in the roost. "They said something about propaganda," she said. "I have always suspected that," said the rooster, and he went around the barnyard next day telling everybody that the very fine gander was a dangerous bird, more than likely a hawk in gander's clothing. A small brown hen remembered a time when at a great distance she had seen the gander talking with some hawks in the forest. "They were up to no good," she said. A duck remembered that the gander had once told him he did not believe in anything. "He said to hell with the flag, too," said the duck. A guinea hen recalled that she had once seen somebody who looked very much like the gander throw something that looked a great deal like a bomb. Finally everybody snatched up sticks and stones and descended on the gander's house. He was strutting in his front yard, singing to his children and his wife. "There he is!"

everybody cried. "Hawk-lover! Unbeliever! Flag-hater! Bomb-thrower!" So they set upon him and drove him out of the country.

Moral: Anybody who you or your wife thinks is going to overthrow the government by violence must be driven out of the country.

The Owl Who Was God 1940

Once upon a starless midnight there was an owl who sat on the branch of an oak tree. Two ground moles tried to slip quietly by, unnoticed. "You!" said the owl. "Who?" they quavered, in fear and astonishment, for they could not believe it was possible for anyone to see them in that thick darkness. "You two!" said the owl. The moles hurried away and told the other creatures of the field and forest that the owl was the greatest and wisest of all animals because he could see in the dark and because he could answer any question. "I'll see about that," said a secretary bird, and he called on the owl one night when it was again very dark. "How many claws am I holding up?" said the secretary bird. "Two," said the owl, and that was right. "Can you give me another expression for 'that is to say' or 'namely'?" asked the secretary bird. "To wit," said the owl. "Why does a lover call on his love?" asked the secretary bird. "To woo," said the owl.[1]

The secretary bird hastened back to the other creatures and reported that the owl was indeed the greatest and wisest animal in the world because he could see in the dark and because he could answer any question. "Can he see in the daytime, too?" asked a red fox. "Yes," echoed a dormouse and a French poodle. "Can he see in the daytime, too?" All the other creatures laughed loudly at this silly question, and they set upon the red fox and his friends and drove them out of the region. Then they sent a messenger to the owl and asked him to be their leader.

When the owl appeared among the animals it was high noon and the sun was shining brightly. He walked very slowly, which gave him an appearance of great dignity, and he peered about him with large, staring eyes, which gave him an air of tremendous importance. "He's God!" screamed a Plymouth Rock hen. And the others took up the cry "He's God!" So they followed him wherever he went and when he began to bump into things they began to bump into things, too. Finally he came to a concrete highway and he started up the middle of it and all the other creatures followed him. Presently a hawk, who was acting as outrider, observed a truck coming toward them at fifty miles an hour, and he reported to the secretary bird and the secretary bird reported to the owl. "There's danger ahead," said the secretary bird. "To wit?" said the owl. The secretary bird told

---

[1] Thurber punningly alludes to the Winter section of the famous lyric that concludes Shakespeare's *Love's Labour's Lost:* "Then nightly sings the staring owl — / Tu-whit, / Tu-who. . . . "

him. "Aren't you afraid?" he asked. "Who?" said the owl calmly, for he could not see the truck. "He's God!" cried all the creatures again, and they were still crying "He's God!" when the truck hit them and ran them down. Some of the animals were merely injured, but most of them, including the owl, were killed.

Moral: You can fool too many of the people too much of the time.

The Unicorn in the Garden   1940

Once upon a sunny morning a man who sat in a breakfast nook looked up from his scrambled eggs to see a white unicorn with a golden horn quietly cropping the roses in the garden. The man went up to the bedroom where his wife was still asleep and woke her. "There's a unicorn in the garden," he said. "Eating roses." She opened one unfriendly eye and looked at him. "The unicorn is a mythical beast," she said, and turned her back on him. The man walked slowly downstairs and out into the garden. The unicorn was still there; he was now browsing among the tulips. "Here, unicorn," said the man, and he pulled up a lily and gave it to him. The unicorn ate it gravely. With a high heart, because there was a unicorn in his garden, the man went upstairs and roused his wife again. "The unicorn," he said, "ate a lily." His wife sat up in bed and looked at him, coldly. "You are a booby," she said, "and I am going to have you put in the booby-hatch." The man, who had never liked the words "booby" and "booby-hatch," and who liked them even less on a shining morning when there was a unicorn in the garden, thought for a moment. "We'll see about that," he said. He walked over to the door. "He has a golden horn in the middle of his forehead," he told her. Then he went back to the garden to watch the unicorn; but the unicorn had gone away. The man sat down among the roses and went to sleep.

As soon as the husband had gone out of the house, the wife got up and dressed as fast as she could. She was very excited and there was a gloat in her eye. She telephoned the police and she telephoned a psychiatrist; she told them to hurry to her house and bring a strait-jacket. When the police and the psychiatrist arrived they sat down in chairs and looked at her, with great interest. "My husband," she said, "saw a unicorn this morning." The police looked at the psychiatrist and the psychiatrist looked at the police. "He told me it ate a lily," she said. The psychiatrist looked at the police and the police looked at the psychiatrist. "He told me it had a golden horn in the middle of its forehead," she said. At a solemn signal from the psychiatrist, the police leaped from their chairs and seized the wife. They had a hard time subduing her, for she put up a terrific struggle, but they finally subdued her. Just as they got her into the strait-jacket, the husband came back into the house.

"Did you tell your wife you saw a unicorn?" asked the police. "Of course not," said the husband. "The unicorn is a mythical beast." "That's all I wanted to know," said the psychiatrist. "Take her away. I'm sorry, sir, but your wife is as crazy as a jay bird." So they took her away, cursing and screaming, and shut her up in an institution. The husband lived happily ever after.

Moral: Don't count your boobies until they are hatched.

For Analysis

1. To what traditional tale does "The Little Girl and the Wolf" allude? How does the allusion affect your expectations? Is the moral's force limited to the events in the fable? Explain.

2. Discuss the political implications of "The Very Proper Gander." Do the remedies embedded in the American system of law always prevent such injustice? Explain.

3. What institutions of American society are addressed in "The Owl Who Was God"? Consider the animals' ironic misunderstanding of the owl's replies, and the consequences of that misunderstanding. To what well-known epigraph does the moral allude?

4. How would you characterize the husband and wife of "The Unicorn in the Garden"? How does Thurber persuade you to side with the husband?

On Style

1. Puns and dramatic irony (see "Glossary of Literary Terms") drive the wit in these pieces. Explain how these devices function in the fables.

2. What determines the owl's replies to his questioners?

3. Why are your expectations thwarted in "The Little Girl and the Wolf"?

4. What misunderstanding initiates the proper gander's downfall?

Making Connections

1. Consider the morals attached to these fables. Can you suggest either a literary work or an event from your own experience that validates each of them? Explain.

2. Are you aware of recent national security issues (in the United States or elsewhere) that reflect the events and moral of "The Very Proper Gander"? Explain.

Writing Topics

1. Write a Thurberesque treatment of a well-known fairy tale or folktale illustrating a moral quite different from that of the original story.

2. Write a critical analysis of these fables, focusing on Thurber's use of puns and dramatic irony.

Martin Luther King Jr. (1929–1968)

Letter from Birmingham Jail[1] 1963

M y Dear Fellow Clergymen:

While confined here in the Birmingham city jail, I came across your recent statement calling my present activities "unwise and untimely." Seldom do I pause to answer criticism of my work and ideas. If I sought to answer all the criticisms that cross my desk, my secretaries would have little time for anything other than such correspondence in the course of the day, and I would have no time for constructive work. But since I feel that you are men of genuine good will and that your criticisms are sincerely set forth, I want to try to answer your statement in what I hope will be patient and reasonable terms.

I think I should indicate why I am here in Birmingham, since you have been influenced by the view which argues against "outsiders coming in." I have the honor of serving as president of the Southern Christian Leadership Conference, an organization operating in every southern state, with headquarters in Atlanta, Georgia. We have some eighty-five affiliated organizations across the South, and one of them is the Alabama Christian Movement for Human Rights. Frequently we share staff, educational, and financial resources with our affiliates. Several months ago the affiliate here in Birmingham asked us to be on call to engage in a nonviolent direct-action program if such were deemed necessary. We readily consented, and when the hour came we lived up to our promise. So I, along with several members of my staff, am here because I was invited here. I am here because I have organizational ties here.

But more basically, I am in Birmingham because injustice is here. Just as the prophets of the eighth century B.C. left their villages and carried their "thus saith the Lord" far beyond the boundaries of their home towns, and just as the Apostle Paul left his village of Tarsus[2] and carried the gospel of Jesus Christ to

---

[1] This response to a published statement by eight fellow clergymen from Alabama (Bishop C. C. J. Carpenter, Bishop Joseph A. Durick, Rabbi Hilton L. Grafman, Bishop Paul Hardin, Bishop Holan B. Harmon, the Reverend George M. Murray, the Reverend Edward V. Ramage, and the Reverend Earl Stallings) was composed under somewhat constricting circumstances. Begun on the margins of the newspaper in which the statement appeared while I was in jail, the letter was continued on scraps of writing paper supplied by a friendly Negro trusty, and concluded on a pad my attorneys were eventually permitted to leave me. Although the text remains in substance unaltered, I have indulged in the author's prerogative of polishing it for publication. [King's note]

[2] Birthplace of St. Paul, in present-day Turkey.

the far corners of the Greco-Roman world, so am I compelled to carry the gospel of freedom beyond my own home town. Like Paul, I must constantly respond to the Macedonian call for aid.[3]

Moreover, I am cognizant of the interrelatedness of all communities and states. I cannot sit idly by in Atlanta and not be concerned about what happens in Birmingham. Injustice anywhere is a threat to justice everywhere. We are caught in an inescapable network of mutuality, tied in a single garment of destiny. Whatever affects one directly, affects all indirectly. Never again can we afford to live with the narrow, provincial "outside agitator" idea. Anyone who lives inside the United States can never be considered an outsider anywhere within its bounds.

You deplore the demonstrations taking place in Birmingham. But your state- 5 ment, I am sorry to say, fails to express a similar concern for the conditions that brought about the demonstrations. I am sure that none of you would want to rest content with the superficial kind of social analysis that deals merely with effects and does not grapple with the underlying causes. It is unfortunate that demonstrations are taking place in Birmingham, but it is even more unfortunate that the city's white power structure left the Negro community with no alternative.

In any nonviolent campaign there are four basic steps: collection of the facts to determine whether injustices exist; negotiation; self-purification; and direct action. We have gone through all these steps in Birmingham. There can be no gainsaying the fact that racial injustice engulfs this community. Birmingham is probably the most thoroughly segregated city in the United States. Its ugly record of brutality is widely known. Negroes have experienced grossly unjust treatment in the courts. There have been more unsolved bombings of Negro homes and churches in Birmingham than in any other city in the nation. These are the hard, brutal facts of the case. On the basis of these conditions, Negro leaders sought to negotiate with the city fathers. But the latter consistently refused to engage in good-faith negotiation.

Then, last September, came the opportunity to talk with leaders of Birmingham's economic community. In the course of the negotiations, certain promises were made by the merchants — for example, to remove the stores' humiliating racial signs. On the basis of these promises, the Reverend Fred Shuttlesworth and the leaders of the Alabama Christian Movement for Human Rights agreed to a moratorium on all demonstrations. As the weeks and months went by, we realized that we were the victims of a broken promise. A few signs, briefly removed, returned; the others remained.

As in so many past experiences, our hopes had been blasted, and the shadow of deep disappointment settled upon us. We had no alternative except to prepare for direct action, whereby we would present our very bodies as a means of

---

[3] St. Paul was frequently called upon to aid the Christian community in Macedonia.

laying our case before the conscience of the local and the national community. Mindful of the difficulties involved, we decided to undertake a process of self-purification. We began a series of workshops on nonviolence, and we repeatedly asked ourselves: "Are you able to accept blows without retaliating?" "Are you able to endure the ordeal of jail?" We decided to schedule our direct-action program for the Easter season, realizing that except for Christmas, this is the main shopping period of the year. Knowing that a strong economic-withdrawal program would be the by-product of direct action, we felt that this would be the best time to bring pressure to bear on the merchants for the needed change.

Then it occurred to us that Birmingham's mayoral election was coming up in March, and we speedily decided to postpone action until after election-day. When we discovered that the Commissioner of Public Safety, Eugene "Bull" Connor, had piled up enough votes to be in the run-off, we decided again to postpone action until the day after the run-off so that the demonstrations could not be used to cloud the issues. Like many others, we waited to see Mr. Connor defeated, and to this end we endured postponement after postponement. Having aided in this community need, we felt that our direct-action program could be delayed no longer.

You may well ask, "Why direct action? Why sit-ins, marches, and so forth?   10 Isn't negotiation a better path?" You are quite right in calling for negotiation. Indeed, this is the very purpose of direct action. Nonviolent direct action seeks to create such a crisis and foster such a tension that a community which has constantly refused to negotiate is forced to confront the issue. It seeks so to dramatize the issue that it can no longer be ignored. My citing the creation of tension as part of the work of the nonviolent-resister may sound rather shocking. But I must confess that I am not afraid of the word "tension." I have earnestly opposed violent tension, but there is a type of constructive, nonviolent tension which is necessary for growth. Just as Socrates[4] felt that it was necessary to create a tension in the mind so that individuals could rise from the bondage of myths and half-truths to the unfettered realm of creative analysis and objective appraisal, so must we see the need for nonviolent gadflies to create the kind of tension in society that will help men rise from the dark depths of prejudice and racism to the majestic heights of understanding and brotherhood.

The purpose of our direct-action program is to create a situation so crisis-packed that it will inevitably open the door to negotiation. I therefore concur with you in your call for negotiation. Too long has our beloved Southland been bogged down in a tragic effort to live in monologue rather than dialogue.

One of the basic points in your statement is that the action that I and my associates have taken in Birmingham is untimely. Some have asked: "Why didn't you give the new city administration time to act?" The only answer that I can give to this query is that the new Birmingham administration must be prodded about as

---

[4] Socrates (469–399 B.C.), a Greek philosopher who often pretended ignorance in arguments to expose the errors in his opponent's reasoning.

much as the outgoing one, before it will act. We are sadly mistaken if we feel that the election of Albert Boutwell as mayor will bring the millennium to Birmingham. While Mr. Boutwell is a much more gentle person than Mr. Connor, they are both segregationists, dedicated to maintenance of the status quo. I have hoped that Mr. Boutwell will be reasonable enough to see the futility of massive resistance to desegregation. But he will not see this without pressure from devotees of civil rights. My friends, I must say to you that we have not made a single gain in civil rights without determined legal and nonviolent pressure. Lamentably, it is an historical fact that privileged groups seldom give up their privileges voluntarily. Individuals may see the moral light and voluntarily give up their unjust posture; but, as Reinhold Niebuhr[5] has reminded us, groups tend to be more immoral than individuals.

We know through painful experience that freedom is never voluntarily given by the oppressor; it must be demanded by the oppressed. Frankly, I have yet to engage in a direct-action campaign that was "well timed" in the view of those who have not suffered unduly from the disease of segregation. For years now I have heard the word "Wait!" It rings in the ear of every Negro with piercing familiarity. This "Wait" has almost always meant "Never." We must come to see, with one of our distinguished jurists, that "justice too long delayed is justice denied."

We have waited for more than 340 years for our constitutional and God-given rights. The nations of Asia and Africa are moving with jetlike speed toward gaining political independence, but we still creep at horse-and-buggy pace toward gaining a cup of coffee at a lunch counter. Perhaps it is easy for those who have never felt the stinging darts of segregation to say, "Wait." But when you have seen vicious mobs lynch your mothers and fathers at will and drown your sisters and brothers at whim; when you have seen hate-filled policemen curse, kick, and even kill your black brothers and sisters; when you see the vast majority of your twenty million Negro brothers smothering in an airtight cage of poverty in the midst of an affluent society; when you suddenly find your tongue twisted and your speech stammering as you seek to explain to your six-year-old daughter why she can't go to the public amusement park that has just been advertised on television, and see tears welling up in her eyes when she is told that Funtown is closed to colored children, and see ominous clouds of inferiority beginning to form in her little mental sky, and see her beginning to distort her personality by developing an unconscious bitterness toward white people; when you have to concoct an answer for a five-year-old son who is asking, "Daddy, why do white people treat colored people so mean?"; when you take a cross-country drive and find it necessary to sleep night after night in the uncomfortable corners of your automobile because no motel will accept you; when you are humiliated day in and day out by nagging signs reading "white" and "colored"; when your first name becomes "nigger," your middle name

---

[5] Reinhold Niebuhr (1892–1971), American philosopher and theologian.

becomes "boy" (however old you are) and your last name becomes "John," and your wife and mother are never given the respected title "Mrs."; when you are harried by day and haunted by night by the fact that you are a Negro, living constantly at tiptoe stance, never quite knowing what to expect next, and are plagued with inner fears and outer resentments; when you are forever fighting a degenerating sense of "nobodiness" — then you will understand why we find it difficult to wait. There comes a time when the cup of endurance runs over, and men are no longer willing to be plunged into the abyss of despair. I hope, sirs, you can understand our legitimate and unavoidable impatience.

You express a great deal of anxiety over our willingness to break laws. This is 15 certainly a legitimate concern. Since we so diligently urge people to obey the Supreme Court's decision of 1954 outlawing segregation in the public schools, at first glance it may seem rather paradoxical for us consciously to break laws. One may well ask: "How can you advocate breaking some laws and obeying others?" The answer lies in the fact that there are two types of laws: just and unjust. I would be the first to advocate obeying just laws. One has not only a legal but a moral responsibility to obey just laws. Conversely, one has a moral responsibility to disobey unjust laws. I would agree with St. Augustine that "an unjust law is no law at all."

Now, what is the difference between the two? How does one determine whether a law is just or unjust? A just law is a man-made code that squares with the moral law or the law of God. An unjust law is a code that is out of harmony with the moral law. To put it in the terms of St. Thomas Aquinas: An unjust law is a human law that is not rooted in eternal law and natural law. Any law that uplifts human personality is just. Any law that degrades human personality is unjust. All segregation statutes are unjust because segregation distorts the soul and damages the personality. It gives the segregator a false sense of superiority and the segregated a false sense of inferiority. Segregation, to use the terminology of the Jewish philosopher Martin Buber, substitutes an "I-it" relationship for an "I-thou" relationship and ends up relegating persons to the status of things. Hence segregation is not only politically, economically, and sociologically unsound, it is morally wrong and sinful. Paul Tillich has said that sin is separation. Is not segregation an existential expression of man's tragic separation, his awful estrangement, his terrible sinfulness? Thus it is that I can urge men to obey the 1954 decision of the Supreme Court, for it is morally right; and I can urge them to disobey segregation ordinances, for they are morally wrong.

Let us consider a more concrete example of just and unjust laws. An unjust law is a code that a numerical or power majority group compels a minority group to obey but does not make binding on itself. This is *difference* made legal. By the same token, a just law is a code that a majority compels a minority to follow and that it is willing to follow itself. This is *sameness* made legal.

Let me give another explanation. A law is unjust if it is inflicted on a minority that, as a result of being denied the right to vote, had no part in enacting or devising the law. Who can say that the legislature of Alabama which set up that state's segregation laws was democratically elected? Throughout Alabama all sorts of devious methods are used to prevent Negroes from becoming registered voters, and there are some counties in which, even though Negroes constitute a majority of the population, not a single Negro is registered. Can any law enacted under such circumstances be considered democratically structured?

Sometimes a law is just on its face and unjust in its application. For instance, I have been arrested on a charge of parading without a permit. Now, there is nothing wrong in having an ordinance which requires a permit for a parade. But such an ordinance becomes unjust when it is used to maintain segregation and to deny citizens the First-Amendment privilege of peaceful assembly and protest.

I hope you are able to see the distinction I am trying to point out. In no sense 20 do I advocate evading or defying the law, as would the rabid segregationist. That would lead to anarchy. One who breaks an unjust law must do so openly, lovingly, and with a willingness to accept the penalty. I submit that an individual who breaks a law that conscience tells him is unjust, and who willingly accepts the penalty of imprisonment in order to arouse the conscience of the community over its injustice, is in reality expressing the highest respect for law.

Of course, there is nothing new about this kind of civil disobedience. It was evidenced sublimely in the refusal of Shadrach, Meshach, and Abednego to obey the laws of Nebuchadnezzar, on the ground that a higher moral law was at stake.[6] It was practiced superbly by the early Christians, who were willing to face hungry lions and the excruciating pain of chopping blocks rather than submit to certain unjust laws of the Roman Empire. To a degree, academic freedom is a reality today because Socrates practiced civil disobedience. In our own nation, the Boston Tea Party represented a massive act of civil disobedience.

We should never forget that everything Adolf Hitler did in Germany was "legal" and everything the Hungarian freedom fighters did in Hungary was "illegal." It was "illegal" to aid and comfort a Jew in Hitler's Germany. Even so, I am sure that, had I lived in Germany at the time, I would have aided and comforted my Jewish brothers. If today I lived in a Communist country where certain principles dear to the Christian faith are suppressed, I would openly advocate disobeying that country's anti-religious laws.

I must make two honest confessions to you, my Christian and Jewish brothers. First, I must confess that over the past few years I have been gravely disappointed with the white moderate. I have almost reached the regrettable conclusion that the Negro's great stumbling block in his stride toward freedom is not the white Citizen's Counciler[7] or the Ku Klux Klanner, but the white moderate, who is more devoted to "order" than to justice; who prefers a negative peace which is the absence of tension to a positive peace which is the presence

---

[6] See Daniel 1:7–3:30.

[7] White Citizen's Councils sprang up in the South after 1954 (the year the Supreme Court declared segregated education unconstitutional) to fight against desegregation.

of justice; who constantly says, "I agree with you in the goal you seek, but I cannot agree with your methods of direct action"; who paternalistically believes he can set the timetable for another man's freedom; who lives by a mythical concept of time and who constantly advises the Negro to wait for a "more convenient season." Shallow understanding from people of good will is more frustrating than absolute misunderstanding from people of ill will. Lukewarm acceptance is much more bewildering than outright rejection.

I had hoped that the white moderate would understand that law and order exist for the purpose of establishing justice and that when they fail in this purpose they become the dangerously structured dams that block the flow of social progress. I had hoped that the white moderate would understand that the present tension in the South is a necessary phase of the transition from an obnoxious negative peace, in which the Negro passively accepted his unjust plight, to a substantive and positive peace, in which all men will respect the dignity and worth of human personality. Actually, we who engage in nonviolent direct action are not the creators of tension. We merely bring to the surface the hidden tension that is already alive. We bring it out in the open, where it can be seen and dealt with. Like a boil that can never be cured so long as it is covered up but must be opened with all its ugliness to the natural medicines of air and light, injustice must be exposed, with all the tension its exposure creates, to the light of human conscience and the air of national opinion, before it can be cured.

In your statement you assert that our actions, even though peaceful, must be 25 condemned because they precipitate violence. But is this a logical assertion? Isn't this like condemning a robbed man because his possession of money precipitated the evil act of robbery? Isn't this like condemning Socrates because his unswerving commitment to truth and his philosophical inquiries precipitated the act by the misguided populace in which they made him drink hemlock? Isn't this like condemning Jesus because his unique God-consciousness and never-ceasing devotion to God's will precipitated the evil act of crucifixion? We must come to see that, as the federal courts have consistently affirmed, it is wrong to urge an individual to cease his efforts to gain his basic constitutional rights because the quest may precipitate violence. Society must protect the robbed and punish the robber.

I had also hoped that the white moderate would reject the myth concerning time in relation to the struggle for freedom. I have just received a letter from a white brother in Texas. He writes: "All Christians know that the colored people will receive greater equal rights eventually, but it is possible that you are in too great a religious hurry. It has taken Christianity almost two thousand years to accomplish what it has. The teachings of Christ take time to come to earth." Such an attitude stems from a tragic misconception of time, from the strangely irrational notion that there is something in the very flow of time that will inevitably cure all ills. Actually, time itself is neutral; it can be used either destructively or constructively. More and more I feel that the people of ill will have used time much more effectively than have the people of good will. We will have to repent in this generation not merely for the hateful words and actions of the bad people, but for the appalling silence of the good people. Human progress never rolls in on wheels of inevitability; it comes through the tireless efforts of men willing to be co-workers with God, and without this hard work, time itself becomes an ally of the forces of social stagnation. We must use time creatively, in the knowledge that the time is always ripe to do right. Now is the time to make real the promise of democracy and transform our pending national elegy into a creative psalm of brotherhood. Now is the time to lift our national policy from the quicksand of racial injustice to the solid rock of human dignity.

You speak of our activity in Birmingham as extreme. At first I was rather disappointed that fellow clergymen would see my nonviolent efforts as those of an extremist. I began thinking about the fact that I stand in the middle of two opposing forces in the Negro community. One is a force of complacency, made up in part of Negroes, who, as a result of long years of oppression, are so drained of self-respect and a sense of "somebodiness" that they have adjusted to segregation; and in part of a few middle-class Negroes who, because of a degree of academic and economic security and because in some ways they profit by segregation, have become insensitive to the problems of the masses. The other force is one of bitterness and hatred, and it comes perilously close to advocating violence. It is expressed in the various black nationalist groups that are springing up across the nation, the largest and best-known being Elijah Muhammad's Muslim movement.[8] Nourished by the Negro's frustration over the continued existence of racial discrimination, this movement is made up of people who have lost faith in America, who have absolutely repudiated Christianity, and who have concluded that the white man is an incorrigible "devil."

I have tried to stand between these two forces, saying that we need emulate neither the "do-nothingism" of the complacent nor the hatred and despair of the black nationalist. For there is the more excellent way of love and nonviolent protest. I am grateful to God that, through the influence of the Negro church, the way of nonviolence became an integral part of our struggle.

If this philosophy had not emerged, by now many streets of the South would, I am convinced, be flowing with blood. And I am further convinced that if our white brothers dismiss as "rabble-rousers" and "outside agitators" those of us who employ nonviolent direct action, and if they refuse to support our non-violent efforts, millions of Negroes will, out of frustration and despair, seek solace and security in black-nationalist ideologies—a development that would inevitably lead to a frightening racial nightmare.

Oppressed people cannot remain oppressed forever. The yearning for free- 30 dom eventually manifests itself, and that is what has happened to the American Negro. Something within has reminded him of his birthright of freedom, and something without has reminded him that it can be gained. Consciously or

---

[8] Elijah Muhammad (1897–1975), leader of the Nation of Islam, a black Muslim religious group that rejected integration and called upon blacks to fight to establish their own nation.

unconsciously, he has been caught up by the *Zeitgeist*,[9] and with his black brothers of Africa and his brown and yellow brothers of Asia, South America, and the Caribbean, the United States Negro is moving with a sense of great urgency toward the promised land of racial justice. If one recognizes this vital urge that has engulfed the Negro community, one should readily understand why public demonstrations are taking place. The Negro has many pent-up resentments and latent frustrations, and he must release them. So let him march; let him make prayer pilgrimages to the city hall; let him go on freedom rides[10]—and try to understand why he must do so. If his repressed emotions are not released in nonviolent ways, they will seek expression through violence; this is not a threat but a fact of history. So I have not said to my people, "Get rid of your discontent." Rather, I have tried to say that this normal and healthy discontent can be channeled into the creative outlet of nonviolent direct action. And now this approach is being termed extremist.

But though I was initially disappointed at being categorized as an extremist, as I continued to think about the matter I gradually gained a measure of satisfaction from the label. Was not Jesus an extremist for love: "Love your enemies, bless them that curse you, do good to them that hate you, and pray for them that despitefully use you, and persecute you." Was not Amos an extremist for justice: "Let justice roll down like waters and righteousness like an ever-flowing stream." Was not Paul an extremist for the Christian gospel: "I bear in my body the marks of the Lord Jesus." Was not Martin Luther an extremist: "Here I stand; I cannot do otherwise, so help me God." And John Bunyan: "I will stay in jail to the end of my days before I make a butchery of my conscience." And Abraham Lincoln: "This nation cannot survive half slave and half free." And Thomas Jefferson: "We hold these truths to be self-evident, that all men are created equal. . . . " So the question is not whether we will be extremists, but what kind of extremists we will be. Will we be extremists for the preservation of injustice or for the extension of justice? In that dramatic scene on Calvary's hill three men were crucified. We must never forget that all three were crucified for the same crime—the crime of extremism. Two were extremists for immorality, and thus fell below their environment. The other, Jesus Christ, was an extremist for love, truth, and goodness, and thereby rose above his environment. Perhaps the South, the nation, and the world are in dire need of creative extremists.

I had hoped that the white moderate would see this need. Perhaps I was too optimistic; perhaps I expected too much. I suppose I should have realized that few members of the oppressor race can understand the deep groans and passionate yearnings of the oppressed race, and still fewer have the vision to see that injustice must be rooted out by strong, persistent, and determined action. I am thankful, however, that some of our white brothers in the South have

---

[9] The spirit of the time.

[10] In 1961, hundreds of blacks and whites, under the direction of the Congress of Racial Equality (CORE), deliberately violated laws in southern states that required segregation in buses and bus terminals.

grasped the meaning of this social revolution and committed themselves to it. They are still all too few in quantity, but they are big in quality. Some — such as Ralph McGill, Lillian Smith, Harry Golden, James McBride Dabbs, Ann Braden, and Sarah Patton Boyle — have written about our struggle in eloquent and prophetic terms. Others have marched with us down nameless streets of the South. They have languished in filthy, roach-infested jails, suffering the abuse and brutality of policemen who view them as "dirty nigger-lovers." Unlike so many of their moderate brothers and sisters, they have recognized the urgency of the moment and sensed the need for powerful "action" antidotes to combat the disease of segregation.

Let me take note of my other major disappointment. I have been so greatly disappointed with the white church and its leadership. Of course, there are some notable exceptions. I am not unmindful of the fact that each of you has taken some significant stands on this issue. I commend you, Reverend Stallings, for your Christian stand on this past Sunday, in welcoming Negroes to your worship service on a nonsegregated basis. I commend the Catholic leaders of this state for integrating Spring Hill College several years ago.

But despite these notable exceptions, I must honestly reiterate that I have been disappointed with the church. I do not say this as one of those negative critics who can always find something wrong with the church. I say this as a minister of the gospel, who loves the church; who was nurtured in its bosom; who has been sustained by its spiritual blessings and who will remain true to it as long as the cord of life shall lengthen.

When I was suddenly catapulted into the leadership of the bus protest in 35 Montgomery, Alabama, a few years ago, I felt we would be supported by the white church. I felt that the white ministers, priests, and rabbis of the South would be among our strongest allies. Instead, some have been outright opponents, refusing to understand the freedom movement and misrepresenting its leaders; all too many others have been more cautious than courageous and have remained silent behind the anesthetizing security of stained-glass windows.

In spite of my shattered dreams, I came to Birmingham with the hope that the white religious leadership of this community would see the justice of our cause and, with deep moral concern, would serve as the channel through which our just grievances could reach the power structure. I had hoped that each of you would understand. But again I have been disappointed.

I have heard numerous southern religious leaders admonish their worshipers to comply with a desegregation decision because it is the law, but I have longed to hear white ministers declare: "Follow this decree because integration is morally right and because the Negro is your brother." In the midst of blatant injustices inflicted upon the Negro, I have watched white churchmen stand on the sideline and mouth pious irrelevancies and sanctimonious trivialities. In the midst of a mighty struggle to rid our nation of racial and economic injustice, I have heard many ministers say: "Those are social issues, with which the gospel has no real concern." And I have watched many churches commit themselves to a completely otherworldly religion which makes a strange, unBiblical distinction between body and soul, between the sacred and the secular.

I have traveled the length and breadth of Alabama, Mississippi, and all the other southern states. On sweltering summer days and crisp autumn mornings I have looked at the South's beautiful churches with their lofty spires pointing heavenward. I have beheld the impressive outlines of her massive religious-education buildings. Over and over I have found myself asking: "What kind of people worship here? Who is their God? Where were their voices when the lips of Governor Barnett dripped with words of interposition and nullification? Where were they when Governor Wallace gave a clarion call for defiance and hatred? Where were their voices of support when bruised and weary Negro men and women decided to rise from the dark dungeons of complacency to the bright hills of creative protest?"

Yes, these questions are still in mind. In deep disappointment I have wept over the laxity of the church. But be assured that my tears have been tears of love. There can be no deep disappointment where there is not deep love. Yes, I love the church. How could I do otherwise? I am in the rather unique position of being the son, the grandson, and the great-grandson of preachers. Yes, I see the church as the body of Christ. But, oh! How we have blemished and scarred the body through social neglect and through fear of being nonconformists.

There was a time when the church was very powerful — in the time when the 40
early Christians rejoiced at being deemed worthy to suffer for what they believed. In those days the church was not merely a thermometer that transformed the mores of society. Whenever the early Christians entered a town, the people in power became disturbed and immediately sought to convict the Christians for being "disturbers of the peace" and "outside agitators." But the Christians pressed on, in the conviction that they were "a colony of heaven," called to obey God rather than man. Small in number, they were big in commitment. They were too God-intoxicated to be "astronomically intimidated." By their effort and example they brought an end to such ancient evils as infanticide and gladiatorial contests.

Things are different now. So often the contemporary church is a weak, ineffectual voice with an uncertain sound. So often it is an archdefender of the status quo. Far from being disturbed by the presence of the church, the power structure of the average community is consoled by the church's silent — and often even vocal — sanction of things as they are.

But the judgment of God is upon the church as never before. If today's church does not recapture the sacrificial spirit of the early church, it will lose its authenticity, forfeit the loyalty of millions, and be dismissed as an irrelevant social club with no meaning for the twentieth century. Every day I meet young people whose disappointment with the church has turned into outright disgust.

Perhaps I have once again been too optimistic. Is organized religion too inextricably bound to the status quo to save our nation and the world? Perhaps I must turn my faith to the inner spiritual church, the church within the church, as the true *ekklesia*[11] and the hope of the world. But again I am thankful to God that some noble souls from the ranks of organized religion have broken loose from the paralyzing chains of conformity and joined us as active partners in the struggle for freedom. They have left their secure congregations and walked the streets of Albany, Georgia, with us. They have gone down the highways of the South on tortuous rides for freedom. Yes, they have gone to jail with us. Some have been dismissed from their churches, have lost the support of their bishops and fellow ministers. But they have acted in the faith that right defeated is stronger than evil triumphant. Their witness has been the spiritual salt that has preserved the true meaning of the gospel in these troubled times. They have carved a tunnel of hope through the dark mountain of disappointment.

I hope that the church as a whole will meet the challenge of this decisive hour. But even if the church does not come to the aid of justice, I have no despair about the future. I have no fear about the outcome of our struggle in Birmingham, even if our motives are at present misunderstood. We will reach the goal of freedom in Birmingham and all over the nation, because the goal of America is freedom. Abused and scorned though we may be, our destiny is tied up with America's destiny. Before the pilgrims landed at Plymouth, we were here. Before the pen of Jefferson etched the majestic words of the Declaration of Independence across the pages of history, we were here. For more than two centuries our forebears labored in this country without wages; they made cotton king; they built the homes of their masters while suffering gross injustice and shameful humiliation — and yet out of a bottomless vitality they continued to thrive and develop. If the inexpressible cruelties of slavery could not stop us, the opposition we now face will surely fail. We will win our freedom because the sacred heritage of our nation and the eternal will of God are embodied in our echoing demands.

Before closing I feel impelled to mention one other point in your state- 45 ment that has troubled me profoundly. You warmly commended the Birmingham police force for keeping "order" and "preventing violence." I doubt that you would have so warmly commended the police force if you had seen its dogs sinking their teeth into unarmed, nonviolent Negroes. I doubt that you would so quickly commend the policemen if you were to observe their ugly and inhumane treatment of Negroes here in the city jail; if you were to watch them push and curse old Negro women and young Negro girls; if you were to see them slap and kick old Negro men and young boys; if you were to observe them, as they did on two occasions, refuse to give us food because we wanted to sing our grace together. I cannot join you in your praise of the Birmingham police department.

---

[11] The Greek New Testament word for the early Christian church.

It is true that the police have exercised a degree of discipline in handling the demonstrators. In this sense they have conducted themselves rather "nonviolently" in public. But for what purpose? To preserve the evil system of segregation. Over the past few years I have consistently preached that nonviolence demands that the means we use must be as pure as the ends we seek. I have tried to make clear that it is wrong to use immoral means to attain moral ends. But now I must affirm that it is just as wrong, or perhaps even more so, to use moral means to preserve immoral ends. Perhaps Mr. Connor and his policemen have been rather nonviolent in public, as was Chief Pritchett in Albany, Georgia, but they have used the moral means of nonviolence to maintain the immoral end of racial injustice. As T. S. Eliot[12] has said, "The last temptation is the greatest treason: To do the right deed for the wrong reason."

I wish you had commended the Negro sit-inners and demonstrators of Birmingham for their sublime courage, their willingness to suffer, and their amazing discipline in the midst of great provocation. One day the South will recognize its real heroes. They will be the James Merediths,[13] with the noble sense of purpose that enables them to face jeering and hostile mobs, and with the agonizing loneliness that characterizes the life of the pioneer. They will be old, oppressed, battered Negro women, symbolized in a seventy-two-year-old woman in Montgomery, Alabama, who rose up with a sense of dignity and with her people decided not to ride segregated buses, and who responded with ungrammatical profundity to one who inquired about her weariness: "My feets is tired, but my soul is at rest." They will be the young high school and college students, the young ministers of the gospel and a host of their elders, courageously and nonviolently sitting in at lunch counters and willingly going to jail for conscience' sake. One day the South will know that when these disinherited children of God sat down at lunch counters, they were in reality standing up for what is best in the American dream and for the most sacred values in our Judaeo-Christian heritage, thereby bringing our nation back to those great wells of democracy which were dug deep by the founding fathers in their formulation of the Constitution and the Declaration of Independence.

Never before have I written so long a letter. I'm afraid it is much too long to take your precious time. I can assure you that it would have been much shorter if I had been writing from a comfortable desk, but what else can one do when he is alone in a narrow jail cell, other than write long letters, think long thoughts, and pray long prayers?

If I have said anything in this letter that overstates the truth and indicates an unreasonable impatience, I beg you to forgive me. If I have said anything that understates the truth and indicates my having a patience that allows me to settle for anything less than brotherhood, I beg God to forgive me.

I hope this letter finds you strong in the faith. I hope that circumstances will 50 soon make it possible for me to meet each of you, not as an integrationist or a

---

[12] Thomas Stearns Eliot (1888–1965), American-born poet.
[13] James Meredith was the first black to be admitted as a student at the University of Mississippi.

civil-rights leader but as a fellow clergyman and a Christian brother. Let us all hope that the dark clouds of a racial prejudice will soon pass away and the deep fog of misunderstanding will be lifted from our fear-drenched communities, and in some not too distant tomorrow the radiant stars of love and brotherhood will shine over our great nation with all their scintillating beauty.

Yours for the cause of Peace and Brotherhood,
Martin Luther King Jr.

For Analysis

1. What is King's definition of "civil disobedience"?

2. Summarize and explain the argument King makes in paragraph 46 about "means" and "ends."

3. Those opposed to civil disobedience frequently argue that in a democratic society, change should be pursued through legislation and the courts because if people are allowed to disobey laws with which they disagree, there will be chaos and violence. How does King seek to allay those fears?

4. How does King deal with the charge that he is an outsider meddling in the affairs of others?

5. What are the "four basic steps" (para. 6) in a nonviolent campaign, according to King?

6. What is King's answer to his critics who urge negotiation instead of direct action?

On Style

1. Readers have often found King's **tone** and **style** strongly influenced by pulpit oratory in its eloquence, elevated **diction,** biblical allusions, and didacticism. Select one or two paragraphs from the essay, and show how these qualities are reflected.

2. Rewrite some of King's sentences by eliminating the **metaphors,** and comment on the effects of the change (see, for example, the metaphors in paras. 14, 26, 43, and 50).

3. Characterize King's tone. Throughout the essay, does the tone change to any significant degree? Explain.

Making Connections

1. Does your own experience bear out King's distinction (para. 10) between "violent" and "nonviolent" tension?

2. Have you ever been in a situation in which you were required to obey what you considered an unjust law? If so, describe the law, why you felt it was unjust, and the course of action you chose.

3. Jonathan Swift uses satire in "A Modest Proposal" to protest the injustice of British rule in Ireland. King adopts a direct personal tone to convey his position. How are these contrasting approaches appropriate for each author's purpose?

4. What do you imagine King's reaction would be to Audre Lorde's poem "Power" (p. 1127)?

Writing Topics

1. King offers a philosophical justification for civil disobedience (paras. 15–22), at the heart of which is his distinction between a just and an unjust law. Defend or take issue with that distinction.

2. In your opinion, has the history of race relations in America since King's assassination in 1968 strengthened or weakened his arguments on the necessity and value of civil disobedience?

LOOKING DEEPER:
From History to Literature

During the 1950s and 1960s, black citizens of the American South engaged in a great struggle to win the civil rights accorded to other U.S. citizens as a matter of course. That struggle nurtured many leaders, but none as charismatic and eloquent as Martin Luther King Jr., who wrote, from his Birmingham jail cell, the essay at the center of this investigation of one interaction between literature and history. The documents collected here reveal that the seeds of the conflict were planted at the very founding of the Republic. Article I, Section 2, of the U.S. Constitution defined slaves as three-fifths of a person when it established the rules that governed the congressional House of Representatives. The Supreme Court, in 1856, found in the Constitution the grounds for denying Dred Scott, a slave who had been taken by his owner into a free territory, the dignity of his own humanity, as is delineated in the excerpted transcript from that case. After the Civil War, the Fourteenth Amendment to the Constitution (1868) redefined the idea of citizenship to include "all persons born or naturalized in the United States," but the resistance of the defeated Confederate states led to the formulation of the so-called Jim Crow laws — named after an African American character in minstrel shows — that endured well past the middle of the twentieth century. Examples of these laws are included in this section.

When the "freedom riders" came into the Deep South in the 1960s to organize black citizens, conduct voter-registration drives, and demonstrate against unfair laws as well as unfair treatment under the law, many white communities responded fiercely and violently. On Good Friday, April 12, 1963, Martin Luther King Jr. was arrested for participating in a peaceful protest parade that was held without a permit. On April 13, a group of "liberal" white clergymen published a letter — included here, in an article reprinted from the *Birmingham News* — urging restraint, cautioning against "outsiders," and advising the local African American community to turn to the courts for redress of their grievances. King's famous reply appeared on April 16. After a week of negotiations between protest leaders and representatives of the city of Birmingham, the Birmingham Truce Agreement was drafted (May 10, 1963). As can be seen from reading this agreement, included at the end of this section, the terms were very modest; however, it was several years before the city implemented the conditions of the agreement.

Before moving through these documents, read the brief biography of Martin Luther King Jr. (p. 1541). Note that the United States Constitution and Supreme Court decisions can be found at several Web sites. We downloaded the sample list of Jim Crow laws from <http://www.nps.gov/malu /documents/jim_crow_laws.htm>.

from The U.S. Constitution, Article I, Section 2 1787

Representatives and direct Taxes shall be apportioned among the several States which may be included within this Union, according to their respective Numbers, which shall be determined by adding to the whole Number of free Persons, including those bound to Service for a Term of Years, and excluding Indians not taxed, three-fifths of all other Persons. The actual Enumeration shall be made within three Years after the first Meeting of the Congress of the United States, and within every subsequent Term of ten Years, in such Manner as they shall by Law direct. The Number of Representatives shall not exceed one for every thirty Thousand, but each State shall have at Least one Representative; and until such enumeration shall be made, the State of New-Hampshire shall be entitled to chuse three, Massachusetts eight, Rhode-Island and Providence Plantations one, Connecticut five, New-York six, New-Jersey four, Pennsylvania eight, Delaware one, Maryland six, Virginia ten, North-Carolina five, South-Carolina five, and Georgia three.

Questions for Looking Deeper

A class of persons called "indentured servants" were counted as part of a state's population to determine the number of representatives the state could send to Congress, but the Constitution excludes Native Americans from such a count. Can you suggest a reason for that exclusion? Slaves were counted as three-fifths of a person. Can you suggest a reason?

from *Dred Scott v. Sandford* 1856

4. A free negro of the African race, whose ancestors were brought to this country and sold as slaves, is not a "citizen" within the meaning of the Constitution of the United States.

5. When the Constitution was adopted, they were not regarded in any of the States as members of the community which constituted the State, and were not numbered among its "people or citizens." Consequently, the special rights and immunities guaranteed to citizens do not apply to them. And not being "citizens" within the meaning of the Constitution, they are not entitled to sue in that character in a court of the United States, and the Circuit Court has not jurisdiction in such a suit.

6. The only two clauses in the Constitution which point to this race, treat them as persons whom it was morally lawful to deal in as articles of property and to hold as slaves.

7. Since the adoption of the Constitution of the United States, no State can by any subsequent law make a foreigner or any other description of persons citizens of the United States, nor entitle them to the rights and privileges secured to citizens by that instrument.

8. A State, by its laws passed since the adoption of the Constitution, may put a 5
foreigner or any other description of persons upon a footing with its own citizens, as to all the rights and privileges enjoyed by them within its dominion and by its laws. But that will not make him a citizen of the United States, nor entitle him to sue in its courts, nor to any of the privileges and immunities of a citizen in another State.

9. The change in public opinion and feeling in relation to the African race, which has taken place since the adoption of the Constitution, cannot change its construction and meaning, and it must be construed and administered now according to its true meaning and intention when it was formed and adopted.

10. The plaintiff having admitted, by his demurrer to the plea in abatement, that his ancestors were imported from Africa and sold as slaves, he is not a citizen of the State of Missouri according to the Constitution of the United States, and was not entitled to sue in that character in the Circuit Court.

11. This being the case, the judgment of the court below, in favor of the plaintiff on the plea in abatement, was erroneous.

Questions for Looking Deeper

1. In 1857, could a person be a "citizen" of a state but not a "citizen" of the United States? Explain.

2. Is such a distinction possible at present?

3. Do you find a contradiction between the statements in number 5 and Article I, Section 2, of the Constitution? Explain.

4. Research the consequences of the Dred Scott decision either at the library or on the Internet. In an essay, describe the immediate consequences of the decision, and its impact on constitutional amendments in the mid–nineteenth century.

The U.S. Constitution, Amendment XIV 1868

Section 1. All persons born or naturalized in the United States, and subject to the jurisdiction thereof, are citizens of the United States and of the State wherein they reside. No State shall make or enforce any law which shall abridge the privileges or immunities of citizens of the United States; nor shall any State deprive any person of life, liberty, or property, without due process of law; nor deny to any person within its jurisdiction the equal protection of the laws.

Section 2. Representatives shall be apportioned among the several States according to their respective numbers, counting the whole number of persons in each State, excluding Indians not taxed. But when the right to vote at any election for the choice of electors for President and Vice President of the United States, Representatives in Congress, the Executive and Judicial officers of a State, or the members of the Legislature thereof, is denied to any of the male inhabitants of such State, being twenty-one years of age, and citizens of the United States, or in any way abridged, except for participation in rebellion, or other crime, the basis of representation therein shall be reduced in the proportion which the number of such male citizens shall bear to the whole number of male citizens twenty-one years of age in such State.

Section 3. No person shall be a Senator or Representative in Congress, or elector of President and Vice President, or hold any office, civil or military, under the United States, or under any State, who, having previously taken an oath, as a member of Congress, or as an officer of the United States, or as a member of any State legislature, or as an executive or judicial officer of any State, to support the Constitution of the United States, shall have engaged in insurrection or rebellion against the same, or given aid or comfort to the enemies thereof. But Congress may by a vote of two-thirds of each House, remove such disability.

Section 4. The validity of the public debt of the United States, authorized by law, including debts incurred for payment of pensions and bounties for services in suppressing insurrection or rebellion, shall not be questioned. But neither the United States nor any State shall assume or pay any debt or obligation incurred in aid of insurrection or rebellion against the United States, or any claim for the loss or emancipation of any slave; but all such debts, obligations and claims shall be held illegal and void.

Section 5. The Congress shall have power to enforce, by appropriate legislation, the provisions of this article.

Questions for Looking Deeper

1. How did the Fourteenth Amendment affect the precedent established by the Dred Scott decision?

2. How did the Fourteenth Amendment change the composition of the House of Representatives?

3. Why do sections of this amendment speak of "insurrection or rebellion"? What are the amendment's practical consequences for those who engaged in insurrection or rebellion?

4. What affect did the Fourteenth Amendment have on the lives of free northern blacks and former southern slaves?

"Jim Crow" Laws ca. 1880s–1960s

From the 1880s into the 1960s, a majority of American states enforced segregation through "Jim Crow" laws, which often imposed legal punishments on people for consorting with members of another race.

Here is a sampling of laws from various states:

Nurses No person or corporation shall require any white female nurse to nurse in wards or rooms in hospitals, either public or private, in which negro men are placed. *Alabama*

Buses All passenger stations in this state operated by any motor transportation company shall have separate waiting rooms or space and separate ticket windows for the white and colored races. *Alabama*

Railroads The conductor of each passenger train is authorized and required to assign each passenger to the car or the division of the car, when it is divided by a partition, designated for the race to which such passenger belongs. *Alabama*

Restaurants It shall be unlawful to conduct a restaurant or other place for the serving of food in the city, at which white and colored people are served in the same room, unless such white and colored persons are effectually separated by a solid partition extending from the floor upward to a distance of seven feet or higher, and unless a separate entrance from the street is provided for each compartment. *Alabama*

Pool and Billiard Rooms It shall be unlawful for a negro and white person to play together or in company with each other at any game of pool or billiards. *Alabama*

Toilet Facilities, Male   Every employer of white or negro males shall provide for such white or negro males reasonably accessible and separate toilet facilities. *Alabama*

Intermarriage   The marriage of a person of Caucasian blood with a Negro, Mongolian, Malay, or Hindu shall be null and void. *Arizona*

Intermarriage   All marriages between a white person and a negro, or between a white person and a person of negro descent to the fourth generation inclusive, are hereby forever prohibited. *Florida*

Cohabitation   Any negro man and white woman, or any white man and negro woman, who are not married to each other, who shall habitually live in and occupy in the nighttime the same room, shall each be punished by imprisonment not exceeding twelve (12) months, or by fine not exceeding five hundred ($500.00) dollars. *Florida*

Education   The schools for white children and the schools for negro children shall be conducted separately. *Florida*

Juvenile Delinquents   There shall be separate buildings, not nearer than one-fourth mile to each other, one for white boys and one for negro boys. White boys and negro boys shall not, in any manner, be associated together or worked together. *Florida*

Intermarriage   It shall be unlawful for a white person to marry anyone except a white person. Any marriage in violation of this section shall be void. *Georgia*

Burial   The officer in charge shall not bury, or allow to be buried, any colored persons upon ground set apart or used for the burial of white persons. *Georgia*

Amateur Baseball   It shall be unlawful for any amateur white baseball team to play baseball on any vacant lot or baseball diamond within two blocks of a playground devoted to the Negro race, and it shall be unlawful for any amateur colored baseball team to play baseball in any vacant lot or baseball diamond within two blocks of any playground devoted to the white race. *Georgia*

Parks   It shall be unlawful for colored people to frequent any park owned or maintained by the city for the benefit, use, and enjoyment of white persons . . . and unlawful for any white person to frequent any park owned or maintained by the city for the use and benefit of colored persons. *Georgia*

Wine and Beer   All persons licensed to conduct the business of selling beer or wine shall serve either white people exclusively or colored people exclusively and shall not sell to the two races within the same room at any time. *Georgia*

Circus Tickets   All circuses, shows, and tent exhibitions, to which the attendance of more than one race is invited or expected to attend, shall provide for the convenience of its patrons not less than two ticket offices with individual ticket sellers, and not less than two entrances to the said performance, with individual ticket takers and receivers, and in the case of outside or tent performances, the said ticket offices shall not be less than twenty-five (25) feet apart. *Louisiana*

Promotion of Equality   Any person . . . who shall be guilty of printing, publishing, or circulating printed, typewritten, or written matter urging or presenting for public acceptance or general information, arguments or suggestions in favor of social equality or of intermarriage between whites and negroes, shall be guilty of a misdemeanor and subject to fine not exceeding five hundred ($500.00) dollars or imprisonment not exceeding six (6) months or both. *Mississippi*

Prisons   The warden shall see that the white convicts shall have separate apartments for both eating and sleeping from the negro convicts. *Mississippi*

Child Custody   It shall be unlawful for any parent, relative, or other white person in this State, having the control or custody of any white child, by right of guardianship, natural or acquired, or otherwise, to dispose of, give, or surrender such white child permanently into the custody, control, maintenance, or support of a negro. *South Carolina*

Libraries   Any white person of such county may use the county free library under the rules and regulations prescribed by the commissioners court and may be entitled to all the privileges thereof. Said court shall make proper provision for the negroes of said county to be served through a separate branch or branches of the county free library, which shall be administered by [a] custodian of the negro race under the supervision of the county librarian. *Texas*

Education   [The County Board of Education] shall provide schools of two kinds, those for white children and those for colored children. *Texas*

Questions for Looking Deeper

1. Research the term *Jim Crow*. Where does it come from and what does it mean?

2. Jim Crow laws began to appear in the 1880s. Why do you suppose they did not appear earlier?

3. Note that the grass-roots activities for which Martin Luther King Jr. was imprisoned occurred in 1963. Why did the African American community and its allies feel it was necessary to break local laws?

4. Place yourself in the position of an African American southerner in 1950. How would you react to the limitations imposed on you by the Jim Crow laws?

A Call for Unity
from Alabama Clergymen[1] 1963

Leading Protestant, Catholic, and Jewish clerics Friday called on local Negro citizens to withdraw support of racial demonstrations and unite for a peaceful Birmingham.

In a prepared statement, the clergy praised the manner in which the 10 days of demonstrations have been handled by the Birmingham Police Department.

The same clergy were among others who recently issued "An Appeal for Law and Order and Common Sense" in dealing with the racial problems in Alabama.

Saturday's statement was signed by C.C.J. Carpenter, Episcopal Bishop of Alabama; Joseph A. Durick, auxiliary bishop, Catholic Diocese of Mobile-Birmingham; Rabbi Milton Grafman, Temple Emanu-El; Bishop Paul Hardin, Bishop of the Alabama–West Florida Conference of the Methodist Church; Bishop Nolan B. Harmen, Bishop of the North Alabama Conference of the Methodist Church; George M. Murray, Bishop Coadjutor, Episcopal Diocese of Alabama; Edward V. Ramage, moderator, Synod of the Alabama Presbyterian Church in the United States, and the Reverend Earl Stallings, pastor, First Baptist Church of Birmingham.

The text of the statement follows:

"We, the undersigned clergymen are among those who in January issued 'An Appeal for Law and Order and Common Sense' in dealing with the racial problems in Alabama. We expressed understanding that honest convictions in racial matters could properly be pursued in the courts, but urged that decisions of these courts should in the meantime be peacefully obeyed.

"Since that time there had been some evidence of increased forbearance and a willingness to face facts. Responsible citizens have undertaken to work on various problems which cause racial friction and unrest.

"In Birmingham recent public events have given indication that we all have opportunity for a new constructive and realistic approach to racial problems.

"However, we are now confronted by a series of demonstrations by some of our Negro citizens directed and led in part by outsiders. We recognize the natural impatience of people who feel their hopes are slow in being realized. But we are convinced that these demonstrations are unwise and untimely.

"We agree rather with certain local Negro leadership which has called for honest and open negotiation of racial issues in our area.

"And we believe this kind of facing issues can best be accomplished by citizens of our own metropolitan area, white and Negro, meeting with their knowledge and experience of the local situation. All of us need to face that responsibility and find proper channels for its accomplishment.

5

[1] The article appeared in the *Birmingham News* on Saturday, April 13, 1963, under the headline "White clergymen urge local Negroes to withdraw from demonstrations."

"Just as we formerly pointed out that 'hatred and violence have no sanction in   10
our religious and political traditions,' we also point out that such actions as
incite hatred and violence, however technically peaceful those actions may be,
have not contributed to the resolution of our local problems.

"We do not believe that these days of new hope are days when extreme measures are justified in Birmingham.

"We commend the community as a whole, and the local news media and law
enforcement officials in particular, on the calm manner in which these demonstrations have been handled.

"We urge the public to continue to show restraint should the demonstrations
continue, and the law enforcement officials to remain calm and continue to protect our city from violence.

"We further strongly urge our own Negro community to withdraw support
from these demonstrations, and to unite locally in working peacefully for a better Birmingham.

"When rights are consistently denied, a cause should be pressed in the courts   15
and negotiations among local leaders, and not in the streets.

"We appeal to both our white and Negro citizenry to observe the principles of
law and order and common sense."

Questions for Looking Deeper

1. Do you agree with the Alabama clergymen's view that "honest convictions in
racial matters could properly be pursued in the courts"? Explain.

2. If the courts do not provide a means to redress grievances, what are the
alternatives?

3. What do you suppose were the "racial matters" the clergymen were speaking of?

4. Do you find their views on "outsiders" persuasive? Explain.

5. The clergymen, at one point, say that "extreme measures" are not justified. What
do you suppose they mean by "extreme measures"? Are there any circumstances that
would justify extreme measures? Explain.

The Birmingham Truce Agreement   1963

1. Within 3 days after close of demonstrations, fitting rooms will be
desegregated.

2. Within 30 days after the city government is established by court order, signs
on wash rooms, rest rooms and drinking fountains will be removed.

3. Within 60 days after the city government is established by court order, a program of lunchroom counter desegregation will be commenced.

4. When the city government is established by court order, a program of upgrading Negro employment will be continued and there will be meetings with responsible local leadership to consider further steps.

Within 60 days from the court order determining Birmingham's city govern- 5 ment, the employment program will include at least one sales person or cashier.

Within 15 days from the cessation of demonstrations, a Committee on Racial Problems and Employment composed of members of the Senior Citizens' Committee will be established, with a membership made public and the publicly announced purpose of establishing liaison with members of the Negro community to carry out a program of up-grading and improving employment opportunities with the Negro citizens of the Birmingham community.

Questions for Looking Deeper

1. Do you feel that the Birmingham Truce Agreement represented total victory for the demonstrators? Explain.

2. Research the behavior of the Birmingham city government after May 10, 1963 (the date this agreement was reached). Did the government meet the terms of the truce agreement? Explain.

Randall Robinson   (b. 1941)

Can a Black Family
Be a Legal Nuisance?   1998

I have arrived from segregationist Virginia to attend Harvard Law School. Our first-year class of more than five hundred students is divided into four sections. My section is sitting through a torts lecture given by young professor Charles Fried. Tall and bespectacled, Professor Fried was born in Prague, Czechoslovakia, in 1935, was educated at Princeton and Oxford and Columbia, and will become Solicitor General of the United States under President Ronald Reagan.

With what seems to be affected formality, Professor Fried is holding forth from the well of the Austin lecture hall on the notion of nuisance as an actionable tort. Among the listeners are five black students, including Henry Sanders of Bay Minette, Alabama, who will become an Alabama state senator, and Rudolph Pierce of Boston, who will become a Massachusetts judge. There are one hundred and twenty-one white students in the large hall. Seated halfway up the ascending bowl to Professor Fried's left is William Weld, a future Republican governor of Massachusetts. At eye level with Professor Fried and to his right is Samuel Berger, who like Messrs. Sanders, Pierce, and Weld will find his way into public service, eventually advising President William Jefferson Clinton from the post of Assistant to the President for National Security Affairs. To Mr. Berger's right and two rows behind sits Mark Joseph Green, late of Cornell University and Great Neck, New York. By the mid-1990s Mr. Green will have nailed down a position as New York City's public advocate and a statewide reputation as a liberal Democrat.

Professor Fried is superciliously droning on in a vaguely British accent about how the visitation of annoying or unpleasant conditions upon a neighborhood (grating noise or belching smoke, for example) can constitute a tort or cause of action for a civil lawsuit.

"Can anyone think of an actionable nuisance we haven't touched on today?" asks Professor Fried.

"What about black people moving into a neighborhood?" suggests Mark 5
Joseph Green, liberal Democrat of Cornell University and Great Neck, New York.

A thoughtful discussion ensues. Henry Sanders looks at me. We five blacks in fact all look at each other. Our faces betray little. In any case, the privileged young white scholars are oblivious. There are legal arguments to be mustered, pro and con. The discussion of whether or not the mere presence of blacks constitutes an inherent nuisance swirls around the five blacks. We say nothing. We cannot dignify insult with reasoned rebuttal. The choice is between ventilated rage and silence. We choose silence.

Mr. Green does not prevail and is foreclosed from extending his argument. Encouraged, he might have made Harvard Law School a plaintiff in a theoretical nuisance suit against the twenty-five blacks admitted to its class of 1970.

Doubtless Mr. Green will not remember his attempt to expand the definition of nuisance as a tort. Thirty years later I will not have forgotten.

For Analysis

1. Why does Robinson devote more than half of this very short essay (paras. 1–2) to describing the jobs that his professor and some of his classmates will secure in the future?

2. What is it that "the privileged young white scholars are oblivious" to (para. 6)?

3. Explain the second sentence of paragraph 7: "Encouraged, he might have made Harvard Law School a plaintiff in a theoretical nuisance suit against the twenty-five blacks admitted to its class of 1970." How would you describe its tone?

4. What do you suppose Robinson wants to illustrate by recounting this experience?

5. Is the final paragraph effective? Explain.

On Style

Characterize the **tone** of this essay.

Making Connections

1. Compare and contrast Robinson's reaction to the class discussion with the reaction of the Younger family to the visit of Mr. Lindner in Hansberry's *A Raisin in the Sun* (p. 867, Act II, Scene 3) and the reaction of Marguerite Johnson to the white commencement speaker in Angelou's "Graduation in Stamps" (p. 1000).

2. Compare the varying responses to social injustice of King in "Letter from Birmingham Jail" (p. 634) and Swift in "A Modest Proposal" (p. 615) with Robinson's in this essay.

Writing Topics

1. Describe an experience where you decided not to "dignify insult with reasoned rebuttal" (para. 6).

2. Contrast Robinson's reaction to racism with Audre Lorde's reaction to power in her poem "Power" (p. 1127).

LOOKING BACK:
Further Questions for Thinking and Writing

1. What support do the works in this section offer for Emily Dickinson's assertion that "Much Madness is divinest Sense"? **Writing Topic:** The central characters in Herman Melville's "Bartleby the Scrivener" and Harlan Ellison's " 'Repent, Harlequin!' Said the Ticktockman" are viewed by society as mad. How might it be argued that they exhibit "divinest sense"?

2. In a number of these works, a single individual rebels against society and suffers defeat or death. Are these works therefore pessimistic and despairing? If not, what is the purpose of the rebellions, and why do the authors choose to bring their characters to such ends? **Writing Topic:** Compare two works from this section that offer support for the idea that a single individual can have a decisive effect on society.

3. Examine some of the representatives of established order — the lawyer in "Bartleby the Scrivener," Creon in *Antigonê,* the Ticktockman — and discuss what attitudes they share and how effectively they function as spokespeople for law and order. **Writing Topic:** Compare and evaluate the kinds of order that each represents.

4. William Butler Yeats's "Easter 1916," Lawrence Ferlinghetti's "In Goya's Greatest Scenes" (p. 1399), and Carolyn Forché's "The Colonel" are poems about political struggle against oppressive rulers. In what ways are the poems similar? In what ways are they different? **Writing Topic:** Select the poem that makes the most powerful and effective case on behalf of the oppressed, and write an argument defending your choice.

5. Most of us live out our lives in the ordinary and humdrum world that is rejected in poems such as William Wordsworth's "The World Is Too Much with Us" and W. H. Auden's "The Unknown Citizen." Can these poems be said to be calls to social irresponsibility? **Writing Topic:** Consider whether "we" in Wordsworth's poem and the unknown citizen are simply objects of scorn or whether they deserve sympathy and perhaps even respect.

6. Characters in several of the works in this section — the Harlequin in " 'Repent, Harlequin!' Said the Ticktockman," Bartleby in "Bartleby the Scrivener," Dave in "The Man Who Was Almost a Man," and Antigonê in *Antigonê* — are rebels. What similarities do you find among these rebels? **Writing Topic:** Explain how the attitudes and actions of these characters constitute an attack on the status quo.

7. Many works in this section deal explicitly with the relationship between the individual and the state. What similarities of outlook do you find among them? **Writing Topic:** Compare and contrast the way that relationship is perceived in Harlan Ellison's " 'Repent, Harlequin!' Said the Ticktockman" and Martin Luther King Jr.'s "Letter from Birmingham Jail."

Culture and Identity

At Connie's Inn, 1974, by Romare Bearden.

America is not a melting pot. It is a sizzling cauldron.
— BARBARA ANN MIKULSKI

Without knowing what I am and why I am here, life is impossible.
— LEO TOLSTOY

I speak to the black experience, but I am always talking about the human condition — about what we can endure, dream, fail at, and still survive.
— MAYA ANGELOU

The best is to consider that we have a home somewhere, and only then does one really love the world.
— HUGO OF ST. VICTOR

I keep trying to recapture myself at different periods of my life and it is impossible because even as I write, I change.
— ERICA JONG

And at the moment the overwhelming majority of our people out there feel that people get along better, take more of a common interest in the life of the community, when they share a common background. I want you to believe me when I tell you that race prejudice simply doesn't enter into it.
— LORRAINE HANSBERRY

What do you do when you discover you like parts of the role you're trying to escape?
— MARILYN FRENCH

Historically, a group of people bound together by kinship and geography will form a society that exhibits a *culture* — common language, behavioral rules, traditions, skills, mores, religion, and art that define the civilization of that group. Literary works, including folklore and myth, are inseparable from the particular human society from which they emerge.

Until relatively recently, with the invention of trains, automobiles, and airplanes, travel over long distances was difficult. Instant communication — the telephone, the computer network — is an innovation of our time. Originally, information about other societies could be heard only as far away as a human could shout. Letters helped transmit ideas and cultural values over time and distance, but no more quickly than a horse could gallop or a ship could sail. For thousands of years cultures lived in relative isolation from each other and, hence, tended to develop distinctive traits and values. Within China, for instance, we discover numerous well-defined cultures: the Uighurs of the northwest, the coastal Chinese of Shanghai, the Tibetan mountain people, the Szechwanese of the southwest. They eat different foods, they practice different religions, they speak different dialects.

Though technological advances have made the world seem smaller and, generally, ended the geographical isolation of various cultures, those advances have not diminished the powerful cultural distinctions that mark societies all over the world. In fact, modern communication and transport have sometimes served to bring cultures into conflict. The works in this section, varied as they are, share a preoccupation with the connection between culture and identity. Some of them, such as Louise Erdrich's "The Red Convertible" and George Orwell's "Shooting an Elephant," examine the devastating consequences of cultural imperialism. Others, such as Maya Angelou's "Graduation in Stamps" and Jamaica Kincaid's "Girl," focus on the way dominant cultural stereotypes distort and undermine the sense of self of those who are different. Chinua Achebe's "Marriage Is a Private Affair" examines the assault of cultural assimilation on tradition.

The works in this section demonstrate how powerfully culture shapes identity. They reveal the tension generated by interacting cultures, and offer insight into the conflicts that usually emerge. But these works also provide an opportunity for us to step outside the bounds and bonds of our own culture and to experience just how complex, diverse, and interesting the human condition can be.

LOOKING AHEAD:
Questions for Thinking and Writing

As you read the selections in this section, consider the questions that follow. You may want to write out your thoughts informally — in a journal if you are keeping one — as a way of preparing to respond to the selections. Or you may wish to make one of these questions the basis for a formal essay.

1. What cultural tradition(s) do you come from? Describe that tradition as fully as you can. Do you feel that you live in or out of the cultural mainstream? Explain.

2. Except for Native Americans, the people of the United States descended from or arrived as citizens of foreign cultures. Is there, nonetheless, an American culture? Explain. America was once called a cultural "melting pot." Now it is sometimes called a cultural "salad." Which metaphor strikes you as more apt? Explain.

3. Do economic considerations affect culture? Are the rich (aside from their wealth) different from the poor? Explain. Does education strengthen or weaken traditional culture? Explain.

4. What are some of the positive and negative associations you have with the values in the cultural traditions you come from? Is the preservation of these traditional cultural values a good thing or a bad thing? Explain.

Fiction

William Faulkner   (1897–1962)

A Rose for Emily   1931

I

When Miss Emily Grierson died, our whole town went to her funeral: the men through a sort of respectful affection for a fallen monument, the women mostly out of curiosity to see the inside of her house, which no one save an old manservant — a combined gardener and cook — had seen in at least ten years.

It was a big, squarish frame house that had once been white, decorated with cupolas and spires and scrolled balconies in the heavily lightsome style of the seventies, set on what had once been our most select street. But garages and cotton gins had encroached and obliterated even the august names of that neighborhood; only Miss Emily's house was left, lifting its stubborn and coquettish decay above the cotton wagons and the gasoline pumps — an eyesore among eyesores. And now Miss Emily had gone to join the representatives of those august names where they lay in the cedar-bemused cemetery among the ranked and anonymous graves of Union and Confederate soldiers who fell at the battle of Jefferson.

Alive, Miss Emily had been a tradition, a duty, and a care; a sort of hereditary obligation upon the town, dating from that day in 1894 when Colonel Sartoris, the mayor — he who fathered the edict that no Negro woman should appear on the streets without an apron — remitted her taxes, the dispensation dating from the death of her father on into perpetuity. Not that Miss Emily would have accepted charity. Colonel Sartoris invented an involved tale to the effect that Miss Emily's father had loaned money to the town, which the town, as a matter of business, preferred this way of repaying. Only a man of Colonel Sartoris' generation and thought could have invented it, and only a woman could have believed it.

When the next generation, with its more modern ideas, became mayors and aldermen, this arrangement created some little dissatisfaction. On the first of the year they mailed her a tax notice. February came, and there was no reply. They wrote her a formal letter, asking her to call at the sheriff's office at her convenience. A week later the mayor wrote her himself, offering to call or to send his car for her, and received in reply a note on paper of an archaic shape, in a thin, flowing calligraphy in faded ink, to the effect that she no longer went out at all. The tax notice was also enclosed, without comment.

They called a special meeting of the Board of Aldermen. A deputation waited 5 upon her, knocked at the door through which no visitor had passed since she ceased giving china-painting lessons eight or ten years earlier. They were admitted by the old Negro into a dim hall from which a stairway mounted into still more shadow. It smelled of dust and disuse — a close, dank smell. The Negro led them into the parlor. It was furnished in heavy, leather-covered furniture. When the Negro opened the blinds of one window, they could see that the leather was cracked; and when they sat down, a faint dust rose sluggishly about their thighs, spinning with slow motions in the single sun-ray. On a tarnished gilt easel before the fireplace stood a crayon portrait of Miss Emily's father.

They rose when she entered — a small, fat woman in black, with a thin gold chain descending to her waist and vanishing into her belt, leaning on an ebony cane with a tarnished gold head. Her skeleton was small and spare; perhaps that was why what would have been merely plumpness in another was obesity in her. She looked bloated, like a body long submerged in motionless water, and of that pallid hue. Her eyes, lost in the fatty ridges of her face, looked like two small pieces of coal pressed into a lump of dough as they moved from one face to another while the visitors stated their errand.

She did not ask them to sit. She just stood in the door and listened quietly until the spokesman came to a stumbling halt. Then they could hear the invisible watch ticking at the end of the gold chain.

Her voice was dry and cold. "I have no taxes in Jefferson. Colonel Sartoris explained it to me. Perhaps one of you can gain access to the city records and satisfy yourselves."

"But we have. We are the city authorities, Miss Emily. Didn't you get a notice from the sheriff, signed by him?"

"I received a paper, yes," Miss Emily said. "Perhaps he considers himself the 10 sheriff . . . I have no taxes in Jefferson."

"But there is nothing on the books to show that, you see. We must go by the — "

"See Colonel Sartoris." (Colonel Sartoris had been dead almost ten years.) "I have no taxes in Jefferson. Tobe!" The Negro appeared. "Show these gentlemen out."

II

So she vanquished them, horse and foot, just as she had vanquished their fathers thirty years before about the smell. That was two years after her father's death and a short time after her sweetheart — the one we believed would marry her — had deserted her. After her father's death she went out very little; after her sweetheart went away, people hardly saw her at all. A few of the ladies had the temerity to call, but were not received, and the only sign of life about the place was the Negro man — a young man then — going in and out with a market basket.

"Just as if a man — any man — could keep a kitchen properly," the ladies said; so they were not surprised when the smell developed. It was another link between the gross, teeming world and the high and mighty Griersons.

A neighbor, a woman, complained to the mayor, Judge Stevens, eighty years 15 old.

"But what will you have me do about it, madam?" he said.

"Why, send her word to stop it," the woman said. "Isn't there a law?"

"I'm sure that won't be necessary," Judge Stevens said. "It's probably just a snake or a rat that nigger of hers killed in the yard. I'll speak to him about it."

The next day he received two more complaints, one from a man who came in diffident deprecation. "We really must do something about it, Judge. I'd be the last one in the world to bother Miss Emily, but we've got to do something." That night the Board of Aldermen met — three graybeards and one younger man, a member of the rising generation.

"It's simple enough," he said. "Send her word to have her place cleaned up. 20 Give her a certain time to do it in, and if she don't . . ."

"Dammit, sir," Judge Stevens said, "will you accuse a lady to her face of smelling bad?"

So the next night, after midnight, four men crossed Miss Emily's lawn and slunk about the house like burglars, sniffing along the base of the brickwork and at the cellar openings while one of them performed a regular sowing motion with his hand out of a sack slung from his shoulder. They broke open the cellar door and sprinkled lime there, and in all the outbuildings. As they recrossed the lawn, a window that had been dark was lighted and Miss Emily sat in it, the light behind her, and her upright torso motionless as that of an idol. They crept quietly across the lawn and into the shadow of the locusts that lined the street. After a week or two the smell went away.

That was when people had begun to feel really sorry for her. People in our town, remembering how old lady Wyatt, her great-aunt, had gone completely crazy at last, believed that the Griersons held themselves a little too high for what they really were. None of the young men were quite good enough for Miss Emily and such. We had long thought of them as a tableau, Miss Emily a slender figure in white in the background, her father a spraddled silhouette in the foreground, his back to her and clutching a horsewhip, the two of them framed by the back-flung front door. So when she got to be thirty and was still single, we were not pleased exactly, but vindicated; even with insanity in the family she wouldn't have turned down all of her chances if they had really materialized.

When her father died, it got about that the house was all that was left to her; and in a way, people were glad. At last they could pity Miss Emily. Being left alone, and a pauper, she had become humanized. Now she too would know the old thrill and the old despair of a penny more or less.

The day after his death all the ladies prepared to call at the house and offer 25 condolence and aid, as is our custom. Miss Emily met them at the door, dressed as usual and with no trace of grief on her face. She told them that her father was not dead. She did that for three days, with the ministers calling on her, and the doctors, trying to persuade her to let them dispose of the body. Just as they were about to resort to law and force, she broke down, and they buried her father quickly.

We did not say she was crazy then. We believed she had to do that. We remembered all the young men her father had driven away, and we knew that with nothing left, she would have to cling to that which had robbed her, as people will.

III

She was sick for a long time. When we saw her again, her hair was cut short, making her look like a girl, with a vague resemblance to those angels in colored church windows — sort of tragic and serene.

The town had just let the contracts for paving the sidewalks, and in the summer after her father's death they began the work. The construction company came with niggers and mules and machinery, and a foreman named Homer Barron, a Yankee — a big, dark, ready man, with a big voice and eyes lighter than his face. The little boys would follow in groups to hear him cuss the niggers, and the niggers singing in time to the rise and fall of picks. Pretty soon he knew everybody in town. Whenever you heard a lot of laughing anywhere about the square, Homer Barron would be in the center of the group. Presently we began to see him and Miss Emily on Sunday afternoons driving in the yellow-wheeled buggy and the matched team of bays from the livery stable.

At first we were glad that Miss Emily would have an interest, because the ladies all said, "Of course a Grierson would not think seriously of a Northerner, a day laborer." But there were still others, older people, who said that even grief could not cause a real lady to forget *noblesse oblige* — without calling it *noblesse oblige*. They just said, "Poor Emily. Her kinsfolk should come to her." She had some kin in Alabama; but years ago her father had fallen out with them over the estate of old lady Wyatt, the crazy woman, and there was no communication between the two families. They had not even been represented at the funeral.

And as soon as the old people said, "Poor Emily," the whispering began. "Do you suppose it's really so?" they said to one another. "Of course it is. What else could . . ." This behind their hands; rustling of craned silk and satin behind jalousies closed upon the sun of Sunday afternoon as the thin, swift clop-clop-clop of the matched team passed: "Poor Emily."

She carried her head high enough — even when we believed that she was fallen. It was as if she demanded more than ever the recognition of her dignity as the last Grierson; as if it had wanted that touch of earthiness to reaffirm her imperviousness. Like when she bought the rat poison, the arsenic. That was over a year after they had begun to say "Poor Emily," and while the two female cousins were visiting her.

"I want some poison," she said to the druggist. She was over thirty then, still a slight woman, though thinner than usual, with cold, haughty black eyes in a face the flesh of which was strained across the temples and about the eye-sockets as you imagine a lighthouse-keeper's face ought to look. "I want some poison," she said.

"Yes, Miss Emily. What kind? For rats and such? I'd recom — "

"I want the best you have. I don't care what kind."

The druggist named several. "They'll kill anything up to an elephant. But 35 what you want is — "

"Arsenic," Miss Emily said. "Is that a good one?"

"Is . . . arsenic? Yes, ma'am. But what you want — "

"I want arsenic."

The druggist looked down at her. She looked back at him, erect, her face like a strained flag. "Why, of course," the druggist said. "If that's what you want. But the law requires you to tell what you are going to use it for."

Miss Emily just stared at him, her head tilted back in order to look him eye 40 for eye, until he looked away and went and got the arsenic and wrapped it up. The Negro delivery boy brought her package; the druggist didn't come back. When she opened the package at home there was written on the box, under the skull and bones: "For rats."

IV

So the next day we all said, "She will kill herself"; and we said it would be the best thing. When she had first begun to be seen with Homer Barron, we had said, "She will marry him." Then we said, "She will persuade him yet," because Homer himself had remarked — he liked men, and it was known that he drank with the younger men in the Elks' Club — that he was not a marrying man. Later we said, "Poor Emily" behind the jalousies as they passed on Sunday afternoon in the glittering buggy, Miss Emily with her head high and Homer Barron with his hat cocked and a cigar in his teeth, reins and whip in a yellow glove.

Then some of the ladies began to say that it was a disgrace to the town and a bad example to the young people. The men did not want to interfere, but at last the ladies forced the Baptist minister — Miss Emily's people were Episcopal — to call upon her. He would never divulge what happened during that interview, but he refused to go back again. The next Sunday they again drove about the streets, and the following day the minister's wife wrote to Miss Emily's relations in Alabama.

So she had blood-kin under her roof again and we sat back to watch developments. At first nothing happened. Then we were sure that they were to be married. We learned that Miss Emily had been to the jeweler's and ordered a man's toilet set in silver, with the letters H.B. on each piece. Two days later we learned that she had bought a complete outfit of men's clothing, including a nightshirt, and we said, "They are married." We were really glad. We were glad because the two female cousins were even more Grierson than Miss Emily had ever been.

So we were not surprised when Homer Barron — the streets had been finished some time since — was gone. We were a little disappointed that there was not a public blowing-off, but we believed that he had gone on to prepare for Miss Emily's coming, or to give her a chance to get rid of the cousins. (By that time it was a cabal, and we were all Miss Emily's allies to help circumvent the cousins.) Sure enough, after another week they departed. And, as we had expected all along, within three days Homer Barron was back in town. A neighbor saw the Negro man admit him at the kitchen door at dusk one evening.

And that was the last we saw of Homer Barron. And of Miss Emily for some 45 time. The Negro man went in and out with the market basket, but the front door remained closed. Now and then we would see her at the window for a moment, as the men did that night when they sprinkled the lime, but for almost six months she did not appear on the streets. Then we knew that this was to be expected too; as if that quality of her father which had thwarted her woman's life so many times had been too virulent and too furious to die.

When we next saw Miss Emily, she had grown fat and her hair was turning gray. During the next few years it grew grayer and grayer until it attained an even pepper-and-salt iron-gray, when it ceased turning. Up to the day of her death at seventy-four it was still that vigorous iron-gray, like the hair of an active man.

From that time on her front door remained closed, save during a period of six or seven years, when she was about forty, during which she gave lessons in china-painting. She fitted up a studio in one of the downstairs rooms, where the daughters and granddaughters of Colonel Sartoris' contemporaries were sent to her with the same regularity and in the same spirit that they were sent to church on Sundays with a twenty-five-cent piece for the collection plate. Meanwhile her taxes had been remitted.

Then the newer generation became the backbone and the spirit of the town, and the painting pupils grew up and fell away and did not send their children to her with boxes of color and tedious brushes and pictures cut from the ladies' magazines. The front door closed upon the last one and remained closed for good. When the town got free postal delivery, Miss Emily alone refused to let them fasten the metal numbers above her door and attach a mailbox to it. She would not listen to them.

Daily, monthly, yearly we watched the Negro grow grayer and more stooped, going in and out with the market basket. Each December we sent her a tax notice, which would be returned by the post office a week later, unclaimed. Now and then we would see her in one of the downstairs windows — she had evidently shut up the top floor of the house — like the carven torso of an idol in a niche, looking or not looking at us, we could never tell which. Thus she passed from generation to generation — dear, inescapable, impervious, tranquil, and perverse.

And so she died. Fell ill in the house filled with dust and shadows, with only a 50 doddering Negro man to wait on her. We did not even know she was sick; we had long since given up trying to get any information from the Negro. He talked to no one, probably not even to her, for his voice had grown harsh and rusty, as if from disuse.

She died in one of the downstairs rooms, in a heavy walnut bed with a curtain, her gray head propped on a pillow yellow and moldy with age and lack of sunlight.

V

The Negro met the first of the ladies at the front door and let them in, with their hushed, sibilant voices and their quick, curious glances, and then he disappeared. He walked right through the house and out the back and was not seen again.

The two female cousins came at once. They held the funeral on the second day, with the town coming to look at Miss Emily beneath a mass of bought flowers, with the crayon face of her father musing profoundly above the bier and the ladies sibilant and macabre; and the very old men — some in their brushed Confederate uniforms — on the porch and the lawn, talking of Miss Emily as if she had been a contemporary of theirs, believing they had danced with her and courted her perhaps, confusing time with its mathematical progression, as the old do, to whom all the past is not a diminishing road but, instead, a huge meadow which no winter ever quite touches, divided from them now by the narrow bottle-neck of the most recent decade of years.

Already we knew that there was one room in that region above stairs which no one had seen in forty years, and which would have to be forced. They waited until Miss Emily was decently in the ground before they opened it.

The violence of breaking down the door seemed to fill this room with pervading dust. A thin, acrid pall as of the tomb seemed to lie everywhere upon this room decked and furnished as for a bridal: upon the valance curtains of faded rose color, upon the rose-shaded lights, upon the dressing table, upon the delicate array of crystal and the man's toilet things backed with tarnished silver, silver so tarnished that the monogram was obscured. Among them lay a collar and tie, as if they had just been removed, which, lifted, left upon the surface a pale crescent in the dust. Upon a chair hung the suit, carefully folded; beneath it the two mute shoes and the discarded socks. 55

The man himself lay in the bed.

For a long while we just stood there, looking down at the profound and fleshless grin. The body had apparently once lain in the attitude of an embrace, but now the long sleep that outlasts love, that conquers even the grimace of love, had cuckolded him. What was left of him, rotted beneath what was left of the nightshirt, had become inextricable from the bed in which he lay; and upon him and upon the pillow beside him lay that even coating of the patient and biding dust.

Then we noticed that in the second pillow was the indentation of a head. One of us lifted something from it, and leaning forward, that faint and invisible dust dry and acrid in the nostrils, we saw a long strand of iron-gray hair.

For Analysis

1. Why does Faulkner title the narrative "A Rose for Emily"?

2. At the end of section two, the narrator says, "We remembered all the young men her father had driven away." What is the significance of this statement? How would you characterize Emily's relationship with her father? Her father's relationship with the town?

3. In section three, we learn that "the ladies all said, 'Of course a Grierson would not think seriously of a Northerner, a day laborer.' " Why not? What are Emily's alternatives?

4. What is the effect of the final paragraph?

On Style

1. Why do you suppose the narrator uses the pronoun "we"? The narrator often speaks of "the town." What does "the town" signify?

2. Reread the description of Emily's house in the second paragraph. What does that description suggest to you?

3. What does the author accomplish by not presenting the story in chronological order?

Making Connections

1. Consider your own relationship with your parents. Does it parallel or differ from Emily's relationship with her father? Explain.

2. In this story the town is sometimes treated like one of the **protagonists**: the narrator refers to himself as "we," and "the town" has significant opinions and reactions. Have you ever lived in a social setting that dictated your behavior? Explain.

Writing Topics

1. Write a brief essay discussing the role of time in this story. How does the town's response to the Griersons in general, and Emily in particular, change as time passes?

2. Write an essay arguing for or against the assertion that Emily's father determined the course of her life.

James Baldwin   (1924–1987)

Sonny's Blues   1957

I read about it in the paper, in the subway, on my way to work. I read it, and I couldn't believe it, and I read it again. Then perhaps I just stared at it, at the newsprint spelling out his name, spelling out the story. I stared at it in the swinging lights of the subway car, and in the faces and bodies of the people, and in my own face, trapped in the darkness which roared outside.

It was not to be believed and I kept telling myself that, as I walked from the subway station to the high school. And at the same time I couldn't doubt it. I was scared, scared for Sonny. He became real to me again. A great block of ice got settled in my belly and kept melting there slowly all day long, while I taught my classes algebra. It was a special kind of ice. It kept melting, sending trickles of ice water all up and down my veins, but it never got less. Sometimes it hardened and seemed to expand until I felt my guts were going to come spilling out or that I was going to choke or scream. This would always be at a moment when I was remembering some specific thing Sonny had once said or done.

When he was about as old as the boys in my classes his face had been bright and open, there was a lot of copper in it; and he'd had wonderfully direct brown eyes, and great gentleness and privacy. I wondered what he looked like now. He had been picked up, the evening before, in a raid on an apartment downtown, for peddling and using heroin.

I couldn't believe it: but what I mean by that is that I couldn't find any room for it anywhere inside me. I had kept it outside me for a long time. I hadn't wanted to know. I had had suspicions, but I didn't name them, I kept putting them away. I told myself that Sonny was wild, but he wasn't crazy. And he'd always been a good boy, he hadn't ever turned hard or evil or disrespectful, the way kids can, so quick, so quick, especially in Harlem. I didn't want to believe that I'd ever see my brother going down, coming to nothing, all that light in his face gone out, in the condition I'd already seen so many others. Yet it had happened and here I was, talking about algebra to a lot of boys who might, every one of them for all I knew, be popping off needles every time they went to the head. Maybe it did more for them than algebra could.

I was sure that the first time Sonny had ever had horse,[1] he couldn't have 5 been much older than these boys were now. These boys, now, were living as we'd been living then, they were growing up with a rush and their heads bumped abruptly against the low ceiling of their actual possibilities. They were

[1] Heroin.

674

filled with rage. All they really knew were two darknesses, the darkness of their lives, which was now closing in on them, and the darkness of the movies, which had blinded them to that other darkness, and in which they now, vindictively, dreamed, at once more together than they were at any other time, and more alone.

When the last bell rang, the last class ended, I let out my breath. It seemed I'd been holding it for all that time. My clothes were wet — I may have looked as though I'd been sitting in a steam bath, all dressed up, all afternoon. I sat alone in the classroom a long time. I listened to the boys outside, downstairs, shouting and cursing and laughing. Their laughter struck me for perhaps the first time. It was not the joyous laughter which — God knows why — one associates with children. It was mocking and insular, its intent to denigrate. It was disenchanted, and in this, also, lay the authority of their curses. Perhaps I was listening to them because I was thinking about my brother and in them I heard my brother. And myself.

One boy was whistling a tune, at once very complicated and very simple, it seemed to be pouring out of him as though he were a bird, and it sounded very cool and moving through all that harsh, bright air, only just holding its own through all those other sounds.

I stood up and walked over to the window and looked down into the courtyard. It was the beginning of the spring and the sap was rising in the boys. A teacher passed through them every now and again, quickly, as though he or she couldn't wait to get out of that courtyard, to get those boys out of their sight and off their minds. I started collecting my stuff. I thought I'd better get home and talk to Isabel.

The courtyard was almost deserted by the time I got downstairs. I saw this boy standing in the shadow of a doorway, looking just like Sonny. I almost called his name. Then I saw that it wasn't Sonny, but somebody we used to know, a boy from around our block. He'd been Sonny's friend. He'd never been mine, having been too young for me, and, anyway, I'd never liked him. And now, even though he was a grown-up man, he still hung around that block, still spent hours on the street corners, was always high and raggy. I used to run into him from time to time and he'd often work around to asking me for a quarter or fifty cents. He always had some real good excuse, too, and I always gave it to him. I don't know why.

But now, abruptly, I hated him. I couldn't stand the way he looked at me, partly like a dog, partly like a cunning child. I wanted to ask him what the hell he was doing in the school courtyard.

He sort of shuffled over to me, and he said, "I see you got the papers. So you already know about it."

"You mean about Sonny? Yes, I already know about it. How come they didn't get you?"

He grinned. It made him repulsive and it also brought to mind what he'd looked like as a kid. "I wasn't there. I stay away from them people."

"Good for you." I offered him a cigarette and I watched him through the smoke. "You come all the way down here just to tell me about Sonny?"

"That's right." He was sort of shaking his head and his eyes looked strange, as though they were about to cross. The bright sun deadened his damp dark brown skin and it made his eyes look yellow and showed up the dirt in his kinked hair. He smelled funky. I moved a little away from him and I said, "Well, thanks. But I already know about it and I got to get home." 15

"I'll walk you a little ways," he said. We started walking. There were a couple of kids still loitering in the courtyard and one of them said goodnight to me and looked strangely at the boy beside me.

"What're you going to do?" he asked me. "I mean, about Sonny?"

"Look. I haven't seen Sonny for over a year, I'm not sure I'm going to do anything. Anyway, what the hell *can* I do?"

"That's right," he said quickly, "ain't nothing you can do. Can't much help old Sonny no more, I guess."

It was what I was thinking and so it seemed to me he had no right to say it. 20

"I'm surprised at Sonny, though," he went on — he had a funny way of talking, he looked straight ahead as though he were talking to himself — "I thought Sonny was a smart boy, I thought he was too smart to get hung."

"I guess he thought so too," I said sharply, "and that's how he got hung. And how about you? You're pretty goddamn smart, I bet."

Then he looked directly at me, just for a minute. "I ain't smart," he said. "If I was smart, I'd have reached for a pistol a long time ago."

"Look. Don't tell *me* your sad story, if it was up to me, I'd give you one." Then I felt guilty — guilty, probably, for never having supposed that the poor bastard *had* a story of his own, much less a sad one, and I asked, quickly, "What's going to happen to him now?"

He didn't answer this. He was off by himself some place. 25

"Funny thing," he said, and from his tone we might have been discussing the quickest way to get to Brooklyn, "when I saw the papers this morning, the first thing I asked myself was if I had anything to do with it. I felt sort of responsible."

I began to listen more carefully. The subway station was on the corner, just before us, and I stopped. He stopped, too. We were in front of a bar and he ducked slightly, peering in, but whoever he was looking for didn't seem to be there. The juke box was blasting away with something black and bouncy and I half watched the barmaid as she danced her way from the juke box to her place behind the bar. And I watched her face as she laughingly responded to something someone said to her, still keeping time to the music. When she smiled one saw the little girl, one sensed the doomed, still-struggling woman beneath the battered face of the semi-whore.

"I never *give* Sonny nothing," the boy said finally, "but a long time ago I come to school high and Sonny asked me how it felt." He paused, I couldn't bear to watch him, I watched the barmaid, and I listened to the music which seemed to be causing the pavement to shake. "I told him it felt great." The music stopped, the barmaid paused and watched the juke box until the music began again. "It did."

All this was carrying me some place I didn't want to go. I certainly didn't want to know how it felt. It filled everything, the people, the houses, the music, the dark, quicksilver barmaid, with menace; and this menace was their reality.

"What's going to happen to him now?" I asked again. 30

"They'll send him away some place and they'll try to cure him." He shook his head. "Maybe he'll even think he's kicked the habit. Then they'll let him loose" — he gestured, throwing his cigarette into the gutter. "That's all."

"What do you mean, that's *all*?"

But I knew what he meant.

"I *mean*, that's *all*." He turned his head and looked at me, pulling down the corners of his mouth. "Don't you know what I mean?" he asked, softly.

"How the hell *would* I know what you mean?" I almost whispered it, I don't 35 know why.

"That's right," he said to the air, "how would *he* know what I mean?" He turned toward me again, patient and calm, and yet I somehow felt him shaking, shaking as though he were going to fall apart. I felt that ice in my guts again, the dread I'd felt all afternoon; and again I watched the barmaid, moving about the bar, washing glasses, and singing. "Listen. They'll let him out and then it'll just start all over again. That's what I mean."

"You mean — they'll let him out. And then he'll just start working his way back in again. You mean he'll never kick the habit. Is that what you mean?"

"That's right," he said, cheerfully. "*You* see what I mean."

"Tell me," I said at last, "why does he want to die? He must want to die, he's killing himself, why does he want to die?"

He looked at me in surprise. He licked his lips. "He don't want to die. He 40 wants to live. Don't nobody want to die, ever."

Then I wanted to ask him — too many things. He could not have answered, or if he had, I could not have borne the answers. I started walking. "Well, I guess it's none of my business."

"It's going to be rough on old Sonny," he said. We reached the subway station. "This is your station?" he asked. I nodded. I took one step down. "Damn!" he said, suddenly. I looked up at him. He grinned again. "Damn it if I didn't leave all my money home. You ain't got a dollar on you, have you? Just for a couple of days, is all."

All at once something inside gave and threatened to come pouring out of me. I didn't hate him any more. I felt that in another moment I'd start crying like a child.

"Sure," I said. "Don't sweat." I looked in my wallet and didn't have a dollar, I only had a five. "Here," I said. "That hold you?"

He didn't look at it — he didn't want to look at it. A terrible, closed look came 45 over his face, as though he were keeping the number on the bill a secret from him and me. "Thanks," he said, and now he was dying to see me go. "Don't worry about Sonny. Maybe I'll write him or something."

"Sure," I said. "You do that. So long."

"Be seeing you," he said. I went on down the steps.

. . .

And I didn't write Sonny or send him anything for a long time. When I finally did, it was just after my little girl died, and he wrote me back a letter which made me feel like a bastard.

Here's what he said:

> Dear brother,
>
> You don't know how much I needed to hear from you. I wanted to write you many a time but I dug how much I must have hurt you and so I didn't write. But now I feel like a man who's been trying to climb up out of some deep, real deep and funky hole and just saw the sun up there, outside. I got to get outside.
>
> I can't tell you much about how I got here. I mean I don't know how to tell you. I guess I was afraid of something or I was trying to escape from something and you know I have never been very strong in the head (smile). I'm glad Mama and Daddy are dead and can't see what's happened to their son and I swear if I'd known what I was doing I would never have hurt you so, you and a lot of other fine people who were nice to me and who believed in me.
>
> I don't want you to think it had anything to do with me being a musician. It's more than that. Or maybe less than that. I can't get anything straight in my head down here and I try not to think about what's going to happen to me when I get outside again. Sometime I think I'm going to flip and *never* get outside and sometime I think I'll come straight back. I tell you one thing, though, I'd rather blow my brains out than go through this again. But that's what they all say, so they tell me. If I tell you when I'm coming to New York and if you could meet me, I sure would appreciate it. Give my love to Isabel and the kids and I was sure sorry to hear about little Gracie. I wish I could be like Mama and say the Lord's will be done, but I don't know it seems to me that trouble is the one thing that never does get stopped and I don't know what good it does to blame it on the Lord. But maybe it does some good if you believe it.
>
> Your brother,
> Sonny

Then I kept in constant touch with him and I sent him whatever I could and I   50
went to meet him when he came back to New York. When I saw him many things I thought I had forgotten came flooding back to me. This was because I had begun, finally, to wonder about Sonny, about the life that Sonny lived inside. This life, whatever it was, had made him older and thinner and it had deepened the distant stillness in which he had always moved. He looked very unlike my baby brother. Yet, when he smiled, when we shook hands, the baby brother I'd never known looked out from the depths of his private life, like an animal waiting to be coaxed into the light.

"How you been keeping?" he asked me.

"All right. And you?"

"Just fine." He was smiling all over his face. "It's good to see you again."

"It's good to see you."

The seven years' difference in our ages lay between us like a chasm: I won-   55
dered if these years would ever operate between us as a bridge. I was remembering, and it made it hard to catch my breath, that I had been there when he

was born; and I had heard the first words he had ever spoken. When he started to walk, he walked from our mother straight to me. I caught him just before he fell when he took the first steps he ever took in this world.

"How's Isabel?"

"Just fine. She's dying to see you."

"And the boys?"

"They're fine, too. They're anxious to see their uncle."

"Oh, come on. You know they don't remember me."   60

"Are you kidding? Of course they remember you."

He grinned again. We got into a taxi. We had a lot to say to each other, far too much to know how to begin.

As the taxi began to move, I asked, "You still want to go to India?"

He laughed. "You still remember that. Hell, no. This place is Indian enough for me."

"It used to belong to them," I said.   65

And he laughed again. "They damn sure knew what they were doing when they got rid of it."

Years ago, when he was around fourteen, he'd been all hipped on the idea of going to India. He read books about people sitting on rocks, naked, in all kinds of weather, but mostly bad, naturally, and walking barefoot through hot coals and arriving at wisdom. I used to say that it sounded to me as though they were getting away from wisdom as fast as they could. I think he sort of looked down on me for that.

"Do you mind," he asked, "if we have the driver drive alongside the park? On the west side — I haven't seen the city in so long."

"Of course not," I said. I was afraid that I might sound as though I were humoring him, but I hoped he wouldn't take it that way.

So we drove along, between the green of the park and the stony, lifeless ele- 70
gance of hotels and apartment buildings, toward the vivid, killing streets of our childhood. These streets hadn't changed, though housing projects jutted up out of them now like rocks in the middle of a boiling sea. Most of the houses in which we had grown up had vanished, as had the stores from which we had stolen, the basements in which we had first tried sex, the rooftops from which we had hurled tin cans and bricks. But houses exactly like the houses of our past yet dominated the landscape, boys exactly like the boys we once had been found themselves smothering in these houses, came down into the streets for light and air and found themselves encircled by disaster. Some escaped the trap, most didn't. Those who got out always left something of themselves behind, as some animals amputate a leg and leave it in the trap. It might be said, perhaps, that I had escaped, after all, I was a school teacher; or that Sonny had, he hadn't lived in Harlem for years. Yet, as the cab moved uptown through streets which seemed, with a rush, to darken with dark people, and as I covertly studied Sonny's face, it came to me that what we both were seeking through our separate cab windows was that part of ourselves which had been left behind. It's always at the hour of trouble and confrontation that the missing member aches.

We hit 110th Street and started rolling up Lenox Avenue. And I'd known this avenue all my life, but it seemed to me again, as it had seemed on the day I'd first heard about Sonny's trouble, filled with a hidden menace which was its very breath of life.

"We almost there," said Sonny.

"Almost." We were both too nervous to say anything more.

We live in a housing project. It hasn't been up long. A few days after it was up it seemed uninhabitably new, now, of course, it's already rundown. It looks like a parody of the good, clean, faceless life — God knows the people who live in it do their best to make it a parody. The beat-looking grass lying around isn't enough to make their lives green, the hedges will never hold out the streets, and they know it. The big windows fool no one, they aren't big enough to make space out of no space. They don't bother with the windows, they watch the TV screen instead. The playground is most popular with the children who don't play at jacks, or skip rope, or roller skate, or swing, and they can be found in it after dark. We moved in partly because it's not too far from where I teach, and partly for the kids; but it's really just like the houses in which Sonny and I grew up. The same things happen, they'll have the same things to remember. The moment Sonny and I started into the house I had the feeling that I was simply bringing him back into the danger he had almost died trying to escape.

Sonny has never been talkative. So I don't know why I was sure he'd be dying 75 to talk to me when supper was over the first night. Everything went fine, the oldest boy remembered him, and the youngest boy liked him, and Sonny had remembered to bring something for each of them; and Isabel, who is really much nicer than I am, more open and giving, had gone to a lot of trouble about dinner and was genuinely glad to see him. And she's always been able to tease Sonny in a way that I haven't. It was nice to see her face so vivid again and to hear her laugh and watch her make Sonny laugh. She wasn't, or, anyway, she didn't seem to be, at all uneasy or embarrassed. She chatted as though there were no subject which had to be avoided and she got Sonny past his first, faint stiffness. And thank God she was there, for I was filled with that icy dread again. Everything I did seemed awkward to me, and everything I said sounded freighted with hidden meaning. I was trying to remember everything I'd heard about dope addiction and I couldn't help watching Sonny for signs. I wasn't doing it out of malice. I was trying to find out something about my brother. I was dying to hear him tell me he was safe.

"Safe!" my father grunted, whenever Mama suggested trying to move to a neighborhood which might be safer for children. "Safe, hell! Ain't no place safe for kids, nor nobody."

He always went on like this, but he wasn't, ever, really as bad as he sounded, not even on weekends, when he got drunk. As a matter of fact, he was always on the lookout for "something a little better," but he died before he found it. He died suddenly, during a drunken weekend in the middle of the war, when Sonny was fifteen. He and Sonny hadn't ever got on too well. And this was partly because Sonny was the apple of his father's eye. It was because he loved Sonny so much and was frightened for him, that he was always fighting with him. It doesn't do any good to fight with Sonny. Sonny just moves back, inside himself, where he can't be reached. But the principal reason that they never hit it off is that they were so much alike. Daddy was big and rough and loud-talking, just the opposite of Sonny, but they both had — that same privacy.

Mama tried to tell me something about this, just after Daddy died. I was home on leave from the army.

This was the last time I ever saw my mother alive. Just the same, this picture gets all mixed up in my mind with pictures I had of her when she was younger. The way I always see her is the way she used to be on a Sunday afternoon, say, when the old folks were talking after the big Sunday dinner. I always see her wearing pale blue. She'd be sitting on the sofa. And my father would be sitting in the easy chair, not far from her. And the living room would be full of church folks and relatives. There they sit, in chairs all around the living room, and the night is creeping up outside, but nobody knows it yet. You can see the darkness growing against the windowpanes and you hear the street noises every now and again, or maybe the jangling beat of a tambourine from one of the churches close by, but it's real quiet in the room. For a moment nobody's talking, but every face looks darkening, like the sky outside. And my mother rocks a little from the waist, and my father's eyes are closed. Everyone is looking at something a child can't see. For a minute they've forgotten the children. Maybe a kid is lying on the rug, half asleep. Maybe somebody's got a kid in his lap and is absent-mindedly stroking the kid's head. Maybe there's a kid, quiet and big-eyed, curled up in a big chair in the corner. The silence, the darkness coming, and the darkness in the faces frighten the child obscurely. He hopes that the hand which strokes his forehead will never stop — will never die. He hopes that there will never come a time when the old folks won't be sitting around the living room, talking about where they've come from, and what they've seen, and what's happened to them and their kinfolk.

But something deep and watchful in the child knows that this is bound to 80 end, is already ending. In a moment someone will get up and turn on the light. Then the old folks will remember the children and they won't talk any more that day. And when light fills the room, the child is filled with darkness. He knows that every time this happens he's moved just a little closer to that darkness outside. The darkness outside is what the old folks have been talking about. It's what they've come from. It's what they endure. The child knows that they won't talk any more because if he knows too much about what's happened to *them,* he'll know too much too soon, about what's going to happen to *him.*

The last time I talked to my mother, I remember I was restless. I wanted to get out and see Isabel. We weren't married then and we had a lot to straighten out between us.

There Mama sat, in black, by the window. She was humming an old church song, *Lord, you brought me from a long ways off.* Sonny was out somewhere. Mama kept watching the streets.

"I don't know," she said, "if I'll ever see you again, after you go off from here. But I hope you'll remember the things I tried to teach you."

"Don't talk like that," I said, and smiled. "You'll be here a long time yet."

She smiled, too, but she said nothing. She was quiet for a long time. And I said, "Mama, don't you worry about nothing. I'll be writing all the time, and you be getting the checks. . . ." 85

"I want to talk to you about your brother," she said, suddenly. "If anything happens to me he ain't going to have nobody to look out for him."

"Mama," I said, "ain't nothing going to happen to you *or* Sonny. Sonny's all right. He's a good boy and he's got good sense."

"It ain't a question of his being a good boy," Mama said, "nor of his having good sense. It ain't only the bad ones, nor yet the dumb ones that gets sucked under." She stopped, looking at me. "Your Daddy once had a brother," she said, and she smiled in a way that made me feel she was in pain. "You didn't never know that, did you?"

"No," I said, "I never knew that," and I watched her face.

"Oh, yes," she said, "your Daddy had a brother." She looked out of the win- 90 dow again. "I know you never saw your Daddy cry. But *I* did — many a time, through all these years."

I asked her, "What happened to his brother? How come nobody's ever talked about him?"

This was the first time I ever saw my mother look old.

"His brother got killed," she said, "when he was just a little younger than you are now. I knew him. He was a fine boy. He was maybe a little full of the devil, but he didn't mean nobody no harm."

Then she stopped and the room was silent, exactly as it had sometimes been on those Sunday afternoons. Mama kept looking out into the streets.

"He used to have a job in the mill," she said, "and, like all young folks, he just 95 liked to perform on Saturday nights. Saturday nights, him and your father would drift around to different places, go to dances and things like that, or just sit around with people they knew, and your father's brother would sing, he had a fine voice, and play along with himself on his guitar. Well, this particular Saturday night, him and your father was coming home from some place, and they were both a little drunk and there was a moon that night, it was bright like day. Your father's brother was feeling kind of good, and he was whistling to himself, and he had his guitar slung over his shoulder. They was coming down a hill and beneath them was a road that turned off from the highway. Well, your father's brother, being always kind of frisky, decided to run down this hill, and he did, with that guitar banging and clanging behind him, and he ran across the road, and he was making water behind a tree. And your father was sort of amused at him and he was still coming down the hill, kind of slow. Then he heard a car motor and that same minute his brother stepped from behind the tree, into the road, in the moonlight. And he started to cross the road. And your father started to run down the hill, he says he don't know why. This car was full of white men. They was all drunk, and when they seen your father's brother they let out a great whoop and holler and they aimed the car straight at him. They was having fun, they just wanted to scare him, the way they do sometimes, you know. But they was drunk. And I guess the boy, being drunk, too, and scared, kind of lost his head. By the time he jumped it was too late. Your father says he heard his brother scream when the car rolled over him, and he heard the wood of that guitar when it give, and he heard them strings go flying, and he heard them white men shouting, and the car kept on a-going and it ain't stopped till this day. And, time your father got down the hill, his brother weren't nothing but blood and pulp."

Tears were gleaming on my mother's face. There wasn't anything I could say.

"He never mentioned it," she said, "because I never let him mention it before you children. Your Daddy was like a crazy man that night and for many a night thereafter. He says he never in his life seen anything as dark as that road after the lights of that car had gone away. Weren't nothing, weren't nobody on that road, just your Daddy and his brother and that busted guitar. Oh, yes. Your Daddy never did really get right again. Till the day he died he weren't sure but that every white man he saw was the man that killed his brother."

She stopped and took out her handkerchief and dried her eyes and looked at me.

"I ain't telling you all this," she said, "to make you scared or bitter or to make you hate nobody. I'm telling you this because you got a brother. And the world ain't changed."

I guess I didn't want to believe this. I guess she saw this in my face. She 100
turned away from me, toward the window again, searching those streets.

"But I praise my Redeemer," she said at last, "that He called your Daddy home before me. I ain't saying it to throw no flowers at myself, but, I declare, it keeps me from feeling too cast down to know I helped your father get safely through this world. Your father always acted like he was the roughest, strongest man on earth. And everybody took him to be like that. But if he hadn't had me there — to see his tears!"

She was crying again. Still, I couldn't move. I said, "Lord, Lord, Mama, I didn't know it was like that."

"Oh, honey," she said, "there's a lot that you don't know. But you are going to find out." She stood up from the window and came over to me. "You got to hold on to your brother," she said, "and don't let him fall, no matter what it looks like is happening to him and no matter how evil you gets with him. You going to be evil with him many a time. But don't you forget what I told you, you hear?"

"I won't forget," I said. "Don't you worry, I won't forget. I won't let nothing happen to Sonny."

My mother smiled as though she was amused at something she saw in my 105
face. Then, "You may not be able to stop nothing from happening. But you got to let him know you's *there*."

Two days later I was married, and then I was gone. And I had a lot of things on my mind and I pretty well forgot my promise to Mama until I got shipped home on a special furlough for her funeral.

And, after the funeral, with just Sonny and me alone in the empty kitchen, I tried to find out something about him.

"What do you want to do?" I asked him.

"I'm going to be a musician," he said.

For he had graduated, in the time I had been away, from dancing to the juke   110
box to finding out who was playing what, and what they were doing with it, and he had bought himself a set of drums.

"You mean, you want to be a drummer?" I somehow had the feeling that being a drummer might be all right for other people but not for my brother Sonny.

"I don't think," he said, looking at me very gravely, "that I'll ever be a good drummer. But I think I can play a piano."

I frowned. I'd never played the role of the oldest brother quite so seriously before, had scarcely ever, in fact, *asked* Sonny a damn thing. I sensed myself in the presence of something I didn't really know how to handle, didn't understand. So I made my frown a little deeper as I asked: "What kind of musician do you want to be?"

He grinned. "How many kinds do you think there are?"

"Be *serious*," I said.   115

He laughed, throwing his head back, and then looked at me. "I *am* serious."

"Well, then, for Christ's sake, stop kidding around and answer a serious question. I mean, do you want to be a concert pianist, you want to play classical music and all that, or — or what?" Long before I finished he was laughing again. "For Christ's *sake*, Sonny!"

He sobered, but with difficulty. "I'm sorry. But you sound so — *scared!*" and he was off again.

"Well, you may think it's funny now, baby, but it's not going to be so funny when you have to make your living at it, let me tell you *that*." I was furious because I knew he was laughing at me and I didn't know why.

"No," he said, very sober now, and afraid, perhaps, that he'd hurt me, "I don't   120
want to be a classical pianist. That isn't what interests me. I mean" — he paused, looking hard at me, as though his eyes would help me to understand, and then gestured helplessly, as though perhaps his hand would help — "I mean, I'll have a lot of studying to do, and I'll have to study *everything*, but, I mean, I want to play *with* — jazz musicians." He stopped. "I want to play jazz," he said.

Well, the word had never before sounded as heavy, as real, as it sounded that afternoon in Sonny's mouth. I just looked at him and I was probably frowning a real frown by this time. I simply couldn't see why on earth he'd want to spend his time hanging around nightclubs, clowning around on bandstands, while people pushed each other around a dance floor. It seemed — beneath him, somehow. I had never thought about it before, had never been forced to, but I suppose I had always put jazz musicians in a class with what Daddy called "good-time people."

"Are you *serious*?"

"Hell, *yes,* I'm serious."

He looked more helpless than ever, and annoyed, and deeply hurt.

I suggested, helpfully: "You mean — like Louis Armstrong?"[2]   125

His face closed as though I'd struck him. "No. I'm not talking about none of that old-time, down home crap."

"Well, look, Sonny, I'm sorry, don't get mad. I just don't altogether get it, that's all. Name somebody — you know, a jazz musician you admire."

"Bird."

"Who?"

"Bird! Charlie Parker![3] Don't they teach you nothing in the goddamn army?"   130

I lit a cigarette. I was surprised and then a little amused to discover that I was trembling. "I've been out of touch," I said. "You'll have to be patient with me. Now. Who's this Parker character?"

"He's just one of the greatest jazz musicians alive," said Sonny, sullenly, his hands in his pockets, his back to me. "Maybe *the* greatest," he added, bitterly, "that's probably why *you* never heard of him."

"All right," I said, "I'm ignorant. I'm sorry. I'll go out and buy all the cat's records right away, all right?"

"It don't," said Sonny, with dignity, "make any difference to me. I don't care what you listen to. Don't do me no favors."

I was beginning to realize that I'd never seen him so upset before. With   135 another part of my mind I was thinking that this would probably turn out to be one of those things kids go through and that I shouldn't make it seem important by pushing it too hard. Still, I didn't think it would do any harm to ask: "Doesn't all this take a lot of time? Can you make a living at it?"

He turned back to me and half leaned, half sat, on the kitchen table. "Everything takes time," he said, "and — well, yes, sure, I can make a living at it. But what I don't seem to be able to make you understand is that it's the only thing I want to do."

"Well, Sonny," I said, gently, "you know people can't always do exactly what they *want* to do —"

"*No,* I don't know that," said Sonny, surprising me. "I think people *ought* to do what they want to do, what else are they alive for?"

"You getting to be a big boy," I said desperately, "it's time you started thinking about your future."

"I'm thinking about my future," said Sonny, grimly. "I think about it all the   140 time."

I gave up. I decided, if he didn't change his mind, that we could always talk about it later. "In the meantime," I said, "you got to finish school." We had already decided that he'd have to move in with Isabel and her folks. I knew this

---

[2] Louis "Satchmo" Armstrong (1901–1971) played the trumpet and was one of the most innovative and influential figures in the history of jazz.

[3] Charles "Bird" Parker (1920–1955) was a seminal African American saxophonist and one of the originators of the be-bop style of jazz. Parker was also a heroin addict.

wasn't the ideal arrangement because Isabel's folks are inclined to be dicty[4] and they hadn't especially wanted Isabel to marry me. But I didn't know what else to do. "And we have to get you fixed up at Isabel's."

There was a long silence. He moved from the kitchen table to the window. "That's a terrible idea. You know it yourself."

"Do you have a *better* idea?"

He just walked up and down the kitchen for a minute. He was as tall as I was. He had started to shave. I suddenly had the feeling that I didn't know him at all.

He stopped at the kitchen table and picked up my cigarettes. Looking at me 145 with a kind of mocking, amused defiance, he put one between his lips. "You mind?"

"You smoking already?"

He lit the cigarette and nodded, watching me through the smoke. "I just wanted to see if I'd have the courage to smoke in front of you." He grinned and blew a great cloud of smoke to the ceiling. "It was easy." He looked at my face. "Come on, now. I bet you was smoking at my age, tell the truth."

I didn't say anything but the truth was on my face, and he laughed. But now there was something very strained in his laugh. "Sure. And I bet that ain't all you was doing."

He was frightening me a little. "Cut the crap," I said. "We already decided that you was going to go and live at Isabel's. Now what's got into you all of a sudden?"

"*You* decided it," he pointed out. "*I* didn't decide nothing." He stopped in 150 front of me, leaning against the stove, arms loosely folded. "Look, brother. I don't want to stay in Harlem no more, I really don't." He was very earnest. He looked at me, then over toward the kitchen window. There was something in his eyes I'd never seen before, some thoughtfulness, some worry all his own. He rubbed the muscle of one arm. "It's time I was getting out of here."

"Where do you want to *go*, Sonny?"

"I want to join the army. Or the navy, I don't care. If I say I'm old enough, they'll believe me."

Then I got mad. It was because I was so scared. "You must be crazy. You goddamn fool, what the hell do you want to go and join the *army* for?"

"I just told you. To get out of Harlem."

"Sonny, you haven't even finished *school*. And if you really want to be a musi- 155 cian, how do you expect to study if you're in the *army*?"

He looked at me, trapped, and in anguish. "There's ways. I might be able to work out some kind of deal. Anyway, I'll have the G.I. Bill when I come out."

"*If* you come out." We stared at each other. "Sonny, please. Be reasonable. I know the setup is far from perfect. But we got to do the best we can."

"I ain't learning nothing in school," he said. "Even when I go." He turned away from me and opened the window and threw his cigarette out into the narrow alley. I watched his back. "At least, I ain't learning nothing you'd want me to

---

[4] Snobbish.

learn." He slammed the window so hard I thought the glass would fly out, and turned back to me. "And I'm sick of the stink of these garbage cans!"

"Sonny," I said, "I know how you feel. But if you don't finish school now, you're going to be sorry later that you didn't." I grabbed him by the shoulders. "And you only got another year. It ain't so bad. And I'll come back and I swear I'll help you do *whatever* you want to do. Just try to put up with it till I come back. Will you please do that? For me?"

He didn't answer and he wouldn't look at me.   160

"Sonny. You hear me?"

He pulled away. "I hear you. But you never hear anything *I* say."

I didn't know what to say to that. He looked out of the window and then back at me. "OK," he said, and sighed. "I'll try."

Then I said, trying to cheer him up a little, "They got a piano at Isabel's. You can practice on it."

And as a matter of fact, it did cheer him up for a minute. "That's right," he 165 said to himself. "I forgot that." His face relaxed a little. But the worry, the thoughtfulness, played on it still, the way shadows play on a face which is staring into the fire.

But I thought I'd never hear the end of that piano. At first, Isabel would write me, saying how nice it was that Sonny was so serious about his music and how, as soon as he came in from school, or wherever he had been when he was supposed to be at school, he went straight to that piano and stayed there until suppertime. And, after supper, he went back to that piano and stayed there until everybody went to bed. He was at the piano all day Saturday and all day Sunday. Then he bought a record player and started playing records. He'd play one record over and over again, all day long sometimes, and he'd improvise along with it on the piano. Or he'd play one section of the record, one chord, one change, one progression, then he'd do it on the piano. Then back to the record. Then back to the piano.

Well, I really don't know how they stood it. Isabel finally confessed that it wasn't like living with a person at all, it was like living with sound. And the sound didn't make any sense to her, didn't make any sense to any of them — naturally. They began, in a way, to be afflicted by this presence that was living in their home. It was as though Sonny were some sort of god, or monster. He moved in an atmosphere which wasn't like theirs at all. They fed him and he ate, he washed himself, he walked in and out of their door; he certainly wasn't nasty or unpleasant or rude, Sonny isn't any of those things; but it was as though he were all wrapped up in some cloud, some fire, some vision all his own; and there wasn't any way to reach him.

At the same time, he wasn't really a man yet, he was still a child, and they had to watch out for him in all kinds of ways. They certainly couldn't throw him out. Neither did they dare to make a great scene about that piano because even they dimly sensed, as I sensed, from so many thousands of miles away, that Sonny was at that piano playing for his life.

But he hadn't been going to school. One day a letter came from the school board and Isabel's mother got it — there had, apparently, been other letters but Sonny had torn them up. This day, when Sonny came in, Isabel's mother showed him the letter and asked where he'd been spending his time. And she finally got it out of him that he'd been down in Greenwich Village, with musicians and other characters, in a white girl's apartment. And this scared her and she started to scream at him and what came up, once she began — though she denies it to this day — was what sacrifices they were making to give Sonny a decent home and how little he appreciated it.

Sonny didn't play the piano that day. By evening, Isabel's mother had calmed 170 down but then there was the old man to deal with, and Isabel herself. Isabel says she did her best to be calm but she broke down and started crying. She says she just watched Sonny's face. She could tell, by watching him, what was happening with him. And what was happening was that they penetrated his cloud, they had reached him. Even if their fingers had been a thousand times more gentle than human fingers ever are, he could hardly help feeling that they had stripped him naked and were spitting on that nakedness. For he also had to see that his presence, that music, which was life or death to him, had been torture for them and that they had endured it, not at all for his sake, but only for mine. And Sonny couldn't take that. He can take it a little better today than he could then but he's still not very good at it and, frankly, I don't know anybody who is.

The silence of the next few days must have been louder than the sound of all the music ever played since time began. One morning, before she went to work, Isabel was in his room for something and she suddenly realized that all of his records were gone. And she knew for certain that he was gone. And he was. He went as far as the navy would carry him. He finally sent me a postcard from some place in Greece and that was the first I knew that Sonny was still alive. I didn't see him any more until we were both back in New York and the war had long been over.

He was a man by then, of course, but I wasn't willing to see it. He came by the house from time to time, but we fought almost every time we met. I didn't like the way he carried himself, loose and dreamlike all the time, and I didn't like his friends, and his music seemed to be merely an excuse for the life he led. It sounded just that weird and disordered.

Then we had a fight, a pretty awful fight, and I didn't see him for months. By and by I looked him up, where he was living, in a furnished room in the Village, and I tried to make it up. But there were lots of other people in the room and Sonny just lay on his bed, and he wouldn't come downstairs with me, and he treated these other people as though they were his family and I weren't. So I got mad and then he got mad, and then I told him that he might just as well be dead as live the way he was living. Then he stood up and he told me not to worry about him any more in life, that he *was* dead as far as I was concerned. Then he pushed me to the door and the other people looked on as though nothing were happening, and he slammed the door behind me. I stood in the hallway, staring at the door. I heard somebody laugh in the room and then the tears came to my eyes. I started down the steps, whistling to keep from crying, I kept whistling to myself, *You going to need me, baby, one of these cold, rainy days.*

I read about Sonny's trouble in the spring. Little Grace died in the fall. She was a beautiful little girl. But she only lived a little over two years. She died of polio and she suffered. She had a slight fever for a couple of days, but it didn't seem like anything and we just kept her in bed. And we would certainly have called the doctor, but the fever dropped, she seemed to be all right. So we thought it had just been a cold. Then, one day, she was up, playing, Isabel was in the kitchen fixing lunch for the two boys when they'd come in from school, and she heard Grace fall down in the living room. When you have a lot of children you don't always start running when one of them falls, unless they start scream-ing or something. And, this time, Gracie was quiet. Yet, Isabel says that when she heard that *thump* and then that silence, something happened to her to make her afraid. And she ran to the living room and there was little Grace on the floor, all twisted up, and the reason she hadn't screamed was that she couldn't get her breath. And when she did scream, it was the worst sound, Isabel says, that she'd ever heard in all her life, and she still hears it sometimes in her dreams. Isabel will sometimes wake me up with a low, moaning, strangling sound and I have to be quick to awaken her and hold her to me and where Isabel is weeping against me seems a mortal wound.

I think I may have written Sonny the very day that little Grace was buried. I was sitting in the living room in the dark, by myself, and I suddenly thought of Sonny. My trouble made his real.

One Saturday afternoon, when Sonny had been living with us, or, anyway, been in our house, for nearly two weeks, I found myself wandering aimlessly about the living room, drinking from a can of beer, and trying to work up courage to search Sonny's room. He was out, he was usually out whenever I was home, and Isabel had taken the children to see their grandparents. Suddenly I was standing still in front of the living room window, watching Seventh Avenue. The idea of searching Sonny's room made me still. I scarcely dared to admit to myself what I'd be searching for. I didn't know what I'd do if I found it. Or if I didn't.

On the sidewalk across from me, near the entrance to a barbecue joint, some people were holding an old-fashioned revival meeting. The barbecue cook, wearing a dirty white apron, his conked[5] hair reddish and metallic in the pale sun, and a cigarette between his lips, stood in the doorway, watching them. Kids and older people paused in their errands and stood there, along with some older men and a couple of very tough-looking women who watched everything that happened on the avenue, as though they owned it, or were maybe owned by it. Well, they were watching this, too. The revival was being carried on by three sis-ters in black, and a brother. All they had were their voices and their Bibles and a tambourine. The brother was testifying and while he testified two of the sisters stood together, seeming to say, amen, and the third sister walked around with

175

---

[5] Straightened and greased.

the tambourine outstretched and a couple of people dropped coins into it. Then the brother's testimony ended and the sister who had been taking up the collection dumped the coins into her palm and transferred them to the pocket of her long black robe. Then she raised both hands, striking the tambourine against the air, and then against one hand, and she started to sing. And the two other sisters and the brother joined in.

It was strange, suddenly, to watch, though I had been seeing these meetings all my life. So, of course, had everybody else down there. Yet, they paused and watched and listened and I stood still at the window. "*'Tis the old ship of Zion*," they sang, and the sister with the tambourine kept a steady, jangling beat, "*it has rescued many a thousand!*" Not a soul under the sound of their voices was hearing this song for the first time, not one of them had been rescued. Nor had they seen much in the way of rescue work being done around them. Neither did they especially believe in the holiness of the three sisters and the brother, they knew too much about them, knew where they lived, and how. The woman with the tambourine, whose voice dominated the air, whose face was bright with joy, was divided by very little from the woman who stood watching her, a cigarette between her heavy, chapped lips, her hair a cuckoo's nest, her face scarred and swollen from many beatings, and her black eyes glittering like coal. Perhaps they both knew this, which was why, when, as rarely, they addressed each other, they addressed each other as Sister. As the singing filled the air the watching, listening faces underwent a change, the eyes focusing on something within; the music seemed to soothe a poison out of them; and time seemed, nearly, to fall away from the sullen, belligerent, battered faces, as though they were fleeing back to their first condition, while dreaming of their last. The barbecue cook half shook his head and smiled, and dropped his cigarette and disappeared into his joint. A man fumbled in his pockets for change and stood holding it in his hand impatiently, as though he had just remembered a pressing appointment further up the avenue. He looked furious. Then I saw Sonny, standing on the edge of the crowd. He was carrying a wide, flat notebook with a green cover, and it made him look, from where I was standing, almost like a schoolboy. The coppery sun brought out the copper in his skin, he was very faintly smiling, standing very still. Then the singing stopped, the tambourine turned into a collection plate again. The furious man dropped in his coins and vanished, so did a couple of the women, and Sonny dropped some change in the plate, looking directly at the woman with a little smile. He started across the avenue, toward the house. He has a slow, loping walk, something like the way Harlem hipsters walk, only he's imposed on this his own half-beat. I had never really noticed it before.

I stayed at the window, both relieved and apprehensive. As Sonny disappeared from my sight, they began singing again. And they were still singing when his key turned in the lock.

"Hey," he said.

"Hey, yourself. You want some beer?"

"No. Well, maybe." But he came up to the window and stood beside me, looking out. "What a warm voice," he said.

180

They were singing *If I could only hear my mother pray again!*

"Yes," I said, "and she can sure beat that tambourine."

"But what a terrible song," he said, and laughed. He dropped his notebook on the sofa and disappeared into the kitchen. "Where's Isabel and the kids?"

"I think they went to see their grandparents. You hungry?" 185

"No." He came back into the living room with his can of beer. "You want to come some place with me tonight?"

I sensed, I don't know how, that I couldn't possibly say no. "Sure. Where?"

He sat down on the sofa and picked up his notebook and started leafing through it. "I'm going to sit in with some fellows in a joint in the Village."

"You mean, you're going to play, tonight?"

"That's right." He took a swallow of his beer and moved back to the window. 190 He gave me a sidelong look. "If you can stand it."

"I'll try," I said.

He smiled to himself and we both watched as the meeting across the way broke up. The three sisters and the brother, heads bowed, were singing *God be with you till we meet again.* The faces around them were very quiet. Then the song ended. The small crowd dispersed. We watched the three women and the lone man walk slowly up the avenue.

"When she was singing before," said Sonny, abruptly, "her voice reminded me for a minute of what heroin feels like sometimes — when it's in your veins. It makes you feel sort of warm and cool at the same time. And distant. And — and sure." He sipped his beer, very deliberately not looking at me. I watched his face. "It makes you feel — in control. Sometimes you've got to have that feeling."

"Do you?" I sat down slowly in the easy chair.

"Sometimes." He went to the sofa and picked up his notebook again. "Some 195 people do."

"In order," I asked, "to play?" And my voice was very ugly, full of contempt and anger.

"Well" — he looked at me with great, troubled eyes, as though, in fact, he hoped his eyes would tell me things he could never otherwise say — "they *think* so. And *if* they think so —!"

"And what do *you* think?" I asked.

He sat on the sofa and put his can of beer on the floor. "I don't know," he said, and I couldn't be sure if he were answering my question or pursuing his thoughts. His face didn't tell me. "It's not so much to *play.* It's to *stand* it, to be able to make it at all. On any level." He frowned and smiled: "In order to keep from shaking to pieces."

"But these friends of yours," I said, "they seem to shake themselves to pieces 200 pretty goddamn fast."

"Maybe." He played with the notebook. And something told me that I should curb my tongue, that Sonny was doing his best to talk, that I should listen. "But of course you only know the ones that've gone to pieces. Some don't — or at least they haven't *yet* and that's just about all *any* of us can say." He paused. "And then there are some who just live, really, in hell, and they know it and they see what's happening and they go right on. I don't know." He sighed, dropped the notebook, folded his arms. "Some guys, you can tell from the way they play, they on something *all* the time. And you can see that, well, it makes something real for them. But of course," he picked up his beer from the floor and sipped it and put the can down again, "they *want* to, too, you've got to see that. Even some of them that say they don't — *some,* not all."

"And what about you?" I asked — I couldn't help it. "What about you? Do *you* want to?"

He stood up and walked to the window and remained silent for a long time. Then he sighed. "Me," he said. Then: "While I was downstairs before, on my way here, listening to that woman sing, it struck me all of a sudden how much suffering she must have had to go through — to sing like that. It's *repulsive* to think you have to suffer that much."

I said: "But there's no way not to suffer — is there, Sonny?"

"I believe not," he said and smiled, "but that's never stopped anyone from try- 205
ing." He looked at me. "Has it?" I realized, with this mocking look, that there stood between us, forever, beyond the power of time or forgiveness, the fact that I had held silence — so long! — when he had needed human speech to help him. He turned back to the window. "No, there's no way not to suffer. But you try all kinds of ways to keep from drowning in it, to keep on top of it, and to make it seem — well, like *you.* Like you did something, all right, and now you're suffering for it. You know?" I said nothing. "Well you know," he said, impatiently, "why *do* people suffer? Maybe it's better to do something to give it a reason, *any* reason."

"But we just agreed," I said, "that there's no way not to suffer. Isn't it better, then, just to — take it?"

"But nobody just takes it," Sonny cried, "that's what I'm telling you! *Every-body* tries not to. You're just hung up on the *way* some people try — it's not *your* way!"

The hair on my face began to itch, my face felt wet. "That's not true," I said, "that's not true. I don't give a damn what other people do, I don't even care how they suffer. I just care how *you* suffer." And he looked at me. "Please believe me," I said, "I don't want to see you — die — trying not to suffer."

"I won't," he said, flatly, "die trying not to suffer. At least, not any faster than anybody else."

"But there's no need," I said, trying to laugh, "is there? in killing yourself." 210

I wanted to say more, but I couldn't. I wanted to talk about will power and how life could be — well, beautiful. I wanted to say that it was all within; but was it? or, rather, wasn't that exactly the trouble? And I wanted to promise that I would never fail him again. But it would all have sounded — empty words and lies.

So I made the promise to myself and prayed that I would keep it.

"It's terrible sometimes, inside," he said, "that's what's the trouble. You walk these streets, black and funky and cold, and there's not really a living ass to talk to, and there's nothing shaking, and there's no way of getting it out — that storm inside. You can't talk it and you can't make love with it, and when you finally try to get with it and play it, you realize *nobody's* listening. So *you've* got to listen. You got to find a way to listen."

And then he walked away from the window and sat on the sofa again, as though all the wind had suddenly been knocked out of him. "Sometimes you'll do *anything to play,* even cut your mother's throat." He laughed and looked at me. "Or your brother's." Then he sobered. "Or your own." Then: "Don't worry. I'm all right now and I think I'll *be* all right. But I can't forget — where I've been. I don't mean just the physical place I've been, I mean where I've *been.* And *what* I've been."

"What have you been, Sonny?" I asked. 215

He smiled — but sat sideways on the sofa, his elbow resting on the back, his fingers playing with his mouth and chin, not looking at me. "I've been something I didn't recognize, didn't know I could be. Didn't know anybody could be." He stopped, looking inward, looking helplessly young, looking old. "I'm not talking about it now because I feel *guilty* or anything like that — maybe it would be better if I did, I don't know. Anyway, I can't really talk about it. Not to you, not to anybody," and now he turned and faced me. "Sometimes, you know, and it was actually when I was most *out* of the world, I felt that I was in it, that I was *with* it, really, and I could play or I didn't really have to *play,* it just came out of me, it was there. And I don't know how I played, thinking about it now, but I know I did awful things, those times, sometimes, to people. Or it wasn't that I *did* anything to them — it was that they weren't real." He picked up the beer can; it was empty; he rolled it between his palms: "And other times — well, I needed a fix, I needed to find a place to lean, I needed to clear a space to *listen* — and I couldn't find it, and I — went crazy, I did terrible things to *me,* I was terrible *for* me." He began pressing the beer can between his hands, I watched the metal begin to give. It glittered, as he played with it like a knife, and I was afraid he would cut himself, but I said nothing. "Oh well. I can never tell you. I was all by myself at the bottom of something, stinking and sweating and crying and shaking, and I smelled it, you know? *my* stink, and I thought I'd die if I couldn't get away from it and yet, all the same, I knew that everything I was doing was just locking me in with it. And I didn't know," he paused, still flattening the beer can, "I didn't know, I still *don't* know, something kept telling me that maybe it was good to smell your own stink, but I didn't think that *that* was what I'd been trying to do — and — who can stand it?" and he abruptly dropped the ruined beer can, looking at me with a small, still smile, and then rose, walking to the window as though it were the lodestone rock. I watched his face, he watched the avenue. "I couldn't tell you when Mama died — but the reason I wanted to leave Harlem so bad was to get away from drugs. And then, when I ran away, that's what I was running from — really. When I came back, nothing had changed, *I* hadn't changed, I was just — older." And he stopped, drumming with his fingers on the windowpane. The sun had vanished, soon darkness would fall. I watched his face. "It can come again," he said, almost as though speaking to himself. Then he turned to me. "It can come again," he repeated. "I just want you to know that."

"All right," I said, at last. "So it can come again. All right."

He smiled, but the smile was sorrowful. "I had to try to tell you," he said.

"Yes," I said. "I understand that."

"You're my brother," he said, looking straight at me, and not smiling at all.   220

"Yes," I repeated, "yes. I understand that."

He turned back to the window, looking out. "All that hatred down there," he said, "all that hatred and misery and love. It's a wonder it doesn't blow the avenue apart."

We went to the only nightclub on a short, dark street, downtown. We squeezed through the narrow, chattering, jampacked bar to the entrance of the big room, where the bandstand was. And we stood there for a moment, for the lights were very dim in this room and we couldn't see. Then, "Hello, boy," said the voice and an enormous black man, much older than Sonny or myself, erupted out of all that atmospheric lighting and put an arm around Sonny's shoulder. "I been sitting right here," he said, "waiting for you."

He had a big voice, too, and heads in the darkness turned toward us.

Sonny grinned and pulled a little away, and said, "Creole, this is my brother. I   225
told you about him."

Creole shook my hand. "I'm glad to meet you, son," he said, and it was clear that he was glad to meet me *there,* for Sonny's sake. And he smiled, "You got a real musician in *your* family," and he took his arm from Sonny's shoulder and slapped him, lightly, affectionately, with the back of his hand.

"Well. Now I've heard it all," said a voice behind us. This was another musician, and a friend of Sonny's, a coal-black, cheerful-looking man, built close to the ground. He immediately began confiding to me, at the top of his lungs, the most terrible things about Sonny, his teeth gleaming like a lighthouse and his laugh coming up out of him like the beginning of an earthquake. And it turned out that everyone at the bar knew Sonny, or almost everyone; some were musicians, working there, or nearby, or not working, some were simply hangers-on, and some were there to hear Sonny play. I was introduced to all of them and they were all very polite to me. Yet, it was clear that, for them, I was only Sonny's brother. Here, I was in Sonny's world. Or, rather: his kingdom. Here, it was not even a question that his veins bore royal blood.

They were going to play soon and Creole installed me, by myself, at a table in a dark corner. Then I watched them, Creole, and the little black man, and Sonny, and the others, while they horsed around, standing just below the bandstand. The light from the bandstand spilled just a little short of them and, watching them laughing and gesturing and moving about, I had the feeling that they, nevertheless, were being most careful not to step into that circle of light too suddenly; that if they moved into the light too suddenly, without thinking, they would perish in flame. Then, while I watched, one of them, the small, black man, moved into the light and crossed the bandstand and started fooling around with his drums. Then — being funny and being, also, extremely ceremonious — Creole took Sonny by the arm and led him to the piano. A woman's voice called Sonny's name and a few hands started clapping. And Sonny, also being funny and being ceremonious, and so touched, I think, that he could have cried, but neither hiding it nor showing it, riding it like a man, grinned, and put both hands to his heart and bowed from the waist.

Creole then went to the bass fiddle and a lean, very bright-skinned brown man jumped up on the bandstand and picked up his horn. So there they were, and the atmosphere on the bandstand and in the room began to change and tighten. Someone stepped up to the microphone and announced them. Then there were all kinds of murmurs. Some people at the bar shushed others. The waitress ran around, frantically getting in the last orders, guys and chicks got closer to each other, and the lights on the bandstand, on the quartet, turned to a kind of indigo. Then they all looked different there. Creole looked about him for the last time, as though he were making certain that all his chickens were in the coop, and then he — jumped and struck the fiddle. And there they were.

All I know about music is that not many people ever really hear it. And even then, on the rare occasions when something opens within, and the music enters, what we mainly hear, or hear corroborated, are personal, private, vanishing evocations. But the man who creates the music is hearing something else, is dealing with the roar rising from the void and imposing order on it as it hits the air. What is evoked in him, then, is of another order, more terrible because it has no words, and triumphant, too, for that same reason. And his triumph, when he triumphs, is ours. I just watched Sonny's face. His face was troubled, he was working hard, but he wasn't with it. And I had the feeling that, in a way, everyone on the bandstand was waiting for him, both waiting for him and pushing him along. But as I began to watch Creole, I realized that it was Creole who held them all back. He had them on a short rein. Up there, keeping the beat with his whole body, wailing on the fiddle, with his eyes half closed, he was listening to everything, but he was listening to Sonny. He was having a dialogue with Sonny. He wanted Sonny to leave the shoreline and strike out for the deep water. He was Sonny's witness that deep water and drowning were not the same thing — he had been there, and he knew. And he wanted Sonny to know. He was waiting for Sonny to do the things on the keys which would let Creole know that Sonny was in the water.

And, while Creole listened, Sonny moved, deep within, exactly like someone in torment. I had never before thought of how awful the relationship must be between the musician and his instrument. He has to fill it, this instrument, with the breath of life, his own. He has to make it do what he wants it to do. And a piano is just a piano. It's made out of so much wood and wires and little hammers and big ones, and ivory. While there's only so much you can do with it, the only way to find this out is to try; to try and make it do everything.

And Sonny hadn't been near a piano for over a year. And he wasn't on much better terms with his life, not the life that stretched before him now. He and the piano stammered, started one way, got scared, stopped; started another way, panicked, marked time, started again; then seemed to have found a direction, panicked again, got stuck. And the face I saw on Sonny I'd never seen before.

230

Everything had been burned out of it, and, at the same time, things usually hidden were being burned in, by the fire and fury of the battle which was occurring in him up there.

Yet, watching Creole's face as they neared the end of the first set, I had the feeling that something had happened, something I hadn't heard. Then they finished, there was scattered applause, and then, without an instant's warning, Creole started into something else, it was almost sardonic, it was *Am I Blue.*[6] And, as though he commanded, Sonny began to play. Something began to happen. And Creole let out the reins. The dry, low, black man said something awful on the drums, Creole answered, and the drums talked back. Then the horn insisted, sweet and high, slightly detached perhaps, and Creole listened, commenting now and then, dry, and driving, beautiful and calm and old. Then they all came together again, and Sonny was part of the family again. I could tell this from his face. He seemed to have found, right there beneath his fingers, a damn brand-new piano. It seemed that he couldn't get over it. Then, for a while, just being happy with Sonny, they seemed to be agreeing with him that brand-new pianos certainly were a gas.

Then Creole stepped forward to remind them that what they were playing was the blues. He hit something in all of them, he hit something in me, myself, and the music tightened and deepened, apprehension began to beat the air. Creole began to tell us what the blues were all about. They were not about anything very new. He and his boys up there were keeping it new, at the risk of ruin, destruction, madness, and death, in order to find new ways to make us listen. For, while the tale of how we suffer, and how we are delighted, and how we may triumph is never new, it always must be heard. There isn't any other tale to tell, it's the only light we've got in all this darkness.

And this tale, according to that face, that body, those strong hands on those strings, has another aspect in every country, and a new depth in every generation. Listen, Creole seemed to be saying, listen. Now these are Sonny's blues. He made the little black man on the drums know it, and the bright, brown man on the horn. Creole wasn't trying any longer to get Sonny in the water. He was wishing him Godspeed. Then he stepped back, very slowly, filling the air with the immense suggestion that Sonny speak for himself.

Then they all gathered around Sonny and Sonny played. Every now and again one of them seemed to say, amen. Sonny's fingers filled the air with life, his life. But that life contained so many others. And Sonny went all the way back, he really began with the spare, flat statement of the opening phrase of the song. Then he began to make it his. It was very beautiful because it wasn't hurried and it was no longer a lament. I seemed to hear with what burning he had made it his, and what burning we had yet to make it ours, how we could cease lamenting. Freedom lurked around us and I understood, at last, that he could help us to be free if we would listen, that he would never be free until we did. Yet, there

235

[6] One of the standard tunes in the jazz/blues repertoire.

was no battle in his face now, I heard what he had gone through, and would continue to go through until he came to rest in earth. He had made it his: that long line, of which we knew only Mama and Daddy. And he was giving it back, as everything must be given back, so that, passing through death, it can live forever. I saw my mother's face again, and felt, for the first time, how the stones of the road she had walked on must have bruised her feet. I saw the moonlit road where my father's brother died. And it brought something else back to me, and carried me past it, I saw my little girl again and felt Isabel's tears again, and I felt my own tears begin to rise. And I was yet aware that this was only a moment, that the world waited outside, as hungry as a tiger, and that trouble stretched above us, longer than the sky.

Then it was over. Creole and Sonny let out their breath, both soaking wet, and grinning. There was a lot of applause and some of it was real. In the dark, the girl came by and I asked her to take drinks to the bandstand. There was a long pause, while they talked up there in the indigo light and after awhile I saw the girl put a Scotch and milk on top of the piano for Sonny. He didn't seem to notice it, but just before they started playing again, he sipped from it and looked toward me, and nodded. Then he put it back on top of the piano. For me, then, as they began to play again, it glowed and shook above my brother's head like the very cup of trembling.[7]

For Analysis

1. Explain the title.

2. What is the relation between the opening events and the end of the story?

3. What function does the narrator's encounter with Sonny's friend at the beginning of the story (paras. 9–47) serve?

4. Does the story offer any explanation for Sonny's addiction? Explain.

5. What adjectives would you use to characterize the narrator? Does he change in the course of the story? Explain.

6. What conclusions does the narrator come to about drugs and addiction?

7. What does the final sentence mean?

On Style

1. Discuss the imagery of darkness in the story.

2. What effects does Baldwin achieve by rearranging the order of events?

3. Discuss the effectiveness of the narrator's description of Sonny's music (para. 236 to the end).

---

[7] See the Old Testament, Isaiah 51:17, 22–23: "Awake, awake, stand up, O Jerusalem, which hast drunk at the hand of the Lord the cup of his fury; thou hast drunken the dregs of the cup of trembling, and wrung them out. . . . Behold, I have taken out of thine hand the cup of trembling, even the dregs of the cup of my fury; thou shalt no more drink it again: But I will put it into the hand of them that afflict thee. . . .

Making Connections

1. Compare and contrast the way racism is portrayed in this story with its portrayal in James Alan McPherson's "A Loaf of Bread" (p. 409).

2. Like this story, Major Jackson's poem "Euphoria" (p. 184) deals with drug addicition. What similarities do you find between them in their handling of this subject? What differences?

3. Franz Kafka's "A Hunger Artist" (p. 362) is also about an artist and the process of artistic creation. What similarities or differences do you find between Kafka's story and Baldwin's?

Writing Topics

1. What does this story have to say about the sources of creativity?

2. Discuss the significance of the narrator's observations on the revival meeting (paras. 176–177) to the theme of the story.

Chinua Achebe   (b. 1930)

Marriage Is a Private Affair   1972

"Have you written to your dad yet?" asked Nene one afternoon as she sat with Nnaemeka in her room at 16 Kasanga Street, Lagos.[1]

"No. I've been thinking about it. I think it's better to tell him when I get home on leave!"

"But why? Your leave is such a long way off yet — six whole weeks. He should be let into our happiness now."

Nnaemeka was silent for a while, and then began very slowly as if he groped for his words: "I wish I were sure it would be happiness to him."

"Of course it must," replied Nene, a little surprised. "Why shouldn't it?"   5

"You have lived in Lagos all your life, and you know very little about people in remote parts of the country."

"That's what you always say. But I don't believe anybody will be so unlike other people that they will be unhappy when their sons are engaged to marry."

"Yes. They are most unhappy if the engagement is not arranged by them. In our case it's worse — you are not even an Ibo."

This was said so seriously and so bluntly that Nene could not find speech immediately. In the cosmopolitan atmosphere of the city it had always seemed to her something of a joke that a person's tribe could determine whom he married.

At last she said, "You don't really mean that he will object to your marrying   10 me simply on that account? I had always thought you Ibos were kindly disposed to other people."

"So we are. But when it comes to marriage, well, it's not quite so simple. And this," he added, "is not peculiar to the Ibos. If your father were alive and lived in the heart of Ibibio-land he would be exactly like my father."

"I don't know. But anyway, as your father is so fond of you, I'm sure he will forgive you soon enough. Come on then, be a good boy and send him a nice lovely letter . . ."

"It would not be wise to break the news to him by writing. A letter will bring it upon him with a shock. I'm quite sure about that."

"All right, honey, suit yourself. You know your father."

As Nnaemeka walked home that evening he turned over in his mind the dif-   15 ferent ways of overcoming his father's opposition, especially now that he had gone and found a girl for him. He had thought of showing his letter to Nene but decided on second thoughts not to, at least for the moment. He read it again

[1] The former capital of Nigeria, Lagos is the largest city in sub-Saharan Africa.

when he got home and couldn't help smiling to himself. He remembered Ugoye quite well, an Amazon of a girl who used to beat up all the boys, himself included, on the way to the stream, a complete dunce at school.

> I have found a girl who will suit you admirably — Ugoye Nweke, the eldest daughter of our neighbour, Jacob Nweke. She has a proper Christian upbringing. When she stopped schooling some years ago her father (a man of sound judgment) sent her to live in the house of a pastor where she has received all the training a wife could need. Her Sunday School teacher has told me that she reads her Bible very fluently. I hope we shall begin negotiations when you come home in December.

On the second evening of his return from Lagos Nnaemeka sat with his father under a cassia tree. This was the old man's retreat where he went to read his Bible when the parching December sun had set and a fresh, reviving wind blew on the leaves.[2]

"Father," began Nnaemeka suddenly, "I have come to ask forgiveness."

"Forgiveness? For what, my son?" he asked in amazement.

"It's about this marriage question."

"Which marriage question?"

"I can't — we must — I mean it is impossible for me to marry Nweke's 20 daughter."

"Impossible? Why?" asked his father.

"I don't love her."

"Nobody said you did. Why should you?" he asked.

"Marriage today is different . . ."

"Look here, my son," interrupted his father, "nothing is different. What one 25 looks for in a wife are a good character and a Christian background."

Nnaemeka saw there was no hope along the present line of argument.

"Moreover," he said, "I am engaged to marry another girl who has all of Ugoye's good qualities, and who . . ."

His father did not believe his ears. "What did you say?" he asked slowly and disconcertingly.

"She is a good Christian," his son went on, "and a teacher in a Girls' School in Lagos."

"Teacher, did you say? If you consider that a qualification for a good wife I 30 should like to point out to you, Emeka, that no Christian woman should teach. St. Paul in his letter to the Corinthians says that women should keep silence." He rose slowly from his seat and paced forwards and backwards. This was his pet subject, and he condemned vehemently those church leaders who encouraged women to teach in their schools. After he had spent his emotion on a long homily he at last came back to his son's engagement, in a seemingly milder tone.

"Whose daughter is she, anyway?"

"She is Nene Atang."

---

[2] Although traditional Ibo religion centers on ancestor and nature worship, many Ibos became Christians under British colonial and missionary influence.

"What!" All the mildness was gone again. "Did you say Neneataga, what does that mean?"

"Nene Atang from Calabar. She is the only girl I can marry." This was a very rash reply and Nnaemeka expected the storm to burst. But it did not. His father merely walked away into his room. This was most unexpected and perplexed Nnaemeka. His father's silence was infinitely more menacing than a flood of threatening speech. That night the old man did not eat.

When he sent for Nnaemeka a day later he applied all possible ways of dissua- 35 sion. But the young man's heart was hardened, and his father eventually gave him up as lost.

"I owe it to you, my son, as a duty to show you what is right and what is wrong. Whoever put this idea into your head might as well have cut your throat. It is Satan's work." He waved his son away.

"You will change your mind, Father, when you know Nene."

"I shall never see her," was the reply. From that night the father scarcely spoke to his son. He did not, however, cease hoping that he would realize how serious was the danger he was heading for. Day and night he put him in his prayers.

Nnaemeka, for his own part, was very deeply affected by his father's grief. But he kept hoping that it would pass away. If it had occurred to him that never in the history of his people had a man married a woman who spoke a different tongue, he might have been less optimistic. "It has never been heard," was the verdict of an old man speaking a few weeks later. In that short sentence he spoke for all of his people. This man had come with others to commiserate with Okeke when news went round about his son's behaviour. By that time the son had gone back to Lagos.

"It has never been heard," said the old man again with a sad shake of his head. 40

"What did Our Lord say?" asked another gentleman. "Sons shall rise against their Fathers; it is there in the Holy Book."

"It is the beginning of the end," said another.

The discussion thus tending to become theological, Madubogwu, a highly practical man, brought it down once more to the ordinary level.

"Have you thought of consulting a native doctor about your son?" he asked Nnaemeka's father.

"He isn't sick," was the reply. 45

"What is he then? The boy's mind is diseased and only a good herbalist can bring him back to his right senses. The medicine he requires is *Amalile,* the same that women apply with success to recapture their husbands' straying affection."

"Madubogwu is right," said another gentleman. "This thing calls for medicine."

"I shall not call in a native doctor." Nnaemeka's father was known to be obstinately ahead of his more superstitious neighbours in these matters. "I will not be another Mrs. Ochuba. If my son wants to kill himself let him do it with his own hands. It is not for me to help him."

"But it was her fault," said Madubogwu. "She ought to have gone to an honest herbalist. She was a clever woman, nevertheless."

"She was a wicked murderess," said Jonathan who rarely argued with his 50 neighbours because, he often said, they were incapable of reasoning. "The medicine was prepared for her husband, it was his name they called in its preparation and I am sure it would have been perfectly beneficial to him. It was wicked to put it into the herbalist's food, and say you were only trying it out."

Six months later, Nnaemeka was showing his young wife a short letter from his father:

> It amazes me that you could be so unfeeling as to send me your wedding picture. I would have sent it back. But on further thought I decided just to cut off your wife and send it back to you because I have nothing to do with her. How I wish that I had nothing to do with you either.

When Nene read through this letter and looked at the mutilated picture her eyes filled with tears, and she began to sob.

"Don't cry, my darling," said her husband. "He is essentially good-natured and will one day look more kindly on our marriage." But years passed and that one day did not come.

For eight years, Okeke would have nothing to do with his son, Nnaemeka. Only three times (when Nnaemeka asked to come home and spend his leave) did he write to him.

"I can't have you in my house," he replied on one occasion. "It can be of no 55 interest to me where or how you spend your leave — or your life, for that matter."

The prejudice against Nnaemeka's marriage was not confined to his little village. In Lagos, especially among his people who worked there, it showed itself in a different way. Their women, when they met at their village meeting, were not hostile to Nene. Rather, they paid her such excessive deference as to make her feel she was not one of them. But as time went on, Nene gradually broke through some of this prejudice and even began to make friends among them. Slowly and grudgingly they began to admit that she kept her home much better than most of them.

The story eventually got to the little village in the heart of the Ibo country that Nnaemeka and his young wife were a most happy couple. But his father was one of the few people who knew nothing about this. He always displayed so much temper whenever his son's name was mentioned that everyone avoided it in his presence. By a tremendous effort of will he had succeeded in pushing his son to the back of his mind. The strain had nearly killed him but he had persevered, and won.

Then one day he received a letter from Nene, and in spite of himself he began to glance through it perfunctorily until all of a sudden the expression on his face changed and he began to read more carefully.

. . . Our two sons, from the day they learnt that they have a grandfather, have insisted on being taken to him. I find it impossible to tell them that you will not see them. I implore you to allow Nnaemeka to bring them home for a short time during his leave next month. I shall remain here in Lagos . . .

The old man at once felt the resolution he had built up over so many years falling in. He was telling himself that he must not give in. He tried to steel his heart against all emotional appeals. It was a reenactment of that other struggle. He leaned against a window and looked out. The sky was overcast with heavy black clouds and a high wind began to blow filling the air with dust and dry leaves. It was one of those rare occasions when even Nature takes a hand in a human fight. Very soon it began to rain, the first rain in the year. It came down in large sharp drops and was accompanied by the lightning and thunder which mark a change of season. Okeke was trying hard not to think of his two grandsons. But he knew he was now fighting a losing battle. He tried to hum a favourite hymn but the pattering of large rain drops on the roof broke up the tune. His mind immediately returned to the children. How could he shut his door against them? By a curious mental process he imagined them standing, sad and forsaken, under the harsh angry weather — shut out from his house.

That night he hardly slept, from remorse — and a vague fear that he might   60
die without making it up to them.

For Analysis

1. Describe the various forms the conflict between modernism and tradition takes in this story.

2. Nnaemeka's father, Okeke, rejects a neighbor's suggestion that he call a doctor to treat his son's "sickness" because, we are told, he is "ahead of his more superstitious neighbours" (para. 48). Does the story provide evidence that Okeke is more enlightened than the others in his village? Explain.

On Style

What is the narrator's attitude toward the story he is telling? How does his attitude affect your reading of it?

Making Connections

Like this story, Faulkner's "A Rose for Emily" (p. 666) and Mukherjee's "Orbiting" (p. 704) focus on courtship and marriage to dramatize the theme of cultural conflict. In what ways are the conflicts similar? In what ways different?

Writing Topic

Have you or someone you know experienced family resistance or criticism for forming a relationship with someone from a different cultural background? Write a page explaining how you dealt with the problem.

Bharati Mukherjee   (b. 1940)

Orbiting   1988

On Thanksgiving morning I'm still in my nightgown thinking of Vic when Dad raps on my apartment door. Who's he rolling joints for, who's he initiating now into the wonders of his inner space? What got me on Vic is remembering last Thanksgiving and his famous cranberry sauce with Grand Marnier, which Dad had interpreted as a sign of permanence in my life. A man who cooks like Vic is ready for other commitments. Dad cannot imagine cooking as self-expression. You cook *for* someone. Vic's sauce was a sign of his permanent isolation, if you really want to know.

Dad's come to drop off the turkey. It's a seventeen-pounder. Mr. Vitelli knows to reserve a biggish one for us every Thanksgiving and Christmas. But this November what with Danny in the Marines, Uncle Carmine having to be very careful after the bypass, and Vic taking off for outer space as well, we might as well have made do with one of those turkey rolls you pick out of the freezer. And in other years, Mr. Vitelli would not have given us a frozen bird. We were proud of that, our birds were fresh killed. I don't bring this up to Dad.

"Your mama took care of the thawing," Dad says. "She said you wouldn't have room in your Frigidaire."

"You mean Mom said Rindy shouldn't be living in a dump, right?" Mom has the simple, immigrant faith that children should do better than their parents, and her definition of better is comfortingly rigid. Fair enough — I believed it, too. But the fact is all I can afford is this third-floor studio with an art deco shower. The fridge fits under the kitchenette counter. The room has potential. I'm content with that. And I *like* my job even though it's selling, not designing, jewelry made out of seashells and semiprecious stones out of a boutique in Bellevue Plaza.

Dad shrugs. "You're an adult, Renata." He doesn't try to lower himself into 5 one of my two deck chairs. He was a minor league catcher for a while and his knees went. The fake zebra-skin cushions piled as seats on the rug are out of the question for him. My futon bed folds up into a sofa, but the satin sheets are still lasciviously tangled. My father stands in a slat of sunlight, trying not to look embarrassed.

"Dad, I'd have come to the house and picked it up. You didn't have to make the extra trip out from Verona." A sixty-five-year-old man in wingtips and a Borsalino[1] hugging a wet, heavy bird is so poignant I have to laugh.

---

[1] A stylish brim hat.

"You wouldn't have gotten out of bed until noon, Renata." But Dad smiles. I know what he's saying. He's saying *he's* retired and *he* should be able to stay in bed till noon if he wants to, but he can't and he'd rather drive twenty miles with a soggy bird than read the *Ledger* one more time.

Grumbling and scolding are how we deMarcos express love. It's the North Italian way, Dad used to tell Cindi, Danny, and me when we were kids. Sicilians and Calabrians are emotional; we're contained. Actually, *he's* contained, the way Vic was contained for the most part. Mom's a Calabrian and she was born and raised there. Dad's very American, so Italy's a safe source of pride for him. I once figured it out: *his* father, Arturo deMarco, was a fifteen-week-old fetus when his mother planted her feet on Ellis Island. Dad, a proud son of North Italy, had one big adventure in his life, besides fighting in the Pacific, and that was marrying a Calabrian peasant. He made it sound as though Mom was a Korean or something, and their marriage was a kind of taming of the West, and that everything about her could be explained as a cultural deficiency. Actually, Vic could talk beautifully about his feelings. He'd brew espresso, pour it into tiny blue pottery cups and analyze our relationship. I should have listened. I mean really listened. I thought he was talking about us, but I know now he was only talking incessantly about himself. I put too much faith in mail-order nightgowns and bras.

"Your mama wanted me out of the house," Dad goes on. "She didn't used to be like this, Renata."

Renata and Carla are what we were christened. We changed to Rindy and 10 Cindi in junior high. Danny didn't have to make such leaps, unless you count dropping out of Montclair State and joining the Marines. He was always Danny, or Junior.

I lug the turkey to the kitchen sink where it can drip away at a crazy angle until I have time to deal with it.

"Your mama must have told you girls I've been acting funny since I retired."

"No, Dad, she hasn't said anything about you acting funny." What she *has* said is do we think she ought to call Doc Brunetti and have a chat about Dad? Dad wouldn't have to know. He and Doc Brunetti are, or were, on the same church league bowling team. So is, or was, Vic's dad, Vinny Riccio.

"Your mama thinks a man should have an office to drive to every day. I sat at a desk for thirty-eight years and what did I get? Ask Doc, I'm too embarrassed to say." Dad told me once Doc — his real name was Frankie, though no one ever called him that — had been called Doc since he was six years old and growing up with Dad in Little Italy. There was never a time in his life when Doc wasn't Doc, which made his professional decision very easy. Dad used to say, no one ever called me Adjuster when I was a kid. Why didn't they call me something like Sarge or Teach? Then I would have known better.

I wish I had something breakfasty in my kitchen cupboard to offer him. He 15 wants to stay and talk about Mom, which is the way old married people have. Let's talk about me means: What do you think of Mom? I'll take the turkey over means: When will Rindy settle down? I wish this morning I had bought the

Goodwill sofa for ten dollars instead of letting Vic haul off the fancy deck chairs from Fortunoff's. Vic had flash. He'd left Jersey a long time before he actually took off.

"I can make you tea."

"None of that herbal stuff."

We don't talk about Mom, but I know what he's going through. She's just started to find herself. He's not burned out, he's merely stuck. I remember when Mom refused to learn to drive, wouldn't leave the house even to mail a letter. Her litany those days was: when you've spent the first fifteen years of your life in a mountain village, when you remember candles and gaslight and carrying water from a well, not to mention holding in your water at night because of wolves and the unlit outdoor privy, you *like* being housebound. She used those wolves for all they were worth, as though imaginary wolves still nipped her heels in the Clifton Mall.

Before Mom began to find herself and signed up for a class at Paterson, she used to nag Cindi and me about finding the right men. "Men," she said; she wasn't coy, never. Unembarrassed, she'd tell me about her wedding night, about her first sighting of Dad's "thing" ("Land Ho!" Cindi giggled. "Thar she blows!" I chipped in.) and she'd giggle at our word for it, the common word, and she'd use it around us, never around Dad. Mom's peasant, she's earthy but never coarse. If I could get that across to Dad, how I admire it in men or in women, I would feel somehow redeemed of all my little mistakes with them, with men, with myself. Cindi and Brent were married on a cruise ship by the ship's captain. Tony, Vic's older brother, made a play for me my senior year. Tony's solid now. He manages a funeral home but he's invested in crayfish ponds on the side.

"You don't even own a dining table." Dad sounds petulant. He uses "even" a 20 lot around me. Not just a judgment, but a comparative judgment. Other people have dining tables. *Lots* of dining tables. He softens it a bit, not wanting to hurt me, wanting more for me to judge him a failure. "We've always had a sit-down dinner, hon."

Okay, so traditions change. This year dinner's potluck. So I don't have real furniture. I eat off stack-up plastic tables as I watch the evening news. I drink red wine and heat a pita bread on the gas burner and wrap it around alfalfa sprouts or green linguine. The Swedish knockdown dresser keeps popping its sides because Vic didn't glue it properly. Swedish engineering, he said, doesn't need glue. Think of Volvos, he said, and Ingmar Bergman. He isn't good with directions that come in four languages. At least he wasn't.

"Trust me, Dad." This isn't the time to spring new lovers on him. "A friend made me a table. It's in the basement."

"How about chairs?" Ah, my good father. He could have said, friend? What friend?

Marge, my landlady, has all kinds of junky stuff in the basement. "Jorge and I'll bring up what we need. You'd strain your back, Dad." Shot knees, bad back: daily pain but nothing fatal. Not like Carmine.

"Jorge? Is that the new boyfriend?" 25

Shocking him makes me feel good. It would serve him right if Jorge were my new boyfriend. But Jorge is Marge's other roomer. He gives Marge Spanish lessons, and does the heavy cleaning and the yard work. Jorge has family in El Salvador he's hoping to bring up. I haven't met Marge's husband yet. He works on an offshore oil rig in some emirate with a funny name.

"No, Dad." I explain about Jorge.

"El Salvador!" he repeats. "That means 'the Savior.' " He passes on the information with a kind of awe. It makes Jorge's homeland, which he's shown me pretty pictures of, seem messy and exotic, at the very rim of human comprehension.

After Dad leaves, I call Cindi, who lives fifteen minutes away on Upper Mountainside Road. She's eleven months younger and almost a natural blond, but we're close. Brent wasn't easy for me to take, not at first. He owns a discount camera and electronics store on Fifty-fourth in Manhattan. Cindi met him through Club Med. They sat on a gorgeous Caribbean beach and talked of hogs. His father is an Amish farmer in Kalona, Iowa. Brent, in spite of the obvious hairpiece and the gold chain, is a rebel. He was born Schwartzendruber, but changed his name to Schwartz. Now no one believes the Brent, either. They call him Bernie on the street and it makes everyone more comfortable. His father's never taken their buggy out of the county.

The first time Vic asked me out, he talked of feminism and holism and macrobiotics. Then he opened up on cinema and literature, and I was very impressed, as who wouldn't be? Ro, my current lover, is very different. He picked me up in an uptown singles bar that I and sometimes Cindi go to. He bought me a Cinzano and touched my breast in the dark. He was direct, and at the same time weirdly courtly. I took him home though usually I don't, at first. I learned in bed that night that the tall brown drink with the lemon twist he'd been drinking was Tab.

I went back on the singles circuit even though the break with Vic should have made me cautious. Cindi thinks Vic's a romantic. I've told her how it ended. One Sunday morning in March he kissed me awake as usual. He'd brought in the *Times* from the porch and was reading it. I made us some cinnamon rose tea. We had a ritual, starting with the real estate pages, passing remarks on the latest tacky towers. Not for us, we'd say, the view is terrible! No room for the servants, things like that. And our imaginary children's imaginary nanny. "Hi, gorgeous," I said. He is gorgeous, not strong, but showy. He said, "I'm leaving, babe. New Jersey doesn't do it for me anymore." I said, "Okay, so where're we going?" I had an awful job at the time, taking orders for MCI. Vic said, "I didn't say we, babe." So I asked, "You mean it's over? Just like that?" And he said, "Isn't that the best way? No fuss, no hang-ups." Then I got a little whiny. "But *why*?" I wanted to know. But he was macrobiotic in lots of things, including relationships. Yin and yang, hot and sour, green and yellow. "You know, Rindy, there are *places*. You don't fall off the earth when you leave Jersey, you know. Places you see pictures of and read about. Different weathers, different trees, different everything. Places that get the Cubs on cable instead of the Mets." He

30

was into that. For all the sophisticated things he liked to talk about, he was a very local boy. "Vic," I pleaded, "you're crazy. You need help." "I need help because I want to get out of Jersey? You gotta be kidding!" He stood up and for a moment I thought he would do something crazy, like destroy something, or hurt me. "Don't ever call me crazy, got that? And give me the keys to the van."

He took the van. Danny had sold it to me when the Marines sent him overseas. I'd have given it to him anyway, even if he hadn't asked.

"Cindi, I need a turkey roaster," I tell my sister on the phone.

"I'll be right over," she says. "The brat's driving me crazy."

"Isn't Franny's visit working out?"   35

"I could kill her. I think up ways. How does that sound?"

"Why not send her home?" I'm joking. Franny is Brent's twelve-year-old and he's shelled out a lot of dough to lawyers in New Jersey and Florida to work out visitation rights.

"Poor Brent. He feels so *divided,*" Cindi says. "He shouldn't have to take sides."

I want her to ask who my date is for this afternoon, but she doesn't. It's important to me that she like Ro, that Mom and Dad more than tolerate him.

All over the country, I tell myself, women are towing new lovers home to   40 meet their families. Vic is simmering cranberries in somebody's kitchen and explaining yin and yang. I check out the stuffing recipe. The gravy calls for cream and freshly grated nutmeg. Ro brought me six whole nutmegs in a Ziplock bag from his friend, a Pakistani, who runs a spice store in SoHo.[2] The nuts look hard and ugly. I take one out of the bag and sniff it. The aroma's so exotic my head swims. On an impulse I call Ro.

The phone rings and rings. He doesn't have his own place yet. He has to crash with friends. He's been in the States three months, maybe less. I let it ring fifteen, sixteen, seventeen times.

Finally someone answers. "Yes?" The voice is guarded, the accent obviously foreign even though all I'm hearing is a one-syllable word. Ro has fled here from Kabul. He wants to take classes at NJIT and become an electrical engineer. He says he's lucky his father got him out. A friend of Ro's father, a man called Mumtaz, runs a fried chicken restaurant in Brooklyn in a neighborhood Ro calls "Little Kabul," though probably no one else has ever noticed. Mr. Mumtaz puts the legal immigrants to work as waiters out front. The illegals hide in a backroom as pluckers and gutters.

"Ro? I miss you. We're eating at three, remember?"

"Who is speaking, please?"

So I fell for the accent, but it isn't a malicious error. I *can* tell one Afghan tribe 45 from another now, even by looking at them or by their names. I can make out

---

[2] A neighborhood south of Houston Street in Manhattan.

some Pashto words. "Tell Ro it's Rindy. Please? I'm a friend. He wanted me to call this number."

"Not knowing any Ro."

"Hey, wait. Tell him it's Rindy deMarco."

The guy hangs up on me.

I'm crumbling cornbread into a bowl for the stuffing when Cindi honks half of "King Cotton" from the parking apron in the back. Brent bought her the BMW on the gray market and saved a bundle — once discount, always discount — then spent three hundred dollars to put in a horn that beeps a Sousa march. I wave a potato masher at her from the back window. She doesn't get out of the car. Instead she points to the pan in the back seat. I come down, wiping my hands on a dish towel.

"I should stay and help." Cindi sounds ready to cry. But I don't want her with me when Ro calls back. 50

"You're doing too much already, kiddo." My voice at least sounds comforting. "You promised one veg and the salad."

"I ought to come up and help. That or get drunk." She shifts the stick. When Brent bought her the car, the dealer threw in driving gloves to match the upholstery.

"Get Franny to shred the greens," I call as Cindi backs up the car. "Get her involved."

The phone is ringing in my apartment. I can hear it ring from the second-floor landing.

"Ro?" 55

"You're taking a chance, my treasure. It could have been any other admirer, then where would you be?"

"I don't have any other admirers." Ro is not a conventionally jealous man, not like the types I have known. He's totally unlike any man I have ever known. He wants men to come on to me. Lately when we go to a bar he makes me sit far enough from him so some poor lonely guy thinks I'm looking for action. Ro likes to swagger out of a dark booth as soon as someone buys me a drink. I go along. He comes from a macho culture.

"How else will I know you are as beautiful as I think you are? I would not want an unprized woman," he says. He is asking me for time, I know. In a few more months he'll know I'm something of a catch in my culture, or at least I've never had trouble finding boys. Even Brent Schwartzendruber has begged me to see him alone.

"I'm going to be a little late," Ro says. "I told you about my cousin, Abdul, no?"

Ro has three or four cousins that I know of in Manhattan. They're all named 60 Abdul something. When I think of Abdul, I think of a giant black man with goggles on, running down a court. Abdul is the teenage cousin whom immigration officials nabbed as he was gutting chickens in Mumtaz's backroom. Abdul doesn't have the right papers to live and work in this country, and now he's been locked up in a detention center on Varick Street. Ro's afraid Abdul will be deported back to Afghanistan. If that happens, he'll be tortured.

"I have to visit him before I take the DeCamp bus. He's talking nonsense. He's talking of starting a hunger fast."

"A hunger strike! God!" When I'm with Ro I feel I am looking at America through the wrong end of a telescope. He makes it sound like a police state, with sudden raids, papers, detention centers, deportations, and torture and death waiting in the wings. I'm not a political person. Last fall I wore the Ferraro button because she's a woman and Italian.

"Rindy, all night I've been up and awake. All night I think of your splendid breasts. Like clusters of grapes, I think. I am stroking and fondling your grapes this very minute. My talk gets you excited?"

I tell him to test me, please get here before three. I remind him he can't buy his ticket on the bus.

"We got here too early, didn't we?" Dad stands just outside the door to my 65 apartment, looking embarrassed. He's in his best dark suit, the one he wears every Thanksgiving and Christmas. This year he can't do up the top button of his jacket.

"Don't be so formal, Dad." I give him a showy hug and pull him indoors so Mom can come in.

"As if your papa ever listens to me!" Mom laughs. But she sits primly on the sofa bed in her velvet cloak, with her tote bag and evening purse on her lap. Before Dad started courting her, she worked as a seamstress. Dad rescued her from a sweatshop. He married down, she married well. That's the family story.

"She told me to rush."

Mom isn't in a mood to squabble. I think she's reached the point of knowing she won't have him forever. There was Carmine, at death's door just a month ago. Anything could happen to Dad. She says, "Renata, look what I made! Crostolis." She lifts a cake tin out of her tote bag. The pan still feels warm. And for dessert, I know, there'll be a jar of super-thick, super-rich Death by Chocolate.

The story about Grandma deMarco, Dad's mama, is that every Thanksgiving 70 she served two full dinners, one American with the roast turkey, candied yams, pumpkin pie, the works, and another with Grandpa's favorite pastas.

Dad relaxes. He appoints himself bartender. "Don't you have more ice cubes, sweetheart?"

I tell him it's good Glenlivet. He shouldn't ruin it with ice, just a touch of water if he must. Dad pours sherry in Vic's pottery espresso cups for his women. Vic made them himself, and I used to think they were perfect blue jewels. Now I see they're lumpy, uneven in color.

"Go change into something pretty before Carla and Brent come." Mom believes in dressing up. Beaded dresses lift her spirits. She's wearing a beaded green dress today.

I take the sherry and vanish behind a four-panel screen, the kind long-legged showgirls change behind in black and white movies while their moustached lovers keep talking. My head barely shows above the screen's top, since I'm no long-legged showgirl. My best points, as Ro has said, are my clusters of grapes. Vic found the screen at a country auction in the Adirondacks. It had filled the van. Now I use the panels as a bulletin board and I'm worried Dad'll spot the notice for the next meeting of Amnesty International, which will bother him. He will think the two words stand for draft dodger and communist. I was going to drop my membership, a legacy of Vic, when Ro saw it and approved. Dad goes to the Sons of Italy Anti-Defamation dinners. He met Frank Sinatra at one. He voted for Reagan last time because the Democrats ran an Italian woman.

Instead of a thirties lover, it's my moustached papa talking to me from the 75 other side of the screen. "So where's this dining table?"

"Ro's got the parts in the basement. He'll bring it up, Dad."

I hear them whispering. "Bo? Now she's messing with a Southerner?" and "Shh, it's her business."

I'm just smoothing on my pantyhose when Mom screams for the cops. Dad shouts too, at Mom for her to shut up. It's my fault, I should have warned Ro not to use his key this afternoon.

I peek over the screen's top and see my lover the way my parents see him. He's a slight, pretty man with hazel eyes and a tufty moustache, so whom can he intimidate? I've seen Jews and Greeks, not to mention Sons of Italy, darker-skinned than Ro. Poor Ro resorts to his Kabuli prep-school manners.

"How do you do, Madam! Sir! My name is Roashan." 80

Dad moves closer to Ro but doesn't hold out his hand. I can almost read his mind: *he speaks.* "Come again?" he says, baffled.

I cringe as he spells his name. My parents are so parochial. With each letter he does a graceful dip and bow. "Try it syllable by syllable, sir. Then it is not so hard."

Mom stares past him at me. The screen doesn't hide me because I've strayed too far in to watch the farce. "Renata, you're wearing only your camisole."

I pull my crew neck over my head, then kiss him. I make the kiss really sexy so they'll know I've slept with this man. Many times. And if he asks me, I will marry him. I had not known that till now. I think my mother guesses.

He's brought flowers: four long-stemmed, stylish purple blossoms in a florist's 85 paper cone. "For you, madam." He glides over the dirty broadloom to Mom who fills up more than half the sofa bed. "This is my first Thanksgiving dinner, for which I have much to give thanks, no?"

"He was born in Afghanistan," I explain. But Dad gets continents wrong. He says, "We saw your famine camps on TV. Well, you won't starve this afternoon."

"They smell good," Mom says. "Thank you very much but you shouldn't spend a fortune."

"No, no, madam. What you smell good is my cologne. Flowers in New York have no fragrance."

"His father had a garden estate outside Kabul." I don't want Mom to think he's putting down American flowers, though in fact he is. Along with American fruits, meats, and vegetables. "The Russians bulldozed it," I add.

Dad doesn't want to talk politics. He senses, looking at Ro, this is not the face 90 of Ethiopian starvation. "Well, what'll it be, Roy? Scotch and soda?" I wince. It's not going well.

"Thank you but no. I do not imbibe alcoholic spirits, though I have no objection for you, sir." My lover goes to the fridge and reaches down. He knows just where to find his Tab. My father is quietly livid, staring down at his drink.

In my father's world, grown men bowl in leagues and drink the best whiskey they can afford. Dad whistles "My Way." He must be under stress. That's his usual self-therapy: how would Francis Albert handle this?

"Muslims have taboos, Dad." Cindi didn't marry a Catholic, so he has no right to be upset about Ro, about us.

"Jews," Dad mutters. "So do Jews." He knows because catty-corner from Vitelli's is a kosher butcher. This isn't the time to parade new words before him, like *halal,* the Muslim kosher. An Italian-American man should be able to live sixty-five years never having heard the word, I can go along with that. Ro, fortunately, is cosmopolitan. Outside of pork and booze, he eats anything else I fix.

Brent and Cindi take forever to come. But finally we hear his MG squeal in 95 the driveway. Ro glides to the front window; he seems to blend with the ficus tree and hanging ferns. Dad and I wait by the door.

"Party time!" Brent shouts as he maneuvers Cindi and Franny ahead of him up three flights of stairs. He looks very much the head of the family, a rich man steeply in debt to keep up appearances, to compete, to head off middle age. He's at that age — and Cindi's nowhere near that age — when people notice the difference and quietly judge it. I know these things from Cindi — I'd never guess it from looking at Brent. If he feels divided, as Cindi says he does, it doesn't show. Misery, anxiety, whatever, show on Cindi though; they bring her cheekbones out. When I'm depressed, my hair looks rough, my skin breaks out. Right now, I'm lustrous.

Brent does a lot of whooping and hugging at the door. He even hugs Dad who looks grave and funereal like an old-world Italian gentleman because of his outdated, pinched dark suit. Cindi makes straight for the fridge with her casserole of squash and browned marshmallow. Franny just stands in the middle of the room holding two biggish Baggies of salad greens and vinaigrette in an old Dijon mustard jar. Brent actually bought the mustard in Dijon, a story that Ro is bound to hear and not appreciate. Vic was mean enough last year to tell him that he could have gotten it for more or less the same price at the Italian specialty foods store down on Watchung Plaza. Franny doesn't seem to have her own winter clothes. She's wearing Cindi's car coat over a Dolphins sweatshirt. Her mother moved down to Florida the very day the divorce became final. She's got a Walkman tucked into the pocket of her cords.

"You could have trusted me to make the salad dressing at least," I scold my sister.

Franny gives up the Baggies and the jar of dressing to me. She scrutinizes us — Mom, Dad, me and Ro, especially Ro, as though she can detect something strange about him — but doesn't take off her earphones. A smirk starts twitching her tanned, feral features. I see what she is seeing. Asian men carry their bodies differently, even these famed warriors from the Khyber Pass. Ro doesn't stand like Brent or Dad. His hands hang kind of stiffly from the shoulder joints, and when he moves, his palms are tucked tight against his thighs, his stomach sticks out like a slightly pregnant woman's. Each culture establishes its own manly posture, different ways of claiming space. Ro, hiding among my plants, holds himself in a way that seems both too effeminate and too macho. I hate Franny for what she's doing to me. I am twenty-seven years old, I should be more mature. But I see now how wrong Ro's clothes are. He shows too much white collar and cuff. His shirt and his wool-blend flare-leg pants were made to measure in Kabul. The jacket comes from a discount store on Canal Street, part of a discontinued line of two-trousered suits. I ought to know, I took him there. I want to shake Franny or smash the earphones.

Cindi catches my exasperated look. "Don't pay any attention to her. She's   100 unsociable this weekend. We can't compete with the Depeche Mode."

I intend to compete.

Franny, her eyes very green and very hostile, turns on Brent. "How come she never gets it right, Dad?"

Brent hi-fives his daughter, which embarrasses her more than anyone else in the room. "It's a Howard Jones, hon," Brent tells Cindi.

Franny, close to tears, runs to the front window where Ro's been hanging back. She has an ungainly walk for a child whose support payments specify weekly ballet lessons. She bores in on Ro's hidey hole like Russian artillery. Ro moves back to the perimeter of family intimacy. I have no way of helping yet. I have to set out the dips and Tostitos. Brent and Dad are talking sports, Mom and Cindi are watching the turkey. Dad's going on about the Knicks. He's in despair, so early in the season. He's on his second Scotch. I see Brent try. "What do you think, Roy?" He's doing his best to get my lover involved. "Maybe we'll get lucky, huh? We can always hope for a top draft pick. End up with Patrick Ewing!" Dad brightens. "That guy'll change the game. Just wait and see. He'll fill the lane better than Russell." Brent gets angry, since for some strange Amish reason he's a Celtics fan. So was Vic. "Bird'll make a monkey out of him." He looks to Ro for support.

Ro nods. Even his headshake is foreign. "You are undoubtedly correct,   105 Brent," he says. "I am deferring to your judgment because currently I have not familiarized myself with these practices."

Ro loves squash, but none of my relatives have ever picked up a racket. I want to tell Brent that Ro's skied in St. Moritz, lost a thousand dollars in a casino in Beirut, knows where to buy Havana cigars without getting hijacked. He's sophisticated, he could make monkeys out of us all, but they think he's a retard.

Brent drinks three Scotches to Dad's two; then all three men go down to the basement. Ro and Brent do the carrying, negotiating sharp turns in the stairwell. Dad supervises. There are two trestles and a wide, splintery plywood top. "Try not to take the wall down!" Dad yells.

When they make it back in, the men take off their jackets to assemble the table. Brent's wearing a red lamb's wool turtleneck under his camel hair blazer. Ro unfastens his cuff links — they are 24-karat gold and his father's told him to sell them if funds run low — and pushes up his very white shirt sleeves. There are scars on both arms, scars that bubble against his dark skin, scars like lightning flashes under his thick black hair. Scar tissue on Ro is the color of freshwater pearls. I want to kiss it.

Cindi checks the turkey one more time. "You guys better hurry. We'll be ready to eat in fifteen minutes."

Ro, the future engineer, adjusts the trestles. He's at his best now. He's be- 110 come quite chatty. From under the plywood top, he's holding forth on the Soviet menace in Kabul. Brent may actually have an idea where Afghanistan is, in a general way, but Dad is lost. He's talking of being arrested for handing out pro-American pamphlets on his campus. Dad stiffens at "arrest" and blanks out the rest. He talks of this "so-called leader," this "criminal" named Babrak Karmal and I hear other buzz-words like Kandahār and Pamir, words that might have been Polish to me a month ago, and I can see even Brent is slightly embarrassed. It's his first exposure to Third World passion. He thought only Americans had informed political opinion — other people staged coups out of spite and misery. It's an unwelcome revelation to him that a reasonably educated and rational man like Ro would die for things that he, Brent, has never heard of and would rather laugh about. Ro was tortured in jail. Franny has taken off her earphones. Electrodes, canes, freezing tanks. He leaves nothing out. Something's gotten into Ro.

Dad looks sick. The meaning of Thanksgiving should not be so explicit. But Ro's in a daze. He goes on about how — *inshallah*[3] — his father, once a rich landlord, had stashed away enough to bribe a guard, sneak him out of this cell and hide him for four months in a tunnel dug under a servant's adobe hut until a forged American visa could be bought. Franny's eyes are wide, Dad joins Mom on the sofa bed, shaking his head. Jail, bribes, forged, what is this? I can read his mind. "For six days I must orbit one international airport to another," Ro is saying. "The main trick is having a valid ticket, that way the airline has to carry you, even if the country won't take you in. Colombo, Seoul, Bombay, Geneva, Frankfurt, I know too too well the transit lounges of many airports. We travel the world with our gym bags and prayer rugs, unrolling them in the transit lounges. The better airports have special rooms."

Brent tries to ease Dad's pain. "Say, buddy," he jokes, "you wouldn't be ripping us off, would you?"

---

[3] "God willing." Here, it is apparently used to mean "Thank God."

Ro snakes his slender body from under the makeshift table. He hasn't been watching the effect of his monologue. "I am a working man," he says stiffly. I have seen his special permit. He's one of the lucky ones, though it might not last. He's saving for NJIT. Meantime he's gutting chickens to pay for room and board in Little Kabul. He describes the gutting process. His face is transformed as he sticks his fist into imaginary roasters and grabs for gizzards, pulls out the squishy stuff. He takes an Afghan dagger out of the pocket of his pants. You'd never guess, he looks like such a victim. "This," he says, eyes glinting. "This is all I need."

"Cool," Franny says.

"Time to eat," Mom shouts. "I made the gravy with the nutmeg as you said, 115 Renata."

I lead Dad to the head of the table. "Everyone else sit where you want to."

Franny picks out the chair next to Ro before I can put Cindi there. I want Cindi to know him, I want her as an ally.

Dad tests the blade of the carving knife. Mom put the knife where Dad always sits when she set the table. He takes his thumb off the blade and pushes the switch. "That noise makes me feel good."

But I carry in the platter with the turkey and place it in front of Ro. "I want you to carve," I say.

He brings out his dagger all over again. Franny is practically licking his fin- 120 gers. "You mean this is a professional job?"

We stare fascinated as my lover slashes and slices, swiftly, confidently, at the huge, browned, juicy breast. The dagger scoops out flesh.

Now I am the one in a daze. I am seeing Ro's naked body as though for the first time, his nicked, scarred, burned body. In his body, the blemishes seem embedded, more beautiful, like wood. I am seeing character made manifest. I am seeing Brent and Dad for the first time, too. They have their little scars, things they're proud of, football injuries and bowling elbows they brag about. Our scars are so innocent; they are invisible and come to us from rough-housing gone too far. Ro hates to talk about his scars. If I trace the puckered tissue on his left thigh and ask "How, Ro?" he becomes shy, dismissive: a pack of dogs attacked him when he was a boy. The skin on his back is speckled and lumpy from burns, but when I ask he laughs. A crazy villager whacked him with a burning stick for cheekiness, he explains. He's ashamed that he comes from a culture of pain.

The turkey is reduced to a drying, whitened skeleton. On our plates, the slices are symmetrical, elegant. I realize all in a rush how much I love this man with his blemished, tortured body. I will give him citizenship if he asks. Vic was beautiful, but Vic was self-sufficient. Ro's my chance to heal the world.

I shall teach him how to walk like an American, how to dress like Brent but better, how to fill up a room as Dad does instead of melting and blending but sticking out in the Afghan way. In spite of the funny way he holds himself and the funny way he moves his head from side to side when he wants to say yes, Ro is Clint Eastwood, scarred hero and survivor. Dad and Brent are children. I realize Ro's the only circumcised man I've slept with.

Mom asks, "Why are you grinning like that, Renata?"   125

For Analysis

1. During the conversation with her father early in the story, Renata thinks: "This isn't the time to spring new lovers on him" (para. 22). What is she referring to?

2. Characterize Renata's previous lover, Vic. What relevance do her comments about him have to the theme of the story?

3. What do Brent and Renata's father talk about before dinner? What does Ro talk about? What do you make of the differences in their interests?

4. How do the various members of Renata's family feel about Ro? How does the family express its disapproval of Renata's choice of a boyfriend? How does Renata react to her family's disapproval?

5. What does the title mean?

6. Are Renata's expectations, described in paragraph 124, realistic? Explain.

On Style

Analyze the ways in which the **first-person narration** shapes the **theme** of this story.

Making Connections

1. What similarities and differences do you find between this story and Chinua Achebe's "Marriage Is a Private Affair" (p. 699)?

2. Have you ever been witness to the kind of cultural conflict dealt with in this story? Have you ever found yourself the outsider? Describe the experience.

Writing Topic

Write an essay analyzing how this story dramatizes the ways in which cultural barriers prevent Renata's family from seeing who Ro really is.

Alice Walker   (b. 1944)

Everyday Use   1973

For Your Grandmama

I will wait for her in the yard that Maggie and I made so clean and wavy yesterday afternoon. A yard like this is more comfortable than most people know. It is not just a yard. It is like an extended living room. When the hard clay is swept clean as a floor and the fine sand around the edges lined with tiny, irregular grooves anyone can come and sit and look up into the elm tree and wait for the breezes that never come inside the house.

Maggie will be nervous until after her sister goes: she will stand hopelessly in corners homely and ashamed of the burn scars down her arms and legs, eyeing her sister with a mixture of envy and awe. She thinks her sister has held life always in the palm of one hand, that "no" is a word the world never learned to say to her.

You've no doubt seen those TV shows where the child who has "made it" is confronted, as a surprise, by her own mother and father, tottering in weakly from backstage. (A pleasant surprise, of course: What would they do if parent and child came on the show only to curse out and insult each other?) On TV mother and child embrace and smile into each other's faces. Sometimes the mother and father weep, the child wraps them in her arms and leans across the table to tell how she would not have made it without their help. I have seen these programs.

Sometimes I dream a dream in which Dee and I are suddenly brought together on a TV program of this sort. Out of a dark and soft-seated limousine I am ushered into a bright room filled with many people. There I meet a smiling, gray, sporty man like Johnny Carson who shakes my hand and tells me what a fine girl I have. Then we are on the stage and Dee is embracing me with tears in her eyes. She pins on my dress a large orchid, even though she has told me once that she thinks orchids are tacky flowers.

In real life I am a large, big-boned woman with rough, man-working hands. 5 In the winter I wear flannel nightgowns to bed and overalls during the day. I can kill and clean a hog as mercilessly as a man. My fat keeps me hot in zero weather. I can work outside all day, breaking ice to get water for washing. I can eat pork liver cooked over the open fire minutes after it comes steaming from the hog. One winter I knocked a bull calf straight in the brain between the eyes with a sledge hammer and had the meat hung up to chill before nightfall. But of course all this does not show on television. I am the way my daughter would want me to be: a hundred pounds lighter, my skin like an uncooked barley pancake. My hair glistens in the hot bright lights. Johnny Carson has much to do to keep up with my quick and witty tongue.

But that is a mistake. I know even before I wake up. Who ever knew a Johnson with a quick tongue? Who can even imagine me looking a strange white man in the eye? It seems to me I have talked to them always with one foot raised in flight, with my head turned in whichever way is farthest from them. Dee, though. She would always look anyone in the eye. Hesitation was no part of her nature.

"How do I look, Mama?" Maggie says, showing just enough of her thin body enveloped in pink skirt and red blouse for me to know she's there, almost hidden by the door.

"Come out into the yard," I say.

Have you ever seen a lame animal, perhaps a dog run over by some careless person rich enough to own a car, sidle up to someone who is ignorant enough to be kind to him? That is the way my Maggie walks. She has been like this, chin on chest, eyes on ground, feet in shuffle, ever since the fire that burned the other house to the ground.

Dee is lighter than Maggie, with nicer hair and a fuller figure. She's a woman   10 now, though sometimes I forget. How long ago was it that the other house burned? Ten, twelve years? Sometimes I can still hear the flames and feel Maggie's arms sticking to me, her hair smoking and her dress falling off her in little black papery flakes. Her eyes seemed stretched open, blazed open by the flames reflected in them. And Dee. I see her standing off under the sweet gum tree she used to dig gum out of; a look of concentration on her face as she watched the last dingy gray board of the house fall in toward the red-hot brick chimney. Why don't you do a dance around the ashes? I'd wanted to ask her. She had hated the house that much.

I used to think she hated Maggie, too. But that was before we raised the money, the church and me, to send her to Augusta to school. She used to read to us without pity; forcing words, lies, other folks' habits, whole lives upon us two, sitting trapped and ignorant underneath her voice. She washed us in a river of make-believe, burned us with a lot of knowledge we didn't necessarily need to know. Pressed us to her with the serious way she read, to shove us away at just the moment, like dimwits, we seemed about to understand.

Dee wanted nice things. A yellow organdy dress to wear to her graduation from high school; black pumps to match a green suit she'd made from an old suit somebody gave me. She was determined to stare down any disaster in her efforts. Her eyelids would not flicker for minutes at a time. Often I fought off the temptation to shake her. At sixteen she had a style of her own: and knew what style was.

I never had an education myself. After second grade the school was closed down. Don't ask me why: in 1927 colored asked fewer questions than they do now. Sometimes Maggie reads to me. She stumbles along good-naturedly but can't see well. She knows she is not bright. Like good looks and money, quickness passed her by. She will marry John Thomas (who has mossy teeth in an earnest face) and then I'll be free to sit here and I guess just sing church songs to myself. Although I never was a good singer. Never could carry a tune. I was always better at a man's job. I used to love to milk till I was hoofed in the side in '49. Cows are soothing and slow and don't bother you, unless you try to milk them the wrong way.

I have deliberately turned my back on the house. It is three rooms, just like the one that burned, except the roof is tin; they don't make shingle roofs any more. There are no real windows, just some holes cut in the sides, like the port-holes in a ship, but not round and not square, with rawhide holding the shutters up on the outside. This house is in a pasture, too, like the other one. No doubt when Dee sees it she will want to tear it down. She wrote me once that no mat-ter where we "choose" to live, she will manage to come see us. But she will never bring her friends. Maggie and I thought about this and Maggie asked me, "Mama, when did Dee ever *have* any friends?"

She had a few. Furtive boys in pink shirts hanging about on washday after   15 school. Nervous girls who never laughed. Impressed with her they worshiped the well-turned phrase, the cute shape, the scalding humor that erupted like bubbles in lye. She read to them.

When she was courting Jimmy T she didn't have much time to pay to us, but turned all her faultfinding power on him. He *flew* to marry a cheap gal from a family of ignorant flashy people. She hardly had time to recompose herself.

When she comes I will meet — but there they are!

Maggie attempts to make a dash for the house, in her shuffling way, but I stay her with my hand. "Come back here," I say. And she stops and tries to dig a well in the sand with her toe.

It is hard to see them clearly through the strong sun. But even the first glimpse of leg out of the car tells me it is Dee. Her feet were always neat-looking, as if God himself had shaped them with a certain style. From the other side of the car comes a short, stocky man. Hair is all over his head a foot long and hanging from his chin like a kinky mule tail. I hear Maggie suck in her breath. "Uhnnnh," is what it sounds like. Like when you see the wriggling end of a snake just in front of your foot on the road. "Uhnnnh."

Dee next. A dress down to the ground, in this hot weather. A dress so loud it   20 hurts my eyes. There are yellows and oranges enough to throw back the light of the sun. I feel my whole face warming from the heat waves it throws out. Ear-rings, too, gold and hanging down to her shoulders. Bracelets dangling and making noises when she moves her arm up to shake the folds of the dress out of her armpits. The dress is loose and flows, and as she walks closer, I like it. I hear Maggie go "Uhnnnh" again. It is her sister's hair. It stands straight up like the wool on a sheep. It is black as night and around the edges are two long pigtails that rope about like small lizards disappearing behind her ears.

"Wa-su-zo-Tean-o!" she says, coming on in that gliding way the dress makes her move. The short stocky fellow with the hair to his navel is all grinning and he follows up with "Asalamalakim, my mother and sister!" He moves to hug Mag-gie but she falls back, right up against the back of my chair. I feel her trembling there and when I look up I see the perspiration falling off her chin.

"Don't get up," says Dee. Since I am stout it takes something of a push. You can see me trying to move a second or two before I make it. She turns, showing white heels through her sandals, and goes back to the car. Out she peeks next with a Polaroid. She stoops down quickly and lines up picture after picture of me sitting there in front of the house with Maggie cowering behind me. She never takes a shot without making sure the house is included. When a cow comes nibbling around the edge of the yard she snaps it and me and Maggie *and* the house. Then she puts the Polaroid in the back seat of the car, and comes up and kisses me on the forehead.

Meanwhile Asalamalakim is going through motions with Maggie's hand. Maggie's hand is as limp as a fish, and probably as cold, despite the sweat, and she keeps trying to pull it back. It looks like Asalamalakim wants to shake hands but wants to do it fancy. Or maybe he don't know how people shake hands. Anyhow, he soon gives up on Maggie.

"Well," I say. "Dee."

"No, Mama," she says. "Not 'Dee,' Wangero Leewanika Kemanjo!" 25

"What happened to 'Dee'?" I wanted to know.

"She's dead," Wangero said. "I couldn't bear it any longer being named after the people who oppress me."

"You know as well as me you was named after your aunt Dicie," I said. Dicie is my sister. She named Dee. We called her "Big Dee" after Dee was born.

"But who was *she* named after?" asked Wangero.

"I guess after Grandma Dee," I said. 30

"And who was she named after?" asked Wangero.

"Her mother," I said, and saw Wangero was getting tired. "That's about as far back as I can trace it," I said. Though, in fact, I probably could have carried it back beyond the Civil War through the branches.

"Well," said Asalamalakim, "there you are."

"Uhnnnh," I heard Maggie say.

"There I was not," I said, "before 'Dicie' cropped up in our family, so why 35 should I try to trace it that far back?"

He just stood there grinning, looking down on me like somebody inspecting a Model A car. Every once in a while he and Wangero sent eye signals over my head.

"How do you pronounce this name?" I asked.

"You don't have to call me by it if you don't want to," said Wangero.

"Why shouldn't I?" I asked. "If that's what you want us to call you, we'll call you."

"I know it might sound awkward at first," said Wangero. 40

"I'll get used to it," I said. "Ream it out again."

Well, soon we got the name out of the way. Asalamalakim had a name twice as long and three times as hard. After I tripped over it two or three times he told me to just call him Hakim-a-barber. I wanted to ask him was he a barber, but I didn't really think he was, so I didn't ask.

"You must belong to those beef-cattle peoples down the road," I said. They said "Asalamalakim" when they met you, too, but they didn't shake hands. Always too busy: feeding the cattle, fixing the fences, putting up salt-lick shelters, throwing down hay. When the white folks poisoned some of the herd the men stayed up all night with rifles in their hands. I walked a mile and a half just to see the sight.

Hakim-a-barber said, "I accept some of their doctrines, but farming and raising cattle is not my style." (They didn't tell me, and I didn't ask, whether Wangero [Dee] had really gone and married him.)

We sat down to eat and right away he said he didn't eat collards and pork was   45
unclean. Wangero, though, went on through the chitlins and corn bread, the greens and everything else. She talked a blue streak over the sweet potatoes. Everything delighted her. Even the fact that we still used the benches her daddy made for the table when we couldn't afford to buy chairs.

"Oh, Mama!" she cried. Then turned to Hakim-a-barber. "I never knew how lovely these benches are. You can feel the rump prints," she said, running her hands underneath her and along the bench. Then she gave a sigh and her hand closed over Grandma Dee's butter dish. "That's it!" she said. "I knew there was something I wanted to ask you if I could have." She jumped up from the table and went over in the corner where the churn stood, the milk in its clabber by now. She looked at the churn and looked at it.

"This churn top is what I need," she said. "Didn't Uncle Buddy whittle it out of a tree you all used to have?"

"Yes," I said.

"Uh huh," she said happily. "And I want the dasher, too."

"Uncle Buddy whittle that, too?" asked the barber.   50

Dee (Wangero) looked up at me.

"Aunt Dee's first husband whittled the dash," said Maggie so low you almost couldn't hear her. "His name was Henry, but they called him Stash."

"Maggie's brain is like an elephant's," Wangero said, laughing. "I can use the churn top as a centerpiece for the alcove table," she said, sliding a plate over the churn, "and I'll think of something artistic to do with the dasher."

When she finished wrapping the dasher the handle stuck out. I took it for a moment in my hands. You didn't even have to look close to see where hands pushing the dasher up and down to make butter had left a kind of sink in the wood. In fact, there were a lot of small sinks; you could see where thumbs and fingers had sunk into the wood. It was beautiful light yellow wood, from a tree that grew in the yard where Big Dee and Stash had lived.

After dinner Dee (Wangero) went to the trunk at the foot of my bed and   55
started rifling through it. Maggie hung back in the kitchen over the dishpan. Out came Wangero with two quilts. They had been pieced by Grandma Dee and then Big Dee and me had hung them on the quilt frames on the front porch and quilted them. One was in the Lone Star pattern. The other was Walk Around the Mountain. In both of them were scraps of dresses Grandma Dee had worn fifty and more years ago. Bits and pieces of Grandpa Jarrell's Paisley shirts. And one teeny faded blue piece, about the size of a penny matchbox, that was from Great Grandpa Ezra's uniform that he wore in the Civil War.

"Mama," Wangero said sweet as a bird. "Can I have these old quilts?"

I heard something fall in the kitchen, and a minute later the kitchen door slammed.

"Why don't you take one or two of the others?" I asked. "These old things was just done by me and Big Dee from some tops your grandma pieced before she died."

"No," said Wangero. "I don't want those. They are stitched around the borders by machine."

"That'll make them last better," I said.   60

"That's not the point," said Wangero. "These are all pieces of dresses Grandma used to wear. She did all this stitching by hand. Imagine!" She held the quilts securely in her arms, stroking them.

"Some of the pieces, like those lavender ones, come from old clothes her mother handed down to her," I said, moving up to touch the quilts. Dee (Wangero) moved back just enough so that I couldn't reach the quilts. They already belonged to her.

"Imagine!" she breathed again, clutching them closely to her bosom.

"The truth is," I said, "I promised to give them quilts to Maggie, for when she marries John Thomas."

She gasped like a bee had stung her.   65

"Maggie can't appreciate these quilts!" she said. "She'd probably be backward enough to put them to everyday use."

"I reckon she would," I said. "God knows I been saving 'em for long enough with nobody using 'em. I hope she will!" I didn't want to bring up how I had offered Dee (Wangero) a quilt when she went away to college. Then she had told me they were old-fashioned, out of style.

"But they're *priceless!*" she was saying now, furiously; for she has a temper. "Maggie would put them on the bed and in five years they'd be in rags. Less than that!"

"She can always make some more," I said. "Maggie knows how to quilt."

Dee (Wangero) looked at me with hatred. "You just will not understand. The   70
point is these quilts, *these* quilts!"

"Well," I said, stumped. "What would *you* do with them?"

"Hang them," she said. As if that was the only thing you *could* do with quilts.

Maggie by now was standing in the door. I could almost hear the sound her feet made as they scraped over each other.

"She can have them, Mama," she said, like somebody used to never winning anything, or having anything reserved for her. "I can 'member Grandma Dee without the quilts."

I looked at her hard. She had filled her bottom lip with checkerberry snuff   75
and it gave her face a kind of dopey, hangdog look. It was Grandma Dee and Big Dee who taught her how to quilt herself. She stood there with her scarred hands hidden in the folds of her skirt. She looked at her sister with something like fear but she wasn't mad at her. This was Maggie's portion. This was the way she knew God to work.

When I looked at her like that something hit me in the top of my head and ran down to the soles of my feet. Just like when I'm in church and the spirit of

God touches me and I get happy and shout. I did something I never had done before: hugged Maggie to me, then dragged her on into the room, snatched the quilts out of Miss Wangero's hands and dumped them into Maggie's lap. Maggie just sat there on my bed with her mouth open.

"Take one or two of the others," I said to Dee.

But she turned without a word and went out to Hakim-a-barber.

"You just don't understand," she said, as Maggie and I came out to the car.

"What don't I understand?" I wanted to know.   80

"Your heritage," she said. And then she turned to Maggie, kissed her, and said, "You ought to try to make something of yourself, too, Maggie. It's really a new day for us. But from the way you and Mama still live you'd never know it."

She put on some sunglasses that hid everything above the tip of her nose and her chin.

Maggie smiled; maybe at the sunglasses. But a real smile, not scared. After we watched the car dust settle I asked Maggie to bring me a dip of snuff. And then the two of us sat there just enjoying, until it was time to go in the house and go to bed.

For Analysis

1. What are the narrator's outstanding traits, her weaknesses and her strengths?

2. How would you characterize the narrator's feelings about her daughter Dee? About her daughter Maggie?

3. How would you characterize the narrator's descriptions of herself? Are her actions consistent with the kind of person she says she is? Explain.

4. Why does the narrator recall the burning of the house? How does this event from the past help the reader understand the present action?

5. What are the sources of the story's humor?

6. What does Dee's boyfriend, Asalamalakim, represent?

7. Why does the narrator give the quilts to Maggie?

8. Explain the title. What is the meaning of the subtitle, "For Your Grandmama"?

On Style

1. Examine the function of the quilts as a **symbol**.

2. Analyze the way in which Walker creates the sense of a narrator speaking spontaneously though in fact the story is carefully structured.

Making Connections

Compare Dee in this story, Hulga in Flannery O'Connor's "Good Country People" (p. 118), and Miss Moore in Bambara's "The Lesson" (p. 134) as characters whose intellectual and educational superiority enables them to unsettle the tranquillity of those around them.

Writing Topics

1. Analyze the opening two paragraphs of the story, showing how they set the **tone** and establish the tension of the story.

2. Write an essay analyzing the **conflict** in this story and the way it is resolved. Is the resolution satisfying?

Barry Holstun Lopez (b. 1945)

Winter Count 1973: Geese, They Flew Over in a Storm 1981

He followed the bellboy off the elevator, through a foyer with forlorn leather couches, noting how low the ceiling was, with its white plaster flowers in bas-relief — and that there were no windows. He followed him down a long corridor dank with an air of fugitives, past dark, impenetrable doors. At the distant end of the next corridor he saw gray thunderheads and the black ironwork of a fire escape. The boy slowed down and reached out to slide a thick key into the lock and he heard the sudden alignment of steel tumblers and their ratchet click. The door swung open and the boy entered, with the suitcase bouncing against the crook at the back of his knee.

He tipped the boy, having no idea what amount was now thought proper. The boy departed, leaving the room sealed off as if in a vacuum. The key with the ornate brass fob lay on a glass table. The man stood by the bed with his hands folded at his lips as though in prayer. Slowly he cleared away the drapes, the curtains and the blinds and stared out at the bare sky. Wind whipped rain in streaks across the glass. He had never been to New Orleans. It was a vague streamer blowing in his memory, like a boyhood acquaintance with Lafcadio Hearn. Natchez Trace. Did Choctaw live here? he wondered. Or Chitamacha? Before them, worshippers of the sun.

He knew the plains better. Best. The high plains north of the Platte River.

He took off his shoes and lay on the bed. He was glad for the feel of the candlewick bedspread. Or was it chenille? He had had this kind of spread on his bed when he was a child. He removed his glasses and pinched the bridge of his nose. In all these years he had delivered so few papers, had come to enjoy much more listening to them, to the stories unfolding in them. It did not matter to him that the arguments were so abstruse they were all but impregnable, that the thought in them would turn to vapor, an arrested breath. He came to hear a story unfold, to regard its shape and effect. He thought one unpacked history, that it came like pemmican in a parfleche and was to be consumed in a hard winter.

The wind sucked at the windows and released them suddenly to rattle in their 5 metal frames. It made him think of home, of the Sand Hills. He lay motionless on the bed and thought of the wind. Crow men racing naked in an April rain, with their hair, five-foot-long black banners, spiraling behind, splashing on the muscled rumps of white horses with brown ears.

1847 One man alone defended the Hat in a fight with the Crow

1847 White buffalo, Dusk killed it

1847 Daughter of Turtle Head, her clothes caught fire and she was burned up

1847 Three men who were women came

He got up and went to his bag. He took out three stout willow sticks and bound them as a tripod. From its apex he hung a beaded bag of white elk hide with long fringe. The fringe was wrinkled from having been folded against itself in his suit pocket.

1891 Medicine bundles, police tore them open

What did they want from him? A teacher. He taught, he did not write papers. He told the story of people coming up from the Tigris-Euphrates, starting there. Other years he would start in a different place — Olduvai, Afar Valley. Or in Tierra del Fuego with the Onas. He could as easily start in the First World of the Navajo. The point, he told his students, was not this. There was no point. It was a slab of meat. It was a rhythm to dance to. It was a cloak that cut the wind when it blew hard enough to crack your soul.

1859 Ravens froze, fell over

1804 Heavy spring snow. Even the dogs went snow-blind

He slept. In his rumpled suit. In the flat, reflected storm light his face appeared ironed smooth. The wind fell away from the building and he dreamed.

For a moment he was lost. Starlight Room. Tarpon Room. Oak Room. He was due — he thought suddenly of aging, of illness: *when our children, they had strangulations of the throat,* of the cure for *any* illness as he scanned the long program — in the Creole Room. He was due in the Creole Room. Roger Callahan, Nebraska State College: "Winter Counts from the Dakota, the Crow and the Blackfeet: Personal Histories." Jesus, he thought, why had he come? He had been asked. They had asked.

"Aha, Roger."

"I'm on time? I got — "

"You come right this way. I want you in front here. Everyone is very excited, very excited, you know. We're very glad you came. And how is Margaret?"

"Yes — . Margaret died. She died two years ago."

10

1837 Straight Calf took six horses from the Crow and gave them to Blue Cloud
Woman's father and took her

1875 White Hair, he was killed in a river by an Omaha man

1943 John Badger Heart killed in an automobile crash

He did not hear the man. He sat. The histories began to cover him over like
willows, thick as creek willows, and he reached out to steady himself in the pool
of time.

He listened patiently to the other papers. Edward Rice Phillips, Purdue: 15
"The Okipa Ceremony and Mandan Sexual Habits." The Mandan, he thought,
they were all dead. Who would defend them? Renata Morrison, University of
Texas: "The Role of Women in Northern Plains Religious Ceremonials."

1818 Sparrow Woman promised the Sun Dance in winter if the Cree didn't find us

1872 Comes Out of the Water, she ran off the Assiniboine horses

1904 Moving Gently, his sister hung herself

He tried to listen, but the words fell away like tumbled leaves. Cottonwoods.
Winters so bad they would have to cut down cottonwood trees for the horses to
eat. *So cold we got water from beaver holes only.* And years when they had to eat
the horses. *We killed our ponies and ate them. No buffalo.*

Inside the windowless room (he could not remember which floor the elevator
had opened on) everyone was seated in long rows. From the first row he could
not see anyone. He shifted in his seat and his leather bag fell with a slap against
the linoleum floor. How long had he been carrying papers from one place to
another like this? He remembered a friend's poem about a snowy owl dead
behind glass in a museum, no more to soar, to hunch and spread his wings and
tail and fall silent as moonlight.

1809 Blue feathers found on the ground from unknown birds

1811 Weasel Sits Down came into camp with blue feathers tied in his hair

There was distant applause, like dry brush rattling in the wind.

Years before, defense of theory had concerned him. Not now. "I've thrown
away everything that is no good," he told a colleague one summer afternoon on
his porch, as though shouting over the roar of a storm. "I can no longer think of
anything worse than proving you are right." He took what was left and he went
on from there.

1851 No meat in camp. A man went to look for buffalo and was killed by two Arapaho

1854 The year they dragged the Arapaho's head through camp

". . . and my purpose in aligning these four examples is to clearly demonstrate 20
an irrefutable, or what I consider an irrefutable, relationship: the Arikara
never . . ."

When he was a boy his father had taken him one April morning to watch
whooping cranes on estuaries of the Platte, headed for Alberta. The morning
was crucial in the unfolding of his own life.

> 1916 My father drives east for hours in silence. We walk out into a field covered all
> over with river fog. The cranes, just their legs are visible

His own count would be personal, more personal, as though he were the only
one.

> 1918 Father, shot dead. Argonne forest

The other years came around him now like soft velvet noses of horses touching his arms in the dark.

". . . while the Cheyenne, contrary to what Greenwold has had to say on this
point but reinforcing what has been stated previously by Gregg and Houston,
were more inclined . . ."

He wished for something to hold, something to touch, to strip leaves bare- 25
handed from a chokecherry branch or to hear rain falling on the surface of a
lake. In this windowless room he ached.

> 1833 Stars blowing around like snow. Some fall to the earth

> 1856 Reaches into the Enemy's Tipi has a dream and can't speak

> 1869 Fire Wagon, it comes

Applause.

He stood up and walked in quiet shoes to the stage. (Once in the middle of
class he had stopped to explain his feeling about walking everywhere in silence.)
He set his notes on the podium and covered them with his hands. In a clear
voice, without apology for his informality or a look at his papers, he unfolded the
winter counts of the Sioux warrior Blue Thunder, of the Blackfeet Bad Head,
and of the Crow Extends His Paw. He stated that these were personal views of
history, sometimes metaphorical, bearing on a larger, tribal history. He spoke of
the confusion caused by translators who had tried to force agreement among
several winter counts or who mistook mythic time for some other kind of real
time. He concluded by urging less contention. "As professional historians, we
have too often subordinated one system to another and forgotten all together
the individual view, the poetic view, which is as close to the truth as the consensus. Or it can be as distant."

He felt the necklace of hawk talons pressing against his clavicles under the
weight of his shirt.

The applause was respectful, thin, distracted. As he stepped away from the podium he realized it was perhaps foolish to have accepted the invitation. He could no longer make a final point. He had long ago lost touch with the definitive, the awful distance of reason. He wanted to go back to the podium. You can only tell the story as it was given to you, he wanted to say. Do not lie. Do not make it up.

He hesitated for a moment at the edge of the stage. He wished he were back 30 in Nebraska with his students, to warn them: it is too dangerous for everyone to have the same story. The same things do not happen to everyone.

He passed through the murmuring crowd, through a steel fire door, down a hallway, up a flight of stairs, another, and emerged into palms in the lobby.

> 1823 A man, he was called Fifteen Horses, who was heyoka, a contrary, sacred clown, ran at the Crow backwards, shooting arrows at his own people. The Crow shot him in midair like a quail. He couldn't fool them

He felt the edge of self-pity, standing before a plate-glass window as wide as the spread of his arms and as tall as his house. He watched the storm that still raged, which he could not hear, which he had not been able to hear, bend trees to breaking, slash the surface of Lake Pontchartrain and raise air boiling over the gulf beyond. "Everything is held together with stories," he thought. "That is all that is holding us together, stories and compassion."

He turned quickly from the cold glass and went up in the silent elevator and ordered dinner. When it came, he threw back the drapes and curtains and opened the windows. The storm howled through his room and roared through his head. He breathed the wet air deep into his lungs. In the deepest distance, once, he heard the barking-dog sounds of geese, running like horses before a prairie thunderstorm.

For Analysis

1. Examine the diction of the opening paragraph, the objects that are described, and the adjectives that are used to characterize them. What kind of tone do they establish?

2. Why does Roger Callahan prefer listening to papers rather than delivering them?

3. Why do you suppose Roger Callahan carries a medicine bag and wears a hawk-talon necklace?

4. Who do you imagine Margaret was (paras. 12–13)? What is the relevance of the brief dialogue about her?

5. How does Callahan's own "count" of his father fit into the pattern of the narrative? How does it help explain the power Callahan feels counts have?

6. Is there any relationship between Callahan and the last winter count anecdote about the "contrary" who ran backwards (para. 31)? Explain.

On Style

1. What is the effect of the various counts that punctuate the narrative? What connections are there among them and the narrative?

2. The story is comprised of various levels of narrative: (1) the narrative voice telling the story, (2) the various counts, (3) flashbacks, and (4) Roger Callahan's reading of his paper. Examine the way Lopez weaves these different narrative levels into a coherent story.

Making Connections

Compare this story and Louise Erdrich's "The Red Convertible" (p. 732) as celebrations of Native American culture within the context of the dominant American culture. Do these very different stories embody, in a broad sense, similar views about Native American culture? In what sense do these stories criticize the dominant culture?

Writing Topics

1. In an essay, expand on Callahan's statement to his colleague: " 'I can no longer think of anything worse than proving you are right' " (para. 19).

2. Keeping in mind the contrast between Native American historical observations and the scholarly papers being read at the academic meeting, discuss Callahan's concluding remark to the audience: "As professional historians, we have too often subordinated one system to another and forgotten all together the individual view, the poetic view, which is as close to the truth as the consensus. Or it can be as distant" (para. 27).

Jamaica Kincaid (b. 1949)

Girl (1983)

Wash the white clothes on Monday and put them on the stone heap; wash the color clothes on Tuesday and put them on the clothesline to dry; don't walk barehead in the hot sun; cook pumpkin fritters in very hot sweet oil; soak your little clothes right after you take them off; when buying cotton to make yourself a nice blouse, be sure that it doesn't have gum on it, because that way it won't hold up well after a wash; soak salt fish overnight before you cook it; is it true that you sing benna[1] in Sunday school?; always eat your food in such a way that it won't turn someone else's stomach; on Sundays try to walk like a lady and not like the slut you are so bent on becoming; don't sing benna in Sunday school; you mustn't speak to wharf-rat boys, not even to give directions; don't eat fruits on the street — flies will follow you; *but I don't sing benna on Sundays at all and never in Sunday school;* this is how to sew on a button; this is how to make a button-hole for the button you have just sewed on; this is how to hem a dress when you see the hem coming down and so to prevent yourself from look-ing like the slut I know you are so bent on becoming; this is how you iron your father's khaki shirt so that it doesn't have a crease; this is how you iron your father's khaki pants so that they don't have a crease; this is how you grow okra — far from the house, because okra tree harbors red ants; when you are growing dasheen,[2] make sure it gets plenty of water or else it makes your throat itch when you are eating it; this is how you sweep a corner; this is how you sweep a whole house; this is how you sweep a yard; this is how you smile to someone you don't like too much; this is how you set a table for dinner with an important guest; this is how you smile to someone you don't like at all; this is how you smile to someone you like completely; this is how you set a table for tea; this is how you set a table for dinner; this is how you set a table for lunch; this is how you set a table for breakfast; this is how to behave in the presence of men who don't know you very well, and this way they won't recognize immediately the slut I have warned you against becoming; be sure to wash every day, even if it is with your own spit; don't squat down to play marbles — you are not a boy, you know; don't pick people's flowers — you might catch something; don't throw stones at blackbirds, because it might not be a blackbird at all; this is how to make a bread pudding; this is how to make doukona;[3] this is how to make pepper pot; this is how to make a good medicine for a cold; this is how to make a good medicine to

[1] Calypso music.
[2] Taro root.
[3] Spicy plantain pudding.

730

throw away a child before it even becomes a child; this is how to catch a fish; this is how to throw back a fish you don't like, and that way something bad won't fall on you; this is how to bully a man; this is how a man bullies you; this is how to love a man, and if this doesn't work there are other ways, and if they don't work don't feel too bad about giving up; this is how to spit up in the air if you feel like it, and this is how to move quick so that it doesn't fall on you; this is how to make ends meet; always squeeze bread to make sure it's fresh; *but what if the baker won't let me feel the bread?*; you mean to say that after all you are really going to be the kind of woman who the baker won't let near the bread? 40

For Analysis

1. What does the title of this short piece suggest?

2. Who is the speaker? To whom is she speaking?

3. What kind of "girl" is the advice intended to produce?

4. What is the speaker's biggest fear?

5. Are the two responses of the girl spoken aloud to the speaker, or are they only the girl's thoughts? Explain.

6. What do the two responses from the girl suggest about her relationship to the speaker?

On Style

1. What effect does Kincaid achieve by making the story a virtually uninterrupted flow of the speaker's advice to the girl?

2. What is the effect of the seemingly random juxtaposition of subjects, as, for example, "this is how to make a good medicine for a cold; this is how to make a good medicine to throw away a child before it even becomes a child" (ll. 32–34)?

3. Which elements of conventional fiction — plot, character, setting, suspense, and so forth — do you find in this dialogue?

4. Characterize the **tone** of this story.

Making Connections

1. Compare the girl in this story with Sylvia, the narrator of Toni Cade Bambara's "The Lesson" (p. 134).

2. Characterize the parent in this story and then compare him or her with the parent in Peter Meinke's poem "Advice to My Son" (p. 171). How do they differ? Do they share any qualities?

Writing Topics

1. List the advice you received from your parents and other elders, and write a paragraph in imitation of Kincaid's piece.

2. Examine closely the details that constitute the advice in this story. What kind of society and culture do these details seem to suggest?

Louise Erdrich (b. 1954)

The Red Convertible 1984

Lyman Lamartine

I was the first one to drive a convertible on my reservation. And of course it was red, a red Olds. I owned that car along with my brother Henry Junior. We owned it together until his boots filled with water on a windy night and he bought out my share. Now Henry owns the whole car, and his youngest brother Lyman (that's myself), Lyman walks everywhere he goes.

How did I earn enough money to buy my share in the first place? My own talent was I could always make money. I had a touch for it, unusual in a Chippewa. From the first I was different that way, and everyone recognized it. I was the only kid they let in the American Legion Hall to shine shoes, for example, and one Christmas I sold spiritual bouquets for the mission door to door. The nuns let me keep a percentage. Once I started, it seemed the more money I made the easier the money came. Everyone encouraged it. When I was fifteen I got a job washing dishes at the Joliet Café, and that was where my first big break happened.

It wasn't long before I was promoted to bussing tables, and then the short-order cook quit and I was hired to take her place. No sooner than you know it I was managing the Joliet. The rest is history. I went on managing. I soon became part owner, and of course there was no stopping me then. It wasn't long before the whole thing was mine.

After I'd owned the Joliet for one year, it blew over in the worst tornado ever seen around here. The whole operation was smashed to bits. A total loss. The fryalator was up in a tree, the grill torn in half like it was paper. I was only sixteen. I had it all in my mother's name, and I lost it quick, but before I lost it I had every one of my relatives, and their relatives, to dinner, and I also bought that red Olds I mentioned, along with Henry.

The first time we saw it! I'll tell you when we first saw it. We had gotten a ride 5 up to Winnipeg, and both of us had money. Don't ask me why, because we never mentioned a car or anything, we just had all our money. Mine was cash, a big bankroll from the Joliet's insurance. Henry had two checks — a week's extra pay for being laid off, and his regular check from the Jewel Bearing Plant.

We were walking down Portage anyway, seeing the sights, when we saw it. There it was, parked, large as life. Really as *if* it was alive. I thought of the word *repose,* because the car wasn't simply stopped, parked, or whatever. That car reposed, calm and gleaming, a FOR SALE sign in its left front window. Then, before we had thought it over at all, the car belonged to us and our pockets were empty. We had just enough money for gas back home.

732

We went places in that car, me and Henry. We took off driving all one whole summer. We started off toward the Little Knife River and Mandaree in Fort Berthold and then we found ourselves down in Wakpala somehow, and then suddenly we were over in Montana on the Rocky Boys, and yet the summer was not even half over. Some people hang on to details when they travel, but we didn't let them bother us and just lived our everyday lives here to there.

I do remember this one place with willows. I remember I laid under those trees and it was comfortable. So comfortable. The branches bent down all around me like a tent or a stable. And quiet, it was quiet, even though there was a powwow close enough so I could see it going on. The air was not too still, not too windy either. When the dust rises up and hangs in the air around the dancers like that, I feel good. Henry was asleep with his arms thrown wide. Later on, he woke up and we started driving again. We were somewhere in Montana, or maybe on the Blood Reserve — it could have been anywhere. Anyway it was where we met the girl.

All her hair was in buns around her ears, that's the first thing I noticed about her. She was posed alongside the road with her arm out, so we stopped. That girl was short, so short her lumber shirt looked comical on her, like a nightgown. She had jeans on and fancy moccasins and she carried a little suitcase.

"Hop on in," says Henry. So she climbs in between us.   10

"We'll take you home," I says. "Where do you live?"

"Chicken," she says.

"Where the hell's that?" I ask her.

"Alaska."

"Okay," says Henry, and we drive.   15

We got up there and never wanted to leave. The sun doesn't truly set there in summer, and the night is more a soft dusk. You might doze off, sometimes, but before you know it you're up again, like an animal in nature. You never feel like you have to sleep hard or put away the world. And things would grow up there. One day just dirt or moss, the next day flowers and long grass. The girl's name was Susy. Her family really took to us. They fed us and put us up. We had our own tent to live in by their house, and the kids would be in and out of there all day and night. They couldn't get over me and Henry being brothers, we looked so different. We told them we knew we had the same mother, anyway.

One night Susy came in to visit us. We sat around in the tent talking of this thing and that. The season was changing. It was getting darker by that time, and the cold was even getting just a little mean. I told her it was time for us to go. She stood up on a chair.

"You never seen my hair," Susy said.

That was true. She was standing on a chair, but still, when she unclipped her buns the hair reached all the way to the ground. Our eyes opened. You couldn't tell how much hair she had when it was rolled up so neatly. Then my brother Henry did something funny. He went up to the chair and said, "Jump on my shoulders." So she did that, and her hair reached down past his waist, and he started twirling, this way and that, so her hair was flung out from side to side.

"I always wondered what it was like to have long pretty hair," Henry says. 20 Well we laughed. It was a funny sight, the way he did it. The next morning we got up and took leave of those people.

On to greener pastures, as they say. It was down through Spokane and across Idaho then Montana and very soon we were racing the weather right along under the Canadian border through Columbus, Des Lacs, and then we were in Bottineau County and soon home. We'd made most of the trip, that summer, without putting up the car hood at all. We got home just in time, it turned out, for the army to remember Henry had signed up to join it.

I don't wonder that the army was so glad to get my brother that they turned him into a Marine. He was built like a brick outhouse anyway. We liked to tease him that they really wanted him for his Indian nose. He had a nose big and sharp as a hatchet, like the nose on Red Tomahawk, the Indian who killed Sitting Bull, whose profile is on signs all along the North Dakota highways. Henry went off to training camp, came home once during Christmas, then the next thing you know we got an overseas letter from him. It was 1970, and he said he was stationed up in the northern hill country. Whereabouts I did not know. He wasn't such a hot letter writer, and only got off two before the enemy caught him. I could never keep it straight, which direction those good Vietnam soldiers were from.

I wrote him back several times, even though I didn't know if those letters would get through. I kept him informed all about the car. Most of the time I had it up on blocks in the yard or half taken apart, because that long trip did a hard job on it under the hood.

I always had good luck with numbers, and never worried about the draft myself. I never even had to think about what my number was. But Henry was never lucky in the same way as me. It was at least three years before Henry came home. By then I guess the whole war was solved in the government's mind, but for him it would keep on going. In those years I'd put his car into almost perfect shape. I always thought of it as his car while he was gone, even though when he left he said, "Now it's yours," and threw me his key.

"Thanks for the extra key," I'd say. "I'll put it up in your drawer just in case I 25 need it." He laughed.

When he came home, though, Henry was very different, and I'll say this: the change was no good. You could hardly expect him to change for the better, I know. But he was quiet, so quiet, and never comfortable sitting still anywhere but always up and moving around. I thought back to times we'd sat still for whole afternoons, never moving a muscle, just shifting our weight along the ground, talking to whoever sat with us, watching things. He'd always had a joke, then, too, and now you couldn't get him to laugh, or when he did it was more the sound of a man choking, a sound that stopped up the throats of other people around him. They got to leaving him alone most of the time, and I didn't blame them. It was a fact: Henry was jumpy and mean.

I'd bought a color TV set for my mom and the rest of us while Henry was away. Money still came very easy. I was sorry I'd ever bought it though, because of Henry. I was also sorry I'd bought color, because with black-and-white the pictures seem older and farther away. But what are you going to do? He sat in front of it, watching it, and that was the only time he was completely still. But it was the kind of stillness that you see in a rabbit when it freezes and before it will bolt. He was not easy. He sat in his chair gripping the armrests with all his might, as if the chair itself was moving at a high speed and if he let go at all he would rocket forward and maybe crash right through the set.

Once I was in the room watching TV with Henry and I heard his teeth click at something. I looked over, and he'd bitten through his lip. Blood was going down his chin. I tell you right then I wanted to smash that tube to pieces. I went over to it but Henry must have known what I was up to. He rushed from his chair and shoved me out of the way, against the wall. I told myself he didn't know what he was doing.

My mom came in, turned the set off real quiet, and told us she had made something for supper. So we went and sat down. There was still blood going down Henry's chin, but he didn't notice it and no one said anything, even though every time he took a bit of his bread his blood fell onto it until he was eating his own blood mixed in with the food.

While Henry was not around we talked about what was going to happen to 30 him. There were no Indian doctors on the reservation, and my mom was afraid of trusting Old Man Pillager because he courted her long ago and was jealous of her husbands. He might take revenge through her son. We were afraid that if we brought Henry to a regular hospital they would keep him.

"They don't fix them in those places," Mom said; "they just give them drugs."

"We wouldn't get him there in the first place," I agreed, "so let's just forget about it."

Then I thought about the car.

Henry had not even looked at the car since he'd gotten home, though like I said, it was in tip-top condition and ready to drive. I thought the car might bring the old Henry back somehow. So I bided my time and waited for my chance to interest him in the vehicle.

One night Henry was off somewhere. I took myself a hammer. I went out to 35 that car and I did a number on its underside. Whacked it up. Bent the tail pipe double. Ripped the muffler loose. By the time I was done with the car it looked worse than any typical Indian car that has been driven all its life on reservation roads, which they always say are like government promises — full of holes. It just about hurt me, I'll tell you that! I threw dirt in the carburetor and I ripped all the electric tape off the seats. I made it look just as beat up as I could. Then I sat back and waited for Henry to find it.

Still, it took him over a month. That was all right, because it was just getting warm enough, not melting, but warm enough to work outside.

"Lyman," he says, walking in one day, "that red car looks like shit."

"Well it's old," I says. "You got to expect that."

"No way!" says Henry. "That car's a classic! But you went and ran the piss right out of it, Lyman, and you know it don't deserve that. I kept that car in A-one shape. You don't remember. You're too young. But when I left, that car was running like a watch. Now I don't even know if I can get it to start again, let alone get it anywhere near its old condition."

"Well you try," I said, like I was getting mad, "but I say it's a piece of junk."   40

Then I walked out before he could realize I knew he'd strung together more than six words at once.

After that I thought he'd freeze himself to death working on that car. He was out there all day, and at night he rigged up a little lamp, ran a cord out the window, and had himself some light to see by while he worked. He was better than he had been before, but that's still not saying much. It was easier for him to do the things the rest of us did. He ate more slowly and didn't jump up and down during the meal to get this or that or look out the window. I put my hand in the back of the TV set, I admit, and fiddled around with it good, so that it was almost impossible now to get a clear picture. He didn't look at it very often anyway. He was always out with that car or going off to get parts for it. By the time it was really melting outside, he had it fixed.

I had been feeling down in the dumps about Henry around this time. We had always been together before. Henry and Lyman. But he was such a loner now that I didn't know how to take it. So I jumped at the chance one day when Henry seemed friendly. It's not that he smiled or anything. He just said, "Let's take that old shitbox for a spin." Just the way he said it made me think he could be coming around.

We went out to the car. It was spring. The sun was shining very bright. My only sister, Bonita, who was just eleven years old, came out and made us stand together for a picture. Henry leaned his elbow on the red car's windshield, and he took his other arm and put it over my shoulder, very carefully, as though it was heavy for him to lift and he didn't want to bring the weight down all at once.

"Smile," Bonita said, and he did.   45

That picture, I never look at it anymore. A few months ago, I don't know why, I got his picture out and tacked it on the wall. I felt good about Henry at the time, close to him. I felt good having his picture on the wall, until one night when I was looking at television. I was a little drunk and stoned. I looked up at the wall and Henry was staring at me. I don't know what it was, but his smile had changed, or maybe it was gone. All I know is I couldn't stay in the same room with that picture. I was shaking. I got up, closed the door, and went into the kitchen. A little later my friend Ray came over and we both went back into that room. We put the picture in a brown bag, folded the bag over and over tightly, then put it way back in a closet.

I still see that picture now, as if it tugs at me, whenever I pass that closet door. The picture is very clear in my mind. It was so sunny that day Henry had to squint against the glare. Or maybe the camera Bonita held flashed like a mirror, blinding him, before she snapped the picture. My face is right out in the sun, big and round. But he might have drawn back, because the shadows on his face are deep as holes. There are two shadows curved like little hooks around the ends of his smile, as if to frame it and try to keep it there — that one, first smile that looked like it might have hurt his face. He has his field jacket on and the worn-in clothes he'd come back in and kept wearing ever since. After Bonita took the picture, she went into the house and we got into the car. There was a full cooler in the trunk. We started off, east, toward Pembina and the Red River because Henry said he wanted to see the high water.

The trip over there was beautiful. When everything starts changing, drying up, clearing off, you feel like your whole life is starting. Henry felt it, too. The top was down and the car hummed like a top. He'd really put it back in shape, even the tape on the seats was very carefully put down and glued back in layers. It's not that he smiled again or even joked, but his face looked to me as if it was clear, more peaceful. It looked as though he wasn't thinking of anything in particular except the bare fields and windbreaks and houses we were passing.

The river was high and full of winter trash when we got there. The sun was still out, but it was colder by the river. There were still little clumps of dirty snow here and there on the banks. The water hadn't gone over the banks yet, but it would, you could tell. It was just at its limit, hard swollen glossy like an old gray scar. We made ourselves a fire, and we sat down and watched the current go. As I watched it I felt something squeezing inside me and tightening and trying to let go all at the same time. I knew I was not just feeling it myself; I knew I was feeling what Henry was going through at that moment. Except that I couldn't stand it, the closing and opening. I jumped to my feet. I took Henry by the shoulders and I started shaking him. "Wake up," I says, "wake up, wake up, wake up!" I didn't know what had come over me. I sat down beside him again.

His face was totally white and hard. Then it broke, like stones break all of a 50 sudden when water boils up inside them.

"I know it," he says. "I know it. I can't help it. It's no use."

We start talking. He said he knew what I'd done with the car. It was obvious it had been whacked out of shape and not just neglected. He said he wanted to give the car to me for good now, it was no use. He said he'd fixed it just to give it back and I should take it.

"No way," I says, "I don't want it."

"That's okay," he says, "you take it."

"I don't want it, though," I says back to him, and then to emphasize, just to 55 emphasize, you understand, I touch his shoulder. He slaps my hand off.

"Take that car," he says.

"No," I say, "make me," I say, and then he grabs my jacket and rips the arm loose. That jacket is a class act, suede with tags and zippers. I push Henry backwards, off the log. He jumps up and bowls me over. We go down in a clinch and come up swinging hard, for all we're worth, with our fists. He socks my jaw so hard I feel like it swings loose. Then I'm at his ribcage and land a good one under his chin so his head snaps back. He's dazzled. He looks at me and I look at him and then his eyes are full of tears and blood and at first I think he's crying. But no, he's laughing. "Ha! Ha!" he says. "Ha! Ha! Take good care of it."

"Okay," I says, "okay, no problem. Ha! Ha!"

I can't help it, and I start laughing, too. My face feels fat and strange, and after a while I get a beer from the cooler in the trunk, and when I hand it to Henry he takes his shirt and wipes my germs off. "Hoof-and-mouth disease," he says. For some reason this cracks me up, and so we're really laughing for a while, and then we drink all the rest of the beers one by one and throw them in the river and see how far, how fast, the current takes them before they fill up and sink.

"You want to go on back?" I ask after a while. "Maybe we could snag a couple 60
nice Kashpaw girls."

He says nothing. But I can tell his mood is turning again.

"They're all crazy, the girls up here, every damn one of them."

"You're crazy too," I say, to jolly him up. "Crazy Lamartine boys!"

He looks as though he will take this wrong at first. His face twists, then clears, and he jumps up on his feet. "That's right!" he says. "Crazier 'n hell. Crazy Indians!"

I think it's the old Henry again. He throws off his jacket and starts swinging 65
his legs out from the knees like a fancy dancer. He's down doing something between a grouse dance and a bunny hop, no kind of dance I ever saw before, but neither has anyone else on all this green growing earth. He's wild. He wants to pitch whoopee! He's up and at me and all over. All this time I'm laughing so hard, so hard my belly is getting tied up in a knot.

"Got to cool me off!" he shouts all of a sudden. Then he runs over to the river and jumps in.

There's boards and other things in the current. It's so high. No sound comes from the river after the splash he makes, so I run right over. I look around. It's getting dark. I see he's halfway across the water already, and I know he didn't swim there but the current took him. It's far. I hear his voice, though, very clearly across it.

"My boots are filling," he says.

He says this in a normal voice, like he just noticed and he doesn't know what to think of it. Then he's gone. A branch comes by. Another branch. And I go in.

By the time I get out of the river, off the snag I pulled myself onto, the sun is 70
down. I walk back to the car, turn on the high beams, and drive it up the bank. I put it in first gear and then I take my foot off the clutch. I get out, close the door, and watch it plow softly into the water. The headlights reach in as they go down, searching, still lighted even after the water swirls over the back end. I wait. The wires short out. It is all finally dark. And then there is only the water, the sound of it going and running and going and running and running.

For Analysis

1. What sort of person is Lyman?

2. Why does Lyman feel that *repose* is the precise word to describe the red convertible the first time he saw it?

3. Characterize Susy's family. Is there any thematic significance to the generosity this Alaskan family extends to the brothers? Explain.

4. How does the episode about Susy's hair relate to the **theme** of the story?

5. What function does the fifth section (paras. 30–41) serve?

6. Does it make a difference that it is the Vietnam War rather than, say, World War II that Henry never recovers from? Explain.

7. What is the significance of the fight over the car in the seventh section (paras. 48–69)?

8. Why does Lyman send the red convertible rolling down the bank and into the river?

9. Is the fact that Lyman and Henry are Native Americans incidental or central to the meaning of this story? Explain.

On Style

1. What is the **theme** that unifies the eight sections of this story?

2. Why does Lyman adopt the third-person **point of view** in referring to himself in the opening paragraph?

3. The only exception to the straightforward chronological narrative occurs in the sixth section of the story (paras. 46–47), when Lyman moves forward in time to describe the photograph taken by his sister and his feelings about it. What purpose does this interruption serve?

Making Connections

1. How might Tim O'Brien's story "The Things They Carried" (p. 1360) help explain Henry's character?

2. Compare the reasons for Henry's withdrawal from life with those of Brown in Nathaniel Hawthorne's "Young Goodman Brown" (p. 80) or those of Bartleby in Herman Melville's "Bartleby the Scrivener" (p. 334).

Writing Topics

1. Write an essay showing how section four (paras. 21–29), dealing with Henry and the Vietnam War, is pivotal in stating the theme of the story and in shifting to a **tone** more appropriate to the impending tragedy.

2. In what ways is it significant that Lyman and Henry are Native Americans?

Sherman Alexie   (b. 1966)

This Is What It Means to Say Phoenix, Arizona   1993

Just after Victor lost his job at the BIA,[1] he also found out that his father had died of a heart attack in Phoenix, Arizona. Victor hadn't seen his father in a few years, only talked to him on the telephone once or twice, but there still was a genetic pain, which was soon to be pain as real and immediate as a broken bone.

Victor didn't have any money. Who does have money on a reservation, except the cigarette and fireworks salespeople? His father had a savings account waiting to be claimed, but Victor needed to find a way to get to Phoenix. Victor's mother was just as poor as he was, and the rest of his family didn't have any use at all for him. So Victor called the Tribal Council.

"Listen," Victor said. "My father just died. I need some money to get to Phoenix to make arrangements."

"Now, Victor," the council said. "You know we're having a difficult time financially."

"But I thought the council had special funds set aside for stuff like this."   5

"Now, Victor, we do have some money available for the proper return of tribal members' bodies. But I don't think we have enough to bring your father all the way back from Phoenix."

"Well," Victor said. "It ain't going to cost all that much. He had to be cremated. Things were kind of ugly. He died of a heart attack in his trailer and nobody found him for a week. It was really hot, too. You get the picture."

"Now, Victor, we're sorry for your loss and the circumstances. But we can really only afford to give you one hundred dollars. "

"That's not even enough for a plane ticket."

"Well, you might consider driving down to Phoenix."   10

"I don't have a car. Besides, I was going to drive my father's pickup back up here."

"Now, Victor," the council said. "We're sure there is somebody who could drive you to Phoenix. Or is there somebody who could lend you the rest of the money?"

"You know there ain't nobody around with that kind of money."

"Well, we're sorry, Victor, but that's the best we can do."

---

[1] The Bureau of Indian Affairs is the U.S. government bureau responsible for the administration of federal programs for federally recognized Indian tribes.

Victor accepted the Tribal Council's offer. What else could he do? So he 15 signed the proper papers, picked up his check, and walked over to the Trading Post to cash it.

While Victor stood in line, he watched Thomas Builds-the-Fire standing near the magazine rack, talking to himself. Like he always did. Thomas was a storyteller that nobody wanted to listen to. That's like being a dentist in a town where everybody has false teeth.

Victor and Thomas Builds-the-Fire were the same age, had grown up and played in the dirt together. Ever since Victor could remember, it was Thomas who always had something to say.

Once, when they were seven years old, when Victor's father still lived with the family, Thomas closed his eyes and told Victor this story: "Your father's heart is weak. He is afraid of his own family. He is afraid of you. Late at night he sits in the dark. Watches the television until there's nothing but that white noise. Sometimes he feels like he wants to buy a motorcycle and ride away. He wants to run and hide. He doesn't want to be found."

Thomas Builds-the-Fire had known that Victor's father was going to leave, knew it before anyone. Now Victor stood in the Trading Post with a one-hundred-dollar check in his hand, wondering if Thomas knew that Victor's father was dead, if he knew what was going to happen next.

Just then Thomas looked at Victor, smiled, and walked over to him. 20

"Victor, I'm sorry about your father," Thomas said.

"How did you know about it?" Victor asked.

"I heard it on the wind. I heard it from the birds. I felt it in the sunlight. Also, your mother was just in here crying."

"Oh," Victor said and looked around the Trading Post. All the other Indians stared, surprised that Victor was even talking to Thomas. Nobody talked to Thomas anymore because he told the same damn stories over and over again. Victor was embarrassed, but he thought that Thomas might be able to help him. Victor felt a sudden need for tradition.

"I can lend you the money you need," Thomas said suddenly. "But you have 25 to take me with you."

"I can't take your money," Victor said. "I mean, I haven't hardly talked to you in years. We're not really friends anymore."

"I didn't say we were friends. I said you had to take me with you."

"Let me think about it."

Victor went home with his one hundred dollars and sat at the kitchen table. He held his head in his hands and thought about Thomas Builds-the-Fire, remembered little details, tears and scars, the bicycle they shared for a summer, so many stories.

Thomas Builds-the-Fire sat on the bicycle, waited in Victor's yard. He was ten 30 years old and skinny. His hair was dirty because it was the Fourth of July.

"Victor," Thomas yelled. "Hurry up. We're going to miss the fireworks."

After a few minutes, Victor ran out of his house, jumped the porch railing, and landed gracefully on the sidewalk.

"And the judges award him a 9.95, the highest score of the summer," Thomas said, clapped, laughed.

"That was perfect, cousin," Victor said. "And it's my turn to ride the bike."

Thomas gave up the bike and they headed for the fairgrounds. It was nearly 35 dark and the fireworks were about to start.

"You know," Thomas said. "It's strange how us Indians celebrate the Fourth of July. It ain't like it was *our* independence everybody was fighting for."

"You think about things too much," Victor said. "It's just supposed to be fun. Maybe Junior will be there."

"Which Junior? Everybody on this reservation is named Junior."

And they both laughed.

The fireworks were small, hardly more than a few bottle rockets and a fountain. 40 But it was enough for two Indian boys. Years later, they would need much more.

Afterwards, sitting in the dark, fighting off mosquitoes, Victor turned to Thomas Builds-the-Fire.

"Hey," Victor said. "Tell me a story."

Thomas closed his eyes and told this story: "There were these two Indian boys who wanted to be warriors. But it was too late to be warriors in the old way. All the horses were gone. So the two Indian boys stole a car and drove to the city. They parked the stolen car in front of the police station and then hitchhiked back home to the reservation. When they got back, all their friends cheered and their parents' eyes shone with pride. *You were very brave,* everybody said to the two Indian boys. *Very brave.*"

"Ya-hey," Victor said. "That's a good one. I wish I could be a warrior."

"Me, too," Thomas said.   45

They went home together in the dark, Thomas on the bike now, Victor on foot. They walked through shadows and light from streetlamps.

"We've come a long ways," Thomas said. "We have outdoor lighting."

"All I need is the stars," Victor said. "And besides, you still think about things too much."

They separated then, each headed for home, both laughing all the way.

Victor sat at his kitchen table. He counted his one hundred dollars again and 50 again. He knew he needed more to make it to Phoenix and back. He knew he needed Thomas Builds-the-Fire. So he put his money in his wallet and opened the front door to find Thomas on the porch.

"Ya-hey, Victor," Thomas said. "I knew you'd call me."

Thomas walked into the living room and sat down on Victor's favorite chair.

"I've got some money saved up," Thomas said. "It's enough to get us down there, but you have to get us back."

"I've got this hundred dollars," Victor said. "And my dad had a savings account I'm going to claim."

"How much in your dad's account?"   55
"Enough. A few hundred."
"Sounds good. When we leaving?"

When they were fifteen and had long since stopped being friends, Victor and Thomas got into a fistfight. That is, Victor was really drunk and beat Thomas up for no reason at all. All the other Indian boys stood around and watched it happen. Junior was there and so were Lester, Seymour, and a lot of others. The beating might have gone on until Thomas was dead if Norma Many Horses hadn't come along and stopped it.

"Hey, you boys," Norma yelled and jumped out of her car. "Leave him alone."

If it had been someone else, even another man, the Indian boys would've just   60
ignored the warnings. But Norma was a warrior. She was powerful. She could have picked up any two of the boys and smashed their skulls together. But worse than that, she would have dragged them all over to some tipi and made them listen to some elder tell a dusty old story.

The Indian boys scattered, and Norma walked over to Thomas and picked him up.

"Hey, little man, are you okay?" she asked.

Thomas gave her a thumbs up.

"Why they always picking on you?"

Thomas shook his head, closed his eyes, but no stories came to him, no words   65
or music. He just wanted to go home, to lie in his bed and let his dreams tell his stories for him.

Thomas Builds-the-Fire and Victor sat next to each other in the airplane, coach section. A tiny white woman had the window seat. She was busy twisting her body into pretzels. She was flexible.

"I have to ask," Thomas said, and Victor closed his eyes in embarrassment.

"Don't," Victor said.

"Excuse me, miss," Thomas asked. "Are you a gymnast or something?"

"There's no something about it," she said. "I was first alternate on the 1980   70
Olympic team."

"Really?" Thomas asked.

"Really."

"I mean, you used to be a world-class athlete?" Thomas asked.

"My husband still thinks I am."

Thomas Builds-the-Fire smiled. She was a mental gymnast, too. She pulled   75
her leg straight up against her body so that she could've kissed her kneecap.

"I wish I could do that," Thomas said.

Victor was ready to jump out of the plane. Thomas, that crazy Indian storyteller with ratty old braids and broken teeth, was flirting with a beautiful Olympic gymnast. Nobody back home on the reservation would ever believe it.

"Well," the gymnast said. "It's easy. Try it."

Thomas grabbed at his leg and tried to pull it up into the same position as the gymnast. He couldn't even come close, which made Victor and the gymnast laugh.

"Hey," she asked. "You two are Indian, right?" 80

"Full-blood," Victor said.

"Not me," Thomas said. "I'm half magician on my mother's side and half clown on my father's."

They all laughed.

"What are your names?" she asked.

"Victor and Thomas." 85

"Mine is Cathy. Pleased to meet you all."

The three of them talked for the duration of the flight. Cathy the gymnast complained about the government, how they screwed the 1980 Olympic team by boycotting.[2]

"Sounds like you all got a lot in common with Indians," Thomas said.

Nobody laughed.

After the plane landed in Phoenix and they had all found their way to the ter- 90 minal, Cathy the gymnast smiled and waved good-bye.

"She was really nice," Thomas said.

"Yeah, but everybody talks to everybody on airplanes," Victor said. "It's too bad we can't always be that way."

"You always used to tell me I think too much," Thomas said. "Now it sounds like you do."

"Maybe I caught it from you."

"Yeah." 95

Thomas and Victor rode in a taxi to the trailer where Victor's father died.

"Listen," Victor said as they stopped in front of the trailer. "I never told you I was sorry for beating you up that time."

"Oh, it was nothing. We were just kids and you were drunk."

"Yeah, but I'm still sorry."

"That's all right." 100

Victor paid for the taxi and the two of them stood in the hot Phoenix summer. They could smell the trailer.

"This ain't going to be nice," Victor said. "You don't have to go in."

"You're going to need help."

Victor walked to the front door and opened it. The stink rolled out and made them both gag. Victor's father had lain in that trailer for a week in hundred-degree temperatures before anyone found him. And the only reason anyone found him was because of the smell. They needed dental records to identify him. That's exactly what the coroner said. They needed dental records.

"Oh, man," Victor said. "I don't know if I can do this." 105

"Well, then don't."

---

[2] The United States withdrew from the 1980 Olympics in Moscow to protest the Soviet Union's invasion of Afghanistan in 1979.

"But there might be something valuable in there."

"I thought his money was in the bank."

"It is. I was talking about pictures and letters and stuff like that."

"Oh," Thomas said as he held his breath and followed Victor into the trailer.   110

When Victor was twelve, he stepped into an underground wasp nest. His foot was caught in the hole, and no matter how hard he struggled, Victor couldn't pull free. He might have died there, stung a thousand times, if Thomas Builds-the-Fire had not come by.

"Run," Thomas yelled and pulled Victor's foot from the hole. They ran then, hard as they ever had, faster than Billy Mills, faster than Jim Thorpe, faster than the wasps could fly.

Victor and Thomas ran until they couldn't breathe, ran until it was cold and dark outside, ran until they were lost and it took hours to find their way home. All the way back, Victor counted his stings.

"Seven," Victor said. "My lucky number."

Victor didn't find much to keep in the trailer. Only a photo album and a   115
stereo. Everything else had that smell stuck in it or was useless anyway.

"I guess this is all," Victor said. "It ain't much."

"Better than nothing," Thomas said.

"Yeah, and I do have the pickup."

"Yeah," Thomas said. "It's in good shape."

"Dad was good about that stuff."   120

"Yeah, I remember your dad."

"Really?" Victor asked. "What do you remember?"

Thomas Builds-the-Fire closed his eyes and told this story: "I remember when I had this dream that told me to go to Spokane, to stand by the Falls in the middle of the city and wait for a sign. I knew I had to go there but I didn't have a car. Didn't have a license. I was only thirteen. So I walked all the way, took me all day, and I finally made it to the Falls. I stood there for an hour waiting. Then your dad came walking up. *What the hell are you doing here?* he asked me. I said, *Waiting for a vision.* Then your father said, *All you're going to get here is mugged.* So he drove me over to Denny's, bought me dinner, and then drove me home to the reservation. For a long time I was mad because I thought my dreams had lied to me. But they didn't. Your dad was my vision. *Take care of each other* is what my dreams were saying. *Take care of each other.*"

Victor was quiet for a long time. He searched his mind for memories of his father, found the good ones, found a few bad ones, added it all up, and smiled.

"My father never told me about finding you in Spokane," Victor said.   125

"He said he wouldn't tell anybody. Didn't want me to get in trouble. But he said I had to watch out for you as part of the deal."

"Really?"

"Really. Your father said you would need the help. He was right."

"That's why you came down here with me, isn't it?" Victor asked.

"I came because of your father." 130

Victor and Thomas climbed into the pickup, drove over to the bank, and claimed the three hundred dollars in the savings account.

Thomas Builds-the-Fire could fly.

Once, he jumped off the roof of the tribal school and flapped his arms like a crazy eagle. And he flew. For a second, he hovered, suspended above all the other Indian boys who were too smart or too scared to jump.

"He's flying," Junior yelled, and Seymour was busy looking for the trick wires or mirrors. But it was real. As real as the dirt when Thomas lost altitude and crashed to the ground.

He broke his arm in two places. 135

"He broke his wing," Victor chanted, and the other Indian boys joined in, made it a tribal song.

"He broke his wing, he broke his wing, he broke his wing," all the Indian boys chanted as they ran off, flapping their wings, wishing they could fly, too. They hated Thomas for his courage, his brief moment as a bird. Everybody has dreams about flying. Thomas flew.

One of his dreams came true for just a second, just enough to make it real.

Victor's father, his ashes, fit in one wooden box with enough left over to fill a cardboard box.

"He always was a big man," Thomas said. 140

Victor carried part of his father and Thomas carried the rest out to the pickup. They set him down carefully behind the seats, put a cowboy hat on the wooden box and a Dodgers cap on the cardboard box. That's the way it was supposed to be.

"Ready to head back home?" Victor asked.

"It's going to be a long drive."

"Yeah, take a couple days, maybe."

"We can take turns," Thomas said. 145

"Okay," Victor said, but they didn't take turns. Victor drove for sixteen hours straight north, made it halfway up Nevada toward home before he finally pulled over.

"Hey, Thomas," Victor said. "You got to drive for a while."

"Okay."

Thomas Builds-the-Fire slid behind the wheel and started off down the road. All through Nevada, Thomas and Victor had been amazed at the lack of animal life, at the absence of water, of movement.

"Where is everything?" Victor had asked more than once. 150

Now when Thomas was finally driving they saw the first animal, maybe the only animal in Nevada. It was a long-eared jackrabbit.

"Look," Victor yelled. "It's alive."

Thomas and Victor were busy congratulating themselves on their discovery when the jackrabbit darted out into the road and under the wheels of the pickup.

"Stop the goddamn car," Victor yelled, and Thomas did stop, backed the pickup to the dead jackrabbit.

"Oh, man, he's dead," Victor said as he looked at the squashed animal.   155

"Really dead."

"The only thing alive in this whole state and we just killed it."

"I don't know," Thomas said. "I think it was suicide."

Victor looked around the desert, sniffed the air, felt the emptiness and loneliness, and nodded his head.

"Yeah," Victor said. "It had to be suicide."   160

"I can't believe this," Thomas said. "You drive for a thousand miles and there ain't even any bugs smashed on the windshield. I drive for ten seconds and kill the only living thing in Nevada."

"Yeah," Victor said. "Maybe I should drive."

"Maybe you should."

Thomas Builds-the-Fire walked through the corridors of the tribal school by himself. Nobody wanted to be anywhere near him because of all those stories. Story after story.

Thomas closed his eyes and this story came to him: "We are all given one   165 thing by which our lives are measured, one determination. Mine are the stories which can change or not change the world. It doesn't matter which as long as I continue to tell the stories. My father, he died on Okinawa in World War II, died fighting for this country, which had tried to kill him for years. My mother, she died giving birth to me, died while I was still inside her. She pushed me out into the world with her last breath. I have no brothers or sisters. I have only my stories which came to me before I even had the words to speak. I learned a thousand stories before I took my first thousand steps. They are all I have. It's all I can do."

Thomas Builds-the-Fire told his stories to all those who would stop and listen. He kept telling them long after people had stopped listening.

Victor and Thomas made it back to the reservation just as the sun was rising. It was the beginning of a new day on earth, but the same old shit on the reservation.

"Good morning," Thomas said.

"Good morning."

The tribe was waking up, ready for work, eating breakfast, reading the news-   170 paper, just like everybody else does. Willene LeBret was out in her garden wearing a bathrobe. She waved when Thomas and Victor drove by.

"Crazy Indians made it," she said to herself and went back to her roses.

Victor stopped the pickup in front of Thomas Builds-the-Fire's HUD house.[3] They both yawned, stretched a little, shook dust from their bodies.

[3] The Department of Housing and Urban Development, an agency of the federal government, provides subsidized housing for low-income persons.

"I'm tired," Victor said.

"Of everything," Thomas added.

They both searched for words to end the journey. Victor needed to thank 175
Thomas for his help, for the money, and make the promise to pay it all back.

"Don't worry about the money," Thomas said. "It don't make any difference
anyhow."

"Probably not, enit?"

"Nope."

Victor knew that Thomas would remain the crazy storyteller who talked to
dogs and cars, who listened to the wind and pine trees. Victor knew that he
couldn't really be friends with Thomas, even after all that had happened. It was
cruel but it was real. As real as the ashes, as Victor's father, sitting behind the
seats.

"I know how it is," Thomas said. "I know you ain't going to treat me any better 180
than you did before. I know your friends would give you too much shit about it."

Victor was ashamed of himself. Whatever happened to the tribal ties, the
sense of community? The only real thing he shared with anybody was a bottle
and broken dreams. He owed Thomas something, anything.

"Listen," Victor said and handed Thomas the cardboard box which contained
half of his father. "I want you to have this."

Thomas took the ashes and smiled, closed his eyes, and told this story: "I'm
going to travel to Spokane Falls one last time and toss these ashes into the water.
And your father will rise like a salmon, leap over the bridge, over me, and find
his way home. It will be beautiful. His teeth will shine like silver, like a rainbow.
He will rise, Victor, he will rise."

Victor smiled.

"I was planning on doing the same thing with my half," Victor said. "But I 185
didn't imagine my father looking anything like a salmon. I thought it'd be like
cleaning the attic or something. Like letting things go after they've stopped having any use."

"Nothing stops, cousin," Thomas said. "Nothing stops."

Thomas Builds-the-Fire got out of the pickup and walked up his driveway.
Victor started the pickup and began the drive home.

"Wait," Thomas yelled suddenly from his porch. "I just got to ask one favor."

Victor stopped the pickup, leaned out the window, and shouted back. "What
do you want?"

"Just one time when I'm telling a story somewhere, why don't you stop and 190
listen?" Thomas asked.

"Just once?"

"Just once."

Victor waved his arms to let Thomas know that the deal was good. It was a fair
trade, and that was all Victor had ever wanted from his whole life. So Victor
drove his father's pickup toward home while Thomas went into his house,
closed the door behind him, and heard a new story come to him in the silence
afterwards.

For Analysis

1. Explain the title. What does "This" refer to?

2. When they were boys, Victor would chide Thomas for thinking too much. Why did he do so? What is it that Thomas thinks about?

3. What is the significance of the conversation Thomas has with Cathy, the Olympic gymnast, during the plane ride to Phoenix?

4. Why has Thomas evoked such dislike and hostility from Victor and others of the tribe?

5. Why is Victor drawn to Thomas despite the embarrassment he feels at being seen with the reservation pariah?

6. The narrator interrupts the flashback describing the Fourth of July celebration to remark: "Years later, they would need much more" (para. 40). Does the narrative, which takes place years after this event, throw light on the meaning of this comment? Explain.

7. How does Victor change in the course of the story?

8. Explain the final sentence.

On Style

1. Discuss how each of the flashbacks relates to the present narrative.

2. How would you characterize the **style** of this story?

Making Connections

1. Compare this story and Ernest Hemingway's "A Clean, Well-Lighted Place" (p. 105) as stories that rely heavily on dialogue rather than narration.

2. What similarities and differences do you find between this story and Louise Erdrich's "The Red Convertible" (p. 732) in their depiction of reservation Indians?

Writing Topics

1. This story, taken from Alexie's book *The Lone Ranger and Tonto Fistfight in Heaven,* is the basis for the 1998 movie *Smoke Signals* (available on video). Write a paper on the way in which the story has been expanded and changed for the film version. (See "Looking Deeper: From Fiction to Film," p. 750.)

2. Analyze the ways in which Alexie creates a comic tone in this story.

LOOKING DEEPER:
From Fiction to Film

Sherman Alexie's "This Is What It Means to Say Phoenix, Arizona" appears in *The Lone Ranger and Tonto Fistfight in Heaven* (1993), a collection of loosely connected short pieces in which certain characters reappear from time to time. When Alexie adapted the story into the screenplay for *Smoke Signals,* he incorporated numerous incidents from other parts of the collection, and invented still others to flesh out his ideas and establish his screenplay's structure. Thus, looking deeper into the transformation from original story to screenplay to film reveals three quite different entities. It is instructive to examine the differences. (The film *Smoke Signals* [1997] was distributed by Miramax Films and can be rented at most video stores. The screenplay was published by Hyperion [1998] and contains an introduction and production notes by Alexie. The original short-story collection [Atlantic Monthly Press, 1993] is still available at bookstores and libraries.)

In his introduction to the screenplay, Alexie points out that "screenplays are more like poetry than like fiction. Screenplays rely on imagery to carry the narrative, rather than the other way around. And screenplays have form. Like sonnets, actually. Just as there are expectations of form, meter, and rhyme in a sonnet, there are the same kinds of expectations for screenplays" (x).

Those who write about the art of the screenplay are more precise in their definitions and advice. They point out that screenplays must have *plot, character, conflict, crisis, climax, exposition,* and *dialogue.* (It should not surprise you that this list corresponds very closely to the parts of a drama defined by Aristotle in *The Poetics* (p. 234), long before movie screens existed.) If the differences between a screenplay and a narrative tale are relatively easy to perceive, the more subtle (but nonetheless real) differences between a screenplay and a drama are quite significant and will occupy some of our attention.

Syd Field, in his influential book *Screenplay: The Foundations of Screenwriting* (Dell Publishing, 1994), points out that the paradigm of a screenplay reveals a *beginning,* which is the "setup"; a *middle,* which embodies a "confrontation"; and an *end,* which provides the "resolution." Another commentator speaks of the kinds of conflict that must be resolved: "conflict between a person and society; conflict between a person and his or her self; conflict between one person and another; and conflict between a person and nature." Alexie's short story animates at least two conflicts — Victor's feelings about his alcoholic father, who abandoned the family, and his feelings about Thomas, who, in some respects, is also a son of the dead man. In addition, both the story and the film touch on Victor's feelings about being a reservation Indian. After reading the story, reading excerpts from the screenplay, and viewing the film, you might ask yourself which most successfully depicts and resolves these conflicts.

In the story, Victor and Thomas fly to Phoenix; in the film, they travel there by bus. Both versions, however, include the encounter with the female gymnast (paras. 66–90 in the story). Here is the screenplay version.

Sherman Alexie (b. 1966)

from the screenplay for
Smoke Signals, Scenes 37–42 1998

37 ◆ INT. BUS — DAY

ANGLE ON Thomas and Victor standing at the front of the bus, staring down the rows.

Thomas's glass jar piggy bank has been about half drained of money.

THOMAS AND VICTOR'S POV on the TEN PEOPLE *aboard the bus, a mixture of odd types: Two old couples that look to be traveling together; a young mother and her young son; two cowboys; a man in a military uniform; a pretty young woman traveling alone.*

Everybody is white.

They are all craning their necks, peering out from their seats, to stare at the two long-haired Indians climbing on the bus.

ANGLE ON Thomas and Victor walking down the aisle toward CAMERA.

REVERSE ANGLE ON Thomas and Victor walking down the aisle as all heads swivel to follow their walk toward the back of the bus.

Victor leads Thomas to a pair of seats near the back of the bus.

Victor sits at the window, Thomas on the aisle.

Thomas smiles at the very small white woman, the GYMNAST, blond, mid-thirties, directly across the aisle.

She doesn't smile.

She just looks at Thomas.

She's busy contouring her body into various pretzel-like positions.

Thomas, nodding his head, turns back toward Victor, who is also watching the Gymnast's contortions.

Victor looks at Thomas with a how-the-hell-should-I-know look.

38 ◆ INT. BUS DRIVER'S SEAT — DAY

The Bus Driver settles into his seat and puts the bus into gear.

39 ◆ EXT. BUS STOP — DAY

The bus pulls away from the stop.

40 ◆ INT. THOMAS'S AND VICTOR'S SEATS — DAY

The Gymnast is still twisting her body into strange shapes.

Thomas is staring at her.

He looks back at Victor and smiles.

Thomas *(whispering).*   I have to ask.
Victor *(whispering).*   No, Thomas.

Thomas ignores Victor, turns back to the Gymnast, leans across the aisle, and speaks to her.

Thomas.   Hey, you're pretty flexible.

The Gymnast looks at him without expression.

Thomas.   Are you a gymnast or something?
Gymnast.   I was an alternate on the 1980 Olympic team.

Thomas turns back to Victor to share the news, but Victor has closed his eyes, embarrassed, pretending to be asleep.

Thomas looks back to the Gymnast.

Thomas smiles.

The Gymnast pulls her leg straight up against her body so that she could kiss her kneecap.

Thomas.   Jeez, I wish I could do that.

Victor opens his eyes and looks at Thomas, disgusted.

The Gymnast looks at Thomas with a slight smile.

Gymnast.   Well, it's easy. Try it.

Thomas grabs at his leg and tries to pull it up into the same position as the Gymnast.

He can't even come close, but the Gymnast laughs.

Gymnast.   Hey, you're Indian, right?
Thomas.   Yeah, my name is Thomas. And this is Victor. We're Coeur d'Alene Indians.
Gymnast.   My name is Cathy. I'm from Mississippi.

Cathy and Thomas smile at each other.

Thomas offers her a drink of water from his goofy army canteen.

Thomas.   You thirsty?

41 ◆ EXT. HIGHWAY — NORTHERN IDAHO PINE FOREST — AFTERNOON

The bus rolling down the two-lane highway lined with pine forest on either side. Very green.

42 ◆ INT. THOMAS'S AND VICTOR'S SEATS — AFTERNOON

Thomas is engaged in a discussion with Cathy.

Victor is listening.

Cathy *(bitterly).*   I put my whole life into making the Olympics. And then Jimmy Carter took it away.

Thomas.   Jeez, you gymnasts got a lot in common with Indians then, enit?

Cathy.   Yeah, I guess so.

Victor sits up, leans over Thomas toward Cathy.

Victor.   Hey, you were an alternate for the team, right?

Cathy looks at Thomas, then to Victor.

She's wondering what Victor is up to.

Cathy.   Yeah?

Victor.   Well, if you were an alternate, then you'd only compete if somebody was hurt or something, right?

Cathy.   Yeah?

Victor.   Was anybody hurt?

Cathy.   No.

Victor.   Then you weren't really on the team, were you? I mean, it didn't matter if there was a boycott or not. You were staying home anyways, right? *(beat)* You ain't got nothing to complain about, so why don't you just be quiet?

Cathy is very hurt and angry.

She gets up and walks to the front of the bus looking for another seat.

ANGLE ON Thomas and Victor in their seats.

Thomas.   Why'd you do that, Victor? She was nice.

Victor.   Nice, my ass. She was a liar.

Thomas.   No, she wasn't.

Victor.   Yes, she was. Think about it, Thomas. What would a big-shot Olympic gymnast be doing on a bus? Answer me that, Thomas.

Thomas.   I don't know.

Victor.   You know, Thomas, you really need to grow up. Don't you know anything? People are awful. They'll rob you blind if you ain't careful. She was probably trying to con you. You still got your piggy bank?

Thomas.   Yeah.

Victor.   Just remember, Thomas. You can't trust anybody.

Questions for Looking Deeper

1. This excerpt covers Scenes 37 through 42. Why is it necessary to indicate different scenes? Is there any counterpart in the short story to the many notes that define each scene? Explain.

2. Describe the difference in tone between the short story's treatment of this event and the screenplay's. How do you account for the difference?

Sherman Alexie (b. 1966)

from the screenplay for

Smoke Signals, Scene 59[1] 1998

59 ◆ INT. BUS (PRESENT DAY) — DAY

. . . and we SEE through the bus window as Young Victor is chasing the bus.

As the bus increases in speed, Young Victor falls behind and out of FRAME.

We SEE only the empty road and then CAMERA SLOWLY PULLS BACK to reveal the adult Victor sitting in the bus.

ANGLE ON Thomas and Victor.

Thomas. Hey, what do you remember about your Dad?

Victor ignores Thomas.

Thomas. I remember one time we had a fry bread eating contest and he ate fifteen pieces of fry bread. It was cool.

Victor sits up in his seat and looks at Thomas.

Victor. You know, Thomas? I don't know what you're talking about half the time. Why is that?
Thomas. I don't know.
Victor. I mean, you just go on and on talking about nothing. Why can't you have a normal conversation? You're always trying to sound like some damn

---

[1] Alexie, in the Scene Notes at the end of his screenplay, asserts that Scene 59 (excerpted here) is, "without a doubt, my favorite scene in the film." Note that this scene does not appear in the story.

medicine man or something. I mean, how many times have you seen *Dances With Wolves*? A hundred, two hundred times?

Embarrassed, Thomas ducks his head.

Victor *(cont'd).* Oh, jeez, you have seen it that many times, haven't you? Man. Do you think that shit is real? God. Don't you even know how to be a real Indian?
Thomas *(whispering).* I guess not.

Victor is disgusted.

Victor. Well, shit, no wonder. Jeez, I guess I'll have to teach you then, enit?

Thomas nods eagerly.

Victor. First of all, quit grinning like an idiot. Indians ain't supposed to smile like that. Get stoic.

Thomas tries to look serious. He fails.

Victor. No, like this.

Victor gets a very cool look on his face, serious, determined, warriorlike.

Victor. You got to look mean or people won't respect you. White people will run all over you if you don't look mean. You got to look like a warrior. You got to look like you just got back from killing a buffalo.
Thomas. But our tribe never hunted buffalo. We were fishermen.
Victor. What? You want to look like you just came back from catching a fish? It ain't Dances With Salmon, you know? Man, you think a fisherman is tough? Thomas, you got to look like a warrior.

Thomas gets stoic. He's better this time.

Victor. There, that's better. And second, you can't be talking as much as you do. You got to have some mystery. You got to look like you have secrets, you know? Like you're in a secret conversation with the earth or something. You don't talk. You just nod your head.
(beat to nod his head)
See! That makes you look dangerous.

Thomas nods his head.

Victor and Thomas nod back and forth.

Victor.   And third, you got to know how to use your hair.
Thomas.   My hair?
Victor.   Yeah, I mean, look at your hear, all braided up and stuff. You've got to free it.

Victor shakes his hair out very vainly.

He runs his hands through it sexily.

Victor.   See what I mean? An Indian man ain't nothing without his hair. You got to use it.

Thomas slowly fingers his tightly braided hair as Victor talks to him.

Victor.   And last, and most important, you've got to get rid of that suit, Thomas. You just have to.

Thomas looks down at his three-piece suit.

Questions for Looking Deeper

1. Did you find the scene funny? Why?

2. How do you think Alexie feels about the general perception of Indians and their behavior?

Syd Field   (b. 1936)
from Screenplay: The Foundations of Screenwriting   1994

Adapting a novel, book, play, or article into a screenplay is the same as writing an original screenplay. "To adapt" means to transpose from one medium to another. *Adaptation* is defined as the ability "to make fit or suitable by changing, or adjusting" — modifying something to create a change in structure, function, and form, which produces a better adjustment.

Put another way, a novel is a novel, a play a play, a screenplay a screenplay. Adapting a book into a screenplay means to change one (a book) into the other (a screenplay), not superimpose one onto the other. Not a filmed novel or a filmed stage play. They are two different forms. An apple and an orange.

When you *adapt* a novel, play, article, or even a song into a screenplay, you are changing one form into another. You are writing a screenplay *based on other material*.

In essence, however, you are still writing an original screenplay. And you must approach it the same way.

A novel usually deals with the internal life of someone, the character's thoughts, feelings, emotions, and memories occurring within the *mindscape* of dramatic action. In a novel, you can write the same scene in a sentence, a paragraph, a page, or chapter, describing the internal dialogue, the thoughts, feelings, and impressions of the character. A novel usually takes place inside the character's head.

A play, on the other hand, is told in words, and thoughts, feelings, and events are described in dialogue on a stage locked within the boundaries of the proscenium arch. A play deals with the *language* of dramatic action.

A screenplay deals with *externals,* with details — the ticking of a clock, a child playing in an empty street, a car turning the corner. A screenplay is a story told with pictures, placed within the context of dramatic structure. . . .

An adaptation must be viewed as an original screenplay. It only *starts* from the novel, book, play, article, or song. That is *source* material, the starting point. Nothing more.

When you adapt a novel, you are not obligated to remain faithful to the original material.

Question for Looking Deeper

Now that you've read a scene adapted from a story, and read an account of what adaptation entails, try your skill. Choose a scene or two from a favorite story in the text (or poem, for that matter) and write a screenplay adaptation.

Emily Dickinson   (1830–1886)

What Soft —
Cherubic Creatures —   ca. 1862

What Soft — Cherubic Creatures —
These Gentlewomen are —
One would as soon assault a Plush —
Or violate a Star —

Such Dimity Convictions —
A Horror so refined
Of freckled Human Nature —
Of Deity — ashamed —

It's such a common-Glory —
A Fisherman's — Degree —   10
Redemption — Brittle Lady —
Be so — ashamed of Thee —

Paul Laurence Dunbar   (1872–1906)

We Wear the Mask   1896

We wear the mask that grins and lies,
It hides our cheeks and shades our eyes —
This debt we pay to human guile;
With torn and bleeding hearts we smile,
And mouth with myriad subtleties.

Why should the world be over-wise,
In counting all our tears and sighs?
Nay, let them only see us, while
   We wear the mask.

We smile, but, O great Christ, our cries   10
To thee from tortured souls arise.
We sing, but oh the clay is vile
Beneath our feet, and long the mile;
But let the world dream otherwise,
   We wear the mask!

Robert Frost   (1874–1963)

Departmental 1936

An ant on the table cloth
Ran into a dormant moth
Of many times his size.
He showed not the least surprise.
His business wasn't with such.
He gave it scarcely a touch,
And was off on his duty run.
Yet if he encountered one
Of the hive's enquiry squad
Whose work is to find out God   10
And the nature of time and space,
He would put him onto the case.
Ants are a curious race;
One crossing with hurried tread
The body of one of their dead
Isn't given a moment's arrest—
Seems not even impressed.
But he no doubt reports to any
With whom he crosses antennae,
And they no doubt report   20
To the higher up at court.
Then word goes forth in Formic:
"Death's come to Jerry McCormic,

Our selfless forager Jerry.
Will the special Janizary
Whose office it is to bury
The dead of the commissary
Go bring him home to his people.
Lay him in state on a sepal.
Wrap him for shroud in a petal.   30
Embalm him with ichor of nettle.
This is the word of your Queen."
And presently on the scene
Appears a solemn mortician;
And taking formal position
With feelers calmly atwiddle,
Seizes the dead by the middle,
And heaving him high in air,
Carries him out of there.
No one stands round to stare.   40
It is nobody else's affair.
It couldn't be called ungentle.
But how thoroughly departmental.

For Analysis

1. What comment does this poem make on human society? Is ant society a good metaphor for human society? Explain.

2. How do the **diction** and **rhyme** help establish the **tone?**

Writing Topic

How does the diction in this poem convey the speaker's attitude toward the social order he describes?

Amy Lowell   (1874–1925)

Patterns   1916

I walk down the garden-paths,
And all the daffodils
Are blowing, and the bright blue squills.
I walk down the patterned garden-paths
In my stiff, brocaded gown.
With my powdered hair and jeweled fan,

I too am a rare
Pattern. As I wander down
The garden-paths.

My dress is richly figured,   10
And the train
Makes a pink and silver stain
On the gravel, and the thrift
Of the borders.
Just a plate of current fashion,
Tripping by in high-heeled, ribboned shoes.
Not a softness anywhere about me,
Only whalebone and brocade.
And I sink on a seat in the shade
Of a lime tree. For my passion   20
Wars against the stiff brocade.
The daffodils and squills
Flutter in the breeze
As they please.
And I weep;
For the lime-tree is in blossom
And one small flower has dropped upon my bosom.

And the plashing of waterdrops
In the marble fountain
Comes down the garden-paths.   30
The dripping never stops.
Underneath my stiffened gown
Is the softness of a woman bathing in a marble basin,
A basin in the midst of hedges grown
So thick, she cannot see her lover hiding,
But she guesses he is near,
And the sliding of the water
Seems the stroking of a dear
Hand upon her.
What is Summer in a fine brocaded gown!   40
I should like to see it lying in a heap upon the ground.
All the pink and silver crumpled up on the ground.

I would be the pink and silver as I ran along the paths,
And he would stumble after,
Bewildered by my laughter.
I should see the sun flashing from his sword-hilt and the buckles
        on his shoes.

I would choose
To lead him in a maze along the patterned paths,
A bright and laughing maze for my heavy-booted lover.
Till he caught me in the shade,   50
And the buttons of his waistcoat bruised my body as he clasped me,
Aching, melting, unafraid.
With the shadows of the leaves and the sundrops,
And the plopping of the waterdrops,
All about us in the open afternoon —
I am very like to swoon
With the weight of this brocade,
For the sun sifts through the shade.

Underneath the fallen blossom
In my bosom   60
Is a letter I have hid.
It was brought to me this morning by a rider from the Duke.
"Madam, we regret to inform you that Lord Hartwell
Died in action Thursday se'nnight."[1]
As I read it in the white, morning sunlight,
The letters squirmed like snakes.
"Any answer, Madam," said my footman.
"No," I told him.
"See that the messenger takes some refreshment.
No, no answer."   70
And I walked into the garden,
Up and down the patterned paths,
In my stiff, correct brocade.
The blue and yellow flowers stood up proudly in the sun,
Each one.
I stood upright too,
Held rigid to the pattern
By the stiffness of my gown;
Up and down I walked,
Up and down.   80

In a month he would have been my husband.
In a month, here, underneath this lime,
We would have broke the pattern;
He for me, and I for him,
He as Colonel, I as Lady,

---

[1] Seven nights (i.e., a week) ago.

On this shady seat.
He had a whim
That sunlight carried blessing.
And I answered, "It shall be as you have said."
Now he is dead.   90

In Summer and in Winter I shall walk
Up and down
The patterned garden-paths
In my stiff, brocaded gown.
The squills and daffodils
Will give place to pillared roses, and to asters, and to snow.
I shall go
Up and down
In my gown.
Gorgeously arrayed,   100
Boned and stayed.
And the softness of my body will be guarded from embrace
By each button, hook, and lace.
For the man who should loose me is dead,
Fighting with the Duke in Flanders,[2]
In a pattern called a war.
Christ! What are patterns for?

For Analysis

1. What period of time does the poem seem to be set in? Explain.

2. Identify the various kinds of patterns in the poem.

3. In line 83, the speaker refers to the pattern "We would have broke." What is that pattern? How might it have been broken?

4. Does the poem provide an answer to the question the speaker asks in the final line? Explain.

Writing Topics

1. Describe a pattern in your family that has limited your life.

2. Describe a societal pattern that has limited your life.

3. Write an essay in which you argue that patterns, while perhaps limiting, are necessary.

---

[2] A region of Belgium where battles were fought during wars in the eighteenth, nineteenth, and twentieth centuries.

Ezra Pound (1885–1972)

Portrait d'une Femme[1] 1926

Your mind and you are our Sargasso Sea,[2]
London has swept about you this score years
And bright ships left you this or that in fee:
Ideas, old gossip, oddments of all things,
Strange spars of knowledge and dimmed wares of price.
Great minds have sought you — lacking someone else.
You have been second always. Tragical?
No. You preferred it to the usual thing:
One dull man, dulling and uxorious,
One average mind — with one thought less, each year.   10
Oh, you are patient, I have seen you sit
Hours, where something might have floated up.
And now you pay one. Yes, you richly pay.
You are a person of some interest, one comes to you
And takes strange gain away:
Trophies fished up; some curious suggestion;
Fact that leads nowhere; and a tale or two,
Pregnant with mandrakes,[3] or with something else
That might prove useful and yet never proves,
That never fits a corner or shows use,   20
Or finds its hour upon the loom of days:
The tarnished, gaudy, wonderful old work;
Idols and ambergris and rare inlays,
These are your riches, your great store; and yet
For all this sea-hoard of deciduous things,
Strange woods half sodden, and new brighter stuff:
In the slow float of different light and deep,
No! there is nothing! In the whole and all,
Nothing that's quite your own.
Yet this is you.   30

---

[1] Portrait of a Lady.

[2] A relatively calm area of water in the North Atlantic Ocean where the currents deposit masses of seaweed, which collect flotsam and jetsam.

[3] A European plant. Its fleshy, forked root, resembling the human form, was thought to have magical properties, including the power to promote conception in women. Compare John Donne's reference to this plant in his poem "Song" (p. 1101).

For Analysis

1. What picture of the lady emerges from the first five lines of the poem? Is that picture modified or only amplified in the rest of the poem? Explain.

2. Is this a love poem? Explain.

3. Characterize the diction of the poem.

4. Explain line 7. Identify and explain the paradoxes in the poem. What do they tell us about the speaker's feelings?

5. One critic has called this a distinguished poem that fails to realize its full potential because it is written in blank verse. Does Pound't use of this very old English poetic meter as well as the elevated and even antiquated diction weaken what Pound is trying to say? Explain.

Writing Topic

Write an essay in which you create a brief biography of the woman Pound describes, including her background, social position, education, and any other aspect of her that interests you.

T. S. Eliot (1888–1965)

The Love Song of J. Alfred Prufrock 1917

S'io credessi che mia risposta fosse
a persona che mai tornasse al mondo,
questa fiamma staria senza più scosse.
Ma per ciò che giammai di questo fondo
non tornò vivo alcun, s'i'odo il vero,
senza tema d'infamia ti rispondo.[1]

Let us go then, you and I,
When the evening is spread out against the sky
Like a patient etherized upon a table;
Let us go, through certain half-deserted streets,

---

[1] From Dante, *Inferno*, XXVII, 61–66. The speaker is Guido da Montefeltro, who is imprisoned in a flame in the level of Hell reserved for false counselors. He tells Dante and Virgil, "If I thought my answer were given to one who might return to the world, this flame would stay without further movement. But since from this depth none has ever returned alive, if what I hear is true, I answer you without fear of infamy."

The muttering retreats
Of restless nights in one-night cheap hotels
And sawdust restaurants with oyster shells:
Streets that follow like a tedious argument
Of insidious intent
To lead you to an overwhelming question . . .   10
Oh, do not ask, "What is it?"
Let us go and make our visit.

In the room the women come and go
Talking of Michelangelo.

The yellow fog that rubs its back upon the windowpanes,
The yellow smoke that rubs its muzzle on the windowpanes
Licked its tongue into the corners of the evening,
Lingered upon the pools that stand in drains,
Let fall upon its back the soot that falls from chimneys,
Slipped by the terrace, made a sudden leap,   20
And seeing that it was a soft October night,
Curled once about the house, and fell asleep.

And indeed there will be time
For the yellow smoke that slides along the street,
Rubbing its back upon the windowpanes;
There will be time, there will be time
To prepare a face to meet the faces that you meet;
There will be time to murder and create,
And time for all the works and days of hands
That lift and drop a question on your plate;   30
Time for you and time for me,
And time yet for a hundred indecisions,
And for a hundred visions and revisions,
Before the taking of a toast and tea.

In the room the women come and go
Talking of Michelangelo.

And indeed there will be time
To wonder, "Do I dare?" and, "Do I dare?"
Time to turn back and descend the stair,
With a bald spot in the middle of my hair —   40
(They will say: "How his hair is growing thin!")
My morning coat, my collar mounting firmly to the chin,
My necktie rich and modest, but asserted by a simple pin —

(They will say: "But how his arms and legs are thin!")
Do I dare
Disturb the universe?
In a minute there is time
For decisions and revisions which a minute will reverse.

For I have known them all already, known them all —
Have known the evenings, mornings, afternoons,   50
I have measured out my life with coffee spoons;
I know the voices dying with a dying fall
Beneath the music from a farther room.
    So how should I presume?

And I have known the eyes already, known them all —
The eyes that fix you in a formulated phrase,
And when I am formulated, sprawling on a pin,
When I am pinned and wriggling on the wall,
Then how should I begin
To spit out all the butt-ends of my days and ways?   60
    And how should I presume?

And I have known the arms already, known them all —
Arms that are braceleted and white and bare
(But in the lamplight, downed with light brown hair!)
Is it perfume from a dress
That makes me so digress?
Arms that lie along a table, or wrap about a shawl.
    And should I then presume?
    And how should I begin?

                    .   .   .   .

Shall I say, I have gone at dusk through narrow streets   70
And watched the smoke that rises from the pipes
Of lonely men in shirt-sleeves, leaning out of windows? . . .

I should have been a pair of ragged claws
Scuttling across the floors of silent seas.

                    .   .   .   .

And the afternoon, the evening, sleeps so peacefully!
Smoothed by long fingers,
Asleep . . . tired . . . or it malingers,
Stretched on the floor, here beside you and me.
Should I, after tea and cakes and ices,
Have the strength to force the moment to its crisis?   80

But though I have wept and fasted, wept and prayed,
Though I have seen my head (grown slightly bald) brought in upon a platter,[2]
I am no prophet — and here's no great matter;
I have seen the moment of my greatness flicker,
And I have seen the eternal Footman hold my coat, and snicker,
And in short, I was afraid.

And would it have been worth it, after all,
After the cups, the marmalade, the tea,
Among the porcelain, among some talk of you and me,
Would it have been worth while,   90
To have bitten off the matter with a smile,
To have squeezed the universe into a ball
To roll it toward some overwhelming question,
To say: "I am Lazarus,[3] come from the dead,
Come back to tell you all, I shall tell you all" —
If one, settling a pillow by her head,
    Should say: "That is not what I meant at all.
    That is not it, at all."

And would it have been worth it, after all,
Would it have been worth while,   100
After the sunsets and the dooryards and the sprinkled streets,
After the novels, after the teacups, after the skirts that trail along the floor —
And this, and so much more? —
It is impossible to say just what I mean!
But as if a magic lantern threw the nerves in patterns on a screen:
Would it have been worth while
If one, settling a pillow or throwing off a shawl,
And turning toward the window, should say:
    "That is not it at all,
    That is not what I meant, at all."   110

               .   .   .   .

No! I am not Prince Hamlet, nor was meant to be;
Am an attendant lord, one that will do
To swell a progress,° start a scene or two,   state journey
Advise the prince; no doubt, an easy tool,
Deferential, glad to be of use,
Politic, cautious, and meticulous;
Full of high sentence,° but a bit obtuse;   sententiousness

---

[2] Like the head of John the Baptist. See Matthew 14:3–12.
[3] See John 11:1–14 and Luke 16:19–26.

At times, indeed, almost ridiculous —
Almost, at times, the Fool.

I grow old . . . I grow old . . .   120
I shall wear the bottoms of my trousers rolled.°   cuffed

Shall I part my hair behind? Do I dare to eat a peach?
I shall wear white flannel trousers, and walk upon the beach.
I have heard the mermaids singing, each to each.

I do not think that they will sing to me.

I have seen them riding seaward on the waves
Combing the white hair of the waves blown back
When the wind blows the water white and black.

We have lingered in the chambers of the sea
By sea-girls wreathed with seaweed red and brown   130
Till human voices wake us, and we drown.

For Analysis

1. This poem may be understood as a stream of consciousness passing through the mind of Prufrock. The "you and I" of line 1 may be different aspects of his personality. Or perhaps the "you and I" is parallel to Guido who speaks the epigraph and Dante to whom he tells the story that resulted in his damnation — hence, "you" is the reader and "I" is Prufrock. The poem is disjointed because it proceeds by psychological rather than logical stages. To what social class does Prufrock belong? How does Prufrock respond to the attitudes and values of his class? Does he change in the course of the poem?

2. Line 92 provides a good example of literary allusion (see the last stanza of Marvell's "To His Coy Mistress," p. 1104). How does an awareness of the allusion contribute to the reader's response to the stanza here?

3. What might the song of the mermaids (l. 124) signify, and why does Prufrock think they will not sing to him (l. 125)?

4. T. S. Eliot once said that some poetry "can communicate without being understood." Is this such a poem?

Writing Topic

What sort of man is J. Alfred Prufrock? How does the poet establish his characteristics?

E. E. Cummings   (1894–1962)

the Cambridge ladies who live in furnished souls   1923

the Cambridge ladies who live in furnished souls
are unbeautiful and have comfortable minds
(also, with the church's protestant blessings
daughters, unscented shapeless spirited)
they believe in Christ and Longfellow, both dead,
are invariably interested in so many things —
at the present writing one still finds
delighted fingers knitting for the is it Poles?
perhaps. While permanent faces coyly bandy
scandal of Mrs. N. and Professor D.   10
. . . the Cambridge ladies do not care, above
Cambridge if sometimes in its box of
sky lavender and cornerless, the
moon rattles like a fragment of angry candy

For Analysis
1. What **images** does the poet use to describe "the Cambridge ladies"? What do the images suggest?

2. What is the effect of the interruption "is it" in line 8?

3. In the final lines, the moon seems to protest against the superficiality of these women. What is the effect of comparing the moon to a fragment of candy?

On Style
Describe the **tone** of this poem.

Writing Topics
1. Compare this poem with Emily Dickinson's "What Soft — Cherubic Creatures — " (p. 759).

2. This poem **satirizes** the behavior of the Cambridge ladies. How *should* they behave?

Langston Hughes   (1902–1967)

Dinner Guest: Me   1965

I know I am
The Negro Problem
Being wined and dined,
Answering the usual questions
That come to white mind
Which seeks demurely
To probe in polite way
The why and wherewithal
Of darkness U.S.A. —
Wondering how things got this way   10
In current democratic night,
Murmuring gently
Over *fraises du bois*,
"I'm so ashamed of being white."

The lobster is delicious,
The wine divine,
And center of attention
At the damask table, mine.
To be a Problem on
Park Avenue at eight   20
Is not so bad.
Solutions to the Problem,
Of course, wait.

Henry Reed   (1914–1986)

Naming of Parts   1946

Today we have naming of parts. Yesterday,
We had daily cleaning. And tomorrow morning
We shall have what to do after firing. But today,
Today we have naming of parts. Japonica
Glistens like coral in all of the neighboring gardens,
   And today we have naming of parts.

This is the lower sling swivel. And this
Is the upper sling swivel, whose use you will see,
When you are given your slings. And this is the piling swivel,
Which in your case you have not got. The branches   10
Hold in the gardens their silent, eloquent gestures,
    Which in our case we have not got.

This is the safety-catch, which is always released
With an easy flick of the thumb. And please do not let me
See anyone using his finger. You can do it quite easy
If you have any strength in your thumb. The blossoms
Are fragile and motionless, never letting anyone see
    Any of them using their finger.

And this you can see is the bolt. The purpose of this
Is to open the breech, as you see. We can slide it   20
Rapidly backwards and forwards: we call this
Easing the spring. And rapidly backwards and forwards
The early bees are assaulting and fumbling the flowers:
    They call it easing the Spring.

They call it easing the Spring: it is perfectly easy
If you have any strength in your thumb: like the bolt,
And the breech, and the cocking-piece, and the point of balance,
Which in our case we have not got; and the almond-blossom
Silent in all of the gardens and the bees going backwards and forwards,
    For today we have naming of parts.   30

For Analysis

1. The poem has two speakers. Identify their voices, and characterize the speakers.

2. The last line of each stanza repeats a phrase from within the stanza. What is the effect of the repetition?

Writing Topic

This poem incorporates a subtle underlying sexuality. Trace the language that generates it. What function does that sexuality serve in the poem?

M. Carl Holman (1919–1988)

Mr. Z 1967

Taught early that his mother's skin was the sign of error,
He dressed and spoke the perfect part of honor;
Won scholarships, attended the best schools,
Disclaimed kinship with jazz and spirituals;
Chose prudent, raceless views for each situation,
Or when he could not cleanly skirt dissension,
Faced up to the dilemma, firmly seized
Whatever ground was Anglo-Saxonized.

In diet, too, his practice was exemplary:
Of pork in its profane forms he was wary;   10
Expert in vintage wines, sauces and salads,
His palate shrank from cornbread, yams and collards.

He was as careful whom he chose to kiss:
His bride had somewhere lost her Jewishness,
But kept her blue eyes; an Episcopalian
Prelate proclaimed them matched chameleon.
Choosing the right addresses, here, abroad,
They shunned those places where they might be barred;
Even less anxious to be asked to dine
Where hosts catered to kosher accent or exotic skin.   20

And so he climbed, unclogged by ethnic weights,
An airborne plant, flourishing without roots.
Not one false note was struck — until he died:
His subtly grieving widow could have flayed
The obit writers, ringing crude changes on a clumsy phrase:
"One of the most distinguished members of his race."

For Analysis

1. Explain the title of this poem. What might "Z" stand for?

2. What is the significance of the description of Mr. Z's wife?

3. In what sense is the comment of the final line the only "false note" in an otherwise successful and exemplary life?

On Style
Describe the use of **irony** in this poem.

Writing Topics
1. Describe an experience you have had in which you successfully conformed to a set of expectations in order to achieve a goal, only to discover that you were denied that goal.

2. If you have lived as a minority (ethnic, religious, racial, or other) in a community, describe the pressures you felt to conform, and the costs (social, economic, or emotional) of your attempts or your refusal to conform.

Anne Sexton   (1928–1974)

Cinderella   1971

You always read about it:
the plumber with twelve children
who wins the Irish Sweepstakes.
From toilets to riches.
That story.

Or the nursemaid,
some luscious sweet from Denmark
who captures the oldest son's heart.
From diapers to Dior.
That story.   10

Or a milkman who serves the wealthy,
eggs, cream, butter, yogurt, milk,
the white truck like an ambulance
who goes into real estate
and makes a pile.
From homogenized to martinis at lunch.

Or the charwoman
who is on the bus when it cracks up
and collects enough from the insurance.
From mops to Bonwit Teller.   20
That story.

Once
the wife of a rich man was on her deathbed
and she said to her daughter Cinderella:
Be devout. Be good. Then I will smile
down from heaven in the seam of a cloud.
The man took another wife who had
two daughters, pretty enough
but with hearts like blackjacks.
Cinderella was their maid.   30
She slept on the sooty hearth each night
and walked around looking like Al Jolson.
Her father brought presents home from town,
jewels and gowns for the other women
but the twig of a tree for Cinderella.
She planted that twig on her mother's grave
and it grew to a tree where a white dove sat.
Whenever she wished for anything the dove
would drop it like an egg upon the ground.
The bird is important, my dears, so heed him.   40

Next came the ball, as you all know.
It was a marriage market.
The prince was looking for a wife.
All but Cinderella were preparing
and gussying up for the big event.
Cinderella begged to go too.
Her stepmother threw a dish of lentils
into the cinders and said: Pick them
up in an hour and you shall go.
The white dove brought all his friends;   50
all the warm wings of the fatherland came,
and picked up the lentils in a jiffy.
No, Cinderella, said the stepmother,
you have no clothes and cannot dance.
That's the way with stepmothers.

Cinderella went to the tree at the grave
and cried forth like a gospel singer:
Mama! Mama! My turtledove,
send me to the prince's ball!
The bird dropped down a golden dress   60
and delicate little gold slippers.
Rather a large package for a simple bird.
So she went. Which is no surprise.

Her stepmother and sisters didn't
recognize her without her cinder face
and the prince took her hand on the spot
and danced with no other the whole day.

As nightfall came she thought she'd better
get home. The prince walked her home
and she disappeared into the pigeon house   70
and although the prince took an axe and broke
it open she was gone. Back to her cinders.
These events repeated themselves for three days.
However on the third day the prince
covered the palace steps with cobbler's wax
and Cinderella's gold shoe stuck upon it.

Now he would find whom the shoe fit
and find his strange dancing girl for keeps.
He went to their house and the two sisters
were delighted because they had lovely feet.   80
The eldest went into a room to try the slipper on
but her big toe got in the way so she simply
sliced it off and put on the slipper.
The prince rode away with her until the white dove
told him to look at the blood pouring forth.

That is the way with amputations.
They don't just heal up like a wish.
The other sister cut off her heel
but the blood told as blood will.
The prince was getting tired.   90
He began to feel like a shoe salesman
but he gave it one last try.
This time Cinderella fit into the shoe
like a love letter into its envelope.

At the wedding ceremony
the two sisters came to curry favor
and the white dove pecked their eyes out.
Two hollow spots were left
like soup spoons.

Cinderella and the prince   100
lived, they say, happily ever after,
like two dolls in a museum case

never bothered by diapers or dust,
never arguing over the timing of an egg,
never telling the same story twice,
never getting a middle-aged spread,
their darling smiles pasted on for eternity.
Regular Bobbsey Twins.[1]
That story.

For Analysis

1. Where does one usually find the first four "stories" mentioned in the poem? Why do such stories interest readers?

2. Do you remember your feelings as a child in response to the story of Cinderella — particularly to Cinderella's success? How are those feelings modified by the last stanza?

Writing Topic

The language and formal structure of this poem resemble prose. Through examination of the image patterns and individual lines, describe the qualities that make the piece a poem.

Etheridge Knight   (1933–1991)

Hard Rock Returns to Prison from the Hospital for the Criminal Insane   1968

Hard Rock was "known not to take no shit
From nobody," and he had the scars to prove it:
Split purple lips, lumped ears, welts above
His yellow eyes, and one long scar that cut
Across his temple and plowed through a thick
Canopy of kinky hair.

Cinderella
    [1] The ever-cheerful central figures in a series of children's books.

The WORD was that Hard Rock wasn't a mean nigger
Anymore, that the doctors had bored a hole in his head,
Cut out part of his brain, and shot electricity
Through the rest. When they brought Hard Rock back,   10
Handcuffed and chained, he was turned loose,
Like a freshly gelded stallion, to try his new status.
And we all waited and watched, like Indians at a corral,
To see if the WORD was true.

As we waited we wrapped ourselves in the cloak
Of his exploits: "Man, the last time, it took eight
Screws to put him in the Hole." "Yeah, remember when he
Smacked the captain with his dinner tray?" "He set
The record for time in the Hole — 67 straight days!"
"Ol Hard Rock! man, that's one crazy nigger."   20
And then the jewel of a myth that Hard Rock had once bit
A screw on the thumb and poisoned him with syphilitic spit.

The testing came, to see if Hard Rock was really tame.
A hillbilly called him a black son of a bitch
And didn't lose his teeth, a screw who knew Hard Rock
From before shook him down and barked in his face.
And Hard Rock did *nothing*. Just grinned and looked silly,
His eyes empty like knot holes in a fence.

And even after we discovered that it took Hard Rock
Exactly 3 minutes to tell you his first name,   30
We told ourselves that he had just wised up,
Was being cool; but we could not fool ourselves for long,
And we turned away, our eyes on the ground. Crushed.

He had been our Destroyer, the doer of things
We dreamed of doing but could not bring ourselves to do,
The fears of years, like a biting whip,
Had cut grooves too deeply across our backs.

Felix Mnthali   (b. 1933)

The Stranglehold of English Lit.   1961

(For Molara Ogundipe-Leslie)

Those questions, sister,
those questions
        stand
        stab
        jab
        and gore
too close to the centre!

For if we had asked
why Jane Austen's people[1]
carouse all day   10
and do no work

would Europe in Africa
have stood
the test of time?
and would she still maul
the flower of our youth
in the south?
Would she?

Your elegance of deceit,
Jane Austen,   20
lulled the sons and daughters
of the dispossessed
into a calf-love
with irony and satire
around imaginary people.

While history went on mocking
the victims of branding irons
and sugar-plantations

[1] Characters in the novels of Jane Austen (1775–1817), a standard author in English literature courses. Her ironic domestic comedies are peopled with English country gentlefolk who, apparently, do not have to work for a living.

780

that made Jane Austen's people
wealthy beyond compare!   30

Eng. Lit., my sister,
was more than a cruel joke —
it was the heart
of alien conquest.

How could questions be asked
at Makerere and Ibadan,
Dakar and Ford Hare[2] —
with Jane Austen
at the centre?
How could they be answered?   40

For Analysis

1. Some would argue that studying Jane Austen is appropriate because her work embodies "universal" values. Does the speaker in the poem agree? Explain.

2. In the fifth stanza (ll. 26–30), the poet moves from derision to attack; discuss the issues Mnthali seems to have raised in this stanza.

3. Do you agree with the assertion of the sixth stanza (ll. 31–34)? Explain.

Writing Topic

Discuss the political and cultural implications of the poem's title.

Yevgeny Yevtushenko   (b. 1933)

I Would Like   trans. 1962

I would like
            to be born
                        in every country,
have a passport
            for them all,
to throw
            all foreign offices
                        into panic,

The Stranglehold of English Lit.
  [2] The sites of major African universities whose students, among others, participated in Africa's struggle to free itself from European domination.

be every fish
        in every ocean   10
and every dog
        along the path.
I don't want to bow down
          before any idols
or play at being
        an Orthodox church hippy,
but I would like to plunge
          deep into Lake Baikal[1]
and surface snorting
        somewhere,   20
            why not in the Mississippi?
In my beloved universe
          I would like
to be a lonely weed,
        but not a delicate Narcissus[2]
kissing his own mug
        in the mirror.
I would like to be
        any of God's creatures
right down to the last mangy hyena —   30
but never a tyrant
        or even the cat of a tyrant.
I would like to be
        reincarnated as a man
           in any circumstance:
a victim of Paraguayan prison tortures,
a homeless child in the slums of Hong Kong,
a living skeleton in Bangladesh,
a holy beggar in Tibet,
a black in Cape Town,   40
but never
      in the image of Rambo
The only people whom I hate
          are the hypocrites —
pickled hyenas
       in heavy syrup.
I would like to lie
        under the knives of all the surgeons in the world,
be hunchbacked, blind,
        suffer all kinds of diseases,   50
            wounds and scars,

---

[1] A large lake in Siberia, just north of Mongolia.
[2] In Greek myth, a beautiful youth who pined away for love of his own reflection and was changed into a flower.

be a victim of war,
                  or a sweeper of cigarette butts,
just so a filthy microbe of superiority
                         doesn't creep inside.
I would not like to be in the elite,
nor of course,
               in the cowardly herd,
nor be a guard-dog of that herd,
nor a shepherd,
                sheltered by that herd.   60
And I would like happiness,
                   but not at the expense of the unhappy,
and I would like freedom,
                   but not at the expense of the unfree.
I would like to love
             all the women in the world,
and I would like to be a woman, too —
                    just once. . . .
Men have been diminished   70
                by Mother Nature.
Suppose she'd given motherhood
                  to men?
If an innocent child
            stirred
               below his heart,
man would probably
             not be so cruel.
I would like to be man's daily bread —
say,   80
     a cup of rice
              for a Vietnamese woman in mourning,
cheap wine
           in a Neapolitan workers' trattoria,[3]
or a tiny tube of cheese
               in orbit round the moon:
let them eat me,
            let them drink me,
only let my death
              be of some use.   90
I would like to belong to all times,
                   shock all history so much
that it would be amazed
               what a smart aleck I was.

---

[3] A small inexpensive restaurant in Italy.

I would like to bring Nefertiti
to Pushkin in a troika.[4]
I would like to increase
the space of a moment
a hundredfold,
so that in the same moment   100
I could drink vodka with fishermen in Siberia
and sit together with Homer,
Dante,
Shakespeare,
and Tolstoy,
drinking anything,
except of course,
Coca-Cola,
— dance to the tom-toms in the Congo,
— strike at Renault,   110
— chase a ball with Brazilian boys
at Copacabana Beach.
I would like
to know every language,
the secret waters under the earth,
and do all kinds of work at once.
I would make sure
that one Yevtushenko was merely a poet,
the second — an underground fighter,
somewhere,   120
I couldn't say where
for security reasons,
the third — a student at Berkeley,
the fourth — a jolly Georgian[5] drinker,
and the fifth —
maybe a teacher of Eskimo children in Alaska,
the sixth —
a young president,
somewhere, say even in Sierra Leone,
the seventh —   130
would still be shaking a rattle in his stroller,
and the tenth . . .
the hundredth . . .
the millionth . . .
For me it's not enough to be myself,

[4] Nefertiti was a famously beautiful fourteenth-century B.C. queen of Egypt. Aleksandr Sergeyevich Pushkin (1799–1837) was, perhaps, the greatest Russian writer and poet of his time. A troika is a Russian vehicle drawn by a team of three horses.

[5] Georgia is one of the republics that made up the former Soviet Union. It lies along the east coast of the Black Sea.

let me be everyone!

Every creature

usually has a double,

but God was stingy

with the carbon paper,   140

and in his Paradise Publishing Company

made a unique copy of me.

But I shall muddle up

all God's cards —

I shall confound God!

I shall be in a thousand copies

to the end of my days,

so that the earth buzzes with me,

and computers go berserk

in the world census of me.   150

I would like to fight on all your barricades,

humanity,

dying each night

an exhausted moon,

and being resurrected each morning

like a newborn sun,

with an immortal soft spot

on my skull.

And when I die,

a smart-aleck Siberian François Villon,[6]   160

do not lay me in the earth

of France

or Italy,

but in our Russian, Siberian earth,

on a still green hill,

where I first felt

that I was

everyone.

For Analysis

1. The poet declares that he would like to be a certain kind of person. What kind of person? What specific **images** lead you to your judgment?

2. What kind of person does he *not* wish to be? What images support your conclusion?

3. Discuss the images that address chronological time. Discuss those that address geographical distance. Discuss those that address a sort of chain of being among creatures, moving from "low" to "high." How does Yevtushenko use these images to define his social and political views?

[6] A French balladeer, born in 1431, who was often in trouble with the law.

Writing Topic
In an essay, characterize the poet's notion of an ideal person, and speculate on how that person would get along in the real world. Do you accept, or would you modify, Yevtushenko's ideal? Explain.

Wole Soyinka   (b. 1934)

Telephone Conversation 1960

The price seemed reasonable, location
Indifferent. The landlady swore she lived
Off premises. Nothing remained
But self-confession. "Madam," I warned,
"I hate a wasted journey — I am African."
Silence. Silenced transmission of
Pressurized good-breeding. Voice, when it came,
Lipstick coated, long gold-rolled
Cigarette-holder pipped. Caught I was, foully.
"HOW DARK?" . . . I had not misheard. . . . "ARE YOU LIGHT   10
OR VERY DARK?" Button B. Button A. Stench
Of rancid breath of public hide-and-speak.
Red booth. Red pillar-box.[1] Red double-tiered
Omnibus squelching tar. It *was* real! Shamed
By ill-mannered silence, surrender
Pushed dumbfoundment to beg simplification.
Considerate she was, varying the emphasis —
"ARE YOU DARK? OR VERY LIGHT?" Revelation came.
"You mean — like plain or milk chocolate?"
Her assent was clinical, crushing in its light   20
Impersonality. Rapidly, wave-length adjusted.
I chose. "West African sepia" — and as afterthought,
"Down in my passport." Silence for spectroscopic
Flight of fancy, till truthfulness clanged her accent
Hard on the mouthpiece. "WHAT'S THAT?" conceding
"DON'T KNOW WHAT THAT IS." "Like brunette."
"THAT'S DARK, ISN'T IT?" "Not altogether.
Facially, I am brunette, but madam, you should see

---

[1] British public phones, whose booths were painted red, had one button which had to be depressed when a connection was made, and a second one that allowed the caller to disconnect. "Red pillar-box" refers to the public mailbox.

The rest of me. Palm of my hand, soles of my feet
Are a peroxide blonde. Friction, caused — 30
Foolishly madam — by sitting down, has turned
My bottom raven black — One moment madam!" — sensing
Her receiver rearing on the thunderclap
About my ears — "Madam," I pleaded, "wouldn't you rather
See for yourself?"

For Analysis

1. Aware of the racism of the culture in which he lives, the speaker volunteers to the landlady that he is African in order to avoid "a wasted journey" (l. 5). Why, then, is he so taken aback when she asks him how dark he is?

2. Describe the meaning and tone of the speaker's comment, "Caught I was, foully" (l. 9).

3. Explain the pun in line 12.

4. What does "It" refer to in line 14?

Writing Topic

How would the landlady have answered the speaker's question at the end of the poem, and how might she have justified her response?

Linda Hogan   (b. 1947)

First Light   1991

In early morning
I forget I'm in this world
with crooked chiefs
who make federal deals.

In the first light
I remember who rewards me for living,
not bosses
but singing birds and blue sky.

I know I can bathe and stretch,
make jewelry and love 10
the witch and wise woman
living inside, needing to be silenced
and put at rest for work's long day.

In the first light
I offer cornmeal
and tobacco.
I say hello to those who came before me,
and to birds
under the eaves,
and budding plants.   20

I know the old ones are here.
And every morning I remember the song
about how buffalo left through a hole in the sky
and how the grandmothers look out from those holes
watching over us
from there and from there.

For Robin

For Analysis

1. Explain what "this world" of line 2 is.

2. Who are the "crooked chiefs" (l. 3)? What is a "federal" deal (l. 4)? Is the speaker part of the world of chiefs and federal deals?

3. Why does the speaker offer cornmeal and tobacco?

4. Explain the title.

Writing Topic

Write an essay in which you speculate on who the poet is and what might have led her to write this poem.

Judith Ortiz Cofer   (b. 1952)

Latin Women Pray   1987

Latin women pray
In incense sweet churches
They pray in Spanish to an Anglo God
With a Jewish heritage.
And this Great White Father
Imperturbable in his marble pedestal
Looks down upon his brown daughters
Votive candles shining like lust
In his all seeing eyes
Unmoved by their persistent prayers.   10

Yet year after year
Before his image they kneel
Margarita Josefina Maria and Isabel
All fervently hoping
That if not omnipotent
At least he be bilingual.

Taslima Nasrin   (b. 1962)

Things Cheaply Had[1]   1991

In the market nothing can be had as cheap as women.
If they get a small bottle of *alta*[2] for their feet
   they spend three nights sleepless for sheer joy.
If they get a few bars of soap to scrub their skin
   and some scented oil for their hair
they become so submissive that they scoop out
   chunks of their flesh
to be sold in the flea market twice a week.
If they get a jewel for their nose
   they lick feet for seventy days or so,   10
a full three and a half months
   if it's a single striped sari.[3]

Even the mangy cur of the house barks now and then,
and over the mouths of women cheaply had
   there's a lock
a golden lock.

Things Cheaply Had
 [1] Translated from the Bengali by Carolyne Wright with Mohammad Nurul Huda and the author.
 [2] *Alta,* or lac-dye, is a red liquid with which South Asian women decorate the borders of their feet on ceremonial occasions, such as weddings and dance performances. *Alta* is more in vogue among Hindus, but Bangladeshi women also use it, and it can be seen on the feet of Muslim heroines and harem women in Moghul miniature paintings. [Translator's note.]
 [3] An outer garment worn chiefly by women of India and Pakistan, consisting of a length of cloth wrapped around the waist at one end and draped over the shoulder or head at the other.

Drama

Arthur Miller   (b. 1915)

Death of a Salesman   1949

*Certain Private Conversations in Two Acts
and a Requiem*

CAST

Willy Loman	**Uncle Ben**
Linda	**Howard Wagner**
Biff	**Jenny**
Happy	**Stanley**
Bernard	**Miss Forsythe**
The Woman	**Letta**
Charley	

Scene: *The action takes place in Willy Loman's house and yard and in various places he visits in the New York and Boston of today.*

  Throughout the play, in the stage directions, left and right mean stage left and stage right.

Act I

A melody is heard, played upon a flute. It is small and fine, telling of grass and trees and the horizon. The curtain rises.

  Before us is the Salesman's house. We are aware of towering, angular shapes behind it, surrounding it on all sides. Only the blue light of the sky falls upon the house and forestage; the surrounding area shows an angry glow of orange. As more light appears, we see a solid vault of apartment houses around the small, fragile-seeming home. An air of the dream clings to the place, a dream rising out of reality. The kitchen at center seems actual enough, for there is a kitchen table with three chairs, and a refrigerator. But no other fixtures are seen. At the back of the kitchen there is a draped entrance, which leads to the living-room. To the right of the kitchen, on a level raised two feet, is a bedroom furnished only with a brass bedstead and a straight chair. On a shelf over the bed a silver athletic trophy stands. A window opens onto the apartment house at the side.

Behind the kitchen, on a level raised six and a half feet, is the boys' bedroom, at present barely visible. Two beds are dimly seen, and at the back of the room a dormer window. (This bedroom is above the unseen living-room.) At the left a stairway curves up to it from the kitchen.

The entire setting is wholly or, in some places, partially transparent. The roof-line of the house is one-dimensional; under and over it we see the apartment buildings. Before the house lies an apron, curving beyond the forestage into the orchestra. This forward area serves as the back yard as well as the locale of all Willy's imaginings and of his city scenes. Whenever the action is in the present the actors observe the imaginary wall-lines, entering the house only through its door at the left. But in the scenes of the past these boundaries are broken, and characters enter or leave a room by stepping "through" a wall onto the forestage.

From the right, Willy Loman, the Salesman, enters, carrying two large sample cases. The flute plays on. He hears but is not aware of it. He is past sixty years of age, dressed quietly. Even as he crosses the stage to the doorway of the house, his exhaustion is apparent. He unlocks the door, comes into the kitchen, and thankfully lets his burden down, feeling the soreness of his palms. A word-sigh escapes his lips — it might be "Oh, boy, oh, boy." He closes the door, then carries his cases out into the living-room, through the draped kitchen doorway.

Linda, his wife, has stirred in her bed at the right. She gets out and puts on a robe, listening. Most often jovial, she has developed an iron repression of her exceptions to Willy's behavior — she more than loves him, she admires him, as though his mercurial nature, his temper, his massive dreams and little cruelties, served her only as sharp reminders of the turbulent longings within him, long-ings which she shares but lacks the temperament to utter and follow to their end.

Linda *(hearing Willy outside the bedroom, calls with some trepidation).* Willy!

Willy. It's all right. I came back.

Linda. Why? What happened? *(Slight pause.)* Did something happen, Willy?

Willy. No, nothing happened.

Linda. You didn't smash the car, did you?

Willy *(with casual irritation).* I said nothing happened. Didn't you hear me?

Linda. Don't you feel well?

Willy. I'm tired to the death. *(The flute has faded away. He sits on the bed beside her, a little numb.)* I couldn't make it. I just couldn't make it, Linda.

Linda (*very carefully, delicately*).   Where were you all day? You look terrible.

Willy.   I got as far as a little above Yonkers. I stopped for a cup of coffee. Maybe it was the coffee.

Linda.   What?

Willy (*after a pause*).   I suddenly couldn't drive any more. The car kept going off onto the shoulder, y'know?

Linda (*helpfully*).   Oh. Maybe it was the steering again. I don't think Angelo knows the Studebaker.

Willy.   No, it's me, it's me. Suddenly I realize I'm goin' sixty miles an hour and I don't remember the last five minutes. I'm — I can't seem to — keep my mind to it.

Linda.   Maybe it's your glasses. You never went for your new glasses.

Willy.   No, I see everything. I came back ten miles an hour. It took me nearly four hours from Yonkers.

Linda (*resigned*).   Well, you'll just have to take a rest, Willy, you can't continue this way.

Willy.   I just got back from Florida.

Linda.   But you didn't rest your mind. Your mind is overactive, and the mind is what counts, dear.

Willy.   I'll start out in the morning. Maybe I'll feel better in the morning. (*She is taking off his shoes.*) These goddam arch supports are killing me.

Linda.   Take an aspirin. Should I get you an aspirin? It'll soothe you.

Willy (*with wonder*).   I was driving along, you understand? And I was fine. I was even observing the scenery. You can imagine, me looking at scenery, on the road every week of my life. But it's so beautiful up there, Linda, the trees are so thick, and the sun is warm. I opened the windshield and just let the warm air bathe over me. And then all of a sudden I'm goin' off the road! I'm tellin' ya, I absolutely forgot I was driving. If I'd've gone the other way over the white line I might've killed somebody. So I went on again — and five minutes later I'm dreamin' again, and I nearly — (*He presses two fingers against his eyes.*) I have such thoughts, I have such strange thoughts.

Linda.   Willy, dear. Talk to them again. There's no reason why you can't work in New York.

Willy.   They don't need me in New York. I'm the New England man. I'm vital in New England.

Linda.   But you're sixty years old. They can't expect you to keep traveling every week.

Willy.   I'll have to send a wire to Portland. I'm supposed to see Brown and Morrison tomorrow morning at ten o'clock to show the line. Goddammit, I could sell them! (*He starts putting on his jacket.*)

Linda (*taking the jacket from him*).   Why don't you go down to the place tomorrow and tell Howard you've simply got to work in New York? You're too accommodating, dear.

Willy.   If old man Wagner was alive I'd a been in charge of New York now! That man was a prince, he was a masterful man. But that boy of his, that

Howard, he don't appreciate. When I went north the first time, the Wagner Company didn't know where New England was!

Linda. Why don't you tell those things to Howard, dear?

Willy *(encouraged).* I will, I definitely will. Is there any cheese?

Linda. I'll make you a sandwich.

Willy. No, go to sleep. I'll take some milk. I'll be up right away. The boys in?

Linda. They're sleeping. Happy took Biff on a date tonight.

Willy *(interested).* That so?

Linda. It was so nice to see them shaving together, one behind the other, in the bathroom. And going out together. You notice? The whole house smells of shaving lotion.

Willy. Figure it out. Work a lifetime to pay off a house. You finally own it, and there's nobody to live in it.

Linda. Well, dear, life is a casting off. It's always that way.

Willy. No, no, some people — some people accomplish something. Did Biff say anything after I went this morning?

Linda. You shouldn't have criticized him, Willy, especially after he just got off the train. You mustn't lose your temper with him.

Willy. When the hell did I lose my temper? I simply asked him if he was making any money. Is that a criticism?

Linda. But, dear, how could he make any money?

Willy *(worried and angered).* There's such an undercurrent in him. He became a moody man. Did he apologize when I left this morning?

Linda. He was crestfallen, Willy. You know how he admires you. I think if he finds himself, then you'll both be happier and not fight any more.

Willy. How can he find himself on a farm? Is that a life? A farmhand? In the beginning, when he was young, I thought, well, a young man, it's good for him to tramp around, take a lot of different jobs. But it's more than ten years now and he has yet to make thirty-five dollars a week!

Linda. He's finding himself, Willy.

Willy. Not finding yourself at the age of thirty-four is a disgrace!

Linda. Shh!

Willy. The trouble is he's lazy, goddammit!

Linda. Willy, please!

Willy. Biff is a lazy bum!

Linda. They're sleeping. Get something to eat. Go on down.

Willy. Why did he come home? I would like to know what brought him home.

Linda. I don't know. I think he's still lost, Willy. I think he's very lost.

Willy. Biff Loman is lost. In the greatest country in the world a young man with such — personal attractiveness, gets lost. And such a hard worker. There's one thing about Biff — he's not lazy.

Linda. Never.

Willy *(with pity and resolve).* I'll see him in the morning; I'll have a nice talk with him. I'll get him a job selling. He could be big in no time. My God! Remember how they used to follow him around in high school? When he smiled at one of them their faces lit up. When he walked down the street . . . *(He loses himself in reminiscences.)*

Linda *(trying to bring him out of it).*   Willy, dear, I got a new kind of American-type cheese today. It's whipped.

Willy.   Why do you get American when I like Swiss?

Linda.   I just thought you'd like a change —

Willy.   I don't want a change! I want Swiss cheese. Why am I always being contradicted?

Linda *(with a covering laugh).*   I thought it would be a surprise.

Willy.   Why don't you open a window in here, for God's sake?

Linda *(with infinite patience).*   They're all open, dear.

Willy.   The way they boxed us in here. Bricks and windows, windows and bricks.

Linda.   We should've bought the land next door.

Willy.   The street is lined with cars. There's not a breath of fresh air in the neighborhood. The grass don't grow any more, you can't raise a carrot in the back yard. They should've had a law against apartment houses. Remember those two beautiful elm trees out there? When I and Biff hung the swing between them?

Linda.   Yeah, like being a million miles from the city.

Willy.   They should've arrested the builder for cutting those down. They massacred the neighborhood. *(Lost.)* More and more I think of those days, Linda. This time of year it was lilac and wisteria. And then the peonies would come out, and the daffodils. What fragrance in this room!

Linda.   Well, after all, people had to move somewhere.

Willy.   No, there's more people now.

Linda.   I don't think there's more people. I think —

Willy.   There's more people! That's what's ruining this country! Population is getting out of control. The competition is maddening! Smell the stink from that apartment house! And another one on the other side . . . How can they whip cheese?

On Willy's last line, Biff and Happy raise themselves up in their beds, listening.

Linda.   Go down, try it. And be quiet.

Willy *(turning to Linda, guiltily).*   You're not worried about me, are you, sweetheart?

Biff.   What's the matter?

Happy.   Listen!

Linda.   You've got too much on the ball to worry about.

Willy.   You're my foundation and my support, Linda.

Linda.   Just try to relax, dear. You make mountains out of molehills.

Willy.   I won't fight with him any more. If he wants to go back to Texas, let him go.

Linda.   He'll find his way.

Willy.   Sure. Certain men just don't get started till later in life. Like Thomas Edison, I think. Or B. F. Goodrich. One of them was deaf. *(He starts for the bedroom doorway.)* I'll put my money on Biff.

Linda.   And Willy — if it's warm Sunday we'll drive in the country. And we'll open the windshield, and take lunch.

Willy.   No, the windshields don't open on the new cars.

Linda.   But you opened it today.

Willy.   Me? I didn't. *(He stops.)* Now isn't that peculiar! Isn't that a remarkable — *(He breaks off in amazement and fright as the flute is heard distantly.)*

Linda.   What, darling?

Willy.   That is the most remarkable thing.

Linda.   What, dear?

Willy.   I was thinking of the Chevy. *(Slight pause.)* Nineteen twenty-eight . . . when I had that red Chevy — *(Breaks off.)* That funny? I coulda sworn I was driving that Chevy today.

Linda.   Well, that's nothing. Something must've reminded you.

Willy.   Remarkable. Ts. Remember those days? The way Biff used to simonize that car? The dealer refused to believe there was eighty thousand miles on it. *(He shakes his head.)* Heh! *(To Linda.)* Close your eyes, I'll be right up. *(He walks out of the bedroom.)*

Happy *(to Biff).*   Jesus, maybe he smashed up the car again!

Linda *(calling after Willy).*   Be careful on the stairs, dear! The cheese is on the middle shelf! *(She turns, goes over to the bed, takes his jacket, and goes out of the bedroom.)*

Light has risen on the boys' room. Unseen, Willy is heard talking to himself, "Eighty thousand miles," and a little laugh. Biff gets out of bed, comes downstage a bit, and stands attentively. Biff is two years older than his brother Happy, well built, but in these days bears a worn air and seems less self-assured. He has succeeded less, and his dreams are stronger and less acceptable than Happy's. Happy is tall, powerfully made. Sexuality is like a visible color on him, or a scent that many women have discovered. He, like his brother, is lost, but in a different way, for he has never allowed himself to turn his face toward defeat and is thus more confused and hard-skinned, although seemingly more content.

Happy *(getting out of bed).*   He's going to get his license taken away if he keeps that up. I'm getting nervous about him, y'know, Biff?

Biff.   His eyes are going.

Happy.   No, I've driven with him. He sees all right. He just doesn't keep his mind on it. I drove into the city with him last week. He stops at a green light and then it turns red and he goes. *(He laughs.)*

Biff.   Maybe he's color-blind.

Happy.   Pop? Why he's got the finest eye for color in the business. You know that.

Biff *(sitting down on his bed).*   I'm going to sleep.

Happy.   You're not still sour on Dad, are you, Biff?

Biff.   He's all right, I guess.

Willy *(underneath them, in the living-room).*   Yes, sir, eighty thousand miles — eighty-two thousand!

Biff.   You smoking?

Happy *(holding out a pack of cigarettes).*   Want one?

Biff *(taking a cigarette).*   I can never sleep when I smell it.

Willy.   What a simonizing job, heh!

Happy *(with deep sentiment).*   Funny, Biff, y'know? Us sleeping in here again? The old beds. *(He pats his bed affectionately.)* All the talk that went across those two beds, huh? Our whole lives.

Biff.   Yeah. Lotta dreams and plans.

Happy *(with a deep and masculine laugh).*   About five hundred women would like to know what was said in this room.

They share a soft laugh.

Biff.   Remember that big Betsy something — what the hell was her name — over on Bushwick Avenue?

Happy *(combing his hair).*   With the collie dog!

Biff.   That's the one. I got you in there, remember?

Happy.   Yeah, that was my first time — I think. Boy, there was a pig! *(They laugh, almost crudely.)* You taught me everything I know about women. Don't forget that.

Biff.   I bet you forgot how bashful you used to be. Especially with girls.

Happy.   Oh, I still am, Biff.

Biff.   Oh, go on.

Happy.   I just control it, that's all. I think I got less bashful and you got more so. What happened, Biff? Where's the old humor, the old confidence? *(He shakes Biff's knee. Biff gets up and moves restlessly about the room.)* What's the matter?

Biff.   Why does Dad mock me all the time?

Happy.   He's not mocking you, he —

Biff.   Everything I say there's a twist of mockery on his face. I can't get near him.

Happy.   He just wants you to make good, that's all. I wanted to talk to you about Dad for a long time, Biff. Something's — happening to him. He — talks to himself.

Biff.   I noticed that this morning. But he always mumbled.

Happy.   But not so noticeable. It got so embarrassing I sent him to Florida. And you know something? Most of the time he's talking to you.

Biff.   What's he say about me?

Happy.   I can't make it out.

Biff.   What's he say about me?

Happy.   I think the fact that you're not settled, that you're still kind of up in the air . . .

Biff.   There's one or two other things depressing him, Happy.

Happy.   What do you mean?

Biff.   Never mind. Just don't lay it all to me.

Happy.   But I think if you just got started — I mean — is there any future for you out there?

Biff.   I tell ya, Hap, I don't know what the future is. I don't know — what I'm supposed to want.

Happy.   What do you mean?

Biff.   Well, I spent six or seven years after high school trying to work myself up. Shipping clerk, salesman, business of one kind or another. And it's a measly manner of existence. To get on that subway on the hot mornings in summer. To devote your whole life to keeping stock, or making phone calls, or selling or buying. To suffer fifty weeks of the year for the sake of a two-week vacation, when all you really desire is to be outdoors, with your shirt off. And always to have to get ahead of the next fella. And still — that's how you build a future.

Happy.   Well, you really enjoy it on a farm? Are you content out there?

Biff (*with rising agitation*).   Hap, I've had twenty or thirty different kinds of jobs since I left home before the war, and it always turns out the same. I just realized it lately. In Nebraska when I herded cattle, and the Dakotas, and Arizona, and now in Texas. It's why I came home now, I guess, because I realized it. This farm I work on, it's spring there now, see? And they've got about fifteen new colts. There's nothing more inspiring or — beautiful than the sight of a mare and a new colt. And it's cool there now, see? Texas is cool now, and it's spring. And whenever spring comes to where I am, I suddenly get the feeling, my God, I'm not gettin' anywhere! What the hell am I doing, playing around with horses, twenty-eight dollars a week! I'm thirty-four years old, I oughta be makin' my future. That's when I come running home. And now, I get here, and I don't know what to do with myself. (*After a pause.*) I've always made a point of not wasting my life, and everytime I come back here I know that all I've done is to waste my life.

Happy.   You're a poet, you know that, Biff? You're a — you're an idealist!

Biff.   No, I'm mixed up very bad. Maybe I oughta get married. Maybe I oughta get stuck into something. Maybe that's my trouble. I'm like a boy. I'm not married. I'm not in business, I just — I'm like a boy. Are you content, Hap? You're a success, aren't you? Are you content?

Happy.   Hell, no!

Biff.   Why? You're making money, aren't you?

Happy (*moving about with energy, expressiveness*).   All I can do now is wait for the merchandise manager to die. And suppose I get to be merchandise manager? He's a good friend of mine, and he just built a terrific estate on Long Island. And he lived there about two months and sold it, and now he's building another one. He can't enjoy it once it's finished. And I know that's just what I would do. I don't know what the hell I'm workin' for. Sometimes I sit in my apartment — all alone. And I think of the rent I'm paying. And it's crazy. But then, it's what I always wanted. My own apartment, a car, and plenty of women. And still, goddammit, I'm lonely.

Biff (*with enthusiasm*).   Listen, why don't you come out West with me?

Happy.   You and I, heh?

Biff.   Sure, maybe we could buy a ranch. Raise cattle, use our muscles. Men built like we are should be working out in the open.

Happy (*avidly*).   The Loman Brothers, heh?

Biff (*with vast affection*).   Sure, we'd be known all over the counties!

Happy (*enthralled*).   That's what I dream about, Biff. Sometimes I want to just rip my clothes off in the middle of the store and outbox that goddam merchandise manager. I mean I can outbox, outrun, and outlift anybody in that store, and I have to take orders from those common, petty sons-of-bitches till I can't stand it any more.

Biff.   I'm tellin' you, kid, if you were with me I'd be happy out there.

Happy (*enthused*).   See, Biff, everybody around me is so false that I'm constantly lowering my ideals . . .

Biff.   Baby, together we'd stand up for one another, we'd have someone to trust.

Happy.   If I were around you —

Biff.   Hap, the trouble is we weren't brought up to grub for money. I don't know how to do it.

Happy.   Neither can I!

Biff.   Then let's go!

Happy.   The only thing is — what can you make out there?

Biff.   But look at your friend. Builds an estate and then hasn't the peace of mind to live in it.

Happy.   Yeah, but when he walks into the store the waves part in front of him. That's fifty-two thousand dollars a year coming through the revolving door, and I got more in my pinky finger than he's got in his head.

Biff.   Yeah, but you just said —

Happy.   I gotta show some of those pompous, self-important executives over there that Hap Loman can make the grade. I want to walk into the store the way he walks in. Then I'll go with you, Biff. We'll be together yet, I swear. But take those two we had tonight. Now weren't they gorgeous creatures?

Biff.   Yeah, yeah, most gorgeous I've had in years.

Happy.   I get that any time I want, Biff. Whenever I feel disgusted. The trouble is, it gets like bowling or something. I just keep knockin' them over and it doesn't mean anything. You still run around a lot?

Biff.   Naa. I'd like to find a girl — steady, somebody with substance.

Happy.   That's what I long for.

Biff.   Go on! You'd never come home.

Happy. I would! Somebody with character, with resistance! Like Mom, y'know? You're gonna call me a bastard when I tell you this. That girl Charlotte I was with tonight is engaged to be married in five weeks. (*He tries on his new hat.*)

Biff. No kiddin'!

Happy. Sure, the guy's in line for the vice-presidency of the store. I don't know what gets into me, maybe I just have an overdeveloped sense of competition or something, but I went and ruined her, and furthermore I can't get rid of her. And he's the third executive I've done that to. Isn't that a crummy characteristic? And to top it all, I go to their weddings! (*Indignantly, but laughing.*) Like I'm not supposed to take bribes. Manufacturers offer me a hundred-dollar bill now and then to throw an order their way. You know how honest I am, but it's like this girl, see. I hate myself for it. Because I don't want the girl, and, still, I take it and — I love it!

Biff. Let's go to sleep.

Happy. I guess we didn't settle anything, heh?

Biff. I just got one idea that I think I'm going to try.

Happy. What's that?

Biff. Remember Bill Oliver?

Happy. Sure, Oliver is very big now. You want to work for him again?

Biff. No, but when I quit he said something to me. He put his arm on my shoulder, and he said, "Biff, if you ever need anything, come to me."

Happy. I remember that. That sounds good.

Biff. I think I'll go to see him. If I could get ten thousand or even seven or eight thousand dollars I could buy a beautiful ranch.

Happy. I bet he'd back you. 'Cause he thought highly of you, Biff. I mean, they all do. You're well liked, Biff. That's why I say to come back here, and we both have the apartment. And I'm tellin' you, Biff, any babe you want . . .

Biff. No, with a ranch I could do the work I like and still be something. I just wonder though. I wonder if Oliver still thinks I stole that carton of basketballs.

Happy. Oh, he probably forgot that long ago. It's almost ten years. You're too sensitive. Anyway, he didn't really fire you.

Biff. Well, I think he was going to. I think that's why I quit. I was never sure whether he knew or not. I know he thought the world of me, though. I was the only one he'd let lock up the place.

Willy (*below*). You gonna wash the engine, Biff?

Happy. Shh!

Biff looks at Happy, who is gazing down, listening. Willy is mumbling in the parlor.

Happy. You hear that?

They listen. Willy laughs warmly.

Biff *(growing angry)*.   Doesn't he know Mom can hear that?
Willy.   Don't get your sweater dirty, Biff!

A look of pain crosses Biff's face.

Happy.   Isn't that terrible? Don't leave again, will you? You'll find a job here. You gotta stick around. I don't know what to do about him, it's getting embarrassing.
Willy.   What a simonizing job!
Biff.   Mom's hearing that!
Willy.   No kiddin', Biff, you got a date? Wonderful!
Happy.   Go on to sleep. But talk to him in the morning, will you?
Biff *(reluctantly getting into bed)*.   With her in the house. Brother!
Happy *(getting into bed)*.   I wish you'd have a good talk with him.

The light on their room begins to fade.

Biff *(to himself in bed)*.   That selfish, stupid . . .
Happy.   Sh . . . Sleep, Biff.

Their light is out. Well before they have finished speaking, Willy's form is dimly seen below in the darkened kitchen. He opens the refrigerator, searches in there, and takes out a bottle of milk. The apartment houses are fading out, and the entire house and surroundings become covered with leaves. Music insinuates itself as the leaves appear.

Willy.   Just wanna be careful with those girls, Biff, that's all. Don't make any promises. No promises of any kind. Because a girl, y'know, they always believe what you tell 'em, and you're very young, Biff, you're too young to be talking seriously to girls.

Light rises on the kitchen. Willy, talking, shuts the refrigerator door and comes downstage to the kitchen table. He pours milk into a glass. He is totally immersed in himself, smiling faintly.

Willy.   Too young entirely, Biff. You want to watch your schooling first. Then when you're all set, there'll be plenty of girls for a boy like you. *(He smiles broadly at a kitchen chair.)* That so? The girls pay for you? *(He laughs.)* Boy, you must really be makin' a hit.

Willy is gradually addressing — physically — a point offstage, speaking through the wall of the kitchen, and his voice has been rising in volume to that of a normal conversation.

Willy.   I been wondering why you polish the car so careful. Ha! Don't leave the hubcaps, boys. Get the chamois to the hubcaps. Happy, use newspaper on the windows, it's the easiest thing. Show him how to do it, Biff! You see, Happy? Pad it up, use it like a pad. That's it, that's it, good work. You're doin' all right, Hap. (*He pauses, then nods in approbation for a few seconds, then looks upward.*) Biff, first thing we gotta do when we get time is clip that big branch over the house. Afraid it's gonna fall in a storm and hit the roof. Tell you what. We get a rope and sling her around, and then we climb up there with a couple of saws and take her down. Soon as you finish the car, boys, I wanna see ya. I got a surprise for you, boys.

Biff (*offstage*).   Whatta ya got, Dad?

Willy.   No, you finish first. Never leave a job till you're finished — remember that. (*Looking toward the "big trees."*) Biff, up in Albany I saw a beautiful hammock. I think I'll buy it next trip, and we'll hang it right between those two elms. Wouldn't that be something? Just swingin' there under those branches. Boy, that would be . . .

Young Biff and Young Happy appear from the direction Willy was addressing. Happy carries rags and a pail of water. Biff, wearing a sweater with a block "S," carries a football.

Biff (*pointing in the direction of the car offstage*).   How's that, Pop, professional?

Willy.   Terrific. Terrific job, boys. Good work, Biff.

Happy.   Where's the surprise, Pop?

Willy.   In the back seat of the car.

Happy.   Boy! (*He runs off.*)

Biff.   What is it, Dad? Tell me, what'd you buy?

Willy (*laughing, cuffs him*).   Never mind, something I want you to have.

Biff (*turns and starts off*).   What is it, Hap?

Happy (*offstage*).   It's a punching bag!

Biff.   Oh, Pop!

Willy.   It's got Gene Tunney's signature on it!

Happy runs onstage with a punching bag.

Biff.   Gee, how'd you know we wanted a punching bag?

Willy.   Well, it's the finest thing for the timing.

Happy (*lies down on his back and pedals with his feet*).   I'm losing weight, you notice, Pop?

Willy (*to Happy*).   Jumping rope is good too.

Biff.   Did you see the new football I got?

Willy (*examining the ball*).   Where'd you get a new ball?

Biff.   The coach told me to practice my passing.

Willy.   That so? And he gave you the ball, heh?

Biff.   Well, I borrowed it from the locker room. (*He laughs confidentially.*)

Willy (*laughing with him at the theft*).   I want you to return that.

Happy.   I told you he wouldn't like it!

Biff (*angrily*).   Well, I'm bringing it back!

Willy (*stopping the incipient argument, to Happy*).   Sure, he's gotta practice with a regulation ball, doesn't he? (*To Biff.*) Coach'll probably congratulate you on your initiative!

Biff.   Oh, he keeps congratulating my initiative all the time, Pop.

Willy.   That's because he likes you. If somebody else took that ball there'd be an uproar. So what's the report, boys, what's the report?

Biff.   Where'd you go this time, Dad? Gee we were lonesome for you.

Willy (*pleased, puts an arm around each boy and they come down to the apron*).   Lonesome, heh?

Biff.   Missed you every minute.

Willy.   Don't say? Tell you a secret, boys. Don't breathe it to a soul. Someday I'll have my own business, and I'll never have to leave home any more.

Happy.   Like Uncle Charley, heh?

Willy.   Bigger than Uncle Charley! Because Charley is not — liked. He's liked, but he's not — well liked.

Biff.   Where'd you go this time, Dad?

Willy.   Well, I got on the road, and I went north to Providence. Met the Mayor.

Biff.   The Mayor of Providence!

Willy.   He was sitting in the hotel lobby.

Biff.   What'd he say?

Willy.   He said, "Morning!" And I said, "You got a fine city here, Mayor." And then he had coffee with me. And then I went to Waterbury. Waterbury is a fine city. Big clock city, the famous Waterbury clock. Sold a nice bill there. And then Boston — Boston is the cradle of the Revolution. A fine city. And a couple of other towns in Mass., and on to Portland and Bangor and straight home!

Biff.   Gee, I'd love to go with you sometime, Dad.

Willy.   Soon as summer comes.

Happy.   Promise?

Willy.   You and Hap and I, and I'll show you all the towns. America is full of beautiful towns and fine, upstanding people. And they know me, boys, they know me up and down New England. The finest people. And when I bring you fellas up, there'll be open sesame for all of us, 'cause one thing, boys: I have friends. I can park my car in any street in New England, and the cops protect it like their own. This summer, heh?

Biff and Happy (*together*).   Yeah! You bet!

Willy.   We'll take our bathing suits.

Happy.   We'll carry your bags, Pop!

Willy.   Oh, won't that be something! Me comin' into the Boston stores with you boys carryin' my bags. What a sensation!

Biff is prancing around, practicing passing the ball.

Willy.   You nervous, Biff, about the game?

Biff.   Not if you're gonna be there.

Willy.   What do they say about you in school, now that they made you captain?

Happy.   There's a crowd of girls behind him everytime the classes change.

Biff *(taking Willy's hand).*   This Saturday, Pop, this Saturday — just for you, I'm going to break through for a touchdown.

Happy.   You're supposed to pass.

Biff.   I'm takin' one play for Pop. You watch me, Pop, and when I take off my helmet, that means I'm breakin' out. Then you watch me crash through that line!

Willy *(kisses Biff).*   Oh, wait'll I tell this in Boston!

Bernard enters in knickers. He is younger than Biff, earnest and loyal, a worried boy.

Bernard.   Biff, where are you? You're supposed to study with me today.

Willy.   Hey, looka Bernard. What're you lookin' so anemic about, Bernard?

Bernard.   He's gotta study, Uncle Willy. He's got Regents next week.

Happy *(tauntingly, spinning Bernard around).*   Let's box, Bernard!

Bernard.   Biff! *(He gets away from Happy.)* Listen, Biff, I heard Mr. Birnbaum say that if you don't start studyin' math, he's gonna flunk you, and you won't graduate. I heard him!

Willy.   You better study with him, Biff. Go ahead now.

Bernard.   I heard him!

Biff.   Oh, Pop, you didn't see my sneakers! *(He holds up a foot for Willy to look at.)*

Willy.   Hey, that's a beautiful job of printing!

Bernard *(wiping his glasses).*   Just because he printed University of Virginia on his sneakers doesn't mean they've got to graduate him, Uncle Willy!

Willy *(angrily).*   What're you talking about? With scholarships to three universities they're gonna flunk him?

Bernard.   But I heard Mr. Birnbaum say —

Willy.   Don't be a pest, Bernard! *(To his boys.)* What an anemic!

Bernard.   Okay, I'm waiting for you in my house, Biff.

Bernard goes off. The Lomans laugh.

Willy.   Bernard is not well liked, is he?

Biff.   He's liked, but he's not well liked.

Happy.   That's right, Pop.

Willy.   That's just what I mean. Bernard can get the best marks in school, y'understand, but when he gets out in the business world, y'understand, you are going to be five times ahead of him. That's why I thank Almighty God you're both built like Adonises.[1] Because the man who makes an appearance in the business world, the man who creates personal interest, is the man who gets ahead. Be liked and you will never want. You take me, for instance. I never have to wait in line to see a buyer. "Willy Loman is here!" That's all they have to know, and I go right through.

Biff. Did you knock them dead, Pop?

Willy. Knocked 'em cold in Providence, slaughtered 'em in Boston.

Happy (*on his back, pedaling again*). I'm losing weight, you notice, Pop?

Linda enters, as of old, a ribbon in her hair, carrying a basket of washing.

Linda (*with youthful energy*). Hello, dear!

Willy. Sweetheart!

Linda. How'd the Chevy run?

Willy. Chevrolet, Linda, is the greatest car ever built. (*To the boys.*) Since when do you let your mother carry wash up the stairs?

Biff. Grab hold there, boy!

Happy. Where to, Mom?

Linda. Hang them up on the line. And you better go down to your friends, Biff. The cellar is full of boys. They don't know what to do with themselves.

Biff. Ah, when Pop comes home they can wait!

Willy (*laughs appreciatively*). You better go down and tell them what to do, Biff.

Biff. I think I'll have them sweep out the furnace room.

Willy. Good work, Biff.

Biff (*goes through wall-line of kitchen to doorway at back and calls down*). Fellas! Everybody sweep out the furnace room! I'll be right down!

Voices. All right! Okay, Biff.

Biff. George and Sam and Frank, come out back! We're hangin' up the wash! Come on, Hap, on the double! (*He and Happy carry out the basket.*)

Linda. The way they obey him!

Willy. Well, that's training, the training. I'm tellin' you, I was sellin' thousands and thousands, but I had to come home.

Linda. Oh, the whole block'll be at that game. Did you sell anything?

Willy. I did five hundred gross in Providence and seven hundred gross in Boston.

Linda. No! Wait a minute, I've got a pencil. (*She pulls pencil and paper out of her apron pocket.*) That makes your commission . . . Two hundred — my God! Two hundred and twelve dollars!

Willy. Well, I didn't figure it yet, but . . .

Linda. How much did you do?

Willy. Well, I — I did — about a hundred and eighty gross in Providence. Well, no — it came to — roughly two hundred gross on the whole trip.

---

[1] In Greek mythology, Adonis was a young man known for his good looks and favored by Aphrodite, goddess of love and beauty.

Linda (*without hesitation*).   Two hundred gross. That's . . . (*She figures.*)

Willy.   The trouble was that three of the stores were half closed for inventory in Boston. Otherwise I woulda broke records.

Linda.   Well, it makes seventy dollars and some pennies. That's very good.

Willy.   What do we owe?

Linda.   Well, on the first there's sixteen dollars on the refrigerator —

Willy.   Why sixteen?

Linda.   Well, the fan belt broke, so it was a dollar eighty.

Willy.   But it's brand new.

Linda.   Well, the man said that's the way it is. Till they work themselves in, y'know.

They move through the wall-line into the kitchen.

Willy.   I hope we didn't get stuck on that machine.

Linda.   They got the biggest ads of any of them!

Willy.   I know, it's a fine machine. What else?

Linda.   Well, there's nine-sixty for the washing machine. And for the vacuum cleaner there's three and a half due on the fifteenth. Then the roof, you got twenty-one dollars remaining.

Willy.   It don't leak, does it?

Linda.   No, they did a wonderful job. Then you owe Frank for the carburetor.

Willy.   I'm not going to pay that man! That goddam Chevrolet, they ought to prohibit the manufacture of that car!

Linda.   Well, you owe him three and a half. And odds and ends, comes to around a hundred and twenty dollars by the fifteenth.

Willy.   A hundred and twenty dollars! My God, if business don't pick up I don't know what I'm gonna do!

Linda.   Well, next week you'll do better.

Willy.   Oh, I'll knock 'em dead next week. I'll go to Hartford. I'm very well liked in Hartford. You know, the trouble is, Linda, people don't seem to take to me.

They move onto the forestage.

Linda.   Oh, don't be foolish.

Willy.   I know it when I walk in. They seem to laugh at me.

Linda.   Why? Why would they laugh at you? Don't talk that way, Willy.

Willy moves to the edge of the stage. Linda goes into the kitchen and starts to darn stockings.

Willy.   I don't know the reason for it, but they just pass me by. I'm not noticed.

Linda.   But you're doing wonderful, dear. You're making seventy to a hundred dollars a week.

Willy. But I gotta be at it ten, twelve hours a day. Other men — I don't know — they do it easier. I don't know why — I can't stop myself — I talk too much. A man oughta come in with a few words. One thing about Charley. He's a man of few words, and they respect him.

Linda. You don't talk too much, you're just lively.

Willy (*smiling*). Well, I figure, what the hell, life is short, a couple of jokes. (*To himself.*) I joke too much! (*The smile goes.*)

Linda. Why? You're —

Willy. I'm fat. I'm very — foolish to look at, Linda. I didn't tell you, but Christmas time I happened to be calling on F. H. Stewarts, and a salesman I know, as I was going in to see the buyer I heard him say something about — walrus. And I — I cracked him right across the face. I won't take that. I simply will not take that. But they do laugh at me. I know that.

Linda. Darling . . .

Willy. I gotta overcome it. I know I gotta overcome it. I'm not dressing to advantage, maybe.

Linda. Willy, darling, you're the handsomest man in the world —

Willy. Oh, no, Linda.

Linda. To me you are. (*Slight pause.*) The handsomest.

From the darkness is heard the laughter of a woman. Willy doesn't turn to it, but it continues through Linda's lines.

Linda. And the boys, Willy. Few men are idolized by their children the way you are.

Music is heard as behind a scrim, to the left of the house, The Woman, dimly seen, is dressing.

Willy (*with great feeling*). You're the best there is, Linda, you're a pal, you know that? On the road — on the road I want to grab you sometimes and just kiss the life outa you.

The laughter is loud now, and he moves into a brightening area at the left, where The Woman has come from behind the scrim and is standing, putting on her hat, looking into a "mirror" and laughing.

Willy. 'Cause I get so lonely — especially when business is bad and there's nobody to talk to. I get the feeling that I'll never sell anything again, that I won't make a living for you, or a business, a business for the boys. (*He talks through The Woman's subsiding laughter; The Woman primps at the "mirror."*) There's so much I want to make for —

The Woman. Me? You didn't make me, Willy. I picked you.

Willy (*pleased*). You picked me?

The Woman (*who is quite proper-looking, Willy's age*). I did. I've been sitting at that desk watching all the salesmen go by, day in, day out. But you've got such a sense of humor, and we do have such a good time together, don't we?

Willy. Sure, sure. (*He takes her in his arms.*) Why do you have to go now?

The Woman. It's two o'clock . . .

Willy. No, come on in! (*He pulls her.*)

The Woman. . . . my sisters'll be scandalized. When'll you be back?

Willy. Oh, two weeks about. Will you come up again?

The Woman. Sure thing. You do make me laugh. It's good for me. (*She squeezes his arm, kisses him.*) And I think you're a wonderful man.

Willy. You picked me, heh?

The Woman. Sure. Because you're so sweet. And such a kidder.

Willy. Well, I'll see you next time I'm in Boston.

The Woman. I'll put you right through to the buyers.

Willy (*slapping her bottom*). Right. Well, bottoms up!

The Woman (*slaps him gently and laughs*). You just kill me, Willy. (*He suddenly grabs her and kisses her roughly.*) You kill me. And thanks for the stockings. I love a lot of stockings. Well, good night.

Willy. Good night. And keep your pores open!

The Woman. Oh, Willy!

The Woman bursts out laughing, and Linda's laughter blends in. The Woman disappears into the dark. Now the area at the kitchen table brightens. Linda is sitting where she was at the kitchen table, but now is mending a pair of her silk stockings.

Linda. You are, Willy. The handsomest man. You've got no reason to feel that —

Willy (*coming out of The Woman's dimming area and going over to Linda*). I'll make it all up to you, Linda, I'll —

Linda. There's nothing to make up, dear. You're doing fine, better than —

Willy (*noticing her mending*). What's that?

Linda. Just mending my stockings. They're so expensive —

Willy (*angrily, taking them from her*). I won't have you mending stockings in this house! Now throw them out!

Linda puts the stockings in her pocket.

Bernard (*entering on the run*). Where is he? If he doesn't study!

Willy (*moving to the forestage, with great agitation*). You'll give him the answers!

Bernard. I do, but I can't on a Regents! That's a state exam! They're liable to arrest me!

Willy. Where is he? I'll whip him, I'll whip him!

Linda. And he'd better give back that football, Willy, it's not nice.

Willy. Biff! Where is he? Why is he taking everything?

Linda. He's too rough with the girls, Willy. All the mothers are afraid of him!

Willy. I'll whip him!

Bernard. He's driving the car without a license!

The Woman's laugh is heard.

Willy. Shut up!

Linda. All the mothers —

Willy. Shut up!

Bernard (*backing quietly away and out*). Mr. Birnbaum says he's stuck up.

Willy. Get outa here!

Bernard. If he doesn't buckle down he'll flunk math! (*He goes off.*)

Linda. He's right, Willy, you've gotta —

Willy (*exploding at her*). There's nothing the matter with him! You want him to be a worm like Bernard? He's got spirit, personality . . .

As he speaks, Linda, almost in tears, exits into the living-room. Willy is alone in the kitchen, wilting and staring. The leaves are gone. It is night again, and the apartment houses look down from behind.

Willy. Loaded with it. Loaded! What is he stealing? He's giving it back, isn't he? Why is he stealing? What did I tell him? I never in my life told him anything but decent things.

Happy in pajamas has come down the stairs; Willy suddenly becomes aware of Happy's presence.

Happy. Let's go now, come on.

Willy (*sitting down at the kitchen table*). Huh! Why did she have to wax the floors herself? Everytime she waxes the floors she keels over. She knows that!

Happy. Shh! Take it easy. What brought you back tonight?

Willy. I got an awful scare. Nearly hit a kid in Yonkers. God! Why didn't I go to Alaska with my brother Ben that time! Ben! That man was a genius, that man was success incarnate! What a mistake! He begged me to go.

Happy. Well, there's no use in —

Willy. You guys! There was a man started with the clothes on his back and ended up with diamond mines!

Happy. Boy, someday I'd like to know how he did it.

Willy. What's the mystery? The man knew what he wanted and went out and got it! Walked into a jungle, and comes out, the age of twenty-one, and he's rich! The world is an oyster, but you don't crack it open on a mattress!

Happy. Pop, I told you I'm gonna retire you for life.

Willy. You'll retire me for life on seventy goddam dollars a week? And your women and your car and your apartment, and you'll retire me for life! Christ's sake, I couldn't get past Yonkers today! Where are you guys, where are you? The woods are burning! I can't drive a car!

Charley has appeared in the doorway. He is a large man, slow of speech, laconic, immovable. In all he says, despite what he says, there is pity, and, now, trepidation. He has a robe over pajamas, slippers on his feet. He enters the kitchen.

Charley. Everything all right?
Happy. Yeah, Charley, everything's . . .
Willy. What's the matter?
Charley. I heard some noise. I thought something happened. Can't we do something about the walls? You sneeze in here, and in my house hats blow off.
Happy. Let's go to bed, Dad. Come on.

Charley signals to Happy to go.

Willy. You go ahead, I'm not tired at the moment.
Happy *(to Willy).* Take it easy, huh? *(He exits.)*
Willy. What're you doin' up?
Charley *(sitting down at the kitchen table opposite Willy).* Couldn't sleep good. I had a heartburn.
Willy. Well, you don't know how to eat.
Charley. I eat with my mouth.
Willy. No, you're ignorant. You gotta know about vitamins and things like that.
Charley. Come on, let's shoot. Tire you out a little.
Willy *(hesitantly).* All right. You got cards?
Charley *(taking a deck from his pocket).* Yeah, I got them. Someplace. What is it with those vitamins?
Willy *(dealing).* They build up your bones. Chemistry.
Charley. Yeah, but there's no bones in a heartburn.
Willy. What are you talkin' about? Do you know the first thing about it?
Charley. Don't get insulted.
Willy. Don't talk about something you don't know anything about.

They are playing. Pause.

Charley. What're you doin' home?
Willy. A little trouble with the car.
Charley. Oh. *(Pause.)* I'd like to take a trip to California.
Willy. Don't say.
Charley. You want a job?
Willy. I got a job, I told you that. *(After a slight pause.)* What the hell are you offering me a job for?
Charley. Don't get insulted.
Willy. Don't insult me.
Charley. I don't see no sense in it. You don't have to go on this way.

Willy.   I got a good job. (*Slight pause.*) What do you keep comin' in here for?

Charley.   You want me to go?

Willy (*after a pause, withering*).   I can't understand it. He's going back to Texas again. What the hell is that?

Charley.   Let him go.

Willy.   I got nothin' to give him, Charley, I'm clean, I'm clean.

Charley.   He won't starve. None a them starve. Forget about him.

Willy.   Then what have I got to remember?

Charley.   You take it too hard. To hell with it. When a deposit bottle is broken you don't get your nickel back.

Willy.   That's easy enough for you to say.

Charley.   That ain't easy for me to say.

Willy.   Did you see the ceiling I put up in the living-room?

Charley.   Yeah, that's a piece of work. To put up a ceiling is a mystery to me. How do you do it?

Willy.   What's the difference?

Charley.   Well, talk about it.

Willy.   You gonna put up a ceiling?

Charley.   How could I put up a ceiling?

Willy.   Then what the hell are you bothering me for?

Charley.   You're insulted again.

Willy.   A man who can't handle tools is not a man. You're disgusting.

Charley.   Don't call me disgusting, Willy.

Uncle Ben, carrying a valise and an umbrella, enters the forestage from around the right corner of the house. He is a stolid man, in his sixties, with a mustache and an authoritative air. He is utterly certain of his destiny, and there is an aura of far places about him. He enters exactly as Willy speaks.

Willy.   I'm getting awfully tired, Ben.

Ben's music is heard. Ben looks around at everything.

Charley.   Good, keep playing; you'll sleep better. Did you call me Ben?

Ben looks at his watch.

Willy.   That's funny. For a second there you reminded me of my brother Ben.

Ben.   I only have a few minutes. (*He strolls, inspecting the place. Willy and Charley continue playing.*)

Charley.   You never heard from him again, heh? Since that time?

Willy.   Didn't Linda tell you? Couple of weeks ago we got a letter from his wife in Africa. He died.

Charley.   That so.

Ben (*chuckling*).   So this is Brooklyn, eh?

Charley. Maybe you're in for some of his money.

Willy. Naa, he had seven sons. There's just one opportunity I had with that man . . .

Ben. I must make a train, William. There are several properties I'm looking at in Alaska.

Willy. Sure, sure! If I'd gone with him to Alaska that time, everything would've been totally different.

Charley. Go on, you'd froze to death up there.

Willy. What're you talking about?

Ben. Opportunity is tremendous in Alaska, William. Surprised you're not up there.

Willy. Sure, tremendous.

Charley. Heh?

Willy. There was the only man I ever met who knew the answers.

Charley. Who?

Ben. How are you all?

Willy (*taking a pot, smiling*). Fine, fine.

Charley. Pretty sharp tonight.

Ben. Is mother living with you?

Willy. No, she died a long time ago.

Charley. Who?

Ben. That's too bad. Fine specimen of a lady, Mother.

Willy (*to Charley*). Heh?

Ben. I'd hoped to see the old girl.

Charley. Who died?

Ben. Heard anything from Father, have you?

Willy (*unnerved*). What do you mean, who died?

Charley (*taking a pot*). What're you talkin' about?

Ben (*looking at his watch*). William, it's half-past eight!

Willy (*as though to dispel his confusion he angrily stops Charley's hand*). That's my build!

Charley. I put the ace —

Willy. If you don't know how to play the game I'm not gonna throw my money away on you!

Charley (*rising*). It was my ace, for God's sake!

Willy. I'm through, I'm through!

Ben. When did Mother die?

Willy. Long ago. Since the beginning you never knew how to play cards.

Charley (*picks up the cards and goes to the door*). All right! Next time I'll bring a deck with five aces.

Willy. I don't play that kind of game!

Charley (*turning to him*). You ought to be ashamed of yourself!

Willy. Yeah?

Charley. Yeah! (*He goes out.*)

Willy (*slamming the door after him*). Ignoramus!

Ben (*as Willy comes toward him through the wall-line of the kitchen*). So you're William.

Willy (*shaking Ben's hand*). Ben! I've been waiting for you so long! What's the answer? How did you do it?

Ben. Oh, there's a story in that.

Linda enters the forestage, as of old, carrying the wash basket.

Linda. Is this Ben?

Ben (*gallantly*). How do you do, my dear.

Linda. Where've you been all these years? Willy's always wondered why you —

Willy (*pulling Ben away from her impatiently*). Where is Dad? Didn't you follow him? How did you get started?

Ben. Well, I don't know how much you remember.

Willy. Well, I was just a baby, of course, only three or four years old —

Ben. Three years and eleven months.

Willy. What a memory, Ben!

Ben. I have many enterprises, William, and I have never kept books.

Willy. I remember I was sitting under the wagon in — was it Nebraska?

Ben. It was South Dakota, and I gave you a bunch of wild flowers.

Willy. I remember you walking away down some open road.

Ben (*laughing*). I was going to find Father in Alaska.

Willy. Where is he?

Ben. At that age I had a very faulty view of geography, William. I discovered after a few days that I was heading due south, so instead of Alaska, I ended up in Africa.

Linda. Africa!

Willy. The Gold Coast!

Ben. Principally diamond mines.

Linda. Diamond mines!

Ben. Yes, my dear. But I've only a few minutes —

Willy. No! Boys! Boys! (*Young Biff and Happy appear.*) Listen to this. This is your Uncle Ben, a great man! Tell my boys, Ben!

Ben. Why, boys, when I was seventeen I walked into the jungle, and when I was twenty-one I walked out. (*He laughs.*) And by God I was rich.

Willy (*to the boys*). You see what I been talking about? The greatest things can happen!

Ben (*glancing at his watch*). I have an appointment in Ketchikan Tuesday week.

Willy. No, Ben! Please tell about Dad. I want my boys to hear. I want them to know the kind of stock they spring from. All I remember is a man with a big beard, and I was in Mamma's lap, sitting around a fire, and some kind of high music.

Ben. His flute. He played the flute.

Willy. Sure, the flute, that's right!

New music is heard, a high, rollicking tune.

Ben. Father was a very great and a very wild-hearted man. We would start in Boston, and he'd toss the whole family into the wagon, and then he'd drive the team right across the country; through Ohio, and Indiana, Michigan, Illinois, and all the Western states. And we'd stop in the towns and sell the flutes that he'd made on the way. Great inventor, Father. With one gadget he made more in a week than a man like you could make in a lifetime.

Willy. That's just the way I'm bringing them up, Ben — rugged, well liked, all-around.

Ben. Yeah? *(To Biff.)* Hit that, boy — hard as you can. *(He pounds his stomach.)*

Biff. Oh, no, sir!

Ben *(taking boxing stance).* Come on, get to me. *(He laughs.)*

Willy. Go to it, Biff! Go ahead, show him!

Biff. Okay! *(He cocks his fists and starts in.)*

Linda *(to Willy).* Why must he fight, dear?

Ben *(sparring with Biff).* Good boy! Good boy!

Willy. How's that, Ben, heh?

Happy. Give him the left, Biff!

Linda. Why are you fighting?

Ben. Good boy! *(Suddenly comes in, trips Biff, and stands over him, the point of his umbrella poised over Biff's eye.)*

Linda. Look out, Biff!

Biff. Gee!

Ben *(patting Biff's knee).* Never fight fair with a stranger, boy. You'll never get out of the jungle that way. *(Taking Linda's hand and bowing):* It was an honor and a pleasure to meet you, Linda.

Linda *(withdrawing her hand coldly, frightened).* Have a nice — trip.

Ben *(to Willy).* And good luck with your — what do you do?

Willy. Selling.

Ben. Yes. Well . . . *(He raises his hand in farewell to all.)*

Willy. No, Ben, I don't want you to think . . . *(He takes Ben's arm to show him.)* It's Brooklyn, I know, but we hunt too.

Ben. Really, now.

Willy. Oh, sure, there's snakes and rabbits and — that's why I moved out here. Why, Biff can fell any one of these trees in no time! Boys! Go right over to where they're building the apartment house and get some sand. We're gonna rebuild the entire front stoop now! Watch this, Ben!

Biff. Yes, sir! On the double, Hap!

Happy *(as he and Biff run off).* I lost weight, Pop, you notice?

Charley enters in knickers, even before the boys are gone.

Charley.   Listen, if they steal any more from that building the watchman'll put the cops on them!
Linda (*to Willy*).   Don't let Biff . . .

Ben laughs lustily.

Willy.   You shoulda seen the lumber they brought home last week. At least a dozen six-by-tens worth all kinds a money.
Charley.   Listen, if that watchman —
Willy.   I gave them hell, understand. But I got a couple of fearless characters there.
Charley.   Willy, the jails are full of fearless characters.
Ben (*clapping Willy on the back, with a laugh at Charley*).   And the stock exchange, friend!
Willy (*joining in Ben's laughter*).   Where are the rest of your pants?
Charley.   My wife bought them.
Willy.   Now all you need is a golf club and you can go upstairs and go to sleep. (*To Ben.*) Great athlete! Between him and his son Bernard they can't hammer a nail!
Bernard (*rushing in*).   The watchman's chasing Biff!
Willy (*angrily*).   Shut up! He's not stealing anything!
Linda (*alarmed, hurrying off left*).   Where is he? Biff, dear! (*She exits.*)
Willy (*moving toward the left, away from Ben*).   There's nothing wrong. What's the matter with you?
Ben.   Nervy boy. Good!
Willy (*laughing*).   Oh, nerves of iron, that Biff!
Charley.   Don't know what it is. My New England man comes back and he's bleedin', they murdered him up there.
Willy.   It's contacts, Charley, I got important contacts!
Charley (*sarcastically*).   Glad to hear it, Willy. Come in later, we'll shoot a little casino. I'll take some of your Portland money. (*He laughs at Willy and exits.*)
Willy (*turning to Ben*).   Business is bad, it's murderous. But not for me, of course.
Ben.   I'll stop by on my way back to Africa.
Willy (*longingly*).   Can't you stay a few days? You're just what I need, Ben, because I — I have a fine position here, but I — well, Dad left when I was such a baby and I never had a chance to talk to him and I still feel — kind of temporary about myself.
Ben.   I'll be late for my train.

They are at opposite ends of the stage.

Willy.   Ben, my boys — can't we talk? They'd go into the jaws of hell for me, see, but I —

Ben.   William, you're being first-rate with your boys. Outstanding, manly chaps!

Willy (*hanging on to his words*).   Oh, Ben, that's good to hear! Because sometimes I'm afraid that I'm not teaching them the right kind of — Ben, how should I teach them?

Ben (*giving great weight to each word, and with a certain vicious audacity*).   William, when I walked into the jungle, I was seventeen. When I walked out I was twenty-one. And, by God, I was rich! (*He goes off into darkness around the right corner of the house.*)

Willy.   . . . was rich! That's just the spirit I want to imbue them with! To walk into a jungle! I was right! I was right! I was right!

Ben is gone, but Willy is still speaking to him as Linda, in nightgown and robe, enters the kitchen, glances around for Willy, then goes to the door of the house, looks out, and sees him. Comes down to his left. He looks at her.

Linda.   Willy, dear? Willy?

Willy.   I was right!

Linda.   Did you have some cheese? (*He can't answer.*) It's very late, darling. Come to bed, heh?

Willy (*looking straight up*).   Gotta break your neck to see a star in this yard.

Linda.   You coming in?

Willy.   Whatever happened to that diamond watch fob? Remember? When Ben came from Africa that time? Didn't he give me a watch fob with a diamond in it?

Linda.   You pawned it, dear. Twelve, thirteen years ago. For Biff's radio correspondence course.

Willy.   Gee, that was a beautiful thing. I'll take a walk.

Linda.   But you're in your slippers.

Willy (*starting to go around the house at the left*).   I was right! I was! (*Half to Linda, as he goes, shaking his head.*) What a man! There was a man worth talking to. I was right!

Linda (*calling after Willy*).   But in your slippers, Willy!

Willy is almost gone when Biff, in his pajamas, comes down the stairs and enters the kitchen.

Biff.   What is he doing out there?

Linda.   Sh!

Biff.   God Almighty, Mom, how long has he been doing this?

Linda.   Don't, he'll hear you.

Biff.   What the hell is the matter with him?

Linda. It'll pass by morning.

Biff. Shouldn't we do anything?

Linda. Oh, my dear, you should do a lot of things, but there's nothing to do, so go to sleep.

Happy comes down the stairs and sits on the steps.

Happy. I never heard him so loud, Mom.

Linda. Well, come around more often; you'll hear him. (*She sits down at the table and mends the lining of Willy's jacket.*)

Biff. Why didn't you ever write me about this, Mom?

Linda. How would I write to you? For over three months you had no address.

Biff. I was on the move. But you know I thought of you all the time. You know that, don't you, pal?

Linda. I know, dear, I know. But he likes to have a letter. Just to know that there's still a possibility for better things.

Biff. He's not like this all the time, is he?

Linda. It's when you come home he's always the worst.

Biff. When I come home?

Linda. When you write you're coming, he's all smiles, and talks about the future, and — he's just wonderful. And then the closer you seem to come, the more shaky he gets, and then, by the time you get here, he's arguing, and he seems angry at you. I think it's just that maybe he can't bring himself to — to open up to you. Why are you so hateful to each other? Why is that?

Biff (*evasively*). I'm not hateful, Mom.

Linda. But you no sooner come in the door than you're fighting!

Biff. I don't know why. I mean to change. I'm tryin', Mom, you understand?

Linda. Are you home to stay now?

Biff. I don't know. I want to look around, see what's doin'.

Linda. Biff, you can't look around all your life, can you?

Biff. I just can't take hold, Mom. I can't take hold of some kind of a life.

Linda. Biff, a man is not a bird, to come and go with the springtime.

Biff. Your hair . . . (*He touches her hair.*) Your hair got so gray.

Linda. Oh, it's been gray since you were in high school. I just stopped dyeing it, that's all.

Biff. Dye it again, will ya? I don't want my pal looking old. (*He smiles.*)

Linda. You're such a boy! You think you can go away for a year and . . . You've got to get it into your head now that one day you'll knock on this door and there'll be strange people here —

Biff. What are you talking about? You're not even sixty, Mom.

Linda. But what about your father?

Biff (*lamely*). Well, I meant him too.

Happy. He admires Pop.

Linda. Biff, dear, if you don't have any feeling for him, then you can't have any feeling for me.

Biff. Sure I can, Mom.

Linda. No. You can't just come to see me, because I love him. (*With a threat, but only a threat, of tears.*) He's the dearest man in the world to me, and I won't have anyone making him feel unwanted and low and blue. You've got to make up your mind now, darling, there's no leeway any more. Either he's your father and you pay him that respect, or else you're not to come here. I know he's not easy to get along with — nobody knows that better than me — but . . .

Willy (*from the left, with a laugh*). Hey, hey, Biffo!

Biff (*starting to go out after Willy*). What the hell is the matter with him? (*Happy stops him.*)

Linda. Don't — don't go near him!

Biff. Stop making excuses for him! He always, always wiped the floor with you. Never had an ounce of respect for you.

Happy. He's always had respect for —

Biff. What the hell do you know about it?

Happy (*surlily*). Just don't call him crazy!

Biff. He's got no character — Charley wouldn't do this. Not in his own house — spewing out that vomit from his mind.

Happy. Charley never had to cope with what he's got to.

Biff. People are worse off than Willy Loman. Believe me, I've seen them!

Linda. Then make Charley your father, Biff. You can't do that, can you? I don't say he's a great man. Willy Loman never made a lot of money. His name was never in the paper. He's not the finest character that ever lived. But he's a human being, and a terrible thing is happening to him. So attention must be paid. He's not to be allowed to fall into his grave like an old dog. Attention, attention must be finally paid to such a person. You called him crazy —

Biff. I didn't mean —

Linda. No, a lot of people think he's lost his — balance. But you don't have to be very smart to know what his trouble is. The man is exhausted.

Happy. Sure!

Linda. A small man can be just as exhausted as a great man. He works for a company thirty-six years this March, opens up unheard-of territories to their trademark, and now in his old age they take his salary away.

Happy (*indignantly*). I didn't know that, Mom.

Linda. You never asked, my dear! Now that you get your spending money someplace else you don't trouble your mind with him.

Happy. But I gave you money last —

Linda. Christmas time, fifty dollars! To fix the hot water it cost ninety-seven fifty! For five weeks he's been on straight commission, like a beginner, an unknown!

Biff. Those ungrateful bastards!

Linda. Are they any worse than his sons? When he brought them business, when he was young, they were glad to see him. But now his old friends, the old buyers that loved him so and always found some order to hand him in a pinch — they're all dead, retired. He used to be able to make six, seven calls a day in Boston. Now he takes his valises out of the car and puts them back and takes them out again and he's exhausted. Instead of walking he talks now. He drives seven hundred miles, and when he gets there no one knows him any more, no one welcomes him. And what goes through a man's mind, driving seven hundred miles home without having earned a cent? Why shouldn't he talk to himself? Why? When he has to go to Charley and borrow fifty dollars a week and pretend to me that it's his pay? How long can that go on? How long? You see what I'm sitting here and waiting for? And you tell me he has no character? The man who never worked a day but for your benefit? When does he get the medal for that? Is this his reward — to turn around at the age of sixty-three and find his sons, who he loved better than his life, one a philandering bum —

Happy. Mom!

Linda. That's all you are, my baby! (*To Biff.*) And you! What happened to the love you had for him? You were such pals! How you used to talk to him on the phone every night! How lonely he was till he could come home to you!

Biff. All right, Mom. I'll live here in my room, and I'll get a job. I'll keep away from him, that's all.

Linda. No, Biff. You can't stay here and fight all the time.

Biff. He threw me out of this house, remember that.

Linda. Why did he do that? I never knew why.

Biff. Because I know he's a fake and he doesn't like anybody around who knows!

Linda. Why a fake? In what way? What do you mean?

Biff. Just don't lay it all at my feet. It's between me and him — that's all I have to say. I'll chip in from now on. He'll settle for half my pay check. He'll be all right. I'm going to bed. (*He starts for the stairs.*)

Linda. He won't be all right.

Biff (*turning on the stairs, furiously*). I hate this city and I'll stay here. Now what do you want?

Linda. He's dying, Biff.

Happy turns quickly to her, shocked.

Biff (*after a pause*). Why is he dying?

Linda. He's been trying to kill himself.

Biff (*with great horror*). How?

Linda. I live from day to day.

Biff. What're you talking about?

Linda. Remember I wrote you that he smashed up the car again? In February?

Biff. Well?

Linda. The insurance inspector came. He said that they have evidence. That all these accidents in the last year — weren't — weren't — accidents.

Happy. How can they tell that? That's a lie.

Linda.   It seems there's a woman . . . (*She takes a breath as*):
  { **Biff** (*sharply but contained*).   What woman?
  { **Linda** (*simultaneously*). . . . and this woman . . .
Linda.   What?
Biff.   Nothing. Go ahead.
Linda.   What did you say?
Biff.   Nothing. I just said what woman?
Happy.   What about her?
Linda.   Well, it seems she was walking down the road and saw his car. She says that he wasn't driving fast at all, and that he didn't skid. She says he came to that little bridge, and then deliberately smashed into the railing, and it was only the shallowness of the water that saved him.
Biff.   Oh, no, he probably just fell asleep again.
Linda.   I don't think he fell asleep.
Biff.   Why not?
Linda.   Last month . . . (*With great difficulty.*) Oh, boys, it's so hard to say a thing like this! He's just a big stupid man to you, but I tell you there's more good in him than in many other people. (*She chokes, wipes her eyes.*) I was looking for a fuse. The lights blew out, and I went down the cellar. And behind the fuse box — it happened to fall out — was a length of rubber pipe — just short.
Happy.   No kidding?
Linda.   There's a little attachment on the end of it. I knew right away. And sure enough, on the bottom of the water heater there's a new little nipple on the gas pipe.
Happy (*angrily*).   That — jerk.
Biff.   Did you have it taken off?
Linda.   I'm — I'm ashamed to. How can I mention it to him? Every day I go down and take away that little rubber pipe. But, when he comes home, I put it back where it was. How can I insult him that way? I don't know what to do. I live from day to day, boys. I tell you, I know every thought in his mind. It sounds so old-fashioned and silly, but I tell you he put his whole life into you and you've turned your backs on him. (*She is bent over in chair, weeping, her face in her hands.*) Biff, I swear to God! Biff, his life is in your hands!
Happy (*to Biff*).   How do you like that damned fool!
Biff (*kissing her*).   All right, pal, all right. It's all settled now. I've been remiss. I know that, Mom. But now I'll stay, and I swear to you, I'll apply myself. (*Kneeling in front of her, in a fever of self-reproach.*) It's just — you see, Mom, I don't fit in business. Not that I won't try. I'll try, and I'll make good.
Happy.   Sure you will. The trouble with you in business was you never tried to please people.
Biff.   I know, I —
Happy.   Like when you worked for Harrison's. Bob Harrison said you were tops, and then you go and do some damn fool thing like whistling whole songs in the elevator like a comedian.

Biff (*against Happy*).   So what? I like to whistle sometimes.

Happy.   You don't raise a guy to a responsible job who whistles in the elevator!

Linda.   Well, don't argue about it now.

Happy.   Like when you'd go off and swim in the middle of the day instead of taking the line around.

Biff (*his resentment rising*).   Well, don't you run off? You take off sometimes, don't you? On a nice summer day?

Happy.   Yeah, but I cover myself!

Linda.   Boys!

Happy.   If I'm going to take a fade the boss can call any number where I'm supposed to be and they'll swear to him that I just left. I'll tell you something that I hate to say, Biff, but in the business world some of them think you're crazy.

Biff (*angered*).   Screw the business world!

Happy.   All right, screw it! Great, but cover yourself!

Linda.   Hap, Hap!

Biff.   I don't care what they think! They've laughed at Dad for years, and you know why? Because we don't belong in this nuthouse of a city! We should be mixing cement on some open plain, or — or carpenters. A carpenter is allowed to whistle!

Willy walks in from the entrance of the house, at left.

Willy.   Even your grandfather was better than a carpenter. (*Pause. They watch him.*) You never grew up. Bernard does not whistle in the elevator, I assure you.

Biff (*as though to laugh Willy out of it*).   Yeah, but you do, Pop.

Willy.   I never in my life whistled in an elevator! And who in the business world thinks I'm crazy?

Biff.   I didn't mean it like that, Pop. Now don't make a whole thing out of it, will ya?

Willy.   Go back to the West! Be a carpenter, a cowboy, enjoy yourself!

Linda.   Willy, he was just saying —

Willy.   I heard what he said!

Happy (*trying to quiet Willy*).   Hey, Pop, come on now . . .

Willy (*continuing over Happy's line*).   They laugh at me, heh? Go to Filene's, go to the Hub, go to Slattery's, Boston. Call out the name Willy Loman and see what happens! Big shot!

Biff.   All right, Pop.

Willy.   Big!

Biff.   All right!

Willy.   Why do you always insult me?

Biff.   I didn't say a word. (*To Linda.*) Did I say a word?

Linda.   He didn't say anything, Willy.

Willy (*going to the doorway of the living-room*).   All right, good night, good night.

Linda. Willy, dear, he just decided . . .

Willy *(to Biff).* If you get tired hanging around tomorrow, paint the ceiling I put up in the living-room.

Biff. I'm leaving early tomorrow.

Happy. He's going to see Bill Oliver, Pop.

Willy *(interestedly).* Oliver? For what?

Biff *(with reserve, but trying, trying).* He always said he'd stake me. I'd like to go into business, so maybe I can take him up on it.

Linda. Isn't that wonderful?

Willy. Don't interrupt. What's wonderful about it? There's fifty men in the City of New York who'd stake him. *(To Biff.)* Sporting goods?

Biff. I guess so. I know something about it and —

Willy. He knows something about it! You know sporting goods better than Spalding, for God's sake! How much is he giving you?

Biff. I don't know, I didn't even see him yet, but —

Willy. Then what're you talkin' about?

Biff *(getting angry).* Well, all I said was I'm gonna see him, that's all!

Willy *(turning away).* Ah, you're counting your chickens again.

Biff *(starting left for the stairs).* Oh, Jesus, I'm going to sleep!

Willy *(calling after him).* Don't curse in this house!

Biff *(turning).* Since when did you get so clean?

Happy *(trying to stop them).* Wait a . . .

Willy. Don't use that language to me! I won't have it!

Happy *(grabbing Biff, shouts).* Wait a minute! I got an idea. I got a feasible idea. Come here, Biff, let's talk this over now, let's talk some sense here. When I was down in Florida last time, I thought of a great idea to sell sporting goods. It just came back to me. You and I, Biff — we have a line, the Loman Line. We train a couple of weeks, and put on a couple of exhibitions, see?

Willy. That's an idea!

Happy. Wait! We form two basketball teams, see? Two water-polo teams. We play each other. It's a million dollars' worth of publicity. Two brothers, see? The Loman Brothers. Displays in the Royal Palms — all the hotels. And banners over the ring and the basketball court: "Loman Brothers." Baby, we could sell sporting goods!

Willy. That is a one-million-dollar idea!

Linda. Marvelous!

Biff. I'm in great shape as far as that's concerned.

Happy. And the beauty of it is, Biff, it wouldn't be like a business. We'd be out playin' ball again . . .

Biff *(enthused).* Yeah, that's . . .

Willy. Million-dollar . . .

Happy. And you wouldn't get fed up with it, Biff. It'd be the family again. There'd be the old honor, and comradeship, and if you wanted to go off for a swim or somethin' — well, you'd do it! Without some smart cooky gettin' up ahead of you!

Willy.   Lick the world! You guys together could absolutely lick the civilized world.

Biff.   I'll see Oliver tomorrow. Hap, if we could work that out . . .

Linda.   Maybe things are beginning to —

Willy *(wildly enthused, to Linda).*   Stop interrupting! *(To Biff.)* But don't wear sport jacket and slacks when you see Oliver.

Biff.   No, I'll —

Willy.   A business suit, and talk as little as possible, and don't crack any jokes.

Biff.   He did like me. Always liked me.

Linda.   He loved you!

Willy *(to Linda).*   Will you stop! *(To Biff.)* Walk in very serious. You are not applying for a boy's job. Money is to pass. Be quiet, fine, and serious. Everybody likes a kidder, but nobody lends him money.

Happy.   I'll try to get some myself, Biff. I'm sure I can.

Willy.   I see great things for you kids, I think your troubles are over. But remember, start big and you'll end big. Ask for fifteen. How much you gonna ask for?

Biff.   Gee, I don't know —

Willy.   And don't say "Gee." "Gee" is a boy's word. A man walking in for fifteen thousand dollars does not say "Gee!"

Biff.   Ten, I think, would be top though.

Willy.   Don't be so modest. You always started too low. Walk in with a big laugh. Don't look worried. Start off with a couple of your good stories to lighten things up. It's not what you say, it's how you say it — because personality always wins the day.

Linda.   Oliver always thought the highest of him —

Willy.   Will you let me talk?

Biff.   Don't yell at her, Pop, will ya?

Willy *(angrily).*   I was talking, wasn't I?

Biff.   I don't like you yelling at her all the time, and I'm tellin' you, that's all.

Willy.   What're you, takin' over this house?

Linda.   Willy —

Willy *(turning on her).*   Don't take his side all the time, goddammit!

Biff *(furiously).*   Stop yelling at her!

Willy *(suddenly pulling on his cheek, beaten down, guilt ridden).*   Give my best to Bill Oliver — he may remember me. *(He exits through the living-room doorway.)*

Linda *(her voice subdued).*   What'd you have to start that for? *(Biff turns away.)* You see how sweet he was as soon as you talked hopefully? *(She goes over to Biff.)* Come up and say good night to him. Don't let him go to bed that way.

Happy.   Come on, Biff, let's buck him up.

Linda.   Please, dear. Just say good night. It takes so little to make him happy. Come. *(She goes through the living-room doorway, calling upstairs from within the living-room.)* Your pajamas are hanging in the bathroom, Willy!

Happy (*looking toward where Linda went out*).   What a woman! They broke the mold when they made her. You know that, Biff?

Biff.   He's off salary. My God, working on commission!

Happy.   Well, let's face it: he's no hot-shot selling man. Except that sometimes, you have to admit, he's a sweet personality.

Biff (*deciding*).   Lend me ten bucks, will ya? I want to buy some new ties.

Happy.   I'll take you to a place I know. Beautiful stuff. Wear one of my striped shirts tomorrow.

Biff.   She got gray. Mom got awful old. Gee, I'm gonna go in to Oliver tomorrow and knock him for a —

Happy.   Come on up. Tell that to Dad. Let's give him a whirl. Come on.

Biff (*steamed up*).   You know, with ten thousand bucks, boy!

Happy (*as they go into the living-room*).   That's the talk, Biff, that's the first time I've heard the old confidence out of you! (*From within the living-room, fading off.*) You're gonna live with me, kid, and any babe you want just say the word . . . (*The last lines are hardly heard. They are mounting the stairs to their parents' bedroom.*)

Linda (*entering her bedroom and addressing Willy, who is in the bathroom. She is straightening the bed for him*).   Can you do anything about the shower? It drips.

Willy (*from the bathroom*).   All of a sudden everything falls to pieces! Goddam plumbing, oughta be sued, those people. I hardly finished putting it in and the thing . . . (*His words rumble off.*)

Linda.   I'm just wondering if Oliver will remember him. You think he might?

Willy (*coming out of the bathroom in his pajamas*).   Remember him? What's the matter with you, you crazy? If he'd've stayed with Oliver he'd be on top by now! Wait'll Oliver gets a look at him. You don't know the average caliber any more. The average young man today — (*he is getting into bed*) — is got a caliber of zero. Greatest thing in the world for him was to bum around.

Biff and Happy enter the bedroom. Slight pause.

Willy (*stops short, looking at Biff*).   Glad to hear it, boy.

Happy.   He wanted to say good night to you, sport.

Willy (*to Biff*).   Yeah. Knock him dead, boy. What'd you want to tell me?

Biff.   Just take it easy, Pop. Good night. (*He turns to go.*)

Willy (*unable to resist*).   And if anything falls off the desk while you're talking to him — like a package or something — don't you pick it up. They have office boys for that.

Linda.   I'll make a big breakfast —

Willy.   Will you let me finish? (*To Biff.*) Tell him you were in the business in the West. Not farm work.

Biff.   All right, Dad.

Linda.   I think everything —

Willy *(going right through her speech).*   And don't undersell yourself. No less than fifteen thousand dollars.

Biff *(unable to bear him).*   Okay. Good night, Mom. *(He starts moving.)*

Willy.   Because you got a greatness in you, Biff, remember that. You got all kinds a greatness . . . *(He lies back, exhausted. Biff walks out.)*

Linda *(calling after Biff).*   Sleep well, darling!

Happy.   I'm gonna get married, Mom. I wanted to tell you.

Linda.   Go to sleep, dear.

Happy *(going).*   I just wanted to tell you.

Willy.   Keep up the good work. *(Happy exits.)* God . . . remember that Ebbets Field game? The championship of the city?

Linda.   Just rest. Should I sing to you?

Willy.   Yeah. Sing to me. *(Linda hums a soft lullaby.)* When that team came out — he was the tallest, remember?

Linda.   Oh, yes. And in gold.

Biff enters the darkened kitchen, takes a cigarette, and leaves the house. He comes downstage into a golden pool of light. He smokes, staring at the night.

Willy.   Like a young god. Hercules — something like that. And the sun, the sun all around him. Remember how he waved to me? Right up from the field, with the representatives of three colleges standing by? And the buyers I brought, and the cheers when he came out — Loman, Loman, Loman! God Almighty, he'll be great yet. A star like that, magnificent, can never really fade away!

The light on Willy is fading. The gas heater begins to glow through the kitchen wall, near the stairs, a blue flame beneath red coils.

Linda *(timidly).*   Willy dear, what has he got against you?

Willy.   I'm so tired. Don't talk any more.

Biff slowly returns to the kitchen. He stops, stares toward the heater.

Linda.   Will you ask Howard to let you work in New York?

Willy.   First thing in the morning. Everything'll be all right.

Biff reaches behind the heater and draws out a length of rubber tubing. He is horrified and turns his head toward Willy's room, still dimly lit, from which the strains of Linda's desperate but monotonous humming rise.

Willy *(staring through the window into the moonlight).*   Gee, look at the moon moving between the buildings!

Biff wraps the tubing around his hand and quickly goes up the stairs.

Curtain

Act II

Music is heard, gay and bright. The curtain rises as the music fades away. Willy, in shirt sleeves, is sitting at the kitchen table, sipping coffee, his hat in his lap. Linda is filling his cup when she can.

Willy.   Wonderful coffee. Meal in itself.
Linda.   Can I make you some eggs?
Willy.   No. Take a breath.
Linda.   You look so rested, dear.
Willy.   I slept like a dead one. First time in months. Imagine, sleeping till ten on a Tuesday morning. Boys left nice and early, heh?
Linda.   They were out of here by eight o'clock.
Willy.   Good work!
Linda.   It was so thrilling to see them leaving together. I can't get over the shaving lotion in this house!
Willy *(smiling).*   Mmm —
Linda.   Biff was very changed this morning. His whole attitude seemed to be hopeful. He couldn't wait to get downtown to see Oliver.
Willy.   He's heading for a change. There's no question, there simply are certain men that take longer to get — solidified. How did he dress?
Linda.   His blue suit. He's so handsome in that suit. He could be a — anything in that suit!

Willy gets up from the table. Linda holds his jacket for him.

Willy.   There's no question, no question at all. Gee, on the way home tonight I'd like to buy some seeds.
Linda *(laughing).*   That'd be wonderful. But not enough sun gets back there. Nothing'll grow any more.
Willy.   You wait, kid, before it's all over we're gonna get a little place out in the country, and I'll raise some vegetables, a couple of chickens . . .
Linda.   You'll do it yet, dear.

Willy walks out of his jacket. Linda follows him.

Willy.   And they'll get married, and come for a weekend. I'd build a little guest house. 'Cause I got so many fine tools, all I'd need would be a little lumber and some peace of mind.

Linda (*joyfully*).   I sewed the lining . . .

Willy.   I could build two guest houses, so they'd both come. Did he decide how much he's going to ask Oliver for?

Linda (*getting him into the jacket*).   He didn't mention it, but I imagine ten or fifteen thousand. You going to talk to Howard today?

Willy.   Yeah. I'll put it to him straight and simple. He'll just have to take me off the road.

Linda.   And Willy, don't forget to ask for a little advance, because we've got the insurance premium. It's the grace period now.

Willy.   That's a hundred . . . ?

Linda.   A hundred and eight, sixty-eight. Because we're a little short again.

Willy.   Why are we short?

Linda.   Well, you had the motor job on the car . . .

Willy.   That goddam Studebaker!

Linda.   And you got one more payment on the refrigerator . . .

Willy.   But it just broke again!

Linda.   Well, it's old, dear.

Willy.   I told you we should've bought a well-advertised machine. Charley bought a General Electric and it's twenty years old and it's still good, that son-of-a-bitch.

Linda.   But, Willy —

Willy.   Whoever heard of a Hastings refrigerator? Once in my life I would like to own something outright before it's broken! I'm always in a race with the junkyard! I just finished paying for the car and it's on its last legs. The refrigerator consumes belts like a goddam maniac. They time those things. They time them so when you finally paid for them, they're used up.

Linda (*buttoning up his jacket as he unbuttons it*).   All told, about two hundred dollars would carry us, dear. But that includes the last payment on the mortgage. After this payment, Willy, the house belongs to us.

Willy.   It's twenty-five years!

Linda.   Biff was nine years old when we bought it.

Willy.   Well, that's a great thing. To weather a twenty-five year mortgage is —

Linda.   It's an accomplishment.

Willy.   All the cement, the lumber, the reconstruction I put in this house! There ain't a crack to be found in it any more.

Linda.   Well, it served its purpose.

Willy.   What purpose? Some stranger'll come along, move in, and that's that. If only Biff would take this house, and raise a family . . . (*He starts to go.*) Good-by, I'm late.

Linda (*suddenly remembering*).   Oh, I forgot! You're supposed to meet them for dinner.

Willy.   Me?

Linda.   At Frank's Chop House on Forty-eighth near Sixth Avenue.

Willy.   Is that so! How about you?

Linda.   No, just the three of you. They're gonna blow you to a big meal!

Willy.   Don't say! Who thought of that?

Linda.   Biff came to me this morning, Willy, and he said, "Tell Dad, we want to blow him to a big meal." Be there six o'clock. You and your two boys are going to have dinner.

Willy.   Gee whiz! That's really somethin'. I'm gonna knock Howard for a loop, kid. I'll get an advance, and I'll come home with a New York job. Goddammit, now I'm gonna do it!

Linda.   Oh, that's the spirit, Willy!

Willy.   I will never get behind a wheel the rest of my life!

Linda.   It's changing, Willy, I can feel it changing!

Willy.   Beyond a question. G'by, I'm late. (*He starts to go again.*)

Linda (*calling after him as she runs to the kitchen table for a handkerchief*). You got your glasses?

Willy (*feels for them, then comes back in*).   Yeah, yeah, got my glasses.

Linda (*giving him the handkerchief*).   And a handkerchief.

Willy.   Yeah, handkerchief.

Linda.   And your saccharine?

Willy.   Yeah, my saccharine.

Linda.   Be careful on the subway stairs.

She kisses him, and a silk stocking is seen hanging from her hand. Willy notices it.

Willy.   Will you stop mending stockings? At least while I'm in the house. It gets me nervous. I can't tell you. Please.

Linda hides the stocking in her hand as she follows Willy across the forestage in front of the house.

Linda.   Remember, Frank's Chop House.

Willy (*passing the apron*).   Maybe beets would grow out there.

Linda (*laughing*).   But you tried so many times.

Willy.   Yeah. Well, don't work hard today. (*He disappears around the right corner of the house.*)

Linda.   Be careful!

As Willy vanishes, Linda waves to him. Suddenly the phone rings. She runs across the stage and into the kitchen and lifts it.

Linda.   Hello? Oh, Biff! I'm so glad you called, I just . . . Yes, sure, I just told him. Yes, he'll be there for dinner at six o'clock, I didn't forget. Listen, I was just dying to tell you. You know that little rubber pipe I told you about? That he connected to the gas heater? I finally decided to go down the cellar this morning and take it away and destroy it. But it's gone! Imagine? He took it away himself, it isn't there! (*She listens.*) When? Oh, then you took it. Oh — nothing, it's just that I'd hoped he'd taken it away himself. Oh, I'm not worried, darling, because this morning he left in such high spirits, it was like the old days! I'm not afraid any more. Did Mr. Oliver see you? . . . Well, you wait there then. And make a nice impression on him, darling. Just don't perspire too much before you see him. And have a nice time with Dad. He may have big news too! . . . That's right, a New York job. And be sweet to him tonight, dear. Be loving to him. Because he's only a little boat looking for a harbor. (*She is trembling with sorrow and joy.*) Oh, that's wonderful, Biff, you'll save his life. Thanks, darling. Just put your arm around him when he comes into the restaurant. Give him a smile. That's the boy . . . Good-by, dear. . . . You got your comb? . . . That's fine. Good-by, Biff dear.

In the middle of her speech, Howard Wagner, thirty-six, wheels in a small typewriter table on which is a wire-recording machine and proceeds to plug it in. This is on the left forestage. Light slowly fades on Linda as it rises on Howard. Howard is intent on threading the machine and only glances over his shoulder as Willy appears.

Willy. Pst! Pst!
Howard. Hello, Willy, come in.
Willy. Like to have a little talk with you, Howard.
Howard. Sorry to keep you waiting. I'll be with you in a minute.
Willy. What's that, Howard?
Howard. Didn't you ever see one of these? Wire recorder.
Willy. Oh. Can we talk a minute?
Howard. Records things. Just got delivery yesterday. Been driving me crazy, the most terrific machine I ever saw in my life. I was up all night with it.
Willy. What do you do with it?
Howard. I bought it for dictation, but you can do anything with it. Listen to this. I had it home last night. Listen to what I picked up. The first one is my daughter. Get this. (*He flicks the switch and "Roll Out the Barrel" is heard being whistled.*) Listen to that kid whistle.
Willy. That is lifelike, isn't it?
Howard. Seven years old. Get that tone.
Willy. Ts, ts. Like to ask a little favor if you . . .

The whistling breaks off, and the voice of Howard's daughter is heard.

His Daughter. "Now you, Daddy."
Howard. She's crazy for me! (*Again the same song is whistled.*) That's me! Ha! (*He winks.*)

Willy. You're very good!

The whistling breaks off again. The machine runs silent for a moment.

Howard. Sh! Get this now, this is my son.

His Son. "The capital of Alabama is Montgomery; the capital of Arizona is Phoenix; the capital of Arkansas is Little Rock; the capital of California is Sacramento . . ." *(and on, and on).*

Howard *(holding up five fingers).* Five years old, Willy!

Willy. He'll make an announcer some day!

His Son *(continuing).* "The capital . . ."

Howard. Get that — alphabetical order! *(The machine breaks off suddenly.)* Wait a minute. The maid kicked the plug out.

Willy. It certainly is a —

Howard. Sh, for God's sake!

His Son. "It's nine o'clock, Bulova watch time. So I have to go to sleep."

Willy. That really is —

Howard. Wait a minute! The next is my wife.

They wait.

Howard's Voice. "Go on, say something." *(Pause.)* "Well, you gonna talk?"

His Wife. "I can't think of anything."

Howard's Voice. "Well, talk — it's turning."

His Wife *(shyly, beaten).* "Hello." *(Silence.)* "Oh, Howard, I can't talk into this . . ."

Howard *(snapping the machine off).* That was my wife.

Willy. That is a wonderful machine. Can we —

Howard. I tell you, Willy, I'm gonna take my camera, and my bandsaw, and all my hobbies, and out they go. This is the most fascinating relaxation I ever found.

Willy. I think I'll get one myself.

Howard. Sure, they're only a hundred and a half. You can't do without it. Supposing you wanna hear Jack Benny, see? But you can't be at home at that hour. So you tell the maid to turn the radio on when Jack Benny comes on, and this automatically goes on with the radio . . .

Willy. And when you come home you . . .

Howard. You can come home twelve o'clock, one o'clock, any time you like, and you get yourself a Coke and sit yourself down, throw the switch, and there's Jack Benny's program in the middle of the night!

Willy. I'm definitely going to get one. Because lots of time I'm on the road, and I think to myself, what I must be missing on the radio!

Howard. Don't you have a radio in the car?

Willy. Well, yeah, but who ever thinks of turning it on?

Howard.   Say, aren't you supposed to be in Boston?

Willy.   That's what I want to talk to you about, Howard. You got a minute? (*He draws a chair in from the wing.*)

Howard.   What happened? What're you doing here?

Willy.   Well . . .

Howard.   You didn't crack up again, did you?

Willy.   Oh, no. No . . .

Howard.   Geez, you had me worried there for a minute. What's the trouble?

Willy.   Well, tell you the truth, Howard. I've come to the decision that I'd rather not travel any more.

Howard.   Not travel! Well, what'll you do?

Willy.   Remember, Christmas time, when you had the party here? You said you'd try to think of some spot for me here in town.

Howard.   With us?

Willy.   Well, sure.

Howard.   Oh, yeah, yeah. I remember. Well, I couldn't think of anything for you, Willy.

Willy.   I tell ya, Howard. The kids are all grown up, y'know. I don't need much any more. If I could take home — well, sixty-five dollars a week, I could swing it.

Howard.   Yeah, but Willy, see I —

Willy.   I tell ya why, Howard. Speaking frankly and between the two of us, y'know — I'm just a little tired.

Howard.   Oh, I could understand that, Willy. But you're a road man, Willy, and we do a road business. We've only got a half-dozen salesmen on the floor here.

Willy.   God knows, Howard, I never asked a favor of any man. But I was with the firm when your father used to carry you in here in his arms.

Howard.   I know that, Willy, but —

Willy.   Your father came to me the day you were born and asked me what I thought of the name of Howard, may he rest in peace.

Howard.   I appreciate that, Willy, but there just is no spot here for you. If I had a spot I'd slam you right in, but I just don't have a single solitary spot.

He looks for his lighter. Willy has picked it up and gives it to him. Pause.

Willy (*with increasing anger*).   Howard, all I need to set my table is fifty dollars a week.

Howard.   But where am I going to put you, kid?

Willy.   Look, it isn't a question of whether I can sell merchandise, is it?

Howard.   No, but it's a business, kid, and everybody's gotta pull his own weight.

Willy (*desperately*).   Just let me tell you a story, Howard —

Howard.   'Cause you gotta admit, business is business.

Willy (*angrily*).   Business is definitely business, but just listen for a minute.

You don't understand this. When I was a boy — eighteen, nineteen — I was already on the road. And there was a question in my mind as to whether selling had a future for me. Because in those days I had a yearning to go to Alaska. See, there were three gold strikes in one month in Alaska, and I felt like going out. Just for the ride, you might say.

Howard (*barely interested*).   Don't say.

Willy.   Oh, yeah, my father lived many years in Alaska. He was an adventurous man. We've got quite a little streak of self-reliance in our family. I thought I'd go out with my older brother and try to locate him, and maybe settle in the North with the old man. And I was almost decided to go, when I met a salesman in the Parker House. His name was Dave Singleman. And he was eighty-four years old, and he'd drummed merchandise in thirty-one states. And old Dave, he'd go up to his room, y'understand, put on his green velvet slippers — I'll never forget — and pick up his phone and call the buyers, and without ever leaving his room, at the age of eighty-four, he made his living. And when I saw that, I realized that selling was the greatest career a man could want. 'Cause what could be more satisfying than to be able to go, at the age of eighty-four, into twenty or thirty different cities, and pick up a phone, and be remembered and loved and helped by so many different people? Do you know? when he died — and by the way he died the death of a salesman, in his green velvet slippers in the smoker of the New York, New Haven, and Hartford, going into Boston — when he died, hundreds of salesmen and buyers were at his funeral. Things were sad on a lotta trains for months after that. (*He stands up. Howard has not looked at him.*) In those days there was personality in it, Howard. There was respect, and comradeship, and gratitude in it. Today, it's all cut and dried, and there's no chance for bringing friendship to bear — or personality. You see what I mean? They don't know me any more.

Howard (*moving away, to the right*).   That's just the thing, Willy.

Willy.   If I had forty dollars a week — that's all I'd need. Forty dollars, Howard.

Howard.   Kid, I can't take blood from a stone, I —

Willy (*desperation is on him now*).   Howard, the year Al Smith[2] was nominated, your father came to me and —

Howard (*starting to go off*).   I've got to see some people, kid.

Willy (*stopping him*).   I'm talking about your father! There were promises made across this desk! You mustn't tell me you've got people to see — I put thirty-four years into this firm, Howard, and now I can't pay my insurance! You can't eat the orange and throw the peel away — a man is not a piece of fruit! (*After a pause.*) Now pay attention. Your father — in 1928 I had a big year. I averaged a hundred and seventy dollars a week in commissions.

Howard (*impatiently*).   Now, Willy, you never averaged —

Willy (*banging his hand on the desk*).   I averaged a hundred and seventy dollars a week in the year of 1928! And your father came to me — or rather, I

---

[2] The Democratic candidate for president in 1928; he lost to Herbert Hoover.

was in the office here — it was right over this desk — and he put his hand on my shoulder —

Howard (*getting up*).   You'll have to excuse me, Willy, I gotta see some people. Pull yourself together. (*Going out.*) I'll be back in a little while.

On Howard's exit, the light on his chair grows very bright and strange.

Willy.   Pull myself together! What the hell did I say to him? My God, I was yelling at him! How could I! (*Willy breaks off, staring at the light, which occupies the chair, animating it. He approaches this chair, standing across the desk from it.*) Frank, Frank, don't you remember what you told me that time? How you put your hand on my shoulder, and Frank . . . (*He leans on the desk and as he speaks the dead man's name he accidentally switches on the recorder, and instantly*):

Howard's Son.   ". . . of New York is Albany. The capital of Ohio is Cincinnati, the capital of Rhode Island is . . . " (*The recitation continues.*)

Willy (*leaping away with fright, shouting*).   Ha! Howard! Howard! Howard!

Howard (*rushing in*).   What happened?

Willy (*pointing at the machine, which continues nasally, childishly, with the capital cities*).   Shut it off! Shut it off!

Howard (*pulling the plug out*).   Look, Willy . . .

Willy (*pressing his hands to his eyes*).   I gotta get myself some coffee. I'll get some coffee . . .

Willy starts to walk out. Howard stops him.

Howard (*rolling up the cord*).   Willy, look . . .

Willy.   I'll go to Boston.

Howard.   Willy, you can't go to Boston for us.

Willy.   Why can't I go?

Howard.   I don't want you to represent us. I've been meaning to tell you for a long time now.

Willy.   Howard, are you firing me?

Howard.   I think you need a good long rest, Willy.

Willy.   Howard —

Howard.   And when you feel better, come back, and we'll see if we can work something out.

Willy.   But I gotta earn money, Howard. I'm in no position to —

Howard.   Where are your sons? Why don't your sons give you a hand?

Willy.   They're working on a very big deal.

Howard.   This is no time for false pride, Willy. You go to your sons and you tell them that you're tired. You've got two great boys, haven't you?

Willy.   Oh, no question, no question, but in the meantime . . .

Howard.   Then that's that, heh?

Willy.   All right, I'll go to Boston tomorrow.

Howard.   No, no.

Willy.   I can't throw myself on my sons. I'm not a cripple!

Howard.   Look, kid, I'm busy this morning.

Willy (*grasping Howard's arm*).   Howard, you've got to let me go to Boston!

Howard (*hard, keeping himself under control*).   I've got a line of people to see this morning. Sit down, take five minutes, and pull yourself together, and then go home, will ya? I need the office, Willy. (*He starts to go, turns, remembering the recorder, starts to push off the table holding the recorder.*) Oh, yeah. Whenever you can this week, stop by and drop off the samples. You'll feel better, Willy, and then come back and we'll talk. Pull yourself together, kid, there's people outside.

Howard exits, pushing the table off left. Willy stares into space, exhausted. Now the music is heard — Ben's music — first distantly, then closer, closer. As Willy speaks, Ben enters from the right. He carries valise and umbrella.

Willy.   Oh, Ben, how did you do it? What is the answer? Did you wind up the Alaska deal already?

Ben.   Doesn't take much time if you know what you're doing. Just a short business trip. Boarding ship in an hour. Wanted to say good-by.

Willy.   Ben, I've got to talk to you.

Ben (*glancing at his watch*).   Haven't the time, William.

Willy (*crossing the apron to Ben*).   Ben, nothing's working out. I don't know what to do.

Ben.   Now, look here, William. I've bought timberland in Alaska and I need a man to look after things for me.

Willy.   God, timberland! Me and my boys in those grand outdoors!

Ben.   You've a new continent at your doorstep, William. Get out of these cities, they're full of talk and time payments and courts of law. Screw on your fists and you can fight for a fortune up there.

Willy.   Yes, yes! Linda, Linda!

Linda enters as of old, with the wash.

Linda.   Oh, you're back?

Ben.   I haven't much time.

Willy.   No, wait! Linda, he's got a proposition for me in Alaska.

Linda.   But you've got — (*To Ben.*) He's got a beautiful job here.

Willy.   But in Alaska, kid, I could —

Linda.   You're doing well enough, Willy!

Ben (*to Linda*).   Enough for what, my dear?

Linda (*frightened of Ben and angry at him*).   Don't say those things to him! Enough to be happy right here, right now. (*To Willy, while Ben laughs.*) Why must everybody conquer the world? You're well liked, and the boys love you, and someday — *(to Ben)* — why, old man Wagner told him just the other day that if he keeps it up he'll be a member of the firm, didn't he, Willy?

Willy. Sure, sure. I am building something with this firm, Ben, and if a man is building something he must be on the right track, mustn't he?

Ben. What are you building? Lay your hand on it. Where is it?

Willy *(hesitantly)*. That's true, Linda, there's nothing.

Linda. Why? *(To Ben.)* There's a man eighty-four years old —

Willy. That's right, Ben, that's right. When I look at that man I say, what is there to worry about?

Ben. Bah!

Willy. It's true, Ben. All he has to do is go into any city, pick up the phone, and he's making his living and you know why?

Ben *(picking up his valise)*. I've got to go.

Willy *(holding Ben back)*. Look at this boy!

Biff, in his high school sweater, enters carrying suitcase. Happy carries Biff's shoulder guards, gold helmet, and football pants.

Willy. Without a penny to his name, three great universities are begging for him, and from there the sky's the limit, because it's not what you do, Ben. It's who you know and the smile on your face! It's contacts, Ben, contacts! The whole wealth of Alaska passes over the lunch table at the Commodore Hotel, and that's the wonder, the wonder of this country, that a man can end with diamonds here on the basis of being liked! *(He turns to Biff.)* And that's why when you get out on that field today it's important. Because thousands of people will be rooting for you and loving you. *(To Ben, who has again begun to leave.)* And Ben! when he walks into a business office his name will sound out like a bell and all the doors will open to him! I've seen it, Ben, I've seen it a thousand times! You can't feel it with your hand like timber, but it's there!

Ben. Good-by, William.

Willy. Ben, am I right? Don't you think I'm right? I value your advice.

Ben. There's a new continent at your doorstep, William. You could walk out rich. Rich! *(He is gone.)*

Willy. We'll do it here, Ben! You hear me? We're gonna do it here!

Young Bernard rushes in. The gay music of the Boys is heard.

Bernard. Oh, gee, I was afraid you left already!

Willy. Why? What time is it?

Bernard. It's half-past one!

Willy. Well, come on, everybody! Ebbets Field next stop! Where's the pennants? *(He rushes through the wall-line of the kitchen and out into the living-room.)*

Linda *(to Biff).* Did you pack fresh underwear?
Biff *(who has been limbering up).* I want to go!
Bernard. Biff, I'm carrying your helmet, ain't I?
Happy. I'm carrying the helmet.
Bernard. How am I going to get in the locker room?
Linda. Let him carry the shoulder guards. *(She puts her coat and hat on in the kitchen.)*
Bernard. Can I, Biff? 'Cause I told everybody I'm going to be in the locker room.
Happy. In Ebbets Field it's the clubhouse.
Bernard. I meant the clubhouse. Biff!
Happy. Biff!
Biff *(grandly, after a slight pause).* Let him carry the shoulder guards.
Happy *(as he gives Bernard the shoulder guards).* Stay close to us now.

Willy rushes in with the pennants.

Willy *(handing them out).* Everybody wave when Biff comes out on the field. *(Happy and Bernard run off.)* You set now, boy?

The music has died away.

Biff. Ready to go, Pop. Every muscle is ready.
Willy *(at the edge of the apron).* You realize what this means?
Biff. That's right, Pop.
Willy *(feeling Biff's muscles).* You're comin' home this afternoon captain of the All-Scholastic Championship Team of the City of New York.
Biff. I got it, Pop. And remember, pal, when I take off my helmet, that touchdown is for you.
Willy. Let's go! *(He is starting out, with his arm around Biff, when Charley enters, as of old, in knickers.)* I got no room for you, Charley.
Charley. Room? For what?
Willy. In the car.
Charley. You goin' for a ride? I wanted to shoot some casino.
Willy *(furiously).* Casino! *(Incredulously.)* Don't you realize what today is?
Linda. Oh, he knows, Willy. He's just kidding you.
Willy. That's nothing to kid about!
Charley. No, Linda, what's goin' on?
Linda. He's playing in Ebbets Field.
Charley. Baseball in this weather?
Willy. Don't talk to him. Come on, come on! *(He is pushing them out.)*
Charley. Wait a minute, didn't you hear the news?
Willy. What?
Charley. Don't you listen to the radio? Ebbets Field just blew up.

Willy.   You go to hell! (*Charley laughs. Pushing them out.*) Come on, come on! We're late.

Charley (*as they go*).   Knock a homer, Biff, knock a homer!

Willy (*the last to leave, turning to Charley*).   I don't think that was funny, Charley. This is the greatest day of his life.

Charley.   Willy, when are you going to grow up?

Willy.   Yeah, heh? When this game is over, Charley, you'll be laughing out of the other side of your face. They'll be calling him another Red Grange. Twenty-five thousand a year.

Charley (*kidding*).   Is that so?

Willy.   Yeah, that's so.

Charley.   Well, then, I'm sorry, Willy. But tell me something.

Willy.   What?

Charley.   Who is Red Grange?

Willy.   Put up your hands. Goddam you, put up your hands!

Charley, chuckling, shakes his head and walks away, around the left corner of the stage. Willy follows him. The music rises to a mocking frenzy.

Willy.   Who the hell do you think you are, better than everybody else? You don't know everything, you big, ignorant, stupid . . . Put up your hands!

Light rises, on the right side of the forestage, on a small table in the reception room of Charley's office. Traffic sounds are heard. Bernard, now mature, sits whistling to himself. A pair of tennis rackets and an overnight bag are on the floor beside him.

Willy (*offstage*).   What are you walking away for? Don't walk away! If you're going to say something say it to my face! I know you laugh at me behind my back. You'll laugh out of the other side of your goddam face after this game. Touchdown! Touchdown! Eighty thousand people! Touchdown! Right between the goal posts.

Bernard is a quiet, earnest, but self-assured young man. Willy's voice is coming from right upstage now. Bernard lowers his feet off the table and listens. Jenny, his father's secretary, enters.

Jenny (*distressed*).   Say, Bernard, will you go out in the hall?

Bernard.   What is that noise? Who is it?

Jenny.   Mr. Loman. He just got off the elevator.

Bernard (*getting up*).   Who's he arguing with?

Jenny.   Nobody. There's nobody with him. I can't deal with him any more, and your father gets all upset everytime he comes. I've got a lot of typing to do, and your father's waiting to sign it. Will you see him?

Willy *(entering).*   Touchdown! Touch — *(He sees Jenny.)* Jenny, Jenny, good to see you. How're ya? Workin'? Or still honest?

Jenny.   Fine. How've you been feeling?

Willy.   Not much any more, Jenny. Ha, ha! *(He is surprised to see the rackets.)*

Bernard.   Hello, Uncle Willy.

Willy *(almost shocked).*   Bernard! Well, look who's here! *(He comes quickly, guiltily, to Bernard and warmly shakes his hand.)*

Bernard.   How are you? Good to see you.

Willy.   What are you doing here?

Bernard.   Oh, just stopped by to see Pop. Get off my feet till my train leaves. I'm going to Washington in a few minutes.

Willy.   Is he in?

Bernard.   Yes, he's in his office with the accountant. Sit down.

Willy *(sitting down).*   What're you going to do in Washington?

Bernard.   Oh, just a case I've got there, Willy.

Willy.   That so? *(Indicating the rackets.)* You going to play tennis there?

Bernard.   I'm staying with a friend who's got a court.

Willy.   Don't say. His own tennis court. Must be fine people, I bet.

Bernard.   They are, very nice. Dad tells me Biff's in town.

Willy *(with a big smile).*   Yeah, Biff's in. Working on a very big deal, Bernard.

Bernard.   What's Biff doing?

Willy.   Well, he's been doing very big things in the West. But he decided to establish himself here. Very big. We're having dinner. Did I hear your wife had a boy?

Bernard.   That's right. Our second.

Willy.   Two boys! What do you know!

Bernard.   What kind of a deal has Biff got?

Willy.   Well, Bill Oliver — very big sporting-goods man — he wants Biff very badly. Called him in from the West. Long distance, carte blanche, special deliveries. Your friends have their own private tennis court?

Bernard.   You still with the old firm, Willy?

Willy *(after a pause).*   I'm — I'm overjoyed to see how you made the grade, Bernard, overjoyed. It's an encouraging thing to see a young man really — really — Looks very good for Biff — very — *(He breaks off, then.)* Bernard — *(He is so full of emotion, he breaks off again.)*

Bernard.   What is it, Willy?

Willy *(small and alone).*   What — what's the secret?

Bernard.   What secret?

Willy.   How — how did you? Why didn't he ever catch on?

Bernard.   I wouldn't know that, Willy.

Willy *(confidentially, desperately).*   You were his friend, his boyhood friend. There's something I don't understand about it. His life ended after that Ebbets Field game. From the age of seventeen nothing good ever happened to him.

Bernard.   He never trained himself for anything.

Willy. But he did, he did. After high school he took so many correspondence courses. Radio mechanics; television; God knows what, and never made the slightest mark.

Bernard (*taking off his glasses*). Willy, do you want to talk candidly?

Willy (*rising, faces Bernard*). I regard you as a very brilliant man, Bernard. I value your advice.

Bernard. Oh, the hell with the advice, Willy. I couldn't advise you. There's just one thing I've always wanted to ask you. When he was supposed to graduate, and the math teacher flunked him —

Willy. Oh, that son-of-a-bitch ruined his life.

Bernard. Yeah, but, Willy, all he had to do was go to summer school and make up that subject.

Willy. That's right, that's right.

Bernard. Did you tell him not to go to summer school?

Willy. Me? I begged him to go. I ordered him to go!

Bernard. Then why wouldn't he go?

Willy. Why? Why! Bernard, that question has been trailing me like a ghost for the last fifteen years. He flunked the subject, and laid down and died like a hammer hit him!

Bernard. Take it easy, kid.

Willy. Let me talk to you — I got nobody to talk to. Bernard, Bernard, was it my fault? Y'see? It keeps going around in my mind, maybe I did something to him. I got nothing to give him.

Bernard. Don't take it so hard.

Willy. Why did he lay down? What is the story there? You were his friend!

Bernard. Willy, I remember, it was June, and our grades came out. And he'd flunked math.

Willy. That son-of-a-bitch!

Bernard. No, it wasn't right then. Biff just got very angry, I remember, and he was ready to enroll in summer school.

Willy (*surprised*). He was?

Bernard. He wasn't beaten by it at all. But then, Willy, he disappeared from the block for almost a month. And I got the idea that he'd gone up to New England to see you. Did he have a talk with you then?

Willy stares in silence.

Bernard. Willy?

Willy (*with a strong edge of resentment in his voice*). Yeah, he came to Boston. What about it?

Bernard. Well, just that when he came back — I'll never forget this, it always mystifies me. Because I'd thought so well of Biff, even though he'd always taken advantage of me. I loved him, Willy, y'know? And he came back after that month and took his sneakers — remember those sneakers with "University of Virginia" printed on them? He was so proud of those, wore them every day. And he took them down in the cellar, and burned them up in the furnace. We had a fist fight. It lasted at least half an hour. Just the two of us, punching each other down the cellar, and crying right through it. I've often thought of how strange it was that I knew he'd given up his life. What happened in Boston, Willy?

Willy looks at him as at an intruder.

Bernard.   I just bring it up because you asked me.

Willy *(angrily).*   Nothing. What do you mean, "What happened?" What's that got to do with anything?

Bernard.   Well, don't get sore.

Willy.   What are you trying to do, blame it on me? If a boy lays down is that my fault?

Bernard.   Now, Willy, don't get —

Willy.   Well, don't — don't talk to me that way! What does that mean, "What happened?"

Charley enters. He is in his vest, and he carries a bottle of bourbon.

Charley.   Hey, you're going to miss that train. *(He waves the bottle.)*

Bernard.   Yeah, I'm going. *(He takes the bottle.)* Thanks, Pop. *(He picks up his rackets and bag.)* Good-by, Willy, and don't worry about it. You know. "If at first you don't succeed . . ."

Willy.   Yes, I believe in that.

Bernard.   But sometimes, Willy, it's better for a man just to walk away.

Willy.   Walk away?

Bernard.   That's right.

Willy.   But if you can't walk away?

Bernard *(after a slight pause).*   I guess that's when it's tough. *(Extending his hand.)* Good-by, Willy.

Willy *(shaking Bernard's hand).*   Good-by, boy.

Charley *(an arm on Bernard's shoulder).*   How do you like this kid? Gonna argue a case in front of the Supreme Court.

Bernard *(protesting).*   Pop!

Willy *(genuinely shocked, pained, and happy).*   No! The Supreme Court!

Bernard.   I gotta run. 'By, Dad!

Charley.   Knock 'em dead, Bernard!

Bernard goes off.

Willy *(as Charley takes out his wallet).*   The Supreme Court! And he didn't even mention it!

Charley *(counting out money on the desk).*   He don't have to — he's gonna do it.

Willy. And you never told him what to do, did you? You never took any interest in him.

Charley. My salvation is that I never took any interest in any thing. There's some money — fifty dollars. I got an accountant inside.

Willy. Charley, look . . . (*With difficulty.*) I got my insurance to pay. If you can manage it — I need a hundred and ten dollars.

Charley doesn't reply for a moment; merely stops moving.

Willy. I'd draw it from my bank but Linda would know, and I . . .

Charley. Sit down, Willy.

Willy (*moving toward the chair*). I'm keeping an account of everything, remember. I'll pay every penny back. (*He sits.*)

Charley. Now listen to me, Willy.

Willy. I want you to know I appreciate . . .

Charley (*sitting down on the table*). Willy, what're you doin'? What the hell is goin' on in your head?

Willy. Why? I'm simply . . .

Charley. I offered you a job. You can make fifty dollars a week. And I won't send you on the road.

Willy. I've got a job.

Charley. Without pay? What kind of a job is a job without pay? (*He rises.*) Now, look, kid, enough is enough. I'm no genius but I know when I'm being insulted.

Willy. Insulted!

Charley. Why don't you want to work for me?

Willy. What's the matter with you? I've got a job.

Charley. Then what're you walkin' in here every week for?

Willy (*getting up*). Well, if you don't want me to walk in here —

Charley. I am offering you a job.

Willy. I don't want your goddam job!

Charley. When the hell are you going to grow up?

Willy (*furiously*). You big ignoramus, if you say that to me again I'll rap you one! I don't care how big you are! (*He's ready to fight.*)

Pause.

Charley (*kindly, going to him*). How much do you need, Willy?

Willy. Charley, I'm strapped. I'm strapped. I don't know what to do. I was just fired.

Charley. Howard fired you?

Willy. That snotnose. Imagine that? I named him. I named him Howard.

Charley. Willy, when're you gonna realize that them things don't mean anything? You named him Howard, but you can't sell that. The only thing you got in this world is what you can sell. And the funny thing is that you're a sales-man, and you don't know that.

Willy. I've always tried to think otherwise, I guess. I always felt that if a man was impressive, and well liked, that nothing —

Charley. Why must everybody like you? Who liked J. P. Morgan? Was he impressive? In a Turkish bath he'd look like a butcher. But with his pockets on he was very well liked. Now listen, Willy, I know you don't like me, and nobody can say I'm in love with you, but I'll give you a job because — just for the hell of it, put it that way. Now what do you say?

Willy. I — I just can't work for you, Charley.

Charley. What're you, jealous of me?

Willy. I can't work for you, that's all, don't ask me why.

Charley (*angered, takes out more bills*). You been jealous of me all your life, you damned fool! Here, pay your insurance. (*He puts the money in Willy's hand.*)

Willy. I'm keeping strict accounts.

Charley. I've got some work to do. Take care of yourself. And pay your insur-ance.

Willy (*moving to the right*). Funny, y'know? After all the highways, and the trains, and the appointments, and the years, you end up worth more dead than alive.

Charley. Willy, nobody's worth nothin' dead. (*After a slight pause.*) Did you hear what I said?

Willy stands still, dreaming.

Charley. Willy!

Willy. Apologize to Bernard for me when you see him. I didn't mean to argue with him. He's a fine boy. They're all fine boys, and they'll end up big — all of them. Someday they'll all play tennis together. Wish me luck, Charley. He saw Bill Oliver today.

Charley. Good luck.

Willy (*on the verge of tears*). Charley, you're the only friend I got. Isn't that a remarkable thing? (*He goes out.*)

Charley. Jesus!

Charley stares after him a moment and follows. All light blacks out. Suddenly raucous music is heard, and a red glow rises behind the screen at right. Stanley, a young waiter, appears, carrying a table, followed by Happy, who is carrying two chairs.

Stanley (*putting the table down*). That's all right, Mr. Loman, I can handle it myself. (*He turns and takes the chairs from Happy and places them at the table.*)

Happy (*glancing around*).   Oh, this is better.

Stanley.   Sure, in the front there you're in the middle of all kinds a noise. Whenever you got a party, Mr. Loman, you just tell me and I'll put you back here. Y'know, there's a lotta people they don't like it private, because when they go out they like to see a lotta action around them because they're sick and tired to stay in the house by theirself. But I know you, you ain't from Hackensack. You know what I mean?

Happy (*sitting down*).   So how's it coming, Stanley?

Stanley.   Ah, it's a dog's life. I only wish during the war they'd a took me in the Army. I coulda been dead by now.

Happy.   My brother's back, Stanley.

Stanley.   Oh, he come back, heh? From the Far West.

Happy.   Yeah, big cattle man, my brother, so treat him right. And my father's coming too.

Stanley.   Oh, your father too!

Happy.   You got a couple of nice lobsters?

Stanley.   Hundred per cent, big.

Happy.   I want them with the claws.

Stanley.   Don't worry, I don't give you no mice. (*Happy laughs.*) How about some wine? It'll put a head on the meal.

Happy.   No. You remember, Stanley, that recipe I brought you from overseas? With the champagne in it?

Stanley.   Oh, yeah, sure. I still got it tacked up yet in the kitchen. But that'll have to cost a buck apiece anyways.

Happy.   That's all right.

Stanley.   What'd you, hit a number or somethin'?

Happy.   No, it's a little celebration. My brother is — I think he pulled off a big deal today. I think we're going into business together.

Stanley.   Great! That's the best for you. Because a family business, you know what I mean? — that's the best.

Happy.   That's what I think.

Stanley.   'Cause what's the difference? Somebody steals? It's in the family. Know what I mean? (*Sotto voce.*[3]) Like this bartender here. The boss is goin' crazy what kinda leak he's got in the cash register. You put it in but it don't come out.

Happy (*raising his head*).   Sh!

Stanley.   What?

Happy.   You notice I wasn't lookin' right or left, was I?

Stanley.   No.

Happy.   And my eyes are closed.

Stanley.   So what's the — ?

Happy.   Strudel's comin'.

Stanley (*catching on, looks around*).   Ah, no, there's no —

---

[3] "Softly" in Italian.

He breaks off as a furred, lavishly dressed girl enters and sits at the next table. Both follow her with their eyes.

Stanley.   Geez, how'd ya know?

Happy.   I got radar or something. (*Staring directly at her profile.*) Ooooooooo . . . Stanley.

Stanley.   I think that's for you, Mr. Loman.

Happy.   Look at that mouth. Oh, God. And the binoculars.

Stanley.   Geez, you got a life, Mr. Loman.

Happy.   Wait on her.

Stanley (*going to the girl's table*).   Would you like a menu, ma'am?

Girl.   I'm expecting someone, but I'd like a —

Happy.   Why don't you bring her — excuse me, miss, do you mind? I sell champagne, and I'd like you to try my brand. Bring her a champagne, Stanley.

Girl.   That's awfully nice of you.

Happy.   Don't mention it. It's all company money. (*He laughs.*)

Girl.   That's a charming product to be selling, isn't it?

Happy.   Oh, gets to be like everything else. Selling is selling, y'know.

Girl.   I suppose.

Happy.   You don't happen to sell, do you?

Girl.   No, I don't sell.

Happy.   Would you object to a compliment from a stranger? You ought to be on a magazine cover.

Girl (*looking at him a little archly*).   I have been.

Stanley comes in with a glass of champagne.

Happy.   What'd I say before, Stanley? You see? She's a cover girl.

Stanley.   Oh, I could see, I could see.

Happy (*to the Girl*).   What magazine?

Girl.   Oh, a lot of them. (*She takes the drink.*) Thank you.

Happy.   You know what they say in France, don't you? "Champagne is the drink of the complexion" — Hya, Biff!

Biff has entered and sits with Happy.

Biff.   Hello, kid. Sorry I'm late.

Happy.   I just got here. Uh, Miss — ?

Girl.   Forsythe.

Happy.   Miss Forsythe, this is my brother.

Biff.   Is Dad here?

Happy.   His name is Biff. You might've heard of him. Great football player.

Girl.   Really? What team?

Happy.   Are you familiar with football?

Girl.   No, I'm afraid I'm not.

Happy.   Biff is quarterback with the New York Giants.

Girl.   Well, that is nice, isn't it? (*She drinks.*)

Happy.   Good health.

Girl.   I'm happy to meet you.

Happy.   That's my name. Hap. It's really Harold, but at West Point they called me Happy.

Girl (*now really impressed*).   Oh, I see. How do you do? (*She turns her profile.*)

Biff.   Isn't Dad coming?

Happy.   You want her?

Biff.   Oh, I could never make that.

Happy.   I remember the time that idea would never come into your head. Where's the old confidence, Biff?

Biff.   I just saw Oliver —

Happy.   Wait a minute. I've got to see that old confidence again. Do you want her? She's on call.

Biff.   Oh, no. (*He turns to look at the Girl.*)

Happy.   I'm telling you. Watch this. (*Turning to the Girl.*) Honey? (*She turns to him.*) Are you busy?

Girl.   Well, I am . . . but I could make a phone call.

Happy.   Do that, will you, honey? And see if you can get a friend. We'll be here for a while. Biff is one of the greatest football players in the country.

Girl (*standing up*).   Well, I'm certainly happy to meet you.

Happy.   Come back soon.

Girl.   I'll try.

Happy.   Don't try, honey, try hard.

The Girl exits. Stanley follows, shaking his head in bewildered admiration.

Happy.   Isn't that a shame now? A beautiful girl like that? That's why I can't get married. There's not a good woman in a thousand. New York is loaded with them, kid!

Biff.   Hap, look —

Happy.   I told you she was on call!

Biff (*strangely unnerved*).   Cut it out, will ya? I want to say something to you.

Happy.   Did you see Oliver?

Biff.   I saw him all right. Now look, I want to tell Dad a couple of things and I want you to help me.

Happy.   What? Is he going to back you?

Biff.   Are you crazy? You're out of your goddam head, you know that?

Happy.   Why? What happened?

Biff (*breathlessly*).   I did a terrible thing today, Hap. It's been the strangest day I ever went through. I'm all numb, I swear.

Happy.   You mean he wouldn't see you?

Biff.   Well, I waited six hours for him, see? All day. Kept sending my name in. Even tried to date his secretary so she'd get me to him, but no soap.

Happy. Because you're not showin' the old confidence, Biff. He remembered you, didn't he?

Biff (*stopping Happy with a gesture*). Finally, about five o'clock, he comes out. Didn't remember who I was or anything. I felt like such an idiot, Hap.

Happy. Did you tell him my Florida idea?

Biff. He walked away. I saw him for one minute. I got so mad I could've torn the walls down! How the hell did I ever get the idea I was a salesman there? I even believed myself that I'd been a salesman for him! And then he gave me one look and — I realized what a ridiculous lie my whole life has been! We've been talking in a dream for fifteen years. I was a shipping clerk.

Happy. What'd you do?

Biff (*with great tension and wonder*). Well, he left, see. And the secretary went out. I was all alone in the waiting-room. I don't know what came over me, Hap. The next thing I know I'm in his office — paneled walls, everything. I can't explain it. I — Hap, I took his fountain pen.

Happy. Geez, did he catch you?

Biff. I ran out. I ran down all eleven flights. I ran and ran and ran.

Happy. That was an awful dumb — what'd you do that for?

Biff (*agonized*). I don't know, I just — wanted to take something, I don't know. You gotta help me, Hap, I'm gonna tell Pop.

Happy. You crazy? What for?

Biff. Hap, he's got to understand that I'm not the man somebody lends that kind of money to. He thinks I've been spiting him all these years and it's eating him up.

Happy. That's just it. You tell him something nice.

Biff. I can't.

Happy. Say you got a lunch date with Oliver tomorrow.

Biff. So what do I do tomorrow?

Happy. You leave the house tomorrow and come back at night and say Oliver is thinking it over. And he thinks it over for a couple of weeks, and gradually it fades away and nobody's the worse.

Biff. But it'll go on forever!

Happy. Dad is never so happy as when he's looking forward to something!

Willy enters.

Happy. Hello, scout!

Willy. Gee, I haven't been here in years!

Stanley has followed Willy in and sets a chair for him. Stanley starts off but Happy stops him.

Happy. Stanley!

Stanley stands by, waiting for an order.

Biff (*going to Willy with guilt, as to an invalid*).   Sit down, Pop. You want a drink?

Willy.   Sure, I don't mind.

Biff.   Let's get a load on.

Willy.   You look worried.

Biff.   N-no. (*To Stanley.*) Scotch all around. Make it doubles.

Stanley.   Doubles, right. (*He goes.*)

Willy.   You had a couple already, didn't you?

Biff.   Just a couple, yeah.

Willy.   Well, what happened, boy? (*Nodding affirmatively, with a smile.*) Everything go all right?

Biff (*takes a breath, then reaches out and grasps Willy's hand.*) Pal . . . (*He is smiling bravely, and Willy is smiling too.*) I had an experience today.

Happy.   Terrific, Pop.

Willy.   That so? What happened?

Biff (*high, slightly alcoholic, above the earth*).   I'm going to tell you everything from first to last. It's been a strange day. (*Silence. He looks around, composes himself as best he can, but his breath keeps breaking the rhythm of his voice.*) I had to wait quite a while for him, and —

Willy.   Oliver.

Biff.   Yeah, Oliver. All day, as a matter of cold fact. And a lot of — instances — facts, Pop, facts about my life came back to me. Who was it, Pop? Who ever said I was a salesman with Oliver?

Willy.   Well, you were.

Biff.   No, Dad, I was a shipping clerk.

Willy.   But you were practically —

Biff (*with determination*).   Dad, I don't know who said it first, but I was never a salesman for Bill Oliver.

Willy.   What're you talking about?

Biff.   Let's hold on to the facts tonight, Pop. We're not going to get anywhere bullin' around. I was a shipping clerk.

Willy (*angrily*).   All right, now listen to me —

Biff.   Why don't you let me finish?

Willy.   I'm not interested in stories about the past or any crap of that kind because the woods are burning, boys, you understand? There's a big blaze going on all around. I was fired today.

Biff (*shocked*).   How could you be?

Willy.   I was fired, and I'm looking for a little good news to tell your mother, because the woman has waited and the woman has suffered. The gist of it is that I haven't got a story left in my head, Biff. So don't give me a lecture about facts and aspects. I am not interested. Now what've you got to say to me?

Stanley enters with three drinks. They wait until he leaves.

Willy.   Did you see Oliver?

Biff. Jesus, Dad!

Willy. You mean you didn't go up there?

Happy. Sure he went up there.

Biff. I did. I — saw him. How could they fire you?

Willy *(on the edge of his chair).* What kind of a welcome did he give you?

Biff. He won't even let you work on commission?

Willy. I'm out! *(Driving.)* So tell me, he gave you a warm welcome?

Happy. Sure, Pop, sure!

Biff *(driven).* Well, it was kind of —

Willy. I was wondering if he'd remember you. *(To Happy.)* Imagine, man doesn't see him for ten, twelve years and gives him that kind of a welcome!

Happy. Damn right!

Biff *(trying to return to the offensive).* Pop, look —

Willy. You know why he remembered you, don't you? Because you impressed him in those days.

Biff. Let's talk quietly and get this down to the facts, huh?

Willy *(as though Biff had been interrupting).* Well, what happened? It's great news, Biff. Did he take you into his office or'd you talk in the waiting-room?

Biff. Well, he came in, see, and —

Willy *(with a big smile).* What'd he say? Betcha he threw his arm around you.

Biff. Well, he kinda —

Willy. He's a fine man. *(To Happy.)* Very hard man to see, y'know.

Happy *(agreeing).* Oh, I know.

Willy *(to Biff).* Is that where you had the drinks?

Biff. Yeah, he gave me a couple of — no, no!

Happy *(cutting in).* He told him my Florida idea.

Willy. Don't interrupt. *(To Biff.)* How'd he react to the Florida idea?

Biff. Dad, will you give me a minute to explain?

Willy. I've been waiting for you to explain since I sat down here! What happened? He took you into his office and what?

Biff. Well — I talked. And — and he listened, see.

Willy. Famous for the way he listens, y'know. What was his answer?

Biff. His answer was — *(He breaks off, suddenly angry.)* Dad, you're not letting me tell you what I want to tell you!

Willy *(accusing, angered).* You didn't see him, did you?

Biff. I did see him!

Willy. What'd you insult him or something? You insulted him, didn't you?

Biff. Listen, will you let me out of it, will you just let me out of it!

Happy. What the hell!

Willy. Tell me what happened!

Biff *(to Happy).* I can't talk to him!

A single trumpet note jars the ear. The light of green leaves stains the house, which holds the air of night and a dream. Young Bernard enters and knocks on the door of the house.

Young Bernard (*frantically*).   Mrs. Loman, Mrs. Loman!

Happy.   Tell him what happened!

Biff (*to Happy*).   Shut up and leave me alone!

Willy.   No, no! You had to go and flunk math!

Biff.   What math? What're you talking about?

Young Bernard.   Mrs. Loman, Mrs. Loman!

Linda appears in the house, as of old.

Willy (*wildly*).   Math, math, math!

Biff.   Take it easy, Pop!

Young Bernard.   Mrs. Loman!

Willy (*furiously*).   If you hadn't flunked you'd've been set by now!

Biff.   Now, look, I'm gonna tell you what happened, and you're going to listen to me.

Young Bernard.   Mrs. Loman!

Biff.   I waited six hours —

Happy.   What the hell are you saying?

Biff.   I kept sending in my name but he wouldn't see me. So finally he . . . (*He continues unheard as light fades low on the restaurant.*)

Young Bernard.   Biff flunked math!

Linda.   No!

Young Bernard.   Birnbaum flunked him! They won't graduate him!

Linda.   But they have to. He's gotta go to the university. Where is he? Biff! Biff!

Young Bernard.   No, he left. He went to Grand Central.

Linda.   Grand — You mean he went to Boston!

Young Bernard.   Is Uncle Willy in Boston?

Linda.   Oh, maybe Willy can talk to the teacher. Oh, the poor, poor boy!

Light on house area snaps out.

Biff (*at the table, now audible, holding up a gold fountain pen*). . . . so I'm washed up with Oliver, you understand? Are you listening to me?

Willy (*at a loss*).   Yeah, sure. If you hadn't flunked —

Biff.   Flunked what? What're you talking about?

Willy.   Don't blame everything on me! I didn't flunk math — you did! What pen?

Happy.   That was awful dumb, Biff, a pen like that is worth —

Willy (*seeing the pen for the first time*).   You took Oliver's pen?

Biff (*weakening*).   Dad, I just explained it to you.

Willy.   You stole Bill Oliver's fountain pen!

Biff.   I didn't exactly steal it! That's just what I've been explaining to you!

Happy.   He had it in his hand and just then Oliver walked in, so he got nervous and stuck it in his pocket!

Willy.   My God, Biff!

Biff.   I never intended to do it, Dad!

Operator's Voice.   Standish Arms, good evening!

Willy (*shouting*).   I'm not in my room!

Biff (*frightened*).   Dad, what's the matter? (*He and Happy stand up.*)

Operator.   Ringing Mr. Loman for you!

Willy.   I'm not there, stop it!

Biff (*horrified, gets down on one knee before Willy*).   Dad, I'll make good, I'll make good. (*Willy tries to get to his feet. Biff holds him down.*) Sit down now.

Willy.   No, you're no good, you're no good for anything.

Biff.   I am, Dad, I'll find something else, you understand? Now don't worry about anything. (*He holds up Willy's face.*) Talk to me, Dad.

Operator.   Mr. Loman does not answer. Shall I page him?

Willy (*attempting to stand, as though to rush and silence the Operator*).   No, no, no!

Happy.   He'll strike something, Pop.

Willy.   No, no . . .

Biff (*desperately, standing over Willy*).   Pop, listen! Listen to me! I'm telling you something good. Oliver talked to his partner about the Florida idea. You listening? He — he talked to his partner, and he came to me . . . I'm going to be all right, you hear? Dad, listen to me, he said it was just a question of the amount!

Willy.   Then you . . . got it?

Happy.   He's gonna be terrific, Pop!

Willy (*trying to stand*).   Then you got it, haven't you? You got it! You got it!

Biff (*agonized, holds Willy down*).   No, no. Look, Pop. I'm supposed to have lunch with them tomorrow. I'm just telling you this so you'll know that I can still make an impression, Pop. And I'll make good somewhere, but I can't go tomorrow, see?

Willy.   Why not? You simply —

Biff.   But the pen, Pop!

Willy.   You give it to him and tell him it was an oversight!

Happy.   Sure, have lunch tomorrow!

Biff.   I can't say that —

Willy.   You were doing a crossword puzzle and accidentally used his pen!

Biff.   Listen, kid, I took those balls years ago, now I walk in with his fountain pen? That clinches it, don't you see? I can't face him like that! I'll try elsewhere.

Page's Voice.   Paging Mr. Loman!

Willy.   Don't you want to be anything?

Biff.   Pop, how can I go back?

Willy.   You don't want to be anything, is that what's behind it?

Biff (*now angry at Willy for not crediting his sympathy*).   Don't take it that way! You think it was easy walking into that office after what I'd done to him? A team of horses couldn't have dragged me back to Bill Oliver!

Willy. Then why'd you go?

Biff. Why did I go? Why did I go! Look at you! Look at what's become of you!

Off left, The Woman laughs.

Willy. Biff, you're going to lunch tomorrow, or —

Biff. I can't go. I've got no appointment!

Happy. Biff, for . . . !

Willy. Are you spiting me?

Biff. Don't take it that way! Goddammit!

Willy (*strikes Biff and falters away from the table*). You rotten little louse! Are you spiting me?

The Woman. Someone's at the door, Willy!

Biff. I'm no good, can't you see what I am?

Happy (*separating them*). Hey, you're in a restaurant! Now cut it out, both of you! (*The girls enter.*) Hello, girls, sit down.

The Woman laughs, off left.

Miss Forsythe. I guess we might as well. This is Letta.

The Woman. Willy, are you going to wake up?

Biff (*ignoring Willy*). How're ya, miss, sit down. What do you drink?

Miss Forsythe. Letta might not be able to stay long.

Letta. I gotta get up very early tomorrow. I got jury duty. I'm so excited! Were you fellows ever on a jury?

Biff. No, but I been in front of them! (*The girls laugh.*) This is my father.

Letta. Isn't he cute? Sit down with us, Pop.

Happy. Sit him down, Biff!

Biff (*going to him*). Come on, slugger, drink us under the table. To hell with it! Come on, sit down, pal.

On Biff's last insistence, Willy is about to sit.

The Woman (*now urgently*). Willy, are you going to answer the door!

The Woman's call pulls Willy back. He starts right, befuddled.

Biff. Hey, where are you going?

Willy. Open the door.

Biff. The door?

Willy. The washroom . . . the door . . . where's the door?

Biff (*leading Willy to the left*). Just go straight down.

Willy moves left.

The Woman. Willy, Willy, are you going to get up, get up, get up, get up?

Willy exits left.

Letta. I think it's sweet you bring your daddy along.

Miss Forsythe. Oh, he isn't really your father!

Biff (*at left, turning to her resentfully*). Miss Forsythe, you've just seen a prince walk by. A fine, troubled prince. A hard-working, unappreciated prince. A pal, you understand? A good companion. Always for his boys.

Letta. That's so sweet.

Happy. Well, girls, what's the program? We're wasting time. Come on, Biff. Gather round. Where would you like to go?

Biff. Why don't you do something for him?

Happy. Me!

Biff. Don't you give a damn for him, Hap?

Happy. What're you talking about? I'm the one who —

Biff. I sense it, you don't give a good goddamn about him. (*He takes the rolled-up hose from his pocket and puts it on the table in front of Happy.*) Look what I found in the cellar, for Christ's sake. How can you bear to let it go on?

Happy. Me? Who goes away? Who runs off and —

Biff. Yeah, but he doesn't mean anything to you. You could help him — I can't! Don't you understand what I'm talking about? He's going to kill himself, don't you know that?

Happy. Don't I know it! Me!

Biff. Hap, help him! Jesus . . . help him . . . Help me, help me, I can't bear to look at his face! (*Ready to weep, he hurries out, up right.*)

Happy (*starting after him*). Where are you going?

Miss Forsythe. What's he so mad about?

Happy. Come on, girls, we'll catch up with him.

Miss Forsythe (*as Happy pushes her out*). Say, I don't like that temper of his!

Happy. He's just a little overstrung, he'll be all right!

Willy (*off left, as The Woman laughs*). Don't answer! Don't answer!

Letta. Don't you want to tell your father —

Happy. No, that's not my father. He's just a guy. Come on, we'll catch Biff, and, honey, we're going to paint this town! Stanley, where's the check! Hey, Stanley!

They exit. Stanley looks toward left.

Stanley (*calling to Happy indignantly*). Mr. Loman! Mr. Loman!

Stanley picks up a chair and follows them off. Knocking is heard off left. The Woman enters, laughing. Willy follows her. She is in a black slip; he is buttoning his shirt. Raw, sensuous music accompanies their speech.

Willy. Will you stop laughing? Will you stop?

The Woman. Aren't you going to answer the door? He'll wake the whole hotel.

Willy. I'm not expecting anybody.

The Woman. Whyn't you have another drink, honey, and stop being so damn self-centered?

Willy. I'm so lonely.

The Woman. You know you ruined me, Willy? From now on, whenever you come to the office, I'll see that you go right through to the buyers. No waiting at my desk any more, Willy. You ruined me.

Willy. That's nice of you to say that.

The Woman. Gee, you are self-centered! Why so sad? You are the saddest, self-centeredest soul I ever did see-saw. *(She laughs. He kisses her.)* Come on inside, drummer boy. It's silly to be dressing in the middle of the night. *(As knocking is heard.)* Aren't you going to answer the door?

Willy. They're knocking on the wrong door.

The Woman. But I felt the knocking. And he heard us talking in here. Maybe the hotel's on fire!

Willy *(his terror rising).* It's a mistake.

The Woman. Then tell him to go away!

Willy. There's nobody there.

The Woman. It's getting on my nerves, Willy. There's somebody standing out there and it's getting on my nerves!

Willy *(pushing her away from him).* All right, stay in the bathroom here, and don't come out. I think there's a law in Massachusetts about it, so don't come out. It may be that new room clerk. He looked very mean. So don't come out. It's a mistake, there's no fire.

The knocking is heard again. He takes a few steps away from her, and she vanishes into the wing. The light follows him, and now he is facing Young Biff, who carries a suitcase. Biff steps toward him. The music is gone.

Biff. Why didn't you answer?

Willy. Biff! What are you doing in Boston?

Biff. Why didn't you answer? I've been knocking for five minutes, I called you on the phone —

Willy. I just heard you. I was in the bathroom and had the door shut. Did anything happen home?

Biff. Dad — I let you down.

Willy. What do you mean?

Biff. Dad . . .

Willy. Biffo, what's this about? *(Putting his arm around Biff.)* Come on, let's go downstairs and get you a malted.

Biff. Dad, I flunked math.

Willy. Not for the term?

Biff. The term. I haven't got enough credits to graduate.

Willy. You mean to say Bernard wouldn't give you the answers?

Biff. He did, he tried, but I only got a sixty-one.

Willy. And they wouldn't give you four points?

Biff. Birnbaum refused absolutely. I begged him, Pop, but he won't give me those points. You gotta talk to him before they close the school. Because if he saw the kind of man you are, and you just talked to him in your way, I'm sure he'd come through for me. The class came right before practice, see, and I didn't go enough. Would you talk to him? He'd like you, Pop. You know the way you could talk.

Willy. You're on. We'll drive right back.

Biff. Oh, Dad, good work! I'm sure he'll change it for you!

Willy. Go downstairs and tell the clerk I'm checkin' out. Go right down.

Biff. Yes, sir! See, the reason he hates me, Pop — one day he was late for class so I got up at the blackboard and imitated him. I crossed my eyes and talked with a lithp.

Willy (laughing). You did? The kids like it?

Biff. They nearly died laughing!

Willy. Yeah? What'd you do?

Biff. The thquare root of thixthy twee is . . . (Willy bursts out laughing; Biff joins him.) And in the middle of it he walked in!

Willy laughs and The Woman joins in offstage.

Willy (without hesitation). Hurry downstairs and —

Biff. Somebody in there?

Willy. No, that was next door.

The Woman laughs offstage.

Biff. Somebody got in your bathroom!

Willy. No, it's the next room, there's a party —

The Woman (enters, laughing. She lisps this): Can I come in? There's something in the bathtub, Willy, and it's moving!

Willy looks at Biff, who is staring open-mouthed and horrified at The Woman.

Willy. Ah — you better go back to your room. They must be finished painting by now. They're painting her room so I let her take a shower here. Go back, go back . . . (He pushes her.)

The Woman (resisting). But I've got to get dressed, Willy, I can't —

Willy. Get out of here! Go back, go back . . . (Suddenly striving for the ordinary): This is Miss Francis, Biff, she's a buyer. They're painting her room. Go back, Miss Francis, go back . . .

The Woman. But my clothes, I can't go out naked in the hall!

Willy (pushing her offstage). Get outa here! Go back, go back!

Biff slowly sits down on his suitcase as the argument continues offstage.

The Woman.   Where's my stockings? You promised me stockings, Willy!

Willy.   I have no stockings here!

The Woman.   You had two boxes of size nine sheers for me, and I want them!

Willy.   Here, for God's sake, will you get outa here!

The Woman (*enters holding a box of stockings*).   I just hope there's nobody in the hall. That's all I hope. (*To Biff.*) Are you football or baseball?

Biff.   Football.

The Woman (*angry, humiliated*).   That's me too. G'night. (*She snatches her clothes from Willy, and walks out.*)

Willy (*after a pause*).   Well, better get going. I want to get to the school first thing in the morning. Get my suits out of the closet. I'll get my valise. (*Biff doesn't move.*) What's the matter? (*Biff remains motionless, tears falling.*) She's a buyer. Buys for J. H. Simmons. She lives down the hall — they're painting. You don't imagine — (*He breaks off. After a pause.*) Now listen, pal, she's just a buyer. She sees merchandise in her room and they have to keep it looking just so . . . (*Pause. Assuming command.*) All right, get my suits. (*Biff doesn't move.*) Now stop crying and do as I say. I gave you an order. Biff, I gave you an order! Is that what you do when I give you an order? How dare you cry! (*Putting his arm around Biff.*) Now look, Biff, when you grow up you'll understand about these things. You mustn't — you mustn't overemphasize a thing like this. I'll see Birnbaum first thing in the morning.

Biff.   Never mind.

Willy (*getting down beside Biff*).   Never mind! He's going to give you those points. I'll see to it.

Biff.   He wouldn't listen to you.

Willy.   He certainly will listen to me. You need those points for the U. of Virginia.

Biff.   I'm not going there.

Willy.   Heh? If I can't get him to change that mark you'll make it up in summer school. You've got all summer to —

Biff (*his weeping breaking from him*).   Dad . . .

Willy (*infected by it*).   Oh, my boy . . .

Biff.   Dad . . .

Willy.   She's nothing to me, Biff. I was lonely, I was terribly lonely.

Biff.   You — you gave her Mama's stockings! (*His tears break through and he rises to go.*)

Willy (*grabbing for Biff*).   I gave you an order!

Biff.   Don't touch me, you — liar!

Willy.   Apologize for that!

Biff.   You fake! You phony little fake! You fake! (*Overcome, he turns quickly and weeping fully goes out with his suitcase. Willy is left on the floor on his knees.*)

Willy.   I gave you an order! Biff, come back here or I'll beat you! Come back here! I'll whip you!

Stanley comes quickly in from the right and stands in front of Willy.

Willy *(shouts at Stanley).*   I gave you an order . . :
Stanley.   Hey, let's pick it up, pick it up, Mr. Loman. *(He helps Willy to his feet.)* Your boys left with the chippies. They said they'll see you home.

A second waiter watches some distance away.

Willy.   But we were supposed to have dinner together.

Music is heard, Willy's theme.

Stanley.   Can you make it?
Willy.   I'll — sure, I can make it. *(Suddenly concerned about his clothes.)* Do I — I look all right?
Stanley.   Sure, you look all right. *(He flicks a speck off Willy's lapel.)*
Willy.   Here — here's a dollar.
Stanley.   Oh, your son paid me. It's all right.
Willy *(putting it in Stanley's hand).*   No, take it. You're a good boy.
Stanley.   Oh, no, you don't have to . . .
Willy.   Here — here's some more, I don't need it any more. *(After a slight pause.)* Tell me — is there a seed store in the neighborhood?
Stanley.   Seeds? You mean like to plant?

As Willy turns, Stanley slips the money back into his jacket pocket.

Willy.   Yes. Carrots, peas . . .
Stanley.   Well, there's hardware stores on Sixth Avenue, but it may be too late now.
Willy *(anxiously).*   Oh, I'd better hurry. I've got to get some seeds. *(He starts off to the right.)* I've got to get some seeds, right away. Nothing's planted. I don't have a thing in the ground.

Willy hurries out as the light goes down. Stanley moves over to the right after him, watches him off. The other waiter has been staring at Willy.

Stanley *(to the waiter).*   Well, whatta you looking at?

The waiter picks up the chairs and moves off right. Stanley takes the table and follows him. The light fades on this area. There is a long pause, the sound of the flute coming over. The light gradually rises on the kitchen, which is empty. Happy appears at the door of the house, followed by Biff. Happy is carrying a large bunch of long-stemmed roses. He enters the kitchen, looks around for Linda. Not seeing her, he turns to Biff, who is just outside the house door, and makes a gesture with his hands, indicating "Not here, I guess." He looks into the living-room and freezes. Inside, Linda, unseen, is seated, Willy's coat on her lap. She rises ominously and quietly and moves toward Happy, who backs up into the kitchen, afraid.

Happy. Hey, what're you doing up? (*Linda says nothing but moves toward him implacably.*) Where's Pop? (*He keeps backing to the right, and now Linda is in full view in the doorway to the living-room.*) Is he sleeping?
Linda. Where were you?
Happy (*trying to laugh it off*). We met two girls, Mom, very fine types. Here, we brought you some flowers. (*Offering them to her.*) Put them in your room, Ma.

She knocks them to the floor at Biff's feet. He has now come inside and closed the door behind him. She stares at Biff, silent.

Happy. Now what'd you do that for? Mom, I want you to have some flowers —
Linda (*cutting Happy off, violently to Biff*). Don't you care whether he lives or dies?
Happy (*going to the stairs*). Come upstairs, Biff.
Biff (*with a flare of disgust, to Happy*). Go away from me! (*To Linda.*) What do you mean, lives or dies? Nobody's dying around here, pal.
Linda. Get out of my sight! Get out of here!
Biff. I wanna see the boss.
Linda. You're not going near him!
Biff. Where is he? (*He moves into the living-room and Linda follows.*)
Linda (*shouting after Biff*). You invite him for dinner. He looks forward to it all day — (*Biff appears in his parents' bedroom, looks around, and exits.*) — and then you desert him there. There's no stranger you'd do that to!
Happy. Why? He had a swell time with us. Listen, when I — (*Linda comes back into the kitchen*) — desert him I hope I don't outlive the day!
Linda. Get out of here!
Happy. Now look, Mom . . .
Linda. Did you have to go to women tonight? You and your lousy rotten whores!

Biff re-enters the kitchen.

Happy. Mom, all we did was follow Biff around trying to cheer him up! (*To Biff.*) Boy, what a night you gave me!
Linda. Get out of here, both of you, and don't come back! I don't want you tormenting him any more. Go on now, get your things together! (*To Biff.*) You can sleep in his apartment. (*She starts to pick up the flowers and stops herself.*) Pick up this stuff, I'm not your maid any more. Pick it up, you bum, you!

Happy turns his back to her in refusal. Biff slowly moves over and gets down on his knees, picking up the flowers.

Linda. You're a pair of animals! Not one, not another living soul would have had the cruelty to walk out on that man in a restaurant!

Biff (*not looking at her*). Is that what he said?

Linda. He didn't have to say anything. He was so humiliated he nearly limped when he came in.

Happy. But, Mom, he had a great time with us —

Biff (*cutting him off violently*). Shut up!

Without another word, Happy goes upstairs.

Linda. You! You didn't even go in to see if he was all right!

Biff (*still on the floor in front of Linda, the flowers in his hand; with self-loathing*). No. Didn't. Didn't do a damned thing. How do you like that, heh? Left him babbling in a toilet.

Linda. You louse. You . . .

Biff. Now you hit it on the nose! (*He gets up, throws the flowers in the wastebasket.*) The scum of the earth, and you're looking at him!

Linda. Get out of here!

Biff. I gotta talk to the boss, Mom. Where is he?

Linda. You're not going near him. Get out of this house!

Biff (*with absolute assurance, determination*). No. We're gonna have an abrupt conversation, him and me.

Linda. You're not talking to him!

Hammering is heard from outside the house, off right. Biff turns toward the noise.

Linda (*suddenly pleading*). Will you please leave him alone?

Biff. What's he doing out there?

Linda. He's planting the garden!

Biff (*quietly*). Now? Oh, my God!

Biff moves outside, Linda following. The light dies down on them and comes up on the center of the apron as Willy walks into it. He is carrying a flashlight, a hoe, and a handful of seed packets. He raps the top of the hoe sharply to fix it firmly, and then moves to the left, measuring off the distance with his foot. He holds the flashlight to look at the seed packets, reading off the instructions. He is in the blue of night.

Willy. Carrots . . . quarter-inch apart. Rows . . . one-foot rows. (*He measures it off.*) One foot. (*He puts down a package and measures off.*) Beets. (*He puts down another package and measures again.*) Lettuce. (*He reads the package, puts it down.*) One foot — (*He breaks off as Ben appears at the right and moves slowly down to him.*) What a proposition, ts, ts. Terrific, terrific. 'Cause she's suffered, Ben, the woman has suffered. You understand me? A man can't go out the way he came in, Ben, a man has got to add up to something. You can't, you can't — (*Ben moves toward him as though to interrupt.*) You gotta consider, now. Don't answer so quick. Remember, it's a guaranteed twenty-thousand-dollar proposition. Now look, Ben, I want you to go through the ins and outs of this thing with me. I've got nobody to talk to, Ben, and the woman has suffered, you hear me?

Ben (*standing still, considering*). What's the proposition?

Willy. It's twenty thousand dollars on the barrelhead. Guaranteed, gilt-edged, you understand?

Ben. You don't want to make a fool of yourself. They might not honor the policy.

Willy. How can they dare refuse? Didn't I work like a coolie to meet every premium on the nose? And now they don't pay off? Impossible!

Ben. It's called a cowardly thing, William.

Willy. Why? Does it take more guts to stand here the rest of my life ringing up a zero?

Ben (*yielding*). That's a point, William. (*He moves, thinking, turns.*) And twenty thousand — that *is* something one can feel with the hand, it is there.

Willy (*now assured, with rising power*). Oh, Ben, that's the whole beauty of it! I see it like a diamond, shining in the dark, hard and rough, that I can pick up and touch in my hand. Not like — like an appointment! This would not be another damned-fool appointment, Ben, and it changes all the aspects. Because he thinks I'm nothing, see, and so he spites me. But the funeral — (*Straightening up.*) Ben, that funeral will be massive! They'll come from Maine, Massachusetts, Vermont, New Hampshire! All the old-timers with the strange license plates — that boy will be thunder-struck, Ben, because he never realized — I am known! Rhode Island, New York, New Jersey — I am known, Ben, and he'll see it with his eyes once and for all. He'll see what I am, Ben! He's in for a shock, that boy!

Ben (*coming to the edge of the garden*). He'll call you a coward.

Willy (*suddenly fearful*). No, that would be terrible.

Ben. Yes. And a damned fool.

Willy. No, no, he mustn't, I won't have that! (*He is broken and desperate.*)

Ben. He'll hate you William.

The gay music of the Boys is heard.

Willy. Oh, Ben, how do we get back to all the great times? Used to be so full of light, and comradeship, the sleigh-riding in winter, and the ruddiness on his cheeks. And always some kind of good news coming up, always something nice coming up ahead. And never even let me carry the valises in the house, and simonizing, simonizing that little red car! Why, why can't I give him something and not have him hate me?

Ben. Let me think about it. (*He glances at his watch.*) I still have a little time. Remarkable proposition, but you've got to be sure you're not making a fool of yourself.

Ben drifts off upstage and goes out of sight. Biff comes down from the left.

Willy (*suddenly conscious of Biff, turns and looks up at him, then begins picking up the packages of seeds in confusion*).   Where the hell is that seed? (*Indignantly.*) You can't see nothing out here! They boxed in the whole goddamn neighborhood!

Biff.   There are people all around here. Don't you realize that?

Willy.   I'm busy. Don't bother me.

Biff (*taking the hoe from Willy*).   I'm saying good-by to you, Pop. (*Willy looks at him, silent, unable to move.*) I'm not coming back any more.

Willy.   You're not going to see Oliver tomorrow?

Biff.   I've got no appointment, Dad.

Willy.   He put his arm around you, and you've got no appointment?

Biff.   Pop, get this now, will you? Everytime I've left it's been a fight that sent me out of here. Today I realized something about myself and I tried to explain it to you and I — I think I'm just not smart enough to make any sense out of it for you. To hell with whose fault it is or anything like that. (*He takes Willy's arm.*) Let's just wrap it up, heh? Come on in, we'll tell Mom. (*He gently tries to pull Willy to left.*)

Willy (*frozen, immobile, with guilt in his voice*).   No, I don't want to see her.

Biff.   Come on! (*He pulls again, and Willy tries to pull away.*)

Willy (*highly nervous*).   No, no, I don't want to see her.

Biff (*tries to look into Willy's face, as if to find the answer there*).   Why don't you want to see her?

Willy (*more harshly now*).   Don't bother me, will you?

Biff.   What do you mean, you don't want to see her? You don't want them calling you yellow, do you? This isn't your fault; it's me, I'm a bum. Now come inside! (*Willy strains to get away.*) Did you hear what I said to you?

Willy pulls away and quickly goes by himself into the house. Biff follows.

Linda (*to Willy*).   Did you plant, dear?

Biff (*at the door, to Linda*).   All right, we had it out. I'm going and I'm not writing any more.

Linda (*going to Willy in the kitchen*).   I think that's the best way, dear. 'Cause there's no use drawing it out, you'll just never get along.

Willy doesn't respond.

Biff.   People ask where I am and what I'm doing, you don't know, and you don't care. That way it'll be off your mind and you can start brightening up again. All right? That clears it, doesn't it? (*Willy is silent, and Biff goes to him.*) You gonna wish me luck, scout? (*He extends his hand.*) What do you say?

Linda.   Shake his hand, Willy.

Willy (*turning to her, seething with hurt*).   There's no necessity to mention the pen at all, y'know.

Biff (*gently*).   I've got no appointment, Dad.

Willy (*erupting fiercely*).   He put his arm around . . . ?

Biff.   Dad, you're never going to see what I am, so what's the use of arguing? If I strike oil I'll send you a check. Meantime forget I'm alive.

Willy (*to Linda*).   Spite, see?

Biff.   Shake hands, Dad.

Willy.   Not my hand.

Biff.   I was hoping not to go this way.

Willy.   Well, this is the way you're going. Good-by.

Biff looks at him a moment, then turns sharply and goes to the stairs.

Willy (*stops him with*).   May you rot in hell if you leave this house!

Biff (*turning*).   Exactly what is it that you want from me?

Willy.   I want you to know, on the train, in the mountains, in the valleys, wherever you go, that you cut down your life for spite!

Biff.   No, no.

Willy.   Spite, spite, is the word of your undoing! And when you're down and out, remember what did it. When you're rotting somewhere beside the railroad tracks, remember, and don't you dare blame it on me!

Biff.   I'm not blaming it on you!

Willy.   I won't take the rap for this, you hear?

Happy comes down the stairs and stands on the bottom step, watching.

Biff.   That's just what I'm telling you!

Willy (*sinking into a chair at the table, with full accusation*).   You're trying to put a knife in me — don't think I don't know what you're doing!

Biff.   All right, phony! Then let's lay it on the line. (*He whips the rubber tube out of his pocket and puts it on the table.*)

Happy.   You crazy —

Linda.   Biff! (*She moves to grab the hose, but Biff holds it down with his hand.*)

Biff.   Leave it there! Don't move it!

Willy (*not looking at it*).   What is that?

Biff.   You know goddam well what that is.

Willy (*caged, wanting to escape*).   I never saw that.

Biff.   You saw it. The mice didn't bring it into the cellar! What is this supposed to do, make a hero out of you? This supposed to make me sorry for you?

Willy.   Never heard of it.

Biff.   There'll be no pity for you, you hear it? No pity!

Willy (*to Linda.*)   You hear the spite!

Biff.   No, you're going to hear the truth — what you are and what I am!

Linda.   Stop it!

Willy.   Spite!

Happy (*coming down toward Biff*).   You cut it now!

Biff (*to Happy*).   The man don't know who we are! The man is gonna know!
  (*To Willy.*) We never told the truth for ten minutes in this house!
Happy.   We always told the truth!
Biff (*turning on him*).   You big blow, are you the assistant buyer? You're one of
  the two assistants to the assistant, aren't you?
Happy.   Well, I'm practically —
Biff.   You're practically full of it! We all are! And I'm through with it. (*To
  Willy.*) Now hear this, Willy, this is me.
Willy.   I know you!
Biff.   You know why I had no address for three months? I stole a suit in Kansas
  City and I was in jail. (*To Linda, who is sobbing.*) Stop crying. I'm through with it.

Linda turns away from them, her hands covering her face.

Willy.   I suppose that's my fault!
Biff.   I stole myself out of every good job since high school!
Willy.   And whose fault is that?
Biff.   And I never got anywhere because you blew me so full of hot air I could
  never stand taking orders from anybody! That's whose fault it is!
Willy.   I hear that!
Linda.   Don't, Biff!
Biff.   It's goddam time you heard that! I had to be boss big shot in two weeks,
  and I'm through with it!
Willy.   Then hang yourself! For spite, hang yourself!
Biff.   No! Nobody's hanging himself, Willy! I ran down eleven flights with a
  pen in my hand today. And suddenly I stopped, you hear me? And in the
  middle of that office building, do you hear this? I stopped in the middle of
  that building and I saw — the sky. I saw the things that I love in this world.
  The work and the food and time to sit and smoke. And I looked at the pen and
  said to myself, what the hell am I grabbing this for? Why am I trying to
  become what I don't want to be? What am I doing in an office, making a contemptuous, begging fool of myself, when all I want is out there, waiting for
  me the minute I say I know who I am! Why can't I say that, Willy? (*He tries to
  make Willy face him, but Willy pulls away and moves to the left.*)
Willy (*with hatred, threateningly*).   The door of your life is wide open!
Biff.   Pop! I'm a dime a dozen, and so are you!
Willy (*turning on him now in an uncontrolled outburst*).   I am not a dime a
  dozen! I am Willy Loman, and you are Biff Loman!

*Biff starts for Willy, but is blocked by Happy. In his fury, Biff seems on the verge
of attacking his father.*

Biff.   I am not a leader of men, Willy, and neither are you. You were never anything but a hard-working drummer who landed in the ash can like all the rest
  of them! I'm one dollar an hour, Willy! I tried seven states and couldn't raise

it. A buck an hour! Do you gather my meaning? I'm not bringing home any prizes any more, and you're going to stop waiting for me to bring them home!

Willy (*directly to Biff*).   You vengeful, spiteful mutt!

Biff breaks from Happy. Willy, in fright, starts up the stairs. Biff grabs him.

Biff (*at the peak of his fury*).   Pop, I'm nothing! I'm nothing, Pop. Can't you understand that? There's no spite in it any more. I'm just what I am, that's all.

Biff's fury has spent itself, and he breaks down, sobbing, holding on to Willy, who dumbly fumbles for Biff's face.

Willy (*astonished*).   What're you doing? What're you doing? (*To Linda.*) Why is he crying?

Biff (*crying, broken*).   Will you let me go, for Christ's sake? Will you take that phony dream and burn it before something happens? (*Struggling to contain himself, he pulls away and moves to the stairs.*) I'll go in the morning. Put him — put him to bed. (*Exhausted, Biff moves up the stairs to his room.*)

Willy (*after a long pause, astonished, elevated*).   Isn't that — isn't that remarkable? Biff — he likes me!

Linda.   He loves you, Willy!

Happy (*deeply moved*).   Always did, Pop.

Willy.   Oh, Biff! (*Staring wildly.*) He cried! Cried to me. (*He is choking with his love, and now cries out his promise.*) That boy — that boy is going to be magnificent!

Ben appears in the light just outside the kitchen.

Ben.   Yes, outstanding, with twenty thousand behind him.

Linda (*sensing the racing of his mind, fearfully, carefully*).   Now come to bed, Willy. It's all settled now.

Willy (*finding it difficult not to rush out of the house*).   Yes, we'll sleep. Come on. Go to sleep, Hap.

Ben.   And it does take a great kind of a man to crack the jungle.

In accents of dread, Ben's idyllic music starts up.

Happy (*his arm around Linda*).   I'm getting married, Pop, don't forget it. I'm changing everything. I'm gonna run that department before the year is up. You'll see, Mom. (*He kisses her.*)

Ben.   The jungle is dark but full of diamonds, Willy.

Willy turns, moves, listening to Ben.

Linda.   Be good. You're both good boys, just act that way, that's all.

Happy.   'Night, Pop. (*He goes upstairs.*)

Linda (*to Willy*).   Come, dear.

Ben (*with greater force*).   One must go in to fetch a diamond out.

Willy (*to Linda, as he moves slowly along the edge of the kitchen, toward the door*).   I just want to get settled down, Linda. Let me sit alone for a little.

Linda (*almost uttering her fear*).   I want you upstairs.

Willy (*taking her in his arms*).   In a few minutes, Linda. I couldn't sleep right now. Go on, you look awful tired. (*He kisses her.*)

Ben.   Not like an appointment at all. A diamond is rough and hard to the touch.

Willy.   Go on now. I'll be right up.

Linda.   I think this is the only way, Willy.

Willy.   Sure, it's the best thing.

Ben.   Best thing!

Willy.   The only way. Everything is gonna be — go on, kid, get to bed. You look so tired.

Linda.   Come right up.

Willy.   Two minutes.

Linda goes into the living-room, then reappears in her bedroom. Willy moves just outside the kitchen door.

Willy.   Loves me. (*Wonderingly.*) Always loved me. Isn't that a remarkable thing? Ben, he'll worship me for it!

Ben (*with promise*).   It's dark there, but full of diamonds.

Willy.   Can you imagine that magnificence with twenty thousand dollars in his pocket?

Linda (*calling from her room*).   Willy! Come up!

Willy (*calling into the kitchen*).   Yes! Yes. Coming! It's very smart, you realize that, don't you, sweetheart? Even Ben sees it. I gotta go, baby. 'By! 'By! (*Going over to Ben, almost dancing.*) Imagine? When the mail comes he'll be ahead of Bernard again!

Ben.   A perfect proposition all around.

Willy.   Did you see how he cried to me? Oh, if I could kiss him, Ben!

Ben.   Time, William, time!

Willy.   Oh, Ben, I always knew one way or another we were gonna make it, Biff and I!

Ben (*looking at his watch*).   The boat. We'll be late. (*He moves slowly off into the darkness.*)

Willy (*elegiacally, turning to the house*).   Now when you kick off, boy, I want a seventy-yard boot, and get right down the field under the ball, and when you hit, hit low and hit hard, because it's important, boy. (*He swings around and faces the audience.*) There's all kinds of important people in the stands, and the first thing you know . . . (*Suddenly realizing he is alone.*) Ben! Ben, where do I . . . ? (*He makes a sudden movement of search.*) Ben, how do I . . . ?

Linda (*calling*).   Willy, you coming up?

Willy (*uttering a gasp of fear, whirling about as if to quiet her*).   Sh! (*He turns around as if to find his way; sounds, faces, voices, seem to be swarming in* *upon him and he flicks at them, crying.*) Sh! Sh! (*Suddenly music, faint and high, stops him. It rises in intensity, almost to an unbearable scream. He goes up and down on his toes, and rushes off around the house.*) Shhh!

Linda. Willy?

There is no answer. Linda waits. Biff gets up off his bed. He is still in his clothes. Happy sits up. Biff stands listening.

Linda (*with real fear*). Willy, answer me! Willy!

There is the sound of a car starting and moving away at full speed.

Linda. No!
Biff (*rushing down the stairs*). Pop!

As the car speeds off, the music crashes down in a frenzy of sound, which becomes the soft pulsation of a single cello string. Biff slowly returns to his bedroom. He and Happy gravely don their jackets. Linda slowly walks out of her room. The music has developed into a dead march. The leaves of day are appearing over everything. Charley and Bernard, somberly dressed, appear and knock on the kitchen door. Biff and Happy slowly descend the stairs to the kitchen as Charley and Bernard enter. All stop a moment when Linda, in clothes of mourning, bearing a little bunch of roses, comes through the draped doorway into the kitchen. She goes to Charley and takes his arm. Now all move toward the audience, through the wall-line of the kitchen. At the limit of the apron, Linda lays down the flowers, kneels, and sits back on her heels. All stare down at the grave.

Requiem

Charley. It's getting dark, Linda.

Linda doesn't react. She stares at the grave.

Biff. How about it, Mom? Better get some rest, heh? They'll be closing the gate soon.

Linda makes no move. Pause.

Happy (*deeply angered*). He had no right to do that. There was no necessity for it. We would've helped him.
Charley (*grunting*). Hmmm.
Biff. Come along, Mom.
Linda. Why didn't anybody come?
Charley. It was a very nice funeral.

Linda. But where are all the people he knew? Maybe they blame him.

Charley. Naa. It's a rough world, Linda. They wouldn't blame him.

Linda. I can't understand it. At this time especially. First time in thirty-five years we were just about free and clear. He only needed a little salary. He was even finished with the dentist.

Charley. No man only needs a little salary.

Linda. I can't understand it.

Biff. There were a lot of nice days. When he'd come home from a trip; or on Sundays, making the stoop; finishing the cellar; putting on the new porch; when he built the extra bathroom; and put up the garage. You know something, Charley, there's more of him in that front stoop than in all the sales he ever made.

Charley. Yeah. He was a happy man with a batch of cement.

Linda. He was so wonderful with his hands.

Biff. He had the wrong dreams. All, all, wrong.

Happy (*almost ready to fight Biff*). Don't say that!

Biff. He never knew who he was.

Charley (*stopping Happy's movement and reply. To Biff*). Nobody dast blame this man. You don't understand: Willy was a salesman. And for a salesman, there is no rock bottom to the life. He don't put a bolt to a nut, he don't tell you the law or give you medicine. He's a man way out there in the blue, riding on a smile and a shoeshine. And when they start not smiling back — that's an earthquake. And then you get yourself a couple of spots on your hat, and you're finished. Nobody dast blame this man. A salesman is got to dream, boy. It comes with the territory.

Biff. Charley, the man didn't know who he was.

Happy (*infuriated*). Don't say that!

Biff. Why don't you come with me, Happy?

Happy. I'm not licked that easily. I'm staying right in this city, and I'm gonna beat this racket! (*He looks at Biff, his chin set.*) The Loman Brothers!

Biff. I know who I am, kid.

Happy. All right, boy. I'm gonna show you and everybody else that Willy Loman did not die in vain. He had a good dream. It's the only dream you can have — to come out number-one man. He fought it out here, and this is where I'm gonna win it for him.

Biff (*with a hopeless glance at Happy, bends toward his mother*). Let's go, Mom.

Linda. I'll be with you in a minute. Go on, Charley. (*He hesitates.*) I want to, just for a minute. I never had a chance to say good-by.

Charley moves away, followed by Happy. Biff remains a slight distance up and left of Linda. She sits there, summoning herself. The flute begins, not far away, playing behind her speech.

Linda. Forgive me, dear. I can't cry. I don't know what it is, but I can't cry. I don't understand it. Why did you ever do that? Help me. Willy, I can't cry. It seems to me that you're just on another trip. I keep expecting you. Willy, dear,

I can't cry. Why did you do it? I search and search and I search, and I can't understand it, Willy. I made the last payment on the house today. Today, dear. And there'll be nobody home. (*A sob rises in her throat.*) We're free and clear. (*Sobbing more fully, released.*) We're free. (*Biff comes slowly toward her.*) We're free . . . We're free . . .

Biff lifts her to her feet and moves out up right with her in his arms. Linda sobs quietly. Bernard and Charley come together and follow them, followed by Happy. Only the music of the flute is left on the darkening stage as over the house the hard towers of the apartment buildings rise into sharp focus, and

The Curtain Falls

For Analysis

1. What is Linda's role in the tragedy of Willy? Do you admire her?

2. In what ways are Biff and Happy similar? In what ways different? Is Biff, as Willy asserts, a failure? Explain.

3. Which of the brothers is most likely to become another Willy Loman? Explain.

4. What does Ben represent to Willy? Are we meant to see Ben as Willy sees him? Explain.

5. The play contains many references to the outdoors, the West, working with one's hands. What purpose do these references serve?

On Style

1. Consider the first long stage direction in which Miller describes a **setting** that can move from the present to the past on stage before the audience. The film version of the play simply alternated between the two time periods. Some critics have argued that the ability of the film to realistically re-create the different times damaged the play by diminishing the significant presence of the past in the Loman household. Discuss the difference between the methods, and defend your choice of the better method.

2. The last paragraph of the first stage direction describes Linda. Comment on the parts of the stage direction that cannot be translated into dramatic action. Why do you suppose Miller wrote of Linda as he did?

Making Connections

1. Compare the depiction of the family in this play with that in Tennessee Williams's *The Glass Menagerie* (p. 243).

2. Use the following comment by Arthur Miller as the basis for a comparison of this play with Sophocles' *Oedipus Rex* (p. 186) and *Antigonê* (p. 467): " . . . I think the tragic feeling is evoked in us when we are in the presence of a character who is ready to lay down his life, if need be, to secure one thing — his sense of personal dignity."

Writing Topics

1. In an essay, either support or refute the assertion that Willy is a victim of the American Dream.

2. Argue for or against the view that Biff's treatment of Willy is justified.

Lorraine Hansberry   (1930–1965)

A Raisin in the Sun 1959

CHARACTERS (in order of appearance)

Ruth Younger
Travis Younger
Walter Lee Younger, brother
Beneatha Younger
Lena Younger, Mama
Joseph Asagai
George Murchison
Mrs. Johnson
Karl Lindner
Bobo
Moving Men

The action of the play is set in Chicago's Southside, sometime between World War II and the present.

Act I

Scene 1. *(Friday morning.)*

The Younger living room would be a comfortable and well-ordered room if it were not for a number of indestructible contradictions to this state of being. Its furnishings are typical and undistinguished and their primary feature now is that they have clearly had to accommodate the living of too many people for too many years — and they are tired. Still, we can see that at some time, a time probably no longer remembered by the family (except perhaps for Mama), the furnishings of this room were actually selected with care and love and even hope — and brought to this apartment and arranged with taste and pride.

That was a long time ago. Now the once loved pattern of the couch upholstery has to fight to show itself from under acres of crocheted doilies and couch covers which have themselves finally come to be more important than the upholstery.

And here a table or a chair has been moved to disguise the worn places in the carpet; but the carpet has fought back by showing its weariness, with depressing uniformity, elsewhere on its surface.

Weariness has, in fact, won in this room. Everything has been polished, washed, sat on, used, scrubbed too often. All pretenses but living itself have long since vanished from the very atmosphere of this room.

Moreover, a section of this room, for it is not really a room unto itself, though the landlord's lease would make it seem so, slopes backward to provide a small kitchen area, where the family prepares the meals that are eaten in the living room proper, which must also serve as dining room. The single window that has been provided for these "two" rooms is located in this kitchen area. The sole natural light the family may enjoy in the course of a day is only that which fights its way through this little window.

At left, a door leads to a bedroom which is shared by Mama and her daughter, Beneatha. At right, opposite, is a second room (which in the beginning of the life of this apartment was probably a breakfast room) which serves as a bedroom for Walter and his wife, Ruth.

Time: Sometime between World War II and the present.

Place: Chicago's Southside.

At Rise: It is morning dark in the living room. Travis is asleep on the make-down bed at center. An alarm clock sounds from within the bedroom at right, and presently Ruth enters from that room and closes the door behind her. She crosses sleepily toward the window. As she passes her sleeping son she reaches down and shakes him a little. At the window she raises the shade and a dusky Southside morning light comes in feebly. She fills a pot with water and puts it on to boil. She calls to the boy, between yawns, in a slightly muffled voice.

Ruth is about thirty. We can see that she was a pretty girl, even exceptionally so, but now it is apparent that life has been little that she expected, and disappointment has already begun to hang in her face. In a few years, before thirty-five even, she will be known among her people as a "settled woman."

She crosses to her son and gives him a good, final, rousing shake.

Ruth.   Come on now, boy, it's seven thirty! (*Her son sits up at last, in a stupor of sleepiness.*) I say hurry up, Travis! You ain't the only person in the world got to use a bathroom! (*The child, a sturdy, handsome little boy of ten or eleven, drags himself out of the bed and almost blindly takes his towels and "today's clothes" from drawers and a closet and goes out to the bathroom, which is in an outside hall and which is shared by another family or families on the same floor. Ruth crosses to the bedroom door at right and opens it and calls in to her husband.*) Walter Lee! . . . It's after seven thirty! Lemme see you do some waking up in there now! (*She waits.*) You better get up from there, man! It's after seven thirty I tell you. (*She waits again.*) All right, you just go ahead and lay there and next thing you know Travis be finished and Mr. Johnson'll be in there and you'll be fussing and cussing round here like a madman! And be late too! (*She waits, at the end of patience.*) Walter Lee — it's time for you to GET UP!

She waits another second and then starts to go into the bedroom, but is apparently satisfied that her husband has begun to get up. She stops, pulls the door to, and returns to the kitchen area. She wipes her face with a moist cloth and runs her fingers through her sleep-disheveled hair in a vain effort and ties an apron around her housecoat. The bedroom door at right opens and her husband stands in the doorway in his pajamas, which are rumpled and mismated. He is a lean, intense young man in his middle thirties, inclined to quick nervous movements and erratic speech habits — and always in his voice there is a quality of indictment.

Walter. Is he out yet?

Ruth. What you mean *out*? He ain't hardly got in there good yet.

Walter (*wandering in, still more oriented to sleep than to a new day*). Well, what was you doing all that yelling for if I can't even get in there yet? (*Stopping and thinking.*) Check coming today?

Ruth. They *said* Saturday and this is just Friday and I hopes to God you ain't going to get up here first thing this morning and start talking to me 'bout no money — 'cause I 'bout don't want to hear it.

Walter. Something the matter with you this morning?

Ruth. No — I'm just sleepy as the devil. What kind of eggs you want?

Walter. Not scrambled. (*Ruth starts to scramble eggs.*) Paper come? (*Ruth points impatiently to the rolled up* Tribune *on the table, and he gets it and spreads it out and vaguely reads the front page.*) Set off another bomb yesterday.

Ruth (*maximum indifference*). Did they?

Walter (*looking up*). What's the matter with you?

Ruth. Ain't nothing the matter with me. And don't keep asking me that this morning.

Walter. Ain't nobody bothering you. (*Reading the news of the day absently again.*) Say Colonel McCormick is sick.

Ruth (*affecting tea-party interest*). Is he now? Poor thing.

Walter (*sighing and looking at his watch*). Oh, me. (*He waits.*) Now what is that boy doing in that bathroom all this time? He just going to have to start getting up earlier. I can't be being late to work on account of him fooling around in there.

Ruth (*turning on him*). Oh, no he ain't going to be getting up no earlier no such thing! It ain't his fault that he can't get to bed no earlier nights 'cause he got a bunch of crazy good-for-nothing clowns sitting up running their mouths in what is supposed to be his bedroom after ten o'clock at night . . .

Walter. That's what you mad about, ain't it? The things I want to talk about with my friends just couldn't be important in your mind, could they?

He rises and finds a cigarette in her handbag on the table and crosses to the little window and looks out, smoking and deeply enjoying this first one.

Ruth (*almost matter of factly, a complaint too automatic to deserve emphasis*). Why you always got to smoke before you eat in the morning?

Walter (*at the window*). Just look at 'em down there . . . Running and racing to work . . . (*He turns and faces his wife and watches her a moment at the stove, and then, suddenly.*) You look young this morning, baby.

Ruth (*indifferently*). Yeah?

Walter. Just for a second — stirring them eggs. Just for a second it was — you looked real young again. (*He reaches for her; she crosses away. Then, drily.*) It's gone now — you look like yourself again!

Ruth. Man, if you don't shut up and leave me alone.

Walter (*looking out to the street again*). First thing a man ought to learn in life is not to make love to no colored woman first thing in the morning. You all some eeeevil people at eight o'clock in the morning.

Travis appears in the hall doorway, almost fully dressed and quite wide awake now, his towels and pajamas across his shoulders. He opens the door and signals for his father to make the bathroom in a hurry.

Travis (*watching the bathroom*). Daddy, come on!

Walter gets his bathroom utensils and flies out to the bathroom.

Ruth. Sit down and have your breakfast, Travis.

Travis. Mama, this is Friday. (*Gleefully.*) Check coming tomorrow, huh?

Ruth. You get your mind off money and eat your breakfast.

Travis (*eating*). This is the morning we supposed to bring the fifty cents to school.

Ruth. Well, I ain't got no fifty cents this morning.

Travis. Teacher say we have to.

Ruth. I don't care what teacher say. I ain't got it. Eat your breakfast, Travis.

Travis. I *am* eating.

Ruth. Hush up now and just eat!

The boy gives her an exasperated look for her lack of understanding, and eats grudgingly.

Travis. You think Grandmama would have it?

Ruth. No! And I want you to stop asking your grandmother for money, you hear me?

Travis (*outraged*). Gaaaleee! I don't ask her, she just gimme it sometimes!

Ruth. Travis Willard Younger — I got too much on me this morning to be —

Travis.   Maybe Daddy —
Ruth.   *Travis!*

The boy hushes abruptly. They are both quiet and tense for several seconds.

Travis *(presently).*   Could I maybe go carry some groceries in front of the supermarket for a little while after school then?
Ruth.   Just hush, I said. *(Travis jabs his spoon into his cereal bowl viciously, and rests his head in anger upon his fists.)* If you through eating, you can get over there and make up your bed.

The boy obeys stiffly and crosses the room, almost mechanically, to the bed and more or less folds the bedding into a heap, then angrily gets his books and cap.

Travis *(sulking and standing apart from her unnaturally).*   I'm gone.
Ruth *(looking up from the stove to inspect him automatically).*   Come here. *(He crosses to her and she studies his head.)* If you don't take this comb and fix this here head, you better! *(Travis puts down his books with a great sigh of oppression, and crosses to the mirror. His mother mutters under her breath about his "slubbornness.")* 'Bout to march out of here with that head looking just like chickens slept in it! I just don't know where you get your slubborn ways . . . And get your jacket, too. Looks chilly out this morning.
Travis *(with conspicuously brushed hair and jacket).*   I'm gone.
Ruth.   Get carfare and milk money — *(Waving one finger.)* — and not a single penny for no caps, you hear me?
Travis *(with sullen politeness).*   Yes'm.

He turns in outrage to leave. His mother watches after him as in his frustration he approaches the door almost comically. When she speaks to him, her voice has become a very gentle tease.

Ruth *(mocking; as she thinks he would say it).*   Oh, Mama makes me so mad sometimes, I don't know what to do! *(She waits and continues to his back as he stands stock-still in front of the door.)* I wouldn't kiss that woman good-bye for nothing in this world this morning! *(The boy finally turns around and rolls his eyes at her, knowing the mood has changed and he is vindicated; he does not, however, move toward her yet.)* Not for nothing in this world! *(She finally laughs aloud at him and holds out her arms to him and we see that it is a way between them, very old and practiced. He crosses to her and allows her to embrace him warmly but keeps his face fixed with masculine rigidity. She holds him back from her presently and looks at him and runs her fingers over the features of his face. With utter gentleness —.)* Now — whose little old angry man are you?
Travis *(the masculinity and gruffness start to fade at last).*   Aw gaalee — Mama . . .

Ruth (*mimicking*).   Aw — gaaaaalleeeee, Mama! (*She pushes him, with rough playfulness and finality, toward the door.*) Get on out of here or you going to be late.

Travis (*in the face of love, new aggressiveness*).   Mama, could I *please* go carry groceries?

Ruth.   Honey, it's starting to get so cold evenings.

Walter (*coming in from the bathroom and drawing a make-believe gun from a make-believe holster and shooting at his son*).   What is it he wants to do?

Ruth.   Go carry groceries after school at the supermarket.

Walter.   Well, let him go . . .

Travis (*quickly, to the ally*).   I *have* to — she won't gimme the fifty cents . . .

Walter (*to his wife only*).   Why not?

Ruth (*simply, and with flavor*).   'Cause we don't have it.

Walter (*to Ruth only*).   What you tell the boy things like that for? (*Reaching down into his pants with a rather important gesture.*) Here, son —

He hands the boy the coin, but his eyes are directed to his wife's. Travis takes the money happily.

Travis.   Thanks, Daddy.

He starts out. Ruth watches both of them with murder in her eyes. Walter stands and stares back at her with defiance, and suddenly reaches into his pocket again on an afterthought.

Walter (*without even looking at his son, still staring hard at his wife*).   In fact, here's another fifty cents . . . Buy yourself some fruit today — or take a taxi-cab to school or something!

Travis.   Whoopee —

He leaps up and clasps his father around the middle with his legs, and they face each other in mutual appreciation; slowly Walter Lee peeks around the boy to catch the violent rays from his wife's eyes and draws his head back as if shot.

Walter.   You better get down now — and get to school, man.

Travis (*at the door*).   O.K. Good-bye.

He exits.

Walter (*after him, pointing with pride*).   That's *my* boy. (*She looks at him in disgust and turns back to her work.*) You know what I was thinking 'bout in the bathroom this morning?

Ruth.   No.

Walter.   How come you always try to be so pleasant!

Ruth. What is there to be pleasant 'bout!

Walter. You want to know what I was thinking 'bout in the bathroom or not!

Ruth. I know what you thinking 'bout.

Walter (*ignoring her*). 'Bout what me and Willy Harris was talking about last night.

Ruth (*immediately — a refrain*). Willy Harris is a good-for-nothing loudmouth.

Walter. Anybody who talks to me has got to be a good-for-nothing loud-mouth, ain't he? And what you know about who is just a good-for-nothing loudmouth? Charlie Atkins was just a "good-for-nothing loudmouth" too, wasn't he! When he wanted me to go in the dry-cleaning business with him. And now — he's grossing a hundred thousand a year. A hundred thousand dollars a year! You still call *him* a loudmouth!

Ruth (*bitterly*). Oh, Walter Lee . . .

She folds her head on her arms over the table.

Walter (*rising and coming to her and standing over her*). You tired, ain't you? Tired of everything. Me, the boy, the way we live — this beat-up hole — everything. Ain't you? (*She doesn't look up, doesn't answer.*) So tired — moaning and groaning all the time, but you wouldn't do nothing to help, would you? You couldn't be on my side that long for nothing, could you?

Ruth. Walter, please leave me alone.

Walter. A man needs for a woman to back him up . . .

Ruth. Walter —

Walter. Mama would listen to you. You know she listen to you more than she do me and Bennie. She think more of you. All you have to do is just sit down with her when you drinking your coffee one morning and talking 'bout things like you do and — (*He sits down beside her and demonstrates graphically what he thinks her methods and tone should be.*) — you just sip your coffee, see, and say easy like that you been thinking 'bout that deal Walter Lee is so interested in, 'bout the store and all, and sip some more coffee, like what you saying ain't really that important to you — And the next thing you know, she be listening good and asking you questions and when I come home — I can tell her the details. This ain't no fly-by-night proposition, baby. I mean we fig-ured it out, me and Willy and Bobo.

Ruth (*with a frown*). Bobo?

Walter. Yeah. You see, this little liquor store we got in mind cost seventy-five thousand and we figured the initial investment on the place be 'bout thirty thousand, see. That be ten thousand each. Course, there's a couple of hun-dred you got to pay so's you don't spend your life just waiting for them clowns to let your license get approved —

Ruth. You mean graft?

Walter (*frowning impatiently*). Don't call it that. See there, that just goes to show you what women understand about the world. Baby, don't *nothing* hap-pen for you in the world 'less you pay *somebody* off!

Ruth. Walter, leave me alone! *(She raises her head and stares at him vigorously — then says, more quietly.)* Eat your eggs, they gonna be cold.

Walter *(straightening up from her and looking off).* That's it. There you are. Man say to his woman: I got me a dream. His woman say: Eat your eggs. *(Sadly, but gaining in power.)* Man say: I got to take hold of this here world, baby! And a woman will say: Eat your eggs and go to work. *(Passionately now.)* Man say: I got to change my life, I'm choking to death, baby! And his woman say — *(In utter anguish as he brings his fists down on his thighs.)* — Your eggs is getting cold!

Ruth *(softly).* Walter, that ain't none of our money.

Walter *(not listening at all or even looking at her).* This morning, I was lookin' in the mirror and thinking about it . . . I'm thirty-five years old; I been married eleven years and I got a boy who sleeps in the living room — *(Very, very quietly.)* — and all I got to give him is stories about how rich white people live . . .

Ruth. Eat your eggs, Walter.

Walter *(slams the table and jumps up).* — DAMN MY EGGS — DAMN ALL THE EGGS THAT EVER WAS!

Ruth. Then go to work.

Walter *(looking up at her).* See — I'm trying to talk to you 'bout myself — *(Shaking his head with the repetition.)* — and all you can say is eat them eggs and go to work.

Ruth *(wearily).* Honey, you never say nothing new. I listen to you every day, every night and every morning, and you never say nothing new. *(Shrugging.)* So you would rather *be* Mr. Arnold than be his chauffeur. So — I would *rather* be living in Buckingham Palace.

Walter. That is just what is wrong with the colored woman in this world . . . Don't understand about building their men up and making 'em feel like they somebody. Like they can do something.

Ruth *(drily, but to hurt).* There *are* colored men who do things.

Walter. No thanks to the colored woman.

Ruth. Well, being a colored woman, I guess I can't help myself none.

She rises and gets the ironing board and sets it up and attacks a huge pile of rough-dried clothes, sprinkling them in preparation for the ironing and then rolling them into tight fat balls.

Walter *(mumbling).* We one group of men tied to a race of women with small minds!

His sister Beneatha enters. She is about twenty, as slim and intense as her brother. She is not as pretty as her sister-in-law, but her lean, almost intellectual face has a handsomeness of its own. She wears a bright-red flannel nightie, and her thick hair stands wildly about her head. Her speech is a mixture of many things; it is different from the rest of the family's insofar as education has per-

meated her sense of English — and perhaps the Midwest rather than the South has finally — at last — won out in her inflection; but not altogether, because over all of it is a soft slurring and transformed use of vowels which is the decided influence of the Southside. She passes through the room without looking at either Ruth or Walter and goes to the outside door and looks, a little blindly, out to the bathroom. She sees that it has been lost to the Johnsons. She closes the door with a sleepy vengeance and crosses to the table and sits down a little defeated.

Beneatha. I am going to start timing those people.

Walter. You should get up earlier.

Beneatha *(her face in her hands. She is still fighting the urge to go back to bed).* Really — would you suggest dawn? Where's the paper?

Walter *(pushing the paper across the table to her as he studies her almost clinically, as though he has never seen her before).* You a horrible-looking chick at this hour.

Beneatha *(drily).* Good morning, everybody.

Walter *(senselessly).* How is school coming?

Beneatha *(in the same spirit).* Lovely. Lovely. And you know, biology is the greatest. *(Looking up at him.)* I dissected something that looked just like you yesterday.

Walter. I just wondered if you've made up your mind and everything.

Beneatha *(gaining in sharpness and impatience).* And what did I answer yesterday morning — and the day before that?

Ruth *(from the ironing board, like someone disinterested and old).* Don't be so nasty, Bennie.

Beneatha *(still to her brother).* And the day before that and the day before that!

Walter *(defensively).* I'm interested in you. Something wrong with that? Ain't many girls who decide —

Walter and Beneatha *(in unison).* — "to be a doctor."

Silence.

Walter. Have we figured out yet just exactly how much medical school is going to cost?

Ruth. Walter Lee, why don't you leave that girl alone and get out of here to work?

Beneatha *(exits to the bathroom and bangs on the door).* Come on out of there, please!

She comes back into the room.

Walter *(looking at his sister intently).* You know the check is coming tomorrow.

Beneatha (*turning on him with a sharpness all her own*).   That money belongs to Mama, Walter, and it's for her to decide how she wants to use it. I don't care if she wants to buy a house or a rocket ship or just nail it up somewhere and look at it. It's hers. Not ours — *hers.*

Walter (*bitterly*).   Now ain't that fine! You just got your mother's interest at heart, ain't you, girl? You such a nice girl — but if Mama got that money she can always take a few thousand and help you through school too — can't she?

Beneatha.   I have never asked anyone around here to do anything for me!

Walter.   No! And the line between asking and just accepting when the time comes is big and wide — ain't it!

Beneatha (*with fury*).   What do you want from me, Brother — that I quit school or just drop dead, which!

Walter.   I don't want nothing but for you to stop acting holy 'round here. Me and Ruth done made some sacrifices for you — why can't you do something for the family?

Ruth.   Walter, don't be dragging me in it.

Walter.   You are in it — Don't you get up and go work in somebody's kitchen for the last three years to help put clothes on her back?

Ruth.   Oh, Walter — that's not fair . . .

Walter.   It ain't that nobody expects you to get on your knees and say thank you, Brother; thank you, Ruth; thank you, Mama — and thank you, Travis, for wearing the same pair of shoes for two semesters —

Beneatha (*dropping to her knees*).   Well — I *do* — all right? — thank everybody! And forgive me for ever wanting to be anything at all! (*Pursuing him on her knees across the floor.*) FORGIVE ME, FORGIVE ME, FORGIVE ME!

Ruth.   Please stop it! Your mama'll hear you.

Walter.   Who the hell told you you had to be a doctor? If you so crazy 'bout messing 'round with sick people — then go be a nurse like other women — or just get married and be quiet . . .

Beneatha.   Well — you finally got it said . . . It took you three years but you finally got it said. Walter, give up; leave me alone — it's Mama's money.

Walter.   *He was my father, too!*

Beneatha.   So what? He was mine, too — and Travis' grandfather — but the insurance money belongs to Mama. Picking on me is not going to make her give it to you to invest in any liquor stores — (*Under breath, dropping into a chair.*) — and I for one say, God bless Mama for that!

Walter (*to Ruth*).   See — did you hear? Did you hear!

Ruth.   Honey, please go to work.

Walter.   Nobody in this house is ever going to understand me.

Beneatha.   Because you're a nut.

Walter.   Who's a nut?

Beneatha.   You — you are a nut. Thee is mad, boy.

Walter (*looking at his wife and his sister from the door, very sadly*).   The world's most backward race of people, and that's a fact.

Beneatha *(turning slowly in her chair).* And then there are all those prophets who would lead us out of the wilderness — *(Walter slams out of the house.)* — into the swamps!

Ruth. Bennie, why you always gotta be pickin' on your brother? Can't you be a little sweeter sometimes? *(Door opens. Walter walks in. He fumbles with his cap, starts to speak, clears throat, looks everywhere but at Ruth. Finally:)*

Walter *(to Ruth).* I need some money for carfare.

Ruth *(looks at him, then warms; teasing, but tenderly).* Fifty cents? *(She goes to her bag and gets money.)* Here — take a taxi!

Walter exits. Mama enters. She is a woman in her early sixties, full-bodied and strong. She is one of those women of a certain grace and beauty who wear it so unobtrusively that it takes a while to notice. Her dark-brown face is surrounded by the total whiteness of her hair, and, being a woman who has adjusted to many things in life and overcome many more, her face is full of strength. She has, we can see, wit and faith of a kind that keep her eyes lit and full of interest and expectancy. She is, in a word, a beautiful woman. Her bearing is perhaps most like the noble bearing of the women of the Hereros of Southwest Africa — rather as if she imagines that as she walks she still bears a basket or a vessel upon her head. Her speech, on the other hand, is as careless as her carriage is precise — she is inclined to slur everything — but her voice is perhaps not so much quiet as simply soft.

Mama. Who that 'round here slamming doors at this hour?

She crosses through the room, goes to the window, opens it, and brings in a feeble little plant growing doggedly in a small pot on the window sill. She feels the dirt and puts it back out.

Ruth. That was Walter Lee. He and Bennie was at it again.

Mama. My children and they tempers. Lord, if this little old plant don't get more sun than it's been getting it ain't never going to see spring again. *(She turns from the window.)* What's the matter with you this morning, Ruth? You looks right peaked. You aiming to iron all them things? Leave some for me. I'll get to 'em this afternoon. Bennie honey, it's too drafty for you to be sitting 'round half dressed. Where's your robe?

Beneatha. In the cleaners.

Mama. Well, go get mine and put it on.

Beneatha. I'm not cold, Mama, honest.

Mama. I know — but you so thin . . .

Beneatha *(irritably).* Mama, I'm not cold.

Mama *(seeing the make-down bed as Travis has left it).* Lord have mercy, look at that poor bed. Bless his heart — he tries, don't he?

She moves to the bed Travis has sloppily made up.

Ruth.   No — he don't half try at all 'cause he knows you going to come along behind him and fix everything. That's just how come he don't know how to do nothing right now — you done spoiled that boy so.

Mama *(folding bedding).*   Well — he's a little boy. Ain't supposed to know 'bout housekeeping. My baby, that's what he is. What you fix for his breakfast this morning?

Ruth *(angrily).*   I feed my son, Lena!

Mama.   I ain't meddling — *(Under breath; busy-bodyish.)* I just noticed all last week he had cold cereal, and when it starts getting this chilly in the fall a child ought to have some hot grits or something when he goes out in the cold —

Ruth *(furious).*   I gave him hot oats — is that all right!

Mama.   I ain't meddling. *(Pause.)* Put a lot of nice butter on it? *(Ruth shoots her an angry look and does not reply.)* He likes lots of butter.

Ruth *(exasperated).*   Lena —

Mama *(to Beneatha. Mama is inclined to wander conversationally sometimes).*   What was you and your brother fussing 'bout this morning?

Beneatha.   It's not important, Mama.

She gets up and goes to look out at the bathroom, which is apparently free, and she picks up her towels and rushes out.

Mama.   What was they fighting about?

Ruth.   Now you know as well as I do.

Mama *(shaking her head).*   Brother still worrying hisself sick about that money?

Ruth.   You know he is.

Mama.   You had breakfast?

Ruth.   Some coffee.

Mama.   Girl, you better start eating and looking after yourself better. You almost thin as Travis.

Ruth.   Lena —

Mama.   Un-hunh?

Ruth.   What are you going to do with it?

Mama.   Now don't you start, child. It's too early in the morning to be talking about money. It ain't Christian.

Ruth.   It's just that he got his heart set on that store —

Mama.   You mean that liquor store that Willy Harris want him to invest in?

Ruth.   Yes —

Mama.   We ain't no business people, Ruth. We just plain working folks.

Ruth.   Ain't nobody business people till they go into business. Walter Lee say colored people ain't never going to start getting ahead till they start gambling on some different kinds of things in the world — investments and things.

Mama.   What done got into you, girl? Walter Lee done finally sold you on investing.

Ruth.   No. Mama, something is happening between Walter and me. I don't know what it is — but he needs something — something I can't give him any more. He needs this chance, Lena.

Mama (*frowning deeply*).   But liquor, honey —

Ruth.   Well — like Walter say — I spec people going to always be drinking themselves some liquor.

Mama.   Well — whether they drinks it or not ain't none of my business. But whether I go into business selling it to 'em *is*, and I don't want that on my ledger this late in life. (*Stopping suddenly and studying her daughter-in-law.*) Ruth Younger, what's the matter with you today? You look like you could fall over right there.

Ruth.   I'm tired.

Mama.   Then you better stay home from work today.

Ruth.   I can't stay home. She'd be calling up the agency and screaming at them, "My girl didn't come in today — send me somebody! My girl didn't come in!" Oh, she just have a fit . . .

Mama.   Well, let her have it. I'll just call her up and say you got the flu —

Ruth (*laughing*).   Why the flu?

Mama.   'Cause it sounds respectable to 'em. Something white people get, too. They know 'bout the flu. Otherwise they think you been cut up or something when you tell 'em you sick.

Ruth.   I got to go in. We need the money.

Mama.   Somebody would of thought my children done all but starved to death the way they talk about money here late. Child, we got a great big old check coming tomorrow.

Ruth (*sincerely, but also self-righteously*).   Now that's your money. It ain't got nothing to do with me. We all feel like that — Walter and Bennie and me — even Travis.

Mama (*thoughtfully, and suddenly very far away*).   Ten thousand dollars —

Ruth.   Sure is wonderful.

Mama.   Ten thousand dollars.

Ruth.   You know what you should do, Miss Lena? You should take yourself a trip somewhere. To Europe or South America or someplace —

Mama (*throwing up her hands at the thought*).   Oh, child!

Ruth.   I'm serious. Just pack up and leave! Go on away and enjoy yourself some. Forget about the family and have yourself a ball for once in your life —

Mama (*drily*).   You sound like I'm just about ready to die. Who'd go with me? What I look like wandering 'round Europe by myself?

Ruth.   Shoot — these here rich white women do it all the time. They don't think nothing of packing up they suitcases and piling on one of them big steamships and — swoosh! — they gone, child.

Mama.   Something always told me I wasn't no rich white woman.

Ruth.   Well — what are you going to do with it then?

Mama.   I ain't rightly decided. *(Thinking. She speaks now with emphasis.)* Some of it got to be put away for Beneatha and her schoolin' — and ain't nothing going to touch that part of it. Nothing. *(She waits several seconds, trying to make up her mind about something, and looks at Ruth a little tentatively before going on.)* Been thinking that we maybe could meet the notes on a little old two-story somewhere, with a yard where Travis could play in the summertime, if we use part of the insurance for a down payment and everybody kind of pitch in. I could maybe take on a little day work again, few days a week —

Ruth *(studying her mother-in-law furtively and concentrating on her ironing, anxious to encourage without seeming to).*   Well, Lord knows, we've put enough rent into this here rat trap to pay for four houses by now . . .

Mama *(looking up at the words "rat trap" and then looking around and leaning back and sighing — in a suddenly reflective mood —).*   "Rat trap" — yes, that's all it is. *(Smiling.)* I remember just as well the day me and Big Walter moved in here. Hadn't been married but two weeks and wasn't planning on living here no more than a year. *(She shakes her head at the dissolved dream.)* We was going to set away, little by little, don't you know, and buy a little place out in Morgan Park. We had even picked out the house. *(Chuckling a little.)* Looks right dumpy today. But Lord, child, you should know all the dreams I had 'bout buying that house and fixing it up and making me a little garden in the back — *(She waits and stops smiling.)* And didn't none of it happen.

Dropping her hands in a futile gesture.

Ruth *(keeps her head down, ironing).*   Yes, life can be a barrel of disappointments, sometimes.

Mama.   Honey, Big Walter would come in here some nights back then and slump down on that couch there and just look at the rug, and look at me and look at the rug and then back at me — and I'd know he was down then . . . really down. *(After a second very long and thoughtful pause; she is seeing back to times that only she can see.)* And then, Lord, when I lost that baby — little Claude — I almost thought I was going to lose Big Walter too. Oh, that man grieved hisself! He was one man to love his children.

Ruth.   Ain't nothin' can tear at you like losin' your baby.

Mama.   I guess that's how come that man finally worked hisself to death like he done. Like he was fighting his own war with this here world that took his baby from him.

Ruth.   He sure was a fine man, all right. I always liked Mr. Younger.

Mama.   Crazy 'bout his children! God knows there was plenty wrong with Walter Younger — hard-headed, mean, kind of wild with women — plenty wrong with him. But he sure loved his children. Always wanted them to have something — be something. That's where Brother gets all these notions, I reckon. Big Walter used to say, he'd get right wet in the eyes sometimes, lean his head back with the water standing in his eyes and say, "Seem like God didn't see fit to give the black man nothing but dreams — but He did give us children to make them dreams seem worthwhile." (*She smiles.*) He could talk like that, don't you know.

Ruth.   Yes, he sure could. He was a good man, Mr. Younger.

Mama.   Yes, a fine man — just couldn't never catch up with his dreams, that's all.

Beneatha comes in, brushing her hair and looking up to the ceiling, where the sound of a vacuum cleaner has started up.

Beneatha.   What could be so dirty on that woman's rugs that she has to vacuum them every single day?

Ruth.   I wish certain young women 'round here who I could name would take inspiration about certain rugs in a certain apartment I could also mention.

Beneatha (*shrugging*).   How much cleaning can a house need, for Christ's sakes.

Mama (*not liking the Lord's name used thus*).   Bennie!

Ruth.   Just listen to her — just listen!

Beneatha.   Oh, God!

Mama.   If you use the Lord's name just one more time —

Beneatha (*a bit of a whine*).   Oh, Mama —

Ruth.   Fresh — just fresh as salt, this girl!

Beneatha (*drily*).   Well — if the salt loses its savor —

Mama.   Now that will do. I just ain't going to have you 'round here reciting the scriptures in vain — you hear me?

Beneatha.   How did I manage to get on everybody's wrong side by just walking into a room?

Ruth.   If you weren't so fresh —

Beneatha.   Ruth, I'm twenty years old.

Mama.   What time you be home from school today?

Beneatha.   Kind of late. (*With enthusiasm.*) Madeline is going to start my guitar lessons today.

Mama and Ruth look up with the same expression.

Mama.   Your *what* kind of lessons?

Beneatha.   Guitar.

Ruth.   Oh, Father!

Mama.   How come you done taken it in your mind to learn to play the guitar?

Beneatha.   I just want to, that's all.

Mama (*smiling*).   Lord, child, don't you know what to do with yourself? How long it going to be before you get tired of this now — like you got tired of that little play-acting group you joined last year? (*Looking at Ruth.*) And what was it the year before that?

Ruth. The horseback-riding club for which she bought that fifty-five-dollar riding habit that's been hanging in the closet ever since!

Mama (*to Beneatha*). Why you got to flit so from one thing to another, baby?

Beneatha (*sharply*). I just want to learn to play the guitar. Is there anything wrong with that?

Mama. Ain't nobody trying to stop you. I just wonders sometimes why you has to flit so from one thing to another all the time. You ain't never done nothing with all that camera equipment you brought home —

Beneatha. I don't flit! I — I experiment with different forms of expression —

Ruth. Like riding a horse?

Beneatha. — People have to express themselves one way or another.

Mama. What is it you want to express?

Beneatha (*angrily*). Me! (*Mama and Ruth look at each other and burst into raucous laughter.*) Don't worry — I don't expect you to understand.

Mama (*to change the subject*). Who you going out with tomorrow night?

Beneatha (*with displeasure*). George Murchison again.

Mama (*pleased*). Oh — you getting a little sweet on him?

Ruth. You ask me, this child ain't sweet on nobody but herself — (*Under breath.*) Express herself!

They laugh.

Beneatha. Oh — I like George all right, Mama. I mean I like him enough to go out with him and stuff, but —

Ruth (*for devilment*). What does *and stuff* mean?

Beneatha. Mind your own business.

Mama. Stop picking at her now, Ruth. (*She chuckles — then a suspicious sudden look at her daughter as she turns in her chair for emphasis.*) What DOES it mean?

Beneatha (*wearily*). Oh, I just mean I couldn't ever really be serious about George. He's — he's so shallow.

Ruth. Shallow — what do you mean he's shallow? He's *rich!*

Mama. Hush, Ruth.

Beneatha. I know he's rich. He knows he's rich, too.

Ruth. Well — what other qualities a man got to have to satisfy you, little girl?

Beneatha. You wouldn't even begin to understand. Anybody who married Walter could not possibly understand.

Mama (*outraged*). What kind of way is that to talk about your brother?

Beneatha. Brother is a flip — let's face it.

Mama (*to Ruth, helplessly*). What's a flip?

Ruth (*glad to add kindling*). She's saying he's crazy.

Beneatha. Not crazy. Brother isn't really crazy yet — he — he's an elaborate neurotic.

Mama. Hush your mouth!

Beneatha. As for George. Well. George looks good — he's got a beautiful car and he takes me to nice places and, as my sister-in-law says, he is probably the richest boy I will ever get to know and I even like him sometimes — but if the Youngers are sitting around waiting to see if their little Bennie is going to tie up the family with the Murchisons, they are wasting their time.

Ruth. You mean you wouldn't marry George Murchison if he asked you someday? That pretty, rich thing? Honey, I knew you was odd —

Beneatha. No I would not marry him if all I felt for him was what I feel now. Besides, George's family wouldn't really like it.

Mama. Why not?

Beneatha. Oh, Mama — The Murchisons are honest-to-God-real-*live*-rich colored people, and the only people in the world who are more snobbish than rich white people are rich colored people. I thought everybody knew that. I've met Mrs. Murchison. She's a scene!

Mama. You must not dislike people 'cause they well off, honey.

Beneatha. Why not? It makes just as much sense as disliking people 'cause they are poor, and lots of people do that.

Ruth (*a wisdom-of-the-ages manner. To Mama*). Well, she'll get over some of this —

Beneatha. Get over it? What are you talking about, Ruth? Listen, I'm going to be a doctor. I'm not worried about who I'm going to marry yet — if I ever get married.

Mama and Ruth. *If!*

Mama. Now, Bennie —

Beneatha. Oh, I probably will . . . but first I'm going to be a doctor, and George, for one, still thinks that's pretty funny. I couldn't be bothered with that. I am going to be a doctor and everybody around here better understand that!

Mama (*kindly*). 'Course you going to be a doctor, honey, God willing.

Beneatha (*drily*). God hasn't got a thing to do with it.

Mama. Beneatha — that just wasn't necessary.

Beneatha. Well — neither is God. I get sick of hearing about God.

Mama. Beneatha!

Beneatha. I mean it! I'm just tired of hearing about God all the time. What has He got to do with anything? Does He pay tuition?

Mama. You 'bout to get your fresh little jaw slapped!

Ruth. That's just what she needs, all right!

Beneatha. Why? Why can't I say what I want to around here, like everybody else?

Mama. It don't sound nice for a young girl to say things like that — you wasn't brought up that way. Me and your father went to trouble to get you and Brother to church every Sunday.

Beneatha. Mama, you don't understand. It's all a matter of ideas, and God is just one idea I don't accept. It's not important. I am not going out and be immoral or commit crimes because I don't believe in God. I don't even think about it. It's just that I get tired of Him getting credit for all the things the human race achieves through its own stubborn effort. There simply is no blasted God — there is only man and it is *He* who makes miracles!

Mama absorbs this speech, studies her daughter, and rises slowly and crosses to Beneatha and slaps her powerfully across the face. After, there is only silence and the daughter drops her eyes from her mother's face, and Mama is very tall before her.

Mama. Now — you say after me, in my mother's house there is still God. (*There is a long pause and Beneatha stares at the floor wordlessly. Mama repeats the phrase with precision and cool emotion.*) In my mother's house there is still God.
Beneatha. In my mother's house there is still God.

A long pause.

Mama (*walking away from Beneatha, too disturbed for triumphant posture. Stopping and turning back to her daughter*). There are some ideas we ain't going to have in this house. Not long as I am at the head of this family.
Beneatha. Yes, ma'am.

Mama walks out of the room.

Ruth (*almost gently, with profound understanding*). You think you a woman, Bennie — but you still a little girl. What you did was childish — so you got treated like a child.
Beneatha. I see. (*Quietly.*) I also see that everybody thinks it's all right for Mama to be a tyrant. But all the tyranny in the world will never put a God in the heavens!

She picks up her books and goes out. Pause.

Ruth (*goes to Mama's door*). She said she was sorry.
Mama (*coming out, going to her plant*). They frightens me, Ruth. My children.
Ruth. You got good children, Lena. They just a little off sometimes — but they're good.
Mama. No — there's something come down between me and them that don't let us understand each other and I don't know what it is. One done almost lost his mind thinking 'bout money all the time and the other done commence to talk about things I can't seem to understand in no form or fashion. What is it that's changing, Ruth?

Ruth (*soothingly, older than her years*).   Now . . . you taking it all too seriously. You just got strong-willed children and it takes a strong woman like you
to keep 'em in hand.

Mama (*looking at her plant and sprinkling a little water on it*).   They spirited
all right, my children. Got to admit they got spirit — Bennie and Walter. Like
this little old plant that ain't never had enough sunshine or nothing — and
look at it . . .

She has her back to Ruth, who has had to stop ironing and lean against
something and put the back of her hand to her forehead.

Ruth (*trying to keep Mama from noticing*).   You . . . sure . . . loves that little
old thing, don't you? . . .

Mama.   Well, I always wanted me a garden like I used to see sometimes at the
back of the houses down home. This plant is close as I ever got to having one.
(*She looks out of the window as she replaces the plant.*) Lord, ain't nothing as
dreary as the view from this window on a dreary day, is there? Why ain't you
singing this morning, Ruth? Sing that "No Ways Tired." That song always lifts
me up so — (*She turns at last to see that Ruth has slipped quietly to the floor,*
in a state of semiconsciousness.) Ruth! Ruth honey — what's the matter with
you . . . Ruth!

Curtain.

Scene 2. (*The following morning.*)

It is the following morning; a Saturday morning, and house cleaning is in
progress at the Youngers'. Furniture has been shoved hither and yon and Mama
is giving the kitchen-area walls a washing down. Beneatha, in dungarees, with a
handkerchief tied around her face, is spraying insecticide into the cracks in the
walls. As they work, the radio is on and a Southside disk-jockey program is
inappropriately filling the house with a rather exotic saxophone blues. Travis,
the sole idle one, is leaning on his arms, looking out of the window.

Travis.   Grandmama, that stuff Bennie is using smells awful. Can I go downstairs, please?

Mama.   Did you get all them chores done already? I ain't seen you doing
much.

Travis.   Yes'm — finished early. Where did Mama go this morning?

Mama (*looking at Beneatha*).   She had to go on a little errand.

The phone rings. Beneatha runs to answer it and reaches it before Walter, who
has entered from bedroom.

Travis. Where?

Mama. To tend to her business.

Beneatha. Haylo . . . *(Disappointed.)* Yes, he is. *(She tosses the phone to Walter, who barely catches it.)* It's Willie Harris again.

Walter *(as privately as possible under Mama's gaze).* Hello, Willie. Did you get the papers from the lawyer? . . . No, not yet. I told you the mailman doesn't get here till ten-thirty . . . No, I'll come there . . . Yeah! Right away. *(He hangs up and goes for his coat.)*

Beneatha. Brother, where did Ruth go?

Walter *(as he exits).* How should I know!

Travis. Aw come on, Grandma. Can I go outside?

Mama. Oh, I guess so. You stay right in front of the house, though, and keep a good lookout for the postman.

Travis. Yes'm. *(He darts into bedroom for stickball and bat, reenters, and sees Beneatha on her knees spraying under sofa with behind upraised. He edges closer to the target, takes aim, and lets her have it. She screams.)* Leave them poor little cockroaches alone, they ain't bothering you none! *(He runs as she swings the spraygun at him viciously and playfully.)* Grandma! Grandma!

Mama. Look out there, girl, before you be spilling some of that stuff on that child!

Travis *(safely behind the bastion of Mama).* That's right — look out, now! *(He exits.)*

Beneatha *(drily).* I can't imagine that it would hurt him — it has never hurt the roaches.

Mama. Well, little boys' hides ain't as tough as Southside roaches. You better get over there behind the bureau. I seen one marching out of there like Napoleon yesterday.

Beneatha. There's really only one way to get rid of them, Mama —

Mama. How?

Beneatha. Set fire to this building! Mama, where did Ruth go?

Mama *(looking at her with meaning).* To the doctor, I think.

Beneatha. The doctor? What's the matter? *(They exchange glances.)* You don't think —

Mama *(with her sense of drama).* Now I ain't saying what I think. But I ain't never been wrong 'bout a woman neither.

The phone rings.

Beneatha *(at the phone).* Hay-lo . . . *(Pause, and a moment of recognition.)* Well — when did you get back! . . . And how was it? . . . Of course I've missed you — in my way . . . This morning? No . . . house cleaning and all that and Mama hates it if I let people come over when the house is like this . . . You *have?* Well, that's different . . . What is it — Oh, what the hell, come on over . . . Right, see you then. *Arrivederci.*

She hangs up.

Mama (*who has listened vigorously, as is her habit*).   Who is that you inviting over here with this house looking like this? You ain't got the pride you was born with!

Beneatha.   Asagai doesn't care how houses look, Mama — he's an intellectual.

Mama.   *Who?*

Beneatha.   Asagai — Joseph Asagai. He's an African boy I met on campus. He's been studying in Canada all summer.

Mama.   What's his name?

Beneatha.   Asagai, Joseph. Ah-sah-guy . . . He's from Nigeria.

Mama.   Oh, that's the little country that was founded by slaves way back . . .

Beneatha.   No, Mama — that's Liberia.

Mama.   I don't think I never met no African before.

Beneatha.   Well, do me a favor and don't ask him a whole lot of ignorant questions about Africans. I mean, do they wear clothes and all that —

Mama.   Well, now, I guess if you think we so ignorant 'round here maybe you shouldn't bring your friends here —

Beneatha.   It's just that people ask such crazy things. All anyone seems to know about when it comes to Africa is Tarzan —

Mama (*indignantly*).   Why should I know anything about Africa?

Beneatha.   Why do you give money at church for the missionary work?

Mama.   Well, that's to help save people.

Beneatha.   You mean save them from *heathenism* —

Mama (*innocently*).   Yes.

Beneatha.   I'm afraid they need more salvation from the British and the French.

Ruth comes in forlornly and pulls off her coat with dejection. They both turn to look at her.

Ruth (*dispiritedly*).   Well, I guess from all the happy faces — everybody knows.

Beneatha.   You pregnant?

Mama.   Lord have mercy, I sure hope it's a little old girl. Travis ought to have a sister.

Beneatha and Ruth give her a hopeless look for this grandmotherly enthusiasm.

Beneatha.   How far along are you?

Ruth.   Two months.

Beneatha.   Did you mean to? I mean did you plan it or was it an accident?

Mama.   What do you know about planning or not planning?

Beneatha.   Oh, Mama.

Ruth (*wearily*).   She's twenty years old, Lena.

Beneatha.   Did you plan it, Ruth?

Ruth.   Mind your own business.

Beneatha.   It is my business — where is he going to live, on the *roof*? (*There is silence following the remark as the three women react to the sense of it.*) Gee — I didn't mean that, Ruth, honest. Gee, I don't feel like that at all. I — I think it is wonderful.

Ruth (*dully*).   Wonderful.

Beneatha.   Yes — really.

Mama (*looking at Ruth, worried*).   Doctor say everything going to be all right?

Ruth (*far away*).   Yes — she says everything is going to be fine . . .

Mama (*immediately suspicious*).   "She" — What doctor you went to?

Ruth folds over, near hysteria.

Mama (*worriedly hovering over Ruth*).   Ruth honey — what's the matter with you — you sick?

Ruth has her fists clenched on her thighs and is fighting hard to suppress a scream that seems to be rising in her.

Beneatha.   What's the matter with her, Mama?

Mama (*working her fingers in Ruth's shoulders to relax her*).   She be all right. Women gets right depressed sometimes when they get her way. (*Speaking softly, expertly, rapidly.*) Now you just relax. That's right . . . just lean back, don't think 'bout nothing at all . . . nothing at all —

Ruth.   I'm all right . . .

The glassy-eyed look melts and then she collapses into a fit of heavy sobbing. The bell rings.

Beneatha.   Oh, my God — that must be Asagai.

Mama (*to Ruth*).   Come on now, honey. You need to lie down and rest awhile . . . then have some nice hot food.

They exit, Ruth's weight on her mother-in-law. Beneatha, herself profoundly disturbed, opens the door to admit a rather dramatic-looking young man with a large package.

Asagai.   Hello, Alaiyo —

Beneatha (*holding the door open and regarding him with pleasure*).   Hello . . . (*Long pause.*) Well — come in. And please excuse everything. My mother was very upset about my letting anyone come here with the place like this.

Asagai *(coming into the room).* You look disturbed too . . . Is something wrong?

Beneatha *(still at the door, absently).* Yes . . . we've all got acute ghetto-itus. *(She smiles and comes toward him, finding a cigarette and sitting.)* So — sit down! No! Wait! *(She whips the spraygun off sofa where she had left it and puts the cushions back. At last perches on arm of sofa. He sits.)* So, how was Canada?

Asagai *(a sophisticate).* Canadian.

Beneatha *(looking at him).* Asagai, I'm very glad you are back.

Asagai *(looking back at her in turn).* Are you really?

Beneatha. Yes — very.

Asagai. Why? — you were quite glad when I went away. What happened?

Beneatha. You went away.

Asagai. Ahhhhhhhh.

Beneatha. Before — you wanted to be so serious before there was time.

Asagai. How much time must there be before one knows what one feels?

Beneatha *(stalling this particular conversation. Her hands pressed together, in a deliberately childish gesture).* What did you bring me?

Asagai *(handing her the package).* Open it and see.

Beneatha *(eagerly opening the package and drawing out some records and the colorful robes of a Nigerian woman).* Oh Asagai! . . . You got them for me! . . . How beautiful . . . and the records too! *(She lifts out the robes and runs to the mirror with them and holds the drapery up in front of herself.)*

Asagai *(coming to her at the mirror).* I shall have to teach you how to drape it properly. *(He flings the material about her for the moment and stands back to look at her.)* Ah — *Oh-pay-gay-day, oh-gbah-mu-shay. (A Yoruba exclamation for admiration.)* You wear it well . . . very well . . . mutilated hair and all.

Beneatha *(turning suddenly).* My hair — what's wrong with my hair?

Asagai *(shrugging).* Were you born with it like that?

Beneatha *(reaching up to touch it).* No . . . of course not.

She looks back to the mirror, disturbed.

Asagai *(smiling).* How then?

Beneatha. You know perfectly well how . . . as crinkly as yours . . . that's how.

Asagai. And it is ugly to you that way?

Beneatha *(quickly).* Oh, no — not ugly . . . *(More slowly, apologetically.)* But it's so hard to manage when it's, well — raw.

Asagai. And so to accommodate that — you mutilate it every week?

Beneatha. It's not mutilation!

Asagai *(laughing aloud at her seriousness).* Oh . . . please! I am only teasing you because you are so very serious about these things. *(He stands back from her and folds his arms across his chest as he watches her pulling at her hair and frowning in the mirror.)* Do you remember the first time you met me at school? . . . *(He laughs.)* You came up to me and you said — and I thought you were the most serious little thing I had ever seen — you said: *(He imitates her.)* "Mr. Asagai — I want very much to talk with you. About Africa. You see, Mr. Asagai, I am looking for my *identity!*"

He laughs.

Beneatha *(turning to him, not laughing).*   Yes —

Her face is quizzical, profoundly disturbed.

Asagai *(still teasing and reaching out and taking her face in his hands and turning her profile to him).*   Well . . . it is true that this is not so much a profile of a Hollywood queen as perhaps a queen of the Nile — *(A mock dismissal of the importance of the question.)* But what does it matter? Assimilationism is so popular in your country.

Beneatha *(wheeling, passionately, sharply).*   I am not an assimilationist!

Asagai *(the protest hangs in the room for a moment and Asagai studies her, his laughter fading).*   Such a serious one. *(There is a pause.)* So — you like the robes? You must take excellent care of them — they are from my sister's personal wardrobe.

Beneatha *(with incredulity).*   You — you sent all the way home — for me?

Asagai *(with charm).*   For you — I would do much more . . . Well, that is what I came for. I must go.

Beneatha.   Will you call me Monday?

Asagai.   Yes . . . We have a great deal to talk about. I mean about identity and time and all that.

Beneatha.   Time?

Asagai.   Yes. About how much time one needs to know what one feels.

Beneatha.   You see! You never understood that there is more than one kind of feeling which can exist between a man and a woman — or, at least, there should be.

Asagai *(shaking his head negatively but gently).*   No. Between a man and a woman there need be only one kind of feeling. I have that for you . . . Now even . . . right this moment . . .

Beneatha.   I know — and by itself — it won't do. I can find that anywhere.

Asagai.   For a woman it should be enough.

Beneatha.   I know — because that's what it says in all the novels that men write. But it isn't. Go ahead and laugh — but I'm not interested in being someone's little episode in America or — *(With feminine vengeance.)* — one of them! *(Asagai has burst into laughter again.)* That's funny as hell, huh!

Asagai.   It's just that every American girl I have known has said that to me. White — black — in this you are all the same. And the same speech, too!

Beneatha *(angrily).*   Yuk, yuk, yuk!

Asagai. It's how you can be sure that the world's most liberated women are not liberated at all. You all talk about it too much!

Mama enters and is immediately all social charm because of the presence of a guest.

Beneatha. Oh — Mama — this is Mr. Asagai.
Mama. How do you do?
Asagai *(total politeness to an elder).* How do you do, Mrs. Younger. Please forgive me for coming at such an outrageous hour on a Saturday.
Mama. Well, you are quite welcome. I just hope you understand that our house don't always look like this. *(Chatterish.)* You must come again. I would love to hear all about — *(Not sure of the name.)* — your country. I think it's so sad the way our American Negroes don't know nothing about Africa 'cept Tarzan and all that. And all that money they pour into these churches when they ought to be helping you people over there drive out them French and Englishmen done taken away your land.

The mother flashes a slightly superior look at her daughter upon completion of the recitation.

Asagai *(taken aback by this sudden and acutely unrelated expression of sympathy).* Yes . . . yes . . .
Mama *(smiling at him suddenly and relaxing and looking him over).* How many miles is it from here to where you come from?
Asagai. Many thousands.
Mama *(looking at him as she would Walter).* I bet you don't half look after yourself, being away from your mama either. I spec you better come 'round here from time to time to get yourself some decent homecooked meals . . .
Asagai *(moved).* Thank you. Thank you very much. *(They are all quiet, then —)* Well . . . I must go. I will call you Monday, Alaiyo.
Mama. What's that he call you?
Asagai. Oh — "Alaiyo." I hope you don't mind. It is what you would call a nickname, I think. It is a Yoruba word. I am a Yoruba.
Mama *(looking at Beneatha).* I — I thought he was from — *(Uncertain.)*
Asagai *(understanding).* Nigeria is my country. Yoruba is my tribal origin —
Beneatha. You didn't tell us what Alaiyo means . . . for all I know, you might be calling me Little Idiot or something . . .
Asagai. Well . . . let me see . . . I do not know how just to explain it . . . The sense of a thing can be so different when it changes languages.
Beneatha. You're evading.
Asagai. No — really it is difficult . . . *(Thinking.)* It means . . . it means One for Whom Bread — Food — Is Not Enough. *(He looks at her.)* Is that all right?
Beneatha *(understanding, softly).* Thank you.

Mama (*looking from one to the other and not understanding any of it*). Well . . . that's nice . . . You must come see us again — Mr. —
Asagai. Ah-sah-guy . . .
Mama. Yes . . . Do come again.
Asagai. Good-bye.

He exits.

Mama (*after him*). Lord, that's a pretty thing just went out here! (*Insinuatingly, to her daughter.*) Yes, I guess I see why we done commence to get so interested in Africa 'round here. Missionaries my aunt Jenny!

She exits.

Beneatha. Oh, Mama! . . .

She picks up the Nigerian dress and holds it up to her in front of the mirror again. She sets the headdress on haphazardly and then notices her hair again and clutches at it and then replaces the headdress and frowns at herself. Then she starts to wriggle in front of the mirror as she thinks a Nigerian woman might. Travis enters and stands regarding her.

Travis. What's the matter, girl, you cracking up?
Beneatha. Shut up.

She pulls the headdress off and looks at herself in the mirror and clutches at her hair again and squinches her eyes as if trying to imagine something. Then, suddenly, she gets her raincoat and kerchief and hurriedly prepares for going out.

Mama (*coming back into the room*). She's resting now. Travis, baby, run next door and ask Miss Johnson to please let me have a little kitchen cleanser. This here can is empty as Jacob's kettle.
Travis. I just came in.
Mama. Do as you told. (*He exits and she looks at her daughter.*) Where you going?
Beneatha (*halting at the door*). To become a queen of the Nile!

She exits in a breathless blaze of glory. Ruth appears in the bedroom doorway.

Mama. Who told you to get up?
Ruth. Ain't nothing wrong with me to be lying in no bed for. Where did Bennie go?
Mama (*drumming her fingers*). Far as I could make out — to Egypt. (*Ruth just looks at her.*) What time is it getting to?

Ruth. Ten twenty. And the mailman going to ring that bell this morning just like he done every morning for the last umpteen years.

Travis comes in with the cleanser can.

Travis. She say to tell you that she don't have much.
Mama (*angrily*). Lord, some people I could name sure is tight-fisted! (*Directing her grandson.*) Mark two cans of cleanser on the list there. If she that hard up for kitchen cleanser, I sure don't want to forget to get her none!
Ruth. Lena — maybe the woman is just short on cleanser —
Mama (*not listening*). — Much baking powder as she done borrowed from me all these years, she could of done gone into the baking business!

The bell sounds suddenly and sharply and all three are stunned — serious and silent — midspeech. In spite of all the other conversations and distractions of the morning, this is what they have been waiting for, even Travis, who looks helplessly from his mother to his grandmother. Ruth is the first to come to life again.

Ruth (*to Travis*). Get down them steps, boy!

Travis snaps to life and flies out to get the mail.

Mama (*her eyes wide, her hand to her breast*). You mean it done really come?
Ruth (*excited*). Oh, Miss Lena!
Mama (*collecting herself*). Well . . . I don't know what we all so excited about 'round here for. We known it was coming for months.
Ruth. That's a whole lot different from having it come and being able to hold it in your hands . . . a piece of paper worth ten thousand dollars . . . (*Travis bursts back into the room. He holds the envelope high above his head, like a little dancer, his face is radiant and he is breathless. He moves to his grandmother with sudden slow ceremony and puts the envelope into her hands. She accepts it, and then merely holds it and looks at it.*) Come on! Open it . . . Lord have mercy, I wish Walter Lee was here!
Travis. Open it, Grandmama!
Mama (*staring at it*). Now you all be quiet. It's just a check.
Ruth. Open it . . .
Mama (*still staring at it*). Now don't act silly . . . We ain't never been no people to act silly 'bout no money —
Ruth (*swiftly*). We ain't never had none before — OPEN IT!

Mama finally makes a good strong tear and pulls out the thin blue slice of paper and inspects it closely. The boy and his mother study it raptly over Mama's shoulders.

Mama. *Travis! (She is counting off with doubt.)* Is that the right number of zeros?

Travis. Yes'm . . . ten thousand dollars. Gaalee, grandmama, you rich.

Mama *(She holds the check away from her, still looking at it. Slowly her face sobers into a mask of unhappiness).* Ten thousand dollars. *(She hands it to Ruth.)* Put it away somewhere, Ruth. *(She does not look at Ruth; her eyes seem to be seeing something somewhere very far off.)* Ten thousand dollars they give you. Ten thousand dollars.

Travis *(to his mother, sincerely).* What's the matter with Grandmama — don't she want to be rich?

Ruth *(distractedly).* You go on out and play now, baby. *(Travis exits. Mama starts wiping dishes absently, humming intently to herself. Ruth turns to her, with kind exasperation.)* You've gone and got yourself upset.

Mama *(not looking at her).* I spec if it wasn't for you all . . . I would just put that money away or give it to the church or something.

Ruth. Now what kind of talk is that. Mr. Younger would just be plain mad if he could hear you talking foolish like that.

Mama *(stopping and staring off).* Yes . . . he sure would. *(Sighing.)* We got enough to do with that money, all right. *(She halts then, and turns and looks at her daughter-in-law hard; Ruth avoids her eyes and Mama wipes her hands with finality and starts to speak firmly to Ruth.)* Where did you go today, girl?

Ruth. To the doctor.

Mama *(impatiently).* Now, Ruth . . . you know better than that. Old Doctor Jones is strange enough in his way but there ain't nothing 'bout him make somebody slip and call him "she" — like you done this morning.

Ruth. Well, that's what happened — my tongue slipped.

Mama. You went to see that woman, didn't you?

Ruth *(defensively, giving herself away).* What woman you talking about?

Mama *(angrily).* That woman who —

Walter enters in great excitement.

Walter. Did it come?

Mama *(quietly).* Can't you give people a Christian greeting before you start asking about money?

Walter *(to Ruth).* Did it come? *(Ruth unfolds the check and lays it quietly before him, watching him intently with thoughts of her own. Walter sits down and grasps it close and counts off the zeros.)* Ten thousand dollars — *(He turns suddenly, frantically to his mother and draws some papers out of his breast pocket.)* Mama — look. Old Willy Harris put everything on paper —

Mama. Son — I think you ought to talk to your wife . . . I'll go on out and leave you alone if you want —

Walter. I can talk to her later — Mama, look —

Mama. Son —

Walter. WILL SOMEBODY PLEASE LISTEN TO ME TODAY!

Mama (*quietly*). I don't 'low no yellin' in this house, Walter Lee, and you know it — (*Walter stares at them in frustration and starts to speak several times.*) And there ain't going to be no investing in no liquor stores.

Walter. But, Mama, you ain't even looked at it.

Mama. I don't aim to have to speak on that again.

A long pause.

Walter. You ain't looked at it and you don't aim to have to speak on that again? You ain't even looked at it and *you* have decided — (*Crumpling his papers.*) Well, *you* tell that to my boy tonight when you put him to sleep on the living-room couch . . . (*Turning to Mama and speaking directly to her.*) Yeah — and tell it to my wife, Mama, tomorrow when she has to go out of here to look after somebody else's kids. And tell it to *me*, Mama, every time we need a new pair of curtains and I have to watch *you* go out and work in somebody's kitchen. Yeah, you tell me then!

Walter starts out.

Ruth. Where you going?

Walter. I'm going out!

Ruth. Where?

Walter. Just out of this house somewhere —

Ruth (*getting her coat*). I'll come too.

Walter. I don't want you to come!

Ruth. I got something to talk to you about, Walter.

Walter. That's too bad.

Mama (*still quietly*). Walter Lee — (*She waits and he finally turns and looks at her.*) Sit down.

Walter. I'm a grown man, Mama.

Mama. Ain't nobody said you wasn't grown. But you still in my house and my presence. And as long as you are — you'll talk to your wife civil. Now sit down.

Ruth (*suddenly*). Oh, let him go on out and drink himself to death! He makes me sick to my stomach! (*She flings her coat against him and exits to bedroom.*)

Walter (*violently flinging the coat after her*). And you turn mine too, baby! (*The door slams behind her.*) That was my biggest mistake —

Mama (*still quietly*). Walter, what is the matter with you?

Walter. Matter with me? Ain't nothing the matter with *me*!

Mama. Yes there is. Something eating you up like a crazy man. Something more than me not giving you this money. The past few years I been watching it happen to you. You get all nervous acting and kind of wild in the eyes — (*Walter jumps up impatiently at her words.*) I said sit there now, I'm talking to you!

Walter. Mama — I don't need no nagging at me today.

Mama. Seem like you getting to a place where you always tied up in some kind of knot about something. But if anybody ask you 'bout it you just yell at 'em and bust out the house and go out and drink somewheres. Walter Lee, people can't live with that. Ruth's a good, patient girl in her way — but you getting to be too much. Boy, don't make the mistake of driving that girl away from you.

Walter. Why — what she do for me?

Mama. She loves you.

Walter. Mama — I'm going out. I want to go off somewhere and be by myself for a while.

Mama. I'm sorry 'bout your liquor store, son. It just wasn't the thing for us to do. That's what I want to tell you about —

Walter. I got to go out, Mama —

He rises.

Mama. It's dangerous, son.

Walter. What's dangerous?

Mama. When a man goes outside his home to look for peace.

Walter (*beseechingly*). Then why can't there never be no peace in this house then?

Mama. You done found it in some other house?

Walter. No — there ain't no woman! Why do women always think there's a woman somewhere when a man gets restless. (*Picks up the check.*) Do you know what this money means to me? Do you know what this money can do for us? (*Puts it back.*) Mama — Mama — I want so many things . . .

Mama. Yes, son —

Walter. I want so many things that they are driving me kind of crazy . . . Mama — look at me.

Mama. I'm looking at you. You a good-looking boy. You got a job, a nice wife, a fine boy, and —

Walter. A job. (*Looks at her.*) Mama, a job? I open and close car doors all day long. I drive a man around in his limousine and I say, "Yes, sir; no, sir; very good, sir; shall I take the Drive, sir?" Mama, that ain't no kind of job . . . that ain't nothing at all. (*Very quietly.*) Mama, I don't know if I can make you understand.

Mama. Understand what, baby?

Walter (*quietly*). Sometimes it's like I can see the future stretched out in front of me — just plain as day. The future, Mama. Hanging over there at the edge of my days. Just waiting for me — a big, looming blank space — full of *nothing*. Just waiting for *me*. But it don't have to be. (*Pause. Kneeling beside her chair.*) Mama — sometimes when I'm downtown and I pass them cool, quiet-looking restaurants where them white boys are sitting back and talking 'bout things . . . sitting there turning deals worth millions of dollars . . . sometimes I see guys don't look much older than me —

Mama.   Son — how come you talk so much 'bout money?

Walter *(with immense passion).*   Because it is life, Mama!

Mama *(quietly).*   Oh — *(Very quietly.)* So now it's life. Money is life. Once upon a time freedom used to be life — now it's money. I guess the world really do change . . .

Walter.   No — it was always money, Mama. We just didn't know about it.

Mama.   No . . . something has changed. *(She looks at him.)* You something new, boy. In my time we was worried about not being lynched and getting to the North if we could and how to stay alive and still have a pinch of dignity too . . . Now here come you and Beneatha — talking 'bout things we ain't never even thought about hardly, me and your daddy. You ain't satisfied or proud of nothing we done. I mean that you had a home; that we kept you out of trouble till you was grown; that you don't have to ride to work on the back of nobody's streetcar — You my children — but how different we done become.

Walter *(a long beat. He pats her hand and gets up).*   You just don't understand, Mama, you just don't understand.

Mama.   Son — do you know your wife is expecting another baby? *(Walter stands, stunned, and absorbs what his mother has said.)* That's what she wanted to talk to you about. *(Walter sinks down into a chair.)* This ain't for me to be telling — but you ought to know. *(She waits.)* I think Ruth is thinking 'bout getting rid of that child.

Walter *(slowly understanding).*   — No — no — Ruth wouldn't do that.

Mama.   When the world gets ugly enough — a woman will do anything for her family. *The part that's already living.*

Walter.   You don't know Ruth, Mama, if you think she would do that.

Ruth opens the bedroom door and stands there a little limp.

Ruth *(beaten).*   Yes I would too, Walter. *(Pause.)* I gave her a five-dollar down payment.

There is total silence as the man stares at his wife and the mother stares at her son.

Mama *(presently).*   Well — *(Tightly.)* Well — son, I'm waiting to hear you say something . . . *(She waits.)* I'm waiting to hear how you be your father's son. Be the man he was . . . *(Pause. The silence shouts.)* Your wife say she going to destroy your child. And I'm waiting to hear you talk like him and say we a people who give children life, not who destroys them — *(She rises.)* I'm waiting to see you stand up and look like your daddy and say we done give up one baby to poverty and that we ain't going to give up nary another one . . . I'm waiting.

Walter. Ruth — *(He can say nothing.)*

Mama. If you a son of mine, tell her! *(Walter picks up his keys and his coat and walks out. She continues, bitterly.)* You . . . you are a disgrace to your father's memory. Somebody get me my hat!

Curtain.

Act II

Scene 1.

Time: Later the same day.

At rise: Ruth is ironing again. She has the radio going. Presently Beneatha's bedroom door opens and Ruth's mouth falls and she puts down the iron in fascination.

Ruth. What have we got on tonight!

Beneatha *(emerging grandly from the doorway so that we can see her thoroughly robed in the costume Asagai brought).* You are looking at what a well-dressed Nigerian woman wears — *(She parades for Ruth, her hair completely hidden by the headdress; she is coquettishly fanning herself with an ornate oriental fan, mistakenly more like Butterfly than any Nigerian that ever was.)* Isn't it beautiful? *(She promenades to the radio and, with an arrogant flourish, turns off the good loud blues that is playing.)* Enough of this assimilationist junk! *(Ruth follows her with her eyes as she goes to the phonograph and puts on a record and turns and waits ceremoniously for the music to come up. Then, with a shout —)* OCOMOGOSIAY!

Ruth jumps. The music comes up, a lovely Nigerian melody. Beneatha listens, enraptured, her eyes far way — "back to the past." She begins to dance. Ruth is dumfounded.

Ruth. What kind of dance is that?

Beneatha. A folk dance.

Ruth *(Pearl Bailey).* What kind of folks do that, honey?

Beneatha. It's from Nigeria. It's a dance of welcome.

Ruth. Who you welcoming?

Beneatha. The men back to the village.

Ruth. Where they been?

Beneatha. How should I know — out hunting or something. Anyway, they are coming back now . . .

Ruth. Well, that's good.
Beneatha (*with the record*).

Alundi, alundi
Alundi alunya
Jop pu a jeepua
Ang gu sooooooooooo
Ai yai yae . . .
Ayehaye — alundi . . .

Walter comes in during this performance; he has obviously been drinking. He leans against the door heavily and watches his sister, at first with distaste. Then his eyes look off — "back to the past" — as he lifts both his fists to the roof, screaming.

Walter. YEAH . . . AND ETHIOPIA STRETCH FORTH HER HANDS AGAIN! . . .
Ruth (*drily, looking at him*). Yes — and Africa sure is claiming her own tonight. (*She gives them both up and starts ironing again.*)
Walter (*all in a drunken, dramatic shout*). Shut up! . . . I'm diggin them drums . . . them drums move me! . . . (*He makes his weaving way to his wife's face and leans in close to her.*) In my *heart of hearts* — (*He thumps his chest.*) — I am much warrior!
Ruth (*without even looking up*). In your heart of hearts you are much drunkard.
Walter (*coming away from her and starting to wander around the room, shouting*). Me and Jomo . . . (*Intently, in his sister's face. She has stopped dancing to watch him in this unknown mood.*) That's my man, Kenyatta. (*Shouting and thumping his chest.*) FLAMING SPEAR! HOT DAMN! (*He is suddenly in possession of an imaginary spear and actively spearing enemies all over the room.*) OCOMOGOSIAY . . .
Beneatha (*to encourage Walter, thoroughly caught up with this side of him*). OCOMOGOSIAY, FLAMING SPEAR!
Walter. THE LION IS WAKING . . . OWIMOWEH!

He pulls his shirt open and leaps up on the table and gestures with his spear.

Beneatha. OWIMOWEH!
Walter (*on the table, very far gone, his eyes pure glass sheets. He sees what we cannot, that he is a leader of his people, a great chief, a descendant of Chaka, and that the hour to march has come*). Listen, my black brothers —
Beneatha. OCOMOGOSIAY!
Walter. — Do you hear the waters rushing against the shores of the coastlands —
Beneatha. OCOMOGOSIAY!

Walter. — Do you hear the screeching of the cocks in yonder hills beyond where the chiefs meet in council for the coming of the mighty war —
Beneatha. OCOMOGOSIAY!

And now the lighting shifts subtly to suggest the world of Walter's imagination, and the mood shifts from pure comedy. It is the inner Walter speaking: the Southside chauffeur has assumed an unexpected majesty.

Walter. — Do you hear the beating of the wings of the birds flying low over the mountains and the low places of our land —
Beneatha. OCOMOGOSIAY!
Walter. — Do you hear the singing of the women, singing the war songs of our fathers to the babies in the great houses? Singing the sweet war songs! *(The doorbell rings.)* OH, DO YOU HEAR, MY *BLACK* BROTHERS!
Beneatha *(completely gone).* We hear you, Flaming Spear —

Ruth shuts off the phonograph and opens the door. George Murchison enters.

Walter. Telling us to prepare for the GREATNESS OF THE TIME! *(Lights back to normal. He turns and sees George.)* Black Brother!

He extends his hand for the fraternal clasp.

George. Black Brother, hell!
Ruth *(having had enough, and embarrassed for the family).* Beneatha, you got company — what's the matter with you? Walter Lee Younger, get down off that table and stop acting like a fool . . .

Walter comes down off the table suddenly and makes a quick exit to the bathroom.

Ruth. He's had a little to drink . . . I don't know what her excuse is.
George *(to Beneatha).* Look honey, we're going to the theater — we're not going to be *in* it . . . so go change, huh?

Beneatha looks at him and slowly, ceremoniously, lifts her hands and pulls off the headdress. Her hair is close-cropped and unstraightened. George freezes mid-sentence and Ruth's eyes all but fall out of her head.

George. What in the name of —
Ruth *(touching Beneatha's hair).* Girl, you done lost your natural mind? Look at your head!
George. What have you done to your head — I mean your hair!
Beneatha. Nothing — except cut it off.
Ruth. Now that's the truth — it's what ain't been done to it! You expect this boy to go out with you with your head all nappy like that?

Beneatha *(looking at George).* That's up to George. If he's ashamed of his heritage —

George. Oh, don't be so proud of yourself, Bennie — just because you look eccentric.

Beneatha. How can something that's natural be eccentric?

George. That's what being eccentric means — being natural. Get dressed.

Beneatha. I don't like that, George.

Ruth. Why must you and your brother make an argument out of everything people say?

Beneatha. Because I hate assimilationist Negroes!

Ruth. Will somebody please tell me what assimila-whoever means!

George. Oh, it's just a college girl's way of calling people Uncle Toms — but that isn't what it means at all.

Ruth. Well, what does it mean?

Beneatha *(cutting George off and staring at him as she replies to Ruth).* It means someone who is willing to give up his own culture and submerge himself completely in the dominant, and in this case *oppressive* culture!

George. Oh, dear, dear, dear! Here we go! A lecture on the African past! On our Great West African Heritage! In one second we will hear all about the great Ashanti empires; the great Songhay civilizations; and the great sculpture of Bénin — and then some poetry in the Bantu — and the whole monologue will end with the word *heritage!* *(Nastily.)* Let's face it, baby, your heritage is nothing but a bunch of raggedy-assed spirituals and some grass huts!

Beneatha. GRASS HUTS! *(Ruth crosses to her and forcibly pushes her toward the bedroom.)* See there . . . you are standing there in your splendid ignorance talking about people who were the first to smelt iron on the face of the earth! *(Ruth is pushing her through the door.)* The Ashanti were performing surgical operations when the English — *(Ruth pulls the door to, with Beneatha on the other side, and smiles graciously at George. Beneatha opens the door and shouts the end of the sentence defiantly at George.)* — were still tattooing themselves with blue dragons! *(She goes back inside.)*

Ruth. Have a seat, George. *(They both sit. Ruth folds her hands rather primly on her lap, determined to demonstrate the civilization of the family.)* Warm, ain't it? I mean for September. *(Pause.)* Just like they always say about Chicago weather: if it's too hot or cold for you, just wait a minute and it'll change. *(She smiles happily at this cliché of clichés.)* Everybody say it's got to do with them bombs and things they keep setting off. *(Pause.)* Would you like a nice cold beer?

George. No, thank you. I don't care for beer. *(He looks at his watch.)* I hope she hurries up.

Ruth. What time is the show?

George. It's an eight-thirty curtain. That's just Chicago, though. In New York standard curtain time is eight forty.

He is rather proud of this knowledge.

Ruth (*properly appreciating it*).   You get to New York a lot?
George (*offhand*).   Few times a year.
Ruth.   Oh — that's nice. I've never been to New York.

Walter enters. We feel he has relieved himself, but the edge of unreality is still with him.

Walter.   New York ain't got nothing Chicago ain't. Just a bunch of hustling people all squeezed up together — being "Eastern."

He turns his face into a screw of displeasure.

George.   Oh — you've been?
Walter.   *Plenty* of times.
Ruth (*shocked at the lie*).   Walter Lee Younger!
Walter (*staring her down*).   Plenty! (*Pause.*) What we got to drink in this house? Why don't you offer this man some refreshment. (*To George.*) They don't know how to entertain people in this house, man.
George.   Thank you — I don't really care for anything.
Walter (*feeling his head; sobriety coming*).   Where's Mama?
Ruth.   She ain't come back yet.
Walter (*looking Murchison over from head to toe, scrutinizing his carefully casual tweed sports jacket over cashmere V-neck sweater over soft eyelet shirt and tie, and soft slacks, finished off with white buckskin shoes*).   Why all you college boys wear them faggoty-looking white shoes?
Ruth.   Walter Lee!

George Murchison ignores the remark.

Walter (*to Ruth*).   Well, they look crazy as hell — white shoes, cold as it is.
Ruth (*crushed*).   You have to excuse him —
Walter.   No he don't! Excuse me for what? What you always excusing me for! I'll excuse myself when I needs to be excused! (*A pause.*) They look as funny as them black knee socks Beneatha wears out of here all the time.
Ruth.   It's the college *style*, Walter.
Walter.   Style, hell. She looks like she got burnt legs or something!
Ruth.   Oh, Walter —
Walter (*an irritable mimic*).   Oh, Walter! Oh, Walter! (*To Murchison.*) How's your old man making out? I understand you all going to buy that big hotel on the Drive? (*He finds a beer in the refrigerator, wanders over to Murchison, sipping and wiping his lips with the back of his hand, and straddling a chair backwards to talk to the other man.*) Shrewd move. Your old man is all right, man. (*Tapping his head and half winking for emphasis.*) I mean he knows how to operate. I mean he thinks *big*, you know what I mean, I mean for a *home*, you know? But I think he's kind of running out of ideas now. I'd like to

talk to him. Listen, man, I got some plans that could turn this city upside down. I mean think like he does. *Big.* Invest big, gamble big, hell, lose *big* if you have to, you know what I mean. It's hard to find a man on this whole Southside who understands my kind of thinking — you dig? (*He scrutinizes Murchison again, drinks his beer, squints his eyes and leans in close, confidential, man to man.*) Me and you ought to sit down and talk sometimes, man. Man, I got me some ideas . . .

Murchison (*with boredom*). Yeah — sometimes we'll have to do that, Walter.

Walter (*understanding the indifference, and offended*). Yeah — well, when you get the time, man. I know you a busy little boy.

Ruth. Walter, please —

Walter (*bitterly, hurt*). I know ain't nothing in this world as busy as you colored college boys with your fraternity pins and white shoes . . .

Ruth (*covering her face with humiliation*). Oh, Walter Lee —

Walter. I see you all all the time — with the books tucked under your arms — going to your (*British A — a mimic.*) "clahsses." And for what! What the hell you learning over there? Filling up your heads — (*Counting off on his fingers.*) — with the sociology and the psychology — but they teaching you how to be a man? How to take over and run the world? They teaching you how to run a rubber plantation or a steel mill? Naw — just to talk proper and read books and wear them faggoty-looking white shoes . . .

George (*looking at him with distaste, a little above it all*). You're all wacked up with bitterness, man.

Walter (*intently, almost quietly, between the teeth, glaring at the boy*). And you — ain't you bitter, man? Ain't you just about had it yet? Don't you see no stars gleaming that you can't reach out and grab? You happy? — You contented son-of-a-bitch — you happy? You got it made? Bitter? Man, I'm a volcano. Bitter? Here I am a giant — surrounded by ants! Ants who can't even understand what it is the giant is talking about.

Ruth (*passionately and suddenly*). Oh, Walter — ain't you with nobody!

Walter (*violently*). No! 'Cause ain't nobody with me! Not even my own mother!

Ruth. Walter, that's a terrible thing to say!

Beneatha enters, dressed for the evening in a cocktail dress and earrings, hair natural.

George. Well — hey — (*Crosses to Beneatha; thoughtful, with emphasis, since this is a reversal.*) You look great!

Walter (*seeing his sister's hair for the first time*). What's the matter with your head?

Beneatha (*tired of the jokes now*). I cut it off, Brother.

Walter (*coming close to inspect it and walking around her*). Well, I'll be damned. So that's what they mean by the African bush . . .

Beneatha.   Ha ha. Let's go, George.

George (*looking at her*).   You know something? I like it. It's sharp. I mean it really is. (*Helps her into her wrap.*)

Ruth.   Yes — I think so, too. (*She goes to the mirror and starts to clutch at her hair.*)

Walter.   Oh no! You leave yours alone, baby. You might turn out to have a pin-shaped head or something!

Beneatha.   See you all later.

Ruth.   Have a nice time.

George.   Thanks. Good night. (*Half out the door, he reopens it. To Walter.*) Good night, Prometheus!

Beneatha and George exit.

Walter (*to Ruth*).   Who is Prometheus?

Ruth.   I don't know. Don't worry about it.

Walter (*in fury, pointing after George*).   See there — they get to a point where they can't insult you man to man — they got to go talk about something ain't nobody never heard of!

Ruth.   How do you know it was an insult? (*To humor him.*) Maybe Prometheus is a nice fellow.

Walter.   Prometheus! I bet there ain't even no such thing! I bet that simple-minded clown —

Ruth.   Walter —

She stops what she is doing and looks at him.

Walter (*yelling*).   Don't start!

Ruth.   Start what?

Walter.   Your nagging! Where was I? Who was I with? How much money did I spend?

Ruth (*plaintively*).   Walter Lee — why don't we just try to talk about it . . .

Walter (*not listening*).   I been out talking with people who understand me. People who care about the things I got on my mind.

Ruth (*wearily*).   I guess that means people like Willy Harris.

Walter.   Yes, people like Willy Harris.

Ruth (*with a sudden flash of impatience*).   Why don't you all just hurry up and go into the banking business and stop talking about it!

Walter.   Why? You want to know why? 'Cause we all tied up in a race of people that don't know how to do nothing but moan, pray and have babies!

The line is too bitter even for him and he looks at her and sits down.

Ruth.   Oh, Walter . . . (*Softly.*) Honey, why can't you stop fighting me?

Walter (*without thinking*).   Who's fighting you? Who even cares about you?

This line begins the retardation of his mood.

Ruth. Well — *(She waits a long time, and then with resignation starts to put away her things.)* I guess I might as well go on to bed . . . *(More or less to herself.)* I don't know where we lost it . . . but we have . . . *(Then, to him.)* I — I'm sorry about this new baby, Walter. I guess maybe I better go on and do what I started . . . I guess I just didn't realize how bad things was with us . . . I guess I just didn't really realize — *(She starts out to the bedroom and stops.)* You want some hot milk?

Walter. Hot milk?

Ruth. Yes — hot milk.

Walter. Why hot milk?

Ruth. 'Cause after all that liquor you come home with you ought to have something hot in your stomach.

Walter. I don't want no milk.

Ruth. You want some coffee then?

Walter. No, I don't want no coffee. I don't want nothing hot to drink. *(Almost plaintively.)* Why you always trying to give me something to eat?

Ruth *(standing and looking at him helplessly)*. What *else* can I give you, Walter Lee Younger?

She stands and looks at him and presently turns to go out again. He lifts his head and watches her going away from him in a new mood which began to emerge when he asked her "Who cares about you?"

Walter. It's been rough, ain't it, baby? *(She hears and stops but does not turn around and he continues to her back.)* I guess between two people there ain't never as much understood as folks generally thinks there is. I mean like between me and you — *(She turns to face him.)* How we gets to the place where we scared to talk softness to each other. *(He waits, thinking hard himself.)* Why you think it got to be like that? *(He is thoughtful, almost as a child would be.)* Ruth, what is it gets into people ought to be close?

Ruth. I don't know, honey. I think about it a lot.

Walter. On account of you and me, you mean? The way things are with us. The way something done come down between us.

Ruth. There ain't so much between us, Walter . . . Not when you come to me and try to talk to me. Try to be with me . . . a little even.

Walter *(total honesty)*. Sometimes . . . sometimes . . . I don't even know how to try.

Ruth. Walter —

Walter. Yes?

Ruth *(coming to him, gently and with misgiving, but coming to him)*. Honey . . . life don't have to be like this. I mean sometimes people can do things so that things are better . . . You remember how we used to talk when Travis was born . . . about the way we were going to live . . . the kind of house . . . (*She is stroking his head.*) Well, it's all starting to slip away from us . . .

He turns her to him and they look at each other and kiss, tenderly and hungrily. The door opens and Mama enters — Walter breaks away and jumps up. A beat.

Walter.   Mama, where have you been?

Mama.   My — them steps is longer than they used to be. Whew! (*She sits down and ignores him.*) How you feeling this evening, Ruth?

Ruth shrugs, disturbed at having been interrupted and watching her husband knowingly.

Walter.   Mama, where have you been all day?

Mama (*still ignoring him and leaning on the table and changing to more comfortable shoes*). Where's Travis?

Ruth.   I let him go out earlier and he ain't come back yet. Boy, is he going to get it!

Walter.   Mama!

Mama (*as if she has heard him for the first time*).   Yes, son?

Walter.   Where did you go this afternoon?

Mama.   I went downtown to tend to some business that I had to tend to.

Walter.   What kind of business?

Mama.   You know better than to question me like a child, Brother.

Walter (*rising and bending over the table*).   Where were you, Mama? (*Bringing his fists down and shouting.*) Mama, you didn't go do something with that insurance money, something crazy?

The front door opens slowly, interrupting him, and Travis peeks his head in, less than hopefully.

Travis (*to his mother*).   Mama, I —

Ruth.   "Mama I" nothing! You're going to get it, boy! Get on in that bedroom and get yourself ready!

Travis.   But I —

Mama.   Why don't you all never let the child explain hisself.

Ruth.   Keep out of it now, Lena.

Mama clamps her lips together, and Ruth advances toward her son menacingly.

Ruth.   A thousand times I have told you not to go off like that —

Mama (*holding out her arms to her grandson*).   Well — at least let me tell him something. I want him to be the first one to hear . . . Come here, Travis. (*The boy obeys, gladly.*) Travis — (*She takes him by the shoulder and looks into his face.*) — you know that money we got in the mail this morning?

Travis. Yes'm —

Mama. Well — what you think your grandmama gone and done with that money?

Travis. I don't know, Grandmama.

Mama (*putting her finger on his nose for emphasis*). She went out and she bought you a house! (*The explosion comes from Walter at the end of the revelation and he jumps up and turns away from all of them in a fury. Mama continues, to Travis.*) You glad about the house? It's going to be yours when you get to be a man.

Travis. Yeah — I always wanted to live in a house.

Mama. All right, gimme some sugar then — (*Travis puts his arms around her neck as she watches her son over the boy's shoulder. Then, to Travis, after the embrace.*) Now when you say your prayers tonight, you thank God and your grandfather — 'cause it was him who give you the house — in his way.

Ruth (*taking the boy from Mama and pushing him toward the bedroom*). Now you get out of here and get ready for your beating.

Travis. Aw, Mama —

Ruth. Get on in there — (*Closing the door behind him and turning radiantly to her mother-in-law.*) So you went and did it!

Mama (*quietly, looking at her son with pain*). Yes, I did.

Ruth (*raising both arms classically*). PRAISE GOD! (*Looks at Walter a moment, who says nothing. She crosses rapidly to her husband.*) Please, honey — let me be glad . . . you be glad too. (*She has laid her hands on his shoulders, but he shakes himself free of her roughly, without turning to face her.*) Oh, Walter . . . a home . . . a home. (*She comes back to Mama.*) Well — where is it? How big is it? How much it going to cost?

Mama. Well —

Ruth. When we moving?

Mama (*smiling at her*). First of the month.

Ruth (*throwing back her head with jubilance*). Praise God!

Mama (*tentatively, still looking at her son's back turned against her and Ruth*). It's — it's a nice house too . . . (*She cannot help speaking directly to him. An imploring quality in her voice, her manner, makes her almost like a girl now.*) Three bedrooms — nice big one for you and Ruth . . . Me and Beneatha still have to share our room, but Travis have one of his own — and (*With difficulty.*) I figure if the — new baby — is a boy, we could get one of them double-decker outfits . . . And there's a yard with a little patch of dirt where I could maybe get to grow me a few flowers . . . And a nice big basement . . .

Ruth. Walter honey, be glad —

Mama (*still to his back, fingering things on the table*). 'Course I don't want to make it sound fancier than it is . . . It's just a plain little old house — but it's made good and solid — and it will be *ours*. Walter Lee — it makes a difference in a man when he can walk on floors that belong to *him* . . .

Ruth. Where is it?

Mama (*frightened at this telling*).   Well — well — it's out there in Clybourne Park —

Ruth's radiance fades abruptly, and Walter finally turns slowly to face his mother with incredulity and hostility.

Ruth.   Where?

Mama (*matter-of-factly*).   Four o six Clybourne Street, Clybourne Park.

Ruth.   Clybourne Park? Mama, there ain't no colored people living in Clybourne Park.

Mama (*almost idiotically*).   Well, I guess there's going to be some now.

Walter (*bitterly*).   So that's the peace and comfort you went out and bought for us today!

Mama (*raising her eyes to meet his finally*).   Son — I just tried to find the nicest place for the least amount of money for my family.

Ruth (*trying to recover from the shock*).   Well — well — 'course I ain't one never been 'fraid of no crackers, mind you — but — well, wasn't there no other houses nowhere?

Mama.   Them houses they put up for colored in them areas way out all seem to cost twice as much as other houses. I did the best I could.

Ruth (*struck senseless with the news, in its various degrees of goodness and trouble, she sits a moment, her fists propping her chin in thought, and then she starts to rise, bringing her fists down with vigor, the radiance spreading from cheek to cheek again*). Well — well — All I can say is — if this is my time in life — MY TIME — to say good-bye — (*And she builds with momentum as she starts to circle the room with an exuberant, almost tearfully happy release.*) — to these Goddamned cracking walls! — (*She pounds the walls.*) — and these marching roaches! — (*She wipes at an imaginary army of marching roaches.*) — and this cramped little closet which ain't now or never was no kitchen! . . . then I say it loud and good, HALLELUJAH! AND GOOD-BYE MISERY . . . I DON'T NEVER WANT TO SEE YOUR UGLY FACE AGAIN! (*She laughs joyously, having practically destroyed the apartment, and flings her arms up and lets them come down happily, slowly, reflectively, over her abdomen, aware for the first time perhaps that the life therein pulses with happiness and not despair.*) Lena?

Mama (*moved, watching her happiness*).   Yes, honey?

Ruth (*looking off*).   Is there — is there a whole lot of sunlight?

Mama (*understanding*).   Yes, child, there's a whole lot of sunlight.

Long pause.

Ruth (*collecting herself and going to the door of the room Travis is in*). Well — I guess I better see 'bout Travis. (*To Mama.*) Lord, I sure don't feel like whipping nobody today!

She exits.

Mama *(the mother and son are left alone now and the mother waits a long time, considering deeply, before she speaks).* Son — you — you understand what I done, don't you? *(Walter is silent and sullen.)* I — I just seen my family falling apart today . . . just falling to pieces in front of my eyes . . . We couldn't of gone on like we was today. We was going backwards 'stead of forwards — talking 'bout killing babies and wishing each other was dead . . . When it gets like that in life — you just got to do something different, push on out and do something bigger . . . *(She waits.)* I wish you say something, son . . . I wish you'd say how deep inside you you think I done the right thing —

Walter *(crossing slowly to his bedroom door and finally turning there and speaking measuredly).* What you need me to say you done right for? *You* the head of this family. You run our lives like you want to. It was your money and you did what you wanted with it. So what you need for me to say it was all right for? *(Bitterly, to hurt her as deeply as he knows is possible.)* So you butchered up a dream of mine — you — who always talking 'bout your children's dreams . . .

Mama. Walter Lee —

He just closes the door behind him. Mama sits alone, thinking heavily.

Curtain.

Scene 2.

Time: Friday night, a few weeks later.

At rise: Packing crates mark the intention of the family to move. Beneatha and George come in, presumably from an evening out again.

George. O.K. . . . O.K., whatever you say . . . *(They both sit on the couch. He tries to kiss her. She moves away.)* Look, we've had a nice evening; let's not spoil it, huh? . . .

He again turns her head and tries to nuzzle in and she turns away from him, not with distaste but with momentary lack of interest; in a mood to pursue what they were talking about.

Beneatha. I'm *trying* to talk to you.

George. We always talk.

Beneatha. Yes — and I love to talk.

George *(exasperated; rising).* I know it and I don't mind it sometimes . . . I want you to cut it out, see — The moody stuff, I mean. I don't like it. You're a

nice-looking girl . . . all over. That's all you need, honey, forget the atmosphere. Guys aren't going to go for the atmosphere — they're going to go for
what they see. Be glad for that. Drop the Garbo routine. It doesn't go with
you. As for myself, I want a nice — *(Groping.)* — simple *(Thoughtfully.)* —
sophisticated girl . . . not a poet — O.K.?

He starts to kiss her, she rebuffs him again and he jumps up.

Beneatha.   Why are you angry, George?
George.   Because this is stupid! I don't go out with you to discuss the nature
of "quiet desperation" or to hear all about your thoughts — because the
world will go on thinking what it thinks regardless —
Beneatha.   Then why read books? Why go to school?
George *(with artificial patience, counting on his fingers).*   It's simple. You
read books — to learn facts — to get grades — to pass the course — to get a
degree. That's all — it has nothing to do with thoughts.

A long pause.

Beneatha.   I see. *(He starts to sit.)* Good night, George.

George looks at her a little oddly, and starts to exit. He meets Mama coming in.

George.   Oh — hello, Mrs. Younger.
Mama.   Hello, George, how you feeling?
George.   Fine — fine, how are you?
Mama.   Oh, a little tired. You know them steps can get you after a day's work.
You all have a nice time tonight?
George.   Yes — a fine time. A fine time.
Mama.   Well, good night.
George.   Good night. *(He exits. Mama closes the door behind her.)*
Mama.   Hello, honey. What you sitting like that for?
Beneatha.   I'm just sitting.
Mama.   Didn't you have a nice time?
Beneatha.   No.
Mama.   No? What's the matter?
Beneatha.   Mama, George is a fool — honest. *(She rises.)*
Mama *(hustling around unloading the packages she has entered with. She
stops).*   Is he, baby?
Beneatha.   Yes.

Beneatha makes up Travis's bed as she talks.

Mama.   You sure?
Beneatha.   Yes.

Mama. Well — I guess you better not waste your time with no fools.

Beneatha looks up at her mother, watching her put groceries in the refrigerator. Finally she gathers up her things and starts into the bedroom. At the door she stops and looks back at her mother.

Beneatha. Mama —
Mama. Yes, baby —
Beneatha. Thank you.
Mama. For what?
Beneatha. For understanding me this time.

She exits quickly and the mother stands, smiling a little, looking at the place where Beneatha just stood. Ruth enters.

Ruth. Now don't you fool with any of this stuff, Lena —
Mama. Oh, I just thought I'd sort a few things out. Is Brother here?
Ruth. Yes.
Mama (*with concern*). Is he —
Ruth (*reading her eyes*). Yes.

Mama is silent and someone knocks on the door. Mama and Ruth exchange weary and knowing glances and Ruth opens it to admit the neighbor, Mrs. Johnson,[1] who is a rather squeaky wide-eyed lady of no particular age, with a newspaper under her arm.

Mama (*changing her expression to acute delight and a ringing cheerful greeting*). Oh — hello there, Johnson.
Johnson (*this is a woman who decided long ago to be enthusiastic about EVERYTHING in life and she is inclined to wave her wrist vigorously at the height of her exclamatory comments*). Hello there, yourself! H'you this evening, Ruth?
Ruth (*not much of a deceptive type*). Fine, Mis' Johnson, h'you?
Johnson. Fine. (*Reaching out quickly, playfully, and patting Ruth's stomach.*) Ain't you starting to poke out none yet! (*She mugs with delight at the over familiar remark and her eyes dart around looking at the crates and packing preparation; Mama's face is a cold sheet of endurance.*) Oh, ain't we getting ready round here, though! Yessir! Lookathere! I'm telling you the Youngers is really getting ready to "move on up a little higher!" — Bless God!
Mama (*a little drily, doubting the total sincerity of the Blesser*). Bless God.
Johnson. He's good, ain't He?
Mama. Oh yes, He's good.

---

[1] This character and the scene of her visit were cut from the original production and early editions of the play.

Johnson.   I mean sometimes He works in mysterious ways . . . but He works, don't He!

Mama *(the same).*   Yes, he does.

Johnson.   I'm just soooooo happy for y'all. And this here child — *(About Ruth.)* looks like she could just pop open with happiness, don't she. Where's all the rest of the family?

Mama.   Bennie's gone to bed —

Johnson.   Ain't no . . . *(The implication is pregnancy.)* sickness done hit you — I hope . . . ?

Mama.   No — she just tired. She was out this evening.

Johnson *(all is a coo, an emphatic coo).*   Aw — ain't that lovely. She still going out with the little Murchison boy?

Mama *(drily).*   Ummmm huh.

Johnson.   That's lovely. You sure got lovely children, Younger. Me and Isaiah talks all the time 'bout what fine children you was blessed with. We sure do.

Mama.   Ruth, give Mis' Johnson a piece of sweet potato pie and some milk.

Johnson.   Oh honey, I can't stay hardly a minute — I just dropped in to see if there was anything I could do. *(Accepting the food easily.)* I guess y'all seen the news what's all over the colored paper this week . . .

Mama.   No — didn't get mine yet this week.

Johnson *(lifting her head and blinking with the spirit of catastrophe).*   You mean you ain't read 'bout them colored people that was bombed out their place out there?

Ruth straightens with concern and takes the paper and reads it. Johnson notices her and feeds commentary.

Johnson.   Ain't it something how bad these here white folks is getting here in Chicago! Lord, getting so you think you right down in Mississippi! *(With a tremendous and rather insincere sense of melodrama.)* 'Course I thinks it's wonderful how our folk keeps on pushing out. You hear some of these Negroes round here talking 'bout how they don't go where they ain't wanted and all that — but not me, honey! *(This is a lie.)* Wilhemenia Othella Johnson goes anywhere, any time she feels like it! *(With head movement for emphasis.)* Yes I do! Why if we left it up to these here crackers, the poor niggers wouldn't have nothing — *(She clasps her hand over her mouth.)* Oh, I always forgets you don't 'low that word in your house.

Mama *(quietly, looking at her).*   No — I don't 'low it.

Johnson *(vigorously again).*   Me neither! I was just telling Isaiah yesterday when he come using it in front of me — I said, "Isaiah, it's just like Mis' Younger says all the time — "

Mama.   Don't you want some more pie?

Johnson.   No — no thank you; this was lovely. I got to get on over home and have my midnight coffee. I hear some people say it don't let them sleep but I finds I can't close my eyes right lessen I done had that laaaast cup of coffee . . . (*She waits. A beat. Undaunted.*) My Goodnight coffee, I calls it!

Mama (*with much eye-rolling and communication between herself and Ruth*). Ruth, why don't you give Mis' Johnson some coffee.

Ruth gives Mama an unpleasant look for her kindness.

Johnson (*accepting the coffee*). Where's Brother tonight?

Mama. He's lying down.

Johnson. Mmmmmmm, he sure gets his beauty rest, don't he? Good-looking man. Sure is a good-looking man! (*Reaching out to pat Ruth's stomach again.*) I guess that's how come we keep on having babies around here. (*She winks at Mama.*) One thing 'bout Brother, he always know how to have a *good* time. And soooooo ambitious! I bet it was his idea y'all moving out to Clybourne Park. Lord — I bet this time next month y'all's names will have been in the papers plenty — (*Holding up her hands to mark off each word of the headline she can see in front of her.*) "NEGROES INVADE CLYBOURNE PARK — BOMBED!"

Mama (*she and Ruth look at the woman in amazement*). We ain't exactly moving out there to get bombed.

Johnson. Oh honey — you know I'm praying to God every day that don't nothing like that happen! But you have to think of life like it is — and these here Chicago peckerwoods is some baaaad peckerwoods.

Mama (*wearily*). We done thought about all that Mis' Johnson.

Beneatha comes out of the bedroom in her robe and passes through to the bathroom. Mrs. Johnson turns.

Johnson. Hello there, Bennie!

Beneatha (*crisply*). Hello, Mrs. Johnson.

Johnson. How is school?

Beneatha (*crisply*). Fine, thank you. (*She goes out.*)

Johnson (*insulted*). Getting so she don't have much to say to nobody.

Mama. The child was on her way to the bathroom.

Johnson. I know — but sometimes she act like ain't got time to pass the time of day with nobody ain't been to college. Oh — I ain't criticizing her none. It's just — you know how some of our young people gets when they get a little education. (*Mama and Ruth say nothing, just look at her.*) Yes — well. Well, I guess I better get on home. (*Unmoving.*) 'Course I can understand how she must be proud and everything — being the only one in the family to make something of herself. I know just being a chauffeur ain't never satisfied Brother none. He shouldn't feel like that, though. Ain't nothing wrong with being a chauffeur.

Mama. There's plenty wrong with it.

Johnson. What?

Mama. Plenty. My husband always said being any kind of a servant wasn't a fit thing for a man to have to be. He always said a man's hands was made to make things, or to turn the earth with — not to drive nobody's car for 'em — or — (*She looks at her own hands.*) carry they slop jars. And my boy is just like him — he wasn't meant to wait on nobody.

Johnson (*rising, somewhat offended*). Mmmmmmmmm. The Youngers is too much for me! (*She looks around.*) You sure one proud-acting bunch of colored folks. Well — I always thinks like Booker T. Washington said that time — "Education has spoiled many a good plow hand" —

Mama. Is that what old Booker T. said?

Johnson. He sure did.

Mama. Well, it sounds just like him. The fool.

Johnson (*indignantly*). Well — he was one of our great men.

Mama. Who said so?

Johnson (*nonplussed*). You know, me and you ain't never agreed about some things, Lena Younger. I guess I better be going —

Ruth (*quickly*). Good night.

Johnson. Good night. Oh — (*Thrusting it at her.*) You can keep the paper! (*With a trill.*) 'Night.

Mama. Good night, Mis' Johnson.

Mrs. Johnson exits.

Ruth. If ignorance was gold . . .

Mama. Shush. Don't talk about folks behind their backs.

Ruth. You do.

Mama. I'm old and corrupted. (*Beneatha enters.*) You was rude to Mis' Johnson, Beneatha, and I don't like it at all.

Beneatha (*at her door*). Mama, if there are two things we, as a people, have got to overcome, one is the Ku Klux Klan — and the other is Mrs. Johnson. (*She exits.*)

Mama. Smart aleck.

The phone rings.

Ruth. I'll get it.

Mama. Lord, ain't this a popular place tonight.

Ruth (*at the phone*). Hello — Just a minute. (*Goes to door.*) Walter, it's Mrs. Arnold. (*Waits. Goes back to the phone. Tense.*) Hello. Yes, this is his wife speaking . . . He's lying down now. Yes . . . well, he'll be in tomorrow. He's been very sick. Yes — I know we should have called, but we were so sure he'd be able to come in today. Yes — yes, I'm very sorry. Yes . . . Thank you very much. (*She hangs up. Walter is standing in the doorway of the bedroom behind her.*) That was Mrs. Arnold.

Walter (*indifferently*). Was it?

Ruth. She said if you don't come in tomorrow that they are getting a new man . . .

Walter. Ain't that sad — ain't that crying sad.

Ruth. She said Mr. Arnold has had to take a cab for three days . . . Walter, you ain't been to work for three days! (*This is a revelation to her.*) Where you been, Walter Lee Younger? (*Walter looks at her and starts to laugh.*) You're going to lose your job.

Walter. That's right . . . (*He turns on the radio.*)

Ruth. Oh, Walter, and with your mother working like a dog every day —

A steamy, deep blues pours into the room.

Walter. That's sad too — Everything is sad.

Mama. What you been doing for these three days, son?

Walter. Mama — you don't know all the things a man what got leisure can find to do in this city . . . What's this — Friday night? Well — Wednesday I borrowed Willy Harris' car and I went for a drive . . . just me and myself and I drove and drove . . . Way out . . . way past South Chicago, and I parked the car and I sat and looked at the steel mills all day long. I just sat in the car and looked at them big black chimneys for hours. Then I drove back and I went to the Green Hat. (*Pause.*) And Thursday — Thursday I borrowed the car again and I got in it and I pointed it the other way and I drove the other way — for hours — way, way up to Wisconsin, and I looked at the farms. I just drove and looked at the farms. Then I drove back and I went to the Green Hat. (*Pause.*) And today — today I didn't get the car. Today I just walked. All over the Southside. And I looked at the Negroes and they looked at me and finally I just sat down on the curb at Thirty-ninth and South Parkway and I just sat there and watched the Negroes go by. And then I went to the Green Hat. You all sad? You all depressed? And you know where I am going right now —

Ruth goes out quietly.

Mama. Oh, Big Walter, is this the harvest of our days?

Walter. You know what I like about the Green Hat? I like this little cat they got there who blows a sax . . . He blows. He talks to me. He ain't but 'bout five feet tall and he's got a conked head and his eyes is always closed and he's all music —

Mama (*rising and getting some papers out of her handbag*). Walter —

Walter. And there's this other guy who plays the piano . . . and they got a sound. I mean they can work on some music . . . They got the best little combo in the world in the Green Hat . . . You can just sit there and drink and listen to them three men play and you realize that don't nothing matter worth a damn, but just being there —

Mama. I've helped do it to you, haven't I, son? Walter I been wrong.

Walter. Naw — you ain't never been wrong about nothing, Mama.

Mama. Listen to me, now. I say I been wrong, son. That I been doing to you what the rest of the world been doing to you. (*She turns off the radio.*) Walter — (*She stops and he looks up slowly at her and she meets his eyes pleadingly.*) What you ain't never understood is that I ain't got nothing, don't own nothing, ain't never really wanted nothing that wasn't for you. There ain't nothing as precious to me . . . There ain't nothing worth holding on to, money, dreams, nothing else — if it means — if it means it's going to destroy my boy. (*She takes an envelope out of her handbag and puts it in front of him and he watches her without speaking or moving.*) I paid the man thirty-five hundred dollars down on the house. That leaves sixty-five hundred dollars. Monday morning I want you to take this money and take three thousand dollars and put it in a savings account for Beneatha's medical schooling. The rest you put in a checking account — with your name on it. And from now on any penny that come out of it or that go in it is for you to look after. For you to decide. (*She drops her hands a little helplessly.*) It ain't much, but it's all I got in the world and I'm putting it in your hands. I'm telling you to be the head of this family from now on like you supposed to be.

Walter (*stares at the money*). You trust me like that, Mama?

Mama. I ain't never stop trusting you. Like I ain't never stop loving you.

She goes out, and Walter sits looking at the money on the table. Finally, in a decisive gesture, he gets up, and, in mingled joy and desperation, picks up the money. At the same moment, Travis enters for bed.

Travis. What's the matter, Daddy? You drunk?

Walter (*sweetly, more sweetly than we have ever known him*). No, Daddy ain't drunk. Daddy ain't going to never be drunk again . . .

Travis. Well, good night, Daddy.

The father has come from behind the couch and leans over, embracing his son.

Walter. Son, I feel like talking to you tonight.

Travis. About what?

Walter. Oh, about a lot of things. About you and what kind of man you going to be when you grow up . . . Son — son, what do you want to be when you grow up?

Travis. A bus driver.

Walter (*laughing a little*). A what? Man, that ain't nothing to want to be!

Travis. Why not?

Walter. 'Cause, man — it ain't big enough — you know what I mean.

Travis. I don't know then. I can't make up my mind. Sometimes Mama asks me that too. And sometimes when I tell her I just want to be like you — she says she don't want me to be like that and sometimes she says she does. . . .

Walter (*gathering him up in his arms*).   You know what, Travis? In seven years you going to be seventeen years old. And things is going to be very different with us in seven years, Travis. . . . One day when you are seventeen I'll come home — home from my office downtown somewhere —

Travis.   You don't work in no office, Daddy.

Walter.   No — but after tonight. After what your daddy gonna do tonight, there's going to be offices — a whole lot of offices. . . .

Travis.   What you gonna do tonight, Daddy?

Walter.   You wouldn't understand yet, son, but your daddy's gonna make a transaction . . . a business transaction that's going to change our lives. . . . That's how come one day when you 'bout seventeen years old I'll come home and I'll be pretty tired, you know what I mean, after a day of conferences and secretaries getting things wrong the way they do . . . 'cause an executive's life is hell, man — (*The more he talks the farther away he gets.*) And I'll pull the car up on the driveway . . . just a plain black Chrysler, I think, with white walls — no — black tires. More elegant. Rich people don't have to be flashy . . . though I'll have to get something a little sportier for Ruth — maybe a Cadillac convertible to do her shopping in. . . . And I'll come up the steps to the house and the gardener will be clipping away at the hedges and he'll say, "Good evening, Mr. Younger." And I'll say, "Hello, Jefferson, how are you this evening?" And I'll go inside and Ruth will come downstairs and meet me at the door and we'll kiss each other and she'll take my arm and we'll go up to your room to see you sitting on the floor with the catalogues of all the great schools in America around you. . . . All the great schools in the world! And — and I'll say, all right son — it's your seventeenth birthday, what is it you've decided? . . . Just tell me where you want to go to school and you'll *go*. Just tell me, what it is you want to be — and you'll *be* it. . . . Whatever you want to be — Yessir! (*He holds his arms open for Travis.*) You just name it, son . . . (*Travis leaps into them.*) and I hand you the world!

Walter's voice has risen in pitch and hysterical promise and on the last line he lifts Travis high.

Blackout.

Scene 3.

Time. Saturday, moving day, one week later.

Before the curtain rises, Ruth's voice, a strident, dramatic church alto, cuts through the silence.

It is, in the darkness, a triumphant surge, a penetrating statement of expectation: "Oh, Lord, I don't feel no ways tired! Children, oh, glory hallelujah!"

As the curtain rises we see that Ruth is alone in the living room, finishing up the family's packing. It is moving day. She is nailing crates and tying cartons.

Beneatha enters, carrying a guitar case, and watches her exuberant sister-in-law.

Ruth. Hey!

Beneatha *(putting away the case).* Hi.

Ruth *(pointing at a package).* Honey — look in that package there and see what I found on sale this morning at the South Center. *(Ruth gets up and moves to the package and draws out some curtains.)* Lookahere — hand-turned hems!

Beneatha. How do you know the window size out there?

Ruth *(who hadn't thought of that).* Oh — Well, they bound to fit something in the whole house. Anyhow, they was too good a bargain to pass up. *(Ruth slaps her head, suddenly remembering something.)* Oh, Bennie — I meant to put a special note on that carton over there. That's your mama's good china and she wants 'em to be very careful with it.

Beneatha. I'll do it.

Beneatha finds a piece of paper and starts to draw large letters on it.

Ruth. You know what I'm going to do soon as I get in that new house?

Beneatha. What?

Ruth. Honey — I'm going to run me a tub of water up to here . . . *(With her fingers practically up to her nostrils.)* And I'm going to get in it — and I am going to sit . . . and sit . . . and sit in that hot water and the first person who knocks to tell *me* to hurry up and come out —

Beneatha. Gets shot at sunrise.

Ruth *(laughing happily).* You said it, sister! *(Noticing how large Beneatha is absent-mindedly making the note):* Honey, they ain't going to read that from no airplane.

Beneatha *(laughing herself).* I guess I always think things have more emphasis if they are big, somehow.

Ruth *(looking up at her and smiling).* You and your brother seem to have that as a philosophy of life. Lord, that man — done changed so 'round here. You know — you know what we did last night? Me and Walter Lee?

Beneatha. What?

Ruth *(smiling to herself).* We went to the movies. *(Looking at Beneatha to see if she understands.)* We went to the movies. You know the last time me and Walter went to the movies together?

Beneatha. No.

Ruth. Me neither. That's how long it been. *(Smiling again.)* But we went last night. The picture wasn't much good, but that didn't seem to matter. We went — and we held hands.

Beneatha. Oh, Lord!

Ruth. We held hands — and you know what?

Beneatha. What?

Ruth.   When we come out of the show it was late and dark and all the stores and things was closed up . . . and it was kind of chilly and there wasn't many people on the streets . . . and we was still holding hands, me and Walter.

Beneatha.   You're killing me.

Walter enters with a large package. His happiness is deep in him; he cannot keep still with his newfound exuberance. He is singing and wiggling and snapping his fingers. He puts his package in a corner and puts a phonograph record, which he has brought in with him, on the record player. As the music, soulful and sensuous, comes up he dances over to Ruth and tries to get her to dance with him. She gives in at last to his raunchiness and in a fit of giggling allows herself to be drawn into his mood. They dip and she melts into his arms in a classic, body-melting "slow drag."

Beneatha (*regarding them a long time as they dance, then drawing in her breath for a deeply exaggerated comment which she does not particularly mean*). Talk about — oldddddddddd-fashionedddddddd — Negroes!

Walter (*stopping momentarily*).   What kind of Negroes?

He says this in fun. He is not angry with her today, nor with anyone. He starts to dance with his wife again.

Beneatha.   Old-fashioned.

Walter (*as he dances with Ruth*).   You know, when these *New Negroes* have their convention — (*Pointing at his sister.*) — that is going to be the chairman of the Committee on Unending Agitation. (*He goes on dancing, then stops.*) Race, race, race! . . . Girl, I do believe you are the first person in the history of the entire human race to successfully brainwash yourself. (*Beneatha breaks up and he goes on dancing. He stops again, enjoying his tease.*) Damn, even the N double A C P takes a holiday sometimes! (*Beneatha and Ruth laugh. He dances with Ruth some more and starts to laugh and stops and pantomimes someone over an operating table.*) I can just see that chick someday looking down at some poor cat on an operating table and before she starts to slice him, she says . . . (*Pulling his sleeves back maliciously.*) "By the way, what are your views on civil rights down there? . . ."

He laughs at her again and starts to dance happily. The bell sounds.

Beneatha.   Sticks and stones may break my bones but . . . words will never hurt me!

Beneatha goes to the door and opens it as Walter and Ruth go on with the clowning. Beneatha is somewhat surprised to see a quiet-looking middle-aged white man in a business suit holding his hat and a briefcase in his hand and consulting a small piece of paper.

Man.   Uh — how do you do, miss. I am looking for a Mrs. — *(He looks at the slip of paper.)* Mrs. Lena Younger? *(He stops short, struck dumb at the sight of the oblivious Walter and Ruth.)*

Beneatha *(smoothing her hair with slight embarrassment).*   Oh — yes, that's my mother. Excuse me. *(She closes the door and turns to quiet the other two.)* Ruth! Brother! *(Enunciating precisely but soundlessly: "There's a white man at the door!" They stop dancing, Ruth cuts off the phonograph, Beneatha opens the door. The man casts a curious quick glance at all of them.)* Uh — come in please.

Man *(coming in).*   Thank you.

Beneatha.   My mother isn't here just now. Is it business?

Man.   Yes . . . well, of a sort.

Walter *(freely, the Man of the House).*   Have a seat. I'm Mrs. Younger's son. I look after most of her business matters.

Ruth and Beneatha exchange amused glances.

Man *(regarding Walter, and sitting).*   Well — My name is Karl Lindner . . .

Walter *(stretching out his hand).*   Walter Younger. This is my wife — *(Ruth nods politely.)* — and my sister.

Lindner.   How do you do.

Walter *(amiably, as he sits himself easily on a chair, leaning forward on his knees with interest and looking expectantly into the newcomer's face).*   What can we do for you, Mr. Lindner!

Lindner *(some minor shuffling of the hat and briefcase on his knees).*   Well — I am a representative of the Clybourne Park Improvement Association —

Walter *(pointing).*   Why don't you sit your things on the floor?

Lindner.   Oh — yes. Thank you. *(He slides the briefcase and hat under the chair.)* And as I was saying — I am from the Clybourne Park Improvement Association and we have had it brought to our attention at the last meeting that you people — or at least your mother — has bought a piece of residential property at — *(He digs for the slip of paper again.)* — four o six Clybourne Street . . .

Walter.   That's right. Care for something to drink? Ruth, get Mr. Lindner a beer.

Lindner *(upset for some reason).*   Oh — no, really. I mean thank you very much, but no thank you.

Ruth *(innocently).*   Some coffee?

Lindner.   Thank you, nothing at all.

Beneatha is watching the man carefully.

Lindner.   Well, I don't know how much you folks know about our organization. *(He is a gentle man; thoughtful and somewhat labored in his manner.)* It is one of these community organizations set up to look after — oh, you know, things like block upkeep and special projects and we also have what we call our New Neighbors Orientation Committee . . .

Beneatha *(drily).*   Yes — and what do they do?

Lindner *(turning a little to her and then returning the main force to Walter).* Well — it's what you might call a sort of welcoming committee, I guess. I mean they, we — I'm the chairman of the committee — go around and see the new people who move into the neighborhood and sort of give them the lowdown on the way we do things out in Clybourne Park.

Beneatha *(with appreciation of the two meanings, which escape Ruth and Walter).*   Un-huh.

Lindner.   And we also have the category of what the association calls — *(He looks elsewhere.)* — uh — special community problems . . .

Beneatha.   Yes — and what are some of those?

Walter.   Girl, let the man talk.

Lindner *(with understated relief).*   Thank you. I would sort of like to explain this thing in my own way. I mean I want to explain to you in a certain way.

Walter.   Go ahead.

Lindner.   Yes. Well. I'm going to try to get right to the point. I'm sure we'll all appreciate that in the long run.

Beneatha.   Yes.

Walter.   Be still now!

Lindner.   Well —

Ruth *(still innocently).*   Would you like another chair — you don't look comfortable.

Lindner *(more frustrated than annoyed).*   No, thank you very much. Please. Well — to get right to the point, I — *(A great breath, and he is off at last.)* I am sure you people must be aware of some of the incidents which have happened in various parts of the city when colored people have moved into certain areas — *(Beneatha exhales heavily and starts tossing a piece of fruit up and down in the air.)* Well — because we have what I think is going to be a unique type of organization in American community life — not only do we deplore that kind of thing — but we are trying to do something about it. *(Beneatha stops tossing and turns with a new and quizzical interest to the man.)* We feel — *(gaining confidence in his mission because of the interest in the faces of the people he is talking to.)* — we feel that most of the trouble in this world, when you come right down to it — *(He hits his knee for emphasis.)* — most of the trouble exists because people just don't sit down and talk to each other.

Ruth *(nodding as she might in church, pleased with the remark).*   You can say that again, mister.

Lindner *(more encouraged by such affirmation).*   That we don't try hard enough in this world to understand the other fellow's problem. The other guy's point of view.

Ruth. Now that's right.

Beneatha and Walter merely watch and listen with genuine interest.

Lindner. Yes — that's the way we feel out in Clybourne Park. And that's why I was elected to come here this afternoon and talk to you people. Friendly like, you know, the way people should talk to each other and see if we couldn't find some way to work this thing out. As I say, the whole business is a matter of *caring* about the other fellow. Anybody can see that you are a nice family of folks, hard working and honest I'm sure. *(Beneatha frowns slightly, quizzically, her head tilted regarding him.)* Today everybody knows what it means to be on the outside of *something*. And of course, there is always somebody who is out to take advantage of people who don't always understand.

Walter. What do you mean?

Lindner. Well — you see our community is made up of people who've worked hard as the dickens for years to build up that little community. They're not rich and fancy people; just hard-working, honest people who don't really have much but those little homes and a dream of the kind of community they want to raise their children in. Now, I don't say we are perfect and there is a lot wrong in some of the things they want. But you've got to admit that a man, right or wrong, has the right to want to have the neighborhood he lives in a certain kind of way. And at the moment the overwhelming majority of our people out there feel that people get along better, take more of a common interest in the life of the community, when they share a common background. I want you to believe me when I tell you that race prejudice simply doesn't enter into it. It is a matter of the people of Clybourne Park believing, rightly or wrongly, as I say, that for the happiness of all concerned that our Negro families are happier when they live in their *own* communities.

Beneatha *(with a grand and bitter gesture).* This, friends, is the Welcoming Committee!

Walter *(dumfounded, looking at Lindner).* Is this what you came marching all the way over here to tell us?

Lindner. Well, now we've been having a fine conversation. I hope you'll hear me all the way through.

Walter *(tightly).* Go ahead, man.

Lindner. You see — in the face of all the things I have said, we are prepared to make your family a very generous offer . . .

Beneatha. Thirty pieces and not a coin less!

Walter. Yeah?

Lindner *(putting on his glasses drawing a form out of the briefcase).* Our association is prepared, through the collective effort of our people, to buy the house from you at a financial gain to your family.

Ruth. Lord have mercy, ain't this the living gall!

Walter. All right, you through?

Lindner.   Well, I want to give you the exact terms of the financial arrangement —
Walter.   We don't want to hear no exact terms of no arrangements. I want to
know if you got any more to tell us 'bout getting together?
Lindner (*taking off his glasses*).   Well — I don't suppose that you feel . . . .
Walter.   Never mind how I feel — you got any more to say 'bout how people
ought to sit down and talk to each other? . . . Get out of my house, man.

He turns his back and walks to the door.

Lindner (*looking around at the hostile faces and reaching and assembling his
hat and briefcase*).   Well — I don't understand why you people are reacting
this way. What do you think you are going to gain by moving into a neighborhood where you just aren't wanted and where some elements — well —
people can get awful worked up when they feel that their whole way of life
and everything they've ever worked for is threatened.
Walter.   Get out.
Lindner (*at the door, holding a small card*).   Well — I'm sorry it went like
this.
Walter.   Get out.
Lindner (*almost sadly regarding Walter*).   You just can't force people to
change their hearts, son.

*He turns and puts his card on a table and exits. Walter pushes the door to with
stinging hatred, and stands looking at it. Ruth just sits and Beneatha just stands.
They say nothing. Mama and Travis enter.*

Mama.   Well — this all the packing got done since I left out of here this morning. I testify before God that my children got all the energy of the *dead!* What
time the moving men due?
Beneatha.   Four o'clock. You had a caller, Mama.

She is smiling, teasingly.

Mama.   Sure enough — who?
Beneatha (*her arms folded saucily*).   The Welcoming Committee.

Walter and Ruth giggle.

Mama (*innocently*).   Who?
Beneatha.   The Welcoming Committee. They said they're sure going to be
glad to see you when you get there.
Walter (*devilishly*).   Yeah, they said they can't hardly wait to see your face.

Laughter.

Mama (*sensing their facetiousness*).   What's the matter with you all?

Walter.   Ain't nothing the matter with us. We just telling you 'bout the gentle-man who came to see you this afternoon. From the Clybourne Park Improve-ment Association.

Mama.   What he want?

Ruth (*in the same mood as Beneatha and Walter*).   To welcome you, honey.

Walter.   He said they can't hardly wait. He said the one thing they don't have, that they just *dying* to have out there is a fine family of fine colored people! (*To Ruth and Beneatha.*) Ain't that right!

Ruth (*mockingly*).   Yeah! He left his card —

Beneatha (*handing card to Mama*).   In case.

Mama reads and throws it on the floor — understanding and looking off as she draws her chair up to the table on which she has put her plant and some sticks and some cord.

Mama.   Father, give us strength. (*Knowingly — and without fun.*) Did he threaten us?

Beneatha.   Oh — Mama — they don't do it like that any more. He talked Brotherhood. He said everybody ought to learn how to sit down and hate each other with good Christian fellowship.

She and Walter shake hands to ridicule the remark.

Mama (*sadly*).   Lord, protect us . . .

Ruth.   You should hear the money those folks raised to buy the house from us. All we paid and then some.

Beneatha.   What they think we going to do — eat 'em?

Ruth.   No, honey, marry 'em.

Mama (*shaking her head*).   Lord, Lord, Lord . . .

Ruth.   Well — that's the way the crackers crumble. (*A beat.*) Joke.

Beneatha (*laughingly noticing what her mother is doing*).   Mama, what are you doing?

Mama.   Fixing my plant so it won't get hurt none on the way . . .

Beneatha.   Mama, you going to take *that* to the new house?

Mama.   Un-huh —

Beneatha.   That raggedy-looking old thing?

Mama (*stopping and looking at her*).   It expresses ME!

Ruth (*with delight, to Beneatha*).   So there, Miss Thing!

Walter comes to Mama suddenly and bends down behind her and squeezes her in his arms with all his strength. She is overwhelmed by the suddenness of it and, though delighted, her manner is like that of Ruth and Travis.

Mama.   Look out now, boy! You make me mess up my thing here!

Walter *(his face lit, he slips down on his knees beside her, his arms still about her).*   Mama . . . you know what it means to climb up in the chariot?
Mama *(gruffly, very happy).*   Get on away from me now . . .
Ruth *(near the gift-wrapped package, trying to catch Walter's eye).*   Psst —
Walter.   What the old song say, Mama . . .
Ruth.   Walter — Now?

She is pointing at the package.

Walter *(speaking the lines, sweetly, playfully, in his mother's face).*

I got wings . . . you got wings . . .
All God's Children got wings . . .

Mama.   Boy — get out of my face and do some work . . .
Walter.

When I get to heaven gonna put on my wings,
Gonna fly all over God's heaven . . .

Beneatha *(teasingly, from across the room).*   Everybody talking 'bout heaven ain't going there!
Walter *(to Ruth, who is carrying the box across to them).*   I don't know, you think we ought to give her that . . . Seems to me she ain't been very appreciative around here.
Mama *(eying the box, which is obviously a gift).*   What is that?
Walter *(taking it from Ruth and putting it on the table in front of Mama).*   Well — what you all think? Should we give it to her?
Ruth.   Oh — she was pretty good today.
Mama.   I'll good you —

She turns her eyes to the box again.

Beneatha.   Open it, Mama.

She stands up, looks at it, turns and looks at all of them, and then presses her hands together and does not open the package.

Walter *(sweetly).*   Open it, Mama. It's for you. (*Mama looks in his eyes. It is the first present in her life without its being Christmas. Slowly she opens her package and lifts out, one by one, a brand-new sparkling set of gardening tools. Walter continues, prodding.*) Ruth made up the note — read it . . .
Mama *(picking up the card and adjusting her glasses).*   "To our own Mrs. Miniver — Love from Brother, Ruth, and Beneatha." Ain't that lovely . . .
Travis *(tugging at his father's sleeve).*   Daddy, can I give her mine now?
Walter.   All right, son. (*Travis flies to get his gift.*)
Mama.   Now I don't have to use my knives and forks no more . . .

Walter. Travis didn't want to go in with the rest of us, Mama. He got his own. (*Somewhat amused.*) We don't know what it is . . .

Travis (*racing back in the room with a large hatbox and putting it in front of his grandmother*). Here!

Mama. Lord have mercy, baby. You done gone and bought your grandmother a hat?

Travis (*very proud*). Open it!

She does and lifts out an elaborate, but very elaborate, wide gardening hat, and all the adults break up at the sight of it.

Ruth. Travis, honey, what is that?

Travis (*who thinks it is beautiful and appropriate*). It's a gardening hat! Like the ladies always have on in the magazines when they work in their gardens.

Beneatha (*giggling fiercely*). Travis — we were trying to make Mama Mrs. Miniver — not Scarlett O'Hara!

Mama (*indignantly*). What's the matter with you all! This here is a beautiful hat! (*Absurdly.*) I always wanted me one just like it!

She pops it on her head to prove it to her grandson, and the hat is ludicrous and considerably oversized.

Ruth. Hot dog! Go, Mama!

Walter (*doubled over with laughter*). I'm sorry, Mama — but you look like you ready to go out and chop you some cotton sure enough!

They all laugh except Mama, out of deference to Travis's feelings.

Mama (*gathering the boy up to her*). Bless your heart — this is the prettiest hat I ever owned — (*Walter, Ruth, and Beneatha chime in — noisily, festively, and insincerely congratulating Travis on his gift.*) What are we all standing around here for? We ain't finished packin' yet. Bennie, you ain't packed one book.

The bell rings.

Beneatha. That couldn't be the movers . . . it's not hardly two good yet —

Beneatha goes into her room. Mama starts for door.

Walter (*turning, stiffening*). Wait — wait — I'll get it.

He stands and looks at the door.

Mama. You expecting company, son?

Walter (*just looking at the door*).   Yeah — yeah . . .

Mama looks at Ruth, and they exchange innocent and unfrightened glances.

Mama (*not understanding*).   Well, let them in, son.
Beneatha (*from her room*).   We need some more string.
Mama.   Travis — you run to the hardware and get me some string cord.

Mama goes out and Walter turns and looks at Ruth. Travis goes to a dish for money.

Ruth.   Why don't you answer the door, man?
Walter (*suddenly bounding across the floor to embrace her*).   'Cause some-times it hard to let the future begin! (*Stooping down in her face.*)

I got wings! You got wings!
All God's children got wings!

He crosses to the door and throws it open. Standing there is a very slight little man in a not-too-prosperous business suit and with haunted frightened eyes and a hat pulled down tightly, brim up, around his forehead. Travis passes between the men and exits. Walter leans deep in the man's face, still in his jubilance.

When I get to heaven gonna put on my wings,
Gonna fly all over God's heaven . . .

The little man just stares at him.

Heaven —

Suddenly he stops and looks past the little man into the empty hallway.

Where's Willy, man?
Bobo.   He ain't with me.
Walter (*not disturbed*).   Oh — come on in. You know my wife.
Bobo (*dumbly, taking off his hat*).   Yes — h'you, Miss Ruth.
Ruth (*quietly, a mood apart from her husband already, seeing Bobo*).   Hello, Bobo.
Walter.   You right on time today . . . Right on time. That's the way! (*He slaps Bobo on his back.*) Sit down . . . lemme hear.

Ruth stands stiffly and quietly in back of them, as though somehow she senses death, her eyes fixed on her husband.

Bobo (*his frightened eyes on the floor, his hat in his hands*).   Could I please get a drink of water, before I tell you about it, Walter Lee?

Walter does not take his eyes off the man. Ruth goes blindly to the tap and gets a glass of water and brings it to Bobo.

Walter.   There ain't nothing wrong, is there?

Bobo.   Lemme tell you —

Walter.   Man — didn't nothing go wrong?

Bobo.   Lemme tell you — Walter Lee. *(Looking at Ruth and talking to her more than to Walter.)* You know how it was. I got to tell you how it was. I mean first I got to tell you how it was all the way . . . I mean about the money I put in, Walter Lee . . .

Walter *(with taut agitation now).*   What about the money you put in?

Bobo.   Well — it wasn't much as we told you — me and Willy — *(He stops.)* I'm sorry, Walter. I got a bad feeling about it. I got a real bad feeling about it . . .

Walter.   Man, what you telling me about all this for? . . . Tell me what happened in Springfield . . .

Bobo.   Springfield.

Ruth *(like a dead woman).*   What was supposed to happen in Springfield?

Bobo *(to her).*   This deal that me and Walter went into with Willy — Me and Willy was going to go down to Springfield and spread some money 'round so's we wouldn't have to wait so long for the liquor license . . . That's what we were going to do. Everybody said that was the way you had to do, you understand, Miss Ruth?

Walter.   Man — what happened down there?

Bobo *(a pitiful man, near tears).*   I'm trying to tell you, Walter.

Walter *(screaming at him suddenly).*   THEN TELL ME, GODDAMMIT . . . WHAT'S THE MATTER WITH YOU?

Bobo.   Man . . . I didn't go to no Springfield, yesterday.

Walter *(halted, life hanging in the moment).*   Why not?

Bobo *(the long way, the hard way to tell).*   'Cause I didn't have no reasons to . . .

Walter.   Man, what are you talking about!

Bobo.   I'm talking about the fact that when I got to the train station yesterday morning — eight o'clock like we planned . . . Man — *Willy didn't never show up.*

Walter.   Why . . . where was he . . . where is he?

Bobo.   That's what I'm trying to tell you . . . I don't know . . . I waited six hours . . . I called his house . . . and I waited . . . six hours . . . I waited in that train station six hours . . . *(Breaking into tears.)* That was all the extra money I had in the world . . . *(Looking up at Walter with the tears running down his face.)* Man, *Willy is gone.*

Walter.   Gone, what you mean Willy is gone? Gone where? You mean he went by himself. You mean he went off to Springfield by himself — to take care of getting the license — *(Turns and looks anxiously at Ruth.)* You mean maybe he didn't want too many people in on the business down there? *(Looks to*

Ruth again, as before.) You know Willy got his own ways. *(Looks back to Bobo.)* Maybe you was late yesterday and he just went on down there without you. Maybe — maybe — he's been callin' you at home tryin' to tell you what happened or something. Maybe — maybe — he just got sick. He's somewhere — he's got to be somewhere. We just got to find him — me and you got to find him. *(Grabs Bobo senselessly by the collar and starts to shake him.)* We got to!

Bobo *(in sudden angry, frightened agony).* What's the matter with you, Walter! *When a cat take off with your money he don't leave you no road maps!*

Walter *(turning madly, as though he is looking for Willy in the very room).* Willy! . . . Willy . . . don't do it . . . Please don't do it . . . Man, not with that money . . . Man, please, not with that money . . . Oh, God . . . Don't let it be true . . . *(He is wandering around, crying out for Willy and looking for him or perhaps for help from God.)* Man . . . I trusted you . . . Man, I put my life in your hands . . . *(He starts to crumple down on the floor as Ruth just covers her face in horror. Mama opens the door and comes into the room, with Beneatha behind her.)* Man . . . *(He starts to pound the floor with his fists, sobbing wildly.)* THAT MONEY IS MADE OUT OF MY FATHER'S FLESH —

Bobo *(standing over him helplessly).* I'm sorry, Walter . . . *(only Walter's sobs reply. Bobo puts on his hat.)* I had my life staked on this deal, too . . .

He exits.

Mama *(to Walter).* Son — *(She goes to him, bends down to him, talks to his bent head.)* Son . . . Is it gone? Son, I gave you sixty-five hundred dollars. Is it gone? All of it? Beneatha's money too?

Walter *(lifting his head slowly).* Mama . . . I never . . . went to the bank at all . . .

Mama *(not wanting to believe him).* You mean . . . your sister's school money . . . you used that too . . . Walter? . . .

Walter. Yessss! All of it . . . It's all gone . . .

There is total silence. Ruth stands with her face covered with her hands; Beneatha leans forlornly against a wall, fingering a piece of red ribbon from the mother's gift. Mama stops and looks at her son without recognition and then, quite without thinking about it, starts to beat him senselessly in the face. Beneatha goes to them and stops it.

Beneatha. Mama!

Mama stops and looks at both of her children and rises slowly and wanders vaguely, aimlessly away from them.

Mama. I seen . . . him . . . night after night . . . come in . . . and look at that rug . . . and then look at me . . . the red showing in his eyes . . . the veins moving in his head . . . I seen him grow thin and old before he was forty . . . working and working and working like somebody's old horse . . . killing himself . . . and you — you give it all away in a day — (*She raises her arms to strike him again.*)

Beneatha. Mama —

Mama. Oh, God . . . (*She looks up to Him.*) Look down here — and show me the strength.

Beneatha. Mama —

Mama (*folding over*). Strength . . .

Beneatha (*plaintively*). Mama . . .

Mama. Strength!

Curtain.

Act III

Time: An hour later.

At curtain, there is a sullen light of gloom in the living room, gray light not unlike that which began the first scene of Act I. At left we can see Walter within his room, alone with himself. He is stretched out on the bed, his shirt out and open, his arms under his head. He does not smoke, he does not cry out, he merely lies there, looking up at the ceiling, much as if he were alone in the world.

In the living room Beneatha sits at the table, still surrounded by the now almost ominous packing crates. She sits looking off. We feel that this is a mood struck perhaps an hour before, and it lingers now, full of the empty sound of profound disappointment. We see on a line from her brother's bedroom the sameness of their attitudes. Presently the bell rings and Beneatha rises without ambition or interest in answering. It is Asagai, smiling broadly, striding into the room with energy and happy expectation and conversation.

Asagai. I came over . . . I had some free time. I thought I might help with the packing. Ah, I like the look of packing crates! A household in preparation for a journey! It depresses some people . . . but for me . . . it is another feeling. Something full of the flow of life, do you understand? Movement, progress . . . It makes me think of Africa.

Beneatha. Africa!

Asagai. What kind of a mood is this? Have I told you how deeply you move me?

Beneatha. He gave away the money, Asagai . . .

Asagai. Who gave away what money?

Beneatha. The insurance money. My brother gave it away.

Asagai. Gave it away?

Beneatha. He made an investment! With a man even Travis wouldn't have trusted with his most worn-out marbles.

Asagai. And it's gone?

Beneatha. Gone!

Asagai. I'm very sorry . . . And you, now?

Beneatha. Me? . . . Me? . . . Me, I'm nothing . . . Me. When I was very small . . . we used to take our sleds out in the wintertime and the only hills we had were the ice-covered stone steps of some houses down the street. And we used to fill them in with snow and make them smooth and slide down them all day . . . and it was very dangerous, you know . . . far too steep . . . and sure enough one day a kid named Rufus came down too fast and hit the sidewalk and we saw his face just split open right there in front of us . . . And I remember standing there looking at his bloody open face thinking that was the end of Rufus. But the ambulance came and they took him to the hospital and they fixed the broken bones and they sewed it all up . . . and the next time I saw Rufus he just had a little line down the middle of his face . . . I never got over that . . .

Asagai. What?

Beneatha. That that was what one person could do for another, fix him up — sew up the problem, make him all right again. That was the most marvelous thing in the world . . . I wanted to do that. I always thought it was the one concrete thing in the world that a human being could do. Fix up the sick, you know — and make them whole again. This was truly being God . . .

Asagai. You wanted to be God?

Beneatha. No — I wanted to cure. It used to be so important to me. I wanted to cure. It used to matter. I used to care. I mean about people and how their bodies hurt . . .

Asagai. And you've stopped caring?

Beneatha. Yes — I think so.

Asagai. Why?

Beneatha (*bitterly*). Because it doesn't seem deep enough, close enough to what ails mankind! It was a child's way of seeing things — or an idealist's.

Asagai. Children see things very well sometimes — and idealists even better.

Beneatha. I know that's what you think. Because you are still where I left off. You with all your talk and dreams about Africa! You still think you can patch up the world. Cure the Great Sore of Colonialism — (*Loftily, mocking it.*) with the Penicillin of Independence —!

Asagai. Yes!

Beneatha. Independence *and then what?* What about all the crooks and thieves and just plain idiots who will come into power and steal and plunder the same as before — only now they will be black and do it in the name of the new Independence — WHAT ABOUT THEM?!

Asagai. That will be the problem for another time. First we must get there.

Beneatha. And where does it end?

Asagai. End? Who even spoke of an end? To life? To living?

Beneatha. An end to misery! To stupidity! Don't you see there isn't any real progress, Asagai, there is only one large circle that we march in, around and around, each of us with our own little picture in front of us — our own little mirage that we think is the future.

Asagai. That is the mistake.

Beneatha. What?

Asagai. What you just said — about the circle. It isn't a circle — it is simply a long line — as in geometry, you know, one that reaches into infinity. And because we cannot see the end — we also cannot see how it changes. And it is very odd but those who see the changes — who dream, who will not give up — are called idealists . . . and those who see only the circle — we call *them* the "realists"!

Beneatha. Asagai, while I was sleeping in that bed in there, people went out and took the future right out of my hands! And nobody asked me, nobody consulted me — they just went out and changed my life!

Asagai. Was it your money?

Beneatha. What?

Asagai. Was it your money he gave away?

Beneatha. It belonged to all of us.

Asagai. But did you earn it? Would you have had it at all if your father had not died?

Beneatha. No.

Asagai. Then isn't there something wrong in a house — in a world — where all dreams, good or bad, must depend on the death of a man? I never thought to see *you* like this, Alaiyo. You! Your brother made a mistake and you are grateful to him so that now you can give up the ailing human race on account of it! You talk about what good is struggle, what good is anything! Where are we all going and why are we bothering!

Beneatha. AND YOU CANNOT ANSWER IT!

Asagai *(shouting over her).* I LIVE THE ANSWER! *(Pause.)* In my village at home it is the exceptional man who can even read a newspaper . . . or who ever sees a book at all. I will go home and much of what I will have to say will seem strange to the people of my village. But I will teach and work and things will happen, slowly and swiftly. At times it will seem that nothing changes at all . . . and then again the sudden dramatic events which make history leap into the future. And then quiet again. Retrogression even. Guns, murder, revolution. And I even will have moments when I wonder if the quiet was not better than all that death and hatred. But I will look about my village at the illiteracy and disease and ignorance and I will not wonder long. And perhaps . . . perhaps I will be a great man . . . I mean perhaps I will hold on to the substance of truth and find my way always with the right course . . . and perhaps for it I will be butchered in my bed some night by the servants of empire . . .

Beneatha. *The martyr!*

Asagai *(he smiles).* . . . or perhaps I shall live to be a very old man, respected and esteemed in my new nation . . . And perhaps I shall hold office and this is what I'm trying to tell you, Alaiyo: perhaps the things I believe now for my country will be wrong and outmoded, and I will not understand and do terrible things to have things my way or merely to keep my power. Don't you see that there will be young men and women — not British soldiers then, but my own black countrymen — to step out of the shadows some evening and slit my then useless throat? Don't you see they have always been there . . . that they always will be. And that such a thing as my own death will be an advance? They who might kill me even . . . actually replenish all that I was.

Beneatha.   Oh, Asagai, I know all that.

Asagai.   Good! Then stop moaning and groaning and tell me what you plan to do.

Beneatha.   Do?

Asagai.   I have a bit of a suggestion.

Beneatha.   What?

Asagai (*rather quietly for him*).   That when it is all over — that you come home with me —

Beneatha (*staring at him and crossing away with exasperation*).   Oh — Asagai — at this moment you decide to be romantic!

Asagai (*quickly understanding the misunderstanding*).   My dear, young creature of the New World — I do not mean across the city — I mean across the ocean: home — to Africa.

Beneatha (*slowly understanding and turning to him with murmured amazement*). To Africa?

Asagai.   Yes! . . . (*smiling and lifting his arms playfully.*) Three hundred years later the African Prince rose up out of the seas and swept the maiden back across the middle passage over which her ancestors had come —

Beneatha (*unable to play*).   To — to Nigeria?

Asagai.   Nigeria. Home. (*Coming to her with genuine romantic flippancy.*) I will show you our mountains and our stars; and give you cool drinks from gourds and teach you the old songs and the ways of our people — and, in time, we will pretend that — (*Very softly.*) — you have only been away for a day. Say that you'll come — (*He swings her around and takes her full in his arms in a kiss which proceeds to passion.*)

Beneatha (*pulling away suddenly*).   You're getting me all mixed up —

Asagai.   Why?

Beneatha.   Too many things — too many things have happened today. I must sit down and think. I don't know what I feel about anything right this minute.

She promptly sits down and props her chin on her fist.

Asagai (*charmed*).   All right, I shall leave you. No — don't get up. (*Touching her, gently, sweetly.*) Just sit awhile and think . . . Never be afraid to sit awhile and think. (*He goes to door and looks at her.*) How often I have looked at you and said, "Ah — so this is what the New World hath finally wrought . . ."

He exits. Beneatha sits on alone. Presently Walter enters from his room and starts to rummage through things, feverishly looking for something. She looks up and turns in her seat.

Beneatha *(hissingly).* Yes — just look at what the New World hath wrought! . . . Just look! *(She gestures with bitter disgust.)* There he is! *Monsieur le petit bourgeois noir*[2] — himself! There he is — Symbol of a Rising Class! Entrepreneur! Titan of the system! *(Walter ignores her completely and continues frantically and destructively looking for something and hurling things to floor and tearing things out of their place in his search. Beneatha ignores the eccentricity of his actions and goes on with the monologue of insult.)* Did you dream of yachts on Lake Michigan, Brother? Did you see yourself on that Great Day sitting down at the Conference Table, surrounded by all the mighty bald-headed men in America? All halted, waiting, breathless, waiting for your pronouncements on industry? Waiting for you — Chairman of the Board! *(Walter finds what he is looking for — a small piece of white paper — and pushes it in his pocket and puts on his coat and rushes out without ever having looked at her. She shouts after him.)* I look at you and I see the final triumph of stupidity in the world!

The door slams and she returns to just sitting again. Ruth comes quickly out of Mama's room.

Ruth. Who was that?
Beneatha. Your husband.
Ruth. Where did he go?
Beneatha. Who knows — maybe he has an appointment at U.S. Steel.
Ruth *(anxiously, with frightened eyes).* You didn't say nothing bad to him, did you?
Beneatha. Bad? Say anything bad to him? No — I told him he was a sweet boy and full of dreams and everything is strictly peachy keen, as the ofay kids say!

Mama enters from her bedroom. She is lost, vague, trying to catch hold, to make some sense of her former command of the world, but it still eludes her. A sense of waste overwhelms her gait; a measure of apology rides on her shoulders. She goes to her plant, which has remained on the table, looks at it, picks it up and takes it to the window sill and sits it outside, and she stands and looks at it a long moment. Then she closes the window, straightens her body with effort and turns around to her children.

Mama. Well — ain't it a mess in here, though? *(A false cheerfulness, a beginning of something.)* I guess we all better stop moping around and get some work done. All this unpacking and everything we got to do. *(Ruth raises her*

---

[2] Mr. Black Bourgeoisie (French).

head slowly in response to the sense of the line; and Beneatha in similar manner turns very slowly to look at her mother.) One of you all better call the moving people and tell 'em not to come.

Ruth.   Tell 'em not to come?

Mama.   Of course, baby. Ain't no need in 'em coming all the way here and having to go back. They charges for that too. *(She sits down, fingers to her brow, thinking.)* Lord, ever since I was a little girl, I always remembers people saying, "Lena — Lena Eggleston, you aims too high all the time. You needs to slow down and see life a little more like it is. Just slow down some." That's what they always used to say down home — "Lord, that Lena Eggleston is a high-minded thing. She'll get her due one day!"

Ruth.   No, Lena . . .

Mama.   Me and Big Walter just didn't never learn right.

Ruth.   Lena, no! We gotta go. Bennie — tell her . . .

She rises and crosses to Beneatha with her arms outstretched. Beneatha doesn't respond.

Tell her we can still move . . . the notes ain't but a hundred and twenty-five a month. We got four grown people in this house — we can work . . .

Mama *(to herself).*   Just aimed too high all the time —

Ruth *(turning and going to Mama fast — the words pouring out with urgency and desperation).*   Lena — I'll work . . . I'll work twenty hours a day in all the kitchens in Chicago . . . I'll strap my baby on my back if I have to and scrub all the floors in America and wash all the sheets in America if I have to — but we got to MOVE! We got to get OUT OF HERE!!

Mama reaches out absently and pats Ruth's hand.

Mama.   No — I sees things differently now. Been thinking 'bout some of the things we could do to fix this place up some. I seen a second-hand bureau over on Maxwell Street just the other day that could fit right there. *(She points to where the new furniture might go. Ruth wanders away from her.)* Would need some new handles on it and then a little varnish and it look like something brand-new. And — we can put up them new curtains in the kitchen . . . Why this place be looking fine. Cheer us all up so that we forget trouble ever come . . . *(To Ruth.)* And you could get some nice screens to put up in your room round the baby's bassinet . . . *(She looks at both of them pleadingly.)* Sometimes you just got to know when to give up some things . . . and hold on to what you got . . .

Walter enters from the outside, looking spent and leaning against the door, his coat hanging from him.

Mama.   Where you been, son?

Walter *(breathing hard).*   Made a call.

Mama.   To who, son?

Walter.   To The Man. *(He heads for his room.)*

Mama.   What man, baby?

Walter *(stops in the door).*   The Man, Mama. Don't you know who The Man is?

Ruth.   Walter Lee?

Walter.   *The Man.* Like the guys in the streets say — The Man. Captain Boss — Mistuh Charley . . . Old Cap'n Please Mr. Bossman . . .

Beneatha *(suddenly).*   Lindner!

Walter.   That's right! That's good. I told him to come right over.

Beneatha *(fiercely, understanding).*   For what? What do you want to see him for!

Walter *(looking at his sister).*   We going to do business with him.

Mama.   What you talking 'bout, son?

Walter.   Talking 'bout life, Mama. You all always telling me to see life like it is. Well — I laid in there on my back today . . . and I figured it out. Life just like it is. Who gets and who don't get. *(He sits down with his coat on and laughs.)* Mama, you know it's all divided up. Life is. Sure enough. Between the takers and the "tooken." *(He laughs.)* I've figured it out finally. *(He looks around at them.)* Yeah. Some of us always getting "tooken." *(He laughs.)* People like Willy Harris, they don't never get "tooken." And you know why the rest of us do? 'Cause we all mixed up. Mixed up bad. We get to looking 'round for the right and the wrong; and we worry about it and cry about it and stay up nights trying to figure out 'bout the wrong and the right of things all the time . . . And all the time, man, them takers is out there operating, just taking and taking. Willy Harris? Shoot — Willy Harris don't even count. He don't even count in the big scheme of things. But I'll say one thing for old Willy Harris . . . he's taught me something. He's taught me to keep my eye on what counts in this world. Yeah — *(Shouting out a little.)* Thanks, Willy!

Ruth.   What did you call that man for, Walter Lee?

Walter.   Called him to tell him to come on over to the show. Gonna put on a show for the man. Just what he wants to see. You see, Mama, the man came here today and he told us that them people out there where you want us to move — well they so upset they willing to pay us *not* to move! *(He laughs again.)* And — and oh, Mama — you would of been proud of the way me and Ruth and Bennie acted. We told him to get out . . . Lord have mercy! We told the man to get out! Oh, we was some proud folks this afternoon, yeah. *(He lights a cigarette.)* We were still full of that old-time stuff . . .

Ruth *(coming toward him slowly).*   You talking 'bout taking them people's money to keep us from moving in that house?

Walter.   I ain't just talking 'bout it, baby — I'm telling you that's what's going to happen!

Beneatha.   Oh, God! Where is the bottom! Where is the real honest-to-God bottom so he can't go any farther!

Walter. See — that's the old stuff. You and that boy that was here today. You all want everybody to carry a flag and a spear and sing some marching songs, huh? You wanna spend your life looking into things and trying to find the right and the wrong part, huh? Yeah. You know what's going to happen to that boy someday — he'll find himself sitting in a dungeon, locked in forever — and the takers will have the key! Forget it, baby! There ain't no causes — there ain't nothing but taking in this world, and he who takes most is smartest — and it don't make a damn bit of difference *how*.

Mama. You making something inside me cry, son. Some awful pain inside me.

Walter. Don't cry, Mama. Understand. That white man is going to walk in that door able to write checks for more money than we ever had. It's important to him and I'm going to help him . . . I'm going to put on the show, Mama.

Mama. Son — I come from five generations of people who was slaves and sharecroppers — but ain't nobody in my family never let nobody pay 'em no money that was a way of telling us we wasn't fit to walk the earth. We ain't never been that poor. (*Raising her eyes and looking at him.*) We ain't never been that — dead inside.

Beneatha. Well — we are dead now. All the talk about dreams and sunlight that goes on in this house. It's all dead now.

Walter. What's the matter with you all! I didn't make this world! It was give to me this way! Hell, yes, I want me some yachts someday! Yes, I want to hang some real pearls 'round my wife's neck. Ain't she supposed to wear no pearls? Somebody tell me — tell me, who decides which women is suppose to wear pearls in this world. I tell you I am a *man* — and I think my wife should wear some pearls in this world!

This last line hangs a good while and Walter begins to move about the room. The word "Man" has penetrated his consciousness; he mumbles it to himself repeatedly between strange agitated pauses as he moves about.

Mama. Baby, how you going to feel on the inside?

Walter. Fine! . . . Going to feel fine . . . a man . . .

Mama. You won't have nothing left then, Walter Lee.

Walter (*coming to her*). I'm going to feel fine, Mama. I'm going to look that son-of-a-bitch in the eyes and say — (*He falters.*) — and say, "All right, Mr. Lindner — (*He falters even more.*) — that's *your* neighborhood out there! You got the right to keep it like you want! You got the right to have it like you want! Just write the check and — the house is yours." And — and I am going to say — (*His voice almost breaks.*) "And you — you people just put the money in my hand and you won't have to live next to this bunch of stinking niggers! . . ." (*He straightens up and moves away from his mother, walking around the room.*) And maybe — maybe I'll just get down on my black knees . . . (*He does so; Ruth and Bennie and Mama watch him in frozen horror.*) "Captain, Mistuh, Bossman — (*Groveling and grinning and wringing* *his hands in profoundly anguished imitation of the slow-witted movie stereo-type.)* A-hee-hee-hee! Oh, yassuh boss! Yasssssuh! Great white — *(Voice breaking, he forces himself to go on.)* — Father, just gi' ussen de money, fo' God's sake, and we's — we's ain't gwine come out deh and dirty up yo' white folks neighborhood . . ." *(He breaks down completely.)* And I'll feel fine! Fine! FINE! *(He gets up and goes into the bedroom.)*

Beneatha. That is not a man. That is nothing but a toothless rat.

Mama. Yes — death done come in this here house. *(She is nodding, slowly, reflectively.)* Done come walking in my house on the lips of my children. You what supposed to be my beginning again. You — what supposed to be my harvest. *(To Beneatha.)* You — you mourning your brother?

Beneatha. He's no brother of mine.

Mama. What you say?

Beneatha. I said that that individual in that room is no brother of mine.

Mama. That's what I thought you said. You feeling like you better than he is today? *(Beneatha does not answer.)* Yes? What you tell him a minute ago? That he wasn't a man? Yes? You give him up for me? You done wrote his epitaph too — like the rest of the world? Well, who give you the privilege?

Beneatha. Be on my side for once! You saw what he just did, Mama! You saw him — down on his knees. Wasn't it you who taught me to despise any man who would do that? Do what he's going to do?

Mama. Yes — I taught you that. Me and your daddy. But I thought I taught you something else too . . . I thought I taught you to love him.

Beneatha. Love him? There is nothing left to love.

Mama. There is *always* something left to love. And if you ain't learned that, you ain't learned nothing. *(Looking at her.)* Have you cried for that boy today? I don't mean for yourself and for the family 'cause we lost the money. I mean for him: what he been through and what it done to him. Child, when do you think is the time to love somebody the most? When they done good and made things easy for everybody? Well then, you ain't through learning — because that ain't the time at all. It's when he's at his lowest and can't believe in hisself 'cause the world done whipped him so! When you starts measuring somebody, measure him right, child, measure him right. Make sure you done taken into account what hills and valleys he come through before he got to wherever he is.

Travis bursts into the room at the end of the speech, leaving the door open.

Travis. Grandmama — the moving men are downstairs! The truck just pulled up.

Mama *(turning and looking at him).* Are they, baby? They downstairs?

She sighs and sits. Lindner appears in the doorway. He peers in and knocks lightly, to gain attention, and comes in. All turn to look at him.

Lindner *(hat and briefcase in hand).* Uh — hello . . .

Ruth crosses mechanically to the bedroom door and opens it and lets it swing open freely and slowly as the lights come up on Walter within, still in his coat, sitting at the far corner of the room. He looks up and out through the room to Lindner.

Ruth. He's here.

A long minute passes and Walter slowly gets up.

Lindner *(coming to the table with efficiency, putting his briefcase on the table and starting to unfold papers and unscrew fountain pens).* Well, I certainly was glad to hear from you people. *(Walter has begun the trek out of the room, slowly and awkwardly, rather like a small boy, passing the back of his sleeve across his mouth from time to time.)* Life can really be so much simpler than people let it be most of the time. Well — with whom do I negotiate? You, Mrs. Younger, or your son here? *(Mama sits with her hands folded on her lap and her eyes closed as Walter advances. Travis goes closer to Lindner and looks at the papers curiously.)* Just some official papers, sonny.

Ruth. Travis, you go downstairs —

Mama *(opening her eyes and looking into Walter's).* No. Travis, you stay right here. And you make him understand what you doing, Walter Lee. You teach him good. Like Willy Harris taught you. You show where our five generations done come to. *(Walter looks from her to the boy, who grins at him innocently.)* Go ahead, son — *(She folds her hands and closes her eyes.)* Go ahead.

Walter *(at last crosses to Lindner, who is reviewing the contract).* Well, Mr. Lindner. *(Beneatha turns away.)* We called you — *(There is a profound, simple groping quality in his speech.)* — because, well, me and my family *(He looks around and shifts from one foot to the other.)* Well — we are very plain people . . .

Lindner. Yes —

Walter. I mean — I have worked as a chauffeur most of my life — and my wife here, she does domestic work in people's kitchens. So does my mother. I mean — we are plain people . . .

Lindner. Yes, Mr. Younger —

Walter *(really like a small boy, looking down at his shoes and then up at the man).* And — uh — well, my father, well, he was a laborer most of his life. . . .

Lindner *(absolutely confused).* Uh, yes — yes, I understand. *(He turns back to the contract.)*

Walter *(a beat; staring at him).* And my father — *(With sudden intensity.)* My father almost *beat a man to death* once because this man called him a bad name or something, you know what I mean?

Lindner *(looking up, frozen).* No, no, I'm afraid I don't —

Walter *(a beat. The tension hangs; then Walter steps back from it).* Yeah. Well — what I mean is that we come from people who had a lot of *pride*. I mean — we are very proud people. And that's my sister over there and she's going to be a doctor — and we are very proud —

Lindner. Well — I am sure that is very nice, but —

Walter.   What I am telling you is that we called you over here to tell you that we are very proud and that this — (*Signaling to Travis.*) Travis, come here. (*Travis crosses and Walter draws him before him facing the man.*) This is my son, and he makes the sixth generation our family in this country. And we have all thought about your offer —

Lindner.   Well, good . . . good —

Walter.   And we have decided to move into our house because my father — my father — he earned it for us brick by brick. (*Mama has her eyes closed and is rocking back and forth as though she were in church, with her head nodding the Amen yes.*) We don't want to make no trouble for nobody or fight no causes, and we will try to be good neighbors. And that's *all* we got to say about that. (*He looks the man absolutely in the eyes.*) We don't want your money. (*He turns and walks away.*)

Lindner (*looking around at all of them*).   I take it then — that you have decided to occupy . . .

Beneatha.   That's what the man said.

Lindner (*to Mama in her reverie*).   Then I would like to appeal to you, Mrs. Younger. You are older and wiser and understand things better I am sure . . .

Mama.   I am afraid you don't understand. My son said we was going to move and there ain't nothing left for me to say. (*Briskly.*) You know how these young folks is nowadays, mister. Can't do a thing with 'em! (*As he opens his mouth, she rises.*) Good-bye.

Lindner (*folding up his materials*).   Well — if you are that final about it . . . there is nothing left for me to say. (*He finishes, almost ignored by the family, who are concentrating on Walter Lee. At the door Lindner halts and looks around.*) I sure hope you people know what you're getting into.

He shakes his head and exits.

Ruth (*looking around and coming to life*).   Well, for God's sake — if the moving men are here — LET'S GET THE HELL OUT OF HERE!

Mama (*into action*).   Ain't it the truth! Look at all this here mess. Ruth, put Travis' good jacket on him . . . Walter Lee, fix your tie and tuck your shirt in, you look like somebody's hoodlum! Lord have mercy, where is my plant? (*She flies to get it amid the general bustling of the family, who are deliberately trying to ignore the nobility of the past moment.*) You all start on down . . . Travis child, don't go empty-handed . . . Ruth, where did I put that box with my skillets in it? I want to be in charge of it myself . . . I'm going to make us the biggest dinner we ever ate tonight . . . Beneatha, what's the matter with them stockings? Pull them things up, girl . . .

The family starts to file out as two moving men appear and begin to carry out the heavier pieces of furniture, bumping into the family as they move about.

Beneatha.   Mama, Asagai asked me to marry him today and go to Africa —

Mama (*in the middle of her getting-ready activity*).   He did? You ain't old enough to marry nobody — (*Seeing the moving men lifting one of her chairs precariously.*) Darling, that ain't no bale of cotton, please handle it so we can sit in it again! I had that chair twenty-five years . . .

The movers sigh with exasperation and go on with their work.

Beneatha (*girlishly and unreasonably trying to pursue the conversation*).   To go to Africa, Mama — be a doctor in Africa . . .
Mama (*distracted*).   Yes, baby —
Walter.   *Africa!* What he want you to go to Africa for?
Beneatha.   To practice there . . .
Walter.   Girl, if you don't get all them silly ideas out your head! You better marry yourself a man with some loot . . .
Beneatha (*angrily, precisely as in the first scene of the play*).   What have you got to do with who I marry!
Walter.   Plenty. Now I think George Murchison —
Beneatha.   *George Murchison!* I wouldn't marry him if he was Adam and I was Eve!

Walter and Beneatha go out yelling at each other vigorously and the anger is loud and real till their voices diminish. Ruth stands at the door and turns to Mama and smiles knowingly.

Mama (*fixing her hat at last*).   Yeah — they something all right, my children . . .
Ruth.   Yeah — they're something. Let's go, Lena.
Mama (*stalling, starting to look around at the house*).   Yes — I'm coming. Ruth —
Ruth.   Yes?
Mama (*quietly, woman to woman*).   He finally come into his manhood today, didn't he? Kind of like a rainbow after the rain . . .
Ruth (*biting her lip lest her own pride explode in front of Mama*).   Yes, Lena.

Walter's voice calls for them raucously.

Walter (*off stage*).   Y'all come on! These people charges by the hour, you know!
Mama (*waving Ruth out vaguely*).   All right, honey — go on down. I be down directly.

Ruth hesitates, then exits. Mama stands, at last alone in the living room, her plant on the table before her as the lights start to come down. She looks around at all the walls and ceilings and suddenly, despite herself, while the children call below, a great heaving thing rises in her and she puts her fist to her mouth to stifle it, takes a final desperate look, pulls her coat about her, pats her hat, and goes out. The lights dim down. The door opens and she comes back in, grabs her plant, and goes out for the last time.

Curtain.

For Analysis

1. In what ways does the opening dialogue between Ruth and Walter establish the major themes of the play?

2. Characterize the shared values and dreams that give the family its cohesiveness.

3. Describe Walter's view of women. Is his view validated by the actions of the women? Explain.

4. Describe the contrast between Beneatha's two suitors, George Murchison and Asagai, and explain how it contributes to the theme of the play.

5. What is the significance of Mama's plant?

6. In what ways does the dialogue between Beneatha and Asagai that opens Act III advance the theme of the play and prepare us for the ending?

7. Mr. Lindner asserts that "the overwhelming majority of our people out there feel that people get along better, take more of a common interest in the life of the community, when they share a common background" (Act II, Scene 3). Is this a reasonable argument? Is Mr. Lindner a racist? Explain.

8. In what sense is this play a celebration of African American life and culture?

On Style

1. Characterize the speech patterns of the main characters. What function do the differences in **diction** serve? Is there any relationship between a character's diction and his or her moral standing in the play? Explain.

2. Even though he is dead, Big Walter is an important presence in the play. Examine the ways in which his presence is created, and explain what he represents.

Making Connections

1. Compare the way in which the characters in this play react to Mr. Lindner with the way Randall Robinson and his fellow black students react to the class discussion in "Can a Black Family Be a Legal Nuisance?" (p. 659).

2. Compare and contrast the dynamics of family life in this play with those of the families in Tennessee Williams's *The Glass Menagerie* (p. 243) and Alice Walker's "Everyday Use" (p. 717). Which family do you think is more successful in coping with its problems? Explain.

Writing Topics

1. Argue for or against the proposition that this play, written over four decades ago, is dated in its portrayal of black life and race relations.

2. Read the Langston Hughes poem "Harlem" (p. 448), from which the title of the play is taken, and write an essay describing why you think Hansberry used one of its lines as the title for her play.

3. Describe the significance of money in the play.

4. Write an essay in which you speculate on what happens to the members of the Younger family once they have moved into their new home.

Athol Fugard   (b. 1932)

"MASTER HAROLD"
. . . and the Boys   1982

CHARACTERS

Hally
Sam
Willie

The St. George's Park Tea Room on a wet and windy Port Elizabeth afternoon.

Tables and chairs have been cleared and are stacked on one side except for one which stands apart with a single chair. On this table a knife, fork, spoon and side plate in anticipation of a simple meal, together with a pile of comic books.

Other elements: a serving counter with a few stale cakes under glass and a not very impressive display of sweets, cigarettes and cool drinks, etc.; a few cardboard advertising handouts — Cadbury's Chocolate, Coca-Cola — and a blackboard on which an untrained hand has chalked up the prices of Tea, Coffee, Scones, Milkshakes — all flavors — and Cool Drinks; a few sad ferns in pots; a telephone; an old-style jukebox.

There is an entrance on one side and an exit into a kitchen on the other.

Leaning on the solitary table, his head cupped in one hand as he pages through one of the comic books, is Sam. A black man in his mid-forties. He wears the white coat of a waiter. Behind him on his knees, mopping down the floor with a bucket of water and a rag, is Willie. Also black and about the same age as Sam. He has his sleeves and trousers rolled up.

The Year: 1950

Willie *(Singing as he works).*   "She was scandalizin' my name,
   She took my money
   She called me honey
   But she was scandalizin' my name.
   Called it love but was playin' a game . . ."

(He gets up and moves the bucket. Stands thinking for a moment, then, raising his arms to hold an imaginary partner, he launches into an intricate ballroom

943

dance step. Although a mildly comic figure, he reveals a reasonable degree of accomplishment)

Hey, Sam.

(Sam, absorbed in the comic book, does not respond)

Hey, Boet[1] Sam!

(Sam looks up)

I'm getting it. The quickstep. Look now and tell me. *(He repeats the step)* Well?

Sam *(Encouragingly)*.   Show me again.

Willie.   Okay, count for me.

Sam.   Ready?

Willie.   Ready.

Sam.   Five, six, seven, eight . . . *(Willie starts to dance)* A-n-d one two three four . . . and one two three four. . . . *(Ad libbing as Willie dances)* Your shoulders, Willie . . . your shoulders! Don't look down! Look happy, Willie! Relax, Willie!

Willie *(Desperate but still dancing)*.   I am relax.

Sam.   No, you're not.

Willie *(He falters)*.   Ag no man, Sam! Mustn't talk. You make me make mistakes.

Sam.   But you're too stiff.

Willie.   Yesterday I'm not straight . . . today I'm too stiff!

Sam.   Well, you are. You asked me and I'm telling you.

Willie.   Where?

Sam.   Everywhere. Try to glide through it.

Willie.   Glide?

Sam.   Ja, make it smooth. And give it more style. It must look like you're enjoying yourself.

Willie *(Emphatically)*.   I wasn't.

Sam.   Exactly.

Willie.   How can I enjoy myself? No straight, too stiff and now it's also glide, give it more style, make it smooth. . . . Haai! Is hard to remember all those things, Boet Sam.

Sam.   That's your trouble. You're trying too hard.

Willie.   I try hard because it *is* hard.

Sam.   But don't let me see it. The secret is to make it look easy. Ballroom must look happy, Willie, not like hard work. It must . . . Ja! . . . it must look like romance.

---

[1] Afrikaans, meaning "brother."

Willie. Now another one! What's romance?

Sam. Love story with happy ending. A handsome man in tails, and in his arms, smiling at him, a beautiful lady in evening dress!

Willie. Fred Astaire, Ginger Rogers.

Sam. You got it. Tapdance or ballroom, it's the same. Romance. In two weeks' time when the judges look at you and Hilda, they must see a man and a woman who are dancing their way to a happy ending. What I saw was you holding her like you were frightened she was going to run away.

Willie. Ja! Because that is what she wants to do! I got no romance left for Hilda anymore, Boet Sam.

Sam. Then pretend. When you put your arms around Hilda, imagine she is Ginger Rogers.

Willie. With no teeth? You try.

Sam. Well, just remember, there's only two weeks left.

Willie. I know, I know! *(To the jukebox)* I do it better with music. You got sixpence for Sarah Vaughan?

Sam. That's a slow foxtrot. You're practicing the quickstep.

Willie. I'll practice slow foxtrot.

Sam *(Shaking his head).* It's your turn to put money in the jukebox.

Willie. I only got bus fare to go home. *(He returns disconsolately to his work)* Love story and happy ending! She's doing it all right, Boet Sam, but is not me she's giving happy endings. Fuckin' whore! Three nights now she doesn't come practice. I wind up gramophone, I get record ready and I sit and wait. What happens? Nothing. Ten o'clock I start dancing with my pillow. You try and practice romance by yourself, Boet Sam. Struesgod,[2] she doesn't come tonight I take back my dress and ballroom shoes and I find me new partner. Size twenty-six. Shoes size seven. And now she's also making trouble for me with the baby again. Reports me to Child Wellfed, that I'm not giving her money. She lies! Every week I am giving her money for milk. And how do I know is my baby? Only his hair looks like me. She's fucking around all the time I turn my back. Hilda Samuels is a bitch! *(Pause)* Hey, Sam!

Sam. Ja.

Willie. You listening?

Sam. Ja.

Willie. So what you say?

Sam. About Hilda?

Willie. Ja.

Sam. When did you last give her a hiding?

Willie *(Reluctantly).* Sunday night.

Sam. And today is Thursday.

Willie *(He knows what's coming).* Okay.

---

[2] Regional slang, meaning "As true as God." A mild oath.

Sam. Hiding on Sunday night, then Monday, Tuesday and Wednesday she doesn't come to practice . . . and you are asking me why?

Willie. I said okay, Boet Sam!

Sam. You hit her too much. One day she's going to leave you for good.

Willie. So? She makes me the hell-in too much.

Sam (*Emphasizing his point*). *Too* much and *too* hard. You had the same trouble with Eunice.

Willie. Because she also make the hell-in, Boet Sam. She never got the steps right. Even the waltz.

Sam. Beating her up every time she makes a mistake in the waltz? (*Shaking his head*) No, Willie! That takes the pleasure out of ballroom dancing.

Willie. Hilda is not too bad with the waltz, Boet Sam. Is the quickstep where the trouble starts.

Sam (*Teasing him gently*). How's your pillow with the quickstep?

Willie (*Ignoring the tease*). Good! And why? Because it got no legs. That's her trouble. She can't move them quick enough, Boet Sam. I start the record and before halfway Count Basie is already winning. Only time we catch up with him is when gramophone runs down.

(*Sam laughs*)

Haaikona,[3] Boet Sam, is not funny.

Sam (*Snapping his fingers*). I got it! Give her a handicap.

Willie. What's that?

Sam. Give her a ten-second start and then let Count Basie go. Then I put my money on her. Hot favorite in the Ballroom Stakes: Hilda Samuels ridden by Willie Malopo.

Willie (*Turning away*). I'm not talking to you no more.

Sam (*Relenting*). Sorry, Willie . . .

Willie. It's finish between us.

Sam. Okay, okay . . . I'll stop.

Willie. You can also fuck off.

Sam. Willie, listen! I want to help you!

Willie. No more jokes?

Sam. I promise.

Willie. Okay. Help me.

Sam (*His turn to hold an imaginary partner*). Look and learn. Feet together. Back straight. Body relaxed. Right hand placed gently in the small of her back and wait for the music. Don't start worrying about making mistakes or the judges or the other competitors. It's just you, Hilda and the music, and you're going to have a good time. What Count Basie do you play?

Willie. "You the cream in my coffee, you the salt in my stew."

---

[3] Zulu word, meaning "Don't"; here meaning "Don't laugh."

Sam. Right. Give it to me in strict tempo.
Willie. Ready?
Sam. Ready.
Willie. A-n-d . . . (*Singing*)
  "You the cream in my coffee.
  You the salt in my stew.
  You will always be my necessity.
  I'd be lost without you. . . ." (*etc.*)

(*Sam launches into the quickstep. He is obviously a much more accomplished dancer than Willie. Hally enters. A seventeen-year-old white boy. Wet raincoat and school case. He stops and watches Sam. The demonstration comes to an end with a flourish. Applause from Hally and Willie*)

Hally. Bravo! No question about it. First place goes to Mr. Sam Semela.
Willie (*In total agreement*). You was gliding with style, Boet Sam.
Hally (*Cheerfully*). How's it, chaps?
Sam. Okay, Hally.
Willie (*Springing to attention like a soldier and saluting*). At your service, Master Harold!
Hally. Not long to the big event, hey!
Sam. Two weeks.
Hally. You nervous?
Sam. No.
Hally. Think you stand a chance?
Sam. Let's just say I'm ready to go out there and dance.
Hally. It looked like it. What about you, Willie?

(*Willie groans*)

  What's the matter?
Sam. He's got leg trouble.
Hally (*Innocently*). Oh, sorry to hear that, Willie.
Willie. Boet Sam! You promised. (*Willie returns to his work*)

(*Hally deposits his school case and takes off his raincoat. His clothes are a little neglected and untidy: black blazer with school badge, gray flannel trousers in need of an ironing, khaki shirt and tie, black shoes. Sam has fetched a towel for Hally to dry his hair*)

Hally. God, what a lousy bloody day. It's coming down cats and dogs out there. Bad for business, chaps . . . (*Conspiratorial whisper*) . . . but it also means we're in for a nice quiet afternoon.
Sam. You can speak loud. Your Mom's not here.

Hally. Out shopping?

Sam. No. The hospital.

Hally. But it's Thursday. There's no visiting on Thursday afternoons. Is my Dad okay?

Sam. Sounds like it. In fact, I think he's going home.

Hally (*Stopped short by Sam's remark*). What do you mean?

Sam. The hospital phoned.

Hally. To say what?

Sam. I don't know. I just heard your Mom talking.

Hally. So what makes you say he's going home?

Sam. It sounded as if they were telling her to come and fetch him.

(*Hally thinks about what Sam has said for a few seconds*)

Hally. When did she leave?

Sam. About an hour ago. She said she would phone you. Want to eat?

(*Hally doesn't respond*)

Hally, want your lunch?

Hally. I suppose so. (*His mood has changed*) What's on the menu? . . . as if I don't know.

Sam. Soup, followed by meat pie and gravy.

Hally. Today's?

Sam. No.

Hally. And the soup?

Sam. Nourishing pea soup.

Hally. Just the soup. (*The pile of comic books on the table*) And these?

Sam. For your Dad. Mr. Kempston brought them.

Hally. You haven't been reading them, have you?

Sam. Just looking.

Hally (*Examining the comics*). Jungle Jim . . . Batman and Robin . . . Tarzan . . . God, what rubbish! Mental pollution. Take them away.

(*Sam exits waltzing into the kitchen. Hally turns to Willie*)

Hally. Did you hear my Mom talking on the telephone, Willie?

Willie. No, Master Hally. I was at the back.

Hally. And she didn't say anything to you before she left?

Willie. She said I must clean the floors.

Hally. I mean about my Dad.

Willie. She didn't say anything to me about him, Master Hally.

Hally (*With conviction*). No! It can't be. They said he needed at least another three weeks of treatment. Sam's definitely made a mistake. (*Rummages*

through his school case, finds a book and settles down at the table to read) So,
Willie!

Willie.   Yes, Master Hally! Schooling okay today?

Hally.   Yes, okay. . . . *(He thinks about it)* . . . No, not really. Ag, what's the difference? I don't care. And Sam says you've got problems.

Willie.   Big problems.

Hally.   Which leg is sore?

(Willie groans)

Both legs.

Willie.   There is nothing wrong with my legs. Sam is just making jokes.

Hally.   So then you *will* be in the competition.

Willie.   Only if I can find me a partner.

Hally.   But what about Hilda?

Sam *(Returning with a bowl of soup).*   She's the one who's got trouble with her
legs.

Hally.   What sort of trouble, Willie?

Sam.   From the way he describes it, I think the lady has gone a bit lame.

Hally.   Good God! Have you taken her to see a doctor?

Sam.   I think a vet would be better.

Hally.   What do you mean?

Sam.   What do you call it again when a racehorse goes very fast?

Hally.   Gallop?

Sam.   That's it!

Willie.   Boet Sam!

Hally.   "A gallop down the homestretch to the winning post." But what's that
got to do with Hilda?

Sam.   Count Basie always gets there first.

(Willie lets fly with his slop rag. It misses Sam and hits Hally)

Hally *(Furious).*   For Christ's sake, Willie! What the hell do you think you're
doing!

Willie.   Sorry, Master Hally, but it's him. . . .

Hally.   Act your bloody age! *(Hurls the rag back at Willie)* Cut out the nonsense now and get on with your work. And you too, Sam. Stop fooling around.

(Sam moves away)

No. Hang on. I haven't finished! Tell me exactly what my Mom said.

Sam.   I have. "When Hally comes, tell him I've gone to the hospital and I'll
phone him."

Hally.   She didn't say anything about taking my Dad home?

Sam.   No. It's just that when she was talking on the phone . . .

Hally *(Interrupting him).*   No, Sam. They can't be discharging him. She would have said so if they were. In any case, we saw him last night and he wasn't in good shape at all. Staff nurse even said there was talk about taking more X-rays. And now suddenly today he's better? If anything, it sounds more like a bad turn to me . . . which I sincerely hope it isn't. Hang on . . . how long ago did you say she left?

Sam.   Just before two . . . *(His wrist watch)* . . . hour and a half.

Hally.   I know how to settle it. *(Behind the counter to the telephone. Talking as he dials)* Let's give her ten minutes to get to the hospital, ten minutes to load him up, another ten, at the most, to get home and another ten to get him inside. Forty minutes. They should have been home for at least half an hour already. *(Pause — he waits with the receiver to his ear)* No reply, chaps. And you know why? Because she's at his bedside in hospital helping him pull through a bad turn. You definitely heard wrong.

Sam.   Okay.

(As far as Hally is concerned, the matter is settled. He returns to his table, sits down and divides his attention between the book and his soup. Sam is at his school case and picks up a textbook)

Modern Graded Mathematics for Standards Nine and Ten. *(Opens it at random and laughs at something he sees)* Who is this supposed to be?

Hally.   Old fart-face Prentice.

Sam.   Teacher?

Hally.   Thinks he is. And believe me, that is not a bad likeness.

Sam.   Has he seen it?

Hally.   Yes.

Sam.   What did he say?

Hally.   Tried to be clever, as usual. Said I was no Leonardo da Vinci and that bad art had to be punished. So, six of the best, and his are bloody good.

Sam.   On your bum?

Hally.   Where else? The days when I got them on my hands are gone forever, Sam.

Sam.   With your trousers down!

Hally.   No. He's not quite that barbaric.

Sam.   That's the way they do it in jail.

Hally *(Flicker of morbid interest).*   Really?

Sam.   Ja. When the magistrate sentences you to "strokes with a light cane."

Hally.   Go on.

Sam.   They make you lie down on a bench. One policeman pulls down your trousers and holds your ankles, another one pulls your shirt over your head and holds your arms . . .

Hally.   Thank you! That's enough.

Sam.   . . . and the one that gives you the strokes talks to you gently and for a long time between each one. (*He laughs*)

Hally.   I've heard enough, Sam! Jesus! It's a bloody awful world when you come to think of it. People can be real bastards.

Sam.   That's the way it is, Hally.

Hally.   It doesn't *have* to be that way. There is something called progress, you know. We don't exactly burn people at the stake anymore.

Sam.   Like Joan of Arc.

Hally.   Correct. If she was captured today, she'd be given a fair trial.

Sam.   And then the death sentence.

Hally (*A world-weary-sigh*).   I know, I know! I oscillate between hope and despair for this world as well, Sam. But things will change, you wait and see. One day somebody is going to get up and give history a kick up the backside and get it going again.

Sam.   Like who?

Hally (*After thought*).   They're called social reformers. Every age, Sam, has got its social reformer. My history book is full of them.

Sam.   So where's ours?

Hally.   Good question. And I hate to say it, but the answer is: I don't know. Maybe he hasn't even been born yet. Or is still only a babe in arms at his mother's breast. God, what a thought.

Sam.   So we just go on waiting.

Hally.   Ja, looks like it. (*Back to his soup and the book*)

Sam (*Reading from the textbook*).   "Introduction: In some mathematical problems only the magnitude . . ." (*He mispronounces the word "magnitude"*)

Hally (*Correcting him without looking up*).   Magnitude.

Sam.   What's it mean?

Hally.   How big it is. The size of the thing.

Sam (*Reading*).   ". . . magnitude of the quantities is of importance. In other problems we need to know whether these quantities are negative or positive. For example, where there is a debit or credit bank balance . . ."

Hally.   Whether you're broke or not.

Sam.   ". . . whether the temperature is above or below Zero . . ."

Hally.   Naught degrees. Cheerful state of affairs! No cash and you're freezing to death. Mathematics won't get you out of that one.

Sam.   "All these quantities are called . . ." (*Spelling the word*) . . . s-c-a-l . . .

Hally.   Scalars.

Sam.   Scalars! (*Shaking his head with a laugh*) You understand all that?

Hally (*Turning a page*).   No. And I don't intend to try.

Sam.   So what happens when the exams come?

Hally.   Failing a maths exam isn't the end of the world, Sam. How many times have I told you that examination results don't measure intelligence?

Sam.   I would say about as many times as you've failed one of them.

Hally (*Mirthlessly*).   Ha, ha, ha.

Sam (*Simultaneously*).   Ha, ha, ha.

Hally.   Just remember Winston Churchill didn't do particularly well at school.

Sam.   You've also told me that one many times.

Hally.   Well, it just so happens to be the truth.

Sam (*Enjoying the word*).   Magnitude! Magnitude! Show me how to use it.

Hally (*After thought*).   An intrepid social reformer will not be daunted by the magnitude of the task he has undertaken.

Sam (*Impressed*).   Couple of jaw-breakers in there!

Hally.   I gave you three for the price of one. Intrepid, daunted and magnitude. I did that once in an exam. Put five of the words I had to explain in one sentence. It was half a page long.

Sam.   Well, I'll put my money on you in the English exam.

Hally.   Piece of cake. Eighty percent without even trying.

Sam (*Another textbook from Hally's case*).   And history?

Hally.   So-so. I'll scrape through. In the fifties if I'm lucky.

Sam.   You didn't do too badly last year.

Hally.   Because we had World War One. That at least had some action. You try to find that in the South African Parliamentary system.

Sam (*Reading from the history textbook*).   "Napoleon and the principle of equality." Hey! This sounds interesting. "After concluding peace with Britain in 1802, Napoleon used a brief period of calm to in-sti-tute . . ."

Hally.   Introduce.

Sam.   ". . . many reforms. Napoleon regarded all people as equal before the law and wanted them to have equal opportunities for advancement. All ves-ti-ges of the feu-dal system with its oppression of the poor were abolished." Vestiges, feudal system and abolished. I'm all right on oppression.

Hally.   I'm thinking. He swept away . . . abolished . . . the last remains . . . vestiges . . . of the bad old days . . . feudal system.

Sam.   Ha! There's the social reformer we're waiting for. He sounds like a man of some magnitude.

Hally.   I'm not so sure about that. It's a damn good title for a book, though. A man of magnitude!

Sam.   He sounds pretty big to me, Hally.

Hally.   Don't confuse historical significance with greatness. But maybe I'm being a bit prejudiced. Have a look in there and you'll see he's two chapters long. And hell! . . . has he only got dates, Sam, all of which you've got to remember! This campaign and that campaign, and then, because of all the fighting, the next thing is we get Peace Treaties all over the place. And what's the end of the story? Battle of Waterloo, which he loses. Wasn't worth it. No, I don't know about him as a man of magnitude.

Sam.   Then who would you say was?

Hally.   To answer that, we need a definition of greatness, and I suppose that would be somebody who . . . somebody who benefited all mankind.

Sam.   Right. But like who?

Hally (*He speaks with total conviction*).   Charles Darwin. Remember him? That big book from the library. *The Origin of the Species.*

Sam.   Him?

Hally.   Yes. For his Theory of Evolution.

Sam.   You didn't finish it.

Hally.   I ran out of time. I didn't finish it because my two weeks was up. But I'm going to take it out again after I've digested what I read. It's safe. I've hidden it away in the Theology section. Nobody ever goes in there. And anyway who are you to talk? You hardly even looked at it.

Sam.   I tried. I looked at the chapters in the beginning and I saw one called "The Struggle for an Existence." Ah ha, I thought. At last! But what did I get? Something called the mistiltoe which needs the apple tree and there's too many seeds and all are going to die except one . . . ! No, Hally.

Hally (*Intellectually outraged*).   What do you mean, No! The poor man had to start somewhere. For God's sake, Sam, he revolutionized science. Now we know.

Sam.   What?

Hally.   Where we come from and what it all means.

Sam.   And that's a benefit to mankind? Anyway, I still don't believe it.

Hally.   God, you're impossible. I showed it to you in black and white.

Sam.   Doesn't mean I got to believe it.

Hally.   It's the likes of you that kept the Inquisition in business. It's called bigotry. Anyway, that's my man of magnitude. Charles Darwin! Who's yours?

Sam (*Without hesitation*).   Abraham Lincoln.

Hally.   I might have guessed as much. Don't get sentimental, Sam. You've never been a slave, you know. And anyway we freed your ancestors here in South Africa long before the Americans. But if you want to thank somebody on their behalf, do it to Mr. William Wilberforce.[4] Come on. Try again. I want a real genius.

(*Now enjoying himself, and so is Sam. Hally goes behind the counter and helps himself to a chocolate*)

Sam.   William Shakespeare.

Hally (*No enthusiasm*).   Oh. So you're also one of them, are you? You're basing that opinion on only one play, you know. You've only read my *Julius Caesar* and even I don't understand half of what they're talking about. They should do what they did with the old Bible: bring the language up to date.

Sam.   That's all you've got. It's also the only one *you've* read.

Hally.   I know. I admit it. That's why I suggest we reserve our judgment until we've checked up on a few others. I've got a feeling, though, that by the end

---

[4] William Wilberforce (1759–1833), an English statesman whose vigorous opposition to slavery led to the Emancipation Act of 1833 that ended slavery in the British Empire.

of this year one is going to be enough for me, and I can give you the names of twenty-nine other chaps in the Standard Nine class of the Port Elizabeth Technical College who feel the same. But if you want him, you can have him. My turn now. (*Pacing*) This is a damned good exercise, you know! It started off looking like a simple question and here it's got us really probing into the intellectual heritage of our civilization.

Sam. So who is it going to be?

Hally. My next man . . . and he gets the title on two scores: social reform and literary genius . . . is Leo Nikolaevich Tolstoy.

Sam. That Russian.

Hally. Correct. Remember the picture of him I showed you?

Sam. With the long beard.

Hally (*Trying to look like Tolstoy*). And those burning, visionary eyes. My God, the face of a social prophet if ever I saw one! And remember my words when I showed it to you? Here's a *man*, Sam!

Sam. Those were words, Hally.

Hally. Not many intellectuals are prepared to shovel manure with the peasants and then go home and write a "little book" called *War and Peace*. Incidentally, Sam, he was somebody else who, to quote, ". . . did not distinguish himself scholastically."

Sam. Meaning?

Hally. He was also no good at school.

Sam. Like you and Winston Churchill.

Hally (*Mirthlessly*). Ha, ha, ha.

Sam (*Simultaneously*). Ha, ha, ha.

Hally. Don't get clever, Sam. That man freed his serfs of his own free will.

Sam. No argument. He was a somebody, all right. I accept him.

Hally. I'm sure Count Tolstoy will be very pleased to hear that. Your turn. Shoot. (*Another chocolate from behind the counter*) I'm waiting, Sam.

Sam. I've got him.

Hally. Good. Submit your candidate for examination.

Sam. Jesus.

Hally (*Stopped him dead in his tracks*). Who?

Sam. Jesus Christ.

Hally. Oh, come on, Sam!

Sam. The Messiah.

Hally. Ja, but still . . . No, Sam. Don't let's get started on religion. We'll just spend the whole afternoon arguing again. Suppose I turn around and say Mohammed?

Sam. All right.

Hally. You can't have them both on the same list!

Sam. Why not? You like Mohammed, I like Jesus.

Hally. I *don't* like Mohammed. I never have. I was merely being hypothetical.

As far as I'm concerned, the Koran is as bad as the Bible. No. Religion is out! I'm not going to waste my time again arguing with you about the existence of God. You know perfectly well I'm an atheist . . . and I've got homework to do.

Sam.   Okay, I take him back.

Hally.   You've got time for one more name.

Sam (*After thought*).   I've got one I know we'll agree on. A simple straightforward great Man of Magnitude . . . and no arguments. And *he* really *did* benefit all mankind.

Hally.   I wonder. After your last contribution I'm beginning to doubt whether anything in the way of an intellectual agreement is possible between the two of us. Who is he?

Sam.   Guess.

Hally.   Socrates? Alexandre Dumas? Karl Marx? Dostoevsky? Nietzsche?

(*Sam shakes his head after each name*)

Give me a clue.

Sam.   The letter P is important . . .

Hally.   Plato!

Sam.   . . . and his name begins with an F.

Hally.   I've got it. Freud and Psychology.

Sam.   No. I didn't understand him.

Hally.   That makes two of us.

Sam.   Think of mouldy apricot jam.

Hally (*After a delighted laugh*).   Penicillin and Sir Alexander Fleming! And the title of the book: *The Microbe Hunters.* (*Delighted*) Splendid, Sam! Splendid. For once we are in total agreement. The major breakthrough in medical science in the Twentieth Century. If it wasn't for him, we might have lost the Second World War. It's deeply gratifying, Sam, to know that I haven't been wasting my time in talking to you. (*Strutting around proudly*) Tolstoy may have educated his peasants, but I've educated you.

Sam.   Standard Four to Standard Nine.

Hally.   Have we been at it as long as that?

Sam.   Yep. And my first lesson was geography.

Hally (*Intrigued*).   Really? I don't remember.

Sam.   My room there at the back of the old Jubilee Boarding House. I had just started working for your Mom. Little boy in short trousers walks in one afternoon and asks me seriously: "Sam, do you want to see South Africa?" Hey man! Sure I wanted to see South Africa!

Hally.   Was that me?

Sam.   . . . So the next thing I'm looking at a map you had just done for homework. It was your first one and you were very proud of yourself.

Hally.   Go on.

Sam. Then came my first lesson. "Repeat after me, Sam: Gold in the Transvaal, mealies in the Free State, sugar in Natal and grapes in the Cape." I still know it!

Hally. Well, I'll be buggered. So that's how it all started.

Sam. And your next map was one with all the rivers and the mountains they came from. The Orange, the Vaal, the Limpopo, the Zambezi . . .

Hally. You've got a phenomenal memory!

Sam. You should be grateful. That is why you started passing your exams. You tried to be better than me.

(They laugh together. Willie is attracted by the laughter and joins them)

Hally. The old Jubilee Boarding House. Sixteen rooms with board and lodging, rent in advance and one week's notice. I haven't thought about it for donkey's years . . . and I don't think that's an accident. God, was I glad when we sold it and moved out. Those years are not remembered as the happiest ones of an unhappy childhood.

Willie *(Knocking on the table to imitate a woman's voice).* "Hally, are you there?"

Hally. Who's that supposed to be?

Willie. "What you doing in there, Hally? Come out at once!"

Hally *(To Sam).* What's he talking about?

Sam. Don't you remember?

Willie. "Sam, Willie . . . is he in there with you boys?"

Sam. Hiding away in our room when your mother was looking for you.

Hally *(Another good laugh).* Of course! I used to crawl and hide under your bed! But finish the story, Willie. Then what used to happen? You chaps would give the game away by telling her I was in there with you. So much for friendship.

Sam. We couldn't lie to her. She knew.

Hally. Which meant I got another rowing for hanging around the "servants' quarters." I think I spent more time in there with you chaps than anywhere else in that dump. And do you blame me? Nothing but bloody misery wherever you went. Somebody was always complaining about the food, or my mother was having a fight with Micky Nash because she'd caught her with a petty officer in her room. Maud Meiring was another one. Remember those two? They were prostitutes, you know. Soldiers and sailors from the troopships. Bottom fell out of the business when the war ended. God, the flotsam and jetsam that life washed up on our shores! No joking, if it wasn't for your room, I would have been the first certified ten-year-old in medical history. Ja, the memories are coming back now. Walking home from school and thinking: "What can I do this afternoon?" Try out a few ideas, but sooner or later I'd end up in there with you fellows. I bet you I could still find my way to your room with my eyes closed. *(He does exactly that)* Down the corridor . . . telephone on the right, which my Mom keeps locked because somebody is using it on the sly and not paying . . . past the kitchen and unappetizing cooking smells . . . around the corner into the backyard, hold my breath again because there are more smells coming when I pass your lavatory, then into that little passageway, first door on the right and into your room. How's that?

Sam. Good. But, as usual, you forgot to knock.

Hally. Like that time I barged in and caught you and Cynthia . . . at it. Remember? God, was I embarrassed! I didn't know what was going on at first.

Sam. Ja, that taught you a lesson.

Hally. And about a lot more than knocking on doors, I'll have you know, and I don't mean geography either. Hell, Sam, couldn't you have waited until it was dark?

Sam. No.

Hally. Was it that urgent?

Sam. Yes, and if you don't believe me, wait until your time comes.

Hally. No, thank you. I am not interested in girls. *(Back to his memories . . . Using a few chairs he recreates the room as he lists the items)* A gray little wall . . . and I now know why the mattress sags so much! . . . Willie's bed . . . it's propped up on bricks because one leg is broken . . . that wobbly little table with the washbasin and jug of water . . . Yes! . . . stuck to the wall above it are some pin-up pictures from magazines. Joe Louis . . .

Willie. Brown Bomber. World Title. *(Boxing pose)* Three rounds and knockout.

Hally. Against who?

Sam. Max Schmeling.

Hally. Correct. I can also remember Fred Astaire and Ginger Rogers, and Rita Hayworth in a bathing costume which always made me hot and bothered when I looked at it. Under Willie's bed is an old suitcase with all his clothes in a mess, which is why I never hide there. Your things are neat and tidy in a trunk next to your bed, and on it there is a picture of you and Cynthia in your ballroom clothes, your first silver cup for third place in a competition and an old radio which doesn't work anymore. Have I left out anything?

Sam. No.

Hally. Right, so much for the stage directions. Now the characters. *(Sam and Willie move to their appropriate positions in the bedroom)* Willie is in bed, under his blankets with his clothes on, complaining non-stop about something, but we can't make out a word of what he's saying because he's got his head under the blankets as well. You're on your bed trimming your toenails with a knife — not a very edifying sight — and as for me . . . What am I doing?

Sam. You're sitting on the floor giving Willie a lecture about being a good loser while you get the checker board and pieces ready for a game. Then you go to Willie's bed, pull off the blankets and make him play with you first because you know you're going to win, and that gives you the second game with me.

Hally. And you certainly were a bad loser, Willie!

Willie. Haai!

Hally. Wasn't he, Sam? And so slow! A game with you almost took the whole afternoon. Thank God I gave up trying to teach you how to play chess.

Willie. You and Sam cheated.

Hally. I never saw Sam cheat, and mine were mostly the mistakes of youth.

Willie. Then how is it you two was always winning?

Hally. Have you ever considered the possibility, Willie, that it was because we were better than you?

Willie. Every time better?

Hally. Not every time. There were occasions when we deliberately let you win a game so that you would stop sulking and go on playing with us. Sam used to wink at me when you weren't looking to show me it was time to let you win.

Willie. So then you two didn't play fair.

Hally. It was for your benefit, Mr. Malopo, which is more than being fair. It was an act of self-sacrifice. *(To Sam)* But you know what my best memory is, don't you?

Sam. No.

Hally. Come on, guess. If your memory is so good, you must remember it as well.

Sam. We got up to a lot of tricks in there, Hally.

Hally. This one was special, Sam.

Sam. I'm listening.

Hally. It started off looking like another of those useless nothing-to-do after-noons. I'd already been down to Main Street looking for adventure, but nothing had happened. I didn't feel like climbing trees in the Donkin Park or pretending I was a private eye and following a stranger . . . so as usual: See what's cooking in Sam's room. This time it was you on the floor. You had two thin pieces of wood and you were smoothing them down with a knife. It didn't look particularly interesting, but when I asked you what you were doing, you just said, "Wait and see, Hally. Wait . . . and see" . . . in that secret sort of way of yours, so I knew there was a surprise coming. You teased me, you bugger, by being deliberately slow and not answering my questions!

(Sam laughs)

And whistling while you worked away! God, it was infuriating! I could have brained you! It was only when you tied them together in a cross and put that down on the brown paper that I realized what you were doing. "Sam is making a kite?" And when I asked you and you said "Yes" . . . ! *(Shaking his head with disbelief)* The sheer audacity of it took my breath away. I mean, seriously, what the hell does a black man know about flying a kite? I'll be honest with you, Sam, I had no hopes for it. If you think I was excited and happy, you got another guess coming. In fact, I was shit-scared that we were going to make fools of ourselves. When we left the boarding house to go up onto the hill, I was praying quietly that there wouldn't be any other kids around to laugh at us.

Sam *(Enjoying the memory as much as Hally).*   Ja, I could see that.

Hally.   I made it obvious, did I?

Sam.   Ja. You refused to carry it.

Hally.   Do you blame me? Can you remember what the poor thing looked like? Tomato-box wood and brown paper! Flour and water for glue! Two of my mother's old stockings for a tail, and then all those bits and pieces of string you made me tie together so that we could fly it! Hell, no, that was now only asking for a miracle to happen.

Sam.   Then the big argument when I told you to hold the string and run with it when I let go.

Hally.   I was prepared to run, all right, but straight back to the boarding house.

Sam *(Knowing what's coming).*   So what happened?

Hally.   Come on, Sam, you remember as well as I do.

Sam.   I want to hear it from you.

(Hally pauses. He wants to be as accurate as possible)

Hally.   You went a little distance from me down the hill, you held it up ready to let it go. . . . "This is it," I thought. "Like everything else in my life, here comes another fiasco." Then you shouted, "Go, Hally!" and I started to run. *(Another pause)* I don't know how to describe it, Sam. Ja! The miracle happened! I was running, waiting for it to crash to the ground, but instead suddenly there was something alive behind me at the end of the string, tugging at it as if it wanted to be free. I looked back . . . *(Shakes his head)* . . . I still can't believe my eyes. It was flying! Looping around and trying to climb even higher into the sky. You shouted to me to let it have more string. I did, until there was none left and I was just holding that piece of wood we had tied it to. You came up and joined me. You were laughing.

Sam.   So were you. And shouting, "It works, Sam! We've done it!"

Hally.   And we had! I was so proud of us! It was the most splendid thing I had ever seen. I wished there were hundreds of kids around to watch us. The part that scared me, though, was when you showed me how to make it dive down to the ground and then just when it was on the point of crashing, swoop up again!

Sam.   You didn't want to try yourself.

Hally.   Of course not! I would have been suicidal if anything had happened to it. Watching you do it made me nervous enough. I was quite happy just to see it up there with its tail fluttering behind it. You left me after that, didn't you? You explained how to get it down, we tied it to the bench so that I could sit and watch it, and you went away. I wanted you to stay, you know. I was a little scared of having to look after it by myself.

Sam (*Quietly*).   I had work to do, Hally.

Hally.   It was sort of sad bringing it down, Sam. And it looked sad again when it was lying there on the ground. Like something that had lost its soul. Just tomato-box wood, brown paper and two of my mother's old stockings! But, hell, I'll never forget that first moment when I saw it up there. I had a stiff neck the next day from looking up so much.

(*Sam laughs. Hally turns to him with a question he never thought of asking before*)

Why did you make that kite, Sam?

Sam (*Evenly*).   I can't remember.

Hally.   Truly?

Sam.   Too long ago, Hally.

Hally.   Ja, I suppose it was. It's time for another one, you know.

Sam.   Why do you say that?

Hally.   Because it feels like that. Wouldn't be a good day to fly it, though.

Sam.   No. You can't fly kites on rainy days.

Hally (*He studies Sam. Their memories have made him conscious of the man's presence in his life*).   How old are you, Sam?

Sam.   Two score and five.

Hally.   Strange, isn't it?

Sam.   What?

Hally.   Me and you.

Sam.   What's strange about it?

Hally.   Little white boy in short trousers and a black man old enough to be his father flying a kite. It's not every day you see that.

Sam.   But why strange? Because the one is white and the other black?

Hally.   I don't know. Would have been just as strange, I suppose, if it had been me and my Dad . . . cripple man and a little boy! Nope! There's no chance of me flying a kite without it being strange. (*Simple statement of fact — no self-pity*) There's a nice little short story there. "The Kite-Flyers." But we'd have to find a twist in the ending.

Sam.   Twist?

Hally.   Yes. Something unexpected. The way it ended with us was too straight-forward . . . me on the bench and you going back to work. There's no drama in that.

Willie.   And me?

Hally.   You?

Willie.   Yes me.

Hally.   You want to get into the story as well, do you? I got it! Change the title: "Afternoons in Sam's Room" . . . expand it and tell all the stories. It's on its way to being a novel. Our days in the old Jubilee. Sad in a way that they're over. I almost wish we were still in that little room.

Sam. We're still together.

Hally. That's true. It's just that life felt the right size in there . . . not too big and not too small. Wasn't so hard to work up a bit of courage. It's got so bloody complicated since then.

(The telephone rings. Sam answers it)

Sam. St. George's Park Tea Room . . . Hello, Madam . . . Yes, Madam, he's here . . . Hally, it's your mother.

Hally. Where is she phoning from?

Sam. Sounds like the hospital. It's a public telephone.

Hally *(Relieved).* You see! I told you. *(The telephone)* Hello, Mom . . . Yes . . . Yes no fine. Everything's under control here. How's things with poor old Dad? . . . Has he had a bad turn? . . . What? . . . Oh, God! . . . Yes, Sam told me, but I was sure he'd made a mistake. But what's this all about, Mom? He didn't look at all good last night. How can he get better so quickly? . . . Then very obviously you must say no. Be firm with him. You're the boss. . . . You know what it's going to be like if he comes home. . . . Well then, don't blame me when I fail my exams at the end of the year. . . . Yes! How am I expected to be fresh for school when I spend half the night massaging his gammy leg? . . . So am I! . . . So tell him a white lie. Say Dr. Colley wants more X-rays of his stump. Or bribe him. We'll sneak in double tots of brandy in future. . . . What? . . . Order him to get back into bed at once! If he's going to behave like a child, treat him like one. . . . All right, Mom! I was just trying to . . . I'm sorry. . . . I said I'm sorry. . . . Quick, give me your number. I'll phone you back. *(He hangs up and waits a few seconds)* Here we go again! *(He dials)* I'm sorry, Mom. . . . Okay . . . But now listen to me carefully. All it needs is for you to put your foot down. Don't take no for an answer. . . . Did you hear me? And whatever you do, don't discuss it with him. . . . Because I'm frightened you'll give in to him. . . . Yes, Sam gave me lunch. . . . I ate all of it! . . . No, Mom, not a soul. It's still raining here. . . . Right, I'll tell them. I'll just do some homework and then lock up. . . . But remember now, Mom. Don't listen to anything he says. And phone me back and let me know what happens. . . . Okay. Bye, Mom. *(He hangs up. The men are staring at him)* My Mom says that when you're finished with the floors you must do the windows. *(Pause)* Don't misunderstand me, chaps. All I want is for him to get better. And if he was, I'd be the first person to say: "Bring him home." But he's not, and we can't give him the medical care and attention he needs at home. That's what hospitals are there for. *(Brusquely)* So don't just stand there! Get on with it!

(Sam clears Hally's table)

You heard right. My Dad wants to go home.

Sam.   Is he better?

Hally (*Sharply*).   No! How the hell can he be better when last night he was groaning with pain? This is not an age of miracles!

Sam.   Then he should stay in hospital.

Hally (*Seething with irritation and frustration*).   Tell me something I don't know, Sam. What the hell do you think I was saying to my Mom? All I can say is fuck-it-all.

Sam.   I'm sure he'll listen to your Mom.

Hally.   You don't know what she's up against. He's already packed his shaving kit and pajamas and is sitting on his bed with his crutches, dressed and ready to go. I know him when he gets in that mood. If she tries to reason with him, we've had it. She's no match for him when it comes to a battle of words. He'll tie her up in knots. (*Trying to hide his true feelings*)

Sam.   I suppose it gets lonely for him in there.

Hally.   With all the patients and nurses around? Regular visits from the Salvation Army? Balls! It's ten times worse for him at home. I'm at school and my mother is here in the business all day.

Sam.   He's at least got you at night.

Hally (*Before he can stop himself*).   And we've got him! Please! I don't want to talk about it anymore. (*Unpacks his school case, slamming down books on the table*) Life is just a plain bloody mess, that's all. And people are fools.

Sam.   Come on, Hally.

Hally.   Yes, they are! They bloody well deserve what they get.

Sam.   Then don't complain.

Hally.   Don't try to be clever, Sam. It doesn't suit you. Anybody who thinks there's nothing wrong with this world needs to have his head examined. Just when things are going along all right, without fail someone or something will come along and spoil everything. Somebody should write that down as a fundamental law of the Universe. The principle of perpetual disappointment. If there is a God who created this world, he should scrap it and try again.

Sam.   All right, Hally, all right. What you got for homework?

Hally.   Bullshit, as usual. (*Opens an exercise book and reads*) "Write five hundred words describing an annual event of cultural or historical significance."

Sam.   That should be easy enough for you.

Hally.   And also plain bloody boring. You know what he wants, don't you? One of their useless old ceremonies. The commemoration of the 1820 Settlers, or if it's going to be culture, Carols by Candlelight every Christmas.

Sam.   It's an impressive sight. Make a good description, Hally. All those candles glowing in the dark and the people singing hymns.

Hally.   And it's called religious hysteria. (*Intense irritation*) Please, Sam! Just leave me alone and let me get on with it. I'm not in the mood for games this afternoon. And remember my Mom's orders . . . you're to help Willie with the windows. Come on now, I don't want any more nonsense in here.

Sam.   Okay, Hally, okay.

(Hally settles down to his homework; determined preparations . . . pen, ruler, exercise book, dictionary, another cake . . . all of which will lead to nothing.)

(Sam waltzes over to Willie and starts to replace tables and chairs. He practices a ballroom step while doing so. Willie watches. When Sam is finished, Willie tries) Good! But just a little bit quicker on the turn and only move in to her after she's crossed over. What about this one?

(Another step. When Sam is finished, Willie again has a go)

Much better. See what happens when you just relax and enjoy yourself? Remember that in two weeks' time and you'll be all right.

Willie. But I haven't got partner, Boet Sam.

Sam. Maybe Hilda will turn up tonight.

Willie. No, Boet Sam. *(Reluctantly)* I gave her a good hiding.

Sam. You mean a bad one.

Willie. Good bad one.

Sam. Then you mustn't complain either. Now you pay the price for losing your temper.

Willie. I also pay two pounds ten shilling entrance fee.

Sam. They'll refund you if you withdraw now.

Willie *(Appalled).* You mean, don't dance?

Sam. Yes.

Willie. No! I wait too long and I practice too hard. If I find me new partner, you think I can be ready in two weeks? I ask Madam for my leave now and we practice every day.

Sam. Quickstep non-stop for two weeks. World record, Willie, but you'll be mad at the end.

Willie. No jokes, Boet Sam.

Sam. I'm not joking.

Willie. So then what?

Sam. Find Hilda. Say you're sorry and promise you won't beat her again.

Willie. No.

Sam. Then withdraw. Try again next year.

Willie. No.

Sam. Then I give up.

Willie. Haaikona, Boet Sam, you can't.

Sam. What do you mean, I can't? I'm telling you: I give up.

Willie *(Adamant).* No! *(Accusingly)* It was you who start me ballroom dancing.

Sam. So?

Willie. Before that I use to be happy. And is you and Miriam who bring me to Hilda and say here's partner for you.

Sam. What are you saying, Willie?

Willie. You!

Sam. But me what? To blame?

Willie. Yes.

Sam. Willie . . . ? *(Bursts into laughter)*

Willie. And now all you do is make jokes at me. You wait. When Miriam leaves you is my turn to laugh. Ha! Ha! Ha!

Sam *(He can't take Willie seriously any longer).* She can leave me tonight! I know what to do. *(Bowing before an imaginary partner)* May I have the pleasure? *(He dances and sings)*
"Just a fellow with his pillow . . .
Dancin' like a willow . . .
In an autumn breeze . . ."

Willie. There you go again!

(Sam goes on dancing and singing)

Boet Sam!

Sam. There's the answer to your problem! Judges' announcement in two weeks' time: "Ladies and gentlemen, the winner in the open section . . . Mr. Willie Malopo and his pillow!"

(This is too much for a now really angry Willie. He goes for Sam, but the latter is too quick for him and puts Hally's table between the two of them)

Hally *(Exploding).* For Christ's sake, you two!

Willie *(Still trying to get at Sam).* I donner you, Sam! Struesgod!

Sam *(Still laughing).* Sorry, Willie . . . Sorry . . .

Hally. Sam! Willie! *(Grabs his ruler and gives Willie a vicious whack on the bum)* How the hell am I supposed to concentrate with the two of you behaving like bloody children!

Willie. Hit him too!

Hally. Shut up, Willie.

Willie. He started jokes again.

Hally. Get back to your work. You too, Sam. *(His ruler)* Do you want another one, Willie?

(Sam and Willie return to their work. Hally uses the opportunity to escape from his unsuccessful attempt at homework. He struts around like a little despot, ruler in hand, giving vent to his anger and frustration)

Suppose a customer had walked in then? Or the Park Superintendent. And seen the two of you behaving like a pair of hooligans. That would have been the end of my mother's license, you know. And your jobs! Well, this is the end of it. From now on there will be no more of your ballroom nonsense in here. This is a business establishment, not a bloody New Brighton dancing school.

I've been far too lenient with the two of you. (*Behind the counter for a green cool drink and a dollop of ice cream. He keeps up his tirade as he prepares it*) But what really makes me bitter is that I allow you chaps a little freedom in here when business is bad and what do you do with it? The foxtrot! Specially you, Sam. There's more to life than trotting around a dance floor and I thought at least you knew it.

Sam. It's a harmless pleasure, Hally. It doesn't hurt anybody.

Hally. It's also a rather simple one, you know.

Sam. You reckon so? Have you ever tried?

Hally. Of course not.

Sam. Why don't you? Now.

Hally. What do you mean? Me dance?

Sam. Yes. I'll show you a simple step — the waltz — then you try it.

Hally. What will that prove?

Sam. That it might not be as easy as you think.

Hally. I didn't say it was easy. I said it was simple — like in simple-minded, meaning mentally retarded. You can't exactly say it challenges the intellect.

Sam. It does other things.

Hally. Such as?

Sam. Make people happy.

Hally (*The glass in his hand*). So do American cream sodas with ice cream. For God's sake, Sam, you're not asking me to take ballroom dancing serious, are you?

Sam. Yes.

Hally (*Sigh of defeat*). Oh well, so much for trying to give you a decent education. I've obviously achieved nothing.

Sam. You still haven't told me what's wrong with admiring something that's beautiful and then trying to do it yourself.

Hally. Nothing. But we happen to be talking about a foxtrot, not a thing of beauty.

Sam. But that is just what I'm saying. If you were to see two champions doing, two masters of the art . . . !

Hally. Oh, God, I give up. So now it's also art!

Sam. Ja.

Hally. There's a limit, Sam. Don't confuse art and entertainment.

Sam. So then what is art?

Hally. You want a definition?

Sam. Ja.

Hally (*He realizes he has got to be careful. He gives the matter a lot of thought before answering*). Philosophers have been trying to do that for centuries. What is Art? What is Life? But basically I suppose it's . . . the giving of meaning to matter.

Sam. Nothing to do with beautiful?

Hally. It goes beyond that. It's the giving of form to the formless.

Sam. Ja, well, maybe it's not art, then. But I still say it's beautiful.

Hally.   I'm sure the word you mean to use is entertaining.

Sam *(Adamant)*.   No. Beautiful. And if you want proof, come along to the Centenary Hall in New Brighton in two weeks' time.

(The mention of the Centenary Hall draws Willie over to them)

Hally.   What for? I've seen the two of you prancing around in here often enough.

Sam *(He laughs)*.   This isn't the real thing, Hally. We're just playing around in here.

Hally.   So? I can use my imagination.

Sam.   And what do you get?

Hally.   A lot of people dancing around and having a so-called good time.

Sam.   That all?

Hally.   Well, basically it is that, surely.

Sam.   No, it isn't. Your imagination hasn't helped you at all. There's a lot more to it than that. We're getting ready for the championships, Hally, not just another dance. There's going to be a lot of people, all right, and they're going to have a good time, but they'll only be spectators, sitting around and watching. It's just the competitors out there on the dance floor. Party decorations and fancy lights all around the walls! The ladies in beautiful evening dresses!

Hally.   My mother's got one of those, Sam, and quite frankly, it's an embarrassment every time she wears it.

Sam *(Undeterred)*.   Your imagination left out the excitement.

(Hally scoffs)

Oh, yes. The finalists are not going to be out there just to have a good time. One of those couples will be the 1950 Eastern Province Champions. And your imagination left out the music.

Willie.   Mr. Elijah Gladman Guzana and his Orchestral Jazzonions.

Sam.   The sound of the big band, Hally. Trombone, trumpet, tenor and alto sax. And then, finally, your imagination also left out the climax of the evening when the dancing is finished, the judges have stopped whispering among themselves and the Master of Ceremonies collects their scorecards and goes up onto the stage to announce the winners.

Hally.   All right. So you make it sound like a bit of a do. It's an occasion. Satisfied?

Sam *(Victory)*.   So you admit that!

Hally.   Emotionally yes, intellectually no.

Sam.   Well, I don't know what you mean by that, all I'm telling you is that it is going to be *the* event of the year in New Brighton. It's been sold out for two weeks already. There's only standing room left. We've got competitors coming from Kingwilliamstown, East London, Port Alfred.

(Hally starts pacing thoughtfully)

Hally. Tell me a bit more.

Sam. I thought you weren't interested . . . intellectually.

Hally (*Mysteriously*). I've got my reasons.

Sam. What do you want to know?

Hally. It takes place every year?

Sam. Yes. But only every third year in New Brighton. It's East London's turn to have the championships next year.

Hally. Which, I suppose, makes it an even more significant event.

Sam. Ah ha! We're getting somewhere. Our "occasion" is now a "significant event."

Hally. I wonder.

Sam. What?

Hally. I wonder if I would get away with it.

Sam. But what?

Hally (*To the table and his exercise book*). "Write five hundred words describing an annual event of cultural or historical significance." Would I be stretching poetic license a little too far if I called your ballroom championships a cultural event?

Sam. You mean . . . ?

Hally. You think we could get five hundred words out of it, Sam?

Sam. Victor Sylvester has written a whole book on ballroom dancing.

Willie. You going to write about it, Master Hally?

Hally. Yes, gentlemen, that is precisely what I am considering doing. Old Doc Bromely — he's my English teacher — is going to argue with me, of course. He doesn't like natives. But I'll point out to him that in strict anthropological terms the culture of a primitive black society includes its dancing and singing. To put my thesis in a nutshell: The war-dance has been replaced by the waltz. But it still amounts to the same thing: the release of primitive emotions through movement. Shall we give it a go?

Sam. I'm ready.

Willie. Me also.

Hally. Ha! This will teach the old bugger a lesson. (*Decision taken*) Right. Let's get ourselves organized. (*This means another cake on the table. He sits*) I think you've given me enough general atmosphere, Sam, but to build the tension and suspense I need facts. (*Pencil poised*)

Willie. Give him facts, Boet Sam.

Hally. What you call the climax . . . how many finalists?

Sam. Six couples.

Hally (*Making notes*). Go on. Give me the picture.

Sam. Spectators seated right around the hall. (*Willie becomes a spectator*)

Hally. . . . and it's a full house.

Sam. At one end, on the stage, Gladman and his Orchestral Jazzonions. At the other end is a long table with the three judges. The six finalists go onto the dance floor and take up their positions. When they are ready and the spectators have settled down, the Master of Ceremonies goes to the microphone. To start with, he makes some jokes to get the people laughing . . .

Hally.   Good touch! (*As he writes*) ". . . creating a relaxed atmosphere which will change to one of tension and drama as the climax is approached."

Sam (*Onto a chair to act out the M.C.*).   "Ladies and gentlemen, we come now to the great moment you have all been waiting for this evening. . . . The finals of the 1950 Eastern Province Open Ballroom Dancing Championships. But first let me introduce the finalists! Mr. and Mrs. Welcome Tchabalala from Kingwilliamstown . . ."

Willie (*He applauds after every name*).   Is when the people clap their hands and whistle and make a lot of noise, Master Hally.

Sam.   "Mr. Mulligan Njikelane and Miss Nomhle Nkonyeni of Grahamstown; Mr. and Mrs. Norman Nchinga from Port Alfred; Mr. Fats Bokolane and Miss Dina Plaatjies from East London; Mr. Sipho Dugu and Mrs. Mable Magada from Peddie; and from New Brighton our very own Mr. Willie Malopo and Miss Hilda Samuels."

(*Willie can't believe his ears. He abandons his role as spectator and scrambles in position as a finalist*)

Willie.   Relaxed and ready to romance!

Sam.   The applause dies down. When everybody is silent, Gladman lifts up his sax, nods at the Orchestral Jazzonions . . .

Willie.   Play the jukebox please, Boet Sam!

Sam.   I also only got bus fare, Willie.

Hally.   Hold it, everybody. (*Heads for the cash register behind the counter*) How much is in the till, Sam?

Sam.   Three shillings. Hally . . . your Mom counted it before she left.

(*Hally hesitates*)

Hally.   Sorry, Willie. You know how she carried on the last time I did it. We'll just have to pool our combined imaginations and hope for the best. (*Returns to the table*) Back to work. How are the points scored, Sam?

Sam.   Maximum of ten points each for individual style, deportment, rhythm and general appearance.

Willie.   Must I start?

Hally.   Hold it for a second, Willie. And penalties?

Sam.   For what?

Hally.   For doing something wrong. Say you stumble or bump into somebody . . . do they take off any points?

Sam (*Aghast*).   Hally . . . !

Hally.   When you're dancing. If you and your partner collide into another couple.

(*Hally can get no further. Sam has collapsed with laughter. He explains to Willie*)

Sam.   If me and Miriam bump into you and Hilda . . .

(Willie joins him in another good laugh)

Hally, Hally . . . !

Hally *(Perplexed).*   Why? What did I say?

Sam.   There's no collisions out there, Hally. Nobody trips or stumbles or bumps into anybody else. That's what that moment is all about. To be one of those finalists on that dance floor is like . . . like being in a dream about a world in which accidents don't happen.

Hally *(Genuinely moved by Sam's image).*   Jesus, Sam! That's beautiful!

Willie *(Can endure waiting no longer).*   I'm starting! *(Willie dances while Sam talks)*

Sam.   Of course it is. That's what I've been trying to say to you all afternoon. And it's beautiful because that is what we want life to be like. But instead, like you said, Hally, we're bumping into each other all the time. Look at the three of us this afternoon: I've bumped into Willie, the two of us have bumped into you, you've bumped into your mother, she bumping into your Dad. . . . None of us knows the steps and there's no music playing. And it doesn't stop with us. The whole world is doing it all the time. Open a newspaper and what do you read? America has bumped into Russia, England is bumping into India, rich man bumps into poor man. Those are big collisions, Hally. They make for a lot of bruises. People get hurt in all that bumping, and we're sick and tired of it now. It's been going on for too long. Are we never going to get it right! . . . Learn to dance life like champions instead of always being just a bunch of beginners at it?

Hally *(Deep and sincere admiration of the man).*   You've got a vision, Sam!

Sam.   Not just me. What I'm saying to you is that everybody's got it. That's why there's only standing room left for the Centenary Hall in two weeks' time. For as long as the music lasts, we are going to see six couples get it right, the way we want life to be.

Hally.   But is that the best we can do, Sam . . . watch six finalists dreaming about the way it should be?

Sam.   I don't know. But it starts with that. Without the dream we won't know what we're going for. And anyway I reckon there are a few people who have got past just dreaming about it and are trying for something real. Remember that thing we read once in the paper about the Mahatma Gandhi? Going without food to stop those riots in India?

Hally.   You're right. He certainly was trying to teach people to get the steps right.

Sam.   And the Pope.

Hally.   Yes, he's another one. Our old General Smuts as well, you know. He's also out there dancing. You know, Sam, when you come to think of it, that's what the United Nations boils down to . . . a dancing school for politicians!

Sam.   And let's hope they learn.

Hally (*A little surge of hope*).   You're right. We mustn't despair. Maybe there's some hope for mankind after all. Keep it up, Willie. (*Back to his table with determination*) This is a lot bigger than I thought. So what have we got? Yes, our title: "A World Without Collisions."

Sam.   That sounds good! "A World Without Collisions."

Hally.   Subtitle: "Global Politics on the Dance Floor." No. A bit too heavy, hey? What about "Ballroom Dancing as a Political Vision"?

(*The telephone rings. Sam answers it*)

Sam.   St. George's Park Tea Room . . . Yes, Madam . . . Hally, it's your Mom.

Hally (*Back to reality*).   Oh, God, yes! I'd forgotten all about that. Shit! Remember my words, Sam? Just when you're enjoying yourself, someone or something will come along and wreck everything.

Sam.   You haven't heard what she's got to say yet.

Hally.   Public telephone?

Sam.   No.

Hally.   Does she sound happy or unhappy?

Sam.   I couldn't tell. (*Pause*) She's waiting, Hally.

Hally (*To the telephone*).   Hello, Mom . . . No, everything is okay here. Just doing my homework. . . . What's your news? . . . You've what? . . . (*Pause. He takes the receiver away from his ear for a few seconds. In the course of Hally's telephone conversation, Sam and Willie discreetly position the stacked tables and chairs. Hally places the receiver back to his ear*) Yes, I'm still here. Oh, well, I give up now. Why did you do it, Mom? . . . Well, I just hope you know what you've let us in for. . . . (*Loudly*) I said I hope you know what you've let us in for! It's the end of the peace and quiet we've been having. (*Softly*) Where is he? (*Normal voice*) He can't hear us from in there. But for God's sake, Mom, what happened? I told you to be firm with him. . . . Then you and the nurses should have held him down, taken his crutches away. . . . I know only too well he's my father! . . . I'm not being disrespectful, but I'm sick and tired of emptying stinking chamberpots full of phlegm and piss. . . . Yes, I do! When you're not there, he asks *me* to do it. . . . If you really want to know the truth, that's why I've got no appetite for my food. . . . Yes! There's a lot of things you don't know about. For your information, I still haven't got that science textbook I need. And you know why? He borrowed the money you gave me for it. . . . Because I didn't want to start another fight between you two. . . . He says that every time. . . . All right, Mom! (*Viciously*) Then just remember to start hiding your bag away again, because he'll be at your purse before long for money for booze. And when he's well enough to come down here, you better keep an eye on the till as well, because that is going to develop a leak. . . . Then don't complain to me when he starts his old tricks. . . . Yes, you do. I get it from you on one side and from him on the other, and it makes life hell for me. I'm not going to be the peacemaker anymore. I'm warning you now: when the two of you start fighting again, I'm leaving home. . . . Mom, if you start crying, I'm going to put down the receiver. . . . Okay . . . (*Lowering* *his voice to a vicious whisper)* Okay, Mom. I heard you. *(Desperate)* No. . . . Because I don't want to. I'll see him when I get home! Mom! . . . *(Pause. When he speaks again, his tone changes completely. It is not simply pretense. We sense a genuine emotional conflict)* Welcome home, chum! . . . What's that? . . . Don't be silly, Dad. You being home is just about the best news in the world. . . . I bet you are. Bloody depressing there with everybody going on about their ailments, hey! . . . How you feeling? . . . Good . . . Here as well, pal. Coming down cats and dogs. . . . That's right. Just the day for a kip and a toss in your old Uncle Ned. . . . Everything's just hunky-dory on my side, Dad. . . . Well, to start with, there's a nice pile of comics for you on the counter. . . . Yes, old Kemple brought them in. *Batman and Robin, Submariner* . . . just your cup of tea . . . I will. . . . Yes, we'll spin a few yarns tonight. . . . Okay, chum, see you in a little while. . . . No, I promise. I'll come straight home. . . . *(Pause — his mother comes back on the phone)* Mom? Okay. I'll lock up now. . . . What? . . . Oh, the brandy . . . Yes, I'll remember! . . . I'll put it in my suitcase now, for God's sake. I know well enough what will happen if he doesn't get it. . . . *(Places a bottle of brandy on the counter)* I *was* kind to him, Mom. I didn't say anything nasty! . . . All right. Bye. *(End of telephone conversation. A desolate Hally doesn't move. A strained silence)*

Sam *(Quietly)*.   That sounded like a bad bump, Hally.

Hally *(Having a hard time controlling his emotions. He speaks carefully)*. Mind your own business, Sam.

Sam.   Sorry. I wasn't trying to interfere. Shall we carry on? Hally? *(He indicates the exercise book. No response from Hally)*

Willie *(Also trying)*.   Tell him about when they give out the cups, Boet Sam.

Sam.   Ja! That's another big moment. The presentation of the cups after the winners have been announced. You've got to put that in.

(Still no response from Hally)

Willie.   A big silver one, Master Hally, called floating trophy for the champions.

Sam.   We always invite some big-shot personality to hand them over. Guest of honor this year is going to be His Holiness Bishop Jabulani of the All African Free Zionist Church.

(Hally gets up abruptly, goes to his table and tears up the page he was writing on)

Hally.   So much for a bloody world without collisions.

Sam.   Too bad. It was on its way to being a good composition.

Hally.   Let's stop bullshitting ourselves, Sam.

Sam.   Have we been doing that?

Hally.   Yes! That's what all our talk about a decent world has been . . . just so much bullshit.

Sam.   We did say it was still only a dream.

Hally. And a bloody useless one at that. Life's a fuck-up and it's never going to change.

Sam. Ja, maybe that's true.

Hally. There's no maybe about it. It's a blunt and brutal fact. All we've done this afternoon is waste our time.

Sam. Not if we'd got your homework done.

Hally. I don't give a shit about my homework, so, for Christ's sake, just shut up about it. (*Slamming books viciously into his school case*) Hurry up now and finish your work. I want to lock up and get out of here. (*Pause*) And then go where? Home-sweet-fucking-home. Jesus, I hate that word.

(*Hally goes to the counter to put the brandy bottle and comics in his school case. After a moment's hesitation, he smashes the bottle of brandy. He abandons all further attempts to hide his feelings. Sam and Willie work away as unobtrusively as possible*)

Do you want to know what is really wrong with your lovely little dream, Sam? It's not just that we are all bad dancers. That does happen to be perfectly true, but there's much more to it than just that. You left out the cripples.

Sam. Hally!

Hally (*Now totally reckless*). Ja! Can't leave them out, Sam. That's why we always end up on our backsides on the dance floor. They're also out there dancing . . . like a bunch of broken spiders trying to do the quickstep! (*An ugly attempt at laughter*) When you come to think of it, it's a bloody comical sight. I mean, it's bad enough on two legs . . . but one and a pair of crutches! Hell, no, Sam. That's guaranteed to turn that dance floor into a shambles. Why you shaking your head? Picture it, man. For once this afternoon let's use our imaginations sensibly.

Sam. Be careful, Hally.

Hally. Of what? The truth? I seem to be the only one around here who is pre-pared to face it. We've had the pretty dream, it's time now to wake up and have a good long look at the way things really are. Nobody knows the steps, there's no music, the cripples are also out there tripping up everybody and trying to get into the act, and it's all called the All-Comers-How-to-Make-a-Fuckup-of-Life Championships. (*Another ugly laugh*) Hang on, Sam! The best bit is still coming. Do you know what the winner's trophy is? A beautiful big chamber-pot with roses on the side, and it's full to the brim with piss. And guess who I think is going to be this year's winner.

Sam (*Almost shouting*). Stop now!

Hally (*Suddenly appalled by how far he has gone*). Why?

Sam. Hally? It's your father you're talking about.

Hally. So?

Sam. Do you know what you've been saying?

(*Hally can't answer. He is rigid with shame. Sam speaks to him sternly*)

No, Hally, you mustn't do it. Take back those words and ask for forgiveness! It's a terrible sin for a son to mock his father with jokes like that. You'll be punished if you carry on. Your father is your father, even if he is a . . . cripple man.

Willie.   Yes, Master Hally. Is true what Sam say.

Sam.   I understand how you are feeling, Hally, but even so . . .

Hally.   No, you don't!

Sam.   I think I do.

Hally.   And I'm telling you you don't. Nobody does. (*Speaking carefully as his shame turns to rage at Sam*) It's your turn to be careful, Sam. Very careful! You're treading on dangerous ground. Leave me and my father alone.

Sam.   I'm not the one who's been saying things about him.

Hally.   What goes on between me and my Dad is none of your business!

Sam.   Then don't tell me about it. If that's all you've got to say about him, I don't want to hear.

(*For a moment Hally is at a loss for a response*)

Hally.   Just get on with your bloody work and shut up.

Sam.   Swearing at me won't help you.

Hally.   Yes, it does! Mind your own fucking business and shut up!

Sam.   Okay. If that's the way you want it, I'll stop trying.

(*He turns away. This infuriates Hally even more*)

Hally.   Good. Because what you've been trying to do is meddle in something you know nothing about. All that concerns you in here, Sam, is to try and do what you get paid for — keep the place clean and serve the customers. In plain words, just get on with your job. My mother is right. She's always warning me about allowing you to get too familiar. Well this time you've gone too far. It's going to stop right now.

(*No response from Sam*)

You're only a servant in here, and don't forget it.

(*Still no response. Hally is trying hard to get one*)

And as far as my father is concerned, all you need to remember is that he is your boss.

Sam (*Needled at last*).   No, he isn't. I get paid by your mother.

Hally.   Don't argue with me, Sam!

Sam.   Then don't say he's my boss.

Hally.   He's a white man and that's good enough for you.

Sam.   I'll try to forget you said that.

Hally. Don't! Because you won't be doing me a favor if you do. I'm telling you to remember it.

(*A pause. Sam pulls himself together and makes one last effort*)

Sam. Hally, Hally . . . ! Come on now. Let's stop before it's too late. You're right. We *are* on dangerous ground. If we're not careful, somebody is going to get hurt.
Hally. It won't be me.
Sam. Don't be so sure.
Hally. I don't know what you're talking about, Sam.
Sam. Yes, you do.
Hally (*Furious*). Jesus, I wish you would stop trying to tell me what I do and what I don't know.

(*Sam gives up. He turns to Willie*)

Sam. Let's finish up.
Hally. Don't turn your back on me! I haven't finished talking.

(*He grabs Sam by the arm and tries to make him turn around. Sam reacts with a flash of anger*)

Sam. Don't do that, Hally! (*Facing the boy*) All right, I'm listening. Well? What do you want to say to me?
Hally (*Pause as Hally looks for something to say*). To begin with, why don't you also start calling me Master Harold, like Willie.
Sam. Do you mean that?
Hally. Why the hell do you think I said it?
Sam. And if I don't?
Hally. You might just lose your job.
Sam (*Quietly and very carefully*). If you make me say it once, I'll never call you anything else again.
Hally. So? (*The boy confronts the man*) Is that meant to be a threat?
Sam. Just telling you what will happen if you make me do that. You must decide what it means to you.
Hally. Well, I have. It's good news. Because that is exactly what Master Harold wants from now on. Think of it as a little lesson in respect, Sam, that's long overdue, and I hope you remember it as well as you do your geography. I can tell you now that somebody who will be glad to hear I've finally given it to you will be my Dad. Yes! He agrees with my Mom. He's always going on about it as well. "You must teach the boys to show you more respect, my son."
Sam. So now you can stop complaining about going home. Everybody is going to be happy tonight.
Hally. That's perfectly correct. You see, you mustn't get the wrong idea about me and my Dad, Sam. We also have our good times together. Some bloody

good laughs. He's got a marvelous sense of humor. Want to know what our favorite joke is? He gives out a big groan, you see, and says: "It's not fair, is it, Hally?" Then I have to ask: "What, chum?" And then he says: "A nigger's arse" . . . and we both have a good laugh.

(The men stare at him with disbelief)

What's the matter, Willie? Don't you catch the joke? You always were a bit slow on the uptake. It's what is called a pun. You see, fair means both light in color and to be just and decent. *(He turns to Sam)* I thought *you* would catch it, Sam.

Sam.   Oh ja, I catch it all right.

Hally.   But it doesn't appeal to your sense of humor.

Sam.   Do you really laugh?

Hally.   Of course.

Sam.   To please him? Make him feel good?

Hally.   No, for heaven's sake! I laugh because I think it's a bloody good joke.

Sam.   You're really trying hard to be ugly, aren't you? And why drag poor old Willie into it? He's done nothing to you except show you the respect you want so badly. That's also not being fair, you know . . . and *I* mean just or decent.

Willie.   It's all right, Sam. Leave it now.

Sam.   It's me you're after. You should just have said "Sam's arse" . . . because that's the one you're trying to kick. Anyway, how do you know it's not fair? You've never seen it. Do you want to? *(He drops his trousers and underpants and presents his backside for Hally's inspection)* Have a good look. A real Basuto arse . . . which is about as nigger as they can come. Satisfied? *(Trousers up)* Now you can make your Dad even happier when you go home tonight. Tell him I showed you my arse and he is quite right. It's not fair. And if it will give him an even better laugh next time, I'll also let *him* have a look. Come, Willie, let's finish up and go.

(Sam and Willie start to tidy up the tea room. Hally doesn't move. He waits for a moment when Sam passes him)

Hally *(Quietly)*.   Sam . . .

(Sam stops and looks expectantly at the boy. Hally spits in his face. A long and heartfelt groan from Willie. For a few seconds Sam doesn't move)

Sam *(Taking out a handkerchief and wiping his face)*.   It's all right, Willie.

(To Hally)

Ja, well, you've done it . . . Master Harold. Yes, I'll start calling you that from now on. It won't be difficult anymore. You've hurt yourself, Master Harold. I saw it coming. I warned you, but you wouldn't listen. You've just hurt yourself *bad*. And you're a coward, Master Harold. The face you should be spitting in is your father's . . . but you used mine, because you think you're safe inside your fair skin . . . and this time I don't mean just or decent. *(Pause, then moving violently towards Hally)* Should I hit him, Willie?

Willie *(Stopping Sam).*   No, Boet Sam.

Sam *(Violently).*   Why not?

Willie.   It won't help, Boet Sam.

Sam.   I don't want to help! I want to hurt him.

Willie.   You also hurt yourself.

Sam.   And if he had done it to you, Willie?

Willie.   Me? Spit at me like I was a dog? *(A thought that had not occurred to him before. He looks at Hally)* Ja. Then I want to hit him. I want to hit him hard!

(A dangerous few seconds as the men stand staring at the boy. Willie turns away shaking his head)

But maybe all I do is go cry at the back. He's little boy, Boet Sam. Little *white* boy. Long trousers now, but he's still little boy.

Sam *(His violence ebbing away into defeat as quickly as it flooded).*   You're right. So go on, then: groan again, Willie. You do it better than me. *(To Hally)* You don't know all of what you've just done . . . Master Harold. It's not just that you've made me feel dirtier than I've ever been in my life . . . I mean, how do I wash off yours and your father's filth? . . . I've also failed. A long time ago I promised myself I was going to try and do something, but you've just shown me . . . Master Harold . . . that I've failed. *(Pause)* I've also got a memory of a little white boy when he was still wearing short trousers and a black man, but they're not flying a kite. It was the old Jubilee days, after dinner one night. I was in my room. You came in and just stood against the wall, looking down at the ground, and only after I'd asked you what you wanted, what was wrong, I don't know how many times, did you speak and even then so softly I almost didn't hear you. "Sam, please help me to go and fetch my Dad." Remember? He was dead drunk on the floor of the Central Hotel Bar. They'd phoned for your Mom, but you were the only one at home. And do you remember how we did it? You went in first by yourself to ask permission for me to go into the bar. Then I loaded him onto my back like a baby and carried him back to the boarding house with you following behind carrying his crutches. *(Shaking his head as he remembers)* A crowded Main Street with all the people watching a little white boy following his drunk father on a nigger's back! I felt for that little boy . . . Master Harold. I felt for him. After that we still had to clean him up, remember? He'd messed in his trousers, so we had to clean him up and get him into bed.

Hally *(Great pain).*   I love him, Sam.

Sam.   I know you do. That's why I tried to stop you from saying these things about him. It would have been so simple if you could have just despised him for being a weak man. But he's your father. You love him and you're ashamed of him. You're ashamed of so much! . . . And now that's going to include yourself. That was the promise I made to myself: to try and stop that happening. (*Pause*) After we got him to bed you came back with me to my room and sat in a corner and carried on just looking down at the ground. And for days after that! You hadn't done anything wrong, but you went around as if you owed the world an apology for being alive. I didn't like seeing that! That's not the way a boy grows up to be a man! . . . But the one person who should have been teaching you what that means was the cause of your shame. If you really want to know, that's why I made you that kite. I wanted you to look up, be proud of something, of yourself . . . (*Bitter smile at the memory*) . . . and you certainly were that when I left you with it up there on the hill. Oh, ja . . . something else! . . . If you ever do write it as a short story, there *was* a twist in our ending. I couldn't sit down there and stay with you. It was a "Whites Only" bench. You were too young, too excited to notice then. But not anymore. If you're not careful . . . Master Harold . . . you're going to be sitting up there by yourself for a long time to come, and there won't be a kite in the sky. (*Sam has got nothing more to say. He exits into the kitchen, taking off his waiter's jacket*)

Willie. Is bad. Is all all bad in here now.

Hally (*Books into his school case, raincoat on*). Willie . . . (*It is difficult to speak*) Will you lock up for me and look after the keys?

Willie. Okay.

(*Sam returns. Hally goes behind the counter and collects the few coins in the cash register. As he starts to leave . . .*)

Sam. Don't forget the comic books.

(*Hally returns to the counter and puts them in his case. He starts to leave again*)

Sam (*To the retreating back of the boy*). Stop . . . Hally . . .

(*Hally stops, but doesn't turn to face him*)

Hally . . . I've got no right to tell you what being a man means if I don't behave like one myself, and I'm not doing so well at that this afternoon. Should we try again, Hally?

Hally. Try what?

Sam. Fly another kite, I suppose. It worked once, and this time I need it as much as you do.

Hally. It's still raining, Sam. You can't fly kites on rainy days, remember.

Sam. So what do we do? Hope for better weather tomorrow?

Hally (*Helpless gesture*). I don't know. I don't know anything anymore.

Sam. You sure of that, Hally? Because it would be pretty hopeless if that was true. It would mean nothing has been learnt in here this afternoon, and there was a hell of a lot of teaching going . . . one way or the other. But anyway, I don't believe you. I reckon there's one thing you know. You don't *have* to sit up there by yourself. You know what that bench means now, and you can leave it any time you choose. All you've got to do is stand up and walk away from it.

(Hally leaves. Willie goes up quietly to Sam)

Willie. Is okay, Boet Sam. You see. Is . . . *(He can't find any better words)* . . . is going to be okay tomorrow. *(Changing his tone)* Hey, Boet Sam! *(He is trying hard)* You right. I think about it and you right. Tonight I find Hilda and say sorry. And make promise I won't beat her no more. You hear me, Boet Sam?

Sam. I hear you, Willie.

Willie. And when we practice I relax and romance with her from beginning to end. Non-stop! You watch! Two weeks' time: "First prize for promising new-comers: Mr. Willie Malopo and Miss Hilda Samuels." *(Sudden impulse)* To hell with it! I walk home. *(He goes to the jukebox, puts in a coin and selects a record. The machine comes to life in the gray twilight, blushing its way through a spectrum of soft, romantic colors)* How did you say it, Boet Sam? Let's dream. *(Willie sways with the music and gestures for Sam to dance)*

(Sarah Vaughan sings)

> "Little man you're crying,
> I know why you're blue,
> Someone took your kiddy car away;
> Better go to sleep now,
> Little man you've had a busy day." *(etc. etc.)*

You lead. I follow.

(The men dance together)

> "Johnny won your marbles,
> Tell you what we'll do;
> Dad will get you new ones right away;
> Better go to sleep now,
> Little man you've had a busy day."

For Analysis

1. Does Hally's brutal attack on Sam at the end of the play come as a surprise? Explain.

2. What is the relevance of the stories about whippings that Hally and Sam exchange?

3. Why does the kite figure so powerfully in Hally's memory?

4. What bearing does Hally's feelings about his father have on his relationship with Sam?

5. Is the ending of the play optimistic or pessimistic? Explain.

On Style
1. Although this play addresses the political oppression embodied in the recently ended apartheid system in the Union of South Africa, it also examines the qualities of fatherhood. How does the playwright reveal Hally's attitude toward his biological father?

2. Who is Hally's spiritual father, and how is the audience made aware of that relationship?

Making Connections
What circumstances might cause you to look to a friend rather than your father or mother as a confidant and protector?

Writing Topics
1. Analyze the opening dialogue between Sam and Willie (up to the appearance of Hally), and show how it establishes the mood and major themes of the play.

2. Write an essay discussing Hally's attitude toward his father and toward Sam.

Essays

Virginia Woolf   (1882–1941)

What If Shakespeare Had Had a Sister?[1]   1928

It was disappointing not to have brought back in the evening some important statement, some authentic fact. Women are poorer than men because — this or that. Perhaps now it would be better to give up seeking for the truth, and receiving on one's head an avalanche of opinion hot as lava, discoloured as dishwater. It would be better to draw the curtains; to shut out distractions; to light the lamp; to narrow the enquiry and to ask the historian, who records not opinions but facts, to describe under what conditions women lived, not throughout the ages, but in England, say in the time of Elizabeth.

For it is a perennial puzzle why no woman wrote a word of that extraordinary literature when every other man, it seemed, was capable of song or sonnet. What were the conditions in which women lived, I asked myself; for fiction, imaginative work that is, is not dropped like a pebble upon the ground, as science may be; fiction is like a spider's web, attached ever so lightly perhaps, but still attached to life at all four corners. Often the attachment is scarcely perceptible; Shakespeare's plays, for instance, seem to hang there complete by themselves. But when the web is pulled askew, hooked up at the edge, torn in the middle, one remembers that these webs are not spun in midair by incorporeal creatures, but are the work of suffering human beings, and are attached to grossly material things, like health and money and the houses we live in.

[1] *A Room of One's Own,* from which this essay is taken, is based on two lectures Woolf delivered on women and literature at Newnham College and Girton College, Cambridge University. In the opening chapter, Woolf declares that without "money and a room of her own," a woman cannot write fiction. In the following chapter, she recounts her unsuccessful attempt to turn up information at the British Library on the lives of women. This essay is from Chapter 3, from which a few passages are omitted. It ends with the concluding paragraph of the book.

980

I went, therefore, to the shelf where the histories stand and took down one of the latest, Professor Trevelyan's *History of England*. Once more I looked up Women, found "position of," and turned to the pages indicated. "Wife-beating," I read, "was a recognized right of man, and was practiced without shame by high as well as low. . . . Similarly," the historian goes on, "the daughter who refused to marry the gentleman of her parents' choice was liable to be locked up, beaten and flung about the room, without any shock being inflicted on public opinion. Marriage was not an affair of personal affection, but of family avarice, particularly in the 'chivalrous' upper classes. . . . Betrothal often took place while one or both of the parties was in the cradle, and marriage when they were scarcely out of the nurses' charge." That was about 1470, soon after Chaucer's time. The next reference to the position of women is some two hundred years later, in the time of the Stuarts. "It was still the exception for women of the upper and middle class to choose their own husbands, and when the husband had been assigned, he was lord and master, so far at least as law and custom could make him. Yet even so," Professor Trevelyan concludes, "neither Shakespeare's women nor those of authentic seventeenth-century memoirs, like the Verneys and the Hutchinsons, seem wanting in personality and character." Certainly, if we consider it, Cleopatra must have had a way with her; Lady Macbeth, one would suppose, had a will of her own; Rosalind, one might conclude, was an attractive girl. Professor Trevelyan is speaking no more than the truth when he remarks that Shakespeare's women do not seem wanting in personality and character. Not being a historian, one might go even further and say that women have burnt like beacons in all the works of all the poets from the beginning of time — Clytemnestra, Antigone, Cleopatra, Lady Macbeth, Phèdre, Cressida, Rosalind, Desdemona, the Duchess of Malfi, among the dramatists; then among the prose writers: Millamant, Clarissa, Becky Sharp, Anna Karenina, Emma Bovary, Madame de Guermantes[2] — the names flock to mind, nor do they recall women "lacking in personality and character." Indeed, if woman had no existence save in the fiction written by men, one would imagine her a person of the utmost importance; very various; heroic and mean; splendid and sordid; infinitely beautiful and hideous in the extreme; as great as a man, some think even greater. But this is woman in fiction. In fact, as Professor Trevelyan points out, she was locked up, beaten and flung about the room.

A very queer, composite being thus emerges. Imaginatively she is of the highest importance; practically she is completely insignificant. She pervades poetry from cover to cover; she is all but absent from history. She dominates the lives of kings and conquerors in fiction; in fact she was the slave of any boy whose parents forced a ring upon her finger. Some of the most inspired words, some of the most profound thoughts in literature fell from her lips; in real life she could hardly read, could scarcely spell, and was the property of her husband.

It was certainly an odd monster that one made up by reading the historians 5

---

[2] Female characters from great works of literature.

first and the poets afterwards — a worm winged like an eagle; the spirit of life and beauty in a kitchen chopping up suet. But these monsters, however amusing to the imagination, have no existence in fact. What one must do to bring her to life was to think poetically and prosaically at one and the same moment, thus keeping in touch with fact — that she is Mrs. Martin, aged thirty-six, dressed in blue, wearing a black hat and brown shoes; but not losing sight of fiction either — that she is a vessel in which all sorts of spirits and forces are coursing and flashing perpetually. The moment, however, that one tries this method with the Elizabethan woman, one branch of illumination fails; one is held up by the scarcity of facts. One knows nothing detailed, nothing perfectly true and substantial about her. History scarcely mentions her. And I turned to Professor Trevelyan again to see what history meant to him. I found by looking at his chapter headings that it meant —

"The Manor Court and the Methods of Open-field Agriculture . . . The Cistercians and Sheep-farming . . . The Crusades . . . The University . . . The House of Commons . . . The Hundred Years' War . . . The Wars of the Roses . . . The Renaissance Scholars . . . The Dissolution of the Monasteries . . . Agrarian and Religious Strife . . . The Origin of English Seapower . . . The Armada . . ." and so on. Occasionally an individual woman is mentioned, an Elizabeth, or a Mary; a queen or a great lady. But by no possible means could middle-class women with nothing but brains and character at their command have taken part in any one of the great movements which, brought together, constitute the historian's view of the past. Nor shall we find her in any collection of anecdotes. Aubrey hardly mentions her.[3] She never writes her own life and scarcely keeps a diary; there are only a handful of her letters in existence. She left no plays or poems by which we can judge her . . . Here am I asking why women did not write poetry in the Elizabethan age, and I am not sure how they were educated; whether they were taught to write; whether they had sitting-rooms to themselves; how many women had children before they were twenty-one; what, in short, they did from eight in the morning till eight at night. They had no money evidently; according to Professor Trevelyan they were married whether they liked it or not before they were out of the nursery, at fifteen or sixteen very likely. It would have been extremely odd, even upon this showing, had one of them suddenly written the plays of Shakespeare, I concluded, and I thought of that old gentleman, who is dead now, but was a bishop, I think, who declared that it was impossible for any woman, past, present, or to come, to have the genius of Shakespeare. He wrote to the papers about it. He also told a lady who applied to him for information that cats do not as a matter of fact go to heaven, though they have, he added, souls of a sort. How much thinking those old gentlemen used to save one! How the borders of ignorance shrank back at their approach! Cats do not go to heaven. Women cannot write the plays of Shakespeare.

---

[3] John Aubrey (1626–1697), author of *Brief Lives*, a biographical work.

Be that as it may, I could not help thinking, as I looked at the works of Shake-speare on the shelf, that the bishop was right at least in this; it would have been impossible, completely and entirely, for any woman to have written the plays of Shakespeare in the age of Shakespeare. Let me imagine, since facts are so hard to come by, what would have happened had Shakespeare had a wonderfully gifted sister, called Judith, let us say. Shakespeare himself went, very probably — his mother was an heiress — to the grammar school, where he may have learnt Latin — Ovid, Virgil and Horace — and the elements of grammar and logic. He was, it is well known, a wild boy who poached rabbits, perhaps shot a deer, and had, rather sooner than he should have done, to marry a woman in the neighbourhood, who bore him a child rather quicker than was right. That escapade sent him to seek his fortune in London. He had, it seemed, a taste for the theatre; he began by holding horses at the stage door. Very soon he got work in the theatre, became a successful actor, and lived in the hub of the universe, meeting everybody, knowing everybody, practising his art on the boards, exer-cising his wits in the streets, and even getting access to the palace of the queen. Meanwhile his extraordinarily gifted sister, let us suppose, remained at home. She was as adventurous, as imaginative, as agog to see the world as he was. But she was not sent to school. She had no chance of learning grammar and logic, let alone of reading Horace and Virgil. She picked up a book now and then, one of her brother's perhaps, and read a few pages. But then her parents came in and told her to mend the stockings or mind the stew and not moon about with books and papers. They would have spoken sharply but kindly, for they were substantial people who knew the conditions of life for a woman and loved their daughter — indeed, more likely than not she was the apple of her father's eye. Perhaps she scribbled some pages up in an apple loft on the sly, but was careful to hide them or set fire to them. Soon, however, before she was out of her teens, she was to be betrothed to the son of a neighbouring wool-stapler. She cried out that marriage was hateful to her, and for that she was severely beaten by her father. Then he ceased to scold her. He begged her instead not to hurt him, not to shame him in this matter of her marriage. He would give her a chain of beads or a fine petticoat, he said; and there were tears in his eyes. How could she dis-obey him? How could she break his heart? The force of her own gift alone drove her to it. She made up a small parcel of her belongings, let herself down by a rope one summer's night and took the road to London. She was not seven-teen. The birds that sang in the hedge were not more musical than she was. She had the quickest fancy, a gift like her brother's, for the tune of words. Like him, she had a taste for the theatre. She stood at the stage door; she wanted to act, she said. Men laughed in her face. The manager — a fat, loose-lipped man — guffawed. He bellowed something about poodles dancing and women acting — no woman, he said, could possibly be an actress.[4] He hinted — you can imagine what. She could get no training in her craft. Could she even seek her dinner in a

---

[4] In Shakespeare's day, women's roles were played by boys.

tavern or roam the streets at midnight? Yet her genius was for fiction and lusted to feed abundantly upon the lives of men and women and the study of their ways. At last — for she was very young, oddly like Shakespeare the poet in her face, with the same grey eyes and rounded brows — at last Nick Greene the actor-manager took pity on her; she found herself with child by that gentleman and so — who shall measure the heat and violence of the poet's heart when caught and tangled in a woman's body? — killed herself one winter's night and lies buried at some cross-roads where the omnibuses now stop outside the Elephant and Castle.[5]

That, more or less, is how the story would run, I think, if a woman in Shakespeare's day had had Shakespeare's genius. But for my part, I agree with the deceased bishop, if such he was — it is unthinkable that any woman in Shakespeare's day should have had Shakespeare's genius. For genius like Shakespeare's is not born among labouring, uneducated, servile people. It was not born in England among the Saxons and the Britons. It is not born today among the working classes. How, then, could it have been born among women whose work began, according to Professor Trevelyan, almost before they were out of the nursery, who were forced to it by their parents and held to it by all the power of law and custom? Yet genius of a sort must have existed among women as it must have existed among the working classes. Now and again an Emily Brontë or a Robert Burns blazes out and proves its presence.[6] But certainly it never got itself on to paper. When, however, one reads of a witch being ducked, of a woman possessed by devils, of a wise woman selling herbs, or even of a very remarkable man who had a mother, then I think we are on the track of a lost novelist, a suppressed poet, of some mute and inglorious[7] Jane Austen, some Emily Brontë who dashed her brains out on the moor or moped and mowed about the highways crazed with the torture that her gift had put her to. Indeed, I would venture to guess that Anon, who wrote so many poems without signing them, was often a woman. It was a woman Edward Fitzgerald,[8] I think, suggested who made the ballads and the folk-songs, crooning them to her children, beguiling her spinning with them, or the length of the winter's night.

This may be true or it may be false — who can say? — but what is true in it, so it seemed to me, reviewing the story of Shakespeare's sister as I had made it, is that any woman born with a great gift in the sixteenth century would certainly have gone crazed, shot herself, or ended her days in some lonely cottage outside the village, half witch, half wizard, feared and mocked at. For it needs little skill in psychology to be sure that a highly gifted girl who had tried to use her gift for poetry would have been so thwarted and hindered by other people, so tortured and pulled asunder by her own contrary instincts, that she must

---

[5] A tavern.

[6] Emily Brontë (1818–1848), English novelist, and Robert Burns (1759–1796), Scottish poet.

[7] Thomas Gray's description in "Elegy Written in a Country Churchyard" of a peasant whose underdeveloped poetic genius might be as powerful as the great John Milton's.

[8] Edward FitzGerald (1809–1883), translator and poet.

have lost her health and sanity to a certainty. No girl could have walked to London and stood at a stage door and forced her way into the presence of actor-managers without doing herself a violence and suffering an anguish which may have been irrational — for chastity may be a fetish invented by certain societies for unknown reasons — but were none the less inevitable. Chastity had then, it has even now, a religious importance in a woman's life, and has so wrapped itself round with nerves and instincts that to cut it free and bring it to the light of day demands courage of the rarest. To have lived a free life in London in the sixteenth century would have meant for a woman who was poet and playwright a nervous stress and dilemma which might well have killed her. Had she survived, whatever she had written would have been twisted and deformed, issuing from a strained and morbid imagination. And undoubtedly, I thought, looking at the shelf where there are no plays by women, her work would have gone unsigned. That refuge she would have sought certainly. It was the relic of the sense of chastity that dictated anonymity to women even so late as the nineteenth century. Currer Bell, George Eliot, George Sand,[9] all the victims of inner strife as their writings prove, sought ineffectively to veil themselves by using the name of a man. Thus they did homage to the convention, which if not implanted by the other sex was liberally encouraged by them (the chief glory of a woman is not to be talked of, said Pericles,[10] himself a much-talked-of man), that publicity in women is detestable. . . .

That woman, then, who was born with a gift of poetry in the sixteenth century, was an unhappy woman, a woman at strife against herself. All the conditions of her life, all her own instincts, were hostile to the state of mind which is needed to set free whatever is in the brain. But what is the state of mind that is most propitious to the act of creation, I asked? Can one come by any notion of the state that furthers and makes possible that strange activity? Here I opened the volume containing the Tragedies of Shakespeare. What was Shakespeare's state of mind, for instance, when he wrote *Lear* and *Antony and Cleopatra*? It was certainly the state of mind most favourable to poetry that there has ever existed. But Shakespeare himself said nothing about it. We only know casually and by chance that he "never blotted a line."[11] Nothing indeed was ever said by the artist himself about his state of mind until the eighteenth century perhaps. Rousseau[12] perhaps began it. At any rate, by the nineteenth century self-consciousness had developed so far that it was the habit for men of letters to describe their minds in confessions and autobiographies. Their lives also were written, and their letters were printed after their deaths. Thus, though we do not know what Shakespeare went through when he wrote *Lear,* we do know what Carlyle went through when he wrote the *French Revolution;* what

10

---

[9] The pseudonyms of Charlotte Brontë (1816–1855) and Mary Ann Evans (1819–1880), English novelists, and Amandine Aurore Lucie Dupin (1804–1876), French novelist.

[10] Pericles (d. 429 B.C.), Athenian statesman and general.

[11] According to Ben Jonson, Shakespeare's contemporary.

[12] Jean-Jacques Rousseau (1712–1778), French philosopher, author of *The Confessions of Jean-Jacques Rousseau.*

Flaubert went through when he wrote *Madame Bovary;* what Keats was going through when he tried to write poetry against the coming of death and the indifference of the world.

And one gathers from this enormous modern literature of confession and self-analysis that to write a work of genius is almost always a feat of prodigious difficulty. Everything is against the likelihood that it will come from the writer's mind whole and entire. Generally material circumstances are against it. Dogs will bark; people will interrupt; money must be made; health will break down. Further, accentuating all these difficulties and making them harder to bear is the world's notorious indifference. It does not ask people to write poems and novels and histories; it does not need them. It does not care whether Flaubert finds the right word or whether Carlyle scrupulously verifies this or that fact. Naturally, it will not pay for what it does not want. And so the writer, Keats, Flaubert, Carlyle, suffers, especially in the creative years of youth, every form of distraction and discouragement. A curse, a cry of agony, rises from those books of analysis and confession. "Mighty poets in their misery dead"[13] — that is the burden of their song. If anything comes through in spite of this, it is a miracle, and probably no book is born entire and uncrippled as it was conceived.

But for women, I thought, looking at the empty shelves, these difficulties were infinitely more formidable. In the first place, to have a room of her own, let alone a quiet room or a sound-proof room, was out of the question, unless her parents were exceptionally rich or very noble, even up to the beginning of the nineteenth century. Since her pin money, which depended on the good will of her father, was only enough to keep her clothed, she was debarred from such alleviations as came even to Keats or Tennyson or Carlyle, all poor men, from a walking tour, a little journey to France, from the separate lodging which, even if it were miserable enough, sheltered them from the claims and tyrannies of their families. Such material difficulties were formidable; but much worse were the immaterial. The indifference of the world which Keats and Flaubert and other men of genius have found so hard to bear was in her case not indifference but hostility. The world did not say to her as it said to them, Write if you choose; it makes no difference to me. The world said with a guffaw, Write? What's the good of your writing? . . .

I told you in the course of this paper that Shakespeare had a sister; but do not look for her in Sir Sidney Lee's life of the poet. She died young — alas, she never wrote a word. She lies buried where the omnibuses now stop, opposite the Elephant and Castle. Now my belief is that this poet who never wrote a word and was buried at the cross-roads still lives. She lives in you and me, and in many other women who are not here tonight, for they are washing up the dishes and putting the children to bed. But she lives; for great poets do not die; they are continuing presences; they need only the opportunity to walk among us in the flesh. This opportunity, as I think, it is now coming within your power to give

[13] From William Wordsworth's poem "Resolution and Independence."

her. For my belief is that if we live another century or so — I am talking of the common life which is the real life and not of the little separate lives which we live as individuals — and have five hundred a year each of us and rooms of our own; if we have the habit of freedom and the courage to write exactly what we think; if we escape a little from the common sitting-room and see human beings not always in their relation to each other but in relation to reality; and the sky, too, and the trees or whatever it may be in themselves; if we look past Milton's bogey, for no human being should shut out the view; if we face the fact, for it is a fact, that there is no arm to cling to, but that we go alone and that our relation is to the world of reality and not only to the world of men and women, then the opportunity will come and the dead poet who was Shakespeare's sister will put on the body which she has so often laid down. Drawing her life from the lives of the unknown who were her forerunners, as her brother did before her, she will be born. As for her coming without that preparation, without that effort on our part, without that determination that when she is born again she shall find it possible to live and write her poetry, that we cannot expect, for that would be impossible. But I maintain that she would come if we worked for her, and that so to work, even in poverty and obscurity, is worth while.

For Analysis

1. How does Woolf explain the contrast between the women of fact and women as they have been portrayed in fiction?

2. What answers do historians provide to the "perennial puzzle" Woolf mentions in the first sentence of the second paragraph? What generalizations might we make about the meaning of "history" on the basis of Woolf's research into the status of women?

3. Analyze the effect of Woolf's concluding remarks about the bishop (para. 6): "Cats do not go to heaven. Women cannot write the plays of Shakespeare." Then consider her later comment (para. 8), "I agree with the deceased bishop, if such he was — it is unthinkable that any woman in Shakespeare's day should have had Shakespeare's genius." Does this contradict what she has been saying?

4. Explain the link Woolf makes (para. 9) between chastity and the problem of the gifted woman writer.

On Style

1. How would you describe Woolf's general **tone** throughout the essay? Where and for what purpose does she adopt an **ironic** tone?

2. In what ways does the first part of Woolf's essay prepare the reader to accept her imagined life of Shakespeare's sister?

Making Connections

1. Among the women who "have burnt like beacons" (para. 3) in the works of great male writers, Woolf cites Antigonê in Sophocles' *Antigonê* (p. 467) and Desdemona in Shakespeare's *Othello* (p. 1144). Do you agree with her assessment of these two women? Might Woolf have included Nora in Henrik Ibsen's *A Doll's House* (p. 499) and Mama in Lorraine Hansberry's *A Raisin in the Sun* (p. 867)? Explain.

2. What do you suppose Woolf would think of Mrs. Peters and Mrs. Hale in Susan Glaspell's *Trifles* (p. 1236) and Calixta in Kate Chopin's "The Storm" (p. 1016)?

Writing Topics

1. Do you believe that our culture has changed so significantly in its attitudes toward women that Woolf's arguments have lost their relevance? Write an essay explaining why or why not.

2. Speculate on why it was the case that, while being economically as dependent on men as servants throughout much of Western history, women were sometimes portrayed in fiction as being "as great as a man, some think even greater" (para. 3).

Zora Neale Hurston   (1891–1960)

How It Feels to Be Colored Me   1928

I am colored but I offer nothing in the way of extenuating circumstances except the fact that I am the only Negro in the United States whose grandfather on the mother's side was *not* an Indian chief.

I remember the very day that I became colored. Up to my thirteenth year I lived in the little Negro town of Eatonville, Florida. It is exclusively a colored town. The only white people I knew passed through the town going to or coming from Orlando. The native whites rode dusty horses, the Northern tourists chugged down the sandy village road in automobiles. The town knew the Southerners and never stopped cane chewing when they passed. But the Northerners were something else again. They were peered at cautiously from behind the curtains by the timid. The more venturesome would come out on the porch to watch them go past and got just as much pleasure out of the tourists as the tourists got out of the village.

The front porch might seem a daring place for the rest of the town, but it was a gallery seat for me. My favorite place was atop the gate-post. Proscenium box[1] for a born first-nighter. Not only did I enjoy the show, but I didn't mind the actors knowing that I liked it. I usually spoke to them in passing. I'd wave at them and when they returned my salute, I would say something like this: "Howdy-do-well-I-thank-you-where-you-goin'?" Usually automobile or the horse paused at this, and after a queer exchange of compliments, I would probably "go a piece of the way" with them, as we say in farthest Florida. If one of my family happened to come to the front in time to see me, of course negotiations would be rudely broken off. But even so, it is clear that I was the first "welcome-to-our-state" Floridian, and I hope the Miami Chamber of Commerce will please take notice.

During this period, white people differed from colored to me only in that they rode through town and never lived there. They liked to hear me "speak pieces" and sing and wanted to see me dance the parse-me-la, and gave me generously of their small silver for doing these things, which seemed strange to me for I wanted to do them so much that I needed bribing to stop. Only they didn't know it. The colored people gave no dimes. They deplored any joyful tendencies in me, but I was their Zora nevertheless. I belonged to them, to the nearby hotels, to the county — everybody's Zora.

---

[1] A box seat close to the stage.

But changes came in the family when I was thirteen, and I was sent to school in Jacksonville. I left Eatonville, the town of the oleanders, as Zora. When I disembarked from the river-boat at Jacksonville, she was no more. It seemed that I had suffered a sea change. I was not Zora of Orange County any more, I was now a little colored girl. I found it out in certain ways. In my heart as well as in the mirror, I became a fast brown — warranted not to rub nor run.

But I am not tragically colored. There is no great sorrow dammed up in my soul, nor lurking behind my eyes. I do not mind at all. I do not belong to the sobbing school of Negrohood who hold that nature somehow has given them a lowdown dirty deal and whose feelings are all hurt about it. Even in the helter-skelter skirmish that is my life, I have seen that the world is to the strong regardless of a little pigmentation more or less. No, I do not weep at the world — I am too busy sharpening my oyster knife.

Someone is always at my elbow reminding me that I am the granddaughter of slaves. It fails to register depression with me. Slavery is sixty years in the past. The operation was successful and the patient is doing well, thank you. The terrible struggle that made me an American out of a potential slave said "On the line!" The Reconstruction said "Get set!"; and the generation before said "Go!" I am off to a flying start and I must not halt in the stretch to look behind and weep. Slavery is the price I paid for civilization, and the choice was not with me. It is a bully adventure and worth all that I have paid through my ancestors for it. No one on earth ever had a greater chance for glory. The world to be won and nothing to be lost. It is thrilling to think — to know that for any act of mine, I shall get twice as much praise or twice as much blame. It is quite exciting to hold the center of the national stage, with the spectators not knowing whether to laugh or to weep.

The position of my white neighbor is much more difficult. No brown specter pulls up a chair beside me when I sit down to eat. No dark ghost thrusts its leg against mine in bed. The game of keeping what one has is never so exciting as the game of getting.

I do not always feel colored. Even now I often achieve the unconscious Zora of Eatonville before the Hegira.[2] I feel most colored when I am thrown against a sharp white background.

For instance at Barnard. "Beside the waters of the Hudson" I feel my race. Among the thousand white persons, I am a dark rock surged upon, and over-swept, but through it all, I remain myself. When covered by the waters, I am; and the ebb but reveals me again.

Sometimes it is the other way around. A white person is set down in our midst, but the contrast is just as sharp for me. For instance, when I sit in the drafty basement that is The New World Cabaret[3] with a white person, my color

---

[2] A flight or journey to a better place.
[3] A Harlem night club popular in the 1920s.

comes. We enter chatting about any little nothing that we have in common and are seated by the jazz waiters. In the abrupt way that jazz orchestras have, this one plunges into a number. It loses no time in circumlocutions, but gets right down to business. It constricts the thorax and splits the heart with its tempo and narcotic harmonics. This orchestra grows rambunctious, rears on its hind legs and attacks the tonal veil with primitive fury, rending it, clawing it until it breaks through to the jungle beyond. I follow those heathen — follow them exultingly. I dance wildly inside myself; I yell within, I whoop; I shake my assegai[4] above my head, I hurl it true to the mark *yeeeeooww!* I am in the jungle and living in the jungle way. My face is painted red and yellow and my body is painted blue. My pulse is throbbing like a war drum. I want to slaughter something — give pain, give death to what, I do not know. But the piece ends. The men of the orchestra wipe their lips and rest their fingers. I creep back slowly to the veneer we call civilization with the last tone and find the white friend sitting motionless in his seat — smoking calmly.

"Good music they have here," he remarks, drumming the table with his fingertips.

Music. The great blobs of purple and red emotion have not touched him. He has only heard what I felt. He is far away and I see him but dimly across the ocean and the continent that have fallen between us. He is so pale with his whiteness then and I am *so* colored.

At certain times I have no race, I am *me*. When I set my hat at a certain angle and saunter down Seventh Avenue, Harlem City, feeling as snooty as the lions in front of the Forty-Second Street Library, for instance. So far as my feelings are concerned, Peggy Hopkins Joyce on the Boule Mich[5] with her gorgeous raiment, stately carriage, knees knocking together in a most aristocratic manner, has nothing on me. The cosmic Zora emerges. I belong to no race nor time. I am the eternal feminine with its string of beads.

I have no separate feeling about being an American citizen and colored. I am 15 merely a fragment of the Great Soul that surges within the boundaries. My country, right or wrong.

Sometimes, I feel discriminated against, but it does not make me angry. It merely astonishes me. How *can* any deny themselves the pleasure of my company? It's beyond me.

But in the main, I feel like a brown bag of miscellany propped against a wall. Against a wall in company with other bags, white, red and yellow. Pour out the contents, and there is discovered a jumble of small things priceless and worthless. A first-water diamond, an empty spool, bits of broken glass, lengths of string, a key to a door long since crumbled away, a rusty knife-blade, old shoes

---

[4] An iron-tipped spear used by the Bantu peoples of Africa.

[5] Peggy Hopkins Joyce (1893–1957) was a media icon of her day, celebrated for her beauty and succession of rich husbands. Boule Mich, short for Boulevard St. Michel, is a famous street on the Left Bank in Paris.

saved for a road that never was and never will be, a nail bent under the weight of things too heavy for any nail, a dried flower or two still a little fragrant. In your hand is the brown bag. On the ground before you is the jumble it held — so much like the jumble in the bags, could they be emptied, that all might be dumped in a single heap and the bags refilled without altering the content of any greatly. A bit of colored glass more or less would not matter. Perhaps that is how the Great Stuffer of Bags filled them in the first place — who knows?

For Analysis

1. Describe the **tone** established in the opening paragraph. Is that tone maintained throughout? Explain.

2. What does Hurston mean by the first sentence of paragraph 6?

3. Describe Hurston's feelings about her African ancestry.

4. What does Hurston mean in paragraph 7 when she says, "Slavery is the price I paid for civilization"?

5. What point is Hurston making in paragraph 7? Is it a convincing one?

On Style

1. How do the four sections of the essay relate to one another?

2. How does Hurston's use of **metaphoric** language and imagery help her develop her argument?

Making Connections

1. Compare Hurston's feelings about the connection between her racial/cultural identity and who she is with those of Jamaica Kincaid in "Girl" (p. 730) and Maya Angelou in "Graduation in Stamps" (p. 1000).

2. Compare the meaning of jazz music in this essay with its meaning in James Baldwin's "Sonny's Blues" (p. 674).

Writing Topics

1. Describe Hurston's sense of what it means to be black.

2. Write an essay either supporting or taking issue with Hurston's declaration that "At certain times I have no race, I am *me*" (para. 14).

3. Use the following famous passage from W. E. B. Dubois's book *The Souls of Black Folk* (1903) as the basis for an analysis of Hurston's essay.

> It is a peculiar sensation, this double-consciousness, this sense of always looking at one's self through the eyes of others, of measuring one's soul by the tape of a world that looks on in amused contempt and pity. One ever feels his two-ness — an American, a Negro; two souls, two thoughts, two unreconciled strivings; two warring ideals in one dark body, whose dogged strength alone keeps it from being torn asunder.

George Orwell (1903–1950)

Shooting an Elephant 1936

In Moulmein, in lower Burma, I was hated by large numbers of people — the only time in my life that I have been important enough for this to happen to me. I was sub-divisional police officer of the town, and in an aimless, petty kind of way anti-European feeling was very bitter. No one had the guts to raise a riot, but if a European woman went through the bazaars alone somebody would probably spit betel juice over her dress. As a police officer I was an obvious target and was baited whenever it seemed safe to do so. When a nimble Burman tripped me up on the football field and the referee (another Burman) looked the other way, the crowd yelled with hideous laughter. This happened more than once. In the end the sneering yellow faces of young men that met me everywhere, the insults hooted after me when I was at a safe distance, got badly on my nerves. The young Buddhist priests were the worst of all. There were several thousands of them in the town and none of them seemed to have anything to do except stand on street corners and jeer at Europeans.

All this was perplexing and upsetting. For at that time I had already made up my mind that imperialism was an evil thing and the sooner I chucked up my job and got out of it the better. Theoretically — and secretly, of course — I was all for the Burmese and all against their oppressors, the British. As for the job I was doing, I hated it more bitterly than I can perhaps make clear. In a job like that you see the dirty work of Empire at close quarters. The wretched prisoners huddling in the stinking cages of the lock-ups, the grey, cowed faces of the long-term convicts, the scarred buttocks of the men who had been flogged with bamboos — all these oppressed me with an intolerable sense of guilt. But I could get nothing into perspective. I was young and ill-educated and I had had to think out my problems in the utter silence that is imposed on every Englishman in the East. I did not even know that the British Empire is dying, still less did I know that it is a great deal better than the younger empires that are going to supplant it. All I knew was that I was stuck between my hatred of the empire I served and my rage against the evil-spirited little beasts who tried to make my job impossible. With one part of my mind I thought of the British[1] as an unbreakable tyranny, as something clamped down, *in saecula saeculorum*,[2] upon the will of prostrate peoples; with another part I thought that the greatest joy in the world would be to drive a bayonet into a Buddhist priest's guts. Feelings like

[1] The imperial British government of India and Burma.
[2] For eternity.

these are the normal by-products of imperialism; ask any Anglo-Indian official, if you can catch him off duty.

One day something happened which in a roundabout way was enlightening. It was a tiny incident in itself, but it gave me a better glimpse than I had had before of the real nature of imperialism — the real motive for which despotic governments act. Early one morning the sub-inspector at a police station the other end of the town rang me up on the 'phone and said that an elephant was ravaging the bazaar. Would I please come and do something about it? I did not know what I could do, but I wanted to see what was happening and I got on to a pony and started out. I took my rifle, an old .44 Winchester and much too small to kill an elephant, but I thought the noise might be useful *in terrorem*. Various Burmans stopped me on the way and told me about the elephant's doings. It was not, of course, a wild elephant, but a tame one which had gone "must." It had been chained up, as tame elephants always are when their attack of "must" is due, but on the previous night it had broken its chain and escaped. Its mahout,[3] the only person who could manage it when it was in that state, had set out in pursuit, but had taken the wrong direction and was now twelve hours' journey away, and in the morning the elephant had suddenly reappeared in the town. The Burmese population had no weapons and were quite helpless against it. It had already destroyed somebody's bamboo hut, killed a cow and raided some fruit-stalls and devoured the stock; also it had met the municipal rubbish van and, when the driver jumped out and took to his heels, had turned the van over and inflicted violences upon it.

The Burmese sub-inspector and some Indian constables were waiting for me in the quarter where the elephant had been seen. It was a very poor quarter, a labyrinth of squalid bamboo huts, thatched with palm-leaf, winding all over a steep hillside. I remember that it was a cloudy, stuffy morning at the beginning of the rains. We began questioning the people as to where the elephant had gone and, as usual, failed to get any definite information. That is invariably the case in the East; a story always sounds clear enough at a distance, but the nearer you get to the scene of events the vaguer it becomes. Some of the people said that the elephant had gone in one direction, some said that he had gone in another, some professed not even to have heard of any elephant. I had almost made up my mind that the whole story was a pack of lies, when we heard yells a little distance away. There was a loud, scandalized cry of "Go away, child! Go away this instant!" and an old woman with a switch in her hand came round the corner of a hut, violently shooing away a crowd of naked children. Some more women followed, clicking their tongues and exclaiming; evidently there was something that the children ought not to have seen. I rounded the hut and saw a man's dead body sprawling in the mud. He was an Indian, a black Dravidian coolie, almost naked, and he could not have been dead many minutes. The people said that the elephant had come suddenly upon him round the corner of

---

[3] The keeper and driver of an elephant.

the hut, caught him with its trunk, put its foot on his back and ground him into the earth. This was the rainy season and the ground was soft, and his face had scored a trench a foot deep and a couple of yards long. He was lying on his belly with arms crucified and head sharply twisted to one side. His face was coated with mud, the eyes wide open, the teeth bared and grinning with an expression of unendurable agony. (Never tell me, by the way, that the dead look peaceful. Most of the corpses I have seen look devilish.) The friction of the great beast's foot had stripped the skin from his back as neatly as one skins a rabbit. As soon as I saw the dead man I sent an orderly to a friend's house nearby to borrow an elephant rifle. I had already sent back the pony, not wanting it to go mad with fright and throw me if it smelt the elephant.

The orderly came back in a few minutes with a rifle and five cartridges, and meanwhile some Burmans had arrived and told us that the elephant was in the paddy fields below, only a few hundred yards away. As I started forward practically the whole population of the quarter flocked out of the houses and followed me. They had seen the rifle and were all shouting excitedly that I was going to shoot the elephant. They had not shown much interest in the elephant when he was merely ravaging their homes, but it was different now that he was going to be shot. It was a bit of fun to them, as it would be to an English crowd; besides they wanted the meat. It made me vaguely uneasy. I had no intention of shooting the elephant — I had merely sent for the rifle to defend myself if necessary — and it is always unnerving to have a crowd following you. I marched down the hill, looking and feeling a fool, with the rifle over my shoulders and an ever-growing army of people jostling at my heels. At the bottom, when you got away from the huts, there was a metalled road and beyond that a miry waste of paddy fields a thousand yards across, not yet ploughed but soggy from the first rains and dotted with coarse grass. The elephant was standing eight yards from the road, his left side towards us. He took not the slightest notice of the crowd's approach. He was tearing up branches of grass, beating them against his knees to clean them and stuffing them into his mouth. 5

I had halted on the road. As soon as I saw the elephant I knew with perfect certainty that I ought not to shoot him. It is a serious matter to shoot a working elephant — it is comparable to destroying a huge and costly piece of machinery — and obviously one ought not to do it if it can possibly be avoided. And at that distance, peacefully eating, the elephant looked no more dangerous than a cow. I thought then and I think now that his attack of "must" was already passing off; in which case he would merely wander harmlessly about until the mahout came back and caught him. Moreover, I did not in the least want to shoot him. I decided that I would watch him for a little while to make sure that he did not turn savage again, and then go home.

But at that moment I glanced round at the crowd that had followed me. It was an immense crowd, two thousand at the least and growing every minute. It blocked the road for a long distance on either side. I looked at the sea of yellow faces above the garish clothes — faces all happy and excited over this bit of fun, all certain that the elephant was going to be shot. They were watching me as they would watch a conjurer about to perform a trick. They did not like me, but with the magical rifle in my hands I was momentarily worth watching. And suddenly I realized that I should have to shoot the elephant after all. The people expected it of me and I had got to do it; I could feel their two thousand wills pressing me forward, irresistibly. And it was at this moment, as I stood there with the rifle in my hands, that I first grasped the hollowness, the futility of the white man's dominion in the East. Here was I, the white man with his gun, standing in front of the unarmed native crowd — seemingly the leading actor of the piece; but in reality I was only an absurd puppet pushed to and fro by the will of those yellow faces behind. I perceived in this moment that when the white man turns tyrant it is his own freedoms that he destroys. He becomes a sort of hollow, posing dummy, the conventionalized figure of a sahib. For it is the condition of his rule that he shall spend his life in trying to impress the "natives," and so in every crisis he has got to do what the "natives" expect of him. He wears a mask, and his face grows to fit it. I had got to shoot the elephant. I had committed myself to doing it when I sent for the rifle. A sahib has got to act like a sahib; he has got to appear resolute, to know his own mind and do definite things. To come all that way, rifle in hand, with two thousand people marching at my heels, and then to trail feebly away, having done nothing — no, that was impossible. The crowd would laugh at me. And my whole life, every white man's life in the East, was one long struggle not to be laughed at.

But I did not want to shoot the elephant. I watched him beating his bunch of grass against his knees, with that preoccupied grandmotherly air that elephants have. It seemed to me that it would be murder to shoot him. At that age I was not squeamish about killing animals, but I had never shot an elephant and never wanted to. (Somehow it always seems worse to kill a *large* animal.) Besides, there was the beast's owner to be considered. Alive, the elephant was worth at least a hundred pounds; dead, he would only be worth the value of his tusks, five pounds, possibly. But I had to act quickly. I turned to some experienced-looking Burmans who had been there when we arrived, and asked them how the elephant had been behaving. They all said the same thing: he took no notice of you if you left him alone, but he might charge if you went too close to him.

It was perfectly clear to me what I ought to do. I ought to walk up to within, say, twenty-five yards of the elephant and test his behavior. If he charged, I could shoot; if he took no notice of me, it would be safe to leave him until the mahout came back. But also I knew that I was going to do no such thing. I was a poor shot with a rifle and the ground was soft mud into which one would sink at every step. If the elephant charged and I missed him, I should have about as much chance as a toad under a steam-roller. But even then I was not thinking particularly of my own skin, only of the watchful yellow faces behind. For at that moment, with the crowd watching me, I was not afraid in the ordinary sense, as I would have been if I had been alone. A white man mustn't be frightened in front of "natives"; and so, in general, he isn't frightened. The sole thought in my mind was that if anything went wrong those two thousand Burmans would see me pursued, caught, trampled on and reduced to a grinning corpse like that Indian up the hill. And if that happened it was quite probable that some of them would laugh. That would never do. There was only one alternative. I shoved the cartridges into the magazine and lay down on the road to get a better aim.

The crowd grew very still, and a deep, low, happy sigh, as of people who see   10
the theatre curtain go up at last, breathed from innumerable throats. They were going to have their bit of fun after all. The rifle was a beautiful German thing with cross-hair sights. I did not then know that in shooting an elephant one would shoot to cut an imaginary bar running from ear-hole to ear-hole. I ought, therefore, as the elephant was sideways on, to have aimed straight at his ear-hole; actually I aimed several inches in front of this, thinking the brain would be further forward.

When I pulled the trigger I did not hear the bang or feel the kick — one never does when a shot goes home — but I heard the devilish roar of glee that went up from the crowd. In that instant, in too short a time, one would have thought, even for the bullet to get there, a mysterious, terrible change had come over the elephant. He neither stirred nor fell, but every line of his body had altered. He looked suddenly stricken, shrunken, immensely old, as though the frightful impact of the bullet had paralysed him without knocking him down. At last, after what seemed a long time — it might have been five seconds, I dare say — he sagged flabbily to his knees. His mouth slobbered. An enormous senility seemed to have settled upon him. One could have imagined him thousands of years old. I fired again into the same spot. At the second shot he did not collapse but climbed with desperate slowness to his feet and stood weakly upright, with legs sagging and head drooping. I fired a third time. That was the shot that did for him. You could see the agony of it jolt his whole body and knock the last remnant of strength from his legs. But in falling he seemed for a moment to rise, for as his hind legs collapsed beneath him he seemed to tower upward like a huge rock toppling, his trunk reaching skywards like a tree. He trumpeted, for the first and only time. And then down he came, his belly towards me, with a crash that seemed to shake the ground even where I lay.

I got up. The Burmans were already racing past me across the mud. It was obvious that the elephant would never rise again, but he was not dead. He was breathing very rhythmically with long rattling gasps, his great mound of a side painfully rising and falling. His mouth was wide open — I could see far down into caverns of pale pink throat. I waited a long time for him to die, but his breathing did not weaken. Finally I fired my two remaining shots into the spot where I thought his heart must be. The thick blood welled out of him like red velvet, but still he did not die. His body did not even jerk when the shots hit him, the tortured breathing continued without a pause. He was dying, very slowly and in great agony, but in some world remote from me where not even a bullet could damage him further. I felt that I had got to put an end to that dreadful noise. It seemed dreadful to see the great beast lying there, powerless to move and yet powerless to die, and not even to be able to finish him. I sent back for my small rifle and poured shot after shot into his heart and down his throat. They seemed to make no impression. The tortured gasps continued as steadily as the ticking of a clock.

In the end I could not stand it any longer and went away. I heard later that it took him half an hour to die. Burmans were bringing dahs[4] and baskets even before I left, and I was told they had stripped his body almost to the bones by the afternoon.

Afterwards, of course, there were endless discussions about the shooting of the elephant. The owner was furious, but he was only an Indian and could do nothing. Besides, legally I had done the right thing, for a mad elephant has to be killed, like a mad dog, if its owner fails to control it. Among the Europeans opinion was divided. The older men said I was right, the younger men said it was a damn shame to shoot an elephant for killing a coolie, because an elephant was worth more than any damn Coringhee coolie. And afterwards I was very glad that the coolie had been killed; it put me legally in the right and it gave me a sufficient pretext for shooting the elephant. I often wondered whether any of the others grasped that I had done it solely to avoid looking a fool.

For Analysis

1. Examine carefully paragraphs 11 and 12, in which Orwell describes the death of the elephant. Is the reader meant to take the passage only literally, or can a case be made that the elephant's death is imbued with symbolic meaning? Explain.

2. Orwell tells us repeatedly that his sympathies are with the Burmese. Yet he describes them as "evil-spirited little beasts" (para. 2). How might this ambivalence be explained?

3. What does the experience described in paragraph 7 teach Orwell?

4. Do you agree with Orwell's rationalization that under the circumstances he had no choice but "to shoot the elephant" (para. 7)?

5. What is your reaction to Orwell's final comment, "I was very glad that the coolie had been killed; it put me legally in the right and it gave me a sufficient pretext for shooting the elephant. I often wondered whether any of the others grasped that I had done it solely to avoid looking a fool"?

On Style

Midway through the essay (para. 7), Orwell discloses the significance the event had for him. Why does he disclose it then rather than save it for the conclusion?

Making Connections

1. Compare this essay with Jonathan Swift's "A Modest Proposal" (p. 615) in the techniques and arguments used to attack imperialism.

[4] Knives.

2. While they are dissimilar in subject matter, this story and Toni Cade Bambara's "The Lesson" (p. 134) culminate in climactic events that change the **protagonists**. Compare those events and their effect on the two protagonists.

Writing Topics

1. In a brief paragraph, summarize the lesson Orwell learned from his experience.

2. What does Orwell conclude regarding the position of foreign authorities in a hostile country?

3. Describe a situation in which you were required to behave in an official capacity that contradicted your personal beliefs.

Maya Angelou   (b. 1928)

Graduation in Stamps   1970

The children in Stamps trembled visibly with anticipation. Some adults were excited too, but to be certain the whole young population had come down with graduation epidemic. Large classes were graduating from both the grammar school and the high school. Even those who were years removed from their own day of glorious release were anxious to help with preparations as a kind of dry run. The junior students who were moving into the vacating classes' chairs were tradition-bound to show their talents for leadership and management. They strutted through the school and around the campus exerting pressure on the lower grades. Their authority was so new that occasionally if they pressed a little too hard it had to be overlooked. After all, next term was coming, and it never hurt a sixth grader to have a play sister in the eighth grade, or a tenth-year student to be able to call a twelfth grader Bubba. So all was endured in a spirit of shared understanding. But the graduating classes themselves were the nobility. Like travelers with exotic destinations on their minds, the graduates were remarkably forgetful. They came to school without their books, or tablets or even pencils. Volunteers fell over themselves to secure replacements for the missing equipment. When accepted, the willing workers might or might not be thanked, and it was of no importance to the pregraduation rites. Even teachers were respectful of the now quiet and aging seniors, and tended to speak to them, if not as equals, as beings only slightly lower than themselves. After tests were returned and grades given, the student body, which acted like an extended family, knew who did well, who excelled, and what piteous ones had failed.

Unlike the white high school, Lafayette County Training School distinguished itself by having neither lawn, nor hedges, nor tennis court, nor climbing ivy. Its two buildings (main classrooms, the grade school and home economics) were set on a dirt hill with no fence to limit either its boundaries or those of bordering farms. There was a large expanse to the left of the school which was used alternately as a baseball diamond or a basketball court. Rusty hoops on the swaying poles represented the permanent recreational equipment, although bats and balls could be borrowed from the P.E. teacher if the borrower was qualified and if the diamond wasn't occupied.

Over this rocky area relieved by a few shady tall persimmon trees the graduating class walked. The girls often held hands and no longer bothered to speak to the lower students. There was a sadness about them, as if this old world was not their home and they were bound for higher ground. The boys, on the other hand, had become more friendly, more outgoing. A decided change from the closed attitude they projected while studying for finals. Now they seemed not ready to give up the old school, the familiar paths and classrooms. Only a small percentage would be continuing on to college — one of the South's A & M (agricultural and mechanical) schools, which trained Negro youths to be carpenters, farmers, handymen, masons, maids, cooks and baby nurses. Their future rode heavily on their shoulders, and blinded them to the collective joy that had pervaded the lives of the boys and girls in the grammar school graduating class.

Parents who could afford it had ordered new shoes and ready-made clothes for themselves from Sears and Roebuck or Montgomery Ward. They also engaged the best seamstresses to make the floating graduating dresses and to cut down secondhand pants which would be pressed to a military slickness for the important event.

Oh, it was important, all right. Whitefolks would attend the ceremony, and 5 two or three would speak of God and home, and the Southern way of life, and Mrs. Parsons, the principal's wife, would play the graduation march while the lower-grade graduates paraded down the aisles and took their seats below the platform. The high school seniors would wait in empty classrooms to make their dramatic entrance.

In the Store I was the person of the moment. The birthday girl. The center. Bailey had graduated the year before, although to do so he had had to forfeit all pleasures to make up for his time lost in Baton Rouge.

My class was wearing butter-yellow piqué dresses, and Momma launched out on mine. She smocked the yoke into tiny crisscrossing puckers, then shirred the rest of the bodice. Her dark fingers ducked in and out of the lemony cloth as she embroidered raised daisies around the hem. Before she considered herself finished she had added a crocheted cuff on the puff sleeves, and a pointy crocheted collar.

I was going to be lovely. A walking model of all the various styles of fine hand sewing and it didn't worry me that I was only twelve years old and merely graduating from the eighth grade. Besides, many teachers in Arkansas Negro schools had only that diploma and were licensed to impart wisdom.

The days had become longer and more noticeable. The faded beige of former times had been replaced with strong and sure colors. I began to see my classmates' clothes, their skin tones, and the dust that waved off pussy willows. Clouds that lazed across the sky were objects of great concern to me. Their shiftier shapes might have held a message that in my new happiness and with a little bit of time I'd soon decipher. During that period I looked at the arch of heaven so religiously my neck kept a steady ache. I had taken to smiling more often, and my jaws hurt from the unaccustomed activity. Between the two physical sore spots, I suppose I could have been uncomfortable, but that was not the case. As a member of the winning team (the graduation class of 1940) I had outdistanced unpleasant sensations by miles. I was headed for the freedom of open fields.

Youth and social approval allied themselves with me and we trammeled 10 memories of slights and insults. The wind of our swift passage remodeled my features. Lost tears were pounded to mud and then to dust. Years of withdrawal were brushed aside and left behind, as hanging ropes of parasitic moss.

My work alone had awarded me a top place and I was going to be one of the first called in the graduating ceremonies. On the classroom blackboard, as well as on the bulletin board in the auditorium, there were blue stars and white stars and red stars. No absences, no tardiness, and my academic work was among the best of the year. I could say the preamble to the Constitution even faster than Bailey. We timed ourselves often: "We the people of the United States in order to form a more perfect union . . ." I had memorized the Presidents of the United States from Washington to Roosevelt in chronological as well as alphabetical order.

My hair pleased me too. Gradually the black mass had lengthened and thickened, so that it kept at last to its braided pattern, and I didn't have to yank my scalp off when I tried to comb it.

Louise and I had rehearsed the exercises until we tired out ourselves. Henry Reed was class valedictorian. He was a small, very black boy with hooded eyes, a long, broad nose and an oddly shaped head. I had admired him for years because each term he and I vied for the best grades in our class. Most often he bested me, but instead of being disappointed I was pleased that we shared top places between us. Like many Southern Black children, he lived with his grandmother, who was as strict as Momma and as kind as she knew how to be. He was courteous, respectful and soft-spoken to elders, but on the playground he chose to play the roughest games. I admired him. Anyone, I reckoned, sufficiently afraid or sufficiently dull could be polite. But to be able to operate at a top level with both adults and children was admirable.

His valedictory speech was entitled "To Be or Not to Be." The rigid tenth-grade teacher had helped him to write it. He'd been working on the dramatic stresses for months.

The weeks until graduation were filled with heady activities. A group of small 15 children were to be presented in a play about buttercups and daisies and bunny rabbits. They could be heard throughout the building practicing their hops and their little songs that sounded like silver bells. The older girls (non-graduates, of course) were assigned the task of making refreshments for the night's festivities. A tangy scent of ginger, cinnamon, nutmeg and chocolate wafted around the home economics building as the budding cooks made samples for themselves and their teachers.

In every corner of the workshop, axes and saws split fresh timber as the woodshop boys made sets and stage scenery. Only the graduates were left out of the general bustle. We were free to sit in the library at the back of the building or look in quite detachedly, naturally, on the measures being taken for our event.

Even the minister preached on graduation the Sunday before. His subject was, "Let your light so shine that men will see your good works and praise your Father, Who is in Heaven." Although the sermon was purported to be addressed to us, he used the occasion to speak to backsliders, gamblers, and general ne'er-do-wells. But since he had called our names at the beginning of the service we were mollified.

Among Negroes the tradition was to give presents to children going only from one grade to another. How much more important this was when the person was graduating at the top of the class. Uncle Willie and Momma had sent away for a Mickey Mouse watch like Bailey's. Louise gave me four embroidered handkerchiefs. (I gave her three crocheted doilies.) Mrs. Sneed, the minister's wife, made me an underskirt to wear for graduation, and nearly every customer gave me a nickel or maybe even a dime with the instruction "Keep on moving to high ground," or some such encouragement.

Amazingly the great day finally dawned and I was out of bed before I knew it. I threw open the back door to see it more clearly, but Momma said, "Sister, come away from that door and put your robe on."

I hoped the memory of that morning would never leave me. Sunlight was 20 itself still young, and the day had none of the insistence maturity would bring it in a few hours. In my robe and barefoot in the backyard, under cover of going to see about my new beans, I gave myself up to the gentle warmth and thanked God that no matter what evil I had done in my life He had allowed me to live to see this day. Somewhere in my fatalism I had expected to die, accidentally, and never have the chance to walk up the stairs in the auditorium and gracefully receive my hard-earned diploma. Out of God's merciful bosom I had won reprieve.

Bailey came out in his robe and gave me a box wrapped in Christmas paper. He said he had saved his money for months to pay for it. It felt like a box of chocolates, but I knew Bailey wouldn't save money to buy candy when we had all we could want under our noses.

He was as proud of the gift as I. It was a soft-leather-bound copy of a collection of poems by Edgar Allan Poe, or, as Bailey and I called him, "Eap." I turned to "Annabel Lee" and we walked up and down the garden rows, the cool dirt between our toes, reciting the beautifully sad lines.

Momma made a Sunday breakfast although it was only Friday. After we finished the blessing, I opened my eyes to find the watch on my plate. It was a dream of a day. Everything went smoothly and to my credit, I didn't have to be reminded or scolded for anything. Near evening I was too jittery to attend to chores, so Bailey volunteered to do all before his bath.

Days before, we had made a sign for the Store and as we turned out the lights Momma hung the cardboard over the doorknob. It read clearly: CLOSED, GRADUATION.

My dress fitted perfectly and everyone said that I looked like a sunbeam in it. 25 On the hill, going toward the school, Bailey walked behind with Uncle Willie, who muttered, "Go on, Ju." He wanted him to walk ahead with us because it embarrassed him to have to walk so slowly. Bailey said he'd let the ladies walk together, and the men would bring up the rear. We all laughed, nicely.

Little children dashed by out of the dark like fireflies. Their crepe-paper dresses and butterfly wings were not made for running and we heard more than one rip, dryly, and the regretful "uh uh" that followed.

The school blazed without gaiety. The windows seemed cold and unfriendly from the lower hill. A sense of ill-fated timing crept over me, and if Momma hadn't reached for my hand I would have drifted back to Bailey and Uncle Willie, and possibly beyond. She made a few slow jokes about my feet getting cold, and tugged me along to the now-strange building.

Around the front steps, assurance came back. There were my fellow "greats," the graduating class. Hair brushed back, legs oiled, new dresses and pressed pleats, fresh pocket handkerchiefs and little handbags, all homesewn. Oh, we were up to snuff, all right. I joined my comrades and didn't even see my family go in to find seats in the crowded auditorium.

The school band struck up a march and all classes filed in as had been rehearsed. We stood in front of our seats, as assigned, and on a signal from the choir director, we sat. No sooner had this been accomplished than the band started to play the national anthem. We rose again and sang the song, after which we recited the pledge of allegiance. We remained standing for a brief minute before the choir director and the principal signaled to us, rather desperately I thought, to take our seats. The command was so unusual that our carefully rehearsed and smooth-running machine was thrown off. For a full minute we fumbled for our chairs and bumped into each other awkwardly. Habits change or solidify under pressure, so in our state of nervous tension we had been ready to follow our usual assembly pattern: the American National Anthem, then the pledge of allegiance, then the song every Black person I knew called the Negro National Anthem. All done in the same key, with the same passion and most often standing on the same foot.

Finding my seat at last, I was overcome with a presentiment of worse things 30 to come. Something unrehearsed, unplanned, was going to happen, and we were going to be made to look bad. I distinctly remember being explicit in the choice of pronoun. It was "we," the graduating class, the unit, that concerned me then.

The principal welcomed "parents and friends" and asked the Baptist minister to lead us in prayer. His invocation was brief and punchy, and for a second I thought we were getting back on the high road to right action. When the principal came back to the dais, however, his voice had changed. Sounds always affected me profoundly and the principal's voice was one of my favorites. During assembly it melted and lowed weakly into the audience. It had not been in my plan to listen to him, but my curiosity was piqued and I straightened up to give him my attention.

He was talking about Booker T. Washington, our "late great leader," who said we can be as close as the fingers on the hand, etc. . . . Then he said a few vague things about friendship and the friendship of kindly people to those less fortunate than themselves. With that his voice nearly faded, thin, away. Like a river diminishing to a stream and then to a trickle. But he cleared his throat and said, "Our speaker tonight, who is also our friend, came from Texarkana to deliver the commencement address, but due to the irregularity of the train schedule, he's going to, as they say, 'speak and run.'" He said that we understood and wanted the man to know that we were most grateful for the time he was able to give us and then something about how we were willing always to adjust to another's program, and without more ado — "I give you Mr. Edward Donleavy."

Not one but two white men came through the door offstage. The shorter one walked to the speaker's platform, and the tall one moved over to the center seat and sat down. But that was our principal's seat, and already occupied. The dislodged gentleman bounced around for a long breath or two before the Baptist minister gave him his chair, then with more dignity than the situation deserved, the minister walked off the stage.

Donleavy looked at the audience once (on reflection, I'm sure that he wanted only to reassure himself that we were really there), adjusted his glasses and began to read from a sheaf of papers.

He was glad "to be here and to see the work going on just as it was in the 35 other schools."

At the first "Amen" from the audience I willed the offender to immediate death by choking on the word. But Amen's and Yes, sir's began to fall around the room like rain through a ragged umbrella.

He told us of the wonderful changes we children in Stamps had in store. The Central School (naturally, the white school was Central) had already been granted improvements that would be in use in the fall. A well-known artist was coming from Little Rock to teach art to them. They were going to have the newest microscopes and chemistry equipment for their laboratory. Mr. Donleavy didn't leave us long in the dark over who made these improvements available to Central High. Nor were we to be ignored in the general betterment scheme he had in mind.

He said that he had pointed out to people at a very high level that one of the first-line football tacklers at Arkansas Agricultural and Mechanical College had graduated from good old Lafayette County Training School. Here fewer Amen's were heard. Those few that did break through lay dully in the air with the heaviness of habit.

He went on to praise us. He went on to say how he had bragged that "one of the best basketball players at Fisk sank his first ball right here at Lafayette County Training School."

The white kids were going to have a chance to become Galileos and Madame 40 Curies and Edisons and Gaugins, and our boys (the girls weren't even in on it) would try to be Jesse Owenses and Joe Louises.

Owens and the Brown Bomber were great heroes in our world, but what school official in the white-goddom of Little Rock had the right to decide that those two men must be our only heroes? Who decided that for Henry Reed to become a scientist he had to work like George Washington Carver, as a boot-black, to buy a lousy microscope? Bailey was obviously always going to be too small to be an athlete, so which concrete angel glued to what country seat had decided that if my brother wanted to become a lawyer he had to first pay penance for his skin by picking cotton and hoeing corn and studying correspondence books at night for twenty years?

The man's dead words fell like bricks around the auditorium and too many settled in my belly. Constrained by hard-learned manners I couldn't look behind me, but to my left and right the proud graduating class of 1940 had dropped their heads. Every girl in my row had found something new to do with her handkerchief. Some folded the tiny squares into love knots, some into triangles, but most were wadding them, then pressing them flat on their yellow laps.

On the dais, the ancient tragedy was being replayed. Professor Parsons sat, a sculptor's reject, rigid. His large, heavy body seemed devoid of will or willingness, and his eyes said he was no longer with us. The other teachers examined the flag (which was draped stage right) or their notes, or the windows which opened on our now-famous playing diamond.

Graduation, the hush-hush magic time of frills and gifts and congratulations and diplomas, was finished for me before my name was called. The accomplishment was nothing. The meticulous maps, drawn in three colors of ink, learning and spelling decasyllabic words, memorizing the whole of *The Rape of Lucrece* — it was nothing. Donleavy had exposed us.

We were maids and farmers, handymen and washerwomen, and anything   45 higher that we aspired to was farcical and presumptuous. Then I wished that Gabriel Prosser and Nat Turner had killed all whitefolks in their beds and that Abraham Lincoln had been assassinated before the signing of the Emancipation Proclamation, and that Harriet Tubman had been killed by that blow on her head and Christopher Columbus had drowned in the *Santa Maria*.

It was awful to be Negro and have no control over my life. It was brutal to be young and already trained to sit quietly and listen to charges brought against my color and no chance of defense. We should all be dead. I thought I should like to see us all dead, one on top of the other. A pyramid of flesh with the whitefolks on the bottom, as the broad base, then the Indians with their silly tomahawks and tepees and wigwams and treaties, the Negroes with their mops and recipes and cotton sacks and spirituals sticking out of their mouths. The Dutch children should all tumble in their wooden shoes and break their necks. The French should choke to death on the Louisiana Purchase (1803) while silkworms ate all the Chinese with their stupid pigtails. As a species, we were an abomination. All of us.

Donleavy was running for election, and assured our parents that if he won we could count on having the only colored paved playing field in that part of Arkansas. Also — he never looked up to acknowledge the grunts of acceptance — also, we were bound to get some new equipment for the home economics building and the workshop.

He finished, and since there was no need to give any more than the most perfunctory thank-you's, he nodded to the men on the stage, and the tall white man who was never introduced joined him at the door. They left with the attitude that now they were off to something really important. (The graduation ceremonies at Lafayette County Training School had been a mere preliminary.)

The ugliness they left was palpable. An uninvited guest who wouldn't leave. The choir was summoned and sang a modern arrangement of "Onward, Christian Soldiers," with new words pertaining to graduates seeking their place in the world. But it didn't work. Elouise, the daughter of the Baptist minister, recited "Invictus," and I could have cried at the impertinence of "I am the master of my fate, I am the captain of my soul."

My name had lost its ring of familiarity and I had to be nudged to go and 50 receive my diploma. All my preparations had fled. I neither marched up to the stage like a conquering Amazon, nor did I look in the audience for Bailey's nod of approval. Marguerite Johnson, I heard the name again, my honors were read, there were noises in the audience of appreciation, and I took my place on the stage as rehearsed.

I thought about colors I hated: ecru, puce, lavender, beige and black.

There was shuffling and rustling around me, then Henry Reed was giving his valedictory address, "To Be or Not to Be." Hadn't he heard the whitefolks? We couldn't *be*, so the question was a waste of time. Henry's voice came out clear and strong. I feared to look at him. Hadn't he got the message? There was no "nobler in the mind" for Negroes because the world didn't think we had minds, and they let us know it. "Outrageous fortune"? Now, that was a joke. When the ceremony was over I had to tell Henry Reed some things. That is, if I still cared. Not "rub," Henry, "erase." "A, there's the erase." Us.

Henry had been a good student in elocution. His voice rose on tides of promise and fell on waves of warnings. The English teacher had helped him to create a sermon winging through Hamlet's soliloquy. To be a man, a doer, a builder, a leader, or to be a tool, an unfunny joke, a crusher of funky toadstools. I marveled that Henry could go through with the speech as if we had a choice.

I had been listening and silently rebutting each sentence with my eyes closed; then there was a hush, which in an audience warns that something unplanned is happening. I looked up and saw Henry Reed, the conservative, the proper, the A student, turn his back to the audience and turn to us (the proud graduating class of 1940) and sing, nearly speaking.

Lift ev'ry voice and sing
Till earth and heaven ring
Ring with the harmonies of Liberty . . .

It was the poem written by James Weldon Johnson. It was the music composed by J. Rosamond Johnson. It was the Negro National Anthem. Out of habit we were singing it.

Our mothers and fathers stood in the dark hall and joined the hymn of en- 55 couragement. A kindergarten teacher led the small children onto the stage and the buttercups and daisies and bunny rabbits marked time and tried to follow:

Stony the road we trod
Bitter the chastening rod
Felt in the days when hope, unborn, had died.
Yet with a steady beat
Have we not our weary feet
Come to the place for which our fathers sighed?

Every child I knew had learned that song with his ABC's and along with "Jesus Loves Me This I Know." But I personally had never heard it before. Never heard the words, despite the thousands of times I had sung them. Never thought they had anything to do with me.

On the other hand, the words of Patrick Henry had made such an impression on me that I had been able to stretch myself tall and trembling and say, "I know not what course others may take, but as for me, give me liberty or give me death."

And now I heard, really for the first time:

We have come over a way that with tears has been watered,
We have come, treading our path through the blood of the slaughtered.

While echoes of the song shivered in the air, Henry Reed bowed his head, said "Thank you," and returned to his place in the line. The tears that slipped down many faces were not wiped away in shame.

We were on top again. As always, again. We survived. The depths had been 60 icy and dark, but now a bright sun spoke to our souls. I was no longer simply a member of the proud graduating class of 1940; I was a proud member of the wonderful, beautiful Negro race.

Oh, Black known and unknown poets, how often have your auctioned pains sustained us? Who will compute the lonely nights made less lonely by your songs, or the empty pots made less tragic by your tales?

If we were a people much given to revealing secrets, we might raise monuments and sacrifice to the memories of our poets, but slavery cured us of that weakness. It may be enough, however, to have it said that we survive in exact relationship to the dedication of our poets (include preachers, musicians and blues singers).

For Analysis

1. Describe the **tone** established in the long opening paragraph.

2. How does the second paragraph relate to and extend the subject matter of the opening paragraph?

3. The title of Henry's speech is taken from Hamlet's famous soliloquy in Act III, Scene 1, of Shakespeare's play. How does this **allusion** contribute to the essay's **theme**?

4. Explain the opening sentence of paragraph 43: "On the dais, the ancient tragedy was being replayed."

5. Explain the meaning of the final sentence of paragraph 44: "Donleavy had exposed us."

6. Is the optimism of the final paragraph warranted? Explain.

On Style

1. How does the first part of the essay prepare us for the **tone** of protest in the latter part?

2. Analyze the function of paragraph 46, beginning "It was awful to be Negro and have no control over my life."

Making Connections

1. Compare Angelou's experience of racism with Randall Robinson's in "Can a Black Family Be a Legal Nuisance?" (p. 659).

2. What qualities do Marguerite Johnson and Sylvia, the narrator of Toni Cade Bambara's story "The Lesson" (p. 134), share?

Writing Topics

1. Describe and analyze the changes the speaker undergoes in the course of the essay.

2. Describe an occasion when you experienced stereotyping. Describe the nature of the stereotype, your reaction to it, and the consequences it had on your life.

LOOKING BACK:
Further Questions for Thinking and Writing

1. Bharati Mukherjee's "Orbiting" is told from the daughter's **point of view**, while Alice Walker's "Everyday Use" is told from the mother's point of view. How might the stories differ if the viewpoints were reversed? How would the parents see their daughter's situation in "Orbiting," and how would the educated daughter see her mother's situation in "Everyday Use"? **Writing Topic:** In each of these stories, the daughter has broken away from the parents' culture. Describe the nature of each break. Have the daughters acted constructively or destructively? Explain.

2. Felix Mnthali's "The Stranglehold of English Lit." examines one culture's imposition of values on another. Consider M. Carl Holman's "Mr. Z" and Amy Lowell's "Patterns" in the light of Mnthali's observations. How do these poems demonstrate the effect of cultural imperialism? **Writing Topic:** Examine a literary work included in this book, and explore how that work fails to embody (or violates) the cultural values of your own tradition.

3. Explain how Virginia Woolf's observations in "What If Shakespeare Had Had a Sister?" illuminate Emily's situation in William Faulkner's "A Rose for Emily." **Writing Topic:** In an essay, argue for or against the proposition that women have achieved absolute equality in the United States.

4. Anne Sexton's "Cinderella," Amy Lowell's "Patterns," E. E. Cummings's "the Cambridge ladies who live in furnished souls," and Emily Dickinson's "What Soft — Cherubic Creatures — " all address certain culturally determined behavior patterns among women. Describe the behavior depicted in these poems. How do the authors feel about the behavior? What devices reveal the authors' attitudes? **Writing Topic:** Define the social tradition that produced the women in these poems. Either defend that tradition as crucial to the social order, or offer a cultural variation that would give women a different social role.

5. The speakers in Yevgeny Yevtushenko's "I Would Like" and T. S. Eliot's "The Love Song of J. Alfred Prufrock" exhibit quite different attitudes about their identities. Describe each speaker's attitude toward his identity, and identify which aspects of the poems define those attitudes. In what sense are the speakers' identities culturally determined? **Writing Topic:** In an imaginative essay, describe each speaker's early life, and suggest what cultural forces shaped them.

6. Many of the works in this section deal with the tension and conflict that result when a minority culture is threatened or overpowered by another, dominant culture. **Writing Topic:** Examine the nature of that conflict in Louise Erdrich's "The Red Convertible," Barry Holstun Lopez's "Winter Count 1973," and Bharati Mukherjee's "Orbiting."

7. Some of the works in this section focus on intergenerational tensions within a culture. **Writing Topic:** Compare such tensions in William Faulkner's "A Rose for Emily," Chinua Achebe's "Marriage Is a Private Affair," and Alice Walker's "Everyday Use."

8. The struggle of women to achieve equality is the subject of many works in this section. **Writing Topic:** Examine some of the feminist works in this section. What, if any, common threads do you find running through them, either in content or in the use of literary devices?

9. Homer in William Faulkner's "A Rose for Emily," Prufrock in T. S. Eliot's "The Love Song of J. Alfred Prufrock," Ro in Bharati Mukherjee's "Orbiting," and Callahan in Barry Holstun Lopez's "Winter Count 1973" are all, in some sense, cultural outsiders. **Writing Topic:** Compare their positions in the dominant culture, the resulting conflicts or tensions, and the strategies they employ in dealing with their status.

Love and Hate

Room in New York, 1932, by Edward Hopper.

Love is nothing but joy accompanied with the idea of an eternal cause,
and hatred is nothing but sorrow with
the accompanying idea of an external cause.
— Baruch Spinoza

We love too much, hate in the same extreme.
— Homer

The only reason I hated him was that I had needed him so much.
That's when I found out about need.
It goes much better with hate than with love.
— Lois Gould

The basic formula for all sin is: frustrated or neglected love.
— Franz Werfel

The worst, the least curable hatred is that
which has superseded deep love.
— Euripides

Love, friendship, respect do not unite people as much as
a common hatred of something.
— Anton Chekhov

This generation, slack as it is and slow, proves that hatred is the best love
to bestow . . . Hate! Hate!
— Henrik Ibsen

Love and death, it is often noted, are the two great themes of literature. Many of the literary works we have placed in the sections "Innocence and Experience," "Conformity and Rebellion," and "Culture and Identity" speak of love and death as well. But in those works, other thematic interests dominate. In this section, we gather a number of works in which love and hate are thematically central.

The rosy conception of love presented in many popular and sentimental stories does not prepare us for the complicated reality we face. We know that the course of true love never runs smooth, but in those popular stories the obstacles that hinder the lovers are simple and external. If the young lover can land the high-paying job or convince the beloved's parents that he or she is worthy despite social differences, all will be well. But love in life is rarely that simple. The external obstacles may be insuperable, or the obstacles may lie deep within the personality. The major obstacle may well be an individual's difficult and painful effort to understand that he or she has been deceived by an immature or sentimental conception of love.

In this age of psychological awareness, the claims of the flesh are well recognized. But psychology teaches us, as well, to recognize the aggressive aspect of the human condition. The omnipresent selfishness that civilization attempts to check may be aggressively violent as well as lustful. Thus, on one hand, we have the simple eroticism of Kate Chopin's "The Storm" and, on the other, the macabre experience of Gilman's narrator in "The Yellow Wallpaper." And Matthew Arnold in "Dover Beach" finds love the only refuge from a chaotic world in which "ignorant armies clash by night."

The cliché has it that love and hate are closely related, and much evidence supports this proposition. But why should love and hate, seeming opposites, lie so close together in the emotional lives of men and women? We are all egos, separate from each other. And as separate individuals, we develop elaborate behavior mechanisms that defend us from each other. But the erotic love relationship differs from other relationships in that it may be defined as a rejection of separateness. The common metaphor speaks of two lovers as joining, as merging into one. That surrender of the "me" to join in an "us" leaves lovers uniquely vulnerable to psychic injury. In short, the defenses are down, and the self-esteem of each of the lovers depends importantly on the behavior of the other. If the lover is betrayed by the beloved, the emotional consequences are uniquely disastrous — hence the peculiarly close relationship between passionate hatred and erotic love.

Words like *love* and *hate* are so general that poets rarely use them except as one term in a metaphor designed to project sharply some aspect of emotional life. The simple sexuality in poems such as Andrew Marvell's "To His Coy Mistress" and Christopher Marlowe's "The Passionate Shepherd to His Love" may be juxtaposed with the hatred and violence generated in *Othello* by sexual jealousy or with the quick reprisal of the slighted Barbara Allan. And Shakespeare's description of lust in "Th' expense of spirit in a waste of shame" notes an aspect of love quite overlooked by Edmund Waller in his song "Go, Lovely Rose!"

Perhaps more than anything, the works in this section celebrate the elemental impulses of men and women that run counter to those rational formulations by which we govern our lives. We pursue Othello's love for Desdemona and Iago's hate for Othello and arrive at an irreducible mystery, for neither Othello's love nor Iago's hate yields satisfactorily to rational explanation. Reason does not tell us why Othello and Desdemona love one another or why Iago hates rather than honors Othello.

Love is an act of faith springing from our deep-seated need to join with another human being not only in physical nakedness but in emotional and spiritual nakedness as well. While hate is a denial of that faith and, therefore, a retreat into spiritual isolation, love is an attempt to break out of the isolation.

LOOKING AHEAD:
Questions for Thinking and Writing

As you read the selections in this section, consider the following questions. You may want to write out your thoughts informally in a journal or notebook as a way of preparing to respond to the selections, or you may wish to make one of these questions the basis for a formal essay.

1. What is love? What is the source of your definition (literature, personal observation, discussions with those you trust)? Have you ever been in love? How did you know? Do you know someone who is in love? How has it changed that person?

2. Have you ever truly hated someone or something? Describe the circumstances, and characterize your hatred.

3. Do you believe that love and hate are closely related? Have you experienced a change from love to hatred, or do you know someone who has? Explain.

4. There are different kinds of love — love of family, of humankind, of a cause. Characterize several different kinds of love, and examine your own motives and behavior in different love relationships. Is it possible that certain kinds of love necessarily generate certain hatreds? Explain.

Fiction

Kate Chopin   (1851–1904)

The Storm   1898

I

The leaves were so still that even Bibi thought it was going to rain. Bobinôt, who was accustomed to converse on terms of perfect equality with his little son, called the child's attention to certain sombre clouds that were rolling with sinister intention from the west, accompanied by a sullen, threatening roar. They were at Friedheimer's store and decided to remain there till the storm had passed. They sat within the door on two empty kegs. Bibi was four years old and looked very wise.

"Mama'll be 'fraid, yes," he suggested with blinking eyes.

"She'll shut the house. Maybe she got Sylvie helpin' her this evenin'," Bobinôt responded reassuringly.

"No; she ent got Sylvie. Sylvie was helpin' her yistiday," piped Bibi.

Bobinôt arose and going across to the counter purchased a can of shrimps, of which Calixta was very fond. Then he returned to his perch on the keg and sat stolidly holding the can of shrimps while the storm burst. It shook the wooden store and seemed to be ripping great furrows in the distant field. Bibi laid his little hand on his father's knee and was not afraid.

II

Calixta, at home, felt no uneasiness for their safety. She sat at a side window sewing furiously on a sewing machine. She was greatly occupied and did not notice the approaching storm. But she felt very warm and often stopped to mop her face on which the perspiration gathered in beads. She unfastened her white sacque at the throat. It began to grow dark, and suddenly realizing the situation she got up hurriedly and went about closing windows and doors.

Out on the small front gallery she had hung Bobinôt's Sunday clothes to air and she hastened out to gather them before the rain fell. As she stepped outside, Alcée Laballière rode in at the gate. She had not seen him very often since her marriage, and never alone. She stood there with Bobinôt's coat in her hands, and the big rain drops began to fall. Alcée rode his horse under the shelter of a side projection where the chickens had huddled and there were plows and a harrow piled up in the corner.

"May I come and wait on your gallery till the storm is over, Calixta?" he asked.

"Come 'long in, M'sieur Alcée."

His voice and her own startled her as if from a trance, and she seized Bo- 10
binôt's vest. Alcée, mounting to the porch, grabbed the trousers and snatched Bibi's braided jacket that was about to be carried away by a sudden gust of wind. He expressed an intention to remain outside, but it was soon apparent that he might as well have been out in the open: the water beat in upon the boards in driving sheets, and he went inside, closing the door after him. It was even necessary to put something beneath the door to keep the water out.

"My! what a rain! It's good two years sence it rain' like that," exclaimed Calixta as she rolled up a piece of bagging and Alcée helped her to thrust it beneath the crack.

She was a little fuller of figure than five years before when she married; but she had lost nothing of her vivacity. Her blue eyes still retained their melting quality; and her yellow hair, dishevelled by the wind and rain, kinked more stubbornly than ever about her ears and temples.

The rain beat upon the low, shingled roof with a force and clatter that threatened to break an entrance and deluge them there. They were in the dining room — the sitting room — the general utility room. Adjoining was her bed room, with Bibi's couch along side her own. The door stood open, and the room with its white, monumental bed, its closed shutters, looked dim and mysterious.

Alcée flung himself into a rocker and Calixta nervously began to gather up from the floor the lengths of a cotton sheet which she had been sewing.

"If this keeps up, *Dieu sait*[1] if the levees goin' to stan' it!" she exclaimed. 15

"What have you got to do with the levees?"

"I got enough to do! An' there's Bobinôt with Bibi out in that storm — if he only didn' left Friedheimer's!"

"Let us hope, Calixta, that Bobinôt's got sense enough to come in out of a cyclone."

She went and stood at the window with a greatly disturbed look on her face. She wiped the frame that was clouded with moisture. It was stiflingly hot. Alcée got up and joined her at the window, looking over her shoulder. The rain was coming down in sheets obscuring the view of far-off cabins and enveloping the distant wood in a gray mist. The playing of the lightning was incessant. A bolt struck a tall chinaberry tree at the edge of the field. It filled all visible space with a blinding glare and the crash seemed to invade the very boards they stood upon.

Calixta put her hands to her eyes, and with a cry, staggered backward. Alcée's 20

---

[1] God knows.

arm encircled her, and for an instant he drew her close and spasmodically to him.

"*Bonté!*"[2] she cried, releasing herself from his encircling arm and retreating from the window, "the house'll go next! If I only knew w'ere Bibi was!" She would not compose herself; she would not be seated. Alcée clasped her shoulders and looked into her face. The contact of her warm, palpitating body when he had unthinkingly drawn her into his arms, had aroused all the old-time infatuation and desire for her flesh.

"Calixta," he said, "don't be frightened. Nothing can happen. The house is too low to be struck, with so many tall trees standing about. There! aren't you going to be quiet? say, aren't you?" He pushed her hair back from her face that was warm and steaming. Her lips were as red and moist as pomegranate seed. Her white neck and a glimpse of her full, firm bosom disturbed him powerfully. As she glanced up at him the fear in her liquid blue eyes had given place to a drowsy gleam that unconsciously betrayed a sensuous desire. He looked down into her eyes and there was nothing for him to do but to gather her lips in a kiss. It reminded him of Assumption.[3]

"Do you remember — in Assumption, Calixta?" he asked in a low voice broken by passion. Oh! she remembered; for in Assumption he had kissed her and kissed and kissed her; until his senses would well nigh fail, and to save her he would resort to a desperate flight. If she was not an immaculate dove in those days, she was still inviolate; a passionate creature whose very defenselessness had made her defense, against which his honor forbade him to prevail. Now — well, now — her lips seemed in a manner free to be tasted, as well as her round, white throat and her whiter breasts.

They did not heed the crashing torrents, and the roar of the elements made her laugh as she lay in his arms. She was a revelation in that dim, mysterious chamber; as white as the couch she lay upon. Her firm, elastic flesh that was knowing for the first time its birthright, was like a creamy lily that the sun invites to contribute its breath and perfume to the undying life of the world.

The generous abundance of her passion, without guile or trickery, was like a white flame which penetrated and found response in depths of his own sensuous nature that had never yet been reached.

When he touched her breasts they gave themselves up in quivering ecstasy, inviting his lips. Her mouth was a fountain of delight. And when he possessed her, they seemed to swoon together at the very borderland of life's mystery.

He stayed cushioned upon her, breathless, dazed, enervated, with his heart beating like a hammer upon her. With one hand she clasped his head, her lips lightly touching his forehead. The other hand stroked with a soothing rhythm his muscular shoulders.

[2] An exclamation: Goodness!

[3] A holiday commemorating the ascent of the Virgin Mary to heaven. Assumption is also the name of a Louisiana parish (county) where Calixta and Alcée had had a rendezvous in an earlier story.

The growl of the thunder was distant and passing away. The rain beat softly upon the shingles, inviting them to drowsiness and sleep. But they dared not yield.

The rain was over; and the sun was turning the glistening green world into a palace of gems. Calixta, on the gallery, watched Alcée ride away. He turned and smiled at her with a beaming face; and she lifted her pretty chin in the air and laughed aloud.

III

Bobinôt and Bibi, trudging home, stopped without at the cistern to make them-   30
selves presentable.

"My! Bibi, w'at will yo' mama say! You ought to be ashame'. You oughtn' put on those good pants. Look at 'em! An' that mud on yo' collar! How you got that mud on yo' collar, Bibi? I never saw such a boy!" Bibi was the picture of pathetic resignation. Bobinôt was the embodiment of serious solicitude as he strove to remove from his own person and his son's the signs of their tramp over heavy roads and through wet fields. He scraped the mud off Bibi's bare legs and feet with a stick and carefully removed all traces from his heavy brogans. Then, prepared for the worst — the meeting with an over-scrupulous housewife, they entered cautiously at the back door.

Calixta was preparing supper. She had set the table and was dripping coffee at the hearth. She sprang up as they came in.

"Oh, Bobinôt! You back! My! but I was uneasy. W'ere you been during the rain? An' Bibi? he ain't wet? he ain't hurt?" She had clasped Bibi and was kissing him effusively. Bobinôt's explanations and apologies which he had been composing all along the way, died on his lips as Calixta felt him to see if he were dry, and seemed to express nothing but satisfaction at their safe return.

"I brought you some shrimps, Calixta," offered Bobinôt, hauling the can from his ample side pocket and laying it on the table.

"Shrimps! Oh, Bobinôt! you too good fo' anything!" and she gave him a   35
smacking kiss on the cheek that resounded. "*J'vous réponds,*[4] we'll have a feas' to night! umph-umph!"

Bobinôt and Bibi began to relax and enjoy themselves, and when the three seated themselves at table they laughed much and so loud that anyone might have heard them as far away as Laballière's.

IV

Alcée Laballière wrote to his wife, Clarisse, that night. It was a loving letter, full of tender solicitude. He told her not to hurry back, but if she and the babies liked it at Biloxi, to stay a month longer. He was getting on nicely; and though he

[4] I'm telling you.

missed them, he was willing to bear the separation a while longer — realizing that their health and pleasure were the first things to be considered.

V

As for Clarisse, she was charmed upon receiving her husband's letter. She and the babies were doing well. The society was agreeable; many of her old friends and acquaintances were at the bay. And the first free breath since her marriage seemed to restore the pleasant liberty of her maiden days. Devoted as she was to her husband, their intimate conjugal life was something which she was more than willing to forego for a while.

So the storm passed and everyone was happy.

For Analysis

1. Aside from the child Bibi, there are four characters in this story — two married couples. How did you respond to each of those characters? What are the sources for your reactions?

2. How do the characters in the story feel about themselves? About each other? On what evidence in the story do you base your response?

3. Discuss the title of the story.

On Style

1. During the second half of the nineteenth century, certain American writers, including Kate Chopin, evoked a sense of region in their work. What region of the country provides the **setting** for this story? How do you know?

2. What aspects of this story's **style** contribute to its realism?

3. Discuss the first part of the story, analyzing the stylistic differences between the first paragraph and the exchange between Bobinôt and Bibi that follows it.

Making Connections

1. Contrast this story with Irwin Shaw's "The Girls in Their Summer Dresses" (p. 1034). Which strikes you as more "realistic"?

2. How might your response to this story differ if it had been written by a man? Explain.

Writing Topics

1. Write an essay on modern marriage, using this story to support your analysis.

2. Comment on the story's final line. Is "the storm" literal or symbolic? If everyone is "happy," do you believe they have the right to be?

Charlotte Perkins Gilman   (1860–1935)

The Yellow Wallpaper   1892

It is very seldom that mere ordinary people like John and myself secure ancestral halls for the summer.

A colonial mansion, a hereditary estate, I would say a haunted house and reach the height of romantic felicity — but that would be asking too much of fate!

Still I will proudly declare that there is something queer about it.

Else, why should it be let so cheaply? And why have stood so long untenanted?

John laughs at me, of course, but one expects that.   5

John is practical in the extreme. He has no patience with faith, an intense horror of superstition, and he scoffs openly at any talk of things not to be felt and seen and put down in figures.

John is a physician, and *perhaps* — (I would not say it to a living soul, of course, but this is dead paper and a great relief to my mind) — *perhaps* that is one reason I do not get well faster.

You see, he does not believe I am sick! And what can one do?

If a physician of high standing, and one's own husband, assures friends and relatives that there is really nothing the matter with one but temporary nervous depression — a slight hysterical tendency — what is one to do?

My brother is also a physician, and also of high standing, and he says the same   10
thing.

So I take phosphates or phosphites — whichever it is, and tonics, and air and exercise, and journeys, and am absolutely forbidden to "work" until I am well again.

Personally, I disagree with their ideas.

Personally, I believe that congenial work, with excitement and change, would do me good.

But what is one to do?

I did write for a while in spite of them; but it *does* exhaust me a good deal —   15
having to be so sly about it, or else meet with heavy opposition.

I sometimes fancy that in my condition if I had less opposition and more society and stimulus — but John says the very worst thing I can do is to think about my condition, and I confess it always makes me feel bad.

So I will let it alone and talk about the house.

The most beautiful place! It is quite alone, standing well back from the road, quite three miles from the village. It makes me think of English places that you

1021

read about, for there are hedges and walls and gates that lock, and lots of separate little houses for the gardeners and people.

There is a *delicious* garden! I never saw such a garden — large and shady, full of box-bordered paths, and lined with long grape-covered arbors with seats under them.

There were greenhouses, too, but they are all broken now.   20

There was some legal trouble, I believe, something about the heirs and co-heirs; anyhow, the place has been empty for years.

That spoils my ghostliness, I am afraid, but I don't care — there is something strange about the house — I can feel it.

I even said so to John one moonlight evening, but he said what I felt was a draught, and shut the window.

I get unreasonably angry with John sometimes. I'm sure I never used to be so sensitive. I think it is due to this nervous condition.

But John says if I feel so I shall neglect proper self-control; so I take pains to   25
control myself — before him, at least, and that makes me very tired.

I don't like our room a bit. I wanted one downstairs that opened onto the piazza and had roses all over the window, and such pretty old-fashioned chintz hangings! But John would not hear of it.

He said there was only one window and not room for two beds, and no near room for him if he took another.

He is very careful and loving, and hardly lets me stir without special direction.

I have a schedule prescription for each hour in the day; he takes all care from me, and so I feel basely ungrateful not to value it more.

He said we came here solely on my account, that I was to have perfect rest   30
and all the air I could get. "Your exercise depends on your strength, my dear," said he, "and your food somewhat on your appetite; but air you can absorb all the time." So we took the nursery at the top of the house.

It is a big, airy room, the whole floor nearly, with windows that look all ways, and air and sunshine galore. It was a nursery first, and then playroom and gymnasium, I should judge, for the windows are barred for little children, and there are rings and things in the walls.

The paint and paper look as if a boys' school had used it. It is stripped off — the paper — in great patches all around the head of my bed, about as far as I can reach, and in a great place on the other side of the room low down. I never saw a worse paper in my life. One of those sprawling, flamboyant patterns committing every artistic sin.

It is dull enough to confuse the eye in following, pronounced enough constantly to irritate and provoke study, and when you follow the lame uncertain curves for a little distance they suddenly commit suicide — plunge off at outrageous angles, destroy themselves in unheard-of contradictions.

The color is repellent, almost revolting; a smouldering unclean yellow, strangely faded by the slow-turning sunlight. It is a dull yet lurid orange in some places, a sickly sulphur tint in others.

No wonder the children hated it! I should hate it myself if I had to live in this 35
room long.

There comes John, and I must put this away — he hates to have me write a
word.

We have been here two weeks, and I haven't felt like writing before, since
that first day.

I am sitting by the window now, up in this atrocious nursery, and there is
nothing to hinder my writing as much as I please, save lack of strength.

John is away all day, and even some nights when his cases are serious.

I'm glad my case is not serious! 40

But these nervous troubles are dreadfully depressing.

John does not know how much I really suffer. He knows there is no reason to
suffer, and that satisfies him.

Of course it is only nervousness. It does weigh on me so not to do my duty in
any way!

I meant to be such a help to John, such a real rest and comfort, and here I am
a comparative burden already!

Nobody would believe what an effort it is to do what little I am able — to 45
dress and entertain, and order things.

It is fortunate Mary is so good with the baby. Such a dear baby!

And yet I *cannot* be with him, it makes me so nervous.

I suppose John never was nervous in his life. He laughs at me so about this
wallpaper!

At first he meant to repaper the room, but afterward he said that I was letting
it get the better of me, and that nothing was worse for a nervous patient than to
give way to such fancies.

He said that after the wallpaper was changed it would be the heavy bed- 50
stead, and then the barred windows, and then that gate at the head of the stairs,
and so on.

"You know the place is doing you good," he said, "and really, dear, I don't care
to renovate the house just for a three months' rental."

"Then do let us go downstairs," I said. "There are such pretty rooms there."

Then he took me in his arms and called me a blessed little goose, and said
he would go down to the cellar, if I wished, and have it whitewashed into the
bargain.

But he is right enough about the beds and windows and things.

It is as airy and comfortable a room as anyone need wish, and, of course, I 55
would not be so silly as to make him uncomfortable just for a whim.

I'm really getting quite fond of the big room, all but that horrid paper.

Out of one window I can see the garden — those mysterious deep-shaded
arbors, the riotous old-fashioned flowers, and bushes and gnarly trees.

Out of another I get a lovely view of the bay and a little private wharf belonging to the estate. There is a beautiful shaded lane that runs down there from the

house. I always fancy I see people walking in these numerous paths and arbors, but John has cautioned me not to give way to fancy in the least. He says that with my imaginative power and habit of story-making, a nervous weakness like mine is sure to lead to all manner of excited fancies, and that I ought to use my will and good sense to check the tendency. So I try.

I think sometimes that if I were only well enough to write a little it would relieve the press of ideas and rest me.

But I find I get pretty tired when I try.   60

It is so discouraging not to have any advice and companionship about my work. When I get really well, John says we will ask Cousin Henry and Julia down for a long visit; but he says he would as soon put fireworks in my pillow-case as to let me have those stimulating people about now.

I wish I could get well faster.

But I must not think about that. This paper looks to me as if it *knew* what a vicious influence it had!

There is a recurrent spot where the pattern lolls like a broken neck and two bulbous eyes stare at you upside down.

I get positively angry with the impertinence of it and the everlastingness. Up   65
and down and sideways they crawl, and those absurd, unblinking eyes are everywhere. There is one place where two breadths didn't match, and the eyes go all up and down the line, one a little higher than the other.

I never saw so much expression in an inanimate thing before, and we all know how much expression they have! I used to lie awake as a child and get more entertainment and terror out of blank walls and plain furniture than most children could find in a toy-store.

I remember what a kindly wink the knobs of our big old bureau used to have, and there was one chair that always seemed like a strong friend.

I used to feel that if any of the other things looked too fierce I could always hop into that chair and be safe.

The furniture in this room is no worse than inharmonious, however, for we had to bring it all from downstairs. I suppose when this was used as a playroom they had to take the nursery things out, and no wonder! I never saw such ravages as the children have made here.

The wallpaper, as I said before, is torn off in spots, and it sticketh closer than   70
a brother — they must have had perseverance as well as hatred.

Then the floor is scratched and gouged and splintered, the plaster itself is dug out here and there, and this great heavy bed, which is all we found in the room, looks as if it had been through the wars.

But I don't mind it a bit — only the paper.

There comes John's sister. Such a dear girl as she is, and so careful of me! I must not let her find me writing.

She is a perfect and enthusiastic housekeeper, and hopes for no better profession. I verily believe she thinks it is the writing which made me sick!

But I can write when she is out, and see her a long way off from these   75
windows.

There is one that commands the road, a lovely shaded winding road, and one that just looks off over the country. A lovely country, too, full of great elms and velvet meadows.

This wallpaper has a kind of sub-pattern in a different shade, a particularly irritating one, for you can only see it in certain lights, and not clearly then.

But in the places where it isn't faded and where the sun is just so — I can see a strange, provoking, formless sort of figure that seems to skulk about behind that silly and conspicuous front design.

There's sister on the stairs!

Well, the Fourth of July is over! The people are all gone and I am tired out. 80 John thought it might do me good to see a little company, so we just had Mother and Nellie and the children down for a week.

Of course I didn't do a thing. Jennie sees to everything now.

But it tired me all the same.

John says if I don't pick up faster he shall send me to Weir Mitchell in the fall.

But I don't want to go there at all. I had a friend who was in his hands once, and she says he is just like John and my brother, only more so!

Besides, it is such an undertaking to go so far. 85

I don't feel as if it was worthwhile to turn my hand over for anything, and I'm getting dreadfully fretful and querulous.

I cry at nothing, and cry most of the time.

Of course I don't when John is here, or anybody else, but when I am alone.

And I am alone a good deal just now. John is kept in town very often by serious cases, and Jennie is good and lets me alone when I want her to.

So I walk a little in the garden or down that lovely lane, sit on the porch under 90 the roses, and lie down up here a good deal.

I'm getting really fond of the room in spite of the wallpaper. Perhaps *because* of the wallpaper.

It dwells in my mind so!

I lie here on this great immovable bed — it is nailed down, I believe — and follow that pattern about by the hour. It is as good as gymnastics, I assure you. I start, we'll say, at the bottom, down in the corner over there where it has not been touched, and I determine for the thousandth time that I *will* follow that pointless pattern to some sort of a conclusion.

I know a little of the principle of design, and I know this thing was not arranged on any laws of radiation, or alternation, or repetition, or symmetry, or anything else that I ever heard of.

It is repeated, of course, by the breadths, but not otherwise. 95

Looked at in one way, each breadth stands alone; the bloated curves and flourishes — a kind of "debased Romanesque" with delirium tremens — go waddling up and down in isolated columns of fatuity.

But, on the other hand, they connect diagonally, and the sprawling outlines run off in great slanting waves of optic horror, like a lot of wallowing sea-weeds in full chase.

The whole thing goes horizontally, too, at least it seems so, and I exhaust myself in trying to distinguish the order of its going in that direction.

They have used a horizontal breadth for a frieze, and that adds wonderfully to the confusion.

There is one end of the room where it is almost intact, and there, when the crosslights fade and the low sun shines directly upon it, I can almost fancy radiation after all, — the interminable grotesque seems to form around a common center and rush off in headlong plunges of equal distraction. 100

It makes me tired to follow it. I will take a nap, I guess.

I don't know why I should write this.

I don't want to.

I don't feel able.

And I know John would think it absurd. But I *must* say what I feel and think 105 in some way — it is such a relief!

But the effort is getting to be greater than the relief.

Half the time now I am awfully lazy, and lie down ever so much. John says I musn't lose my strength, and has me take cod liver oil and lots of tonics and things, to say nothing of ale and wine and rare meat.

Dear John! He loves me very dearly, and hates to have me sick. I tried to have a real earnest reasonable talk with him the other day, and tell him how I wish he would let me go and make a visit to Cousin Henry and Julia.

But he said I wasn't able to go, nor able to stand it after I got there; and I did not make out a very good case for myself, for I was crying before I had finished.

It is getting to be a great effort for me to think straight. Just this nervous 110 weakness, I suppose.

And dear John gathered me up in his arms, and just carried me upstairs and laid me on the bed, and sat by me and read to me till it tired my head.

He said I was his darling and his comfort and all he had, and that I must take care of myself for his sake, and keep well.

He says no one but myself can help me out of it, that I must use my will and self-control and not let any silly fancies run away with me.

There's one comfort — the baby is well and happy, and does not have to occupy this nursery with the horrid wallpaper.

If we had not used it, that blessed child would have! What a fortunate escape! 115 Why, I wouldn't have a child of mine, an impressionable little thing, live in such a room for worlds.

I never thought of it before, but it is lucky that John kept me here after all; I can stand it so much easier than a baby, you see.

Of course I never mention it to them any more — I am too wise — but I keep watch of it all the same.

There are things in that wallpaper that nobody knows but me, or ever will.

Behind that outside pattern the dim shapes get clearer every day.

It is always the same shape, only very numerous. 120

And it is like a woman stooping down and creeping about behind that pattern.

I don't like it a bit. I wonder — I begin to think — I wish John would take me away from here!

It is so hard to talk with John about my case, because he is so wise, and because he loves me so.

But I tried it last night.

It was moonlight. The moon shines in all around just as the sun does.

I hate to see it sometimes, it creeps so slowly, and always comes in by one   125
window or another.

John was asleep and I hated to waken him, so I kept still and watched the moonlight on that undulating wallpaper till I felt creepy.

The faint figure behind seemed to shake the pattern, just as if she wanted to get out.

I got up softly and went to feel and see if the paper *did* move, and when I came back John was awake.

"What is it, little girl?" he said. "Don't go walking about like that — you'll get cold."

I thought it was a good time to talk, so I told him that I really was not gaining   130
here, and that I wished he would take me away.

"Why, darling!" said he, "Our lease will be up in three weeks, and I can't see how to leave before.

"The repairs are not done at home, and I cannot possibly leave town just now. Of course if you were in any danger, I could and would, but you really are better, dear, whether you can see it or not. I am a doctor, dear, and I know. You are gaining flesh and color, your appetite is better, I feel really much easier about you."

"I don't weigh a bit more," said I, "nor as much; and my appetite may be better in the evening when you are here but it is worse in the morning when you are away!"

"Bless her little heart!" said he with a big hug, "She shall be as sick as she pleases! But now let's improve the shining hours by going to sleep, and talk about it in the morning!"

"And you won't go away?" I asked gloomily.   135

"Why, how can I, dear? It is only three weeks more and then we will take a nice little trip of a few days while Jennie is getting the house ready. Really, dear, you are better!"

"Better in body perhaps — " I began, and stopped short, for he sat up straight and looked at me with such a stern, reproachful look that I could not say another word.

"My darling," said he, "I beg of you, for my sake and for our child's sake, as well as for your own, that you will never for one instant let that idea enter your mind! There is nothing so dangerous, so fascinating, to a temperament like yours. It is a false and foolish fancy. Can you trust me as a physician when I tell you so?"

So of course I said no more on that score, and we went to sleep before long. He thought I was asleep first, but I wasn't, and lay there for hours trying to decide whether that front pattern and the back pattern really did move together or separately.

On a pattern like this, by daylight, there is a lack of sequence, a defiance of law, that is a constant irritant to a normal mind.

The color is hideous enough, and unreliable enough, and infuriating enough, but the pattern is torturing.

You think you have mastered it, but just as you get well under way in following, it turns a back-somersault and there you are. It slaps you in the face, knocks you down, and tramples upon you. It is like a bad dream.

The outside pattern is a florid arabesque, reminding one of a fungus. If you can imagine a toadstool in joints, an interminable string of toadstools, budding and sprouting in endless convolutions — why, that is something like it.

That is, sometimes!

There is one marked peculiarity about this paper, a thing nobody seems to notice but myself, and that is that it changes as the light changes.

When the sun shoots in through the east window — I always watch for that first long, straight ray — it changes so quickly that I never can quite believe it.

That is why I watch it always.

By moonlight — the moon shines in all night when there is a moon — I wouldn't know it was the same paper.

At night in any kind of light, in twilight, candlelight, lamplight, and worst of all by moonlight, it becomes bars! The outside pattern, I mean, and the woman behind it is as plain as can be.

I didn't realize for a long time what the thing was that showed behind, that dim sub-pattern, but now I am quite sure it is a woman.

By daylight she is subdued, quiet. I fancy it is the pattern that keeps her so still. It is so puzzling. It keeps me quiet by the hour.

I lie down ever so much now. John says it is good for me, and to sleep all I can.

Indeed he started the habit by making me lie down for an hour after each meal.

It is a very bad habit, I am convinced, for you see, I don't sleep.

And that cultivates deceit, for I don't tell them I'm awake — oh, no!

The fact is I am getting a little afraid of John.

He seems very queer sometimes, and even Jennie has an inexplicable look.

It strikes me occasionally, just as a scientific hypothesis, that perhaps it is the paper!

I have watched John when he did not know I was looking, and come into the room suddenly on the most innocent excuses, and I've caught him several times *looking at the paper!* And Jennie too. I caught Jennie with her hand on it once.

She didn't know I was in the room, and when I asked her in a quiet, a very quiet voice, with the most restrained manner possible, what she was doing with the paper — she turned around as if she had been caught stealing, and looked quite angry — asked me why I should frighten her so!

Then she said that the paper stained everything it touched, that she had found yellow smooches on all my clothes and John's and she wished we would be more careful!

Did not that sound innocent? But I know she was studying that pattern, and I am determined that nobody shall find it out but myself!

Life is very much more exciting now than it used to be. You see, I have something more to expect, to look forward to, to watch. I really do eat better, and am more quiet than I was.

John is so pleased to see me improve! He laughed a little the other day, and said I seemed to be flourishing in spite of my wallpaper.

I turned it off with a laugh. I had no intention of telling him it was *because* of 165
the wallpaper — he would make fun of me. He might even want to take me away.

I don't want to leave now until I have found it out. There is a week more, and I think that will be enough.

I'm feeling so much better!

I don't sleep much at night, for it is so interesting to watch developments; but I sleep a good deal in the daytime.

In the daytime it is tiresome and perplexing.

There are always new shoots on the fungus, and new shades of yellow all over 170
it. I cannot keep count of them, though I have tried conscientiously.

It is the strangest yellow, that wallpaper! It makes me think of all the yellow things I ever saw — not beautiful ones like buttercups, but old, foul, bad yellow things.

But there is something else about that paper — the smell! I noticed it the moment we came into the room, but with so much air and sun it was not bad. Now we have had a week of fog and rain, and whether the windows are open or not, the smell is here.

It creeps all over the house.

I find it hovering in the dining-room, skulking in the parlor, hiding in the hall, lying in wait for me on the stairs.

It gets into my hair.   175

Even when I go to ride, if I turn my head suddenly and surprise it — there is that smell!

Such a peculiar odor, too! I have spent hours in trying to analyze it, to find what it smelled like.

It is not bad — at first — and very gentle, but quite the subtlest, most enduring odor I ever met.

In this damp weather it is awful. I wake up in the night and find it hanging over me.

It used to disturb me at first. I thought seriously of burning the house — to 180
reach the smell.

But now I am used to it. The only thing I can think of that it is like is the *color* of the paper! A yellow smell.

There is a very funny mark on this wall, low down, near the mopboard. A streak that runs round the room. It goes behind every piece of furniture, except the bed, a long, straight, even *smooch,* as if it had been rubbed over and over.

I wonder how it was done and who did it, and what they did it for. Round and round and round — round and round and round — it makes me dizzy!

I really have discovered something at last.

Through watching so much at night, when it changes so, I have finally 185 found out.

The front pattern *does* move — and no wonder! The woman behind shakes it!

Sometimes I think there are a great many women behind, and sometimes only one, and she crawls around fast, and her crawling shakes it all over.

Then in the very bright spots she keeps still, and in the very shady spots she just takes hold of the bars and shakes them hard.

And she is all the time trying to climb through. But nobody could climb through that pattern — it strangles so; I think that is why it has so many heads.

They get through, and then the pattern strangles them off and turns them 190 upside down and makes their eyes white!

If those heads were covered or taken off it would not be half so bad.

I think that woman gets out in the daytime!

And I'll tell you why — privately — I've seen her!

I can see her out of every one of my windows!

It is the same woman, I know, for she is always creeping, and most women do 195 not creep by daylight.

I see her in that long shaded lane, creeping up and down. I see her in those dark grape arbors, creeping all around the garden.

I see her on that long road under the trees, creeping along, and when a carriage comes she hides under the blackberry vines.

I don't blame her a bit. It must be very humiliating to be caught creeping by daylight!

I always lock the door when I creep by daylight. I can't do it at night, for I know John would suspect something at once.

And John is so queer now that I don't want to irritate him. I wish he would 200 take another room! Besides, I don't want anybody to get that woman out at night but myself.

I often wonder if I could see her out of all the windows at once.

But, turn as fast as I can, I can only see out of one at one time.

And though I always see her, she *may* be able to creep faster than I can turn! I have watched her sometimes away off in the open country, creeping as fast as a cloud shadow in a high wind.

If only that top pattern could be gotten off from the under one! I mean to try it, little by little.

I have found out another funny thing, but I shan't tell it this time! It does not 205 do to trust people too much.

There are only two more days to get this paper off, and I believe John is beginning to notice. I don't like the look in his eyes.

And I hear him ask Jennie a lot of professional questions about me. She had a very good report to give.

She said I slept a good deal in the daytime.

John knows I don't sleep very well at night, for all I'm so quiet!

He asked me all sorts of questions, too, and pretended to be very loving and 210 kind.

As if I couldn't see through him!

Still, I don't wonder he acts so, sleeping under this paper for three months.

It only interests me, but I feel sure John and Jennie are secretly affected by it.

Hurrah! This is the last day, but it is enough. John is to stay in town over night, and won't be out until this evening.

Jennie wanted to sleep with me — the sly thing; but I told her I should un- 215 doubtedly rest better for a night all alone.

That was clever, for really I wasn't alone a bit! As soon as it was moonlight and that poor thing began to crawl and shake the pattern, I got up and ran to help her.

I pulled and she shook. I shook and she pulled, and before morning we had peeled off yards of that paper.

A strip about as high as my head and half around the room.

And then when the sun came and that awful pattern began to laugh at me, I declared I would finish it to-day!

We go away to-morrow, and they are moving all my furniture down again to 220 leave things as they were before.

Jennie looked at the wall in amazement, but I told her merrily that I did it out of pure spite at the vicious thing.

She laughed and said she wouldn't mind doing it herself, but I must not get tired.

How she betrayed herself that time!

But I am here, and no person touches this paper but Me — not *alive!*

She tried to get me out of the room — it was too patent! But I said it was so 225 quiet and empty and clean now that I believed I would lie down again and sleep all I could, and not to wake me even for dinner — I would call when I woke.

So now she is gone, and the servants are gone, and the things are gone, and there is nothing left but that great bedstead nailed down, with the canvas mattress we found on it.

We shall sleep downstairs to-night, and take the boat home to-morrow.

I quite enjoy the room, now it is bare again.

How those children did tear about here!

This bedstead is fairly gnawed!   230

But I must get to work.

I have locked the door and thrown the key down into the front path.

I don't want to go out, and I don't want to have anybody come in, till John comes.

I want to astonish him.

I've got a rope up here that even Jennie did not find. If that woman does get 235
out, and tries to get away, I can tie her!

But I forgot I could not reach far without anything to stand on!

This bed will *not* move!

I tried to lift and push it until I was lame, and then I got so angry I bit off a
little piece at one corner — but it hurt my teeth.

Then I peeled off all the paper I could reach standing on the floor. It sticks
horribly and the pattern just enjoys it! All those strangled heads and bulbous
eyes and waddling fungus growths just shriek with derision!

I am getting angry enough to do something desperate. To jump out of the 240
window would be admirable exercise, but the bars are too strong even to try.

Besides I wouldn't do it. Of course not. I know well enough that a step like
that is improper and might be misconstrued.

I don't like to *look* out of the windows even — there are so many of those
creeping women, and they creep so fast.

I wonder if they all come out of that wallpaper as I did?

But I am securely fastened now by my well-hidden rope — you don't get *me*
out in the road there!

I suppose I shall have to get back behind the pattern when it comes night, 245
and that is hard!

It is so pleasant to be out in this great room and creep around as I please!

I don't want to go outside. I won't, even if Jennie asks me to.

For outside you have to creep on the ground, and everything is green instead
of yellow.

But here I can creep smoothly on the floor, and my shoulder just fits in that
long smooch around the wall, so I cannot lose my way.

Why, there's John at the door! 250

It is no use, young man, you can't open it!

How he does call and pound!

Now he's crying to Jennie for an axe.

It would be a shame to break down that beautiful door!

"John, dear!" said I in the gentlest voice, "The key is down by the front steps, 255
under a plantain leaf!"

That silenced him for a few moments.

Then he said — very quietly indeed, "Open the door, my darling!"

"I can't," said I. "The key is down by the front door under a plantain leaf!"
And then I said it again, several times, very gently and slowly, and said it so often
that he had to go and see, and he got it of course, and came in. He stopped short
by the door.

"What is the matter?" he cried. "For God's sake, what are you doing!"

I kept on creeping just the same, but I looked at him over my shoulder. 260

"I've got out at last," said I, "in spite of you and Jane. And I've pulled off most
of the paper, so you can't put me back!"

Now why should that man have fainted? But he did, and right across my path
by the wall, so that I had to creep over him every time!

For Analysis

1. Why have the narrator and her husband John rented the mansion?

2. In the opening paragraphs, what tone does the narrator's description of the mansion establish?

3. Describe the character of John. Does the narrator's view of him change in the course of the story? Explain.

4. After telling us that her husband John is a physician, the narrator adds that "*perhaps . . . that is one reason I do not get well faster*" (para. 7). What does she mean by this comment?

5. How does the narrator's description of what she sees in the outside world reflect her inner state?

6. Who is Jennie? What is her function in the story?

7. The narrator both accepts her husband's control over her and yet disobeys him by secretly continuing to write. What effect does writing have on her? Is her husband correct in his judgment that writing will hinder her recovery?

8. What evidence does the story provide to explain the narrator's present state?

9. Can it be argued that, on some level, the narrator refuses to recover? Explain.

10. In what ways does the wallpaper embody the **theme** of the story?

On Style

1. Discuss the **images** and **figurative language** used by the narrator. What do they tell us about her?

2. Analyze the ways by which Gilman achieves suspense.

Making Connections

1. Compare the marriage relationship in this story with the marriage in Ibsen's play *A Doll's House* (p. 499).

2. Compare and contrast the narrator in this story with Laura in Tennessee Williams's play *The Glass Menagerie* (p. 243) and Emily Grierson in William Faulkner's story "A Rose for Emily" (p. 666) as examples of women wounded by a patriarchal society.

3. Compare the wallpaper in this story with the bird cage in Susan Glaspell's play *Trifles* (p. 1236) as **symbols**. In what ways are they similar? In what ways different? Which do you find more effective? Explain.

4. Considered as a horror story, in what ways is Gilman's narrative similar to Edgar Allan Poe's "The Cask of Amontillado" (p. 1280)? In what ways is it different?

Writing Topics

1. Analyze the way **irony** is used in this story.

2. Write an essay in which you imaginatively reconstruct the early life of the narrator, including her marriage, to explain her illness.

3. Write an essay describing the aptness of wallpaper to symbolize the life of the narrator.

4. In a paragraph, explain why we never learn the narrator's name.

Irwin Shaw   (1913–1984)

The Girls in Their Summer Dresses 1939

Fifth Avenue was shining in the sun when they left the Brevoort.[1] The sun was warm, even though it was February, and everything looked like Sunday morning — the buses and the well-dressed people walking slowly in couples and the quiet buildings with the windows closed.

Michael held Frances' arm tightly as they walked toward Washington Square[2] in the sunlight. They walked lightly, almost smiling, because they had slept late and had a good breakfast and it was Sunday. Michael unbuttoned his coat and let it flap around him in the mild wind.

"Look out," Frances said as they crossed Eighth Street. "You'll break your neck." Michael laughed and Frances laughed with him.

"She's not so pretty," Frances said. "Anyway, not pretty enough to take a chance of breaking your neck."

Michael laughed again. "How did you know I was looking at her?"   5

Frances cocked her head to one side and smiled at her husband under the brim of her hat. "Mike, darling," she said.

"O.K.," he said. "Excuse me."

Frances patted his arm lightly and pulled him along a little faster toward Washington Square. "Let's not see anybody all day," she said. "Let's just hang around with each other. You and me. We're always up to our neck in people, drinking their Scotch or drinking our Scotch; we only see each other in bed. I want to go out with my husband all day long. I want him to talk only to me and listen only to me."

"What's to stop us?" Michael asked.

"The Stevensons. They want us to drop by around one o'clock and they'll   10 drive us into the country."

"The cunning Stevensons," Mike said. "Transparent. They can whistle. They can go driving in the country by themselves."

"Is it a date?"

"It's a date."

Frances leaned over and kissed him on the tip of the ear.

"Darling," Michael said, "this is Fifth Avenue."   15

[1] The Brevoort was a New York hotel on lower Fifth Avenue. At the time that this story was written, the Brevoort's bar was famous as a gathering place for literary people.
[2] A park at the south end of Fifth Avenue.

"Let me arrange a program," Frances said. "A planned Sunday in New York for a young couple with money to throw away."

"Go easy."

"First let's go to the Metropolitan Museum of Art," Frances suggested, because Michael had said during the week he wanted to go. "I haven't been there in three years and there're at least ten pictures I want to see again. Then we can take the bus down to Radio City and watch them skate. And later we'll go down to Cavanagh's and get a steak as big as a blacksmith's apron, with a bottle of wine, and after that there's a French picture at the Filmarte that everybody says — say, are you listening to me?"

"Sure," he said. He took his eyes off the hatless girl with the dark hair, cut dancer-style like a helmet, who was walking past him.

"That's the program for the day," Frances said flatly. "Or maybe you'd just 20 rather walk up and down Fifth Avenue."

"No," Michael said. "Not at all."

"You always look at other women," Frances said. "Everywhere. Every damned place we go."

"No, darling," Michael said, "I look at everything. God gave me eyes and I look at women and men in subway excavations and moving pictures and the little flowers of the field. I casually inspect the universe."

"You ought to see the look in your eye," Frances said, "as you casually inspect the universe on Fifth Avenue."

"I'm a happily married man." Michael pressed her elbow tenderly. "Example 25 for the whole twentieth century — Mr. and Mrs. Mike Loomis. Hey, let's have a drink," he said, stopping.

"We just had breakfast."

"Now listen, darling," Mike said, choosing his words with care, "it's a nice day and we both felt good and there's no reason why we have to break it up. Let's have a nice Sunday."

"All right. I don't know why I started this. Let's drop it. Let's have a good time."

They joined hands consciously and walked without talking among the baby carriages and the old Italian men in their Sunday clothes and the young women with Scotties in Washington Square Park.

"At least once a year everyone should go to the Metropolitan Museum of 30 Art," Frances said after a while, her tone a good imitation of the tone she had used at breakfast and at the beginning of their walk. "And it's nice on Sunday. There're a lot of people looking at the pictures and you get the feeling maybe Art isn't on the decline in New York City, after all — "

"I want to tell you something," Michael said very seriously. "I have not touched another woman. Not once. In all the five years."

"All right," Frances said.

"You believe that, don't you?"

"All right."

They walked between the crowded benches, under the scrubby city-park 35 trees.

"I try not to notice it," Frances said, "but I feel rotten inside, in my stomach, when we pass a woman and you look at her and I see that look in your eye and that's the way you looked at me the first time. In Alice Maxwell's house. Standing there in the living room, next to the radio, with a green hat on and all those people."

"I remember the hat," Michael said.

"The same look," Frances said. "And it makes me feel bad. It makes me feel terrible."

"Sh-h-h, please, darling, sh-h-h."

"I think I would like a drink now," Frances said. 40

They walked over to a bar on Eighth Street, not saying anything, Michael automatically helping her over curbstones and guiding her past automobiles. They sat near a window in the bar and the sun streamed in and there was a small, cheerful fire in the fireplace. A little Japanese waiter came over and put down some pretzels and smiled happily at them.

"What do you order after breakfast?" Michael asked.

"Brandy, I suppose," Frances said.

"Courvoisier," Michael told the waiter. "Two Courvoisiers."

The waiter came with the glasses and they sat drinking the brandy in the sun- 45 light. Michael finished half his and drank a little water.

"I look at women," he said. "Correct. I don't say it's wrong or right. I look at them. If I pass them on the street and I don't look at them, I'm fooling you, I'm fooling myself."

"You look at them as though you want them," Frances said, playing with her brandy glass. "Every one of them."

"In a way," Michael said, speaking softly and not to his wife, "in a way that's true. I don't do anything about it, but it's true."

"I know it. That's why I feel bad."

"Another brandy," Michael called. "Waiter, two more brandies." 50

He sighed and closed his eyes and rubbed them gently with his fingers. "I love the way women look. One of the things I like best about New York is the battalions of women. When I first came to New York from Ohio that was the first thing I noticed, the million wonderful women, all over the city. I walked around with my heart in my throat."

"A kid," Frances said. "That's a kid's feeling."

"Guess again," Michael said. "Guess again. I'm older now. I'm a man getting near middle age, putting on a little fat, and I still love to walk along Fifth Avenue at three o'clock on the east side of the street between Fiftieth and Fifty-seventh Streets. They're all out then, shopping, in their furs and their crazy hats, everything all concentrated from all over the world into seven blocks — the best furs, the best clothes, the handsomest women, out to spend money and feeling good about it."

The Japanese waiter put the two drinks down, smiling with great happiness.

"Everything is all right?" he asked.   55

"Everything is wonderful," Michael said.

"If it's just a couple of fur coats," Frances said, "and forty-five dollar hats — "

"It's not the fur coats. Or the hats. That's just the scenery for that particular kind of woman. Understand," he said, "you don't have to listen to this."

"I want to listen."

"I like the girls in the offices. Neat with their eyeglasses, smart, chipper, 60 knowing what everything is about. I like the girls on Forty-fourth Street at lunchtime, the actresses, all dressed up on nothing a week. I like the salesgirls in the stores, paying attention to you first because you're a man, leaving the lady customers waiting. I got all this stuff accumulated in me because I've been thinking about it for ten years and now you've asked for it and here it is."

"Go ahead," Frances said.

"When I think of New York City, I think of all the girls on parade in the city. I don't know whether it's something special with me or whether every man in the city walks around with the same feeling inside him, but I feel as though I'm at a picnic in this city. I like to sit near the women in the theatres, the famous beauties who've taken six hours to get ready and look it. And the young girls at the football games, with the red cheeks, and when the warm weather comes, the girls in their summer dresses." He finished his drink. "That's the story."

Frances finished her drink and swallowed two or three times extra. "You say you love me?"

"I love you."

"I'm pretty, too," Frances said. "As pretty as any of them."   65

"You're beautiful," Michael said.

"I'm good for you," Frances said, pleading. "I've made a good wife, a good housekeeper, a good friend. I'd do any damn thing for you."

"I know," Michael said. He put his hand out and grasped hers.

"You'd like to be free to — " Frances said.

"Sh-h-h."   70

"Tell the truth." She took her hand away from under his.

Michael flicked the edge of his glass with his finger. "O.K.," he said gently. "Sometimes I feel I would like to be free."

"Well," Frances said, "any time you say."

"Don't be foolish." Michael swung his chair around to her side of the table and patted her thigh.

She began to cry silently into her handkerchief, bent over just enough so that 75 nobody else in the bar would notice. "Someday," she said, crying, "you're going to make a move."

Michael didn't say anything. He sat watching the bartender slowly peel a lemon.

"Aren't you?" Frances asked harshly. "Come on, tell me. Talk. Aren't you?"

"Maybe," Michael said. He moved his chair back again. "How the hell do I know?"

"You know," Frances persisted. "Don't you know?"

"Yes," Michael said after a while, "I know." 80

Frances stopped crying then. Two or three snuffles into the handkerchief and she put it away and her face didn't tell anything to anybody. "At least do me one favor," she said.

"Sure."

"Stop talking about how pretty this woman is or that one. Nice eyes, nice breasts, a pretty figure, good voice." She mimicked his voice. "Keep it to yourself. I'm not interested."

Michael waved to the waiter. "I'll keep it to myself," he said.

Frances flicked the corners of her eyes. "Another brandy," she told the waiter. 85

"Two," Michael said.

"Yes, ma'am, yes, sir," said the waiter, backing away.

Frances regarded Michael coolly across the table. "Do you want me to call the Stevensons?" she asked. "It'll be nice in the country."

"Sure," Michael said. "Call them."

She got up from the table and walked across the room toward the telephone. 90 Michael watched her walk, thinking what a pretty girl, what nice legs.

For Analysis

1. How does Frances react to Michael's roving eyes?

2. When Michael admits, "Sometimes I feel I would like to be free" (para. 72), what is Frances's response? Do you feel her response is justified?

3. Why do you suppose Michael suggests they have a drink? Why does Frances agree? What causes Frances to order a third drink?

4. What is the significance of their decision to spend the afternoon with the Stevensons?

5. What effect does the final sentence of the story create?

On Style

1. How does the author's description of Fifth Avenue and the weather affect your initial response to the narrative?

2. When Frances and Michael order their third brandies, the waiter responds while "backing away." What does that movement suggest?

Making Connections

Have you ever experienced the sort of sexual jealousy that animates this story? On reflection, was your response appropriate?

Writing Topics

1. Kate Chopin's "The Storm" deals with sexual infidelity in marriage. Contrast the relationship between spouses in that story and in this one.

2. Is Frances's anger justified, or do you support Michael?

Alice Munro (b. 1931)

How I Met My Husband 1974

We heard the plane come over at noon, roaring through the radio news, and we were sure it was going to hit the house, so we all ran out into the yard. We saw it come over the treetops, all red and silver, the first close-up plane I ever saw. Mrs. Peebles screamed.

"Crash landing," their little boy said. Joey was his name.

"It's okay," said Dr. Peebles. "He knows what he's doing." Dr. Peebles was only an animal doctor, but had a calming way of talking, like any doctor.

This was my first job — working for Dr. and Mrs. Peebles, who had bought an old house out on the Fifth Line, about five miles out of town. It was just when the trend was starting of town people buying up old farms, not to work them but to live on them.

We watched the plane land across the road, where the fairgrounds used to be. 5 It did make a good landing field, nice and level for the old race track, and the barns and display sheds torn down now for scrap lumber so there was nothing in the way. Even the old grandstand bays had burned.

"All right," said Mrs. Peebles, snappy as she always was when she got over her nerves. "Let's go back in the house. Let's not stand here gawking like a set of farmers."

She didn't say that to hurt my feelings. It never occurred to her.

I was just setting the dessert down when Loretta Bird arrived, out of breath, at the screen door.

"I thought it was going to crash into the house and kill youse all!"

She lived on the next place and the Peebleses thought she was a country- 10 woman, they didn't know the difference. She and her husband didn't farm, he worked on the roads and had a bad name for drinking. They had seven children and couldn't get credit at the HiWay Grocery. The Peebleses made her welcome, not knowing any better, as I say, and offered her dessert.

Dessert was never anything to write home about, at their place. A dish of Jell-O or sliced bananas or fruit out of a tin. "Have a house without a pie, be ashamed until you die," my mother used to say, but Mrs. Peebles operated differently.

Loretta Bird saw me getting the can of peaches.

"Oh, never mind," she said. "I haven't got the right kind of a stomach to trust what comes out of those tins, I can only eat home canning."

I could have slapped her. I bet she never put down fruit in her life.

"I know what he's landed here for," she said. "He's got permission to use the 15 fairgrounds and take people up for rides. It costs a dollar. It's the same fellow

1039

who was over at Palmerston last week and was up the lakeshore before that. I wouldn't go up, if you paid me."

"I'd jump at the chance," Dr. Peebles said. "I'd like to see this neighborhood from the air."

Mrs. Peebles said she would just as soon see it from the ground. Joey said he wanted to go and Heather did, too. Joey was nine and Heather was seven.

"Would you, Edie?" Heather said.

I said I didn't know. I was scared, but I never admitted that, especially in front of children I was taking care of.

"People are going to be coming out here in their cars raising dust and tram- 20 pling your property, if I was you I would complain," Loretta said. She hooked her legs around the chair rung and I knew we were in for a lengthy visit. After Dr. Peebles went back to his office or out on his next call and Mrs. Peebles went for her nap, she would hang around me while I was trying to do the dishes. She would pass remarks about the Peebleses in their own house.

"She wouldn't find time to lay down in the middle of the day, if she had seven kids like I got."

She asked me did they fight and did they keep things in the dresser drawer not to have babies with. She said it was a sin if they did. I pretended I didn't know what she was talking about.

I was fifteen and away from home for the first time. My parents had made the effort and sent me to high school for a year, but I didn't like it. I was shy of strangers and the work was hard, they didn't make it nice for you or explain the way they do now. At the end of the year the averages were published in the paper, and mine came out at the very bottom, 37 percent. My father said that's enough and I didn't blame him. The last thing I wanted, anyway, was to go on and end up teaching school. It happened the very day the paper came out with my disgrace in it, Dr. Peebles was staying at our place for dinner, having just helped one of our cows have twins, and he said I looked smart to him and his wife was looking for a girl to help. He said she felt tied down, with the two children, out in the country. I guess she would, my mother said, being polite, though I could tell from her face she was wondering what on earth it would be like to have only two children and no barn work, and then to be complaining.

When I went home I would describe to them the work I had to do, and it made everybody laugh. Mrs. Peebles had an automatic washer and dryer, the first I ever saw. I have had those in my own home for such a long time now it's hard to remember how much of a miracle it was to me, not having to struggle with the wringer and hang up and haul down. Let alone not having to heat water. Then there was practically no baking. Mrs. Peebles said she couldn't make pie crust, the most amazing thing I ever heard a woman admit. I could, of course, and I could make light biscuits and a white cake and dark cake, but they didn't want it, she said they watched their figures. The only thing I didn't like about working there, in fact, was feeling half hungry a lot of the time. I used to bring back a box of doughnuts made out at home, and hide them under my bed.

The children found out, and I didn't mind sharing, but I thought I better bind them to secrecy.

The day after the plane landed Mrs. Peebles put both children in the car and   25
drove over to Chesley, to get their hair cut. There was a good woman then at Chesley for doing hair. She got hers done at the same place, Mrs. Peebles did, and that meant they would be gone a good while. She had to pick a day Dr. Peebles wasn't going out into the country, she didn't have her own car. Cars were still in short supply then, after the war.

I loved being left in the house alone, to do my work at leisure. The kitchen was all white and bright yellow, with fluorescent lights. That was before they ever thought of making the appliances all different colors and doing the cupboards like dark old wood and hiding the lighting. I loved light. I loved the double sink. So would anybody new-come from washing dishes in a dishpan with a rag-plugged hole on an oilcloth-covered table by light of a coal-oil lamp. I kept everything shining.

The bathroom too. I had a bath in there once a week. They wouldn't have minded if I took one oftener, but to me it seemed like asking too much, or maybe risking making it less wonderful. The basin and the tub and the toilet were all pink, and there were glass doors with flamingos painted on them, to shut off the tub. The light had a rosy cast and the mat sank under your feet like snow, except that it was warm. The mirror was three-way. With the mirror all steamed up and the air like a perfume cloud, from things I was allowed to use, I stood up on the side of the tub and admired myself naked, from three directions. Sometimes I thought about the way we lived out at home and the way we lived here and how one way was so hard to imagine when you were living the other way. But I thought it was still a lot easier, living the way we lived at home, to picture something like this, the painted flamingos and the warmth and the soft mat, than it was anybody knowing only things like this to picture how it was the other way. And why was that?

I was through my jobs in no time, and had the vegetables peeled for supper and sitting in cold water besides. Then I went into Mrs. Peebles' bedroom. I had been in there plenty of times, cleaning, and I always took a good look in her closet, at the clothes she had hanging there. I wouldn't have looked in her drawers, but a closet is open to anybody. That's a lie. I would have looked in drawers, but I would have felt worse doing it and been more scared she could tell.

Some clothes in her closet she wore all the time, I was quite familiar with them. Others she never put on, they were pushed to the back. I was disappointed to see no wedding dress. But there was one long dress I could just see the skirt of, and I was hungering to see the rest. Now I took note of where it hung and lifted it out. It was satin, a lovely weight on my arm, light bluish-green in color, almost silvery. It had a fitted, pointed waist and a full skirt and an off-the-shoulder fold hiding the little sleeves.

Next thing was easy. I got out of my own things and slipped it on. I was slim-   30
mer at fifteen than anybody would believe who knows me now and the fit was beautiful. I didn't, of course, have a strapless bra on, which was what it needed,

I just had to slide my straps down my arms under the material. Then I tried pinning up my hair, to get the effect. One thing led to another. I put on rouge and lipstick and eyebrow pencil from her dresser. The heat of the day and the weight of the satin and all the excitement made me thirsty, and I went out to the kitchen, got-up as I was, to get a glass of ginger ale with ice cubes from the refrigerator. The Peebleses drank ginger ale, or fruit drinks, all day, like water, and I was getting so I did too. Also there was no limit on ice cubes, which I was so fond of I would even put them in a glass of milk.

I turned from putting the ice tray back and saw a man watching me through the screen. It was the luckiest thing in the world I didn't spill the ginger ale down the front of me then and there.

"I never meant to scare you. I knocked but you were getting the ice out, you didn't hear me."

I couldn't see what he looked like, he was dark the way somebody is pressed up against a screen door with the bright daylight behind them. I only knew he wasn't from around here.

"I'm from the plane over there. My name is Chris Watters and what I was wondering was if I could use that pump."

There was a pump in the yard. That was the way the people used to get their 35
water. Now I noticed he was carrying a pail.

"You're welcome," I said. "I can get it from the tap and save you pumping." I guess I wanted him to know we had piped water, didn't pump ourselves.

"I don't mind the exercise." He didn't move, though, and finally he said, "Were you going to a dance?"

Seeing a stranger there had made me entirely forget how I was dressed.

"Or is that the way ladies around here generally get dressed up in the afternoon?"

I didn't know how to joke back then. I was too embarrassed. 40

"You live here? Are you the lady of the house?"

"I'm the hired girl."

Some people change when they find that out, their whole way of looking at you and speaking to you changes, but his didn't.

"Well, I just wanted to tell you you look very nice. I was so surprised when I looked in the door and saw you. Just because you looked so nice and beautiful."

I wasn't even old enough then to realize how out of the common it is, for a 45
man to say something like that to a woman, or somebody he is treating like a woman. For a man to say a word like *beautiful*. I wasn't old enough to realize or to say anything back, or in fact to do anything but wish he would go away. Not that I didn't like him, but just that it upset me so, having him look at me, and me trying to think of something to say.

He must have understood. He said good-bye, and thanked me, and went and started filling his pail from the pump. I stood behind the Venetian blinds in the dining room, watching him. When he had gone, I went into the bedroom and took the dress off and put it back in the same place. I dressed in my own clothes and took my hair down and washed my face, wiping it on Kleenex, which I threw in the wastebasket.

The Peebleses asked me what kind of man he was. Young, middle-aged, short, tall? I couldn't say.

"Good-looking?" Dr. Peebles teased me.

I couldn't think a thing but that he would be coming to get his water again, he would be talking to Dr. or Mrs. Peebles, making friends with them, and he would mention seeing me that first afternoon, dressed up. Why not mention it? He would think it was funny. And no idea of the trouble it would get me into.

After supper the Peebleses drove into town to go to a movie. She wanted to   50 go somewhere with her hair fresh done. I sat in my bright kitchen wondering what to do, knowing I would never sleep. Mrs. Peebles might not fire me, when she found out, but it would give her a different feeling about me altogether. This was the first place I ever worked but I really had picked up things about the way people feel when you are working for them. They like to think you aren't curious. Not just that you aren't dishonest, that isn't enough. They like to feel you don't notice things, that you don't think or wonder about anything but what they liked to eat and how they liked things ironed, and so on. I don't mean they weren't kind to me, because they were. They had me eat my meals with them (to tell the truth I expected to, I didn't know there were families who don't) and sometimes they took me along in the car. But all the same.

I went up and checked on the children being asleep and then I went out. I had to do it. I crossed the road and went in the old fairgrounds gate. The plane looked unnatural sitting there, and shining with the moon. Off at the far side of the fairgrounds, where the bush was taking over, I saw his tent.

He was sitting outside it smoking a cigarette. He saw me coming.

"Hello, were you looking for a plane ride? I don't start taking people up till tomorrow." Then he looked again and said, "Oh, it's you. I didn't know you without your long dress on."

My heart was knocking away, my tongue was dried up. I had to say something. But I couldn't. My throat was closed and I was like a deaf-and-dumb.

"Did you want to ride? Sit down. Have a cigarette."   55

I couldn't even shake my head to say no, so he gave me one.

"Put it in your mouth or I can't light it. It's a good thing I'm used to shy ladies."

I did. It wasn't the first time I had smoked a cigarette, actually. My girl friend out home, Muriel Lowe, used to steal them from her brother.

"Look at your hand shaking. Did you just want to have a chat, or what?"

In one burst I said, "I wisht you wouldn't say anything about that dress."   60

"What dress? Oh, the long dress."

"It's Mrs. Peebles'."

"Whose? Oh, the lady you work for? Is that it? She wasn't home so you got dressed up in her dress, eh? You got dressed up and played queen. I don't blame you. You're not smoking the cigarette right. Don't just puff. Draw it in. Did anybody ever show you how to inhale? Are you scared I'll tell on you? Is that it?"

I was so ashamed at having to ask him to connive this way I couldn't nod. I just looked at him and he saw *yes*.

"Well I won't. I won't in the slightest way mention it or embarrass you. I give 65 you my word of honor."

Then he changed the subject, to help me out, seeing I couldn't even thank him.

"What do you think of this sign?"

It was a board sign lying practically at my feet.

SEE THE WORLD FROM THE SKY. ADULTS $1.00, CHILDREN 50¢. QUALIFIED PILOT.

"My old sign was getting pretty beat up, I thought I'd make a new one. That's 70 what I've been doing with my time today."

The lettering wasn't all that handsome, I thought. I could have done a better one in half an hour.

"I'm not an expert at sign making."

"It's very good," I said.

"I don't need it for publicity, word of mouth is usually enough. I turned away two carloads tonight. I felt like taking it easy. I didn't tell them ladies were dropping in to visit me."

Now I remembered the children and I was scared again, in case one of them 75 had waked up and called me and I wasn't there.

"Do you have to go so soon?"

I remembered some manners. "Thank you for the cigarette."

"Don't forget. You have my word of honor."

I tore off across the fairgrounds, scared I'd see the car heading home from town. My sense of time was mixed up, I didn't know how long I'd been out of the house. But it was all right, it wasn't late, the children were asleep. I got in bed myself and lay thinking what a lucky end to the day, after all, and among things to be grateful for I could be grateful Loretta Bird hadn't been the one who caught me.

The yard and borders didn't get trampled, it wasn't as bad as that. All the 80 same it seemed very public, around the house. The sign was on the fairgrounds gate. People came mostly after supper but a good many in the afternoon, too. The Bird children all came without fifty cents between them and hung on the gate. We got used to the excitement of the plane coming in and taking off, it wasn't excitement anymore. I never went over, after that one time, but would see him when he came to get his water. I would be out on the steps doing sitting-down work, like preparing vegetables, if I could.

"Why don't you come over? I'll take you up in my plane."

"I'm saving my money," I said, because I couldn't think of anything else.

"For what? For getting married?"

I shook my head.

"I'll take you up for free if you come sometime when it's slack. I thought you 85 would come, and have another cigarette."

I made a face to hush him, because you never could tell when the children would be sneaking around the porch, or Mrs. Peebles herself listening in the house. Sometimes she came out and had a conversation with him. He told her things he hadn't bothered to tell me. But then I hadn't thought to ask. He told her he had been in the war, that was where he learned to fly a plane, and now he couldn't settle down to ordinary life, this was what he liked. She said she couldn't imagine anybody liking such a thing. Though sometimes, she said, she was almost bored enough to try anything herself, she wasn't brought up to living in the country. It's all my husband's idea, she said. This was news to me.

"Maybe you ought to give flying lessons," she said.

"Would you take them?"

She just laughed.

Sunday was a busy flying day in spite of it being preached against from two 90 pulpits. We were all sitting out watching. Joey and Heather were over on the fence with the Bird kids. Their father had said they could go, after their mother saying all week they couldn't.

A car came down the road past the parked cars and pulled up right in the drive. It was Loretta Bird who got out, all importance, and on the driver's side another woman got out, more sedately. She was wearing sunglasses.

"This is a lady looking for the man that flies the plane," Loretta Bird said. "I heard her inquire in the hotel coffee shop where I was having a Coke and I brought her out."

"I'm sorry to bother you," the lady said. "I'm Alice Kelling, Mr. Watters' fiancée."

This Alice Kelling had on a pair of brown and white checked slacks and a yellow top. Her bust looked to me rather low and bumpy. She had a worried face. Her hair had had a permanent, but had grown out, and she wore a yellow band to keep it off her face. Nothing in the least pretty or even young-looking about her. But you could tell from how she talked she was from the city, or educated, or both.

Dr. Peebles stood up and introduced himself and his wife and me and asked 95 her to be seated.

"He's up in the air right now, but you're welcome to sit and wait. He gets his water here and he hasn't been yet. He'll probably take his break about five."

"That is him, then?" said Alice Kelling, wrinkling and straining at the sky.

"He's not in the habit of running out on you, taking a different name?" Dr. Peebles laughed. He was the one, not his wife, to offer iced tea. Then she sent me into the kitchen to fix it. She smiled. She was wearing sunglasses too.

"He never mentioned his fiancée," she said.

I loved fixing iced tea with lots of ice and slices of lemon in tall glasses. I ought 100 to have mentioned before, Dr. Peebles was an abstainer, at least around the house, or I wouldn't have been allowed to take the place. I had to fix a glass for Loretta Bird too, though it galled me, and when I went out she had settled in my lawn chair, leaving me the steps.

"I knew you was a nurse when I first heard you in that coffee shop."

"How would you know a thing like that?"

"I get my hunches about people. Was that how you met him, nursing?"

"Chris? Well yes. Yes, it was."

"Oh, were you overseas?" said Mrs. Peebles.   105

"No, it was before he went overseas. I nursed him when he was stationed at Centralia and had a ruptured appendix. We got engaged and then he went overseas. My, this is refreshing, after a long drive."

"He'll be glad to see you," Dr. Peebles said. "It's a rackety kind of life, isn't it, not staying one place long enough to really make friends."

"Youse've had a long engagement," Loretta Bird said.

Alice Kelling passed that over. "I was going to get a room at the hotel, but when I was offered directions I came on out. Do you think I could phone them?"

"No need," Dr. Peebles said. "You're five miles away from him if you stay at   110 the hotel. Here, you're right across the road. Stay with us. We've got rooms on rooms, look at this big house."

Asking people to stay, just like that, is certainly a country thing, and maybe seemed natural to him now, but not to Mrs. Peebles, from the way she said, oh yes, we have plenty of room. Or to Alice Kelling, who kept protesting, but let herself be worn down. I got the feeling it was a temptation to her, to be that close. I was trying for a look at her ring. Her nails were painted red, her fingers were freckled and wrinkled. It was a tiny stone. Muriel Lowe's cousin had one twice as big.

Chris came to get his water, late in the afternoon just as Dr. Peebles had predicted. He must have recognized the car from a way off. He came smiling.

"Here I am chasing after you to see what you're up to," called Alice Kelling. She got up and went to meet him and they kissed, just touched, in front of us.

"You're going to spend a lot on gas that way," Chris said.

Dr. Peebles invited Chris to stay for supper, since he had already put up the   115 sign that said: NO MORE RIDES TILL 7 P.M. Mrs. Peebles wanted it served in the yard, in spite of the bugs. One thing strange to anybody from the country is this eating outside. I had made a potato salad earlier and she had made a jellied salad, that was one thing she could do, so it was just a matter of getting those out, and some sliced meat and cucumbers and fresh leaf lettuce. Loretta Bird hung around for some time saying, "Oh, well, I guess I better get home to those yappers," and, "It's so nice just sitting here, I sure hate to get up," but nobody invited her, I was relieved to see, and finally she had to go.

That night after rides were finished Alice Kelling and Chris went off somewhere in her car. I lay awake till they got back. When I saw the car lights sweep my ceiling I got up to look down on them through the slats of my blind. I don't know what I thought I was going to see. Muriel Lowe and I used to sleep on her front veranda and watch her sister and her sister's boy friend saying good night. Afterward we couldn't get to sleep, for longing for somebody to kiss us and rub up against us and we would talk about suppose you were out in a boat with a boy and he wouldn't bring you in to shore unless you did it, or what if somebody got you trapped in a barn, you would have to, wouldn't you, it wouldn't be your fault. Muriel said her two girl cousins used to try with a toilet paper roll that one of them was a boy. We wouldn't do anything like that; just lay and wondered.

All that happened was that Chris got out of the car on one side and she got out on the other and they walked off separately — him toward the fairgrounds and her toward the house. I got back in bed and imagined about me coming home with him, not like that.

Next morning Alice Kelling got up late and I fixed a grapefruit for her the way I had learned and Mrs. Peebles sat down with her to visit and have another cup of coffee. Mrs. Peebles seemed pleased enough now, having company. Alice Kelling said she guessed she better get used to putting in a day just watching Chris take off and come down, and Mrs. Peebles said she didn't know if she should suggest it because Alice Kelling was the one with the car, but the lake was only twenty-five miles away and what a good day for a picnic.

Alice Kelling took her up on the idea and by eleven o'clock they were in the car, with Joey and Heather and a sandwich lunch I had made. The only thing was that Chris hadn't come down, and she wanted to tell him where they were going.

"Edie'll go over and tell him," Mrs. Peebles said. "There's no problem."   120

Alice Kelling wrinkled her face and agreed.

"Be sure and tell him we'll be back by five!"

I didn't see that he would be concerned about knowing this right away, and I thought of him eating whatever he ate over there, alone, cooking on his camp stove, so I got to work and mixed up a crumb cake and baked it, in between the other work I had to do; then, when it was a bit cooled, wrapped it in a tea towel. I didn't do anything to myself but take off my apron and comb my hair. I would like to have put some makeup on, but I was too afraid it would remind him of the way he first saw me, and that would humiliate me all over again.

He had come and put another sign on the gate: NO RIDES THIS P.M. APOLO-GIES. I worried that he wasn't feeling well. No sign of him outside and the tent flap was down. I knocked on the pole.

"Come in," he said, in a voice that would just as soon have said *Stay out.*   125

I lifted the flap.

"Oh, it's you. I'm sorry. I didn't know it was you."

He had been just sitting on the side of the bed, smoking. Why not at least sit and smoke in the fresh air?

"I brought a cake and hope you're not sick," I said.

"Why would I be sick? Oh — that sign. That's all right. I'm just tired of talk-   130 ing to people. I don't mean you. Have a seat." He pinned back the tent flap. "Get some fresh air in here."

I sat on the edge of the bed, there was no place else. It was one of those fold-up cots, really: I remembered and gave him his fiancée's message.

He ate some of the cake. "Good."

"Put the rest away for when you're hungry later."

"I'll tell you a secret. I won't be around here much longer."

"Are you getting married?"   135

"Ha ha. What time did you say they'd be back?"

"Five o'clock."

"Well, by that time, this place will have seen the last of me. A plane can get further than a car." He unwrapped the cake and ate another piece of it, absent-mindedly.

"Now you'll be thirsty."

"There's some water in the pail."   140

"It won't be very cold. I could bring some fresh. I could bring some ice from the refrigerator."

"No," he said. "I don't want you to go. I want a nice long time of saying good-bye to you."

He put the cake away carefully and sat beside me and started those little kisses, so soft, I can't ever let myself think about them, such kindness in his face and lovely kisses, all over my eyelids and neck and ears, all over, then me kissing back as well as I could (I had only kissed a boy on a dare before, and kissed my own arms for practice) and we lay back on the cot and pressed together, just gently, and he did some other things, not bad things or not in a bad way. It was lovely in the tent, that smell of grass and hot tent cloth with the sun beating down on it, and he said, "I wouldn't do you any harm for the world." Once, when he had rolled on top of me and we were sort of rocking together on the cot, he said softly, "Oh, no," and freed himself and jumped up and got the water pail. He splashed some of it on his neck and face, and the little bit left, on me lying there.

"That's to cool us off, miss."

When we said good-bye I wasn't at all sad, because he held my face and said,   145
"I'm going to write you a letter. I'll tell you where I am and maybe you can come and see me. Would you like that? Okay then. You wait." I was really glad I think to get away from him, it was like he was piling presents on me I couldn't get the pleasure of till I considered them alone.

No consternation at first about the plane being gone. They thought he had taken somebody up, and I didn't enlighten them. Dr. Peebles had phoned he had to go to the country, so there was just us having supper, and then Loretta Bird thrusting her head in the door and saying, "I see he's took off."

"What?" said Alice Kelling, and pushed back her chair.

"The kids come and told me this afternoon he was taking down his tent. Did he think he'd run through all the business there was round here? He didn't take off without letting you know, did he?"

"He'll send me word," Alice Kelling said. "He'll probably phone tonight. He's terribly restless, since the war."

"Edie, he didn't mention to you, did he?" Mrs. Peebles said. "When you took   150
over the message?"

"Yes," I said. So far so true.

"Well why didn't you say?" All of them were looking at me. "Did he say where he was going?"

"He said he might try Bayfield," I said. What made me tell such a lie? I didn't intend it.

"Bayfield, how far is that?" said Alice Kelling.

Mrs. Peebles said. "Thirty, thirty-five miles." 155

"That's not far. Oh, well, that's really not far at all. It's on the lake, isn't it?"

You'd think I'd be ashamed of myself, setting her on the wrong track. I did it to give him more time, whatever time he needed. I lied for him, and also, I have to admit, for me. Women should stick together and not do things like that. I see that now, but didn't then. I never thought of myself as being in any way like her, or coming to the same troubles, ever.

She hadn't taken her eyes off me. I thought she suspected my lie.

"When did he mention this to you?"

"Earlier." 160

"When you were over at the plane?"

"Yes."

"You must've stayed and had a chat." She smiled at me, not a nice smile. "You must've stayed and had a little visit with him."

"I took a cake," I said, thinking that telling some truth would spare me telling the rest.

"We didn't have a cake," said Mrs. Peebles rather sharply. 165

"I baked one."

Alice Kelling said, "That was very friendly of you."

"Did you get permission?" said Loretta Bird. "You never know what these girls'll do next," she said. "It's not they mean harm so much, as they're ignorant."

"The cake is neither here nor there," Mrs. Peebles broke in. "Edie, I wasn't aware you knew Chris that well."

I didn't know what to say. 170

"I'm not surprised," Alice Kelling said in a high voice. "I knew by the look of her as soon as I saw her. We get them at the hospital all the time." She looked hard at me with her stretched smile. "Having their babies. We have to put them in a special ward because of their diseases. Little country tramps. Fourteen and fifteen years old. You should see the babies they have, too."

"There was a bad woman here in town had a baby that pus was running out of its eyes," Loretta Bird put in.

"Wait a minute," said Mrs. Peebles. "What is this talk? Edie. What about you and Mr. Watters? Were you intimate with him?"

"Yes," I said. I was thinking of us lying on the cot and kissing, wasn't that intimate? And I would never deny it.

They were all one minute quiet, even Loretta Bird. 175

"Well," said Mrs. Peebles. "I am surprised. I think I need a cigarette. This is the first of any such tendencies I've seen in her," she said, speaking to Alice Kelling, but Alice Kelling was looking at me.

"Loose little bitch." Tears ran down her face. "Loose little bitch, aren't you? I knew as soon as I saw you. Men despise girls like you. He just made use of you and went off, you know that, don't you? Girls like you are just nothing, they're just public conveniences, just filthy little rags!"

"Oh, now," said Mrs. Peebles.

"Filthy," Alice Kelling sobbed. "Filthy little rags!"

"Don't get yourself upset," Loretta Bird said. She was swollen up with plea-   180
sure at being in on this scene. "Men are all the same."

"Edie, I'm very surprised," Mrs. Peebles said. "I thought your parents were so strict. You don't want to have a baby, do you?"

I'm still ashamed of what happened next. I lost control, just like a six-year-old, I started howling. "You don't get a baby from just doing that!"

"You see. Some of them are that ignorant," Loretta Bird said.

But Mrs. Peebles jumped up and caught my arms and shook me.

"Calm down. Don't get hysterical. Calm down. Stop crying. Listen to me. Lis-   185
ten. I'm wondering, if you know what being intimate means. Now tell me. What did you think it meant?"

"Kissing," I howled.

She let go. "Oh, Edie. Stop it. Don't be silly. It's all right. It's all a misunderstanding. Being intimate means a lot more than that. Oh, I *wondered*."

"She's trying to cover up, now," said Alice Kelling. "Yes. She's not so stupid. She sees she got herself in trouble."

"I believe her," Mrs. Peebles said. "This is an awful scene."

"Well there is one way to find out," said Alice Kelling, getting up. "After all, I   190
am a nurse."

Mrs. Peebles drew a breath and said, "No. No. Go to your room, Edie. And stop that noise. This is too disgusting."

I heard the car start in a little while. I tried to stop crying, pulling back each wave as it started over me. Finally I succeeded, and lay heaving on the bed.

Mrs. Peebles came and stood in the doorway.

"She's gone," she said. "That Bird woman too. Of course, you know you should never have gone near that man and that is the cause of all this trouble. I have a headache. As soon as you can, go and wash your face in cold water and get at the dishes and we will not say any more about this."

Nor we didn't. I didn't figure out till years later the extent of what I had been   195
saved from. Mrs. Peebles was not very friendly to me afterward, but she was fair. Not very friendly is the wrong way of describing what she was. She had never been very friendly. It was just that now she had to see me all the time and it got on her nerves, a little.

As for me, I put it all out of my mind like a bad dream and concentrated on waiting for my letter. The mail came every day except Sunday, between one-thirty and two in the afternoon, a good time for me because Mrs. Peebles was always having her nap. I would get the kitchen all cleaned and then go up to the mailbox and sit in the grass, waiting. I was perfectly happy, waiting, I forgot all about Alice Kelling and her misery and awful talk and Mrs. Peebles and her chilliness and the embarrassment of whether she had told Dr. Peebles and the face of Loretta Bird, getting her fill of other people's troubles. I was always smiling when the mailman got there, and continued smiling even after he gave me the mail and I saw today wasn't the day. The mailman was a Carmichael. I knew by his face because there are a lot of Carmichaels living out by us and so many of them have a sort of sticking-out top lip. So I asked his name (he was a young man, shy, but good-humored, anybody could ask him anything) and then I said, "I knew by your face!" He was pleased by that and always glad to see me and got a little less shy. "You've got the smile I've been waiting on all day!" he used to holler out the car window.

It never crossed my mind for a long time a letter might not come. I believed in it coming just like I believed the sun would rise in the morning. I just put off my hope from day to day, and there was the goldenrod out around the mailbox and the children gone back to school, and the leaves turning, and I was wearing a sweater when I went to wait. One day walking back with the hydro bill stuck in my hand, that was all, looking across at the fairgrounds with the full-blown milkweed and dark teasels, so much like fall, it just struck me: *No letter was ever going to come.* It was an impossible idea to get used to. No, not impossible. If I thought about Chris's face when he said he was going to write to me, it was impossible, but if I forgot that and thought about the actual tin mailbox, empty, it was plain and true. I kept on going to meet the mail, but my heart was heavy now like a lump of lead. I only smiled because I thought of the mailman counting on it, and he didn't have an easy life, with the winter driving ahead.

Till it came to me one day there were women doing this with their lives, all over. There were women just waiting and waiting by mailboxes for one letter or another. I imagined me making this journey day after day and year after year, and my hair starting to go gray, and I thought, I was never made to go on like that. So I stopped meeting the mail. If there were women all through life waiting, and women busy and not waiting, I knew which I had to be. Even though there might be things the second kind of women have to pass up and never know about, it still is better.

I was surprised when the mailman phoned the Peebleses' place in the evening and asked for me. He said he missed me. He asked if I would like to go to Goderich, where some well-known movie was on, I forget now what. So I said yes, and I went out with him for two years and he asked me to marry him, and we were engaged a year more while I got my things together, and then we did marry. He always tells the children the story of how I went after him by sitting by the mailbox every day, and naturally I laugh and let him, because I like for people to think what pleases them and makes them happy.

For Analysis

1. How does the author establish Edie's superiority over the other women in the story?

2. Is Edie better off with the mailman than she would have been with the pilot? Explain.

3. Consider the impact of Edie's assertion: "If there were women all through life waiting, and women busy and not waiting, I knew which I had to be" (para. 198). Which sort did she have to be? Do you agree with her? Explain.

4. Should Edie correct her husband's misunderstanding of her motives for waiting at the mailbox? Why or why not?

On Style
1. The story is told from Edie's **point of view** — but as a reminiscence. Do you find this technique effective? For instance, how might the story differ if it were told from the viewpoint of a fifteen-year-old girl rather than a mature wife and mother?

2. Aside from Edie, which woman in the story is characterized most realistically? Least realistically? Explain.

Making Connections
1. Compare Edie's behavior with Calixta's in Kate Chopin's "The Storm" (p. 1016).

2. Which of Edie's suitors exhibits the characteristics of the man in Pam Houston's "How to Talk to a Hunter" (p. 1077)?

Writing Topic
Use this story as a focal point in an essay on the differences between idealized romantic love and the qualities of realistic marriages and family relationships.

Raymond Carver   (1938–1988)

What We Talk about When We Talk about Love   1981

My friend Mel McGinnis was talking. Mel McGinnis is a cardiologist, and sometimes that gives him the right.

The four of us were sitting around his kitchen table drinking gin. Sunlight filled the kitchen from the big window behind the sink. There were Mel and me and his second wife, Teresa — Terri, we called her — and my wife, Laura. We lived in Albuquerque then. But we were all from somewhere else.

There was an ice bucket on the table. The gin and the tonic water kept going around, and we somehow got on the subject of love. Mel thought real love was nothing less than spiritual love. He said he'd spent five years in a seminary before quitting to go to medical school. He said he still looked back on those years in the seminary as the most important years in his life.

Terri said the man she lived with before she lived with Mel loved her so much he tried to kill her. Then Terri said, "He beat me up one night. He dragged me around the living room by my ankles. He kept saying, 'I love you, I love you, you bitch.' He went on dragging me around the living room. My head kept knocking on things." Terri looked around the table. "What do you do with love like that?"

She was a bone-thin woman with a pretty face, dark eyes, and brown hair that 5 hung down her back. She liked necklaces made of turquoise, and long pendant earrings.

"My God, don't be silly. That's not love, and you know it," Mel said. "I don't know what you'd call it, but I sure know you wouldn't call it love."

"Say what you want to, but I know it was," Terri said. "It may sound crazy to you, but it's true just the same. People are different, Mel. Sure, sometimes he may have acted crazy. Okay. But he loved me. In his own way maybe, but he loved me. There was love there, Mel. Don't say there wasn't."

Mel let out his breath. He held his glass and turned to Laura and me. "The man threatened to kill me," Mel said. He finished his drink and reached for the gin bottle. "Terri's a romantic. Terri's of the kick-me-so-I'll-know-you-love-me school. Terri, hon, don't look that way." Mel reached across the table and touched Terri's cheek with his fingers. He grinned at her.

"Now he wants to make up," Terri said.

"Make up what?" Mel said. "What is there to make up? I know what I know. 10 That's all."

"How'd we get started on this subject, anyway?" Terri said. She raised her glass and drank from it. "Mel always has love on his mind," she said. "Don't you, honey?" She smiled, and I thought that was the last of it.

"I just wouldn't call Ed's behavior love. That's all I'm saying, honey," Mel said. "What about you guys?" Mel said to Laura and me. "Does that sound like love to you?"

"I'm the wrong person to ask," I said. "I didn't even know the man. I've only heard his name mentioned in passing. I wouldn't know. You'd have to know the particulars. But I think what you're saying is that love is an absolute."

Mel said, "The kind of love I'm talking about is. The kind of love I'm talking about, you don't try to kill people."

Laura said, "I don't know anything about Ed, or anything about the situation. 15 But who can judge anyone else's situation?"

I touched the back of Laura's hand. She gave me a quick smile. I picked up Laura's hand. It was warm, the nails polished, perfectly manicured. I encircled the broad wrist with my fingers, and I held her.

"When I left, he drank rat poison," Terri said. She clasped her arms with her hands. "They took him to the hospital in Sante Fe. That's where we lived then, about ten miles out. They saved his life. But his gums went crazy from it. I mean they pulled away from his teeth. After that, his teeth stood out like fangs. My God," Terri said. She waited a minute, then let go of her arms and picked up her glass.

"What people won't do!" Laura said.

"He's out of the action now," Mel said. "He's dead."

Mel handed me the saucer of limes. I took a section, squeezed it over my 20 drink, and stirred the ice cubes with my finger.

"It gets worse," Terri said. "He shot himself in the mouth. But he bungled that too. Poor Ed," she said. Terri shook her head.

"Poor Ed nothing," Mel said. "He was dangerous."

Mel was forty-five years old. He was tall and rangy with curly soft hair. His face and arms were brown from the tennis he played. When he was sober, his gestures, all his movements, were precise, very careful.

"He did love me though, Mel. Grant me that," Terri said. "That's all I'm asking. He didn't love me the way you love me. I'm not saying that. But he loved me. You can grant me that, can't you?"

"What do you mean, he bungled it?" I said. 25

Laura leaned forward with her glass. She put her elbows on the table and held her glass in both hands. She glanced from Mel to Terri and waited with a look of bewilderment on her open face, as if amazed that such things happened to people you were friendly with.

"How'd he bungle it when he killed himself?" I said.

"I'll tell you what happened," Mel said. "He took this twenty-two pistol he'd bought to threaten Terri and me with. Oh, I'm serious, the man was always threatening. You should have seen the way we lived in those days. Like fugitives. I even bought a gun myself. Can you believe it? A guy like me? But I did.

I bought one for self-defense and carried it in the glove compartment. Sometimes I'd have to leave the apartment in the middle of the night. To go to the hospital, you know? Terri and I weren't married then, and my first wife had the house and kids, the dog, everything, and Terri and I were living in this apartment here. Sometimes, as I say, I'd get a call in the middle of the night and have to go in to the hospital at two or three in the morning. It'd be dark out there in the parking lot, and I'd break into a sweat before I could even get to my car. I never knew if he was going to come up out of the shrubbery or from behind a car and start shooting. I mean, the man was crazy. He was capable of wiring a bomb, anything. He used to call my service at all hours and say he needed to talk to the doctor, and when I'd return the call, he'd say, 'Son of a bitch, your days are numbered.' Little things like that. It was scary, I'm telling you."

"I still feel sorry for him," Terri said.

"It sounds like a nightmare," Laura said. "But what exactly happened after he   30
shot himself?"

Laura is a legal secretary. We'd met in a professional capacity. Before we knew it, it was a courtship. She's thirty-five, three years younger than I am. In addition to being in love, we like each other and enjoy one another's company. She's easy to be with.

"What happened?" Laura said.

Mel said, "He shot himself in the mouth in his room. Someone heard the shot and told the manager. They came in with a passkey, saw what had happened, and called an ambulance. I happened to be there when they brought him in, alive but past recall. The man lived for three days. His head swelled up to twice the size of a normal head. I'd never seen anything like it, and I hope I never do again. Terri wanted to go in and sit with him when she found out about it. We had a fight over it. I didn't think she should see him like that. I didn't think she should see him, and I still don't."

"Who won the fight?" Laura said.

"I was in the room with him when he died," Terri said. "He never came up   35
out of it. But I sat with him. He didn't have anyone else."

"He was dangerous," Mel said. "If you call that love, you can have it."

"It was love," Terri said. "Sure, it's abnormal in most people's eyes. But he was willing to die for it. He did die for it."

"I sure as hell wouldn't call it love," Mel said. "I mean, no one knows what he did it for. I've seen a lot of suicides, and I couldn't say anyone ever knew what they did it for."

Mel put his hands behind his neck and tilted his chair back. "I'm not interested in that kind of love," he said. "If that's love, you can have it."

Terri said, "We were afraid. Mel even made a will out and wrote to his brother   40
in California who used to be a Green Beret. Mel told him who to look for if something happened to him."

Terri drank from her glass. She said, "But Mel's right — we lived like fugitives. We were afraid. Mel was, weren't you, honey? I even called the police at one point, but they were no help. They said they couldn't do anything until Ed actually did something. Isn't that a laugh?" Terri said.

She poured the last of the gin into her glass and waggled the bottle. Mel got up from the table and went to the cupboard. He took down another bottle.

"Well, Nick and I know what love is," Laura said. "For us, I mean," Laura said. She bumped my knee with her knee. "You're supposed to say something now," Laura said, and turned her smile on me.

For an answer, I took Laura's hand and raised it to my lips. I made a big production out of kissing her hand. Everyone was amused.

"We're lucky," I said.   45

"You guys," Terri said. "Stop that now. You're making me sick. You're still on the honeymoon, for God's sake. You're still gaga, for crying out loud. Just wait. How long have you been together now? How long has it been? A year? Longer than a year?"

"Going on a year and a half," Laura said, flushed and smiling.

"Oh, now," Terri said. "Wait a while."

She held her drink and gazed at Laura.

"I'm only kidding," Terri said.   50

Mel opened the gin and went around the table with the bottle.

"Here, you guys," he said. "Let's have a toast. I want to propose a toast. A toast to love. To true love," Mel said.

We touched glasses.

"To love," we said.

Outside in the backyard, one of the dogs began to bark. The leaves of the   55
aspen that leaned past the window ticked against the glass. The afternoon sun was like a presence in this room, the spacious light of ease and generosity. We could have been anywhere, somewhere enchanted. We raised our glasses again and grinned at each other like children who had agreed on something forbidden.

"I'll tell you what real love is," Mel said. "I mean, I'll give you a good example. And then you can draw your own conclusions." He poured more gin into his glass. He added an ice cube and a sliver of lime. We waited and sipped our drinks. Laura and I touched knees again. I put a hand on her warm thigh and left it there.

"What do any of us really know about love?" Mel said. "It seems to me we're just beginners at love. We say we love each other and we do, I don't doubt it. I love Terri and Terri loves me, and you guys love each other too. You know the kind of love I'm talking about now. Physical love, that impulse that drives you to someone special, as well as love of the other person's being, his or her essence, as it were. Carnal love and, well, call it sentimental love, the day-to-day caring about the other person. But sometimes I have a hard time accounting for the fact that I must have loved my first wife too. But I did, I know I did. So I suppose I am like Terri in that regard. Terri and Ed." He thought about it and then he went on. "There was a time when I thought I loved my first wife more than life itself. But now I hate her guts. I do. How do you explain that? What happened to that love? What happened to it, is what I'd like to know. I wish someone could tell me. Then there's Ed. Okay, we're back to Ed. He loves Terri so much he tries to kill her and he winds up killing himself." Mel stopped talking and swallowed from his glass. "You guys have been together eighteen months and you love each other. It shows all over you. You glow with it. But you both loved other people before you met each other. You've both been married before, just like us. And you probably loved other people before that too, even. Terri and I have been together five years, been married for four. And the terrible thing, the terrible thing is, but the good thing too, the saving grace, you might say, is that if something happened to one of us — excuse me for saying this — but if something happened to one of us tomorrow I think the other one, the other person, would grieve for a while, you know, but then the surviving party would go out and love again, have someone else soon enough. All this, all of this love we're talking about, it would just be a memory. Maybe not even a memory. Am I wrong? Am I way off base? Because I want you to set me straight if you think I'm wrong. I want to know. I mean, I don't know anything, and I'm the first one to admit it."

"Mel, for God's sake," Terri said. She reached out and took hold of his wrist. "Are you getting drunk? Honey? Are you drunk?"

"Honey, I'm just talking," Mel said. "All right? I don't have to be drunk to say what I think. I mean, we're all just talking, right?" Mel said. He fixed his eyes on her.

"Sweetie, I'm not criticizing," Terri said.   60

She picked up her glass.

"I'm not on call today," Mel said. "Let me remind you of that. I am not on call," he said.

"Mel, we love you," Laura said.

Mel looked at Laura. He looked at her as if he could not place her, as if she was not the woman she was.

"Love you too, Laura," Mel said. "And you, Nick, love you too. You know   65 something?" Mel said. "You guys are our pals," Mel said.

He picked up his glass.

Mel said, "I was going to tell you about something. I mean, I was going to prove a point. You see, this happened a few months ago, but it's still going on right now, and it ought to make us feel ashamed when we talk like we know what we're talking about when we talk above love."

"Come on now," Terri said. "Don't talk like you're drunk if you're not drunk."

"Just shut up for once in your life," Mel said very quietly. "Will you do me a favor and do that for a minute? So as I was saying, there's this old couple who had this car wreck out on the interstate. A kid hit them and they were all torn to shit and nobody was giving them much chance to pull through."

Terri looked at us and then back at Mel. She seemed anxious, or maybe that's   70 too strong a word.

Mel was handing the bottle around the table.

"I was on call that night," Mel said. "It was May or maybe it was June. Terri and I had just sat down to dinner when the hospital called. There'd been this thing out on the interstate. Drunk kid, teenager, plowed his dad's pickup into this camper with this old couple in it. They were up in their mid-seventies, that couple. The kid — eighteen, nineteen, something — he was DOA. Taken the steering wheel through his sternum. The old couple, they were alive, you understand. I mean, just barely. But they had everything. Multiple fractures, internal injuries, hemorrhaging, contusions, lacerations, the works, and they each of them had themselves concussions. They were in a bad way, believe me. And, of course, their age was two strikes against them. I'd say she was worse off than he was. Ruptured spleen along with everything else. Both kneecaps broken. But they'd been wearing their seatbelts and, God knows, that's what saved them for the time being."

"Folks, this is an advertisement for the National Safety Council," Terri said. "This is your spokesman, Dr. Melvin R. McGinnis, talking." Terri laughed. "Mel," she said, "sometimes you're just too much. But I love you, hon," she said.

"Honey, I love you," Mel said.

He leaned across the table. Terri met him halfway. They kissed. 75

"Terri's right," Mel said as he settled himself again. "Get those seatbelts on. But seriously, they were in some shape, those oldsters. By the time I got down there, the kid was dead, as I said. He was off in a corner, laid out on a gurney. I took one look at the old couple and told the ER nurse to get me a neurologist and an orthopedic man and a couple of surgeons down there right away."

He drank from his glass. "I'll try to keep this short," he said. "So we took the two of them up to the OR and worked like fuck on them most of the night. They had these incredible reserves, those two. You see that once in a while. So we did everything that could be done, and toward morning we're giving them a fifty-fifty chance, maybe less than that for her. So here they are, still alive the next morning. So, okay, we move them into the ICU, which is where they both kept plugging away at it for two weeks, hitting it better and better on all the scopes. So we transfer them out to their own room."

Mel stopped talking. "Here," he said, "let's drink this cheapo gin the hell up. Then we're going to dinner, right? Terri and I know a new place. That's where we'll go, to this new place we know about. But we're not going until we finish up this cut-rate, lousy gin."

Terri said, "We haven't actually eaten there yet. But it looks good. From the outside, you know."

"I like food," Mel said. "If I had it to do all over again, I'd be a chef, you 80 know? Right, Terri?" Mel said.

He laughed. He fingered the ice in his glass.

"Terri knows," he said. "Terri can tell you. But let me say this. If I could come back again in a different life, a different time and all, you know what? I'd like to come back as a knight. You were pretty safe wearing all that armor. It was all right being a knight until gunpowder and muskets and pistols came along."

"Mel would like to ride a horse and carry a lance," Terri said.

"Carry a woman's scarf with you everywhere," Laura said.

"Or just a woman," Mel said. 85

"Shame on you," Laura said.

Terri said, "Suppose you came back as a serf. The serfs didn't have it so good in those days," Terri said.

"The serfs never had it good," Mel said. "But I guess even the knights were vessels to someone. Isn't that the way it worked? But then everyone is always a vessel to someone. Isn't that right? Terri? But what I liked about knights, besides their ladies, was that they had that suit of armor, you know, and they couldn't get hurt very easy. No cars in those days, you know? No drunk teenagers to tear into your ass."

"Vassals," Terri said.

"What?" Mel said. 90

"Vassals," Terri said. "They were called vassals, not vessels."

"Vassals, vessels," Mel said, "what the fuck's the difference? You knew what I meant anyway. All right," Mel said. "So I'm not educated. I learned my stuff. I'm a heart surgeon, sure, but I'm just a mechanic. I go in and I fuck around and I fix things. Shit," Mel said.

"Modesty doesn't become you," Terri said.

"He's just a humble sawbones," I said. "But sometimes they suffocated in all that armor, Mel. They'd even have heart attacks if it got too hot and they were too tired and worn out. I read somewhere that they'd fall off their horses and not be able to get up because they were too tired to stand with all that armor on them. They got trampled by their own horses sometimes."

"That's terrible," Mel said. "That's a terrible thing, Nicky. I guess they'd just 95 lay there and wait until somebody came along and made a shish kebab out of them."

"Some other vessel," Terri said.

"That's right," Mel said. "Some vassal would come along and spear the bastard in the name of love. Or whatever the fuck it was they fought over in those days."

"Same things we fight over these days," Terri said.

Laura said, "Nothing's changed."

The color was still high in Laura's cheeks. Her eyes were bright. She brought 100 her glass to her lips.

Mel poured himself another drink. He looked at the label closely as if studying a long row of numbers. Then he slowly put the bottle down on the table and slowly reached for the tonic water.

"What about the old couple?" Laura said. "You didn't finish that story you started."

Laura was having a hard time lighting her cigarette. Her matches kept going out.

The sunshine inside the room was different now, changing, getting thinner. But the leaves outside the window were still shimmering, and I stared at the pattern they made on the panes and on the Formica counter. They weren't the same patterns, of course.

"What about the old couple?" I said.

"Older but wiser," Terri said.

Mel stared at her.

Terri said, "Go on with your story, hon. I was only kidding. Then what happened?"

"Terri, sometimes," Mel said.

"Please, Mel," Terri said. "Don't always be so serious, sweetie. Can't you take a joke?"

"Where's the joke?" Mel said.

He held his glass and gazed steadily at his wife.

"What happened?" Laura said.

Mel fastened his eyes on Laura. He said, "Laura, if I didn't have Terri and if I didn't love her so much, and if Nick wasn't my best friend, I'd fall in love with you, I'd carry you off, honey," he said.

"Tell your story," Terri said. "Then we'll go to that new place, okay?"

"Okay," Mel said. "Where was I?" he said. He stared at the table and then he began again.

"I dropped in to see each of them every day, sometimes twice a day if I was up doing other calls anyway. Casts and bandages, head to foot, the both of them. You know, you've seen it in the movies. That's just the way they looked, just like in the movies. Little eye-holes and nose-holes and mouth-holes. And she had to have her legs slung up on top of it. Well, the husband was very depressed for the longest while. Even after he found out that his wife was going to pull through, he was still very depressed. Not about the accident, though. I mean, the accident was one thing, but it wasn't everything. I'd get up to his mouth-hole, you know, and he'd say no, it wasn't the accident exactly but it was because he couldn't see her through his eye-holes. He said that was what was making him feel so bad. Can you imagine? I'm telling you, the man's heart was breaking because he couldn't turn his goddamn head and *see* his goddamn wife."

Mel looked around the table and shook his head at what he was going to say.

"I mean, it was killing the old fart just because he couldn't *look* at the fucking woman."

We all looked at Mel.

"Do you see what I'm saying?" he said.

Maybe we were a little drunk by then. I know it was hard keeping things in focus. The light was draining out of the room, going back through the window where it had come from. Yet nobody made a move to get up from the table to turn on the overhead light.

"Listen," Mel said. "Let's finish this fucking gin. There's about enough left here for one shooter all around. Then let's go eat. Let's go to the new place."

"He's depressed," Terri said. "Mel, why don't you take a pill?"

105

110

115

120

Mel shook his head. "I've taken everything there is."   125

"We all need a pill now and then," I said.

"Some people are born needing them," Terri said.

She was using her finger to rub at something on the table. Then she stopped rubbing.

"I think I want to call my kids," Mel said. "Is that all right with everybody? I'll call my kids," he said.

Terri said, "What if Marjorie answers the phone? You guys, you've heard us   130 on the subject of Marjorie? Honey, you know you don't want to talk to Marjorie. It'll make you feel even worse."

"I don't want to talk to Marjorie," Mel said. "But I want to talk to my kids."

"There isn't a day goes by that Mel doesn't say he wishes she'd get married again. Or else die," Terri said. "For one thing," Terri said, "she's bankrupting us. Mel says it's just to spite him that she won't get married again. She has a boyfriend who lives with her and the kids, so Mel is supporting the boyfriend too."

"She's allergic to bees," Mel said. "If I'm not praying she'll get married again, I'm praying she'll get herself stung to death by a swarm of fucking bees."

"Shame on you," Laura said.

"Bzzzzzzz," Mel said, turning his fingers into bees and buzzing them at Terri's   135 throat. Then he let his hands drop all the way to his sides.

"She's vicious," Mel said. "Sometimes I think I'll go up there dressed like a beekeeper. You know, that hat that's like a helmet with the plate that comes down over your face, the big gloves, and the padded coat? I'll knock on the door and let loose a hive of bees in the house. But first I'd make sure the kids were out, of course."

He crossed one leg over the other. It seemed to take him a lot of time to do it. Then he put both feet on the floor and leaned forward, elbows on the table, his chin cupped in his hands.

"Maybe I won't call the kids, after all. Maybe it isn't such a hot idea. Maybe we'll just go eat. How does that sound?"

"Sounds fine to me," I said. "Eat or not eat. Or keep drinking. I could head right on out into the sunset."

"What does that mean, honey?" Laura said.   140

"It just means what I said," I said. "It means I could just keep going. That's all it means."

"I could eat something myself," Laura said. "I don't think I've ever been so hungry in my life. Is there something to nibble on?"

"I'll put out some cheese and crackers," Terri said.

But Terri just sat there. She did not get up to get anything.

Mel turned his glass over. He spilled it out on the table.   145

"Gin's gone," Mel said.

Terri said, "Now what?"

I could hear my heart beating. I could hear everyone's heart. I could hear the human noise we sat there making, not one of us moving, not even when the room went dark.

For Analysis

1. How would you characterize the relationship between Mel and Terri? Between Nick and Laura?

2. What is your reaction to Mel? Is he likable? What does his profession — a scientist and a cardiologist — represent?

3. Do you agree with Mel or Terri about Ed? Explain.

4. What is the significance of Mel's account of the old couple injured in an accident?

5. Do Mel's feelings about his ex-wife parallel Ed's feelings about Terri? Explain.

On Style

1. The story begins in the sunlight of midday and ends in darkness. How does this transition affect our understanding of what the story says about love and marriage?

2. Identify the elements in Carver's style that suggest Mel's increasing drunkenness.

3. Are the assertions in the last paragraph literal or **figurative**? Explain.

Making Connections

1. Have you ever come to hate someone you once loved or wanted to injure someone you once cherished? Given the circumstances, can you justify your feelings?

2. Compare the marital relationships in this story with those in Kate Chopin's "The Storm" (p. 1016) and Irwin Shaw's "The Girls in Their Summer Dresses" (p. 1034). Which relationships, in your opinion, offer the most realistic view of marriage?

Writing Topic

In an essay, examine the various relationships in the story: Nick and Laura, Mel and Terri, Terri and Ed, Mel and his ex-wife Marjorie, and the injured old couple. Conclude with a comment on "what we talk about when we talk about love."

Joyce Carol Oates   (b. 1938)

Where Are You Going, Where Have You Been?   1970

For Bob Dylan[1]

Her name was Connie. She was fifteen and she had a quick nervous giggling habit of craning her neck to glance into mirrors, or checking other people's faces to make sure her own was all right. Her mother, who noticed everything and knew everything and who hadn't much reason any longer to look at her own face, always scolded Connie about it. "Stop gawking at yourself, who are you? You think you're so pretty?" she would say. Connie would raise her eyebrows at these familiar complaints and look right through her mother, into a shadowy vision of herself as she was right at that moment: she knew she was pretty and that was everything. Her mother had been pretty once too, if you could believe those old snapshots in the album, but now her looks were gone and that was why she was always after Connie.

"Why don't you keep your room clean like your sister? How've you got your hair fixed — what the hell stinks? Hair spray? You don't see your sister using that junk."

Her sister June was twenty-four and still lived at home. She was a secretary in the high school Connie attended, and if that wasn't bad enough — with her in the same building — she was so plain and chunky and steady that Connie had to hear her praised all the time by her mother and her mother's sisters. June did this, June did that, she saved money and helped clean the house and cooked and Connie couldn't do a thing, her mind was all filled with trashy daydreams. Their father was away at work most of the time and when he came home he wanted supper and he read the newspaper at supper and after supper he went to bed. He didn't bother talking much to them, but around his bent head Connie's mother kept picking at her until Connie wished her mother was dead and she herself was dead and it was all over. "She makes me want to throw up some-times," she complained to her friends. She had a high, breathless, amused voice which made everything she said sound a little forced, whether it was sincere or not.

There was one good thing: June went places with girl friends of hers, girls who were just as plain and steady as she, and so when Connie wanted to do that her mother had no objections. The father of Connie's best girl friend drove the

---

[1] Bob Dylan (b. 1941) is an influential folk-rock musician and songwriter. Oates has commented that she had Dylan's song "It's All Over Now, Baby Blue" in mind when she wrote this story.

girls the three miles to town and left them off at a shopping plaza, so that they could walk through the stores or go to a movie, and when he came to pick them up again at eleven he never bothered to ask what they had done.

They must have been familiar sights, walking around that shopping plaza in 5 their shorts and flat ballerina slippers that always scuffed the sidewalk, with charm bracelets jingling on their thin wrists; they would lean together to whisper and laugh secretly if someone passed by who amused or interested them. Connie had long dark blond hair that drew anyone's eye to it, and she wore part of it pulled up on her head and puffed out and the rest of it she let fall down her back. She wore a pull-over jersey blouse that looked one way when she was at home and another way when she was away from home. Everything about her had two sides to it, one for home and one for anywhere that was not home: her walk that could be childlike and bobbing, or languid enough to make anyone think she was hearing music in her head, her mouth which was pale and smirking most of the time, but bright and pink on these evenings out, her laugh which was cynical and drawling at home — "Ha, ha, very funny" — but high-pitched and nervous anywhere else, like the jingling of the charms on her bracelet.

Sometimes they did go shopping or to a movie, but sometimes they went across the highway, ducking fast across the busy road, to a drive-in restaurant where older kids hung out. The restaurant was shaped like a big bottle, though squatter than a real bottle, and on its cap was a revolving figure of a grinning boy who held a hamburger aloft. One night in mid-summer they ran across, breathless with daring, and right away someone leaned out a car window and invited them over, but it was just a boy from high school they didn't like. It made them feel good to be able to ignore him. They went up through the maze of parked and cruising cars to the bright-lit, fly-infested restaurant, their faces pleased and expectant as if they were entering a sacred building that loomed out of the night to give them what haven and what blessing they yearned for. They sat at the counter and crossed their legs at the ankles, their thin shoulders rigid with excitement, and listened to the music that made everything so good: the music was always in the background like music at a church service, it was something to depend upon.

A boy named Eddie came in to talk with them. He sat backwards on his stool, turning himself jerkily around in semi-circles and then stopping and turning again, and after a while he asked Connie if she would like something to eat. She said she did and so she tapped her friend's arm on her way out — her friend pulled her face up into a brave droll look — and Connie said she would meet her at eleven, across the way. "I just hate to leave her like that," Connie said earnestly, but the boy said that she wouldn't be alone for long. So they went out to his car and on the way Connie couldn't help but let her eyes wander over the windshields and faces all around her, her face gleaming with a joy that had nothing to do with Eddie or even this place; it might have been the music. She drew her shoulders up and sucked in her breath with the pure pleasure of being alive, and just at that moment she happened to glance at a face just a few feet from hers. It was a boy with shaggy black hair, in a convertible jalopy painted gold. He stared at her and then his lips widened into a grin. Connie slit her eyes at him and turned away, but she couldn't help glancing back and there he was still watching her. He wagged a finger and laughed and said, "Gonna get you, baby," and Connie turned away without Eddie noticing anything.

She spent three hours with him, at the restaurant where they ate hamburgers and drank Cokes in wax cups that were always sweating, and then down an alley a mile or so away, and when he left her off at five to eleven only the movie house was still open at the plaza. Her girl friend was there, talking with a boy. When Connie came up the two girls smiled at each other and Connie said, "How was the movie?" and the girl said, "*You* should know." They rode off with the girl's father, sleepy and pleased, and Connie couldn't help but look at the darkened shopping plaza with its big empty parking lot and its signs that were faded and ghostly now, and over at the drive-in restaurant where cars were still circling tirelessly. She couldn't hear the music at this distance.

Next morning June asked her how the movie was and Connie said, "So-so."

She and that girl and occasionally another girl went several times a week that   10 way, and the rest of the time Connie spent around the house — it was summer vacation — getting in her mother's way and thinking, dreaming, about the boys she met. But all the boys fell back and dissolved into a single face that was not even a face, but an idea, a feeling, mixed up with the urgent insistent pounding of the music and the humid night air of July. Connie's mother kept dragging her back to the daylight by finding things for her to do or saying, suddenly, "What's this about the Pettinger girl?"

And Connie would say nervously, "Oh, her. That dope." She always drew thick clear lines between herself and such girls, and her mother was simple and kindly enough to believe her. Her mother was so simple, Connie thought, that it was maybe cruel to fool her so much. Her mother went scuffling around the house in old bedroom slippers and complained over the telephone to one sister about the other, then the other called up and the two of them complained about the third one. If June's name was mentioned her mother's tone was approving, and if Connie's name was mentioned it was disapproving. This did not really mean she disliked Connie and actually Connie thought that her mother preferred her to June because she was prettier, but the two of them kept up a pretense of exasperation, a sense that they were tugging and struggling over something of little value to either of them. Sometimes, over coffee, they were almost friends, but something would come up — some vexation that was like a fly buzzing suddenly around their heads — and their faces went hard with contempt.

One Sunday Connie got up at eleven — none of them bothered with church — and washed her hair so that it could dry all day long, in the sun. Her parents and sister were going to a barbecue at an aunt's house and Connie said no, she wasn't interested, rolling her eyes to let her mother know just what she thought of it. "Stay home alone then," her mother said sharply. Connie sat out back in a lawn chair and watched them drive away, her father quiet and bald, hunched around so that he could back the car out, her mother with a look that was still angry and not at all softened through the windshield, and in the back seat poor old June all dressed up as if she didn't know what a barbecue was, with all the running yelling kids and the flies. Connie sat with her eyes closed in the sun, dreaming and dazed with the warmth about her as if this were a kind of love, the caresses of love, and her mind slipped over onto thoughts of the boy she had been with the night before and how nice he had been, how sweet it always was, not the way someone like June would suppose but sweet, gentle, the way it was in movies and promised in songs; and when she opened her eyes she hardly knew where she was, the back yard ran off into weeds and a fence-line of trees and behind it the sky was perfectly blue and still. The asbestos "ranch house" that was now three years old still startled her — it looked small. She shook her head as if to get awake.

It was too hot. She went inside the house and turned on the radio to drown out the quiet. She sat on the edge of her bed, barefoot, and listened for an hour and a half to a program called XYZ Sunday Jamboree, record after record of hard, fast, shrieking songs she sang along with, interspersed by exclamations from "Bobby King": "An' look here you girls at Napoleon's — Son and Charley want you to pay real close attention to this song coming up!"

And Connie paid close attention herself, bathed in a glow of slow-pulsed joy that seemed to rise mysteriously out of the music itself and lay languidly about the airless little room, breathed in and breathed out with each gentle rise and fall of her chest.

After a while she heard a car coming up the drive. She sat up at once, startled, 15 because it couldn't be her father so soon. The gravel kept crunching all the way in from the road — the driveway was long — and Connie ran to the window. It was a car she didn't know. It was an open jalopy, painted a bright gold that caught the sunlight opaquely. Her heart began to pound and her fingers snatched at her hair, checking it, and she whispered "Christ. Christ," wondering how bad she looked. The car came to a stop at the side door and the horn sounded four short taps as if this were a signal Connie knew.

She went into the kitchen and approached the door slowly, then hung out the screen door, her bare toes curling down off the step. There were two boys in the car and now she recognized the driver: he had shaggy, shabby black hair that looked crazy as a wig and he was grinning at her.

"I ain't late, am I?" he said.

"Who the hell do you think you are?" Connie said.

"Toldja I'd be out, didn't I?"

"I don't even know who you are." 20

She spoke sullenly, careful to show no interest or pleasure, and he spoke in a fast bright monotone. Connie looked past him to the other boy, taking her time. He had fair brown hair, with a lock that fell onto his forehead. His sideburns gave him a fierce, embarrassed look, but so far he hadn't even bothered to glance at her. Both boys wore sunglasses. The driver's glasses were metallic and mirrored everything in miniature.

"You wanta come for a ride?" he said.

Connie smirked and let her hair fall loose over one shoulder.

"Don'tcha like my car? New paint job," he said. "Hey."

"What?"   25

"You're cute."

She pretended to fidget, chasing flies away from the door.

"Don'tcha believe me, or what?" he said.

"Look, I don't even know who you are," Connie said in disgust.

"Hey, Ellie's got a radio, see. Mine's broke down." He lifted his friend's arm   30
and showed her the little transistor the boy was holding, and now Connie began
to hear the music. It was the same program that was playing inside the house.

"Bobby King?" she said.

"I listen to him all the time. I think he's great."

"He's kind of great," Connie said reluctantly.

"Listen, that guy's *great*. He knows where the action is."

Connie blushed a little, because the glasses made it impossible for her to see   35
just what this boy was looking at. She couldn't decide if she liked him or if he
was just a jerk, and so she dawdled in the doorway and wouldn't come down or
go back inside. She said, "What's all that stuff painted on your car?"

"Can'tcha read it?" He opened the door very carefully, as if he was afraid it
might fall off. He slid out just as carefully, planting his feet firmly on the ground,
the tiny metallic world in his glasses slowing down like gelatine hardening and
in the midst of it Connie's bright green blouse. "This here is my name, to begin
with," he said. ARNOLD FRIEND was written in tarlike black letters on the
side, with a drawing of a round grinning face that reminded Connie of a pumpkin, except it wore sunglasses. "I wanta introduce myself, I'm Arnold Friend
and that's my real name and I'm gonna be your friend, honey, and inside the
car's Ellie Oscar, he's kinda shy." Ellie brought his transistor radio up to his
shoulder and balanced it there. "Now these numbers are a secret code, honey,"
Arnold Friend explained. He read off the numbers 33, 19, 17 and raised his eyebrows at her to see what she thought of that, but she didn't think much of it.
The left rear fender had been smashed and around it was written on the gleaming gold background: DONE BY CRAZY WOMAN DRIVER. Connie had to
laugh at that. Arnold Friend was pleased at her laughter and looked up at her.
"Around the other side's a lot more — you wanta come and see them?"

"No."

"Why not?"

"Why should I?"

"Don'tcha wanta see what's on the car? Don'tcha wanta go for a ride?"   40

"I don't know."

"Why not?"

"I got things to do."

"Like what?"

"Things."   45

He laughed as if she had said something funny. He slapped his thighs. He was
standing in a strange way, leaning back against the car as if he were balancing

himself. He wasn't tall, only an inch or so taller than she would be if she came down to him. Connie liked the way he was dressed, which was the way all of them dressed: tight faded jeans stuffed into black, scuffed boots, a belt that pulled his waist in and showed how lean he was, and a white pull-over shirt that was a little soiled and showed the hard small muscles of his arms and shoulders. He looked as if he possibly did hard work, lifting and carrying things. Even his neck looked muscular. And his face was a familiar face, somehow: the jaw and chin and cheeks slightly darkened, because he hadn't shaved for a day or two, and the nose long and hawk-like, sniffing as if she were a treat he was going to gobble up and it was all a joke.

"Connie, you ain't telling the truth. This is your day set aside for a ride with me and you know it," he said, still laughing. The way he straightened and recovered from his fit of laughing showed that it had been all fake.

"How do you know what my name is?" she said suspiciously.

"It's Connie."

"Maybe and maybe not." 50

"I know my Connie," he said, wagging his finger. Now she remembered him even better, back at the restaurant, and her cheeks warmed at the thought of how she sucked in her breath just at the moment she passed him — how she must have looked to him. And he had remembered her. "Ellie and I came out here especially for you," he said. "Ellie can sit in back. How about it?"

"Where?"

"Where what?"

"Where're we going?"

He looked at her. He took off the sunglasses and she saw how pale the skin 55 around his eyes was, like holes that were not in shadow but instead in light. His eyes were chips of broken glass that catch the light in an amiable way. He smiled. It was as if the idea of going for a ride somewhere, to some place, was a new idea to him.

"Just for a ride, Connie sweetheart."

"I never said my name was Connie," she said.

"But I know what it is. I know your name and all about you, lots of things," Arnold Friend said. He had not moved yet but stood still leaning back against the side of his jalopy. "I took a special interest in you, such a pretty girl, and found out all about you like I know your parents and sister are gone somewheres and I know where and how long they're going to be gone, and I know who you were with last night, and your best girl friend's name is Betty. Right?"

He spoke in a simple lilting voice, exactly as if he were reciting the words to a song. His smile assured her that everything was fine. In the car, Ellie turned up the volume on his radio and did not bother to look around at them.

"Ellie can sit in the back seat," Arnold Friend said. He indicated his friend 60 with a casual jerk of his chin, as if Ellie did not count and she should not bother with him.

"How'd you find out all that stuff?" Connie said.

"Listen: Betty Schultz and Tony Fitch and Jimmy Pettinger and Nancy Pettinger," he said, in a chant. "Raymond Stanley and Bob Hutter — "

"Do you know all those kids?"

"I know everybody."

"Look, you're kidding. You're not from around here."   65

"Sure."

"But — how come we never saw you before?"

"Sure you saw me before," he said. He looked down at his boots, as if he were a little offended. "You just don't remember."

"I guess I'd remember you," Connie said.

"Yeah?" He looked up at this, beaming. He was pleased. He began to mark   70
time with the music from Ellie's radio, tapping his fists lightly together. Connie looked away from his smile to the car, which was painted so bright it almost hurt her eyes to look at it. She looked at that name, ARNOLD FRIEND. And up at the front fender was an expression that was familiar — MAN THE FLYING SAUCERS. It was an expression kids had used the year before, but didn't use this year. She looked at it for a while as if the words meant something to her that she did not yet know.

"What're you thinking about? Huh?" Arnold Friend demanded. "Not worried about your hair blowing around in the car, are you?"

"No."

"Think I maybe can't drive good?"

"How do I know?"

"You're a hard girl to handle. How come?" he said. "Don't you know I'm your   75
friend? Didn't you see me put my sign in the air when you walked by?"

"What sign?"

"My sign." And he drew an X in the air, leaning out toward her. They were maybe ten feet apart. After his hand fell back to his side, the X was still in the air, almost visible. Connie let the screen door close and stood perfectly still inside it, listening to the music from her radio and the boy's blend together. She stared at Arnold Friend. He stood there so stiffly relaxed, pretending to be relaxed, with one hand idly on the door handle as if he were keeping himself up that way and had no intention of ever moving again. She recognized most things about him, the tight jeans that showed his thighs and buttocks and the greasy leather boots and the tight shirt, and even that slippery friendly smile of his, that sleepy dreamy smile that all the boys used to get across ideas they didn't want to put into words. She recognized all this and also the singsong way he talked, slightly mocking, kidding, but serious and a little melancholy, and she recognized the way he tapped one fist against the other in homage to the perpetual music behind him. But all these things did not come together.

She said suddenly, "Hey, how old are you?"

His smile faded. She could see then that he wasn't a kid, he was much older — thirty, maybe more. At this knowledge her heart began to pound faster.

"That's a crazy thing to ask. Can'tcha see I'm your own age?"   80

"Like hell you are."

"Or maybe a couple years older, I'm eighteen."

"Eighteen?" she said doubtfully.

He grinned to reassure her and lines appeared at the corners of his mouth. His teeth were big and white. He grinned so broadly his eyes became slits and she saw how thick the lashes were, thick and black as if painted with a black tar-like material. Then he seemed to become embarrassed, abruptly, and looked over his shoulder at Ellie. "*Him,* he's crazy," he said. "Ain't he a riot, he's a nut, a real character." Ellie was still listening to the music. His sunglasses told nothing about what he was thinking. He wore a bright orange shirt unbuttoned halfway to show his chest, which was a pale, bluish chest and not muscular like Arnold Friend's. His shirt collar was turned up all around and the very tips of the collar pointed out past his chin as if they were protecting him. He was pressing the transistor radio up against his ear and sat there in a kind of daze, right in the sun.

"He's kinda strange," Connie said. 85

"Hey, she says you're kinda strange! Kinda strange!" Arnold Friend cried. He pounded on the car to get Ellie's attention. Ellie turned for the first time and Connie saw with shock that he wasn't a kid either — he had a fair, hairless face, cheeks reddened slightly as if the veins grew too close to the surface of his skin, the face of a forty-year-old baby. Connie felt a wave of dizziness rise in her at this sight and she stared at him as if waiting for something to change the shock of the moment, make it all right again. Ellie's lips kept shaping words, mum-bling along, with the words blasting in his ear.

"Maybe you two better go away," Connie said faintly.

"What? How come?" Arnold Friend cried. "We come out here to take you for a ride. It's Sunday." He had the voice of the man on the radio now. It was the same voice, Connie thought. "Don'tcha know it's Sunday all day and honey, no matter who you were with last night today you're with Arnold Friend and don't you forget it! — Maybe you better step out here," he said, and this last was in a different voice. It was a little flatter, as if the heat was finally getting to him.

"No. I got things to do."

"Hey." 90

"You two better leave."

"We ain't leaving until you come with us."

"Like hell I am — "

"Connie, don't fool around with me. I mean, I mean, don't fool *around,*" he said, shaking his head. He laughed incredulously. He placed his sunglasses on top of his head, carefully, as if he were indeed wearing a wig, and brought the stems down behind his ears. Connie stared at him, another wave of dizziness and fear rising in her so that for a moment he wasn't even in focus but was just a blur, standing there against his gold car, and she had the idea that he had driven up the driveway all right but had come from nowhere before that and belonged nowhere and that everything about him and even about the music that was so familiar to her was only half real.

"If my father comes and sees you — "

"He ain't coming. He's at the barbecue."

"How do you know that?"

"Aunt Tillie's. Right now they're — uh — they're drinking. Sitting around," he said vaguely, squinting as if he were staring all the way to town and over to Aunt Tillie's backyard. Then the vision seemed to get clear and he nodded energetically. "Yeah. Sitting around. There's your sister in a blue dress, huh? And high heels, the poor sad bitch — nothing like you, sweetheart! And your mother's helping some fat woman with the corn, they're cleaning the corn — husking the corn — "

"What fat woman?" Connie cried.

"How do I know what fat woman. I don't know every goddam fat woman in the world!" Arnold Friend laughed.

"Oh, that's Mrs. Hornby. . . . Who invited her?" Connie said. She felt a little light-headed. Her breath was coming quickly.

"She's too fat. I don't like them fat. I like them the way you are, honey," he said, smiling sleepily at her. They stared at each other for awhile, through the screen door. He said softly, "Now what you're going to do is this: you're going to come out that door. You're going to sit up front with me and Ellie's going to sit in the back, the hell with Ellie, right? This isn't Ellie's date. You're my date. I'm your lover, honey."

"What? You're crazy — "

"Yes, I'm your lover. You don't know what that is but you will," he said. "I know that too. I know all about you. But look: it's real nice and you couldn't ask for nobody better than me, or more polite. I always keep my word. I'll tell you how it is, I'm always nice at first, the first time. I'll hold you so tight you won't think you have to try to get away or pretend anything because you'll know you can't. And I'll come inside you where it's all secret and you'll give in to me and you'll love me — "

"Shut up! You're crazy!" Connie said. She backed away from the door. She put her hands against her ears as if she'd heard something terrible, something not meant for her. "People don't talk like that, you're crazy," she muttered. Her heart was almost too big now for her chest and its pumping made sweat break out all over her. She looked out to see Arnold Friend pause and then take a step toward the porch lurching. He almost fell. But, like a clever drunken man, he managed to catch his balance. He wobbled in high boots and grabbed hold of one of the porch posts.

"Honey?" he said. "You still listening?"

"Get the hell out of here!"

"Be nice, honey. Listen."

"I'm going to call the police — "

He wobbled again and out of the side of his mouth came a fast spat curse, an aside not meant for her to hear. But even this "Christ!" sounded forced. Then he began to smile again. She watched this smile come, awkward as if he were

95

100

105

110

smiling from inside a mask. His whole face was a mask, she thought wildly, tanned down onto his throat but then running out as if he had plastered make-up on his face but had forgotten about his throat.

"Honey — ? Listen, here's how it is. I always tell the truth and I promise you this: I ain't coming in the house after you."

"You better not! I'm going to call the police if you — if you don't — "

"Honey," he said, talking right through her voice, "honey, I'm not coming in there but you are coming out here. You know why?"

She was panting. The kitchen looked like a place she had never seen before, some room she had run inside but which wasn't good enough, wasn't going to help her. The kitchen window had never had a curtain, after three years, and there were dishes in the sink for her to do — probably — and if you ran your hand across the table you'd probably feel something sticky there.

"You listening, honey? Hey?"   115

" — going to call the police — "

"Soon as you touch the phone I don't need to keep my promise and can come inside. You won't want that."

She rushed forward and tried to lock the door. Her fingers were shaking. "But why lock it," Arnold Friend said gently, talking right into her face. "It's just a screen door. It's just nothing." One of his boots was at a strange angle, as if his foot wasn't in it. It pointed out to the left, bent at the ankle. "I mean, anybody can break through a screen door and glass and wood and iron or anything else he needs to, anybody at all and specially Arnold Friend. If the place got lit up with a fire honey you'd come running out into my arms, right into my arms and safe at home — like you knew I was your lover and'd stopped fooling around. I don't mind a nice shy girl but I don't like no fooling around." Part of those words were spoken with a slight rhythmic lilt, and Connie somehow recognized them — the echo of a song from last year, about a girl rushing into her boy friend's arms and coming home again —

Connie stood barefoot on the linoleum floor, staring at him. "What do you want?" she whispered.

"I want you," he said.   120

"What?"

"Seen you that night and thought, that's the one, yes sir. I never needed to look any more."

"But my father's coming back. He's coming to get me. I had to wash my hair first — " She spoke in a dry, rapid voice, hardly raising it for him to hear.

"No, your daddy is not coming and yes, you had to wash your hair and you washed it for me. It's nice and shining and all for me, I thank you, sweetheart," he said, with a mock bow, but again he almost lost his balance. He had to bend and adjust his boots. Evidently his feet did not go all the way down; the boots must have been stuffed with something so that he would seem taller. Connie stared out at him and behind him Ellie in the car, who seemed to be looking off toward Connie's right, into nothing. This Ellie said, pulling the words out of the air one after another as if he were just discovering them, "You want me to pull out the phone?"

"Shut your mouth and keep it shut," Arnold Friend said, his face red from 125 bending over or maybe from embarrassment because Connie had seen his boots. "This ain't none of your business."

"What — what are you doing? What do you want?" Connie said. "If I call the police they'll get you, they'll arrest you — "

"Promise was not to come in unless you touch that phone, and I'll keep that promise," he said. He resumed his erect position and tried to force his shoulders back. He sounded like a hero in a movie, declaring something important. He spoke too loudly and it was as if he were speaking to someone behind Connie. "I ain't made plans for coming in that house where I don't belong but just for you to come out to me, the way you should. Don't you know who I am?"

"You're crazy," she whispered. She backed away from the door but did not want to go into another part of the house, as if this would give him permission to come through the door. "What do you . . . You're crazy, you . . ."

"Huh? What're you saying, honey?"

Her eyes darted everywhere in the kitchen. She could not remember what it 130 was, this room.

"This is how it is, honey: you come out and we'll drive away, have a nice ride. But if you don't come out we're gonna wait till your people come home and then they're all going to get it."

"You want that telephone pulled out?" Ellie said. He held the radio away from his ear and grimaced, as if without the radio the air was too much for him.

"I toldja shut up, Ellie," Arnold Friend said, "you're deaf, get a hearing aid, right? Fix yourself up. This little girl's no trouble and's gonna be nice to me, so Ellie keep to yourself, this ain't your date — right? Don't hem in on me. Don't hog. Don't crush. Don't bird dog. Don't trail me," he said in a rapid meaningless voice, as if he were running through all the expressions he'd learned but was no longer sure which one of them was in style, then rushing on to new ones, making them up with his eyes closed, "Don't crawl under my fence, don't squeeze in my chipmunk hole, don't sniff my glue, suck my popsicle, keep your own greasy fingers on yourself!" He shaded his eyes and peered in at Connie, who was backed against the kitchen table. "Don't mind him honey he's just a creep. He's a dope. Right? I'm the boy for you and like I said you come out here nice like a lady and give me your hand, and nobody else gets hurt, I mean, your nice old bald-headed daddy and your mummy and your sister in her high heels. Because listen: why bring them in this?"

"Leave me alone," Connie whispered.

"Hey, you know that old woman down the road, the one with the chickens 135 and stuff — you know her?"

"She's dead!"

"Dead? What? You know her?" Arnold Friend said.

"She's dead — "

"Don't you like her?"

"She's dead — she's — she isn't here any more — " 140

"But don't you like her, I mean, you got something against her? Some grudge or something?" Then his voice dipped as if he were conscious of a rudeness. He touched the sunglasses perched on top of his head as if to make sure they were still there. "Now you be a good girl."

"What are you going to do?"

"Just two things, or maybe three," Arnold Friend said. "But I promise it won't last long and you'll like me that way you get to like people you're close to. You will. It's all over for you here, so come on out. You don't want your people in any trouble, do you?"

She turned and bumped against a chair or something, hurting her leg, but she ran into the back room and picked up the telephone. Something roared in her ear, a tiny roaring, and she was so sick with fear that she could do nothing but listen to it — the telephone was clammy and very heavy and her fingers groped down to the dial but were too weak to touch it. She began to scream into the phone, into the roaring. She cried out, she cried for her mother, she felt her breath start jerking back and forth in her lungs as if it were something Arnold Friend were stabbing her with again and again with no tenderness. A noisy sorrowful wailing rose all about her and she was locked inside it the way she was locked inside that house.

After a while she could hear again. She was sitting on the floor with her wet 145
back against the wall.

Arnold Friend was saying from the door, "That's a good girl. Put the phone back."

She kicked the phone away from her.

"No, honey. Pick it up. Put it back right."

She picked it up and put it back. The dial tone stopped.

"That's a good girl. Now come outside." 150

She was hollow with what had been fear, but what was now just an emptiness. All that screaming had blasted it out of her. She sat, one leg cramped under her, and deep inside her brain was something like a pinpoint of light that kept going and would not let her relax. She thought, I'm not going to see my mother again. She thought, I'm not going to sleep in my bed again. Her bright green blouse was all wet.

Arnold Friend said, in a gentle-loud voice that was like a stage voice, "The place where you came from ain't there any more, and where you had in mind to go is cancelled out. This place you are now — inside your daddy's house — is nothing but a cardboard box I can knock down any time. You know that and always did know it. You hear me?"

She thought, I have got to think. I have to know what to do.

"We'll go out to a nice field, out in the country here where it smells so nice and it's sunny," Arnold Friend said. "I'll have my arms around you so you won't need to try to get away and I'll show you what love is like, what it does. The hell with this house! It looks solid all right," he said. He ran a fingernail down the screen and the noise did not make Connie shiver, as it would have the day before. "Now put your hand on your heart, honey. Feel that? That feels solid too but we know better, be nice to me, be sweet like you can because what else is there for a girl like you but to be sweet and pretty and give in? — and get away before her people come back?"

She felt her pounding heart. Her hand seemed to enclose it. She thought for 155 the first time in her life that it was nothing that was hers, that belonged to her, but just a pounding, living thing inside this body that wasn't really hers either.

"You don't want them to get hurt," Arnold Friend went on. "Now get up, honey. Get up all by yourself."

She stood up.

"Now turn this way. That's right. Come over here to me — Ellie, put that away, didn't I tell you? You dope. You miserable creepy dope," Arnold said. His words were not angry but only part of an incantation. The incantation was kindly. "Now come out through the kitchen to me honey and let's see a smile, try it, you're a brave sweet little girl and now they're eating corn and hotdogs cooked to bursting over an outdoor fire, and they don't know one thing about you and never did and honey, you're better than them because not a one of them would have done this for you."

Connie felt the linoleum under her feet; it was cool. She brushed her hair back out of her eyes. Arnold Friend let go of the post tentatively and opened his arms for her, his elbows pointing in toward each other and his wrists limp, to show that this was an embarrassed embrace and a little mocking, he didn't want to make her self-conscious.

She put out her hand against the screen. She watched herself push the door 160 slowly open as if she were safe back somewhere in the other doorway, watching this body and this head of long hair moving out into the sunlight where Arnold Friend waited.

"My sweet little blue-eyed girl," he said, in a half-sung sigh that had nothing to do with her brown eyes but was taken up just the same by the vast sunlit reaches of the land behind him and on all sides of him, so much land that Connie had never seen before and did not recognize except to know that she was going to it.

For Analysis

1. Characterize Connie in your own words. What are the sources of her values? What sort of love experience does she imagine?

2. When she agrees to go with Eddie, what do you suppose they did in the "alley a mile or so away" (para. 8)?

3. How does Arnold Friend differ from Eddie?

4. How does Arnold know so much about Connie and her family? Is his knowledge acquired supernaturally? What might that suggest about his nature?

5. Suggest some reason for the attention paid in the story to Arnold's boots.

6. What effect does Ellie's repeated proposal that he pull out the phone have on your understanding of Arnold and Ellie's motives?

7. Does Connie go to Arnold simply to protect her family from his threats? Explain.

8. What is going to happen to Connie? Give reasons for your response.

On Style

The story is told as a **third-person** narrative — yet it is limited, essentially, to Connie's viewpoint. Would multiple viewpoints — her mother's, June's, Eddie's, her friend's, Arnold's — enhance or impair the story's impact? Defend your answer.

Making Connections

1. Can you remember and describe the sexual attitudes you held when you were fifteen? In what ways were they similar to or different from Connie's?

2. Music seems to generate an imaginative world that Connie would like to inhabit. What sort of music does she apparently enjoy? What sort of emotional world does that music describe? Familiarize yourself with Bob Dylan's music, and comment on how it might differ from Connie's preferred style of music.

3. Compare Arnold Friend with Manley Pointer in Flannery O'Connor's "Good Country People" (p. 118).

Writing Topics

1. Does your experience support the proposition that some women find dangerous and unstable men more attractive than gentle and kind men? Support your arguments with allusions to this and other stories you have read.

2. Using evidence from the story, argue that Arnold Friend is an incarnation of the devil or some other fairy-tale villain.

Pam Houston   (b. 1962)

How to Talk to a Hunter   1990

When he says "Skins or blankets?" it will take you a moment to realize that he's asking which you want to sleep under. And in your hesitation he'll decide that he wants to see your skin wrapped in the big black moosehide. He carried it, he'll say, soaking wet and heavier than a dead man, across the tundra for two — was it hours or days or weeks? But the payoff, now, will be to see it fall across one of your white breasts. It's December, and your skin is never really warm, so you will pull the bulk of it around you and pose for him, pose for his camera, without having to narrate this moose's death.

You will spend every night in this man's bed without asking yourself why he listens to top-forty country. Why he donated money to the Republican party. Why he won't play back his messages while you are in the room. You are there so often the messages pile up. Once, you noticed the bright green counter reading as high as fifteen.

He will have lured you here out of a careful independence that you spent months cultivating; though it will finally be winter, the dwindling daylight and the threat of Christmas, that makes you give in. Spending nights with this man means suffering the long face of your sheep dog, who likes to sleep on your bed, who worries when you don't come home. But the hunter's house is so much warmer than yours, and he'll give you a key, and just like a woman, you'll think that means something. It will snow hard for thirteen straight days. Then it will really get cold. When it is sixty below there will be no wind and no clouds, just still air and cold sunshine. The sun on the windows will lure you out of bed, but he'll pull you back under. The next two hours he'll devote to your body. With his hands, with his tongue, he'll express what will seem to you like the most eternal of loves. Like the house key, this is just another kind of lie. Even in bed; especially in bed, you and he cannot speak the same language. The machine will answer the incoming calls. From under an ocean of passion and hide and hair you'll hear a woman's muffled voice between the beeps.

Your best female friend will say, "So what did you think? That a man who sleeps under a dead moose is capable of commitment?"

This is what you learned in college: A man desires the satisfaction of his 5 desire; a woman desires the condition of desiring.

The hunter will talk about spring in Hawaii, summer in Alaska. The man who says he was always better at math will form the sentences so carefully it will be impossible to tell if you are included in these plans. When he asks you if you would like to open a small guest ranch way out in the country, understand that this is a rhetorical question. Label these conversations future perfect, but don't expect the present to catch up with them. Spring is an inconceivable distance from the December days that just keep getting shorter and gray.

He'll ask you if you've ever shot anything, if you'd like to, if you ever thought about teaching your dog to retrieve. Your dog will like him too much, will drop the stick at his feet every time, will roll over and let the hunter scratch his belly.

One day he'll leave you sleeping to go split wood or get the mail and his phone will ring again. You'll sit very still while a woman who calls herself something like Patty Coyote leaves a message on his machine: she's leaving work, she'll say, and the last thing she wanted to hear was the sound of his beautiful voice. Maybe she'll talk only in rhyme. Maybe the counter will change to sixteen. You'll look a question at the mule deer on the wall, and the dark spots on either side of his mouth will tell you he shares more with this hunter than you ever will. One night, drunk, the hunter told you he was sorry for taking that deer, that every now and then there's an animal that isn't meant to be taken, and he should have known that deer was one.

Your best male friend will say, "No one who needs to call herself Patty Coyote can hold a candle to you, but why not let him sleep alone a few nights, just to make sure?"

The hunter will fill your freezer with elk burger, venison sausage, organic 10 potatoes, fresh pecans. He'll tell you to wear your seat belt, to dress warmly, to drive safely. He'll say you are always on his mind, that you're the best thing that's ever happened to him, that you make him glad that he's a man.

Tell him it don't come easy, tell him freedom's just another word for nothing left to lose.

These are the things you'll know without asking: The coyote woman wears her hair in braids. She uses words like "howdy." She's man enough to shoot a deer.

A week before Christmas you'll rent *It's a Wonderful Life* and watch it together, curled on your couch, faces touching. Then you'll bring up the word "monogamy." He'll tell you how badly he was hurt by your predecessor. He'll tell you he couldn't be happier spending every night with you. He'll say there's just a few questions he doesn't have the answers for. He'll say he's just scared and confused. Of course this isn't exactly what he means. Tell him you understand. Tell him you are scared too. Tell him to take all the time he needs. Know that you could never shoot an animal, and be glad of it.

Your best female friend will say, "You didn't tell him you loved him, did you?" Don't even tell her the truth. If you do, you'll have to tell her that he said this: "I feel exactly the same way."

Your best male friend will say, "Didn't you know what would happen when 15 you said the word 'commitment'?"
But that isn't the word that you said.
He'll say, "Commitment, monogamy, it all means just one thing."

The coyote woman will come from Montana with the heavier snows. The hunter will call you on the day of the solstice to say he has a friend in town and can't see you. He'll leave you hanging your Christmas lights; he'll give new meaning to the phrase "longest night of the year." The man who has said he's not so good with words will manage to say eight things about his friend without using a gender-determining pronoun. Get out of the house quickly. Call the most understanding person you know that will let you sleep in his bed.

Your best female friend will say, "So what did you think? That he was capable of living outside his gender?"

When you get home in the morning there's a candy tin on your pillow. Santa, 20 obese and grotesque, fondles two small children on the lid. The card will say something like, From your not-so-secret admirer. Open it. Examine each carefully made truffle. Feed them, one at a time, to the dog. Call the hunter's machine. Tell him you don't speak chocolate.

Your best female friend will say, "At this point, what is it about him that you could possibly find appealing?"

Your best male friend will say, "Can't you understand that this is a good sign? Can't you understand that this proves how deep he's in with you?" Hug your best male friend. Give him the truffles the dog wouldn't eat.

Of course the weather will cooperate with the coyote woman. The highways will close, she will stay another night. He'll tell her he's going to work so he can come and see you. He'll even leave her your number and write "Me at Work" on the yellow pad of paper by his phone. Although you shouldn't, you'll have to be there. It will be you and your nauseous dog and your half-trimmed tree all waiting for him like a series of questions.

This is what you learned in graduate school: In every assumption is contained the possibility of its opposite.

In your kitchen he'll hug you like you might both die there. Sniff him for coy- 25 ote. Don't hug him back.

He will say whatever he needs to win. He'll say it's just an old friend. He'll say the visit was all the friend's idea. He'll say the night away from you has given him time to think about how much you mean to him. Realize that nothing short of sleeping alone will ever make him realize how much you mean to him. He'll say that if you can just be a little patient, some good will come out of this for the two of you after all. He still won't use a gender-specific pronoun.

Put your head in your hands. Think about what it means to be patient. Think about the beautiful, smart, strong, clever woman you thought he saw when he looked at you. Pull on your hair. Rock your body back and forth. Don't cry.

He'll say that after holding you it doesn't feel right holding anyone else. For "holding," substitute "fucking." Then take it as a compliment.

He will get frustrated and rise to leave. He may or may not be bluffing. Stall for time. Ask a question he can't immediately answer. Tell him you want to make love on the floor. When he tells you your body is beautiful, say, "I feel exactly the same way." Don't, under any circumstances, stand in front of the door.

Your best female friend will say, "They lie to us, they cheat on us, and we love 30 them more for it." She'll say, "It's our fault. We raise them to be like that."

Tell her it can't be your fault. You've never raised anything but dogs.

The hunter will say it's late and he has to go home to sleep. He'll emphasize the last word in the sentence. Give him one kiss that he'll remember while he's fucking the coyote woman. Give him one kiss that ought to make him cry if he's capable of it, but don't notice when he does. Tell him to have a good night.

Your best male friend will say, "We all do it. We can't help it. We're self-destructive. It's the old bad-boy routine. You have a male dog, don't you?"

The next day the sun will be out and the coyote woman will leave. Think about how easy it must be for the coyote woman and a man who listens to top-forty country. The coyote woman would never use a word like "monogamy"; the coyote woman will stay gentle on his mind.

If you can, let him sleep alone for at least one night. If you can't, invite him 35 over to finish trimming your Christmas tree. When he asks how you are, tell him you think it's a good idea to keep your sense of humor during the holidays.

Plan to be breezy and aloof and full of interesting anecdotes about all the other men you've ever known. Plan to be hotter than ever before in bed, and a little cold out of it. Remember that necessity is the mother of invention. Be flexible.

First, he will find the faulty bulb that's been keeping all the others from lighting. He will explain in great detail the most elementary electrical principles. You will take turns placing the ornaments you and other men, he and other women, have spent years carefully choosing. Under the circumstances, try to let this be a comforting thought.

He will thin the clusters of tinsel you put on the tree. He'll say something ambiguous like, Next year you should string popcorn and cranberries. Finally, his arm will stretch just high enough to place the angel on the top of the tree.

Your best female friend will say, "Why can't you ever fall in love with a man who will be your friend?"

Your best male friend will say, "You ought to know this by now: Men always   40 cheat on the best women."

This is what you learned in the pop psychology book: Love means letting go of fear.

Play Willie Nelson's "Pretty Paper." He'll ask you to dance, and before you can answer he'll be spinning you around your wood stove, he'll be humming in your ear. Before the song ends he'll be taking off your clothes, setting you lightly under the tree, hovering above you with tinsel in his hair. Through the spread of the branches the all-white lights you insisted on will shudder and blur, outlining the ornaments he brought: a pheasant, a snow goose, a deer.

The record will end. Above the crackle of the wood stove and the rasp of the hunter's breathing you'll hear one long low howl break the quiet of the frozen night: your dog, chained and lonely and cold. You'll wonder if he knows enough to stay in his dog house. You'll wonder if he knows that the nights are getting shorter now.

For Analysis

1. What is the difference between the male friend's advice and the female friend's advice? Which advice is more accurate and useful? Explain.

2. The second paragraph, with three unasked questions, characterizes both the hunter and the narrator. What do the questions reveal about each of them? What is the significance of the order of the questions?

3. Describe the difference between the narrator and the "coyote woman." What does the narrator think of the coyote woman? What specific advice does the narrator give about talking to a hunter?

4. What is the significance of the narrator lying to her best female friend?

5. Why does the story end with the narrator's thoughts about the dog?

On Style

The story is written as if it were a series of notes or journal entries. How does that **style** and the **tone** of these notes affect your response to the story?

Making Connections

1. Does the relationship in this story remind you of any of your own or your friends' courtship experiences? Explain.

2. Compare and contrast the narrator of this story with Frances in Irwin Shaw's "The Girls in Their Summer Dresses" (p. 1034). What traits do the hunter and Michael share? Explain.

Writing Topic

In an essay, and, perhaps, drawing on your own experiences, analyze Houston's assertions about the differences between what men and women expect from a relationship.

Sappho (ca. 610–ca. 580 B.C.)

With His Venom[1]

With his venom

Irresistible
and bittersweet

that loosener
of limbs, Love

reptile-like
strikes me down

Anonymous

Bonny Barbara Allan

It was in and about the Martinmas[1] time,
    When the green leaves were a falling,
That Sir John Graeme, in the West Country,
    Fell in love with Barbara Allan.

With His Venom
    [1] Translated by Mary Barnard.
Bonny Barbara Allan
    [1] November 11.

He sent his man down through the town,
   To the place where she was dwelling:
"O haste and come to my master dear,
   Gin° ye be Barbara Allan."   *if*

O hooly,° hooly rose she up,   *slowly*
   To the place where he was lying,   10
And when she drew the curtain by:
   "Young man, I think you're dying."

"O it's I'm sick, and very, very sick,
   And 'tis a' for Barbara Allan."
"O the better for me ye s'° never be,   *ye shall*
   Tho your heart's blood were a-spilling."

"O dinna° ye mind,° young man," said she,   *don't/remember*
   "When ye was in the tavern a drinking,
That ye made the healths gae° round and round,   *go*
   And slighted Barbara Allan?"   20

He turned his face unto the wall,
   And death was with him dealing:
"Adieu, adieu, my dear friends all,
   And be kind to Barbara Allan."

And slowly, slowly raise she up,
   And slowly, slowly left him,
And sighing said she could not stay,
   Since death of life had reft him.

She had not gane a mile but twa,
   When she heard the dead-bell ringing,   30
And every jow° that the dead-bell geid,°   *stroke/gave*
   It cried, "Woe to Barbara Allan!"

"O mother, mother, make my bed!
   O make it saft and narrow!
Since my love died for me to-day,
   I'll die for him to-morrow."

LOOKING DEEPER:
From Poetry to Song

Each of the arts works in its own way. Though we may use the same term in dealing with different art forms, the meanings of our terms may not carry over from one form to another: clearly, the "movement" of a poem is something different from the "movement" of a dance or symphony. And some terms do not carry over at all: poetry can employ didacticism and paradox but music cannot. The medium of poetry is language. Inseparable from language is meaning. Words refer to things and concepts and feelings.

We know that the meaning of poetry involves more than the dictionary definitions of words (see "Reading Poetry," pp. 11–19). The dictionary offers little help when we try to understand how rhyme, rhythm, meter, or alliteration contribute to the "meaning" of a poem. The poet William Butler Yeats tells us that the job of the poet is "to articulate sweet sounds together." The meaning of these words (including the metaphoric use of *sweet*) poses no problem, though we would probably find it difficult to explain the pleasing effect of the alliteration in "sweet sounds."

Alliteration is the musical equivalent of the meanings words convey, an example of sound supporting sense. The music of a poem is felt when one reads silently, but musical effect is given fuller play when the poem is read aloud. A printed poem is static and unchanging. Read aloud, it takes on new meanings. When recited by different readers, it can reveal a range of possible interpretations. Alliteration, assonance, consonance, as well as tempo, emphasis, pause — even pitch, tone, and timbre — all contribute to our understanding. Read poorly, the sweet sounds of the poem may turn sour; read sensitively, the sweet sounds are music.

This section is devoted to joining sounds to words. You will want to bring to these poems and songs the same approaches and techniques of analysis you have been applying to poetry all along. Do they exhibit the richness of language — metaphor, simile, symbol, connotative language, and so forth — you have been looking for in poems? Can you make a convincing case that though the centuries may change, the themes of love songs do not? What common literary devices do you find across the ages? As poetry, do some of the poems strike you as more successful than others? Why? Above all, does your judgment change after you have listened to the words *and* the music?[1]

---

[1] Whenever possible we have included titles of recordings that can be easily purchased through record stores and online music sellers. Many online sellers provide actual tracks of the songs that can be listened to at no cost on the Web.

When sung to instrumental accompaniment, do the words tend to become assimilated by the music and thereby take on a richness of effect that they do not have on the printed page? Finally, is it fair to make judgments about the words of a song when divorced from the music?

As you try to answer these questions, keep in mind that with two exceptions, all the poems in this section either were written as songs to be accompanied by a melody or, in the case of the earlier poems, were quickly set to music. They were the pop tunes of their day. The two exceptions are W. S. Gilbert's "To Phoebe" and C. Day-Lewis's "Song," which, as far as we know, have not been set to music. We include them as examples of the anti-love poem, which could not exist without the tradition of the love song.

Christopher Marlowe (1564–1593)
The Passionate Shepherd to His Love[1] 1600

Come live with me and be my love,
And we will all the pleasures prove
That valleys, groves, hills, and fields,
Woods, or steepy mountain yields.

And we will sit upon the rocks,
Seeing the shepherds feed their flocks,
By shallow rivers to whose falls
Melodious birds sing madrigals.

And I will make thee beds of roses
And a thousand fragrant posies,   10
A cap of flowers, and a kirtle°   skirt
Embroidered all with leaves of myrtle;

A gown made of the finest wool
Which from our pretty lambs we pull;
Fair lined slippers for the cold,
With buckles of the purest gold;

---

[1] The melody for Marlowe's song was published as early as 1603. That four-hundred-year-old melody can be heard on the Web at <*www.contemplator.com/folk6/livewme.html*>.

A belt of straw and ivy buds,
With coral clasps and amber studs:
And if these pleasures may thee move,
Come live with me, and be my love.   20

The shepherds' swains shall dance and sing
For thy delight each May morning:
If these delights thy mind may move,
Then live with me and be my love.

Sir Walter Raleigh   (1554–1618)
The Nymph's Reply
to the Shepherd[1]   1600

If all the world and love were young,
And truth in every shepherd's tongue,
These pretty pleasures might me move
To live with thee and be thy love.

Time drives the flocks from field to fold,
When rivers rage and rocks grow cold,
And Philomel° becometh dumb;   the nightingale
The rest complains of cares to come.

The flowers do fade, and wanton fields
To wayward winter reckoning yields;   10
A honey tongue, a heart of gall,
Is fancy's spring, but sorrow's fall.

Thy gowns, thy shoes, thy beds of roses,
Thy cap, thy kirtle, and thy posies
Soon break, soon wither, soon forgotten —
In folly ripe, in reason rotten.

Thy belt of straw and ivy buds,
Thy coral clasps and amber studs,
All these in me no means can move
To come to thee and be thy love.   20

[1] Available on CD, *Voices from the Lost Realms* (Albany Records, 1994), composed by William Mayer, performed by New Calliope Singers, conducted by Peter Schubert.

But could youth last and love still breed,
Had joys no date° nor age no need,   end
Then these delights my mind might move
To live with thee and be thy love.

C. Day-Lewis   (1904–1972)
Song   1935

Come, live with me and be my love,
And we will all the pleasures prove
Of peace and plenty, bed and board,
That chance employment may afford.

I'll handle dainties on the docks
And thou shalt read of summer frocks:
At evening by the sour canals
We'll hope to hear some madrigals.

Care on thy maiden brow shall put
A wreath of wrinkles, and thy foot   10
Be shod with pain: not silken dress
But toil shall tire thy loveliness.

Hunger shall make thy modest zone
And cheat fond death of all but bone —
If these delights thy mind may move,
Then live with me and be my love.

Questions for Looking Deeper

1. Marlowe adopts a common convention of his day, the pastoral tradition, to make his plea. Raleigh's answer follows the same tradition, while Day-Lewis's rendering utilizes modern imagery. Which of the two responses to Marlowe is more convincing?

2. In what ways do Raleigh's and Day-Lewis's rejection of Marlowe's arguments agree? In what ways do they differ?

3. What other poems in this section support the thesis that Marlowe's poem is an early example of themes common to love songs across the ages?

4. Compare the love-song lyrics of any of your favorite pop groups or singers to these poems in terms of their thematic similarities. Considered only as poems — written words on the page — how do your favorite modern lyrics compare to these earlier songs?

William Shakespeare (1564–1616)
It Was a Lover and His Lass[1] 1600

It was a lover and his lass,
   With a hey, and a ho, and a hey nonny no,
That o'er the green corn fields did pass
   In spring time, the only pretty ring time,
   When birds do sing, hey ding a ding a ding:
   Sweet lovers love the spring.

Between the acres of the rye,
   With a hey, and a ho, and a hey nonny no,
These pretty country fools would lie,
   In spring time, the only pretty ring time,   10
   When birds do sing, hey ding a ding a ding:
   Sweet lovers love the spring.

This carol they began that hour,
   With a hey, and a ho, and a hey nonny no,
How that a life was but a flower
   In spring time, the only pretty ring time,
   When birds do sing, hey ding a ding a ding:
   Sweet lovers love the spring.

Then pretty lovers take the time
   With a hey, and a ho, and a hey nonny no,   20
For love is crownèd with the prime
   In spring time, the only pretty ring time,
   When birds do sing, hey ding a ding a ding:
   Sweet lovers love the spring.

Questions for Looking Deeper

1. Like Marlowe's "The Passionate Shepherd to His Love," Shakespeare adopts the pastoral convention for his song. Unlike Marlowe's poem, however, "It Was a Lover and His Lass" was conceived as a song (it comes from Shakespeare's play *As You Like It*). What elements of the poem suggest that it is meant to be sung?

2. What evidence from the poem would you use to argue that the poem is more than a simple song filled with repetition and nonsense syllables?

3. Who is the speaker?

[1] Available on CD, *Songs and Dances from Shakespeare* (Saydisc, 1995), composed by Thomas Morley, performed by the Broadside Band, conducted by Jeremy Barlow.

4. Norman Ault's book *Elizabethan Lyrics* includes many of the songs from Shakespeare's plays. Examine some of these songs, and compare them to "It Was a Lover and His Lass."

Ben Jonson   (1572–1637)
Song, To Celia[1]   1616

Drink to me only with thine eyes,
   And I will pledge with mine;
Or leave a kiss but in the cup,
   And I'll not look for wine.
The thirst that from the soul doth rise
   Doth ask a drink divine;
But might I of Jove's nectar sup,
   I would not change for thine.
I sent thee late a rosy wreath,
   Not so much honoring thee   10
As giving it a hope, that there
   It could not withered be.
But thou thereon didst only breathe,
   And sent'st it back to me;
Since when it grows, and smells, I swear,
   Not of itself but thee.

Questions for Looking Deeper

1. This celebrated song (often printed with the first line as its title) defines love in spiritual terms. Like John Donne's "A Valediction: Forbidding Mourning" (p. 1102), it pays its compliments not to the lady's physical beauty but to her spiritual depth. Can you find any other poems in this section that celebrate spiritual love? Are you familiar with any modern song lyrics that do? If so, compare them with Jonson's song in terms of the images they use to define spirituality.

2. Does the imagery of Jonson's song in any way suggest physical love?

---

[1] Available on CD, *Murmurs of the Heart* (Quicksilver Records, 1999), composed and performed by Roscoe Lee Brown.

Robert Herrick (1591–1674)
To the Virgins, to Make Much of Time[1] 1648

Gather ye rosebuds while ye may,
 Old Time is still a-flying;
And this same flower that smiles today,
 Tomorrow will be dying.

The glorious lamp of heaven, the sun,
 The higher he's a-getting,
The sooner will his race be run,
 And nearer he's to setting.

That age is best which is the first,
 When youth and blood are warmer;   10
But being spent, the worse, and worst
 Times still succeed the former.

Then be not coy, but use your time;
 And while ye may, go marry:
For having lost but once your prime,
 You may for ever tarry.

Questions for Looking Deeper

1. This poem belongs to an important sub-genre of love poetry called *carpe diem* (see "Glossary of Literary Terms"). Another example is Edmund Waller's "Go, Lovely Rose!" (p. 1103). Andrew Marvell's "To His Coy Mistress" (p. 1104) is perhaps the most famous example of the type, which flourished in seventeenth- and eighteenth-century England. Examine other examples of carpe-diem poems (many can be found in Norman Ault's *Elizabethan Lyrics* and Philip Ledger's *The Oxford Book of English Madrigals*), and compile a report on their distinguishing characteristics.

2. Bring to class examples of modern carpe-diem songs to compare with Herrick's and Marvell's poems.

3. Is John Donne's poem "The Flea" a carpe-diem poem? Explain.

---

[1] Available on CD, *In Praise of Woman* (Hyperion, 1994), composed by Madeleine Dring with Graham Johnson, Anthony Rolfe-Johnson.

Sir John Suckling   (1609–1642)
Song   1659

Why so pale and wan, fond° lover?   foolish
   Prithee, why so pale?
Will, when looking well can't move her,
   Looking ill prevail?
   Prithee, why so pale?

Why so dull and mute, young sinner?
   Prithee, why so mute?
Will, when speaking well can't win her,
   Saying nothing do't?
   Prithee, why so mute?   10

Quit, quit, for shame; this will not move,
   This cannot take her.
If of herself she will not love,
   Nothing can make her:
   The devil take her!

Questions for Looking Deeper

1. While the carpe-diem theme and the lament of the spurned lover have been the dominant themes of love songs through the ages, Suckling's poem is another recognizable type of love poem: the angry response to unrequited love. Sappho's "With His Venom" (p. 1083) makes it clear that the emotion is about as old as love itself. Who is the speaker? Why is he angry with the "fond lover"?

2. What are the attitudes toward love and women that underlie this poem and John Donne's "Song" (p. 1101)?

3. Examine the following poems, all written by women: Edna St. Vincent Millay's "Love Is Not All" (p. 1111), Dorothy Parker's "One Perfect Rose" (p. 1111), Denise Levertov's "The Mutes" (p. 1120), Anne Sexton's "The Farmer's Wife" (p. 1122), Adrienne Rich's "Living in Sin" (p. 1123), and Sharon Olds's "The Victims" (p. 1132). In what sense might it be said that these poems constitute an answer to the love poems written by men?

W. S. Gilbert (1836–1911)
To Phoebe 1865

"Gentle, modest little flower
   Sweet epitome of May
Love me but for half-an-hour,
   Love me, love me, little fay."
Sentences so fiercely flaming
   In your tiny shell-like ear,
I should always be exclaiming
   If I loved you, PHOEBE dear!

"Smiles that thrill from any distance
   Shed upon me while I sing!   10
Please ecstaticize existence,
   Love me, oh, thou fairy thing!"
Words like these, outpouring sadly,
   You'd perpetually hear,
If I loved you, fondly, madly; —
   But I do not, PHOEBE dear!

Questions for Looking Deeper

1. Examine the earlier love poems in this section and show how Gilbert's poem draws on the conventions established by those poems to make its point.

2. Compare this poem with Shakespeare's Sonnet 130 (p. 1098), Thomas Campion's "I Care Not for These Ladies" (p. 1099), and Dorothy Parker's "One Perfect Rose" (p. 1111) in the way each uses the conventions of love poetry for humor and satire. What modern love songs do you know that use these conventions in the same way?

Paul Simon (b. 1941)
Scarborough Fair/Canticle[1] 1966

Are you going to Scarborough Fair:
Parsley, sage, rosemary and thyme.
Remember me to one who lives there.
She once was a true love of mine.

On the side of a hill in the deep forest green.
Tracing of sparrow on snow-crested brown.
Blankets and bedclothes the child of the mountain
Sleeps unaware of the clarion call.

Tell her to make me a cambric shirt:
Parsley, sage, rosemary and thyme;   10
Without no seams nor needle work,
Then she'll be a true love of mine.

On the side of a hill a sprinkling of leaves.
Washes the grave with silvery tears.
A soldier cleans and polishes a gun.
Sleeps unaware of the clarion call.

Tell her to find me an acre of land:
Parsley, sage, rosemary and thyme;
Between the salt water and the sea strand,
Then she'll be a true love of mine.   20

War bellows blazing in scarlet battalions.
Generals order their soldiers to kill.
And to fight for a cause they've long ago forgotten.

Tell her to reap it with a sickle of leather:
Parsley, sage, rosemary and thyme;
And gather it all in a bunch of heather,
Then she'll be a true love of mine.

---

[1] Available on CD, *The Best of Simon and Garfunkel* (Sony/Columbia, 1999), written by Paul Simon and performed by Paul Simon and Art Garfunkel.

Questions for Looking Deeper

1. This song is an impressive achievement in many ways, a modern song with the feel of an ancient ballad. The haunting quality of Simon's music strengthens the ballad feel. Simon's song appears to be about love and seems to tell a story, though it is difficult to be sure what the essential narrative is. Compare "Bonny Barbara Allen" (p. 1083) and "Edward" (p. 1378) with Simon's song in terms of narrative clarity and diction.

2. Using the resources of the Internet, look up the lyrics of some of your favorite songs. Do you find lyrics you do not understand? Does that make any difference in your enjoyment of the song? Explain. What does this suggest to you about the relationship of words to songs?

Aimee Mann   (b. 1960)
Save Me [1]   1999

You look like
A perfect fit
For a girl in need
Of a tourniquet
But can you save me
Come on and save me
If you could save me
From the ranks
Of the freaks
Who suspect   10
They could never love anyone

'Cause I can tell
You know what it's like
The long farewell
Of the hunger strike
But can you save me
Come on and save me
If you could save me
From the ranks

---

[1] Available on CD, *Magnolia: Music from the Motion Picture [Soundtrack]* (Wea/Warner Brothers, 1999), written and performed by Aimee Mann.

Of the freaks
Who suspect
They could never love anyone   20

You struck me dumb
Like radium
Like Peter Pan
Or Superman
You will come
To save me
Why don't you save me
Come on and save me   30
From the ranks
Of the freaks
Who suspect
They could never love anyone

Questions for Looking Deeper

1. In what sense is this a love song? How does it differ from more traditional love songs?

2. This is one of the songs Aimee Mann wrote for the film *Magnolia* (1999). According to director/screenwriter Paul Thomas Anderson, Mann's music was one of the inspirations for the film. View the film and discuss the song's thematic relevance.

3. Examine other Aimee Mann lyrics (many of them can be found on the Internet at <*http://lyricsearch.net/*>), and characterize her typical themes and writing style.

William Shakespeare   (1564–1616)

Sonnets   1609

18

Shall I compare thee to a summer's day?
Thou art more lovely and more temperate:
Rough winds do shake the darling buds of May,
And summer's lease hath all too short a date:
Sometime too hot the eye of heaven shines,
And often is his gold complexion dimmed;
And every fair from fair sometimes declines,
By chance or nature's changing course untrimmed;
But thy eternal summer shall not fade,
Nor lose possession of that fair thou ow'st,°   owns
Nor shall death brag thou wander'st in his shade,   11
When in eternal lines to time thou grow'st:
    So long as men can breathe, or eyes can see,
    So long lives this, and this gives life to thee.

For Analysis

1. Why does the speaker in the poem argue that "a summer's day" is an inappropriate **metaphor** for his beloved?

2. What is "this" in line 14?

29

When, in disgrace with fortune and men's eyes,
I all alone beweep my outcast state
And trouble deaf heaven with my bootless cries
And look upon myself and curse my fate,
Wishing me like to one more rich in hope,
Featured like him, like him with friends possessed,
Desiring this man's art and that man's scope,
With what I most enjoy contented least;
Yet in these thoughts myself almost despising,
Haply I think on thee, and then my state,   10
Like to the lark at break of day arising
From sullen earth, sings hymns at heaven's gate;
    For thy sweet love remembered such wealth brings
    That then I scorn to change my state with kings.

129

Th' expense of spirit in a waste of shame
Is lust in action; and till action, lust
Is perjured, murderous, bloody, full of blame,
Savage, extreme, rude, cruel, not to trust;
Enjoyed no sooner but despiséd straight;
Past reason hunted; and no sooner had,
Past reason hated, as a swallowed bait,
On purpose laid to make the taker mad:
Mad in pursuit, and in possession so;
Had, having, and in quest to have, extreme;   10
A bliss in proof,° and proved, a very woe;   experience
Before, a joy proposed; behind, a dream.
    All this the world well knows; yet none knows well
    To shun the heaven that leads men to this hell.

For Analysis

1. Paraphrase "Th' expense of spirit in a waste of shame / Is lust in action."

2. Describe the sound patterns and metrical variations in lines 3 and 4. What do they contribute to the "sense" of the lines?

Writing Topic

How do the sound patterns, the variations in **meter**, and the **paradox** in the final **couplet** contribute to the sense of this sonnet?

130

My mistress' eyes are nothing like the sun;
Coral is far more red than her lips' red;
If snow be white, why then her breasts are dun;
If hairs be wires, black wires grow on her head.
I have seen roses damasked,° red and white,   variegated
But no such roses see I in her cheeks;
And in some perfumes is there more delight
Than in the breath that from my mistress reeks.
I love to hear her speak, yet well I know
That music hath a far more pleasing sound;   10
I grant I never saw a goddess go;
My mistress, when she walks, treads on the ground.
    And yet, by heaven, I think my love as rare
    As any she belied with false compare.[1]

Sonnet 130
  [1] I.e., as any woman misrepresented with false comparisons.

Thomas Campion   (1567–1620)

I Care Not for These Ladies 1601

I care not for these ladies,
That must be wooed and prayed:
Give me kind Amaryllis,[1]
The wanton country maid.
Nature art disdaineth,
Her beauty is her own.
    Who, when we court and kiss,
    She cries, "Forsooth, let go!"
    But when we come where comfort is,
    She never will say no.   10

If I love Amaryllis,
She gives me fruit and flowers:
But if we love these ladies,
We must give golden showers.
Give them gold, that sell love,
Give me the nut-brown lass,
    Who, when we court and kiss,
    She cries, "Forsooth, let go!"
    But when we come where comfort is,
    She never will say no.   20

These ladies must have pillows,
And beds by strangers wrought;
Give me a bower of willows,
Of moss and leaves unbought,
And fresh Amaryllis,
With milk and honey fed;
    Who, when we court and kiss,
    She cries, "Forsooth, let go!"
    But when we come where comfort is,
    She never will say no.   30

[1] A conventional name for a country girl in pastoral poetry.

John Donne (1572–1631)

The Flea 1633

Mark but this flea, and mark in this,
How little that which thou deniest me is;
It sucked me first, and now sucks thee,
And in this flea our two bloods mingled be;
Thou know'st that this cannot be said
A sin, nor shame, nor loss of maidenhead,
 Yet this enjoys before it woo,
 And pampered swells with one blood made of two,
 And this, alas, is more than we would do.

Oh stay, three lives in one flea spare,   10
Where we almost, yea more than married, are.
This flea is you and I, and this
Our marriage bed and marriage temple is;
Though parents grudge, and you, we are met,
And cloistered in these living walls of jet,
 Though use° make you apt to kill me   custom
 Let not to that, self-murder added be,
 And sacrilege, three sins in killing three.

Cruel and sudden, hast thou since
Purpled thy nail, in blood of innocence?   20
Wherein could this flea guilty be,
Except in that drop which it sucked from thee?
Yet thou triumph'st, and say'st that thou
Find'st not thy self nor me the weaker now;
 'Tis true, then learn how false fears be;
 Just so much honor, when thou yield'st to me,
 Will waste, as this flea's death took life from thee.

For Analysis

1. What does the woman addressed in this poem deny the poet (l. 2)?

2. What is the woman about to do at the beginning of the second stanza? What argument does the poet use to save the flea?

3. How does the poet turn the flea's life and death to his own purposes?

Writing Topic

In a paragraph, discuss your response to Donne's use of a flea to animate a seduction poem.

Song 1633

Go and catch a falling star
    Get with child a mandrake root,[1]
Tell me where all past years are,
    Or who cleft the Devil's foot,
Teach me to hear mermaids singing,
Or to keep off envy's stinging,
        And find
        What wind
Serves to advance an honest mind.

If thou be'st born to strange sights,   10
    Things invisible to see,
Ride ten thousand days and nights,
    Till age snow white hairs on thee,
Thou, when thou return'st, wilt tell me
    All strange wonders that befell thee,
        And swear
        Nowhere
Lives a woman true, and fair.

If thou findst one, let me know,
    Such a pilgrimage were sweet —   20
    Yet do not, I would not go,
    Though at next door we might meet;
Though she were true, when you met her,
    And last, till you write your letter,
        Yet she
        Will be
False, ere I come, to two or three.

For Analysis

1. The first five lines set tasks for the reader. How would you characterize those tasks?

2. The tasks set in the remaining lines of the stanza seem different. Characterize the difference.

3. In the second stanza, how does the poet emphasize the difficulty of finding a woman both "true, and fair"?

Writing Topics

1. Does this poem reveal that Donne is a male chauvinist? Explain.

2. Describe the poetic devices Donne employs to make his point.

---

[1] A forked root associated with fertility and thought to have magical powers.

A Valediction: Forbidding Mourning 1633

As virtuous men pass mildly away,
    And whisper to their souls to go,
Whilst some of their sad friends do say
    The breath goes now, and some say, No;

So let us melt, and make no noise,
    No tear-floods, nor sigh-tempests move,
'Twere profanation of our joys
    To tell the laity our love.

Moving of th' earth° brings harms and fears,   *earthquake*
    Men reckon what it did and meant;   10
But trepidation of the spheres,
    Though greater far, is innocent.[1]

Dull sublunary° lovers' love   *under the moon*
    (Whose soul is sense) cannot admit
Absence, because it doth remove
    Those things which elemented it.

But we by a love so much refined
    That our selves know not what it is,
Inter-assuréd of the mind,
    Care less, eyes, lips, and hands to miss.   20

Our two souls therefore, which are one,
    Though I must go, endure not yet
A breach, but an expansion,
    Like gold to airy thinness beat.

If they be two, they are two so
    As stiff twin compasses are two;
Thy soul, the fixed foot, makes no show
    To move, but doth, if th' other do.

And though it in the center sit,
    Yet when the other far doth roam,   30
It leans and harkens after it,
    And grows erect, as that comes home.

[1] The movement of the heavenly spheres is harmless.

Such wilt thou be to me, who must
 Like th' other foot, obliquely run;
Thy firmness makes my circle just,
 And makes me end where I begun.

For Analysis

1. Two kinds of love are described in this poem — spiritual and physical. How does the **simile** drawn in the first two stanzas help define the differences between them?

2. How does the contrast between earthquakes and the movement of the spheres in stanza three further develop the contrast between the two types of love?

3. Explain the comparison between a drawing compass and the lovers in the last three stanzas.

Edmund Waller   (1606–1687)

Go, Lovely Rose!   1645

 Go, lovely rose!
Tell her that wastes her time and me
 That now she knows,
When I resemble° her to thee,   compare
How sweet and fair she seems to be.

 Tell her that's young,
And shuns to have her graces spied,
 That hadst thou sprung
In deserts, where no men abide,
Thou must have uncommended died.   10

 Small is the worth
Of beauty from the light retired;
 Bid her come forth,
Suffer herself to be desired,
And not blush so to be admired.

 Then die! that she
The common fate of all things rare
 May read in thee;
How small a part of time they share
That are so wondrous sweet and fair!   20

Andrew Marvell   (1621–1678)

To His Coy Mistress 1681

Had we but world enough, and time,
This coyness, lady, were no crime.
We would sit down, and think which way
To walk, and pass our long love's day.
Thou by the Indian Ganges' side
Shouldst rubies find; I by the tide
Of Humber would complain. I would
Love you ten years before the flood,
And you should, if you please, refuse
Til the conversion of the Jews.   10
My vegetable love should grow
Vaster than empires and more slow;
An hundred years should go to praise
Thine eyes, and on thy forehead gaze;
Two hundred to adore each breast,
But thirty thousand to the rest;
An age at least to every part,
And the last age should show your heart.
For, lady, you deserve this state,
Nor would I love at lower rate.   20
    But at my back I always hear
Time's wingéd chariot hurrying near;
And yonder all before us lie
Deserts of vast eternity.
Thy beauty shall no more be found,
Nor, in thy marble vault, shall sound
My echoing song; then worms shall try
That long-preserved virginity,
And your quaint honor turn to dust,
And into ashes all my lust: 30
The grave's a fine and private place,
But none, I think, do there embrace.
    Now therefore, while the youthful hue
Sits on thy skin like morning dew,
And while thy willing soul transpires
At every pore with instant fires,
Now let us sport us while we may,
And now, like amorous birds of prey,
Rather at once our time devour   39
Than languish in his slow-chapped° power.   slow-jawed

1104

Let us roll our strength and all
Our sweetness up into one ball,
And tear our pleasures with rough strife
Thorough° the iron gates of life: through
Thus, though we cannot make our sun
Stand still, yet we will make him run.

For Analysis

1. State the argument of the poem (see ll. 1–2, 21–22, 33–34).

2. Compare the figures of speech in the first verse paragraph with those in the last. How do they differ?

3. Characterize the attitude toward life recommended by the poet.

Writing Topic

In what ways does the conception of love in this poem differ from that in John Donne's "A Valediction: Forbidding Mourning" (p. 1102)? In your discussion, consider the **imagery** in both poems.

William Blake   (1757–1827)

A Poison Tree   1794

I was angry with my friend:
I told my wrath, my wrath did end.
I was angry with my foe:
I told it not, my wrath did grow.

And I watered it in fears,
Night & morning with my tears;
And I sunnéd it with smiles,
And with soft deceitful wiles.

And it grew both day and night,
Till it bore an apple bright.   10
And my foe beheld it shine,
And he knew that it was mine,

And into my garden stole,
When the night had veil'd the pole;
In the morning glad I see
My foe outstretched beneath the tree.

For Analysis

1. Is anything gained from the parallel readers might draw between this tree and the tree in the Garden of Eden? Explain.

2. Can you articulate what the "poison" is?

3. Does your own experience verify the first stanza of the poem?

Robert Burns   (1759–1796)

A Red, Red Rose   1796

O My Luve's like a red, red rose,
  That's newly sprung in June;
O My Luve's like a melodie
  That's sweetly played in tune.

As fair art thou, my bonnie lass,
  So deep in luve am I;
And I will luve thee still, my dear,
  Til a' the seas gang dry.

Till a' the seas gang dry, my dear,
  And the rocks melt wi' the sun: 10
O I will love thee still, my dear,
  While the sands o' life shall run.

And fare thee weel, my only luve,
  And fare thee weel awhile!
And I will come again, my luve,
  Though it were ten thousand mile.

Walt Whitman   (1819–1892)

from
Song of Myself   1855

11

Twenty-eight young men bathe by the shore,
Twenty-eight young men and all so friendly;
Twenty-eight years of womanly life and all so lonesome.

She owns the fine house by the rise of the bank,
She hides handsome and richly drest aft the blinds of the window.

Which of the young men does she like the best?
Ah the homeliest of them is beautiful to her.

Where are you off to, lady? for I see you,
You splash in the water there, yet stay stock still in your room.

Dancing and laughing along the beach came the twenty-ninth bather,   10
The rest did not see her, but she saw them and loved them.

The beards of the young men glisten'd with wet, it ran from their long
      hair,
Little streams pass'd all over their bodies.

An unseen hand also pass'd over their bodies,
It descended tremblingly from their temples and ribs.

The young men float on their backs, their white bellies bulge to the sun,
      they do not ask who seizes fast to them,
They do not know who puffs and declines with pendant and bending
      arch,
They do not think whom they souse with spray.

Matthew Arnold (1822–1888)

Dover Beach 1867

The sea is calm tonight.
The tide is full, the moon lies fair
Upon the straits; on the French coast the light
Gleams and is gone; the cliffs of England stand,
Glimmering and vast, out in the tranquil bay.
Come to the window, sweet is the night-air!
Only, from the long line of spray
Where the sea meets the moon-blanched land,
Listen! you hear the grating roar
Of pebbles which the waves draw back, and fling,   10
At their return, up the high strand,
Begin, and cease, and then again begin,
With tremulous cadence slow, and bring
The eternal note of sadness in.

Sophocles long ago
Heard it on the Aegean, and it brought
Into his mind the turbid ebb and flow
Of human misery; we
Find also in the sound a thought,
Hearing it by this distant northern sea.   20

The Sea of Faith
Was once, too, at the full, and round earth's shore
Lay like the folds of a bright girdle furled.
But now I only hear
Its melancholy, long, withdrawing roar,
Retreating, to the breath
Of the night-wind, down the vast edges drear
And naked shingles° of the world.   pebble beaches

Ah, love, let us be true
To one another! for the world, which seems   30
To lie before us like a land of dreams,
So various, so beautiful, so new,
Hath really neither joy, nor love, nor light,
Nor certitude, nor peace, nor help for pain;
And we are here as on a darkling plain
Swept with confused alarms of struggle and flight,
Where ignorant armies clash by night.

Emily Dickinson (1830–1886)

Mine Enemy is growing old ca. 1881

Mine Enemy is growing old —
I have at last Revenge —
The Palate of the Hate departs —
If any would avenge

Let him be quick—the Viand flits —
It is a faded Meat —
Anger as soon as fed is dead —
'Tis starving makes it fat —

For Analysis
Explain the **paradox** contained in the last two lines.

Writing Topic
Compare this poem with William Blake's "A Poison Tree" (p. 1105).

Gerard Manley Hopkins (1844–1889)

Pied Beauty 1877

Glory be to God for dappled things —
  For skies of couple-colour as a brinded° cow;   brindled
    For rose-moles all in stipple upon trout that swim;
Fresh-firecoal chestnut-falls;[1] finches' wings;
  Landscape plotted and pieced[2] — fold, fallow, and plough;
    And all trades, their gear and tackle, and trim.°   equipment
All things counter,° original, spare, strange;   contrasted
  Whatever is fickle, freckled (who knows how?)
    With swift, slow; sweet, sour; adazzle, dim;
He fathers-forth whose beauty is past change: 10
        Praise him.

Pied Beauty
  [1] Fallen chestnuts, with the outer husks removed, colored like fresh fire coal.
  [2] Reference to the variegated pattern of land put to different uses.

William Butler Yeats   (1865–1939)

Politics 1939

*In our time the destiny of man presents its meaning
in political terms.* — Thomas Mann

How can I, that girl standing there,
My attention fix
On Roman or on Russian
Or on Spanish politics?
Yet here's a travelled man that knows
What he talks about,
And there's a politician
That has read and thought,
And maybe what they say is true
Of war and war's alarms,   10
But O that I were young again
And held her in my arms!

Robert Frost   (1874–1963)

Fire and Ice 1923

Some say the world will end in fire,
Some say in ice,
From what I've tasted of desire
I hold with those who favor fire.
But if it had to perish twice,
I think I know enough of hate
To say that for destruction ice
Is also great
And would suffice.

Edna St. Vincent Millay (1892–1950)

Love Is Not All 1931

Love is not all: it is not meat nor drink
Nor slumber nor a roof against the rain;
Nor yet a floating spar to men that sink
And rise and sink and rise and sink again;
Love can not fill the thickened lung with breath,
Nor clean the blood, nor set the fractured bone;
Yet many a man is making friends with death
Even as I speak, for lack of love alone.
It well may be that in a difficult hour,
Pinned down by pain and moaning for release,   10
Or nagged by want past resolution's power,
I might be driven to sell your love for peace,
Or trade the memory of this night for food.
It well may be. I do not think I would.

Dorothy Parker (1893–1967)

One Perfect Rose 1926

A single flow'r he sent me, since we met.
    All tenderly his messenger he chose;
Deep-hearted, pure, with scented dew still wet —
    One perfect rose.

I knew the language of the floweret;
    "My fragile leaves," it said, "his heart enclose."
Love long has taken for his amulet
    One perfect rose.

Why is it no one ever sent me yet
    One perfect limousine, do you suppose?   10
Ah no, it's always just my luck to get
    One perfect rose.

E. E. Cummings (1894–1962)

if everything happens that can't be done 1944

if everything happens that can't be done
(and anything's righter
than books
could plan)
the stupidest teacher will almost guess
(with a run
skip
around we go yes)
there's nothing as something as one

one hasn't a why or because or although   10
(and buds know better
than books
don't grow)
one's anything old being everything new
(with a what
which
around we come who)
one's everyanything so

so world is a leaf so tree is a bough
(and birds sing sweeter   20
than books
tell how)
so here is away and so your is a my
(with a down
up
around again fly)
forever was never till now

now i love you and you love me
(and books are shuter
than books   30
can be)
and deep in the high that does nothing but fall
(with a shout
each

around we go all)
there's somebody calling who's we

we're anything brighter than even the sun
(we're everything greater
than books
might mean)   40
we're everyanything more than believe
(with a spin
leap
alive we're alive)
we're wonderful one times one

For Analysis

1. What fundamental contrast is stated by the poem?

2. Lines 2–4 and 6–8 of each stanza could be printed as single lines. Why do you think Cummings decided to print them as he does?

3. What common attitude toward lovers is expressed by the last lines of the stanzas?

4. Is the poem **free verse** or formal verse?

Writing Topic

What relation do the parenthetical lines in each stanza bear to the poem as a whole?

when serpents bargain for the right to squirm 1923

when serpents bargain for the right to squirm
and the sun strikes to gain a living wage —
when thorns regard their roses with alarm
and rainbows are insured against old age

when every thrush may sing no new moon in
if all screech-owls have not okayed his voice
— and any wave signs on the dotted line
or else an ocean is compelled to close

when the oak begs permission of the birch
to make an acorn — valleys accuse their   10
mountains of having altitude — and march
denounces april as a saboteur

then we'll believe in that incredible
unanimal mankind (and not until)

Theodore Roethke   (1908–1963)

My Papa's Waltz   1948

The whiskey on your breath
Could make a small boy dizzy;
But I hung on like death:
Such waltzing was not easy.

We romped until the pans
Slid from the kitchen shelf;
My mother's countenance
Could not unfrown itself.

The hand that held my wrist
Was battered on one knuckle;   10
At every step you missed
My right ear scraped a buckle.

You beat time on my head
With a palm caked hard by dirt,
Then waltzed me off to bed
Still clinging to your shirt.

For Analysis

1. Why is iambic trimeter an appropriate **meter** for this poem?

2. Identify the details that reveal the kind of person the father is.

3. How would you characterize the boy's feelings about his father? The father's about
the boy?

Writing Topic

Robert Hayden's "Those Winter Sundays" (p. 1118) and Sylvia Plath's "Daddy"
(p. 1124) also deal with a child's feelings about a parent. Compare one of them with
this poem.

I Knew a Woman 1958

I knew a woman, lovely in her bones,
When small birds sighed, she would sigh back at them;
Ah, when she moved, she moved more ways than one:
The shapes a bright container can contain!
Of her choice virtues only gods should speak,
Or English poets who grew up on Greek
(I'd have them sing in chorus, cheek to cheek).

How well her wishes went! She stroked my chin,
She taught me Turn, and Counter-turn, and Stand;
She taught me Touch, that undulant white skin;   10
I nibbled meekly from her proffered hand;
She was the sickle; I, poor I, the rake,
Coming behind her for her pretty sake
(But what prodigious mowing we did make).

Love likes a gander, and adores a goose:
Her full lips pursed, the errant note to seize;
She played it quick, she played it light and loose;
My eyes, they dazzled at her flowing knees;
Her several parts could keep a pure repose,
Or one hip quiver with a mobile nose   20
(She moved in circles, and those circles moved).

Let seed be grass, and grass turn into hay:
I'm martyr to a motion not my own;
What's freedom for? To know eternity.
I swear she cast a shadow white as stone.
But who would count eternity in days?
These old bones live to learn her wanton ways:
(I measure time by how a body sways).

For Analysis

1. How would you characterize the rhyme scheme of this poem?

2. What does the third line of the first stanza mean?

3. Describe the two principal images in the second stanza.

Writing Topic

In an essay, describe the role of motion in this celebration of a woman's beauty.

Elizabeth Bishop   (1911–1979)

One Art   1976

The art of losing isn't hard to master;
so many things seem filled with the intent
to be lost that their loss is no disaster.

Lose something every day. Accept the fluster
of lost door keys, the hour badly spent.
The art of losing isn't hard to master.

Then practice losing farther, losing faster:
places, and names, and where it was you meant
to travel. None of these will bring disaster.

I lost my mother's watch. And look! my last, or   10
next-to-last, of three loved houses went.
The art of losing isn't hard to master.

I lost two cities, lovely ones. And, vaster,
some realms I owned, two rivers, a continent.
I miss them, but it wasn't a disaster.

— Even losing you (the joking voice, a gesture
I love) I shan't have lied. It's evident
the art of losing's not too hard to master
though it may look like (*Write* it!) like disaster.

May Sarton   (1912–1995)

AIDS   1988

We are stretched to meet a new dimension
Of love, a more demanding range
Where despair and hope must intertwine.
How grow to meet it? Intention
Here can neither move nor change
The raw truth. Death is on the line.
It comes to separate and estrange

Lover from lover in some reckless design.
Where do we go from here?

Fear.   Fear.   Fear.   Fear.   10

Our world has never been more stark
Or more in peril.
It is very lonely now in the dark.
Lonely and sterile.

And yet in the simple turn of a head
Mercy lives. I heard it when someone said
"I must go now to a dying friend.
Every night at nine I tuck him into bed,
And give him a shot of morphine,"
And added, "I go where I have never been."   20
I saw he meant into a new discipline
He had not imagined before, and a new grace.

Every day now we meet it face to face.
Every day now devotion is the test.
Through the long hours, the hard, caring nights
We are forging a new union. We are blest.
As closed hands open to each other
Closed lives open to strange tenderness.
We are learning the hard way how to mother.
Who says it is easy? But we have the power.   30
I watch the faces deepen all around me.
It is the time of change, the saving hour.
The word is not fear, the word we live,
But an old word suddenly made new,
As we learn it again, as we bring it alive:

Love.   Love.   Love.   Love.

For Analysis

1. Paraphrase the first three lines.
2. Explain the difference between "separate" and "estrange" (l. 7).
3. What is the meaning of "reckless design" (l. 8)?
4. What does the speaker mean by "new discipline" (l. 21) and "new grace" (l. 22)?
5. Who are the "We" of line 26, and why are they "blest"?

Writing Topic

Argue either for or against the assertion that the specter of AIDS has brought about a "time of change," and that fear is giving way to love.

Robert Hayden (1913–1980)

Those Winter Sundays 1975

Sundays too my father got up early
and put his clothes on in the blueblack cold,
then with cracked hands that ached
from labor in the weekday weather made
banked fires blaze. No one ever thanked him.

I'd wake and hear the cold splintering, breaking.
When the rooms were warm, he'd call,
and slowly I would rise and dress,
fearing the chronic angers of that house,

Speaking indifferently to him,   10
who had driven out the cold
and polished my good shoes as well.
What did I know, what did I know
of love's austere and lonely offices?

Anthony Hecht (b. 1923)

The Dover Bitch 1968

A Criticism of Life

So there stood Matthew Arnold and this girl
With the cliffs of England crumbling away behind them,
And he said to her, "Try to be true to me,
And I'll do the same for you, for things are bad
All over, etc., etc."

Well now, I knew this girl. It's true she had read
Sophocles in a fairly good translation
And caught that bitter allusion to the sea,
But all the time he was talking she had in mind
The notion of what his whiskers would feel like   10
On the back of her neck. She told me later on
That after a while she got to looking out
At the lights across the channel, and really felt sad,
Thinking of all the wine and enormous beds
And blandishments in French and the perfumes.
And then she got really angry. To have been brought
All the way down from London, and then be addressed
As a sort of mournful cosmic last resort
Is really tough on a girl, and she was pretty.
Anyway, she watched him pace the room   20
And finger his watch-chain and seem to sweat a bit,
And then she said one or two unprintable things.
But you mustn't judge her by that. What I mean to say is,
She's really all right. I still see her once in a while
And she always treats me right. We have a drink
And I give her a good time, and perhaps it's a year
Before I see her again, but there she is,
Running to fat, but dependable as they come,
And sometimes I bring her a bottle of *Nuit d'Amour.*

For Analysis

1. This poem is a response to Matthew Arnold's "Dover Beach," which appears on p. 1108 in this section. Arnold's poem is often read as a pained response to the breakdown of religious tradition and social and political order in the mid-nineteenth century. Is this poem, in contrast, optimistic? Is the relationship between the speaker and the girl at the end of the poem admirable? Explain.

2. Do you suppose Hecht was moved to write this poem out of admiration for "Dover Beach"? Explain.

Writing Topic

What is the fundamental difference between the speaker's conception of love in Arnold's poem and "the girl's" conception of love as reported in this poem?

Denise Levertov   (1923–1997)

The Mutes   1967

Those groans men use
passing a woman on the street
or on the steps of the subway

to tell her she is a female
and their flesh knows it,

are they a sort of tune,
an ugly enough song, sung
by a bird with a slit tongue

but meant for music?

Or are they the muffled roaring   10
of deafmutes trapped in a building that is
slowly filling with smoke?

Perhaps both.

Such men most often
look as if groan were all they could do,
yet a woman, in spite of herself,

knows it's a tribute:
if she were lacking all grace
they'd pass her in silence:

so it's not only to say she's   20
a warm hole. It's a word

in grief-language, nothing to do with
primitive, not an ur-language;[1]
language stricken, sickened, cast down

in decrepitude. She wants to
throw the tribute away, disgusted, and can't,

---

[1] Primordial language.

it goes on buzzing in her ear,
it changes the pace of her walk,
the torn posters in echoing corridors   30

spell it out, it
quakes and gnashes as the train comes in.
Her pulse sullenly

had picked up speed,
but the cars slow down and
jar to a stop while her understanding

keeps on translating:
'Life after life after life goes by

without poetry,
without seemliness,   40
without love.'

For Analysis

1. Explain the title.

2. Why does the tribute go on "buzzing in her ear" (l. 28)?

3. Is this poem an attack on men? Explain.

<u>Carolyn Kizer</u>   (b. 1925)

Bitch   1984

Now, when he and I meet, after all these years,
I say to the bitch inside me, don't start growling.
He isn't a trespasser anymore,
Just an old acquaintance tipping his hat.
My voice says, "Nice to see you,"
As the bitch starts to bark hysterically.
He isn't an enemy now,
Where are your manners, I say, as I say,
"How are the children? They must be growing up."
At a kind word from him, a look like the old days,   10
The bitch changes her tone: she begins to whimper.

She wants to snuggle up to him, to cringe.
Down, girl! Keep your distance
Or I'll give you a taste of the choke-chain.
"Fine, I'm just fine," I tell him.
She slobbers and grovels.
After all, I am her mistress. She is basically loyal.
It's just that she remembers how she came running
Each evening, when she heard his step;
How she lay at his feet and looked up adoringly   20
Though he was absorbed in his paper;
Or, bored with her devotion, ordered her to the kitchen
Until he was ready to play.
But the small careless kindnesses
When he'd had a good day, or a couple of drinks,
Come back to her now, seem more important
Than the casual cruelties, the ultimate dismissal.
"It's nice to know you are doing so well," I say.
He couldn't have taken you with him;
You were too demonstrative, too clumsy,   30
Not like the well-groomed pets of his new friends.
"Give my regards to your wife," I say. You gag
As I drag you off by the scruff,
Saying, "Goodbye! Goodbye! Nice to have seen you again."

For Analysis

1. Who is being addressed in lines 13 and 14?

2. In what ways does the title suit the poem? Consider the **tone** of "Bitch," as well as the many connotations of the word, in answering this question.

3. What is "the ultimate dismissal" referred to in line 27?

4. How would you describe the speaker's present feelings about her former relationship?

Anne Sexton   (1928–1974)

The Farmer's Wife   1960

From the hodge porridge
of their country lust,
their local life in Illinois,
where all their acres look
like a sprouting broom factory,

they name just ten years now
that she has been his habit;
as again tonight he'll say
honey bunch let's go
and she will not say how there   10
must be more to living
than this brief bright bridge
of the raucous bed or even
the slow braille touch of him
like a heavy god grown light,
that old pantomime of love
that she wants although
it leaves her still alone,
built back again at last,
minds apart from him, living   20
her own self in her own words
and hating the sweat of the house
they keep when they finally lie
each in separate dreams
and then how she watches him,
still strong in the blowzy bag
of his usual sleep while
her young years bungle past
their same marriage bed
and she wishes him cripple, or poet,   30
or even lonely, or sometimes,
better, my lover, dead.

Adrienne Rich   (b. 1929)

Living in Sin   1955

She had thought the studio would keep itself;
no dust upon the furniture of love.
Half heresy, to wish the taps less vocal,
the panes relieved of grime. A plate of pears,
a piano with a Persian shawl, a cat
stalking the picturesque amusing mouse
had risen at his urging.
Not that at five each separate stair would writhe
under the milkman's tramp; that morning light
so coldly would delineate the scraps   10

of last night's cheese and three sepulchral bottles;
that on the kitchen shelf among the saucers
a pair of beetle-eyes would fix her own —
Envoy from some village in the moldings . . .
Meanwhile, he, with a yawn,
sounded a dozen notes upon the keyboard,
declared it out of tune, shrugged at the mirror,
rubbed at his beard, went out for cigarettes;
while she, jeered by the minor demons,
pulled back the sheets and made the bed and found   20
a towel to dust the table-top,
and let the coffee-pot boil over on the stove.
By evening she was back in love again,
though not so wholly but throughout the night
she woke sometimes to feel the daylight coming
like a relentless milkman up the stairs.

Sylvia Plath   (1932–1963)

Daddy 1965

You do not do, you do not do
Any more, black shoe
In which I have lived like a foot
For thirty years, poor and white,
Barely daring to breathe or Achoo.

Daddy, I have had to kill you,
You died before I had time —
Marble-heavy, a bag full of God,
Ghastly statue with one gray toe
Big as a Frisco seal   10

And a head in the freakish Atlantic
Where it pours bean green over blue
In the waters off beautiful Nauset.
I used to pray to recover you.
Ach, du.[1]

Daddy
[1] German for "Oh, you."

In the German tongue, in the Polish town
Scraped flat by the roller
Of wars, wars, wars.
But the name of the town is common.
My Polack friend

20

Says there are a dozen or two.
So I never could tell where you
Put your foot, your root,
I never could talk to you.
The tongue stuck in my jaw.

It stuck in a barb wire snare.
Ich, ich, ich, ich,[2]
I could hardly speak.
I thought every German was you.
And the language obscene

30

An engine, an engine
Chuffing me off like a Jew.
A Jew to Dachau, Auschwitz, Belsen.
I began to talk like a Jew.
I think I may well be a Jew.

The snows of the Tyrol, the clear beer of Vienna
Are not very pure or true.
With my gypsy ancestress and my weird luck
And my Taroc pack and my Taroc pack
I may be a bit of a Jew.

40

I have always been scared of *you*,
With your Luftwaffe,[3] your gobbledygoo.
And your neat mustache
And your Aryan eye, bright blue.
Panzer-man,[4] panzer-man, O You —

Not God but a swastika
So black no sky could squeak through.
Every woman adores a Fascist,
The boot in the face, the brute
Brute heart of a brute like you.

50

[2] German for "I, I, I, I."
[3] Name of the German air force during World War II.
[4] *Panzer* refers to German armored divisions during World War II.

You stand at the blackboard, daddy,
In the picture I have of you,
A cleft in your chin instead of your foot
But no less a devil for that, no not
Any less the black man who

Bit my pretty red heart in two.
I was ten when they buried you.
At twenty I tried to die
And get back, back, back to you.
I thought even the bones would do   60

But they pulled me out of the sack,
And they stuck me together with glue.
And then I knew what to do.
I made a model of you,
A man in black with a Meinkampf⁵ look

And a love of the rack and the screw.
And I said I do, I do.
So daddy, I'm finally through.
The black telephone's off at the root,
The voices just can't worm through.   70

If I've killed one man, I've killed two —
The vampire who said he was you
And drank my blood for a year,
Seven years, if you want to know.
Daddy, you can lie back now.

There's a stake in your fat black heart
And the villagers never liked you.
They are dancing and stamping on you.
They always *knew* it was you.
Daddy, daddy, you bastard, I'm through.   80

For Analysis

1. How do the allusions to Nazism function in the poem?

2. Does the poem exhibit the speaker's love for her father or her hatred of him? Explain.

3. What sort of man does the speaker marry (see stanzas 13 and 14)?

---

⁵ *My Struggle,* the title of Adolf Hitler's autobiography.

4. How does the speaker characterize her husband and her father in the last two stanzas? Might the "Daddy" of the last line of the poem refer to something more than the speaker's father? Explain.

Writing Topics

1. What is the effect of the peculiar structure, idiosyncratic **rhyme**, unusual words (such as *achoo, gobbledygoo*), and repetitions in the poem?

2. What emotional associations does the title "Daddy" possess? Are those associations reinforced or contradicted by the poem?

Audre Lorde   (1934–1992)

Power[1]   1978

The difference between poetry and rhetoric
is being
ready to kill
yourself
instead of your children.

I am trapped on a desert of raw gunshot wounds
and a dead child dragging his shattered black
face off the edge of my sleep
blood from his punctured cheeks and shoulders
is the only liquid for miles and my stomach   10
churns at the imagined taste while
my mouth splits into dry lips
without loyalty or reason
thirsting for the wetness of his blood
as it sinks into the whiteness
of the desert where I am lost
without imagery or magic
trying to make power out of hatred and destruction

Power
[1] "'Power' . . . is a poem written about Clifford Glover, the ten-year-old Black child shot by a cop who was acquitted by a jury on which a Black woman sat. In fact, the day I heard on the radio that O'Shea had been acquitted, I was going across town on Eighty-eighth Street and I had to pull over. A kind of fury rose up in me; the sky turned red. I felt so sick. I felt as if I would drive this car into a wall, into the next person I saw. So I pulled over. I took out my journal just to air some of my fury, to get it out of my fingertips. Those expressed feelings are that poem" (Audre Lorde, "My Words Will Be There," in *Black Women Writers* (1950–1980), ed. Mari Evans, New York, 1983, p. 266).

trying to heal my dying son with kisses
only the sun will bleach his bones quicker.   20

The policeman who shot down a 10-year-old in Queens[2]
stood over the boy with his cop shoes in childish blood
and a voice said "Die you little motherfucker" and
there are tapes to prove that. At his trial
this policeman said in his own defense
"I didn't notice the size or nothing else
only the color." and
there are tapes to prove that, too.

Today that 37-year-old white man with 13 years of police forcing
has been set free   30
by 11 white men who said they were satisfied
justice had been done
and one black woman who said
"They convinced me" meaning
they had dragged her 4′ 10″ black woman's frame
over the hot coals of four centuries of white male approval
until she let go the first real power she ever had
and lined her own womb with cement
to make a graveyard for our children.

I have not been able to touch the destruction within me.   40
But unless I learn to use
the difference between poetry and rhetoric
my power too will run corrupt as poisonous mold
or lie limp and useless as an unconnected wire
and one day I will take my teenaged plug
and connect it to the nearest socket
raping an 85-year-old white woman
who is somebody's mother
and as I beat her senseless and set a torch to her bed
a greek chorus will be singing in ¾ time[3]   50
"Poor thing. She never hurt a soul. What beasts they are."

---

[2] A borough of New York City.
[3] In classical Greek tragedy, a chorus chanted in response to the action in the play. Three-quarter time is waltz rhythm.

Lucille Clifton   (b. 1936)

There Is a Girl Inside   1977

there is a girl inside.
she is randy as a wolf.
she will not walk away
and leave these bones
to an old woman.

she is a green tree
in a forest of kindling.
she is a green girl
in a used poet.

she has waited   10
patient as a nun
for the second coming,
when she can break through gray hairs
into blossom

and her lovers will harvest
honey and thyme
and the woods will be wild
with the damn wonder of it.

For Analysis

1. Who is the "girl" of this poem? What is she "inside" of?

2. What are the "bones" of the first stanza? What does the speaker's statement that she will not defer to an old woman tell us about her?

3. Describe the prevailing **metaphor** of the poem.

Writing Topic

In an essay, discuss the appropriateness of the **images** Clifton uses to make her point.

Valediction   1966

Lady with the frilled blouse
And simple tartan skirt,
Since you have left the house
Its emptiness has hurt
All thought. In your presence
Time rode easy, anchored
On a smile; but absence
Rocked love's balance, unmoored
The days. They buck and bound
Across the calendar   10
Pitched from the quiet sound
Of your flower-tender
Voice. Need breaks on my strand;
You've gone, I am at sea.
Until you resume command
Self is in mutiny.

For Analysis

1. What is the central figure of speech (beginning in the middle of line 5) that animates this poem?

2. How are *time, love's balance,* and *the days* affected by the lady's behavior?

3. What sort of voice would a "flower-tender / Voice" (ll. 12–13) be?

Writing Topic

Write an essay or a poem, serious or humorous, in which you use an extended
metaphor to describe a fundamental emotion or experience — for example, how
falling in love is like racing a car, or how the anguish of separation is like a visit to a
dentist, or how attending classes is like a long hike through a desert.

Billy Collins   (b. 1941)

Sonnet   1999

All we need is fourteen lines, well, thirteen now,
and after this one just a dozen
to launch a little ship on love's storm-tossed seas,
then only ten more left like rows of beans.

How easily it goes unless you get Elizabethan[1]
and insist the iambic bongos must be played
and rhymes positioned at the ends of lines,
one for every station of the cross.
But hang on here while we make the turn
into the final six where all will be resolved,   10
where longing and heartache will find an end,
where Laura will tell Petrarch[2] to put down his pen,
take off those crazy medieval tights,
blow out the lights, and come at last to bed.

Sharon Olds   (b. 1942)

Sex without Love   1984

How do they do it, the ones who make love
without love? Beautiful as dancers,
gliding over each other like ice skaters
over the ice, fingers hooked
inside each other's bodies, faces
red as steak, wine, wet as the
children at birth whose mothers are going to
give them away. How do they come to the
come to the   come to the   God   come to the
still waters, and not love   10
the one who came there with them, light
rising slowly as steam off their joined
skin? These are the true religious,
the purists, the pros, the ones who will not
accept a false Messiah, love the
priest instead of the God. They do not
mistake the lover for their own pleasure,
they are like great runners: they know they are alone
with the road surface, the cold, the wind,

Sonnet
[1] The entry for **sonnet** in the "Glossary of Literary Terms" (p. 1580) distinguishes between the Elizabethan and the Italian, or Petrarchan, sonnet.
[2] Francesco Petrarca (1304–1374), who employed the sonnet form named for him. Laura was the idealized woman he celebrated in his sonnets.

the fit of their shoes, their over-all cardio-   20
vascular health — just factors, like the partner
in the bed, and not the truth, which is the
single body alone in the universe
against its own best time.

For Analysis

1. Characterize the speaker's attitude toward "the ones who make love without love" (ll. 1–2).

2. Who are the "These" of line 13?

3. What is the effect of the repetitions in lines 8 and 9?

4. What does "factors" of line 21 refer to?

5. Put into your own words the "truth" referred to in the final three lines. Is the speaker using the word straightforwardly or ironically? Explain.

The Victims   1984

When Mother divorced you, we were glad. She took it and
took it, in silence, all those years and then
kicked you out, suddenly, and her
kids loved it. Then you were fired, and we
grinned inside, the way people grinned when
Nixon's helicopter lifted off the South
Lawn for the last time. We were tickled
to think of your office taken away,
your secretaries taken away,
your lunches with three double bourbons,   10
your pencils, your reams of paper. Would they take your
suits back, too, those dark
carcasses hung in your closet, and the black
noses of your shoes with their large pores?
She had taught us to take it, to hate you and take it
until we pricked with her for your
annihilation, Father. Now I
pass the bums in doorways, the white
slugs of their bodies gleaming through slits in their
suits of compressed silt, the stained   20
flippers of their hands, the underwater
fire of their eyes, ships gone down with the
lanterns lit, and I wonder who took it and

took it from them in silence until they had
given it all away and had nothing
left but this.

For Analysis

1. Characterize the **tone** of this poem. Who are the victims?

2. Identify and analyze the effects of the **metaphors** the speaker uses in the final lines to describe the "bums."

3. How does the speaker's description of the bums clarify her feelings about her father?

Deborah Pope   (b. ?)

Getting Through   1995

Like a car stuck in gear,
a chicken too stupid to tell
its head is gone,
or sound ratcheting on
long after the film
has jumped the reel,
or a phone
ringing and ringing
in the house they have all
moved away from,   10
through rooms where dust
is a deepening skin,
and the locks unneeded,
so I go on loving you,
my heart blundering on,
a muscle spilling out
what is no longer wanted,
and my words hurtling past,
like a train off its track,
toward a boarded-up station,   20
closed for years,
like some last speaker
of a beautiful language
no one else can hear.

Molly Peacock (b. 1947)

Say You Love Me 1989

What happened earlier I'm not sure of.
Of course he was drunk, but often he was.
His face looked like a ham on a hook above

me — I was pinned to the chair because
he'd hunkered over me with arms like jaws
pried open by the chair arms. "Do you love

me?" he began to sob. "Say you love me!"
I held out. I was probably fifteen.
What had happened? Had my mother — had she

said or done something? Or had he just been   10
drinking too long after work? "He'll get *mean,*"
my sister hissed, "just *tell* him." I brought my knee

up to kick him, but was too scared. Nothing
could have got the words out of me then. Rage
shut me up, yet "DO YOU?" was beginning

to peel, as of live layers of skin, age
from age from age from him until he gazed
through hysteria as a wet baby thing

repeating, "Do you love me? Say you do,"
in baby chokes, only loud, for they came   20
from a man. There wouldn't be a rescue

from my mother, still at work. The same
choking sobs said, "Love me, love me," and my game
was breaking down because I couldn't do

anything, not escape into my own
refusal, *I won't, I won't,* not fantasize
a kind, rich father, not fill the narrowed zone,

empty except for confusion until the size
of my fear ballooned as I saw his eyes,
blurred, taurean° — my sister screamed — unknown,   bull-like

1134

unknown to me, a voice rose and leveled   31
off, "I love you," I said. *"Say 'I love you,*
Dad!' " "I love you, Dad," I whispered, leveled

by defeat into a cardboard image, untrue,
unbending. I was surprised I could move
as I did to get up, but he stayed, burled

onto the chair — my monstrous fear — she screamed,
my sister, "Dad, the phone! Go answer it!"
The phone wasn't ringing, yet he seemed

to move toward it, and I ran. He had a fit —   40
"It's not ringing!" — but I was at the edge of it
as he collapsed into the chair and blamed

both of us at a distance. No, the phone
was not ringing. There was no world out there,
so there we remained, completely alone.

For Analysis

1. Is the speaker a child or an adult? Explain.

2. How do the **images** of the sixth stanza capture the speaker's feelings?

3. When the speaker finally capitulates to her father's demand, she describes herself in lines 33 to 35 as "leveled / by defeat into a cardboard image, untrue, / unbending." What does she mean?

4. Explain what the speaker means by "my game" (l. 23).

Writing Topic

What would motivate a parent, even a drunken one, to make the kind of demand the father makes on his daughter?

Wyatt Prunty   (b. 1947)

Learning the Bicycle   2000

for Heather

The older children pedal past
Stable as little gyros, spinning hard
To supper, bath, and bed, until at last
We also quit, silent and tired

Beside the darkening yard where trees
Now shadow up instead of down.
Their predictable lengths can only tease
Her as, head lowered, she walks her bike alone
Somewhere between her wanting to ride
And her certainty she will always fall.   10

Tomorrow, though I will run behind,
Arms out to catch her, she'll tilt then balance wide
Of my reach, till distance makes her small,
Smaller, beyond the place I stop and know
That to teach her I had to follow
And when she learned to let her go.

For Analysis
1. Describe the form and rhyme scheme of this poem. How does it differ from a **sonnet?**

2. What does the speaker learn from the experience of teaching his daughter to ride a bicycle?

Writing Topic
Write an analysis of the poem's formal structure, noting how the poem turns somewhat at lines 5, 9, and 11. How does the poem's organization and rhyme scheme mimic a typical sonnet?

The Actuarial Wife 2000

for Patty

About their chances for divorce
She says, "Slim —
Because the one who leaves
Will have to take the children."

About their children,
She says,
"We should have waited until
They were older to have them."

But most about her husband's smoking.
He's fifty now, and, taking stock   10
Of all they have, she stands outside
The blue haze through which he angles down
Into his favorite easy chair
Like an accurate punt, perfect hang time,

To read the morning paper over coffee
And start another pack of Luckies, stubbed
Emphatically, like punctuation marks
Down through an urgent argument.
She clarifies their options for retirement:
"Darling, if one of us dies,   20
I'm going to live in Paris."

David St. John   (b. 1949)

My Friend   1994

My friend, a man I love as wholly,
    As deeply as the brother neither of us
        Ever had, my friend, who once
Greeted me at the door of his carriage house —
        Having not seen each other in seven years —
    Saying only, as he turned to place
The needle into the grooves of Mahler's unfinished 10th,
    "*Listen* to this! It's just like the *Four Quartets!*"[1]
        His head, tilted slightly back
As we listened in silence, his black scarf looped loosely   10
    Around his neck, not an affectation, simply
Because of the cold in the carriage house he'd redone
        With everything but heat,
    The wind slicing off the East River, the mansion
In front of us lit up brilliantly that night
        By chandelier and firelight — my friend,
    Whom I love as deeply as any friend, called
This morning to report the sleet blanketing the East,
        To ask about the color of the sunlight
Sweeping the beaches of California; I tell him, "A lot   20
        Like the green of ice at night,
    Or the orange of the hair of that girl who once
Lived downstairs from you, in Cleveland. . . ."
        My friend, who said nothing for a moment,
    My friend, who had always lived the pure, whole
Solitude of Rilke,[2] though he fell in love

---

[1] Four poems by T. S. Eliot (1888–1965), written between 1940 and 1942, that were collected
and published as *Four Quartets* in 1943. Critics assert that the themes of the poems reveal an
"orchestration of related themes in successive movements."
[2] Rainer Maria Rilke (1875–1926) was an Austrian lyric poet.

As often and as desperately as Rilke,
　　Began to talk about his recent engagement, now
Past, though still not quite a memory, simply a subject
　　　　Yet too mystifying to be ignored,　　　　　　　　　　30
To a debutante, half-British, that is, an American deb
　　With an overlay of aristocratic parquet —
Albeit with an Italian given name — a stunning woman
　　　　He had loved desperately, silently,
　　　　　　The way Rilke loved
　　The sky at evening as the cloud-laced sunset
Dusted the high ragged peaks of Switzerland . . .
　　　　Yet, after a pause, he began
Again to talk, about some new acquaintances, two
　　Young ladies, both painters (of course),　　　　　　　　40
Who seemed to enjoy his company as a pair; that is,
　　　　The two of them, both of the young
Ladies, preferred him as a garnish
　　To their own extravagances — for example,
　　　　They'd welcomed him into their bath one
Evening when he came to visit, only to find them lathering
　　　　Each other tenderly. And though quite
Clearly desiring the company of each other to his alone,
　　They were tolerant, he said, even welcoming,
　　　　As the one reached up her hand　　　　　　　　　　50
And invited him into the froth of the square black tub.
　　And now this had, he reported, been
　　　　Going on for several weeks this way, perhaps longer,
He couldn't be clear about those kinds
　　　　Of details, though about other, more
Intriguing things, his memory was exact. The very night before,
　　He recalled, as the two young women painted
　　　　His naked torso slowly into a tuxedo of pastel
Watercolors, they'd both wisely proposed the following:
　　A joint — triadic — marriage for one month　　　　　　60
As they traveled, all three, through Italy and France,
　　　　A journey to visit all of the Holy Places
　　　　　　Of Art, as well as
The grandparents of the one, Delphine — about whom Constance,
　　The younger, had heard so many stories — at their home
　　　　In the hills overlooking the beaches of Nice.
　　My friend, a quiet man, a man who remains as
Precise, in his reckonings, as a jewel cutter, a man whose
　　　　Charm could seduce the Medusa,[3] was,

---

[3] In Greek myth, the Gorgon Medusa had serpents for hair, huge teeth, protruding tongue, and an ugly face. Those who looked at her were turned to stone.

He confessed, totally at a loss, bewildered, delighted,   70
   Terrified, exhausted — mainly, he said, exhausted
      From the constellations of couplings
   He'd been exercising, recognizing in the process
He was, as they say, as he said, really not quite so young
     As he'd once been, though certainly still
       As eager for invention
As any artist who takes his life work, well, seriously . . .
   And as we talked about old times, old friends, our
Old lives being somehow perpetually rearranged, at last
     He stopped me, saying, "Christ, you know —   80
   I can't *believe* how much the world has changed. . . ."

Susan Musgrave   (b. 1951)

Right through the Heart 1982

and out the other side,
pumping like a bitch in heat,
beast with two backs,[1] the
left and right ventricles.

It has to be love
when it goes straight through;
no bone can stop it,
no barb impede its journey.

When it happens you have to bleed,
you want to kiss and hold on   10

despite all the messy blood
you want to embrace it.

You want it to last forever,
you want to own it.
You want to take love's tiny life
in your hands

and crush it to death before it dies.

[1] See *Othello,* Act I, Scene 1, lines 115–16, p. 1147.

For Analysis

1. What goes "Right through the Heart?"

2. How are the "left and right ventricles" characterized?

3. Explain the **paradox** of the last three lines.

Writing Topic

Analyze the last three lines of this poem in an essay on the dangers of unbounded passion.

Gary Soto   (b. 1952)

Oranges   1987

The first time I walked
With a girl, I was twelve,
Cold, and weighted down
With two oranges in my jacket.
December. Frost cracking
Beneath my steps, my breath
Before me, then gone,
As I walked toward
Her house, the one whose
Porch light burned yellow   10
Night and day, in any weather.
A dog barked at me, until
She came out pulling
At her gloves, face bright
With rouge. I smiled,
Touched her shoulder, and led
Her down the street, across
A used car lot and a line
Of newly planted trees,
Until we were breathing   20
Before a drugstore. We
Entered, the tiny bell
Bringing a saleslady
Down a narrow aisle of goods.
I turned to the candies
Tiered like bleachers,
And asked what she wanted —
Light in her eyes, a smile
Starting at the corners

Of her mouth. I fingered 30
A nickel in my pocket,
And when she lifted a chocolate
That cost a dime,
I didn't say anything.
I took the nickel from
My pocket, then an orange,
And set them quietly on
The counter. When I looked up,
The lady's eyes met mine,
And held them, knowing 40
Very well what it was all
About.

      Outside,
A few cars hissing past,
Fog hanging like old
Coats between the trees.
I took my girl's hand
In mine for two blocks,
Then released it to let
Her unwrap the chocolate. 50
I peeled my orange
That was so bright against
The gray of December
That, from some distance,
Someone might have thought
I was making a fire in my hands.

Tony Hoagland   (b. 1953)

The Dog Years 1998

when it seemed every girl I dated
had a friend —
a Sheena or a Scoop, Jerome or Mr. Bones —
a four-legged, longtime furry pal

whose single-minded, tail-shaking
devotion to his mistress
caused me a certain pang,
knowing his relationship with her

would outlast mine;
that he would still be here,   10
jumping on the furniture
long after I was just a memory

beside the toothbrush rack, another
anecdotal mugshot
in the history book of non-commitment.
Still, that animal and I would often,

of a sunny afternoon, promenade together,
sniffing at the pants of strangers,
one of us pausing
while the other peed,   20

having in common both
a short attention span
and an insatiable appetite
for the love of womankind.

How perplexing for that dog
it must have been
when at the midnight hour
it was me, not him,

admitted to the fresh
bower of her bed —   30
and more than once,
in the warm, aromatic dark

full of animal mysteries
and spiritual facts,
I myself felt baffled by my luck,
like a sinner who has woken up

inexplicably in heaven,
while far off in the background
some poor wretch
who had lived by all the rules   40

howled and scratched at the shut door.

Mary Karr (b. 1954)

Revenge of the Ex-Mistress 1996

Dear X —
Finally met your wife
in Beef & Beer.
She hates it that you let me
pierce your ear, and time
you lost to me she guessed.
Still, we fell in love.
Please send her clothes
to my address. Best
wishes, no regrets.   10
           — Another X

Kate Gleason (b. 1956)

After Fighting for Hours 1997

When all else fails
we fall to making love,
our bodies like the pioneers
in rough covered wagons
whose oxen strained to cross the Rockies
until their hearts gave out trying,
those pioneers who had out-survived
fever, hunger, a run of broken luck,
those able-bodied men and women
who simply unlocked the animals   10
from their yokes, and taking
the hitches in their own hands, pulled
by the sheer desire of their bodies
their earthly goods over the divide.

Drama

William Shakespeare   (1564–1616)

Othello   ca. 1604

CHARACTERS

Duke of Venice
Brabantio, a Senator
Senators
Gratiano, Brother to Brabantio
Lodovico, Kinsman to Brabantio
Othello, a noble Moor; in the service of the Venetian State
Cassio, his Lieutenant
Iago, his Ancient
Roderigo, a Venetian Gentleman

Montano, Othello's predecessor in the Government of Cyprus
Clown, Servant to Othello
Desdemona, Daughter to Brabantio, and Wife to Othello
Emilia, Wife to Iago
Bianca, Mistress to Cassio
Sailor, Officers, Gentlemen, Messengers, Musicians, Heralds, Attendants

Scene

For the first Act, in Venice; during the rest of the Play, at a Sea-port in Cyprus

Act I

Scene 1.   Venice. A Street.

(Enter Roderigo and Iago)

Roderigo.   Tush! Never tell me; I take it much unkindly
  That thou, Iago, who has had my purse
  As if the strings were thine, shouldst know of this.[1]

[1] I.e., Othello's successful courtship of Desdemona.

Iago. 'Sblood,[2] but you will not hear me:
    If ever I did dream of such a matter,
    Abhor me.
Roderigo.   Thou told'st me thou didst hold him[3] in thy hate.
Iago.   Despise me if I do not. Three great ones of the city,
    In personal suit to make me his lieutenant,
    Off-capp'd[4] to him; and, by the faith of man,
    I know my price, I am worth no worse a place;   10
    But he, as loving his own pride and purposes,
    Evades them, with a bombast circumstance[5]
    Horribly stuff'd with epithets of war;
    And, in conclusion,
    Nonsuits[6] my mediators;[7] for, 'Certes,'[8] says he,
    'I have already chosen my officer.'
    And what was he?
    Forsooth, a great arithmetician,
    One Michael Cassio, a Florentine,
    A fellow almost damn'd in a fair wife;[9]   20
    That never set a squadron in the field,
    Nor the division of a battle knows
    More than a spinster; unless[10] the bookish theoric,[11]
    Wherein the toged consuls can propose
    As masterly as he: mere prattle, without practice,
    Is all his soldiership. But he, sir, had the election;
    And I — of whom his eyes had seen the proof
    At Rhodes, at Cyprus, and on other grounds
    Christian and heathen — must be be-lee'd[12] and calm'd
    By debitor and creditor; this counter-caster,[13]   30
    He, in good time, must his lieutenant be,
    And I — God bless the mark! — his Moorship's ancient.[14]
Roderigo.   By heaven, I rather would have been his hangman.
Iago.   Why, there's no remedy: 'tis the curse of service,
    Preferment goes by letter and affection,
    Not by the old gradation,[15] where each second
    Stood heir to the first. Now, sir, be judge yourself,
    Whe'r[16] I in any just term am affin'd[17]
    To love the Moor.

---

  [2] By God's blood.   [3] I.e., Othello.   [4] Took off their caps.   [5] Pompous wordiness, circumlocution.   [6] Turns down.   [7] Spokesmen.   [8] In truth.   [9] A much debated phrase. In the Italian source the Captain (i.e., Cassio) was married, and it may be that Shakespeare originally intended Bianca to be Cassio's wife but later changed his mind and failed to alter the phrase here accordingly. Or perhaps Iago simply sneers at Cassio as a notorious ladies' man.   [10] Except.   [11] Theory.   [12] Left without wind for my sails.   [13] Bookkeeper (*cf.* "arithmetician" above).   [14] Ensign (but Iago's position in the play seems to be that of Othello's aide-de-camp).   [15] Seniority.   [16] Whether.   [17] Obliged.

Roderigo.   I would not follow him then.
Iago.   O! sir, content you;   40
  I follow him to serve my turn upon him;
  We cannot all be masters, nor all masters
  Cannot be truly follow'd. You shall mark
  Many a duteous and knee-crooking knave,
  That, doting on his own obsequious bondage,
  Wears out his time, much like his master's ass,
  For nought but provender, and when he's old, cashier'd;
  Whip me such honest knaves. Others there are
  Who, trimm'd in forms and visages of duty,
  Keep yet their hearts attending on themselves,   50
  And, throwing but shows of service on their lords,
  Do well thrive by them, and when they have lin'd their coats
  Do themselves homage: these fellows have some soul;
  And such a one do I profess myself. For, sir,
  It is as sure as you are Roderigo,
  Were I the Moor, I would not be Iago:
  In following him, I follow but myself;
  Heaven is my judge, not I for love and duty,
  But seeming so, for my peculiar end:
  For when my outward action doth demonstrate   60
  The native act and figure of my heart
  In compliment extern,[18] 'tis not long after
  But I will wear my heart upon my sleeve
  For daws to peck at: I am not what I am.
Roderigo.   What a full fortune does the thick-lips owe,[19]
  If he can carry 't thus!
Iago.   Call up her father;
  Rouse him, make after him, poison his delight,
  Proclaim him in the streets, incense her kinsmen,
  And, though he in a fertile climate dwell,[20]
  Plague him with flies; though that his joy be joy,   70
  Yet throw such changes of vexation on 't
  As it may lose some colour.
Roderigo.   Here is her father's house; I'll call aloud.
Iago.   Do; with like timorous[21] accent and dire yell
  As when, by night and negligence, the fire
  Is spied in populous cities.
Roderigo.   What, ho! Brabantio: Signior Brabantio, ho!
Iago.   Awake! what, ho! Brabantio! thieves! thieves! thieves!
  Look to your house, your daughter, and your bags!
  Thieves! thieves!   80

---

[18] External show.   [19] Own.   [20] I.e., is fortunate.   [21] Frightening.

(Enter Brabantio, above, at a window.)

Brabantio.   What is the reason of this terrible summons?
  What is the matter there?
Roderigo.   Signior, is all your family within?
Iago.   Are your doors lock'd?
Brabantio.   Why? wherefore ask you this?
Iago.   'Zounds![22] sir, you're robb'd; for shame, put on your gown;
  Your heart is burst, you have lost half your soul;
  Even now, now, very now, an old black ram
  Is tupping[23] your white ewe. Arise, arise!
  Awake the snorting[24] citizens with the bell,
  Or else the devil will make a grandsire of you.   90
  Arise, I say.
Brabantio.   What! have you lost your wits?
Roderigo.   Most reverend signior, do you know my voice?
Brabantio.   Not I, what are you?
Roderigo.   My name is Roderigo.
Brabantio.   The worser welcome:
  I have charg'd thee not to haunt about my doors:
  In honest plainness thou hast heard me say
  My daughter is not for thee; and now, in madness,
  Being full of supper and distempering draughts,
  Upon malicious knavery dost thou come
  To start my quiet.   100
Roderigo.   Sir, sir, sir!
Brabantio.   But thou must needs be sure
  My spirit and my place[25] have in them power
  To make this bitter to thee.
Roderigo.   Patience, good sir.
Brabantio.   What tell'st thou me of robbing? this is Venice;
  My house is not a grange.[26]
Roderigo.   Most grave Brabantio,
  In simple and pure soul I come to you.
Iago.   'Zounds! sir, you are one of those that will not serve God if the devil bid
  you. Because we come to do you service and you think we are ruffians, you'll
  have your daughter covered with a Barbary horse; you'll have your nephews
  neigh to you; you'll have coursers for cousins and gennets[27] for germans.[28] 110
Brabantio.   What profane wretch art thou?
Iago.   I am one, sir, that comes to tell you, your daughter and the Moor are
  now making the beast with two backs.
Brabantio.   Thou art a villain.

---

[22] By God's wounds.   [23] Copulating.   [24] Snoring.   [25] Position.   [26] Isolated farmhouse.
[27] Spanish horses.   [28] Blood relations.

Iago. You are — a senator.

Brabantio. This thou shalt answer; I know thee, Roderigo.

Roderigo. Sir, I will answer any thing. But, I beseech you,
If 't be your pleasure and most wise consent, —
As partly, I find, it is, — that your fair daughter,
At this odd-even[29] and dull watch o' the night,
Transported with no worse nor better guard   120
But with a knave of common hire, a gondolier,
To the gross clasps of a lascivious Moor, —
If this be known to you, and your allowance,[30]
We then have done you bold and saucy wrongs;
But if you know not this, my manners tell me
We have your wrong rebuke. Do not believe
That, from[31] the sense of all civility,
I thus would play and trifle with your reverence:
Your daughter, if you have not given her leave,
I say again, hath made a gross revolt;   130
Tying her duty, beauty, wit and fortunes
In[32] an extravagant[33] and wheeling stranger
Of here and every where. Straight satisfy yourself:
If she be in her chamber or your house,
Let loose on me the justice of the state
For thus deluding you.

Brabantio. Strike on the tinder, ho!
Give me a taper! call up all my people!
This accident[34] is not unlike my dream;
Belief of it oppresses me already.
Light, I say! light!   *(Exit, from above.)*

Iago. Farewell, for I must leave you: 140
It seems not meet nor wholesome to my place
To be produc'd,[35] as, if I stay, I shall,
Against the Moor; for I do know the state,
However this may gall him with some check,[36]
Cannot with safety cast him; for he's embark'd
With such loud reason to the Cyprus wars, —
Which even now stand in act, — that, for their souls,
Another of his fathom[37] they have none,
To lead their business; in which regard,
Though I do hate him as I do hell-pains,   150
Yet, for necessity of present life,
I must show out a flag and sign of love,

---

[29] Between night and morning.   [30] By your approval.   [31] Away from.   [32] To.   [33] Expatriate.   [34] Happening.   [35] I.e., as a witness.   [36] Restraining adversity.   [37] Caliber, ability.

Which is indeed but sign. That you shall surely find him,
Lead to the Sagittary[38] the raised search;
And there will I be with him. So, farewell. *(Exit.)*

(Enter below, Brabantio, and servants with torches.)

Brabantio. It is too true an evil: gone she is,
And what's to come of my despised time
Is nought but bitterness. Now, Roderigo,
Where didst thou see her? O, unhappy girl!
With the Moor, sayst thou? Who would be a father! 160
How didst thou know 'twas she? O, she deceives me
Past thought. What said she to you? Get more tapers!
Raise all my kindred! Are they married, think you?
Roderigo. Truly, I think they are.
Brabantio. O heaven! How got she out? O treason of the blood:
Fathers, from hence trust not your daughters' minds
By what you see them act. Are there not charms
By which the property of youth and maidhood
May be abus'd? Have you not read, Roderigo,
Of some such thing?
Roderigo. Yes, sir, I have indeed. 170
Brabantio. Call up my brother. O! that you had had her.
Some one way, some another! Do you know
Where we may apprehend her and the Moor?
Roderigo. I think I can discover him, if you please
To get good guard and go along with me.
Brabantio. Pray you, lead on. At every house I'll call;
I may command at most. Get weapons, ho!
And raise some special officers of night.
On, good Roderigo; I'll deserve[39] your pains. *(Exeunt.)*

Scene 2. Another Street.

(Enter Othello, Iago, and Attendants, with torches.)

Iago. Though in the trade of war I have slain men,
Yet do I hold it very stuff o' the conscience
To do no contriv'd murder: I lack iniquity
Sometimes to do me service. Nine or ten times
I had thought to have yerk'd[40] him here under the ribs.
Othello. 'Tis better as it is.

---

[38] The name of an inn (?).   [39] I.e., reward.   [40] Stabbed.

Iago.   Nay, but he prated,
  And spoke such scurvy and provoking terms
  Against your honour
  That, with the little godliness I have,
  I did full hard forbear him. But, I pray, sir,   10
  Are you fast married? Be assur'd of this,
  That the magnifico[41] is much belov'd,
  And hath in his effect a voice potential
  As double[42] as the duke's; he will divorce you,
  Or put upon you what restraint and grievance
  The law — with all his might to enforce it on —
  Will give him cable.[43]
Othello.   Let him do his spite:
  My services which I have done the signiory[44]
  Shall out-tongue his complaints. 'Tis yet to know,[45]
  Which when I know that boasting is an honour   20
  I shall promulgate, I fetch my life and being
  From men of royal siege, and my demerits[46]
  May speak unbonneted[47] to as proud a fortune
  As this[48] that I have reach'd; for know, Iago,
  But that I love the gentle Desdemona,
  I would not my unhoused[49] free condition
  Put into circumscription and confine
  For the sea's worth. But, look! what lights come yond?
Iago.   Those are the raised[50] father and his friends:
  You were best[51] go in.
Othello.   Not I; I must be found: 30
  My parts, my title, and my perfect[52] soul
  Shall manifest me rightly. Is it they?
Iago.   By Janus,[53] I think no.

(Enter Cassio and certain Officers, with torches.)

Othello.   The servants of the duke, and my lieutenant.
  The goodness of the night upon you, friends!
  What is the news?
Cassio.   The duke does greet you, general,
  And he requires your haste-post-haste appearance,
  Even on the instant.

---

[41] One of the grandees, or rulers, of Venice; here, Brabantio.   [42] Iago means that Brabantio's influence equals that of the Doge's with his double vote.   [43] I.e., scope.   [44] The Venetian government.   [45] I.e., the signiory does not as yet know.   [46] Merits.   [47] I.e., as equals.   [48] I.e., that of Desdemona's family.   [49] Unconfined.   [50] Aroused.   [51] Had better.   [52] Untroubled by a bad conscience.   [53] The two-faced Roman god of portals and doors and (hence) of beginnings and ends.

Othello.   What is the matter, think you?
Cassio.   Something from Cyprus, as I may divine.
   It is a business of some heat;[54] the galleys   40
   Have sent a dozen sequent[55] messengers
   This very night at one another's heels,
   And many of the consuls,[56] rais'd and met,
   Are at the duke's already. You have been hotly call'd for;
   When, being not at your lodging to be found,
   The senate hath sent about three several[57] quests
   To search you out.
Othello.   'Tis well I am found by you.
   I will but spend a word here in the house,
   And go with you.   *(Exit.)*
Cassio.   Ancient, what makes he here?
Iago.   Faith, he to-night hath boarded a land carrack;[58]   50
   If it prove lawful prize, he's made for ever.
Cassio.   I do not understand.
Iago.   He's married.
Cassio.   To who?

(Re-enter Othello.)

Iago.   Marry,[59] to — Come, captain, will you go?
Othello.   Have with you.
Cassio.   Here comes another troop to seek for you.
Iago.   It is Brabantio. General, be advis'd;
   He comes to bad intent.

(Enter Brabantio, Roderigo, and Officers, with torches and weapons.)

Othello.   Holla! stand there!
Roderigo.   Signior, it is the Moor.
Brabantio.   Down with him, thief!

(They draw on both sides.)

Iago.   You, Roderigo! Come, sir, I am for you.[60]
Othello.   Keep up your bright swords, for the dew will rust them.
   Good signior, you shall more command with years   60
   Than with your weapons.
Brabantio.   O thou foul thief! where hast thou stow'd my daughter?
   Damn'd as thou art, thou hast enchanted her;

---

[54] Urgency.   [55] Following one another.   [56] I.e., senators.   [57] Separate.   [58] Treasure ship.   [59] By the Virgin Mary.   [60] Let you and me fight.

For I'll refer me to all things of sense,
If she in chains of magic were not bound,
Whether a maid so tender, fair, and happy,
So opposite to marriage that she shunn'd
The wealthy curled darlings of our nation,
Would ever have, to incur a general mock,
Run from her guardage to the sooty bosom   70
Of such a thing as thou; to fear, not to delight.
Judge me the world, if 'tis not gross in sense[61]
That thou hast practis'd on her with foul charms,
Abus'd her delicate youth with drugs or minerals
That weaken motion:[62] I'll have 't disputed on;
'Tis probable, and palpable to thinking.
I therefore apprehend and do attach[63] thee
For an abuser of the world, a practiser
Of arts inhibited and out of warrant.[64]
Lay hold upon him: if he do resist,   80
Subdue him at his peril.

Othello.   Hold your hands,
Both you of my inclining,[65] and the rest:
Were it my cue to fight, I should have known it
Without a prompter. Where will you that I go
To answer this your charge?

Brabantio.   To prison; till fit time
Of law and course of direct session[66]
Call thee to answer.

Othello.   What if I do obey?
How may the duke be therewith satisfied,
Whose messengers are here about my side,
Upon some present[67] business of the state   90
To bring me to him?

Officer.   'Tis true, most worthy signior;
The duke's in council, and your noble self,
I am sure, is sent for.

Brabantio.   How! the duke in council!
In this time of the night! Bring him away.
Mine's not an idle cause: the duke himself,
Or any of my brothers of the state,[68]
Cannot but feel this wrong as 'twere their own;
For if such actions may have passage free,
Bond-slaves and pagans shall our statesmen be.   *(Exeunt.)*

---

[61] Obvious.   [62] Normal reactions.   [63] Arrest.   [64] Prohibited and illegal.   [65] Party.
[66] Normal process of law.   [67] Immediate, pressing.   [68] Fellow senators.

Scene 3.   A Council Chamber.

(The Duke and Senators sitting at a table. Officers attending.)

Duke.   There is no composition[69] in these news
  That gives them credit.
First Senator.   Indeed, they are disproportion'd;
  My letters say a hundred and seven galleys.
Duke.   And mine, a hundred and forty.
Second Senator.   And mine, two hundred:
  But though they jump[70] not on a just[71] account, —
  As in these cases, where the aim[72] reports,
  'Tis oft with difference, — yet do they all confirm
  A Turkish fleet, and bearing up to Cyprus.
Duke.   Nay, it is possible enough to judgment:
  I do not so secure me in[73] the error,
  But the main article[74] I do approve[75]   10
  In fearful sense.
Sailor *(within)*.   What, ho! what, ho! what, ho!
Officer.   A messenger from the galleys.

(Enter a Sailor.)

Duke.   Now, what's the business?
Sailor.   The Turkish preparation makes for Rhodes;
  So was I bid report here to the state
  By Signior Angelo.
Duke.   How say you by this change?
First Senator.   This cannot be
  By no[76] assay[77] of reason; 'tis a pageant[78]
  To keep us in false gaze.[79] When we consider
  The importancy of Cyprus to the Turk,   20
  And let ourselves again but understand,
  That as it more concerns the Turk than Rhodes,
  So may he with more facile question bear[80] it,
  For that it stands not in such warlike brace,[81]
  But altogether lacks the abilities
  That Rhodes is dress'd in: if we make thought of this,
  We must not think the Turk is so unskilful
  To leave that latest which concerns him first,
  Neglecting an attempt of ease and gain,
  To wake and wage a danger profitless.   30

[69] Consistency, agreement.   [70] Coincide.   [71] Exact.   [72] Conjecture.   [73] Draw comfort from.   [74] Substance.   [75] Believe.   [76] Any.   [77] Test.   [78] (Deceptive) show.   [79] Looking in the wrong direction.   [80] More easily capture.   [81] State of defense.

Duke. Nay, in all confidence, he's not for Rhodes.
Officer. Here is more news.

(Enter a Messenger.)

Messenger. The Ottomites,[82] reverend and gracious,
    Steering with due course toward the isle of Rhodes,
    Have there injointed[83] them with an after fleet.[84]
First Senator. Ay, so I thought. How many, as you guess?
Messenger. Of thirty sail; and now they do re-stem[85]
    Their backward course, bearing with frank appearance
    Their purposes toward Cyprus. Signior Montano,
    Your trusty and most valiant servitor,   40
    With his free duty[86] recommends[87] you thus,
    And prays you to believe him.
Duke. 'Tis certain then, for Cyprus.
    Marcus Luccicos, is not he in town?
First Senator. He's now in Florence.
Duke. Write from us to him; post-post-haste dispatch.
First Senator. Here comes Brabantio and the valiant Moor.

(Enter Brabantio, Othello, Iago, Roderigo, and Officers.)

Duke. Valiant Othello, we must straight employ you
    Against the general enemy Ottoman.
    (To Brabantio) I did not see you; welcome, gentle signior;   50
    We lack'd your counsel and your help to-night.
Brabantio. So did I yours. Good your Grace, pardon me;
    Neither my place nor aught I heard of business
    Hath rais'd me from my bed, nor doth the general care
    Take hold of me, for my particular grief
    Is of so flood-gate[88] and o'erbearing nature
    That it engluts and swallows other sorrows
    And it is still itself.
Duke.   Why, what's the matter?
Brabantio. My daughter! O! my daughter.
Duke.   ⎫
Senators.   ⎬   Dead?
          ⎭
Brabantio.   Ay, to me;
    She is abus'd, stol'n from me, and corrupted   60
    By spells and medicines bought of mountebanks;
    For nature so preposterously to err,

---

[82] Turks.   [83] Joined.   [84] Fleet that followed after.   [85] Steer again.   [86] Unqualified expressions of respect.   [87] Informs.   [88] Torrential.

Being not deficient, blind, or lame of sense,
Sans[89] witchcraft could not.

Duke.   Whoe'er he be that in this foul proceeding
Hath thus beguil'd your daughter of herself
And you of her, the bloody book of law
You shall yourself read in the bitter letter
After your own sense; yea, though our proper[90] son
Stood[91] in your action.[92]

Brabantio.   Humbly I thank your Grace.   70
Here is the man, this Moor; whom now, it seems,
Your special mandate for the state affairs
Hath hither brought.

Duke.   ⎫
Senators. ⎬   We are very sorry for it.
            ⎭

Duke (*to Othello*).   What, in your own part, can you say to this?

Brabantio.   Nothing, but this is so.

Othello.   Most potent, grave, and reverend signiors,
My very noble and approv'd[93] good masters,
That I have ta'en away this old man's daughter,
It is most true; true, I have married her:
The very head and front of my offending   80
Hath this extent, no more. Rude am I in my speech,
And little bless'd with the soft phrase of peace;
For since these arms of mine had seven years' pith,[94]
Till now some nine moons wasted,[95] they have us'd
Their dearest action in the tented field;
And little of this great world can I speak,
More than pertains to feats of broil and battle;
And therefore little shall I grace my cause
In speaking for myself. Yet, by your gracious patience,
I will a round[96] unvarnish'd tale deliver   90
Of my whole course of love; what drugs, what charms,
What conjuration, and what mighty magic,
For such proceeding I am charg'd withal,
I won his daughter.

Brabantio.   A maiden never bold;
Of spirit so still and quiet, that her motion
Blush'd at herself;[97] and she, in spite of nature,
Of years, of country, credit, every thing,
To fall in love with what she fear'd to look on!
It is a judgment maim'd and most imperfect

---

[89] Without.   [90] Own.   [91] Were accused.   [92] Suit.   [93] Tested (by past experience).
[94] Strength.   [95] Past.   [96] Blunt.   [97] I.e. (her modesty was such that) she blushed at her own emotions; or: she could not move without blushing.

That will confess[98] perfection so could err   100
Against all rules of nature, and must be driven
To find out practices of cunning hell,
Why this should be. I therefore vouch again
That with some mixtures powerful o'er the blood,
Or with some dram conjur'd to this effect,
He wrought upon her.
Duke.   To vouch this, is no proof,
Without more certain and more overt test
Than these thin habits[99] and poor likelihoods
Of modern[100] seeming do prefer against him.
First Senator.   But, Othello, speak: 110
Did you by indirect and forced courses
Subdue and poison this young maid's affections;
Or came it by request and such fair question[101]
As soul to soul affordeth?
Othello.   I do beseech you;
Send for the lady to the Sagittary,
And let her speak of me before her father:
If you do find me foul in her report,
The trust, the office I do hold of you,
Not only take away, but let your sentence
Even fall upon my life.
Duke.   Fetch Desdemona hither.   120
Othello.   Ancient, conduct them; you best know the place.

(Exeunt Iago and Attendants.)

And, till she come, as truly as to heaven
I do confess the vices of my blood,
So justly to your grave ears I'll present
How I did thrive in this fair lady's love,
And she in mine.
Duke.   Say it, Othello.
Othello.   Her father lov'd me; oft invited me;
Still[102] question'd me the story of my life
From year to year, the battles, sieges, fortunes   130
That I have pass'd.
I ran it through, even from my boyish days
To the very moment that he bade me tell it;
Wherein I spake of most disastrous chances,
Of moving accidents by flood and field,

---

[98] Assert.   [99] Weak appearances.   [100] Commonplace.   [101] Conversation.   [102] Always,
regularly.

Of hair-breadth 'scapes i' the imminent deadly breach,
Of being taken by the insolent foe
And sold to slavery, of my redemption thence
And portance[103] in my travel's history;
Wherein of antres[104] vast and deserts idle,[105]   140
Rough quarries, rocks, and hills whose heads touch heaven,
It was my hint[106] to speak, such was the process;
And of the Cannibals that each other eat,
The Anthropophagi,[107] and men whose heads
Do grow beneath their shoulders. This to hear
Would Desdemona seriously incline;
But still the house-affairs would draw her thence;
Which ever as she could with haste dispatch,
She'd come again, and with a greedy ear
Devour up my discourse. Which I observing,   150
Took once a pliant[108] hour, and found good means
To draw from her a prayer of earnest heart
That I would all my pilgrimage dilate,[109]
Whereof by parcels[110] she had something heard,
But not intentively:[111] I did consent;
And often did beguile her of her tears,
When I did speak of some distressful stroke
That my youth suffer'd. My story being done,
She gave me for my pains a world of sighs:
She swore, in faith, 'twas strange, 'twas passing[112] strange;   160
'Twas pitiful, 'twas wondrous pitiful:
She wish'd she had not heard it, yet she wish'd
That heaven had made her[113] such a man; she thank'd me,
And bade me, if I had a friend that lov'd her,
I should but teach him how to tell my story,
And that would woo her. Upon this hint I spake.
She lov'd me for the dangers I had pass'd,
And I lov'd her that she did pity them.
This only is the witchcraft I have us'd:
Here comes the lady; let her witness it.   170

(*Enter Desdemona, Iago, and Attendants.*)

Duke.   I think this tale would win my daughter too.
   Good Brabantio,
   Take up this mangled matter at the best;

---

[103] Behavior.   [104] Caves.   [105] Empty, sterile.   [106] Opportunity.   [107] Man-eaters.
[108] Suitable.   [109] Relate in full.   [110] Piecemeal.   [111] In sequence.   [112] Surpassing.
[113] Direct object; not "for her."

Men do their broken weapons rather use
Than their bare hands.

Brabantio. I pray you, hear her speak:
If she confess that she was half the wooer,
Destruction on my head, if my bad blame
Light on the man! Come hither, gentle mistress:
Do you perceive in all this noble company
Where most you owe obedience?

Desdemona. My noble father,   180
I do perceive here a divided duty:
To you I am bound for life and education;
My life and education both do learn[114] me
How to respect you; you are the lord of duty,
I am hitherto your daughter: but here's my husband;
And so much duty as my mother show'd
To you, preferring you before her father,
So much I challenge[115] that I may profess
Due to the Moor my lord.

Brabantio. God be with you! I have done.
Please it your Grace, on to the state affairs;   190
I had rather to adopt a child than get it.
Come hither, Moor:
I here do give thee that with all my heart
Which, but thou hast[116] already, with all my heart
I would keep from thee. For your sake,[117] jewel,
I am glad at soul I have no other child;
For thy escape would teach me tyranny,
To hang clogs on them. I have done, my lord.

Duke. Let me speak like yourself and lay a sentence,[118]
Which as a grize[119] or step, may help these lovers   200
Into your favour.
When remedies are past, the griefs are ended
By seeing the worst, which[120] late on hopes depended.
To mourn a mischief that is past and gone
Is the next way to draw new mischief on.
What cannot be preserv'd when Fortune takes,
Patience her injury a mockery makes.[121]
The robb'd that smiles steals something from the thief;
He robs himself that spends a bootless grief.

Brabantio. So let the Turk of Cyprus us beguile;   210
We lose it not so long as we can smile.

---

[114] Teach.   [115] Claim as right.   [116] Didn't you have it.   [117] Because of you.   [118] Provide a maxim.   [119] Step.   [120] The antecedent is "griefs."   [121] To suffer an irreparable loss patiently is to make light of injury (i.e., to triumph over adversity).

He bears the sentence[122] well that nothing bears
But the free comfort which from thence he hears;
But he bears both the sentence and the sorrow
That, to pay grief, must of poor patience borrow.
These sentences, to sugar, or to gall,
Being strong on both sides, are equivocal:[123]
But words are words: I never yet did hear
That the bruis'd heart was pierced[124] through the ear.
I humbly beseech you, proceed to the affairs of state.   220

Duke.   The Turk with a most mighty preparation makes for Cyprus. Othello,
the fortitude[125] of the place is best known to you; and though we have there a
substitute of most allowed sufficiency,[126] yet opinion, a sovereign mistress of
effects, throws a more safer voice on you:[127] you must therefore be content to
slubber[128] the gloss of your new fortunes with this more stubborn[129] and boisterous expedition.

Othello.   The tyrant custom, most grave senators,
Hath made the flinty and steel couch of war
My thrice-driven[130] bed of down: I do agnize[131]
A natural and prompt alacrity   230
I find in hardness, and do undertake
These present wars against the Ottomites.
Most humbly therefore bending to your state,[132]
I crave fit disposition[133] for my wife,
Due reference of place and exhibition,[134]
With such accommodation and besort[135]
As levels with[136] her breeding.

Duke.   If you please,
Be 't at her father's.

Brabantio.   I'll not have it so.

Othello.   Nor I.

Desdemona.   Nor I; I would not there reside,   240
To put my father in impatient thoughts
By being in his eye. Most gracious duke,
To my unfolding[137] lend your gracious ear;
And let me find a charter[138] in your voice
To assist my simpleness.

Duke.   What would you, Desdemona?

Desdemona.   That I did love the Moor to live with him,
My downright violence and storm of fortunes

---

[122] (1) Verdict, (2) Maxim.   [123] Sententious comfort (like the Duke's trite maxims) can hurt
as well as soothe.   [124] (1) Lanced (i.e., cured), (2) Wounded.   [125] Strength.   [126] Admitted
competence.   [127] General opinion, which mainly determines action, thinks Cyprus safer with
you in command.   [128] Besmear.   [129] Rough.   [130] Made as soft as possible.   [131] Recognize.
[132] Submitting to your authority.   [133] Disposal.   [134] Provision.   [135] Fitness.   [136] Is proper to.
[137] Explanation.   [138] Permission.

May trumpet to the world; my heart's subdu'd
Even to the very quality of my lord;[139]   250
I saw Othello's visage in his mind,
And to his honours and his valiant parts
Did I my soul and fortunes consecrate.
So that, dear lords, if I be left behind,
A moth of peace, and he go to the war,
The rites[140] for which I love him are bereft me,
And I a heavy interim shall support[141]
By his dear[142] absence. Let me go with him.

Othello.   Let her have your voices.
Vouch with me, heaven, I therefore beg it not   260
To please the palate of my appetite,
Nor to comply with heat, — the young affects[143]
In me defunct, — and proper satisfaction,
But to be free and bounteous to her mind;
And heaven defend[144] your good souls that you think
I will your serious and great business scant
For[145] she is with me. No, when light-wing'd toys
Of feather'd Cupid seel[146] with wanton dulness
My speculative and offic'd instruments,[147]
That[148] my disports corrupt and taint my business,   270
Let housewives make a skillet of my helm,
And all indign[149] and base adversities
Make head against my estimation![150]

Duke.   Be it as you shall privately determine,
Either for her stay or going. The affair cries haste,
And speed must answer it.

First Senator.   You must away to-night.

Othello.   With all my heart.

Duke.   At nine i' the morning here we'll meet again.
Othello, leave some officer behind,
And he shall our commission bring to you;   280
With such things else of quality and respect
As doth import you.[151]

Othello.   So please your Grace, my ancient;
A man he is of honesty and trust:
To his conveyance I assign my wife,
With what else needful your good grace shall think
To be sent after me.

---

[139] I.e., I have become a soldier, like Othello.   [140] I.e., of marriage, or of war, or of both.
[141] Endure.   [142] Closely concerning (i.e., Desdemona).   [143] The passions of youth (hence, here,
immoderate sexual passion).   [144] Forbid.   [145] Because.   [146] Blind (v.) by sewing up the eyelids (a term from falconry).   [147] Reflective and executive faculties and organs.   [148] So that.
[149] Shameful.   [150] Reputation.   [151] Concern.

Duke.   Let it be so.
Good-night to every one. (*To Brabantio*) And, noble signior,
If virtue no delighted[152] beauty lack,
Your son-in-law is far more fair than black.
First Senator.   Adieu, brave Moor! use Desdemona well.   290
Brabantio.   Look to her, Moor, if thou hast eyes to see:
She has deceiv'd her father, and may thee.

(Exeunt Duke, Senators, Officers, &c.)

Othello.   My life upon her faith! Honest Iago,
My Desdemona must I leave to thee:
I prithee, let thy wife attend on her;
And bring them after in the best advantage.[153]
Come, Desdemona; I have but an hour
Of love, of worldly matters and direction,
To spend with thee: we must obey the time.

(Exeunt Othello and Desdemona.)

Roderigo.   Iago!   300
Iago.   What sayst thou, noble heart?
Roderigo.   What will I do, think'st thou?
Iago.   Why, go to bed, and sleep.
Roderigo.   I will incontinently[154] drown myself.
Iago.   Well, if thou dost, I shall never love thee after.
Why, thou silly gentleman!
Roderigo.   It is silliness to live when to live is torment; and then have we a
prescription to die when death is our physician.
Iago.   O! villainous; I have looked upon the world for four times seven years,
and since I could distinguish betwixt a benefit and an injury, I never found
man that knew how to love himself. Ere I would say, I would drown myself for
the love of a guinea-hen, I would change my humanity with a baboon.   312
Roderigo.   What should I do? I confess it is my shame to be so fond;[155] but it is
not in my virtue[156] to amend it.
Iago.   Virtue! a fig! 'tis in ourselves that we are thus, or thus. Our bodies are
our gardens, to the which our wills are gardeners; so that if we will plant
nettles or sow lettuce, set hyssop and weed up thyme, supply it with one gender[157] of herbs or distract it with many, either to have it sterile with idleness or
manured with industry, why, the power and corrigible[158] authority of this lies
in our wills. If the balance of our lives had not one scale of reason to poise

---

[152] Delightful.   [153] Opportunity.   [154] Forthwith.   [155] Infatuated.   [156] Strength.
[157] Kind.   [158] Corrective.

another of sensuality, the blood and baseness of our natures would conduct us to most preposterous conclusions; but we have reason to cool our raging motions, our carnal stings, our unbitted[159] lusts, whereof I take this that you call love to be a sect or scion.[160]   324

Roderigo.   It cannot be.

Iago.   It is merely a lust of the blood and a permission of the will. Come, be a man. Drown thyself! drown cats and blind puppies. I have professed me thy friend, and I confess me knit to thy deserving with cables of perdurable toughness; I could never better stead thee than now. Put money in thy purse; follow these wars; defeat thy favour[161] with a usurped[162] beard; I say, put money in thy purse. It cannot be that Desdemona should long continue her love to the Moor, — put money in thy purse, — nor he his to her. It was a violent commencement in her, and thou shalt see an answerable sequestration;[163] put but money in thy purse. These Moors are changeable in their wills; — fill thy purse with money: — the food that to him now is as luscious as locusts,[164] shall be to him shortly as bitter as coloquintida.[165] She must change for youth: when she is sated with his body, she will find the error of her choice. She must have change, she must: therefore put money in thy purse. If thou wilt needs damn thyself, do it a more delicate way than drowning. Make all the money thou canst. If sanctimony and a frail vow betwixt an erring[166] barbarian and a supersubtle[167] Venetian be not too hard for my wits and all the tribe of hell, thou shalt enjoy her; therefore make money. A pox of drowning thyself! it is clean out of the way: seek thou rather to be hanged in compassing thy joy than to be drowned and go without her.   344

Roderigo.   Wilt thou be fast to my hopes, if I depend on the issue?[168]

Iago.   Thou art sure of me: go, make money. I have told thee often, and I retell thee again and again, I hate the Moor; my cause is hearted; thine hath no less reason. Let us be conjunctive[169] in our revenge against him; if thou canst cuckold him, thou dost thyself a pleasure, me a sport. There are many events in the womb of time which will be delivered. Traverse;[170] go: provide thy money. We will have more of this to-morrow. Adieu.   351

Roderigo.   Where shall we meet i' the morning?

Iago.   At my lodging.

Roderigo.   I'll be with thee betimes.

Iago.   Go to: farewell. Do you hear, Roderigo?

Roderigo.   What say you?

Iago.   No more of drowning, do you hear?

Roderigo.   I am changed. I'll sell all my land.

Iago.   Go to; farewell! put money enough in your purse.   (*Exit Roderigo.*)

Thus do I ever make my fool my purse;   360

For I mine own gain'd knowledge should profane,

---

[159] I.e., uncontrolled.   [160] Offshoot.   [161] Change thy appearance (for the worse?).   [162] Assumed.   [163] Estrangement.   [164] Sweet-tasting fruits (perhaps the carob, the edible seedpod of an evergreen tree in the Mediterranean area).   [165] Purgative derived from a bitter apple. [166] Vagabond.   [167] Exceedingly refined.   [168] Rely on the outcome.   [169] Allied.   [170] March.

If I would time expend with such a snipe[171]
But for my sport and profit. I hate the Moor,
And it is thought abroad[172] that 'twixt my sheets
He has done my office: I know not if 't be true,
But I, for mere suspicion in that kind,
Will do as if for surety.[173] He holds me well;[174]
The better shall my purpose work on him.
Cassio's a proper[175] man; let me see now:
To get his place; and to plume up[176] my will   370
In double knavery; how, how? Let's see:
After some time to abuse Othello's ear
That he[177] is too familiar with his wife:
He hath a person and a smooth dispose[178]
To be suspected; framed[179] to make women false,
The Moor is of a free and open nature,
That thinks men honest that but seem to be so,
And will as tenderly be led by the nose
As asses are.
I have 't; it is engender'd: hell and night   380
Must bring this monstrous birth to the world's light.   (*Exit.*)

Act II

Scene 1.   A Sea-port Town in Cyprus. An open place near the Quay.

(*Enter Montano and two Gentlemen.*)

Montano.   What from the cape can you discern at sea?
First Gentleman.   Nothing at all: it is a high-wrought flood;
   I cannot 'twixt the heaven and the main[180]
   Descry a sail.
Montano.   Methinks the wind hath spoke aloud at land;
   A fuller blast ne'er shook our battlements;
   If it hath ruffian'd so upon the sea,
   What ribs of oak, when mountains melt on them,
   Can hold the mortise?[181] What shall we hear of this?
Second Gentleman.   A segregation[182] of the Turkish fleet;   10
   For do but stand upon the foaming shore,
   The chidden billow seems to pelt the clouds;

---

[171] Dupe.   [172] People think.   [173] As if it were certain.   [174] In high regard.   [175] Handsome.   [176] Make ready.   [177] I.e., Cassio.   [178] Bearing.   [179] Designed, apt.   [180] Ocean.
[181] Hold the joints together.   [182] Scattering.

The wind-shak'd surge, with high and monstrous mane,
Seems to cast water on the burning bear[183]
And quench the guards of the ever-fixed pole:[184]
I never did like[185] molestation view
On the enchafed[186] flood.

Montano.   If that[187] the Turkish fleet
Be not enshelter'd and embay'd, they are drown'd;
It is impossible they bear it out.

(Enter a Third Gentleman.)

Third Gentleman.   News, lad! our wars are done.   20
The desperate tempest hath so bang'd the Turks
That their designment halts;[188] a noble ship of Venice
Hath seen a grievous wrack and suffrance[189]
On most part of their fleet.
Montano.   How! is this true?
Third Gentleman.   The ship is here put in,
A Veronesa;[190] Michael Cassio,
Lieutenant to the warlike Moor Othello,
Is come on shore: the Moor himself's at sea,
And is in full commission here for Cyprus.
Montano.   I am glad on 't; 'tis a worthy governor.   30
Third Gentleman.   But this same Cassio, though he speak of comfort
Touching the Turkish loss, yet he looks sadly
And prays the Moor be safe; for they were parted
With foul and violent tempest.
Montano.   Pray heaven he be;
For I have serv'd him, and the man commands
Like a full soldier. Let's to the sea-side, ho!
As well to see the vessel that's come in
As to throw out our eyes for brave Othello,
Even till we make the main and the aerial blue
An indistinct regard.[191]   40
Third Gentleman.   Come, let's do so;
For every minute is expectancy
Of more arrivance.

(Enter Cassio.)

---

[183] Ursa Minor (the Little Dipper).   [184] Polaris, the North Star, almost directly above the Earth's axis, is part of the constellation of the Little Bear, or Dipper.   [185] Similar.   [186] Agitated.   [187] If.   [188] Plan is stopped.   [189] Damage.   [190] Probably a *type* of ship, rather than a ship from Verona — not only because Verona is an inland city but also because of "a noble ship of Venice" above.   [191] Till our (straining) eyes can no longer distinguish sea and sky.

Cassio. Thanks, you the valiant of this warlike isle,
That so approve the Moor. O! let the heavens
Give him defence against the elements,
For I have lost him on a dangerous sea.
Montano. Is he well shipp'd?
Cassio. His bark is stoutly timber'd, and his pilot
Of very expert and approv'd allowance;[192]   50
Therefore my hopes, not surfeited to death,[193]
Stand in bold cure.[194]

(*Within,* 'A sail! — a sail! — a sail!' *Enter a Messenger.*)

Cassio. What noise?
Messenger. The town is empty; on the brow o' the sea
Stand ranks of people, and they cry 'A sail!'
Cassio. My hopes do shape him for the governor.

(*Guns heard.*)

Second Gentleman. They do discharge their shot of courtesy;
Our friends at least.
Cassio.   I pray you, sir, go forth.
And give us truth who 'tis that is arriv'd.
Second Gentleman. I shall.   (*Exit.*)   60
Montano. But, good lieutenant, is your general wiv'd?
Cassio. Most fortunately: he hath achiev'd a maid
That paragons[195] description and wild fame;
One that excels the quirks[196] of blazoning pens,
And in th' essential vesture of creation[197]
Does tire the ingener.[198]

(*Re-enter Second Gentleman.*)

                     How now! who has put in?
Second Gentleman. 'Tis one Iago, ancient to the general.
Cassio. He has had most favourable and happy speed:
Tempests themselves, high seas, and howling winds,
The gutter'd[199] rocks, and congregated sands,   70
Traitors ensteep'd[200] to clog the guiltless keel,
As having sense of beauty, do omit

---

[192] Admitted and proven to be expert.   [193] Overindulged.   [194] With good chance of being fulfilled.   [195] Exceeds, surpasses.   [196] Ingenuities.   [197] I.e., just as God made her; or: (even in)
the (mere) essence of human nature.   [198] Inventor (i.e., of her praises?).   [199] Jagged; or: submerged.   [200] Submerged.

Their mortal[201] natures, letting go safely by
The divine Desdemona.
Montano.   What is she?
Cassio.   She that I spake of, our great captain's captain,
Left in the conduct of the bold Iago,
Whose footing[202] here anticipates our thoughts
A se'nnight's[203] speed. Great Jove, Othello guard,
And swell his sail with thine own powerful breath,
That he may bless this bay with his tall[204] ship,   80
Make love's quick pants in Desdemona's arms,
Give renew'd fire to our extincted spirits,
And bring all Cyprus comfort!

(Enter Desdemona, Emilia, Iago, Roderigo, and Attendants.)

                              O! behold,
The riches of the ship is come on shore.
Ye men of Cyprus, let her have your knees.
Hail to thee, lady! and the grace of heaven,
Before, behind thee, and on every hand,
Enwheel thee round!
Desdemona.   I thank you, valiant Cassio.
What tidings can you tell me of my lord?
Cassio.   He is not yet arriv'd; nor know I aught   90
But that he's well, and will be shortly here.
Desdemona.   O! but I fear — How lost you company?
Cassio.   The great contention of the sea and skies
Parted our fellowship. But hark! a sail.

(Cry within, 'A sail — a sail!' Guns heard.)

Second Gentleman.   They give their greeting to the citadel:
This likewise is a friend.
Cassio.   See for the news!   *(Exit Gentleman.)*
Good ancient, you are welcome: — *(To Emilia)* welcome, mistress.
Let it not gall your patience, good Iago,
That I extend my manners; 'tis my breeding
That gives me this bold show of courtesy.   *(Kissing her.)*   100
Iago.   Sir, would she give you so much of her lips
As of her tongue she oft bestows on me,
You'd have enough.
Desdemona.   Alas! she has no speech.

---

[201] Deadly.   [202] Landing.   [203] Week's.   [204] Brave.

Iago.   In faith, too much;
 I find it still when I have list[205] to sleep:
 Marry, before your ladyship, I grant,
 She puts her tongue a little in her heart,
 And chides with thinking.[206]

Emilia.   You have little cause to say so.

Iago.   Come on, come on; you are pictures[207] out of doors,   110
 Bells[208] in your parlours, wild cats in your kitchens,
 Saints in your injuries, devils being offended,
 Players[209] in your housewifery,[210] and housewives[211] in your beds.

Desdemona.   O! fie upon thee, slanderer.

Iago.   Nay, it is true, or else I am a Turk:
 You rise to play and go to bed to work.

Emilia.   You shall not write my praise.

Iago.   No, let me not.

Desdemona.   What wouldst thou write of me, if thou shouldst praise me?

Iago.   O gentle lady, do not put me to 't,
 For I am nothing if not critical.   120

Desdemona.   Come on; assay. There's one gone to the harbour?

Iago.   Ay, madam.

Desdemona (*aside*).   I am not merry, but I do beguile
 The thing I am by seeming otherwise.
 (*To Iago.*) Come, how wouldst thou praise me?

Iago.   I am about it; but indeed my invention
 Comes from my pate[212] as birdlime does from frize;[213]
 It plucks out brains and all: but my muse labours
 And thus she is deliver'd.
 If she be fair and wise, fairness and wit,   130
 The one's for use, the other useth it.

Desdemona.   Well prais'd! How if she be black and witty?

Iago.   If she be black,[214] and thereto have a wit,
 She'll find a white that shall her blackness fit.

Desdemona.   Worse and worse.

Emilia.   How if fair and foolish?

Iago.   She never yet was foolish that was fair,
 For even her folly[215] help'd to an heir.

Desdemona.   These are old fond[216] paradoxes to make fools laugh i' the ale-
 house. What miserable praise has thou for her that's foul and foolish?   140

Iago.   There's none so foul and foolish thereunto,
 But does foul pranks which fair and wise ones do.

---

[205] Wish.   [206] I.e., without words.   [207] I.e., made up, "painted."   [208] I.e., jangly.   [209] Triflers, wastrels.   [210] Housekeeping.   [211] (1) Hussies, (2) (unduly) frugal with their sexual favors, (3) businesslike, serious.   [212] Head.   [213] Coarse cloth.   [214] Brunette, dark haired.   [215] Here also, wantonness.   [216] Foolish.

Desdemona. O heavy ignorance! thou praisest the worst best. But what praise couldst thou bestow on a deserving woman indeed, one that, in the authority of her merit, did justly put on the vouch[217] of very malice itself?

Iago.   She that was ever fair and never proud,
Had tongue at will and yet was never loud,
Never lack'd gold and yet went never gay,
Fled from her wish and yet said 'Now I may,'
She that being anger'd, her revenge being nigh,   150
Bade her wrong stay and her displeasure fly,
She that in wisdom never was so frail
To change the cod's head for the salmon's tail,[218]
She that could think and ne'er disclose her mind,
See suitors following and not look behind,
She was a wight, if ever such wight were, —

Desdemona.   To do what?

Iago.   To suckle fools and chronicle small beer.[219]

Desdemona.   O most lame and impotent conclusion! Do not learn of him, Emilia, though he be thy husband. How say you, Cassio? Is he not a most profane and liberal[220] counsellor?   161

Cassio.   He speaks home,[221] madam; you may relish him more in the soldier than in[222] the scholar.

Iago (*aside*).   He takes her by the palm: ay, well said, whisper; with as little a web as this will I ensnare as great a fly as Cassio. Ay, smile upon her, do; I will gyve[223] thee in thine own courtship. You say true, 'tis so, indeed. If such tricks as these strip you out of your lieutenantry, it had been better you had not kissed your three fingers so oft, which now again you are most apt to play the sir [224] in. Very good; well kissed! an excellent courtesy! 'tis so, indeed. Yet again your fingers to your lips? would they were clyster-pipes[225] for your sake! (*A trumpet heard.*) The Moor! I know his trumpet.[226]   171

Cassio.   'Tis truly so.

Desdemona.   Let's meet him and receive him.

Cassio.   Lo! where he comes.

(*Enter Othello and Attendants.*)

Othello.   O my fair warrior!

Desdemona.   My dear Othello!

Othello.   It gives me wonder great as my content
To see you here before me. O my soul's joy!
If after every tempest come such calms,

---

[217] Compel the approval.   [218] To make a foolish exchange (a bawdy secondary meaning is probable).   [219] I.e., keep petty household accounts.   [220] Free-spoken, licentious.   [221] To the mark, aptly.   [222] As . . . as.   [223] Entangle.   [224] Gentleman.   [225] Syringes, enema pipes.   [226] I.e., Othello's distinctive trumpet call.

May the winds blow till they have waken'd death!
And let the labouring bark climb hills of seas   180
Olympus-high, and duck again as low
As hell's from heaven! If it were now to die,
'Twere now to be most happy, for I fear
My soul hath her content so absolute
That not another comfort like to this
Succeeds in unknown fate.
Desdemona.   The heavens forbid
But that our loves and comforts should increase
Even as our days do grow!
Othello.   Amen to that, sweet powers!
I cannot speak enough of this content;   190
It stops me here; it is too much of joy:
And this, and this, the greatest discords be   (*Kissing her.*)
That e'er our hearts shall make!
Iago (*aside*).   O! you are well tun'd now,
But I'll set down[227] the pegs that make this music,
As honest as I am.
Othello.   Come, let us to the castle.
News, friends; our wars are done, the Turks are drown'd.
How does my old acquaintance of this isle?
Honey, you shall be well desir'd[228] in Cyprus;
I have found great love amongst them. O my sweet,
I prattle out of fashion, and I dote   200
In mine own comforts. I prithee, good Iago,
Go to the bay and disembark my coffers.
Bring thou the master to the citadel;
He is a good one, and his worthiness
Does challenge much respect. Come, Desdemona,
Once more well met at Cyprus.

                              (*Exeunt all except Iago and Roderigo.*)

Iago.   Do thou meet me presently at the harbour. Come hither. If thou be'st
valiant, as they say base men being in love have then a nobility in their natures
more than is native to them, list[229] me. The lieutenant to-night watches on the
court of guard:[230] first, I must tell thee this, Desdemona is directly in love
with him.
Roderigo.   With him! Why, 'tis not possible.
Iago.   Lay thy finger thus, and let thy soul be instructed. Mark me with what
violence she first loved the Moor but for bragging and telling her fantastical
lies; and will she love him still for prating? let not thy discreet heart think it.

---

[227] Loosen.   [228] Welcomed.   [229] Listen to.   [230] Guardhouse.

Her eye must be fed; and what delight shall she have to look on the devil?
When the blood is made dull with the act of sport, there should be, again to
inflame it, and to give satiety a fresh appetite, loveliness in favour, sympathy
in years, manners, and beauties; all which the Moor is defective in. Now, for
want of these required conveniences, her delicate tenderness will find itself
abused, begin to heave the gorge,[231] disrelish and abhor the Moor; very nature
will instruct her in it, and compel her to some second choice. Now, sir, this
granted, as it is a most pregnant[232] and unforced position, who stands so eminently in the degree of this fortune as Cassio does? a knave very voluble, no
further conscionable[233] than in putting on the mere form of civil and humane
seeming, for the better compassing of his salt[234] and most hidden loose affection? why, none; why, none: a slipper[235] and subtle knave, a finder-out of occasions, that has an eye can stamp and counterfeit advantages, though true
advantage never present itself; a devilish knave! Besides, the knave is handsome, young, and hath all those requisites in him that folly and green minds
look after; a pestilent complete knave! and the woman hath found him
already.

Roderigo.   I cannot believe that in her; she is full of most blessed condition.

Iago.   Blessed fig's end! the wine she drinks is made of grapes;[236] if she had
been blessed she would never have loved the Moor; blessed pudding! Didst
thou not see her paddle with the palm of his hand? didst not mark that?

Roderigo.   Yes, that I did; but that was but courtesy.

Iago.   Lechery, by this hand! an index[237] and obscure prologue to the history of
lust and foul thoughts. They met so near with their lips, that their breaths
embraced together. Villainous thoughts, Roderigo! when these mutualities so
marshal the way, hard at hand comes the master and main exercise, the incorporate[238] conclusion. Pish![239] But, sir, be you ruled by me: I have brought you
from Venice. Watch you to-night; for the command, I'll lay 't upon you: Cassio
knows you not. I'll not be far from you: do you find some occasion to anger
Cassio, either by speaking too loud, or tainting[240] his discipline; or from what
other course you please, which the time shall more favourably minister.

Roderigo.   Well.

Iago.   Sir, he is rash and very sudden in choler, and haply may strike at you:
provoke him, that he may; for even out of that will I cause these of Cyprus
to mutiny, whose qualification[241] shall come into no true taste again but by
the displanting of Cassio. So shall you have a shorter journey to your desires
by the means I shall then have to prefer[242] them; and the impediment most
profitably removed, without the which there were no expectation of our prosperity.

Roderigo.   I will do this, if I can bring it to any opportunity.

Iago.   I warrant thee. Meet me by and by at the citadel: I must fetch his necessaries ashore. Farewell.

---

[231] Vomit.   [232] Obvious.   [233] Conscientious.   [234] Lecherous.   [235] Slippery.   [236] I.e., she
is only flesh and blood.   [237] Pointer.   [238] Carnal.   [239] Exclamation of disgust.   [240] Disparag-
ing.   [241] Appeasement.   [242] Advance.

Roderigo. Adieu. *(Exit.)*

Iago. That Cassio loves her, I do well believe it;
That she loves him, 'tis apt,[243] and of great credit:[244]   260
The Moor, howbeit that I endure him not,
Is of a constant, loving, noble nature;
And I dare think he'll prove to Desdemona
A most dear[245] husband. Now, I do love her too;
Not out of absolute lust, — though peradventure[246]
I stand accountant[247] for as great a sin, —
But partly led to diet my revenge,
For that I do suspect the lusty Moor
Hath leap'd into my seat; the thought whereof
Doth like a poisonous mineral gnaw my inwards;   270
And nothing can or shall content my soul
Till I am even'd with him, wife for wife;
Or failing so, yet that I put the Moor
At least into a jealousy so strong
That judgment cannot cure. Which thing to do,
If this poor trash[248] of Venice, whom I trash[249]
For his quick hunting, stand the putting-on,[250]
I'll have our Michael Cassio on the hip;
Abuse him to the Moor in the rank garb,[251]
For I fear Cassio with my night-cap too,   280
Make the Moor thank me, love me, and reward me
For making him egregiously an ass
And practising upon his peace and quiet
Even to madness. 'Tis here, but yet confus'd:
Knavery's plain face is never seen till us'd.   *(Exit.)*

Scene 2.   A Street.

(Enter a Herald with a proclamation; people following.)

Herald.   It is Othello's pleasure, our noble and valiant general, that, upon certain tidings now arrived, importing the mere[252] perdition of the Turkish fleet, every man put himself into triumph; some to dance, some to make bonfires, each man to what sport and revels his addiction leads him; for, besides these beneficial news, it is the celebration of his nuptial. So much was his pleasure should be proclaimed. All offices[253] are open, and there is full liberty of feasting from this present hour of five till the bell have told eleven. Heaven bless the isle of Cyprus and our noble general Othello!   *(Exeunt.)*

---

[243] Natural, probable.   [244] Easily believable.   [245] A pun on the word in the sense of expensive.
[246] Perchance, perhaps.   [247] Accountable.   [248] I.e., Roderigo.   [249] Check, control.   [250] Inciting.   [251] Gross manner.   [252] Utter.   [253] Kitchens and storehouses.

Scene 3.   A Hall in the Castle.

(Enter Othello, Desdemona, Cassio, and Attendants.)

Othello.   Good Michael, look you to the guard to-night:
　　Let's teach ourselves that honourable stop,[254]
　　Not to outsport discretion.
Cassio.   Iago hath direction what to do:
　　But, notwithstanding, with my personal[255] eye
　　Will I look to 't.
Othello.　　　　　Iago is most honest.
　　Michael, good-night; to-morrow with your earliest
　　Let me have speech with you. *(To Desdemona.)* Come, my dear love,
　　The purchase made, the fruits are to ensue;
　　That profit's yet to come 'twixt me and you.　　　　　　10
　　Good-night.

　　　　　　　　　(Exeunt Othello, Desdemona, and Attendants.)

(Enter Iago.)

Cassio.   Welcome, Iago; we must to the watch.
Iago.   Not this hour, lieutenant; 'tis not yet ten o' clock. Our general casts
　　us thus early for the love of his Desdemona, who let us not therefore blame;
　　he hath not yet made wanton the night with her, and she is sport for Jove.
Cassio.   She's a most exquisite lady.
Iago.   And, I'll warrant her, full of game.
Cassio.   Indeed, she is a most fresh and delicate creature.
Iago.   What an eye she has! methinks it sounds a parley[256] of provocation.
Cassio.   An inviting eye: and yet methinks right modest.　　　　　　20
Iago.   And when she speaks, is it not an alarum[257] to love?
Cassio.   She is indeed perfection.
Iago.   Well, happiness to their sheets! Come, lieutenant, I have a stoup of
　　wine, and here without are a brace[258] of Cyprus gallants that would fain have a
　　measure to the health of black Othello.
Cassio.   Not to-night, good Iago: I have very poor and unhappy brains for
　　drinking: I could well wish courtesy would invent some other custom of
　　entertainment.
Iago.   O! they are our friends; but one cup: I'll drink for you.　　　　　　29
Cassio.   I have drunk but one cup to-night, and that was craftily qualified[259]

---

[254] Discipline.　　[255] Own.　　[256] Conference.　　[257] Call-to-arms.　　[258] Pair.　　[259] Diluted.

too, and, behold, what innovation[260] it makes here: I am unfortunate in the infirmity, and dare not task my weakness with any more.

Iago. What, man! 'tis a night of revels; the gallants desire it.

Cassio. Where are they?

Iago. Here at the door; I pray you, call them in.

Cassio. I'll do 't; but it dislikes me. *(Exit.)*

Iago. If I can fasten but one cup upon him,
With that which he hath drunk to-night already,
He'll be as full of quarrel and offence
As my young mistress' dog. Now, my sick fool Roderigo,   40
Whom love has turn'd almost the wrong side out,
To Desdemona hath to-night carous'd
Potations pottle-deep;[261] and he's to watch.
Three lads of Cyprus, noble swelling spirits,
That hold their honours in a wary distance,[262]
The very elements[263] of this warlike isle,
Have I to-night fluster'd with flowing cups,
And they watch too. Now, 'mongst this flock of drunkards,
Am I to put our Cassio in some action
That may offend the isle. But here they come.   50
If consequence[264] do but approve my dream,
My boat sails freely, both with wind and stream.

(Re-enter Cassio, with him Montano, and Gentlemen. Servant following with wine.)

Cassio. 'Fore God, they have given me a rouse[265] already.

Montano. Good faith, a little one; not past a pint, as I am a soldier.

Iago. Some wine, ho!
(Sings.) And let me the canakin[266] clink, clink;
    And let me the canakin clink:
    A soldier's a man;
    A life's but a span;
    Why then let a soldier drink.   60
Some wine, boys!

Cassio. 'Fore God, an excellent song.

Iago. I learned it in England, where indeed they are most potent in potting; your Dane, your German, and your swag-bellied[267] Hollander, — drink ho! — are nothing to your English.

Cassio. Is your Englishman so expert in his drinking?

Iago. Why, he drinks you[268] with facility your Dane dead drunk; he sweats not

---

[260] Change, revolution.   [261] Bottoms-up.   [262] Take offense easily.   [263] Types.   [264] Succeeding events.   [265] Drink.   [266] Small cup.   [267] With a pendulous belly.   [268] The "ethical" dative, i.e., you'll see that he drinks.

to overthrow your Almain;[269] he gives your Hollander a vomit ere the next
pottle can be filled.

Cassio.   To the health of our general!   70

Montano.   I am for it, lieutenant; and I'll do you justice.

Iago.   O sweet England!

   (*Sings.*) King Stephen was a worthy peer,
         His breeches cost him but a crown;
       He held them sixpence all too dear,
         With that he call'd the tailor lown.[270]
       He was a wight of high renown,
         And thou art but of low degree:
       'Tis pride that pulls the country down,
         Then take thine auld cloak about thee.   80

Some wine, ho!

Cassio.   Why, this is a more exquisite song than the other.

Iago.   Will you hear 't again?

Cassio.   No; for I hold him to be unworthy of his place that does those things.
Well, God's above all; and there be souls must be saved, and there be souls
must not be saved.

Iago.   It's true, good lieutenant.

Cassio.   For mine own part, — no offence to the general, nor any man of
quality, — I hope to be saved.

Iago.   And so do I too, lieutenant.   90

Cassio.   Ay; but, by your leave, not before me; the lieutenant is to be saved
before the ancient. Let's have no more of this; let's to our affairs. God forgive
us our sins! Gentlemen, let's look to our business. Do not think, gentlemen, I
am drunk: this is my ancient; this is my right hand, and this is my left hand. I
am not drunk now; I can stand well enough, and speak well enough.

All.   Excellent well.

Cassio.   Why, very well, then; you must not think then that I am drunk.

                                       (*Exit.*)

Montano.   To the platform, masters; come, let's set the watch.

Iago.   You see this fellow that is gone before;
He is a soldier fit to stand by Caesar   100
And give direction; and do but see his vice;
'Tis to his virtue a just equinox,[271]
The one as long as the other; 'tis pity of him.
I fear the trust Othello puts him in,
On some odd time of his infirmity,
Will shake this island.

Montano.   But is he often thus?

Iago.   'Tis evermore the prologue to his sleep;

---

[269] German.   [270] Lout, rascal.   [271] Equivalent.

He'll watch the horologe a double set,[272]
If drink rock not his cradle.
Montano.   It were well
The general were put in mind of it.   110
Perhaps he sees it not; or his good nature
Prizes the virtue that appears in Cassio,
And looks not on his evils. Is not this true?

(Enter Roderigo.)

Iago *(aside to him).*   How now, Roderigo!
I pray you, after the lieutenant; go.   *(Exit Roderigo.)*
Montano.   And 'tis great pity that the noble Moor
Should hazard such a place as his own second
With one of an ingraft[273] infirmity;
It were an honest action to say
So to the Moor.
Iago.   Not I, for this fair island: 120
I do love Cassio well, and would do much
To cure him of this evil. But hark! what noise?

(Cry within, 'Help! Help!' Re-enter Cassio, driving in Roderigo.)

Cassio.   You rogue! you rascal!
Montano.   What's the matter, lieutenant?
Cassio.   A knave teach me my duty!
I'll beat the knave into a twiggen[274] bottle.
Roderigo.   Beat me!
Cassio.   Dost thou prate, rogue?

(Striking Roderigo.)

Montano *(staying him).*   Nay, good lieutenant;
I pray you, sir, hold your hand.
Cassio.   Let me go, sir,
Or I'll knock you o'er the mazzard.[275]
Montano.   Come, come; you're drunk.
Cassio.   Drunk!   130

(They fight.)

Iago *(aside to Roderigo).*   Away, I say! go out, and cry a mutiny.
                                                                (Exit Roderigo.)

---

[272] Stand watch twice twelve hours.   [273] Ingrained.   [274] Wicker.   [275] Head.

Nay, good lieutenant! God's will, gentlemen!
Help, ho! Lieutenant! sir! Montano! sir!
Help, masters! Here's a goodly watch indeed!

(*Bell rings.*)

Who's that that rings the bell? Diablo, ho!
The town will rise: God's will! lieutenant, hold!
You will be sham'd for ever.

(*Re-enter Othello and Attendants.*)

Othello.   What is the matter here?
Montano.   'Zounds! I bleed still; I am hurt to the death.

(*He faints.*)

Othello.   Hold, for your lives!   140
Iago.   Hold, ho, lieutenant! Sir! Montano! gentlemen!
Have you forgot all sense of place and duty?
Hold! the general speaks to you; hold for shame!
Othello.   Why, how now, ho! from whence ariseth this?
Are we turn'd Turks, and to ourselves do that
Which heaven hath forbid the Ottomites?
For Christian shame put by this barbarous brawl;
He that stirs next to carve for his own rage
Holds his soul light; he dies upon his motion.
Silence that dreadful bell! it frights the isle   150
From her propriety. What is the matter, masters?
Honest Iago, that look'st dead with grieving,
Speak, who began this? On thy love, I charge thee.
Iago.   I do not know; friends all but now, even now,
In quarter[276] and in terms like bride and groom
Devesting[277] them for bed; and then, but now, —
As if some planet had unwitted men, —
Swords out, and tilting one at other's breast,
In opposition bloody. I cannot speak
Any beginning to this peevish odds,[278]   160
And would in action glorious I had lost
Those legs that brought me to a part of it!
Othello.   How comes it, Michael, you are thus forgot?
Cassio.   I pray you, pardon me; I cannot speak.

---

[276] On duty.   [277] Undressing.   [278] Silly quarrel.

Othello.   Worthy Montano, you were wont be civil;
The gravity and stillness of your youth
The world hath noted, and your name is great
In mouths of wisest censure:[279] what's the matter,
That you unlace[280] your reputation thus
And spend your rich opinion[281] for the name   170
Of a night-brawler? give me answer to it.
Montano.   Worthy Othello, I am hurt to danger;
Your officer, Iago, can inform you,
While I spare speech, which something now offends[282] me,
Of all that I do know; nor know I aught
By me that 's said or done amiss this night,
Unless self-charity be sometimes a vice,
And to defend ourselves it be a sin
When violence assails us.
Othello.   Now, by heaven,
My blood begins my safer guides to rule,   180
And passion, having my best judgment collied,[283]
Assays to lead the way. If I once stir,
Or do but lift this arm, the best of you
Shall sink in my rebuke. Give me to know
How this foul rout began, who set it on;
And he that is approv'd[284] in this offence,
Though he had twinn'd with me — both at a birth —
Shall lose me. What! in a town of war,
Yet wild, the people's hearts brimful of fear,
To manage private and domestic quarrel,   190
In night, and on the court and guard of safety!
'Tis monstrous. Iago, who began 't?
Montano.   If partially affin'd,[285] or leagu'd in office,
Thou dost deliver more or less than truth,
Thou art not soldier.
Iago.   Touch me not so near;
I had rather[286] have this tongue cut from my mouth
Than it should do offence to Michael Cassio;
Yet, I persuade myself, to speak the truth
Shall nothing wrong him. Thus it is, general.
Montano and myself being in speech,   200
There comes a fellow crying out for help,
And Cassio following with determin'd sword
To execute upon him. Sir, this gentleman

---

[279] Judgment.   [280] Undo.   [281] High reputation.   [282] Pains, harms.   [283] Clouded.
[284] Proved (i.e., guilty).   [285] Favorably biased (by ties of friendship, or as Cassio's fellow officer).
[286] More quickly.

Steps in to Cassio, and entreats his pause;
Myself the crying fellow did pursue,
Lest by his clamour, as it so fell out,
The town might fall in fright; he, swift of foot,
Outran my purpose, and I return'd the rather
For that I heard the clink and fall of swords,
And Cassio high in oath, which till to-night   210
I ne'er might say before. When I came back, —
For this was brief, — I found them close together,
At blow and thrust, even as again they were
When you yourself did part them.
More of this matter can I not report:
But men are men; the best sometimes forget:
Though Cassio did some little wrong to him,
As men in rage strike those that wish them best,
Yet, surely Cassio, I believe, receiv'd
From him that fled some strange indignity,   220
Which patience could not pass.
Othello.   I know, Iago.
Thy honesty and love doth mince[287] this matter,
Making it light to Cassio. Cassio, I love thee;
But never more be officer of mine.

(Enter Desdemona, attended.)

Look! if my gentle love be not rais'd up;
(To Cassio.) I'll make thee an example.
Desdemona.   What's the matter?
Othello.   All's well now, sweeting; come away to bed.
Sir, for your hurts, myself will be your surgeon.
Lead him off.   *(Montano is led off.)*
Iago, look with care about the town,   230
And silence those whom this vile brawl distracted.
Come, Desdemona; 'tis the soldier's life,
To have their balmy slumbers wak'd with strife.

(Exeunt all but Iago and Cassio.)

Iago.   What! are you hurt, lieutenant?
Cassio.   Ay; past all surgery.
Iago.   Marry, heaven forbid!
Cassio.   Reputation, reputation, reputation! O! I have lost my reputation. I

---

[287] Tone down.

have lost the immortal part of myself, and what remains is bestial. My reputation, Iago, my reputation!

Iago. As I am an honest man, I thought you had received some bodily wound; there is more offence in that than in reputation. Reputation is an idle and most false imposition;[288] oft got without merit, and lost without deserving: you have lost no reputation at all, unless you repute yourself such a loser. What! man; there are ways to recover the general again; you are but now cast in his mood,[289] a punishment more in policy[290] than in malice; even so as one would beat his offenceless dog to affright an imperious lion. Sue to him again, and he is yours.

Cassio. I will rather sue to be despised than to deceive so good a commander with so slight, so drunken and so indiscreet an officer. Drunk! and speak parrot![291] and squabble, swagger, swear, and discourse fustian[292] with one's own shadow! O thou invisible spirit of wine! if thou hast no name to be known by, let us call thee devil!

Iago. What was he that you followed with your sword? What hath he done to you?

Cassio. I know not.

Iago. Is 't possible?

Cassio. I remember a mass of things, but nothing distinctly; a quarrel, but nothing wherefore. O God! that men should put an enemy in their mouths to steal away their brains; that we should, with joy, pleasance,[293] revel, and applause, transform ourselves into beasts.   260

Iago. Why, but you are now well enough; how came you thus recovered?

Cassio. It hath pleased the devil drunkenness to give place to the devil wrath; one unperfectness shows me another, to make me frankly despise myself.

Iago. Come, you are too severe a moraler. As the time, the place, and the condition of this country stands, I could heartily wish this had not befallen, but since it is as it is, mend it for your own good.

Cassio. I will ask him for my place again; he shall tell me I am a drunkard! Had I as many mouths as Hydra,[294] such an answer would stop them all. To be now a sensible man, by and by a fool, and presently a beast! O strange! Every inordinate cup is unblessed and the ingredient[295] is a devil.   270

Iago. Come, come; good wine is a good familiar creature if it be well used; exclaim no more against it. And, good lieutenant, I think you think I love you.

Cassio. I have well approved it, sir. I drunk!

Iago. You or any man living may be drunk at some time, man. I'll tell you what you shall do. Our general's wife is now the general; I may say so in this respect, for that he hath devoted and given up himself to the contemplation, mark, and denotement of her parts and graces: confess yourself freely to her;

---

[288] Something external.   [289] Dismissed because he is angry.   [290] I.e., more for the sake of the example or to show his fairness.   [291] I.e., without thinking.   [292] I.e., nonsense.   [293] Pleasure.   [294] Many-headed snake in Greek mythology.   [295] Contents.

importune her; she'll help to put you in your place again. She is of so free, so kind, so apt, so blessed a disposition, that she holds it a vice in her goodness not to do more than she is requested. This broken joint between you and her husband entreat her to splinter;[296] and, my fortunes against any lay[297] worth naming, this crack of your love shall grow stronger than it was before.

Cassio.   You advise me well.

Iago.   I protest, in the sincerity of love and honest kindness.

Cassio.   I think it freely; and betimes in the morning I will beseech the virtuous Desdemona to undertake for me. I am desperate of my fortunes if they check me here.

Iago.   You are in the right. Good-night, lieutenant; I must to the watch.

Cassio.   Good-night, honest Iago!   (*Exit.*)

Iago.   And what's he then that says I play the villain?   290
    When this advice is free I give and honest,
    Probal[298] to thinking and indeed the course
    To win the Moor again? For 'tis most easy
    The inclining Desdemona to subdue
    In any honest suit; she's fram'd as fruitful[299]
    As the free elements. And then for her
    To win the Moor, were 't to renounce his baptism,
    All seals and symbols of redeemed sin,
    His soul is so enfetter'd to her love,
    That she may make, unmake, do what she list,   300
    Even as her appetite shall play the god
    With his weak function.[300] How am I then a villain
    To counsel Cassio to this parallel[301] course,
    Directly to his good? Divinity of hell!
    When devils will the blackest sins put on,
    They do suggest at first with heavenly shows,
    As I do now; for while this honest fool
    Plies Desdemona to repair his fortunes,
    And she for him pleads strongly to the Moor,
    I'll pour this pestilence into his ear   310
    That she repeals[302] him for her body's lust;
    And, by how much she strives to do him good,
    She shall undo her credit with the Moor.
    So will I turn her virtue into pitch,
    And out of her own goodness make the net
    That shall enmesh them all.

(*Re-enter Roderigo.*)

---

[296] Bind up with splints.   [297] Wager.   [298] Provable.   [299] Generous.   [300] Faculties.
[301] Purposeful.   [302] I.e., seeks to recall.

Iago.   How now, Roderigo!

Roderigo.   I do follow here in the chase, not like a hound that hunts, but one that fills up the cry.[303] My money is almost spent; I have been to-night exceedingly well cudgelled; and I think the issue will be, I shall have so much experience for my pains; and so, with no money at all and a little more wit, return again to Venice.

Iago.   How poor are they that have not patience!
What wound did ever heal but by degrees?
Thou know'st we work by wit and not by witchcraft,
And wit depends on dilatory time.
Does 't not go well? Cassio hath beaten thee,
And thou by that small hurt hast cashiered Cassio.
Though other things grow fair against the sun,
Yet fruits that blossom first will first be ripe:
Content thyself awhile. By the mass, 'tis morning;   330
Pleasure and action make the hours seem short.
Retire thee; go where thou art billeted:
Away, I say; thou shalt know more hereafter:
Nay, get thee gone. (*Exit Roderigo.*) Two things are to be done,
My wife must move for Cassio to her mistress;
I'll set her on;
Myself the while to draw the Moor apart,
And bring him jump[304] when he may Cassio find
Soliciting his wife: ay, that's the way:
Dull not device by coldness and delay.   (*Exit.*)

Act III

Scene 1.   Cyprus. Before the Castle.

(*Enter Cassio, and some Musicians.*)

Cassio.   Masters, play here, I will content your pains;[305]
Something that's brief; and bid 'Good-morrow, general.'   (*Music.*)

(*Enter Clown.*)

Clown.   Why, masters, have your instruments been in Naples, that they speak i' the nose[306] thus?

---

[303] Pack (hunting term).   [304] At the exact moment.   [305] Reward your efforts.   [306] Naples was notorious for venereal disease, and syphilis was believed to affect the nose.

First Musician.   How, sir, how?

Clown.   Are these, I pray you, wind-instruments?

First Musician.   Ay, marry, are they, sir.

Clown.   O! thereby hangs a tale.

First Musician.   Whereby hangs a tale, sir?

Clown.   Marry, sir, by many a wind-instrument that I know. But, masters, here's money for you; and the general so likes your music, that he desires you, for love's sake, to make no more noise with it.

First Musician.   Well, sir, we will not.

Clown.   If you have any music that may not be heard, to 't again; but, as they say, to hear music the general does not greatly care.

First Musician.   We have none such, sir.

Clown.   Then put up your pipes in your bag, for I'll away.
Go; vanish into air; away! *(Exeunt Musicians.)*

Cassio.   Dost thou hear, mine honest friend?

Clown.   No, I hear not your honest friend; I hear you.   20

Cassio.   Prithee, keep up thy quillets.[307] There's a poor piece of gold for thee. If the gentlewoman that attends the general's wife be stirring, tell her there's one Cassio entreats her a little favour of speech: wilt thou do this?

Clown.   She is stirring, sir: if she will stir hither, I shall seem to notify unto her.

Cassio.   Do, good my friend.   *(Exit Clown.)*

(Enter Iago.)

                    In happy time, Iago.

Iago.   You have not been a-bed, then?

Cassio.   Why, no; the day had broke
Before we parted. I have made bold, Iago,
To send in to your wife; my suit to her
Is, that she will to virtuous Desdemona   30
Procure me some access.

Iago.   I'll send her to you presently;
And I'll devise a mean to draw the Moor
Out of the way, that your converse and business
May be more free.

Cassio.   I humbly thank you for 't.   *(Exit Iago.)*
                    I never knew
A Florentine more kind and honest.[308]

(Enter Emilia.)

Emilia.   Good-morrow, good lieutenant: I am sorry

---

[307] Quibbles.   [308] Cassio means that not even a fellow Florentine could behave to him in a friendlier fashion than does Iago.

For your displeasure,[309] but all will soon be well.
The general and his wife are talking of it,
And she speaks for you stoutly: the Moor replies   40
That he you hurt is of great fame in Cyprus
And great affinity,[310] and that in wholesome wisdom
He might not but refuse you; but he protests he loves you,
And needs no other suitor but his likings
To take the safest occasion by the front[311]
To bring you in again.[312]

Cassio.   Yet, I beseech you,
If you think fit, or that it may be done,
Give me advantage of some brief discourse
With Desdemona alone.

Emilia.   Pray you, come in:
I will bestow you where you shall have time   50
To speak your bosom[313] freely.

Cassio.   I am much bound to you.   (*Exeunt.*)

Scene 2.   A Room in the Castle.

(*Enter Othello, Iago, and Gentlemen.*)

Othello.   These letters give, Iago, to the pilot,
And by him do my duties to the senate;
That done, I will be walking on the works;
Repair there to me.

Iago.   Well, my good lord, I'll do 't.

Othello.   This fortification, gentlemen, shall we see 't?

Gentlemen.   We'll wait upon your lordship.   (*Exeunt.*)

Scene 3.   Before the Castle.

(*Enter Desdemona, Cassio, and Emilia.*)

Desdemona.   Be thou assur'd, good Cassio, I will do
All my abilities in thy behalf.

Emilia.   Good madam, do: I warrant it grieves my husband,
As if the case were his.

Desdemona.   O! that's an honest fellow. Do not doubt, Cassio,
But I will have my lord and you again
As friendly as you were.

---

[309] Disgrace.   [310] Family connection.   [311] Forelock.   [312] Restore you (to Othello's favor).
[313] Heart, inmost thoughts.

Cassio. Bounteous madam,
 Whatever shall become of Michael Cassio,
 He's never any thing but your true servant.
Desdemona. I know 't; I thank you. You do love my lord; 10
 You have known him long; and be you well assur'd
 He shall in strangeness[314] stand no further off
 Than in a politic[315] distance.
Cassio. Ay, but, lady,
 That policy may either last so long,
 Or feed upon such nice[316] and waterish diet,
 Or breed itself so out of circumstance,
 That, I being absent and my place supplied,
 My general will forget my love and service.
Desdemona. Do not doubt[317] that; before Emilia here
 I give thee warrant of thy place. Assure thee, 20
 If I do vow a friendship, I'll perform it
 To the last article; my lord shall never rest;
 I'll watch him tame,[318] and talk him out of patience;
 His bed shall seem a school, his board a shrift;[319]
 I'll intermingle every thing he does
 With Cassio's suit. Therefore be merry, Cassio;
 For thy solicitor shall rather die
 Than give thy cause away.[320]

(Enter Othello and Iago, at a distance.)

Emilia. Madam, here comes my lord.
Cassio. Madam, I'll take my leave. 30
Desdemona. Why, stay, and hear me speak.
Cassio. Madam, not now; I am very ill at ease,
 Unfit for mine own purposes.
Desdemona. Well, do your discretion. *(Exit Cassio.)*
Iago. Ha! I like not that.
Othello. What dost thou say?
Iago. Nothing, my lord: or if — I know not what.
Othello. Was not that Cassio parted from my wife?
Iago. Cassio, my lord? No, sure, I cannot think it,
 That he would steal away so guilty-like,
 Seeing you coming.
Othello. I do believe 'twas he. 40
Desdemona. How now, my lord!

---

[314] Aloofness. [315] I.e., dictated by policy. [316] Slight, trivial. [317] Fear. [318] Outwatch him (i.e., keep him awake) till he submits. [319] Confessional. [320] Abandon your cause.

I have been talking with a suitor here,
A man that languishes in your displeasure.
Othello.   Who is 't you mean?
Desdemona.   Why, your lieutenant, Cassio. Good my lord,
If I have any grace or power to move you,
His present[321] reconciliation take;
For if he be not one that truly loves you,
That errs in ignorance and not in cunning,
I have no judgment in an honest face.   50
I prithee[322] call him back.
Othello.   Went he hence now?
Desdemona.   Ay, sooth; so humbled,
That he hath left part of his grief with me,
To suffer with him. Good love, call him back.
Othello.   Not now, sweet Desdemona; some other time.
Desdemona.   But shall 't be shortly?
Othello.   The sooner, sweet, for you.
Desdemona.   Shall 't be to-night at supper?
Othello.   No, not to-night.
Desdemona.   To-morrow dinner, then?
Othello.   I shall not dine at home;
I meet the captains at the citadel.
Desdemona.   Why, then, to-morrow night; or Tuesday morn;   60
Or Tuesday noon, or night; or Wednesday morn:
I prithee name the time, but let it not
Exceed three days: in faith, he's penitent;
And yet his trespass, in our common reason, —
Save that they say, the wars must make examples
Out of their best, — is not almost[323] a fault
To incur a private check.[324] When shall he come?
Tell me, Othello: I wonder in my soul,
What you could ask me, that I should deny,
Or stand so mammering[325] on. What! Michael Cassio,   70
That came a wooing with you, and so many a time,
When I have spoke of you dispraisingly,
Hath ta'en your part; to have so much to do
To bring him in! Trust me, I could do much, —
Othello.   Prithee, no more; let him come when he will;
I deny thee nothing.
Desdemona.   Why, this is not a boon;
'Tis as I should entreat you wear your gloves,
Or feed on nourishing dishes, or keep you warm,

---

[321] Immediate.   [322] Pray thee.   [323] Hardly.   [324] (Even) a private reprimand.   [325] Shilly-
shallying.

Or sue to you to do a peculiar profit
To your own person: nay, when I have a suit   80
Wherein I mean to touch your love indeed,
It shall be full of poise[326] and difficult weight,
And fearful to be granted.
Othello.   I will deny thee nothing:
Whereon, I do beseech thee, grant me this,
To leave me but a little to myself.
Desdemona.   Shall I deny you? no: farewell, my lord.
Othello.   Farewell, my Desdemona: I'll come to thee straight.
Desdemona.   Emilia, come. Be as your fancies teach you;
Whate'er you be, I am obedient.   *(Exit, with Emilia.)*
Othello.   Excellent wretch![327] Perdition catch my soul,   90
But I do love thee! and when I love thee not,
Chaos is[328] come again.
Iago.   My noble lord, —
Othello.   What dost thou say, Iago?
Iago.   Did Michael Cassio, when you woo'd my lady,
Know of your love?
Othello.   He did, from first to last: why dost thou ask?
Iago.   But for a satisfaction of my thought;
No further harm.
Othello.   Why of thy thought, Iago?
Iago.   I did not think he had been acquainted with her.
Othello.   O! yes; and went between us very oft.   100
Iago.   Indeed!
Othello.   Indeed! ay, indeed; discern'st thou aught in that?
Is he not honest?
Iago.   Honest, my lord?
Othello.   Honest! ay, honest.
Iago.   My lord, for aught I know.
Othello.   What dost thou think?
Iago.   Think, my lord!
Othello.   Think, my lord!
By heaven, he echoes me,
As if there were some monster in his thought
Too hideous to be shown. Thou dost mean something:
I heard thee say but now, thou lik'dst not that,
When Cassio left my wife; what didst not like?   110
And when I told thee he was of my counsel
In my whole course of wooing, thou criedst, 'Indeed!'
And didst contract and purse thy brow together,
As if thou then hadst shut up in thy brain

[326] Weight.   [327] Here, a term of endearment.   [328] Will have.

Some horrible conceit.[329] If thou dost love me,
Show me thy thought.
Iago.   My lord, you know I love you.
Othello.   I think thou dost;
And, for[330] I know thou art full of love and honesty,
And weigh'st thy words before thou givest them breath,
Therefore these stops[331] of thine fright me the more;   120
For such things in a false disloyal knave
Are tricks of custom, but in a man that's just
They are close dilations,[332] working from the heart
That passion cannot rule.
Iago.   For Michael Cassio,
I dare be sworn I think that he is honest.
Othello.   I think so too.
Iago.   Men should be what they seem;
Or those that be not, would they might seem none!
Othello.   Certain men should be what they seem.
Iago.   Why then, I think Cassio's an honest man.
Othello.   Nay, yet there's more in this.   130
I pray thee, speak to me as to thy thinkings,
As thou dost ruminate, and give thy worst of thoughts
The worst of words.
Iago.   Good my lord, pardon me;
Though I am bound to every act of duty,
I am not bound to[333] that all slaves are free to.
Utter my thoughts? Why, say they are vile and false;
As where's that palace whereinto foul things
Sometimes intrude not? who has a breast so pure
But some uncleanly apprehensions[334]
Keep leets and law-days,[335] and in session sit   140
With meditations lawful?
Othello.   Thou dost conspire against thy friend, Iago,
If thou but think'st him wrong'd, and mak'st his ear
A stranger to thy thoughts.
Iago.   I do beseech you,
Though I perchance am vicious in my guess, —
As, I confess, it is my nature's plague
To spy into abuses, and oft my jealousy[336]
Shapes faults that are not, — that your wisdom yet,
From one that so imperfectly conceits,
Would take no notice, nor build yourself a trouble   150

---

[329] Fancy.   [330] Because.   [331] Interruptions, hesitations.   [332] Secret (i.e., involuntary, unconscious) revelations.   [333] Bound with regard to.   [334] Conceptions.   [335] Sittings of the local
courts.   [336] Suspicion.   .

Out of his scattering and unsure observance.
It were not for your quiet nor your good,
Nor for my manhood, honesty, or wisdom,
To let you know my thoughts.
Othello.   What dost thou mean?
Iago.   Good name in man and woman, dear my lord,
Is the immediate jewel of [337] their souls:
Who steals my purse steals trash; 'tis something, nothing;
'Twas mine, 'tis his, and has been slave to thousands;
But he that filches from me my good name
Robs me of that which not enriches him,   160
And makes me poor indeed.
Othello.   By heaven, I'll know thy thoughts.
Iago.   You cannot, if my heart were in your hand;
Nor shall not, whilst 'tis in my custody.
Othello.   Ha!
Iago.   O! beware, my lord, of jealousy;
It is the green-ey'd monster which doth mock
The meat it feeds on: that cuckold [338] lives in bliss
Who, certain of his fate, loves not his wronger;
But, O! what damned minutes tells [339] he o'er
Who dotes, yet doubts; suspects, yet soundly loves!   170
Othello.   O misery!
Iago.   Poor and content is rich, and rich enough,
But riches fineless [340] is as poor as winter
To him that ever fears he shall be poor.
Good heaven, the souls of all my tribe defend
From jealousy!
Othello.   Why, why is this?
Think'st thou I'd make a life of jealousy,
To follow still the changes of the moon
With fresh suspicions? No; to be once in doubt
Is once to be resolved. Exchange me for a goat   180
When I shall turn the business of my soul
To such exsufflicate [341] and blown [342] surmises,
Matching thy inference. 'Tis not to make me jealous
To say my wife is fair, feeds well, loves company,
Is free of speech, sings, plays, and dances well;
Where virtue is, these are more virtuous:
Nor from mine own weak merits will I draw
The smallest fear, or doubt of her revolt;
For she had eyes, and chose me. No, Iago;

---

[337] Jewel closest to.   [338] Husband of an adulterous woman.   [339] Counts.   [340] Boundless.
[341] Spat out (?).   [342] Fly-blown.

I'll see before I doubt; when I doubt, prove; 190
And, on the proof, there is no more but this,
Away at once with love or jealousy!

Iago. I am glad of it; for now I shall have reason
To show the love and duty that I bear you
With franker spirit; therefore, as I am bound,
Receive it from me; I speak not yet of proof.
Look to your wife; observe her well with Cassio;
Wear your eye thus, not jealous nor secure:
I would not have your free and noble nature
Out of self-bounty[343] be abus'd; look to 't: 200
I know our country disposition[344] well;
In Venice they do let heaven see the pranks
They dare not show their husbands; their best conscience
Is not to leave 't undone, but keep 't unknown.

Othello. Dost thou say so?

Iago. She did deceive her father, marrying you;
And when she seem'd to shake and fear your looks,
She lov'd them most.

Othello. And so she did.

Iago. Why, go to,[345] then;
She that so young could give out such a seeming,
To seel her father's eyes up close as oak, 210
He thought 'twas witchcraft; but I am much to blame;
I humbly do beseech you of your pardon
For too much loving you.

Othello. I am bound to thee for ever.

Iago. I see, this hath a little dash'd your spirits.

Othello. Not a jot, not a jot.

Iago. I' faith, I fear it has.
I hope you will consider what is spoke
Comes from my love. But I do see you're mov'd;
I am to pray you not to strain my speech
To grosser issues nor to larger reach
Than to suspicion. 220

Othello. I will not.

Iago. Should you do so, my lord,
My speech should fall into such vile success
As my thoughts aim not at. Cassio's my worthy friend —
My lord, I see you're mov'd.

Othello. No, not much mov'd:
I do not think but Desdemona's honest.[346]

---

[343] Innate generosity. [344] I.e., that of Venice. [345] Colloquialism; here, something like "all right." [346] Chaste.

Iago.   Long live she so! and long live you to think so!

Othello.   And yet, how nature erring from itself, —

Iago.   Ay, there's the point: as, to be bold with you,
    Not to affect many proposed matches
    Of her own clime,[347] complexion, and degree,[348]   230
    Whereto, we see, in all things nature tends;
    Foh! one may smell in such, a will most rank,
    Foul disproportion, thoughts unnatural.
    But pardon me; I do not in position[349]
    Distinctly[350] speak of her, though I may fear
    Her will, recoiling[351] to her better judgment,
    May fall to match you with her country forms
    And happily[352] repent.

Othello.   Farewell, farewell:
    If more thou dost perceive, let me know more;
    Set on thy wife to observe. Leave me, Iago.   240

Iago.   My lord, I take my leave.   *(Going.)*

Othello.   Why did I marry? This honest creature, doubtless,
    Sees and knows more, much more, than he unfolds.

Iago *(returning).*   My lord, I would I might entreat your honour
    To scan this thing no further; leave it to time.
    Although 'tis fit that Cassio have his place,
    For, sure he fills it up with great ability,
    Yet, if you please to hold him off awhile,
    You shall by that perceive him and his means:
    Note if your lady strain his entertainment[353]   250
    With any strong or vehement importunity;
    Much will be seen in that. In the mean time,
    Let me be thought too busy[354] in my fears,
    As worthy cause I have to fear I am,
    And hold her free, I do beseech your honour.

Othello.   Fear not my government.

Iago.   I once more take my leave.   *(Exit.)*

Othello.   This fellow's of exceeding honesty,
    And knows all qualities, with a learned spirit,
    Of human dealings; if I do prove her haggard,[355]   260
    Though that her jesses[356] were my dear heart-strings,
    I'd whistle her off and let her down the wind,[357]
    To prey at fortune. Haply, for I am black,
    And have not those soft parts of conversation

---

[347] Country.   [348] Social rank.   [349] In definite assertion.   [350] Specifically.   [351] Reverting.
[352] Perhaps.   [353] Urge his re-welcome (i.e., to Othello's trust and favor).   [354] Meddlesome.
[355] Wild hawk.   [356] Leather thongs by which the hawk's legs were strapped to the trainer's wrist.
[357] I'd let her go and take care of herself.

That chamberers[358] have, or, for I am declin'd
Into the vale of years — yet that's not much —
She's gone, I am abus'd;[359] and my relief
Must be to loathe her. O curse of marriage!
That we can call these delicate creatures ours,
And not their appetites. I had rather be a toad,   270
And live upon the vapour of a dungeon,
Than keep a corner in the thing I love
For others' uses. Yet, 'tis the plague of great ones;
Prerogativ'd[360] are they less than the base;
'Tis destiny unshunnable, like death:
Even then this forked plague[361] is fated to us
When we do quicken.[362]
                Look! where she comes.
If she be false, O! then heaven mocks itself.
I'll not believe it.

(Re-enter Desdemona and Emilia.)

Desdemona.   How now, my dear Othello!
  Your dinner and the generous[363] islanders   280
  By you invited, do attend your presence.
Othello.   I am to blame.
Desdemona.   Why do you speak so faintly?
  Are you not well?
Othello.   I have a pain upon my forehead here.[364]
Desdemona.   Faith, that's with watching; 'twill away again:
  Let me but bind it hard, within this hour
  It will be well.
Othello.   Your napkin[365] is too little:

(She drops her handkerchief.)

  Let it alone. Come, I'll go in with you.
Desdemona.   I am very sorry that you are not well.

(Exeunt Othello and Desdemona.)

Emilia.   I am glad I have found this napkin;   290
  This was her first remembrance from the Moor;
  My wayward husband hath a hundred times

---

[358] Courtiers; or (more specifically) gallants, frequenters of bed chambers.   [359] Deceived.
[360] Privileged.   [361] I.e., the cuckold's proverbial horns.   [362] Are conceived, come alive.
[363] Noble.   [364] Othello again refers to his cuckoldom.   [365] Handkerchief.

Woo'd me to steal it, but she so loves the token,
For he conjur'd her she should ever keep it,
That she reserves it evermore about her
To kiss and talk to. I'll have the work ta'en out,[366]
And giv 't Iago:
What he will do with it heaven knows, not I;
I nothing but[367] to please his fantasy.[368]

(Enter Iago.)

Iago.   How now! what do you here alone?   300
Emilia.   Do not you chide; I have a thing for you.
Iago.   A thing for me? It is a common thing —
Emilia.   Ha!
Iago.   To have a foolish wife.
Emilia.   O! is that all? What will you give me now
   For that same handkerchief?
Iago.   What handkerchief?
Emilia.   What handkerchief!
   Why, that the Moor first gave to Desdemona:
   That which so often you did bid me steal.
Iago.   Hath stol'n it from her?   310
Emilia.   No, faith; she let it drop by negligence,
   And, to the advantage, I, being there, took 't up.
   Look, here it is.
Iago.   A good wench; give it me.
Emilia.   What will you do with 't, that you have been so earnest
   To have me filch it?
Iago.   Why, what's that to you?   *(Snatches it.)*
Emilia.   If it be not for some purpose of import
   Give 't me again; poor lady! she'll run mad
   When she shall lack it.
Iago.   Be not acknown on 't;[369] I have use for it.
   Go, leave me.   *(Exit Emilia.)*
   I will in Cassio's lodging lose this napkin,
   And let him find it; trifles light as air
   Are to the jealous confirmations strong
   As proofs of holy writ; this may do something.
   The Moor already changes with my poison:
   Dangerous conceits are in their natures poisons,
   Which at the first are scarce found to distaste,[370]

---

[366] Pattern copied.   [367] I.e., only want.   [368] Whim.   [369] You know nothing about it.
[370] Scarce can be tasted.

But with a little act upon the blood,
Burn like the mines of sulphur. I did say so:
Look! where he comes!

(Enter Othello.)

                    Not poppy,[371] nor mandragora,[372]   330
Nor all the drowsy syrups[373] of the world,
Shall ever medicine thee to that sweet sleep
Which thou ow'dst yesterday.
Othello.   Ha! ha! false to me?
Iago.   Why, how now, general! no more of that.
Othello.   Avaunt! be gone! thou hast set me on the rack;
  I swear 'tis better to be much abus'd
  Than but to know 't a little.
Iago.   How now, my lord!
Othello.   What sense had I of her stol'n hours of lust?
  I saw 't not, thought it not, it harm'd not me;
  I slept the next night well, was free and merry;   340
  I found not Cassio's kisses on her lips;
  He that is robb'd, not wanting what is stol'n,
  Let him not know 't, and he's not robb'd at all.
Iago.   I am sorry to hear this.
Othello.   I had been happy, if the general camp,[374]
  Pioners[375] and all, had tasted her sweet body,
  So[376] I had nothing known. O! now, for ever
  Farewell the tranquil mind; farewell content!
  Farewell the plumed troop and the big wars
  That make ambition virtue! O, farewell!   350
  Farewell the neighing steed, and the shrill trump,
  The spirit-stirring drum, the ear-piercing fife,
  The royal banner, and all quality,
  Pride, pomp, and circumstance[377] of glorious war!
  And, O you mortal engines,[378] whose rude throats
  The immortal Jove's dread clamours counterfeit,
  Farewell! Othello's occupation's gone!
Iago.   Is it possible, my lord?
Othello.   Villain, be sure thou prove my love a whore,
  Be sure of it; give me the ocular proof;   360
  Or, by the worth of mine eternal soul,
  Thou hadst been better have been born a dog
  Than answer my wak'd wrath.

---

[371] Opium.   [372] A soporific.   [373] I.e., soporifics.   [374] Whole army.   [375] Lowest rank of
manual laborers in the army.   [376] As long as.   [377] Pageantry.   [378] Deadly artillery.

Iago.   Is 't come to this?
Othello.   Make me to see 't; or, at the least, so prove it,
That the probation[379] bear no hinge nor loop
To hang a doubt on; or woe upon thy life!
Iago.   My noble lord —
Othello.   If thou dost slander her and torture me,
Never pray more; abandon all remorse;
On horror's head horrors accumulate;   370
Do deeds to make heaven weep, all earth amaz'd;
For nothing canst thou to damnation add
Greater than that.
Iago.   O grace! O heaven forgive me!
Are you a man! have you a soul or sense?
God be wi' you; take mine office. O wretched fool!
That liv'st to make thine honesty a vice.
O monstrous world! Take note, take note, O world!
To be direct and honest is not safe.
I thank you for this profit,[380] and, from hence
I'll love no friend, sith[381] love breeds such offence.   380
Othello.   Nay, stay; thou shouldst be honest.
Iago.   I should be wise; for honesty's a fool,
And loses that it works for.
Othello.   By the world,
I think my wife be honest and think she is not;
I think that thou art just and think thou art not.
I'll have some proof. Her name, that was as fresh
As Dian's[382] visage, is now begrim'd and black
As mine own face. If there be cords or knives,
Poison or fire or suffocating streams,
I'll not endure it. Would I were satisfied!   390
Iago.   I see, sir, you are eaten up with passion.
I do repent me that I put it to you.
You would be satisfied?
Othello.   Would! nay, I will.
Iago.   And may; but how? how satisfied, my lord?
Would you, the supervisor,[383] grossly gape on;
Behold her tupp'd?
Othello.   Death and damnation! O!
Iago.   It were a tedious[384] difficulty, I think,
To bring them to that prospect; damn them then,
If ever mortal eyes do see them bolster[385]

---

[379] Proof.   [380] Lesson.   [381] Since.   [382] Diana's, the goddess of the moon.   [383] Observer.
[384] Laborious.   [385] Lie together.

More[386] than their own! What then? how then?   400
What shall I say? Where's satisfaction?
It is impossible you should see this,
Were they as prime[387] as goats, as hot as monkeys,
As salt as wolves in pride,[388] and fools as gross
As ignorance made drunk; but yet, I say,
If imputation, and strong circumstances,
Which lead directly to the door of truth,
Will give you satisfaction, you may have it.

Othello.   Give me a living reason she's disloyal.

Iago.   I do not like the office;   410
But, sith I am enter'd in this cause so far,
Prick'd to 't by foolish honesty and love,
I will go on. I lay with Cassio lately;
And, being troubled with a raging tooth,
I could not sleep.
There are a kind of men so loose of soul
That in their sleeps will mutter their affairs;
One of this kind is Cassio.
In sleep I heard him say, 'Sweet Desdemona,
Let us be wary, let us hide our loves!'   420
And then, sir, would he gripe[389] and wring my hand,
Cry, 'O, sweet creature!' and then kiss me hard,
As if he pluck'd up kisses by the roots,
That grew upon my lips; then laid his leg
Over my thigh, and sigh'd, and kiss'd; and then
Cried, 'Cursed fate, that gave thee to the Moor!'

Othello.   O monstrous! monstrous!

Iago.   Nay, this was but his dream.

Othello.   But this denoted a foregone conclusion:[390]
'Tis a shrewd doubt,[391] though it be but a dream.

Iago.   And this may help to thicken other proofs   430
That do demonstrate thinly.

Othello.   I'll tear her all to pieces.

Iago.   Nay, but be wise; yet we see nothing done;
She may be honest yet. Tell me but this:
Have you not sometimes seen a handkerchief
Spotted with strawberries in your wife's hand?

Othello.   I gave her such a one; 'twas my first gift.

Iago.   I know not that; but such a handkerchief —
I am sure it was your wife's — did I to-day
See Cassio wipe his beard with.

---

[386] Other.   [387] Lustful.   [388] Heat.   [389] Seize.   [390] Previous consummation.   [391] (1) Cursed, (2) Acute, suspicion.

Othello.   If it be that, —

Iago.   If it be that, or any that was hers,   440
It speaks against her with the other proofs.

Othello.   O! that the slave had forty thousand lives;
One is too poor, too weak for my revenge.
Now do I see 'tis true. Look here, Iago;
All my fond love thus do I blow to heaven:
'Tis gone.
Arise, black vengeance, from the hollow hell!
Yield up, O love! thy crown and hearted throne
To tyrannous hate. Swell, bosom, with thy fraught,[392]
For 'tis of aspics'[393] tongues!

Iago.   Yet be content.[394]   450

Othello.   O! blood, blood, blood!

Iago.   Patience, I say; your mind, perhaps, may change.

Othello.   Never, Iago. Like to the Pontic sea,[395]
Whose icy current and compulsive course
Ne'er feels retiring ebb, but keeps due on
To the Propontic and the Hellespont,[396]
Even so my bloody thoughts, with violent pace,
Shall ne'er look back, ne'er ebb to humble love,
Till that a capable[397] and wide revenge
Swallow them up.   *(Kneels.)*
                    Now, by yond marble heaven,   460
In the due reverence of a sacred vow
I here engage my words.

Iago.   Do not rise yet.   *(Kneels.)*
Witness, you ever-burning lights above!
You elements that clip[398] us round about!
Witness, that here Iago doth give up
The execution of his wit, hands, heart,
To wrong'd Othello's service! Let him command,
And to obey shall be in me remorse,[399]
What bloody business ever.[400]   *(They rise.)*

Othello.   I greet thy love,
Not with vain thanks, but with acceptance bounteous,   470
And will upon the instant put thee to 't:
Within these three days let me hear thee say
That Cassio 's not alive.

Iago.   My friend is dead; 'tis done at your request:
But let her live.

---

[392] Burden.   [393] Poisonous snakes.   [394] Patient.   [395] The Black Sea.   [396] The Sea of Marmara, the Dardanelles.   [397] Comprehensive.   [398] Encompass.   [399] Probably a corrupt line; the meaning appears to be: "to obey shall be my solemn obligation."   [400] Soever.

Othello.   Damn her, lewd minx! O, damn her!
  Come, go with me apart; I will withdraw.
  To furnish me with some swift means of death
  For the fair devil. Now art thou my lieutenant.
Iago.   I am your own for ever.   (*Exeunt.*)

Scene 4.   Before the Castle.

(*Enter Desdemona, Emilia, and Clown.*)

Desdemona.   Do you know, sirrah,[401] where Lieutenant Cassio lies?[402]
Clown.   I dare not say he lies any where.
Desdemona.   Why, man?
Clown.   He is a soldier; and for one to say a soldier lies, is stabbing.[403]
Desdemona.   Go to;[404] where lodges he?
Clown.   To tell you where he lodges is to tell you where I lie.
Desdemona.   Can anything be made of this?
Clown.   I know not where he lodges, and for me to devise[405] a lodging, and say
  he lies here or he lies there, were to lie in mine own throat.
Desdemona.   Can you inquire him out, and be edified by report?   10
Clown.   I will catechize the world for him; that is, make questions, and by
  them answer.
Desdemona.   Seek him, bid him come hither; tell him I have moved my lord
  in his behalf, and hope all will be well.
Clown.   To do this is within the compass of man's wit, and therefore I will
  attempt the doing it.   (*Exit.*)
Desdemona.   Where should I lose that handkerchief, Emilia?
Emilia.   I know not, madam.
Desdemona.   Believe me, I had rather have lost my purse
  Full of cruzadoes;[406] and, but my noble Moor   20
  Is true of mind, and made of no such baseness
  As jealous creatures are, it were enough
  To put him to ill thinking.
Emilia.   Is he not jealous?
Desdemona.   Who! he? I think the sun where he was born
  Drew all such humours from him.
Emilia.   Look! where he comes.
Desdemona.   I will not leave him now till Cassio
  Be call'd to him.

(*Enter Othello.*)

---

[401] Common form of address to inferiors.   [402] Lives.   [403] I.e., is cause for stabbing.
[404] Here apparently: "Come on!"   [405] Invent.   [406] Portuguese gold coins.

Desdemona.   How is 't with you, my lord?

Othello.   Well, my good lady. (*Aside.*) O! hardness to dissemble.
How do you, Desdemona?

Desdemona.   Well, my good lord.

Othello.   Give me your hand. This hand is moist,[407] my lady.   30

Desdemona.   It yet has felt no age nor known no sorrow.

Othello.   This argues fruitfulness and liberal[408] heart;
Hot, hot, and moist; this hand of yours requires
A sequester[409] from liberty, fasting and prayer,
Much castigation, exercise devout;
For here 's a young and sweating devil here,
That commonly rebels. 'Tis a good hand,
A frank one.

Desdemona.   You may, indeed, say so;
For 'twas that hand that gave away my heart.   40

Othello.   A liberal hand; the hearts of old gave hands,
But our new heraldry[410] is hands not hearts.

Desdemona.   I cannot speak of this. Come now, your promise.

Othello.   What promise, chuck?[411]

Desdemona.   I have sent to bid Cassio come speak with you.

Othello.   I have a salt and sorry rheum offends me.
Lend me thy handkerchief.

Desdemona.   Here, my lord.

Othello.   That which I gave you.

Desdemona.   I have it not about me.

Othello.   Not?

Desdemona.   No, indeed, my lord.

Othello.   That is a fault.
That handkerchief   50
Did an Egyptian[412] to my mother give;
She was a charmer,[413] and could almost read
The thoughts of people; she told her, while she kept it,
'Twould make her amiable[414] and subdue my father
Entirely to her love, but if she lost it
Or made a gift of it, my father's eye
Should hold her loathed, and his spirits should hunt
After new fancies.[415] She dying gave it me;
And bid me, when my fate would have me wive,
To give it her. I did so; and take heed on 't;   60
Make it a darling like your precious eye;

---

[407] A supposed symptom of a lustful nature.   [408] With overtones of: too free, loose.   [409] Separation.   [410] I.e., new heraldic symbolism (Othello means that the new way is not to give the heart together with the hand).   [411] Common term of endearment.   [412] Gypsy.   [413] Sorceress.   [414] Lovable, desirable.   [415] Loves.

To lose 't or give 't away, were such perdition
As nothing else could match.
Desdemona.   Is 't possible?
Othello.   'Tis true; there 's magic in the web of it;
A sibyl,[416] that had number'd in the world
The sun to course two hundred compasses,
In her prophetic fury sew'd the work;
The worms were hallow'd that did breed the silk,
And it was dy'd in mummy[417] which the skilful
Conserv'd of maidens' hearts.
Desdemona.   Indeed! is 't true?   70
Othello.   Most veritable; therefore look to 't well.
Desdemona.   Then would to heaven that I had never seen it!
Othello.   Ha! wherefore?
Desdemona.   Why do you speak so startingly and rash?
Othello.   Is 't lost? is 't gone? speak, is it out o' the way?
Desdemona.   Heaven bless us!
Othello.   Say you?
Desdemona.   It is not lost; but what an if[418] it were?
Othello.   How!
Desdemona.   I say, it is not lost.
Othello.   Fetch 't, let me see 't!   80
Desdemona.   Why, so I can, sir, but I will not now.
   This is a trick to put me from my suit:
   Pray you let Cassio be receiv'd again.
Othello.   Fetch me the handkerchief; my mind misgives.
Desdemona.   Come, come;
   You'll never meet a more sufficient[419] man.
Othello.   The handkerchief!
Desdemona.   I pray, talk[420] me of Cassio.
Othello.   The handkerchief!
Desdemona.   A man that all his time
   Hath founded his good fortunes on your love,
   Shar'd dangers with you, —   90
Othello.   The handkerchief!
Desdemona.   In sooth, you are to blame.
Othello.   Away!   (*Exit.*)
Emilia.   Is not this man jealous?
Desdemona.   I ne'er saw this before.
   Sure, there's some wonder in this handkerchief;
   I am most unhappy in the loss of it.

---

[416] Prophetess.   [417] Drug (medicinal or magic) derived from embalmed bodies.   [418] If.
[419] Adequate.   [420] Talk to.

Emilia. 'Tis not a year or two shows us a man;
    They are all but stomachs, and we all but[421] food;
    They eat us hungerly, and when they are full   100
    They belch us. Look you! Cassio and my husband.

(Enter Iago and Cassio.)

Iago. There is no other way; 'tis she must do 't:
    And, lo! the happiness;[422] go and importune her.
Desdemona. How now, good Cassio! what 's the news with you?
Cassio. Madam, my former suit: I do beseech you
    That by your virtuous means I may again
    Exist, and be a member of his love
    Whom I with all the office[423] of my heart
    Entirely honour; I would not be delay'd.
    If my offence be of such mortal kind   110
    That nor my service past, nor present sorrows,
    Nor purpos'd merit in futurity,
    Can ransom me into his love again,
    But to know so must be my benefit;
    So shall I clothe me in a forc'd content,
    And shut myself up in some other course
    To fortune's alms.
Desdemona.   Alas! thrice-gentle Cassio!
    My advocation is not now in tune;
    My lord is not my lord, nor should I know him,
    Were he in favour[424] as in humour alter'd.   120
    So help me every spirit sanctified,
    As I have spoken for you all my best
    And stood within the blank of[425] his displeasure
    For my free speech. You must awhile be patient;
    What I can do I will, and more I will
    Than for myself I dare: let that suffice you.
Iago. Is my lord angry?
Emilia.   He went hence but now,
    And certainly in strange unquietness.
Iago. Can he be angry? I have seen the cannon,
    When it hath blown his ranks[426] into the air,   130
    And, like the devil, from his very arm
    Puff'd his own brother; and can he be angry?

---

[421] Only . . . only.   [422] "What luck!"   [423] Duty.   [424] Appearance.   [425] As the target for.
[426] I.e., his soldiers.

Something of moment[427] then; I will go meet him;
There's matter in 't indeed, if he be angry.
Desdemona.   I prithee, do so. *(Exit Iago.)* Something, sure, of state,[428]
Either from Venice, or some unhatch'd[429] practice
Made demonstrable here in Cyprus to him,
Hath puddled[430] his clear spirit; and, in such cases
Men's natures wrangle with inferior things,
Though great ones are their object. 'Tis even so;   140
For let our finger ache, and it indues[431]
Our other healthful members even to that sense
Of pain. Nay, we must think men are not gods,
Nor of them look for such observancy[432]
As fits the bridal.[433] Beshrew me much, Emilia,
I was — unhandsome warrior as I am —
Arraigning his unkindness with[434] my soul;
But now I find I had suborn'd the witness,[435]
And he 's indicted falsely.
Emilia.   Pray heaven it be state matters, as you think,   150
And no conception,[436] nor no jealous toy[437]
Concerning you.
Desdemona.   Alas the day! I never gave him cause.
Emilia.   But jealous souls will not be answer'd so;
They are not ever jealous for the cause,
But jealous for they are jealous; 'tis a monster
Begot upon itself, born on itself.
Desdemona.   Heaven keep that monster from Othello's mind!
Emilia.   Lady, amen.
Desdemona.   I will go seek him. Cassio, walk hereabout;   160
If I do find him fit, I'll move your suit
And seek to effect it to my uttermost.
Cassio.   I humbly thank your ladyship.

(Exeunt Desdemona and Emilia.)

(Enter Bianca.)

Bianca.   Save you, friend Cassio!
Cassio.   What make you from home?
How is it with you, my most fair Bianca?
I' faith, sweet love, I was coming to your house.

---

[427] Important.   [428] Public affairs.   [429] Abortive or budding plot.   [430] Muddied.   [431] Brings, leads.   [432] Attention.   [433] Wedding.   [434] To.   [435] I.e., caused my soul to bring in wrong charges.   [436] Fancy, supposition.   [437] Fancy.

Bianca.   And I was going to your lodging, Cassio.
   What! keep a week away? seven days and nights?
   Eight score eight hours? and lovers' absent hours,
   More tedious than the dial eight score times?   170
   O weary reckoning!
Cassio.   Pardon me, Bianca,
   I have this while with leaden thoughts been press'd;
   But I shall, in a more continuate[438] time,
   Strike off[439] this score of absence. Sweet Bianca,

(Giving her Desdemona's handkerchief.)

   Take me this work out.
Bianca.   O Cassio! whence came this?
   This is some token from a newer friend;
   To the felt absence now I feel a cause;
   Is 't come to this? Well, well.
Cassio.   Go to, woman!
   Throw your vile guesses in the devil's teeth,
   From whence you have them. You are jealous now   180
   That this is from some mistress, some remembrance:
   No, in good troth, Bianca.
Bianca.   Why, whose is it?
Cassio.   I know not, sweet; I found it in my chamber.
   I like the work well; ere it be demanded, —[440]
   As like enough it will, — I'd have it copied;
   Take it and do 't; and leave me for this time.
Bianca.   Leave you! wherefore?
Cassio.   I do attend here on[441] the general,
   And think it no addition,[442] nor my wish,
   To have him see me woman'd.
Bianca.   Why, I pray you?   190
Cassio.   Not that I love you not.
Bianca.   But that you do not love me.
   I pray you, bring me on the way a little
   And say if I shall see you soon at night.
Cassio.   'Tis but a little way that I can bring you,
   For I attend here; but I'll see you soon.
Bianca.   'Tis very good; I must be circumstanc'd.[443]   *(Exeunt.)*

---

[438] Uninterrupted.   [439] Cancel (i.e., make up for).   [440] Asked for.   [441] Wait for.   [442] Advantage, credit.   [443] Governed by circumstances.

Act IV

Scene 1.   Cyprus. Before the Castle.

(Enter Othello and Iago.)

Iago.   Will you think so?
Othello.   Think so, Iago!
Iago.   What!
  To kiss in private?
Othello.   An unauthoriz'd kiss.
Iago.   Or to be naked with her friend a-bed
  An hour or more, not meaning any harm?
Othello.   Naked a-bed, Iago, and not mean harm?
  It is hypocrisy against the devil:[444]
  They that mean virtuously, and yet do so,
  The devil their virtue tempts, and they tempt heaven.
Iago.   If they do nothing, 'tis a venial slip;
  But if I give my wife a handkerchief, —   10
Othello.   What then?
Iago.   Why, then, 'tis hers, my lord; and, being hers,
  She may, I think, bestow 't on any man.
Othello.   She is protectress of her honour too;
  May she give that?
Iago.   Her honour is an essence that 's not seen;
  They have it very oft that have it not:[445]
  But for the handkerchief, —
Othello.   By heaven, I would most gladly have forgot it: —
  Thou said'st, — O! it comes o'er my memory,   20
  As doth the raven[446] o'er the infected house,
  Boding to all, — he had my handkerchief.
Iago.   Ay, what of that?
Othello.   That's not so good now.
Iago.   What,
  If I had said I had seen him do you wrong?
  Or heard him say, as knaves be such abroad,[447]
  Who having, by their own importunate suit,
  Or voluntary dotage[448] of some mistress,
  Convinced or supplied them,[449] cannot choose
  But they must blab.

---

[444] I.e., by not committing the sin which the situation invites.   [445] I.e., some unchaste women are thought chaste.   [446] (1) A bad omen, (2) A carrier of the plague.   [447] As there are some such in the world.   [448] Foolish affection.   [449] Overcome (their reluctance) or satisfied (their desires).

Othello.   Hath he said any thing?

Iago.   He hath, my lord; but be you well assur'd,   30
No more than he'll unswear.

Othello.   What hath he said?

Iago.   Faith, that he did — I know not what he did.

Othello.   What? what?

Iago.   Lie —

Othello.   With her?

Iago.   With her, on her; what you will.

Othello.   Lie with her; lie on her! We say, lie on her, when they belie her. Lie with her! that's fulsome. Handkerchief, — confessions, — handkerchief! To confess, and be hanged for his labour. First, to be hanged, and then to confess: I tremble at it. Nature would not invest herself in such shadowing passion without some instruction.[450] It is not words that shake me thus. Pish! Noses, ears, and lips. Is it possible? — Confess! — Handkerchief! — O devil!

(Falls in a trance.)

Iago.   Work on,
My medicine, work! Thus credulous fools are caught;
And many worthy and chaste dames even thus,
All guiltless, meet reproach. What, ho! my lord!
My lord, I say! Othello!

(Enter Cassio.)

                    How now, Cassio!

Cassio.   What's the matter?

Iago.   My lord is fallen into an epilepsy;[451]
This is his second fit; he had one yesterday.

Cassio.   Rub him about the temples.

Iago.   No, forbear;   50
The lethargy[452] must have his quiet course,
If not, he foams at mouth, and by and by
Breaks out to savage madness. Look! he stirs;
Do you withdraw yourself a little while,
He will recover straight; when he is gone,
I would on great occasion[453] speak with you.   *(Exit Cassio.)*
How is it, general? have you not hurt your head?

Othello.   Dost thou mock me?[454]

Iago.   I mock you! no, by heaven.
Would you would bear your fortune like a man!

---

[450] I would not fall into such passion unless there were some real grounds for it.   [451] Seizure, fit.   [452] Coma.   [453] Important matter.   [454] Another allusion to the cuckold's horns.

Othello.   A horned man's a monster and a beast.   60

Iago.   There's many a beast then, in a populous city,
And many a civil[455] monster.

Othello.   Did he confess it?

Iago.   Good sir, be a man;
Think every bearded fellow that's but yok'd
May draw[456] with you; there's millions now alive
That nightly lie in those unproper[457] beds
Which they dare swear peculiar;[458] your case is better.
O! 'tis the spite of hell, the fiend's arch-mock,
To lip[459] a wanton in a secure[460] couch,
And to suppose her chaste. No, let me know;   70
And knowing what I am, I know what she shall be.

Othello.   O! thou art wise; 'tis certain.

Iago.   Stand you awhile apart;
Confine yourself but in a patient list.[461]
Whilst you were here o'erwhelmed with your grief, —
A passion most unsuiting such a man, —
Cassio came hither; I shifted him away,
And laid good 'scuse upon your ecstasy;[462]
Bade him anon return and here speak with me;
The which he promis'd. Do but encave yourself,
And mark the fleers, the gibes, and notable scorns,   80
That dwell in every region of his face;
For I will make him tell the tale anew,
Where, how, how oft, how long ago, and when
He hath, and is again to cope[463] your wife:
I say, but mark his gesture. Marry, patience;
Or I shall say you are all in all in spleen,[464]
And nothing of a man.

Othello.   Dost thou hear, Iago?
I will be found most cunning in my patience;
But — dost thou hear? — most bloody.

Iago.   That's not amiss:
But yet keep time[465] in all. Will you withdraw?   *(Othello goes apart.)*
Now will I question Cassio of Bianca,
A housewife[466] that by selling her desires
Buys herself bread and clothes; it is a creature
That dotes on Cassio; as 'tis the strumpet's plague
To beguile many and be beguil'd by one.

---

[455] Citizen.   [456] I.e., pull the burden of cuckoldom.   [457] Not exclusively their own.   [458] Exclusively their own.   [459] Kiss.   [460] I.e., without suspicion of having a rival.   [461] Bounds of patience.   [462] Derangement, trance.   [463] Close with.   [464] Completely overcome by passion.   [465] Maintain control.   [466] Hussy.

He, when he hears of her, cannot refrain
From the excess of laughter. Here he comes:

(Re-enter Cassio.)

As he shall smile, Othello shall go mad;
And his unbookish[467] jealousy must construe
Poor Cassio's smiles, gestures, and light behaviour   100
Quite in the wrong. How do you now, lieutenant?

Cassio.   The worser that you give me the addition[468]
Whose want[469] even kills me.

Iago.   Ply Desdemona well, and you are sure on 't.
(Speaking lower.) Now, if this suit lay in Bianca's power,
How quickly should you speed!

Cassio.   Alas! poor caitiff![470]

Othello.   Look! how he laughs already!

Iago.   I never knew woman love man so.

Cassio.   Alas! poor rogue, I think i' faith, she loves me.

Othello.   Now he denies it faintly, and laughs it out.   110

Iago.   Do you hear, Cassio?

Othello.   Now he importunes him
To tell it o'er: go to; well said, well said.

Iago.   She gives it out that you shall marry her;
Do you intend it?

Cassio.   Ha, ha, ha!

Othello.   Do you triumph, Roman?[471] do you triumph?

Cassio.   I marry her! what? a customer?[472] I prithee, bear some charity to my
wit;[473] do not think it so unwholesome. Ha, ha, ha!

Othello.   So, so, so, so. They laugh that win.[474]

Iago.   Faith, the cry goes that you shall marry her.   120

Cassio.   Prithee, say true.

Iago.   I am a very villain else.

Othello.   Have you scored me?[475] Well.

Cassio.   This is the monkey's own giving out: she is persuaded I will marry her,
out of her own love and flattery, not out of my promise.

Othello.   Iago beckons me;[476] now he begins the story.

Cassio.   She was here even now; she haunts me in every place. I was the other
day talking on the sea-bank with certain Venetians, and thither comes this
bauble,[477] and, by this hand, she falls me thus about my neck; —

Othello.   Crying, 'O dear Cassio!' as it were; his gesture imports it.   130

---

[467] Unpracticed, naive.   [468] Title.   [469] The want of which.   [470] Wretch.   [471] I.e., one who
triumphs (?).   [472] Courtesan, prostitute.   [473] Give me credit for some sense.   [474] "He who
laughs last laughs longest" (?).   [475] Wounded, defaced (?); or: settled my account (?).   [476] Signals.   [477] Plaything.

Cassio. So hangs and lolls and weeps upon me; so hales[478] and pulls me; ha, ha, ha!

Othello. Now he tells how she plucked him to my chamber. O! I see that nose of yours, but not the dog I shall throw it to.

Cassio. Well, I must leave her company.

Iago. Before me![479] look, where she comes.

Cassio. 'Tis such another fitchew![480] marry, a perfumed one.

(Enter Bianca.)

What do you mean by this haunting of me?

Bianca. Let the devil and his dam haunt you! What did you mean by that same handkerchief you gave me even now? I was a fine fool to take it. I must take out the work! A likely piece of work, that you should find it in your chamber, and not know who left it there! This is some minx's token, and I must take out the work! There, give it your hobby-horse;[481] wheresoever you had it I'll take out no work on 't.

Cassio. How now, my sweet Bianca! how now, how now!

Othello. By heaven, that should be[482] my handkerchief!

Bianca. An you'll come to supper to-night, you may; an you will not, come when you are next prepared[483] for.　　　　　　　　　　　　　　　*(Exit.)*

Iago. After her, after her.

Cassio. Faith, I must; she'll rail in the street else.　　　　　　　　　150

Iago. Will you sup there?

Cassio. Faith, I intend so.

Iago. Well, I may chance to see you, for I would very fain[484] speak with you.

Cassio. Prithee come; will you?

Iago. Go to; say no more.　　　　　　　　　　　　　　　*(Exit Cassio.)*

Othello *(advancing).* How shall I murder him, Iago?

Iago. Did you perceive how he laughed at his vice?

Othello. O! Iago!

Iago. And did you see the handkerchief?

Othello. Was that mine?　　　　　　　　　　　　　　　160

Iago. Yours, by this hand; and to see how he prizes the foolish woman your wife! she gave it him, and he hath given it his whore.

Othello. I would have him nine years a-killing. A fine woman! a fair woman! a sweet woman!

Iago. Nay, you must forget that.

Othello. Ay, let her rot, and perish, and be damned to-night; for she shall not live. No, my heart is turned to stone; I strike it, and it hurts my hand. O! the

---

[478] Hauls.　　[479] An exclamation of surprise.　　[480] Polecat, noted both for its strong smell and for its lechery.　　[481] Harlot.　　[482] I.e., I think that is.　　[483] Expected (Bianca means that if he does not come that night, she will never want to see him again).　　[484] Gladly.

world hath not a sweeter creature; she might lie by an emperor's side and
command him tasks.

Iago. Nay, that's not your way.[485] 170

Othello. Hang her! I do but say what she is. So delicate with her needle! An
admirable musician! O, she will sing the savageness out of a bear. Of so high
and plenteous wit and invention!

Iago. She's the worse for all this.

Othello. O! a thousand, a thousand times. And then, of so gentle a condition![486]

Iago. Ay, too gentle.[487]

Othello. Nay, that's certain; — but yet the pity of it, Iago!
O! Iago, the pity of it, Iago!

Iago. If you are so fond over her iniquity, give her patent to offend; for, if it
touch not you, it comes near nobody.

Othello. I will chop her into messes.[488] Cuckold me!

Iago. O! 'tis foul in her.

Othello. With mine officer!

Iago. That's fouler.

Othello. Get me some poison, Iago; this night: I'll not expostulate with her,
lest her body and beauty unprovide my mind again.[489] This night, Iago.

Iago. Do it not with poison, strangle her in her bed, even the bed she hath
contaminated.

Othello. Good, good; the justice of it pleases; very good. 190

Iago. And for Cassio, let me be his undertaker;[490] you shall hear more by
midnight.

Othello. Excellent good. (*A trumpet within.*) What trumpet is that same?

Iago. Something from Venice, sure. 'Tis Lodovico,
Come from the duke; and see, your wife is with him.

(*Enter Lodovico, Desdemona, and Attendants.*)

Lodovico. God save you, worthy general!

Othello.   With all my heart, sir.

Lodovico. The duke and senators of Venice greet you.

(*Gives him a packet.*)

Othello. I kiss the instrument of their pleasures.

(*Opens the packet, and reads.*)

---

[485] Proper course. [486] So much the high-born lady. [487] I.e., yielding. [488] Bits. [489] Unsettle my intention. [490] Dispatcher.

Desdemona.   And what's the news, good cousin Lodovico?

Iago.   I am very glad to see you, signior;   200
  Welcome to Cyprus.

Lodovico.   I thank you. How does Lieutenant Cassio?

Iago.   Lives, sir.

Desdemona.   Cousin, there's fall'n between him and my lord
  An unkind[491] breach; but you shall make all well.

Othello.   Are you sure of that?

Desdemona.   My lord?

Othello (reads).   'This fail you not to do, as you will' —

Lodovico.   He did not call; he's busy in the paper.
  Is there division[492] twixt my lord and Cassio?   210

Desdemona.   A most unhappy one; I would do much
  To atone[493] them, for the love I bear to Cassio.

Othello.   Fire and brimstone!

Desdemona.   My lord?

Othello.   Are you wise?

Desdemona.   What! is he angry?

Lodovico.   May be the letter mov'd him;
  For, as I think, they do command him home,
  Deputing Cassio in his government.

Desdemona.   Trust me, I am glad on 't.

Othello.   Indeed!

Desdemona.   My lord?

Othello.   I am glad to see you mad.

Desdemona.   Why, sweet Othello?

Othello.   Devil!   (Strikes her.)

Desdemona.   I have not deserved this.   220

Lodovico.   My lord, this would not be believ'd in Venice,
  Though I should swear I saw 't; 'tis very much;
  Make her amends, she weeps.

Othello.   O devil, devil!
  If that the earth could teem with woman's tears,
  Each drop she falls[494] would prove a crocodile.[495]
  Out of my sight!

Desdemona.   I will not stay to offend you.   (Going.)

Lodovico.   Truly, an obedient lady;
  I do beseech your lordship, call her back.

Othello.   Mistress!

Desdemona.   My lord?

Othello.   What would you with her, sir?   230

Lodovico.   Why, I, my lord?

---

[491] Unnatural.   [492] Estrangement.   [493] Reconcile.   [494] Lets fall.   [495] The crocodile's tears
were supposed to be hypocritical.

Othello.   Ay; you did wish that I would make her turn:
Sir, she can turn, and turn, and yet go on,
And turn again; and she can weep, sir, weep;
And she's obedient, as you say, obedient,
Very obedient. Proceed you in your tears.
Concerning this, sir — O well-painted passion! —
I am commanded home. Get you away;
I'll send for you anon. Sir, I obey the mandate,
And will return to Venice. Hence! avaunt![496]   *(Exit Desdemona.)*
Cassio shall have my place. And, sir, to-night,
I do entreat that we may sup together;
You are welcome, sir, to Cyprus. Goats and monkeys!   *(Exit.)*
Lodovico.   Is this the noble Moor whom our full senate
Call all-in-all sufficient? is this the noble nature
Whom passion could not shake? whose solid virtue
The shot of accident nor dart of chance
Could neither graze nor pierce?
Iago.   He is much chang'd.
Lodovico.   Are his wits safe? is he not light of brain?
Iago.   He's that he is; I may not breathe my censure.   250
What he might be, if, what he might, he is not,
I would to heaven he were![497]
Lodovico.   What! strike his wife!
Iago.   Faith, that was not so well; yet would I knew
That stroke would prove the worst!
Lodovico.   Is it his use?
Or did the letters work upon his blood,
And new-create this fault?
Iago.   Alas, alas!
It is not honesty in me to speak
What I have seen and known. You shall observe him,
And his own courses[498] will denote him so
That I may save my speech. Do but go after   260
And mark how he continues.
Lodovico.   I am sorry that I am deceiv'd in him.   *(Exeunt.)*

Scene 2.   A Room in the Castle.

(Enter Othello and Emilia.)

Othello.   You have seen nothing, then?
Emilia.   Nor ever heard, nor ever did suspect.

---

[496] Begone!   [497] Another of Iago's gnomic speeches; perhaps approximately: "If now he is not himself, I wish he would be what he could be!"   [498] Actions.

Othello.   Yes, you have seen Cassio and her together.
Emilia.   But then I saw no harm, and then I heard
   Each syllable that breath made up between them.
Othello.   What! did they never whisper?
Emilia.   Never, my lord.
Othello.   Nor send you out o' the way?
Emilia.   Never.
Othello.   To fetch her fan, her gloves, her mask, nor nothing?[499]
Emilia.   Never, my lord.   10
Othello.   That's strange.
Emilia.   I durst, my lord, to wager she is honest,
   Lay down my soul at stake: if you think other,
   Remove your thought; it doth abuse your bosom.
   If any wretch have put this in your head,
   Let heaven requite it with the serpent's curse!
   For, if she be not honest, chaste, and true,
   There's no man happy; the purest of their wives
   Is foul as slander.
Othello.   Bid her come hither; go.   *(Exit Emilia.)*
   She says enough; yet she 's a simple[500] bawd   20
   That cannot say as much. This is a subtle whore,
   A closet lock and key of villainous secrets;
   And yet she 'll kneel and pray; I have seen her do 't.

(Re-enter Emilia with Desdemona.)

Desdemona.   My lord, what is your will?
Othello.   Pray, chuck, come hither.
Desdemona.   What is your pleasure?
Othello.   Let me see your eyes;
   Look in my face.
Desdemona.   What horrible fancy 's this?
Othello *(to Emilia).*   Some of your function,[501] mistress;
   Leave procreants alone and shut the door;
   Cough or cry 'hem' if any body come;
   Your mystery,[502] your mystery; nay, dispatch.   *(Exit Emilia.)*
Desdemona.   Upon my knees, what doth your speech import?
   I understand a fury in your words.
   But not the words.
Othello.   Why, what art thou?
Desdemona.   Your wife, my lord; your true
   And loyal wife.

---

[499] Anything.   [500] Simpleminded.   [501] To your duty, business.   [502] Trade.

Othello.   Come, swear it, damn thyself;
   Lest, being like one of heaven, the devils themselves
   Should fear to seize thee; therefore be double-damn'd;
   Swear thou art honest.
Desdemona.   Heaven doth truly know it.
Othello.   Heaven truly knows that thou art false as hell.
Desdemona.   To whom, my lord? with whom? how am I false?   40
Othello.   Ah! Desdemona; away, away, away!
Desdemona.   Alas, the heavy day! — Why do you weep?
   Am I the motive of these tears, my lord?
   If haply you my father do suspect
   An instrument of this your calling back,
   Lay not your blame on me; if you have lost him,
   Why, I have lost him too.
Othello.   Had it pleas'd heaven
   To try me with affliction, had he rain'd
   All kinds of sores and shames on my bare head,
   Steep'd me in poverty to the very lips,   50
   Given to captivity me and my utmost hopes,
   I should have found in some part of my soul
   A drop of patience; but, alas! to make me
   The fixed figure for the time of scorn[503]
   To point his slow and moving finger at;
   Yet could I bear that too; well, very well:
   But there, where I have garner'd[504] up my heart,
   Where either I must live or bear no life,
   The fountain from the which my current runs
   Or else dries up; to be discarded thence!   60
   Or keep it as a cistern for foul toads
   To knot and gender in![505] Turn thy complexion there,[506]
   Patience, thou young and rose-lipp'd cherubin;
   Ay, there, look grim as hell!
Desdemona.   I hope my noble lord esteems me honest.
Othello.   O! ay; as summer flies are in the shambles,[507]
   That quicken even with blowing. O thou weed!
   Who art so lovely fair and smell'st so sweet
   That the sense aches at thee, would thou hadst ne'er been born.
Desdemona.   Alas! what ignorant sin have I committed?   70
Othello.   Was this fair paper, this most goodly book,
   Made to write 'whore' upon? What committed!
   Committed! O thou public commoner![508]
   I should make very forges of my cheeks,

---

[503] I.e., the scornful world.   [504] Stored.   [505] Bunch up and procreate.   [506] I.e., change your
color to suit the "cistern for foul toads."   [507] Slaughterhouse.   [508] Harlot.

That would to cinders burn up modesty,
Did I but speak thy deeds. What committed!
Heaven stops the nose at it and the moon winks,[509]
The bawdy wind that kisses all it meets
Is hush'd within the hollow mine of earth,
And will not hear it. What committed!   80
Impudent strumpet!
Desdemona.   By heaven, you do me wrong.
Othello.   Are not you a strumpet?
Desdemona.   No, as I am a Christian.
If to preserve this vessel for my lord
From any other foul unlawful touch
Be not to be a strumpet, I am none.
Othello.   What! not a whore?
Desdemona.   No, as I shall be sav'd.
Othello.   Is it possible?
Desdemona.   O! heaven forgive us.
Othello.   I cry you mercy,[510] then;
I took you for that cunning whore of Venice
That married with Othello. You, mistress,   90
That have the office opposite to Saint Peter,
And keep the gate of hell!

(Re-enter Emilia.)

                    You, you, ay, you!
We have done our course; there's money for your pains.
I pray you, turn the key and keep our counsel.   *(Exit.)*
Emilia.   Alas! what does this gentleman conceive?[511]
How do you, madam? how do you, my good lady?
Desdemona.   Faith, half asleep.
Emilia.   Good madam, what 's the matter with my lord?
Desdemona.   With who?
Emilia.   Why, with my lord, madam.   100
Desdemona.   Who is thy lord?
Emilia.   He that is yours, sweet lady.
Desdemona.   I have none; do not talk to me, Emilia;
I cannot weep, nor answer have I none,
But what should go by water.[512] Prithee, to-night
Lay on my bed my wedding sheets: remember:
And call thy husband hither.
Emilia.   Here is a change indeed!   *(Exit.)*

---

[509] Closes her eyes.   [510] Beg your pardon.   [511] Imagine.   [512] Be conveyed by means of tears.

Desdemona.   'Tis meet I should be us'd so, very meet.
How have I been behav'd, that he might stick
The small'st opinion on my least misuse?[513]

(Re-enter Emilia, with Iago.)

Iago.   What is your pleasure, madam? How is it with you?   110
Desdemona.   I cannot tell. Those that do teach young babes
Do it with gentle means and easy tasks;
He might have chid me so; for, in good faith,
I am a child to chiding.
Iago.   What 's the matter, lady?
Emilia.   Alas, Iago, my lord hath so bewhor'd her,
Thrown such despite[514] and heavy terms upon her,
As true hearts cannot bear.
Desdemona.   Am I that name, Iago?
Iago.   What name, fair lady?
Desdemona.   Such as she says my lord did say I was.
Emilia.   He call'd her whore; a beggar in his drink   120
Could not have laid such terms upon his callat.[515]
Iago.   Why did he so?
Desdemona.   I do not know; I am sure I am none such.
Iago.   Do not weep, do not weep. Alas the day!
Emilia.   Has she forsook so many noble matches,
Her father and her country and her friends,
To be call'd whore? would it not make one weep?
Desdemona.   It is my wretched fortune.
Iago.   Beshrew[516] him for it!
How comes this trick upon him?
Desdemona.   Nay, heaven doth know.
Emilia.   I will be hang'd, if some eternal villain,   130
Some busy and insinuating rogue,
Some cogging[517] cozening slave, to get some office,
Have not devis'd this slander; I'll be hang'd else.
Iago.   Fie! there is no such man; it is impossible.
Desdemona.   If any such there be, heaven pardon him!
Emilia.   A halter pardon him, and hell gnaw his bones!
Why should he call her whore? who keeps her company?
What place? what time? what form? what likelihood?
The Moor 's abus'd by some most villainous knave,
Some base notorious knave, some scurvy fellow.   140
O heaven! that such companions[518] thou'dst unfold,

---

[513] The least suspicion on my slightest misconduct.   [514] Abuse.   [515] Slut.   [516] Curse.
[517] Cheating.   [518] Fellows (derogatory).

And put in every honest hand a whip
To lash the rascals naked through the world,
Even from the east to west!

Iago. Speak within door.

Emilia. O! fie upon them. Some such squire he was
That turn'd your wit the seamy side without,[519]
And made you to suspect me with the Moor.

Iago. You are a fool; go to.

Desdemona. O good Iago,
What shall I do to win my lord again?
Good friend, go to him; for, by this light of heaven,   150
I know not how I lost him. Here I kneel:
If e'er my will did trespass 'gainst his love,
Either in discourse of thought or actual deed,
Or that mine eyes, mine ears, or any sense,
Delighted them[520] in any other form;
Or that I do not yet,[521] and ever did,
And ever will, though he do shake me off
To beggarly divorcement, love him dearly,
Comfort forswear me! Unkindness may do much;
And his unkindness may defeat[522] my life,   160
But never taint my love. I cannot say 'whore':
It does abhor me now I speak the word;
To do the act that might the addition earn
Not the world's mass of vanity could make me.

Iago. I pray you be content, 'tis but his humour;
The business of the state does him offence,
And he does chide with you.

Desdemona. If 'twere no other, —

Iago. 'Tis but so, I warrant.   *(Trumpets.)*
Hark! how these instruments summon to supper;
The messengers of Venice stay the meat: 170
Go in, and weep not; all things shall be well.

        (Exeunt Desdemona and Emilia.)

(Enter Roderigo.)

How now, Roderigo!

Roderigo. I do not find that thou dealest justly with me.

Iago. What in the contrary?[523]

Roderigo. Every day thou daffest me[524] with some device, Iago; and rather, as
it seems to me now, keepest from me all conveniency,[525] than suppliest me

---

[519] Outward.   [520] Found delight.   [521] Still.   [522] Destroy.   [523] I.e., what reason do you
have for saying that?   [524] You put me off.   [525] Favorable circumstances.

with the least advantage of hope. I will indeed no longer endure it, nor am I yet persuaded to put up[526] in peace what already I have foolishly suffered.

Iago. Will you hear me, Roderigo?

Roderigo. Faith, I have heard too much, for your words and performances are no kin together.

Iago. You charge me most unjustly.

Roderigo. With nought but truth. I have wasted myself out of my means. The jewels you have had from me to deliver to Desdemona would half have corrupted a votarist;[527] you have told me she has received them, and returned me expectations and comforts of sudden respect[528] and acquaintance, but I find none.

Iago. Well; go to; very well.

Roderigo. Very well! go to! I cannot go to, man; nor 'tis not very well: by this hand, I say, it is very scurvy, and begin to find myself fobbed[529] in it.   190

Iago. Very well.

Roderigo. I tell you 'tis not very well. I will make myself known to Desdemona; if she will return me my jewels, I will give over my suit and repent my unlawful solicitation; if not, assure yourself I will seek satisfaction of you.

Iago. You have said now.[530]

Roderigo. Ay, and said nothing, but what I protest intendment of doing.

Iago. Why, now I see there's mettle in thee, and even from this instant do build on thee a better opinion than ever before. Give me thy hand, Roderigo; thou hast taken against me a most just exception; but yet, I protest, I have dealt most directly in thy affair.   200

Roderigo. It hath not appeared.

Iago. I grant indeed it hath not appeared, and your suspicion is not without wit and judgment. But, Roderigo, if thou hast that in thee indeed, which I have greater reason to believe now than ever, I mean purpose, courage, and valour, this night show it: if thou the next night following enjoy not Desdemona, take me from this world with treachery and devise engines for[531] my life.

Roderigo. Well, what is it? is it within reason and compass?

Iago. Sir, there is especial commission come from Venice to depute Cassio in Othello's place.   210

Roderigo. Is that true? why, then Othello and Desdemona return again to Venice.

Iago. O, no! he goes into Mauritania, and takes away with him the fair Desdemona, unless his abode be lingered here by some accident; wherein none can be so determinate[532] as the removing of Cassio.

Roderigo. How do you mean, removing of him?

Iago. Why, by making him uncapable of Othello's place; knocking out his brains.

---

[526] Put up with.   [527] Nun.   [528] Immediate consideration.   [529] Cheated.   [530] I.e., "I suppose you're through?" (?); or: "Now you're talking" (?).   [531] Devices against.   [532] Effective.

Roderigo.   And that you would have me do?

Iago.   Ay; if you dare do yourself a profit and a right. He sups to-night with a harlotry,[533] and thither will I go to him; he knows not yet of his honourable fortune. If you will watch his going thence, — which I will fashion to fall out between twelve and one, — you may take him at your pleasure; I will be near to second your attempt, and he shall fall between us. Come, stand not amazed at it, but go along with me; I will show you such a necessity in his death that you shall think yourself bound to put it on him. It is now high supper-time, and the night grows to waste; about it.

Roderigo.   I will hear further reason for this.

Iago.   And you shall be satisfied.   *(Exeunt.)*

Scene 3.   Another Room in the Castle.

(Enter Othello, Lodovico, Desdemona, Emilia, and Attendants.)

Lodovico.   I do beseech you, sir, trouble yourself no further.

Othello.   O! pardon me; 'twill do me good to walk.

Lodovico.   Madam, good-night; I humbly thank your ladyship.

Desdemona.   Your honour is most welcome.

Othello.   Will you walk, sir?
   O! Desdemona, —

Desdemona.   My lord?

Othello.   Get you to bed on the instant; I will be returned forthwith; dismiss
   your attendant there; look it be done.

Desdemona.   I will, my lord.   *(Exeunt Othello, Lodovico, and Attendants.)*

Emilia.   How goes it now? He looks gentler than he did.   10

Desdemona.   He says he will return incontinent;[534]
   He hath commanded me to go to bed,
   And bade me to dismiss you.

Emilia.   Dismiss me!

Desdemona.   It was his bidding; therefore, good Emilia,
   Give me my nightly wearing, and adieu:
   We must not now displease him.

Emilia.   I would you had never seen him.

Desdemona.   So would not I; my love doth so approve him,
   That even his stubbornness,[535] his checks[536] and frowns, —
   Prithee, unpin me, — have grace and favour in them.   20

Emilia.   I have laid those sheets you bade me on the bed.

Desdemona.   All's one.[537] Good faith! how foolish are our minds!
   If I do die before thee, prithee, shroud me
   In one of those same sheets.

---

[533] Harlot.   [534] At once.   [535] Roughness.   [536] Rebukes.   [537] I.e., it doesn't matter.

Emilia.   Come, come, you talk.
Desdemona.   My mother had a maid call'd Barbara;
  She was in love, and he she lov'd prov'd mad[538]
  And did forsake her; she had a song of 'willow';
  An old thing 'twas, but it express'd her fortune,
  And she died singing it; that song to-night
  Will not go from my mind; I have much to do   30
  But to go hang my head all at one side,
  And sing it like poor Barbara. Prithee, dispatch.
Emilia.   Shall I go fetch your night-gown?
Desdemona.   No, unpin me here.
  This Lodovico is a proper man.
Emilia.   A very handsome man.
Desdemona.   He speaks well.
Emilia.   I know a lady in Venice would have walked barefoot to Palestine for a
  touch of his nether lip.
Desdemona (*sings*).
  The poor soul sat sighing by a sycamore tree,
    Sing all a green willow;   40
  Her hand on her bosom, her head on her knee,
    Sing willow, willow, willow:
  The fresh streams ran by her, and murmur'd her moans;
    Sing willow, willow, willow:
  Her salt tears fell from her and soften'd the stones; —

  Lay by these: —
    Sing willow, willow, willow:

  Prithee, hie thee;[539] he 'll come anon. —

    Sing all a green willow must be my garland.
      Let nobody blame him, his scorn I approve, —   50
  Nay, that's not next. Hark! who is it that knocks?
Emilia.   It is the wind.
Desdemona.
  I call'd my love false love; but what said he then?
    Sing willow, willow, willow:
  If I court moe[540] women, you 'll couch with moe men.

  So, get thee gone; good-night. Mine eyes do itch;
  Doth that bode weeping?
Emilia.   'Tis neither here nor there.
Desdemona.   I have heard it said so. O! these men, these men!

---

[538] Wild.   [539] Hurry.   [540] More.

Dost thou in conscience think, tell me, Emilia,
That there be women do abuse their husbands   60
In such gross kind?
Emilia.   There be some such, no question.
Desdemona.   Wouldst thou do such a deed for all the world?
Emilia.   Why, would not you?
Desdemona.   No, by this heavenly light!
Emilia.   Nor I neither by this heavenly light;
I might do 't as well i' the dark.
Desdemona.   Wouldst thou do such a deed for all the world?
Emilia.   The world is a huge thing; 'tis a great price
For a small vice.
Desdemona.   In troth, I think thou wouldst not.
Emilia.   In troth, I think I should, and undo 't when I had done. Marry, I
would not do such a thing for a joint-ring,[541] nor measures of lawn,[542] nor for
gowns, petticoats, nor caps, nor any petty exhibition;[543] but for the whole
world, who would not make her husband a cuckold to make him a monarch? I
should venture purgatory for 't.
Desdemona.   Beshrew me, if I would do such a wrong
For the whole world.
Emilia.   Why, the wrong is but a wrong i' the world; and having the world for
your labour, 'tis a wrong in your own world, and you might quickly make it
right.
Desdemona.   I do not think there is any such woman.
Emilia.   Yes, a dozen; and as many to the vantage,[544] as   80
Would store[545] the world they played for.
But I do think it is their husbands' faults
If wives do fall. Say that they slack their duties,
And pour our treasures into foreign laps,
Or else break out in peevish jealousies,
Throwing restraint upon us; or say they strike us,
Or scant[546] our former having[547] in despite;
Why, we have galls;[548] and though we have some grace,
Yet have we some revenge. Let husbands know
Their wives have sense like them; they see and smell,   90
And have their palates both for sweet and sour,
As husbands have. What is it that they do
When they change us for others? Is it sport?[549]
I think it is; and doth affection breed it?
I think it doth; is 't frailty that thus errs?
It is so too; and have not we affections,
Desires for sport, and frailty, as men have?

---

[541] Ring made in separable halves.   [542] Fine linen.   [543] Offer, gift.   [544] Over and above.
[545] Populate.   [546] Reduce.   [547] Allowance.   [548] Spirits, temper.   [549] Lust, sexual enjoyment.

Then, let them use us well; else let them know,
The ills we do, their ills instruct us so.
Desdemona.   Good-night, good night; heaven me such usage[550] send,   100
Not to pick bad from bad, but by bad mend!   (*Exeunt.*)

Act V

Scene 1.   Cyprus. A Street.

(*Enter Iago and Roderigo.*)

Iago.   Here, stand behind this bulk,[551] straight will he come:
Wear thy good rapier bare, and put it home.
Quick, quick; fear nothing; I 'll be at thy elbow.
It makes us, or it mars us; think on that,
And fix most firm thy resolution.
Roderigo.   Be near at hand; I may miscarry in 't.
Iago.   Here, at thy hand: be bold, and take thy stand.   (*Retires.*)
Roderigo.   I have no great devotion to the deed;
And yet he has given me satisfying reasons:
'Tis but a man gone: forth, my sword; he dies.   10
Iago.   I have rubb'd this young quat[552] almost to the sense,[553]
And he grows angry. Now, whether he kill Cassio,
Or Cassio him, or each do kill the other,
Every way makes my gain: live Roderigo,
He calls me to a restitution large
Of gold and jewels that I bobb'd[554] from him,
As gifts to Desdemona;
It must not be: if Cassio do remain,
He hath a daily beauty in his life
That makes me ugly: and, besides, the Moor   20
May unfold me to him; there stand I in much peril.
No, he must die. But so;[555] I hear him coming.

(*Enter Cassio.*)

Roderigo.   I know his gait; 'tis he. Villain, thou diest!

(*Makes a pass at Cassio.*)

---

[550] Habits (?), treatment (?).   [551] Jutting part of a wall.   [552] Pimple.   [553] To the quick.
[554] Swindled.   [555] I.e., that's the only way.

Cassio.   That thrust had been mine enemy indeed
    But that my coat is better than thou know'st;
    I will make proof of thine.

(Draws, and wounds Roderigo.)

Roderigo.   O! I am slain.

(Iago from behind wounds Cassio in the leg, and exit.)

Cassio.   I am maim'd for ever. Help, ho! murder! murder!   *(Falls.)*

(Enter Othello, at a distance.)

Othello.   The voice of Cassio: Iago keeps his word.
Roderigo.   O! villain that I am!
Othello.   It is e'en so.
Cassio.   O, help, ho! light! a surgeon!   30
Othello.   'Tis he: O brave Iago, honest and just!
    That hast such noble sense of thy friend's wrong;
    Thou teachest me. Minion,[556] your dear lies dead,
    And your unblest fate hies; strumpet, I come!
    Forth of my heart those charms, thine eyes, are blotted;
    Thy bed lust-stain'd shall with lust's blood be spotted.   *(Exit.)*

(Enter Lodovico and Gratiano, at a distance.)

Cassio.   What ho! no watch? no passage?[557] murder! murder!
Gratiano.   'Tis some mischance; the cry is very direful.
Cassio.   O, help!
Lodovico.   Hark!   40
Roderigo.   O wretched villain!
Lodovico.   Two or three groans: it is a heavy[558] night;
    These may be counterfeits; let 's think 't unsafe
    To come in to the cry[559] without more help.
Roderigo.   Nobody come? then shall I bleed to death.
Lodovico.   Hark!

(Re-enter Iago, with a light.)

Gratiano.   Here 's one comes in his shirt, with light and weapons.
Iago.   Who 's there? whose noise is this that cries on murder?

---

[556] (Cassio's) darling, i.e., Desdemona.   [557] Passer-by.   [558] Dark.   [559] Where the cry comes
from.

Lodovico.   We do not know.
Iago.   Did not you hear a cry?
Cassio.   Here, here! for heaven's sake, help me.
Iago.   What's the matter?   50
Gratiano.   This is Othello's ancient, as I take it.
Lodovico.   The same indeed; a very valiant fellow.
Iago.   What are you here that cry so grievously?
Cassio.   Iago? O! I am spoil'd, undone by villains!
   Give me some help.
Iago.   O me, lieutenant! what villains have done this?
Cassio.   I think that one of them is hereabout,
   And cannot make away.
Iago.   O treacherous villains!
   (*To Lodovico and Gratiano.*) What are you there? come in, and
   give some help.   60
Roderigo.   O! help me here.
Cassio.   That's one of them.
Iago.   O murderous slave! O villain!

(*Stabs Roderigo.*)

Roderigo.   O damn'd Iago! O inhuman dog!
Iago.   Kill men i' the dark! Where be these bloody thieves?
   How silent is this town! Ho! murder! murder!
   What may you be? are you of good or evil?
Lodovico.   As you shall prove us, praise us.
Iago.   Signior Lodovico?
Lodovico.   He, sir.
Iago.   I cry you mercy. Here 's Cassio hurt by villains.   70
Gratiano.   Cassio!
Iago.   How is it, brother?
Cassio.   My leg is cut in two.
Iago.   Marry, heaven forbid.
   Light, gentlemen; I 'll bind it with my shirt.

(*Enter Bianca.*)

Bianca.   What is the matter, ho? who is 't that cried?
Iago.   Who is 't that cried!
Bianca.   O my dear Cassio! my sweet Cassio!
   O Cassio, Cassio, Cassio!
Iago.   O notable strumpet! Cassio, may you suspect
   Who they should be that have thus mangled you?   80
Cassio.   No.
Gratiano.   I am sorry to find you thus; I have been to seek you.

Iago.   Lend me a garter. So. O! for a chair,
  To bear him easily hence!
Bianca.   Alas; he faints! O Cassio, Cassio, Cassio!
Iago.   Gentlemen all, I do suspect this trash[560]
  To be a party in this injury.
  Patience awhile, good Cassio. Come, come.
  Lend me a light. Know we this face, or no?
  Alas! my friend and my dear countryman,   90
  Roderigo? no: yes, sure, O heaven! Roderigo.
Gratiano.   What! of Venice?
Iago.   Even he, sir, did you know him?
Gratiano.   Know him! ay.
Iago.   Signior Gratiano? I cry you gentle pardon;
  These bloody accidents must excuse my manners,
  That so neglected you.
Gratiano.   I am glad to see you.
Iago.   How do you, Cassio? O! a chair, a chair!
Gratiano.   Roderigo!

(A chair brought in.)

Iago.   He, he, 'tis he, — O! that 's well said; the chair:
  Some good men bear him carefully from hence;   100
  I 'll fetch the general's surgeon. *(To Bianca.)* For you, mistress,
  Save you your labour. He that lies slain here, Cassio,
  Was my dear friend. What malice was between you?
Cassio.   None in the world; nor do I know that man.
Iago *(to Bianca).*   What! look you pale? O! bear him out o' the air —

(Cassio and Roderigo are borne off.)

  Stay you, good gentlemen. Look you pale, mistress? —
  Do you perceive the gastness[561] of her eye?
  Nay, if you stare, we shall hear more anon.
  Behold her well; I pray you, look upon her.
  Do you see, gentlemen? nay, guiltiness will speak   110
  Though tongues were out of use.

(Enter Emilia.)

Emilia.   'Las! what 's the matter? what 's the matter, husband?
Iago.   Cassio hath here been set on in the dark

---

[560] I.e., Bianca.   [561] Terror.

By Roderigo and fellows that are 'scaped:
He 's almost slain, and Roderigo dead.

Emilia.   Alas! good gentleman; alas! good Cassio!

Iago.   This is the fruit of whoring. Prithee, Emilia,
Go know of Cassio where he supp'd to-night.
(To Bianca.) What! do you shake at that?

Bianca.   He supp'd at my house; but I therefore shake not.   120

Iago.   O! did he so? I charge you, go with me.

Emilia.   Fie, fie, upon thee, strumpet!

Bianca.   I am no strumpet, but of life as honest
As you that thus abuse me.

Emilia.   As I! foh! fie upon thee!

Iago.   Kind gentlemen, let 's go see poor Cassio dress'd.[562]
Come, mistress, you must tell 's another tale.
Emilia, run you to the citadel,
And tell my lord and lady what hath happ'd.
Will you go on afore? *(Aside.)* This is the night
That either makes me or fordoes[563] me quite.   *(Exeunt.)*

Scene 2.   A Bedchamber in the Castle. Desdemona in bed asleep. A light burning.

(Enter Othello.)

Othello.   It is the cause,[564] it is the cause, my soul;
Let me not name it to you, you chaste stars!
It is the cause. Yet I 'll not shed her blood,
Nor scar that whiter skin of hers than snow,
And smooth as monumental alabaster.
Yet she must die, else she 'll betray more men.
Put out the light, and then put out the light:
If I quench thee, thou flaming minister,[565]
I can again thy former light restore,
Should I repent me; but once put out thy light,   10
Thou cunning'st[566] pattern of excelling nature,
I know not where is that Promethean[567] heat
That can thy light relume.[568] When I have pluck'd the rose,
I cannot give it vital growth again,
It needs must wither: I 'll smell it on the tree. *(Kisses her.)*
O balmy breath, that dost almost persuade

---

[562] Bandaged.   [563] Ruins.   [564] I.e., Desdemona's unchastity (Othello means that the severity of the punishment is required by the nature of her sin).   [565] I.e., the candle.   [566] Most intricately wrought.   [567] In Greek mythology the demigod Prometheus stole fire from the gods and gave it to man.   [568] Relight.

Justice to break her sword! One more, one more.
Be thus when thou art dead, and I will kill thee,
And love thee after. One more, and this the last:
So sweet was ne'er so fatal. I must weep,   20
But they are cruel tears; this sorrow 's heavenly,
It strikes where it doth love. She wakes.

Desdemona.   Who 's there? Othello?

Othello.   Ay, Desdemona.

Desdemona.   Will you come to bed, my lord?

Othello.   Have you pray'd to-night, Desdemona?

Desdemona.   Ay, my lord.

Othello.   If you bethink yourself of any crime
Unreconcil'd as yet to heaven and grace,
Solicit for it straight.

Desdemona.   Alas! my lord, what may you mean by that?

Othello.   Well, do it, and be brief; I will walk by:569   30
I would not kill thy unprepared spirit;
No; heaven forfend!570 I would not kill thy soul.

Desdemona.   Talk you of killing?

Othello.   Ay, I do.

Desdemona.   Then heaven
Have mercy on me!

Othello.   Amen! with all my heart.

Desdemona.   If you say so, I hope you will not kill me.

Othello.   Hum!

Desdemona.   And yet I fear you; for you are fatal then
When your eyes roll so. Why I should fear I know not,
Since guiltiness I know not; but yet I feel I fear.

Othello.   Think on thy sins.

Desdemona.   They are loves I bear to you.   40

Othello.   Ay, and for that thou diest.

Desdemona.   That death's unnatural that kills for loving.
Alas! why gnaw you so your nether lip?
Some bloody passion shakes your very frame;
These are portents,571 but yet, I hope, I hope
They do not point on me.

Othello.   Peace, and be still!

Desdemona.   I will so. What 's the matter?

Othello.   That handkerchief which I so lov'd and gave thee
Thou gav'st to Cassio.

Desdemona.   No, by my life and soul!
Send for the man and ask him.

---

569 Nearby.   570 Forbid.   571 Omens.

Othello.   Sweet soul, take heed,   50
  Take heed of perjury; thou 'rt on thy death-bed.
Desdemona.   Ay, but not yet to die.
Othello.   Yes, presently;[572]
  Therefore confess thee freely of thy sin;
  For to deny each article with oath
  Cannot remove nor choke the strong conception[573]
  That I do groan withal. Thou art to die.
Desdemona.   Then Lord have mercy on me!
Othello.   I say, amen.
Desdemona.   And have you mercy too! I never did
  Offend you in my life; never lov'd Cassio
  But with such general warranty[574] of heaven   60
  As I might love; I never gave him token.
Othello.   By heaven, I saw my handkerchief in 's hand.
  O perjur'd woman! thou dost stone[575] my heart,
  And mak'st me call what I intend to do
  A murder, which I thought a sacrifice:
  I saw the handkerchief.
Desdemona.   He found it then;
  I never gave it him. Send for him hither;
  Let him confess a truth.
Othello.   He had confessed.
Desdemona.   What, my lord?
Othello.   That he hath us'd thee.
Desdemona.   How? Unlawfully?
Othello.   Ay.   70
Desdemona.   He will not say so.
Othello.   No; his mouth is stopp'd:
  Honest Iago hath ta'en order for 't.[576]
Desdemona.   O! my fear interprets. What! is he dead?
Othello.   Had all his hairs been lives, my great revenge
  Had stomach[577] for them all.
Desdemona.   Alas! he is betray'd and I undone.
Othello.   Out, strumpet! Weep'st thou for him to my face?
Desdemona.   O! banish me, my lord, but kill me not!
Othello.   Down, strumpet!
Desdemona.   Kill me to-morrow; let me live to-night!   80
Othello.   Nay, if you strive, —
Desdemona.   But half an hour!
Othello.   Being done, there is no pause.
Desdemona.   But while I say one prayer!

---

[572] At once.   [573] Belief.   [574] Permission.   [575] Turn to stone.   [576] Taken steps.   [577] Appetite.

Othello. It is too late. (*He smothers her.*)

Emilia (*within*). My lord, my lord! what, ho! my lord, my lord!

Othello. What noise is this? Not dead? Not yet quite dead?
I that am cruel am yet merciful;
I would not have thee linger in thy pain.
So, so.

Emilia (*within*). What, ho! my lord, my lord!

Othello. Who's there?

Emilia (*within*). O! good my lord, I would speak a word with you! 90

Othello. Yes; 'tis Emilia: by and by.[578] She's dead.
'Tis like[579] she comes to speak of Cassio's death;
The noise was high. Ha! no more moving?
Still as the grave. Shall she come in? were 't good?[580]
I think she stirs again: no. What 's best to do?
If she come in she'll sure speak to my wife:
My wife! my wife! what wife? I have no wife;
O, insupportable! O heavy hour!
Methinks it should be now a huge eclipse
Of sun and moon, and that the affrighted globe 100
Should yawn[581] at alteration.

Emilia (*within*). I do beseech you
That I may speak with you, O! good my lord.

Othello. I had forgot thee: O! come in, Emilia:
Soft, by and by: let me the curtains draw.
Where art thou? (*Unlocks the door.*)

(*Enter Emilia.*)

What 's the matter with thee now?

Emilia. O! my good lord, yonder 's foul murder done.

Othello. What! now?

Emilia. But now, my lord.

Othello. It is the very error[582] of the moon;
She comes more near the earth than she was wont, 110
And makes men mad.

Emilia. Cassio, my lord, has kill'd a young Venetian
Call'd Roderigo.

Othello. Roderigo kill'd!
And Cassio kill'd?

Emilia. No, Cassio is not kill'd.

Othello. Not Cassio kill'd! then murder 's out of tune,
And sweet revenge grows harsh.

---

[578] I.e., "just a moment."   [579] Likely.   [580] Would that be wise.   [581] Open up (as in an earth-quake).   [582] Straying.

Desdemona.   O! falsely, falsely murder'd.

Emilia.   Alas! what cry is that?

Othello.   That! what?

Emilia.   Out, and alas! that was my lady's voice:
Help! Help, ho! help! O lady, speak again!   120
Sweet Desdemona! O! sweet mistress, speak.

Desdemona.   A guiltless death I die.

Emilia.   O! who hath done this deed?

Desdemona.   Nobody; I myself; farewell:
Commend me to my kind lord. O! farewell!   *(Dies.)*

Othello.   Why, how should she be murder'd?

Emilia.   Alas! who knows?

Othello.   You heard her say herself it was not I.

Emilia.   She said so; I must needs report the truth.

Othello.   She 's like a liar gone to burning hell;
'Twas I that kill'd her.

Emilia.   O! the more angel she,   130
And you the blacker devil.

Othello.   She turn'd to folly, and she was a whore.

Emilia.   Thou dost belie her, and thou art a devil.

Othello.   She was false as water.

Emilia.   Thou art rash as fire to say
That she was false! O! she was heavenly true.

Othello.   Cassio did tup her; ask thy husband else.
O! I were damn'd beneath all depth in hell
But that I did proceed[583] upon just grounds
To this extremity. Thy husband knew it all.

Emilia.   My husband!   140

Othello.   Thy husband.

Emilia.   That she was false to wedlock?

Othello.   Ay, with Cassio. Nay, had she been true,
If heaven would make me such another world
Of one entire and perfect chrysolite,[584]
I'd not have sold her for it.

Emilia.   My husband!

Othello.   Ay, 'twas he that told me first:
An honest man he is, and hates the slime
That sticks on filthy deeds.

Emilia.   My husband!

Othello.   What needs this iterance,[585] woman? I say thy husband.   150

Emilia.   O mistress! villany hath made mocks with love.
My husband say that she was false!

---

[583] Had I not proceeded.   [584] Topaz.   [585] Repetition.

Othello.   He, woman;
  I say, thy husband: dost understand the word?
  My friend, thy husband, honest, honest Iago.
Emilia.   If he say so, may his pernicious soul
  Rot half a grain a day! he lies to the heart:
  She was too fond of her most filthy bargain.[586]
Othello.   Ha!
Emilia.   Do thy worst:
  This deed of thine is no more worthy heaven   160
  Than thou wast worthy her.
Othello.   Peace! you were best.[587]
Emilia.   Thou hast not half the power to do me harm
  As I have to be hurt. O gull! O dolt!
  As ignorant as dirt! thou hast done a deed, —
  I care not for thy sword; I'll make thee known,
  Though I lost twenty lives. Help! help, ho! help!
  The Moor has kill'd my mistress! murder! murder!

(Enter Montano, Gratiano, Iago, and others.)

Montano.   What is the matter? How now, general!
Emilia.   O! are you come, Iago? you have done well,
  That men must lay their murders on your neck.   170
Gratiano.   What is the matter?
Emilia.   Disprove this villain if thou be'st a man:
  He says thou told'st him that his wife was false.
  I know thou didst not, thou 'rt not such a villain.
  Speak, for my heart is full.
Iago.   I told him what I thought, and told no more
  Than what he found himself was apt and true.
Emilia.   But did you ever tell him she was false?
Iago.   I did.
Emilia.   You told a lie, an odious damned lie;   180
  Upon my soul, a lie, a wicked lie;
  She false with Cassio! Did you say with Cassio?
Iago.   With Cassio, mistress. Go to, charm[588] your tongue.
Emilia.   I will not charm my tongue; I am bound to speak.
  My mistress here lies murder'd in her bed.
All.   O heavens forfend!
Emilia.   And your reports have set the murder on.
Othello.   Nay, stare not, masters; it is true, indeed.
Gratiano.   'Tis a strange truth.
Montano.   O monstrous act!

---

[586] I.e., Othello.   [587] You'd better be quiet.   [588] I.e., into silence.

Emilia.   Villany! villany! villany!   190
   I think upon 't, I think, I smell 't; O villany!
   I thought so then;[589] I'll kill myself for grief.
   O! villany, villany!
Iago.   What! are you mad? I charge you, get you home.
Emilia.   Good gentlemen, let me have leave to speak:
   'Tis proper I obey him, but not now.
   Perchance, Iago, I will ne'er go home.
Othello.   O! O! O!   *(Falls on the bed.)*
Emilia.   Nay, lay thee down and roar,
   For thou hast kill'd the sweetest innocent
   That e'er did lift up eye.
Othello.   O! she was foul.   *(Rises.)*
   I scarce did know you, uncle. There lies your niece,
   Whose breath, indeed, these hands have newly stopp'd:
   I know this act shows terrible and grim.
Gratiano.   Poor Desdemona! I am glad thy father 's dead.
   Thy match was mortal to him, and pure grief
   Shore[590] his old thread in twain: did he live now,
   This sight would make him do a desperate turn,
   Yea, curse his better angel from his side,
   And fall to reprobation.[591]
Othello.   'Tis pitiful; but yet Iago knows   210
   That she with Cassio hath the act of shame
   A thousand times committed; Cassio confess'd it:
   And she did gratify[592] his amorous works
   With that recognizance and pledge of love
   Which I first gave her. I saw it in his hand:
   It was a handkerchief, an antique token
   My father gave my mother.
Emilia.   O heaven! O heavenly powers!
Iago.   Come, hold your peace.
Emilia.   'Twill out, 'twill out; I hold my peace, sir? no;
   No, I will speak as liberal as the north;[593]   220
   Let heaven and men and devils, let them all,
   All, all, cry shame against me, yet I'll speak.
Iago.   Be wise, and get you home.
Emilia.   I will not.

(Iago threatens to stab Emilia.)

---

[589] *Cf.* "I will be hang'd, if some eternal villain, / Some busy and insinuating rogue, / Some cogging cozening slave, to get some office, / Have not devis'd this slander; . . ." (IV, 2, 130 ff.). Emilia means not that she guessed Iago's guilt but that she rightly guessed the slanderer's motive. [590] Cut.   [591] Damnation.   [592] Reward.   [593] I.e., the north wind (?), the supposedly free-spoken people of north England (?).

Gratiano.   Fie!
  Your sword upon a woman!
Emilia. O thou dull Moor! that handkerchief thou speak'st of
  I found by fortune and did give my husband;
  For often, with a solemn earnestness,
  More than, indeed, belong'd to such a trifle,
  He begg'd of me to steal it.
Iago.   Villainous whore!
Emilia.   She give it Cassio! no, alas! I found it,   230
  And I did give 't my husband.
Iago.   Filth, thou liest!
Emilia.   By heaven, I do not, I do not, gentlemen.
  O murderous coxcomb![594] what should such a fool
  Do with so good a wife?
Othello.   Are there no stones[595] in heaven
  But what serve for the thunder? Precious villain!

(He runs at Iago. Iago stabs Emilia.)

Gratiano.   The woman falls; sure, he has kill'd his wife.   *(Exit Iago.)*
Emilia.   Ay, ay; O! lay me by my mistress' side.
Gratiano.   He 's gone; but his wife 's kill'd.
Montano.   'Tis a notorious[596] villain. Take you this weapon,
  Which I have here recover'd from the Moor.   240
  Come, guard the door without; let him not pass,
  But kill him rather. I'll after that same villain,
  For 'tis a damned slave.   *(Exeunt Montano and Gratiano.)*
Othello.   I am not valiant neither,
  But every puny whipster[597] gets my sword.
  But why should honour outlive honesty?
  Let it go all.
Emilia.   What did thy song bode, lady?
  Hark, canst thou hear me? I will play the swan,
  And die in music: —
  (Sings.)   Willow, willow, willow.
  Moor, she was chaste; she lov'd thee, cruel Moor;
  So come my soul to bliss as I speak true;   250
  So speaking as I think, I die, I die.   *(Dies.)*
Othello.   I have another weapon in this chamber;
  It is a sword of Spain, the ice-brook's temper.[598]
  O! here it is. Uncle, I must come forth.

---

[594] Idiot.   [595] I.e., thunderbolts (to strike Iago down).   [596] Notable.   [597] I.e., a small boy whipping a top.   [598] Tempered in icy water (or the reference may be to Innsbruck, famed for the quality of its steel, but this hardly fits "a sword of Spain").

Gratiano (*within*). If thou attempt it, it will cost thee dear:
  Thou hast no weapon, and perforce must suffer.
Othello. Look in upon me then, and speak with me,
  Or, naked[599] as I am, I will assault thee.

(Re-enter Gratiano.)

Gratiano. What is the matter?
Othello.   Behold! I have a weapon;
  A better never did itself sustain   260
  Upon a soldier's thigh: I have seen the day,
  That with this little arm, and this good sword,
  I have made my way through more impediments
  Than twenty times your stop: but, O vain boast!
  Who can control his fate? 'tis not so now.
  Be not afraid, though you do see me weapon'd;
  Here is my journey's end, here is my butt,[600]
  And very sea-mark of my utmost sail.[601]
  Do you go back dismay'd? 'tis a lost fear;
  Man but a rush[602] against Othello's breast,   270
  And he retires. Where should Othello go?
  Now how dost thou look now? O ill-starr'd wench!
  Pale as thy smock! when we shall meet at compt,[603]
  This look of thine will hurl my soul from heaven,
  And fiends will snatch at it. Cold, cold, my girl!
  Even like thy chastity.
  O! cursed, cursed slave. Whip me, ye devils,
  From the possession of this heavenly sight!
  Blow me about in winds! roast me in sulphur!
  Wash me in steep-down gulfs of liquid fire!   280
  O Desdemona! Desdemona! dead!
  Oh! Oh! Oh!

(Enter Lodovico, Montano, Cassio carried in a chair, and Officers with Iago, prisoner.)

Lodovico. Where is this rash and most unfortunate man?
Othello. That's he that was Othello; here I am.
Lodovico. Where is that viper? bring the villain forth.
Othello. I look down towards his feet;[604] but that 's a fable.
  If that thou be'st a devil, I cannot kill thee.   *(Wounds Iago.)*
Lodovico. Wrench his sword from him.   *(Othello is disarmed.)*

---

[599] Unarmed.   [600] Goal, end, limit.   [601] Destination of my farthest journey.   [602] Wield but
a reed.   [603] On the day of judgment.   [604] I.e., for the Devil's cloven hoof.

Iago.   I bleed, sir; but not kill'd.

Othello.   I am not sorry neither; I'd have thee live;
For, in my sense,[605] 'tis happiness to die.   290

Lodovico.   O thou Othello! that wert once so good,
Fall'n in the practice[606] of a damned slave,[607]
What shall be said to thee?

Othello.   Why, any thing:
An honourable murderer, if you will;
For nought did I in hate, but all in honour.

Lodovico.   This wretch hath part confess'd his villany:
Did you and he consent in Cassio's death?

Othello.   Ay.

Cassio.   Dear general, I never gave you cause.

Othello.   I do believe it, and I ask your pardon.   300
Will you, I pray, demand that demi-devil
Why he hath thus ensnar'd my soul and body?

Iago.   Demand me nothing: what you know, you know:
From this time forth I never will speak word.

Lodovico.   What! not to pray?

Gratiano.   Torments will ope[608] your lips.

Othello.   Well, thou dost best.

Lodovico.   Sir, you shall understand what hath befall'n,
Which, as I think, you know not. Here is a letter
Found in the pocket of the slain Roderigo,
And here another; the one of them imports   310
The death of Cassio to be undertook
By Roderigo.

Othello.   O villain!

Cassio.   Most heathenish and most gross!

Lodovico.   Now here's another discontented paper,
Found in his pocket too; and this, it seems,
Roderigo meant to have sent this damned villain,
But that, belike,[609] Iago in the interim[610]
Came in and satisfied him.

Othello.   O the pernicious caitiff!
How came you, Cassio, by that handkerchief
That was my wife's?

Cassio.   I found it in my chamber;   320
And he himself confess'd but even now
That there he dropp'd it for a special purpose
Which wrought to his desire.

Othello.   O fool! fool! fool!

---

[605] The way I feel.   [606] Plot, machination.   [607] I.e., Iago.   [608] Open.   [609] Most likely.
[610] In the meantime.

Cassio.   There is besides in Roderigo's letter
How he upbraids Iago that he made him
Brave me upon the watch; whereon it came
That I was cast:[611] and even but now he spake,
After long seeming dead, Iago hurt him,
Iago set him on.

Lodovico.   You must forsake this room and go with us;   330
Your power and your command is taken off,
And Cassio rules in Cyprus. For this slave,
If there be any cunning cruelty
That can torment him much and hold him long,
It shall be his. You shall close prisoner rest,
Till that the nature of your fault be known
To the Venetian state. Come, bring him away.

Othello.   Soft you; a word or two before you go.
I have done the state some service, and they know 't;
No more of that. I pray you, in your letters,   340
When you shall these unlucky deeds relate,
Speak of me as I am; nothing extenuate,
Nor set down aught[612] in malice: then, must you speak
Of one that lov'd not wisely but too well;
Of one not easily jealous, but, being wrought,
Perplex'd[613] in the extreme; of one whose hand
Like the base Indian,[614] threw a pearl away
Richer than all his tribe; of one whose subdu'd[615] eyes
Albeit unused to the melting mood,
Drop tears as fast as the Arabian trees   350
Their med'cinable gum. Set you down this;
And say besides, that in Aleppo once,
Where a malignant and a turban'd Turk
Beat a Venetian and traduc'd the state,
I took by the throat the circumcised dog,
And smote him, thus.   *(Stabs himself.)*

Lodovico.   O bloody period![616]

Gratiano.   All that's spoke is marr'd.

Othello.   I kiss'd thee ere I killed thee; no way but this.

                    (Falling upon Desdemona.)
Killing myself to die upon a kiss.   *(Dies.)*

Cassio.   This did I fear, but thought he had no weapon;   360
For he was great of heart.

Lodovico *(to Iago).*   O Spartan dog!
More fell[617] than anguish, hunger, or the sea.

---

[611] Dismissed.   [612] Anything.   [613] Distracted.   [614] The Folio reads "Iudean." Both readings denote the foolish infidel who fails to appreciate the treasure he possesses.   [615] Overcome (by grief).   [616] Ending.   [617] Grim, cruel.

Look on the tragic loading of this bed;
This is thy work; the object poisons sight;
Let it be hid. Gratiano, keep the house,
And seize upon the fortunes of the Moor,
For they succeed on you. To you, lord governor,
Remains the censure of this hellish villain,
The time, the place, the torture; O! enforce it.
Myself will straight aboard, and to the state   370
This heavy act with heavy heart relate.   (*Exeunt.*)

For Analysis

1. In what sense might it be said that Othello is responsible for his own downfall?

2. Do you find the reasons that Iago gives for his actions consistent and convincing?

3. Discuss the functions of the minor characters, such as Roderigo, Bianca, and Emilia.

4. Is the rapidity of Othello's emotional collapse (Act III, Scene 3) plausible? Does his race contribute to his emotional turmoil? Explain.

5. The first part of Act IV, Scene 2 (until Othello exits), is sometimes called the "brothel" scene. What features of Othello's language and behavior justify that designation?

6. Why does Iago kill Roderigo?

7. What are the benefits of moving the main characters to Cyprus rather than setting the drama in Venice?

On Style

1. Compare the speeches of Cassio and Iago in Act II, Scene 1. What do the differences in language and **style** reveal about their characters?

2. Review the play to carefully determine how much time elapses between the arrival in Cyprus and the end of the action. Can you find narrated events that could not possibly have occurred within that time frame? What effect do the chronological inconsistencies have on you? Explain.

Making Connections

1. Place yourself in Othello's position. How would you respond to Iago's machinations? If you were in Desdemona's position, how would you deal with Othello's (apparently) bizarre behavior?

2. Compare Desdemona's hope that her virtue will win out to the hope (or cynicism) of the wives in Irwin Shaw's "The Girls in Their Summer Dresses" (p. 1034) and Raymond Carver's "What We Talk about When We Talk about Love" (p. 1053). Why do you think Desdemona remains submissive?

Writing Topics

1. Write an analysis of the **figurative language** in Iago's soliloquies at the end of Act I and at the end of Act II, Scene 1.

2. Choose a minor character, such as Roderigo, Emilia, or Bianca, and in a carefully reasoned essay, explain how the character contributes to the design of the play.

3. Discuss the relationship between love and hate in this tragedy.

Susan Glaspell   (1882–1948)

Trifles 1916

CHARACTERS

George Henderson, county
  attorney
Henry Peters, sheriff

Lewis Hale, a neighboring farmer
Mrs. Peters
Mrs. Hale

Scene

The kitchen in the now abandoned farmhouse of John Wright, a gloomy kitchen, and left without having been put in order — the walls covered with a faded wall paper. Down right is a door leading to the parlor. On the right wall above this door is a built-in kitchen cupboard with shelves in the upper portion and drawers below. In the rear wall at right, up two steps is a door opening onto stairs leading to the second floor. In the rear wall at left is a door to the shed and from there to the outside. Between these two doors is an old-fashioned black iron stove. Running along the left wall from the shed door is an old iron sink and sink shelf, in which is set a hand pump. Downstage of the sink is an uncurtained window. Near the window is an old wooden rocker. Center stage is an unpainted wooden kitchen table with straight chairs on either side. There is a small chair down right. Unwashed pans under the sink, a loaf of bread outside the breadbox, a dish towel on the table — other signs of incompleted work. At the rear the shed door opens and the Sheriff comes in followed by the County Attorney and Hale. The Sheriff and Hale are men in middle life, the County Attorney is a young man; all are much bundled up and go at once to the stove. They are followed by the two women — the Sheriff's wife, Mrs. Peters, first; she is a slightly wiry woman, with a thin nervous face. Mrs. Hale is larger and would ordinarily be called more comfortable looking, but she is disturbed now and looks fearfully about as she enters. The women have come in slowly, and stand close together near the door.

County Attorney (*at stove rubbing his hands*).   This feels good. Come up to the fire, ladies.
Mrs. Peters (*after taking a step forward*).   I'm not — cold.
Sheriff (*unbuttoning his overcoat and stepping away from the stove to right of table as if to mark the beginning of official business*).   Now, Mr. Hale, before we move things about, you explain to Mr. Henderson just what you saw when you came here yesterday morning.
County Attorney (*crossing down to left of the table*).   By the way, has anything been moved? Are things just as you left them yesterday?

Sheriff (*looking about*). It's just about the same. When it dropped below zero last night I thought I'd better send Frank out this morning to make a fire for us — (*sits right of center table*) no use getting pneumonia with a big case on, but I told him not to touch anything except the stove — and you know Frank.

County Attorney. Somebody should have been left here yesterday.

Sheriff. Oh — yesterday. When I had to send Frank to Morris Center for that man who went crazy — I want you to know I had my hands full yesterday. I knew you could get back from Omaha by today and as long as I went over everything here myself —

County Attorney. Well, Mr. Hale, tell just what happened when you came here yesterday morning.

Hale (*crossing down to above table*). Harry and I started to town with a load of potatoes. We came along the road from my place and as I got here I said, "I'm going to see if I can't get John Wright to go in with me on a party telephone." I spoke to Wright about it once before and he put me off, saying folks talked too much anyway, and all he asked was peace and quiet — I guess you know about how much he talked himself; but I thought maybe if I went to the house and talked about it before his wife, though I said to Harry that I didn't know as what his wife wanted made much difference to John ———

County Attorney. Let's talk about that later, Mr. Hale. I do want to talk about that, but tell now just what happened when you got to the house.

Hale. I didn't hear or see anything; I knocked at the door, and still it was all quiet inside. I knew they must be up, it was past eight o'clock. So I knocked again, and I thought I heard somebody say, "Come in." I wasn't sure. I'm not sure yet, but I opened the door — this door (*indicating the door by which the two women are still standing*) and there in that rocker — (*pointing at it*) sat Mrs. Wright. (*They all look at the rocker down left.*)

County Attorney. What — was she doing?

Hale. She was rockin' back and forth. She had her apron in her hand and was kind of — pleating it.

County Attorney. And how did she — look?

Hale. Well, she looked queer.

County Attorney. How do you mean — queer?

Hale. Well, as if she didn't know what she was going to do next. And kind of done up.

County Attorney (*takes out notebook and pencil and sits left of center table*). How did she seem to feel about your coming?

Hale. Why, I don't think she minded — one way or another. She didn't pay much attention. I said, "How do, Mrs. Wright, it's cold, ain't it?" And she said, "Is it?" — and went on kind of pleating at her apron. Well, I was surprised; she didn't ask me to come up to the stove, or to set down, but just sat there, not even looking at me, so I said, "I want to see John." And then she — laughed. I guess you would call it a laugh. I thought of Harry and the team outside, so I said a little sharp: "Can't I see John?" "No," she says, kind o' dull like. "Ain't he home?" says I. "Yes," says she, "he's home." "Then why can't I see him?" I asked her, out of patience. " 'Cause he's dead," says she. *"Dead?"* says I. She just nodded her head, not getting a bit excited, but rockin' back and forth. "Why — where is he?" says I, not knowing what to say. She just pointed upstairs — like that. *(Himself pointing to the room above.)* I started for the stairs, with the idea of going up there. I walked from there to here — then I says, "Why, what did he die of?" "He died of a rope round his neck," says she, and just went on, pleatin' at her apron. Well, I went out and called Harry. I thought I might — need help. We went upstairs and there he was lyin' ————

County Attorney. I think I'd rather have you go into that upstairs, where you can point it all out. Just go on now with the rest of the story.

Hale. Well, my first thought was to get that rope off. It looked . . . *(stops; his face twitches)* . . . but Harry, he went up to him, and he said, "No, he's dead all right, and we'd better not touch anything." So we went back downstairs. She was still sitting that same way. "Has anybody been notified?" I asked. "No," says she, unconcerned. "Who did this, Mrs. Wright?" said Harry. He said it businesslike — and she stopped pleatin' of her apron. "I don't know," she says. "You don't *know?*" says Harry. "No," says she. "Weren't you sleepin' in the bed with him?" says Harry. "Yes," says she, "but I was on the inside." "Somebody slipped a rope round his neck and strangled him and you didn't wake up?" says Harry. "I didn't wake up," she said after him. We must 'a' looked as if we didn't see how that could be, for after a minute she said, "I sleep sound." Harry was going to ask her more questions but I said maybe we ought to let her tell her story first to the coroner, or the sheriff, so Harry went fast as he could to Rivers' place, where there's a telephone.

County Attorney. And what did Mrs. Wright do when she knew that you had gone for the coroner?

Hale. She moved from the rocker to that chair over there *(pointing to a small chair in the down right corner)* and just sat there with her hands held together and looking down. I got a feeling that I ought to make some conversation, so I said I had come in to see if John wanted to put in a telephone, and at that she started to laugh, and then she stopped and looked at me — scared. *(The County Attorney, who has had his notebook out, makes a note.)* I dunno, maybe it wasn't scared. I wouldn't like to say it was. Soon Harry got back, and then Dr. Lloyd came and you, Mr. Peters, and so I guess that's all I know that you don't.

County Attorney *(rising and looking around).* I guess we'll go upstairs first — and then out to the barn and around there. *(To the Sheriff.)* You're convinced that there was nothing important here — nothing that would point to any motive?

Sheriff. Nothing here but kitchen things.

(The County Attorney, after again looking around the kitchen, opens the door of a cupboard closet in right wall. He brings a small chair from right — gets on it and looks on a shelf. Pulls his hand away, sticky.)

County Attorney.   Here's a nice mess. (*The women draw nearer up center.*)

Mrs. Peters (*to the other woman*).   Oh, her fruit; it did freeze. (*To the Lawyer.*) She worried about that when it turned so cold. She said the fire'd go out and her jars would break.

Sheriff (*rises*).   Well, can you beat the women! Held for murder and worryin' about her preserves.

County Attorney (*getting down from chair*).   I guess before we're through she may have something more serious than preserves to worry about. (*Crosses down right center.*)

Hale.   Well, women are used to worrying over trifles. (*The two women move a little closer together.*)

County Attorney (*with the gallantry of a young politician*).   And yet, for all their worries, what would we do without the ladies? (*The women do not unbend. He goes below the center table to the sink, takes a dipperful of water from the pail, and pouring it into a basin, washes his hands. While he is doing this the Sheriff and Hale cross to cupboard, which they inspect. The County Attorney starts to wipe his hands on the roller towel, turns it for a cleaner place.*) Dirty towels! (*Kicks his foot against the pans under the sink.*) Not much of a housekeeper, would you say, ladies?

Mrs. Hale (*stiffly*).   There's a great deal of work to be done on a farm.

County Attorney.   To be sure. And yet (*with a little bow to her*) I know there are some Dickson County farmhouses which do not have such roller towels.

(*He gives it a pull to expose its full length again.*)

Mrs. Hale.   Those towels get dirty awful quick. Men's hands aren't always as clean as they might be.

County Attorney.   Ah, loyal to your sex, I see. But you and Mrs. Wright were neighbors. I suppose you were friends, too.

Mrs. Hale (*shaking her head*).   I've not seen much of her of late years. I've not been in this house — it's more than a year.

County Attorney (*crossing to women up center*).   And why was that? You didn't like her?

Mrs. Hale.   I liked her all well enough. Farmers' wives have their hands full, Mr. Henderson. And then ———

County Attorney.   Yes ——— ?

Mrs. Hale (*looking about*).   It never seemed a very cheerful place.

County Attorney.   No — it's not cheerful. I shouldn't say she had the home-making instinct.

Mrs. Hale.   Well, I don't know as Wright had, either.

County Attorney.   You mean that they didn't get on very well?

Mrs. Hale.   No, I don't mean anything. But I don't think a place'd be any cheerfuller for John Wright's being in it.

County Attorney.   I'd like to talk more of that a little later. I want to get the lay of things upstairs now.

(He goes past the women to up right where steps lead to a stair door.)

Sheriff.   I suppose anything Mrs. Peters does'll be all right. She was to take in some clothes for her, you know, and a few little things. We left in such a hurry, yesterday.

County Attorney.   Yes, but I would like to see what you take, Mrs. Peters, and keep an eye out for anything that might be of use to us.

Mrs. Peters.   Yes, Mr. Henderson.

(The men leave by up right door to stairs. The women listen to the men's steps on the stairs, then look about the kitchen.)

Mrs. Hale *(crossing left to sink).*   I'd hate to have men coming into my kitchen, snooping around and criticizing.

(She arranges the pans under sink which the Lawyer had shoved out of place.)

Mrs. Peters.   Of course it's no more than their duty.

(Crosses to cupboard up right.)

Mrs. Hale.   Duty's all right, but I guess that deputy sheriff that came out to make the fire might have got a little of this on. *(Gives the roller towel a pull.)* Wish I'd thought of that sooner. Seems mean to talk about her for not having things slicked up when she had to come away in such a hurry.

(Crosses right to Mrs. Peters at cupboard.)

Mrs. Peters *(who has been looking through cupboard, lifts one end of towel that covers a pan).*   She had bread set.

(Stands still.)

Mrs. Hale *(eyes fixed on a loaf of bread beside the breadbox, which is on a low shelf of the cupboard).*   She was going to put this in there. *(Picks up a loaf, abruptly drops it. In a manner of returning to familiar things.)* It's a shame about her fruit. I wonder if it's all gone. *(Gets up on the chair and looks.)* I think there's some here that's all right, Mrs. Peters. Yes — here; *(holding it toward the window)* this is cherries, too. *(Looking again.)* I declare I believe that's the only one. *(Gets down, jar in her hand. Goes to the sink and wipes it off on the outside.)* She'll feel awful bad after all her hard work in the hot weather. I remember the afternoon I put up my cherries last summer.

(She puts the jar on the big kitchen table, center of the room. With a sigh, is about to sit down in the rocking chair. Before she is seated realizes what chair it

is; with a slow look at it, steps back. The chair which she has touched rocks back and forth. Mrs. Peters moves to center table and they both watch the chair rock for a moment or two.)

Mrs. Peters *(shaking off the mood which the empty rocking chair has evoked. Now in a businesslike manner she speaks).* Well I must get those things from the front room closet. *(She goes to the door at the right but, after looking into the other room, steps back.)* You coming with me, Mrs. Hale? You could help me carry them. *(They go in the other room; reappear, Mrs. Peters carrying a dress, petticoat, and skirt, Mrs. Hale following with a pair of shoes.)* My, it's cold in there.

(She puts the clothes on the big table and hurries to the stove.)

Mrs. Hale *(right of center table examining the skirt).* Wright was close. I think maybe that's why she kept so much to herself. She didn't even belong to the Ladies' Aid. I suppose she felt she couldn't do her part, and then you don't enjoy things when you feel shabby. I heard she used to wear pretty clothes and be lively, when she was Minnie Foster, one of the town girls singing in the choir. But that — oh, that was thirty years ago. This all you want to take in?

Mrs. Peters. She said she wanted an apron. Funny thing to want, for there isn't much to get you dirty in jail, goodness knows. But I suppose just to make her feel more natural. *(Crosses to cupboard.)* She said they was in the top drawer in this cupboard. Yes, here. And then her little shawl that always hung behind the door. *(Opens stair door and looks.)* Yes, here it is.

(Quickly shuts door leading upstairs.)

Mrs. Hale *(abruptly moving toward her).* Mrs. Peters?
Mrs. Peters. Yes, Mrs. Hale?

(At up right door.)

Mrs. Hale. Do you think she did it?
Mrs. Peters *(in a frightened voice).* Oh, I don't know.
Mrs. Hale. Well, I don't think she did. Asking for an apron and her little shawl. Worrying about her fruit.
Mrs. Peters *(starts to speak, glances up, where footsteps are heard in the room above. In a low voice).* Mr. Peters says it looks bad for her. Mr. Henderson is awful sarcastic in a speech and he'll make fun of her sayin' she didn't wake up.
Mrs. Hale. Well, I guess John Wright didn't wake when they was slipping that rope under his neck.
Mrs. Peters *(crossing slowly to table and placing shawl and apron on table with other clothing).* No, it's strange. It must have been done awful crafty and still. They say it was such a — funny way to kill a man, rigging it all up like that.

Mrs. Hale (*crossing to left of Mrs. Peters at table*).   That's just what Mr. Hale said. There was a gun in the house. He says that's what he can't understand.

Mrs. Peters.   Mr. Henderson said coming out that what was needed for the case was a motive; something to show anger, or — sudden feeling.

Mrs. Hale (*who is standing by the table*).   Well, I don't see any signs of anger around here. (*She puts her hand on the dish towel, which lies on the table, stands looking down at table, one-half of which is clean, the other half messy.*) It's wiped to here. (*Makes a move as if to finish work, then turns and looks at loaf of bread outside the breadbox. Drops towel. In that voice of coming back to familiar things.*) Wonder how they are finding things upstairs. (*Crossing below table to down right.*) I hope she had it a little more red-up[1] up there. You know, it seems kind of *sneaking.* Locking her up in town and then coming out here and trying to get her own house to turn against her!

Mrs. Peters.   But, Mrs. Hale, the law is the law.

Mrs. Hale.   I s'pose 'tis. (*Unbuttoning her coat.*) Better loosen up your things, Mrs. Peters. You won't feel them when you go out.

(*Mrs. Peters takes off her fur tippet, goes to hang it on chair back left of table, stands looking at the work basket on floor near down left window.*)

Mrs. Peters.   She was piecing a quilt.

(*She brings the large sewing basket to the center table and they look at the bright pieces, Mrs. Hale above the table and Mrs. Peters left of it.*)

Mrs. Hale.   It's a log cabin pattern. Pretty, isn't it? I wonder if she was goin' to quilt it or just knot it?

(*Footsteps have been heard coming down the stairs. The Sheriff enters followed by Hale and the County Attorney.*)

Sheriff.   They wonder if she was going to quilt it or just knot it!

(*The men laugh, the women look abashed.*)

County Attorney (*rubbing his hands over the stove*).   Frank's fire didn't do much up there, did it? Well, let's go out to the barn and get that cleared up.

(*The men go outside by up left door.*)

Mrs. Hale (*resentfully*).   I don't know as there's anything so strange, our takin' up our time with little things while we're waiting for them to get the evi-

[1] A slang expression for "make attractive."

dence. (*She sits in chair right of table smoothing out a block with decision.*) I don't see as it's anything to laugh about.

Mrs. Peters (*apologetically*).   Of course they've got awful important things on their minds.

(*Pulls up a chair and joins Mrs. Hale at the left of the table.*)

Mrs. Hale (*examining another block*).   Mrs. Peters, look at this one. Here, this is the one she was working on, and look at the sewing! All the rest of it has been so nice and even. And look at this! It's all over the place! Why, it looks as if she didn't know what she was about!

(*After she has said this they look at each other, then start to glance back at the door. After an instant Mrs. Hale has pulled at a knot and ripped the sewing.*)

Mrs. Peters.   Oh, what are you doing, Mrs. Hale?

Mrs. Hale (*mildly*).   Just pulling out a stitch or two that's not sewed very good. (*Threading a needle.*) Bad sewing always made me fidgety.

Mrs. Peters (*with a glance at door, nervously*).   I don't think we ought to touch things.

Mrs. Hale.   I'll just finish up this end. (*Suddenly stopping and leaning forward.*) Mrs. Peters?

Mrs. Peters.   Yes, Mrs. Hale?

Mrs. Hale.   What do you suppose she was so nervous about?

Mrs. Peters.   Oh — I don't know. I don't know as she was nervous. I sometimes sew awful queer when I'm just tired. (*Mrs. Hale starts to say something, looks at Mrs. Peters, then goes on sewing.*) Well, I must get these things wrapped up. They may be through sooner than we think. (*Putting apron and other things together.*) I wonder where I can find a piece of paper, and string.

(*Rises.*)

Mrs. Hale.   In that cupboard, maybe.

Mrs. Peters (*crosses right looking in cupboard*).   Why, here's a bird-cage. (*Holds it up.*) Did she have a bird, Mrs. Hale?

Mrs. Hale.   Why, I don't know whether she did or not — I've not been here for so long. There was a man around last year selling canaries cheap, but I don't know as she took one; maybe she did. She used to sing real pretty herself.

Mrs. Peters (*glancing around*).   Seems funny to think of a bird here. But she must have had one, or why would she have a cage? I wonder what happened to it?

Mrs. Hale.   I s'pose maybe the cat got it.

Mrs. Peters.   No, she didn't have a cat. She's got that feeling some people have about cats — being afraid of them. My cat got in her room and she was real upset and asked me to take it out.

Mrs. Hale.   My sister Bessie was like that. Queer, ain't it?

Mrs. Peters (*examining the cage*).   Why, look at this door. It's broke. One hinge is pulled apart.

(*Takes a step down to Mrs. Hale's right.*)

Mrs. Hale (*looking too*).   Looks as if someone must have been rough with it.

Mrs. Peters.   Why, yes.

(*She brings the cage forward and puts it on the table.*)

Mrs. Hale (*glancing toward up left door*).   I wish if they're going to find any evidence they'd be about it. I don't like this place.

Mrs. Peters.   But I'm awful glad you came with me, Mrs. Hale. It would be lonesome for me sitting here alone.

Mrs. Hale.   It would, wouldn't it? (*Dropping her sewing.*) But I tell you what I do wish, Mrs. Peters. I wish I had come over sometimes when *she* was here. I — (*looking around the room*) — wish I had.

Mrs. Peters.   But of course you were awful busy, Mrs. Hale — your house and your children.

Mrs. Hale (*rises and crosses left*).   I could've come. I stayed away because it weren't cheerful — and that's why I ought to have come. I — (*looking out left window*) — I've never liked this place. Maybe because it's down in a hollow and you don't see the road. I dunno what it is, but it's a lonesome place and always was. I wish I had come over to see Minnie Foster sometimes. I can see now —

(*Shakes her head.*)

Mrs. Peters (*left of table and above it*).   Well, you mustn't reproach yourself, Mrs. Hale. Somehow we just don't see how it is with other folks until — something turns up.

Mrs. Hale.   Not having children makes less work — but it makes a quiet house, and Wright out to work all day, and no company when he did come in. (*Turning from window.*) Did you know John Wright, Mrs. Peters?

Mrs. Peters.   Not to know him; I've seen him in town. They say he was a good man.

Mrs. Hale.   Yes — good; he didn't drink, and kept his word as well as most, I guess, and paid his debts. But he was a hard man, Mrs. Peters. Just to pass the time of day with him — (*Shivers.*) Like a raw wind that gets to the bone. (*Pauses, her eye falling on the cage.*) I should think she would 'a' wanted a bird. But what do you suppose went with it?

Mrs. Peters.   I don't know, unless it got sick and died.

(*She reaches over and swings the broken door, swings it again, both women watch it.*)

Mrs. Hale. You weren't raised round here, were you? (*Mrs. Peters shakes her head.*) You didn't know — her?

Mrs. Peters. Not till they brought her yesterday.

Mrs. Hale. She — come to think of it, she was kind of like a bird herself — real sweet and pretty, but kind of timid and — fluttery. How — she — did — change. (*Silence: then as if struck by a happy thought and relieved to get back to everyday things. Crosses right above Mrs. Peters to cupboard, replaces small chair used to stand on to its original place down right.*) Tell you what, Mrs. Peters, why don't you take the quilt in with you? It might take up her mind.

Mrs. Peters. Why, I think that's a real nice idea, Mrs. Hale. There couldn't possibly be any objection to it could there? Now, just what would I take? I wonder if her patches are in here — and her things.

(*They look in the sewing basket.*)

Mrs. Hale (*crosses to right of table*). Here's some red. I expect this has got sewing things in it. (*Brings out a fancy box.*) What a pretty box. Looks like something somebody would give you. Maybe her scissors are in here. (*Opens box. Suddenly puts her hand to her nose.*) Why ——— (*Mrs. Peters bends nearer, then turns her face away.*) There's something wrapped up in this piece of silk.

Mrs. Peters. Why, this isn't her scissors.

Mrs. Hale (*lifting the silk*). Oh, Mrs. Peters — it's ———

(*Mrs. Peters bends closer.*)

Mrs. Peters. It's the bird.

Mrs. Hale. But, Mrs. Peters — look at it! Its neck! Look at its neck! It's all — other side *to*.

Mrs. Peters. Somebody — wrung — its — neck.

(*Their eyes meet. A look of growing comprehension, of horror. Steps are heard outside. Mrs. Hale slips box under quilt pieces, and sinks into her chair. Enter Sheriff and County Attorney. Mrs. Peters steps down left and stands looking out of window.*)

County Attorney (*as one turning from serious things to little pleasantries*). Well, ladies, have you decided whether she was going to quilt it or knot it?

(*Crosses to center above table.*)

Mrs. Peters. We think she was going to — knot it.

(*Sheriff crosses to right of stove, lifts stove lid, and glances at fire, then stands warming hands at stove.*)

County Attorney. Well, that's interesting, I'm sure. (*Seeing the bird-cage.*) Has the bird flown?

Mrs. Hale (*putting more quilt pieces over the box*). We think the — cat got it.

County Attorney (*preoccupied*). Is there a cat?

(*Mrs. Hale glances in a quick covert way at Mrs. Peters.*)

Mrs. Peters (*turning from window takes a step in*). Well, not *now*. They're superstitious, you know. They leave.

County Attorney (*to Sheriff Peters, continuing an interrupted conversation*). No sign at all of anyone having come from the outside. Their own rope. Now let's go up again and go over it piece by piece. (*They start upstairs.*) It would have to have been someone who knew just the ———

(*Mrs. Peters sits down left of table. The two women sit there not looking at one another, but as if peering into something and at the same time holding back. When they talk now it is in the manner of feeling their way over strange ground, as if afraid of what they are saying, but as if they cannot help saying it.*)

Mrs. Hale (*hesitatively and in hushed voice*). She liked the bird. She was going to bury it in that pretty box.

Mrs. Peters (*in a whisper*). When I was a girl — my kitten — there was a boy took a hatchet, and before my eyes — and before I could get there ——— (*Covers her face an instant.*) If they hadn't held me back I would have — (*catches herself, looks upstairs where steps are heard, falters weakly*) — hurt him.

Mrs. Hale (*with a slow look around her*). I wonder how it would seem never to have had any children around. (*Pause.*) No, Wright wouldn't like the bird — a thing that sang. She used to sing. He killed that, too.

Mrs. Peters (*moving uneasily*). We don't know who killed the bird.

Mrs. Hale. I knew John Wright.

Mrs. Peters. It was an awful thing was done in this house that night, Mrs. Hale. Killing a man while he slept, slipping a rope around his neck that choked the life out of him.

Mrs. Hale. His neck. Choked the life out of him.

(*Her hand goes out and rests on the bird-cage.*)

Mrs. Peters (*with rising voice*). We don't know who killed him. We don't *know.*

Mrs. Hale (*her own feeling not interrupted*). If there'd been years and years of nothing, then a bird to sing to you, it would be awful — still, after the bird was still.

Mrs. Peters (*something within her speaking*). I know what stillness is. When we homesteaded in Dakota, and my first baby died — after he was two years old, and me with no other then ———

Mrs. Hale *(moving).*   How soon do you suppose they'll be through looking for the evidence?

Mrs. Peters.   I know what stillness is. *(Pulling herself back.)* The law has got to punish crime, Mrs. Hale.

Mrs. Hale *(not as if answering that).*   I wish you'd seen Minnie Foster when she wore a white dress with blue ribbons and stood up there in the choir and sang. *(A look around the room.)* Oh, I *wish* I'd come over here once in a while! That was a crime! That was a crime! Who's going to punish that?

Mrs. Peters *(looking upstairs).*   We mustn't — take on.

Mrs. Hale.   I might have known she needed help! I know how things can be — for women. I tell you, it's queer, Mrs. Peters. We live close together and we live far apart. We all go through the same things — it's all just a different kind of the same thing. *(Brushes her eyes, noticing the jar of fruit, reaches out for it.)* If I was you I wouldn't tell her her fruit was gone. Tell her it *ain't*. Tell her it's all right. Take this in to prove it to her. She — she may never know whether it was broke or not.

Mrs. Peters *(takes the jar, looks about for something to wrap it in; takes petti-coat from the clothes brought from the other room, very nervously begins winding this around the jar. In a false voice).*   My, it's a good thing the men couldn't hear us. Wouldn't they just laugh! Getting all stirred up over a little thing like a — dead canary. As if that could have anything to do with — with — wouldn't they *laugh!*

(The men are heard coming downstairs.)

Mrs. Hale *(under her breath).*   Maybe they would — maybe they wouldn't.

County Attorney.   No, Peters, it's all perfectly clear except a reason for doing it. But you know juries when it comes to women. If there was some definite thing. *(Crosses slowly to above table. Sheriff crosses down right. Mrs. Hale and Mrs. Peters remain seated at either side of table.)* Something to show — something to make a story about — a thing that would connect up with this strange way of doing it ———

(The women's eyes meet for an instant. Enter Hale from outer door.)

Hale *(remaining by door).*   Well, I've got the team around. Pretty cold out there.

County Attorney.   I'm going to stay awhile by myself. *(To the Sheriff.)* You can send Frank out for me, can't you? I want to go over everything. I'm not satisfied that we can't do better.

Sheriff.   Do you want to see what Mrs. Peters is going to take in?

(The Lawyer picks up the apron, laughs.)

County Attorney.   Oh, I guess they're not very dangerous things the ladies have picked out. *(Moves a few things about, disturbing the quilt pieces which* *cover the box. Steps back.)* No, Mrs. Peters doesn't need supervising. For that matter a sheriff's wife is married to the law. Ever think of it that way, Mrs. Peters?

Mrs. Peters.   Not — just that way.

Sheriff *(chuckling).*   Married to the law. *(Moves to down right door to the other room.)* I just want you to come in here a minute, George. We ought to take a look at these windows.

County Attorney *(scoffingly).*   Oh, windows!

Sheriff.   We'll be right out, Mr. Hale.

(Hale goes outside. The Sheriff follows the County Attorney into the room. Then Mrs. Hale rises, hands tight together, looking intensely at Mrs. Peters, whose eyes make a slow turn, finally meeting Mrs. Hale's. A moment Mrs. Hale holds her, then her own eyes point the way to where the box is concealed. Suddenly Mrs. Peters throws back quilt pieces and tries to put the box in the bag she is carrying. It is too big. She opens box, starts to take bird out, cannot touch it, goes to pieces, stands there helpless. Sound of a knob turning in the other room. Mrs. Hale snatches the box and puts it in the pocket of her big coat. Enter County Attorney and Sheriff, who remain down right.)

County Attorney *(crosses to up left door facetiously).*   Well, Henry, at least we found out that she was not going to quilt it. She was going to — what is it you call it, ladies?

Mrs. Hale *(standing center below table facing front, her hand against her pocket).*   We call it — knot it, Mr. Henderson.

Curtain.

For Analysis

1. What is the meaning of the title? Glaspell titled a short-story version of the play "A Jury of Her Peers." Is that a better title than *Trifles*? Explain.

2. What are the major differences between Mrs. Hale and Mrs. Peters?

3. At one point, Mrs. Peters tells Mrs. Hale a childhood story about a boy who killed her kitten. Why is she reminded of this event? What does it tell us about her reaction to the Wrights' marriage?

4. Which of the two women undergoes the most noticeable character development?

5. In what ways do the relationships between the two couples — Mrs. Hale and Mrs. Peters, and Henry Peters and Lewis Hale — change by the end of the play?

6. Do Henry Peters and Lewis Hale change in the course of the play?

7. Why are the men unable to see the clues that become obvious to the women?

8. Can you suggest why Mrs. Wright is the only one identified by her birth name?

On Style

1. What does Glaspell gain by **setting** this drama in rural (rather than urban) America?

2. Are the bird cage and the quilt effective as **symbols**?

3. Analyze the bird cage and quilt in this play and the tarantella dance and party in Henrik Ibsen's *A Doll's House* (p. 499) as symbols that capture an important **theme** in each play.

Making Connections

1. What similarities in attitudes toward women do you find in this play and in Ibsen's *A Doll's House* (p. 499)?

2. Do you think it is fair to say that Mrs. Wright in this play and Laura in Tennessee Williams's *The Glass Menagerie* (p. 243) are people whose lives have been blighted by a patriarchal society that confines women to narrow, stereotypical roles?

Writing Topics

1. Show how the discussion of Mrs. Wright's quilt embodies the major themes of *Trifles*.

2. Argue for or against the proposition that Mrs. Hale and Mrs. Peters are morally obligated to tell the county attorney what they know about the murder.

3. Write a one-page essay using *Trifles* to define realistic drama and Sophocles' *Antigonê* (p. 467) to define poetic drama.

Essays

Paul   (d. ca. A.D. 64)

1 Corinthians 13   ca. 56

If I speak in the tongues of men° and of angels, but have not love, I am a noisy gong or a clanging cymbal. ² And if I have prophetic powers, and understand all mysteries and all knowledge, and if I have all faith, so as to remove mountains, but have not love, I am nothing. ³ If I give away all I have, and if I deliver my body to be burned, but have not love, I gain nothing.

⁴ Love is patient and kind; love is not jealous or boastful; ⁵ it is not arrogant or rude. Love does not insist on its own way; it is not irritable or resentful; ⁶ it does not rejoice at wrong, but rejoices in the right. ⁷ Love bears all things, believes all things, hopes all things, endures all things.

⁸ Love never ends; as for prophesies, they will pass away; as for tongues, they will cease; as for knowledge, it will pass away. ⁹ For our knowledge is imperfect and our prophecy is imperfect; ¹⁰ but when the perfect comes, the imperfect will pass away. ¹¹ When I was a child, I spoke like a child, I thought like a child, I reasoned like a child; when I became a man, I gave up childish ways. ¹² For now we see in a mirror dimly, but then face to face. Now I know in part; then I shall understand fully, even as I have been fully understood. ¹³ So faith, hope, love abide, these three; but the greatest of these is love.

For Analysis

1. How does Paul emphasize the significance of love in verses 1 to 3?

2. What does Paul mean by "now" and "then" in verse 12?

3. In verse 13, Paul mentions "faith, hope, love" as abiding conditions. What do you understand by "faith" and "hope"? What do you think "love" means to Paul?

°Glossolalia, the ecstatic uttering of unintelligible sounds that some interpret as a deeply religious experience.

On Style

Examine Paul's method of argument. Note that his definition of love embodies asser-tions of what love is and, equally important, what it is not. How effective do you find this definition by exclusion? Explain.

Making Connections

How do you think the characters in Raymond Carver's "What We Talk about When We Talk about Love" (p. 1053) would respond to Paul's definition of love or the absence of love?

Writing Topics

1. Read Paul's First Epistle to the Corinthians (preferably in a well-annotated study Bible), and analyze the relationship of Chapter 13 to the rest of the epistle.

2. This text, translated from the original Greek, is taken from the Revised Standard Version of the Bible. Read the same passage in two or three other versions (for example, the King James Version, the Douay Version, the New American Bible), and compare the translations in terms of style and effectiveness.

Erich Fromm   (1900–1980)

Is Love an Art?   1956

Is love an art? Then it requires knowledge and effort. Or is love a pleasant sensation, which to experience is a matter of chance, something one "falls into" if one is lucky? This little book is based on the former premise, while undoubtedly the majority of people today believe in the latter.

Not that people think that love is not important. They are starved for it; they watch endless numbers of films about happy and unhappy love stories, they listen to hundreds of trashy songs about love — yet hardly anyone thinks that there is anything that needs to be learned about love.

This peculiar attitude is based on several premises which either singly or combined tend to uphold it. Most people see the problem of love primarily as that of *being loved*, rather than that of *loving*, of one's capacity to love. Hence the problem to them is how to be loved, how to be lovable. In pursuit of this aim they follow several paths. One, which is especially used by men, is to be successful, to be as powerful and rich as the social margin of one's position permits. Another, used especially by women, is to make oneself attractive, by cultivating one's body, dress, etc. Other ways of making oneself attractive, used both by men and women, are to develop pleasant manners, interesting conversation, to be helpful, modest, inoffensive. Many of the ways to make oneself lovable are the same as those used to make oneself successful, "to win friends and influence people." As a matter of fact, what most people in our culture mean by being lovable is essentially a mixture between being popular and having sex appeal.

A second premise behind the attitude that there is nothing to be learned about love is the assumption that the problem of love is the problem of an *object*, not the problem of a *faculty*. People think that to *love* is simple, but that to find the right object to love — or to be loved by — is difficult. This attitude has several reasons rooted in the development of modern society. One reason is the great change which occurred in the twentieth century with respect to the choice of a "love object." In the Victorian age, as in many traditional cultures, love was mostly not a spontaneous personal experience which then might lead to marriage. On the contrary, marriage was contracted by convention — either by the respective families, or by a marriage broker, or without the help of such intermediaries; it was concluded on the basis of social considerations, and love was supposed to develop once the marriage had been concluded. In the last few generations the concept of romantic love has become almost universal in the Western world. In the United States, while considerations of a conventional nature are not entirely absent, to a vast extent people are in search of "romantic love," of the personal experience of love which then should lead to marriage.

1252

This new concept of freedom in love must have greatly enhanced the importance of the *object* as against the importance of the *function*.

Closely related to this factor is another feature characteristic of contempo- 5 rary culture. Our whole culture is based on the appetite for buying, on the idea of a mutually favorable exchange. Modern man's happiness consists in the thrill of looking at the shop windows, and in buying all that he can afford to buy, either for cash or on installments. He (or she) looks at people in a similar way. For the man an attractive girl — and for the woman an attractive man — are the prizes they are after. "Attractive" usually means a nice package of qualities which are popular and sought after on the personality market. What specifically makes a person attractive depends on the fashion of the time, physically as well as mentally. During the twenties, a drinking and smoking girl, tough and sexy, was attractive; today the fashion demands more domesticity and coyness. At the end of the nineteenth and the beginning of this century, a man had to be aggressive and ambitious — today he has to be social and tolerant — in order to be an attractive "package." At any rate, the sense of falling in love develops usually only with regard to such human commodities as are within reach of one's own possibilities for exchange. I am out for a bargain; the object should be desirable from the standpoint of its social value, and at the same time should want me, considering my overt and hidden assets and potentialities. Two persons thus fall in love when they feel they have found the best object available on the market, considering the limitations of their own exchange values. Often, as in buying real estate, the hidden potentialities which can be developed play a considerable role in this bargain. In a culture in which the marketing orientation prevails, and in which material success is the outstanding value, there is little reason to be surprised that human love relations follow the same pattern of exchange which governs the commodity and the labor market.

The third error leading to the assumption that there is nothing to be learned about love lies in the confusion between the initial experience of *"falling"* in love, and the permanent state of *being* in love, or as we might better say, of "standing" in love. If two people who have been strangers, as all of us are, suddenly let the wall between them break down, and feel close, feel one, this moment of oneness is one of the most exhilarating, most exciting experiences in life. It is all the more wonderful and miraculous for persons who have been shut off, isolated, without love. This miracle of sudden intimacy is often facilitated if it is combined with, or initiated by, sexual attraction and consummation. However, this type of love is by its very nature not lasting. The two persons become well acquainted, their intimacy loses more and more its miraculous character, until their antagonism, their disappointments, their mutual boredom kill whatever is left of the initial excitement. Yet, in the beginning they do not know all this: in fact, they take the intensity of the infatuation, this being "crazy" about each other, for proof of the intensity of their love, while it may only prove the degree of their preceding loneliness.

This attitude — that nothing is easier than to love — has continued to be the prevalent idea about love in spite of the overwhelming evidence to the contrary.

There is hardly any activity, any enterprise, which is started with such tremendous hopes and expectations, and yet, which fails so regularly, as love. If this were the case with any other activity, people would be eager to know the reasons for the failure, and to learn how one could do better — or they would give up the activity. Since the latter is impossible in the case of love, there seems to be only one adequate way to overcome the failure of love — to examine the reasons for this failure, and to proceed to study the meaning of love.

The first step to take is to become aware that *love is an art,* just as living is an art; if we want to learn how to love we must proceed in the same way we have to proceed if we want to learn any other art, say music, painting, carpentry, or the art of medicine or engineering.

What are the necessary steps in learning any art?

The process of learning an art can be divided conveniently into two parts: 10 one, the mastery of the theory; the other, the mastery of the practice. If I want to learn the art of medicine, I must first know the facts about the human body, and about various diseases. When I have all this theoretical knowledge, I am by no means competent in the art of medicine. I shall become a master in this art only after a great deal of practice, until eventually the results of my theoretical knowledge and the results of my practice are blended into one — my intuition, the essence of the mastery of any art. But, aside from learning the theory and practice, there is a third factor necessary to becoming a master in any art — the mastery of the art must be a matter of ultimate concern; there must be nothing else in the world more important than the art. This holds true for music, for medicine, for carpentry — and for love. And, maybe, here lies the answer to the question of why people in our culture try so rarely to learn this art, in spite of their obvious failures: in spite of the deep-seated craving for love, almost everything else is considered to be more important than love: success, prestige, money, power — almost all our energy is used for the learning of how to achieve these aims, and almost none to learn the art of loving.

Could it be that only those things are considered worthy of being learned with which one can earn money or prestige, and that love, which "only" profits the soul, but is profitless in the modern sense, is a luxury we have no right to spend much energy on?

For Analysis

1. In paragraph 3, Fromm speaks of people's attempts to be loved. In his opinion, how do men contrive to be loved? How do women? Do you agree with Fromm's analysis? If not, how would you characterize people's attempts to attract love?

2. In paragraph 4, Fromm describes two distinct elements of love, referred to as "object" and "faculty." What are these, and how are they different?

3. Do you agree with the author's notion that in contemporary Western culture, attractiveness is measured in essentially commercial terms? Explain.

4. What is the difference between "falling" in love and "standing" in love (para. 6)?

5. What three stages are required to master an art? Why does love, so often, remain unmastered?

Making Connections

1. Does Adrienne Rich's poem "Living in Sin" (p. 1123) validate Fromm's ideas? Explain.

2. Discuss Alice Munro's story "How I Met My Husband" (p. 1039) in the context of Fromm's essay.

3. Christopher Marlowe's poem "The Passionate Shepherd to His Love" (p. 1086) and Sir Walter Raleigh's response, "The Nymph's Reply to the Shepherd" (p. 1087), reflect elements in Fromm's essay. Which poem would Fromm prefer? Explain.

Writing Topics

1. Write an analysis of Jill Tweedie's "The Experience" (p. 1256) from the point of view detailed in this essay.

2. Apply Fromm's ideas to an experience you've had with love.

Jill Tweedie   (1936–1993)

The Experience   1979

"Some day my prince will come . . . "

I have no particular qualifications to write about love but then, who has? There are no courses of higher learning offered in the subject except at the University of Life, as they say, and there I have put in a fair amount of work. So I offer my own thoughts, experiences and researches into love in the only spirit possible to such an enterprise — a combination of absolute humility and utter arrogance that will cause the reader either to deride my wrongheadedness or, with luck, to recognize some of the same lessons.

I am a white, Anglo-Saxon, heterosexual, happily married, middle-income female whose experience of what is called love spans forty years of the mid-twentieth century in one of the most fortunate parts of the globe. I mention this because I am profoundly aware of the limits these facts give to my vision; also because, in spite of such advantages, my experience of love has hardly been uplifting and yet, because of them too, I have at least been vouchsafed a glimpse of what love might be, some day.

I took my first steps in what I was told was love when the idea of high romance and living happily ever after still held sway. They said that whatever poisoned apple I might bite would surely be dislodged by a Prince's kiss and I would then rise from all the murderous banalities of living and, enfolded in a strong man's arms, gallop away on a white charger to the better land called love. The way it turned out, this dream of love did not do much to irradiate my life. The ride was nice enough but 'twas better to travel than to arrive and — oh, shame — there was more than one Prince. Of two previous marriages and a variety of other lovings, very little remains and that mostly ugly. However sweet love's initial presence, when it goes it leaves horrid scars. Unlike friendship and other forms of love, the tide of male/female sex love does not ebb imperceptibly, leaving the stones it reveals gleaming and covetable. No. It only shows that what was taken to be precious is simply a bare, dull pebble like any other.

Loving, lovers fill each other's lives, Siamese twins joined at the heart, bees that suck honey from each other's blossoms. When love ebbs, nothing remains. Ex-lovers rarely meet again or write or offer each other even those small kindnesses and comforts that strangers would not withhold. Birthdays, high days and holidays pass unmarked where once they were entered in New Year diaries and planned for months ahead. Photographs of the beloved are discarded or curl up, yellowing, in some dusty drawer. What was once the world becomes a no-man's

1256

land, fenced with barbed wire, where trespassers are prosecuted and even the civilities given a passing acquaintance are forbidden. What was the most intimate — private thoughts, dreams, nightmares and childhood panics soothed in warm arms — are now merely coinage for a pub joke, a hostess flippancy, worth a line or two in the local paper or the old school magazine. Divorced. Separated. Split.

For the first man I thought I loved, and therefore married, I bear, at most, a 5 distant anger for injuries received. For the second I carefully suppress the good times, burying them with the bad. All those hours, weeks, months, years passed in the same bed have vanished, leaving only the traces of an old wound, an ache where a growth was removed.

Was either a part of love, ever? Of a kind. The best we could manage at the time, a deformed seedling planted in fertile ground. The three of us, each of them and me, carried loads on our backs when we met, all the clobber of past generations. This I must do, that you must be, this is good, that is bad, you must, I must, we must. By the time we met, we were already proficient puppeteers, hands stuck up our stage dolls, our real selves well concealed behind the striped canvas. You Punch, me Judy. Me Jane, you Tarzan.

I had a conventional 1940s and 1950s childhood, cut to the pattern of time. I adored and admired my father and my father did not adore or admire me. My mother was there like the curtains and the carpets were there, taken for loving granted in early childhood and then ruthlessly discarded, the living symbol of everything my world did not regard and that I, therefore, did not wish to become. Rejecting her caused a very slight wreckage inside, nothing you'd notice, though transfusions would later be necessary. Powerful unloving father, powerless loving mother. Cliché.

So I did what I could to make my way and married an older man. Love and marriage go together like a horse and carriage. This act imposed certain conditions. First of all, you cannot grow up if you marry a father figure because this is no part of the contract, and besides, growing up is a disagreeable occupation. Then, of course, a continuing virginity of mind, if not of body, is essential because Daddy's girl has never known other men and any evidence of sexual curiosity or, worse, a touch of ribaldry might cause him to withdraw his protection. Indeed, a daughter must not know much of anything at all because Daddy must teach and daughter learn, for ever. Competence, independence, self-sufficiency, talent in anything but the most girlish endeavours, toughness of any kind, is against the rules. Light-heartedness, giggling, little tantrums and a soupçon of mischief are permitted because Daddy is a Daddy, after all, and likes to be amused after a long day or even smack a naughty bum, in his wisdom. My first marriage was a romper room and each day I laid plans to negotiate the next, with my thumb stuck endearingly in my mouth.

To begin with, we both enjoyed the game we didn't know we were playing. He was a proper husband in the eyes of the outside world, protective and admonitory, and I was a proper wife, that is to say, a child; charming and irresponsible.

But quite soon these playful rituals began to harden into concrete, so that we could no longer move, even if we wished, as long as we were together. For a few years I was satisfied enough, the drama of my life absorbed me, it was a stage and I was the star. First a house to play with and later, in case the audience began to cough and fidget, a pregnancy to hold them riveted. Later, like Alice in Wonderland, I came across the cake labelled 'eat me' and whenever my husband was away at work, I ate and I grew. My legs stuck out of the windows, my arms snaked round the doors, my head above an endless neck loomed through the chimney and my heartbeat rocked the room. Each day, just before 5 P.M., I nibbled the other side of Alice's cake and, in the nick of time, shrank to being a little woman again. Hullo, darling, how was your day? Me? Oh, nothing happened. Terrified, I knew that one day I wouldn't make it down again and my husband, returning from work, would fall back in horror at the monster who had taken over his home and push me out into the big wide world.[1]

Writing this now perhaps suggests that I was aware of a pretence and set up   10 my false self knowingly, for reward. Not so. The boundaries given me in girlhood were strictly defined, allowing only minimum growth and that mainly physical. To sprout the titivating secondary sexual characteristics was expected, but woe betide the *enfant terrible* who tried to burst that tight cocoon and emerge as a full-grown adult in mind as well as body. The penalty was ill-defined but all-pervasive, like those sci-fi novels of a postnuclear generation bred to fear the radioactive world above their subterranean tunnels that threatens isolation, mutilation and death. The reward for my self-restraint (in the most literal sense) was a negative one — be good and tractable and you will be looked after — but it was none the less powerful for that. So my real self, or hints of it, was as frightening to me as I feared it would be to my husband, a dark shadow given to emerging at less and less acceptable times. I was Mr. Rochester[2] secure in his mansion but I was also his mad wife in the attic. I had to conceal her existence to preserve my way of life but all the time she was setting matches to the bedding, starting a flame at the hem of the curtains, hoping to burn the mansion down.

Things became more and more schizoid. The demure façade of a prim girl hid a raucous fishwife who folded her massive arms against her chest and cursed. She horrified me, so much so — threatening, as she did, my exile from society — that in spite of increasing marital quarrels and even spurts of pure hatred, never once did I let that fishwife out to hurl the oaths she could have hurled or yelled the truths she knew. How could I, without revealing what I really was, to him and to myself?

The inner split opened wider. When my husband said he loved me, I knew he meant he loved the doll I had created and I accepted his love smugly enough, on her behalf. She was worth it. She wore the right clothes, she said the right things, the span of her waist would bring tears to your eyes and the tiny staccato

---

[1] The allusion to *Alice in Wonderland* refers to a number of affairs Tweedie had during her first marriage.

[2] The hero of Charlotte Brontë's novel *Jane Eyre* (1847), who keeps his insane wife secluded.

of her heels across a floor would melt the sternest heart. She turned her head upon its graceful stem just so and her camellia hands, laced on her lap, could make a stone bleed. She smiled just enough to give a man the wildest expectations and frowned just enough to make him feel safe. This doll is a good doll. This doll is a marriageable doll. This doll is a real doll.

I knew, of course, that my doll self was only a front but it was the one I had deliberately created in response to popular demand. My real self knew all the things the doll did not wish to know. She was human and therefore hopelessly unfeminine, she had no pretty ways. Her voice was harsh, pumped from the guts instead of issuing sweetly from the throat, and every now and then she howled and the doll was forced to look at her face, bare as a picked bone. No wonder the poor dolly gathered up her ruffled skirts and ran shrieking down corridors to find reassurance in a man's eyes. See my soft red lips, my white skin, feel how smooth the shaven legs, smell the scented underarms, tell me you love me, dolly me.

There were, of course, other ways to accommodate the spectre within and other ways became more necessary as the spectre grew stronger and rattled the bars of the cage. My husband was a man of uncertain temper. I was quite aware of this before we married. He came from a country ravaged by war, his home had been destroyed, his brother killed, his family made refugees and he, corralled off the streets of his town, had spent two years starving in the polar wastes of a Russian prison camp. Understandably, he was outside the conventional pale. I was afraid of him.

The fear was seductive. The dolly shook with it at times, was martyred by it. 15 Hit, punched, she fell to the floor and lay, a poor pale victim, her lashes fanned against an appealingly white cheek stained, briefly, dull red. Later, kindly, she accepted the remorse of her attacker, grovelling before her. Yes, I forgive you, she said. And well she might forgive, because down in the dungeon beneath, her other self was quiet for the time being, gorged to quiescence on the thick hot adrenaline provided by the man. A small price to pay.

I do not know how many people stand at the altar repeating the marriage vows and knowing, however unclearly, that what they say is false and what they do calamitous. My doll stood stiffly in her stiff dress, the groom beside her, and there was not a hope for them. Upbringing had set us against each other from the start and each was busily preparing to hammer the other into an appropriate frame. After the service well-wishers launched our raft with champagne; lashed together, not far out, we sank.

Next time, I chose more carefully. The doll, anyway, was aware that her days were numbered. Winning ways must be adjusted if they are to go on being useful and a good actress acknowledges that she has aged out of *ingénue* roles before the casting director says don't call us. Besides, I was no longer enamoured of my puppet and did not want to extend her life much further. She had become more obstacle than defence, the way a wall, originally built to keep enemies out, can come to be a prison keeping you in.

So I let my real self out on probation, to be called in only now and then for discipline. And now I needed a male with all the right worldly appurtenances, whom I could use as a hermit crab uses a shell, to reach full growth without exposing vulnerable flesh. Using him, I could flex my own muscles in safety until they were strong enough to risk exposure.

So I fell in love with my second husband. This time, the emotion was much more powerful because I knew he had seen something of my real self before he took me on. I thought him beautiful, a golden man, flamboyant and seductively hollow, like a rocket into which I could squeeze myself and guide the flight, using his engines. He was so large he filled a room, his laugh set it shaking, his shining head topped everyone, he drew all eyes. In the turmoil of his wake I found breathing space, I could advance or retreat as I chose. He had another desirable asset and that was his lack of self-restraint. He never talked if he could shout, he never saved if he could spend, he was full of tall stories and the drinks were always on him. All of which combined to make him a natural force and nat- ural forces can be harnessed for other ends. By his noisy, infuriating, unpre- dictable, ebullient and blustering existence he made me look, in comparison, a good, calm, reasonable and deeply feminine woman and thus I was able, over the years with him, to allow my real self out for airings in the sure knowledge that though I might not be as adorable as the doll, I was bound to appear more acceptable than I actually was.

There were drawbacks, of course. Originally, the space within our relation- 20 ship was almost entirely taken up with the volume of his ego and I made do in a little left-over corner. He breathed deeply, his lungs fully expanded, and I breathed lightly, in short thin gasps, and there was air enough for both of us. But then things changed. I learned a trade, began to work, worked hard and earned money. Hey, he said, getting a little stuffy in here, isn't it? Sorry, darling, I said. I breathed more deeply and new ideas rushed in. The voices of American women reached me, ideas on women's rights that linked me to the clamour of the out- side world. For the first time I saw myself face to face, recognized myself, realised that I was not my own creation, uniquely formed in special circum- stances, but much of a muchness with other women, a fairly standard female product made by a conveyor-belt society. Inner battles, to be fought for myself alone, became outer battles, to be fought alongside the whole female sex. Release, euphoria. Look, said my husband, I haven't enough room. Neither have I, I said. I would not placate, I would not apologise, I would not give ground any more because I was connected now to a larger army that waged a bigger war, and rescue was at hand. The slaves had revolted and even the most abject gained strength for their individual skirmishes from the growing aware- ness that they were not personally slavish but merely enslaved. My poor man had his problems, too, but I felt no pity, then. The walls of our relationship were closing in, we fought each other as the oxygen gave out and finally I made it into the cold, invigorating fresh air. The dolly died of double pneumonia but I was still alive.

That is a brief sketch of two marriages, founded on something we all called love because we lived in the romantic West and what other reason is allowed for marriage, if not love? On the surface, of course, the upheavals were not so apparent, being thought of as private quarrels, and I have anyway condensed them greatly — they were actually spread over seven years each, the seven years they say it takes a human to replace every cell of body skin. In the lulls between there were good times, when we laughed together and shared quite a deal of tenderness and celebrated the birth of children, and just ordinary times when we went about the business of marriage, the paying of bills, the buying of goods, the cooking and the cleaning and the entertainment of friends, as every couple does. I make very little of them because the world made so much, crowding around the happy wife, the successful husband, and abruptly turning away, turning a blind and embarrassed eye to the sobbing wife and the angry, frustrated husband. Besides, the violence was endemic and perhaps because of that, ignored as much as possible. Each of us thought we were building new houses, especially designed for us, but we didn't know about the quicksand beneath or the death-watch beetles munching the timbers. An all-pervading dishonesty hung over our enterprise. I was not what I pretended and neither were they. I sold my soul for a mess of sacrificial femininity, sugar and spice and all things nice. They built a prison with their own masculinity, so constricting it made them red in the face, choleric. And the impulsion to act on our roles, the sheer effort it took, left little time or energy to investigate small sounds of protest within. What reward, anyway, would there be for such investigation? In fact, only penalties would be paid. Loss of social approval, isolation from friends and family, accusations of bizarre behaviour and, for the woman, selfishness, that sin forbidden to any female unless she be extraordinarily rich, beautiful or old. To let the human being show behind the mask of gender was to risk even madness. They might come and take us away to the funny farm, make arrangements for derangement.

Much safer to be what they wanted, what was considered respectable. Much better to lean heavily upon each other for support and set up a quarrel, some drama, whenever the inner voices grew querulous and needed to be drowned. *Men*, said my mother, wiping my tears away. *Women*, said my father, soothing a husband. They sounded calm and quite pleased. Well, it was all very natural, wasn't it?

Long before all this, in my very first close encounter with the opposite sex, the pattern was laid down. I was ten at the time and jaunted daily back and forth to school on a bus. Every morning a boy was also waiting at the stop, he with his mates and I with mine. I liked the way he looked, I laughed a little louder when he was about. One afternoon, on the way home, it happened. I was sitting right at the front of the bus and he was two rows behind. There came a rustle, sounds of suppressed mirth, a hand stuck itself over my shoulder and thrust a small piece of paper at me. I unfolded it. There upon the graph-lined page were fat letters in pencil. "Dear Girl," said the letters, "I love you."

I read the message and stared out of the window and watched the grass that lined the road grow as green as emeralds, as if a light had been lit under every leaf. An ache started at my chest and spread through every vein until

I was heavy, drugged with glucose, banjaxed° by that most potent of love-surrogates — thick undiluted narcissism. A boy, a stranger, a member of the male sex, encased in his own unknown life, lying on his unknown bed, had thought of me and, by doing so, given me surreality. Until that moment "I" was who I thought I was. From then on for a very long time, "I" was whoever a man thought I was. That pencilled note signalled the end of an autonomy I was not to experience again for many years. As I turned towards that boy, tilting my chin, narrowing my eyes, pulling down my underlip to show my pearly teeth, giving him my first consciously manufactured, all synthetic skin-deep smile, I entered into my flawed inheritance.

Looking back on all this and other episodes of lust and affection, encounters 25 that lasted a week or a year, the picture seems at first glance chaotic and a gloomy sort of chaos at that. Love and failure. By the standards of my time, success in love is measured in bronze and gold and diamonds, anniversaries of the day when love was first publicly seen to be there, at the altar. Thus I am found wanting, like any other whose marriage and relationships have ended in separation, and to be found wanting is meant to induce a sense of failure because those who do not conform must be rendered impotent.

In fact, people of my generation, like all the generations before, have had little chance of success in love of any kind. Many of those who offer the longevity of their marriage as proof of enduring love are often only revealing their own endurance in the face of ravaging compromises and a resulting anaesthesia that has left them half-way dead. In the name of that love they have jettisoned every grace considered admirable in any other part or act of life: honesty, dignity, self-respect, courtesy, kindness, integrity, steadfastness of principle. They have said those things to each other that are unsayable and done those things that are undoable and there is no health in them. They have not been true to themselves and therefore they are false to everyone else, including their children. The man has become and been allowed to become an autocrat, a tin-pot dictator in love's police state. The woman has lowered herself upon the floor to lick his jackboots. Or, sometimes, vice versa. What would never have been permitted strangers is given a free licence under love — abuse, insults, petty denigration, physical attack, intrusions on personal privacy, destruction of personal beliefs, destruction of any other friendships, destruction of sex itself. In order to enter the kingdom of love they have shrunk themselves to the space of less than one and, atrophied in every part, they claim love's crown. Two individuals who could have reached some stature have settled for being pygmies whose life's work, now, is the similar distortion of their offspring.

If love takes any other form than this tight, monogamous, heterosexual, life-long reproductive unit, blessed by the law, the State, the priests and sanctified by gods, it is dismissed as an aberration, hounded as a perversion, insulted as a failure and refused the label "love." The incredible shrinking couple is presented to the world as the central aim and reward of life, a holy grail for which it

°damaged

is never too early to begin searching. Worst of all, we are given to believe that these dwarfish twosomes form the rock upon which all the rest of life is built, from the mental health of children to whole political systems and to remain outside it is to opt out of a cosmic responsibility and threaten the very roots of the human community. Love is all, they say. Love makes the world go round, they say. And you know it's true love, they say, when two people remain together from youth to death.

But you don't and it doesn't and you can't. The truth is that we have not yet created upon this earth the conditions in which true love can exist. Most of us are quite aware that most of mankind's other developments, emotional or technological, have been dependent upon certain prerequisites. Fire had to be discovered before we could develop a taste for cooked food and a pot to cook it in. Mass literacy was only possible after the invention of printing and printing itself depended on the much earlier Chinese discovery of paper-making. The geodesic dome was an absolute impossibility before the computer age. The emotions are based on something of the same rules. Men's lives were not overshadowed by the certainty of death (and this is still so in some primitive tribes) until life itself was safer and death could be seen inevitably to arrive without sudden injury or accident. Unlike his fellow Greeks, Xenophanes[3] was a monotheist, largely because he guessed that the physical characteristics of the earth changed with time and belief in one universal god is dependent upon belief in universal rules. And man can only be said to have become truly self-conscious after Freud's delineation of the unconscious. Just so has love its necessary prerequisites, its birth-time in history, its most favourable climatic conditions.

So for all that we lay claim to an eternal heritage of love, man's bosom companion since the dawn of time, we have got it wrong. We have called other emotions love and they do not smell as sweet. Love itself has been very nearly impossible for most of us most of our history and is only just becoming possible today. I failed in love, like many others, because given the tools I had to hand the work could not be done. More hopelessly still, the very blueprint was flawed, rough sketch of the eventual edifice without a single practical instruction, without a brick or a nail, without a vital part or principle. Dreams are not enough.

For Analysis

1. What function does the **epigraph** to this essay serve?

2. How do Tweedie's first and second husbands differ? Suggest a cause for the divorce in each case.

3. In paragraph 27, Tweedie rather bitterly describes the prevailing social attitudes (those taught to the young) toward love and marriage. Is her bitterness justified? Explain.

---

[3] Greek philosopher (b. ca. 570 B.C.).

4. In paragraph 28, the author asserts that "we have not yet created upon this earth the conditions in which true love can exist." What do you suppose she means by "true love"? Do you agree or disagree? Explain.

On Style

1. *Love* and *hate* are abstract nouns. This essay, however, contains many concrete **images** to exemplify those emotional states. Consider the second sentence of paragraph 11: "The demure façade of a prim girl hid a raucous fishwife who folded her massive arms against her chest and cursed." Do these images effectively evoke a split personality? Explain.

2. Select a half page in the essay, and carefully catalog the concrete images the author uses to exemplify abstract ideas such as love, hate, a wife's duty, a husband's role. Suggest how the concrete images affect your response to Tweedie's argument.

Making Connections

1. Describe the circumstances of a divorce you are familiar with. Was one of the parties clearly at fault? Could (or should) the divorce have been prevented?

2. Describe a successful marriage of a friend, relative, or acquaintance. What makes it successful?

Writing Topics

1. In an essay, define your own understanding of "true love." Describe what you expect to contribute and what you expect your partner to contribute to a love relationship.

2. Using a single page of this essay's text, closely analyze Tweedie's use of **figurative language**. What varieties of imagery does she use to make abstractions concrete?

Maxine Hong Kingston (b. 1940)

No Name Woman 1970

"You must not tell anyone," my mother said, "what I am about to tell you. In China your father had a sister who killed herself. She jumped into the family well. We say that your father has all brothers because it is as if she had never been born.

"In 1924 just a few days after our village celebrated seventeen hurry-up weddings — to make sure that every young man who went 'out on the road' would responsibly come home — your father and his brothers and your grandfather and his brothers and your aunt's new husband sailed for America, the Gold Mountain. It was your grandfather's last trip. Those lucky enough to get contracts waved good-bye from the decks. They fed and guarded the stowaways and helped them off in Cuba, New York, Bali, Hawaii. 'We'll meet in California next year,' they said. All of them sent money home.

"I remember looking at your aunt one day when she and I were dressing; I had not noticed before that she had such a protruding melon of a stomach. But I did not think, 'She's pregnant,' until she began to look like other pregnant women, her shirt pulling and the white tops of her black pants showing. She could not have been pregnant, you see, because her husband had been gone for years. No one said anything. We did not discuss it. In early summer she was ready to have the child, long after the time when it could have been possible.

"The village had also been counting. On the night the baby was to be born the villagers raided our house. Some were crying. Like a great saw, teeth strung with lights, files of people walked zigzag across our land, tearing the rice. Their lanterns doubled in the disturbed black water, which drained away through the broken bunds. As the villagers closed in, we could see that some of them, probably men and women we knew well, wore white masks. The people with long hair hung it over their faces. Women with short hair made it stand up on end. Some had tied white bands around their foreheads, arms, and legs.

"At first they threw mud and rocks at the house. Then they threw eggs and began slaughtering our stock. We could hear the animals scream their deaths — the roosters, the pigs, a last great roar from the ox. Familiar wild heads flared in our night windows; the villagers encircled us. Some of the faces stopped to peer at us, their eyes rushing like searchlights. The hands flattened against the panes, framed heads, and left red prints.

"The villagers broke in the front and the back doors at the same time, even though we had not locked the doors against them. Their knives dripped with the blood of our animals. They smeared blood on the doors and walls. One woman swung a chicken, whose throat she had slit, splattering blood in red arcs about

5

1265

her. We stood together in the middle of our house, in the family hall with the pictures and tables of the ancestors around us, and looked straight ahead.

"At that time the house had only two wings. When the men came back, we would build two more to enclose our courtyard and a third one to begin a second courtyard. The villagers pushed through both wings, even your grandparents' rooms, to find your aunt's, which also mine until the men returned. From this room a new wing for one of the younger families would grow. They ripped up her clothes and shoes and broke her combs, grinding them underfoot. They tore her work from the loom. They scattered the cooking fire and rolled the new weaving in it. We could hear them in the kitchen breaking our bowls and banging the pots. They overturned the great waist-high earthenware jugs; duck eggs, pickled fruits, vegetables burst out and mixed in acrid torrents. The old woman from the next field swept a broom through the air and loosed the spirits-of-the-broom over our heads. 'Pig.' 'Ghost.' 'Pig,' they sobbed and scolded while they ruined our house.

"When they left, they took sugar and oranges to bless themselves. They cut pieces from the dead animals. Some of them took bowls that were not broken and clothes that were not torn. Afterward we swept up the rice and sewed it back up into sacks. But the smells from the spilled preserves lasted. Your aunt gave birth in the pigsty that night. The next morning when I went for the water, I found her and the baby plugging up the family well.

"Don't let your father know that I told you. He denies her. Now that you have started to menstruate, what happened to her could happen to you. Don't humiliate us. You wouldn't like to be forgotten as if you had never been born. The villagers are watchful."

Whenever she had to warn us about life, my mother told stories that ran like 10 this one, a story to grow up on. She tested our strength to establish realities. Those in the emigrant generations who could not reassert brute survival died young and far from home. Those of us in the first American generations have had to figure out how the invisible world the emigrants built around our childhoods fit in solid America.

The emigrants confused the gods by diverting their curses, misleading them with crooked streets and false names. They must try to confuse their offspring as well, who, I suppose, threaten them in similar ways — always trying to get things straight, always trying to name the unspeakable. The Chinese I know hide their names; sojourners take new names when their lives change and guard their real names with silence.

Chinese-Americans, when you try to understand what things in you are Chinese, how do you separate what is peculiar to childhood, to poverty, insanities, one family, your mother who marked your growing with stories, from what is Chinese? What is Chinese tradition and what is the movies?

If I want to learn what clothes my aunt wore, whether flashy or ordinary, I would have to begin, "Remember Father's drowned-in-the-well sister?" I cannot ask that. My mother has told me once and for all the useful parts. She will add nothing unless powered by Necessity, a riverbank that guides her life. She

plants vegetable gardens rather than lawns; she carries the odd-shaped tomatoes home from the fields and eats food left for the gods.

Whenever we did frivolous things, we used up energy; we flew high kites. We
children came up off the ground over the melting cones our parents brought
home from work and the American movie on New Year's Day — *Oh, You Beautiful Doll* with Betty Grable one year, and *She Wore a Yellow Ribbon* with John
Wayne another year. After the one carnival ride each, we paid in guilt; our tired
father counted his change on the dark walk home.

Adultery is extravagance. Could people who hatch their own chicks and eat   15
the embryos and the heads for delicacies and boil the feet in vinegar for party
food, leaving only the gravel, eating even the gizzard lining — could such
people engender a prodigal aunt? To be a woman, to have a daughter in starvation time was a waste enough. My aunt could not have been the lone romantic
who gave up everything for sex. Women in the old China did not choose. Some
man had commanded her to lie with him and be his secret evil. I wonder
whether he masked himself when he joined the raid on her family.

Perhaps she had encountered him in the fields or on the mountain where the
daughters-in-law collected fuel. Or perhaps he first noticed her in the market-
place. He was not a stranger because the village housed no strangers. She had to
have dealings with him other than sex. Perhaps he worked an adjoining field, or
he sold her the cloth for the dress she sewed and wore. His demand must have
surprised, then terrified her. She obeyed him; she always did as she was told.

When the family found a young man in the next village to be her husband, she
had stood tractably beside the best rooster, his proxy, and promised before they
met that she would be his forever. She was lucky that he was her age and she
would be the first wife, an advantage secure now. The night she first saw him,
he had sex with her. Then he left for America. She had almost forgotten what he
looked like. When she tried to envision him, she only saw the black and white
face in the group photograph the men had had taken before leaving.

The other man was not, after all, much different from her husband. They
both gave orders: she followed. "If you tell your family, I'll beat you. I'll kill you.
Be here again next week." No one talked sex, ever. And she might have separated the rapes from the rest of living if only she did not have to buy her oil from
him or gather wood in the same forest. I want her fear to have lasted just as long
as rape lasted so that the fear could have been contained. No drawn-out fear.
But women at sex hazarded birth and hence lifetimes. The fear did not stop but
permeated everywhere. She told the man, "I think I'm pregnant." He organized
the raid against her.

On nights when my mother and father talked about their life back home,
sometimes they mentioned an "outcast table" whose business they still seemed
to be settling, their voices tight. In a commensal tradition, where food is precious, the powerful older people made wrongdoers eat alone. Instead of letting
them start separate new lives like the Japanese, who could become samurais
and geishas, the Chinese family, faces averted but eyes glowering sideways,
hung on to the offenders and fed them leftovers. My aunt must have lived in the

same house as my parents and eaten at an outcast table. My mother spoke about the raid as if she had seen it, when she and my aunt, a daughter-in-law to a different household, should not have been living together at all. Daughters-in-law lived with their husbands' parents, not their own; a synonym for marriage in Chinese is "taking a daughter-in-law." Her husband's parents could have sold her, mortgaged her, stoned her. But they had sent her back to her own mother and father, a mysterious act hinting at disgraces not told me. Perhaps they had thrown her out to deflect the avengers.

She was the only daughter; her four brothers went with her father, husband, and uncles "out on the road" and for some years became western men. When the goods were divided among the family, three of the brothers took land, and the youngest, my father, chose an education. After my grandparents gave their daughter away to her husband's family, they had dispensed all the adventure and all the property. They expected her alone to keep the traditional ways, which her brothers, now among the barbarians, could fumble without detection. The heavy, deep-rooted women were to maintain the past against the flood, safe for returning. But the rare urge west had fixed upon our family, and so my aunt crossed boundaries not delineated in space.

The work of preservation demands that the feelings playing about in one's guts not be turned into action. Just watch their passing like cherry blossoms. But perhaps my aunt, my forerunner, caught in a slow life, let dreams grow and fade and after some months or years went toward what persisted. Fear at the enormities of the forbidden kept her desires delicate, wire and bone. She looked at a man because she liked the way the hair was tucked behind his ears, or she liked the question-mark line of a long torso curving at the shoulder and straight at the hip. For warm eyes or a soft voice or a slow walk — that's all — a few hairs, a line, a brightness, a sound, a pace, she gave up family. She offered us up for a charm that vanished with tiredness, a pigtail that didn't toss when the wind died. Why, the wrong lighting could erase the dearest thing about him.

It could very well have been, however, that my aunt did not take subtle enjoyment of her friend, but, a wild woman, kept rollicking company. Imagining her free with sex doesn't fit, though. I don't know any women like that, or men either. Unless I see her life branching into mine, she gives me no ancestral help.

To sustain her being in love, she often worked at herself in the mirror, guessing at the colors and shapes that would interest him, changing them frequently in order to hit on the right combination. She wanted him to look back.

On a farm near the sea, a woman who tended her appearance reaped a reputation for eccentricity. All the married women blunt-cut their hair in flaps about their ears or pulled it back in tight buns. No nonsense. Neither style blew easily into heart-catching tangles. And at their weddings they displayed themselves in their long hair for the last time. "It brushed the backs of my knees," my mother tells me. "It was braided, and even so, it brushed the backs of my knees."

At the mirror my aunt combined individuality into her bob. A bun could have been contrived to escape into black streamers blowing in the wind or in quiet wisps about her face, but only the older women in our picture album wear buns. She brushed her hair back from her forehead, tucking the flaps behind her ears.

She looped a piece of thread, knotted into a circle between her index fingers and thumbs, and ran the double strand across her forehead. When she closed her fingers as if she were making a pair of shadow geese bite, the string twisted together catching the little hairs. Then she pulled the thread away from her skin, ripping the hairs out neatly, her eyes watering from the needles of pain. Opening her fingers, she cleaned the thread, then rolled it along her hairline and the tops of her eyebrows. My mother did the same to me and my sisters and herself. I used to believe that the expression "caught by the short hairs" meant a captive held with a depilatory string. It especially hurt at the temples, but my mother said we were lucky we didn't have to have our feet bound when we were seven. Sisters used to sit on their beds and cry together, she said, as their mothers or their slave removed the bandages for a few minutes each night and let the blood gush back into their veins. I hope that the man my aunt loved appreciated a smooth brow, that he wasn't just a tits-and-ass man.

Once my aunt found a freckle on her chin, at a spot that the almanac said predestined her for unhappiness. She dug it out with a hot needle and washed the wound with peroxide.

More attention to her looks than these pullings of hairs and pickings at spots would have caused gossip among the villagers. They owned work clothes and good clothes, and they wore good clothes for feasting the new seasons. But since a woman combing her hair hexes beginnings, my aunt rarely found an occasion to look her best. Women looked like great sea snails — the corded wood, babies, and laundry they carried were the whorls on their backs. The Chinese did not admire a bent back; goddesses and warriors stood straight. Still there must have been a marvelous freeing of beauty when a worker laid down her burden and stretched and arched.

Such commonplace loveliness, however, was not enough for my aunt. She dreamed of a lover for the fifteen days of New Year's, the time for families to exchange visits, money, and food. She plied her secret comb. And sure enough she cursed the year, the family, the village, and herself.

Even as her hair lured her imminent lover, many other men looked at her. Uncles, cousins, nephews, brothers would have looked, too, had they been home between journeys. Perhaps they had already been restraining their curiosity, and they left, fearful that their glances, like a field of nesting birds, might be startled and caught. Poverty hurt, and that was their first reason for leaving. But another, final reason for leaving the crowded house was the never-said.

She may have been unusually beloved, the precious only daughter, spoiled 30 and mirror-gazing because of the affection the family lavished on her. When her husband left, they welcomed the chance to take her back from the in-laws; she could live like the little daughter for just a while longer. There are stories that my grandfather was different from other people, "crazy ever since the little Jap bayoneted him in the head." He used to put his naked penis on the dinner table, laughing. And one day he brought home a baby girl, wrapped up inside his brown western-style greatcoat. He had traded one of his sons, probably my father, the youngest, for her. My grandmother made him trade back. When he finally got a daughter of his own, he doted on her. They must have all loved her, except perhaps my father, the only brother who never went back to China, having once been traded for a girl.

Brothers and sisters, newly men and women, had to efface their sexual color and present plain miens. Disturbing hair and eyes, a smile like no other, threatened the ideal of five generations living under one roof. To focus blurs, people shouted face to face and yelled from room to room. The immigrants I know have loud voices, unmodulated to American tones even after years away from the village where they called their friendships out across the fields. I have not been able to stop my mother's screams in public libraries or over telephones. Walking erect (knees straight, toes pointed forward, not pigeon-toed, which is Chinese-feminine) and speaking in an inaudible voice, I have tried to turn myself American-feminine. Chinese communication was loud, public. Only sick people had to whisper. But at the dinner table, where the family members came nearest one another, no one could talk, not the outcasts nor any eaters. Every word that falls from the mouth is a coin lost. Silently they gave and accepted food with both hands. A preoccupied child who took his bowl with one hand got a sideways glare. A complete moment of total attention is due everyone alike. Children and lovers have no singularity here, but my aunt used a secret voice, a separate attentiveness.

She kept the man's name to herself throughout her labor and dying; she did not accuse him that he be punished with her. To save her inseminator's name she gave silent birth.

He may have been somebody in her own household, but intercourse with a man outside the family would have been no less abhorrent. All the village were kinsmen, and the titles shouted in loud country voices never let kinship be forgotten. Any man within visiting distance would have been neutralized as a lover — "brother," "younger brother," "older brother" — 115 relationship titles. Parents researched birth charts probably not so much to assure good fortune as to circumvent incest in a population that has but one hundred surnames. Everybody has eight million relatives. How useless then sexual mannerisms, how dangerous.

As if it came from an atavism deeper than fear, I used to add "brother" silently to boys' names. It hexed the boys, who would or would not ask me to dance, and made them less scary and as familiar and deserving of benevolence as girls.

But, of course, I hexed myself also — no dates. I should have stood up, both arms waving, and shouted out across libraries, "Hey, you! Love me back." I had no idea, though, how to make attraction selective, how to control its direction and magnitude. If I made myself American-pretty so that the five or six Chinese boys in the class fell in love with me, everyone else — the Caucasian, Negro, and Japanese boys — would too. Sisterliness, dignified and honorable, made much more sense.

Attraction eludes control so stubbornly that whole societies designed to organize relationships among people cannot keep order, not even when they bind people to one another from childhood and raise them together. Among the very poor and the wealthy, brothers married their adopted sisters, like doves. Our family allowed some romance, paying adult brides' prices and providing dowries so that their sons and daughters could marry strangers. Marriage promises to turn strangers into friendly relatives — a nation of siblings.

In the village structure, spirits shimmered among the live creatures, balanced and held in equilibrium by time and land. But one human being flaring up into violence could open up a black hole, a maelstrom that pulled in the sky. The frightened villagers, who depended on one another to maintain the real, went to my aunt to show her a personal, physical representation of the break she had made in the "roundness." Misallying couples snapped off the future, which was to be embodied in true offspring. The villagers punished her for acting as if she could have a private life, secret and apart from them.

If my aunt had betrayed the family at a time of large grain yields and peace, when many boys were born, and wings were being built on many houses, perhaps she might have escaped such severe punishment. But the men — hungry, greedy, tired of planting in dry soil, cuckolded — had been forced to leave the village in order to send food-money home. There were ghost plagues, bandit plagues, wars with the Japanese, floods. My Chinese brother and sister had died of an unknown sickness. Adultery, perhaps only a mistake during good times, became a crime when the village needed food.

The round moon cakes and round doorways, the round tables of graduated size that fit one roundness inside another, round windows and rice bowls — these talismans had lost their power to warn this family of the law: a family must be whole, faithfully keeping the descent line by having sons to feed the old and the dead, who in turn look after the family. The villagers came to show my aunt and her lover-in-hiding a broken house. The villagers were speeding up the circling of events because she was too shortsighted to see that her infidelity had already harmed the village, that waves of consequences would return unpredictably, sometimes in disguise, as now, to hurt her. This roundness had to be made coin-sized so that she would see its circumference: punish her at the birth of her baby. Awaken her to the inexorable. People who refused fatalism because they could invent small resources insisted on culpability. Deny accidents and wrest fault from the stars.

After the villagers left, their lanterns now scattering in various directions 40 toward home, the family broke their silence and cursed her. "Aiaa, we're going to die. Death is coming. Death is coming. Look what you've done. You've killed us. Ghost! Dead ghost! Ghost! You've never been born." She ran out into the fields, far enough from the house so that she could no longer hear their voices, and pressed herself against the earth, her own land no more. When she felt the birth coming, she thought that she had been hurt. Her body seized together. "They've hurt me too much," she thought. "This is gall, and it will kill me." With forehead and knees against the earth, her body convulsed and then relaxed. She turned on her back, lay on the ground. The black well of sky and stars went out and out and out forever; her body and her complexity seemed to disappear. She was one of the stars, a bright dot in blackness, without home, without a companion, in eternal cold and silence. An agoraphobia rose in her, speeding higher and higher, bigger and bigger; she would not be able to contain it; there would be no end to fear.

Flayed, unprotected against space, she felt pain return, focusing her body. This pain chilled her — a cold, steady kind of surface pain. Inside, spasmodically, the other pain, the pain of the child, heated her. For hours she lay on the ground, alternately body and space. Sometimes a vision of normal comfort obliterated reality: she saw the family in the evening gambling at the dinner table, the young people massaging their elders' backs. She saw them congratulating one another, high joy on the mornings the rice shoots came up. When these pictures burst, the stars drew yet further apart. Black space opened.

She got to her feet to fight better and remembered that old-fashioned women gave birth in their pigsties to fool the jealous, pain-dealing gods, who do not snatch piglets. Before the next spasms could stop her, she ran to the pigsty, each step a rushing out into emptiness. She climbed over the fence and knelt in the dirt. It was good to have a fence enclosing her, a tribal person alone.

Laboring, this woman who had carried her child as a foreign growth that sickened her every day, expelled it at last. She reached down to touch the hot, wet, moving mass, surely smaller than anything human, and could feel that it was human after all — fingers, toes, nails, nose. She pulled it up on to her belly, and it lay curled there, butt in the air, feet precisely tucked one under the other. She opened her loose shirt and buttoned the child inside. After resting, it squirmed and thrashed and she pushed it up to her breast. It turned its head this way and that until it found her nipple. There, it made little snuffling noises. She clenched her teeth at its preciousness, lovely as a young calf, a piglet, a little dog.

She may have gone to the pigsty as a last act of responsibility: she would protect this child as she had protected its father. It would look after her soul, leaving supplies on her grave. But how would this tiny child without family find her grave when there would be no marker for her anywhere, neither in the earth nor the family hall? No one would give her a family hall name. She had taken the child with her into the wastes. At its birth the two of them had felt the same raw pain of separation, a wound that only the family pressing tight could close. A child with no descent line would not soften her life but only trail after her, ghostlike, begging her to give it purpose. At dawn the villagers on their way to the fields would stand around the fence and look.

Full of milk, the little ghost slept. When it awoke, she hardened her breasts 45 against the milk that crying loosens. Toward morning she picked up the baby and walked to the well.

Carrying the baby to the well shows loving. Otherwise abandon it. Turn its face into the mud. Mothers who love their children take them along. It was probably a girl; there is some hope of forgiveness for boys.

"Don't tell anyone you had an aunt. Your father does not want to hear her name. She has never been born." I have believed that sex was unspeakable and words so strong and fathers so frail that "aunt" would do my father mysterious harm. I have thought that my family, having settled among immigrants who had also been their neighbors in the ancestral land, needed to clean their name, and a wrong word would incite the kinspeople even here. But there is more to this silence: they want me to participate in her punishment. And I have.

In the twenty years since I heard this story I have not asked for details nor said my aunt's name; I do not know it. People who can comfort the dead can also chase after them to hurt them further — a reverse ancestor worship. The real punishment was not the raid swiftly inflicted by the villagers, but the family's deliberately forgetting her. Her betrayal so maddened them, they saw to it that she would suffer forever, even after death. Always hungry, always needing, she would have to beg food from other ghosts, snatch and steal it from those whose living descendants give them gifts. She would have to fight the ghosts massed at crossroads for the buns a few thoughtful citizens leave to decoy her away from village and home so that the ancestral spirits could feast unharassed. At peace, they could act like gods, not ghosts, their descent lines providing them with paper suits and dresses, spirit money, paper houses, paper automobiles, chicken, meat, and rice into eternity — essences delivered up in smoke and flames, steam and incense rising from each rice bowl. In an attempt to make the Chinese care for people outside the family, Chairman Mao encourages us now to give our paper replicas to the spirits of outstanding soldiers and workers, no matter whose ancestors they may be. My aunt remains forever hungry. Goods are not distributed evenly among the dead.

My aunt haunts me — her ghost drawn to me because now, after fifty years of neglect, I alone devote pages of paper to her, though not origamied into houses and clothes. I do not think she always means me well. I am telling on her, and she was a spite suicide, drowning herself in the drinking water. The Chinese are always very frightened of the drowned one, whose weeping ghost, wet hair hanging and skin bloated, waits silently by the water to pull down a substitute.

For Analysis

1. In what sense did the narrator participate in her aunt's punishment?

2. Given the Chinese belief system, what is the No Name Woman's most significant punishment?

3. What evidence in the essay supports the view that the Chinese villagers favored males over females?

4. Why does the woman enter the pigsty to give birth?

5. What factors intensify the ferocity of the villagers' attack on the house?

6. Discuss the significance of the assertion in paragraph 49: "I alone devote pages of paper to her, though not origamied into houses and clothes."

On Style

1. Reread the essay, noting scenes the speaker seems to invent. What reasons might Kingston have for imagining the events that she could not have known?

2. Look up the definition of **parable**. Why does the narrator's mother tell her about her unfortunate aunt? In what sense might this essay be considered a parable?

Making Connections

1. Describe the techniques for warding off demons or ensuring good luck in your own tradition.

2. Can you justify the villagers' communal attack on the house? Defend your response.

3. Some authors, such as Kate Chopin in "The Storm" (p. 1016), seem to treat sexual infidelity casually; others, such as Shakespeare in *Othello* (p. 1144), treat it murderously. Give reasons to support each view.

Writing Topic

Describe the nature of the No Name Woman's sin. Was it a sin against the absent husband of her hastily arranged marriage, against her extended family, against the village, against the gods?

LOOKING BACK:
Further Questions for Thinking and Writing

1. Almost every story in this section incorporates some sexual element. Distinguish among the functions served by the sexual themes and issues of the stories. **Writing Topic:** Contrast the function of sexuality in Kate Chopin's "The Storm" with that in Pam Houston's "How to Talk to a Hunter."

2. Examine the works in this section in terms of the support they provide for the contention that love and hate are closely related emotions. **Writing Topic:** Discuss the relationship between love and hate in Carver's "What We Talk about When We Talk about Love" and Shakespeare's *Othello.*

3. What images are characteristically associated with love in the prose and poetry of this section? What images are associated with hate? **Writing Topic:** Compare the image patterns in Shakespeare's Sonnets 18 and 130 or the image patterns in John Donne's "A Valediction: Forbidding Mourning" and Christopher Marlowe's "The Passionate Shepherd to His Love."

4. The Greeks have three words that can be translated by the English word *love: eros, agape,* and *philia.* Describe the differences among these three types of love. **Writing Topic:** Find a story or poem that you think is representative of each type of love. In analyzing each work, discuss the extent to which the primary notion of love being addressed or celebrated is tempered by the other two types.

5. William Blake's "A Poison Tree," Molly Peacock's "Say You Love Me," Carolyn Kizer's "Bitch," and Sylvia Plath's "Daddy" all seem to describe aspects of hate. Distinguish among the different varieties of hatred expressed in each poem. **Writing Topic:** Compare and contrast the source of the speaker's hatred in two of these poems.

6. Kate Chopin's "The Storm" and Irwin Shaw's "The Girls in Their Summer Dresses" deal with infidelity. Distinguish between the attitudes toward infidelity developed by these stories. **Writing Topic:** Describe the effects of sexual infidelity on the lives of the major characters in each story.

7. Raymond Carver's "What We Talk about When We Talk about Love" and Irwin Shaw's "The Girls in Their Summer Dresses" deal with jealousy. Contrast the sources of the jealousy and the resolution of the problems caused by the jealousy in both stories. **Writing Topic:** Who, in your opinion, has the better reason for being jealous: Mel in Carver's story or Frances in "The Girls in Their Summer Dresses"? Explain.

8. Which works in this section treat love and/or hate in a way that corresponds most closely with your own experience or conception of those emotional states? Which contradict your experience? **Writing Topic:** For each case, isolate the elements in the work that provoke your response, and discuss them in terms of their "truth" or "falsity."

The Presence of Death

The Dead Mother, 1899–1900, by Edvard Munch.

If life is an illusion, then so is death — the greatest of all illusions. If life must not be taken too seriously — then neither must death.

— Samuel Butler

. . . it is old age, rather than death, that is to be contrasted with life. Old age is life's parody, whereas death transforms life into a destiny: in a way it preserves it by giving it the absolute dimension — "As into himself eternity changes him at last." Death does away with time.

— Simone de Beauvoir

The whole of life is but keeping away the thoughts of death.

— Samuel Johnson

I learned early to keep death in my line of sight, to keep it under surveillance, keep it on cleared ground and away from any brush where it might coil unnoticed.

— Joan Didion

Immortality is what nature possesses without effort and without anybody's assistance, and immortality is what the mortals must therefore try to achieve if they want to live up to the world into which they were born, to live up to the things which surround them and to whose company they are admitted for a short while.

— Hannah Arendt

Death is not the greatest of evils; it is worse to want to die, and not be able to.

— Sophocles

The inevitability of death is not implied in the biblical story of creation; it required an act of disobedience before an angry God passed a sentence of hard labor and mortality on humankind: "In the sweat of your face you shall eat bread till you return to the ground, for out of it you were taken; you are dust and to dust you shall return." These words, written down some 2,800 years ago, preserve one ancient explanation for a persistently enigmatic condition of life. Though we cannot know what death is like, from earliest times men and women have attempted to characterize death, to cultivate beliefs about it. The mystery and certainty of death, in every age, make it an important theme for literary art.

Beliefs about the nature of death vary widely. The ancient Jews of the Pentateuch reveal no conception of immortality. Ancient Buddhist writings describe death as a mere translation from one painful life to another in an ongoing process of atonement that only the purest can avoid. The Christians came to conceive of a soul, separate from the body, which at the body's death is freed for a better (or worse) disembodied eternal life. More recently, attitudes about death reflect the great intellectual revolutions that affected all thought. For example, the Darwinian revolution replaced humans, the greatest glory of God's creation, with upright primates whose days are likely to be numbered by the flux between the fire and ice of geological history; and the Freudian revolution robbed men and women of their proudest certainty — the conviction that they possessed a dependable and controlling rational mind. In the context of Western tradition, these ideas serve to diminish us, to mock our self-importance. And, inevitably, these shifts lead us to alter our conception of death.

But despite the impact of intellectual history, death remains invested with a special awe — perhaps because it infallibly mediates between all human differences. For many, death, like birth and marriage, is the occasion for a solemn, reaffirming ritual. Although for Christians death holds promise of a better life hereafter, the belief in immortality does not eliminate sadness and regret. For those for whom there is no immortality, death is nonetheless a ceremonial affair, full of awe, for nothing human is so purely defined, so utterly important, as a life ended. Furthermore, both the religious and the secular see death in moral terms. For both, the killer is hateful. For both, there are some deaths that are deserved, some deaths that human weakness makes inevitable, some deaths that are outrageously unfair. For both, there are courageous deaths that exalt the community and cowardly deaths too embarrassing to recognize.

The speaker in Robert Frost's "Stopping by Woods on a Snowy Evening" gazes into the dark woods filling up with snow, momentarily drawn toward the peace it represents. But Frost's is a secular poem, and the speaker turns back to life. In much religious poetry — John Donne's sonnet "Death, Be Not Proud" is an outstanding example — death is celebrated as a release from a burdensome existence into the eternal happiness of the afterlife.

The view that establishes death as the great leveler, bringing citizens and emperors to the selfsame dust, is apparent in such poems as Shelley's "Ozymandias" and Housman's "To an Athlete Dying Young." This leveling view of death leads easily to the tradition wherein life itself is made absurd by the fact of death. You may remember that Macbeth finally declares that life is "a tale / Told by an idiot, full of sound and fury, / Signifying nothing." And the contemplation of suicide, which the pain and absurdity of life would seem to commend, provokes responses such as Edwin Arlington Robinson's ironic "Richard Cory." Some rage against death — Dylan Thomas in "Do Not Go Gentle into That Good Night"; others caution a quiet resignation — Frost in "After Apple-Picking" and Catherine Davis in "After a Time," her answer to Thomas. Much fine poetry on death is elegiac — it speaks the melancholy response of the living to the fact of death in poems such as A. E. Housman's "To an Athlete Dying Young" and Theodore Roethke's "Elegy for Jane."

In short, literary treatments of death display immense diversity. In Leo Tolstoy's "The Death of Iván Ilých," dying leads to a redemptive awareness. Bessie Head's "Looking for a Rain God" and Leslie Marmon Silko's "The Man to Send Rain Clouds" explore sacrificial death as a means to control nature. In Dylan Thomas's "Do Not Go Gentle into That Good Night," death is an adversary, a thief that must be resisted. In E. E. Cummings's "nobody loses all the time," the comic lightens the weight of death. The inevitability of death and the way one confronts it paradoxically lend to life its meaning and its value.

LOOKING AHEAD:
Questions for Thinking and Writing

As you read the selections in this section, consider the following questions. You may want to write out your thoughts informally in a journal, if you are keeping one, as a way of preparing to respond to the selections, or you may wish to make one of these questions the basis for a formal essay.

1. Has a close relative or friend of yours died? Was the person young or old, vigorous or feeble? How did you feel? How might the circumstances of death alter one's feelings toward death or toward the person who died?

2. Do you believe that some essential part of you will survive the death of your body? On what do you base the belief? How does it alter your feelings about the death of people close to you? How does it alter your own behavior?

3. Are there any circumstances that justify suicide? Explain. If you feel that some suicides are justifiable, would it also be justifiable to help someone end his or her life? Explain.

4. Are there any circumstances that justify killing someone? Explain.

5. Imagine as best you can the circumstances of your own death. Describe them.

Fiction

Edgar Allan Poe   (1809–1849)

The Cask of Amontillado   1846

The thousand injuries of Fortunato I had borne as I best could, but when he ventured upon insult, I vowed revenge. You, who so well know the nature of my soul, will not suppose, however, that I gave utterance to a threat. At *length* I would be avenged; this was a point definitely settled — but the very definitiveness with which it was resolved precluded the idea of risk. I must not only punish, but punish with impunity. A wrong is unredressed when retribution overtakes its redresser. It is equally unredressed when the avenger fails to make himself felt as such to him who has done the wrong.

It must be understood that neither by word nor deed had I given Fortunato cause to doubt my good will. I continued, as was my wont, to smile in his face, and he did not perceive that my smile *now* was at the thought of his immolation.

He had a weak point — this Fortunato — although in other regards he was a man to be respected and even feared. He prided himself on his connoisseurship in wine. Few Italians have the true virtuoso spirit. For the most part their enthusiasm is adopted to suit the time and opportunity to practise imposture upon the British and Austrian *millionnaires*. In painting and gemmary Fortunato, like his countrymen, was a quack, but in the matter of old wines he was sincere. In this respect I did not differ from him materially; — I was skillful in the Italian vintages myself, and bought largely whenever I could.

It was about dusk, one evening during the supreme madness of the carnival season, that I encountered my friend. He accosted me with excessive warmth, for he had been drinking much. The man wore motley. He had on a tight-fitting parti-striped dress, and his head was surmounted by the conical cap and bells. I was so pleased to see him, that I thought I should never have done wringing his hand.

I said to him — "My dear Fortunato, you are luckily met. How remarkably 5 well you are looking to-day! But I have received a pipe[1] of what passes for Amontillado, and I have my doubts."

"How?" said he, "Amontillado? A pipe? Impossible! And in the middle of the carnival!"

"I have my doubts," I replied; "and I was silly enough to pay the full Amontillado price without consulting you in the matter. You were not to be found, and I was fearful of losing a bargain."

"Amontillado!"

"I have my doubts."

"Amontillado!"   10

"And I must satisfy them."

"Amontillado!"

"As you are engaged, I am on my way to Luchesi. If any one has a critical turn, it is he. He will tell me — "

"Luchesi cannot tell Amontillado from Sherry."

"And yet some fools will have it that his taste is a match for your own."   15

"Come, let us go."

"Whither?"

"To your vaults."

"My friend, no; I will not impose upon your good nature. I perceive you have an engagement. Luchesi —"

"I have no engagement; — come."   20

"My friend, no. It is not the engagement, but the severe cold with which I perceive you are afflicted. The vaults are insufferably damp. They are encrusted with nitre."

"Let us go, nevertheless. The cold is merely nothing. Amontillado! You have been imposed upon; and as for Luchesi, he cannot distinguish Sherry from Amontillado."

Thus speaking, Fortunato possessed himself of my arm. Putting on a mask of black silk, and drawing a *roquelaure*[2] closely about my person, I suffered him to hurry me to my palazzo.

There were no attendants at home; they had absconded to make merry in honor of the time. I had told them that I should not return until the morning, and had given them explicit orders not to stir from the house. These orders were sufficient, I well knew, to insure their immediate disappearance, one and all, as soon as my back was turned.

I took from their sconces two flambeaux, and giving one to Fortunato, bowed 25 him through several suites of rooms to the archway that led into the vaults. I passed down a long and winding staircase, requesting him to be cautious as he followed. We came at length to the foot of the descent, and stood together on the damp ground of the catacombs of the Montresors.

[1] Large wine cask.
[2] Short cloak.

The gait of my friend was unsteady, and the bells upon his cap jingled as he strode.

"The pipe," said he.

"It is farther on," said I; "but observe the white web-work which gleams from these cavern walls."

He turned towards me, and looked into my eyes with two filmy orbs that distilled the rheum of intoxication.

"Nitre?" he asked, at length. 30

"Nitre," I replied. "How long have you had that cough?"

"Ugh! ugh! ugh! — ugh! ugh! ugh! — ugh! ugh! ugh! — ugh! ugh! ugh! — ugh! ugh! ugh!"

My poor friend found it impossible to reply for many minutes.

"It is nothing," he said, at last.

"Come," I said, with decision, "we will go back; your health is precious. You 35 are rich, respected, admired, beloved; you are happy, as once I was. You are a man to be missed. For me it is no matter. We will go back; you will be ill, and I cannot be responsible. Besides, there is Luchesi —"

"Enough," he said; "the cough is a mere nothing: it will not kill me. I shall not die of a cough."

"True — true," I replied; "and, indeed, I had no intention of alarming you unnecessarily — but you should use all proper caution. A draught of this Medoc will defend us from the damps."

Here I knocked off the neck of a bottle which I drew from a long row of its fellows that lay upon the mould.

"Drink," I said, presenting him the wine.

He raised it to his lips with a leer. He paused and nodded to me familiarly, 40 while his bells jingled.

"I drink," he said, "to the buried that repose around us."

"And I to your long life."

He again took my arm, and we proceeded.

"These vaults," he said, "are extensive."

"The Montresors," I replied, "were a great and numerous family." 45

"I forget your arms."

"A huge human foot d'or, in a field azure; the foot crushes a serpent rampant whose fangs are imbedded in the heel."

"And the motto?"

"*Nemo me impune lacessit.*"[3]

"Good!" he said. 50

The wine sparkled in his eyes and the bells jingled. My own fancy grew warm with the Medoc. We had passed through walls of piled bones, with casks and puncheons intermingling, into the inmost recesses of the catacombs. I paused again, and this time I made bold to seize Fortunato by an arm above the elbow.

"The nitre!" I said; "see, it increases. It hangs like moss upon the vaults. We

[3] No one dare attack me with impunity (the motto of Scotland).

are below the river's bed. The drops of moisture trickle among the bones. Come, we will go back ere it is too late. Your cough — "

"It is nothing," he said; "let us go on. But first, another draught of the Medoc."

I broke and reached him a flagon of De Grâve. He emptied it at a breath. His eyes flashed with a fierce light. He laughed and threw the bottle upwards with a gesticulation I did not understand.

I looked at him in surprise. He repeated the movement — a grotesque one.   55

"You do not comprehend?" he said.

"Not I," I replied.

"Then you are not of the brotherhood."

"How?"

"You are not of the masons."[4]   60

"Yes, yes," I said; "yes, yes."

"You? Impossible! A mason?"

"A mason," I replied.

"A sign," he said.

"It is this," I answered, producing a trowel from beneath the folds of my   65
roquelaure.

"You jest," he exclaimed, recoiling a few paces. "But let us proceed to the Amontillado."

"Be it so," I said, replacing the tool beneath the cloak, and again offering him my arm. He leaned upon it heavily. We continued our route in search of the Amontillado. We passed through a range of low arches, descended, passed on, and descending again, arrived at a deep crypt, in which the foulness of the air caused our flambeaux rather to glow than flame.

At the most remote end of the crypt there appeared another less spacious. Its walls had been lined with human remains piled to the vault overhead, in the fashion of the great catacombs of Paris. Three sides of this interior crypt were still ornamented in this manner. From the fourth the bones had been thrown down, and lay promiscuously upon the earth, forming at one point a mound of some size. Within the wall thus exposed by the displacing of the bones, we perceived a still interior recess, in depth about four feet, in width three, in height six or seven. It seemed to have been constructed for no especial use within itself, but formed merely the interval between two of the colossal supports of the roof of the catacombs, and was backed by one of their circumscribing walls of solid granite.

It was in vain that Fortunato, uplifting his dull torch, endeavored to pry into the depths of the recess. Its termination the feeble light did not enable us to see.

"Proceed," I said; "herein is the Amontillado. As for Luchesi —"   70

"He is an ignoramus," interrupted my friend, as he stepped unsteadily forward, while I followed immediately at his heels. In an instant he had reached the extremity of the niche, and finding his progress arrested by the rock, stood stupidly bewildered. A moment more and I had fettered him to the granite. In

---

[4] A member of the Freemasons, an international secretive mutual aid society.

its surface were two iron staples, distant from each other about two feet, horizontally. From one of these depended a short chain, from the other a padlock. Throwing the links about his waist, it was but the work of a few seconds to secure it. He was too much astounded to resist. Withdrawing the key I stepped back from the recess.

"Pass your hand," I said, "over the wall; you cannot help feeling the nitre. Indeed it is *very* damp. Once more let me *implore* you to return. No? Then I must positively leave you. But I must first render you all the little attentions in my power."

"The Amontillado!" ejaculated my friend, not yet recovered from his astonishment.

"True," I replied; "the Amontillado."

As I said these words I busied myself among the pile of bones of which I have 75 before spoken. Throwing them aside, I soon uncovered a quantity of building-stone and mortar. With these materials and with the aid of my trowel, I began vigorously to wall up the entrance of the niche.

I had scarcely laid the first tier of the masonry when I discovered that the intoxication of Fortunato had in a great measure worn off. The earliest indication I had of this was a low moaning cry from the depth of the recess. It was *not* the cry of a drunken man. There was then a long and obstinate silence. I laid the second tier, and the third, and the fourth; and then I heard the furious vibrations of the chain. The noise lasted for several minutes, during which, that I might hearken to it with the more satisfaction, I ceased my labors and sat down upon the bones. When at last the clanking subsided, I resumed the trowel, and finished without interruption the fifth, the sixth, and the seventh tier. The wall was now nearly upon a level with my breast. I again paused, and holding the flambeaux over the masonwork, threw a few feeble rays upon the figure within.

A succession of loud and shrill screams, bursting suddenly from the throat of the chained form, seemed to thrust me violently back. For a brief moment I hesitated — I trembled. Unsheathing my rapier, I began to grope with it about the recess; but the thought of an instant reassured me. I placed my hand upon the solid fabric of the catacombs, and felt satisfied. I reapproached the wall. I replied to the yells of him who clamored. I re-echoed — I aided — I surpassed them in volume and in strength. I did this, and the clamorer grew still.

It was now midnight, and my task was drawing to a close. I had completed the eighth, the ninth, and the tenth tier. I had finished a portion of the last and the eleventh; there remained but a single stone to be fitted and plastered in. I struggled with its weight; I placed it partially in its destined position. But now there came from out the niche a low laugh that erected the hairs upon my head. It was succeeded by a sad voice, which I had difficulty in recognizing as that of the noble Fortunato. The voice said —

"Ha! ha! ha! — he! he! he! — a very good joke indeed — an excellent jest. We will have many a rich laugh about it at the palazzo — he! he! he! — over our wine — he! he! he!"

"The Amontillado!" I said. 80

"He! he! he! — he! he! he! — yes, the Amontillado. But is it not getting late? Will not they be awaiting us at the palazzo, the Lady Fortunato and the rest? Let us be gone."

"Yes," I said, "let us be gone."

"*For the love of God, Montresor!*"

"Yes," I said, "for the love of God!"

But to these words I hearkened in vain for a reply. I grew impatient. I called 85 aloud;

"Fortunato!"

No answer. I called again;

"Fortunato!"

No answer still, I thrust a torch through the remaining aperture and let it fall within. There came forth in return only a jingling of the bells. My heart grew sick — on account of the dampness of the catacombs. I hastened to make an end of my labor. I forced the last stone into its position; I plastered it up. Against the new masonry I reerected the old rampart of bones. For the half of a century no mortal has disturbed them. *In pace requiescat!*[5]

For Analysis

1. We are not told how Fortunato insulted Montresor. Would the story be more effective if we knew? Explain.

2. Are there any clues that suggest when and to whom Montresor tells his tale? Explain.

3. How is Montresor able to lure Fortunato into the catacombs?

4. Describe the qualities that Montresor insists on as the characteristics of a successful vengeance.

On Style

1. Characterize the style of this story, particularly the speech of the characters. What effect does the archaic flavor contribute to the tale?

2. Why does Montresor keep mentioning Luchesi?

Making Connections

1. Compare this story with Shirley Jackson's "The Lottery" (p. 386), which also ends with an unexpected and horrible murder. What similarities do you find? What differences?

2. How would you characterize the **theme** of "The Cask of Amontillado"?

Writing Topics

1. In an essay, imagine and describe the circumstances and the nature of Fortunato's insult.

2. Choose a short section of the story, say three or four paragraphs, and carefully analyze the language line by line (particularly insofar as it differs from ordinary colloquial English), and suggest how the unusual language contributes to the story's effect.

---

[5] May he rest in peace.

Leo Tolstoy   (1828–1910)

The Death of Iván Ilých[1] 1886

CHAPTER I

During an interval in the Melvínski trial in the large building of the Law Courts the members and public prosecutor met in Iván Egórovich Shébek's private room, where the conversation turned on the celebrated Krasóvski case. Fëdor Vasílievich warmly maintained that it was not subject to their jurisdiction, Iván Egórovich maintained the contrary, while Peter Ivánovich, not having entered into the discussion at the start, took no part in it but looked through the *Gazette* which had just been handed in.

"Gentlemen," he said, "Iván Ilých has died!"

"You don't say so!"

"Here, read it yourself," replied Peter Ivánovich, handing Fëdor Vasílievich the paper still damp from the press. Surrounded by a black border were the words: "Praskóvya Fëdorovna Goloviná, with profound sorrow, informs relatives and friends of the demise of her beloved husband Iván Ilých Golovín, Member of the Court of Justice, which occurred on February the 4th of this year 1882. The funeral will take place on Friday at one o'clock in the afternoon."

Iván Ilých had been a colleague of the gentlemen present and was liked by 5 them all. He had been ill for some weeks with an illness said to be incurable. His post had been kept open for him, but there had been conjectures that in case of his death Alexéev might receive his appointment, and that either Vínnikov or Shtábel would succeed Alexéev. So on receiving the news of Iván Ilých's death the first thought of each of the gentlemen in that private room was of the changes and promotions it might occasion among themselves or their acquaintances.

"I shall be sure to get Shtábel's place or Vínnikov's," thought Fëdor Vasílievich. "I was promised that long ago, and the promotion means an extra eight hundred rubles a year for me besides the allowance."

"Now I must apply for my brother-in-law's transfer from Kalúga," thought Peter Ivánovich. "My wife will be very glad, and then she won't be able to say that I never do anything for her relations."

"I thought he would never leave his bed again," said Peter Ivánovich aloud. "It's very sad."

"But what really was the matter with him?"

[1] Translated by Aylmer Maude.

"The doctors couldn't say — at least they could, but each of them said some- 10 thing different. When last I saw him I thought he was getting better."

"And I haven't been to see him since the holidays. I always meant to go."

"Had he any property?"

"I think his wife had a little — but something quite trifling."

"We shall have to go to see her, but they live so terribly far away."

"Far away from you, you mean. Everything's far away from your place." 15

"You see, he never can forgive my living on the other side of the river," said Peter Ivánovich, smiling at Shébek. Then, still talking of the distances between different parts of the city, they returned to the Court.

Besides considerations as to the possible transfers and promotions likely to result from Iván Ilých's death, the mere fact of the death of a near acquaintance aroused, as usual, in all who heard of it the complacent feeling that, "it is he who is dead and not I."

Each one thought or felt, "Well, he's dead but I'm alive!" But the more intimate of Iván Ilých's acquaintances, his so-called friends, could not help thinking also that they would now have to fulfill the very tiresome demands of propriety by attending the funeral service and paying a visit of condolence to the widow.

Fëdor Vasílievich and Peter Ivánovich had been his nearest acquaintances. Peter Ivánovich had studied law with Iván Ilých and had considered himself to be under obligations to him.

Having told his wife at dinner-time of Iván Ilých's death, and of his conjecture 20 that it might be possible to get her brother transferred to their circuit, Peter Ivánovich sacrificed his usual nap, put on his evening clothes, and drove to Iván Ilých's house.

At the entrance stood a carriage and two cabs. Leaning against the wall in the hall downstairs near the cloak-stand was a coffin-lid covered with cloth of gold, ornamented with gold cord and tassels, that had been polished up with metal powder. Two ladies in black were taking off their fur cloaks. Peter Ivánovich recognized one of them as Iván Ilých's sister, but the other was a stranger to him. His colleague Schwartz was just coming downstairs, but on seeing Peter Ivánovich enter he stopped and winked at him, as if to say: "Iván Ilých has made a mess of things — not like you and me."

Schwartz's face with his Piccadilly whiskers, and his slim figure in evening dress, had as usual an air of elegant solemnity which contrasted with the playfulness of his character and had a special piquancy here, or so it seemed to Peter Ivánovich.

Peter Ivánovich allowed the ladies to precede him and slowly followed them upstairs. Schwartz did not come down but remained where he was, and Peter Ivánovich understood that he wanted to arrange where they should play bridge that evening. The ladies went upstairs to the widow's room, and Schwartz with seriously compressed lips but a playful look in his eyes, indicated by a twist of his eyebrows the room to the right where the body lay.

Peter Ivánovich, like everyone else on such occasions, entered feeling uncertain what he would have to do. All he knew was that at such times it is always safe to cross oneself. But he was not quite sure whether one should make obeisances while doing so. He therefore adopted a middle course. On entering the room he began crossing himself and made a slight movement resembling a bow. At the same time, as far as the motion of his head and arm allowed, he surveyed the room. Two young men — apparently nephews, one of whom was a high-school pupil — were leaving the room, crossing themselves as they did so. An old woman was standing motionless, and a lady with strangely arched eyebrows was saying something to her in a whisper. A vigorous, resolute Church Reader, in a frock-coat, was reading something in a loud voice with an expression that precluded any contradiction. The butler's assistant, Gerásim, stepping lightly in front of Peter Ivánovich, was strewing something on the floor. Noticing this, Peter Ivánovich was immediately aware of a faint odour of a decomposing body.

The last time he had called on Iván Ilých, Peter Ivánovich had seen Gerásim   25 in the study. Iván Ilých had been particularly fond of him and he was performing the duty of a sick nurse.

Peter Ivánovich continued to make the sign of the cross slightly inclining his head in an intermediate direction between the coffin, the Reader, and the icons on the table in a corner of the room. Afterwards, when it seemed to him that this movement of his arm in crossing himself had gone on too long, he stopped and began to look at the corpse.

The dead man lay, as dead men always lie, in a specially heavy way, his rigid limbs sunk in the soft cushions of the coffin, with the head forever bowed on the pillow. His yellow waxen brow with bald patches over his sunken temples was thrust up in the way peculiar to the dead, the protruding nose seeming to press on the upper lip. He was much changed and had grown even thinner since Peter Ivánovich had last seen him, but, as is always the case with the dead, his face was handsomer and above all more dignified than when he was alive. The expression on the face said that what was necessary had been accomplished, and accomplished rightly. Besides this there was in that expression a reproach and a warning to the living. This warning seemed to Peter Ivánovich out of place, or at least not applicable to him. He felt a certain discomfort and so he hurriedly crossed himself once more and turned and went out of the door — too hurriedly and too regardless of propriety, as he himself was aware.

Schwartz was waiting for him in the adjoining room with legs spread wide apart and both hands toying with his top-hat behind his back. The mere sight of that playful, well-groomed, and elegant figure refreshed Peter Ivánovich. He felt that Schwartz was above all these happenings and would not surrender to any depressing influences. His very look said that this incident of a church service for Iván Ilých could not be a sufficient reason for infringing the order of the session — in other words, that it would certainly not prevent his unwrapping a new pack of cards and shuffling them that evening while a footman placed four fresh candles on the table: in fact, there was no reason for supposing that this incident would hinder their spending the evening agreeably. Indeed he said this in a whisper as Peter Ivánovich passed him, proposing that they should meet for a game at Fëdor Vasílievich's. But apparently Peter Ivánovich was not destined to play bridge that evening. Praskóvya Fëdorovna (a short, fat woman who despite all efforts to the contrary had continued to broaden steadily from her shoulders downwards and who had the same extraordinarily arched eyebrows as the lady who had been standing by the coffin), dressed all in black, her head covered with lace, came out of her own room with some other ladies, conducted them to the room where the dead body lay, and said: "The service will begin immediately. Please go in."

Schwartz, making an indefinite bow, stood still, evidently neither accepting nor declining this invitation. Praskóvya Fëdorovna recognizing Peter Ivánovich, sighed, went close up to him, took his hand, and said: "I know you were a true friend to Iván Ilých . . ." and looked at him awaiting some suitable response. And Peter Ivánovich knew that, just as it had been the right thing to cross himself in that room, so what he had to do here was to press her hand, sigh, and say, "Believe me . . ." So he did all this and as he did it felt that the desired result had been achieved: that both he and she were touched.

"Come with me. I want to speak to you before it begins," said the widow.   30 "Give me your arm."

Peter Ivánovich gave her his arm and they went to the inner rooms, passing Schwartz who winked at Peter Ivánovich compassionately.

"That does for our bridge! Don't object if we find another player. Perhaps you can cut in when you do escape," said his playful look.

Peter Ivánovich sighed still more deeply and despondently, and Praskóvya Fëdorovna pressed his arm gratefully. When they reached the drawing-room, upholstered in pink cretonne and lighted by a dim lamp, they sat down at the table — she on a sofa and Peter Ivánovich on a low pouffe, the springs of which yielded spasmodically under his weight. Praskóvya Fëdorovna had been on the point of warning him to take another seat, but felt that such a warning was out of keeping with her present condition and so changed her mind. As he sat down on the pouffe Peter Ivánovich recalled how Iván Ilých had arranged this room and had consulted him regarding this pink cretonne with green leaves. The whole room was full of furniture and knick-knacks, and on her way to the sofa the lace of the widow's black shawl caught on the carved edge of the table. Peter Ivánovich rose to detach it, and the springs of the pouffe, relieved of his weight, rose also and gave him a push. The widow began detaching her shawl herself, and Peter Ivánovich again sat down, suppressing the rebellious springs of the pouffe under him. But the widow had not quite freed herself and Peter Ivánovich got up again, and again the pouffe rebelled and even creaked. When this was all over she took out a clean cambric handkerchief and began to weep. The episode with the shawl and the struggle with the pouffe had cooled Peter Ivánovich's emotions and he sat there with a sullen look on his face. This awkward situation was interrupted by Sokolóv, Iván Ilých's butler, who came to report that the plot in the cemetery that Praskóvya Fëdorovna had chosen would cost two hundred rubles. She stopped weeping and, looking at Peter

Ivánovich with the air of a victim, remarked in French that it was very hard for her. Peter Ivánovich made a silent gesture signifying his full conviction that it must indeed be so.

"Please smoke," she said in a magnanimous yet crushed voice, and turned to discuss with Sokolóv the price of the plot for the grave.

Peter Ivánovich while lighting his cigarette heard her inquiring very circum-   35
stantially into the price of different plots in the cemetery and finally decide which she would take. When that was done she gave instructions about engaging the choir. Sokolóv then left the room.

"I look after everything myself," she told Peter Ivánovich, shifting the albums that lay on the table; and noticing that the table was endangered by his cigarette-ash, she immediately passed him an ashtray, saying as she did so: "I consider it an affectation to say that my grief prevents my attending to practical affairs. On the contrary, if anything can — I won't say console me, but — distract me, it is seeing to everything concerning him." She again took out her handkerchief as if preparing to cry, but suddenly, as if mastering her feeling, she shook herself and began to speak calmly. "But there is something I want to talk to you about."

Peter Ivánovich bowed, keeping control of the springs of the pouffe, which immediately began quivering under him.

"He suffered terribly the last few days."

"Did he?" said Peter Ivánovich.

"Oh, terribly! He screamed unceasingly, not for minutes but for hours. For   40
the last three days he screamed incessantly. It was unendurable. I cannot understand how I bore it; you could hear him three rooms off. Oh, what I have suffered!"

"Is it possible that he was conscious all that time?" asked Peter Ivánovich.

"Yes," she whispered. "To the last moment. He took leave of us a quarter of an hour before he died, and asked us to take Volódya away."

The thought of the sufferings of this man he had known so intimately, first as a merry little boy, then as a school-mate, and later as a grown-up colleague, suddenly struck Peter Ivánovich with horror, despite an unpleasant consciousness of his own and this woman's dissimulation. He again saw that brow, and that nose pressing down on the lip, and felt afraid for himself.

"Three days of frightful suffering and then death! Why, that might suddenly, at any time, happen to me," he thought, and for a moment felt terrified. But — he did not himself know how — the customary reflection at once occurred to him that this had happened to Iván Ilých and not to him, and that it should not and could not happen to him, and that to think that it could would be yielding to depression which he ought not to do, as Schwartz's expression plainly showed. After which reflection Peter Ivánovich felt reassured, and began to ask with interest about the details of Iván Ilých's death, as though death was an accident natural to Iván Ilých but certainly not to himself.

After many details of the really dreadful physical sufferings Iván Ilých   45
had endured (which details he learnt only from the effect those sufferings had

produced on Praskóvya Fëdorovna's nerves) the widow apparently found it necessary to get to business.

"Oh, Peter Ivánovich, how hard it is! How terribly, terribly hard!" and she again began to weep.

Peter Ivánovich sighed and waited for her to finish blowing her nose. When she had done so he said, "Believe me . . ." and she again began talking and brought out what was evidently her chief concern with him — namely, to question him as to how she could obtain a grant of money from the government on the occasion of her husband's death. She made it appear that she was asking Peter Ivánovich's advice about her pension, but he soon saw that she already knew about that to the minutest detail, more even than he did himself. She knew how much could be got out of the government in consequence of her husband's death, but wanted to find out whether she could not possibly extract something more. Peter Ivánovich tried to think of some means of doing so, but after reflecting for a while and, out of propriety, condemning the government for its niggardliness, he said he thought that nothing more could be got. Then she sighed and evidently began to devise means of getting rid of her visitor. Noticing this, he put out his cigarette, rose, pressed her hand, and went out into the anteroom.

In the dining-room where the clock stood that Iván Ilých had liked so much and had bought at an antique shop, Peter Ivánovich met a priest and a few acquaintances who had come to attend the service, and he recognized Iván Ilých's daughter, a handsome young woman. She was in black and her slim figure appeared slimmer than ever. She had a gloomy, determined, almost angry expression, and bowed to Peter Ivánovich as though he were in some way to blame. Behind her, with the same offended look, stood a wealthy young man, an examining magistrate, whom Peter Ivánovich also knew and who was her fiancé, as he had heard. He bowed mournfully to them and was about to pass into the death-chamber, when from under the stairs appeared the figure of Iván Ilých's school-boy son, who was extremely like his father. He seemed a little Iván Ilých, such as Peter Ivánovich remembered when they studied law together. His tear-stained eyes had in them the look that is seen in the eyes of boys of thirteen or fourteen who are not pure-minded. When he saw Peter Ivánovich he scowled morosely and shamefacedly. Peter Ivánovich nodded to him and entered the death-chamber. The service began: candles, groans, incense, tears, and sobs. Peter Ivánovich stood looking gloomily down at his feet. He did not look once at the dead man, did not yield to any depressing influence, and was one of the first to leave the room. There was no one in the anteroom, but Gerásim darted out of the dead man's room, rummaged with his strong hands among the fur coats to find Peter Ivánovich's and helped him on with it.

"Well, friend Gerásim," said Peter Ivánovich, so as to say something. "It's a sad affair, isn't it?"

"It's God's will. We shall all come to it some day," said Gerásim, displaying his 50 teeth — the even, white teeth of a healthy peasant — and, like a man in the thick of urgent work, he briskly opened the front door, called the coachman, helped Peter Ivánovich into the sledge, and sprang back to the porch as if in readiness for what he had to do next.

Peter Ivánovich found the fresh air particularly pleasant after the smell of incense, the dead body, and carbolic acid.

"Where to, sir?" asked the coachman.

"It's not too late even now. . . . I'll call round on Fëdor Vasílievich."

He accordingly drove there and found them just finishing the first rubber, so that it was quite convenient for him to cut in.

CHAPTER II

Iván Ilých's life had been most simple and most ordinary and therefore most 55 terrible.

He had been a member of the Court of Justice, and died at the age of forty-five. His father had been an official who after serving in various ministries and departments in Petersburg had made the sort of career which brings men to positions from which by reason of their long service they cannot be dismissed, though they are obviously unfit to hold any responsible position, and for whom therefore posts are specially created, which though fictitious carry salaries of from six to ten thousand rubles that are not fictitious, and in receipt of which they live on to a great age.

Such was the Privy Councillor and superfluous member of various superfluous institutions, Ilyá Epímovich Golovín.

He had three sons, of whom Iván Ilých was the second. The eldest son was following in his father's footsteps only in another department, and was already approaching that stage in the service at which a similar sinecure would be reached. The third son was a failure. He had ruined his prospects in a number of positions and was now serving in the railway department. His father and brothers, and still more their wives, not merely disliked meeting him, but avoided remembering his existence unless compelled to do so. His sister had married Baron Greff, a Petersburg official of her father's type. Iván Ilých was *le phénix de la famille*[2] as people said. He was neither as cold and formal as his elder brother nor as wild as the younger, but was a happy mean between them — an intelligent, polished, lively and agreeable man. He had studied with his younger brother at the School of Law, but the latter had failed to complete the course and was expelled when he was in the fifth class. Iván Ilých finished the course well. Even when he was at the School of Law he was just what he remained for the rest of his life: a capable, cheerful, good-natured, and sociable man, though strict in the fulfilment of what he considered to be his duty: and he considered his duty to be what was so considered by those in authority. Neither as a boy nor as a man was he a toady, but from early youth was by nature attracted to people of high station as a fly is drawn to the light, assimilating their ways and views of life and establishing friendly relations with them. All the

[2] The phoenix of the family, here meaning "rare bird" or "prodigy."

enthusiasms of childhood and youth passed without leaving much trace on him; he succumbed to sensuality, to vanity, and latterly among the highest classes to liberalism, but always within limits which his instinct unfailingly indicated to him as correct.

At school he had done things which had formerly seemed to him very horrid and made him feel disgusted with himself when he did them; but when later on he saw that such actions were done by people of good position and that they did not regard them as wrong, he was able not exactly to regard them as right, but to forget about them entirely or not be at all troubled at remembering them.

Having graduated from the School of Law and qualified for the tenth rank of 60 the civil service, and having received money from his father for his equipment, Iván Ilých ordered himself clothes at Scharmer's, the fashionable tailor, hung a medallion inscribed *respice finem*[3] on his watch-chain, took leave of his professor and the prince who was patron of the school, had a farewell dinner with his comrades at Donon's first-class restaurant, and with his new and fashionable portmanteau, linen, clothes, shaving and other toilet appliances, and a travelling rug, all purchased at the best shops, he set off for one of the provinces where, through his father's influence, he had been attached to the Governor as an official for special service.

In the province Iván Ilých soon arranged as easy and agreeable a position for himself as he had had at the School of Law. He performed his official tasks, made his career, and at the same time amused himself pleasantly and decorously. Occasionally he paid official visits to country districts, where he behaved with dignity both to his superiors and inferiors, and performed the duties entrusted to him, which related chiefly to the sectarians,[4] with an exactness and incorruptible honesty of which he could not but feel proud.

In official matters, despite his youth and taste for frivolous gaiety, he was exceedingly reserved, punctilious, and even severe; but in society he was often amusing and witty, and always good-natured, correct in his manner, and *bon enfant*, as the governor and his wife — with whom he was like one of the family — used to say of him.

In the provinces he had an affair with a lady who made advances to the elegant young lawyer, and there was also a milliner; and there were carousals with aides-de-camp who visited the district, and after-supper visits to a certain outlying street of doubtful reputation; and there was too some obsequiousness to his chief and even to his chief's wife, but all this was done with such a tone of good breeding that no hard names could be applied to it. It all came under the heading of the French saying: "Il faut que jeunesse se passe."[5] It was all done with clean hands, in clean linen, with French phrases, and above all among people of the best society and consequently with the approval of people of rank.

[3] Regard the end.
[4] A large sect, whose members were placed under many legal restrictions, which broke away from the Orthodox Church in the seventeenth century.
[5] Youth must have its fling.

So Iván Ilých served for five years and then came a change in his official life. The new and reformed judicial institutions were introduced, and new men were needed. Iván Ilých became such a new man. He was offered the post of Examining Magistrate, and he accepted it though the post was in another province and obliged him to give up the connections he had formed and to make new ones. His friends met to give him a send-off; they had a group-photograph taken and presented him with a silver cigarette-case, and he set off to his new post.

As examining magistrate Iván Ilých was just as *comme il faut*[6] and decorous a   65 man, inspiring general respect and capable of separating his official duties from his private life, as he had been when acting as an official on special service. His duties now as examining magistrate were far more interesting and attractive than before. In his former position it had been pleasant to wear an undress uniform made by Scharmer, and to pass through the crowd of petitioners and officials who were timorously awaiting an audience with the governor, and who envied him as with free and easy gait he went straight into his chief's private room to have a cup of tea and a cigarette with him. But not many people had then been directly dependent on him — only police officials and the sectarians when he went on special missions — and he liked to treat them politely, almost as comrades, as if he were letting them feel that he who had the power to crush them was treating them in this simple, friendly way. There were then but few such people. But now, as an examining magistrate, Iván Ilých felt that everyone without exception, even the most important and self-satisfied, was in his power, and that he need only write a few words on a sheet of paper with a certain heading, and this or that important, self-satisfied person would be brought before him in the role of an accused person or a witness, and if he did not choose to allow him to sit down, would have to stand before him and answer his questions. Iván Ilých never abused his power; he tried on the contrary to soften its expression, but the consciousness of it and of the possibility of softening its effect, supplied the chief interest and attraction of his office. In his work itself, especially in his examinations, he very soon acquired a method of eliminating all considerations irrelevant to the legal aspect of the case, and reducing even the most complicated case to a form in which it would be presented on paper only in its externals, completely excluding his personal opinion of the matter, while above all observing every prescribed formality. The work was new and Iván Ilých was one of the first men to apply the new Code of 1864.[7]

On taking up the post of examining magistrate in a new town, he made new acquaintances and connections, placed himself on a new footing, and assumed a somewhat different tone. He took up an attitude of rather dignified aloofness towards the provincial authorities, but picked out the best circle of legal gentlemen and wealthy gentry living in the town and assumed a tone of slight dissatisfaction with the government, of moderate liberalism, and of enlightened citizenship. At the same time, without at all altering the elegance of his toilet, he ceased shaving his chin and allowed his beard to grow as it pleased.

---

[6] Proper.
[7] Judicial procedures were reformed after the emancipation of the serfs in 1861.

Iván Ilých settled down very pleasantly in this new town. The society there, which inclined towards opposition to the Governor, was friendly, his salary was larger, and he began to play *vint*,[8] which he found added not a little to the pleasure of life, for he had a capacity for cards, played good-humouredly, and calculated rapidly and astutely, so that he usually won.

After living there for two years he met his future wife, Praskóvya Fëdorovna Míkhel, who was the most attractive, clever, and brilliant girl of the set in which he moved, and among other amusements and relaxations from his labours as examining magistrate, Iván Ilých established light and playful relations with her.

While he had been an official on special service he had been accustomed to dance, but now as an examining magistrate it was exceptional for him to do so. If he danced now, he did it as if to show that though he served under the reformed order of things, and had reached the fifth official rank, yet when it came to dancing he could do it better than most people. So at the end of an evening he sometimes danced with Praskóvya Fëdorovna, and it was chiefly during these dances that he captivated her. She fell in love with him. Iván Ilých had at first no definite intention of marrying, but when the girl fell in love with him he said to himself: "Really, why shouldn't I marry?"

Praskóvya Fëdorovna came of a good family, was not bad looking and had 70 some little property. Iván Ilých might have aspired to a more brilliant match, but even this was good. He had his salary, and she, he hoped, would have an equal income. She was well connected, and was a sweet, pretty, and thoroughly correct young woman. To say that Iván Ilých married because he fell in love with Praskóvya Fëdorovna and found that she sympathized with his views of life would be as incorrect as to say that he married because his social circle approved of the match. He was swayed by both these considerations: the marriage gave him personal satisfaction, and at the same time it was considered the right thing by the most highly placed of his associates.

So Iván Ilých got married.

The preparations for marriage and the beginning of married life, with its conjugal caresses, the new furniture, new crockery, and new linen, were very pleasant until his wife became pregnant — so that Iván Ilých had begun to think that marriage would not impair the easy, agreeable, gay and always decorous character of his life, approved of by society and regarded by himself as natural, but would even improve it. But from the first months of his wife's pregnancy, something new, unpleasant, depressing, and unseemly, and from which there was no way of escape, unexpectedly showed itself.

His wife, without any reason — *de gaieté de coeur*[9] as Iván Ilých expressed it to himself — began to disturb the pleasure and propriety of their life. She began to be jealous without any cause, expected him to devote his whole attention to her, found fault with everything, and made coarse and ill-mannered scenes.

At first Iván Ilých hoped to escape from the unpleasantness of this state of affairs by the same easy and decorous relation to life that had served him

---

[8] A card game similar to bridge.
[9] Of a joyous heart. Iván uses the expression ironically.

heretofore: he tried to ignore his wife's disagreeable moods, continued to live in his usual easy and pleasant way, invited friends to his house for a game of cards, and also tried going out to his club or spending his evenings with friends. But one day his wife began upbraiding him so vigorously, using such coarse words, and continued to abuse him every time he did not fulfil her demands, so resolutely and with such evident determination not to give way till he submitted — that is, till he stayed at home and was bored just as she was — that he became alarmed. He now realized that matrimony — at any rate with Praskóvya Fëdorovna — was not always conducive to the pleasures and amenities of life but on the contrary often infringed both comfort and propriety, and that he must therefore entrench himself against such infringement. And Iván Ilých began to seek for means of doing so. His official duties were the one thing that imposed upon Praskóvya Fëdorovna, and by means of his official work and the duties attached to it he began struggling with his wife to secure his own independence.

With the birth of their child, the attempts to feed it and the various failures in doing so, and with the real and imaginary illnesses of mother and child, in which Iván Ilých's sympathy was demanded but about which he understood nothing, the need of securing for himself an existence outside his family life became still more imperative. 75

As his wife grew more irritable and exacting and Iván Ilých transferred the centre of gravity of his life more and more to his official work, so did he grow to like his work better and became more ambitious than before.

Very soon, within a year of his wedding, Iván Ilých had realized that marriage, though it may add some comforts to life, is in fact a very intricate and difficult affair towards which in order to perform one's duty, that is, to lead a decorous life approved of by society, one must adopt a definite attitude just as towards one's official duties.

And Iván Ilých evolved such an attitude towards married life. He only required of it those conveniences — dinner at home, housewife, and bed — which it could give him, and above all that propriety of external forms required by public opinion. For the rest he looked for lighthearted pleasure and propriety, and was very thankful when he found them, but if he met with antagonism and querulousness he at once retired into his separate fenced-off world of official duties, where he found satisfaction.

Iván Ilých was esteemed a good official, and after three years was made Assistant Public Prosecutor. His new duties, their importance, the possibility of indicting and imprisoning anyone he chose, the publicity his speeches received, and the success he had in all these things, made his work still more attractive.

More children came. His wife became more and more querulous and ill-tempered, but the attitude Iván Ilých had adopted towards his home life rendered him almost impervious to her grumbling. 80

After seven years' service in that town he was transferred to another province as Public Prosecutor. They moved, but were short of money and his wife did not like the place they moved to. Though the salary was higher the cost of living was greater, besides which two of their children died and family life became still more unpleasant for him.

Praskóvya Fëdorovna blamed her husband for every inconvenience they encountered in their new home. Most of the conversations between husband and wife, especially as to the children's education, led to topics which recalled former disputes, and those disputes were apt to flare up again at any moment. There remained only those rare periods of amorousness which still came to them at times but did not last long. These were islets at which they anchored for a while and then again set out upon that ocean of veiled hostility which showed itself in their aloofness from one another. This aloofness might have grieved Iván Ilých had he considered that it ought not to exist, but he now regarded the position as normal, and even made it the goal at which he aimed in family life. His aim was to free himself more and more from those unpleasantnesses and to give them a semblance of harmlessness and propriety. He attained this by spending less and less time with his family, and when obliged to be at home he tried to safeguard his position by the presence of outsiders. The chief thing however was that he had his official duties. The whole interest of his life now centered in the official world and that interest absorbed him. The consciousness of his power, being able to ruin anybody he wished to ruin, the importance, even the external dignity of his entry into court, or meetings with his subordinates, his success with superiors and inferiors, and above all his masterly handling of cases, of which he was conscious — all this gave him pleasure and filled his life, together with chats with his colleagues, dinners, and bridge. So that on the whole Iván Ilých's life continued to flow as he considered it should do — pleasantly and properly.

So things continued for another seven years. His eldest daughter was already sixteen, another child had died, and only one son was left, a schoolboy and a subject of dissension. Iván Ilých wanted to put him in the School of Law, but to spite him Praskóvya Fëdorovna entered him at the High School. The daughter had been educated at home and had turned out well: the boy did not learn badly either.

CHAPTER III

So Iván Ilých lived for seventeen years after his marriage. He was already a Public Prosecutor of long standing, and had declined several proposed transfers while awaiting a more desirable post, when an unanticipated and unpleasant occurrence quite upset the peaceful course of his life. He was expecting to be offered the post of presiding judge in a University town, but Happe somehow came to the front and obtained the appointment instead. Iván Ilých became irritable, reproached Happe, and quarreled both with him and with his immediate superiors — who became colder to him and again passed him over when other appointments were made.

This was in 1880, the hardest year of Iván Ilých's life. It was then that it 85 became evident on the one hand that his salary was insufficient for them to live on, and on the other that he had been forgotten, and not only this, but that what was for him the greatest and most cruel injustice appeared to others a quite ordinary occurrence. Even his father did not consider it his duty to help him.

Iván Ilých felt himself abandoned by everyone, and that they regarded his position with a salary of 3,500 rubles as quite normal and even fortunate. He alone knew that with the consciousness of the injustices done him, with his wife's incessant nagging, and with the debts he had contracted by living beyond his means, his position was far from normal.

In order to save money that summer he obtained leave of absence and went with his wife to live in the country at her brother's place.

In the country, without his work, he experienced *ennui* for the first time in his life, and not only *ennui* but intolerable depression, and he decided that it was impossible to go on living like that, and that it was necessary to take energetic measures.

Having passed a sleepless night pacing up and down the veranda, he decided to go to Petersburg and bestir himself, in order to punish those who had failed to appreciate him and to get transferred to another ministry.

Next day, despite many protests from his wife and her brother, he started for Petersburg with the sole object of obtaining a post with a salary of five thousand rubles a year. He was no longer bent on any particular department, or tendency, or kind of activity. All he now wanted was an appointment to another post with a salary of five thousand rubles, either in the administration, in the banks, with the railways, in one of the Empress Márya's Institutions,[10] or even in the customs — but it had to carry with it a salary of five thousand rubles and be in a ministry other than that in which they had failed to appreciate him.

And this quest of Iván Ilých's was crowned with remarkable and unexpected 90
success. At Kursk an acquaintance of his, F. I. Ilyín, got into the first-class carriage, sat down beside Iván Ilých, and told him of a telegram just received by the Governor of Kursk announcing that a change was about to take place in the ministry: Peter Ivánovich was to be superseded by Iván Semënovich.

The proposed change, apart from its significance for Russia, had a special significance for Iván Ilých, because by bringing forward a new man, Peter Petróvich, and consequently his friend Zachár Ivánovich, it was highly favourable for Iván Ilých, since Zachár Ivánovich was a friend and colleague of his.

In Moscow this news was confirmed, and on reaching Petersburg Iván Ilých found Zachár Ivánovich and received a definite promise of an appointment in his former Department of Justice.

A week later he telegraphed to his wife: "Zachár in Miller's place. I shall receive appointment on presentation of report."

Thanks to this change of personnel, Iván Ilých had unexpectedly obtained an appointment in his former ministry which placed him two stages above his former colleagues besides giving him five thousand rubles salary and three thousand five hundred rubles for expenses connected with his removal. All his ill humour towards his former enemies and the whole department vanished, and Iván Ilých was completely happy.

He returned to the country more cheerful and contented than he had been 95

---

[10] A charitable organization founded in the late eighteenth century by the Empress Márya.

for a long time. Praskóvya Fëdorovna also cheered up and a truce was arranged between them. Iván Ilých told of how he had been fêted by everybody in Petersburg, how all those who had been his enemies were put to shame and now fawned on him, how envious they were of his appointment, and how much everybody in Petersburg had liked him.

Praskóvya Fëdorovna listened to all this and appeared to believe it. She did not contradict anything, but only made plans for their life in the town to which they were going. Iván Ilých saw with delight that these plans were his plans, that he and his wife agreed, and that, after a stumble, his life was regaining its due and natural character of pleasant lightheartedness and decorum.

Iván Ilých had come back for a short time only, for he had to take up his new duties on the 10th of September. Moreover, he needed time to settle into the new place, to move all his belongings from the province, and to buy and order many additional things: in a word, to make such arrangements as he had resolved on, which were almost exactly what Praskóvya Fëdorovna too had decided on.

Now that everything had happened so fortunately, and that he and his wife were at one in their aims and moreover saw so little of one another, they got on together better than they had done since the first years of marriage. Iván Ilých had thought of taking his family away with him at once, but the insistence of his wife's brother and her sister-in-law, who had suddenly become particularly amiable and friendly to him and his family, induced him to depart alone.

So he departed, and the cheerful state of mind induced by his success and by the harmony between his wife and himself, the one intensifying the other, did not leave him. He found a delightful house, just the thing both he and his wife had dreamt of. Spacious, lofty reception rooms in the old style, a convenient and dignified study, rooms for his wife and daughter, a study for his son — it might have been specially built for them. Iván Ilých himself superintended the arrangements, chose the wallpapers, supplemented the furniture (preferably with antiques which he considered particularly *comme il faut*), and supervised the upholstering. Everything progressed and progressed and approached the ideal he had set himself: even when things were only half completed they exceeded his expectations. He saw what a refined and elegant character, free from vulgarity, it would all have when it was ready. On falling asleep he pictured to himself how the reception-room would look. Looking at the yet unfinished drawing-room he could see the fireplace, the screen, the what-not, the little chairs dotted here and there, the dishes and plates on the walls, and the bronzes, as they would be when everything was in place. He was pleased by the thought of how his wife and daughter, who shared his taste in this matter, would be impressed by it. They were certainly not expecting as much. He had been particularly successful in finding, and buying cheaply, antiques which gave a particularly aristocratic character to the whole place. But in his letters he intentionally understated everything in order to be able to surprise them. All this so absorbed him that his new duties — though he liked his official work — interested him less than he had expected. Sometimes he even had moments of absent-mindedness during the Court Sessions, and would consider whether he should have straight or curved cornices for his curtains. He was so interested in it all that he often did things himself, rearranging the furniture, or rehanging the curtains. Once when mounting a step-ladder to show the upholsterer, who did not understand, how he wanted the hangings draped, he made a false step and slipped, but being a strong and agile man he clung on and only knocked his side against the knob of the window frame. The bruised place was painful but the pain soon passed, and he felt particularly bright and well just then. He wrote: "I feel fifteen years younger." He thought he would have everything ready by September, but it dragged on till mid-October. But the result was charming not only in his eyes but to everyone who saw it.

In reality it was just what is usually seen in the houses of people of moderate 100 means who want to appear rich, and therefore succeed only in resembling others like themselves: there were damasks, dark wood, plants, rugs, and dull and polished bronzes — all the things people of a certain class have in order to resemble other people of that class. His house was so like the others that it would never have been noticed, but to him it all seemed to be quite exceptional. He was very happy when he met his family at the station and brought them to the newly furnished house all lit up, where a footman in a white tie opened the door into the hall decorated with plants, and when they went on into the drawing room and the study uttering exclamations of delight. He conducted them everywhere, drank in their praises eagerly, and beamed with pleasure. At tea that evening, when Praskóvya Fëdorovna among other things asked him about his fall, he laughed and showed them how he had gone flying and had frightened the upholsterer.

"It's a good thing I'm a bit of an athlete. Another man might have been killed, but I merely knocked myself, just here; it hurts when it's touched, but it's passing off already — it's only a bruise."

So they began living in their new home — in which, as always happens, when they got thoroughly settled in they found they were just one room short — and with the increased income, which as always was just a little (some five hundred rubles) too little, but it was all very nice.

Things went particularly well at first, before everything was finally arranged and while something had still to be done: this thing bought, that thing ordered, another thing moved, and something else adjusted. Though there were some disputes between husband and wife, they were both so well satisfied and had so much to do that it all passed off without any serious quarrels. When nothing was left to arrange it became rather dull and something seemed to be lacking, but they were then making acquaintances, forming habits, and life was growing fuller.

Iván Ilých spent his mornings at the law court and came home to dinner, and at first he was generally in a good humour, though he occasionally became irritable just on account of his house. (Every spot on the tablecloth or the upholstery, and every broken window-blind string, irritated him. He had devoted so much trouble to arranging it all that every disturbance of it distressed him.) But on the whole his life ran its course as he believed life should do: easily, pleasantly, and decorously.

He got up at nine, drank his coffee, read the paper, and then put on his undress uniform and went to the law courts. There the harness in which he worked had already been stretched to fit him and he donned it without a hitch: petitioners, inquiries at the chancery, the chancery itself, and the sittings public and administrative. In all this the thing was to exclude everything fresh and vital, which always disturbs the regular course of official business, and to admit only official relations with people, and then only on official grounds. A man would come, for instance, wanting some information. Iván Ilých, as one in whose sphere the matter did not lie, would have nothing to do with him: but if the man had some business with him in his official capacity, something that could be expressed on officially stamped paper, he would do everything, positively everything he could within the limits of such relations, and in doing so would maintain the semblance of friendly human relations, that is, would observe the courtesies of life. As soon as the official relations ended, so did everything else. Iván Ilých possessed this capacity to separate his real life from the official side of affairs and not mix the two, in the highest degree, and by long practice and natural aptitude had brought it to such a pitch that sometimes, in the manner of a virtuoso, he would even allow himself to let the human and official relations mingle. He let himself do this just because he felt that he could at any time he chose resume the strictly official attitude again and drop the human relation. And he did it all easily, pleasantly, correctly, and even artistically. In the intervals between the sessions he smoked, drank tea, chatted a little about politics, a little about general topics, a little about cards, but most of all about official appointments. Tired, but with the feelings of a virtuoso — one of the first violins who has played his part in an orchestra with precision — he would return home to find that his wife and daughter had been out paying calls, or had a visitor, and that his son had been to school, had done his homework with his tutor, and was duly learning what is taught at High Schools. Everything was as it should be. After dinner, if they had no visitors, Iván Ilých sometimes read a book that was being much discussed at the time, and in the evening settled down to work, that is, read official papers, compared the depositions of witnesses, and noted paragraphs of the Code applying to them. This was neither dull nor amusing. It was dull when he might have been playing bridge, but if no bridge was available it was at any rate better than doing nothing or sitting with his wife. Iván Ilých's chief pleasure was giving little dinners to which he invited men and women of good social position, and just as his drawing-room resembled all other drawing-rooms so did his enjoyable little parties resemble all other such parties.

Once they even gave a dance. Iván Ilých enjoyed it and everything went off well, except that it led to a violent quarrel with his wife about the cakes and sweets. Praskóvya Fëdorovna had made her own plans, but Iván Ilých insisted on getting everything from an expensive confectioner and ordered too many cakes, and the quarrel occurred because some of those cakes were left over and the confectioner's bill came to forty-five rubles. It was a great and disagreeable quarrel. Praskóvya Fëdorovna called him "a fool and an imbecile," and he clutched at his head and made angry allusions to divorce.

But the dance itself had been enjoyable. The best people were there, and Iván Ilých had danced with Princess Trúfonova, a sister of the distinguished founder of the Society "Bear My Burden."

The pleasures connected with his work were pleasures of ambition; his social pleasures were those of vanity; but Iván Ilých's greatest pleasure was playing bridge. He acknowledged that whatever disagreeable incident happened in his life, the pleasure that beamed like a ray of light above everything else was to sit down to bridge with good players, not noisy partners, and of course to four-handed bridge (with five players it was annoying to have to stand out, though one pretended not to mind), to play a clever and serious game (when the cards allowed it) and then to have supper and drink a glass of wine. After a game of bridge, especially if he had won a little (to win a large sum was unpleasant), Iván Ilých went to bed in specially good humour.

So they lived. They formed a circle of acquaintances among the best people and were visited by people of importance and by young folk. In their views as to their acquaintances, husband, wife and daughter were entirely agreed, and tacitly and unanimously kept at arm's length and shook off the various shabby friends and relations who, with much show of affection, gushed into the drawing-room with its Japanese plates on the walls. Soon these shabby friends ceased to obtrude themselves and only the best people remained in the Golovíns' set.

Young men made up to Lisa, and Petríshchev, an examining magistrate and 110 Dmítri Ivanovich Petríshchev's son and sole heir, began to be so attentive to her that Iván Ilých had already spoken to Praskóvya Fëdorovna about it, and considered whether they should not arrange a party for them or get up some private theatricals.

So they lived, and all went well, without change, and life flowed pleasantly.

CHAPTER IV

They were all in good health. It could not be called ill health if Iván Ilých sometimes said that he had a queer taste in his mouth and felt some discomfort in his left side.

But this discomfort increased and, though not exactly painful, grew into a sense of pressure in his side accompanied by ill humour. And his irritability became worse and worse and began to mar the agreeable, easy, and correct life that had established itself in the Golovín family. Quarrels between husband and wife became more and more frequent, and soon the ease and amenity disappeared and even the decorum was barely maintained. Scenes again became frequent, and very few of those islets remained on which husband and wife could meet without explosion. Praskóvya Fëdorovna now had good reason to say that her husband's temper was trying. With characteristic exaggeration she said he had always had a dreadful temper, and that it had needed all her good nature to put up with it for twenty years. It was true that now the quarrels were started by

him. His bursts of temper always came just before dinner, often just as he began
to eat his soup. Sometimes he noticed that a plate or dish was chipped, or the
food was not right, or his son put his elbow on the table, or his daughter's hair
was not done as he liked it, and for all this he blamed Praskóvya Fëdorovna. At
first she retorted and said disagreeable things to him, but once or twice he fell
into such a rage at the beginning of dinner that she realized it was due to some
physical derangement brought on by taking food, and so she restrained herself
and did not answer, but only hurried to get the dinner over. She regarded this
self-restraint as highly praiseworthy. Having come to the conclusion that her
husband had a dreadful temper and made her life miserable, she began to feel
sorry for herself, and the more she pitied herself the more she hated her husband. She began to wish he would die; yet she did not want him to die because
then his salary would cease. And this irritated her against him still more. She
considered herself dreadfully unhappy just because not even his death could
save her, and though she concealed her exasperation, that hidden exasperation
of hers increased his irritation also.

After one scene in which Iván Ilých had been particularly unfair and after
which he had said in explanation that he certainly was irritable but that it was
due to his not being well, she said that if he was ill it should be attended to, and
insisted on his going to see a celebrated doctor.

He went. Everything took place as he had expected and as it always does. 115
There was the usual waiting and the important air assumed by the doctor, with
which he was so familiar (resembling that which he himself assumed in court),
and the sounding and listening, and the questions which called for answers that
were foregone conclusions and were evidently unnecessary, and the look of
importance which implied that "if only you put yourself in our hands we will
arrange everything — we know indubitably how it has to be done, always in the
same way for everybody alike." It was all just as it was in the law courts. The doctor put on just the same air towards him as he himself put on towards an accused
person.

The doctor said that so-and-so indicated that there was so-and-so inside the
patient, but if the investigation of so-and-so did not confirm this, then he must
assume that and that. If he assumed that and that, then . . . and so on. To Iván
Ilých only one question was important: was his case serious or not? But the doctor ignored that inappropriate question. From his point of view it was not the
one under consideration, the real question was to decide between a floating kidney, chronic catarrh, or appendicitis. It was not a question of Iván Ilých's life or
death, but one between a floating kidney and appendicitis. And that question
the doctor solved brilliantly, as it seemed to Iván Ilých, in favour of the appendix, with the reservation that should an examination of the urine give fresh indications the matter would be reconsidered. All this was just what Iván Ilých had
himself brilliantly accomplished a thousand times in dealing with men on trial.
The doctor summed up just as brilliantly, looking over his spectacles triumphantly and even gaily at the accused. From the doctor's summing up Iván
Ilých concluded that things were bad, but that for the doctor, and perhaps for

everybody else, it was a matter of indifference, though for him it was bad. And this conclusion struck him painfully, arousing in him a great feeling of pity for himself and of bitterness towards the doctor's indifference to a matter of such importance.

He said nothing of this, but rose, placed the doctor's fee on the table, and remarked with a sigh: "We sick people probably often put inappropriate questions. But tell me, in general, is this complaint dangerous, or not? . . ."

The doctor looked at him sternly over his spectacles with one eye, as if to say: "Prisoner, if you will not keep to the questions put to you, I shall be obliged to have you removed from the court."

"I have already told you what I consider necessary and proper. The analysis may show something more." And the doctor bowed.

Iván Ilých went out slowly, seated himself disconsolately in his sledge, and   120 drove home. All the way home he was going over what the doctor had said, trying to translate those complicated, obscure, scientific phrases into plain language and find in them an answer to the question: "Is my condition bad? Is it very bad? Or is there as yet nothing much wrong?" And it seemed to him that the meaning of what the doctor had said was that it was very bad. Everything in the streets seemed depressing. The cabmen, the houses, the passers-by, and the shops, were dismal. His ache, this dull gnawing ache that never ceased for a moment, seemed to have acquired a new and more serious significance from the doctor's dubious remarks. Iván Ilých now watched it with a new and oppressive feeling.

He reached home and began to tell his wife about it. She listened, but in the middle of his account his daughter came in with her hat on, ready to go out with her mother. She sat down reluctantly to listen to this tedious story, but could not stand it long, and her mother too did not hear him to the end.

"Well, I am very glad," she said. "Mind now to take your medicine regularly. Give me the prescription and I'll send Gerásim to the chemist's." And she went to get ready to go out.

While she was in the room Iván Ilých had hardly taken time to breathe, but he sighed deeply when she left it.

"Well," he thought, "perhaps it isn't so bad after all."

He began taking his medicine and following the doctor's directions, which   125 had been altered after the examination of the urine. But then it happened that there was a contradiction between the indications drawn from the examination of the urine and the symptoms that showed themselves. It turned out that what was happening differed from what the doctor had told him, and that he had either forgotten, or blundered, or hidden something from him. He could not, however, be blamed for that, and Iván Ilých still obeyed his orders implicitly and at first derived some comfort from doing so.

From the time of his visit to the doctor, Iván Ilých's chief occupation was the exact fulfilment of the doctor's instructions regarding hygiene and the taking of medicine, and the observation of his pain and his excretions. His chief interests came to be people's ailments and people's health. When sickness, deaths, or recoveries were mentioned in his presence, especially when the illness resembled his own, he listened with agitation which he tried to hide, asked questions, and applied what he heard to his own case.

The pain did not grow less, but Iván Ilých made efforts to force himself to think that he was better. And he could do this so long as nothing agitated him. But as soon as he had any unpleasantness with his wife, any lack of success in his official work, or held bad cards at bridge, he was at once acutely sensible of his disease. He had formerly borne such mischances, hoping soon to adjust what was wrong, to master it and attain success, or make a grand slam. But now every mischance upset him and plunged him into despair. He would say to himself: "There now, just as I was beginning to get better and the medicine had begun to take effect, comes this accursed misfortune, or unpleasantness. . . ." And he was furious with the mishap, or with the people who were causing the unpleasantness and killing him, for he felt that this fury was killing him but could not restrain it. One would have thought that it should have been clear to him that this exasperation with circumstances and people aggravated his illness, and that he ought therefore to ignore unpleasant occurrences. But he drew the very opposite conclusion: he said that he needed peace, and he watched for everything that might disturb it and became irritable at the slightest infringement of it. His condition was rendered worse by the fact that he read medical books and consulted doctors. The progress of his disease was so gradual that he could deceive himself when comparing one day with another — the difference was so slight. But when he consulted the doctors it seemed to him that he was getting worse, and even very rapidly. Yet despite this he was continually consulting them.

That month he went to see another celebrity, who told him almost the same as the first had done but put his questions rather differently, and the interview with this celebrity only increased Iván Ilých's doubts and fears. A friend of a friend of his, a very good doctor, diagnosed his illness again quite differently from the others, and though he predicted recovery, his questions and suppositions bewildered Iván Ilých still more and increased his doubts. A homeopathist diagnosed the disease in yet another way, and prescribed medicine which Iván Ilých took secretly for a week. But after a week, not feeling any improvement and having lost confidence both in the former doctor's treatment and in this one's, he became still more despondent. One day a lady acquaintance mentioned a cure effected by a wonder-working icon. Iván Ilých caught himself listening attentively and beginning to believe that it had occurred. This incident alarmed him. "Has my mind really weakened to such an extent?" he asked himself. "Nonsense! It's all rubbish. I mustn't give way to nervous fears but having chosen a doctor must keep strictly to his treatment. That is what I will do. Now it's all settled. I won't think about it, but will follow the treatment seriously till summer, and then we shall see. From now there must be no more of this wavering!" This was easy to say but impossible to carry out. The pain in his side oppressed him and seemed to grow worse and more incessant, while the taste in his mouth grew stranger and stranger. It seemed to him that his breath had a disgusting smell, and he was conscious of a loss of appetite and strength. There was no deceiving himself: something terrible, new, and more important than anything before in his life, was taking place within him of which he alone was aware. Those about him did not understand or would not understand it, but thought everything in the world was going on as usual. That tormented Iván Ilých more than anything. He saw that his household, especially his wife and daughter who were in a perfect whirl of visiting, did not understand anything of it and were annoyed that he was so depressed and so exacting, as if he were to blame for it. Though they tried to disguise it he saw that he was an obstacle in their path, and that his wife had adopted a definite line in regard to his illness and kept to it regardless of anything he said or did. Her attitude was this: "You know," she would say to her friends, "Iván Ilých can't do as other people do, and keep to the treatment prescribed for him. One day he'll take his drops and keep strictly to his diet and go to bed in good time, but the next day unless I watch him he'll suddenly forget his medicine, eat sturgeon — which is forbidden — and sit up playing cards till one o'clock in the morning."

"Oh, come, when was that?" Iván Ilých would ask in vexation. "Only once at Peter Ivánovich's."

"And yesterday with Shébek." 130

"Well, even if I hadn't stayed up, this pain would have kept me awake."

"Be that as it may you'll never get well like that, but will always make us wretched."

Praskóvya Fëdorovna's attitude to Iván Ilých's illness, as she expressed it both to others and to him, was that it was his own fault and was another of the annoyances he caused her. Iván Ilých felt that this opinion escaped her involuntarily — but that did not make it easier for him.

At the law courts too, Iván Ilých noticed, or thought he noticed, a strange attitude towards himself. It sometimes seemed to him that people were watching him inquisitively as a man whose place might soon be vacant. Then again, his friends would suddenly begin to chaff him in a friendly way about his low spirits, as if the awful, horrible, and unheard-of thing that was going on within him, incessantly gnawing at him and irresistibly drawing him away, was a very agreeable subject for jests. Schwartz in particular irritated him by his jocularity, vivacity, and *savoir-faire*, which reminded him of what he himself had been ten years ago.

Friends came to make up a set and they sat down to cards. They dealt, bending 135 the new cards to soften them, and he sorted the diamonds in his hand and found he had seven. His partner said "No trumps" and supported him with two diamonds. What more could be wished for? It ought to be jolly and lively. They would make a grand slam. But suddenly Iván Ilých was conscious of that gnawing pain, that taste in his mouth, and it seemed ridiculous that in such circumstances he should be pleased to make a grand slam.

He looked at his partner Mikháil Mikháylovich, who rapped the table with his strong hand and instead of snatching up the tricks pushed the cards courteously and indulgently towards Iván Ilých that he might have the pleasure of gathering them up without the trouble of stretching out his hand for them. "Does he think I am too weak to stretch out my arm?" thought Iván Ilých, and forgetting what he was doing he over-trumped his partner, missing the grand slam by three tricks. And what was most awful of all was that he saw how upset Mikháil Mikháylovich was about it but did not himself care. And it was dreadful to realize why he did not care.

They all saw that he was suffering and said: "We can stop if you are tired. Take a rest." Lie down? No, he was not at all tired, and he finished the rubber. All were gloomy and silent. Iván Ilých felt that he had diffused this gloom over them and could not dispel it. They had supper and went away, and Iván Ilých was left alone with the consciousness that his life was poisoned and was poisoning the lives of others, and that this poison did not weaken but penetrated more and more deeply into his whole being.

With this consciousness, and with physical pain besides the terror, he must go to bed, often to lie awake the greater part of the night. Next morning he had to get up again, dress, go to the law courts, speak, and write; or if he did not go out, spend at home those twenty-four hours a day each of which was a torture. And he had to live thus all alone on the brink of an abyss, with no one who understood or pitied him.

CHAPTER V

So one month passed and then another. Just before the New Year his brother-in-law came to town and stayed at their house. Iván Ilých was at the law courts and Praskóvya Fëdorovna had gone shopping. When Iván Ilých came home and entered his study he found his brother-in-law there — a healthy, florid man — unpacking his portmanteau himself. He raised his head on hearing Iván Ilých's footsteps and looked up at him for a moment without a word. That stare told Iván Ilých everything. His brother-in-law opened his mouth to utter an exclamation of surprise but checked himself, and that action confirmed it all.

"I have changed, eh?"

140

"Yes, there is a change."

And after that, try as he would to get his brother-in-law to return to the subject of his looks, the latter would say nothing about it. Praskóvya Fëdorovna came home and her brother went out to her. Iván Ilých locked the door and began to examine himself in the glass, first full face, then in profile. He took up a portrait of himself taken with his wife, and compared it with what he saw in the glass. The change in him was immense. Then he bared his arms to the elbow, looked at them, drew the sleeves down again, sat down on an ottoman, and grew blacker than night.

"No, no, this won't do!" he said to himself, and jumped up, went to the table, took up some law papers and began to read them, but could not continue. He unlocked the door and went into the reception-room. The door leading to the drawing room was shut. He approached it on tiptoe and listened.

"No, you are exaggerating!" Praskóvya Fëdorovna was saying.

"Exaggerating! Don't you see it? Why, he's a dead man! Look at his eyes — there's no light in them. But what is it that is wrong with him?"

"No one knows. Nikoláevich (that was another doctor) said something, but I don't know what. And Leshchetítsky (this was the celebrated specialist) said quite the contrary . . ."

Iván Ilých walked away, went to his own room, lay down, and began musing: "The kidney, a floating kidney." He recalled all the doctors had told him of how it detached itself and swayed about. And by an effort of imagination he tried to catch that kidney and arrest it and support it. So little was needed for this, it seemed to him. "No, I'll go to see Peter Ivánovich again." (That was the friend whose friend was a doctor.) He rang, ordered the carriage, and got ready to go.

"Where are you going, Jean?" asked his wife, with a specially sad and exceptionally kind look.

This exceptionally kind look irritated him. He looked morosely at her.

"I must go to see Peter Ivánovich."

He went to see Peter Ivánovich, and together they went to see his friend, the doctor. He was in, and Iván Ilých had a long talk with him.

Reviewing the anatomical and physiological details of what in the doctor's opinion was going on inside him, he understood it all.

There was something, a small thing, in the vermiform appendix. It might all come right. Only stimulate the energy of one organ and check the activity of another, then absorption would take place and everything would come right. He got home rather late for dinner, ate his dinner, and conversed cheerfully, but could not for a long time bring himself to go back to work in his room. At last, however, he went to his study and did what was necessary, but the consciousness that he had put something aside — an important, intimate matter which he would revert to when his work was done — never left him. When he had finished his work he remembered that this intimate matter was the thought of his vermiform appendix. But he did not give himself up to it, and went to the drawing-room for tea. There were callers there, including the examining magistrate who was a desirable match for his daughter, and they were conversing, playing the piano and singing. Iván Ilých, as Praskóvya Fëdorovna remarked, spent that evening more cheerfully than usual, but he never for a moment forgot that he had postponed the important matter of the appendix. At eleven o'clock he said good-night and went to his bedroom. Since his illness he had slept alone in a small room next to his study. He undressed and took up a novel by Zola, but instead of reading it he fell into thought, and in his imagination that desired improvement in the vermiform appendix occurred. There was the absorption and evacuation and the reestablishment of normal activity. "Yes, that's it!" he said to himself. "One need only assist nature, that's all." He remembered his medicine, rose, took it, and lay down on his back watching for the beneficent action of the medicine and for it to lessen the pain. "I need only take it regularly and avoid all injurious influences. I am already feeling better, much better." He began touching his side: it was not painful to the touch. "There, I really don't feel it. It's much better already." He put out the light and turned on his side . . . "The appendix is getting better, absorption is occurring." Suddenly he felt the old, familiar, dull, gnawing pain, stubborn and serious. There was the same familiar loathsome taste in his mouth. His heart sank and he felt dazed. "My God! My God!" he muttered. "Again, again! and it will never cease." And suddenly the matter presented itself in a quite different aspect. "Vermiform appendix! Kidney!" he said to himself. "It's not a question of appendix or kidney, but of life and . . . death. Yes, life was there and now it is going, going and I cannot stop it. Yes. Why deceive myself? Isn't it obvious to everyone but me that I'm dying, and that it's only a question of weeks, days . . . it may happen this moment. There was light and now there is darkness. I was here and now I'm going there! Where?" A chill came over him, his breathing ceased, and he felt only the throbbing of his heart.

"When I am not, what will there be? There will be nothing. Then where shall I be when I am no more? Can this be dying? No, I don't want to!" He jumped up and tried to light the candle, felt for it with trembling hands, dropped candle and candlestick on the floor, and fell back on his pillow.

"What's the use? It makes no difference," he said to himself, staring with   155
wide-open eyes into the darkness. "Death. Yes, death. And none of them know or wish to know it, and they have no pity for me. Now they are playing." (He heard through the door the distant sound of a song and its accompaniment.) "It's all the same to them, but they will die too! Fools! I first, and they later, but it will be the same for them. And now they are merry . . . the beasts!"

Anger choked him and he was agonizingly, unbearably miserable. "It is impossible that all men have been doomed to suffer this awful horror!" He raised himself.

"Something must be wrong. I must calm myself — must think it all over from the beginning." And he again began thinking. "Yes, the beginning of my illness: I knocked my side, but I was still quite well that day and the next. It hurt a little, then rather more. I saw the doctors, then followed despondency and anguish, more doctors, and I drew nearer to the abyss. My strength grew less and I kept coming nearer and nearer, and now I have wasted away and there is no light in my eyes. I think of the appendix — but this is death! I think of mending the appendix, and all the while here is death! Can it really be death?" Again terror seized him and he gasped for breath. He leant down and began feeling for the matches, pressing with his elbow on the stand beside the bed. It was in his way and hurt him, he grew furious with it, pressed on it still harder, and upset it. Breathless and in despair he fell on his back, expecting death to come immediately.

Meanwhile the visitors were leaving. Praskóvya Fëdorovna was seeing them off. She heard something fall and came in.

"What has happened?"

"Nothing. I knocked it over accidentally."   160

She went out and returned with a candle. He lay there panting heavily, like a man who has run a thousand yards, and stared upwards at her with a fixed look.

"What is it, Jean?"

"No . . . o . . . thing. I upset it." ("Why speak of it? She won't understand," he thought.)

And in truth she did not understand. She picked up the stand, lit his candle, and hurried away to see another visitor off. When she came back he still lay on his back, looking upwards.

"What is it? Do you feel worse?"   165

"Yes."

She shook her head and sat down.

"Do you know, Jean, I think we must ask Leshchetítsky to come and see you here."

This meant calling in the famous specialist, regardless of expense. He smiled malignantly and said "No." She remained a little longer and then went up to him and kissed his forehead.

While she was kissing him he hated her from the bottom of his soul and with   170 difficulty refrained from pushing her away.

"Good-night. Please God you'll sleep."

"Yes."

CHAPTER VI

Iván Ilých saw that he was dying, and he was in continual despair.

In the depth of his heart he knew he was dying, but not only was he not accustomed to the thought, he simply did not and could not grasp it.

The syllogism he had learnt from Kiezewetter's Logic:[11] "Caius is a man, men   175 are mortal, therefore Caius is mortal," had always seemed to him correct as applied to Caius, but certainly not as applied to himself. That Caius — man in the abstract — was mortal, was perfectly correct, but he was not Caius, not an abstract man, but a creature quite, quite separate from all others. He had been little Ványa, with a mamma and a papa; with Mítya and Volódya, and the toys, a coachman and a nurse, afterwards with Kátenka and with all the joys, griefs, and delights of childhood, boyhood, and youth. What did Caius know of the smell of that striped leather ball Ványa had been so fond of? Had Caius kissed his mother's hand like that, and did the silk of her dress rustle so for Caius? Had he rioted like that at school when the pastry was bad? Had Caius been in love like that? Could Caius preside at a session as he did? "Caius really was mortal, and it was right for him to die; but for me, little Ványa, Iván Ilých, with all my thoughts and emotions, it's altogether a different matter. It cannot be that I ought to die. That would be too terrible."

Such was his feeling.

"If I had to die like Caius I should have known it was so. An inner voice would have told me so, but there was nothing of the sort in me and I and all my friends felt that our case was quite different from that of Caius. And now here it is!" he

---

[11] Karl Kiezewetter (1766–1819), author of an outline of logic widely used in Russian schools at the time.

said to himself. "It can't be. It's impossible! But here it is. How is this? How is one to understand it?"

He could not understand it, and tried to drive this false, incorrect, morbid thought away and to replace it by other proper and healthy thoughts. But that thought, and not the thought only but the reality itself, seemed to come and confront him.

And to replace that thought he called up a succession of others, hoping to find in them some support. He tried to get back into the former current of thoughts that had once screened the thought of death from him. But strange to say, all that had formerly shut off, hidden, and destroyed, his consciousness of death, no longer had that effect. Iván Ilých now spent most of his time in attempting to re-establish that old current. He would say to himself: "I will take up my duties again — after all I used to live by them." And banishing all doubts he would go to the law courts, enter into conversation with his colleagues, and sit carelessly as was his wont, scanning the crowd with a thoughtful look and leaning both his emaciated arms on the arms of his oak chair; bending over as usual to a colleague and drawing his papers nearer he would interchange whispers with him, and then suddenly raising his eyes and sitting erect would pronounce certain words and open the proceedings. But suddenly in the midst of those proceedings the pain in his side, regardless of the stage the proceedings had reached, would begin its own gnawing work. Iván Ilých would turn his attention to it and try to drive the thought of it away, but without success. *It* would come and stand before him and look at him, and he would be petrified and the light would die out of his eyes, and he would again begin asking himself whether *It* alone was true. And his colleagues and subordinates would see with surprise and distress that he, the brilliant and subtle judge, was becoming confused and making mistakes. He would shake himself, try to pull himself together, manage somehow to bring the sitting to a close, and return home with the sorrowful consciousness that his judicial labours could not as formerly hide from him what he wanted them to hide, and could not deliver him from *It*. And what was worst of all was that *It* drew his attention to itself not in order to make him take some action but only that he should look at *It*, look it straight in the face: look at it and without doing anything, suffer inexpressibly.

And to save himself from this condition Iván Ilých looked for consolations — 180 new screens — and new screens were found and for a while seemed to save him, but then they immediately fell to pieces or rather became transparent, as if *It* penetrated them and nothing could veil *It*.

In these latter days he would go into the drawing-room he had arranged — that drawing-room where he had fallen and for the sake of which (how bitterly ridiculous it seemed) he had sacrificed his life — for he knew that his illness originated with that knock. He would enter and see that something had scratched the polished table. He would look for the cause of this and find that it was the bronze ornamentation of an album, that had got bent. He would take up the expensive album which he had lovingly arranged, and feel vexed with his daughter and her friends for their untidiness — for the album was torn here and there and some of the photographs turned upside down. He would put it carefully in order and bend the ornamentation back into position. Then it would occur to him to place all those things in another corner of the room, near the plants. He could call the footman, but his daughter or wife would come to help him. They would not agree, and his wife would contradict him, and he would dispute and grow angry. But that was all right, for then he did not think about *It*. *It* was invisible.

But then, when he was moving something himself, his wife would say: "Let the servants do it. You will hurt yourself again." And suddenly *It* would flash through the screen and he would see it. It was just a flash, and he hoped it would disappear, but he would involuntarily pay attention to his side. "It sits there as before, gnawing just the same!" And he could no longer forget *It*, but could distinctly see it looking at him from behind the flowers. "What is it all for?"

"It really is so! I lost my life over that curtain as I might have done when storming a fort. Is that possible? How terrible and how stupid. It can't be true! It can't, but it is."

He would go to his study, lie down, and again be alone with *It*: face to face with *It*. And nothing could be done with *It* except to look at it and shudder.

CHAPTER VII

How it happened it is impossible to say because it came about step by step, 185 unnoticed, but in the third month of Iván Ilých's illness, his wife, his daughter, his son, his acquaintances, the doctors, the servants, and above all he himself, were aware that the whole interest he had for other people was whether he would soon vacate his place, and at last release the living from the discomfort caused by his presence and be himself released from his sufferings.

He slept less and less. He was given opium and hypodermic injections of morphine, but this did not relieve him. The dull depression he experienced in a somnolent condition at first gave him a little relief, but only as something new, afterwards it became as distressing as the pain itself or even more so.

Special foods were prepared for him by the doctors' orders, but all those foods became increasingly distasteful and disgusting to him.

For his excretions also special arrangements had to be made, and this was a torment to him every time — a torment from the uncleanliness, the unseemliness, and the smell, and from knowing that another person had to take part in it.

But just through this most unpleasant matter Iván Ilých obtained comfort. Gerásim, the butler's young assistant, always came in to carry the things out. Gerásim was a clean, fresh peasant lad, grown stout on town food and always cheerful and bright. At first the sight of him, in his clean Russian peasant costume, engaged on that disgusting task embarrassed Iván Ilých.

Once when he got up from the commode too weak to draw up his trousers, he 190 dropped into a soft armchair and looked with horror at his bare, enfeebled thighs with the muscles so sharply marked on them.

Gerásim with a firm light tread, his heavy boots emitting a pleasant smell of tar and fresh winter air, came in wearing a clean Hessian apron, the sleeves of his print shirt tucked up over his strong bare young arms; and refraining from looking at his sick master out of consideration for his feelings, and restraining the joy of life that beamed from his face, he went up to the commode.

"Gerásim!" said Iván Ilých in a weak voice.

Gerásim started, evidently afraid he might have committed some blunder, and with a rapid movement turned his fresh, kind, simple young face which just showed the first downy signs of a beard.

"Yes, sir?"

"That must be very unpleasant for you. You must forgive me. I am helpless."   195

"Oh, why, sir," and Gerásim's eyes beamed and he showed his glistening white teeth, "what's a little trouble? It's a case of illness with you, sir."

And his deft strong hands did their accustomed task, and he went out of the room stepping lightly. Five minutes later he as lightly returned.

Iván Ilých was still sitting in the same position in the armchair.

"Gerásim," he said when the latter had replaced the freshly-washed utensil. "Please come here and help me." Gerásim went up to him. "Lift me up. It is hard for me to get up, and I have sent Dmítri away."

Gerásim went up to him, grasped his master with his strong arms deftly but   200 gently, in the same way that he stepped — lifted him, supported him with one hand, and with the other drew up his trousers and would have set him down again, but Iván Ilých asked to be led to the sofa. Gerásim, without an effort and without apparent pressure, led him, almost lifting him, to the sofa and placed him on it.

"Thank you. How easily and well you do it all!"

Gerásim smiled again and turned to leave the room. But Iván Ilých felt his presence such a comfort that he did not want to let him go.

"One thing more, please move up that chair. No, the other one — under my feet. It is easier for me when my feet are raised."

Gerásim brought the chair, set it down gently in place, and raised Iván Ilých's legs on to it. It seemed to Iván Ilých that he felt better while Gerásim was holding up his legs.

"It's better when my legs are higher," he said. "Place that cushion under   205 them."

Gerásim did so. He again lifted the legs and placed them, and again Iván Ilých felt better while Gerásim held his legs. When he set them down Iván Ilých fancied he felt worse.

"Gerásim," he said. "Are you busy now?"

"Not at all, sir," said Gerásim, who had learnt from the townsfolk how to speak to gentlefolk.

"What have you still to do?"

"What have I to do? I've done everything except chopping the logs for tomor-   210 row."

"Then hold my legs up a bit higher, can you?"

"Of course I can. Why not?" And Gerásim raised his master's legs higher and Iván Ilých thought that in that position he did not feel any pain at all.

"And how about the logs?"

"Don't trouble about that, sir. There's plenty of time."

Iván Ilých told Gerásim to sit down and hold his legs, and began to talk to him. And strange to say it seemed to him that he felt better while Gerásim held his legs up. 215

After that Iván Ilých would sometimes call Gerásim and get him to hold his legs on his shoulders, and he liked talking to him. Gerásim did it all easily, willingly, simply, and with a good nature that touched Iván Ilých. Health, strength, and vitality in other people were offensive to him, but Gerásim's strength and vitality did not mortify but soothed him.

What tormented Iván Ilých most was the deception, the lie, which for some reason they all accepted, that he was not dying but was simply ill, and that he only need keep quiet and undergo a treatment and then something very good would result. He however knew that do what they would nothing would come of it, only still more agonizing suffering and death. This deception tortured him — their not wishing to admit what they all knew and what he knew, but wanting to lie to him concerning his terrible condition, and wishing and forcing him to participate in that lie. Those lies — lies enacted over him on the eve of his death and destined to degrade this awful, solemn act to the level of their visitings, their curtains, their sturgeon for dinner — were a terrible agony for Iván Ilých. And strangely enough, many times when they were going through their antics over him he had been within a hairbreadth of calling out to them: "Stop lying! You know and I know that I am dying. Then at least stop lying about it!" But he had never had the spirit to do it. The awful, terrible act of his dying was, he could see, reduced by those about him to the level of a casual, unpleasant, and almost indecorous incident (as if someone entered a drawing-room diffusing an unpleasant odour) and this was done by that very decorum which he had served all his life long. He saw that no one felt for him, because no one even wished to grasp his position. Only Gerásim recognized it and pitied him. And so Iván Ilých felt at ease only with him. He felt comforted when Gerásim supported his legs (sometimes all night long) and refused to go to bed, saying, "Don't you worry, Iván Ilých. I'll get sleep enough later on," or when he suddenly became familiar and exclaimed: "If you weren't sick it would be another matter, but as it is, why should I grudge a little trouble?" Gerásim alone did not lie; everything showed that he alone understood the facts of the case and did not consider it necessary to disguise them, but simply felt sorry for his emaciated and enfeebled master. Once when Iván Ilých was sending him away he even said straight out: "We shall all of us die, so why should I grudge a little trouble?" — expressing the fact that he did not think his work burdensome, because he was doing it for a dying man and hoped someone would do the same for him when his time came.

Apart from this lying, or because of it, what most tormented Iván Ilých was that no one pitied him as he wished to be pitied. At certain moments after prolonged suffering he wished most of all (though he would have been ashamed to confess it) for someone to pity him as a sick child is pitied. He longed to be petted and comforted. He knew he was an important functionary, that he had a beard turning grey, and that therefore what he longed for was impossible, but still he longed for it. And in Gerásim's attitude towards him there was something akin to what he wished for, and so that attitude comforted him. Iván Ilých wanted to weep, wanted to be petted and cried over, and then his colleague Shébek would come, and instead of weeping and being petted, Iván Ilých would assume a serious, severe, and profound air, and by force of habit would express his opinion on a decision of the Court of Cassation and would stubbornly insist on that view. This falsity around him and within him did more than anything else to poison his last days.

CHAPTER VIII

It was morning. He knew it was morning because Gerásim had gone, and Peter the footman had come and put out the candles, drawn back one of the curtains, and begun quietly to tidy up. Whether it was morning or evening, Friday or Sunday, made no difference, it was all just the same: the gnawing, unmitigated, agonizing pain, never ceasing for an instant, the consciousness of life inexorably waning but not yet extinguished, that approach of that ever dreaded and hateful Death which was the only reality, and always the same falsity. What were days, weeks, hours, in such a case?

"Will you have some tea, sir?"   220

"He wants things to be regular, and wishes the gentlefolk to drink tea in the morning," thought Iván Ilých, and only said "No."

"Wouldn't you like to move onto the sofa, sir?"

"He wants to tidy up the room, and I'm in the way. I am uncleanliness and disorder," he thought, and said only:

"No, leave me alone."

The man went on bustling about. Iván Ilých stretched out his hand. Peter 225 came up, ready to help.

"What is it, sir?"

"My watch."

Peter took the watch which was close at hand and gave it to his master.

"Half-past eight. Are they up?"

"No, sir, except Vladímir Ivánich" (the son) "who has gone to school. Pra- 230 skóvya Fëdorovna ordered me to wake her if you asked for her. Shall I do so?"

"No, there's no need to." "Perhaps I'd better have some tea," he thought, and added aloud: "Yes, bring me some tea."

Peter went to the door but Iván Ilých dreaded being left alone. "How can I keep him here? Oh yes, my medicine." "Peter, give me my medicine." "Why not? Perhaps it may still do me some good." He took a spoonful and swallowed it. "No, it won't help. It's all tomfoolery, all deception," he decided as soon as he became aware of the familiar, sickly, hopeless taste. "No, I can't believe in it any longer. But the pain, why this pain? If it would only cease just for a moment!" And he moaned. Peter turned towards him. "It's all right. Go and fetch me some tea."

Peter went out. Left alone Iván Ilých groaned not so much with pain, terrible though that was, as from mental anguish. Always and for ever the same, always these endless days and nights. If only it would come quicker! If only *what* would come quicker? Death, darkness? . . . No, no! Anything rather than death!

When Peter returned with the tea on a tray, Iván Ilých stared at him for a time in perplexity, not realizing who and what he was. Peter was disconcerted by that look and his embarrassment brought Iván Ilých to himself.

"Oh, tea! All right, put it down. Only help me to wash and put on a clean   235
shirt."

And Iván Ilých began to wash. With pauses for rest, he washed his hands and then his face, cleaned his teeth, brushed his hair, and looked in the glass. He was terrified by what he saw, especially by the limp way in which his hair clung to his pallid forehead.

While his shirt was being changed he knew that he would be still more frightened at the sight of his body, so he avoided looking at it. Finally he was ready. He drew on a dressing-gown, wrapped himself in a plaid, and sat down in the armchair to take his tea. For a moment he felt refreshed, but as soon as he began to drink the tea he was again aware of the same taste, and the pain also returned. He finished it with an effort, and then lay down stretching out his legs, and dismissed Peter.

Always the same. Now a spark of hope flashes up, then a sea of despair rages, and always pain; always pain, always despair, and always the same. When alone he had a dreadful and distressing desire to call someone, but he knew beforehand that with others present it would be still worse. "Another dose of morphine — to lose consciousness. I will tell him, the doctor, that he must think of something else. It's impossible, impossible, to go on like this."

An hour and another pass like that. But now there is a ring at the door bell. Perhaps it's the doctor? It is. He comes in fresh, hearty, plump, and cheerful, with that look on his face that seems to say: "There now, you're in a panic about something, but we'll arrange it all for you directly!" The doctor knows this expression is out of place here, but he has put it on once for all and can't take it off — like a man who has put on a frock-coat in the morning to pay a round of calls.

The doctor rubs his hands vigorously and reassuringly.   240

"Brr! How cold it is! There's such a sharp frost; just let me warm myself!" he says, as if it were only a matter of waiting till he was warm, and then he would put everything right.

"Well now, how are you?"

Iván Ilých feels that the doctor would like to say: "Well, how are our affairs?" but that even he feels that this would not do, and says instead: "What sort of a night have you had?"

Iván Ilých looks at him as much as to say: "Are you really never ashamed of lying?" But the doctor does not wish to understand this question, and Iván Ilých says: "Just as terrible as ever. The pain never leaves me and never subsides. If only something . . ."

"Yes, you sick people are always like that. . . . There, now I think I am warm 245 enough. Even Praskóvya Fëdorovna, who is so particular, could find no fault with my temperature. Well, now I can say good-morning," and the doctor presses his patient's hand.

Then, dropping his former playfulness, he begins with a most serious face to examine the patient, feeling his pulse and taking his temperature, and then begins the sounding and auscultation.

Iván Ilých knows quite well and definitely that all this is nonsense and pure deception, but when the doctor, getting down on his knee, leans over him, putting his ear first higher then lower, and performs various gymnastic movements over him with a significant expression on his face, Iván Ilých submits to it all as he used to submit to the speeches of the lawyers, though he knew very well that they were all lying and why they were lying.

The doctor, kneeling on the sofa, is still sounding him when Praskóvya Fëdorovna's silk dress rustles at the door and she is heard scolding Peter for not having let her know of the doctor's arrival.

She comes in, kisses her husband, and at once proceeds to prove that she has been up a long time already, and only owing to a misunderstanding failed to be there when the doctor arrived.

Iván Ilých looks at her, scans her all over, sets against her the whiteness and 250 plumpness and cleanness of her hands and neck, the gloss of her hair, and the sparkle of her vivacious eyes. He hates her with his whole soul. And the thrill of hatred he feels for her makes him suffer from her touch.

Her attitude towards him and his disease is still the same. Just as the doctor had adopted a certain relation to his patient which he could not abandon, so had she formed one towards him — that he was not doing something he ought to do and was himself to blame, and that she reproached him lovingly for this — and she could not now change that attitude.

"You see he doesn't listen to me and doesn't take his medicine at the proper time. And above all he lies in a position that is no doubt bad for him — with his legs up."

She described how he made Gerásim hold his legs up.

The doctor smiled with a contemptuous affability that said: "What's to be done? These sick people do have foolish fancies of that kind, but we must forgive them."

When the examination was over the doctor looked at his watch, and then 255 Praskóvya Fëdorovna announced to Iván Ilých that it was of course as he pleased, but she had sent to-day for a celebrated specialist who would examine him and have a consultation with Michael Danílovich (their regular doctor).

"Please don't raise any objections. I am doing this for my own sake," she said ironically, letting it be felt that she was doing it all for his sake and only said this to leave him no right to refuse. He remained silent, knitting his brows. He felt that he was so surrounded and involved in a mesh of falsity that it was hard to unravel anything.

Everything she did for him was entirely for her own sake, and she told him she was doing for herself what she actually was doing for herself, as if that was so incredible that he must understand the opposite.

At half-past eleven the celebrated specialist arrived. Again the sounding began and the significant conversations in his presence and in another room, about the kidneys and the appendix, and the questions and answers, with such an air of importance that again, instead of the real question of life and death which now alone confronted him, the question arose of the kidney and appendix which were not behaving as they ought to and would now be attacked by Michael Danílovich and the specialist and forced to amend their ways.

The celebrated specialist took leave of him with a serious though not hopeless look, and in reply to the timid question Iván Ilých, with eyes glistening with fear and hope, put to him as to whether there was a chance of recovery, said that he could not vouch for it but there was a possibility. The look of hope with which Iván Ilých watched the doctor out was so pathetic that Praskóvya Fëdorovna, seeing it, even wept as she left the room to hand the doctor his fee.

The gleam of hope kindled by the doctor's encouragement did not last long. 260 The same room, the same pictures, curtains, wall-paper, medicine bottles, were all there, and the same aching suffering body, and Iván Ilých began to moan. They gave him a subcutaneous injection and he sank into oblivion.

It was twilight when he came to. They brought him his dinner and he swallowed some beef tea with difficulty, and then everything was the same again and night was coming on.

After dinner, at seven o'clock, Praskóvya Fëdorovna came into the room in evening dress, her full bosom pushed up by her corset, and with traces of powder on her face. She had reminded him in the morning that they were going to the theater. Sarah Bernhardt was visiting the town and they had a box, which he had insisted on their taking. Now he had forgotten about it and her toilet offended him, but he concealed his vexation when he remembered that he had himself insisted on their securing a box and going because it would be an instructive and aesthetic pleasure for the children.

Praskóvya Fëdorovna came in, self-satisfied but yet with a rather guilty air. She sat down and asked how he was, but, as he saw, only for the sake of asking and not in order to learn about it, knowing that there was nothing to learn — and then went on to what she really wanted to say: that she would not on any account have gone but that the box had been taken and Helen and their daughter were going, as well as Petríshchev (the examining magistrate, their daughter's fiancé) and that it was out of the question to let them go alone; but that she would have much preferred to sit with him for a while; and he must be sure to follow the doctor's orders while she was away.

"Oh, and Fëdor Petróvich" (the fiancé) "would like to come in. May he? And Lisa?"

"All right."

Their daughter came in in full evening dress, her fresh young flesh exposed (making a show of that very flesh which in his own case caused so much suffering), strong, healthy, evidently in love, and impatient with illness, suffering, and death, because they interfered with her happiness.

Fëdor Petróvich came in too, in evening dress, his hair curled *á la Capoul,* a tight stiff collar round his long sinewy neck, an enormous white shirt-front and narrow black trousers tightly stretched over his strong thighs. He had one white glove tightly drawn on, and was holding his opera hat in his hand.

Following him the schoolboy crept in unnoticed, in a new uniform, poor little fellow, and wearing gloves. Terribly dark shadows showed under his eyes, the meaning of which Iván Ilých knew well.

His son had always seemed pathetic to him, and now it was dreadful to see the boy's frightened look of pity. It seemed to Iván Ilých that Vásya was the only one besides Gerásim who understood and pitied him.

They all sat down and again asked how he was. A silence followed. Lisa asked her mother about the opera-glasses, and there was an altercation between mother and daughter as to who had taken them and where they had been put. This occasioned some unpleasantness. 270

Fëdor Petróvich inquired of Iván Ilých whether he had ever seen Sarah Bernhardt. Iván Ilých did not at first catch the question, but then replied: "No, have you seen her before?"

"Yes, in *Adrienne Lecouvreur.*"[12]

Praskóvya Fëdorovna mentioned some roles in which Sarah Bernhardt was particularly good. Her daughter disagreed. Conversation sprang up as to the elegance and realism of her acting — the sort of conversation that is always repeated and is always the same.

In the midst of the conversation Fëdor Petróvich glanced at Iván Ilých and became silent. The others also looked at him and grew silent. Iván Ilých was staring with glittering eyes straight before him, evidently indignant with them. This had to be rectified, but it was impossible to do so. The silence had to be broken, but for a time no one dared to break it and they all became afraid that the conventional deception would suddenly become obvious and the truth become plain to all. Lisa was the first to pluck up courage and break that silence, but by trying to hide what everybody was feeling, she betrayed it.

"Well, if we are going it's time to start," she said, looking at her watch, a present from her father, and with a faint and significant smile at Fëdor Petróvich relating to something known only to them. She got up with a rustle of her dress. 275

They all rose, said good-night, and went away.

When they had gone it seemed to Iván Ilých that he felt better; the falsity had gone with them. But the pain remained — that same pain and that same fear that made everything monotonously alike, nothing harder and nothing easier. Everything was worse.

Again minute followed minute and hour followed hour. Everything remained

[12] A play by the French dramatist Eugène Scribe (1791–1861).

the same and there was no cessation. And the inevitable end of it all became more and more terrible.

"Yes, send Gerásim here," he replied to a question Peter asked.

CHAPTER IX

His wife returned late at night. She came in on tiptoe, but he heard her, opened 280
his eyes, and made haste to close them again. She wished to send Gerásim away and to sit with him herself, but he opened his eyes and said: "No, go away."

"Are you in great pain?"

"Always the same."

"Take some opium."

He agreed and took some. She went away.

Till about three in the morning he was in a state of stupefied misery. It seemed 285
to him that he and his pain were being thrust into a narrow, deep black sack, but though they were pushed further and further in they could not be pushed to the bottom. And this, terrible enough in itself, was accompanied by suffering. He was frightened yet wanted to fall through the sack, he struggled but yet co-operated. And suddenly he broke through, fell, and regained consciousness. Gerásim was sitting at the foot of the bed dozing quietly and patiently, while he himself lay with his emaciated stockinged legs resting on Gerásim's shoulders; the same shaded candle was there and the same unceasing pain.

"Go away, Gerásim," he whispered.

"It's all right, sir. I'll stay a while."

"No. Go away."

He removed his legs from Gerásim's shoulders, turned sideways onto his arm, and felt sorry for himself. He only waited till Gerásim had gone into the next room and then restrained himself no longer but wept like a child. He wept on account of his helplessness, his terrible loneliness, the cruelty of man, the cruelty of God, and the absence of God.

"Why hast Thou done all this? Why hast Thou brought me here? Why, why 290
dost Thou torment me so terribly?"

He did not expect an answer and yet wept because there was no answer and could be none. The pain again grew more acute, but he did not stir and did not call. He said to himself: "Go on! Strike me! But what is it for? What have I done to Thee? What is it for?"

Then he grew quiet and not only ceased weeping but even held his breath and became all attention. It was as though he were listening not to an audible voice but to the voice of his soul, to the current of thoughts arising within him.

"What is it you want?" was the first clear conception capable of expression in words, that he heard.

"What do you want? What do you want?" he repeated to himself.

"What do I want? To live and not to suffer," he answered. 295

And again he listened with such concentrated attention that even his pain did not distract him.

"To live? How?" asked his inner voice.

"Why, to live as I used to — well and pleasantly."

"As you lived before, well and pleasantly?" the voice repeated.

And in imagination he began to recall the best moments of his pleasant life. 300 But strange to say none of those best moments of his pleasant life now seemed at all what they had then seemed — none of them except the first recollections of childhood. There, in childhood, there had been something really pleasant with which it would be possible to live if it could return. But the child who had experienced that happiness existed no longer, it was like a reminiscence of somebody else.

As soon as the period began which had produced the present Iván Ilých, all that had then seemed joys now melted before his sight and turned into something trivial and often nasty.

And the further he departed from childhood and the nearer he came to the present the more worthless and doubtful were the joys. This began with the School of Law. A little that was really good was still found there — there was lightheartedness, friendship, and hope. But in the upper classes there had already been fewer of such good moments. Then during the first years of his official career, when he was in the service of the Governor, some pleasant moments again occurred: they were the memories of love for a woman. Then all became confused and there was still less of what was good; later on again there was still less that was good, and the further he went the less there was. His marriage, a mere accident, then the disenchantment that followed it, his wife's bad breath and the sensuality and hypocrisy: then that deadly official life and those preoccupations about money, a year of it, and two, and ten, and twenty, and always the same thing. And the longer it lasted the more deadly it became. "It is as if I had been going downhill while I imagined I was going up. And that is really what it was. I was going up in public opinion, but to the same extent life was ebbing away from me. And now it is all done and there is only death."

"Then what does it mean? Why? It can't be that life is so senseless and horrible. But if it really has been so horrible and senseless, why must I die and die in agony? There is something wrong!"

"Maybe I did not live as I ought to have done," it suddenly occurred to him. "But how could that be, when I did everything properly?" he replied, and immediately dismissed from his mind this, the sole solution of all the riddles of life and death, as something quite impossible.

"Then what do you want now? To live? Live how? Live as you lived in the law 305 courts when the usher proclaimed 'The judge is coming!' " "The judge is coming, the judge!" he repeated to himself. "Here he is, the judge. But I am not guilty!" he exclaimed angrily. "What is it for?" And he ceased crying, but turning his face to the wall continued to ponder on the same question: Why, and for what purpose, is there all this horror? But however much he pondered he found no answer. And whenever the thought occurred to him, as it often did, that it all resulted from his not having lived as he ought to have done, he at once recalled the correctness of his whole life and dismissed so strange an idea.

CHAPTER X

Another fortnight passed. Iván Ilých now no longer left his sofa. He would not lie in bed but lay on the sofa, facing the wall nearly all the time. He suffered ever the same unceasing agonies and in his loneliness pondered always on the same insoluble question: "What is this? Can it be that it is Death?" And the inner voice answered: "Yes, it is Death."

"Why these sufferings?" And the voice answered, "For no reason — they just are so." Beyond and besides this there was nothing.

From the very beginning of his illness, ever since he had first been to see the doctor, Iván Ilých's life had been divided between two contrary and alternating moods: now it was despair and the expectation of this uncomprehended and terrible death, and now hope and an intently interested observation of the functioning of his organs. Now before his eyes there was only a kidney or an intestine that temporarily evaded its duty, and now only that incomprehensible and dreadful death from which it was impossible to escape.

These two states of mind had alternated from the very beginning of his illness, but the further it progressed the more doubtful and fantastic became the conception of the kidney, and the more real the sense of impending death.

He had but to call to mind what he had been three months before and what 310 he was now, to call to mind with what regularity he had been going downhill, for every possibility of hope to be shattered.

Latterly during that loneliness in which he found himself as he lay facing the back of the sofa, a loneliness in the midst of a populous town and surrounded by numerous acquaintances and relations but that yet could not have been more complete anywhere — either at the bottom of the sea or under the earth — during that terrible loneliness Iván Ilých had lived only in memories of the past. Pictures of his past rose before him one after another. They always began with what was nearest in time and then went back to what was most remote — to his childhood — and rested there. If he thought of the stewed prunes that had been offered him that day, his mind went back to the raw shrivelled French plums of his childhood, their peculiar flavor and the flow of saliva when he sucked their stones, and along with the memory of that taste came a whole series of memories of those days: his nurse, his brother, and their toys. "No, I mustn't think of that. . . . It is too painful," Iván Ilých said to himself, and brought himself back to the present — to the button on the back of the sofa and the creases in its morocco. "Morocco is expensive, but it does not wear well: There had been a quarrel about it. It was a different kind of quarrel and a different kind of morocco that time when we tore father's portfolio and were punished, and mamma brought us some tarts. . . ." And again his thoughts dwelt on his childhood, and again it was painful and he tried to banish them and fix his mind on something else.

Then again together with that chain of memories another series passed through his mind — of how his illness had progressed and grown worse. There also the further back he looked the more life there had been. There had been more of what was good in life and more of life itself. The two merged together. "Just as the pain went on getting worse and worse so my life grew worse and worse," he thought. "There is one bright spot there at the back, at the beginning of life, and afterwards all becomes blacker and blacker and proceeds more and more rapidly — in inverse ratio to the square of the distance from death," thought Iván Ilých. And the example of a stone falling downwards with increasing velocity entered his mind. Life, a series of increasing sufferings, flies, further and further towards its end — the most terrible suffering. "I am flying. . . ." He shuddered, shifted himself, and tried to resist, but was already aware that resistance was impossible, and again with eyes weary of gazing but unable to cease seeing what was before them, he stared at the back of the sofa and waited — awaiting that dreadful fall and shock and destruction.

"Resistance is impossible!" he said to himself. "If I could only understand what it is all for! But that too is impossible. An explanation would be possible if it could be said that I have not lived as I ought to. But it is impossible to say that," and he remembered all the legality, correctitude, and propriety of his life. "That at any rate can certainly not be admitted," he thought, and his lips smiled ironically as if someone could see that smile and be taken in by it. "There is no explanation! Agony, death. . . . What for?"

CHAPTER XI

Another two weeks went by in this way and during that fortnight an event occurred that Iván Ilých and his wife had desired. Petríshchev formally proposed. It happened in the evening. The next day Praskóvya Fëdorovna came into her husband's room considering how best to inform him of it, but that very night there had been a fresh change for the worse in his condition. She found him still lying on the sofa but in a different position. He lay on his back, groaning and staring fixedly straight in front of him.

She began to remind him of his medicines, but he turned his eyes towards 315 her with such a look that she did not finish what she was saying; so great an animosity, to her in particular, did that look express.

"For Christ's sake, let me die in peace!" he said.

She would have gone away, but just then their daughter came in and went up to say good morning. He looked at her as he had done at his wife, and in reply to her inquiry about his health said dryly that he would soon free them all of himself. They were both silent and after sitting with him for a while went away.

"Is it our fault?" Lisa said to her mother. "It's as if we were to blame! I am sorry for papa, but why should we be tortured?"

The doctor came at his usual time. Iván Ilých answered "Yes" and "No," never taking his angry eyes from him, and at last said: "You know you can do nothing for me, so leave me alone."

"We can ease your sufferings." 320

"You can't even do that. Let me be."

The doctor went into the drawing-room and told Praskóvya Fëdorovna that the case was very serious and that the only resource left was opium to allay her husband's sufferings, which must be terrible.

It was true, as the doctor said, that Iván Ilých's physical sufferings were terrible, but worse than the physical sufferings were his mental sufferings which were his chief torture.

His mental sufferings were due to the fact that that night, as he looked at Gerásim's sleepy, good-natured face with its prominent cheek-bones, the question suddenly occurred to him: "What if my whole life has really been wrong?"

It occurred to him that what had appeared perfectly impossible before, 325 namely that he had not spent his life as he should have done, might after all be true. It occurred to him that his scarcely perceptible attempts to struggle against what was considered good by the most highly placed people, those scarcely noticeable impulses which he had immediately suppressed, might have been the real thing, and all the rest false. And his professional duties and the whole arrangement of his life and of his family, and all his social and official interests, might all have been false. He tried to defend all those things to himself and suddenly felt the weakness of what he was defending. There was nothing to defend.

"But if that is so," he said to himself, "and I am leaving this life with the consciousness that I have lost all that was given me and it is impossible to rectify it — what then?"

He lay on his back and began to pass his life in review in quite a new way. In the morning when he saw first his footman, then his wife, then his daughter, and then the doctor, their every word and movement confirmed to him the awful truth that had been revealed to him during the night. In them he saw himself — all that for which he had lived — and saw clearly that it was not real at all, but a terrible and huge deception which had hidden both life and death. This consciousness intensified his physical suffering tenfold. He groaned and tossed about, and pulled at his clothing which choked and stifled him. And he hated them on that account.

He was given a large dose of opium and became unconscious, but at noon his sufferings began again. He drove everybody away and tossed from side to side.

His wife came to him and said:

"Jean, my dear, do this for me. It can't do any harm and often helps. Healthy 330 people often do it."

He opened his eyes wide.

"What? Take communion? Why? It's unnecessary! However. . . ."

She began to cry.

"Yes, do, my dear. I'll send for our priest. He is such a nice man."

"All right. Very well," he muttered. 335

When the priest came and heard his confession, Iván Ilých was softened and seemed to feel a relief from his doubts and consequently from his sufferings, and for a moment there came a ray of hope. He again began to think of the vermiform appendix and the possibility of correcting it. He received the sacrament with tears in his eyes.

When they laid him down again afterwards he felt a moment's ease, and the hope that he might live awoke in him again. He began to think of the operation that had been suggested to him. "To live! I want to live!" he said to himself.

His wife came in to congratulate him after his communion, and when uttering the usual conventional words she added:

"You feel better, don't you?"

Without looking at her he said "Yes."   340

Her dress, her figure, the expression of her face, the tone of her voice, all revealed the same thing. "This is wrong, it is not as it should be. All you have lived for and still live for is falsehood and deception, hiding life and death from you." And as soon as he admitted that thought, his hatred and his agonizing physical suffering again sprang up, and with that suffering a consciousness of the unavoidable, approaching end. And to this was added a new sensation of grinding shooting pain and a feeling of suffocation.

The expression of his face when he uttered that "yes" was dreadful. Having uttered it, he looked her straight in the eyes, turned on his face with a rapidity extraordinary in his weak state and shouted:

"Go away! Go away and leave me alone!"

CHAPTER XII

From that moment the screaming began that continued for three days, and was so terrible that one could not hear it through two closed doors without horror. At the moment he answered his wife he realized that he was lost, that there was no return, that the end had come, the very end, and his doubts were still unsolved and remained doubts.

"Oh! Oh! Oh!" he cried in various intonations. He had begun by screaming "I 345 won't!" and continued screaming on the letter "o."

For three whole days, during which time did not exist for him, he struggled in that black sack into which he was being thrust by an invisible, resistless force. He struggled as a man condemned to death struggles in the hands of the executioner, knowing that he cannot save himself. And every moment he felt that despite all his efforts he was drawing nearer and nearer to what terrified him. He felt that his agony was due to his being thrust into that black hole and still more to his not being able to get right into it. He was hindered from getting into it by his conviction that his life had been a good one. That very justification of his life held him fast and prevented his moving forward, and it caused him most torment of all.

Suddenly some force struck him in the chest and side, making it still harder to breathe, and he fell through the hole and there at the bottom was a light. What had happened to him was like the sensation one sometimes experiences in a railway carriage when one thinks one is going backwards while one is really going forwards and suddenly becomes aware of the real direction.

"Yes, it was all not the right thing," he said to himself, "but that's no matter. It can be done. But what *is* the right thing?" he asked himself, and suddenly grew quiet.

This occurred at the end of the third day, two hours before his death. Just then his schoolboy son had crept softly in and gone up to the bedside. The dying man was still screaming desperately and waving his arms. His hand fell on the boy's head, and the boy caught it, pressed it to his lips, and began to cry.

At that very moment Iván Ilých fell through and caught sight of the light, and   350
it was revealed to him that though his life had not been what it should have been, this could still be rectified. He asked himself, "What *is* the right thing?" and grew still, listening. Then he felt that someone was kissing his hand. He opened his eyes, looked at his son, and felt sorry for him. His wife came up to him and he glanced at her. She was gazing at him open-mouthed, with undried tears on her nose and cheek and a despairing look on her face. He felt sorry for her too.

"Yes, I am making them wretched," he thought. "They are sorry, but it will be better for them when I die." He wished to say this but had not the strength to utter it. "Besides, why speak? I must act," he thought. With a look at his wife he indicated his son and said: "Take him away . . . sorry for him . . . sorry for you too. . . ." He tried to add, "forgive me," but said "forego" and waved his hand, knowing that He whose understanding mattered would understand.

And suddenly it grew clear to him that what had been oppressing him and would not leave him was all dropping away at once from two sides, from ten sides, and from all sides. He was sorry for them, he must act so as not to hurt them: release them and free himself from these sufferings. "How good and how simple!" he thought. "And the pain?" he asked himself. "What has become of it? Where are you, pain?"

He turned his attention to it.

"Yes, here it is. Well, what of it? Let the pain be."

"And death . . . where is it?"   355

He sought his former accustomed fear of death and did not find it. "Where is it? What death?" There was no fear because there was no death.

In place of death there was light.

"So that's what it is!" he suddenly exclaimed aloud. "What joy!"

To him all this happened in a single instant, and the meaning of that instant did not change. For those present his agony continued for another two hours. Something rattled in his throat, his emaciated body twitched, then the gasping and rattle became less and less frequent.

"It is finished!" said someone near him.   360

He heard these words and repeated them in his soul.

"Death is finished," he said to himself. "It is no more!"

He drew in a breath, stopped in the midst of a sigh, stretched out, and died.

For Analysis

1. Discuss the evidence that Ilých's death is a moral judgment — that is, a punishment for his life.

2. Discuss "The Death of Iván Ilých" from the perspective revealed in Paul's 1 Corinthians 13 (p. 1250). What accounts for the change in Ilých's attitude toward his approaching death?

3. How do you respond to the fact that Gerásim, Ilých's peasant servant, is more sympathetic to his condition than Ilých's family?

On Style

Suggest a reason for Tolstoy's decision to begin the story immediately after Ilých's death and then move back to recount the significant episodes of his life.

Making Connections

Compare the significance of death to the characters in this story with the significance of death to the characters in one or two of the following works: D. H. Lawrence's "The Rocking-Horse Winner" (p. 1328), Katherine Anne Porter's "The Jilting of Granny Weatherall" (p. 1340), Leslie Marmon Silko's "The Man to Send Rain Clouds" (p. 1374), and Harvey Fierstein's *On Tidy Endings* (p. 1460).

Writing Topics

1. At the conclusion of the story, Ilých achieves peace and understanding, and the questions that have been torturing him are resolved. He realizes that "though his life had not been what it should have been, this could still be rectified" (para. 350). What does this mean?

2. In an essay, compare and contrast the attitudes of various characters to Ilých's mortal illness. How do his colleagues respond? His wife? His children? His servant Gerásim?

D. H. Lawrence   (1885–1930)

The Rocking-Horse Winner   1926

There was a woman who was beautiful, who started with all the advantages, yet she had no luck. She married for love, and the love turned to dust. She had bonny children, yet she felt they had been thrust upon her, and she could not love them. They looked at her coldly, as if they were finding fault with her. And hurriedly she felt she must cover up some fault in herself. Yet what it was that she must cover up she never knew. Nevertheless, when her children were present, she always felt the centre of her heart go hard. This troubled her, and in her manner she was all the more gentle and anxious for her children, as if she loved them very much. Only she herself knew that at the centre of her heart was a hard little place that could not feel love, no, not for anybody. Everybody else said of her: "She is such a good mother. She adores her children." Only she herself, and her children themselves, knew it was not so. They read it in each other's eyes.

There were a boy and two little girls. They lived in a pleasant house, with a garden, and they had discreet servants, and felt themselves superior to anyone in the neighbourhood.

Although they lived in style, they felt always an anxiety in the house. There was never enough money. The mother had a small income, and the father had a small income, but not nearly enough for the social position which they had to keep up. The father went in to town to some office. But though he had good prospects, these prospects never materialized. There was always the grinding sense of the shortage of money, though the style was always kept up.

At last the mother said: "I will see if *I* can't make something." But she did not know where to begin. She racked her brains, and tried this thing and the other, but could not find anything successful. The failure made deep lines come into her face. Her children were growing up, they would have to go to school. There must be more money, there must be more money. The father, who was always very handsome and expensive in his tastes, seemed as if he never *would* be able to do anything worth doing. And the mother, who had a great belief in herself, did not succeed any better, and her tastes were just as expensive.

And so the house came to be haunted by the unspoken phrase: *There must be more money! There must be more money!* The children could hear it all the time, though nobody said it aloud. They heard it at Christmas, when the expensive and splendid toys filled the nursery. Behind the shining modern rocking-horse, behind the smart doll's-house, a voice would start whispering: "There *must* be more money! There *must* be more money!" And the children would stop playing, to listen for a moment. They would look into each other's eyes, to

5

1328

see if they had all heard. And each one saw in the eyes of the other two that they too had heard. "There *must* be more money! There *must* be more money!"

It came whispering from the springs of the still-swaying rocking-horse, and even the horse, bending his wooden, champing head, heard it. The big doll, sitting so pink and smirking in her new pram,[1] could hear it quite plainly, and seemed to be smirking all the more self-consciously because of it. The foolish puppy, too, that took the place of the teddy-bear, he was looking so extraordinarily foolish for no other reason but that he heard the secret whisper all over the house: "There *must* be more money!"

Yet nobody ever said it aloud. The whisper was everywhere, and therefore no one spoke it. Just as no one ever says: "We are breathing!" in spite of the fact that breath is coming and going all the time.

"Mother," said the boy Paul one day, "why don't we keep a car of our own? Why do we always use uncle's, or else a taxi?"

"Because we're the poor members of the family," said the mother.

"But why *are* we, mother?"   10

"Well — I suppose," she said slowly and bitterly, "it's because your father has no luck."

The boy was silent for some time.

"Is luck money, mother?" he asked rather timidly.

"No, Paul. Not quite. It's what causes you to have money."

"Oh!" said Paul vaguely. "I thought when Uncle Oscar said *filthy lucker,* it   15
meant money."

"*Filthy lucre* does mean money," said the mother. "But it's lucre, not luck."

"Oh!" said the boy. "Then what *is* luck, mother?"

"It's what causes you to have money. If you're lucky you have money. That's why it's better to be born lucky than rich. If you're rich, you may lose your money. But if you're lucky, you will always get more money."

"Oh! Will you? And is father not lucky?"

"Very unlucky, I should say," she said bitterly.   20

The boy watched her with unsure eyes.

"Why?" he asked.

"I don't know. Nobody ever knows why one person is lucky and another unlucky."

"Don't they? Nobody at all? Does *nobody* know?"

"Perhaps God. But He never tells."   25

"He ought to, then. And aren't you lucky either, mother?"

"I can't be, if I married an unlucky husband."

"But by yourself, aren't you?"

"I used to think I was, before I married. Now I think I am very unlucky indeed."

"Why?"   30

"Well — never mind! Perhaps I'm not really," she said.

---

[1] A baby carriage.

The child looked at her, to see if she meant it. But he saw, by the lines of her mouth, that she was only trying to hide something from him.

"Well, anyhow," he said stoutly, "I'm a lucky person."

"Why?" said his mother, with a sudden laugh.

He stared at her. He didn't even know why he had said it.   35

"God told me," he asserted, brazening it out.

"I hope He did, dear!" she said, again with a laugh, but rather bitter.

"He did, mother!"

"Excellent!" said the mother, using one of her husband's exclamations.

The boy saw she did not believe him; or, rather, that she paid no attention to   40 his assertion. This angered him somewhat, and made him want to compel her attention.

He went off by himself, vaguely, in a childish way, seeking for the clue to "luck." Absorbed, taking no heed of other people, he went about with a sort of stealth, seeking inwardly for luck. He wanted luck, he wanted it, he wanted it. When the two girls were playing dolls in the nursery, he would sit on his big rocking-horse, charging madly into space, with a frenzy that made the little girls peer at him uneasily. Wildly the horse careered, the waving dark hair of the boy tossed, his eyes had a strange glare in them. The little girls dared not speak to him.

When he had ridden to the end of his mad little journey, he climbed down and stood in front of his rocking-horse, staring fixedly into its lowered face. Its red mouth was slightly open, its big eye was wide and glassy-bright.

"Now!" he would silently command the snorting steed. "Now, take me to where there is luck! Now take me!"

And he would slash the horse on the neck with the little whip he had asked Uncle Oscar for. He *knew* the horse could take him to where there was luck, if only he forced it. So he would mount again, and start on his furious ride, hoping at last to get there. He knew he could get there.

"You'll break your horse, Paul!" said the nurse.   45

"He's always riding like that! I wish he'd leave off!" said his elder sister Joan.

But he only glared down on them in silence. Nurse gave him up. She could make nothing of him. Anyhow he was growing beyond her.

One day his mother and his Uncle Oscar came in when he was on one of his furious rides. He did not speak to them.

"Hallo, you young jockey! Riding a winner?" said his uncle.

"Aren't you growing too big for a rocking-horse? You're not a very little boy   50 any longer, you know," said his mother.

But Paul only gave a blue glare from his big, rather close-set eyes. He would speak to nobody when he was in full tilt. His mother watched him with an anxious expression on her face.

At last he suddenly stopped forcing his horse into the mechanical gallop, and slid down.

"Well, I got there!" he announced fiercely, his blue eyes still flaring, and his sturdy long legs straddling apart.

"Where did you get to?" asked his mother.

"Where I wanted to go," he flared back at her.   55

"That's right, son!" said Uncle Oscar. "Don't you stop till you get there. What's the horse's name?"

"He doesn't have a name," said the boy.

"Gets on without all right?" asked the uncle.

"Well, he has different names. He was called Sansovino last week."

"Sansovino, eh? Won the Ascot.[2] How did you know his name?"   60

"He always talks about horse-races with Bassett," said Joan.

The uncle was delighted to find that his small nephew was posted with all the racing news. Bassett, the young gardener, who had been wounded in the left foot in the war and had got his present job through Oscar Cresswell, whose batman[3] he had been, was a perfect blade of the "turf."[4] He lived in the racing events, and the small boy lived with him.

Oscar Cresswell got it all from Bassett.

"Master Paul comes and asks me, so I can't do more than tell him, sir," said Bassett, his face terribly serious, as if he were speaking of religious matters.

"And does he ever put anything on a horse he fancies?"   65

"Well — I don't want to give him away — he's a young sport, a fine sport, sir. Would you mind asking him himself? He sort of takes a pleasure in it, and perhaps he'd feel I was giving him away, sir, if you don't mind."

Bassett was serious as a church.

The uncle went back to his nephew and took him off for a ride in the car.

"Say, Paul, old man, do you ever put anything on a horse?" the uncle asked.

The boy watched the handsome man closely.   70

"Why, do you think I oughtn't to?" he parried.

"Not a bit of it! I thought perhaps you might give me a tip for the Lincoln."

The car sped on into the country, going down to Uncle Oscar's place in Hampshire.

"Honour bright?" said the nephew.

"Honour bright, son!" said the uncle.   75

"Well, then, Daffodil."

"Daffodil! I doubt it, sonny. What about Mirza?"

"I only know the winner," said the boy. "That's Daffodil."

"Daffodil, eh?"

There was a pause. Daffodil was an obscure horse comparatively.   80

"Uncle!"

"Yes, son?"

"You won't let it go any further, will you? I promised Bassett."

"Bassett be damned, old man! What's he got to do with it?"

[2] A racetrack in Berkshire, England; also the name of its most celebrated race. The names of other racetracks and races are mentioned throughout the story.

[3] A soldier in the British army assigned to an officer as a servant.

[4] A dashing young man.

"We're partners. We've been partners from the first. Uncle, he lent me my 85 first five shillings, which I lost. I promised him, honour bright, it was only between me and him; only you gave me that ten-shilling note I started winning with, so I thought you were lucky. You won't let it go any further, will you?"

The boy gazed at his uncle from those big, hot, blue eyes, set rather close together. The uncle stirred and laughed uneasily.

"Right you are, son! I'll keep your tip private. Daffodil, eh? How much are you putting on him?"

"All except twenty pounds," said the boy. "I keep that in reserve."

The uncle thought it a good joke.

"You keep twenty pounds in reserve, do you, you young romancer? What are 90 you betting, then?"

"I'm betting three hundred," said the boy, gravely. "But it's between you and me, Uncle Oscar! Honour bright?"

The uncle burst into a roar of laughter.

"It's between you and me all right, you young Nat Gould,"[5] he said, laughing. "But where's your three hundred?"

"Bassett keeps it for me. We're partners."

"You are, are you! And what is Bassett putting on Daffodil?" 95

"He won't go quite as high as I do, I expect. Perhaps he'll go a hundred and fifty."

"What, pennies?" laughed the uncle.

"Pounds," said the child, with a surprised look at his uncle. "Bassett keeps a bigger reserve than I do."

Between wonder and amusement Uncle Oscar was silent. He pursued the matter no further, but he determined to take his nephew with him to the Lincoln races.

"Now, son." he said, "I'm putting twenty on Mirza, and I'll put five for you on 100 any horse you fancy. What's your pick?"

"Daffodil, uncle."

"No, not the fiver on Daffodil!"

"I should if it was my own fiver," said the child.

"Good! Good! Right you are! A fiver for me and a fiver for you on Daffodil."

The child had never been to a race-meeting before, and his eyes were blue 105 fire. He pursed his mouth tight, and watched. A Frenchman just in front had put his money on Lancelot. Wild with excitement, he flayed his arms up and down, yelling *"Lancelot! Lancelot!"* in his French accent.

Daffodil came in first, Lancelot second, Mirza third. The child, flushed and with eyes blazing, was curiously serene. His uncle brought him four five-pound notes, four to one.

"What am I to do with these?" he cried, waving them before the boy's eyes.

"I suppose we'll talk to Bassett," said the boy. "I expect I have fifteen hundred now; and twenty in reserve; and this twenty."

[5] Nathaniel Gould (1857–1919) was an English novelist who wrote prolifically about horse racing.

His uncle studied him for some moments.

"Look here, son!" he said. "You're not serious about Bassett and that fifteen   110
hundred, are you?"

"Yes, I am. But it's between you and me, uncle. Honour bright!"

"Honour bright all right, son! But I must talk to Bassett."

"If you'd like to be a partner, uncle, with Bassett and me, we could all be partners. Only, you'd have to promise, honour bright, uncle, not to let it go beyond
us three. Bassett and I are lucky, and you must be lucky, because it was your ten
shillings I started winning with. . . ."

Uncle Oscar took both Bassett and Paul into Richmond Park for an afternoon, and there they talked.

"It's like this, you see, sir," Bassett said. "Master Paul would get me talking   115
about racing events, spinning yarns, you know, sir. And he was always keen on
knowing if I'd made or if I'd lost. It's about a year since, now, that I put five
shillings on Blush of Dawn for him — and we lost. Then the luck turned, with
the ten shillings he had from you, that we put on Singhalese. And since that time,
it's been pretty steady, all things considering. What do you say, Master Paul?"

"We're all right when we're sure," said Paul. "It's when we're not quite sure
that we go down."

"Oh, but we're careful then," said Bassett.

"But when are you *sure*?" smiled Uncle Oscar.

"It's Master Paul, sir," said Bassett, in a secret, religious voice. "It's as if he had
it from heaven. Like Daffodil, now, for the Lincoln. That was as sure as eggs."

"Did you put anything on Daffodil?" asked Oscar Cresswell.   120

"Yes, sir. I made my bit."

"And my nephew?"

Bassett was obstinately silent, looking at Paul.

"I made twelve hundred, didn't I, Bassett? I told uncle I was putting three
hundred on Daffodil."

"That's right," said Bassett, nodding.   125

"But where's the money?" asked the uncle.

"I keep it safe locked up, sir. Master Paul he can have it any minute he likes to
ask for it."

"What, fifteen hundred pounds?"

"And twenty! And *forty*, that is, with the twenty he made on the course."

"It's amazing!" said the uncle.   130

"If Master Paul offers you to be partners, sir, I would, if I were you; if you'll
excuse me," said Bassett.

Oscar Cresswell thought about it.

"I'll see the money," he said.

They drove home again, and sure enough, Bassett came round to the garden-
house with fifteen hundred pounds in notes. The twenty pounds reserve was left
with Joe Glee, in the Turf Commission deposit.

"You see, it's all right, uncle, when I'm *sure*! Then we go strong, for all we're   135
worth. Don't we, Bassett?"

"We do that, Master Paul."

"And when are you sure?" said the uncle, laughing.

"Oh, well, sometimes I'm *absolutely* sure, like about Daffodil," said the boy; "and sometimes I have an idea; and sometimes I haven't even an idea, have I, Bassett? Then we're careful, because we mostly go down."

"You do, do you! And when you're sure, like about Daffodil, what makes you sure, sonny?"

"Oh, well, I don't know," said the boy uneasily. "I'm sure, you know, uncle; 140 that's all."

"It's as if he had it from heaven, sir," Bassett reiterated.

"I should say so!" said the uncle.

But he became a partner. And when the Leger was coming on, Paul was "sure" about Lively Spark, which was a quite inconsiderable horse. The boy insisted on putting a thousand on the horse, Bassett went for five hundred, and Oscar Cresswell two hundred. Lively Spark came in first, and the betting had been ten to one against him. Paul had made ten thousand.

"You see," he said, "I was absolutely sure of him."

Even Oscar Cresswell had cleared two thousand. 145

"Look here, son," he said, "this sort of thing makes me nervous."

"It needn't, uncle! Perhaps I shan't be sure again for a long time."

"But what are you going to do with your money?" asked the uncle.

"Of course," said the boy, "I started it for mother. She said she had no luck, because father is unlucky, so I thought if *I* was lucky, it might stop whispering."

"What might stop whispering?" 150

"Our house. I *hate* our house for whispering."

"What does it whisper?"

"Why — why" — the boy fidgeted — "why, I don't know. But it's always short of money, you know, uncle."

"I know it, son, I know it."

"You know people send mother writs, don't you, uncle?" 155

"I'm afraid I do," said the uncle.

"And then the house whispers, like people laughing at you behind your back. It's awful, that is! I thought if I was lucky . . ."

"You might stop it," added the uncle.

The boy watched him with big blue eyes, that had an uncanny cold fire in them, and he said never a word.

"Well, then!" said the uncle. "What are we doing?" 160

"I shouldn't like mother to know I was lucky," said the boy.

"Why not, son?"

"She'd stop me."

"I don't think she would."

"Oh!" — and the boy writhed in an odd way — "I *don't* want her to know, 165 uncle."

"All right, son! We'll manage it without her knowing."

They managed it very easily. Paul, at the other's suggestion, handed over five thousand pounds to his uncle, who deposited it with the family lawyer, who was then to inform Paul's mother that a relative had put five thousand pounds into his hands, which sum was to be paid out a thousand pounds at a time, on the mother's birthday, for the next five years.

"So she'll have a birthday present of a thousand pounds for five successive years," said Uncle Oscar. "I hope it won't make it all the harder for her later."

Paul's mother had her birthday in November. The house had been "whispering" worse than ever lately, and, even in spite of his luck, Paul could not bear up against it. He was very anxious to see the effect of the birthday letter, telling his mother about the thousand pounds.

When there were no visitors, Paul now took his meals with his parents, as 170 he was beyond the nursery control. His mother went into town nearly every day. She had discovered that she had an odd knack of sketching furs and dress materials, so she worked secretly in the studio of a friend who was the chief "artist" for the leading drapers. She drew the figures of ladies in furs and ladies in silk and sequins for the newspaper advertisements. This young woman artist earned several thousand pounds a year, but Paul's mother only made several hundreds, and she was again dissatisfied. She so wanted to be first in something, and she did not succeed, even in making sketches for drapery advertisements.

She was down to breakfast on the morning of her birthday. Paul watched her face as she read her letters. He knew the lawyer's letter. As his mother read it, her face hardened and became more expressionless. Than a cold, determined look came on her mouth. She hid the letter under the pile of others, and said not a word about it.

"Didn't you have anything nice in the post for your birthday, mother?" said Paul.

"Quite moderately nice," she said, her voice cold and absent.

She went away to town without saying more.

But in the afternoon Uncle Oscar appeared. He said Paul's mother had had a 175 long interview with the lawyer, asking if the whole five thousand could not be advanced at once, as she was in debt.

"What do you think, uncle?" said the boy.

"I leave it to you, son."

"Oh, let her have it, then! We can get some more with the other," said the boy.

"A bird in the hand is worth two in the bush, laddie!" said Uncle Oscar.

"But I'm sure to *know* for the Grand National; or the Lincolnshire; or else the 180 Derby. I'm sure to know for *one* of them," said Paul.

So Uncle Oscar signed the agreement, and Paul's mother touched the whole five thousand. Then something very curious happened. The voices in the house suddenly went mad, like a chorus of frogs on a spring evening. There were certain new furnishings, and Paul had a tutor. He was *really* going to Eton, his father's school, in the following autumn. There were flowers in the winter, and a blossoming of the luxury Paul's mother had been used to. And yet the voices in the house, behind the sprays of mimosa and almond blossom, and from under the piles of iridescent cushions, simply trilled and screamed in a sort of ecstasy: "There *must* be more money! Oh-h-h; there *must* be more money! Oh, now,

now-w! Now-w-w — there *must* be more money! — more than ever! More than ever!"

It frightened Paul terribly. He studied away at his Latin and Greek with his tutors. But his intense hours were spent with Bassett. The Grand National had gone by: he had not "known," and had lost a hundred pounds. Summer was at hand. He was in agony for the Lincoln. But even for the Lincoln he didn't "know," and he lost fifty pounds. He became wild-eyed and strange, as if something were going to explode in him.

"Let it alone, son! Don't you bother about it!" urged Uncle Oscar. But it was as if the boy couldn't really hear what his uncle was saying.

"I've got to know for the Derby! I've got to know for the Derby!" the child reiterated, his big blue eyes blazing with a sort of madness.

His mother noticed how overwrought he was. 185

"You'd better go to the seaside. Wouldn't you like to go now to the seaside, instead of waiting? I think you'd better," she said, looking down at him anxiously, her heart curiously heavy because of him.

But the child lifted his uncanny blue eyes.

"I couldn't possibly go before the Derby, mother!" he said. "I couldn't possibly!"

"Why not?" she said, her voice becoming heavy when she was opposed. "Why not? You can still go from the seaside to see the Derby with your Uncle Oscar, if that's what you wish. No need for you to wait here. Besides, I think you care too much about these races. It's a bad sign. My family has been a gambling family, and you won't know till you grow up how much damage it has done. But it has done damage. I shall have to send Bassett away, and ask Uncle Oscar not to talk racing to you, unless you promise to be reasonable about it; go away to the seaside and forget it. You're all nerves!"

"I'll do what you like, mother, so long as you don't send me away till after the 190 Derby," the boy said.

"Send you away from where? Just from this house?"

"Yes," he said, gazing at her.

"Why, you curious child, what makes you care about this house so much, suddenly? I never knew you loved it."

He gazed at her without speaking. He had a secret within a secret, something he had not divulged, even to Bassett or to his Uncle Oscar.

But his mother, after standing undecided and a little bit sullen for some 195 moments, said:

"Very well, then! Don't go to the seaside till after the Derby, if you don't wish it. But promise me you won't let your nerves go to pieces. Promise you won't think so much about horse-racing and events, as you call them!"

"Oh, no," said the boy casually. "I won't think much about them, mother. You needn't worry. I wouldn't worry, mother, if I were you."

"If you were me and I were you," said his mother, "I wonder what we *should* do!"

"But you know you needn't worry, mother, don't you?" the boy repeated.

"I should be awfully glad to know it," she said wearily.   200

"Oh, well, you *can,* you know. I mean, you *ought* to know you needn't worry," he insisted.

"Ought I? Then I'll see about it," she said.

Paul's secret of secrets was his wooden horse, that which had no name. Since he was emancipated from a nurse and a nursery-governess, he had had his rocking-horse removed to his own bedroom at the top of the house.

"Surely, you're too big for a rocking-horse!" his mother had remonstrated.

"Well, you see, mother, till I can have a *real* horse, I like to have *some* sort of 205 animal about," had been his quaint answer.

"Do you feel he keeps you company?" she laughed.

"Oh, yes! He's very good, he always keeps me company, when I'm there," said Paul.

So the horse, rather shabby, stood in an arrested prance in the boy's bedroom.

The Derby was drawing near, and the boy grew more and more tense. He hardly heard what was spoken to him, he was very frail, and his eyes were really uncanny. His mother had sudden strange seizures of uneasiness about him. Sometimes, for half-an-hour, she would feel a sudden anxiety about him that was almost anguish. She wanted to rush to him at once, and know he was safe.

Two nights before the Derby, she was at a big party in town, when one of her 210 rushes of anxiety about her boy, her first-born, gripped her heart till she could hardly speak. She fought with the feeling, might and main, for she believed in common-sense. But it was too strong. She had to leave the dance and go downstairs to telephone to the country. The children's nursery-governess was terribly surprised and startled at being rung up in the night.

"Are the children all right, Miss Wilmot?"

"Oh, yes, they are quite all right."

"Master Paul? Is he all right?"'

"He went to bed as right as a trivet. Shall I run up and look at him?"

"No," said Paul's mother reluctantly. "No! Don't trouble. It's all right. Don't 215 sit up. We shall be home fairly soon." She did not want her son's privacy intruded upon.

"Very good," said the governess.

It was about one o'clock when Paul's mother and father drove up to their house. All was still. Paul's mother went to her room and slipped off her white fur cloak. She had told her maid not to wait up for her. She heard her husband downstairs, mixing a whisky-and-soda.

And then, because of the strange anxiety at her heart, she stole upstairs to her son's room. Noiselessly she went along the upper corridor. Was there a faint noise? What was it?

She stood, with arrested muscles, outside his door, listening. There was a strange, heavy, and yet not loud noise. Her heart stood still. It was a soundless noise, yet rushing and powerful. Something huge, in violent, hushed motion. What was it? What in God's name was it? She ought to know. She felt that she knew the noise. She knew what it was.

Yet she could not place it. She couldn't say what it was. And on and on it went, 220 like a madness.

Softly, frozen with anxiety and fear, she turned the door-handle.

The room was dark. Yet in the space near the window, she heard and saw something plunging to and fro. She gazed in fear and amazement.

Then suddenly she switched on the light, and saw her son, in his green pyjamas, madly surging on the rocking-horse. The blaze of light suddenly lit him up, as he urged the wooden horse, and lit her up, as she stood, blonde, in her dress of pale green and crystal, in the doorway.

"Paul!" she cried. "Whatever are you doing?"

"It's Malabar!" he screamed, in a powerful, strange voice. "It's Malabar!" 225

His eyes blazed at her for one strange and senseless second, as he ceased urging his wooden horse. Then he fell with a crash to the ground, and she, all her tormented motherhood flooding upon her, rushed to gather him up.

But he was unconscious, and unconscious he remained, with some brain-fever. He talked and tossed, and his mother sat stonily by his side.

"Malabar! It's Malabar! Bassett, Bassett, I *know*! It's Malabar!"

So the child cried, trying to get up and urge the rocking-horse that gave him his inspiration.

"What does he mean by Malabar?" asked the heart-frozen mother. 230

"I don't know," said the father stonily.

"What does he mean by Malabar?" she asked her brother Oscar.

"It's one of the horses running for the Derby," was the answer.

And, in spite of himself, Oscar Cresswell spoke to Bassett, and himself put a thousand on Malabar: at fourteen to one.

The third day of the illness was critical: they were waiting for a change. The 235 boy, with his rather long, curly hair, was tossing ceaselessly on the pillow. He neither slept nor regained consciousness, and his eyes were like blue stones. His mother sat, feeling her heart had gone, turned actually into a stone.

In the evening, Oscar Cresswell did not come, but Bassett sent a message, saying could he come up for one moment, just one moment? Paul's mother was very angry at the intrusion, but on second thought she agreed. The boy was the same. Perhaps Bassett might bring him to consciousness.

The gardener, a shortish fellow with a little brown moustache, and sharp little brown eyes, tip-toed into the room, touched his imaginary cap to Paul's mother, and stole to the bedside, staring with glittering, smallish eyes, at the tossing, dying child.

"Master Paul!" he whispered. "Master Paul! Malabar came in first all right, a clean win. I did as you told me. You've made over seventy thousand pounds, you have; you've got over eighty thousand. Malabar came in all right, Master Paul."

"Malabar! Malabar! Did I say Malabar, mother? Did I say Malabar? Do you think I'm lucky, mother? I knew Malabar, didn't I? Over eighty thousand pounds! I call that lucky, don't you, mother? Over eighty thousand pounds! I knew, didn't I know I knew! Malabar came in all right. If I ride my horse till I'm sure, then I tell you, Bassett, you can go as high as you like. Did you go for all you were worth, Bassett?"

"I went a thousand on it, Master Paul."   240

"I never told you, mother, that if I can ride my horse, and *get there*, then I'm absolutely sure — oh absolutely! Mother, did I ever tell you? *I am* lucky!"

"No, you never did," said the mother.

But the boy died in the night.

And even as he lay dead, his mother heard her brother's voice saying to her: "My God, Hester, you're eighty-odd thousand to the good, and a poor devil of a son to the bad. But, poor devil, poor devil, he's best gone out of a life where he rides his rocking-horse to find a winner."

For Analysis

1. How do the opening paragraphs establish the tone of the story? Do these paragraphs foreshadow a realistic narrative? Explain.

2. Why is the mother unable to feel love for her children?

3. What does "luck" mean to Paul's mother? To Paul?

4. What does Paul mean when he tells his uncle that he does not want his mother to know that he is "lucky" because "She'd stop me" (paras. 161–163)?

5. When Paul's mother read the letter from the lawyer informing her that she is to receive a thousand pounds for the next five years, "her face hardened and became more expressionless" (para. 171). Why did she react this way?

6. What do Oscar and Bassett represent?

7. In the opening paragraph, we learn that Paul's mother "knew that at the centre of her heart was a hard little place that could not feel love." At the end of the story, as she sits at the bedside of her dying son, she feels as though "her heart had gone, turned actually into a stone" (para. 235). What accounts for this change?

8. What is the meaning of Paul's death?

9. Why is Oscar given the final words in the story?

On Style

1. How does Lawrence make credible the fantastic events of this story?

2. Discuss the use of **irony** in this story.

Making Connections

Compare this story with one of the following stories that also depart from the world of everyday reality and logic to develop their themes: Nathaniel Hawthorne's "Young Goodman Brown" (p. 80), Ursula K. Le Guin's "The Ones Who Walk Away from Omelas" (p. 393), Harlan Ellison's " 'Repent, Harlequin!' Said the Ticktockman" (p. 399), and Bernard Malamud's "Idiots First" (p. 1348).

Writing Topics

1. Discuss the meaning of the rocking-horse.

2. Write an essay on "The Rocking-Horse Winner" as a fairy tale.

3. Describe a family you know that was driven by a destructive obsession.

Katherine Anne Porter (1890–1980)

The Jilting of Granny Weatherall 1930

She flicked her wrist neatly out of Doctor Harry's pudgy careful fingers and pulled the sheet up to her chin. The brat ought to be in knee breeches. Doctoring around the country with spectacles on his nose! "Get along now, take your schoolbooks and go. There's nothing wrong with me."

Doctor Harry spread a warm paw like a cushion on her forehead where the forked green vein danced and made her eyelids twitch. "Now, now, be a good girl, and we'll have you up in no time."

"That's no way to speak to a woman nearly eighty years old just because she's down. I'd have you respect your elders, young man."

"Well, Missy, excuse me." Doctor Harry patted her cheek. "But I've got to warn you, haven't I? You're a marvel, but you must be careful or you're going to be good and sorry."

"Don't tell me what I'm going to be. I'm on my feet now, morally speaking. 5 It's Cornelia. I had to go to bed to get rid of her."

Her bones felt loose, and floated around in her skin, and Doctor Harry floated like a balloon around the foot of the bed. He floated and pulled down his waistcoat and swung his glasses on a cord. "Well, stay where you are, it certainly can't hurt you."

"Get along and doctor your sick," said Granny Weatherall. "Leave a well woman alone. I'll call for you when I want you. . . . Where were you forty years ago when I pulled through milk-leg and double pneumonia? You weren't even born. Don't let Cornelia lead you on," she shouted, because Doctor Harry appeared to float up to the ceiling and out. "I pay my own bills, and I don't throw my money away on nonsense!"

She meant to wave good-by, but it was too much trouble. Her eyes closed of themselves, it was like a dark curtain drawn around the bed. The pillow rose and floated under her, pleasant as a hammock in a light wind. She listened to the leaves rustling outside the window. No, somebody was swishing newspapers: no, Cornelia and Doctor Harry were whispering together. She leaped broad awake, thinking they whispered in her ear.

"She was never like this, *never* like this!" "Well, what can we expect?" "Yes, eighty years old. . . ."

Well, and what if she was? She still had ears. It was like Cornelia to whisper 10 around doors. She always kept things secret in such a public way. She was always being tactful and kind. Cornelia was dutiful; that was the trouble with her. Dutiful and good: "So good and dutiful," said Granny, "that I'd like to spank her." She saw herself spanking Cornelia and making a fine job of it.

1340

"What'd you say, Mother?"

Granny felt her face tying up in hard knots.

"Can't a body think, I'd like to know?"

"I thought you might want something."

"I do. I want a lot of things. First off, go away and don't whisper." 15

She lay and drowsed, hoping in her sleep that the children would keep out and let her rest a minute. It had been a long day. Not that she was tired. It was always pleasant to snatch a minute now and then. There was always so much to be done, let me see: tomorrow.

Tomorrow was far away and there was nothing to trouble about. Things were finished somehow when the time came; thank God there was always a little margin over for peace: then a person could spread out the plan of life and tuck in the edges orderly. It was good to have everything clean and folded away, with the hair brushes and tonic bottles sitting straight on the white embroidered linen: the day started without fuss and the pantry shelves laid out with rows of jelly glasses and brown jugs and white stone-china jars with blue whirligigs and words painted on them: coffee, tea, sugar, ginger, cinnamon, allspice: and the bronze clock with the lion on top nicely dusted off. The dust that lion could collect in twenty-four hours! The box in the attic with all those letters tied up, well she'd have to go through that tomorrow. All those letters — George's letters and John's letters and her letters to them both — lying around for the children to find afterwards made her uneasy. Yes, that would be tomorrow's business. No use to let them know how silly she had been once.

While she was rummaging around she found death in her mind and it felt clammy and unfamiliar. She had spent so much time preparing for death there was no need for bringing it up again. Let it take care of itself now. When she was sixty she had felt very old, finished, and went around making farewell trips to see her children and grandchildren, with a secret in her mind: This is the very last of your mother, children! Then she made her will and came down with a long fever. That was all just a notion like a lot of other things, but it was lucky too, for she had once for all got over the idea of dying for a long time. Now she couldn't be worried. She hoped she had better sense now. Her father had lived to be one hundred and two years old and had drunk a noggin of strong hot toddy on his last birthday. He told the reporters it was his daily habit, and he owed his long life to that. He had made quite a scandal and was very pleased about it. She believed she'd just plague Cornelia a little.

"Cornelia! Cornelia!" No footsteps, but a sudden hand on her cheek. "Bless you, where have you been?"

"Here, mother." 20

"Well, Cornelia, I want a noggin of hot toddy."

"Are you cold, darling?"

"I'm chilly, Cornelia. Lying in bed stops the circulation. I must have told you that a thousand times."

Well, she could just hear Cornelia telling her husband that Mother was getting childish and they'd have to humor her. The thing that most annoyed her was that Cornelia thought she was deaf, dumb, and blind. Little hasty glances and tiny gestures tossed around her and over her head saying, "Don't cross her, let her have her way, she's eighty years old," and she sitting there as if she lived in a thin glass cage. Sometimes Granny almost made up her mind to pack up and move back to her own house where nobody could remind her every minute that she was old. Wait, wait, Cornelia, till your own children whisper behind your back!

In her day she had kept a better house and had got more work done. She wasn't too old yet for Lydia to be driving eighty miles for advice when one of the children jumped the track, and Jimmy still dropped in and talked things over: "Now, Mammy, you've a good business head, I want to know what you think of this? . . ." Old Cornelia couldn't change the furniture around without asking. Little things, little things! They had been so sweet when they were little. Granny wished the old days were back again with the children young and everything to be done over. It had been a hard pull, but not too much for her. When she thought of all the food she had cooked, and all the clothes she had cut and sewed, and all the gardens she had made — well, the children showed it. There they were, made out of her, and they couldn't get away from that. Sometimes she wanted to see John again and point to them and say, Well, I didn't do so badly, did I? But that would have to wait. That was for tomorrow. She used to think of him as a man, but now all the children were older than their father, and he would be a child beside her if she saw him now. It seemed strange and there was something wrong in the idea. Why, he couldn't possibly recognize her. She had fenced in a hundred acres once, digging the post holes herself and clamping the wires with just a negro boy to help. That changed a woman. John would be looking for a young woman with the peaked Spanish comb in her hair and the painted fan. Digging post holes changed a woman. Riding country roads in the winter when women had their babies was another thing: sitting up nights with sick horses and sick negroes and sick children and hardly ever losing one. John, I hardly ever lost one of them! John would see that in a minute, that would be something he could understand, she wouldn't have to explain anything!

It made her feel like rolling up her sleeves and putting the whole place to rights again. No matter if Cornelia was determined to be everywhere at once, there were a great many things left undone in this place. She would start tomorrow and do them. It was good to be strong enough for everything, even if all you made melted and changed and slipped under your hands, so that by the time you finished you almost forgot what you were working for. What was it I set out to do? she asked herself intently, but she could not remember. A fog rose over the valley, she saw it marching across the creek swallowing the trees and moving up the hill like an army of ghosts. Soon it would be at the near edge of the orchard, and then it was time to go in and light the lamps. Come in, children, don't stay out in the night air.

Lighting the lamps had been beautiful. The children huddled up to her and breathed like little calves waiting at the bars in the twilight. Their eyes followed the match and watched the flame rise and settle in a blue curve, then they moved away from her. The lamp was lit, they didn't have to be scared and hang on to mother any more. Never, never, never more. God, for all my life I thank Thee. Without Thee, my God, I could never have done it. Hail, Mary, full of grace.

I want you to pick all the fruit this year and see that nothing is wasted. There's always someone who can use it. Don't let good things rot for want of using. You waste life when you waste good food. Don't let things get lost. It's bitter to lose things. Now, don't let me get to thinking, not when I am tired and taking a little nap before supper. . . .

The pillow rose about her shoulders and pressed against her heart and the memory was being squeezed out of it: oh, push down the pillow, somebody: it would smother her if she tried to hold it. Such a fresh breeze blowing and such a green day with no threats in it. But he had not come, just the same. What does a woman do when she has put on the white veil and set out the white cake for a man and he doesn't come? She tried to remember. No, I swear he never harmed me but in that. He never harmed me but in that . . . and what if he did? There was the day, the day, but a whirl of dark smoke rose and covered it, crept up and over into the bright field where everything was planted so carefully in orderly rows. That was hell, she knew hell when she saw it. For sixty years she had prayed against remembering him and against losing her soul in the deep pit of hell, and now the two things were mingled in one and the thought of him was a smoky cloud from hell that moved and crept in her head when she had just got rid of Doctor Harry and was trying to rest a minute. Wounded vanity, Ellen, said a sharp voice in the top of her mind. Don't let your wounded vanity get the upper hand of you. Plenty of girls get jilted. You were jilted, weren't you? Then stand up to it. Her eyelids wavered and let in streamers of blue-gray light like tissue paper over her eyes. She must get up and pull the shades down or she'd never sleep. She was in bed again and the shades were not down. How could that happen? Better turn over, hide from the light, sleeping in the light gave you nightmares. "Mother, how do you feel now?" and a stinging wetness on her forehead. But I don't like having my face washed in cold water!

Hapsy? George? Lydia? Jimmy? No, Cornelia, and her features were swollen 30 and full of little puddles. "They're coming, darling, they'll all be here soon." Go wash your face, child, you look funny.

Instead of obeying, Cornelia knelt down and put her head on the pillow. She seemed to be talking but there was no sound. "Well, are you tongue-tied? Whose birthday is it? Are you going to give a party?"

Cornelia's mouth moved urgently in strange shapes. "Don't do that, you bother me, daughter."

"Oh, no, Mother, Oh, no. . . . "

Nonsense. It was strange about children. They disputed your every word. "No what, Cornelia?"

"Here's Doctor Harry." 35

"I won't see that boy again. He just left five minutes ago."

"That was this morning, Mother. It's night now. Here's the nurse."

"This is Doctor Harry, Mrs. Weatherall. I never saw you look so young and happy!"

"Ah, I'll never be young again — but I'd be happy if they'd let me lie in peace and get rested."

She thought she spoke up loudly, but no one answered. A warm weight on her forehead, a warm bracelet on her wrist, and a breeze went on whispering, trying to tell her something. A shuffle of leaves in the everlasting hand of God. He blew on them and they danced and rattled. "Mother, don't mind, we're going to give you a little hypodermic." "Look here, daughter, how do ants get in this bed? I saw sugar ants yesterday." Did you send for Hapsy too?

It was Hapsy she really wanted. She had to go a long way back through a great many rooms to find Hapsy standing with a baby on her arm. She seemed to herself to be Hapsy also, and the baby on Hapsy's arm was Hapsy and himself and herself, all at once, and there was no surprise in the meeting. Then Hapsy melted from within and turned flimsy as gray gauze and the baby was a gauzy shadow, and Hapsy came up close and said, "I thought you'd never come," and looked at her very searchingly and said, "You haven't changed a bit!" They leaned forward to kiss, when Cornelia began whispering from a long way off, "Oh, is there anything you want to tell me? Is there anything I can do for you?"

Yes, she had changed her mind after sixty years and she would like to see George. I want you to find George. Find him and be sure to tell him I forgot him. I want him to know I had my husband just the same and my children and my house like any other woman. A good house too and a good husband that I loved and fine children out of him. Better than I hoped for even. Tell him I was given back everything he took away and more. Oh, no, oh, God, no, there was something else besides the house and the man and the children. Oh, surely they were not all? What was it? Something not given back. . . . Her breath crowded down under her ribs and grew into a monstrous frightening shape with cutting edges; it bored up into her head, and the agony was unbelievable. Yes, John, get the doctor now, no more talk, my time has come.

When this one was born it should be the last. The last. It should have been born first, for it was the one she had truly wanted. Everything came in good time. Nothing left out, left over. She was strong. In three days she would be as well as ever. Better. A woman needed milk in her to have her full health.

"Mother, do you hear me?"

"I've been telling you —"

"Mother, Father Connolly's here."

"I went to Holy Communion only last week. Tell him I'm not so sinful as all that."

"Father just wants to speak to you."

He could speak as much as he pleased. It was like him to drop in and inquire about her soul as if it were a teething baby, and then stay on for a cup of tea and a round of cards and gossip. He always had a funny story of some sort, usually about an Irishman who made his little mistakes and confessed them, and the point lay in some absurd thing he would blurt out in the confessional showing his struggles between naive piety and original sin. Granny felt easy about her soul. Cornelia, where are your manners? Give Father Connolly a chair. She had her secret comfortable understanding with a few favorite saints who cleared a straight road to God for her. All as surely signed and sealed as the papers for the new Forty Acres. Forever . . . heirs and assigns forever. Since the day the wedding cake was not cut, but thrown out and wasted. The whole bottom dropped out of the world, and there she was blind and sweating with nothing under her feet and the walls falling away. His hand had caught her under the breast, she had not fallen, there was the freshly polished floor with the green rug on it, just as before. He had cursed like a sailor's parrot and said, "I'll kill him for you." Don't lay a hand on him, for my sake leave something to God. "Now, Ellen, you must believe what I tell you. . . . "

So there was nothing, nothing to worry about any more, except sometimes in 50 the night one of the children screamed in a nightmare, and they both hustled out shaking and hunting for the matches and calling, "There, wait a minute, here we are!" John, get the doctor now, Hapsy's time has come. But there was Hapsy standing by the bed in a white cap. "Cornelia, tell Hapsy to take off her cap, I can't see her plain."

Her eyes opened very wide and the room stood out like a picture she had seen somewhere. Dark colors with the shadows rising towards the ceiling in long angles. The tall black dresser gleamed with nothing on it but John's picture, enlarged from a little one, with John's eyes very black when they should have been blue. You never saw him, so how do you know how he looked? But the man insisted the copy was perfect, it was very rich and handsome. For a picture, yes, but it's not my husband. The table by the bed had a linen cover and a candle and a crucifix. The light was blue from Cornelia's silk lampshades. No sort of light at all, just frippery. You had to live forty years with kerosene lamps to appreciate honest electricity. She felt very strong and she saw Doctor Harry with a rosy nimbus around him.

"You look like a saint, Doctor Harry, and I vow that's as near as you'll ever come to it."

"She's saying something."

"I heard you, Cornelia. What's all this carrying on?"

"Father Connolly's saying —"   55

Cornelia's voice staggered and bumped like a cart in a bad road. It rounded corners and turned back again and arrived nowhere. Granny stepped up in the cart very lightly and reached for the reins, but a man sat beside her and she knew him by his hands, driving the cart. She did not look in his face, for she knew without seeing, but looked instead down the road where the trees leaned over and bowed to each other and a thousand birds were singing a Mass. She felt like singing too, but she put her hand in the bosom of her dress and pulled out a rosary, and Father Connolly murmured Latin in a very solemn voice and tickled her feet. My God, will you stop that nonsense? I'm a married woman.

What if he did run away and leave me to face the priest by myself? I found another a whole world better. I wouldn't have exchanged my husband for anybody except St. Michael himself, and you may tell him that for me with a thank you in the bargain.

Light flashed on her closed eyelids, and a deep roaring shook her. Cornelia, is that lightning? I hear thunder. There's going to be a storm. Close all the windows. Call the children in. . . . "Mother, here we are, all of us." "Is that you, Hapsy?" "Oh, no, I'm Lydia. We drove as fast as we could." Their faces drifted above her, drifted away. The rosary fell out of her hands and Lydia put it back. Jimmy tried to help, their hands fumbled together, and Granny closed two fingers around Jimmy's thumb. Beads wouldn't do, it must be something alive. She was so amazed her thoughts ran round and round. So, my dear Lord, this is my death and I wasn't even thinking about it. My children have come to see me die. But I can't, it's not time. Oh, I always hated surprises. I wanted to give Cornelia the amethyst set — Cornelia, you're to have the amethyst set, but Hapsy's to wear it when she wants, and, Doctor Harry, do shut up. Nobody sent for you. Oh, my dear Lord, do wait a minute. I meant to do something about the Forty Acres, Jimmy doesn't need it and Lydia will later on, with that worthless husband of hers. I meant to finish the altar cloth and send six bottles of wine to Sister Borgia for her dyspepsia. I want to send six bottles of wine to Sister Borgia, Father Connolly, now don't let me forget.

Cornelia's voice made short turns and tilted over and crashed. "Oh, Mother, oh, Mother, oh, Mother. . . . "

"I'm not going, Cornelia. I'm taken by surprise. I can't go."

You'll see Hapsy again. What about her? "I thought you'd never come." 60 Granny made a long journey outward, looking for Hapsy. What if I don't find her? What then? Her heart sank down and down, there was no bottom to death, she couldn't come to the end of it. The blue light from Cornelia's lampshade drew into a tiny point in the center of her brain, it flickered and winked like an eye, quietly it fluttered and dwindled. Granny lay curled down within herself, amazed and watchful, staring at the point of light that was herself; her body was now only a deeper mass of shadow in an endless darkness and this darkness would curl around the light and swallow it up. God, give a sign!

For the second time there was no sign. Again no bridegroom and the priest in the house. She could not remember any other sorrow because this grief wiped them all away. Oh, no, there's nothing more cruel than this — I'll never forgive it. She stretched herself with a deep breath and blew out the light.

For Analysis

1. Characterize Granny Weatherall. What facts about her life does the story provide?

2. Why, after sixty years, does the jilting by George loom so large in Granny's mind? Are we to accept her own strong statements that the pain of the jilting was more than compensated for by the happiness she ultimately found with her husband, her children, and her grandchildren? Defend your response.

3. Who is Hapsy? Why do you suppose she is not present?

4. The final paragraph echoes Christ's parable of the bridegroom (Matthew 25:1–13). Why does Granny connect this final, deep religious grief with the grief she felt when George jilted her?

On Style

1. Why doesn't the author present Granny's final thoughts in an orderly and sequential pattern?

2. Granny is revealed to us not only through her direct thoughts but also through the many images that float through her mind — the "fog" (para. 26), the "breeze blowing" (para. 29), "a whirl of dark smoke" (para. 29), and others. What do these images reveal about Granny?

3. Discuss the significance of Granny's name.

Making Connections

Compare the final hours of Granny Weatherall with those of Tolstoy's Iván Ilých (p. 1286).

Writing Topic

Compare the thoughts and behavior of the dying Granny Weatherall with those of Tolstoy's Iván Ilých. How do their final hours significantly differ?

Bernard Malamud (1914–1986)

Idiots First 1963

The thick ticking of the tin clock stopped. Mendel, dozing in the dark, awoke in fright. The pain returned as he listened. He drew on his cold embittered clothing, and wasted minutes sitting at the edge of the bed.

"Isaac," he ultimately sighed.

In the kitchen, Isaac, his astonished mouth open, held six peanuts in his palm. He placed each on the table. "One . . . two . . . nine."

He gathered each peanut and appeared in the doorway. Mendel, in loose hat and long overcoat, still sat on the bed. Isaac watched with small eyes and ears, thick hair graying the sides of his head.

"Schlaf," he nasally said.   5

"No," muttered Mendel. As if stifling he rose. "Come, Isaac."

He wound his old watch though the sight of the stopped clock nauseated him. Isaac wanted to hold it to his ear.

"No, it's late." Mendel put the watch carefully away. In the drawer he found the little paper bag of crumpled ones and fives and slipped it into his overcoat pocket. He helped Isaac on with his coat.

Isaac looked at one dark window, then at the other. Mendel stared at both   10
blank windows.

They went slowly down the darkly lit stairs, Mendel first, Isaac watching the moving shadows on the wall. To one long shadow he offered a peanut.

"Hungrig."

In the vestibule the old man gazed through the thin glass. The November night was cold and bleak. Opening the door he cautiously thrust his head out. Though he saw nothing he quickly shut the door.

"Ginzburg, that he came to see me yesterday," he whispered in Isaac's ear.
Isaac sucked air.   15

"You know who I mean?"

Isaac combed his chin with his fingers.

"That's the one, with the black whiskers. Don't talk to him or go with him if he asks you."

Isaac moaned.

"Young people he don't bother so much," Mendel said in afterthought.   20

It was suppertime and the street was empty but the store windows dimly lit their way to the corner. They crossed the deserted street and went on. Isaac, with a happy cry, pointed to the three golden balls. Mendel smiled but was exhausted when they got to the pawnshop.

The pawnbroker, a red-bearded man with black horn-rimmed glasses, was eating a whitefish at the rear of the store. He craned his head, saw them, and settled back to sip his tea.

In five minutes he came forward, patting his shapeless lips with a large white handkerchief.

Mendel, breathing heavily, handed him the worn gold watch. The pawnbroker, raising his glasses, screwed in his eyepiece. He turned the watch over once. "Eight dollars."

The dying man wet his cracked lips. "I must have thirty-five."   25

"So go to Rothschild."

"Cost me myself sixty."

"In 1905." The pawnbroker handed back the watch. It had stopped ticking. Mendel wound it slowly. It ticked hollowly.

"Isaac must go to my uncle that he lives in California."

"It's a free country," said the pawnbroker.   30

Isaac, watching a banjo, snickered.

"What's the matter with him?" the pawnbroker asked.

"So let be eight dollars," muttered Mendel, "but where will I get the rest till tonight?"

"How much for my hat and coat?" he asked.

"No sale." The pawnbroker went behind the cage and wrote out a ticket. He   35 locked the watch in a small drawer but Mendel still heard it ticking.

In the street he slipped the eight dollars into the paper bag, then searched in his pockets for a scrap of writing. Finding it, he strained to read the address by the light of the street lamp.

As they trudged to the subway, Mendel pointed to the sprinkled sky.

"Isaac, look how many stars are tonight."

"Eggs," said Isaac.

"First we will go to Mr. Fishbein, after we will eat."   40

They got off the train in upper Manhattan and had to walk several blocks before they located Fishbein's house.

"A regular palace," Mendel murmured, looking forward to a moment's warmth.

Isaac stared uneasily at the heavy door of the house.

Mendel rang. The servant, a man with long sideburns, came to the door and said Mr. and Mrs. Fishbein were dining and could see no one.

"He should eat in peace but we will wait till he finishes."   45

"Come back tomorrow morning. Tomorrow morning Mr. Fishbein will talk to you. He don't do business or charity at this time of the night."

"Charity I am not interested —"

"Come back tomorrow."

"Tell him it's life or death —"

"Whose life or death?"   50

"So if not his, then mine."

"Don't be such a big smart aleck."

"Look me in my face," said Mendel, "and tell me if I got time till tomorrow morning?"

The servant stared at him, then at Isaac, and reluctantly let them in.

The foyer was a vast high-ceilinged room with many oil paintings on the walls, 55 voluminous silken draperies, a thick flowered rug at foot, and a marbled staircase.

Mr. Fishbein, a paunchy bald-headed man with hairy nostrils and small patent leather feet, ran lightly down the stairs, a large napkin tucked under a tuxedo coat button. He stopped on the fifth step from the bottom and examined his visitors.

"Who comes on Friday night to a man that he has guests, to spoil him his supper?"

"Excuse me that I bother you, Mr. Fishbein," Mendel said. "If I didn't come now I couldn't come tomorrow."

"Without more preliminaries, please state your business. I'm a hungry man."

"Hungrig," wailed Isaac. 60

Fishbein adjusted his pince-nez. "What's the matter with him?"

"This is my son Isaac. He is like this all his life."

Isaac mewled.

"I am sending him to California."

"Mr. Fishbein don't contribute to personal pleasure trips." 65

"I am a sick man and he must go tonight on the train to my Uncle Leo."

"I never give to unorganized charity," Fishbein said, "but if you are hungry I will invite you downstairs in my kitchen. We having tonight chicken with stuffed derma."

"All I ask is thirty-five dollars for the train ticket to my uncle in California. I have already the rest."

"Who is your uncle? How old a man?"

"Eighty-one years, a long life to him." 70

Fishbein burst into laughter. "Eighty-one years and you are sending him this halfwit."

Mendel, flailing both arms, cried, "Please, without names."

Fishbein politely conceded.

"Where is open the door there we go in the house," the sick man said. "If you will kindly give me thirty-five dollars, God will bless you. What is thirty-five dollars to Mr. Fishbein? Nothing. To me, for my boy, is everything."

Fishbein drew himself up to his tallest height. 75

"Private contributions I don't make — only to institutions. This is my fixed policy."

Mendel sank to his creaking knees on the rug.

"Please, Mr. Fishbein, if not thirty-five, give maybe twenty."

"Levinson!" Fishbein angrily called.

The servant with the long sideburns appeared at the top of the stairs. 80

"Show this party where is the door — unless he wishes to partake food before leaving the premises."

"For what I got chicken won't cure it," Mendel said.

"This way if you please," said Levinson, descending.

Isaac assisted his father up.

"Take him to an institution," Fishbein advised over the marble balustrade. He 85 ran quickly up the stairs and they were at once outside, buffeted by winds.

The walk to the subway was tedious. The wind blew mournfully. Mendel, breathless, glanced furtively at shadows. Isaac, clutching his peanuts in his frozen fist, clung to his father's side. They entered a small park to rest for a minute on a stone bench under a leafless two-branched tree. The thick right branch was raised, the thin left one hung down. A very pale moon rose slowly. So did a stranger as they approached the bench.

"Gut yuntif" [Happy holiday], he said hoarsely.

Mendel, drained of blood, waved his wasted arms. Isaac yowled sickly. Then a bell chimed and it was only ten. Mendel let out a piercing anguished cry as the bearded stranger disappeared into the bushes. A policeman came running, and though he beat the bushes with his nightstick, could turn up nothing. Mendel and Isaac hurried out of the little park. When Mendel glanced back the dead tree had its thin arm raised, the thick one down. He moaned.

They boarded a trolley, stopping at the home of a former friend, but he had died years ago. On the same block they went into a cafeteria and ordered two fried eggs for Isaac. The tables were crowded except where a heavy-set man sat eating soup with kasha. After one look at him they left in haste, although Isaac wept.

Mendel had another address on a slip of paper but the house was too far away, 90 in Queens, so they stood in a doorway shivering.

What can I do, he frantically thought, in one short hour?

He remembered the furniture in the house. It was junk but might bring a few dollars. "Come, Isaac." They went once more to the pawnbroker's to talk to him, but the shop was dark and an iron gate — rings and gold watches glinting through it — was drawn tight across his place of business.

They huddled behind a telephone pole, both freezing. Isaac whimpered.

"See the big moon, Isaac. The whole sky is white."

He pointed but Isaac wouldn't look. 95

Mendel dreamed for a minute of the sky lit up, long sheets of light in all directions. Under the sky, in California, sat Uncle Leo drinking tea with lemon. Mendel felt warm but woke up cold.

Across the street stood an ancient brick synagogue.

He pounded on the huge door but no one appeared. He waited till he had breath and desperately knocked again. At last there were footsteps within, and the synagogue door creaked open on its massive brass hinges.

A darkly dressed sexton, holding a dripping candle, glared at them.

"Who knocks this time of night with so much noise on the synagogue door?" 100

Mendel told the sexton his troubles. "Please, I would like to speak to the rabbi."

"The rabbi is an old man. He sleeps now. His wife won't let you see him. Go home and come back tomorrow."

"To tomorrow I said goodbye already. I am a dying man."

Though the sexton seemed doubtful he pointed to an old wooden house next door. "In there he lives." He disappeared into the synagogue with his lit candle casting shadows around him.

Mendel, with Isaac clutching his sleeve, went up the wooden steps and rang   105
the bell. After five minutes a big-faced, gray-haired bulky woman came out on the porch with a torn robe thrown over her nightdress. She emphatically said the rabbi was sleeping and could not be waked.

But as she was insisting, the rabbi himself tottered to the door. He listened a minute and said, "Who wants to see me let them come in."

They entered a cluttered room. The rabbi was an old skinny man with bent shoulders and a wisp of white beard. He wore a flannel nightgown and black skullcap; his feet were bare.

"Vey is mir" [Woe is me], his wife muttered. "Put on shoes or tomorrow comes sure pneumonia." She was a woman with a big belly, years younger than her husband. Staring at Isaac, she turned away.

Mendel apologetically related his errand. "All I need more is thirty-five dollars."

"Thirty-five?" said the rabbi's wife. "Why not thirty-five thousand? Who has so   110
much money? My husband is a poor rabbi. The doctors take away every penny."

"Dear friend," said the rabbi, "if I had I would give you."

"I got already seventy," Mendel said, heavy-hearted. "All I need more is thirty-five."

"God will give you," said the rabbi.

"In the grave," said Mendel. "I need tonight. Come, Isaac."

"Wait," called the rabbi.   115

He hurried inside, came out with a fur-lined caftan, and handed it to Mendel.

"Yascha," shrieked his wife, "not your new coat!"

"I got my old one. Who needs two coats for one body?"

"Yascha, I am screaming —"

"Who can go among poor people, tell me, in a new coat?"   120

"Yascha," she cried, "what can this man do with your coat? He needs tonight the money. The pawnbrokers are asleep."

"So let him wake them up."

"No." She grabbed the coat from Mendel.

He held on to a sleeve, wrestling her for the coat. Her I know, Mendel thought. "Shylock," he muttered. Her eyes glittered.

The rabbi groaned and tottered dizzily. His wife cried out as Mendel yanked   125
the coat from her hands.

"Run," cried the rabbi.

"Run, Isaac."

They ran out of the house and down the steps.

"Stop, you thief," called the rabbi's wife.

The rabbi pressed both hands to his temples and fell to the floor.   130

"Help!" his wife wept. "Heart attack! Help!"

But Mendel and Isaac ran through the streets with the rabbi's new fur-lined caftan. After them noiselessly ran Ginzburg.

It was very late when Mendel bought the train ticket in the only booth open.

There was no time to stop for a sandwich so Isaac ate his peanuts and they hurried to the train in the vast deserted station.

"So in the morning," Mendel gasped as they ran, "there comes a man that he   135
sells sandwiches and coffee. Eat but get change. When reaches California the train, will be waiting for you on the station Uncle Leo. If you don't recognize him he will recognize you. Tell him I send best regards."

But when they arrived at the gate to the platform it was shut, the light out.

Mendel, groaning, beat on the gate with his fists.

"Too late," said the uniformed ticket collector, a bulky, bearded man with hairy nostrils and a fishy smell.

He pointed to the station clock. "Already past twelve."

"But I see standing there still the train," Mendel said, hopping in his grief.   140

"It just left — in one more minute."

"A minute is enough. Just open the gate."

"Too late I told you."

Mendel socked his bony chest with both hands. "With my whole heart I beg you this little favor."

"Favors you had enough already. For you the train is gone. You shoulda been   145
dead already at midnight. I told you that yesterday. This is the best I can do."

"Ginzburg!" Mendel shrank from him.

"Who else?" The voice was metallic, eyes glittered, the expression amused.

"For myself," the old man begged, "I don't ask a thing. But what will happen to my boy?"

Ginzburg shrugged slightly. "What will happen happens. This isn't my responsibility. I got enough to think about without worrying about somebody on one cylinder."

"What then is your responsibility?"   150

"To create conditions. To make happen what happens. I ain't in the anthropomorphic business."

"Whatever business you in, where is your pity?"

"This ain't my commodity. The law is the law."

"Which law is this?"

"The cosmic universal law, goddamit, the one I got to follow myself."   155

"What kind of a law is it?" cried Mendel. "For God's sake, don't you understand what I went through in my life with this poor boy? Look at him. For thirty-nine years, since the day he was born, I wait for him to grow up, but he don't. Do you understand what this means in a father's heart? Why don't you let him go to his uncle?" His voice had risen and he was shouting.

Isaac mewled loudly.

"Better calm down or you'll hurt somebody's feelings," Ginzburg said with a wink toward Isaac.

"All my life," Mendel cried, his body trembling, "what did I have? I was poor. I suffered from my health. When I worked I worked too hard. When I didn't work was worse. My wife died a young woman. But I didn't ask from anybody nothing. Now I ask a small favor. Be so kind, Mr. Ginzburg."

The ticket collector was picking his teeth with a match stick.   160

"You ain't the only one, my friend, some got it worse than you. That's how it goes in this country."

"You dog you." Mendel lunged at Ginzburg's throat and began to choke. "You bastard, don't you understand what it means human?"

They struggled nose to nose, Ginzburg, though his astonished eyes bulged, began to laugh. "You pipsqueak nothing. I'll freeze you to pieces."

His eyes lit in rage and Mendel felt an unbearable cold like an icy dagger invading his body, all of his parts shriveling.

Now I die without helping Isaac.   165

A crowd gathered. Isaac yelped in fright.

Clinging to Ginzburg in his last agony, Mendel saw reflected in the ticket collector's eyes the depth of his terror. But he saw that Ginzburg, staring at himself in Mendel's eyes, saw mirrored in them the extent of his own awful wrath. He beheld a shimmering, starry, blinding light that produced darkness.

Ginzburg looked astounded. "Who me?"

His grip on the squirming old man slowly loosened, and Mendel, his heart barely beating, slumped to the ground.

"Go." Ginzburg muttered, "take him to the train."   170

"Let pass," he commanded a guard.

The crowd parted. Isaac helped his father up and they tottered down the steps to the platform where the train waited, lit and ready to go.

Mendel found Isaac a coach seat and hastily embraced him. "Help Uncle Leo, Isaakil. Also remember your father and mother."

"Be nice to him," he said to the conductor. "Show him where everything is."

He waited on the platform until the train began slowly to move. Isaac sat 175 at the edge of his seat, his face strained in the direction of his journey. When the train was gone, Mendel ascended the stairs to see what had become of Ginzburg.

For Analysis

1. What traits does the rabbi embody?

2. What does Ginzburg represent?

3. What is the significance of the fact that Isaac, whom Mendel is determined to provide for before death claims him, is mentally disabled?

4. Mendel wins the battle with Ginzburg. What does that victory signify?

On Style

Discuss the function of **dialect** in this story. How does Malamud convey that Isaac is an "idiot"?

Making Connections

Consider the desperate appeals that Mendel makes to the pawnbroker, the "philanthropist" Fishbein, the rabbi's wife, and the rabbi. What do the differing responses reveal about the human condition? Imagine yourself in Mendel's situation and discuss the likely responses of various people — friends, clergy, family, counselors — to your desperate appeal for help.

Writing Topic

How do the various episodes in this story establish Mendel's character? How do they prepare the reader for the climactic confrontation between Mendel and Ginzburg?

Bessie Head   (1937–1986)

Looking for a Rain God   1977

It is lonely at the lands where the people go to plough. These lands are vast clearings in the bush, and the wild bush is lonely too. Nearly all the lands are within walking distance from the village. In some parts of the bush where the underground water is very near the surface, people made little rest camps for themselves and dug shallow wells to quench their thirst while on their journey to their own lands. They experienced all kinds of things once they left the village. They could rest at shady watering places full of lush, tangled trees with delicate pale-gold and purple wildflowers springing up between soft green moss and the children could hunt around for wild figs and any berries that might be in season. But from 1958, a seven-year drought fell upon the land and even the watering places began to look as dismal as the dry open thornbush country; the leaves of the trees curled up and withered; the moss became dry and hard and, under the shade of the tangled trees, the ground turned a powdery black and white, because there was no rain. People said rather humorously that if you tried to catch the rain in a cup it would only fill a teaspoon. Toward the beginning of the seventh year of drought, the summer had become an anguish to live through. The air was so dry and moisture-free that it burned the skin. No one knew what to do to escape the heat and tragedy was in the air. At the beginning of that summer, a number of men just went out of their homes and hung themselves to death from trees. The majority of the people had lived off crops, but for two years past they had all returned from the lands with only their rolled-up skin blankets and cooking utensils. Only the charlatans, incanters, and witch doctors made a pile of money during this time because people were always turning to them in desperation for little talismans and herbs to rub on the plough for the crops to grow and the rain to fall.

The rains were late that year. They came in early November, with a promise of good rain. It wasn't the full, steady downpour of the years of good rain but thin, scanty, misty rain. It softened the earth and a rich growth of green things sprang up everywhere for the animals to eat. People were called to the center of the village to hear the proclamation of the beginning of the ploughing season; they stirred themselves and whole families began to move off to the lands to plough.

The family of the old man, Mokgobja, were among those who left early for the lands. They had a donkey cart and piled everything onto it, Mokgobja — who was over seventy years old; two girls, Neo and Boseyong; their mother Tiro and an unmarried sister, Nesta; and the father and supporter of the family,

Ramadi, who drove the donkey cart. In the rush of the first hope of rain, the man, Ramadi, and the two women, cleared the land of thornbush and then hedged their vast ploughing area with this same thornbush to protect the future crop from the goats they had brought along for milk. They cleared out and deepened the old well with its pool of muddy water and still in this light, misty rain, Ramadi inspanned two oxen and turned the earth over with a hand plough.

The land was ready and ploughed, waiting for the crops. At night, the earth was alive with insects singing and rustling about in search of food. But suddenly, by mid-November, the rain flew away; the rain clouds fled away and left the sky bare. The sun danced dizzily in the sky, with a strange cruelty. Each day the land was covered in a haze of mist as the sun sucked up the last drop of moisture out of the earth. The family sat down in despair, waiting and waiting. Their hopes had run so high; the goats had started producing milk, which they had eagerly poured on their porridge, now they ate plain porridge with no milk. It was impossible to plant the corn, maize, pumpkin, and watermelon seeds in the dry earth. They sat the whole day in the shadow of the huts and even stopped thinking, for the rain had fled away. Only the children, Neo and Boseyong, were quite happy in their little-girl world. They carried on their game of making house like their mother and chattered to each other in light, soft tones. They made children from sticks around which they tied rags, and scolded them severely in an exact imitation of their own mother. Their voices could be heard scolding the day long: "You stupid thing, when I send you to draw water, why do you spill half of it out of the bucket!" "You stupid thing! Can't you mind the porridge pot without letting the porridge burn!" And then they would beat the rag dolls on their bottoms with severe expressions.

The adults paid no attention to this; they did not even hear the funny chatter; 5 they sat waiting for rain; their nerves were stretched to the breaking-point willing the rain to fall out of the sky. Nothing was important, beyond that. All their animals had been sold during the bad years to purchase food, and of all their herd only two goats were left. It was the women of the family who finally broke down under the strain of waiting for rain. It was really the two women who caused the death of the little girls. Each night they started a weird, high-pitched wailing that began on a low, mournful note and whipped up to a frenzy. Then they would stamp their feet and shout as though they had lost their heads. The men sat quiet and self-controlled; it was important for men to maintain their self control at all times but their nerve was breaking too. They knew the women were haunted by the starvation of the coming year.

Finally, an ancient memory stirred in the old man, Mokgobja. When he was very young and the customs of the ancestors still ruled the land, he had been witness to a rain-making ceremony. And he came alive a little, struggling to recall the details which had been buried by years and years of prayer in a Christian church. As soon as the mists cleared a little, he began consulting in whispers with his youngest son, Ramadi. There was, he said, a certain rain god who accepted only the sacrifice of the bodies of children. Then the rain would fall;

then the crops would grow, he said. He explained the ritual and as he talked, his memory became a conviction and he began to talk with unshakable authority. Ramadi's nerves were smashed by the nightly wailing of the women and soon the two men began whispering with the two women. The children continued their game: "You stupid thing! How could you have lost the money on the way to the shop! You must have been playing again!"

After it was all over and the bodies of the two little girls had been spread across the land, the rain did not fall. Instead, there was a deathly silence at night and the devouring heat of the sun by day. A terror, extreme and deep, overwhelmed the whole family. They packed, rolling up their skin blankets and pots, and fled back to the village.

People in the village soon noted the absence of the two little girls. They had died at the lands and were buried there, the family said. But people noted their ashen, terror-stricken faces and a murmur arose. What had killed the children, they wanted to know? And the family replied they had just died. And people said amongst themselves that it was strange that the two deaths had occurred at the same time. And there was a feeling of great unease at the unnatural looks of the family. Soon the police came around. The family told them the same story of death and burial at the lands. They did not know what the children had died of. So the police asked to see the graves. At this, the mother of the children broke down and told everything.

Throughout that terrible summer the story of the children hung like a dark cloud of sorrow over the village, and the sorrow was not assuaged when the old man and Ramadi were sentenced to death for ritual murder. All they had on the statute books was that ritual murder was against the law and must be stamped out with the death penalty. The subtle story of strain and starvation and breakdown was inadmissible evidence at court; but all the people who lived off the crops knew in their hearts that only a hair's breadth had saved them from sharing a fate similar to that of the Mokgobja family. They could have killed something to make the rain fall.

For Analysis

1. Characterize the lives of the people in the story. What do they live on? What are the consequences of the long drought?

2. How do the two little girls' games affect you as a reader?

3. Consider the story's final paragraph. Do you feel the men should be executed? Explain.

On Style

Examine the language Head uses to describe the two girls. Why are they the only people in the story quoted directly? What reason might Head have to portray the girls this way?

Making Connections

Write an essay reflecting on a crisis in your own life and discuss the "sacrifices" you offered in exchange for a resolution of your problem.

Writing Topic

Find references to human and animal sacrifice in the Hebrew Bible (e.g., Genesis 22, Leviticus 1, and Judges 12:30, 34–40). As well, consider Christianity's view of the crucifixion of Jesus. In an essay, relate the blood sacrifices found in the Judeo-Christian tradition with the events in this story.

Tim O'Brien   (b. 1947)

The Things They Carried   1986

First Lieutenant Jimmy Cross carried letters from a girl named Martha, a junior at Mount Sebastian College in New Jersey. They were not love letters, but Lieutenant Cross was hoping, so he kept them folded in plastic at the bottom of his rucksack. In the late afternoon, after a day's march, he would dig his foxhole, wash his hands under a canteen, unwrap the letters, hold them with the tips of his fingers, and spend the last hour of light pretending. He would imagine romantic camping trips into the White Mountains in New Hampshire. He would sometimes taste the envelope flaps, knowing her tongue had been there. More than anything, he wanted Martha to love him as he loved her, but the letters were mostly chatty, elusive on the matter of love. She was a virgin, he was almost sure. She was an English major at Mount Sebastian, and she wrote beautifully about her professors and roommates and midterm exams, about her respect for Chaucer and her great affection for Virginia Woolf. She often quoted lines of poetry; she never mentioned the war, except to say, Jimmy, take care of yourself. The letters weighed ten ounces. They were signed "Love, Martha," but Lieutenant Cross understood that "Love" was only a way of signing and did not mean what he sometimes pretended it meant. At dusk, he would carefully return the letters to his rucksack. Slowly, a bit distracted, he would get up and move among his men, checking the perimeter, then at full dark he would return to his hole and watch the night and wonder if Martha was a virgin.

The things they carried were largely determined by necessity. Among the necessities or near necessities were P-38 can openers, pocket knives, heat tabs, wrist watches, dog tags, mosquito repellent, chewing gum, candy, cigarettes, salt tablets, packets of Kool-Aid, lighters, matches, sewing kits, Military Payment Certificates, C rations, and two or three canteens of water. Together, these items weighed between fifteen and twenty pounds, depending upon a man's habits or rate of metabolism. Henry Dobbins, who was a big man, carried extra rations; he was especially fond of canned peaches in heavy syrup over pound cake. Dave Jensen, who practiced field hygiene, carried a toothbrush, dental floss, and several hotel-size bars of soap he'd stolen on R&R[1] in Sydney, Australia. Ted Lavender, who was scared, carried tranquilizers until he was shot in the head outside the village of Than Khe in mid-April. By necessity, and because it was SOP,[2] they all carried steel helmets that weighed five pounds including the liner and camouflage cover. They carried the standard fatigue jackets and trousers.

[1] Rest and recreation.
[2] Standard operating procedure.

1360

Very few carried underwear. On their feet they carried jungle boots — 2.1 pounds — and Dave Jensen carried three pairs of socks and a can of Dr. Scholl's foot powder as a precaution against trench foot. Until he was shot, Ted Lavender carried six or seven ounces of premium dope, which for him was a necessity. Mitchell Sanders, the RTO, carried condoms. Norman Bowker carried a diary. Rat Kiley carried comic books. Kiowa, a devout Baptist, carried an illustrated New Testament that had been presented to him by his father, who taught Sunday school in Oklahoma City, Oklahoma. As a hedge against bad times, however, Kiowa also carried his grandmother's distrust of the white man, his grandfather's old hunting hatchet. Necessity dictated. Because the land was mined and booby-trapped, it was SOP for each man to carry a steel-centered, nylon-covered flak jacket, which weighed 6.7 pounds, but which on hot days seemed much heavier. Because you could die so quickly, each man carried at least one large compress bandage, usually in the helmet band for easy access. Because the nights were cold, and because the monsoons were wet, each carried a green plastic poncho that could be used as a raincoat or ground sheet or makeshift tent. With its quilted liner, the poncho weighed almost two pounds, but it was worth every ounce. In April, for instance, when Ted Lavender was shot, they used his poncho to wrap him up, then to carry him across the paddy, then to lift him into the chopper that took him away.

They were called legs or grunts.

To carry something was to "hump" it, as when Lieutenant Jimmy Cross humped his love for Martha up the hills and through the swamps. In its intransitive form, "to hump" meant "to walk," or "to march," but it implied burdens far beyond the intransitive.

Almost everyone humped photographs. In his wallet, Lieutenant Cross carried two photographs of Martha. The first was a Kodachrome snapshot signed "Love," though he knew better. She stood against a brick wall. Her eyes were gray and neutral, her lips slightly open as she stared straight-on at the camera. At night, sometimes, Lieutenant Cross wondered who had taken the picture, because he knew she had boyfriends, because he loved her so much, and because he could see the shadow of the picture taker spreading out against the brick wall. The second photograph had been clipped from the 1968 Mount Sebastian yearbook. It was an action shot — women's volleyball — and Martha was bent horizontal to the floor, reaching, the palms of her hands in sharp focus, the tongue taut, the expression frank and competitive. There was no visible sweat. She wore white gym shorts. Her legs, he thought, were almost certainly the legs of a virgin, dry and without hair, the left knee cocked and carrying her entire weight, which was just over one hundred pounds. Lieutenant Cross remembered touching that left knee. A dark theater, he remembered, and the movie was *Bonnie and Clyde,* and Martha wore a tweed skirt, and during the final scene, when he touched her knee, she turned and looked at him in a sad, sober way that made him pull his hand back, but he would always remember the feel of the tweed skirt and the knee beneath it and the sound of the gunfire that killed Bonnie and Clyde, how embarrassing it was, how slow and oppressive. He remembered kissing her good night at the dorm door. Right then, he thought, he should've done something brave. He should've carried her up the stairs to her room and tied her to the bed and touched that left knee all night long. He should've risked it. Whenever he looked at the photographs, he thought of new things he should've done.

What they carried was partly a function of rank, partly of field specialty.

As a first lieutenant and platoon leader, Jimmy Cross carried a compass, maps, code books, binoculars, and a .45-caliber pistol that weighed 2.9 pounds fully loaded. He carried a strobe light and the responsibility for the lives of his men.

As an RTO, Mitchell Sanders carried the PRC-25 radio, a killer, twenty-six pounds with its battery.

As a medic, Rat Kiley carried a canvas satchel filled with morphine and plasma and malaria tablets and surgical tape and comic books and all the things a medic must carry, including M&M's for especially bad wounds, for a total weight of nearly twenty pounds.

As a big man, therefore a machine gunner, Henry Dobbins carried the M-60, which weighed twenty-three pounds unloaded, but which was almost always loaded. In addition, Dobbins carried between ten and fifteen pounds of ammunition draped in belts across his chest and shoulders.

As PFCs or Spec 4s, most of them were common grunts and carried the standard M-16 gas-operated assault rifle. The weapon weighed 7.5 pounds unloaded, 8.2 pounds with its full twenty-round magazine. Depending on numerous factors, such as topography and psychology, the riflemen carried anywhere from twelve to twenty magazines, usually in cloth bandoliers, adding on another 8.4 pounds at minimum, fourteen pounds at maximum. When it was available, they also carried M-16 maintenance gear — rods and steel brushes and swabs and tubes of LSA oil — all of which weighed about a pound. Among the grunts, some carried the M-79 grenade launcher, 5.9 pounds unloaded, a reasonably light weapon except for the ammunition, which was heavy. A single round weighed ten ounces. The typical load was twenty-five rounds. But Ted Lavender, who was scared, carried thirty-four rounds when he was shot and killed outside Than Khe, and he went down under an exceptional burden, more than twenty pounds of ammunition, plus the flak jacket and helmet and rations and water and toilet paper and tranquilizers and all the rest, plus the unweighed fear. He was dead weight. There was no twitching or flopping. Kiowa, who saw it happen, said it was like watching a rock fall, or a big sandbag or something — just boom, then down — not like the movies where the dead guy rolls around and does fancy spins and goes ass over teakettle — not like that, Kiowa said, the poor bastard just flat-fuck fell. Boom. Down. Nothing else. It was a bright morning in mid-April. Lieutenant Cross felt the pain. He blamed himself. They stripped off Lavender's canteens and ammo, all the heavy things, and Rat Kiley said the obvious, the guy's dead, and Mitchell Sanders used his radio to report

10

one U.S. KIA and to request a chopper. Then they wrapped Lavender in his poncho. They carried him out to a dry paddy, established security, and sat smoking the dead man's dope until the chopper came. Lieutenant Cross kept to himself. He pictured Martha's smooth young face, thinking he loved her more than anything, more than his men, and now Ted Lavender was dead because he loved her so much and could not stop thinking about her. When the dust-off arrived, they carried Lavender aboard. Afterward they burned Than Khe. They marched until dusk, then dug their holes, and that night Kiowa kept explaining how you had to be there, how fast it was, how the poor guy just dropped like so much concrete. Boom-down, he said. Like cement.

In addition to the three standard weapons — the M-60, M-16, and M-79 — they carried whatever presented itself, or whatever seemed appropriate as a means of killing or staying alive. They carried catch-as-catch-can. At various times, in various situations, they carried M-14s and CAR-15s and Swedish Ks and grease guns and captured AK-47s and Chi-Coms and RPGs and Simonov carbines and black-market Uzis and .38-caliber Smith & Wesson handguns and 66 mm LAWs and shotguns and silencers and blackjacks and bayonets and C-4 plastic explosives. Lee Strunk carried a slingshot; a weapon of last resort, he called it. Mitchell Sanders carried brass knuckles. Kiowa carried his grandfather's feathered hatchet. Every third or fourth man carried a Claymore antipersonnel mine — 3.5 pounds with its firing device. They all carried fragmentation grenades — fourteen ounces each. They all carried at least one M-18 colored smoke grenade — twenty-four ounces. Some carried CS or tear-gas grenades. Some carried white-phosphorus grenades. They carried all they could bear, and then some, including a silent awe for the terrible power of the things they carried.

In the first week of April, before Lavender died, Lieutenant Jimmy Cross received a good-luck charm from Martha. It was a simple pebble, an ounce at most. Smooth to the touch, it was a milky-white color with flecks of orange and violet, oval-shaped, like a miniature egg. In the accompanying letter, Martha wrote that she had found the pebble on the Jersey shoreline, precisely where the land touched water at high tide, where things came together but also separated. It was this separate-but-together quality, she wrote, that had inspired her to pick up the pebble and to carry it in her breast pocket for several days, where it seemed weightless, and then to send it through the mail, by air, as a token of her truest feelings for him. Lieutenant Cross found this romantic. But he wondered what her truest feelings were, exactly, and what she meant by separate-but-together. He wondered how the tides and waves had come into play on that afternoon along the Jersey shoreline when Martha saw the pebble and bent down to rescue it from geology. He imagined bare feet. Martha was a poet, with the poet's sensibilities, and her feet would be brown and bare, the toenails unpainted, the eyes chilly and somber like the ocean in March, and though it was painful, he wondered who had been with her that afternoon. He imagined a pair of shadows moving along the strip of sand where things came together but also separated. It was phantom jealousy, he knew, but he couldn't help himself. He loved her so much. On the march, through the hot days of early April, he carried the pebble in his mouth, turning it with his tongue, tasting sea salts and moisture. His mind wandered. He had difficulty keeping his attention on the war. On occasion he would yell at his men to spread out the column, to keep their eyes open, but then he would slip away into daydreams, just pretending, walking barefoot along the Jersey shore, with Martha, carrying nothing. He would feel himself rising. Sun and waves and gentle winds, all love and lightness.

What they carried varied by mission.

When a mission took them to the mountains, they carried mosquito netting, 15 machetes, canvas tarps, and extra bug juice.

If a mission seemed especially hazardous, or if it involved a place they knew to be bad, they carried everything they could. In certain heavily mined AOs, where the land was dense with Toe Poppers and Bouncing Betties, they took turns humping a twenty-eight-pound mine detector. With its headphones and big sensing plate, the equipment was a stress on the lower back and shoulders, awkward to handle, often useless because of the shrapnel in the earth, but they carried it anyway, partly for safety, partly for the illusion of safety.

On ambush, or other night missions, they carried peculiar little odds and ends. Kiowa always took along his New Testament and a pair of moccasins for silence. Dave Jensen carried night-sight vitamins high in carotin. Lee Strunk carried his slingshot; ammo, he claimed, would never be a problem. Rat Kiley carried brandy and M&M's. Until he was shot, Ted Lavender carried the starlight scope, which weighed 6.3 pounds with its aluminum carrying case. Henry Dobbins carried his girlfriend's pantyhose wrapped around his neck as a comforter. They all carried ghosts. When dark came, they would move out single file across the meadows and paddies to their ambush coordinates, where they would quietly set up the Claymores and lie down and spend the night waiting.

Other missions were more complicated and required special equipment. In mid-April, it was their mission to search out and destroy the elaborate tunnel complexes in the Than Khe area south of Chu Lai. To blow the tunnels, they carried one-pound blocks of pentrite high explosives, four blocks to a man, sixty-eight pounds in all. They carried wiring, detonators, and battery-powered clackers. Dave Jensen carried earplugs. Most often, before blowing the tunnels, they were ordered by higher command to search them, which was considered bad news, but by and large they just shrugged and carried out orders. Because he was a big man, Henry Dobbins was excused from tunnel duty. The others would draw numbers. Before Lavender died there were seventeen men in the platoon, and whoever drew the number seventeen would strip off his gear and crawl in head first with a flashlight and Lieutenant Cross's .45-caliber pistol. The rest of them would fan out as security. They would sit down or kneel, not facing the hole, listening to the ground beneath them, imagining cobwebs and ghosts, whatever was down there — the tunnel walls squeezing in — how the flashlight seemed impossibly heavy in the hand and how it was tunnel vision in the very strictest sense, compression in all ways, even time, and how you had to wiggle in — ass and elbows — a swallowed-up feeling — and how you found yourself worrying about odd things — will your flashlight go dead? Do rats carry rabies? If you screamed, how far would the sound carry? Would your buddies hear it? Would they have the courage to drag you out? In some respects, though not many, the waiting was worse than the tunnel itself. Imagination was a killer.

On April 16, when Lee Strunk drew the number seventeen, he laughed and muttered something and went down quickly. The morning was hot and very still. Not good, Kiowa said. He looked at the tunnel opening, then out across a dry paddy toward the village of Than Khe. Nothing moved. No clouds or birds or people. As they waited, the men smoked and drank Kool-Aid, not talking much, feeling sympathy for Lee Strunk but also feeling the luck of the draw. You win some, you lose some, said Mitchell Sanders, and sometimes you settle for a rain check. It was a tired line and no one laughed.

Henry Dobbins ate a tropical chocolate bar. Ted Lavender popped a tranquil- 20
izer and went off to pee.

After five minutes, Lieutenant Jimmy Cross moved to the tunnel, leaned down, and examined the darkness. Trouble, he thought — a cave-in maybe. And then suddenly, without willing it, he was thinking about Martha. The stresses and fractures, the quick collapse, the two of them buried alive under all that weight. Dense, crushing love. Kneeling, watching the hole, he tried to concentrate on Lee Strunk and the war, all the dangers, but his love was too much for him, he felt paralyzed, he wanted to sleep inside her lungs and breathe her blood and be smothered. He wanted her to be a virgin and not a virgin, all at once. He wanted to know her. Intimate secrets — why poetry? Why so sad? Why the grayness in her eyes? Why so alone? Not lonely, just alone — riding her bike across campus or sitting off by herself in the cafeteria. Even dancing, she danced alone — and it was the aloneness that filled him with love. He remembered telling her that one evening. How she nodded and looked away. And how, later, when he kissed her, she received the kiss without returning it, her eyes wide open, not afraid, not a virgin's eyes, just flat and uninvolved.

Lieutenant Cross gazed at the tunnel. But he was not there. He was buried with Martha under the white sand at the Jersey shore. They were pressed together, and the pebble in his mouth was her tongue. He was smiling. Vaguely, he was aware of how quiet the day was, the sullen paddies, yet he could not bring himself to worry about matters of security. He was beyond that. He was just a kid at war, in love. He was twenty-two years old. He couldn't help it.

A few moments later Lee Strunk crawled out of the tunnel. He came up grinning, filthy but alive. Lieutenant Cross nodded and closed his eyes while the others clapped Strunk on the back and made jokes about rising from the dead.

Worms, Rat Kiley said. Right out of the grave. Fuckin' zombie.

The men laughed. They all felt great relief. 25

Spook City, said Mitchell Sanders.

Lee Strunk made a funny ghost sound, a kind of moaning, yet very happy, and right then, when Strunk made that high happy moaning sound, when he went *Ahhooooo,* right then Ted Lavender was shot in the head on his way back from peeing. He lay with his mouth open. The teeth were broken. There was a swollen black bruise under his left eye. The cheekbone was gone. Oh shit, Rat Kiley said, the guy's dead. The guy's dead, he kept saying, which seemed profound — the guy's dead. I mean really.

The things they carried were determined to some extent by superstition. Lieutenant Cross carried his good-luck pebble. Dave Jensen carried a rabbit's foot. Norman Bowker, otherwise a very gentle person, carried a thumb that had been presented to him as a gift by Mitchell Sanders. The thumb was dark brown, rubbery to the touch, and weighed four ounces at most. It had been cut from a VC[3] corpse, a boy of fifteen or sixteen. They'd found him at the bottom of an irrigation ditch, badly burned, flies in his mouth and eyes. The boy wore black shorts and sandals. At the time of his death he had been carrying a pouch of rice, a rifle, and three magazines of ammunition.

You want my opinion, Mitchell Sanders said, there's a definite moral here.

He put his hand on the dead boy's wrist. He was quiet for a time, as if count- 30 ing a pulse, then he patted the stomach, almost affectionately, and used Kiowa's hunting hatchet to remove the thumb.

Henry Dobbins asked what the moral was.

Moral?

You know. *Moral.*

Sanders wrapped the thumb in toilet paper and handed it across to Norman Bowker. There was no blood. Smiling, he kicked the boy's head, watched the flies scatter, and said, It's like with that old TV show — Paladin. Have gun, will travel.

Henry Dobbins thought about it.   35

Yeah, well, he finally said. I don't see no moral.

There it *is,* man.

Fuck off.

They carried USO stationery and pencils and pens. They carried Sterno, safety pins, trip flares, signal flares, spools of wire, razor blades, chewing tobacco, liberated joss sticks and statuettes of the smiling Buddha, candles, grease pencils, *The Stars and Stripes,*[4] fingernail clippers, Psy Ops leaflets, bush hats, bolos, and much more. Twice a week, when the resupply choppers came in, they carried hot chow in green Mermite cans and large canvas bags filled with iced beer and soda pop. They carried plastic water containers, each with a two-gallon capacity. Mitchell Sanders carried a set of starched tiger fatigues for special occasions. Henry Dobbins carried Black Flag insecticide. Dave Jensen carried empty sandbags that could be filled at night for added protection. Lee

---

[3] Viet Cong.
[4] The military's officially sanctioned overseas newspaper.

Strunk carried tanning lotion. Some things they carried in common. Taking turns, they carried the big PRC-77 scrambler radio, which weighed thirty pounds with its battery. They shared the weight of memory. They took up what others could no longer bear. Often, they carried each other, the wounded or weak. They carried infections. They carried chess sets, basketballs, Vietnamese-English dictionaries, insignia of rank, Bronze Stars and Purple Hearts, plastic cards imprinted with the Code of Conduct. They carried diseases, among them malaria and dysentery. They carried lice and ringworm and leeches and paddy algae and various rots and molds. They carried the land itself — Vietnam, the place, the soil — a powdery orange-red dust that covered their boots and fatigues and faces. They carried the sky. The whole atmosphere, they carried it, the humidity, the monsoons, the stink of fungus and decay, all of it, they carried gravity. They moved like mules. By daylight they took sniper fire, at night they were mortared, but it was not battle, it was just the endless march, village to village, without purpose, nothing won or lost. They marched for the sake of the march. They plodded along slowly, dumbly, leaning forward against the heat, unthinking, all blood and bone, simple grunts, soldiering with their legs, toiling up the hills and down into the paddies and across the rivers and up again and down, just humping, one step and then the next and then another, but no volition, no will, because it was automatic, it was anatomy, and the war was entirely a matter of posture and carriage, the hump was everything, a kind of inertia, a kind of emptiness, a dullness of desire and intellect and conscience and hope and human sensibility. Their principles were in their feet. Their calculations were biological. They had no sense of strategy or mission. They searched the villages without knowing what to look for, not caring, kicking over jars of rice, frisking children and old men, blowing tunnels, sometimes setting fires and sometimes not, then forming up and moving on to the next village, then other villages, where it would always be the same. They carried their own lives. The pressures were enormous. In the heat of early afternoon, they would remove their helmets and flak jackets, walking bare, which was dangerous but which helped ease the strain. They would often discard things along the route of march. Purely for comfort, they would throw away rations, blow their Claymores and grenades, no matter, because by nightfall the resupply choppers would arrive with more of the same, then a day or two later still more, fresh watermelons and crates of ammunition and sunglasses and woolen sweaters — the resources were stunning — sparklers for the Fourth of July, colored eggs for Easter. It was the great American war chest — the fruits of science, the smoke-stacks, the canneries, the arsenals at Hartford, the Minnesota forests, the machine shops, the vast fields of corn and wheat — they carried like freight trains; they carried it on their backs and shoulders — and for all the ambiguities of Vietnam, all the mysteries and unknowns, there was at least the single abiding certainty that they would never be at a loss for things to carry.

After the chopper took Lavender away, Lieutenant Jimmy Cross led his men   40
into the village of Than Khe. They burned everything. They shot chickens and dogs, they trashed the village well, they called in artillery and watched the

wreckage, then they marched for several hours through the hot afternoon, and then at dusk, while Kiowa explained how Lavender died, Lieutenant Cross found himself trembling.

He tried not to cry. With his entrenching tool, which weighed five pounds, he began digging a hole in the earth.

He felt shame. He hated himself. He had loved Martha more than his men, and as a consequence Lavender was now dead, and this was something he would have to carry like a stone in his stomach for the rest of the war.

All he could do was dig. He used his entrenching tool like an ax, slashing, feeling both love and hate, and then later, when it was full dark, he sat at the bottom of his foxhole and wept. It went on for a long while. In part, he was grieving for Ted Lavender, but mostly it was for Martha, and for himself, because she belonged to another world, which was not quite real, and because she was a junior at Mount Sebastian College in New Jersey, a poet and a virgin and uninvolved, and because he realized she did not love him and never would.

Like cement, Kiowa whispered in the dark. I swear to God — boom-down. Not a word.

I've heard this, said Norman Bowker.   45

A pisser, you know? Still zipping himself up. Zapped while zipping.

All right, fine. That's enough.

Yeah, but you had to see it, the guy just —

I *heard,* man. Cement. So why not shut the fuck *up?*

Kiowa shook his head sadly and glanced over at the hole where Lieutenant   50
Jimmy Cross sat watching the night. The air was thick and wet. A warm, dense fog had settled over the paddies and there was the stillness that precedes rain.

After a time Kiowa sighed.

One thing for sure, he said. The Lieutenant's in some deep hurt. I mean that crying jag — the way he was carrying on — it wasn't fake or anything, it was real heavy-duty hurt. The man cares.

Sure, Norman Bowker said.

Say what you want, the man does care.

We all got problems.   55

Not Lavender.

No, I guess not, Bowker said. Do me a favor, though.

Shut up?

That's a smart Indian. Shut up.

Shrugging, Kiowa pulled off his boots. He wanted to say more, just to lighten 60
up his sleep, but instead he opened his New Testament and arranged it beneath his head as a pillow. The fog made things seem hollow and unattached. He tried not to think about Ted Lavender, but then he was thinking how fast it was, no drama, down and dead, and how it was hard to feel anything except surprise. It seemed un-Christian. He wished he could find some great sadness, or even anger, but the emotion wasn't there and he couldn't make it happen. Mostly he felt pleased to be alive. He liked the smell of the New Testament under

his cheek, the leather and ink and paper and glue, whatever the chemicals were. He liked hearing the sounds of night. Even his fatigue, it felt fine, the stiff muscles and the prickly awareness of his own body, a floating feeling. He enjoyed not being dead. Lying there, Kiowa admired Lieutenant Jimmy Cross's capacity for grief. He wanted to share the man's pain, he wanted to care as Jimmy Cross cared. And yet when he closed his eyes, all he could think was Boom-down, and all he could feel was the pleasure of having his boots off and the fog curling in around him and the damp soil and the Bible smells and the plush comfort of night.

After a moment Norman Bowker sat up in the dark.

What the hell, he said. You want to talk, *talk*. Tell it to me.

Forget it.

No, man, go on. One thing I hate, it's a silent Indian.

For the most part they carried themselves with poise, a kind of dignity. Now 65 and then, however, there were times of panic, when they squealed or wanted to squeal but couldn't, when they twitched and made moaning sounds and covered their heads and said Dear Jesus and flopped around on the earth and fired their weapons blindly and cringed and sobbed and begged for the noise to stop and went wild and made stupid promises to themselves and to God and to their mothers and fathers, hoping not to die. In different ways, it happened to all of them. Afterward, when the firing ended, they would blink and peek up. They would touch their bodies, feeling shame, then quickly hiding it. They would force themselves to stand. As if in slow motion, frame by frame, the world would take on the old logic — absolute silence, then the wind, then sunlight, then voices. It was the burden of being alive. Awkwardly, the men would reassemble themselves, first in private, then in groups, becoming soldiers again. They would repair the leaks in their eyes. They would check for casualties, call in dust-offs, light cigarettes, try to smile, clear their throats and spit and begin cleaning their weapons. After a time someone would shake his head and say, No lie, I almost shit my pants, and someone else would laugh, which meant it was bad, yes, but the guy had obviously not shit his pants, it wasn't that bad, and in any case nobody would ever do such a thing and then go ahead and talk about it. They would squint into the dense, oppressive sunlight. For a few moments, perhaps, they would fall silent, lighting a joint and tracking its passage from man to man, inhaling, holding in the humiliation. Scary stuff, one of them might say. But then someone else would grin or flick his eyebrows and say, Roger-dodger, almost cut me a new asshole, *almost*.

There were numerous such poses. Some carried themselves with a sort of wistful resignation, others with pride or stiff soldierly discipline or good humor or macho zeal. They were afraid of dying but they were even more afraid to show it.

They found jokes to tell.

They used a hard vocabulary to contain the terrible softness. *Greased,* they'd say. *Offed, lit up, zapped while zipping.* It wasn't cruelty, just stage presence.

They were actors and the war came at them in 3-D. When someone died, it wasn't quite dying, because in a curious way it seemed scripted, and because they had their lines mostly memorized, irony mixed with tragedy, and because they called it by other names, as if to encyst and destroy the reality of death itself. They kicked corpses. They cut off thumbs. They talked grunt lingo. They told stories about Ted Lavender's supply of tranquilizers, how the poor guy didn't feel a thing, how incredibly tranquil he was.

There's a moral here, said Mitchell Sanders.

They were waiting for Lavender's chopper, smoking the dead man's dope.   70

The moral's pretty obvious, Sanders said, and winked. Stay away from drugs. No joke, they'll ruin your day every time.

Cute, said Henry Dobbins.

Mind-blower, get it? Talk about wiggy — nothing left, just blood and brains.

They made themselves laugh.

There it is, they'd say, over and over, as if the repetition itself were an act of 75 poise, a balance between crazy and almost crazy, knowing without going. There it is, which meant be cool, let it ride, because oh yeah, man, you can't change what can't be changed, there it is, there it absolutely and positively and fucking well *is*.

They were tough.

They carried all the emotional baggage of men who might die. Grief, terror, love, longing — these were intangibles, but the intangibles had their own mass and specific gravity, they had tangible weight. They carried shameful memories. They carried the common secret of cowardice barely restrained, the instinct to run or freeze or hide, and in many respects this was the heaviest burden of all, for it could never be put down, it required perfect balance and perfect posture. They carried their reputations. They carried the soldier's greatest fear, which was the fear of blushing. Men killed, and died, because they were embarrassed not to. It was what had brought them to the war in the first place, nothing positive, no dreams of glory or honor, just to avoid the blush of dishonor. They died so as not to die of embarrassment. They crawled into tunnels and walked point and advanced under fire. Each morning, despite the unknowns, they made their legs move. They endured. They kept humping. They did not submit to the obvious alternative, which was simply to close the eyes and fall. So easy, really. Go limp and tumble to the ground and let the muscles unwind and not speak and not budge until your buddies picked you up and lifted you into the chopper that would roar and dip its nose and carry off to the world. A mere matter of falling, yet no one ever fell. It was not courage, exactly; the object was not valor. Rather, they were too frightened to be cowards.

By and large they carried these things inside, maintaining the masks of composure. They sneered at sick call. They spoke bitterly about guys who had found release by shooting off their own toes or fingers. Pussies, they'd say. Candyasses. It was fierce, mocking talk, with only a trace of envy or awe, but even so, the image played itself out behind their eyes.

They imagined the muzzle against flesh. They imagined the quick, sweet pain, then the evacuation to Japan, then a hospital with warm beds and cute geisha nurses.

They dreamed of freedom birds. 80

At night, on guard, staring into the dark, they were carried away by jumbo jets. They felt the rush of takeoff. *Gone!* they yelled. And then velocity, wings and engines, a smiling stewardess — but it was more than a plane, it was a real bird, a big sleek silver bird with feathers and talons and high screeching. They were flying. The weights fell off, there was nothing to bear. They laughed and held on tight, feeling the cold slap of wind and altitude, soaring, thinking *It's over, I'm gone!* — they were naked, they were light and free — it was all lightness, bright and fast and buoyant, light as light, a helium buzz in the brain, a giddy bubbling in the lungs as they were taken up over the clouds and the war, beyond duty, beyond gravity and mortification and global entanglements — *Sin loi!* they yelled, *I'm sorry, motherfuckers, but I'm out of it, I'm goofed, I'm on a space cruise, I'm gone!* — and it was a restful, disencumbered sensation, just riding the light waves, sailing that big silver freedom bird over the mountains and oceans, over America, over the farms and great sleeping cities and cemeteries and highways and the golden arches of McDonald's. It was flight, a kind of fleeing, a kind of falling, falling higher and higher, spinning off the edge of the earth and beyond the sun and through the vast, silent vacuum where there were no burdens and where everything weighed exactly nothing. *Gone!* they screamed, *I'm sorry but I'm gone!* And so at night, not quite dreaming, they gave themselves over to lightness, they were carried, they were purely borne.

On the morning after Ted Lavender died, First Lieutenant Jimmy Cross crouched at the bottom of his foxhole and burned Martha's letters. Then he burned the two photographs. There was a steady rain falling, which made it difficult, but he used heat tabs and Sterno to build a small fire, screening it with his body, holding the photographs over the tight blue flame with the tips of his fingers.

He realized it was only a gesture. Stupid, he thought. Sentimental, too, but mostly just stupid.

Lavender was dead. You couldn't burn the blame.

Besides, the letters were in his head. And even now, without photographs, 85 Lieutenant Cross could see Martha playing volleyball in her white gym shorts and yellow T-shirt. He could see her moving in the rain.

When the fire died out, Lieutenant Cross pulled his poncho over his shoulders and ate breakfast from a can.

There was no great mystery, he decided.

In those burned letters Martha had never mentioned the war, except to say, Jimmy, take care of yourself. She wasn't involved. She signed the letters "Love," but it wasn't love, and all the fine lines and technicalities did not matter.

The morning came up wet and blurry. Everything seemed part of everything else, the fog and Martha and the deepening rain.

It was a war, after all.   90

Half smiling, Lieutenant Jimmy Cross took out his maps. He shook his head hard, as if to clear it, then bent forward and began planning the day's march. In ten minutes, or maybe twenty, he would rouse the men and they would pack up and head west, where the maps showed the country to be green and inviting. They would do what they had always done. The rain might add some weight, but otherwise it would be one more day layered upon all the other days.

He was realistic about it. There was that new hardness in his stomach.

No more fantasies, he told himself.

Henceforth, when he thought about Martha, it would be only to think that she belonged elsewhere. He would shut down the daydreams. This was not Mount Sebastian, it was another world, where there were no pretty poems or midterm exams, a place where men died because of carelessness and gross stupidity. Kiowa was right. Boom-down, and you were dead, never partly dead.

Briefly, in the rain, Lieutenant Cross saw Martha's gray eyes gazing back   95
at him.

He understood.

It was very sad, he thought. The things men carried inside. The things men did or felt they had to do.

He almost nodded at her, but didn't.

Instead he went back to his maps. He was now determined to perform his duties firmly and without negligence. It wouldn't help Lavender, he knew that, but from this point on he would comport himself as a soldier. He would dispose of his good-luck pebble. Swallow it, maybe, or use Lee Strunk's slingshot, or just drop it along the trail. On the march he would impose strict field discipline. He would be careful to send out flank security, to prevent straggling or bunching up, to keep his troops moving at the proper pace and at the proper interval. He would insist on clean weapons. He would confiscate the remainder of Lavender's dope. Later in the day, perhaps, he would call the men together and speak to them plainly. He would accept the blame for what had happened to Ted Lavender. He would be a man about it. He would look them in the eyes, keeping his chin level, and he would issue the new SOPs in a calm, impersonal tone of voice, an officer's voice, leaving no room for argument or discussion. Commencing immediately, he'd tell them, they would no longer abandon equipment along the route of march. They would police up their acts. They would get their shit together, and keep it together, and maintain it neatly and in good working order.

He would not tolerate laxity. He would show strength, distancing himself.   100

Among the men there would be grumbling, of course, and maybe worse, because their days would seem longer and their loads heavier, but Lieutenant Cross reminded himself that his obligation was not to be loved but to lead. He would dispense with love; it was not now a factor. And if anyone quarreled or complained, he would simply tighten his lips and arrange his shoulders in the correct command posture. He might give a curt little nod. Or he might not. He might just shrug and say Carry on, then they would saddle up and form into a column and move out toward the villages of Than Khe.

For Analysis

1. What are the various meanings of "Things" in the title?

2. What is the narrator's attitude toward war? Does his attitude differ from the attitudes of the soldiers he is describing? Explain.

3. How do Lieutenant Cross's thoughts about Martha fit into the overall thematic pattern of the story?

4. What is the attitude of the men toward the enemy?

5. How does O'Brien create suspense?

On Style

1. What are the distinguishing characteristics of O'Brien's **style**?

2. How effective do you find the cataloguing of things as a way to tell this story? Explain.

3. Why are major events, such as the death of Lavender and the destruction of the village of Than Khe, not narrated chronologically?

Making Connections

Compare and contrast O'Brien's perspective on war with that of Wilfred Owen in "Dulce et Decorum Est" (p. 1406). Which do you find to be a more effective antiwar statement? Explain.

Writing Topics

1. Discuss the meaning of heroism in this story.

2. Write an essay showing how Lieutenant Cross's thoughts and feelings about Martha reflect the changes he undergoes in the course of the narrative.

Leslie Marmon Silko   (b. 1948)

The Man to Send Rain Clouds (1981)

They found him under a big cottonwood tree. His Levi jacket and pants were faded light blue so that he had been easy to find. The big cottonwood tree stood apart from a small grove of winterbare cottonwoods which grew in the wide, sandy arroyo. He had been dead for a day or more, and the sheep had wandered and scattered up and down the arroyo. Leon and his brother-in-law, Ken, gathered the sheep and left them in the pen at the sheep camp before they returned to the cottonwood tree. Leon waited under the tree while Ken drove the truck through the deep sand to the edge of the arroyo. He squinted up at the sun and unzipped his jacket — it sure was hot for this time of year. But high and northwest the blue mountains were still in snow. Ken came sliding down the low, crumbling bank about fifty yards down, and he was bringing the red blanket.

Before they wrapped the old man, Leon took a piece of string out of his pocket and tied a small gray feather in the old man's long white hair. Ken gave him the paint. Across the brown wrinkled forehead he drew a streak of white and along the high cheekbones he drew a strip of blue paint. He paused and watched Ken throw pinches of corn meal and pollen into the wind that fluttered the small gray feather. Then Leon painted with yellow under the old man's broad nose, and finally, when he had painted green across the chin, he smiled.

"Send us rain clouds, Grandfather." They laid the bundle in the back of the pickup and covered it with a heavy tarp before they started back to the pueblo.

They turned off the highway onto the sandy pueblo road. Not long after they passed the store and post office they saw Father Paul's car coming toward them. When he recognized their faces he slowed his car and waved them to stop. The young priest rolled down the car window.

"Did you find old Teofilo?" he asked loudly.   5

Leon stopped the truck. "Good morning, Father. We were just out to the sheep camp. Everything is O.K. now."

"Thank God for that. Teofilo is a very old man. You really shouldn't allow him to stay at the sheep camp alone."

"No, he won't do that any more now."

"Well, I'm glad you understand. I hope I'll be seeing you at Mass this week — we missed you last Sunday. See if you can get old Teofilo to come with you." The priest smiled and waved at them as they drove away.

Louise and Teresa were waiting. The table was set for lunch, and the coffee 10 was boiling on the black iron stove. Leon looked at Louise and then at Teresa.

1374

"We found him under a cottonwood tree in the big arroyo near sheep camp. I guess he sat down to rest in the shade and never got up again." Leon walked toward the old man's bed. The red plaid shawl had been shaken and spread carefully over the bed, and a new brown flannel shirt and pair of stiff new Levi's were arranged neatly beside the pillow. Louise held the screen door open while Leon and Ken carried in the red blanket. He looked small and shriveled, and after they dressed him in the new shirt and pants he seemed more shrunken.

It was noontime now because the church bells rang the Angelus. They ate the beans with hot bread, and nobody said anything until after Teresa poured the coffee.

Ken stood up and put on his jacket. "I'll see about the gravediggers. Only the top layer of soil is frozen. I think it can be ready before dark."

Leon nodded his head and finished his coffee. After Ken had been gone for a while, the neighbors and clanspeople came quietly to embrace Teofilo's family and to leave food on the table because the gravediggers would come to eat when they were finished.

The sky in the west was full of pale yellow light. Louise stood outside with her 15 hands in the pockets of Leon's green army jacket that was too big for her. The funeral was over, and the old men had taken their candles and medicine bags and were gone. She waited until the body was laid into the pickup before she said anything to Leon. She touched his arm, and he noticed that her hands were still dusty from the corn meal that she had sprinkled around the old man. When she spoke, Leon could not hear her.

"What did you say? I didn't hear you."

"I said that I had been thinking about something."

"About what?"

"About the priest sprinkling holy water for Grandpa. So he won't be thirsty."

Leon stared at the new moccasins that Teofilo had made for the ceremonial 20 dances in the summer. They were nearly hidden by the red blanket. It was getting colder, and the wind pushed gray dust down the narrow pueblo road. The sun was approaching the long mesa where it disappeared during the winter. Louise stood there shivering and watching his face. Then he zipped up his jacket and opened the truck door. "I'll see if he's there."

Ken stopped the pickup at the church, and Leon got out; and then Ken drove down the hill to the graveyard where people were waiting. Leon knocked at the old carved door with its symbols of the Lamb. While he waited he looked up at the twin bells from the king of Spain with the last sunlight pouring around them in their tower.

The priest opened the door and smiled when he saw who it was. "Come in! What brings you here this evening?"

The priest walked toward the kitchen, and Leon stood with his cap in his hand, playing with the earflaps and examining the living room — the brown sofa, the green armchair, and the brass lamp that hung down from the ceiling by links of chain. The priest dragged a chair out of the kitchen and offered it to Leon.

"No thank you, Father. I only came to ask you if you would bring your holy water to the graveyard."

The priest turned away from Leon and looked out the window at the patio 25 full of shadows and the dining-room windows of the nuns' cloister across the patio. The curtains were heavy, and the light from within faintly penetrated; it was impossible to see the nuns inside eating supper. "Why didn't you tell me he was dead? I could have brought the Last Rites anyway."

Leon smiled. "It wasn't necessary, Father."

The priest stared down at his scuffed brown loafers and the worn hem of his cassock. "For a Christian burial it was necessary."

His voice was distant, and Leon thought that his blue eyes looked tired.

"It's O.K. Father, we just want him to have plenty of water."

The priest sank down into the green chair and picked up a glossy missionary 30 magazine. He turned the colored pages full of lepers and pagans without looking at them.

"You know I can't do that, Leon. There should have been the Last Rites and a funeral Mass at the very least."

Leon put on his green cap and pulled the flaps down over his ears. "It's getting late, Father. I've got to go."

When Leon opened the door Father Paul stood up and said, "Wait." He left the room and came back wearing a long brown overcoat. He followed Leon out the door and across the dim churchyard to the adobe steps in front of the church. They both stooped to fit through the low adobe entrance. And when they started down the hill to the graveyard only half of the sun was visible above the mesa.

The priest approached the grave slowly, wondering how they had managed to dig into the frozen ground, and then he remembered that this was New Mexico, and saw the pile of cold loose sand beside the hole. The people stood close to each other with little clouds of steam puffing from their faces. The priest looked at them and saw a pile of jackets, gloves, and scarves in the yellow, dry tumbleweeds that grew in the graveyard. He looked at the red blanket, not sure that Teofilo was so small, wondering if it wasn't some perverse Indian trick — something they did in March to ensure a good harvest — wondering if maybe old Teofilo was actually at sheep camp corraling the sheep for the night. But there he was, facing into a cold dry wind and squinting at the last sunlight, ready to bury a red wool blanket while the faces of his parishioners were in shadow with the last warmth of the sun on their backs.

His fingers were stiff, and it took him a long time to twist the lid off the holy 35 water. Drops of water fell on the red blanket and soaked into dark icy spots. He sprinkled the grave and the water disappeared almost before it touched the dim, cold sand; it reminded him of something — he tried to remember what it was, because he thought if he could remember he might understand this. He sprinkled more water; he shook the container until it was empty, and the water fell through the light from sundown like August rain that fell while the sun was still shining, almost disappearing before it touched the wilted squash flowers.

The wind pulled at the priest's brown Franciscan robe and swirled away the corn meal and pollen that had been sprinkled on the blanket. They lowered the bundle into the ground, and they didn't bother to untie the stiff pieces of new rope that were tied around the ends of the blanket. The sun was gone, and over on the highway the eastbound lane was full of headlights. The priest walked away slowly. Leon watched him climb the hill, and when he had disappeared within the tall, thick walls, Leon turned to look up at the high blue mountains in the deep snow that reflected a faint red light from the west. He felt good because it was finished, and he was happy about the sprinkling of the holy water; now the old man could send them big thunderclouds for sure.

For Analysis
1. Why do Leon and Ken not tell Father Paul that Teofilo is dead? Why do they later request Father Paul to bring holy water to the funeral?

2. Two rituals associated with death — the Native American and the Roman Catholic — seem to conflict. Why does Teofilo's family seek the priest's help? Why does Father Paul agree to help them?

3. What do rain clouds signify?

4. What reason do you think Silko had for including the detail (in the last paragraph) about the automobile lights on the highway?

5. Why does Leon feel good at the end of the story?

On Style
1. Although the story is mostly told from the point of view of an **omniscient narrator,** at one point we share a character's thoughts. What effect does that shift generate?

2. Contrast the narrative **style** of this story with the style of Poe's "The Cask of Amontillado" (p. 1280) and Tolstoy's "The Death of Iván Ilých" (p. 1286). Some writers use unusual language and sentence structure; some insist on close realistic detail; some use understatement and leave much unsaid. How would you characterize the style of this story? Defend your response.

Making Connections
1. Compare this story with Bessie Head's "Looking for a Rain God" (p. 1356) and Shirley Jackson's "The Lottery" (p. 386). What similarities do you find? What differences?

2. Consider the treatment of death and the nature of funerals in your own experience. Describe the rituals, and suggest what functions they serve.

Writing Topic
Compare the methods for ensuring fertility revealed in "The Lottery," "Looking for a Rain God," "The Man to Send Rain Clouds," and your own religious tradition.

Poetry

Anonymous

Edward

1

"Why does your brand° sae° drap wi' bluid,   sword/so
        Edward, Edward,
Why does your brand sae drap wi' bluid,
    And why sae sad gang° ye, O?"   go
"O I ha'e killed my hawk sae guid,
        Mither, mither,
O I ha'e killed my hawk sae guid,
    And I had nae mair but he, O."

2

"Your hawke's bluid was never sae reid,°   red
        Edward, Edward,   10
Your hawke's bluid was never sae reid,
    My dear son I tell thee, O."
"O I ha'e killed my reid-roan steed,
        Mither, mither,
O I ha'e killed my reid-roan steed,
    That erst was sae fair and free, O."

3

"Your steed was auld, and ye ha'e gat mair,
        Edward, Edward,
Your steed was auld, and ye ha'e gat mair,
    Some other dule° ye drie,° O."   grief/suffer 20
"O I ha'e killed my fader dear,
        Mither, mither,
O I ha'e killed my fader dear,
    Alas, and wae° is me, O!"   woe

4

"And whatten penance wul ye drie for that,
    Edward, Edward?
And whatten penance wul ye drie for that,
  My dear son, now tell me, O?"
"I'll set my feet in yonder boat,
    Mither, mither,   30
I'll set my feet in yonder boat,
  And I'll fare over the sea, O."

5

"And what wul ye do wi' your towers and your ha',
    Edward, Edward?
And what wul ye do wi' your towers and your ha',
  That were sae fair to see, O?"
"I'll let them stand tul they down fa',
    Mither, mither,
I'll let them stand tul they down fa',
  For here never mair maun° I be, O."   must 40

6

"And what wul ye leave to your bairns° and your wife,   children
    Edward, Edward?
And what wul ye leave to your bairns and your wife,
  Whan ye gang over the sea, O?"
"The warlde's° room, let them beg thrae° life,   world's/through
    Mither, mither,
The warlde's room, let them beg thrae life,
  For them never mair wul I see, O."

7

"And what wul ye leave to your ain mither dear,
    Edward, Edward?   50
And what wul ye leave to your ain mither dear,
  My dear son, now tell me, O?"
"The curse of hell frae° me sall° ye bear,   from/shall
    Mither, mither,
The curse of hell frae me sall ye bear,
  Sic° counsels ye gave to me, O."   such

For Analysis

1. Why does the mother reject Edward's answers to her first two questions?

2. Does the poem provide any clues to the murderer's motive?

3. Edward has murdered his father and then bitterly turns away from his mother, wife, and children. What basis is there in the poem for nevertheless sympathizing with Edward?

Writing Topic

What effects are achieved through the question-and-answer technique and the repetition of lines?

William Shakespeare (1564–1616)

Sonnet 1609

73

That time of year thou mayst in me behold
When yellow leaves, or none, or few, do hang
Upon those boughs which shake against the cold,
Bare ruined choirs, where late the sweet birds sang.
In me thou see'st the twilight of such day
As after sunset fadeth in the west;
Which by and by black night doth take away,
Death's second self, that seals up all in rest.
In me thou see'st the glowing of such fire,
That on the ashes of his youth doth lie,   10
As the deathbed whereon it must expire,
Consumed with that which it was nourished by.
This thou perceiv'st, which makes thy love more strong,
To love that well which thou must leave ere long.

Fear No More the Heat o' the Sun 1623

Fear no more the heat o' the sun,[1]
    Nor the furious winter's rages;
Thou thy worldly task hast done,
    Home art gone, and ta'en thy wages:
Golden lads and girls all must,
As chimney-sweepers, come to dust.

Fear no more the frown o' the great;
    Thou art past the tyrant's stroke;
Care no more to clothe and eat;
    To thee the reed is as the oak: 10
The scepter, learning, physic,° must[2]   medicine
All follow this, and come to dust.

Fear no more the lightning flash,
    Nor the all-dreaded thunder stone;[3]
Fear not slander, censure rash;
    Thou hast finished joy and moan:
All lovers young, all lovers must
Consign to° thee, and come to dust.   agree with

No exorciser harm thee!
Nor no witchcraft charm thee!   20
Ghost unlaid forbear thee!
Nothing ill come near thee!
Quiet consummation have;
And renownéd be thy grave!

[1] From *Cymbeline*, Act IV, Scene 2.
[2] I.e., kings, scholars, and physicians.
[3] It was believed that thunder was caused by falling meteorites.

from
Richard II 1595

And nothing can we call our own but death
And that small model of the barren earth
Which serves as paste and cover to our bones.
For God's sake, let us sit upon the ground
And tell sad stories of the death of kings:
How some have been deposed; some slain in war;
Some haunted by the ghosts they have deposed;
Some poison'd by their wives; some sleeping kill'd;
All murder'd: for within the hollow crown
That rounds the mortal temples of a king   10
Keeps Death his court and there the antic sits
Scoffing his state and grinning at his pomp,
Allowing him a breath, a little scene,
To monarchize, be fear'd and kill with looks,
Infusing him with self and vain conceit,
As if this flesh which walls about our life
Were brass impregnable, and humour'd thus
Comes at the last and with a little pin
Bores through his castle wall, and farewell king!

from
Macbeth 1606

She should have died hereafter;
There would have been a time for such a word.
To-morrow, and to-morrow, and to-morrow,
Creeps in this petty pace from day to day
To the last syllable of recorded time,
And all our yesterdays have lighted fools
The way to dusty death. Out, out, brief candle!
Life's but a walking shadow, a poor player
That struts and frets his hour upon the stage
And then is heard no more: it is a tale   10
Told by an idiot, full of sound and fury,
Signifying nothing.

For Analysis
Examine the **images** in this meditation by Macbeth on the meaning of life (he has just received word that Lady Macbeth has died). Do they hold together, or are they con-

fusing? For example, how does the image of the candle (I. 7) relate to the images that precede and follow it?

from
Hamlet 1601

To be, or not to be, that is the question:
Whether 'tis nobler in the mind to suffer
The slings and arrows of outrageous fortune,
Or to take arms against a sea of troubles,
And by opposing end them. To die, to sleep —
No more; and by a sleep to say we end
The heartache, and the thousand natural shocks
That flesh is heir to. 'Tis a consummation
Devoutly to be wished — to die, to sleep —
To sleep, perchance to dream, ay there's the rub;   10
For in that sleep of death what dreams may come
When we have shuffled off this mortal coil°   turmoil
Must give us pause — there's the respect
That makes calamity of so long life.
For who would bear the whips and scorns of time,
Th' oppressor's wrong, the proud man's contumely,
The pangs of despised love, the law's delay,
The insolence of office, and the spurns
That patient merit of th' unworthy takes,
When he himself might his quietus° make   settlement 20
With a bare bodkin°? Who would fardels° bear,   dagger/burdens
To grunt and sweat under a weary life,
But that the dread of something after death,
The undiscovered country, from whose bourn°   realm
No traveller returns, puzzles the will,
And makes us rather bear those ills we have
Than fly to others that we know not of?
Thus conscience° does make cowards of us all;   thought
And thus the native hue of resolution
Is sicklied o'er with the pale cast of thought,   30
And enterprises of great pitch° and moment   degree
With this regard their currents turn awry
And lose the name of action.

For Analysis

1. What does Hamlet conclude about man's fear of death? Does he view it as cowardly and ignoble? Explain.

2. Explain line 28.

John Donne   (1572–1631)

Death, Be Not Proud   1633

Death be not proud, though some have calléd thee
Mighty and dreadful, for thou art not so;
For those whom thou think'st thou dost overthrow
Die not, poor Death, nor yet canst thou kill me.
From rest and sleep, which but thy pictures be,
Much pleasure; then from thee much more must flow,
And soonest our best men with thee do go,
Rest of their bones, and soul's delivery.
Thou art slave to fate, chance, kings, and desperate men,
And dost with poison, war, and sickness dwell,   10
And poppy or charms can make us sleep as well
And better than thy stroke; why swell'st thou then?
One short sleep past, we wake eternally
And death shall be no more; Death, thou shalt die.

Percy Bysshe Shelley   (1792–1822)

Ozymandias[1]   1818

I met a traveller from an antique land
Who said: Two vast and trunkless legs of stone
Stand in the desert . . . Near them, on the sand,
Half sunk, a shattered visage lies, whose frown,
And wrinkled lip, and sneer of cold command,
Tell that its sculptor well those passions read
Which yet survive, stamped on these lifeless things,
The hand that mocked them, and the heart that fed:
And on the pedestal these words appear:
"My name is Ozymandias, king of kings: 10
Look on my works, ye Mighty, and despair!"
Nothing beside remains. Round the decay
Of that colossal wreck, boundless and bare
The lone and level sands stretch far away.

Ozymandias
[1] Egyptian monarch of the thirteenth century B.C., said to have erected a huge statue of himself.

John Keats (1795–1821)

Ode on a Grecian Urn 1820

I

Thou still unravished bride of quietness,
   Thou foster child of silence and slow time,
Sylvan historian, who canst thus express
   A flowery tale more sweetly than our rhyme:
What leaf-fringed legend haunts about thy shape
   Of deities or mortals, or of both,
      In Tempe or the dales of Arcady?[1]
What men or gods are these? What maidens loath?
What mad pursuit? What struggle to escape?
     What pipes and timbrels? What wild ecstasy?　　　10

II

Heard melodies are sweet, but those unheard
   Are sweeter; therefore, ye soft pipes, play on;
Not to the sensual ear, but, more endeared,
   Pipe to the spirit ditties of no tone:
Fair youth, beneath the trees, thou canst not leave
   Thy song, nor ever can those trees be bare;
     Bold Lover, never, never canst thou kiss,
Though winning near the goal — yet, do not grieve;
     She cannot fade, though thou hast not thy bliss,
Forever wilt thou love, and she be fair!　　　20

III

Ah, happy, happy boughs! that cannot shed
   Your leaves, nor ever bid the Spring adieu;
And, happy melodist, unweariéd,
   Forever piping songs forever new;
More happy love! more happy, happy love!
   Forever warm and still to be enjoyed,
     Forever panting, and forever young;

---

[1] Tempe and Arcady are valleys in Greece famous for their beauty. In ancient times, Tempe was regarded as sacred to Apollo.

All breathing human passion far above,[2]
  That leaves a heart high-sorrowful and cloyed,
    A burning forehead, and a parching tongue.   30

IV

Who are these coming to the sacrifice?
  To what green altar, O mysterious priest,
Lead'st thou that heifer lowing at the skies,
  And all her silken flanks with garlands dressed?
What little town by river or sea shore,
  Or mountain-built with peaceful citadel,
    Is emptied of this folk, this pious morn?
And, little town, thy streets forevermore
  Will silent be; and not a soul to tell
    Why thou art desolate, can e'er return.   40

V

O Attic[3] shape! Fair attitude! with brede
  Of marble men and maidens overwrought,
With forest branches and the trodden weed;
  Thou, silent form, dost tease us out of thought
As doth eternity: Cold Pastoral!
  When old age shall this generation waste,
    Thou shalt remain, in midst of other woe
Than ours, a friend to man, to whom thou say'st,
"Beauty is truth, truth beauty, — that is all
  Ye know on earth, and all ye need to know."   50

For Analysis

1. Describe the scene the poet sees depicted on the urn. Describe the scene the poet imagines as a consequence of the scene on the urn.

2. Why are the boughs, the piper, and the lovers happy in stanza 3?

3. Explain the assertion of stanza 2 that "Heard melodies are sweet, but those unheard / Are sweeter."

4. Does the poem support the assertion of the last two lines? What does that assertion mean?

Writing Topic

In what sense might it be argued that this poem is about mortality and immortality? With this in mind, consider the meaning of the phrase "Cold Pastoral!" (l. 45).

---

[2] I.e., far above all breathing human passion.
[3] Athenian, thus simple and graceful.

Matthew Arnold   (1822–1888)

Growing Old   1867

What is it to grow old?
Is it to lose the glory of the form,
The luster of the eye?
Is it for beauty to forego her wreath?
— Yes, but not this alone.

Is it to feel our strength —
Not our bloom only, but our strength — decay?
Is it to feel each limb
Grow stiffer, every function less exact,
Each nerve more loosely strung?   10

Yes, this, and more; but not
Ah, 'tis not what in youth we dreamed 'twould be!
'Tis not to have our life
Mellowed and softened as with sunset glow,
A golden day's decline.

'Tis not to see the world
As from a height, with rapt prophetic eyes,
And heart profoundly stirred;
And weep, and feel the fullness of the past,
The years that are no more.   20

It is to spend long days
And not once feel that we were ever young;
It is to add, immured
In the hot prison of the present, month
To month with weary pain.

It is to suffer this,
And feel but half, and feebly, what we feel.
Deep in our hidden heart
Festers the dull remembrance of a change,
But no emotion — none.   30

It is — last stage of all —
When we are frozen up within, and quite
The phantom of ourselves,
To hear the world applaud the hollow ghost
Which blamed the living man.

Emily Dickinson (1830–1886)

After great pain, a formal feeling comes ca. 1862

After great pain, a formal feeling comes —
The Nerves sit ceremonious, like Tombs —
The stiff Heart questions was it He, that bore,
And Yesterday, or Centuries before?

The Feet, mechanical, go round —
Of Ground, or Air, or Ought —
A Wooden way
Regardless grown,
A Quartz contentment, like a stone —

This is the Hour of Lead —   10
Remembered, if outlived,
As Freezing persons, recollect the Snow —
First — Chill — then Stupor — then the letting go —

For Analysis
Is this poem about physical or psychic pain? Explain.

Writing Topic
What is the meaning of "stiff Heart" (l. 3) and "Quartz contentment" (l. 9)? What part
do they play in the larger pattern of **images** in this poem?

I heard a Fly buzz — when I died ca. 1862

I heard a Fly buzz — when I died —
The Stillness in the Room
Was like the Stillness in the Air —
Between the Heaves of Storm —

The Eyes around — had wrung them dry —
And Breaths were gathering firm
For that last Onset — when the King
Be witnessed — in the Room —

I willed my Keepsakes — Signed away
What portion of me be
Assignable — and then it was
There interposed a Fly —

With Blue — uncertain stumbling Buzz —
Between the light — and me —
And then the Windows failed — and then
I could not see to see —

10

Apparently with no surprise ca. 1884

Apparently with no surprise
To any happy Flower,
The Frost beheads it at its play
In accidental power.
The blond Assassin passes on,
The Sun proceeds unmoved
To measure off another Day
For an Approving God.

A. E. Housman   (1859–1936)

To an Athlete Dying Young 1896

The time you won your town the race
We chaired you through the market place;
Man and boy stood cheering by,
And home we brought you shoulder-high.

Today, the road all runners come,
Shoulder-high we bring you home,
And set you at your threshold down,
Townsman of a stiller town.

Smart lad, to slip betimes away
From fields where glory does not stay,
And early though the laurel grows
It withers quicker than the rose.

10

Eyes the shady night has shut
Cannot see the record cut,
And silence sounds no worse than cheers
After earth has stopped the ears:

Now you will not swell the rout
Of lads that wore their honors out,
Runners whom renown outran
And the name died before the man.   20

So set, before its echoes fade,
The fleet foot on the sill of shade,
And hold to the low lintel up
The still-defended challenge cup.

And round that early-laureled head
Will flock to gaze the strengthless dead
And find unwithered on its curls
The garland briefer than a girl's.

William Butler Yeats   (1865–1939)

Sailing to Byzantium[1]   1927

1

That is no country for old men. The young
In one another's arms, birds in the trees
— Those dying generations — at their song,
The salmon-falls, the mackerel-crowded seas,
Fish, flesh, or fowl, commend all summer long
Whatever is begotten, born, and dies.
Caught in that sensual music all neglect
Monuments of unaging intellect.

2

An aged man is but a paltry thing,
A tattered coat upon a stick, unless   10

Sailing to Byzantium
   [1] Capital of the ancient Eastern Roman Empire, Byzantium (modern Istanbul) is celebrated for its great art, including mosaics (in ll. 17–18, Yeats addresses the figures in one of these mosaics). In *A Vision*, Yeats cites Byzantium as possibly the only civilization that had achieved what he called "Unity of Being" — a state where "religious, aesthetic and practical life were one."

Soul clap its hands and sing, and louder sing
For every tatter in its mortal dress,
Nor is there singing school but studying
Monuments of its own magnificence;
And therefore I have sailed the seas and come
To the holy city of Byzantium.

3

O sages standing in God's holy fire
As in the gold mosaic of a wall,
Come from the holy fire, perne in a gyre,[2]
And be the singing-masters of my soul.   20
Consume my heart away; sick with desire
And fastened to a dying animal
It knows not what it is; and gather me
Into the artifice of eternity.

4

Once out of nature I shall never take
My bodily form from any natural thing,
But such a form as Grecian goldsmiths make
Of hammered gold and gold enameling
To keep a drowsy Emperor awake;[3]
Or set upon a golden bough to sing   30
To lords and ladies of Byzantium
Of what is past, or passing, or to come.

For Analysis

1. This poem incorporates a series of contrasts, among them "That" country and Byzantium, and the real birds of the first stanza and the artificial bird of the final stanza. What others do you find?

2. What are the meanings of "generations" (l. 3)?

3. For what is the poet "sick with desire" (l. 21)?

4. In what sense is eternity an "artifice" (l. 24)?

Writing Topic

In what ways are the **images** of bird and song used throughout this poem?

---

[2] I.e., whirl in a spiral motion. Yeats associated this motion with the cycles of history and the fate of the individual. Here he entreats the sages represented in the mosaic to take him out of the natural world described in the first stanza and into the eternal world of art.

[3] "I have read somewhere," Yeats wrote, "that in the Emperor's palace at Byzantium was a tree made of gold and silver, and artificial birds that sang." The poet wishes to become an artificial bird (a work of art) in contrast to the real birds of the first stanza.

Edwin Arlington Robinson (1869–1935)

Richard Cory 1897

Whenever Richard Cory went down town,
We people on the pavement looked at him:
He was a gentleman from sole to crown,
Clean favored, and imperially slim.

And he was always quietly arrayed,
And he was always human when he talked;
But still he fluttered pulses when he said,
"Good-morning," and he glittered when he walked.

And he was rich — yes, richer than a king —
And admirably schooled in every grace: 10
In fine, we thought that he was everything
To make us wish that we were in his place.

So on we worked, and waited for the light,
And went without the meat, and cursed the bread;
And Richard Cory, one calm summer night,
Went home and put a bullet through his head.

Robert Frost (1874–1963)

After Apple-Picking 1914

My long two-pointed ladder's sticking through a tree
Toward heaven still,
And there's a barrel that I didn't fill
Beside it, and there may be two or three
Apples I didn't pick upon some bough.
But I am done with apple-picking now.
Essence of winter sleep is on the night,
The scent of apples: I am drowsing off.
I cannot rub the strangeness from my sight
I got from looking through a pane of glass   10
I skimmed this morning from the drinking trough
And held against the world of hoary grass.
It melted, and I let it fall and break.

But I was well
Upon my way to sleep before it fell,
And I could tell
What form my dreaming was about to take.
Magnified apples appear and disappear,
Stem end and blossom end,
And every fleck of russet showing clear. 20
My instep arch not only keeps the ache,
It keeps the pressure of a ladder-round.
I feel the ladder sway as the boughs bend.
And I keep hearing from the cellar bin
The rumbling sound
Of load on load of apples coming in.
For I have had too much
Of apple-picking: I am overtired
Of the great harvest I myself desired.
There were ten thousand thousand fruit to touch, 30
Cherish in hand, lift down, and not let fall.
For all
That struck the earth,
No matter if not bruised or spiked with stubble,
Went surely to the cider-apple heap
As of no worth.
One can see what will trouble
This sleep of mine, whatever sleep it is.
Were he not gone,
The woodchuck could say whether it's like his 40
Long sleep, as I describe its coming on,
Or just some human sleep.

For Analysis

1. What does apple-picking symbolize?

2. At the end of the poem, why is the speaker uncertain about what kind of sleep is coming on him?

Nothing Gold Can Stay 1923

Nature's first green is gold,
Her hardest hue to hold.
Her early leaf's a flower;
But only so an hour.
Then leaf subsides to leaf.
So Eden sank to grief,
So dawn goes down to day.
Nothing gold can stay.

For Analysis

1. Does this poem protest or accept the transitoriness of things?

2. Why does Frost use the word "subsides" in line 5 rather than a word like "expands" or "grows"?

3. How are "Nature's first green" (l. 1), "Eden" (l. 6), and "dawn" (l. 7) linked together?

'Out, Out —'¹ 1916

The buzz-saw snarled and rattled in the yard
And made dust and dropped stove-length sticks of wood,
Sweet-scented stuff when the breeze drew across it.
And from there those that lifted eyes could count
Five mountain ranges one behind the other
Under the sunset far into Vermont.
And the saw snarled and rattled, snarled and rattled,
As it ran light, or had to bear a load.
And nothing happened: day was all but done.
Call it a day, I wish they might have said   10
To please the boy by giving him the half hour
That a boy counts so much when saved from work.
His sister stood beside them in her apron
To tell them 'Supper.' At the word, the saw,
As if to prove saws knew what supper meant,
Leaped out at the boy's hand, or seemed to leap —
He must have given the hand. However it was,
Neither refused the meeting. But the hand!
The boy's first outcry was a rueful laugh,
As he swung toward them holding up the hand   20
Half in appeal, but half as if to keep
The life from spilling. Then the boy saw all —
Since he was old enough to know, big boy
Doing a man's work, though a child at heart —
He saw all spoiled. 'Don't let him cut my hand off —
The doctor, when he comes. Don't let him, sister!'
So. But the hand was gone already.
The doctor put him in the dark of ether.
He lay and puffed his lips out with his breath.
And then — the watcher at his pulse took fright.   30
No one believed. They listened at his heart.
Little — less — nothing! — and that ended it.
No more to build on there. And they, since they
Were not the one dead, turned to their affairs.

---

¹ The title is taken from the famous speech of Macbeth upon hearing that his wife has died (*Macbeth*, Act V, Scene 5).

Stopping by Woods on a Snowy Evening 1923

Whose woods these are I think I know.
His house is in the village though;
He will not see me stopping here
To watch his woods fill up with snow.

My little horse must think it queer
To stop without a farmhouse near
Between the woods and frozen lake
The darkest evening of the year.

He gives his harness bells a shake
To ask if there is some mistake.   10
The only other sound's the sweep
Of easy wind and downy flake.

The woods are lovely, dark and deep,
But I have promises to keep,
And miles to go before I sleep,
And miles to go before I sleep.

For Analysis
1. What does the description of the horse tell us about the speaker?
2. What function does the repetition in the last two lines of the poem serve?
3. Why does the speaker refer to the owner of the woods in the opening stanza?

Design 1936

I found a dimpled spider, fat and white,
On a white heal-all, holding up a moth
Like a white piece of rigid satin cloth —
Assorted characters of death and blight
Mixed ready to begin the morning right,
Like the ingredients of a witches' broth —
A snow-drop spider, a flower like a froth,
And dead wings carried like a paper kite.

What had that flower to do with being white,
The wayside blue and innocent heal-all?   10
What brought the kindred spider to that height,
Then steered the white moth thither in the night?
What but design of darkness to appall? —
If design govern in a thing so small.

Writing Topic
Compare this poem with Emily Dickinson's "Apparently with no surprise" (p. 1389).

Antonio Machado   (1875–1939)

Lament of the Virtues and Verses on Account of the Death of Don Guido   1978[1]

It was pneumonia
finally carried away
Don Guido, and so the bells
(*din-dan*) toll for him the whole day.

Died Don Guido
gentleman; when younger
great at gallantry and roistering,
a minor talent in the bullring —
older, his prayers grew longer.

This Sevillan[2] gentleman   10
kept (so they say)
a seraglio, was apt
at managing a horse
and a master
at cooling manzanilla.[3]   [Poem continues on p. 1405.]

Lament of the Virtues and Verses on Account of the Death of Don Guido
  [1] Translated in 1978 by Charles Tomlinson with Henry Gifford.
  [2] A citizen of Seville, a city in southwestern Spain.
  [3] A dry, light, high-quality Spanish sherry wine.

LOOKING DEEPER:
From Art to Literature

The works in this section offer a unique opportunity to reflect on the ways meaning can be conveyed through different media. Most of the poems here are linked with the paintings that inspired them; others appear with paintings thematically similar in their treatment of death. While all these groupings offer an opportunity for rich examination, the ones featuring poems inspired by a particular painting open up even more complex areas for analysis: not only can the painting and the poem be considered independently of each other, but the poem can also be analyzed as a reading of the painting — an interpretation in words of a visual object.

As you read and enter into a dialogue between the works of art and the poems, an interesting approach would be to jot down your reactions to each painting in some detail before reading each accompanying poem. After you have read a poem, compare your reactions to the poet's. Did reading the poem clarify or in any other way alter your response to the painting? Are the poems successful or even comprehensible without reference to the paintings? How are the works alike or different? With paired works, why does the poet choose to emphasize certain details of a painting and ignore others? What accounts for the order in which the poet deals with the details of the painting? Is the poet attempting an accurate and neutral description of the painting or making some judgment about it?

If you wish to look beyond the individual work, you might consider researching one of the poets, with an eye to speculating on why he or she was so moved by the painting as to write about it. Or you might examine the historical context of both the poem and the painting for any illuminating connections.

W. H. Auden   (1907–1973)
Musée des Beaux Arts   1940

About suffering they were never wrong,
The Old Masters: how well they understood
Its human position; how it takes place
While someone else is eating or opening a window or just walking dully along;

How, when the aged are reverently, passionately waiting
For the miraculous birth, there always must be
Children who did not specially want it to happen, skating
On a pond at the edge of the wood:
They never forgot
That even the dreadful martyrdom must run its course   10
Anyhow in a corner, some untidy spot
Where the dogs go on with their doggy life and the torturer's horse
Scratches its innocent behind on a tree.

In Brueghel's *Icarus*,[1] for instance: how everything turns away
Quite leisurely from the disaster; the plowman may
Have heard the splash, the forsaken cry,
But for him it was not an important failure; the sun shone
As it had to on the white legs disappearing into the green
Water; and the expensive delicate ship that must have seen
Something amazing, a boy falling out of the sky,   20
Had somewhere to get to and sailed calmly on.

Landscape with the Fall of Icarus, ca. 1560, by Pieter Brueghel the Elder

---

[1] This poem describes and comments on Pieter Brueghel's painting *Landscape with the Fall of Icarus* (reproduced above). According to myth, Daedalus and his son Icarus made wings, whose feathers they attached with wax, to escape Crete. Icarus flew so near the sun that the wax melted and he fell into the sea.

Questions for Looking Deeper

1. Look up the story of Icarus in an encyclopedia or other reference work. What aspects of the human condition or of human nature does the story embody? How does Brueghel interpret the story? What other interpretations are possible? Compare Anne Sexton's interpretation of the legend in her poem "To a Friend Whose Work Has Come to Triumph," which can be read in her volume *All My Pretty Ones* (1962) or online at *<http://pages.prodigy.net/stesha/toafriend.html>*.

2. Does the poem offer an accurate interpretation of the painting? Explain.

3. Which details of the painting does the poem describe? Does the poet omit details you found important?

Lawrence Ferlinghetti (b. 1919)
In Goya's Greatest Scenes 1958

In Goya's greatest scenes[1] we seem to see
                    the people of the world
    exactly at the moment when
        they first attained the title of
                'suffering humanity'
   They writhe upon the page
            in a veritable rage
                of adversity
    Heaped up
        groaning with babies and bayonets   10
                under cement skies
   in an abstract landscape of blasted trees
      bent statues bats wings and beaks
          slippery gibbets
     cadavers and carnivorous cocks
    and all the final hollering monsters
       of the
             'imagination of disaster'
   they are so bloody real
          it is as if they really still existed   20

   And they do

---

[1] Francisco José de Goya (1746–1828), famous Spanish artist, celebrated for his representations of "suffering humanity."

Only the landscape is changed
They still are ranged along the roads
plagued by legionaires
false windmills and demented roosters

They are the same people
only further from home
on freeways fifty lanes wide
on a concrete continent
spaced with bland billboards
30
illustrating imbecile illusions of happiness
The scene shows fewer tumbrils[2]
but more maimed citizens
in painted cars
and they have strange license plates
and engines
that devour America

The Third of May, 1808, Madrid, 1814, by Francisco de Goya

[2] Carts in which prisoners were conducted to the place of execution.

Questions for Looking Deeper

1. While *The Third of May, 1808, Madrid* commemorates the uprising of the Spanish people against the invading forces of Napoleon, it has come to be seen as a powerful and universal statement against the brutalities of war. (Goya also created a series of eighty-five etchings entitled *The Disasters of War* [1810–1820], which shows how individuals are transformed into "suffering humanity" when they are savaged by war.) There are many Web sites devoted to this great artist, including sites such as *<http://oac.schools.sa.edu.au/goya/disas.html>* and *<http://chomsky.arts.adelaide .edu.au/person/DHart/ResponsesToWar/Art/StudyGuides/Goya.html>*, where the entire series can be viewed. Compare the painting and some of the etchings as views of the disasters of war. What different effects result from the use of color in the painting and of black and white in the etchings?

2. Goya represents suffering and death in their most elemental, physical sense. Do you find Ferlinghetti's transformation of suffering and death from the literal to the metaphoric in the second half of his poem successful? Explain.

Anne Sexton   (1928–1974)
The Starry Night   1961

That does not keep me from having a terrible need of — shall I say the word — religion.
Then I go out at night to paint the stars.
                                        — Vincent van Gogh in a letter to his brother

The town does not exist
except where one black-haired tree slips
up like a drowned woman into the hot sky.
The town is silent. The night boils with eleven stars
Oh starry starry night! This is how
I want to die

It moves. They are all alive.
Even the moon bulges in its orange irons
to push children, like a god from its eye.
The old unseen serpent swallows up the stars.   10
Oh starry starry night! This is how
I want to die:

into that rushing beast of the night,
sucked up by that great dragon, to split
from my life with no flag,
no belly,
no cry.

The Starry Night, 1889, by Vincent van Gogh

Questions for Looking Deeper

1. In what ways does your reaction to the painting agree with Sexton's? In what ways does it differ? Does her poem open your eyes to elements of the painting you had not initially seen? Explain.

2. The first two stanzas of the poem end with the refrain "This is how / I want to die." What does "This" refer to? In what sense might *The Starry Night* be described as a painting about death?

3. Around the time of this painting, van Gogh was much preoccupied with cypress trees. He wrote his brother, "The tree is as beautiful of line and proportion as an Egyptian obelisk. And the green has such a quality of distinction. It is a splash of black in a sunny landscape, but it is one of the most interesting black notes, and the most difficult to hit off exactly that I can imagine." How does Sexton's reference to the cypress tree in the opening lines of her poem relate to her overall reading of the painting?

4. Describe the difference in brush strokes van Gogh uses for the sky and those he uses for the village. How does this difference relate to the painting's theme?

5. *The Starry Night* was painted in the town of Saint-Rémy. Later in the same year, van Gogh did another painting, this one in the town of Arles, to which he gave the same title. Look up this later painting and compare the differences in the painter's handling of light, both natural and artificial.

6. Some of van Gogh's paintings have been described as mystical. Which of these two paintings does the term best fit? Explain. What similarities and differences do you find between the depiction of the village and the sky in the two works?

Donald Finkel   (b. 1929)
The Great Wave: Hokusai   1959

But we will take the problem in its most obscure manifestation, and suppose that our
spectator is an average Englishman. A trained observer, carefully hidden behind a
screen, might notice a dilation in his eyes, even an intake of his breath, perhaps a grunt.
— Herbert Read, *The Meaning of Art*

It is because the sea is blue,
Because Fuji is blue, because the bent blue
Men have white faces, like the snow
On Fuji, like the crest of the wave in the sky the color of their
Boats. It is because the air
Is full of writing, because the wave is still: that nothing
Will harm these frail strangers,
That high over Fuji in an earthcolored sky the fingers
Will not fall; and the blue men
Lean on the sea like snow, and the wave like a mountain leans   10
Against the sky.

       In the painter's sea
All fishermen are safe. All anger bends under his unity.
But the innocent bystander, he merely
'Walks round a corner, thinking of nothing': hidden
Behind a screen we hear his cry.
He stands half in and half out of the world; he is the men,
But he cannot see below Fuji
The shore the color of sky; he is the wave, he stretches
His claws against strangers. He is   20
Not safe, not even from himself. His world is flat.
He fishes a sea full of serpents, he rides his boat
Blindly from wave to wave toward Ararat.

The Great Wave off Kanagawa, 1831–1833, by Katsushika Hokusai

Questions for Looking Deeper

1. The "average Englishman" or indeed any other eyewitness to the actual scene depicted in this print would reasonably assume that the men in the boats are in imminent danger of being drowned by the enoromous, menacing wave about to crash down upon them. Yet that is not how the poet interprets the scene. On what basis does he declare "that nothing / Will harm these frail strangers" (ll. 6–7) and that "In the painter's sea / All fishermen are safe" (ll. 12–13)?

2. What does Finkel mean when he says "In the painters's sea / All fishermen are safe. All anger bends under his unity" (ll. 12–13)? How has the artist's representation of nature changed its reality — that is, eliminated the danger and imposed unity?

3. What does the "innocent bystander" not understand that the poet does? Why is the bystander not safe from himself? In contrast to the world represented by the artist, what kind of world does the bystander inhabit? Why is his sea "full of serpents" (l. 22) and why is his boat headed for Ararat (l. 23)?

4. Finkel's epigraph is taken from a passage that can be found in section 1, paragraph 17, of Herbert Read's *The Meaning of Art* (1968). Read the passage, which defines "the problem," and explain why Finkel uses it to introduce his poem.

5. Compare Finkel's poem with John Keats's "Ode on a Grecian Urn" (p. 1385) for similarities and differences in the way they interpret the visual work that has inspired them to poetry.

When his riches dwindled
it was his obssesion
to think that he ought to think
of settling in quiet possession.
And he settled   20
in a very Spanish way
which was — to marry
a maiden of large fortune
and to repaint his blazons,
to refer to the traditions of
"this house of ours,"
setting a measure
to scandals and amours
and damping down the expenditure on pleasure.

He became, great pagan   30
that he was,
brother in a fraternity;[4]
on Holy Thursday could be seen
disguised
(the immense candle in his hand)
in the long robe of a Nazarene.[5]

Today
you may hear the bell
say that the good Don Guido
with solemn face   40
tomorrow must go
the slow road to the burial place.
For ever and for always
gone, good Don Guido . . .
"What have you left?" some will say —
I ask, "What have you taken
to the world in which you are today?"

Your love for braid
and for silks and gold
and the blood of bulls and the fume that rolled   50
from off the altars.

To good Don Guido and his equipage
bon voyage!

[4] A religious organization.
[5] An early Christian sect.

The here
and the there,
cavalier,
show in your withered face,
confess the infinite:
the nothingness.

Oh the thin cheeks   60
• yellow
and the eyelids, wax,
and the delicate skull
on the bed's pillow!

Oh end of an aristocracy!
The beard on breast
lies limp and hoary,
in the rough serge
of a monk he's dressed;
crossed, the hands that cannot stir   70
and the Andalusian[6] gentleman
on his best behaviour.

For Analysis

1. Characterize Don Guido's behavior as a young man. How does it change as he grows older and poorer?

2. Look up "blazon" (l. 24). Why does Don Guido repaint "his blazons"? What does he mean when he says "this house of ours" (l. 26)?

3. Is Don Guido's life unique — different from the lives of ordinary people? Explain.

Writing Topic

Using the concrete details that animate the poem, describe the changes in Don Guido's belief system and behavior as he grows older, and suggest the reasons for those changes.

Wilfred Owen   (1893–1918)

Dulce et Decorum Est   1920

Bent double, like old beggars under sacks,
Knock-kneed, coughing like hags, we cursed through sludge,
Till on the haunting flares we turned our backs,

Lament of the Virtues and Verses on Account of the Death of Don Guido
   [6] From Andalusia, a region in southern Spain.

And towards our distant rest began to trudge.
Men marched asleep. Many had lost their boots,
But limped on, blood-shod. All went lame, all blind;
Drunk with fatigue; deaf even to the hoots
Of gas-shells dropping softly behind.

Gas! GAS! Quick, boys! — An ecstasy of fumbling,
Fitting the clumsy helmets just in time,   10
But someone still was yelling out and stumbling
And flound'ring like a man in fire or lime. —
Dim through the misty panes and thick green light,
As under a green sea, I saw him drowning.
In all my dreams before my helpless sight
He plunges at me, guttering, choking, drowning.

If in some smothering dreams, you too could pace
Behind the wagon that we flung him in,
And watch the white eyes writhing in his face,
His hanging face, like a devil's sick of sin,   20
If you could hear, at every jolt, the blood
Come gargling from the froth-corrupted lungs
Bitter as the cud
Of vile, incurable sores on innocent tongues, —
My friend, you would not tell with such high zest
To children ardent for some desperate glory,
The old lie: *Dulce et decorum est*
Pro patria mori.[1]

E. E. Cummings   (1894–1962)

nobody loses all the time   1926

nobody loses all the time

i had an uncle named
Sol who was a born failure and
nearly everybody said he should have gone
into vaudeville perhaps because my Uncle Sol could
sing McCann He Was A Diver on Xmas Eve like Hell Itself which
may or may not account for the fact that my Uncle

Dulce et Decorum Est
    [1] A quotation from the Latin poet Horace, "It is sweet and fitting to die for one's country."

Sol indulged in that possibly most inexcusable
of all to use a highfalootin phrase
luxuries that is or to   10
wit farming and be
it needlessly
added

my Uncle Sol's farm
failed because the chickens
ate the vegetables so
my Uncle Sol had a
chicken farm till the
skunks ate the chickens when

my Uncle Sol   20
had a skunk farm but
the skunks caught cold and
died and so
my Uncle Sol imitated the
skunks in a subtle manner

or by drowning himself in the watertank
but somebody who'd given my Uncle Sol a Victor
Victrola and records while he lived presented to
him upon the auspicious occasion of his decease a
scrumptious not to mention splendiferous funeral with   30
tall boys in black gloves and flowers and everything and

i remember we all cried like the Missouri
when my Uncle Sol's coffin lurched because
somebody pressed a button
(and down went
my Uncle
Sol

and started a worm farm)

For Analysis

1. Explain the title.
2. What is the speaker's attitude toward Uncle Sol?

O sweet spontaneous 1923

O sweet spontaneous
earth how often have
the
doting

    fingers of
prurient philosophers pinched
and
poked

thee
, has the naughty thumb   10
of science prodded
thy

    beauty   .how
often have religions taken
thee upon their scraggy knees
squeezing and

buffeting thee that thou mightest conceive
gods
    (but
true   20

to the incomparable
couch of death thy
rhythmic
lover

    thou answerest

them only with

   spring)

For Analysis

1. Analyze the erotic **imagery** in this poem. What does it tell us about the speaker's attitude toward philosophy, science, and religion?

2. What does the speaker mean by calling death earth's "lover" (l. 24)? And why "rhythmic" lover (l. 23)?

3. In what sense is "spring" (l. 27) an answer?

Pablo Neruda   (1904–1973)

The Dead Woman   1972

If suddenly you do not exist,
if suddenly you are not living,
I shall go on living.

I do not dare,
I do not dare to write it,
if you die.

I shall go on living.

Because where a man has no voice,
there, my voice.

Where blacks are beaten,   10
I can not be dead.
When my brothers go to jail
I shall go with them.

When victory,
not my victory
but the great victory
arrives,
even though I am mute I must speak:
I shall see it come even though I am blind.

No, forgive me.   20
If you are not living,
if you, beloved, my love,
if you
have died,
all the leaves will fall on my breast,
it will rain upon my soul night and day,
the snow will burn my heart,
I shall walk with cold and fire and death and snow,
my feet will want to march toward where you sleep,
but   30
I shall go on living,
because you wanted me to be, above all things,
untamable,
and, love, because you know that I am not just one man
but all men.

1410

Theodore Roethke (1908–1963)

Elegy for Jane 1958

My Student, Thrown by a Horse

I remember the neckcurls, limp and damp as tendrils;
And her quick look, a sidelong pickerel smile;
And how, once startled into talk, the light syllables leaped for her,
And she balanced in the delight of her thought,
A wren, happy, tail into the wind,
Her song trembling the twigs and small branches.
The shade sang with her;
The leaves, their whispers turned to kissing;
And the mold sang in the bleached valleys under the rose.

Oh, when she was sad, she cast herself down into such a pure depth,   10
Even a father could not find her:
Scraping her cheek against straw;
Stirring the clearest water.

My sparrow, you are not here,
Waiting like a fern, making a spiny shadow.
The sides of wet stones cannot console me,
Nor the moss, wound with the last light.

If only I could nudge you from this sleep,
My maimed darling, my skittery pigeon.
Over this damp grave I speak the words of my love: 20
I, with no rights in this matter,
Neither father nor lover.

Dylan Thomas   (1914–1953)

Do Not Go Gentle into That Good Night 1952

Do not go gentle into that good night,
Old age should burn and rave at close of day;
Rage, rage against the dying of the light.

Though wise men at their end know dark is right,
Because their words had forked no lightning they
Do not go gentle into that good night.

Good men, the last wave by, crying how bright
Their frail deeds might have danced in a green bay,
Rage, rage against the dying of the light.

Wild men who caught and sang the sun in flight,   10
And learn, too late, they grieved it on its way,
Do not go gentle into that good night.

Grave men, near death, who see with blinding sight
Blind eyes could blaze like meteors and be gay,
Rage, rage against the dying of the light.

And you, my father, there on the sad height,
Curse, bless, me now with your fierce tears, I pray.
Do not go gentle into that good night.
Rage, rage against the dying of the light.

For Analysis

1. What do wise, good, wild, and grave men have in common?

2. Why does the poet use the adjective "gentle" rather than the adverb "gently" in the title?

3. What is the "sad height" (l. 16)?

Philip Larkin   (1922–1985)

Aubade[1]   1977

I work all day, and get half drunk at night.
Waking at four to soundless dark, I stare.
In time the curtain-edges will grow light.
Till then I see what's really always there:
Unresting death, a whole day nearer now;
Making all thought impossible but how
And where and when I shall myself die.
Arid interrogation: yet the dread
Of dying, and being dead,
Flashes afresh to hold and horrify.   10

The mind blanks at the glare. Not in remorse
 — The good not done, the love not given, time
Torn off unused — nor wretchedly because
An only life can take so long to climb
Clear of its wrong beginnings, and may never;
But at the total emptiness for ever,
The sure extinction that we travel to
And shall be lost in always. Not to be here,
Not to be anywhere,
And soon; nothing more terrible, nothing more true.   20

This is a special way of being afraid
No trick dispels. Religion used to try,
That vast moth-eaten musical brocade
Created to pretend we never die,
And specious stuff that says *No rational being
Can fear a thing it will not feel,* not seeing
That this is what we fear — no sight, no sound.
No touch or taste to smell, nothing to think with.
Nothing to love or link with,
The anaesthetic from which none come round.   30

And so it stays just on the edge of vision,
A small unfocused blur, a standing chill
That slows each impulse down to indecision.
Most things may never happen: this one will.
And realisation of it rages out

[1] An aubade is a morning song.

In furnace-fear when we are caught without
People or drink. Courage is no good:
It means not scaring others. Being brave
Lets no one off the grave.
Death is no different whined at than withstood.   40

Slowly light strengthens, and the room takes shape.
It stands plain as a wardrobe, what we know,
Have always known, know that we can't escape,
Yet can't accept. One side will have to go.
Meanwhile telephones crouch, getting ready to ring
In locked-up offices, and all the uncaring
Intricate rented world begins to rouse.
The sky is white as clay, with no sun.
Work has to be done.
Postmen like doctors go from house to house.   50

Catherine Davis   (b. 1924)

After a Time   1961?

After a time, all losses are the same.
One more thing lost is one thing less to lose;
And we go stripped at last the way we came.

Though we shall probe, time and again, our shame,
Who lack the wit to keep or to refuse,
After a time, all losses are the same.

No wit, no luck can beat a losing game;
Good fortune is a reassuring ruse:
And we go stripped at last the way we came.

Rage as we will for what we think to claim,   10
Nothing so much as this bare thought subdues:
After a time, all losses are the same.

The sense of treachery — the want, the blame —
Goes in the end, whether or not we choose,
And we go stripped at last the way we came.

So we, who would go raging, will go tame
When what we have we can no longer use:
After a time, all losses are the same;
And we go stripped at last the way we came.

For Analysis

1. What difference in effect would occur if the **refrain** "After a time" were changed to "When life is done"?

2. Does the meaning of the refrain in lines 3, 9, 15, and 16 change in the course of this poem? Explain.

3. Explain the meaning of "The sense of treachery" (l. 13).

4. Does this poem say that life is meaningless? Explain.

Writing Topic

Compare the form and attitude asserted in this poem with that of Dylan Thomas's "Do Not Go Gentle into That Good Night" (p. 1412).

Maxine Kumin   (b. 1925)

Woodchucks   1972

Gassing the woodchucks didn't turn out right.
The knockout bomb from the Feed and Grain Exchange
was featured as merciful, quick at the bone
and the case we had against them was airtight
both exits shoehorned shut with puddingstone,
but they had a sub-sub-basement out of range.

Next morning they turned up again, no worse
for the cyanide than we for our cigarettes
and state-store Scotch, all of us up to scratch.
They brought down the marigolds as a matter of course   10
and then took over the vegetable patch
nipping the broccoli shoots, beheading the carrots.

The food from our mouths, I said, righteously thrilling
to the feel of the .22, the bullets' neat noses.
I, a lapsed pacifist fallen from grace
puffed with Darwinian pieties for killing,
now drew a bead on the littlest woodchuck's face.
He died down in the everbearing roses.

Ten minutes later I dropped the mother. She
flipflopped in the air and fell, her needle teeth   20
still hooked in a leaf of early Swiss chard.
Another baby next. O one-two-three
the murderer inside me rose up hard,
the hawkeye killer came on stage forthwith.

There's one chuck left. Old wily fellow, he keeps
me cocked and ready day after day after day.
All night I hunt his humped-up form. I dream
I sight along the barrel in my sleep.
If only they'd all consented to die unseen
gassed underground the quiet Nazi way.   30

Edwin Brock   (b. 1927)

Five Ways to Kill a Man   1963

There are many cumbersome ways to kill a man:
you can make him carry a plank of wood
to the top of a hill and nail him to it. To do this
properly you require a crowd of people
wearing sandals, a cock that crows, a cloak
to dissect, a sponge, some vinegar and one
man to hammer the nails home.

Or you can take a length of steel,
shaped and chased° in a traditional way,   ornamented
and attempt to pierce the metal cage he wears.   10
But for this you need white horses,
English trees, men with bows and arrows,
at least two flags, a prince and a
castle to hold your banquet in.

Dispensing with nobility, you may, if the wind
allows, blow gas at him. But then you need
a mile of mud sliced through with ditches,
not to mention black boots, bomb craters,
more mud, a plague of rats, a dozen songs
and some round hats made of steel.   20

In an age of aeroplanes, you may fly
miles above your victim and dispose of him by
pressing one small switch. All you then
require is an ocean to separate you, two
systems of government, a nation's scientists,
several factories, a psychopath and
land that no one needs for several years.

These are, as I began, cumbersome ways
to kill a man. Simpler, direct, and much more neat
is to see that he is living somewhere in the middle   30
of the twentieth century, and leave him there.

Yevgeny Yevtushenko   (b. 1933)

People[1]   trans. 1962

No people are uninteresting.
Their fate is like the chronicle of planets.

Nothing in them is not particular,
and planet is dissimilar from planet.

And if a man lived in obscurity
making his friends in that obscurity
obscurity is not uninteresting.

To each his world is private,
and in that world one excellent minute.

And in that world one tragic minute.   10
These are private.

In any man who dies there dies with him
his first snow and kiss and fight.
It goes with him.

People
    [1] Translated by Robin Milner-Gulland and Peter Levi.

They are left books and bridges
and painted canvas and machinery.

Whose fate is to survive.
But what has gone is also not nothing:

by the rule of the game something has gone.
Not people die but worlds die in them.   20

Whom we knew as faulty, the earth's creatures.
Of whom, essentially, what did we know?

Brother of a brother? Friend of friends?
Lover of lover?

We who knew our fathers
in everything, in nothing.

They perish. They cannot be brought back.
The secret worlds are not regenerated.

And every time again and again
I make my lament against destruction.   30

Mary Oliver (b. 1935)

When Death Comes 1992

When death comes
like the hungry bear in autumn;
when death comes and takes all the bright coins from his purse

to buy me, and snaps the purse shut;
when death comes
like the measle-pox;

when death comes
like an iceberg between the shoulder blades,

I want to step through the door full of curiosity, wondering:
what is it going to be like, that cottage of darkness? 10

And therefore I look upon everything
as a brotherhood and a sisterhood,
and I look upon time as no more than an idea,
and I consider eternity as another possibility,

and I think of each life as a flower, as common
as a field daisy, and as singular,

and each name a comfortable music in the mouth,
tending, as all music does, toward silence,

and each body a lion of courage, and something
precious to the earth. 20

When it's over, I want to say: all my life
I was a bride married to amazement.
I was the bridegroom, taking the world into my arms.

When it's over, I don't want to wonder
if I have made of my life something particular, and real.
I don't want to find myself sighing and frightened,
or full of argument.

I don't want to end up simply having visited this world.

For Analysis

1. This poem turns on a series of **images**. Characterize each image associated with approaching death, evaluating its effectiveness and appropriateness.

2. What is the "cottage of darkness" (l. 10)?

3. What images are associated with life and experience? Do you find them effective? Explain.

4. What is wrong with "simply having visited this world" (l. 28)?

Writing Topic

Lines 24 to 27 express the poet's attitude toward life as its end approaches. In an essay, explain how a life that is "particular, and real," leads naturally to a death that does not generate either sighing and fear, or argument.

Seamus Heaney (b. 1939)

Mid-term Break 1966

I sat all morning in the college sick bay
Counting bells knelling classes to a close.
At two o'clock our neighbors drove me home.

In the porch I met my father crying —
He had always taken funerals in his stride —
And Big Jim Evans saying it was a hard blow.

The baby cooed and laughed and rocked the pram
When I came in, and I was embarrassed
By old men standing up to shake my hand

And tell me they were "sorry for my trouble,"   10
Whispers informed strangers I was the eldest,
Away at school, as my mother held my hand

In hers and coughed out angry tearless sighs.
At ten o'clock the ambulance arrived
With the corpse, stanched and bandaged by the nurses.

Next morning I went up into the room. Snowdrops
And candles soothed the bedside; I saw him
For the first time in six weeks. Paler now,

Wearing a poppy bruise on his left temple,
He lay in the four foot box as in his cot.   20
No gaudy scars, the bumper knocked him clear.

A four foot box, a foot for every year.

For Analysis
1. Although it contains little rhyme, this poem is remarkably musical. Identify the **assonance** and **alliteration** that permeate the poem.

2. What event does the poem describe?

3. How is the poem's title relevant?

Writing Topic
Characterize the family and the society revealed in this short poem.

James Fenton   (b. 1949)

God, A Poem   1984

A nasty surprise in a sandwich,
A drawing-pin caught in your sock,
The limpest of shakes from a hand which
You'd thought would be firm as a rock,

A serious mistake in a nightie,
A grave disappointment all round
Is all that you'll get from th'Almighty,
Is all that you'll get underground.

Oh he *said:* "If you lay off the crumpet
I'll see you alright in the end.   10
Just hang on until the last trumpet.
Have faith in me, chum — I'm your friend."

But if you remind him, he'll tell you:
"I'm sorry, I must have been pissed —
Though your name rings a sort of a bell. You
Should have guessed that I do not exist.

"I didn't exist at Creation,
I didn't exist at the Flood,
And I won't be around for Salvation
To sort out the sheep from the cud —   20

"Or whatever the phrase is. The fact is
In soteriological terms
I'm a crude existential malpractice
And you are a diet of worms.

"You're a nasty surprise in a sandwich.
You're a drawing-pin caught in my sock.
You're the limpest of shakes from a hand which
I'd have thought would be firm as a rock,

"You're a serious mistake in a nightie,
You're a grave disappointment all round —   30
That's all that you are," says th'Almighty,
"And that's all that you'll be underground."

Drama

Samuel Beckett   (1906–1989)

Endgame   1958

A Play in One Act

CHARACTERS

Nagg   **Hamm**
Nell   **Clov**

Bare interior. Gray light. Left and right back, high up, two small windows, curtains drawn. Front right, a door. Hanging near door, its face to wall, a picture. Front left, touching each other, covered with an old sheet, two ashbins. Center, in an armchair on casters, covered with an old sheet, Hamm. Motionless by the door, his eyes fixed on Hamm, Clov. Very red face. Brief tableau.

Clov goes and stands under window left. Stiff, staggering walk. He looks up at window left. He turns and looks at window right. He goes and stands under window right. He looks up at window right. He turns and looks at window left. He goes out, comes back immediately with a small stepladder, carries it over and sets it down under window left, gets up on it, draws back curtain. He gets down, takes six steps (for example) towards window right, goes back for ladder, carries it over and sets it down under window right, gets up on it, draws back curtain. He gets down, takes three steps towards window left, goes back for ladder, carries it over and sets it down under window left, gets up on it, looks out of window. Brief laugh. He gets down, takes one step towards window right, goes back for ladder, carries it over and sets it down under window right, gets up on it, looks out of window. Brief laugh. He gets down, goes with ladder towards ashbins, halts, turns, carries back ladder and sets it down under window right, goes to ashbins, removes sheet covering them, folds it over his arm. He raises one lid, stoops and looks into bin. Brief laugh. He closes lid. Same with other bin. He goes to Hamm, removes sheet covering him, folds it over his arm. In a dressing-gown, a stiff toque on his head, a large blood-stained handkerchief over his face,

Translated from the French by the author.

a whistle hanging from his neck, a rug over his knees, thick socks on his feet, Hamm seems to be asleep. Clov looks him over. Brief laugh. He goes to door, halts, turns towards auditorium.

Clov (*Fixed gaze, tonelessly*).   Finished, it's finished, nearly finished, it must be nearly finished. (*Pause*) Grain upon grain, one by one, and one day, suddenly, there's a heap, a little heap, the impossible heap. (*Pause*) I can't be punished any more. (*Pause*) I'll go now to my kitchen, ten feet by ten feet by ten feet, and wait for him to whistle me. (*Pause*) Nice dimensions, nice proportions, I'll lean on the table, and look at the wall, and wait for him to whistle me. (*He remains a moment motionless, then goes out. He comes back immediately, goes to window right, takes up the ladder and carries it out. Pause. Hamm stirs. He yawns under the handkerchief. He removes the handkerchief from his face. Very red face. Black glasses*)

Hamm.   Me — (*He yawns*) — to play. (*He holds the handkerchief spread out before him*) Old stancher! (*He takes off his glasses, wipes his eyes, his face, the glasses, puts them on again, folds the handkerchief and puts it back neatly in the breast-pocket of his dressing-gown. He clears his throat, joins the tips of his fingers*) Can there be misery — (*He yawns*) — loftier than mine? No doubt. Formerly. But now? (*Pause*) My father? (*Pause*) My mother? (*Pause*) My . . . dog? (*Pause*) Oh I am willing to believe they suffer as much as such creatures can suffer. But does that mean their sufferings equal mine? No doubt. (*Pause*) No, all is a — (*He yawns*) — bsolute, (*Proudly*) the bigger a man is the fuller he is. (*Pause. Gloomily*) And the emptier. (*He sniffs*) Clov! (*Pause*) No, alone. (*Pause*) What dreams! Those forests! (*Pause*) Enough, it's time it ended, in the shelter too. (*Pause*) And yet I hesitate, I hesitate to . . . to end. Yes there it is, it's time it ended and yet I hesitate to — (*He yawns*) — to end. (*Yawns*) God, I'm tired, I'd be better off in bed. (*He whistles. Enter Clov immediately. He halts beside the chair*) You pollute the air! (*Pause*) Get me ready, I'm going to bed.

Clov.   I've just got you up.

Hamm.   And what of it?

Clov.   I can't be getting you up and putting you to bed every five minutes, I have things to do. (*Pause*)

Hamm.   Did you ever see my eyes?

Clov.   No.

Hamm.   Did you never have the curiosity, while I was sleeping, to take off my glasses and look at my eyes?

Clov.   Pulling back the lids? (*Pause*) No.

Hamm.   One of these days I'll show them to you. (*Pause*) It seems they've gone all white. (*Pause*) What time is it?

Clov.   The same as usual.

Hamm (*Gesture towards window right*).   Have you looked?

Clov.   Yes.

Hamm.   Well?

Clov.   Zero.

Hamm.   It'd need to rain.

Clov.   It won't rain. *(Pause)*

Hamm.   Apart from that, how do you feel?

Clov.   I don't complain.

Hamm.   You feel normal?

Clov *(Irritably)*.   I tell you I don't complain.

Hamm.   I feel a little queer. *(Pause)* Clov!

Clov.   Yes.

Hamm.   Have you not had enough?

Clov.   Yes! *(Pause)* Of what?

Hamm.   Of this . . . this . . . thing.

Clov.   I always had. *(Pause)* Not you?

Hamm *(Gloomily)*.   Then there's no reason for it to change.

Clov.   It may end. *(Pause)* All life long the same questions, the same answers.

Hamm.   Get me ready. *(Clov does not move)* Go and get the sheet. *(Clov does not move)* Clov!

Clov.   Yes.

Hamm.   I'll give you nothing more to eat.

Clov.   Then we'll die.

Hamm.   I'll give you just enough to keep you from dying. You'll be hungry all the time.

Clov.   Then we won't die. *(Pause)* I'll go and get the sheet. *(He goes towards the door)*

Hamm.   No! *(Clov halts)* I'll give you one biscuit per day. *(Pause)* One and a half. *(Pause)* Why do you stay with me?

Clov.   Why do you keep me?

Hamm.   There's no one else.

Clov.   There's nowhere else. *(Pause)*

Hamm.   You're leaving me all the same.

Clov.   I'm trying.

Hamm.   You don't love me.

Clov.   No.

Hamm.   You loved me once.

Clov.   Once!

Hamm.   I've made you suffer too much. *(Pause)* Haven't I?

Clov.   It's not that.

Hamm *(Shocked)*.   I haven't made you suffer too much?

Clov.   Yes!

Hamm *(Relieved)*.   Ah you gave me a fright! *(Pause. Coldly)* Forgive me. *(Pause. Louder)* I said, Forgive me.

Clov.   I heard you. *(Pause)* Have you bled?

Hamm.   Less. *(Pause)* Is it not time for my pain-killer?

Clov.   No. *(Pause)*

Hamm.   How are your eyes?

Clov.   Bad.

Hamm. How are your legs?

Clov. Bad.

Hamm. But you can move.

Clov. Yes.

Hamm (*Violently*). Then move! (*Clov goes to back wall, leans against it with his forehead and hands*) Where are you?

Clov. Here.

Hamm. Come back! (*Clov returns to his place beside the chair*) Where are you?

Clov. Here.

Hamm. Why don't you kill me?

Clov. I don't know the combination of the cupboard. (*Pause*)

Hamm. Go and get two bicycle-wheels.

Clov. There are no more bicycle-wheels.

Hamm. What have you done with your bicycle?

Clov. I never had a bicycle.

Hamm. The thing is impossible.

Clov. When there were still bicycles I wept to have one. I crawled at your feet. You told me to go to hell. Now there are none.

Hamm. And your rounds? When you inspected my paupers. Always on foot?

Clov. Sometimes on horse. (*The lid of one of the bins lifts and the hands of Nagg appear, gripping the rim. Then his head emerges. Nightcap. Very white face. Nagg yawns, then listens*) I'll leave you, I have things to do.

Hamm. In your kitchen?

Clov. Yes.

Hamm. Outside of here it's death. (*Pause*) All right, be off. (*Exit Clov. Pause*) We're getting on.

Nagg. Me pap!

Hamm. Accursed progenitor!

Nagg. Me pap!

Hamm. The old folks at home! No decency left! Guzzle, guzzle, that's all they think of. (*He whistles. Enter Clov. He halts beside the chair*) Well! I thought you were leaving me.

Clov. Oh not just yet, not just yet.

Nagg. Me pap!

Hamm. Give him his pap.

Clov. There's no more pap.

Hamm (*To Nagg*). Do you hear that? There's no more pap. You'll never get any more pap.

Nagg. I want me pap!

Hamm. Give him a biscuit. (*Exit Clov*) Accursed fornicator! How are your stumps?

Nagg. Never mind me stumps. (*Enter Clov with biscuit*)

Clov. I'm back again, with the biscuit. (*He gives biscuit to Nagg who fingers it, sniffs it*)

Nagg (*Plaintively*). What is it?

Clov. Spratt's medium.

Nagg (*As before*). It's hard! I can't!

Hamm. Bottle him! (*Clov pushes Nagg back into the bin, closes the lid*)

Clov (*Returning to his place beside the chair*). If age but knew!

Hamm. Sit on him!

Clov. I can't sit.

Hamm. True. And I can't stand.

Clov. So it is.

Hamm. Every man his speciality. (*Pause*) No phone calls? (*Pause*) Don't we laugh?

Clov (*After reflection*). I don't feel like it.

Hamm (*After reflection*). Nor I. (*Pause*) Clov!

Clov. Yes.

Hamm. Nature has forgotten us.

Clov. There's no more nature.

Hamm. No more nature! You exaggerate.

Clov. In the vicinity.

Hamm. But we breathe, we change! We lose our hair, our teeth! Our bloom! Our ideals!

Clov. Then she hasn't forgotten us.

Hamm. But you say there is none.

Clov (*Sadly*). No one that ever lived ever thought so crooked as we.

Hamm. We do what we can.

Clov. We shouldn't. (*Pause*)

Hamm. You're a bit of all right, aren't you?

Clov. A smithereen. (*Pause*)

Hamm. This is slow work. (*Pause*) Is it not time for my pain-killer?

Clov. No. (*Pause*) I'll leave you, I have things to do.

Hamm. In your kitchen?

Clov. Yes.

Hamm. What, I'd like to know.

Clov. I look at the wall.

Hamm. The wall! And what do you see on your wall? Mene, mene?[1] Naked bodies?

Clov. I see my light dying.

Hamm. Your light dying! Listen to that! Well, it can die just as well here, *your* light. Take a look at me and then come back and tell me what you think of *your* light. (*Pause*)

Clov. You shouldn't speak to me like that. (*Pause*)

Hamm (*Coldly*). Forgive me. (*Pause. Louder*) I said, Forgive me.

---

[1] See Daniel 5:25–28. Daniel interprets the handwriting on the wall at the Court of Belshazzar — "Mene, Mene, Tekel, U-pharsin" — to mean "God has numbered the days of your kingdom and brought it to an end; you have been weighed in the balances and found wanting; your kingdom is divided and given to the Medes and Persians."

Clov. I heard you. (*The lid of Nagg's bin lifts. His hands appear, gripping the rim. Then his head emerges. In his mouth the biscuit. He listens*)

Hamm. Did your seeds come up?

Clov. No.

Hamm. Did you scratch round them to see if they had sprouted?

Clov. They haven't sprouted.

Hamm. Perhaps it's still too early.

Clov. If they were going to sprout they would have sprouted. (*Violently*) They'll never sprout! (*Pause. Nagg takes biscuit in his hand*)

Hamm. This is not much fun. (*Pause*) But that's always the way at the end of the day, isn't it, Clov?

Clov. Always.

Hamm. It's the end of the day like any other day, isn't it, Clov?

Clov. Looks like it. (*Pause*)

Hamm (*Anguished*). What's happening, what's happening?

Clov. Something is taking its course. (*Pause*)

Hamm. All right, be off. (*He leans back in his chair, remains motionless. Clov does not move, heaves a great groaning sigh. Hamm sits up*) I thought I told you to be off.

Clov. I'm trying. (*He goes to door, halts*) Ever since I was whelped. (*Exit Clov*)

Hamm. We're getting on. (*He leans back in his chair, remains motionless. Nagg knocks on the lid of the other bin. Pause. He knocks harder. The lid lifts and the hands of Nell appear, gripping the rim. Then her head emerges. Lace cap. Very white face*)

Nell. What is it, my pet? (*Pause*) Time for love?

Nagg. Were you asleep?

Nell. Oh no!

Nagg. Kiss me.

Nell. I can't.

Nagg. Try. (*Their heads strain towards each other, fail to meet, fall apart again*)

Nell. Why this farce, day after day? (*Pause*)

Nagg. I've lost me tooth.

Nell. When?

Nagg. I had it yesterday.

Nell (*Elegiac*). Ah yesterday! (*They turn painfully towards each other*)

Nagg. Can you see me?

Nell. Hardly. And you?

Nagg. What?

Nell. Can you see me?

Nagg. Hardly.

Nell. So much the better, so much the better.

Nagg. Don't say that. (*Pause*) Our sight has failed.

Nell. Yes. (*Pause. They turn away from each other*)

Nagg.   Can you hear me?

Nell.   Yes. And you?

Nagg.   Yes. *(Pause)* Our hearing hasn't failed.

Nell.   Our what?

Nagg.   Our hearing.

Nell.   No. *(Pause)* Have you anything else to say to me?

Nagg.   Do you remember —

Nell.   No.

Nagg.   When we crashed on our tandem and lost our shanks. *(They laugh heartily)*

Nell.   It was in the Ardennes. *(They laugh less heartily)*

Nagg.   On the road to Sedan.[2] *(They laugh still less heartily)* Are you cold?

Nell.   Yes, perished. And you?

Nagg *(Pause)*.   I'm freezing. *(Pause)* Do you want to go in?

Nell.   Yes.

Nagg.   Then go in. *(Nell does not move)* Why don't you go in?

Nell.   I don't know. *(Pause)*

Nagg.   Has he changed your sawdust?

Nell.   It isn't sawdust. *(Pause. Wearily)* Can you not be a little accurate, Nagg?

Nagg.   Your sand then. It's not important.

Nell.   It is important. *(Pause)*

Nagg.   It was sawdust once.

Nell.   Once!

Nagg.   And now it's sand. *(Pause)* From the shore. *(Pause. Impatiently)* Now it's sand he fetches from the shore.

Nell.   Now it's sand.

Nagg.   Has he changed yours?

Nell.   No.

Nagg.   Nor mine. *(Pause)* I won't have it! *(Pause. Holding up the biscuit)* Do you want a bit?

Nell.   No. *(Pause)* Of what?

Nagg.   Biscuit. I've kept you half. *(He looks at the biscuit. Proudly)* Three quarters. For you. Here. *(He proffers the biscuit)* No? *(Pause)* Do you not feel well?

Hamm *(Wearily)*.   Quiet, quiet, you're keeping me awake. *(Pause)* Talk softer. *(Pause)* If I could sleep I might make love. I'd go into the woods. My eyes would see . . . the sky, the earth. I'd run, run, they wouldn't catch me. *(Pause)* Nature! *(Pause)* There's something dripping in my head. *(Pause)* A heart, a heart in my head. *(Pause)*

Nagg *(Soft)*.   Do you hear him? A heart in his head! *(He chuckles cautiously)*

Nell.   One mustn't laugh at those things, Nagg. Why must you always laugh at them?

Nagg.   Not so loud!

---

[2] A city on the Meuse River in northeast France, site of the defeat and capture of Napoleon III in 1870.

Nell (*Without lowering her voice*).   Nothing is funnier than unhappiness, I grant you that. But —

Nagg (*Shocked*).   Oh!

Nell.   Yes, yes, it's the most comical thing in the world. And we laugh, we laugh, with a will, in the beginning. But it's always the same thing. Yes, it's like the funny story we have heard too often, we still find it funny, but we don't laugh any more. (*Pause*) Have you anything else to say to me?

Nagg.   No.

Nell.   Are you quite sure? (*Pause*) Then I'll leave you.

Nagg.   Do you not want your biscuit? (*Pause*) I'll keep it for you. (*Pause*) I thought you were going to leave me.

Nell.   I am going to leave you.

Nagg.   Could you give me a scratch before you go?

Nell.   No. (*Pause*) Where?

Nagg.   In the back.

Nell.   No. (*Pause*) Rub yourself against the rim.

Nagg.   It's lower down. In the hollow.

Nell.   What hollow?

Nagg.   The hollow! (*Pause*) Could you not? (*Pause*) Yesterday you scratched me there.

Nell (*Elegiac*).   Ah yesterday!

Nagg.   Could you not? (*Pause*) Would you like me to scratch you? (*Pause*) Are you crying again?

Nell.   I was trying. (*Pause*)

Hamm.   Perhaps it's a little vein. (*Pause*)

Nagg.   What was that he said?

Nell.   Perhaps it's a little vein.

Nagg.   What does that mean? (*Pause*) That means nothing. (*Pause*) Will I tell you the story of the tailor?

Nell.   No. (*Pause*) What for?

Nagg.   To cheer you up.

Nell.   It's not funny.

Nagg.   It always made you laugh. (*Pause*) The first time I thought you'd die.

Nell.   It was on Lake Como.[3] (*Pause*) One April afternoon. (*Pause*) Can you believe it?

Nagg.   What?

Nell.   That we once went out rowing on Lake Como. (*Pause*) One April afternoon.

Nagg.   We had got engaged the day before.

Nell.   Engaged!

Nagg.   You were in such fits that we capsized. By rights we should have been drowned.

Nell.   It was because I felt happy.

---

[3] A popular lakeside resort area in northwest Italy.

Nagg *(Indignant).*   It was not, it was not, it was my story and nothing else. Happy! Don't you laugh at it still? Every time I tell it. Happy!

Nell.   It was deep, deep. And you could see down to the bottom. So white. So clean.

Nagg.   Let me tell it again. *(Raconteur's voice)* An Englishman, needing a pair of striped trousers in a hurry for the New Year festivities, goes to his tailor who takes his measurements. *(Tailor's voice)* "That's the lot, come back in four days, I'll have it ready." Good. Four days later. *(Tailor's voice)* "So sorry, come back in a week, I've made a mess of the seat." Good, that's all right, a neat seat can be very ticklish. A week later. *(Tailor's voice)* "Frightfully sorry, come back in ten days, I've made a hash of the crotch." Good, can't be helped, a snug crotch is always a teaser. Ten days later. *(Tailor's voice)* "Dreadfully sorry, come back in a fortnight, I've made a balls of the fly." Good, at a pinch, a smart fly is a stiff proposition. *(Pause. Normal voice)* I never told it worse. *(Pause. Gloomy)* I tell this story worse and worse. *(Pause. Raconteur's voice)* Well, to make it short, the bluebells are blowing and he ballockses the buttonholes. *(Customer's voice)* "God damn you to hell, Sir, no, it's indecent, there are limits! In six days, do you hear me, six days, God made the world. Yes Sir, no less Sir, the WORLD! And you are not bloody well capable of making me a pair of trousers in three months!" *(Tailor's voice, scandalized)* "But my dear Sir, my dear Sir, look — (Disdainful gesture, disgustedly) — at the world — (Pause) and look — (Loving gesture, proudly) — at my TROUSERS!" (Pause. He looks at Nell who has remained impassive, her eyes unseeing, breaks into a high forced laugh, cuts it short, pokes his head towards Nell, launches his laugh again)*

Hamm.   Silence! *(Nagg starts, cuts short his laugh)*

Nell.   You could see down to the bottom.

Hamm *(Exasperated).*   Have you not finished? Will you never finish? *(With sudden fury)* Will this never finish? *(Nagg disappears into his bin, closes the lid behind him. Nell does not move. Frenziedly)* My kingdom for a nightman! *(He whistles. Enter Clov)* Clear away this muck! Chuck it in the sea! *(Clov goes to bins, halts)*

Nell.   So white.

Hamm.   What? What's she blathering about? *(Clov stoops, takes Nell's hand, feels her pulse)*

Nell *(To Clov).*   Desert! *(Clov lets go her hand, pushes her back in the bin, closes the lid)*

Clov *(Returning to his place beside the chair).*   She has no pulse.

Hamm.   What was she drivelling about?

Clov.   She told me to go away, into the desert.

Hamm.   Damn busybody! Is that all?

Clov.   No.

Hamm.   What else?

Clov.   I didn't understand.

Hamm.   Have you bottled her?

Clov.   Yes.

Hamm.   Are they both bottled?

Clov.   Yes.

Hamm.   Screw down the lids. (*Clov goes towards door*) Time enough. (*Clov halts*) My anger subsides, I'd like to pee.

Clov (*With alacrity*).   I'll go and get the catheter. (*He goes towards door*)

Hamm.   Time enough. (*Clov halts*) Give me my pain-killer.

Clov.   It's too soon. (*Pause*) It's too soon on top of your tonic, it wouldn't act.

Hamm.   In the morning they brace you up and in the evening they calm you down. Unless it's the other way round. (*Pause*) That old doctor, he's dead naturally?

Clov.   He wasn't old.

Hamm.   But he's dead?

Clov.   Naturally. (*Pause*) You ask *me* that? (*Pause*)

Hamm.   Take me for a little turn. (*Clov goes behind the chair and pushes it forward*) Not too fast! (*Clov pushes chair*) Right round the world! (*Clov pushes chair*) Hug the walls, then back to the center again. (*Clov pushes chair*) I was right in the center, wasn't I?

Clov (*Pushing*).   Yes.

Hamm.   We'd need a proper wheel-chair. With big wheels. Bicycle wheels! (*Pause*) Are you hugging?

Clov (*Pushing*).   Yes.

Hamm (*Groping for wall*).   It's a lie! Why do you lie to me?

Clov (*Bearing closer to wall*).   There! There!

Hamm.   Stop! (*Clov stops chair close to back wall. Hamm lays his hand against wall*) Old wall! (*Pause*) Beyond is the . . . other hell. (*Pause. Violently*) Closer! Closer! Up against!

Clov.   Take away your hand. (*Hamm withdraws his hand. Clov rams chair against wall*) There! (*Hamm leans towards wall, applies his ear to it*)

Hamm.   Do you hear? (*He strikes the wall with his knuckles*) Do you hear? Hollow bricks! (*He strikes again*) All that's hollow! (*Pause. He straightens up. Violently*) That's enough. Back!

Clov.   We haven't done the round.

Hamm.   Back to my place! (*Clov pushes chair back to center*) Is that my place?

Clov.   Yes, that's your place.

Hamm.   Am I right in the center?

Clov.   I'll measure it.

Hamm.   More or less! More or less!

Clov (*Moving chair slightly*).   There!

Hamm.   I'm more or less in the center?

Clov.   I'd say so.

Hamm.   You'd say so! Put me right in the center!

Clov.   I'll go and get the tape.

Hamm.   Roughly! Roughly! (*Clov moves chair slightly*) Bang in the center!

Clov.   There! (*Pause*)

Hamm.   I feel a little too far to the left. (*Clov moves chair slightly*) Now I feel a little too far to the right. (*Clov moves chair slightly*) I feel a little too far forward. (*Clov moves chair slightly*) Now I feel a little too far back. (*Clov moves chair slightly*) Don't stay there (*i.e. behind the chair*), you give me the shivers. (*Clov returns to his place beside the chair*)

Clov.   If I could kill him I'd die happy. (*Pause*)

Hamm.   What's the weather like?

Clov.   As usual.

Hamm.   Look at the earth.

Clov.   I've looked.

Hamm.   With the glass?

Clov.   No need of the glass.

Hamm.   Look at it with the glass.

Clov.   I'll go and get the glass. (*Exit Clov*)

Hamm.   No need of the glass! (*Enter Clov with telescope*)

Clov.   I'm back again, with the glass. (*He goes to window right, looks up at it*) I need the steps.

Hamm.   Why? Have you shrunk? (*Exit Clov with telescope*) I don't like that, I don't like that. (*Enter Clov with ladder, but without telescope*)

Clov.   I'm back again, with the steps. (*He sets down ladder under window right, gets up on it, realizes he has not the telescope, gets down*) I need the glass. (*He goes towards door*)

Hamm (*Violently*).   But you have the glass!

Clov (*Halting, violently*).   No, I haven't the glass! (*Exit Clov*)

Hamm.   This is deadly. (*Enter Clov with telescope. He goes towards ladder*)

Clov.   Things are livening up. (*He gets up on ladder, raises the telescope, lets it fall*) I did it on purpose. (*He gets down, picks up the telescope, turns it on auditorium*) I see . . . a multitude . . . in transports . . . of joy. (*Pause*) That's what I call a magnifier. (*He lowers the telescope, turns towards Hamm*) Well? Don't we laugh?

Hamm (*After reflection*).   I don't.

Clov (*After reflection*).   Nor I. (*He gets up on ladder, turns the telescope on the without*) Let's see. (*He looks, moving the telescope*) Zero . . . (*He looks*) . . . zero . . . (*He looks*) . . . and zero.

Hamm.   Nothing stirs. All is —

Clov.   Zer —

Hamm (*Violently*).   Wait till you're spoken to! (*Normal voice*) All is . . . all is . . . all is what? (*Violently*) All is what?

Clov.   What all is? In a word? Is that what you want to know? Just a moment. (*He turns the telescope on the without, looks, lowers the telescope, turns towards Hamm*) Corpsed. (*Pause*) Well? Content?

Hamm.   Look at the sea.

Clov.   It's the same.

Hamm.   Look at the ocean! (*Clov gets down, takes a few steps towards window left, goes back for ladder, carries it over and sets it down under window* *left, gets up on it, turns the telescope on the without, looks at length. He starts, lowers the telescope, examines it, turns it again on the without)*

Clov.   Never seen anything like that!

Hamm *(Anxious)*.   What? A sail? A fin? Smoke?

Clov *(Looking)*.   The light is sunk.

Hamm *(Relieved)*.   Pah! We all knew that.

Clov *(Looking)*.   There was a bit left.

Hamm.   The base.

Clov *(Looking)*.   Yes.

Hamm.   And now?

Clov *(Looking)*.   All gone.

Hamm.   No gulls?

Clov *(Looking)*.   Gulls!

Hamm.   And the horizon? Nothing on the horizon?

Clov *(Lowering the telescope, turning towards Hamm, exasperated)*.   What in God's name could there be on the horizon? *(Pause)*

Hamm.   The waves, how are the waves?

Clov.   The waves? *(He turns the telescope on the waves)* Lead.

Hamm.   And the sun?

Clov *(Looking)*.   Zero.

Hamm.   But it should be sinking. Look again.

Clov *(Looking)*.   Damn the sun.

Hamm.   Is it night already then?

Clov *(Looking)*.   No.

Hamm.   Then what is it?

Clov *(Looking)*.   Gray. *(Lowering the telescope, turning towards Hamm, louder)* Gray! *(Pause. Still louder)* GRRAY! *(Pause. He gets down, approaches Hamm from behind, whispers in his ear)*

Hamm *(Starting)*.   Gray! Did I hear you say gray?

Clov.   Light black. From pole to pole.

Hamm.   You exaggerate. *(Pause)* Don't stay there, you give me the shivers. *(Clov returns to his place beside the chair)*

Clov.   Why this farce, day after day?

Hamm.   Routine. One never knows. *(Pause)* Last night I saw inside my breast. There was a big sore.

Clov.   Pah! You saw your heart.

Hamm.   No, it was living. *(Pause. Anguished)* Clov!

Clov.   Yes.

Hamm.   What's happening?

Clov.   Something is taking its course. *(Pause)*

Hamm.   Clov!

Clov *(Impatiently)*.   What is it?

Hamm.   We're not beginning to . . . to . . . mean something?

Clov.   Mean something! You and I, mean something! *(Brief laugh)* Ah that's a good one!

Hamm.   I wonder. *(Pause)* Imagine if a rational being came back to earth, wouldn't he be liable to get ideas into his head if he observed us long enough. (*Voice of rational being*) Ah, good, now I see what it is, yes, now I under-stand what they're at! (*Clov starts, drops the telescope and begins to scratch his belly with both hands. Normal voice*) And without going so far as that, we ourselves . . . (*With emotion*) . . . we ourselves . . . at certain moments . . . (*Vehemently*) To think perhaps it won't all have been for nothing!

Clov (*Anguished, scratching himself*). I have a flea!

Hamm.   A flea! Are there still fleas?

Clov.   On me there's one. (*Scratching*) Unless it's a crablouse.

Hamm (*Very perturbed*).   But humanity might start from there all over again! Catch him, for the love of God!

Clov.   I'll go and get the powder. (*Exit Clov*)

Hamm.   A flea! This is awful! What a day! (*Enter Clov with a sprinkling-tin*)

Clov.   I'm back again, with the insecticide.

Hamm.   Let him have it! (*Clov loosens the top of his trousers, pulls it forward and shakes powder into the aperture. He stoops, looks, waits, starts, frenziedly shakes more powder, stoops, looks, waits*)

Clov.   The bastard!

Hamm.   Did you get him?

Clov.   Looks like it. (*He drops the tin and adjusts his trousers*) Unless he's laying doggo.

Hamm.   Laying! Lying you mean. Unless he's *lying* doggo.

Clov.   Ah? One says lying? One doesn't say laying?

Hamm.   Use your head, can't you. If he was laying we'd be bitched.

Clov.   Ah. (*Pause*) What about that pee?

Hamm.   I'm having it.

Clov.   Ah that's the spirit, that's the spirit! (*Pause*)

Hamm (*With ardor*).   Let's go from here, the two of us! South! You can make a raft and the currents will carry us away, far away, to other . . . mammals!

Clov.   God forbid!

Hamm.   Alone, I'll embark alone! Get working on that raft immediately. Tomor-row I'll be gone for ever.

Clov (*Hastening towards door*).   I'll start straight away.

Hamm.   Wait! (*Clov halts*) Will there be sharks, do you think?

Clov.   Sharks? I don't know. If there are there will be. (*He goes towards door*)

Hamm.   Wait! (*Clov halts*) Is it not yet time for my pain-killer?

Clov (*Violently*).   No! (*He goes towards door*)

Hamm.   Wait! (*Clov halts*) How are your eyes?

Clov.   Bad.

Hamm.   But you can see.

Clov.   All I want.

Hamm.   How are your legs?

Clov.   Bad.

Hamm.   But you can walk.

Clov.   I come . . . and go.

Hamm. In my house. *(Pause. With prophetic relish)* One day you'll be blind, like me. You'll be sitting there, a speck in the void, in the dark, for ever, like me. *(Pause)* One day you'll say to yourself, I'm tired, I'll sit down, and you'll go and sit down. Then you'll say, I'm hungry, I'll get up and get something to eat. But you won't get up. You'll say, I shouldn't have sat down, but since I have I'll sit on a little longer, then I'll get up and get something to eat. But you won't get up and you won't get anything to eat. *(Pause)* You'll look at the wall a while, then you'll say, I'll close my eyes, perhaps have a little sleep, after that I'll feel better, and you'll close them. And when you open them again there'll be no wall any more. *(Pause)* Infinite emptiness will be all around you, all the resurrected dead of all the ages wouldn't fill it, and there you'll be like a little bit of grit in the middle of the steppe. *(Pause)* Yes, one day you'll know what it is, you'll be like me, except that you won't have anyone with you, because you won't have had pity on anyone and because there won't be anyone left to have pity on. *(Pause)*

Clov. It's not certain. *(Pause)* And there's one thing you forget.

Hamm. Ah?

Clov. I can't sit down.

Hamm *(Impatiently)*. Well you'll lie down then, what the hell! Or you'll come to a standstill, simply stop and stand still, the way you are now. One day you'll say, I'm tired, I'll stop. What does the attitude matter? *(Pause)*

Clov. So you all want me to leave you.

Hamm. Naturally.

Clov. Then I'll leave you.

Hamm. You can't leave us.

Clov. Then I won't leave you. *(Pause)*

Hamm. Why don't you finish us? *(Pause)* I'll tell you the combination of the cupboard if you promise to finish me.

Clov. I couldn't finish you.

Hamm. Then you won't finish me. *(Pause)*

Clov. I'll leave you, I have things to do.

Hamm. Do you remember when you came here?

Clov. No. Too small, you told me.

Hamm. Do you remember your father?

Clov *(Wearily)*. Same answer. *(Pause)* You've asked me these questions millions of times.

Hamm. I love the old questions. *(With fervor)* Ah the old questions, the old answers, there's nothing like them! *(Pause)* It was I was a father to you.

Clov. Yes. *(He looks at Hamm fixedly)* You were that to me.

Hamm. My house a home for you.

Clov. Yes. *(He looks about him)* This was that for me.

Hamm *(Proudly)*. But for me, *(Gesture towards himself)* no father. But for Hamm, *(Gesture towards surroundings)* no home. *(Pause)*

Clov. I'll leave you.

Hamm. Did you ever think of one thing?

Clov. Never.

Hamm. That here we're down in a hole. *(Pause)* But beyond the hills? Eh? Perhaps it's still green. Eh? *(Pause)* Flora! Pomona! *(Ecstatically)* Ceres![4] *(Pause)* Perhaps you won't need to go very far.

Clov. I can't go very far. *(Pause)* I'll leave you.

Hamm. Is my dog ready?

Clov. He lacks a leg.

Hamm. Is he silky?

Clov. He's a kind of Pomeranian.

Hamm. Go and get him.

Clov. He lacks a leg.

Hamm. Go and get him! *(Exit Clov)* We're getting on. *(Enter Clov holding by one of its three legs a black toy dog)*

Clov. Your dogs are here. *(He hands the dog to Hamm who feels it, fondles it)*

Hamm. He's white, isn't he?

Clov. Nearly.

Hamm. What do you mean, nearly? Is he white or isn't he?

Clov. He isn't. *(Pause)*

Hamm. You've forgotten the sex.

Clov *(Vexed)*. But he isn't finished. The sex goes on at the end. *(Pause)*

Hamm. You haven't put on his ribbon.

Clov *(Angrily)*. But he isn't finished, I tell you! First you finish your dog and then you put on his ribbon! *(Pause)*

Hamm. Can he stand?

Clov. I don't know.

Hamm. Try. *(He hands the dog to Clov who places it on the ground)* Well?

Clov. Wait! *(He squats down and tries to get the dog to stand on its three legs, fails, lets it go. The dog falls on its side)*

Hamm *(Impatiently)*. Well?

Clov. He's standing.

Hamm *(Groping for the dog)*. Where? Where is he? *(Clov holds up the dog in a standing position)*

Clov. There. *(He takes Hamm's hand and guides it towards the dog's head)*

Hamm *(His hand on the dog's head)*. Is he gazing at me?

Clov. Yes.

Hamm *(Proudly)*. As if he were asking me to take him for a walk?

Clov. If you like.

Hamm *(As before)*. Or as if he were begging me for a bone. *(He withdraws his hand)* Leave him like that, standing there imploring me. *(Clov straightens up. The dog falls on its side)*

Clov. I'll leave you.

Hamm. Have you had your visions?

---

[4] Flora is the goddess of flowers; Pomona is the goddess of fruit; Ceres is the goddess of grain and harvests.

Clov. Less.

Hamm. Is Mother Pegg's light on?

Clov. Light! How could anyone's light be on?

Hamm. Extinguished!

Clov. Naturally it's extinguished. If it's not on it's extinguished.

Hamm. No, I mean Mother Pegg.

Clov. But naturally she's extinguished! *(Pause)* What's the matter with you today?

Hamm. I'm taking my course. *(Pause)* Is she buried?

Clov. Buried! Who would have buried her?

Hamm. You.

Clov. Me! Haven't I enough to do without burying people?

Hamm. But you'll bury me.

Clov. No I won't bury you. *(Pause)*

Hamm. She was bonny once, like a flower of the field. *(With reminiscent leer)* And a great one for the men!

Clov. We too were bonny — once. It's a rare thing not to have been bonny — once. *(Pause)*

Hamm. Go and get the gaff. *(Clov goes to door, halts)*

Clov. Do this, do that, and I do it. I never refuse. Why?

Hamm. You're not able to.

Clov. Soon I won't do it any more.

Hamm. You won't be able to any more. *(Exit Clov)* Ah the creatures, the creatures, everything has to be explained to them. *(Enter Clov with gaff)*

Clov. Here's your gaff. Stick it up. *(He gives the gaff to Hamm who, wielding it like a puntpole, tries to move his chair)*

Hamm. Did I move?

Clov. No. *(Hamm throws down the gaff)*

Hamm. Go and get the oilcan.

Clov. What for?

Hamm. To oil the casters.

Clov. I oiled them yesterday.

Hamm. Yesterday! What does that mean? Yesterday!

Clov *(Violently)*. That means that bloody awful day, long ago, before this bloody awful day. I use the words you taught me. If they don't mean anything any more, teach me others. Or let me be silent. *(Pause)*

Hamm. I once knew a madman who thought the end of the world had come. He was a painter — and engraver. I had a great fondness for him. I used to go and see him, in the asylum. I'd take him by the hand and drag him to the window. Look! There! All that rising corn! And there! Look! The sails of the herring fleet! All that loveliness! *(Pause)* He'd snatch away his hand and go back into his corner. Appalled. All he had seen was ashes. *(Pause)* He alone had been spared. *(Pause)* Forgotten. *(Pause)* It appears the case is . . . was not so . . . so unusual.

Clov. A madman? When was that?

Hamm. Oh way back, way back, you weren't in the land of the living.

Clov. God be with the days! *(Pause. Hamm raises his toque)*

Hamm. I had a great fondness for him. *(Pause. He puts on his toque again)* He was a painter — and engraver.

Clov. There are so many terrible things.

Hamm. No, no, there are not so many now. *(Pause)* Clov!

Clov. Yes.

Hamm. Do you not think this has gone on long enough?

Clov. Yes! *(Pause)* What?

Hamm. This . . . this . . . thing.

Clov. I've always thought so. *(Pause)* You not?

Hamm *(Gloomily).* Then it's a day like any other day.

Clov. As long as it lasts. *(Pause)* All life long the same inanities.

Hamm. I can't leave you.

Clov. I know. And you can't follow me. *(Pause)*

Hamm. If you leave me how shall I know?

Clov *(Briskly).* Well you simply whistle me and if I don't come running it means I've left you. *(Pause)*

Hamm. You won't come and kiss me goodbye?

Clov. Oh I shouldn't think so. *(Pause)*

Hamm. But you might be merely dead in your kitchen.

Clov. The result would be the same.

Hamm. Yes, but how would I know, if you were merely dead in your kitchen?

Clov. Well . . . sooner or later I'd start to stink.

Hamm. You stink already. The whole place stinks of corpses.

Clov. The whole universe.

Hamm *(Angrily).* To hell with the universe. *(Pause)* Think of something.

Clov. What?

Hamm. An idea, have an idea. *(Angrily)* A bright idea!

Clov. Ah good. *(He starts pacing to and fro, his eyes fixed on the ground, his hands behind his back. He halts)* The pains in my legs! It's unbelievable! Soon I won't be able to think any more.

Hamm. You won't be able to leave me. *(Clov resumes his pacing)* What are you doing?

Clov. Having an idea. *(He paces)* Ah! *(He halts)*

Hamm. What a brain! *(Pause)* Well?

Clov. Wait! *(He meditates. Not very convinced)* Yes . . . *(Pause. More convinced)* Yes! *(He raises his head)* I have it! I set the alarm. *(Pause)*

Hamm. This is perhaps not one of my bright days, but frankly —

Clov. You whistle me. I don't come. The alarm rings. I'm gone. It doesn't ring. I'm dead. *(Pause)*

Hamm. Is it working? *(Pause. Impatiently)* The alarm, is it working?

Clov. Why wouldn't it be working?

Hamm. Because it's worked too much.

Clov. But it's hardly worked at all.

Hamm *(Angrily).* Then because it's worked too little!

Clov. I'll go and see. *(Exit Clov. Brief ring of alarm off. Enter Clov with alarm-clock. *He holds it against Hamm's ear and releases alarm. They listen to it ringing to the end. Pause)* Fit to wake the dead! Did you hear it?

Hamm.   Vaguely.

Clov.   The end is terrific!

Hamm.   I prefer the middle. *(Pause)* Is it not time for my pain-killer?

Clov.   No! *(He goes to door, turns)* I'll leave you.

Hamm.   It's time for my story. Do you want to listen to my story?

Clov.   No.

Hamm.   Ask my father if he wants to listen to my story. *(Clov goes to bins, raises the lid of Nagg's, stoops, looks into it. Pause. He straightens up)*

Clov.   He's asleep.

Hamm.   Wake him. *(Clov stoops, wakes Nagg with the alarm. Unintelligible words. Clov straightens up)*

Clov.   He doesn't want to listen to your story.

Hamm.   I'll give him a bon-bon. *(Clov stoops. As before)*

Clov.   He wants a sugar-plum.

Hamm.   He'll get a sugar-plum. *(Clov stoops. As before)*

Clov.   It's a deal. *(He goes towards door. Nagg's hands appear, gripping the rim. Then the head emerges. Clov reaches door, turns)* Do you believe in the life to come?

Hamm.   Mine was always that. *(Exit Clov)* Got him that time!

Nagg.   I'm listening.

Hamm.   Scoundrel! Why did you engender me?

Nagg.   I didn't know.

Hamm.   What? What didn't you know?

Nagg.   That it'd be you. *(Pause)* You'll give me a sugar-plum?

Hamm.   After the audition.

Nagg.   You swear?

Hamm.   Yes.

Nagg.   On what?

Hamm.   My honor. *(Pause. They laugh heartily)*

Nagg.   Two.

Hamm.   One.

Nagg.   One for me and one for —

Hamm.   One! Silence! *(Pause)* Where was I? *(Pause. Gloomily)* It's finished, we're finished. *(Pause)* Nearly finished. *(Pause)* There'll be no more speech. *(Pause)* Something dripping in my head, ever since the fontanelles. *(Stifled hilarity of Nagg)* Splash, splash, always on the same spot. *(Pause)* Perhaps it's a little vein. *(Pause)* A little artery. *(Pause. More animated)* Enough of that, it's story time, where was I? *(Pause. Narrative tone)* The man came crawling towards me, on his belly. Pale, wonderfully pale and thin, he seemed on the point of — *(Pause. Normal tone)* No. I've done that bit. *(Pause. Narrative tone)* I calmly filled my pipe — the meerschaum, lit it with . . . let us say a vesta, drew a few puffs. Aah! *(Pause)* Well, what is it *you* want? *(Pause)* It was an extraordinarily bitter day, I remember, zero by the thermometer. But considering it was

Christmas Eve there was nothing . . . extraordinary about that. Seasonable weather, for once in a way. *(Pause)* Well, what ill wind blows you my way? He raised his face to me, black with mingled dirt and tears. *(Pause. Normal tone)* That should do it. *(Narrative tone)* No no, don't look at me, don't look at me. He dropped his eyes and mumbled something, apologies I presume. *(Pause)* I'm a busy man, you know, the final touches, before the festivities, you know what it is. *(Pause. Forcibly)* Come on now, what is the object of this invasion? *(Pause)* It was a glorious bright day, I remember, fifty by the heliometer, but already the sun was sinking down into the . . . down among the dead. *(Normal tone)* Nicely put, that. *(Narrative tone)* Come on now, come on, present your petition and let me resume my labors. *(Pause. Normal tone)* There's English for you. Ah well . . . *(Narrative tone)* It was then he took the plunge. It's my little one, he said. Tsstss, a little one, that's bad. My little boy, he said, as if the sex mattered. Where did he come from? He named the hole. A good half-day, on horse. What are you insinuating? That the place is still inhabited? No, no, not a soul, except himself and the child — assuming he existed. Good. I inquired about the situation at Kov, beyond the gulf. Not a sinner. Good. And you expect me to believe you have left your little one back there, all alone, and alive into the bargain? Come now! *(Pause)* It was a howling wild day, I remember, a hundred by the anemometer. The wind was tearing up the dead pines and sweeping them . . . away. *(Pause. Normal tone)* A bit feeble, that. *(Narrative tone)* Come on, man, speak up, what is it you want from me, I have to put up my holly. *(Pause)* Well to make it short it finally transpired that what he wanted from me was . . . bread for his brat? Bread? But I have no bread, it doesn't agree with me. Good. Then perhaps a little corn? *(Pause. Normal tone)* That should do it. *(Narrative tone)* Corn, yes, I have corn, it's true, in my granaries. But use your head. I give you some corn, a pound, a pound and a half, you bring it back to your child and you make him — if he's still alive — a nice pot of porridge, *(Nagg reacts)* a nice pot and a half of porridge, full of nourishment. Good. The colors come back into his little cheeks — perhaps. And then? *(Pause)* I lost patience. *(Violently)* Use your head, can't you, use your head, you're on earth, there's no cure for that! *(Pause)* It was an exceedingly dry day, I remember, zero by the hygrometer. Ideal weather, for my lumbago. *(Pause. Violently)* But what in God's name do you imagine? That the earth will awake in spring? That the rivers and seas will run with fish again? That there's manna in heaven still for imbeciles like you? *(Pause)* Gradually I cooled down, sufficiently at least to ask him how long he had taken on the way. Three whole days. Good. In what condition he had left the child. Deep in sleep. *(Forcibly)* But deep in what sleep, deep in what sleep already? *(Pause)* Well to make it short I finally offered to take him into my service. He had touched a chord. And then I imagined already that I wasn't much longer for this world. *(He laughs. Pause)* Well? *(Pause)* Well? Here if you were careful you might die a nice natural death, in peace and comfort. *(Pause)* Well? *(Pause)* In the end he asked me would I consent to take in the child as well — if he were still alive. *(Pause)* It was the moment I was waiting for. *(Pause)* Would I consent to take in the child . . . *(Pause)* I can see him still, down on his knees, his hands flat on the ground, glaring at me with his mad eyes, in defiance of my wishes. *(Pause. Normal tone)* I'll soon have finished with this story. *(Pause)* Unless I bring in other characters. *(Pause)* But where would I find them? *(Pause)* Where would I look for them? *(Pause. He whistles. Enter Clov)* Let us pray to God.

Nagg.   Me sugar-plum!

Clov.   There's a rat in the kitchen!

Hamm.   A rat! Are there still rats?

Clov.   In the kitchen there's one.

Hamm.   And you haven't exterminated him?

Clov.   Half. You disturbed us.

Hamm.   He can't get away?

Clov.   No.

Hamm.   You'll finish him later. Let us pray to God.

Clov.   Again!

Nagg.   Me sugar-plum!

Hamm.   God first! *(Pause)* Are you right?

Clov *(Resigned)*.   Off we go.

Hamm *(To Nagg)*.   And you?

Nagg *(Clasping his hands, closing his eyes, in a gabble)*.   Our Father which art —

Hamm.   Silence! In silence! Where are your manners? *(Pause)* Off we go. *(Attitudes of prayer. Silence. Abandoning his attitude, discouraged)* Well?

Clov *(Abandoning his attitude)*.   What a hope! And you?

Hamm.   Sweet damn all! *(To Nagg)* And you?

Nagg.   Wait! *(Pause. Abandoning his attitude)* Nothing doing!

Hamm.   The bastard! He doesn't exist!

Clov.   Not yet.

Nagg.   Me sugar-plum!

Hamm.   There are no more sugar-plums! *(Pause)*

Nagg.   It's natural. After all I'm your father. It's true if it hadn't been me it would have been someone else. But that's no excuse. *(Pause)* Turkish Delight, for example, which no longer exists, we all know that, there is nothing in the world I love more. And one day I'll ask you for some, in return for a kindness, and you'll promise it to me. One must live with the times. *(Pause)* Whom did you call when you were a tiny boy, and were frightened, in the dark? Your mother? No. Me. We let you cry. Then we moved you out of earshot, so that we might sleep in peace. *(Pause)* I was asleep, as happy as a king, and you woke me up to have me listen to you. It wasn't indispensable, you didn't really need to have me listen to you. *(Pause)* I hope the day will come when you'll really need to have me listen to you, and need to hear my voice, any voice. *(Pause)* Yes, I hope I'll live till then, to hear you calling me like when you were a tiny boy, and were frightened, in the dark, and I was your only hope. *(Pause. Nagg knocks on lid of Nell's bin. Pause)* Nell! *(Pause. He knocks louder. Pause. Louder)* Nell! *(Pause. Nagg sinks back into his bin, closes the lid behind him. Pause)*

Hamm.   Our revels now are ended.[5] *(He gropes for the dog)* The dog's gone.

Clov.   He's not a real dog, he can't go.

Hamm *(Groping)*.   He's not there.

Clov.   He's lain down.

Hamm.   Give him up to me. *(Clov picks up the dog and gives it to Hamm. Hamm holds it in his arms. Pause. Hamm throws away the dog)* Dirty brute! *(Clov begins to pick up the objects lying on the ground)* What are you doing?

Clov.   Putting things in order. *(He straightens up. Fervently)* I'm going to clear everything away! *(He starts picking up again)*

Hamm.   Order!

Clov *(Straightening up)*.   I love order. It's my dream. A world where all would be silent and still and each thing in its last place, under the last dust. *(He starts picking up again)*

Hamm *(Exasperated)*.   What in God's name do you think you are doing?

Clov *(Straightening up)*.   I'm doing my best to create a little order.

Hamm.   Drop it! *(Clov drops the objects he has picked up)*

Clov.   After all, there or elsewhere. *(He goes towards door)*

Hamm *(Irritably)*.   What's wrong with your feet?

Clov.   My feet?

Hamm.   Tramp! Tramp!

Clov.   I must have put on my boots.

Hamm.   Your slippers were hurting you? *(Pause)*

Clov.   I'll leave you.

Hamm.   No!

Clov.   What is there to keep me here?

Hamm.   The dialogue. *(Pause)* I've got on with my story. *(Pause)* I've got on with it well. *(Pause. Irritably)* Ask me where I've got to.

Clov.   Oh, by the way, your story?

Hamm *(Surprised)*.   What story?

Clov.   The one you've been telling yourself all your days.

Hamm.   Ah you mean my chronicle?

Clov.   That's the one. *(Pause)*

Hamm *(Angrily)*.   Keep going, can't you, keep going!

Clov.   You've got on with it, I hope.

Hamm *(Modestly)*.   Oh not very far, not very far. *(He sighs)* There are days like that, one isn't inspired. *(Pause)* Nothing you can do about it, just wait for it to come. *(Pause)* No forcing, no forcing, it's fatal. *(Pause)* I've got on with it a little all the same. *(Pause)* Technique, you know. *(Pause. Irritably)* I say I've got on with it a little all the same.

Clov *(Admiringly)*.   Well I never! In spite of everything you were able to get on with it!

---

[5] From Shakespeare, *The Tempest*, Act IV, Scene 1. With this line, Prospero interrupts and ends a pageant featuring pagan fertility figures. Later in the speech, he says, "We are such stuff / As dreams are made on, and our little life / Is rounded with a sleep."

Hamm (*Modestly*).   Oh not very far, you know, not very far, but nevertheless, better than nothing.

Clov.   Better than nothing! Is it possible?

Hamm.   I'll tell you how it goes. He comes crawling on his belly —

Clov.   Who?

Hamm.   What?

Clov.   Who do you mean, he?

Hamm.   Who do I mean! Yet another.

Clov.   Ah him! I wasn't sure.

Hamm.   Crawling on his belly, whining for bread for his brat. He's offered a job as gardener. Before — (*Clov bursts out laughing*) What is there so funny about that?

Clov.   A job as gardener!

Hamm.   Is that what tickles you?

Clov.   It must be that.

Hamm.   It wouldn't be the bread?

Clov.   Or the brat. (*Pause*)

Hamm.   The whole thing is comical, I grant you that. What about having a good guffaw the two of us together?

Clov (*After reflection*).   I couldn't guffaw again today.

Hamm (*After reflection*).   Nor I. (*Pause*) I continue then. Before accepting with gratitude he asks if he may have his little boy with him.

Clov.   What age?

Hamm.   Oh tiny.

Clov.   He would have climbed the trees.

Hamm.   All the little odd jobs.

Clov.   And then he would have grown up.

Hamm.   Very likely. (*Pause*)

Clov.   Keep going, can't you, keep going!

Hamm.   That's all. I stopped there. (*Pause*)

Clov.   Do you see how it goes on.

Hamm.   More or less.

Clov.   Will it not soon be the end?

Hamm.   I'm afraid it will.

Clov.   Pah! You'll make up another.

Hamm.   I don't know. (*Pause*) I feel rather drained. (*Pause*) The prolonged creative effort. (*Pause*) If I could drag myself down to the sea! I'd make a pillow of sand for my head and the tide would come.

Clov.   There's no more tide. (*Pause*)

Hamm.   Go and see is she dead. (*Clov goes to bins, raises the lid of Nell's, stoops, looks into it. Pause*)

Clov.   Looks like it. (*He closes the lid, straightens up. Hamm raises his toque. Pause. He puts it on again*)

Hamm (*With his hand to his toque*).   And Nagg? (*Clov raises lid of Nagg's bin, stoops, looks into it. Pause*)

Clov. Doesn't look like it. (*He closes the lid, straightens up*)

Hamm (*Letting go his toque*). What's he doing? (*Clov raises lid of Nagg's bin, stoops, looks into it. Pause*)

Clov. He's crying. (*He closes lid, straightens up*)

Hamm. Then he's living. (*Pause*) Did you ever have an instant of happiness?

Clov. Not to my knowledge. (*Pause*)

Hamm. Bring me under the window. (*Clov goes towards chair*) I want to feel the light on my face. (*Clov pushes chair*) Do you remember, in the beginning, when you took me for a turn? You used to hold the chair too high. At every step you nearly tipped me out. (*With senile quaver*) Ah great fun, we had, the two of us, great fun. (*Gloomily*) And then we got into the way of it. (*Clov stops the chair under window right*) There already? (*Pause. He tilts back his head*) Is it light?

Clov. It isn't dark.

Hamm (*Angrily*). I'm asking you is it light.

Clov. Yes. (*Pause*)

Hamm. The curtain isn't closed?

Clov. No.

Hamm. What window is it?

Clov. The earth.

Hamm. I knew it! (*Angrily*) But there's no light there! The other! (*Clov pushes chair towards window left*) The earth! (*Clov stops the chair under window left. Hamm tilts back his head*) That's what I call light! (*Pause*) Feels like a ray of sunshine. (*Pause*) No?

Clov. No.

Hamm. It isn't a ray of sunshine I feel on my face?

Clov. No. (*Pause*)

Hamm. Am I very white? (*Pause. Angrily*) I'm asking you am I very white!

Clov. Not more so than usual. (*Pause*)

Hamm. Open the window.

Clov. What for?

Hamm. I want to hear the sea.

Clov. You wouldn't hear it.

Hamm. Even if you opened the window?

Clov. No.

Hamm. Then it's not worthwhile opening it?

Clov. No.

Hamm (*Violently*). Then open it! (*Clov gets up on the ladder, opens the window. Pause*) Have you opened it?

Clov. Yes. (*Pause*)

Hamm. You swear you've opened it?

Clov. Yes. (*Pause*)

Hamm. Well . . . ! (*Pause*) It must be very calm. (*Pause. Violently*) I'm asking you is it very calm!

Clov. Yes.

Hamm.   It's because there are no more navigators. *(Pause)* You haven't much conversation all of a sudden. Do you not feel well?

Clov.   I'm cold.

Hamm.   What month are we? *(Pause)* Close the window, we're going back. *(Clov closes the window, gets down, pushes the chair back to its place, remains standing behind it, head bowed)* Don't stay there, you give me the shivers! *(Clov returns to his place beside the chair)* Father! *(Pause. Louder)* Father! *(Pause)* Go and see did he hear me. *(Clov goes to Nagg's bin, raises the lid, stoops. Unintelligible words. Clov straightens up)*

Clov.   Yes.

Hamm.   Both times? *(Clov stoops. As before)*

Clov.   Once only.

Hamm.   The first time or the second? *(Clov stoops. As before)*

Clov.   He doesn't know.

Hamm.   It must have been the second.

Clov.   We'll never know. *(He closes lid)*

Hamm.   Is he still crying?

Clov.   No.

Hamm.   The dead go fast. *(Pause)* What's he doing?

Clov.   Sucking his biscuit.

Hamm.   Life goes on. *(Clov returns to his place beside the chair)* Give me a rug, I'm freezing.

Clov.   There are no more rugs. *(Pause)*

Hamm.   Kiss me. *(Pause)* Will you not kiss me?

Clov.   No.

Hamm.   On the forehead.

Clov.   I won't kiss you anywhere. *(Pause)*

Hamm *(Holding out his hand)*.   Give me your hand at least. *(Pause)* Will you not give me your hand?

Clov.   I won't touch you. *(Pause)*

Hamm.   Give me the dog. *(Clov looks round for the dog)* No!

Clov.   Do you not want your dog?

Hamm.   No.

Clov.   Then I'll leave you.

Hamm *(Head bowed, absently)*.   That's right. *(Clov goes to door, turns)*

Clov.   If I don't kill that rat he'll die.

Hamm *(As before)*.   That's right. *(Exit Clov. Pause)* Me to play. *(He takes out his handkerchief, unfolds it, holds it spread out before him)* We're getting on. *(Pause)* You weep, and weep, for nothing, so as not to laugh, and little by little . . . you begin to grieve. *(He folds the handkerchief, puts it back in his pocket, raises his head)* All those I might have helped. *(Pause)* Helped! *(Pause)* Saved. *(Pause)* Saved! *(Pause)* The place was crawling with them! *(Pause. Violently)* Use your head, can't you, use your head, you're on earth, there's no cure for that! *(Pause)* Get out of here and love one another! Lick your neighbor as yourself! *(Pause. Calmer)* When it wasn't bread they wanted it was crumpets.

(Pause. Violently) Out of my sight and back to your petting parties! *(Pause)* All that, all that! *(Pause)* Not even a real dog! *(Calmer)* The end is in the beginning and yet you go on. *(Pause)* Perhaps I could go on with my story, end it and begin another. *(Pause)* Perhaps I could throw myself out on the floor. *(He pushes himself painfully off his seat, falls back again)* Dig my nails into the cracks and drag myself forward with my fingers. *(Pause)* It will be the end and there I'll be, wondering what can have brought it on and wondering what can have . . . *(He hesitates)* . . . why it was so long coming. *(Pause)* There I'll be, in the old shelter, along against the silence and . . . *(He hesitates)* the stillness. If I can hold my peace, and sit quiet, it will be all over with sound, and motion, all over and done with. *(Pause)* I'll have called my father and I'll have called my . . . *(He hesitates)* my son. And even twice, or three times, in case they shouldn't have heard me, the first time, or the second. *(Pause)* I'll say to myself, He'll come back. *(Pause)* And then? *(Pause)* And then? *(Pause)* He couldn't, he has gone too far. *(Pause)* And then? *(Pause. Very agitated)* All kinds of fantasies! That I'm being watched! A rat! Steps! Breath held and then . . . *(He breathes out)* Then babble, babble, words, like the solitary child who turns himself into children, two, three, so as to be together, and whisper together, in the dark. *(Pause)* Moment upon moment, pattering down, like the millet grains of . . . *(He hesitates)* . . . that old Greek,[6] and all life long you wait for that to mount up to a life. *(Pause. He opens his mouth to continue, renounces)* Ah let's get it over! *(He whistles. Enter Clov with alarm-clock. He halts beside the chair)* What? Neither gone nor dead?

Clov. In spirit only.

Hamm. Which?

Clov. Both.

Hamm. Gone from me you'd be dead.

Clov. And vice versa.

Hamm. Outside of here it's death! *(Pause)* And the rat?

Clov. He's got away.

Hamm. He can't go far. *(Pause. Anxious)* Eh?

Clov. He doesn't need to go far. *(Pause)*

Hamm. Is it not time for my pain-killer?

Clov. Yes.

Hamm. Ah! At last! Give it to me! Quick! *(Pause)*

Clov. There's no more pain-killer. *(Pause)*

Hamm *(Appalled)*. Good . . . ! *(Pause)* No more pain-killer!

Clov. No more pain-killer. You'll never get any more pain-killer. *(Pause)*

Hamm. But the little round box. It was full!

Clov. Yes. But now it's empty. *(Pause. Clov starts to move about the room. He is looking for a place to put down the alarm-clock)*

Hamm *(Soft)*. What'll I do? *(Pause. In a scream)* What'll I do? *(Clov sees the

---

[6] Identified by Professor Ruby Cohn as Eubulides of Miletus (4th century B.C.), who wrote: "One grain of corn is not a heap. Add a grain and there is yet no heap. When does a heap begin?"

picture, takes it down, stands it on the floor with its face to the wall, hangs up the alarm-clock in its place) What are you doing?

Clov. Winding up.

Hamm. Look at the earth.

Clov. Again!

Hamm. Since it's calling to you.

Clov. Is your throat sore? *(Pause)* Would you like a lozenge? *(Pause)* No. *(Pause)* Pity. *(Clov goes, humming, towards window right, halts before it, looks up at it)*

Hamm. Don't sing.

Clov *(Turning towards Hamm).*   One hasn't the right to sing anymore?

Hamm. No.

Clov. Then how can it end?

Hamm. You want it to end?

Clov. I want to sing.

Hamm. I can't prevent you. *(Pause. Clov turns towards window right)*

Clov. What did I do with that steps? *(He looks around for ladder)* You didn't see that steps? *(He sees it)* Ah, about time. *(He goes towards window left)* Sometimes I wonder if I'm in my right mind. Then it passes over and I'm as lucid as before. *(He gets up on ladder, looks out of window)* Christ, she's under water! *(He looks)* How can that be? *(He pokes forward his head, his hand above his eyes)* It hasn't rained. *(He wipes the pane, looks. Pause)* Ah what a fool I am! I'm on the wrong side! *(He gets down, takes a few steps towards window right)* Under water! *(He goes back for ladder)* What a fool I am! *(He carries ladder towards window right)* Sometimes I wonder if I'm in my right senses. Then it passes off and I'm as intelligent as ever. *(He sets down ladder under window right, gets up on it, looks out of window. He turns towards Hamm)* Any particular sector you fancy? Or merely the whole thing?

Hamm. Whole thing.

Clov. The general effect? Just a moment. *(He looks out of window. Pause)*

Hamm. Clov.

Clov *(Absorbed).*   Mmm.

Hamm. Do you know what it is?

Clov *(As before).*   Mmm.

Hamm. I was never there. *(Pause)* Clov!

Clov *(Turning towards Hamm, exasperated).*   What is it?

Hamm. I was never there.

Clov. Lucky for you. *(He looks out of window)*

Hamm. Absent, always. It all happened without me. I don't know what's happened. *(Pause)* Do you know what's happened? *(Pause)* Clov!

Clov *(Turning towards Hamm, exasperated).*   Do you want me to look at this muckheap, yes or no?

Hamm. Answer me first.

Clov. What?

Hamm. Do you know what's happened?

Clov. When? Where?

Hamm (*Violently*).   When! What's happened? Use your head, can't you! What has happened?

Clov.   What for Christ's sake does it matter? (*He looks out of window*)

Hamm.   I don't know. (*Pause. Clov turns towards Hamm*)

Clov (*Harshly*).   When old Mother Pegg asked you for oil for her lamp and you told her to get out to hell, you knew what was happening then, no? (*Pause*) You know what she died of, Mother Pegg? Of darkness.

Hamm (*Feebly*).   I hadn't any.

Clov (*As before*).   Yes, you had. (*Pause*)

Hamm.   Have you the glass?

Clov.   No, it's clear enough as it is.

Hamm.   Go and get it. (*Pause. Clov casts up his eyes, brandishes his fists. He loses balance, clutches on to the ladder. He starts to get down, halts*)

Clov.   There's one thing I'll never understand. (*He gets down*) Why I always obey you. Can you explain that to me?

Hamm.   No. . . . Perhaps it's compassion. (*Pause*) A kind of great compassion. (*Pause*) Oh you won't find it easy, you won't find it easy. (*Pause. Clov begins to move about the room in search of the telescope*)

Clov.   I'm tired of our goings on, very tired. (*He searches*) You're not sitting on it? (*He moves the chair, looks at the place where it stood, resumes his search*)

Hamm (*Anguished*).   Don't leave me there! (*Angrily Clov restores the chair to its place*) Am I right in the center?

Clov.   You'd need a microscope to find this — (*He sees the telescope*) Ah, about time. (*He picks up the telescope, gets up on the ladder, turns the telescope on the without*)

Hamm.   Give me the dog.

Clov (*Looking*).   Quiet!

Hamm (*Angrily*).   Give me the dog! (*Clov drops the telescope, clasps his hands to his head. Pause. He gets down precipitately, looks for the dog, sees it, picks it up, hastens towards Hamm and strikes him violently on the head with the dog*)

Clov.   There's your dog for you! (*The dog falls to the ground. Pause*)

Hamm.   He hit me!

Clov.   You drive me mad, I'm mad!

Hamm.   If you must hit me, hit me with the ax. (*Pause*) Or with the gaff, hit me with the gaff. Not with the dog. With the gaff. Or with the ax. (*Clov picks up the dog and gives it to Hamm who takes it in his arms*)

Clov (*Imploringly*).   Let's stop playing!

Hamm.   Never! (*Pause*) Put me in my coffin.

Clov.   There are no more coffins.

Hamm.   Then let it end! (*Clov goes towards ladder*) With a bang! (*Clov gets up on ladder, gets down again, looks for telescope, sees it, picks it up, gets up ladder, raises telescope*) Of darkness! And me? Did anyone ever have pity on me?

Clov (*Lowering the telescope, turning towards Hamm*).   What? (*Pause*) Is it me you're referring to?

Hamm (*Angrily*).   An aside, ape! Did you never hear an aside before? (*Pause*) I'm warming up for my last soliloquy.

Clov. I warn you. I'm going to look at this filth since it's an order. But it's the last time. *(He turns the telescope on the without)* Let's see. *(He moves the telescope)* Nothing . . . nothing . . . good . . . good . . . nothing . . . goo — *(He starts, lowers the telescope, examines it, turns it again on the without. Pause)* Bad luck to it!

Hamm. More complications! *(Clov gets down)* Not an underplot, I trust. *(Clov moves ladder nearer window, gets up on it, turns telescope on the without)*

Clov *(Dismayed)*. Looks like a small boy!

Hamm *(Sarcastic)*. A small . . . boy!

Clov. I'll go and see. *(He gets down, drops the telescope, goes towards door, turns)* I'll take the gaff. *(He looks for the gaff, sees it, picks it up, hastens towards door)*

Hamm. No! *(Clov halts)*

Clov. No? A potential procreator?

Hamm. If he exists he'll die there or he'll come here. And if he doesn't . . . *(Pause)*

Clov. You don't believe me? You think I'm inventing? *(Pause)*

Hamm. It's the end, Clov, we've come to the end. I don't need you any more. *(Pause)*

Clov. Lucky for you. *(He goes towards door)*

Hamm. Leave me the gaff. *(Clov gives him the gaff, goes towards door, halts, looks at alarm-clock, takes it down, looks round for a better place to put it, goes to bins, puts it on lid of Nagg's bin. Pause)*

Clov. I'll leave you. *(He goes towards door)*

Hamm. Before you go . . . *(Clov halts near door)* . . . say something.

Clov. There is nothing to say.

Hamm. A few words . . . to ponder . . . in my heart.

Clov. Your heart!

Hamm. Yes. *(Pause. Forcibly)* Yes! *(Pause)* With the rest, in the end, the shadows, the murmurs, all the trouble, to end up with. *(Pause)* Clov. . . . He never spoke to me. Then, in the end, before he went, without my having asked him, he spoke to me. He said . . .

Clov *(Despairingly)*. Ah . . . !

Hamm. Something . . . from your heart.

Clov. My heart!

Hamm. A few words . . . from your heart. *(Pause)*

Clov *(Fixed gaze, tonelessly, towards auditorium)*. They said to me, That's love, yes, yes, not a doubt, now you see how —

Hamm. Articulate!

Clov *(As before)*. How easy it is. They said to me, That's friendship, yes, yes, no question, you've found it. They said to me, Here's the place, stop, raise your head and look at all that beauty. That order! They said to me, Come now, you're not a brute beast, think upon these things and you'll see how all becomes clear. And simple! They said to me, What skilled attention they get, all these dying of their wounds.

Hamm. Enough!

Clov *(As before)*. I say to myself — sometimes, Clov, you must learn to suffer better than that if you want them to weary of punishing you — one day. I say to myself — sometimes, Clov, you must be there better than that if you want them to let you go — one day. But I feel too old, and too far, to form new habits. Good, it'll never end, I'll never go. *(Pause)* Then one day, suddenly, it ends, it changes, I don't understand, it dies, or it's me, I don't understand, that either. I ask the words that remain — sleeping, waking, morning, evening. They have nothing to say. *(Pause)* I open the door of the cell and go. I am so bowed I only see my feet, if I open my eyes, and between my legs a little trail of black dust. I say to myself that the earth is extinguished, though I never saw it lit. *(Pause)* It's easy going. *(Pause)* When I fall I'll weep for happiness. *(Pause. He goes towards door)*

Hamm.   Clov! *(Clov halts, without turning)* Nothing. *(Clov moves on)* Clov! *(Clov halts, without turning)*

Clov.   This is what we call making an exit.

Hamm.   I'm obliged to you, Clov. For your services.

Clov *(Turning, sharply)*.   Ah pardon, it's I am obliged to you.

Hamm.   It's we are obliged to each other. *(Pause. Clov goes towards door)* One thing more. *(Clov halts)* A last favor. *(Exit Clov)* Cover me with the sheet. *(Long pause)* No? Good. *(Pause)* Me to play. *(Pause. Wearily)* Old endgame lost of old, play and lose and have done with losing. *(Pause. More animated)* Let me see. *(Pause)* Ah yes! *(He tries to move the chair, using the gaff as before. Enter Clov, dressed for the road. Panama hat, tweed coat, raincoat over his arm, umbrella, bag. He halts by the door and stands there, impassive and motionless, his eyes fixed on Hamm, till the end. Hamm gives up)* Good. *(Pause)* Discard. *(He throws away the gaff, makes to throw away the dog, thinks better of it)* Take it easy. *(Pause)* And now? *(Pause)* Raise hat. *(He raises his toque)* Peace to our . . . arses. *(Pause)* And put on again. *(He puts on his toque)* Deuce. *(Pause. He takes off his glasses)* Wipe. *(He takes out his handkerchief and, without unfolding it, wipes his glasses)* And put on again. *(He puts on his glasses, puts back the handkerchief in his pocket)* We're coming. A few more squirms like that and I'll call. *(Pause)* A little poetry. *(Pause)* You prayed — *(Pause. He corrects himself)* You CRIED for night; it comes — *(Pause. He corrects himself)* It FALLS: now cry in darkness. *(He repeats, chanting)* You cried for night; it falls: now cry in darkness. *(Pause)* Nicely put, that. *(Pause)* And now? *(Pause)* Moments for nothing, now as always, time was never and time is over, reckoning closed and story ended. *(Pause. Narrative tone)* If he could have his child with him . . . *(Pause)* It was the moment I was waiting for. *(Pause)* You don't want to abandon him? You want him to bloom while you are withering? Be there to solace your last million last moments? *(Pause)* He doesn't realize, all he knows is hunger, and cold, and death to crown it all. But you! You ought to know what the earth is like, nowadays. Oh I put him before his responsibilities! *(Pause. Normal tone)* Well, there we are, there I am, that's enough. *(He raises the whistle to his lips, hesitates, drops it. Pause)* Yes, truly! *(He whistles. Pause. Louder. Pause)* Good. *(Pause)* Father! *(Pause. Louder)* Father! *(Pause)* Good. *(Pause)* We're coming. *(Pause)* And to end up with? *(Pause)* Discard. *(He throws away the dog. He tears the whistle from his neck)* With my compli-

ments. *(He throws whistle towards auditorium. Pause. He sniffs. Soft)* Clov!
(Long pause) No? Good. *(He takes out the handkerchief)* Since that's the way
we're playing it . . . *(He unfolds handkerchief)* . . . let's play it that way . . . *(He
unfolds)* . . . and speak no more about it . . . *(He finishes unfolding)* . . . speak
no more. *(He holds handkerchief spread out before him)* Old stancher! *(Pause)*
You . . . remain. *(Pause. He covers his face with handkerchief, lowers his arms
to armrests, remains motionless. Brief tableau)*

Curtain

For Analysis

1. In chess, the endgame is the last phase of play, and culminates in a checkmate. In
what sense is *Endgame* an appropriate title for this play? What other associations relevant to the events in the play does the word *endgame* suggest?

2. The stage directions at the beginning of the play indicate that a picture hangs with
its face to the wall. What purpose is served by that strange visual effect?

3. Why do you suppose that Nagg and Nell live in garbage cans?

4. What associations do you make with the names of the four characters?

5. What are the relationships among the four characters?

6. What lies outside the shelter? Why are Hamm and Clov upset when Clov sees
something that "looks like a small boy" outside?

7. Early in the play, when Clov attempts a retreat to his kitchen to look at the wall,
Hamm responds with a biblical **allusion:** "The wall! And what do you see on your
wall? Mene, mene?" Read the Book of Daniel, chapter 5, and explain the allusion.

On Style

1. Characterize the dominant emotional **tone** of the play. How do the author's stage
directions and language project that emotional tone?

2. There are comic passages in the play, particularly the speeches and interactions
involving Nagg and Nell. Do those passages damage the dominant mood or reinforce it? Explain.

Making Connections

1. Contrast the effect of this drama with the effect of Tolstoy's "The Death of Iván
Ilých" (p. 1286). Which is more hopeful? Why?

2. Read the speeches from Shakespeare's *Richard II, Macbeth,* and *Hamlet* (pp.
1382–83). Which one best reflects the **tone** of Beckett's play? Explain.

Writing Topic

1. Explain the relationship of the **setting** to the **theme** of the play.

2. In a paragraph or two, suggest what Clov might be seeing when he peers through
the windows.

3. Explain how comic elements in the play reinforce its aura of despair.

4. Look up *entropy* in an encyclopedia. In an essay, critically analyze this play as a
dramatic representation of entropy.

Woody Allen   (b. 1935)

Death Knocks 1968

The play takes place in the bedroom of Nat Ackerman's two-story house, somewhere in Kew Gardens.[1] The carpeting is wall-to-wall. There is a big double bed and a large vanity. The room is elaborately furnished and curtained, and on the walls there are several paintings and a not really attractive barometer. Soft theme music as the curtain rises. Nat Ackerman, a bald, paunchy fifty-seven-year-old dress manufacturer, is lying on the bed finishing off tomorrow's Daily News.[2] *He wears a bathrobe and slippers, and reads by a bed light clipped to the white headboard of the bed. The time is near midnight. Suddenly we hear a noise, and Nat sits up and looks at the window.*

Nat.   What the hell is that?

(Climbing awkwardly through the window is a sombre, caped figure. The intruder wears a black hood and skintight black clothes. The hood covers his head but not his face, which is middle-aged and stark white. He is something like Nat in appearance. He huffs audibly and then trips over the windowsill and falls into the room.)

Death (*for it is no one else*).   Jesus Christ. I nearly broke my neck.
Nat (*watching with bewilderment*).   Who are you?
Death.   Death.
Nat.   Who?
Death.   Death. Listen — can I sit down? I nearly broke my neck. I'm shaking like a leaf.
Nat.   Who *are* you?
Death.   *Death.* You got a glass of water?
Nat.   Death? What do you mean, Death?
Death.   What is wrong with you? You see the black costume and the whitened face?
Nat.   Yeah.
Death.   Is it Halloween?
Nat.   No.
Death.   Then I'm Death. Now can I get a glass of water — or a Fresca?

---

[1] A middle-class neighborhood in the New York City borough of Queens.   [2] The *Daily News* is a tabloid newspaper; the morning edition used to be distributed at about 10 P.M. the previous night.

Nat. If this is some joke —

Death. What kind of joke? You're fifty-seven? Nat Ackerman? One eighteen Pacific Street? Unless I blew it — where's that call sheet? (*He fumbles through pocket, finally producing a card with an address on it. It seems to check.*)

Nat. What do you want with me?

Death. What do I want? What do you think I want?

Nat. You must be kidding. I'm in perfect health.

Death (*unimpressed*). Uh-huh. (*Looking around*) This is a nice place. You do it yourself?

Nat. We had a decorator, but we worked with her.

Death (*looking at picture on the wall*). I love those kids with the big eyes.

Nat. I don't want to go yet.

Death. *You* don't want to go? Please don't start in. As it is, I'm nauseous from the climb.

Nat. What climb?

Death. I climbed up the drainpipe. I was trying to make a dramatic entrance. I see the big windows and you're awake reading. I figure it's worth a shot. I'll climb up and enter with a little — you know . . . (*Snaps fingers*) Meanwhile, I get my heel caught on some vines, the drainpipe breaks, and I'm hanging by a thread. Then my cape begins to tear. Look, let's just go. It's been a rough night.

Nat. You broke my drainpipe?

Death. Broke. It didn't break. It's a little bent. Didn't you hear anything? I slammed into the ground.

Nat. I was reading.

Death. You must have really been engrossed. (*Lifting newspaper Nat was reading*) "NAB COEDS IN POT ORGY." Can I borrow this?

Nat. I'm not finished.

Death. Er — I don't know how to put this to you, pal. . . .

Nat. Why didn't you just ring downstairs?

Death. I'm telling you, I could have, but how does it look? This way I get a little drama going. Something. Did you read "Faust"?

Nat. What?

Death. And what if you had company? You're sitting there with important people. I'm Death — I should ring the bell and traipse right in the front? Where's your thinking?

Nat. Listen, Mister, it's very late.

Death. Yeah. Well, you want to go?

Nat. Go where?

Death. Death. It. The Thing. The Happy Hunting Grounds. (*Looking at his own knee*) Y'know, that's a pretty bad cut. My first job, I'm liable to get gangrene yet.

Nat. Now, wait a minute. I need time. I'm not ready to go.

Death. I'm sorry. I can't help you. I'd like to, but it's the moment.

Nat. How can it be the moment? I just merged with Modiste Originals.

Death.   What's the difference, a couple of bucks more or less.

Nat.   Sure, what do you care? You guys probably have all your expenses paid.

Death.   You want to come along now?

Nat (*studying him*).   I'm sorry, but I cannot believe you're Death.

Death.   Why? What'd you expect — Rock Hudson?

Nat.   No, it's not that.

Death.   I'm sorry if I disappointed you.

Nat.   Don't get upset. I don't know, I always thought you'd be . . . uh . . . taller.

Death.   I'm five seven. It's average for my weight.

Nat.   You look a little like me.

Death.   Who should I look like? I'm your death.

Nat.   Give me some time. Another day.

Death.   I can't. What do you want me to say?

Nat.   One more day. Twenty-four hours.

Death.   What do you need it for? The radio said rain tomorrow.

Nat.   Can't we work out something?

Death.   Like what?

Nat.   You play chess?

Death.   No, I don't.

Nat.   I once saw a picture of you playing chess.

Death.   Couldn't be me, because I don't play chess. Gin rummy, maybe.

Nat.   You play gin rummy?

Death.   Do I play gin rummy? Is Paris a city?

Nat.   You're good, huh?

Death.   Very good.

Nat.   I'll tell you what I'll do —

Death.   Don't make any deals with me.

Nat.   I'll play you gin rummy. If you win, I'll go immediately. If I win, give me some more time. A little bit — one more day.

Death.   Who's got time to play gin rummy?

Nat.   Come on. If you're so good.

Death.   Although I feel like a game . . .

Nat.   Come on. Be a sport. We'll shoot for a half hour.

Death.   I really shouldn't.

Nat.   I got the cards right here. Don't make a production.

Death.   All right, come on. We'll play a little. It'll relax me.

Nat (*getting cards, pad, and pencil*).   You won't regret this.

Death.   Don't give me a sales talk. Get the cards and give me a Fresca and put out something. For God's sake, a stranger drops in, you don't have potato chips or pretzels.

Nat.   There's M&M's downstairs in a dish.

Death.   M&M's. What if the President came? He'd get M&M's too?

Nat.   You're not the President.

Death.   Deal.

(*Nat deals, turns up a five.*)

Nat.   You want to play a tenth of a cent a point to make it interesting?
Death.   It's not interesting enough for you?
Nat.   I play better when money's at stake.
Death.   Whatever you say, Newt.
Nat.   Nat, Nat Ackerman. You don't know my name?
Death.   Newt, Nat — I got such a headache.
Nat.   You want that five?
Death.   No.
Nat.   So pick.
Death (*surveying his hand as he picks*).   Jesus, I got nothing here.
Nat.   What's it like?
Death.   What's what like?

(*Throughout the following, they pick and discard.*)

Nat.   Death.
Death.   What should it be like? You lay there.
Nat.   Is there anything after?
Death.   Aha, you're saving twos.
Nat.   I'm asking. Is there anything after?
Death (*absently*).   You'll see.
Nat.   Oh, then I will actually see something?
Death.   Well, maybe I shouldn't have put it that way. Throw.
Nat.   To get an answer from you is a big deal.
Death.   I'm playing cards.
Nat.   All right, play, play.
Death.   Meanwhile, I'm giving you one card after another.
Nat.   Don't look through the discards.
Death.   I'm not looking. I'm straightening them up. What was the knock card?
Nat.   Four. You ready to knock already?
Death.   Who said I'm ready to knock. All I asked was what was the knock card.
Nat.   And all I asked was is there anything for me to look forward to.
Death.   Play.
Nat.   Can't you tell me anything? Where do we go?
Death.   We? To tell you the truth, *you* fall in a crumpled heap on the floor.
Nat.   Oh, I can't wait for that! Is it going to hurt?
Death.   Be over in a second.
Nat.   Terrific. (*Sighs*) I needed this. A man merges with Modiste Originals . . .
Death.   How's four points?
Nat.   You're knocking?
Death.   Four points is good?

Nat. No, I got two.

Death. You're kidding.

Nat. No, you lose.

Death. Holy Christ, and I thought you were saving sixes.

Nat. No. Your deal. Twenty points and two boxes. Shoot. (*Death deals.*) I must fall on the floor, eh? I can't be standing over the sofa when it happens?

Death. No. Play.

Nat. Why not?

Death. Because you fall on the floor! Leave me alone. I'm trying to concentrate.

Nat. Why must it be on the floor? That's all I'm saying! Why can't the whole thing happen and I'll stand next to the sofa?

Death. I'll try my best. Now can we play?

Nat. That's all I'm saying. You remind me of Moe Lefkowitz. He's also stubborn.

Death. I remind you of Moe Lefkowitz. I'm one of the most terrifying figures you could possibly imagine, and him I remind of Moe Lefkowitz. What is he, a furrier?

Nat. You should be such a furrier. He's good for eighty thousand a year. Passementeries. He's got his own factory. Two points.

Death. What?

Nat. Two points. I'm knocking. What have you got?

Death. My hand is like a basketball score.

Nat. And it's spades.

Death. If you didn't talk so much.

(*They redeal and play on.*)

Nat. What'd you mean before when you said this was your first job?

Death. What does it sound like?

Nat. What are you telling me — that nobody ever went before?

Death. Sure they went. But I didn't take them.

Nat. So who did?

Death. Others.

Nat. There's others?

Death. Sure. Each one has his own personal way of going.

Nat. I never knew that.

Death. Why should you know? Who are you?

Nat. What do you mean who am I? Why — I'm nothing?

Death. Not nothing. You're a dress manufacturer. Where do you come to knowledge of the eternal mysteries?

Nat. What are you talking about? I make a beautiful dollar. I sent two kids through college. One is in advertising, the other's married. I got my own home. I drive a Chrysler. My wife has whatever she wants. Maids, mink coat, vacations. Right now she's at the Eden Roc. Fifty dollars a day because she wants to be near her sister. I'm supposed to join her next week, so what do you think I am — some guy off the street?

Death.   All right. Don't be so touchy.

Nat.   Who's touchy?

Death.   How would you like it if I got insulted quickly?

Nat.   Did I insult you?

Death.   You didn't say you were disappointed in me?

Nat.   What do you expect? You want me to throw you a block party?

Death.   I'm not talking about that. I mean me personally. I'm too short, I'm this, I'm that.

Nat.   I said you looked like me. It's like a reflection.

Death.   All right, deal, deal.

(*They continue to play as music steals in and the lights dim until all is in total darkness. The lights slowly come up again, and now it is later and their game is over. Nat tallies.*)

Nat.   Sixty-eight . . . one-fifty . . . Well, you lose.

Death (*dejectedly looking through the deck*).   I knew I shouldn't have thrown that nine. Damn it.

Nat.   So I'll see you tomorrow.

Death.   What do you mean you'll see me tomorrow?

Nat.   I won the extra day. Leave me alone.

Death.   You were serious?

Nat.   We made a deal.

Death.   Yeah, but —

Nat.   Don't "but" me. I won twenty-four hours. Come back tomorrow.

Death.   I didn't know we were actually playing for time.

Nat.   That's too bad about you. You should pay attention.

Death.   Where am I going to go for twenty-four hours?

Nat.   What's the difference? The main thing is I won an extra day.

Death.   What do you want me to do — walk the streets?

Nat.   Check into a hotel and go to a movie. Take a *schvitz*.[3] Don't make a federal case.

Death.   Add the score again.

Nat.   Plus you owe me twenty-eight dollars.

Death.   *What?*

Nat.   That's right, Buster. Here it is — read it.

Death (*going through pockets*).   I have a few singles — not twenty-eight dollars.

Nat.   I'll take a check.

Death.   From what account?

Nat.   Look who I'm dealing with.

[3] Steam bath.

Death. Sue me. Where do I keep my checking account?

Nat. All right, gimme what you got and we'll call it square.

Death. Listen, I need that money.

Nat. Why should you need money?

Death. What are you talking about? You're going to the Beyond.

Nat. So?

Death. So — you know how far that is?

Nat. So?

Death. So where's gas? Where's tolls?

Nat. We're going by car!

Death. You'll find out. *(Agitatedly)* Look — I'll be back tomorrow, and you'll give me a chance to win the money back. Otherwise I'm in definite trouble.

Nat. Anything you want. Double or nothing we'll play. I'm liable to win an extra week or a month. The way you play, maybe years.

Death. Meantime I'm stranded.

Nat. See you tomorrow.

Death *(being edged to the doorway).* Where's a good hotel? What am I talking about hotel, I got no money. I'll go sit in Bickford's.[4] *(He picks up the News.)*

Nat. Out. Out. That's my paper. *(He takes it back.)*

Death *(exiting).* I couldn't just take him and go. I had to get involved in rummy.

Nat *(calling after him).* And be careful going downstairs. On one of the steps the rug is loose.

(And, on cue, we hear a terrific crash. Nat sighs, then crosses to the bedside table and makes a phone call.)

Nat. Hello, Moe? Me. Listen, I don't know if somebody's playing a joke, or what, but Death was just here. We played a little gin . . . No, *Death.* In person. Or somebody who claims to be Death. But, Moe, he's such a *schlep!*[5]

Curtain

For Analysis

1. Consider the stage direction that opens the play. What sort of household is described?

2. The stage direction describes Nat Ackerman as a dress manufacturer. If you were directing the play, how might you convey that information to your audience? Why do you suppose Allen included the information in a stage direction?

3. Reread the stage directions and identify any others that are literary rather than dramatic tools.

---

[4] Bickford's was a chain of inexpensive all-night cafeterias in New York City.
[5] Boring jerk.

On Style

Characterize the speech patterns of the characters. How do they contribute to the play's effect?

Making Connections

Compare and contrast the **personification** of death in Allen's play with Bernard Mala-mud's use of personification in his story "Idiots First" (p. 1348).

Writing Topic

Either read or rent a video of Ingmar Bergman's *The Seventh Seal*. In an essay, describe the effects of Allen's central allusion in *Death Knocks.*

Harvey Fierstein   (b. 1954)

On Tidy Endings   1987

The curtain rises on a deserted, modern Upper West Side apartment. In the bright daylight that pours in through the windows we can see the living room of the apartment. Far Stage Right is the galley kitchen, next to it the multilocked front door with intercom. Stage Left reveals a hallway that leads to the two bedrooms and baths.

Though the room is still fully furnished (couch, coffee table, etc.), there are boxes stacked against the wall and several photographs and paintings are on the floor leaving shadows on the wall where they once hung. Obviously someone is moving out. From the way the boxes are neatly labeled and stacked, we know that this is an organized person.

From the hallway just outside the door we hear the rattling of keys and two arguing voices:

Jim *(offstage).*   I've got to be home by four. I've got practice.
Marion *(offstage).*   I'll get you to practice, don't worry.
Jim *(offstage).*   I don't want to go in there.
Marion *(offstage).*   Jimmy, don't make Mommy crazy, alright? We'll go inside,
     I'll call Aunt Helen and see if you can go down and play with Robbie.

(The door opens. Marion is a handsome woman of forty. Dressed in a business suit, her hair conservatively combed, she appears to be going to a business meeting. Jim is a boy of eleven. His playclothes are typical, but someone has obviously just combed his hair. Marion recovers the key from the lock.)

Jim.   Why can't I just go down and ring the bell?
Marion.   Because I said so.

(As Marion steps into the room she is struck by some unexpected emotion. She freezes in her path and stares at the empty apartment. Jim lingers by the door.)

Jim.   I'm going downstairs.
Marion.   Jimmy, please.
Jim.   This place gives me the creeps.
Marion.   This was your father's apartment. There's nothing creepy about it.
Jim.   Says you.
Marion.   You want to close the door, please?

(Jim reluctantly obeys.)

1460

Marion. Now, why don't you go check your room and make sure you didn't leave anything.

Jim. It's empty.

Marion. Go look.

Jim. I looked last time.

Marion (*trying to be patient*). Honey, we sold the apartment. You're never going to be here again. Go make sure you have everything you want.

Jim. But Uncle Arthur packed everything.

Marion (*less patiently*). Go make sure.

Jim. There's nothing in there.

Marion (*exploding*). I said make sure!

(*Jim jumps, then realizing that she's not kidding, obeys.*)

Marion. Everything's an argument with that one. (*She looks around the room and breathes deeply. There is sadness here. Under her breath:*) I can still smell you. (*Suddenly not wanting to be alone*) Jimmy? Are you okay?

Jim (*returning*). Nothing. Told you so.

Marion. Uncle Arthur must have worked very hard. Make sure you thank him.

Jim. What for? Robbie says, (*Fey mannerisms*) "They love to clean up things!"

Marion. Sometimes you can be a real joy.

Jim. Did you call Aunt Helen?

Marion. Do I get a break here? (*Approaching the boy understandingly*) Wouldn't you like to say good-bye?

Jim. To who?

Marion. To the apartment. You and your daddy spent a lot of time here together. Don't you want to take one last look around?

Jim. Ma, get a real life.

Marion. "Get a real life." (*Going for the phone*) Nice. Very nice.

Jim. Could you call already?

Marion (*dialing*). Jimmy, what does this look like I'm doing?

(*Jim kicks at the floor impatiently. Someone answers the phone at the other end.*)

Marion (*into the phone*). Helen? Hi, we're upstairs. . . . No, we just walked in the door. Jimmy wants to know if he can come down. . . . Oh, thanks.

(*Hearing that, Jim breaks for the door.*)

Marion (*yelling after him*). Don't run in the halls! And don't play with the elevator buttons!

(*The door slams shut behind him.*)

Marion *(back to the phone)*.   Hi.... No, I'm okay. It's a little weird being here.... No. Not since the funeral, and then there were so many people. Jimmy told me to get "a real life." I don't think I could handle anything realer.... No, please. Stay where you are. I'm fine. The doorman said Arthur would be right back and my lawyer should have been here already.... Well, we've got the papers to sign and a few other odds and ends to clean up. Shouldn't take long.

(The intercom buzzer rings.)

Marion.   Hang on, that must be her. *(Marion goes to the intercom and speaks)* Yes?... Thank you. *(Back to the phone)* Helen? Yeah, it's the lawyer. I'd better go.... Well, I could use a stiff drink, but I drove down. Listen, I'll stop by on my way out. Okay? Okay. 'Bye.

(She hangs up the phone, looks around the room. That uncomfortable feeling returns to her quickly. She gets up and goes to the front door, opens it and looks out. No one there yet. She closes the door, shakes her head knowing that she's being silly and starts back into the room. She looks around, can't make it and retreats to the door. She opens it, looks out, closes it, but stays right there, her hand on the doorknob.
The bell rings. She throws open the door.)

Marion.   That was quick.

(June Lowell still has her finger on the bell. Her arms are loaded with contracts. Marion's contemporary, June is less formal in appearance and more hyper in her manner.)

June.   *That* was quicker. What, were you waiting by the door?
Marion *(embarrassed)*.   No. I was just passing it. Come on in.
June.   Have you got your notary seal?
Marion.   I think so.
June.   Great. Then you can witness. I left mine at the office and thanks to gentrification I'm double-parked downstairs. *(Looking for a place to dump her load)* Where?
Marion *(definitely pointing to the coffee table)*.   Anywhere. You mean you're not staying?
June.   If you really think you need me I can go down and find a parking lot. I think there's one over on Columbus. So, I can go down, park the car in the lot and take a cab back if you really think you need me.
Marion.   Well...?
June.   But you shouldn't have any problems. The papers are about as straightforward as papers get. Arthur is giving you power of attorney to sell the apartment and you're giving him a check for half the purchase price. Everything else is just signing papers that state that you know that you signed the other

papers. Anyway, he knows the deal, his lawyers have been over it all with him, it's just a matter of signatures.

Marion (*not fine*).   Oh, fine.

June.   Unless you just don't want to be alone with him . . . ?

Marion.   With Arthur? Don't be silly.

June (*laying out the papers*).   Then you'll handle it solo? My car thanks you, the parking lot thanks you, and the cab driver that wouldn't have gotten a tip thanks you. Come have a quick look-see.

Marion (*joining her on the couch*).   There are a lot of papers here.

June.   Copies. Not to worry. Start here.

(*Marion starts to read.*)

June.   I ran into Jimmy playing Elevator Operator.

(*Marion jumps.*)

June.   I got him off at the sixth floor. Read on.

Marion.   This is definitely not my day for dealing with him.

(*June gets up and has a look around.*)

June.   I don't believe what's happening to this neighborhood. You made quite an investment when you bought this place.

Marion.   Collin was always very good at figuring out those things.

June.   Well, he sure figured this place right. What, have you tripled your money in ten years?

Marion.   More.

June.   It's a shame to let it go.

Marion.   We're not ready to be a two-dwelling family.

June.   So, sublet it again.

Marion.   Arthur needs the money from the sale.

June.   Arthur got plenty already. I'm not crying for Arthur.

Marion.   I don't hear you starting in again, do I?

June.   Your interests and your wishes are my only concern.

Marion.   Fine.

June.   I still say we should contest Collin's will.

Marion.   June! . . .

June.   You've got a child to support.

Marion.   And a great job, and a husband with a great job. Tell me what Arthur's got.

June.   To my thinking, half of everything that should have gone to you. And more. All of Collin's personal effects, his record collection . . .

Marion.   And I suppose their three years together meant nothing.

June.   When you compare them to your sixteen-year marriage? Not nothing, but not half of everything.

Marion (*trying to change the subject*).   June, who gets which copies?

June.   Two of each to Arthur. One you keep. The originals and anything else
 come back to me. (*Looking around*) I still say you should've sublet the apartment for a year and then sold it. You would've gotten an even better price.
 Who wants to buy an apartment when they know someone died in it. No one.
 And certainly no one wants to buy an apartment when they know the person
 died of AIDS.

Marion (*snapping*).   June. Enough!

June (*catching herself*).   Sorry. That was out of line. Sometimes my mouth
 does that to me. Hey, that's why I'm a lawyer. If my brain worked as fast as my
 mouth I would have gotten a real job.

Marion (*holding out a stray paper*).   What's this?

June.   I forgot. Arthur's lawyer sent that over yesterday. He found it in Collin's
 safety-deposit box. It's an insurance policy that came along with some consulting job he did in Japan. He either forgot about it when he made out his
 will or else he wanted you to get the full payment. Either way, it's yours.

Marion.   Are you sure we don't split this?

June.   Positive.

Marion.   But everything else . . . ?

June.   Hey, Arthur found it, his lawyer sent it to me. Relax, it's all yours. Minus
 my commission, of course. Go out and buy yourself something. Anything else
 before I have to use my cut to pay the towing bill?

Marion.   I guess not.

June (*starting to leave*).   Great. Call me when you get home. (*Stopping at the
 door and looking back*) Look, I know that I'm attacking this a little coldly. I
 am aware that someone you loved has just died. But there's a time and place
 for everything. This is about tidying up loose ends, not holding hands. I hope
 you'll remember that when Arthur gets here. Call me.

(*And she's gone.*)

   (*Marion looks ill at ease to be alone again. She nervously straightens the
papers into neat little piles, looks at them and then remembers:*)

Marion.   Pens. We're going to need pens.

(*At last a chore to be done. She looks in her purse and finds only one. She goes to
the kitchen and opens a drawer where she finds two more. She starts back to
the table with them but suddenly remembers something else. She returns to the
kitchen and begins going through the cabinets until she finds what she's looking
for: a blue Art Deco teapot. Excited to find it, she takes it back to the couch.*
   Guilt strikes. She stops, considers putting it back, wavers, then:)

Marion (*to herself*).   Oh, he won't care. One less thing to pack.

(*She takes the teapot and places it on the couch next to her purse. She is happier.
Now she searches the room with her eyes for any other treasures she may have
overlooked. Nothing here. She wanders off into the bedroom.*

We hear keys outside the front door. Arthur lets himself into the apartment carrying a load of empty cartons and a large shopping bag.

Arthur is in his mid-thirties, pleasant looking though sloppily dressed in work clothes and slightly overweight.

Arthur enters the apartment just as Marion comes out of the bedroom carrying a framed watercolor painting. They jump at the sight of each other.)

Marion. Oh, hi, Arthur. I didn't hear the door.

Arthur *(staring at the painting).* Well hello, Marion.

Marion *(guiltily).* I was going to ask you if you were thinking of taking this painting because if you're not going to then I'll take it. Unless, of course, you want it.

Arthur. No. You can have it.

Marion. I never really liked it, actually. I hate cats. I didn't even like the show. I needed something for my college dorm room. I was never the rock star poster type. I kept it in the back of a closet for years until Collin moved in here and took it. He said he liked it.

Arthur. I do too.

Marion. Well, then you keep it.

Arthur. No. Take it.

Marion. We've really got no room for it. You keep it.

Arthur. I don't want it.

Marion. Well, if you're sure.

Arthur *(seeing the teapot).* You want the teapot?

Marion. If you don't mind.

Arthur. One less thing to pack.

Marion. Funny, but that's exactly what I thought. One less thing to pack. You know, my mother gave it to Collin and me when we moved in to our first apartment. Silly sentimental piece of junk, but you know.

Arthur. That's not the one.

Marion. Sure it is. Hall used to make them for Westinghouse back in the thirties. I see them all the time at antiques shows and I always wanted to buy another, but they ask such a fortune for them.

Arthur. We broke the one your mother gave you a couple of years ago. That's a reproduction. You can get them almost anywhere in the Village for eighteen bucks.

Marion. Really? I'll have to pick one up.

Arthur. Take this one. I'll get another.

Marion. No, it's yours. You bought it.

Arthur. One less thing to pack.

Marion. Don't be silly. I didn't come here to raid the place.

Arthur. Well, was there anything else of Collin's that you thought you might like to have?

Marion. Now I feel so stupid, but actually I made a list. Not for me. But I started thinking about different people; friends, relatives, you know, that might want to have something of Collin's to remember him by. I wasn't sure just what you were taking and what you were throwing out. Anyway, I brought the list. (*Gets it from her purse*) Of course these are only suggestions. You probably thought of a few of these people yourself. But I figured it couldn't hurt to write it all down. Like I said, I don't know what you are planning on keeping.

Arthur (*taking the list*).   I was planning on keeping it all.

Marion.   Oh, I know. But most of these things are silly. Like his high school yearbooks. What would you want with them?

Arthur.   Sure. I'm only interested in his Gay period.

Marion.   I didn't mean it that way. Anyway, you look it over. They're only suggestions. Whatever you decide to do is fine with me.

Arthur (*folding the list*).   It would have to be, wouldn't it. I mean, it's all mine now. He did leave this all to me.

(*Marion is becoming increasingly nervous, but tries to keep a light approach as she takes a small bundle of papers from her bag.*)

Marion.   While we're on the subject of what's yours. I brought a batch of condolence cards that were sent to you care of me. Relatives mostly.

Arthur (*taking them*).   More cards? I'm going to have to have another printing of thank-you notes done.

Marion.   I answered these last week, so you don't have to bother. Unless you want to.

Arthur.   Forge my signature?

Marion.   Of course not. They were addressed to both of us and they're mostly distant relatives or friends we haven't seen in years. No one important.

Arthur.   If they've got my name on them, then I'll answer them myself.

Marion.   I wasn't telling you not to, I was only saying that you don't have to.

Arthur.   I understand.

(*Marion picks up the teapot and brings it to the kitchen.*)

Marion.   Let me put this back.

Arthur.   I ran into Jimmy in the lobby.

Marion.   Tell me you're joking.

Arthur.   I got him to Helen's.

Marion.   He's really racking up the points today.

Arthur.   You know, he still can't look me in the face.

Marion.   He's reacting to all of this in strange ways. Give him time. He'll come around. He's really very fond of you.

Arthur.   I know. But he's at that awkward age: under thirty. I'm sure in twenty years we'll be the best of friends.

Marion.   It's not what you think.

Arthur.   What do you mean?

Marion.   Well, you know.

Arthur.   No I don't know. Tell me.

Marion.   I thought that you were intimating something about his blaming you for Collin's illness and I was just letting you know that it's not true. (*Foot in mouth, she braves on*) We discussed it a lot and . . . uh . . . he understands that his father was sick before you two ever met.

Arthur.   I don't believe this.

Marion.   I'm just trying to say that he doesn't blame you.

Arthur.   First of all, who asked you? Second of all, that's between him and me. And third and most importantly, of course he blames me. Marion, he's eleven years old. You can discuss all you want, but the fact is that his father died of a "fag" disease and I'm the only fag around to finger.

Marion.   My son doesn't use that kind of language.

Arthur.   Forget the language. I'm talking about what he's been through. Can you imagine the kind of crap he's taken from his friends? That poor kid's been chased and chastised from one end of town to the other. He's got to have someone to blame just to survive. He can't blame you, you're all he's got. He can't blame his father; he's dead. So, Uncle Arthur gets the shaft. Fine, I can handle it.

Marion.   You are so wrong, Arthur. I know my son and that is not the way his mind works.

Arthur.   I don't know what you know. I only know what I know. And all I know is what I hear and see. The snide remarks, the little smirks . . . And it's not just the illness. He's been looking for a scapegoat since the day you and Collin first split up. Finally he has one.

Marion (*getting very angry now*).   Wait. Are you saying that if he's going to blame someone it should be me?

Arthur.   I think you should try to see things from his point of view.

Marion.   Where do you get off thinking you're privy to my son's point of view?

Arthur.   It's not that hard to imagine. Life's rolling right along, he's having a happy little childhood, when suddenly one day his father's moving out. No explanations, no reasons, none of the fights that usually accompany such things. Divorce is hard enough for a kid to understand when he's listened to years of battles, but yours?

Marion.   So what should we have done? Faked a few months' worth of fights before Collin moved out?

Arthur.   You could have told him the truth, plain and simple.

Marion.   He was seven years old at the time. How the hell do you tell a seven-year-old that his father is leaving his mother to go sleep with other men?

Arthur.   Well, not like that.

Marion.   You know, Arthur, I'm going to say this as nicely as I can: Butt out. You're not his mother and you're not his father.

Arthur.   Thank you. I wasn't acutely aware of that fact. I will certainly keep that in mind from now on.

Marion.   There's only so much information a child that age can handle.

Arthur.   So it's best that he reach his capacity on the street.

Marion.   He knew about the two of you. We talked about it.

Arthur.   Believe me, he knew before you talked about it. He's young, not stupid.

Marion.   It's very easy for you to stand here and criticize, but there are aspects that you will just never be able to understand. You weren't there. You have no idea what it was like for me. You're talking to someone who thought that a girl went to college to meet a husband. I went to protest rallies because I liked the music. I bought a guitar because I thought it looked good on the bed! This lifestyle, this knowledge that you take for granted, was all a little out of left field for me.

Arthur.   I can imagine.

Marion.   No. I don't think you can. I met Collin in college, married him right after graduation and settled down for a nice quiet life of Kids and Careers. You think I had any idea about this? Talk about life's little surprises. You live with someone for sixteen years, you share your life, your bed, you have a child together, and then you wake up one day and he tells you that to him it's all been a lie. A lie. Try that on for size. Here you are the happiest couple you know, fulfilling your every life fantasy and he tells you he's living a lie.

Arthur.   I'm sure he never said that.

Marion.   Don't be so sure. There was a lot of new ground being broken back then and plenty of it was muddy.

Arthur.   You know that he loved you.

Marion.   What's that supposed to do, make things easier? It doesn't. I was brought up to believe, among other things, that if you had love that was enough. So what if I wasn't everything he wanted. Maybe he wasn't exactly everything I wanted either. So, you know what? You count your blessings and you settle.

Arthur.   No one has to settle. Not him. Not you.

Marion.   Of course not. You can say, "Up yours!" to everything and everyone who depends and needs you, and go off to make yourself happy.

Arthur.   It's not that simple.

Marion.   No. This is simpler. Death is simpler. *(Yelling out)* Happy now?

(They stare at each other. Marion calms the rage and catches her breath. Arthur holds his emotions in check.)

Arthur.   How about a nice hot cup of coffee? Tea with lemon? Hot cocoa with a marshmallow floating in it?

Marion *(laughs)*.   I was wrong. You *are* a mother.

(Arthur goes into the kitchen and starts preparing things. Marion loafs by the doorway.)

Marion.   I lied before. He *was* everything I ever wanted.

(Arthur stops, looks at her, and then changes the subject as he goes on with his work.)

Arthur. When I came into the building and saw Jimmy in the lobby I absolutely freaked for a second. It's amazing how much they look alike. It was like seeing a little miniature Collin standing there.

Marion. I know. He's like Collin's clone. There's nothing of me in him.

Arthur. I always kinda hoped that when he grew up he'd take after me. Not much chance, I guess.

Marion. Don't do anything fancy in there.

Arthur. Please. Anything we can consume is one less thing to pack.

Marion. So you've said.

Arthur. So *we've* said.

Marion. I want to keep seeing you and I want you to see Jim. You're still part of this family. No one's looking to cut you out.

Arthur. Ah, who'd want a kid to grow up looking like me anyway. I had enough trouble looking like this. Why pass on the misery?

Marion. You're adorable.

Arthur. Is that like saying I have a good personality?

Marion. I think you are one of the most naturally handsome men I know.

Arthur. Natural is right, and the bloom is fading.

Marion. All you need is a few good nights' sleep to kill those rings under your eyes.

Arthur. Forget the rings under my eyes, *(Grabbing his middle)* . . . how about the rings around my moon?

Marion. I like you like this.

Arthur. From the time that Collin started using the wheelchair until he died, about six months, I lost twenty-three pounds. No gym, no diet. In the last seven weeks I've gained close to fifty.

Marion. You're exaggerating.

Arthur. I'd prove it on the bathroom scale, but I sold it in working order.

Marion. You'd never know.

Arthur. Marion, *you'd* never know, but ask my belt. Ask my pants. Ask my underwear. Even my stretch socks have stretch marks. I called the ambulance at five A.M., he was gone at nine and by nine-thirty, I was on a first-name basis with Sara Lee. I can quote the business hours of every ice-cream parlor, pizzeria and bakery on the island of Manhattan. I know the location of every twenty-four-hour grocery in the greater New York area, and I have memorized the phone numbers of every Mandarin, Szechuan and Hunan restaurant with free delivery.

Marion. At least you haven't wasted your time on useless hobbies.

Arthur. Are you kidding? I'm opening my own Overeater's Hotline. We'll have to start small, but expansion is guaranteed.

Marion. You're the best, you know that? If I couldn't be everything that Collin wanted then I'm grateful that he found someone like you.

Arthur *(turning on her without missing a beat).* Keep your goddamned gratitude to yourself. I didn't go through any of this for you. So your thanks are out of line. And he didn't find "someone like" me. It was me.

Marion (*frightened*).   I didn't mean . . .

Arthur.   And I wish you'd remember one thing more: He died in my arms, not yours.

(*Marion is totally caught off guard. She stares disbelieving, open-mouthed. Arthur walks past her as he leaves the kitchen with place mats. He puts them on the coffee table. As he arranges the papers and place mats he speaks, never looking at her.*)

Arthur.   Look, I know you were trying to say something supportive. Don't waste your breath. There's nothing you can say that will make any of this easier for me. There's no way for you to help me get through this. And that's your fault. After three years you still have no idea or understanding of who I am. Or maybe you do know but refuse to accept it. I don't know and I don't care. But at least understand, from my point of view, who you are: You are my husband's *ex*-wife. If you like, the mother of *my* stepson. Don't flatter yourself into thinking you're any more than that. And whatever you are, you're certainly not my friend.

(*He stops, looks up at her, then passes her again as he goes back to the kitchen. Marion is shaken, working hard to control herself. She moves toward the couch.*)

Marion.   Why don't we just sign these papers and I'll be out of your way.

Arthur.   Shouldn't you say *I'll* be out of *your* way? After all, I'm not just signing papers, I'm signing away my home.

Marion (*resolved not to fight, she gets her purse*).   I'll leave the papers here. Please have them notarized and returned to my lawyer.

Arthur.   Don't forget my painting.

Marion (*exploding*).   What do you want from me, Arthur?

Arthur (*yelling back*).   I want you the hell out of my apartment! I want you out of my life! And I want you to leave Collin alone!

Marion.   The man's dead. I don't know how much more alone I can leave him.

(*Arthur laughs at the irony, but behind the laughter is something much more desperate.*)

Arthur.   Lots more, Marion. You've got to let him go.

Marion.   For the life of me, I don't know what I did, or what you think I did, for you to treat me like this. But you're not going to get away with it. You will not take your anger out on me. I will not stand here and be badgered and insulted by you. I know you've been hurt and I know you're hurting but you're not the only one who lost someone here.

Arthur (*topping her*).   Yes I am! You didn't just lose him. I did! You lost him five years ago when he divorced you. This is not your moment of grief and loss, it's mine! (*Picking up the bundle of cards and throwing it toward her*)

These condolences do not belong to you, they're mine. (*Tossing her list back to her*) His things are not yours to give away, they're mine! This death does not belong to you, it's mine! Bought and paid for outright. I suffered for it, I bled for it. I was the one who cooked his meals. I was the one who spoon-fed them. I pushed his wheelchair. I carried and bathed him. I wiped his backside and changed his diapers. I breathed life into and wrestled fear out of his heart. I kept him alive for two years longer than any doctor thought possible and when it was time I was the one who prepared him for death.

I paid in full for my place in his life and I will *not* share it with you. We are not the two widows of Collin Redding. Your life was not here. Your husband didn't just die. You've got a son and a life somewhere else. Your husband's sitting, waiting for you at home, wondering, as I am, what the hell you're doing here and why you can't let go.

(*Marion leans back against the couch. She's blown away. Arthur stands staring at her.*)

Arthur (*quietly*).   Let him go, Marion. He's mine. Dead or alive; mine.

(*The teakettle whistles. Arthur leaves the room, goes to the kitchen and pours the water as Marion pulls herself together.*
   Arthur carries the loaded tray back into the living room and sets it down on the coffee table. He sits and pours a cup.)

Arthur.   One marshmallow or two?

(*Marion stares, unsure as to whether the attack is really over or not.*)

Arthur (*placing them in her cup*).   Take three, they're small.

(*Marion smiles and takes the offered cup.*)

Arthur (*campily*).   Now let me tell you how I *really* feel.

(*Marion jumps slightly, then they share a small laugh. Silence as they each gather themselves and sip their refreshments.*)

Marion (*calmly*).   Do you think that I sold the apartment just to throw you out?
Arthur.   I don't care about the apartment . . .
Marion.   . . . Because I really didn't. Believe me.
Arthur.   I know.
Marion.   I knew the expenses here were too much for you, and I knew you couldn't afford to buy out my half . . . I figured if we sold it, that you'd at least have a nice chunk of money to start over with.
Arthur.   You could've given me a little more time.

Marion.   Maybe. But I thought the sooner you were out of here, the sooner you could go on with your life.

Arthur.   Or the sooner you could go on with yours.

Marion.   Maybe. *(Pause to gather her thoughts)* Anyway, I'm not going to tell you that I have no idea what you're talking about. I'd have to be worse than deaf and blind not to have seen the way you've been treated. Or mistreated. When I read Collin's obituary in the newspaper and saw my name and Jimmy's name and no mention of you . . . *(Shakes her head, not knowing what to say)* You know that his secretary was the one who wrote that up and sent it in. Not me. But I should have done something about it and I didn't. I know.

Arthur.   Wouldn't have made a difference. I wrote my own obituary for him and sent it to the smaller papers. They edited me out.

Marion.   I'm sorry. I remember, at the funeral, I was surrounded by all of Collin's family and business associates while you were left with your friends. I knew it was wrong. I knew I should have said something but it felt good to have them around me and you looked like you were holding up . . . Wrong. But saying that it's all my fault for not letting go? . . . There were other people involved.

Arthur.   Who took their cue from you.

Marion.   Arthur, you don't understand. Most people that we knew as a couple had no idea that Collin was Gay right up to his death. And even those that did know only found out when he got sick and the word leaked out that it was AIDS. I don't think I have to tell you how stupid and ill-informed most people are about homosexuality. And AIDS . . . ? The kinds of insane behavior that word inspires? . . .

Those people at the funeral, how many times did they call to see how he was doing over these years? How many of them ever went to see him in the hospital? Did any of them even come here? So, why would you expect them to act any differently after his death?

So, maybe that helps to explain their behavior, but what about mine, right? Well, maybe there is no explanation. Only excuses. And excuse number one is that you're right, I have never really let go of him. And I am jealous of you. Hell, I was jealous of anyone that Collin ever talked to, let alone slept with . . . let alone loved.

The first year, after he moved out, we talked all the time about the different men he was seeing. And I always listened and advised. It was kind of fun. It kept us close. It kept me a part of his intimate life. And the bottom line was always that he wasn't happy with the men he was meeting. So, I was always allowed to hang on to the hope that one day he'd give it all up and come home. Then he got sick.

He called me, told me he was in the hospital and asked if I'd come see him. I ran. When I got to his door there was a sign, INSTRUCTIONS FOR VISITORS OF AN AIDS PATIENT. I nearly died.

Arthur.   He hadn't told you?

Marion. No. And believe me a sign is not the way to find these things out. I was so angry . . . And he was so sick . . . I was sure that he'd die right then. If not from the illness then from the hospital staff's neglect. No one wanted to go near him and I didn't bother fighting with them because I understood that they were scared. I was scared. That whole month in the hospital I didn't let Jimmy visit him once.

You learn.

Well, as you know, he didn't die. And he asked if he could come stay with me until he was well. And I said yes. Of course, yes. Now, here's something I never thought I'd ever admit to anyone: had he asked to stay with me for a few weeks I would have said no. But he asked to stay with me until he was well and knowing there was no cure I said yes. In my craziness I said yes because to me that meant forever. That he was coming back to me forever. Not that I wanted him to die, but I assumed from everything I'd read . . . And we'd be back together for whatever time he had left. Can you understand that?

(Arthur nods.)

Marion *(gathers her thoughts again).* Two weeks later he left. He moved in here. Into this apartment that we had bought as an investment. Never to live in. Certainly never to live apart in. Next thing I knew, the name Arthur starts appearing in every phone call, every dinner conversation.

"Did you see the doctor?"

"Yes. Arthur made sure I kept the appointment."

"Are you going to your folks for Thanksgiving?"

"No. Arthur and I are having some friends over."

I don't know which one of us was more of a coward, he for not telling or me for not asking about you. But eventually you became a given. Then, of course, we met and became what I had always thought of as friends.

(Arthur winces in guilt.)

Marion. I don't care what you say, how could we not be friends with something so great in common: love for one of the most special human beings there ever was. And don't try and tell me there weren't times when you enjoyed my being around as an ally. I can think of a dozen occasions when we ganged up on him, teasing him with our intimate knowledge of his personal habits.

(Arthur has to laugh.)

Marion. Blanket stealing? Snoring? Excess gas, no less? *(Takes a moment to enjoy this truce)* I don't think that my loving him threatened your relationship. Maybe I'm not being truthful with myself. But I don't. I never tried to step between you. Not that I ever had the opportunity. Talk about being joined at the hip! And that's not to say I wasn't jealous. I was. Terribly. Hatefully. But always lovingly. I was happy for Collin because there was no way to deny that he was happy. With everything he was facing, he was happy. Love did that. You did that.

He lit up with you. He came to life. I envied that and all the time you spent together, but more, I watched you care for him (sometimes *overcare* for him), and I was in awe. I could never have done what you did. I never would have survived. I really don't know how you did.

Arthur.   Who said I survived?

Marion.   Don't tease. You did an absolutely incredible thing. It's not as if you met him before he got sick. You entered a relationship that you knew in all probability would end this way and you never wavered.

Arthur.   Of course I did. Don't have me sainted, Marion. But sometimes you have no choice. Believe me, if I could've gotten away from him I would've. But I was a prisoner of love.

(He makes a campy gesture and pose.)

Marion.   Stop.

Arthur.   And there were lots of pluses. I got to quit a job I hated, stay home all day and watch game shows. I met a lot of doctors and learned a lot of big words. *(Arthur jumps up and goes to the pile of boxes where he extracts one and brings it back to the couch)* And then there was all the exciting traveling I got to do. This box has a souvenir from each one of our trips. Wanna see?

(Marion nods. He opens the box and pulls things out one by one.)

Arthur *(continuing)* *(Holding up an old bottle).*   This is from the house we rented in Reno when we went to clear out his lungs. *(Holding handmade potholders)* This is from the hospital in Reno. Collin made them. They had a great arts and crafts program. *(Copper bracelets)* These are from a faith healer in Philly. They don't do much for a fever, but they look great with a green sweater. *(Glass ashtrays)* These are from our first visit to the clinic in France. Such lovely people. *(A Bible)* This is from our second visit to the clinic in France. *(A bead necklace)* A Voodoo doctor in New Orleans. Next time we'll have to get there earlier in the year. I think he sold all the pretty ones at Mardi Gras. *(A tiny piñata)* Then there was Mexico. Black market drugs and empty wallets. *(Now pulling things out at random)* L.A., San Francisco, Houston, Boston . . . We traveled everywhere they offered hope for sale and came home with souvenirs. *(Arthur quietly pulls a few more things out and then begins to put them all back into the box slowly. Softly as he works:)*

Marion, I would have done anything, traveled anywhere to avoid . . . or delay . . . Not just because I loved him so desperately, but when you've lived the way we did for three years . . . the battle becomes your life. (*He looks at her and then away*)

His last few hours were beyond any scenario I had imagined. He hadn't walked in nearly six months. He was totally incontinent. If he spoke two words in a week I was thankful. Days went by without his eyes ever focusing on me. He just stared out at I don't know what. Not the meals as I fed him. Not the TV I played constantly for company. Just out. Or maybe in.

It was the middle of the night when I heard his breathing become labored. His lungs were filling with fluid again. I knew the sound. I'd heard it a hundred times before. So, I called the ambulance and got him to the hospital. They hooked him up to the machines, the oxygen, shot him with morphine and told me that they would do what they could to keep him alive.

But, Marion, it wasn't the machines that kept him breathing. He did it himself. It was that incredible will and strength inside him. Whether it came from his love of life or fear of death, who knows. But he'd been counted out a hundred times and a hundred times he fought his way back.

I got a magazine to read him, pulled a chair up to the side of his bed and holding his hand, I wondered whether I should call Helen to let the cleaning lady in or if he'd fall asleep and I could sneak home for an hour. I looked up from the page and he was looking at me. Really looking right into my eyes. I patted his cheek and said, "Don't worry, honey, you're going to be fine."

But there was something else in his eyes. He wasn't satisfied with that. And I don't know why, I have no idea where it came from, I just heard the words coming out of my mouth, "Collin, do you want to die?" His eyes filled and closed, he nodded his head.

I can't tell you what I was thinking, I'm not sure I was. I slipped off my shoes, lifted his blanket and climbed into bed next to him. I helped him to put his arms around me, and mine around him, and whispered as gently as I could into his ear, "It's alright to let go now. It's time to go on." And he did.

Marion, you've got your life and his son. All I have is an intangible place in a man's history. Leave me that. Respect that.

Marion.   I understand.

(*Arthur suddenly comes to life, running to get the shopping bag that he'd left at the front door.*)

Arthur.   Jeez! With all the screamin' and sad storytelling I forgot something. (*He extracts a bouquet of flowers from the bag*) I brung you flowers and everything.

Marion.   You brought *me* flowers?

Arthur.   Well, I knew you'd never think to bring me flowers and I felt that on an occasion such as this somebody oughta get flowers from somebody.

Marion.   You know, Arthur, you're really making me feel like a worthless piece of garbage.

Arthur.   So what else is new? (*He presents the flowers*) Just promise me one thing: Don't press one in a book. Just stick them in a vase and when they fade just toss them out. No more memorabilia.

Marion.   Arthur, I want to do something for you and I don't know what. Tell me what you want.

Arthur.   I want little things. Not much. I want to be remembered. If you get a Christmas card from Collin's mother, make sure she sent me one too. If his friends call to see how you are, ask if they've called me. Have me to dinner so I can see Jimmy. Let me take him out now and then. Invite me to his wedding.

(*They both laugh.*)

Marion.   You've got it.

Arthur (*clearing the table*).   Let me get all this cold cocoa out of the way. We still have the deed to do.

Marion (*checking her watch*).   And I've got to get Jimmy home in time for practice.

Arthur.   Band practice?

Marion.   Baseball. (*Picking her list off the floor*) About this list, you do what you want.

Arthur.   Believe me, I will. But I promise to consider your suggestions. Just don't rush me. I'm not ready to give it all away. (*Arthur is off to the kitchen with his tray and the phone rings. He answers it in the kitchen*) Hello? . . . just a minute. (*Calling out*) It's your eager Little Leaguer.

(*Marion picks up the living room extension and Arthur hangs his up.*)

Marion (*into phone*).   Hello, honey . . . I'll be done in five minutes. No. You know what? You come up here and get me. . . . No, I said you should come up here. . . . I said I want you to come up here. . . . Because I said so. . . . Thank you.

(*She hangs the receiver.*)

Arthur (*rushing to the papers*).   Alright, where do we start on these?

Marion (*getting out her seal*).   I guess you should just start signing everything and I'll stamp along with you. Keep one of everything on the side for yourself.

Arthur.   Now I feel so rushed. What am I signing?

Marion.   You want to do this another time?

Arthur.   No. Let's get it over with. I wouldn't survive another session like this.

(*He starts to sign and she starts her job.*)

Marion.   I keep meaning to ask you; how are you?

Arthur (*at first puzzled and then*). Oh, you mean my health? Fine. No, I'm fine. I've been tested, and nothing. We were very careful. We took many precautions. Collin used to make jokes about how we should invest in rubber futures.

Marion. I'll bet.

Arthur (*stops what he's doing*). It never occurred to me until now. How about you?

Marion (*not stopping*). Well, we never had sex after he got sick.

Arthur. But before?

Marion (*stopping but not looking up*). I have the antibodies in my blood. No signs that it will ever develop into anything else. And it's been five years so my chances are pretty good that I'm just a carrier.

Arthur. I'm so sorry. Collin never told me.

Marion. He didn't know. In fact, other than my husband and the doctors, you're the only one I've told.

Arthur. You and your husband . . . ?

Marion. Have invested in rubber futures. There'd only be a problem if we wanted to have a child. Which we do. But we'll wait. Miracles happen every day.

Arthur. I don't know what to say.

Marion. Tell me you'll be there if I ever need you.

(*Arthur gets up, goes to her and puts his arms around her. They hold each other. He gently pushes her away to make a joke.*)

Arthur. Sure! Take something else that should have been mine.

Marion. Don't even joke about things like that.

(*The doorbell rings. They pull themselves together.*)

Arthur. You know we'll never get these done today.

Marion. So, tomorrow.

(*Arthur goes to open the door as Marion gathers her things. He opens the door and Jimmy is standing in the hall.*)

Jim. C'mon, Ma. I'm gonna be late.

Arthur. Would you like to come inside?

Jim. We've gotta go.

Marion. Jimmy, come on.

Jim. Ma!

(*She glares. He comes in. Arthur closes the door.*)

Marion (*holding out the flowers*). Take these for Mommy.

Jim (*taking them*).   Can we go?

Marion (*picking up the painting*).   Say good-bye to your Uncle Arthur.

Jim.   'Bye, Arthur. Come on.

Marion.   Give him a kiss.

Arthur.   Marion, don't.

Marion.   Give your uncle a kiss good-bye.

Jim.   He's not my uncle.

Marion.   No. He's a hell of a lot more than your uncle.

Arthur (*offering his hand*).   A handshake will do.

Marion.   Tell Uncle Arthur what your daddy told you.

Jim.   About what?

Marion.   Stop playing dumb. You know.

Arthur.   Don't embarrass him.

Marion.   Jimmy, please.

Jim (*he regards his mother's softer tone and then speaks*).   He said that after me and Mommy he loved you the most.

Marion (*standing behind him*).   Go on.

Jim.   And that I should love you too. And make sure that you're not lonely or very sad.

Arthur.   Thank you.

(*Arthur reaches down to the boy and they hug. Jim gives him a little peck on the cheek and then breaks away.*)

Marion (*going to open the door*).   Alright, kid, you done good. Now let's blow this joint before you muck it up.

(*Jim rushes out the door. Marion turns to Arthur.*)

Marion.   A child's kiss is magic. Why else would they be so stingy with them. I'll call you.

(*Arthur nods understanding. Marion pulls the door closed behind her. Arthur stands quietly as the lights fade to black.*)

NOTE: *If being performed on film, the final image should be of Arthur leaning his back against the closed door on the inside of the apartment and Marion leaning on the outside of the door. A moment of thought and then they both move on.*

For Analysis

1. What is Jimmy's attitude toward homosexuals? How is it revealed?

2. What is June's view on the disposition of Collin's property? On what does she base her opinion?

3. How does Marion's relationship to Arthur change during the play? What causes the change?

4. What do you make of the title of the play?

5. What is the effect of Jimmy's last encounter with Arthur?

6. What, exactly, does Arthur ask for from Marion and her family?

On Style

Carefully reread the first two stage directions. Imagine yourself the director of the play. How would you realize the stage directions: "Obviously someone is moving out. From the way the boxes are neatly labeled and stacked, we know that this is an organized person" and "she appears to be going to a business meeting"?

Making Connections

1. The idea of marriage for gay couples is being hotly debated by governments, the clergy, and the public. What are your feelings on the issue? Are those feelings affected by your response to this play? Explain.

2. Reflect on Nora's marriage to Helmer in Henrik Ibsen's *A Doll's House* (p. 499) and the relationship between Arthur and Collin in this play. Which "marriage" corresponds most closely to your own view of marriage? Explain.

Writing Topic

1. The interaction of Arthur and Marion begins with strained politeness, degenerates into anger, and ends with reconciliation. In an essay, describe the sources of each of these emotional interactions.

2. Did this play in any way affect your attitudes about gay people — or about being gay? Explain.

Essays

John Donne   (1572–1631)

Meditation XVII, from *Devotions upon Emergent Occasions* 1623

Nunc lento sonitu dicunt morieris.
  Now this bell tolling softly for another says to me, Thou must die.

Perchance he for whom this bell tolls may be so ill as that he knows not it tolls for him; and perchance I may think myself so much better than I am, as that they who are about me and see my state may have caused it to toll for me, and I know not that. The church is catholic, universal, so are all her actions; all that she does belongs to all. When she baptizes a child, that action concerns me; for 5 that child is thereby connected to that head which is my head too, and ingrafted into that body whereof I am a member. And when she buries a man, that action concerns me: all mankind is of one author and is one volume; when one man dies, one chapter is not torn out of the book, but translated into a better language; and every chapter must be so translated. God employs several transla- 10 tors; some pieces are translated by age, some by sickness, some by war, some by justice; but God's hand is in every translation, and his hand shall bind up all our scattered leaves again for that library where every book shall lie open to one another. As therefore the bell that rings to a sermon calls not upon the preacher only, but upon the congregation to come, so this bell calls us all; but how much 15 more me, who am brought so near the door by this sickness. There was a contention as far as a suit[1] (in which piety and dignity, religion and estimation, were mingled) which of the religious orders should ring to prayers first in the morning; and it was determined that they should ring first that rose earliest. If we

---

[1] An argument settled by a lawsuit.

understand aright the dignity of this bell that tolls for our evening prayer, we   20
would be glad to make it ours by rising early, in that application, that it might be
ours as well as his whose indeed it is. The bell doth toll for him that thinks it
doth, and though it intermit again, yet from that minute that that occasion
wrought upon him, he is united to God. Who casts not up his eye to the sun
when it rises? but who takes off his eye from a comet when that breaks out?   25
Who bends not his ear to any bell which upon any occasion rings? but who can
remove it from that bell which is passing a piece of himself out of this world? No
man is an island, entire of itself; every man is a piece of the continent, a part of
the main. If a clod be washed away by the sea, Europe is the less, as well as if a
promontory were, as well as if a manor of thy friend's or of thine own were. Any   30
man's death diminishes me, because I am involved in mankind; and therefore
never send to know for whom the bell tolls; it tolls for thee. Neither can we call
this a begging of misery or a borrowing of misery, as though we were not miserable enough of ourselves but must fetch in more from the next house, in taking
upon us the misery of our neighbors. Truly it were an excusable covetousness if   35
we did; for affliction is a treasure, and scarce any man hath enough of it. No man
hath affliction enough that is not matured and ripened by it, and made fit for
God by that affliction. If a man carry treasure in bullion, or in a wedge of gold,
and have none coined into current moneys, his treasure will not defray him as
he travels. Tribulation is treasure in the nature of it, but it is not current money   40
in the use of it, except we get nearer and nearer our home, heaven, by it.
Another man may be sick too, and sick to death, and this affliction may lie in his
bowels as gold in a mine and be of no use to him; but this bell that tells me of his
affliction digs out and applies that gold to me, if by this consideration of
another's danger I take mine own into contemplation and so secure myself by   45
making my recourse to my God, who is our only security.

For Analysis

1. What does Donne mean when he asserts that the death bell "tolls for thee" (l. 32)?

2. Toward the end of his meditation, Donne states that "tribulation is treasure"
(l. 40). What does he mean? What will that treasure purchase?

On Style

Donne is justly admired for his use of **figurative language**. What extended **metaphors**
does he use to characterize humankind and death?

Making Connections

Consider Donne's famous assertion, "No man is an island, entire of itself" (ll. 27–28).
Is the assertion an accurate description of the human condition? Explain.

Writing Topics

1. What does Donne mean when he asserts that "affliction is a treasure" (l. 36)? Do
you agree? Explain.

2. Identify and analyze the figurative language Donne uses to illuminate the human
condition and his attitude toward death.

Mark Twain (1835–1910)

Little Bessie Would Assist Providence[1] 1908

[It is dull, and I need wholesome excitements and distractions; so I will go lightly excursioning along the primrose path of theology.]

Little Bessie was nearly three years old. She was a good child, and not shallow, not frivolous, but meditative and thoughtful, and much given to thinking out the reasons of things and trying to make them harmonize with results. One day she said:

'Mama, why is there so much pain and sorrow and suffering? What is it all for?'

It was an easy question, and mama had no difficulty in answering it:

'It is for our good, my child. In His wisdom and mercy the Lord sends us 5
these afflictions to discipline us and make us better.'

'Is it *He* that sends them?'

'Yes.'

'Does He need *all* of them, mama?'

'Yes, dear, all of them. None of them comes by accident; He alone sends them, and always out of love for us, and to make us better.'

'Isn't it strange?' 10

'Strange? Why, no, I have never thought of it in that way. I have not heard any one call it strange before. It has always seemed natural and right to me, and wise and most kindly and merciful.'

'Who first thought of it like that, mama? Was it you?'

'Oh no, child, I was taught it.'

'Who taught you so, mama?'

'Why, really, I don't know — I can't remember. My mother, I suppose; or the 15
preacher. But it's a thing that everybody knows.'

'Well, anyway, it does seem strange. Did He give Billy Norris the typhus?'

'Yes.'

'What for?'

'Why, to discipline him and make him good.'

'But he died, mama, and so it *couldn't* make him good.' 20

'Well, then, I suppose it was for some other reason. We know it was a *good* reason, whatever it was.'

---

[1] Late in his life, Twain worked and wrote often on what he called "moral ideas." Occasionally, he wrote moral essays in the voice of an inquisitive little girl, Bessie, who pursues her mother with difficult questions.

'What do you think it was, mama?'

'Oh, you ask so many questions! I think it was to discipline his parents.'

'Well, then, it wasn't fair, mama. Why should *his* life be taken away for their sake, when he wasn't doing anything?'

'Oh, *I* don't know! I only know it was for a good and wise and merciful rea- 25 son.'

'What reason, mama?'

'I think — I think — well, it was a judgment; it was to punish them for some sin they had committed.'

'But *he* was the one that was punished, mama. Was that right?'

'Certainly, certainly. He does nothing that isn't right and wise and merciful. You can't understand these things now, dear, but when you are grown up you will understand them, and then you will see that they are just and wise.'

After a pause: 30

'Did He make the roof fall in on the stranger that was trying to save the crippled old woman from the fire, mama?'

'Yes, my child. *Wait!* Don't ask me why, because I don't know. I only know it was to discipline some one, or be a judgment upon somebody, or to show His power.'

'That drunken man that stuck a pitchfork into Mrs. Welch's baby when —'

'Never mind about it, you needn't go into particulars; it was to discipline the child — *that* much is certain, anyway.'

'Mama, Mr. Burgess said in his sermon that billions of little creatures are sent 35 into us to give us cholera, and typhoid, and lockjaw, and more than a thousand other sicknesses and — mama, does He send them?'

'Oh, certainly, child, certainly. Of course.'

'What for?'

'Oh, to *dis*cipline us! Haven't I told you so, over and over again?'

'It's awful cruel, mama! And silly! and if I —'

'Hush, oh *hush!* Do you want to bring the lightning?' 40

'You know the lightning *did* come last week, mama, and struck the new church, and burnt it down. Was it to discipline the church?'

(Wearily) 'Oh, I suppose so.'

'But it killed a hog that wasn't doing anything. Was it to discipline the hog, mama?'

'Dear child, don't you want to run out and play a while? If you would like to —'

'Mama, only think! Mr. Hollister says there isn't a bird, or fish, or reptile, or 45 any other animal that hasn't got an enemy that Providence has sent to bite it and chase it and pester it and kill it and suck its blood and discipline it and make it good and religious. Is that true, mother — because if it is true why did Mr. Hollister laugh at it?'

'That Hollister is a scandalous person, and I don't want you to listen to anything he says.'

'Why, mama, he is very interesting, and *I* think he tries to be good. He says the wasps catch spiders and cram them down into their nests in the ground — *alive,* mama! — and there they live and suffer days and days and days, and the hungry little wasps chewing their legs and gnawing into their bellies all the time, to make them good and religious and praise God for His infinite mercies. *I* think Mr. Hollister is just lovely, and ever so kind; for when I asked him if *he* would treat a spider like that he said he hoped to be damned if he would; and then he — *Dear* mama, have you fainted? I will run and bring help! Now *this* comes of staying in town this hot weather.'

For Analysis

1. What assumptions does Bessie's mother have about the relationship between God and people?

2. Bessie and Mr. Hollister confront the problem addressed in the Old Testament Book of Job and by modern theologians as well: Why do bad things happen to good people? How would you answer the question?

On Style

Do you think Twain's colloquial **style** is suitable for the grave issues he addresses? Why or why not?

Making Connections

Compare this essay with Donne's "Meditation XVII" (p. 1480). Which do you find more persuasive? Defend your response.

Writing Topics

1. Contrast the formal style of Donne's "Meditation XVII" with Twain's colloquial style in this piece.

2. Contrast Donne's religious perspective (revealed in "Meditation XVII") with Twain's.

3. Explain which worldview — the religious or the secular humanist view exhibited in this essay — is more congenial to your own experience.

Jessica Mitford   (1917–1996)

The American Way of Death   1963

O Death, where is thy sting? O grave, where is thy victory?[1] Where, indeed. Many a badly stung survivor, faced with the aftermath of some relative's funeral, has ruefully concluded that the victory has been won hands down by a funeral establishment — in disastrously unequal battle.

Much has been written of late about the affluent society in which we live, and much fun poked at some of the irrational "status symbols" set out like golden snares to trap the unwary consumer at every turn. Until recently, little has been said about the most irrational and weirdest of the lot, lying in ambush for all of us at the end of the road — the modern American funeral.

If the Dismal Traders (as an eighteenth-century English writer calls them) have traditionally been cast in a comic role in literature, a universally recognized symbol of humor from Shakespeare to Dickens to Evelyn Waugh, they have successfully turned the tables in recent years to perpetrate a huge, macabre and expensive practical joke on the American public. It is not consciously conceived as a joke, of course; on the contrary, it is hedged with admirably contrived rationalizations.

Gradually, almost imperceptibly, over the years the funeral men have constructed their own grotesque cloud-cuckooland where the trappings of Gracious Living are transformed, as in a nightmare, into the trappings of Gracious Dying. The same familiar Madison Avenue language, with its peculiar adjectival range designed to anesthetize sales resistance to all sorts of products, has seeped into the funeral industry in a new and bizarre guise. The emphasis is on the same desirable qualities that we have all been schooled to look for in our daily search for excellence: comfort, durability, beauty, craftsmanship. The attuned ear will recognize too the convincing quasi-scientific language, so reassuring even if unintelligible.

So that this too, too solid flesh might not melt, we are offered "solid copper —   5 a quality casket which offers superb value to the client seeking long-lasting protection," or "the Colonial Classic Beauty — 18 gauge lead coated steel, seamless top, lap-jointed welded body construction." Some are equipped with foam rubber, some with innerspring mattresses. Elgin offers "the revolutionary 'Perfect-Posture' bed." Not every casket need have a silver lining, for one may choose between "more than 60 color matched shades, magnificent and unique masterpieces" by the Cheney casket-lining people. Shrouds no longer exist. Instead, you may patronize a grave-wear couturière who promises "handmade original

---

[1] See 1 Corinthians 15:55.

fashions — styles from the best in life for the last memory — dresses, men's suits, negligees, accessories." For the final, perfect grooming: "Nature-Glo — the ultimate in cosmetic embalming." And, where have we heard the phrase "peace of mind protection" before? No matter. In funeral advertising, it is applied to the Wilbert Burial Vault, with its ⅝-inch precast asphalt inner liner plus extra-thick, reinforced concrete — all this "guaranteed by Good House-keeping." Here again the Cadillac, status symbol par excellence, appears in all its gleaming glory, this time transformed into a pastel-colored funeral hearse.

You, the potential customer for all this luxury, are unlikely to read the lyrical descriptions quoted above, for they are culled from *Mortuary Management* and *Casket and Sunnyside,* two of the industry's eleven trade magazines. For you there are ads in your daily newspaper, generally found on the obituary page, stressing dignity, refinement, high-caliber professional service and that intangible quality, *sincerity.* The trade advertisements are, however, instructive, because they furnish an important clue to the frame of mind into which the funeral industry has hypnotized itself.

A new mythology, essential to the twentieth-century American funeral rite, has grown up — or rather has been built up step by step — to justify the peculiar customs surrounding the disposal of our dead. And, just as the witch doctor must be convinced of his own infallibility in order to maintain a hold over his clientele, so the funeral industry has had to "sell itself" on its articles of faith in the course of passing them along to the public.

The first of these is the tenet that today's funeral procedures are founded in "American tradition." The story comes to mind of a sign on the freshly sown lawn of a brand-new Midwest college: "There is a tradition on this campus that students never walk on this strip of grass. This tradition goes into effect next Tuesday." The most cursory look at American funerals of past times will establish this parallel. Simplicity to the point of starkness, the plain pine box, the laying out of the dead by friends and family who also bore the coffin to the grave — these were the hallmarks of the traditional funeral until the end of the nineteenth century.

Secondly, there is a myth that the American public is only being given what it wants — an opportunity to keep up with the Joneses to the end. "In keeping with our high standard of living, there should be an equally high standard of dying," says the past president of the Funeral Directors of San Francisco. "The cost of a funeral varies according to individual taste and the niceties of living the family has been accustomed to." Actually, choice doesn't enter the picture for the average individual, faced, generally for the first time, with the necessity of buying a product of which he is totally ignorant, at a moment when he is least in a position to quibble. In point of fact the cost of a funeral almost always varies, not "according to individual taste" but according to what the traffic will bear.

Thirdly, there is an assortment of myths based on half-digested psychiatric theories. The importance of the "memory picture" is stressed — meaning the last glimpse of the deceased in open casket, done up with the latest in embalming techniques and finished off with a dusting of makeup. A newer one, impres- 10 sively authentic-sounding, is the need for "grief therapy," which is beginning to go over big in mortuary circles. A historian of American funeral directing hints at the grief-therapist idea when speaking of the new role of the undertaker — "the dramaturgic role, in which the undertaker becomes a stage manager to create an appropriate atmosphere and to move the funeral party through a drama in which social relationships are stressed and an emotional catharsis or release is provided through ceremony."

Lastly, a whole new terminology, as ornately shoddy as the satin rayon casket liner, has been invented by the funeral industry to replace the direct and serviceable vocabulary of former times. Undertaker has been supplanted by "funeral director" or "mortician." (Even the classified section of the telephone directory gives recognition to this; in its pages you will find "Undertakers — see Funeral Directors.") Coffins are "caskets"; hearses are "coaches," or "professional cars"; flowers are "floral tributes"; corpses generally are "loved ones," but mortuary etiquette dictates that a specific corpse be referred to by name only — as, "Mr. Jones"; cremated ashes are "cremains." Euphemisms such as "slumber room," "reposing room," and "calcination — the *kindlier* heat" abound in the funeral business.

If the undertaker is the stage manager of the fabulous production that is the modern American funeral, the stellar role is reserved for the occupant of the open casket. The decor, the stagehands, the supporting cast are all arranged for the most advantageous display of the deceased, without which the rest of the paraphernalia would lose its point — *Hamlet* without the Prince of Denmark. It is to this end that a fantastic array of costly merchandise and services is pyramided to dazzle the mourners and facilitate the plunder of the next of kin.

Grief therapy, anyone? But it's going to come high. According to the funeral industry's own figures, the *average* undertaker's bill in 1961 was $708 for casket and "services," to which must be added the cost of a burial vault, flowers, clothing, clergy and musician's honorarium, and cemetery charges. When these costs are added to the undertaker's bill, the total average cost for an adult's funeral is, as we shall see, close to $1,450.

The question naturally arises, *is* this what most people want for themselves and their families? For several reasons, this has been a hard one to answer until recently. It is a subject seldom discussed. Those who have never had to arrange for a funeral frequently shy away from its implications, preferring to take comfort in the thought that sufficient unto the day is the evil thereof. Those who have acquired personal and painful knowledge of the subject would often rather forget about it. Pioneering "Funeral Societies" or "Memorial Associations," dedicated to the principle of dignified funerals at reasonable cost, have existed in a number of communities throughout the country, but their membership has been limited for the most part to the more sophisticated element in the population — university people, liberal intellectuals — and those who, like doctors and lawyers, come up against problems in arranging funerals for their clients.

Some indication of the pent-up resentment felt by vast numbers of people 15 against the funeral interests was furnished by the astonishing response to an article by Roul Tunley, titled "Can You Afford to Die?" in *The Saturday Evening Post* of June 17, 1961. As though a dike had burst, letters poured in from every part of the country to the *Post*, to the funeral societies, to local newspapers. They came from clergymen, professional people, old-age pensioners, trade unionists. Three months after the article appeared, an estimated six thousand had taken pen in hand to comment on some phase of the high cost of dying. Many recounted their own bitter experiences at the hands of funeral directors; hundreds asked for advice on how to establish a consumer organization in communities where none exists; others sought information about pre-need plans. The membership of funeral societies skyrocketed. The funeral industry, finding itself in the glare of public spotlight, has begun to engage in serious debate about its own future course — as well it might.

Is the funeral inflation bubble ripe for bursting? A few years ago, the United States public suddenly rebelled against the trend in the auto industry towards ever more showy cars, with their ostentatious and nonfunctional fins, and a demand was created for compact cars patterned after European models. The all-powerful auto industry, accustomed to *telling* the customer what sort of car he wanted, was suddenly forced to *listen* for a change. Overnight, the little cars became for millions a new kind of status symbol. Could it be that the same cycle is working itself out in the attitude towards the final return of dust to dust, that the American public is becoming sickened by ever more ornate and costly funerals, and that a status symbol of the future may indeed be the simplest kind of "funeral without fins"?

For Analysis

1. What four "articles of faith" (para. 7) does Mitford attribute to the funeral industry?

2. In the final three paragraphs, Mitford speculates about what most people want. Make a list of the assumptions she puts forward. Do you agree with her? Explain.

On Style

Consider the opening sentences of the first and fifth paragraphs. Identify the **allusions** Mitford uses, and comment on how they contribute to her argument.

Making Connections

What other "ornate and costly" (para. 16) cultural customs would you consider open to criticism or ridicule?

Writing Topic

Imitating Mitford's approach and style, write an essay on "The American Way of _____ ." Possible subjects might include high school proms, weddings, football half-time shows, debutante balls, bar mitzvahs or confirmations, or New Year's Eve celebrations.

Melvin I. Urofsky   (b.1939)

Two Scenes from a Hospital 1993

Two things a person does alone, the ancient maxim held, are come into the world and leave it. It is true that for most of human existence, people died by themselves, the victims of predators, war, disease, or aging. As civilization tamed humanity, people died at home, in their own beds, surrounded by loving family who might ease the final pains but could do nothing to delay the death. Only in the recent past have people gone to hospitals to die, and only within the last decade or so has medicine developed drugs, procedures, and technology to hold off death.

These developments raise a host of questions, but in the end they all come down to what does the individual want, and if the individual is incapable of deciding, what does the family want. But there are others who now demand a voice in the decision — doctors, nurses, hospital administrators, insurance companies, and, very often, agents of the state. In most instances, the person dies without interference, since there is still little that medicine can do when age or disease have taken their ultimate toll. But in other situations, instead of death coming peacefully and with dignity, there is conflict and suffering, rage and public controversy.

In these cases, the key issue is who will decide whether or not care should be provided or withheld, whether enormous energy and resources should be expended to delay death, or whether nothing should be done, so that death may have its way. Who decides, and what role, if any, should the law play in this process? These are not easy questions, as can be seen in the following stories.

Rocco Musolino was a big man, one who enjoyed good food and drink and people, a gregarious man who had run a liquor store in College Park, Maryland, until his retirement. He also hated hospitals, and never wanted to end his days in one.[1] To avoid that possibility, Musolino wrote a living will in 1989 in which he specifically declared that if he were terminally ill, he did not want to be kept alive by machine. Aware that if he were really sick he might not be able to make decisions on his own, he also signed a durable power of attorney giving his wife of fifty years, Edith, the authority to make decisions about his care. Repeatedly

---

[1] Rocco Musolino's story is based on an extensive feature by Susan Okie in the *Washington Post,* June 16, 1991. [This, and subsequent notes, are Urofsky's.]

he told his family he did not want to be hooked up to any "damn machine" or "kept alive as a vegetable."

Rocco Musolino had drawn up his living will shortly after he had suffered a 5 major heart attack in 1988. While he was in the hospital at that time doctors had performed a catheterization procedure that revealed that he had severe blockages in the coronary arteries and that one-fourth of his heart muscle was already dead. The damage was so extensive that doctors ruled out coronary bypass surgery.

Musolino had no illusions as to the prognosis of the disease, nor the fact that his diabetes seriously compounded the problem. In the two years following his heart attack, his condition deteriorated to the point that he had difficulty moving around his house. "If he made it to the bathroom, that was a big deal," his daughter Edith Scott said. "He couldn't shave. He would get all out of breath."

On October 24, 1990, following a night of chest pains and difficulty breathing, he told his wife he couldn't stand the pain anymore. She called an ambulance to take him to Georgetown University Medical Center. There his regular cardiologist, Dr. Richard Rubin, examined Musolino, and then called in a surgeon, Dr. Nevin Katz, who told the family that Rocco's only hope lay in bypass surgery, the same procedure that had been ruled out two years earlier.

"He'll die without an operation," Katz told Edith Musolino. "He's got a 50-50 chance with it." The family agreed reluctantly, since it appeared that potential kidney failure would also require dialysis, the type of machine treatment that Musolino had always feared. Musolino stayed in the hospital to undergo tests and build up his strength, and the medical staff scheduled him for bypass surgery on November 12. The night before the operation, Dr. Rubin went in to visit his patient, and later said that Rocco expressed a strong desire to live, even if it meant he might have to go onto dialysis for the rest of his life.

Later that night, Musolino suffered two cardiac arrests but survived, and Rubin and Katz decided to go ahead with the surgery. Rubin called to get Edith Musolino's consent and then wrote in the patient's record: "He is awake and wishes to proceed. He is aware of the risk. I have reviewed the high risk of death (40 percent), high risk of renal failure (long term about 50 percent) with wife and daughter." His daughter later said she could not recall any such discussion.

The operation appeared successful, at least in relieving strain on the heart, 10 but Musolino's kidneys failed, and he required dialysis several times a week. Since he could not breathe without a respirator, his wife reluctantly agreed to a tracheotomy, in which doctors inserted a breathing tube into his neck. In addition to causing constant pain, the breathing tube left Rocco unable to talk.

Musolino remained conscious and aware of what was happening, but his family claims he was never fully alert, and his medical records seem to bear this out. Doctors' notes show that he slept a lot, and often responded to questions only with a grimace. A neurologist who examined him noted that his fluctuating state of consciousness resulted from severe medical problems; if he overcame them, he would probably regain full mental clarity.

But Rocco Musolino did not improve, and as the weeks went on his family concluded that he would never recover. In late November they asked the doctors to put a "Do Not Resuscitate" order on his chart, so that he would not be treated if he suffered another cardiac arrest. Dr. Katz refused. When the family requested that he stop some of the medication, he angrily told them: "I stay awake at night trying to keep your father alive, and you want me to kill him. What is wrong with you people?" Only after his patient's condition deteriorated further did Katz agree to a "DNR" order.

Edith Musolino watched her husband's condition worsen. "Everything that could be wrong with him was wrong with him. I knew he was dying. I knew his body couldn't take any more." She made up her mind in December to ask the hospital to stop the dialysis sessions and to let her husband die in peace.

On December 21, 1990, the hospital's ethics committee met to consider the request, and recommended a psychiatric examination to determine whether Musolino was mentally competent. Under District of Columbia law, if he were declared incompetent, then the durable power of attorney would become operative, and his wife would have the authority to make the medical decisions.

The hospital named Dr. Steven A. Epstein to do the evaluation, and he visited 15 Musolino twice at times when the patient seemed to rally a bit. Epstein's initial report, dated December 27, was inconclusive, and the family pushed for a second evaluation. This time the doctor reported the patient "lethargic and barely responding to voice. Today he clearly cannot make health care decisions on his own." Musolino, he told the family, was not mentally competent.

On New Year's Day 1991, Edith Musolino filed a note in her husband's medical records withdrawing her consent for dialysis. According to her, doctors, hospital administrators, and the hospital's lawyers agreed that she had the authority; they ordered dialysis stopped and removed the tube used to connect Musolino to the machine. Advised that without the treatment he would probably die within a few days, she and her children went to a funeral home and made the necessary arrangements.

They returned to the hospital to learn that Katz had changed his mind, and wanted to restart dialysis. He wrote on January 2, "I cannot in good conscience carry out their request," and he asked the hospital's lawyers and the chairman of the ethics committee to reopen the case.

The family now tried to find another physician or to have Musolino transferred to another hospital that would honor their requests. Katz agreed to turn over the case if the family could find a heart specialist with intensive-care experience. As Scott Musolino reported: "I called so many doctors. No one was willing to touch my father."

The next day Georgetown Hospital's lawyers wrote to the family's attorney informing them that the hospital would seek "emergency temporary guardianship" unless the family agreed to resume dialysis. Edith Musolino felt she had no choice but to agree.

Ten days later, her husband's condition deteriorating, her frustration and 20 anger at the indignities that had been heaped upon him in spite of his express wishes finally erupted in a confrontation with Katz at Rocco's bedside. With her husband's legs and arms twitching, his face grimacing, she demanded of Katz: "What are you trying to prove here? You have made him suffer so much."

Katz asked her what she wanted. She said she wanted another doctor, Taveira Da Silva, the head of the hospital's intensive-care unit, who had earlier agreed to take the case on condition that dialysis be continued. Katz agreed, and the next morning nurses wheeled Rocco to the ICU, where the staff gradually began treating him as a dying patient. While Da Silva described Musolino as "terminal," he nonetheless continued dialysis, even though by this point the patient had become totally disoriented and his arms had to be tied down during the procedure.

His family had reached the end of their patience as well and had agreed that the only way to save Rocco from further indignity was to take him home. At a meeting on January 24, Dr. Da Silva agreed to stop the dialysis if they wanted to do that. A few days later, however, Da Silva finally came to the conclusion the family had reached much earlier — Rocco Musolino had "virtually a fatal, irreversible disease," that no medical care could help, and that the living will, which the hospital and doctors had ignored for three months, should be enforced. He told Edith that he would stop the dialysis and let her husband die in the hospital.

Instead of relief that her husband's long ordeal would soon be over, Edith Musolino felt only anger. "You know, Doctor," she said, "I was beginning not to know who to pray to anymore. Do I pray to you, or do I pray to God?"

On February 2, 1991, Rocco Musolino died, after a stay of 102 days in Georgetown University Medical Center, a place he had never wanted to be and where he and his family had lost all power to decide his fate.

While Rocco Musolino's wife fought to get hospital authorities to stop treat- 25 ing him, halfway across the continent hospital officials were trying to get a patient's family to consent to a cessation of treatment.

On December 14, 1989, Helga Wanglie, an eighty-six-year-old retired school-teacher, tripped on a scatter rug in her home in Minneapolis and fractured her hip. After surgery in a small private hospital, she developed breathing problems and was transferred to Hennepin County Medical Center. There, although on a respirator, she remained fully conscious and alert, writing notes to her husband, since the breathing tube prevented her from talking.

After five months, the hospital weaned her from the respirator in May 1990, and she entered Bethesda Lutheran Hospital across the river in St. Paul, a facility specializing in the care of respiratory ailments. A few days later, her heart stopped suddenly, and by the time doctors and nurses could resuscitate her, she had suffered severe brain damage. An ambulance brought her back to Hennepin Medical in a comatose state, her breathing sustained by a ventilator. When it became clear that doctors could do nothing for Mrs. Wanglie, they spoke with her husband of fifty-three years, Oliver, a retired attorney, about turning off the ventilator.

Although her husband and sons recognized that Helga had no cognition and might never regain consciousness, they would not hear of turning off the machine. His wife had strong religious convictions, Oliver told reporters, and they had talked about the possibility that if anything happened to her, she wanted "everything" done to keep her alive. "She told me, 'Only He who gave me life has the right to take life.' . . . It seems to me [the hospital officials] are trying to play God. Who are they to determine who's to die and who's to live? I take the position that as long as her heart is beating there's life there."

Eight months after readmitting Helga Wanglie and trying to convince her family to stop treatment, Hennepin Medical Center officials announced they would go to court seeking the appointment of a guardian to determine Helga Wanglie's medical treatment. The hospital did not request that the court authorize discontinuing treatment. To the best of my knowledge, no hospital has ever made such a request, nor has there been any case law on it. Rather, the hospital sought the appointment of a "stranger" conservator, that is, one independent of both family and hospital, to make decisions based on the best interests of the patient. The hospital believed that a neutral party would agree with its position.

While in most right-to-die cases it is the patient or the family that wants the   30 hospital to stop treatment, the Wanglie case is the rarely seen other side of the coin. Dr. Michael B. Belzer, the hospital's medical director, said he sympathized with the Wanglie family, but a heartbeat no longer signified life, since machines could artificially do the heart's work. The real question, he believed, was whether the hospital had an obligation to provide "inappropriate medical treatment."

Mrs. Wanglie's medical bills were paid in full by her insurance company, so money was not an issue in the hospital's decision. "This is a pure ethics case," said Dr. Arthur Caplan, director of the Center for Biomedical Ethics at the University of Minnesota. For years, he explained, we've used the "smokescreen of 'Can we afford to do this?' There's been a harder question buried under that layer of blather about money, namely: 'What's the point of medical care?' "

Dr. Belzer noted that Hennepin had the facilities and "the technology to keep fifty Helga Wanglies alive for an indefinite period of time. That would be the easy thing to do. The harder thing is to say just because we can do it, do we have to do it?"

Hennepin Medical Center is a public hospital, one of the best in the upper midwest, and before it could petition a court to appoint a conservator or guardian for Mrs. Wanglie (in order to have consent for turning off the life support), it needed the approval of the county's Board of Commissioners. The board members gave the hospital permission by a 4–3 vote, with the tiebreaker cast by a member who had known the Wanglie family for more than thirty years. It took him a month to make up his mind.

The commissioner, Randy Jackson, said that he finally voted to let the hospital go to the courts because "I don't think this is a decision to be made by a board of elected commissioners who happen to be trustees of the hospital. These are issues that we're going to be confronted with more and more often as medical machinery becomes more and more able to keep people alive."[2]

Hospital attorneys presented their case to county judge Patricia Belois on 35 May 28, 1991, asking her to appoint a conservator to decide Mrs. Wanglie's fate. They did not question her husband's sincerity, but argued instead that her condition was hopeless, and respirators had never been intended to prolong life in such cases.

On July 1, Judge Belois ruled against the hospital and left power to decide decisions on Helga's medical treatment in her husband's hands. "He is in the best position to investigate and act upon Helga Wanglie's conscientious, religious, and moral beliefs." After the decision Oliver Wanglie said "I think she'd be proud of me. She knew where I stood. I have a high regard for the sanctity of human life."[3]

A little while after this decision, Helga Wanglie died.

The key issue is that of who decides what is best for a terminally ill person and what role the law and the courts have in that process. In an ideal world, perhaps, the interests of patients, families, doctors, hospitals, and courts would all coincide. But aside from the fact that this is an imperfect world, the interests of these groups are not necessarily congruent.

For centuries doctors have sworn to uphold life, and now for the first time they are being asked, openly and at times defiantly, what gives them the right to decide other people's fate? Hospitals, caught in a crunch between escalating expenses and new technology, must weigh costs that never before mattered. Moreover, in a society as litigious as ours, doctors and hospitals walk in constant fear that a "wrong" judgment will lead to a ruinous lawsuit. While elective bodies are responsible for broad policy decisions, it is difficult if not impossible to frame legislation in such a way as to cover all contingencies, and so courts must step in to interpret not only what the laws say and mean, but also what the limits of self-autonomy are under both the common law and constitutional protection.

Two things a person does alone, the ancient maxim held: come into the world 40 and leave it. But at the end of the twentieth century, before one can leave this world, he or she may find it necessary to traverse a bewildering legal, moral, and medical maze.

For Analysis

1. Do you think Rocco Musolino's surgeon was justified in putting a "Do Not Resuscitate" order on his patient's chart? Why or why not?

2. Do you think Helga Wanglie's husband and sons were justified in refusing to give permission to turn off the ventilator that was keeping her alive? Explain.

---

[2] *New York Times*, January 10, 1991; *Time*, January 21, 1991, 67.
[3] In re the Conservatorship of Wanglie, No. PX-91-283, Minnesota Dist. Ct., Probate Div. [July 1991].

On Style

Compare and contrast the writing style of this essay with the **style** of Mark Twain's "Little Bessie Would Assist Providence" (p. 1482). Discuss the relationship between style and purpose in these two works.

Making Connections

Examine the relationships between public officials, the courts, doctors, and the family in the case of Helga Wanglie. Then define your own position on how patients in right-to-die cases should be treated.

Writing Topic

In an essay, describe a scene from your own experience of the death of someone close to you.

LOOKING BACK:
Further Questions for Thinking and Writing

1. Although A. E. Housman's "To an Athlete Dying Young" (p. 1389), Pablo Neruda's "The Dead Woman" (p. 1402), and Theodore Roethke's "Elegy for Jane" (p. 1411) employ different poetic forms, they all embody a poetic mode called *elegy*. Define *elegy* in terms of the characteristic tone of these poems. Compare the elegiac tone of these poems. **Writing Topic:** Compare the elegiac tone of one of these poems with the tone of Wilfred Owen's "Dulce et Decorum Est" (p. 1406) or Dylan Thomas's "Do Not Go Gentle into That Good Night" (p. 1412).

2. What figurative language in the prose and poetry of this section is commonly associated with death itself? With dying? Contrast the characteristic imagery of this section with the characteristic imagery of love poetry. **Writing Topic:** Compare the imagery in Shakespeare's Sonnet 18 (p. 1097) with the imagery in Sonnet 73 (p. 1380).

3. In Leo Tolstoy's "The Death of Iván Ilých" (p. 1286) and John Donne's sonnet "Death, Be Not Proud" (p. 1384), death and dying are considered from a religious viewpoint. **Writing Topic:** Discuss whether these works develop a similar attitude toward death or whether the attitudes they develop differ crucially.

4. State the argument against resignation to death made in Dylan Thomas's "Do Not Go Gentle into That Good Night" (p. 1412). State the argument of Catherine Davis's reply, "After a Time" (p. 1414). **Writing Topic:** Using these positions as the basis of your discussion, select for analysis two works that support Thomas's argument and two works that support Davis's.

5. Contrast the attitude toward death revealed in John Donne's "Meditation XVII" (p. 1480) and Mark Twain's "Little Bessie Would Assist Providence" (p. 1482). **Writing Topic:** Analyze the figurative language in each essay. How does style contribute to the contrasting attitudes toward death expressed in these essays?

6. Antonio Machado's "Lament of the Virtues and Verses on Account of the Death of Don Guido" (p. 1396) and James Fenton's "God, A Poem" (p. 1421) both present a grim picture of the human condition, yet they are often funny. What function does humor serve in each work? **Writing Topic:** Which work embodies a more hopeful vision of the human condition? Explain.

7. Which works in this section treat death and dying in a way that corresponds most closely with your own attitudes toward mortality? Which contradict your attitudes? **Writing Topic:** Choose two works, each of which affects you differently, and isolate and discuss the elements responsible for your response.

Appendices

Appendices

Glossary of Critical Approaches

INTRODUCTION

This glossary attempts to define, briefly and in general terms, some major critical approaches to literature. Because literary criticism has to do with the *value* of literature — not with its history — judgments tend to be subjective and disagreements, frequent and even acrimonious. The truth of a work of art is very different from the truth of a mathematical formula. Certainly one's attitudes toward war, religion, sex, and politics are irrelevant to the truth of a formula but quite relevant to one's judgment of a literary work.

Yet any examination of the broad range of literary criticism reveals that groups of critics (and all readers, ultimately, are critics) share certain assumptions about literature. These shared assumptions govern the way critics approach a work, the elements they tend to look for and emphasize, the details they find significant or insignificant, and, finally, the overall value they place on the work.

We do not suggest that one approach is more valid than another or that the lines dividing the various approaches are always clear and distinct. Readers will, perhaps, discover one approach more congenial to their temperament, more "true" to their sense of the world, than another. More likely, they will find themselves utilizing more than one approach in dealing with a single work. Many of the diverse approaches described here actually overlap, and even those critics who champion a single abstract theory often draw on a variety of useful approaches when they write about a particular work.

Formalist critics assume that a literary text remains independent of the writer who created it. The function of the critic, then, is to discover how the author has deployed language to create (or perhaps failed to create) a formal and aesthetically satisfying structure. The influential American formalists of the 1940s and 1950s (the New Critics) were fond of describing literary texts as "autonomous," meaning that political, historical, biographical, and other considerations were always secondary if not irrelevant to any discussion of the work's merits.

Furthermore, formalist critics argue that the various elements of a "great" work interweave to create a seamless whole that embodies "universal" values. Unsurprisingly, the "universal" values formalist critics praise, on close analysis, tend to parallel the moral, political, and cultural ideals of the critics' social class.

But the formalist point of view, cherishing the artwork's structure, spawned its own antithesis — a group of theorists called *deconstructionists*.

1499

These writers argued that language itself was too shifty to support the expectations of formalist criticism. One reader might read a sentence literally, while another might read it ironically. Hence, their "understanding" of the text would be diametrically opposed.

The deconstructionists believe that intelligent readers cannot be expected to ignore those responses that interfere with some "correct" or "desirable" reading of the piece. Given what they see as the notoriously ambiguous and unstable nature of language, deconstructionist critics argue that a literary text can never have a fixed meaning.

While the formalists and deconstructionists wrestle over the philosophy of language and its implications for the nature of literary texts, other critics pursue quite different primary interests. The term *ethical criticism* describes a variety of approaches, all of which argue that literature, like any other human activity, connects to the real world and, consequently, influences real people. If that is so, our appraisal of a work must take into account the ethical and moral values it embodies. Though it sounds simple enough, in reality the task is difficult and often quite controversial. Ethical criticism is the very opposite of the "art for art's sake" approach, best represented by formalist criticism. The formalist critic tries to isolate the work in a timeless world of universal aesthetic considerations; the ethical critic insists on making judgments about whether a work serves values that are "good" or encourages values that are "bad."

Other critical approaches analyze literary works from still other perspectives. *Reader-response* critics assert that a work of art is created as much by its audience as by the artist. For these critics, art has no significant abstract existence: a reader's experience of the work gives birth to it and contributes crucially to its power and value. Further, since each reader embodies a unique set of experiences and values, each reader's response to the work will in some respects be uniquely personal. *Psychoanalytic* criticism, similar to reader-response, is nevertheless distinctive in its application of psychoanalytic principles to works of art. Those principles, originally derived from the work of Sigmund Freud (1856–1939), now often reflect the views of more recent theorists such as Jacques Lacan (1901–1981). There is, finally, the recently emergent approach called *new historical* criticism, which brings historical knowledge to bear on the analysis of literary works in new and sophisticated ways. The result is a sometimes dizzying proliferation of analyses that argue for the relationship between literature and life.

The glossary that follows reveals the widely diverse and often contradictory views expressed by professional theorists and critics.

Deconstruction   This approach grew out of the work of certain twentieth-century European philosophers, notably Jacques Derrida (b. 1930), whose study of language led to the conclusion that since we can know only through the medium of language, and language is unstable and ambiguous, it is impossible to talk about truth and knowledge and meaning in any absolute sense. Verbal structures, these critics maintained, inevitably contained within themselves oppositions. Derrida asserted that in the Western world, language leads us to think in terms of opposites (for example, soul/body, man/woman, master/slave) that imply what he called "a violent hierarchy," with one of the terms (the first) always being superior to the other (the second). The aim of deconstruction is to show that this hierarchy of values cannot be permanent and absolute.

Readers therefore cannot be expected to ignore the oppositions and contradictions in a text just because they do not contribute to some "correct" or "desirable" reading of the piece that might uphold a particular political, social, or cultural view.

Formalism assures us that the successful artist is the master of language and that he or she consciously deploys all its resources to achieve a rich and unified work. Sensitive readers can aspire to a complete understanding of a work undistorted by their own idiosyncrasies, subjective states, or ideological biases.

Rejecting the formalist assumption about authorial control and conscious design, deconstruction attempts to show that by its very nature, language is constantly "saying" more than the writer can control or even know. Thus, a close study of any text (literary or otherwise) will reveal contradictory and irreconcilable elements.

Deconstructionist critics do not necessarily reject the validity of feminist, Marxist, formalist, and other critical approaches. In fact, they often draw on the insights furnished by them. But the deconstructionist critic says that any discourse or critical approach that fails to recognize the inherently shifting and unstable nature of language is bound to produce only a partial if not misleading interpretation. For example, in his study *America the Scrivener: Deconstruction and the Subject of Literary Studies* (1990), Gregory S. Jay finds Emily Grierson, the protagonist of William Faulkner's story "A Rose for Emily" (p. 666), a "puzzle" and warns against simplistic interpretations:

> As feminist subject, her story speaks of a revolutionary subversion of patriarchy; as herself, a figure of racial and class power, Emily also enacts the love affair of patriarchy with its own past, despite all the signs of decline and degradation. She is a split subject, crossed by rival discourses. What the text forces us to think, then, is the complex and ironic alliances between modes of possession and subjection, desire and ownership, identity and position.

Like Marxism and feminism, deconstruction defines itself both as a critical theory of literature and as a philosophy of human values. Hence, it is applicable not only to literature but also to an understanding of the power relations among humans and the societies they create. In insisting that we recognize the way language embodies and supports class, gender, and other biases, deconstruction challenges both the ethnocentrism of political structures and the idea of "universal values" in literary works.

Ethical Criticism Ethical criticism may range from a casual appraisal of a work's moral content to the more rigorous and systematic analysis driven by a coherent set of stated beliefs and assumptions. A *religious* critic (committed to certain moral positions) might attack a work (regardless of its artfulness or brilliance) because it does not condemn adultery. A *feminist* critic might focus on the way literary works devalue women; a *black* critic, on the way they stereotype blacks; a *Marxist* critic, on the way they support class divisions; and a *new historicist* critic, on the way a dominant class interprets history to protect its own interests. But all of them agree that literary works invite ethical judgments. Most of them also agree that literary works must be judged as another means by which a society both defines and perpetuates its political institutions and cultural values. The feminist, the black critic, and the Marxist critics would also agree that the political institutions and cultural values of most Western societies have been carefully designed to serve the interests of a dominant class: white, male, and wealthy.

Ethical criticism takes us out of the comparatively calm, academic world of aesthetic values into the larger world of moral judgments. If a literary work's capacity to promote good or bad behavior becomes the criterion for judging its value, then surely some people will try to suppress works they perceive as morally threatening. It is here that ethical criticism encounters its most vexing and dangerous problem: censorship. The literary critic Wayne Booth, who advocates ethical criticism in his book *The Company We Keep: An Ethics of Fiction* (1988), concedes the danger but notes that teaching itself is a form of censorship in that "we impose our ethical choices on our students when we choose our reading lists."

Feminist Criticism Feminist critics hold that literature is merely one of many expressions of a patriarchal society with a vested interest in keeping women subordinate to men. Thus literature, in the way it portrays gender roles, helps to condition women to accept as normal a society that directs them to become nurses rather than doctors, secretaries rather than attorneys or corporate executives, sex symbols rather than thinkers, elementary school teachers rather than university professors. Beyond this general critique of patriarchy, feminists differ in their detailed analyses. Some have re-examined history to show that a literary canon created by males has slighted and ignored female authors. Others, studying canonical works from a feminist perspective, have come up with fresh readings that challenge conventional interpretations, focusing on how women are empowered in literary texts or through writing literary texts. Some, believing that language itself allows men to impose their power, use literary analyses to expose the gender bias of language. Why, they ask, is the English language so rich in words to describe a quarrelsome, abusive woman (*shrew, harridan, termagant*) but so lacking in comparable terms for men? Some feminists believe that the male bias of language, far deeper than mere words, is actually structural. The constellation of qualities connoted by *masculine* and *feminine,* they say, reveals how deeply the positive (male) and negative (female) values are embedded in the language.

While a psychoanalytic critic might use Freud's Oedipal theories to explain Emily's relationship to Homer Barron in William Faulkner's "A Rose for Emily" (p. 666), the feminist critic Judith Fetterley maintains that the explanation is to be found in the fact that a patriarchal culture instills in us the notion "that men and women are made for each other" and that " 'masculinity' and 'femininity' are the natural reflection of that divinely ordained complement." In a society where there is "a massive differentiation of everything according to sex, one sees that in reality a sexist culture is one in which men and women are not simply incompatible but murderously so. . . . Emily murders Homer Barron because she must at any cost get a man" (*The Resisting Reader: A Feminist Approach to American Fiction,* 1978).

Formalist Criticism Like deconstruction, formalism focuses on the ambiguous and multilayered nature of language but does so to achieve the precisely opposite effect. Formalism assures us that the successful artist is the master of language and consciously deploys all its resources to achieve a rich and unified work. Careful readers can aspire to a complete understanding of a work undistorted by their own idiosyncrasies or subjective states or ideological biases. The formalist rejects the central tenet of the reader-response critic — that a work comes into existence, so to speak, through the interaction of the reader with the work. For the formalist, the work exists independent of any particular reader. The work is a structured and formal aesthetic object comprising such elements as symbol, image, and sound patterns. Political, biographical, or historical considerations not embodied in the work itself are irrelevant.

The formalist sees literature as a sort of Platonic ideal form — immutable and objective. Works close to that ideal are praised for their aesthetic energy and their universality (a characteristic of the greatest literature). Works that do not exhibit this prized formal coherence are dispraised and often dismissed as neither universal nor important. Because formalism focuses on the internal structure of literature above all else, it rejects didactic works — those intended to teach or convey moral observations. During the 1940s and 1950s, when the New Critics (as the formalists were called) dominated academic literary criticism, social protest writing was generally dismissed as subliterary because it lacked the "universality" of great literature. What was important in a work of art was not that it might change people's behavior but that its parts coalesced into a beautiful whole. Consider the following comment by two formalist critics (Caroline Gordon and Allen Tate, *The House of Fiction*, 1950) on Nathaniel Hawthorne's "Young Goodman Brown" (p. 80):

> The dramatic impact would have been stronger if Hawthorne had let the incidents tell their own story: Goodman Brown's behavior to his neighbors and finally to his wife show us that he is a changed man. Since fiction is a kind of shorthand of human behavior and one moment may represent years in a man's life, we would have concluded that the change was to last his entire life. But Hawthorne's weakness for moralizing and his insufficient technical equipment betray him into the anticlimax of the last paragraph.

African American writers and critics, for example, complained that the criterion of universality was merely a way of protecting white, conservative social and political dominance. The New Critics dismissed African American literature that sought to deal with racism and the struggle for equality as mere didacticism or agitprop, not to be compared with the great white literary productions that achieved universal import. In a major work of New Criticism published in 1952, the influential critic R. P. Blackmur dismissed *Native Son*, a powerful and now classic novel about white racism, as "one of those books in which everything is undertaken with seriousness except the writing."

Marxist Criticism The Marxist critic sees literature as one activity among many to be studied and judged in terms of a larger and all-encompassing ideology derived from the economic and political doctrines of Karl Marx (1818–1883). Marxism offers a comprehensive theory about the nature of humans and the way in which a few of them manage to seize control of the means of production and thereby exploit the masses of working people. But Marxism is about more than analysis. As Karl Marx himself said, "It is not enough to analyze society; we must also change it."

The Marxist critic analyzes literary works to show how, wittingly or unwittingly, they support the dominant social class or how they, in some way, contribute to the

struggle against oppression and exploitation. And since the Marxist critic views literature as just one among the variety of human activities that reflect power relations
and class divisions, he or she is likely to be more interested in what a work says than
in its formal structure.

The Marxist argues that one cannot properly understand a literary work unless one
understands how it reflects the relationship between economic production and
social class. Further, this relationship cannot be explored adequately without examining a range of questions that other critical approaches, notably formalism, deem
irrelevant. How does the work relate to the profit-driven enterprise of publishing?
What does the author's biography reveal about his or her class biases? Does the work
accurately portray the class divisions of society? Does the work expose the economic
bases of oppression and advance the cause of liberation?

And since Marxist critics see their duty — indeed, the duty of all responsible and
humane people — as not merely to describe the world but to change it, they judge
literature by the contribution it makes to bringing about revolution or in some way
enlightening its readers about oppression and the necessity for class struggle.

For example, a Marxist critic's analysis of Matthew Arnold's poem "Dover Beach"
(p. 1108) might see it not as a brilliantly structured pattern of images and sounds but
as the predictable end product of a dehumanizing capitalist economy in which a
small class of oligarchs is willing, at whatever cost, to protect its wealth and power.
The Marxist critic, as a materialist who believes that humans make their own history,
would find Arnold's reference to "the eternal note of sadness" (l. 14) a mystic evasion
of the real sources of his alienation and pain: Arnold's misery can be clearly and
unmystically explained by his fearful responses to the socioeconomic conditions of
his time.

Arnold's refusal to face this fact leads him to the conclusion typical of a bourgeois
artist-intellectual who cannot discern the truth. But the cure for Arnold's pain, the
Marxist would argue, cannot be found in a love relationship because relations
between people are determined crucially by socioeconomic conditions. The cure for
the pain he describes so well will be found in the world of action, in the struggle to
create a society that is just and humane. "Dover Beach," the Marxist critic would
conclude, is both a brilliant evocation of the alienation and misery caused by a capitalist economy and a testimony to the inability of a bourgeois intellectual to understand what is responsible for his feelings.

New Historical Criticism   There is nothing "new" about historians drawing on literary works as significant documents to support and illuminate historical analysis; nor
is there anything "new" about literary critics drawing on history to illuminate literary
works. For the historian, Sophocles' *Antigonê* (p. 467) tells us much about the conflict between the old-time religion and the new secularism in fifth-century B.C.
Athens. The literary critic of *Othello* (p. 1144) goes to the historian to understand the
way in which Shakespeare and his contemporaries viewed black Africans. But until
recently, the provinces of the historian and of the literary critics were pretty much
mutually exclusive.

The new historians (influenced by modern theories of language and literature)
began to question the very idea of history as it had been practiced. The historians of
the past tended, for the most part, to think of history in terms of overarching themes
and theses, and attempted to understand it in terms of some perceived *Zeitgeist,* or
"spirit of the times." This kind of history was often linked to nationalism. Hence (for

one example), nineteenth-century Americans created the idea of manifest destiny and then used it to explain and justify eastern settlers' movement west and their attendant atrocities against the Native Americans who resided there. When the Nazis came to power in Germany, they developed the idea that true Germans were descended from a superior Aryan race and then used that idea to deprive "inferior races" of civil rights, of property, and, finally, of life.

More abstractly, the purpose of writing history was to articulate and reinforce the values and beliefs that gave a culture unity. By that means, some new historians note, history became the story (and the ideas and beliefs and culture) of the rich, the powerful, the privileged, the victorious. The new historians see history not as the search for some grand, unifying thesis but as the articulation of the various kinds of discourse that compete with, contradict, overlap, and modify one another in the constant struggle for dominance. Indeed, the new historians, influenced by deconstructionist views of language, came to question the very idea of historical truth.

The new historians also reject the traditional division between history and other disciplines, appropriating to historical studies many kinds of texts — including literary texts — that traditional historians left to others. These critics assert that without an understanding of the historical context that produced it, no work of literature can really be understood; therefore, in their eyes, literature belongs as much to the historian as to the literary critic. Such critics aim at what they call a "thick" description of a literary work, one that brings to bear on a text as much information as can be gathered about every aspect of the author, his work, and his times.

Finally, it should be noted that new historicism has developed only recently and cannot be defined in detail. While its practitioners generally share the fundamental ideas outlined above, they can differ widely in the tools and methodologies they bring to bear on a literary text. That is to say, a new historian may also be a Marxist, feminist, or deconstructionist.

Psychoanalytic Criticism   Psychoanalytic criticism always proceeds from a set of principles that describes the inner life of men and women. Though differing psychological theorists argue for diverse views, all analysts and all psychoanalytic critics assume that the development of the psyche is analogous to the development of the body. Doctors can provide charts indicating physical growth stages; analysts can supply similar charts indicating stages in the growth of the psyche. Sigmund Freud, for all practical purposes, invented psychoanalysis by creating a theoretical model for the human (mostly male) psyche.

The Oedipus complex is a significant element in that model. Freud contends that everyone moves through a childhood stage of erotic attachment to the parent of the opposite sex and an accompanying hostility and aggression against the parent of the same sex, who is seen as a rival. Such feelings, part of the natural biography of the psyche, pass or are effectively controlled in most cases. But sometimes the child grown to adulthood is still strongly gripped by the Oedipal mode, which then may result in neurotic or even psychotic behavior. Freud did not invent the Oedipus complex — he simply described it. It was always there, especially noticeable in the work of great literary artists who, in every era, demonstrate a special insight into the human condition.

Along with Oedipal feelings, the psyche inevitably embodies aggressive feelings — the urge to attack those who exercise authority, who deny us our primal desires. For the young, the authority figure is frequently a parent. Adults must deal with police, government officials, the boss at the office. As far back as the Hebrew Bible story of the tower of Babel and the old Greek myths in which the giant Titans, led by Cronus, overthrow their father, and Zeus and the Olympians subsequently overthrow Cronus, there appears evidence of the rebellion against the parent-authority figure. Freud views that aggressive hostility as another component of the developing psyche. But, in the interest of civilization, society has developed ways to control that aggressiveness.

Freud saw us as divided selves. An unconscious *id* struggles to gratify aggressive and erotic primal urges, while a *superego* (roughly what society calls *conscience*), by producing guilt feelings, struggles to control the id. The *ego* (the self) is defined by the struggle. Thus the Freudian psychoanalytic critic is constantly aware that authors and their characters suffer and resuffer a primal tension that results from the conflict between psychic aggressions and social obligations.

Freud has been succeeded by a number of psychological theorists who present quite different models of the psyche, and recent literary theory has responded to these post-Freudian views. Among the most important are Carl Gustav Jung (1875–1961), who argued that there exists a collective (as well as a racial and individual) unconscious. Residing there are archetypes — original patterns — that emerge into our consciousness in the form of shadowy images that persistently appear and reappear in such literary themes as the search for the father, death and resurrection, the quest, and the double.

The psychoanalytic critic understands literature in terms of the psychic models that Freud and others defined. Originally, such critics tended to analyze literature in an attempt to identify the author's neuroses. More recently, psychoanalytic critics have argued that the patterns they discover in works allow us to tap into and, perhaps, resolve our own neuroses.

Reader-Response Criticism   Reader-response criticism (also called *transactional theory*) emerged in the 1970s as one of the many challenges to formalist principles. Reader-response critics focus on the interaction between the work and the reader, holding that, in a sense, a work exists only when it is experienced by the reader. If the work exists only in the mind of the reader, the reader becomes an active participant in the creative process rather than a passive receptacle for an autonomous work. The creation of a work thus becomes a dynamic enterprise between the reader and the text, each acting on the other. The study of the affective power of a work becomes not a fallacy, as formalism holds, but the central focus of criticism. The task of the critic is to investigate this dynamic relationship between reader and text in order to discover how it works.

We know that various readers respond differently to the same text. In fact, the same reader might respond to the text quite differently at a different time. The reader-response critic wants to know why. In what ways do such conditions as age, gender, upbringing, and race account for differing responses? Does the reader's mood at the time of reading make a difference? If you accept the principles of reader-response criticism, the inevitable conclusion — *reductio ad absurdum,* its critics would say — is that there is no limit to the possible readings of any text. Consequently, many reader-response critics qualify the intense subjectivity of their approach by admitting that an "informed" or "educated" reader is likely to produce a more "valid" reading than an "uninformed" or "uneducated" one.

Gaps or blanks in literary texts provide particular opportunities to readers. Every narrative work omits, for example, periods of time that the reader must fill in. In Nathaniel Hawthorne's "Young Goodman Brown" (p. 80), the author omits all the years of Brown's life between his emergence from the forest and his death. The reader is free to imagine that history. In Sophocles' *Antigonê* (p. 467), we never see Antigonê and her betrothed, Haimon, together. The reader will supply the dynamics of that courtship. The filling in of these blanks enables readers to participate in "creating" a text and reinforces the arguments of reader-response theorists.

Biographical Notes on the Authors

Chinua Achebe (b. 1930) Born in Ogidi, Nigeria, Achebe attended University College, Ibadan (1948–1953), and London University, where he earned a B.A. (1953). After spending some years working in broadcasting in his native country, Achebe began a distinguished academic career as professor of English at Anambra State University of Technology in Enugu. His acclaim as a writer led to many academic appointments and honors, including visiting professorships at the University of Massachusetts at Amherst, the University of Connecticut, and the University of California at Los Angeles. His numerous literary awards include the Commonwealth Poetry Prize (1972) and a Booker Prize nomination for his novel *Anthills of the Savannah* (1988). Although Achebe's native language is Ibo, he writes in English, a language he learned in his youth. Achebe's novels include *Things Fall Apart* (1958), *Arrow of God* (1964), and *Anthills of the Savannah* (1988). He has also published volumes of poetry, short stories, and essays, including the poetry and text for *Another Africa* (1998), a picturebook.

Sherman Alexie (b. 1966) A Spokane/Coeur d'Alene Indian, Sherman Alexie was born on the Spokane Indian Reservation in Wellpinit, Washington. In 1981, he left the reservation school and enrolled in a predominantly white high school, where, according to Alexie, he "kept [his] mouth shut and became a good white Indian." He enrolled at Gonzaga University in Spokane and began to discover his love for literature and his talent for writing. After two years at Gonzaga, he transferred to Washington State University in Pullman, where he began to write seriously. A year after he received his degree, he published two collections of poetry, *The Business of Fancydancing* and *I Would Steal Horses* (both 1992), followed the next year by another poetry collection, *First Indian on the Moon*. Alexie then turned to prose, publishing a volume of loosely related stories dealing with life on the reservation, *The Lone Ranger and Tonto Fistfight in Heaven* (1993). One of the stories in this collection, "This Is What It Means to Say Phoenix, Arizona," provided the basis for the film *Smoke Signals* (1998), which Alexie produced and for which he wrote the screenplay. His many other works include two novels, *Reservation Blues* (1995) and *Indian Killer* (1996), and a collection of short stories, *The Toughest Indian in the World* (2000). About the criticism he has received from members of his reservation, who find his portrayals of Native Americans and reservation life demeaning, Alexie has replied: "I write what I know, and I don't try to mythologize myself, which is what some seem to want, and which some Indian women and men writers are doing, this Earth Mother and Shaman Man thing, trying to create these 'authentic, traditional' Indians. We don't live our lives that way."

Woody Allen (b. 1935)   After being dismissed from both City College of New York and New York University, this precocious and prototypical New Yorker became a television comedy writer at the age of eighteen. He wrote two successful Broadway plays; his first screenplay, *What's New Pussycat?*, appeared in 1965. A dozen years in show business gave him the confidence to set out on his own, and he began performing as a standup comic. Soon after, he embarked on the filmmaking — writing, performing, directing, and producing — career for which he is famous. His talents, and those of the actors and technical group he has brought together as a kind of filmmaking repertory company, account for his reputation as an innovative contributor to cinema history. (His 1977 film, *Annie Hall,* won four Academy Awards.) In his spare time, he plays the clarinet in a Dixieland jazz group at a New York nightspot, and continues to write occasional pieces such as *Death Knocks.*

Maya Angelou (b. 1928)   Angelou was born Marguerite Johnson in St. Louis, Missouri. After the breakup of her parents' marriage, she and her brother lived with her paternal grandmother in Stamps, Arkansas, where she attended public schools. At age eight, she returned to her mother's home, where she was raped by her mother's lover, a trauma that caused her to stop talking for a year. Returned to her grandmother's home, she began reading widely among English and American writers. A mother by the time she was sixteen, Angelou had held jobs as a cook, cocktail waitress, and dancer by her early twenties. Her literary talent was also developing and, encouraged by friends, she published her first book, *I Know Why the Caged Bird Sings* (1970), the story of her first sixteen years. A great critical and commercial success, it was followed by four more autobiographical volumes, each covering a later period of her life: *Gather Together in My Name* (1974), *Singin' and Swingin' and Gettin' Merry Like Christmas* (1976), *The Heart of a Woman* (1981), and *All God's Children Need Traveling Shoes* (1986). The multitalented Angelou has also published fiction, written plays, and contributed to many periodicals. Her poems have been collected in *The Complete Collected Poems of Maya Angelou* (1994). An actress, she also wrote the screenplay for the film *Georgia, Georgia* (1972) and made her debut as a director with the film *Down in the Delta* (1998). In 1993, she recited her poem "On the Pulse of Morning" at the inauguration of President William Jefferson Clinton.

Aristotle (384–322 B.C.)   Aristotle was born in the north of Greece, near Macedonia, which, under Alexander the Great, was to become a dominant power in the region. At seventeen, he became Plato's student at the famous Academy in Athens, and remained there until Plato died in 348 B.C. After serving as a tutor to the young Alexander in Macedonia, he returned to Athens and founded his own school, the Lyceum, where he and his students studied zoology, botany, biology, physics, ethics, logic, music, mathematics, and, of course, literary criticism. His *Poetics* is the first Western effort to create a systematic literary theory. When Alexander died, the Athenians demonstrated so violent a resentment against all things Macedonian that Aristotle left Athens. He died a year later. His intellect and wide-ranging curiosity made him the predominant Greek philosopher, and his influence is still apparent in the modern world.

Matthew Arnold (1822–1888)   Born in Middlesex, England, Arnold attended Rugby School (where his father was headmaster) and studied classics at Oxford University. Following his graduation in 1844, he became a fellow at Oxford and a master at Rugby. In 1851, he was appointed inspector of schools in England and was sent by the government to observe educational systems in Europe. He remained in that post for some thirty-five years. As a poet, Arnold took inspiration from Greek tragedies, Keats, and Wordsworth. His collections include *Empedocles on Etna and Other Poems* (1852). An eminent social and literary critic in his later years, Arnold lectured in America in 1883 and 1886. His essay "The Function of Criticism" sheds light on his transition from poet to critic. Much of his work is collected in *Complete Prose Works* (11 volumes, 1960–1977).

W. H. Auden (1907–1973)   A poet, playwright, translator, librettist, critic, and editor, Wystan Hugh Auden was born in York, England, son of a medical officer and a nurse. He attended Oxford University from 1925 to 1928, then taught, traveled, and moved from faculty to faculty of several universities in the United States (where he became a naturalized citizen in 1946). He won the Pulitzer Prize in 1948 for his collection *The Age of Anxiety,* an expression he coined to describe the 1930s. While his early writing exhibited Marxist sympathies and reflected the excitement of new Freudian psychoanalytic thought, he later embraced Christianity and produced sharply honed verse in the rhyme and meter of traditional forms.

James Baldwin (1924–1987)   Born in New York City, the son of a Harlem minister, Baldwin began preaching as a young teenager. Some years later, he experienced a religious crisis, left the church, and moved to New York City's bohemian Greenwich Village, where he began his career as a writer, supporting himself with menial jobs and publishing occasional articles in journals such as the *Nation* and *Commentary.* By the end of the 1940s, Baldwin's anger over the treatment of African Americans led him into exile in France. There, Baldwin completed his acclaimed first novel, *Go Tell It on the Mountain* (1953), a work for which he drew heavily on his own childhood to depict the lives of members of a Harlem church, focusing on a minister's son.

His next work, *Notes of a Native Son* (1955), a collection of personal, literary, and social essays, secured Baldwin's reputation as a major American writer. Two later collections of essays, *Nobody Knows My Name* (1961) and *The Fire Next Time* (1963), established Baldwin as one of the most powerful voices of the turbulent civil rights movement of the 1960s. But as riots, bombings, and other violence grew more frequent, Baldwin grew increasingly pessimistic over the prospect that white America could ever overcome its racism. That pessimism was deepened by two traumatic events: the 1964 bombing of the Sixteenth Avenue Baptist Church in Birmingham, Alabama, that killed four young girls attending a Sunday-school class, and the assassination of the Reverend Martin Luther King Jr. in 1968. Baldwin began making periodic trips to France, settling there permanently in 1974.

Toni Cade Bambara (1939–1995)   Born in New York City, Bambara was educated there as well as in Italy and Paris. Early in her career she worked as an investigator for the New York State Department of Social Welfare but later devoted herself for many years to teaching and writing. One of the best representatives of a group of African American writers who emerged in the 1960s, Bambara was a consistent civil rights activist, both politically and culturally involved in African American life. Much of her writing focuses on African American women, particularly as they confront experiences that force them to new awareness. She authored several collections of short stories, including *Gorilla, My Love* (1972) and *The Sea Birds Are Still Alive: Collected Stories* (1977), and two novels, *The Salt Eaters* (1980) and *If Blessing Comes* (1987). She also edited a groundbreaking collection of African American women's writing, *The Black Woman: An Anthology* (1970). *Deep Sightings and Rescue Missions: Fiction, Essays, and Conversations* was published in 1996.

Samuel Beckett (1906–1989)   Born in Foxrock, County Dublin, Ireland, Beckett attended Trinity College, Dublin, where he earned a B.A. (1927) and an M.A. (1931) in both French and Italian. He was a lecturer in French at Trinity College (1930–1932), but resigned because "he could not bear the absurdity of teaching to others what he did not know himself." He has been characterized as a lonely and unhappy boy who matured into a lonely and unhappy man. He once proclaimed himself a dead person with no feelings that were human. After extensive travel in England and Europe between 1932 and 1936, during which he supported himself with odd jobs, Beckett settled in Paris. In the early thirties, he helped the nearly blind James Joyce by taking dictation and copying parts of *Finnegan's Wake,* and his close relationship with Joyce is sometimes reflected in his own work. When Beckett visited Joyce, the two men would often sit in sadness and silence. One night, Beckett was almost fatally stabbed by a mugger in Paris. While recovering, he was looked after by Joyce, who brought numerous visitors to his hospital room, among them Suzanne Deschevaux-Dusmesnil, who became his life companion and, ultimately, his wife (1961). From the early 1940s on, his writing consumed most of his energy. During World War II, he was involved with the French resistance movement and remained under cover as a farm-hand in southeastern France. All of Beckett's major works were written in French, though he often translated them into English himself. Though he wrote prolifically after the war ended, his first breakthrough came when *Waiting for Godot* premiered in 1953, and his stature was ensured with *Endgame,* which opened in 1957. He won many awards, including the Nobel Prize for literature in 1969. Beckett was the first absurdist writer to win international fame, and his works have been translated into more than twenty languages. As one observer pointed out, his "characters exist in a terrible dreamlike vacuum, overcome by an overwhelming sense of bewilderment and grief, grotesquely attempting some form of communication, then crawling on endlessly."

Bruce Bennett (b. 1940)   Bennett was born in Philadelphia, Pennsylvania, and began writing poems when he was eight years old. He attended Harvard University as an undergraduate and graduate student, receiving a Ph.D. in English (1967). From 1967 to 1970 he taught at Oberlin College, where he co-founded *Field: Contemporary Poetry and Poetics*. In 1971 he co-founded and co-edited the literary journal *Ploughshares*. In that year he married Renaissance art historian Bonnie Apgar; the couple lived in Florence, Italy, for two years, and return there often. Since 1973, Bennett has taught English and directed creative writing at Wells College in Aurora, New York, where, in 1993, he also became director of the Wells College Book Arts Center. He has published numerous books and chapbooks, including *Navigating the Distances* (1999), which was selected by *Booklist* as "one of the Top Ten Poetry Books of 1999." Bennett writes in a variety of forms and moods, and regards storytelling as a key element of his work. He believes poetry should be accessible, a part of everyone's life, and approvingly quotes William Carlos Williams: "If it ain't pleasure, it ain't a poem." Through public readings and visits to schools, he encourages young people to write poems. X. J. Kennedy has called Bennett a "master fabulist and satirist" and a "parodist *par excellence*," who "often compresses realms of wisdom into tight, economical packages."

Jill Bialosky (b. 1957)   Born in Cleveland, Ohio, she earned a B.A. at Ohio University, an M.A. from the Writing Seminars at Johns Hopkins University, and an M.F.A. from the University of Iowa's Writers' Workshop. *The End of Desire: Poems* (1997), her first collection, was published by Alfred A. Knopf. She co-edited (with Helen Schulman) *Wanting a Child* (1998). Her most recent poems appear in *Subterranean* (2001). She has won, among several other awards, the Elliot Coleman Award in poetry. Currently, she is an editor at W. W. Norton & Company, and lives in New York City.

Elizabeth Bishop (1911–1979)   Bishop was born in Worcester, Massachusetts. Her father died before she was a year old; four years later, when her mother suffered a mental breakdown, Bishop was taken to live with her grandmother in Nova Scotia. Although her mother lived until 1934, Bishop saw her for the last time in 1916, a visit recalled in one of her rare autobiographical stories, "In the Village." Bishop planned to enter Cornell Medical School after graduating from Vassar, but was persuaded by poet Marianne Moore to become a writer. For the next fifteen years, she was a virtual nomad, traveling in Canada, Europe, and North and South America. In 1951, she finally settled in Rio de Janeiro, where she lived for almost twenty years. During the final decade of her life, Bishop continued to travel, but she resumed living in the United States and taught frequently at Harvard University. She was an austere writer, publishing only four slim volumes of poetry: *North and South* (1946); *A Cold Spring* (1955), which won the Pulitzer Prize; *Questions of Travel* (1965); and *Geography III* (1976), which won the National Book Critics' Circle Award. *The Complete Poems, 1927–1979* (1984) was published after her death, as was a collection of her prose. Despite her modest output, she has earned an enduring place of respect among twentieth-century poets.

William Blake (1757–1827)   Born in London to an obscure family, Blake was educated at home until he was ten and then enrolled in a drawing school, advancing ultimately to a formal apprenticeship as an engraver. At an early age, Blake exhibited talent as both an artist and a poet. Throughout his life, he read widely among modern philosophers and poets, and experienced mystical visions that provided him with the inspiration for many of his poems. Blake devised a process he called illuminated printing, which involved the preparation of drawings and decorative frames to complement his poems. He published *Songs of Innocence* (1789) and *Songs of Experience* (1794) in this fashion. These books, as well as the many subsequent works he wrote and illustrated, earned him a reputation as one of the most important artists of his day. Many of Blake's works assert his conviction that the established church and state hinder rather than nurture human freedom and the sense of divine love.

Bertolt Brecht (1898–1956)   Born in Augsburg, Germany, Brecht studied medicine at Munich University but soon turned to writing. Following World War I, he wrote his first play, *Baal* (1918). His second play, *Drums in the Night* (1922), earned him Germany's premier literary prize. During the following years, his reputation grew through his work in the radically staged epic theater. His collaboration with the composer Kurt Weill in 1928 produced *The Threepenny Opera,* still his most popular work. His works during this period were shaped by his Marxist beliefs and his conviction that drama should help advance the interests of the working class. The Nazi takeover of Germany in 1933 forced Brecht and his wife to flee to Scandinavia, where he wrote many poems and epic plays, among them *Mother Courage and Her Children* (1939), *The Life of Galileo* (1939), and *The Good Woman of Setzuan* (1940). In 1941, Brecht and his wife began a six-year stay in Hollywood, California, where he collaborated on several films and a volume of satirical songs, *Hollywood Elegies* (1942). By the late 1940s and early 1950s, Brecht's criticisms of American life and his well-known Marxism led to his being summoned to appear before the U.S. House of Representatives' Committee on Un-American Activities. Within days of that celebrated appearance, Brecht was back in Europe. He settled in East Berlin in 1949, where he remained until his death.

Edwin Brock (b. 1927) Born in London, Brock served two years in the Royal Navy. He was a police officer when he completed his first poetry collection, *An Attempt at Exorcism* (1959). Influenced by American confessional poets, Brock writes about family relationships and childhood memories and sometimes shifts into the linguistic mode of an advertising copywriter (which he became in 1959). Suggesting that all poetry is to some extent autobiographical, Brock argues "that most activity is an attempt to define oneself in one way or another: for me poetry, and only poetry, has provided this self-defining act." His works include over a dozen poetry collections, most recently, *Five Ways to Kill a Man: New and Selected Poems* (1990); a novel, *The Little White God* (1962); and an autobiography, *Here, Now, Always* (1977).

Robert Browning (1812–1889) Born in London, Browning attended a private school and was later tutored at home. After one year as a student of Greek at the University of London, he moved with his family to Hatcham, where he studied, wrote poetry, and practiced writing for the theater. In 1845, he began exchanging poems and letters with the already famous poet Elizabeth Barrett; they eloped in 1846. They moved to Italy, where Browning completed most of his work. When Elizabeth died in 1861, he returned to England and began to establish his own reputation. He is noted especially for his fine dramatic monologues in which a wide range of characters reveals the complexity of human belief and passion. His many volumes of poetry include *Dramatis Personae* (1864) and *The Ring and the Book* (1868–1869).

Robert Burns (1759–1796) Born in Scotland to a family of poor tenant farmers, Burns was working in the fields with his father by age twelve. During these early years, the family moved often in fruitless attempts to improve its lot. Although Burns received formal education only intermittently, he read widely on his own. After the death of his father, Burns and his brother worked vainly to make their farm pay, an effort Burns was able to abandon when his first volume of poetry, *Poems, Chiefly in the Scottish Dialect* (1786) brought him overnight fame. One result of this fame was his appointment as an excise officer, a position that gave him some financial security while he continued to write poetry. Burns's humble origins instilled in him a lifelong sympathy for the poor and downtrodden, the rebels and iconoclasts, as well as a disdain for religion, particularly Calvinism and what he considered the hypocrisy of its "devout" ministers.

Thomas Campion (1567–1620)   Campion spent his early childhood in London, studied at Cambridge, then returned to London in 1586 to study law. It appears that Campion served, for a short time, as a soldier in France. In 1595, he published a collection of Latin poems, *Poemata*. After the publication of this volume, he apparently went abroad to study medicine and, later, music (though it is not known when or where). His first volume of English poems, *A Book of Ayres,* appeared in 1601; the other three volumes appeared between 1601 and 1617. Campion also wrote masques for presentation at court, often composing the music for his own lyrics. Toward the end of his life, he wrote a treatise on music that became a standard text.

Raymond Carver (1938–1988)   Carver was born in Clatskanie, Oregon, the son of a sawmill worker and a mother who did odd jobs. He graduated from high school at age eighteen, and was married and the father of two children before he was twenty. The following years were difficult as he struggled to develop a writing career while supporting a family. While at Chico State College (now California State University at Chico), Carver took a creative writing course that profoundly affected him. He went on to earn a B.A. (1963) from Humboldt State College in Eureka, and spent the following year studying writing at the University of Iowa. As he became known, he began to lecture on English and creative writing at various universities, including the University of Iowa's Writers' Workshop. He taught at Goddard College in Vermont, and was professor of English at Syracuse University from 1980 to 1983. In 1983, he received the Mildred and Harold Strauss Living Award, which allowed him to devote the next five years to writing. His first collection of short stories, *Will You Please Be Quiet, Please?* (1976), was nominated for the National Book Award. Other short-story collections include *What We Talk about When We Talk about Love* (1981) and *Cathedral* (1984). He also published five volumes of poems, among them *Near Klamath* (1968), *Ultramarine* (1986), and *A New Path to the Waterfall* (1989); *No Heroics, Please* (1992) was published posthumously. During the last ten years of his life, Carver lived with the poet and short-story writer Tess Gallagher, whom he married shortly before his death.

Kate Chopin (1851–1904)   Born Kate O'Flaherty in St. Louis, Missouri, Chopin was raised by her mother, grandmother, and great-grandmother, all widows, after her father's death when she was four. In 1870, following her graduation from Sacred Heart Convent, she married Oscar Chopin and moved to New Orleans, where she became a housewife and mother (she had six children). After her husband's death in 1882, she returned to her mother's home in St. Louis and began her career as a writer. Her first novel, *At Fault*

(1890), and her stories, collected in *Bayou Folk* (1894) and *A Night in Acadie* (1897), gained her a reputation as a vivid chronicler of the lives of Creoles and Acadians (Cajuns) in Louisiana. Many of these stories explore a female protagonist's attempts to achieve self-fulfillment. Her novel *The Awakening* (1899) is probably her most ambitious exploration of this theme. It is the story of a woman whose awakening to her passion and inner self leads her to adultery and suicide. The storm of controversy with which this work was met virtually ended Chopin's literary career.

Sandra Cisneros (b. 1954)   Cisneros, the daughter of a Mexican father and a Mexican American mother, grew up in poor neighborhoods of Chicago, where she attended public schools. The only daughter among seven children, Cisneros recalled that because her brothers attempted to control her and expected her to assume a traditional female role, she grew up feeling as if she had "seven fathers." The family's frequent moves, many of them between the United States and Mexico to visit a grandmother, left Cisneros feeling alone and displaced. She found refuge both in reading and in writing poems and stories. In the late 1970s, Cisneros's writing talent earned her admission to the University of Iowa's Writers' Workshop. There, Cisneros observed, "Everyone seemed to have some communal knowledge which I did not have. . . . My classmates were from the best schools in the country. They had been bred as fine hothouse flowers. I was a yellow weed among the city's cracks." This realization led Cisneros to focus her writing on the conflicts and yearnings of her own life and culture. Her writings include four volumes of poetry — *Bad Boys* (1980), *The Rodrigo Poems* (1985), *My Wicked, Wicked Ways* (1987), and *Loose Woman* (1994) — and two volumes of fiction — *The House on Mango Street* (1983) and *Woman Hollering Creek and Other Stories* (1991). She is also the author of a bilingual children's book, *Hairs = Pelitos* (1994). She received a prestigious MacArthur Fellowship in 1995.

Lucille Clifton (b. 1936)   Born in Depew, New York, Clifton attended Howard University (1953–1955) and Fredonia State Teachers College. She worked as a claims clerk in the New York State Division of Employment, Buffalo (1958–1960), and as literature assistant in the Office of Education in Washington, D.C. (1960–1971). In 1969, she received the YM-YWHA Poetry Center Discovery Award, and her first collection, *Good Times,* was selected as one of the ten best books of 1969 by the *New York Times.* From 1971 to 1974 she was poet-in-residence at Coppin State College in Baltimore, and in 1979 she was named poet laureate of the state of Maryland. She has written many collections for children and a free-verse chronicle of five generations of her family, *Generations: A Memoir* (1976). Her most recent volume of poetry is *Blessing the Boats: New and Selected Poems 1988–2000* (2000). Noted for celebrating ordinary people and everyday things, Clifton has said, "I am a black woman poet, and I sound like one."

Judith Ortiz Cofer (b. 1952)   Cofer was born in Hormigueros, Puerto Rico. She earned a B.A. (1974) from Augusta College and an M.A. (1977) from Florida Atlantic University and briefly attended Oxford University. She began her teaching career as a bilingual instructor in Florida public schools and taught at a number of schools, including the University of Miami and the University of Georgia. Her first volume of poems, *Latin Women Pray,* appeared in 1981, and she has since published poetry collections, essays, and a novel. Her recent work includes several multigenre collections of stories, poems, and essays about coming of age in the barrio, including *The Year of Our Revolution: New and Selected Stories and Poems* (1998) and *Woman in Front of the Sun: On Becoming a Writer* (2000). Cofer points out that her family is an important source for her writing. "The place of birth itself becomes a metaphor for the things we must all leave behind; the assimilation of a new culture is the coming into maturity by accepting the terms necessary for survival."

Billy Collins (b. 1941)   Collins was born in New York City and earned a B.A. (1963) from the College of Holy Cross and a Ph.D. (1971) from the University of California at Riverside. He has been teaching at the City University of New York since 1971. *Pokerface,* the first of his several books of poetry, was published in 1977. Collins's later work attracted so much attention that his early poetry books became economically valuable. Consequently, the University of Pittsburgh Press, publisher of *The Art of Drowning* (1995) and *Picnic, Lightning* (1998), at first withheld permission from Random House to reprint earlier poems in Collins's *Sailing around the Room: New and Selected Poems* (2000). The struggle between Random House and the University of Pittsburgh Press over the rights to Collins's work made him sufficiently notorious. He has won several poetry prizes as well as fellowships from the New York Foundation for the Arts, the National Endowment for the Arts, and the Guggenheim Foundation. He commented to one journalist: "I think my work has to do with a sense that we are attempting, all the time, to create a logical, rational path through the day. To the left and right there are an amazing set of distractions that we usually can't afford to follow. But the poet is willing to stop anywhere."

Bernard Cooper (b. 1951)   Cooper was born in Hollywood, California; attended the California Institute of the Arts (M.F.A., 1979); and currently resides in Los Angeles. After graduation, he abandoned visual art and began to write, supporting himself as a shoe salesman. He taught at the UCLA Writer's Program and the Creating Writing program at Antioch University. He has published two collections of memoirs as well as a novel, and his essays have been anthologized in *The Best American Essays* (1988, 1995, 1997) and *The Oxford Book of Literature on Aging.* His most recent book is a collection of short stories, *Guess Again* (2000). Among his awards are the P.E.N./Ernest

Hemingway Award (1991) and the O'Henry Prize (1995). In a recent interview, Cooper asserted that "a good piece of writing causes you to have a sense of identification, even if the experience . . . is remote from your own. When suddenly you feel that you've taken on a completely foreign experience and you're living it to its fullest, it's absolutely transporting. It's one of the greatest pleasures literature can offer."

Stephen Crane (1871–1900)   Born in Newark, New Jersey, the fourteenth and youngest child of a Methodist minister who died when Stephen was nine years old, Crane was raised by his strong-minded mother. His brief college career, first at Lafayette College and then at Syracuse University, was dominated by his interest in baseball; he left college after two semesters and moved on to a bohemian life in New York City. There he wandered through the slums, observing and developing a strong sympathy for the underclass of boozers and prostitutes that inhabited the Bowery. His first novel, *Maggie: A Girl of the Streets* (1893), described the inevitable consequences of grinding poverty — but no publisher would take a chance on Crane's bleak and biting vision. He published it at his own expense, but it found no audience. Without any military experience, and at the age of twenty-four, Crane produced *The Red Badge of Courage* (1895), a novel that made him famous and that became an American classic. For the remainder of his life, he traveled about the world as a writer and war correspondent. He died of a tubercular infection in Badenweiler, Germany. Despite the brevity of his writing career, Crane left behind a substantial volume of work that includes a number of brilliant short stories and innovative poems.

Countee Cullen (1903–1946)   Born Countee L. Porter in New York City, Cullen was adopted by the Reverend and Mrs. Cullen in 1918 and raised in Harlem. He was extraordinarily precocious, and by 1920 his poems had been published in *Poetry,* the *Nation,* and *Harper's.* He published his famous poem "Heritage" in 1925, the year he graduated from New York University. After earning an M.A. in English from Harvard in 1926, he taught French in a junior high school and was assistant editor of the National Urban League's *Opportunity: Journal of Negro Life.* Cullen, along with Langston Hughes and Jean Toomer, was a central figure in the Harlem Renaissance of the 1920s. He received a Guggenheim Fellowship in 1929. In addition to five volumes of poetry, he published a novel, *One Way to Heaven* (1932), which deals with the interaction between upper- and lower-class African Americans in Harlem in the 1920s.

E. E. Cummings (1894–1962)   Born in Cambridge, Massachusetts, Edward Estlin Cummings attended Harvard University (B.A., 1915; M.A., 1916), served as a volunteer ambulance driver in France during World War I, was imprisoned for three months in a French detention camp, served in the

United States Army (1918–1919), and then studied art and painting in Paris (1920–1924). His prose narrative *The Enormous Room* (1922), a recollection of his imprisonment, brought instant acclaim. Several volumes of poetry followed. His experiments with punctuation, line division, and capitalization make his work immediately recognizable. In a letter to young poets published in a high school newspaper, Cummings said, "[N]othing is quite so easy as using words like somebody else. We all of us do exactly this nearly all the time — and whenever we do it, we're not poets."

C. Day-Lewis (1904–1972)   Born in Ireland, son of a minister, Cecil Day-Lewis began writing poetry at age six. He attended Oxford University, taught for seven years, served as editor for the Ministry of Information (1941–1946), and was professor of poetry at Oxford (1951–1956) and visiting professor at Harvard University (1964–1965). His early works — *From Feathers to Iron* (1931) and *The Magnetic Mountain* (1933) — reflect a politically radical ideology, but Lewis mellowed enough to be named poet laureate in 1968. From 1935 to 1964 he wrote nearly two dozen detective novels under the pseudonym Nicholas Blake. He commented, "In my young days, words were my antennae, my touch-stones, my causeway over a quaking bog of mistrust."

Emily Dickinson (1830–1886)   Dickinson, one of three children, was born in Amherst, Massachusetts. Her father was a prominent lawyer. Except for one year away at a nearby college and a trip with her sister to Washington, D.C., to visit her father when he was serving in Congress, she lived out her life, unmarried, in her parents' home. During her trip to Washington, she met the Reverend Charles Wadsworth, a married man, whom she came to characterize as her "dearest earthly friend." Little is known of this relationship except that Dickinson's feelings for Wadsworth were strong. In 1862 Wadsworth moved to San Francisco, an event that coincided with a period of Dickinson's intense poetic creativity. Also in that year, she initiated a literary correspondence with the critic T. W. Higginson, to whom she sent some of her poems for his opinion. Higginson, although he recognized her talent, was puzzled by her startling originality and urged her to write more conventionally. Unable to do so, she concluded, we may surmise, that she would never see her poems through the press. In fact, only seven of her poems were published while she was alive, none of them with her consent. After her death, the extraordinary richness of her imaginative life came to light with the discovery of her more than one thousand lyrics.

Joan Didion (b. 1934)   A fifth-generation Californian, Didion was born in Sacramento and raised in the great central plain of California, an area she often describes nostalgically in her work. As an undergraduate English major at the University of California, Berkeley, she won an essay prize sponsored by *Vogue* magazine. As a result, *Vogue* hired her, and for eight years she lived in

New York City, while she rose to associate features editor. She published her first novel, *Run River,* in 1963 and in the same year married the writer John Gregory Dunne. In 1964 the couple returned to California, where they remained for twenty-five years. Although Didion wrote four more novels, her reputation rests on her essays collected as *Slouching toward Bethlehem* (1968) and *The White Album* (1979). In addition to her work as a columnist, essayist, and fiction writer, she has collaborated with her husband on a number of screenplays. She has focused her trenchant powers of observation in two documentary, book-length studies: *Salvador* (1983) and *Miami* (1987). Her most recent book is the novel *The Last Thing He Wanted* (1996). Her reputation as a prose stylist is reflected in a comment by one critic who asserts that "nobody writes better English prose than Joan Didion. Try to rearrange one of her sentences, and you've realized that the sentence was inevitable, a hologram." Didion characterizes herself as uneasy with abstractions: "I would try to think about the Great Dialectic and I would find myself thinking instead about how the light was falling through the window in an apartment I had on the North Side. How it was hitting the floor."

John Donne (1572–1631) Born in London into a prosperous Roman Catholic family of tradespeople, at a time when England was staunchly anti-Catholic, Donne was forced to leave Oxford University without a degree because of his religion. He studied law and, at the same time, read widely in theology in an attempt to decide whether the Roman or the Anglican Church was the true Catholic Church, a decision he was not able to make for many years. In the meantime, he became known as a witty man of the world and the author of original, often dense, erotic poems. Donne left his law studies, participated in two naval expeditions, and then became secretary to a powerful noble, a job he lost when he was briefly sent to prison for secretly marrying his patron's niece. In 1615, at the age of forty-two, Donne accepted ordination in the Anglican Church. He quickly earned a reputation as one of the greatest preachers of his time. He was Dean of St. Paul's from 1621 until his death. In his later years, Donne repudiated the poetry of his youth.

Paul Laurence Dunbar (1872–1906) The son of former slaves, Dunbar was born in Dayton, Ohio, where he graduated from Dayton High School (1891) and worked for two years as an elevator operator. In 1894, he worked in Chicago at the World's Columbian Exhibition. His first verse collection, *Oak and Ivy,* was published in 1893. William Dean Howells — an eminent editor, author, and critic — encouraged him to write and had him join a lecture bureau in 1896. Dunbar read his own works in the United States and traveled to England in 1897. While Dunbar maintained that African American poetry was not much different from white poetry (and wrote many poems in standard English), he often wrote poems in black dialect that seemed to cater to the racial stereotypes of his white audience. He died of tuberculosis in 1906. His complete works appear in *The Dunbar Reader* (1975).

Stephen Dunn (b. 1939) Dunn was born in New York City and educated at Hofstra University (B.A., 1962), the New School for Social Research, and Syracuse University (M.A., 1970). He played professional basketball for the Williamsport (PA) Billies (1962–1963) but then moved back to New York, where he worked as a copywriter and assistant editor. He began a college teaching career, and is now a professor of creative writing at Stockton State College in New Jersey. His first book of poems, *Five Impersonations,* appeared in 1971, and was followed by several volumes, the most recent being *Walking Light: Essays and Memoirs* (1993), *New and Selected Poems: 1974–1994* (1994), *Loosestrife* (1996), *Riffs and Reciprocities Prose Pairs* (1998), and *Different Hours* (2000). He has won several awards and fellowships, including three National Endowment for the Arts Fellowships, Yaddo Fellowships (1979–89), and a Guggenheim Fellowship (1984–85). His volume *Local Time* was the National Poetry Series winner in 1986; *Different Hours* won the 2001 Pulitzer Prize for poetry.

Lars Eighner (b. 1948) Born in Corpus Christi, Texas, Eighner was two when his parents divorced and he and his mother, a teacher of the deaf, moved to Houston. He became a student at the University of Texas in 1966 but dropped out after three years and took a job as a counselor in a drug-crisis center in Austin. In 1979, he was hired as an attendant at Austin State Hospital but lost his job after quarreling with his supervisor. Unable to support himself by writing stories, he was finally evicted from his Austin home and became a homeless itinerant. By 1990 Eighner, who has described himself as "a homosexual pornographer," had many stories published in obscure gay publications. In 1991, he became more widely known when the *Threepenny Review* published two of his essays on homelessness. The publication in 1993 of *Travels with Lizbeth,* an account of his three years of homelessness, was widely and enthusiastically reviewed. He is the author of two collections of stories, *Bayou Boy* and *B.M.O.C.* (both 1993), as well as *Pawn to Queen Four: A Novel* (1995). Eighner now lives with Lizbeth, his dog, in an apartment in Austin, Texas.

T. S. Eliot (1888–1965) Thomas Stearns Eliot was born in St. Louis, Missouri. His father was president of the Hydraulic Press Brick Company, and his mother was a teacher, social worker, and writer. Educated in private academies, Eliot earned two philosophy degrees at Harvard University (B.A., 1909; M.A., 1910). After graduate study in Paris and England, he worked for eight years as a clerk in Lloyd's Bank in London and became a naturalized British citizen in 1927. He was editor, then director, of Faber & Gwyer Publishers (later Faber & Faber) from 1925 to 1965 and spent time in the United States as a visiting lecturer and scholar. Admirers and detractors alike agree that Eliot was the most imposing and influential poet writing between the world wars. His poems "The Love Song of J. Alfred Prufrock" (1917) and *The Waste Land* (1922) are among his earliest and most famous. Acknowledging his dependence on a preexisting cultural tradition, Eliot explained: "The existing order is complete before the new work arrives; for order to persist after the supervention of novelty, the whole existing order must be altered." Eliot also wrote plays, including *Murder in the Cathedral* (1935) and *The Cocktail Party* (1950). The long-running Broadway musical *Cats* is based on his 1939 verse collection, *Old Possum's Book of Practical Cats*. He won the Nobel Prize for literature in 1948.

Harlan Ellison (b. 1934)   Born in Cleveland, Ohio, Ellison published his first story when he was thirteen. He left Ohio State University after two years and worked at a variety of odd jobs while establishing himself as a writer. In a career spanning over fifty years, he has written or edited sixty-five books and more than seventeen hundred stories, essays, reviews, articles, motion picture scripts, and teleplays. He has won the Hugo Award eight and a half times, the Nebula Award three times, the Edgar Allan Poe Award of the Mystery Writers of America twice, the Bram Stoker Award of Horror Writers of America twice, the World Fantasy Award, the British Fantasy Award, and the Silver Pen for journalism from P.E.N. He is the only scenarist in Hollywood ever to have won the Writers Guild of America award for Most Outstanding Teleplay four times for solo work. His recent books are *The Harlan Ellison Hornbook* (1990); *The City on the Edge of Forever* (1995), the first book publication of his *Star Trek* script in its original (not aired) version; *Slippage: Previously Uncollected, Precariously Poised Stories* (1997); and *The Essential Ellison: A 50 Year Retrospective* (2001). He lives with his wife, Susan, in the Lost Aztec Temple of Mars somewhere in the Los Angeles area.

Louise Erdrich (b. 1954)   Born in Little Falls, Minnesota, Erdrich grew up in Wahpeton, North Dakota, a member of the Turtle Mountain Band of Chippewa. Her grandfather was for many years tribal chair of the reservation where her parents taught in the Bureau of Indian Affairs School. She attended Dartmouth College, earning a degree in anthropology (1976) as well as prizes for fiction and poetry, including the American Academy of Poets Prize. She returned to North Dakota for a brief period of teaching before going on to study creative writing at Johns Hopkins University (M.A., 1979). The following year, she returned to Dartmouth as a writer-in-residence. Her works have appeared in the *New England Review* and *Redbook* as well as such anthologies of Native American writing as *Earth Power Coming* and *That's What She Said: Contemporary Poetry and Fiction by Native American Women*. She has published two collections of poems, *Jacklight* (1984) and *Baptism of Desire* (1989). Her novel *Love Medicine* (1984) won the National Book Critics Circle Award. *The Beet Queen* (1986), *Tracks* (1988), *The Bingo Palace* (1994), and *Tales of Burning Love* (1996) extend the histories of families dealt with in *Love Medicine*. In 1991, Erdrich and her then husband, Michael Dorris — a professor of Native American Studies at Dartmouth — published *The Crown of Columbus,* a collaborative novel about Christopher Columbus's discovery of

America, donating a part of their royalties to American Indian charities. Dorris committed suicide in 1997 after a charge of sexual abuse involving his children was made against him. Erdrich's most recent work is *The Last Report on the Miracles at Little No Horse: A Novel* (2001).

William Faulkner (1897–1962)   Faulkner was born in New Albany, Mississippi, and lived most of his life in Oxford, the seat of the University of Mississippi. Although he did not graduate from high school, he did attend the university as a special student from 1919 to 1921. During this period, he also worked as a janitor, a bank clerk, and a postmaster. His southern forebears had held slaves, served during the Civil War, endured the deprivations of Reconstruction, fought duels, and even wrote the occasional romance of the old South. Faulkner mined these generous layers of history in his work. He created the mythical Yoknapatawpha County in northern Mississippi and traced the destinies of its inhabitants from the colonial era to the middle of the twentieth century in such novels as *The Sound and the Fury* (1929), *Light in August* (1932), and *Absalom, Absalom!* (1936). Further, Faulkner described the decline of the pre–Civil War aristocratic families and the rise of mean-spirited money-grubbers in a trilogy: *The Hamlet* (1940), *The Town* (1957), *The Mansion* (1959). Recognition came late, and Faulkner fought a constant battle to keep afloat financially. During the 1940s, he wrote screenplays in Hollywood, but his achievements brought him the Nobel Prize in 1950.

James Fenton (b. 1949)   Born in Lincoln, England, Fenton earned a B.A. (1970) from Magdalen College, Oxford University. His earliest volumes of verse appeared during his undergraduate years: *Our Western Furniture* (1968) and *Put Thou Thy Tears Into My Bottle* (1969). He wrote for the *New Statesman and Nation,* a leftist weekly magazine, and continued to publish relatively few but always finely crafted poems. Almost half of his collection *Children in Exile: Poems 1968–1984* is light verse, but often those poems move from whimsy to horror. He won the 1984 Geoffrey Faber Memorial Prize for his poetry. He translated the lyrics of Verdi's opera *Rigoletto,* controversially setting the action in the 1950s New York mafia world. He accompanied Redmond O'Hanlon on a remarkable trip to Borneo that served as the source for O'Hanlon's comic travel book *Into the Heart of Borneo* (1984). *Children in Exile*'s appearance in the United States (1985) generated an enthusiastic response to the relatively unknown British poet. More recently, Fenton has published a travel book with political overtones, *All the Wrong Places: Adrift in the Politics of the Pacific Rim* (1988); *Leonardo's Nephew: Essays on Art and Artists* (1998); and *Out of Danger* (1993), a collection of poetry. He was appointed professor of poetry at Oxford University in 1994.

Lawrence Ferlinghetti (b. 1919)   Born Lawrence Ferling, this irreverent writer restored his original family name in 1954. He earned a B.A. in journalism from the University of North Carolina in 1941, served as lieutenant commander in the U.S. Naval Reserve during World War II, then received graduate degrees from Columbia and the University of Paris. He worked briefly as a translator of French before rising to prominence in the San Francisco–based beat literary movement of the 1950s, composed of a group of writers who felt strongly that art should be accessible to all, not just to a small group of intellectuals. Ferlinghetti received great praise from many readers and some critics for his attempts to incorporate American vernacular speech and the rhythms of modern jazz into his writings, while he was roundly attacked by defenders of the status quo. Ferlinghetti has been a prolific writer in all genres. In addition, he co-founded the San Francisco bookstore City Lights and two publishing enterprises, City Lights Books and the Pocket Book Series. In 1998 Ferlinghetti was named San Francisco's first poet laureate. He has published two novels, many plays, and over two dozen volumes of poetry including *How to Paint Sunlight: New Poems* (2001). His early work, *A Coney Island of the Mind* (1958), remains his most popular and best-selling poetry collection.

Syd Field (b. 1936)   Field has published five books on the creation and marketing of screenplays, some of which are used as texts in college-level courses. He has taught at a number of universities, including UCLA and Harvard. He serves as a creative consultant in film to several foreign governments, and is a special consultant to the Film Preservation Project at the Getty Museum in southern California.

Harvey Fierstein (b. 1954)   Fierstein was born in Brooklyn, New York. His father was a handkerchief manufacturer and his mother a school librarian. He began his career in the theater at the age of eleven as a founding actor in the Gallery Players Community Theater in Brooklyn. He earned a B.F.A. from Pratt Institute in 1973 and added writing and producing to his early acting skills as he embarked on a remarkable career. He wrote the three one-act plays that constitute *Torch Song Trilogy* between 1976 and 1979, which were all produced in small theaters; but when he starred in the production that opened in an off-off-Broadway house (1981) and later moved to Broadway, his considerable talents were widely recognized. In fact, he is the first person to win Tony Awards for best actor and best play for the same production. Fierstein has characterized himself as the first "real live, out-of-the-closet queer on Broadway." He pointed out to one critic that Arnold, the homosexual central figure in *Torch Song Trilogy,* is much like us all. "Everyone wants what Arnold wants — an apartment they can afford, a job they don't hate too much, a chance to go to the store once in a while and someone to share it all with." Fierstein wrote the book for the musical version of *La Cage aux Folles* and a number of one-act and full-length plays and television dramas. His work has been recognized with numerous awards in addition to his Tonys. The original producer of *Torch Song Trilogy* illuminated the source of Fierstein's success when he pointed out that "what Harvey proved was that you could use a gay context and a gay experience and speak in universal truths."

Donald Finkel (b. 1929)   Donald Finkel was born in New York City, the son of an attorney. He earned a B.S. (1952) and an M.A. (1953) from Columbia University. In 1956 he married the writer Constance Urdang. Shortly thereafter, Finkel began a university teaching career at the University of Iowa, and in 1960 moved to Washington University in St. Louis where he became poet-in-residence. His interest in Antarctica and exploration produced *Endurance: An Antarctic Idyll* and *Going Under* (1978). The first describes the shipwreck and rescue of Ernest Shackleton's 1914 expedition. The second examines two men who explored Kentucky's Mammoth Cave. His many books, including *Selected Shorter Poems* (1987), *A Splintered Mirror: Chinese Poetry from the Democracy Movement* (1991), and *A Question of Seeing: Poems* (1998), have earned him abundant awards and honors, among them a Guggenheim Fellowship (1967), nomination for a National Book Award (1970), and two nominations for the National Book Critics Circle Award (1975, 1981).

Nick Flynn (b. 1960)   Flynn has worked at an odd variety of jobs, including ship's captain, electrician, and caseworker for homeless adults. He is a member of Columbia University's Writing Project, and spends significant time in New York City public schools introducing young people to poetry. With Shirley McPhillips, he authored *A Note Slipped Under the Door: Teaching from Poems We Love* (2000) — a teachers' guidebook that explores the benefits of using poetry in the classroom. His first book of poems, *Some Ether* (2000), won two awards, and he has won fellowships from the Fine Arts Work Center, Provincetown, MA, and the MacDowell and Millay Colonies. He lives in Brooklyn, NY.

Carolyn Forché (b. 1950)   Born in Detroit, Forché earned a B.A. in international relations and creative writing at Michigan State University in 1972. After graduate study at Bowling Green State University in 1975, she taught at a number of schools, including the University of Arkansas, Vassar College, and Columbia University. She won the Yale Series of Younger Poets Award in 1976 for her first collection, *Gathering the Tribes*. Other honors include a Guggenheim Fellowship and the Lamont Award (1981). Forché was a journalist for Amnesty International in El Salvador in 1983 and Beirut correspondent for the National Public Radio program *All Things Considered*. Her works include the collections of poetry *The Country between Us* (1981) and *The Angel of History* (1994), both embodying her passionate preoccupation with the dehumanizing effects of political repression. She currently teaches in the M.F.A. program in poetry at George Mason University.

Erich Fromm (1900–1980)   Fromm was born in Frankfurt, Germany, into the family of a wine merchant. He earned a Ph.D. from the University of Heidelberg, and completed further post-graduate study at the University of Munich, the Institute of the German Psychoanalytic Society, and the Psychoanalytic Institute of Berlin. In 1934, he immigrated to the United States, where he enjoyed a distinguished and prolific career as a psychoanalyst, philosopher, and writer. He lectured at numerous universities throughout the United States and Mexico, and was an adjunct professor of psychology at New York University (1962–1980), where he founded the Institute of Psychology. He authored and edited more than thirty-five books, among them *The Art of Loving: An Enquiry into the Nature of Love* (1956, reissued 1974). Though his family had produced several rabbis, he gave up his religious convictions and practices because he "just didn't want to participate in any division of the human race, whether religious or political." Fromm helped organize the National Committee for a Sane Nuclear Policy (SANE) in 1957. As a psychologist, he resisted the Freudian model in which the unconscious dominates, focusing instead on the importance of social and economic factors in human behavior.

Robert Frost (1874–1963)   Frost was born in San Francisco but from the age of ten lived in New England. He attended Dartmouth College briefly, became a teacher, but soon decided to resume his formal training and enrolled at Harvard University. He left Harvard after two years without a degree and for several years supported himself and his growing family by tending a farm his grandfather bought for him. When he was not farming, he read and wrote intensively, though he received little recognition. Discouraged by his lack of success, he sold the farm and moved his family to England, where he published his first volumes of poetry, *A Boy's Will* (1913) and *North of Boston* (1914). After three years in England, Frost returned to America a recognized poet. Later volumes, notably *Mountain Interval* (1916), *New Hampshire* (1923), *West-Running Brook* (1928), and *A Further Range* (1936), won Frost numerous awards, including two Pulitzer Prizes, and wide popularity. By the time he delivered his poem "The Gift Outright" at the inauguration of President John F. Kennedy in 1961, Frost had achieved the status of unofficial poet laureate of America, widely revered and beloved for his folksy manner and seemingly artless, accessible poems.

Athol Fugard (b. 1932)   Born in a remote village in South Africa, Fugard grew up in Port Elizabeth, the setting for most of his plays. He attended Cape Town University, spent two years as the only white seaman on a merchant ship in the Far East, then returned to South Africa. In 1958, he moved to Johannesburg where he worked as a court clerk, an experience that made him keenly aware of the injustices of apartheid, the theme of many of his plays. In that same year, he organized a multiracial theater for which he wrote, directed, and acted. Fugard's attacks on apartheid brought him into conflict with the South African government. After his play *Blood Knot* (1961) was produced in England, the government withdrew his passport for four years. His support in 1962 of an international boycott against the South African practice of segregating theater audiences led to further restrictions. The restrictions were relaxed somewhat in 1971, when he was allowed to travel to England to direct his play *Boesman and Lena* (1969). *A Lesson* *from Aloes* won the 1980 New York Drama Critics' Circle Award. *"Master Harold"* . . . *and the Boys* (1982) premiered at the Yale Repertory Theatre and was then taken to Broadway. He is also the author of *Cousins: A Memoir* (1997).

William Schwenck Gilbert (1836–1911)   Born in London, Gilbert attended King's College of London University (B.A., 1856), where he trained for a career as an attorney. He worked as a law clerk, and was called to the bar in 1864. But writing was clearly his first love, and he began writing humorous verse under the pseudonym Bab. In 1861, he produced the first of more than fifty stage plays, and in 1866 began his collaboration with Arthur Sullivan. Together they produced fourteen operettas until the partnership dissolved in 1896. Those celebrated works often revealed and satirized the vanity, hypocrisy, and selfishness of the Victorian English establishment. His legal background led to his appointment as a justice of the peace in 1893.

Charlotte Perkins Gilman (1860–1935)   Charlotte Perkins Gilman was born in Hartford, Connecticut. Shortly after her birth, her father deserted the family. Left with two children to support and scant help from their father, her mother was unable to provide her children with a secure and stable childhood. Gilman attended for a time the Rhode Island School of Design and went on to work as a commercial artist and teacher. In 1884 she married Charles Stetson, an artist. Following the birth of her only child the next year, Gilman was immobilized by a deep depression. At the urging of her husband, she became the patient of S. Weir Mitchell, a physician celebrated for his treatment of female nervous disorders. Gilman found the treatment intolerable and finally abandoned it. In 1888, convinced that her marriage threatened her sanity, she moved with her daughter to California and began her productive career as writer and feminist. In 1900, after her divorce, she married her first cousin George Houghton Gilman, enjoying a happy relationship that lasted until his sudden death thirty-four years later. Among Gilman's many works are *Women and Economics* (1899), *The Home: Its Work and Influence* (1903), and *The Man-Made World* (1911), whose thesis is that war and injustice will be eliminated only when women assume a larger role in national and international affairs. Gilman's fiction includes the novels *Moving the Mountain* (1911), *Herland* (1915), and *With Her in Ourland* (1916). Her autobiography, *The Living of Charlotte Perkins Gilman,* was published posthumously in 1935, the year she committed suicide to avoid suffering the final stages of breast cancer.

Nikki Giovanni (b. 1943)   Born Yolande Cornelia Giovanni Jr. in Knoxville, Tennessee, daughter of a probation officer and a social worker, Giovanni graduated with honors from Fisk University in 1967. She attended the University of Pennsylvania School of Social Work and Columbia School of the Arts, was assistant professor of black studies at Queens College (1968), and associate professor of English at Rutgers University (1968–1970). She is currently a professor of English at Virginia Tech. Giovanni's early work reflects her social activism as an African American college student in the 1960s, while her later works focus on the individual struggle for fulfillment rather than the collective struggle for black empowerment. Her books include *Black Feeling, Black Talk, Black Judgment* (1970), *My House* (1972), and *The Women and the Men* (1975). She is also the author of a collection of essays, *Sacred Cows . . . and Other Edibles* (1988), as well as poetry and fiction for children. Recent publications include *The Selected Poems of Nikki Giovanni, 1968–1995* (1996), *Love Poems* (1997), and *Blues: For All the Changes: New Poems* (1999).

Susan Glaspell (1882–1948)   Born and raised in Davenport, Iowa, Glaspell began her career as a novelist and author of sentimental short stories for popular magazines. By 1915, she had turned her energies to the theater, becoming one of the founders of the Provincetown Players, a group devoted to experimental drama. In 1916, Glaspell moved with the company, now called the Playwright's Theatre, to Greenwich Village in New York, where for two seasons — as writer, director, and actor — she played an important role in a group that came to have a major influence on the development of American drama. *Trifles* was written to be performed with a group of one-act plays by Eugene O'Neill at the company's summer playhouse on Cape Cod. Among her longer plays that embody a feminist perspective are *The Verge* (1921) and *Allison's House* (1931), a Pulitzer Prize–winning drama based on the life of Emily Dickinson. Among more than forty short stories, some twenty plays, and ten novels, Glaspell's best works deal with the theme of the new woman, presenting a protagonist who embodies the American pioneer spirit of independence and freedom.

Kate Gleason (b. 1956)   Kate Gleason's work has appeared in numerous publications, including *Best American Poetry 1997, Boomer Girls,* and *Yearbook of American Poetry.* She has authored two poetry chapbooks: *Making As If to Sing* (1989) and *The Brighter the Deeper* (1995). Among many awards, she has received a New Hampshire State Council on the Arts Fellowship (1998), the New Hampshire Writer's Project Outstanding Emerging Writer Award (1998), and a 1999 National Endowment for the Arts Fellowship for residency at Ragdale Artist's Colony. She has served as a poet-in-the-schools and edited *Peregrine,* a literary journal. She currently teaches creative writing workshops in New Hampshire.

Emma Goldman (1869–1940)   Socialist, anarchist, and feminist, Goldman was born in Russia and immigrated in 1885 to New York City, where she worked in clothing factories and began writing and lecturing on behalf of reform movements, including feminism and birth control. In 1893, she was arrested for inciting a riot after urging a group of unemployed workers to take food by force. In 1919, after serving time in prison for agitating against military conscription and U.S. involvement in World War I, she was deported to Russia, whose revolution in 1917 she had hailed as the dawn of a just society. After two years, she left Russia to travel in a number of countries, including Germany, England, and Canada. In two books, *My Disillusionment with Russia* (1923) and *My Further Disillusionment with Russia* (1924), Goldman announced her break with the Russian regime. She spent her final years in Canada, anxiously awaiting word on her request to end her exile. The request was denied. She died in Canada and is buried in Chicago. Other works include *Anarchism and Other Essays* (1911) and the autobiography *Living My Life* (1931).

Robert Graves (1895–1985)   Graves was born in London, son of an Irish poet. He served in the Royal Welsh Fusiliers during World War I and rose to the rank of captain. He studied at Oxford, and in 1926 was professor of English literature at Cairo University. In 1929, he left his wife and four children to live in Mallorca, Spain, with Laura Riding, an American poet. Controversial in both his personal life and his work, Graves aroused indignation with his translation of *The Rubáiyát of Omar Khayyám,* which departed markedly from the popular Edward Fitzgerald translation (1859). During the late 1950s and 1960s, he taught at Oxford and lectured in the United States. *Goodbye to All That* (1929), his early autobiography, provides a nice insight into the culture that nourished him. Among his numerous works are the influential "historical grammar of poetic myth," *The White Goddess* (1948, 1952), and the historical novels *I, Claudius* (1934) and *Claudius the God* (1934).

Lorraine Hansberry (1930–1965)   Lorraine Hansberry was born into a prosperous, middle-class African American family on the south side of Chicago. When she was seven, her family went to court over an attempt to deny them the right to buy a home in a restricted white neighborhood. Their lawsuit challenging the restrictive covenant was finally decided in their favor by the U.S. Supreme Court. Hansberry later recalled, "Both of my parents were strong-minded, civic-minded, exceptionally race-minded people who made enormous sacrifices on behalf of the struggle for civil rights throughout their lifetimes." After graduating from the segregated public school system of Chicago, she attended the University of Wisconsin and studied at the Art Institute of Chicago and abroad. She soon gave up her artistic plans and moved to New York City to pursue a writing career. She also became politically active in liberal causes. During a protest demonstration at New York University, she met Robert Nemiroff, a white writer and political activist. They married in 1953. Encouraged by her husband, Hansberry finally completed *A Raisin in the Sun,* a play she had been working on for some time. It opened in 1959, becoming the first play written by a black woman to be produced on Broadway.

An immediate success, the play won the New York Drama Critics' Circle Award. A film version, for which she wrote the screenplay, was released in 1961. Her next play, *The Sign in Sidney Brustein's Window* (1964), met with less success. She was working on another play, *Les Blancs,* when she died of cancer (the play was produced in 1970). Although Nemiroff and Hansberry divorced in 1964, he was appointed her literary executor and assembled, from his former wife's writings and words, a dramatic autobiography titled *To Be Young, Gifted, and Black* (1969).

Thomas Hardy (1840–1928)   Hardy was born near Dorchester, in southeastern England (on which he based the Wessex of many of his novels and poems). Hardy worked for the ecclesiastical architect John Hicks from 1856 to 1861. He then moved to London to practice architecture and took evening classes at King's College for six years. In 1867, he gave up architecture to become a full-time writer and after writing short stories and poems, found success as a novelist. *The Mayor of Casterbridge* (1886) and *Tess of the d'Urbervilles* (1891) reveal Hardy's concern for victims of circumstance and his appeal to humanitarian sympathy in readers. After his novel *Jude the Obscure* (1896) was strongly criticized, Hardy set aside prose fiction and returned to poetry — a genre in which he was most prolific and successful after he reached the age of seventy.

Nathaniel Hawthorne (1804–1864)   The son of a merchant sea captain who died in a distant port when Nathaniel was four, Hawthorne grew up in genteel poverty in Massachusetts and Maine. His earliest American ancestor, the magistrate William Hathorne, ordered the whipping of a Quaker woman in Salem. William's son John was one of the three judges at the Salem witch trials of 1692. Aware of his family's role in colonial America, Hawthorne returned to Salem after graduating from Bowdoin College (where future president Franklin Pierce was a friend and classmate), determined to be a writer. He recalled and destroyed copies of his first novel, the mediocre *Fanshawe* (1828). His short stories, often set in Puritan America, revealed a moral complexity that had not troubled his righteous ancestors William and John. His success as an author allowed him to marry Sophia Peabody in 1842 (after a four-year engagement). Though his stories were critically praised, they did not earn much money, and in 1846, he used his political connections with the Democratic Party to obtain a job at the Salem custom house. His dismissal in 1849 (when the Democrats lost) produced both anger and resolve. The result was a great American novel, *The Scarlet Letter* (1850), which made him famous and improved his fortune. Although he was friendly with Emerson and his circle of optimistic transcendentalists (some of whom established the utopian socialist community at Brook Farm), Hawthorne's vision of the human condition was considerably darker. Herman Melville dedicated *Moby Dick* to Hawthorne and characterized him as a man who could say "No" in thunder.

Robert Hayden (1913–1980)   Born in Detroit, Hayden studied at Wayne State University and the University of Michigan (M.A., 1944). In 1946, he joined the faculty of Fisk University. He left Fisk in 1968 for a professorship at the University of Michigan, where he remained until his death. He produced some ten volumes of poetry but did not receive the acclaim many thought he deserved until late in life, with the publication of *Words in the Mourning Time: Poems* (1971). In the 1960s, he aroused some hostility from African Americans who wanted him to express more militancy. But Hayden did not want to be part of what he called a "kind of literary ghetto." He considered his own work "a form of prayer — a prayer for illumination, perfection."

Bessie Head (1937–1986)   Bessie Head was born in Pietermaritzburg, South Africa, the daughter of a racially mixed marriage. She was taken from her white mother, raised by foster parents until she was thirteen, and then placed in an orphanage. She overcame this difficult childhood and trained to be a primary-school teacher. After four years as a teacher, two years as a journalist, and a failed marriage in South Africa, she immigrated to Botswana where she lived for many years in deep poverty. She spent fifteen years in a refugee community at the Bamangwato Development Farm before winning Botswanian citizenship. At the development farm, she continued her distinguished career as a writer, though she had to plead for small advances from her publisher to buy paper to write on. Her writing brought her recognition and prominence, and she represented Botswana at international writers' conferences in the United States, Canada, Europe, and Australia. She died of hepatitis at age forty-nine. Along with several collections of short stories, she published three novels and two historical chronicles of African life. In an interview, Head acknowledged "that the regularity of her life in the refugee community brought her the peace of mind she sought: 'In South Africa, all my life I lived in shattered little bits. All those shattered bits began to grow together here. . . . I have a peace against which all the turmoil is worked out!' "

Seamus Heaney (b. 1939)   Heaney, the eldest of nine children, was born on his family's farm near Belfast in County Derry, Northern Ireland. He attended local schools; earned a degree in English with first-class honors from Queen's University, Belfast; and received a teacher's certificate in English from St. Joseph's College in Belfast. He published his first writings while a student at St. Joseph's and began a career as a teacher. His first volume of poetry, *Death of a Naturalist* (1966), won several prizes and launched Heaney's distinguished career as a poet. His many books include two volumes of essays, *The Government of the Tongue* (1988) and *The Redress of Poetry* (1995), as well as *Selected Poems: 1966–1987* (1990), *The Spirit Level* (1996), *Opened Ground: Selected Poems, 1966–1996* (1998), and *Electric Light* (2001). He has taught at Oxford University, the University of California at Berkeley, and Harvard University. An immensely popular poet, he enjoys the support of a host of "Heaneyboppers" who attend his readings. Several modern critics characterize him as "the most important Irish poet since Yeats." When asked "about his abiding interest in memorializing the people of his life, he replied, 'The elegiac Heaney? There's nothing else.'" In 1995, Heaney was awarded the Nobel Prize for literature.

Anthony Hecht (b. 1923)   Born in New York City, Hecht attended Bard College (B.A., 1944). After three years in the U.S. Army, serving in Europe and Japan, he continued his education at Columbia University (M.A., 1950). Hecht has taught at several universities, including the University of Rochester, where he was professor of poetry and rhetoric in 1967. He is presently a professor in the graduate school of Georgetown University. His awards include a 1951 Prix de Rome; Guggenheim, Rockefeller, and Ford Foundation Fellowships; as well as the Bollingen Prize in Poetry. His first book of poetry, *A Summer of Stones* (1954), was followed by *Hard Hours* (1968), which won a Pulitzer Prize for poetry; *Millions of Strange Shadows* (1977); *Venetian Vespers* (1979); and *The Transparent Man* (1990). His most recent collection of poems is *The Darkness and the Light* (2002). Hecht is also the author of a collection of critical essays, *Obbligati* (1986). Acclaimed for his technical expertise, Hecht was first devoted to traditional poetic forms, and his work was sometimes described as "baroque" and "courtly." More recently, his work has become less decorative.

Ernest Hemingway (1899–1961)   Born in Oak Park, Illinois, Hemingway became a cub reporter after high school. After World War I — during which he was seriously wounded while serving as an ambulance driver — he lived in Paris, a member of a lively and productive expatriate community characterized by Gertrude Stein as "a lost generation." He lived an active life, not only as a writer but as a war correspondent, big game hunter, and fisherman. In such novels as *The Sun Also Rises* (1926), *A Farewell to Arms* (1929), and *For Whom the Bell Tolls* (1940), his fictional characters exhibit a passion for courage and integrity, for grace under pressure. Hemingway's spare, unembellished style reinforced his central theme that one must confront danger and live honorably. He won the Nobel Prize for literature in 1954. In 1961, unable to write because treatment for mental instability affected his memory, he killed himself with the shotgun he had so often used when hunting.

Robert Herrick (1591–1674)   Born in London, Herrick was apprenticed to his uncle, a goldsmith, for ten years until, at age twenty-two, he was sent to Cambridge University in recognition of his academic talents. Little is known of the decade following his graduation from Cambridge, although it seems certain that he associated with a circle of literary artists. In 1629, he was appointed vicar at Dean Prior, Devonshire — a rural parish that the sophisticated and cosmopolitan Herrick looked upon as a kind of exile. Yet, he was fascinated by the pagan elements of local songs and dances, and often drew upon pre-Christian writers for inspiration. His chief work, *Hesperides* (1648), is a collection of some twelve hundred poems — mostly written in Devon-shire — about local scenery, customs, and people.

Tony Hoagland (b. 1953) Tony Hoagland was born in Fort Bragg, North Carolina, and educated at the University of Iowa and the University of Ari-zona. He has taught at many universities, including Kalamazoo College, Michigan, where he was writer-in-residence (summer 1991). Since 1993, he has been a faculty member in the writing program at Warren Wilson College in Asheville, North Carolina, and an instructor at Colby College in Maine. His poems and critical writings have appeared in such publications as *Ploughshares, American Poetry Review,* and the *Pushcart Prize Anthology* (1991). Hoagland's first three collections of poems were chapbooks: *A Change in Plans* (1985), *Talking to Stay Warm* (1986), and *History of Desire* (1990). His first full-length volume of poetry, *Sweet Ruin* (1992), won the Brit-tingham Prize in poetry as well as the Zacharas Award from Emerson College. His most recent volume is *Donkey Gospel* (1998).

Linda Hogan (b. 1947) A Chickasaw, Hogan was born in Denver, Colorado, and educated at the University of Colorado, where she received her M.A. in 1978. For a time, she supported herself with odd jobs and freelance writing. By 1980, her success as a writer led to her appointment as writer-in-residence for the states of Colorado and Oklahoma. In 1982 she became an assistant professor in the TRIBES program at Colorado College, Colorado Springs. She is now associate professor of American Indian studies at the University of Minnesota. In 1980, her play *A Piece of Moon* won the Five Civilized Tribes Playwriting Award, and in 1983 she received the *Stand* magazine fiction award. Her writings include six volumes of poetry: *Calling Myself Home* (1979), *Daughters, I Love You* (1981), *Eclipse* (1983), *Seeing through the Sun* (1985), *Savings* (1991), and *The Book of Medicines* (1993). Her fiction includes two volumes of short stories and three novels, *Mean Spirit* (1990), *Solar Storms* (1995), and *Power* (1999). Her collection of essays, *Dwellings: Reflections on the Natural World* (1995), describes her attempts to "relearn the tribal knowings of thousands of years." Her most recent work is a memoir, *Woman Who Watches Over the World* (2001).

M. Carl Holman (1919–1988) Holman was born in Minter City, Mississippi, and grew up in St. Louis, Missouri. He graduated magna cum laude from Lin-coln University and earned a master's degree from the University of Chicago and a Master of Fine Arts from Yale University, which he attended on a creative-writing scholarship. He taught as an English professor at Hampton University, Lincoln University, and Clark College. For a while, he edited the Atlanta *Inquirer* — a weekly publication that reported on civil rights activities in the South. In 1962, he moved to Washington, D.C., to become an informa-tion officer at the U.S. Civil Rights Commission, becoming its deputy director in 1966. From 1971 to 1988, he served as director of the Urban Coalition, an organization formed after the riots of 1967 for the purpose of forging partnerships between industry and government to promote inner-city development.

Gerard Manley Hopkins (1844–1889)   Raised in London, Hopkins won a scholarship to Balliol College, Oxford University, where he studied classical literature. He converted to Roman Catholicism in 1866 and two years later entered the Jesuit novitiate. In 1877, he was ordained as a Jesuit priest and served in missions in London, Liverpool, Oxford, and Glasgow until 1882. From 1884 to his death in 1889, he was professor of Greek at University College, Dublin. A technically innovative poet, Hopkins saw only three of his poems published during his lifetime but gained posthumous recognition in 1918 when a friend (the poet laureate Robert Bridges) published his complete works. His early poems celebrate the beauty of God's world, but later works reflect his poor health and depression.

A. E. Housman (1859–1936)   Born in Fockbury, England, and an outstanding student, Alfred Edward Housman nonetheless failed his final examinations at Oxford University in 1881 (possibly as a result of emotional chaos caused by his love for a male classmate). Working as a clerk in the patent office in London, he pursued classical studies on his own, earned an M.A., and was appointed to the Chair of Latin at University College, London. In 1910, he became professor of Latin at Cambridge, where he remained until his death in 1936. As a poet, Housman was concerned primarily with the fleetingness of love and the decay of youth. After his first collection, *A Shropshire Lad,* was rejected by several publishers, Housman published it at his own expense in 1896. It gained popularity during World War I, and his 1922 collection, *Last Poems,* was well received. In his lecture "The Name and Nature of Poetry" (1933), Housman argued that poetry should appeal to emotions rather than intellect. *More Poems* (1936) was published posthumously.

Pam Houston (b. 1962)   Houston grew up in New Jersey, the only child of an actress and an unsuccessful businessman. After graduating in English from Denison University in Ohio, she rode across Canada on a bicycle and then down to Colorado, where she worked at various odd jobs, among them bartender and flagwoman on a highway crew. Eventually, she entered a doctoral program at the University of Utah. Her first collection of short stories, *Cowboys Are My Weakness,* was published in 1992. Her stories have also appeared in *Mirabella, Mademoiselle,* the *Mississippi Review,* and *Best American Short Stories,* and her nonfiction has appeared in the *New York Times, Elle,* and *Vogue.* She recently edited *Women on Hunting: Essays, Fiction, and Poetry* (1994) and published a collection of essays, *A Little More about Me* (2000). A licensed river guide and accomplished horsewoman, Houston teaches at many writing conferences and programs in the United States and England. In explaining her pursuit of outdoor and often dangerous activities during her early twenties, she says: "You think I spent three summers leading hunters through Alaska because I like watching guys like David Duke shoot sheep? No. It was because if I didn't go with my boyfriend, somebody else would. I wanted to win."

Langston Hughes (1902–1967)   Hughes was born in Joplin, Missouri. His father was a businessman and lawyer, his mother a teacher. Hughes attended Columbia University, graduated from Lincoln University in 1929, traveled throughout the world, and held many odd jobs as a young man. While Hughes had a long and prolific career as a writer in all genres, he is still remembered as the central figure of the Harlem Renaissance of the 1920s, a movement that committed itself to the examination and celebration of black life in America and its African heritage. He was the Madrid correspondent for the Baltimore *Afro-American* (1937) and a columnist for the Chicago *Defender* (1943–1967) and the New York *Post* (1962–1967). His poems of racial affirmation and protest are often infused with the rhythms of blues and jazz music. He wrote over two dozen plays (many musicalized) and founded the Suitcase Theater (Harlem, 1938), the New Negro Theater (Los Angeles, 1939), and the Skyloft Players (Chicago, 1941). His works include *The Weary Blues* (1926), *Montage of a Dream Deferred* (1951), and *The Panther and the Lash: Poems of Our Times* (1969).

Zora Neale Hurston (1891–1960)   Born in Eatonville, Florida, an African American town, Hurston enjoyed a happy early childhood in a town that spared her from racism and with a mother who instilled a strong sense of self-worth in her. With the death of her mother, she was sent off to boarding school, but was forced to give up her formal education when her father remarried and refused to give her further financial help. She supported herself with odd jobs, managing to earn a high school diploma and enter Howard University in Washington, D.C. Unable to support herself as a full-time student, Hurston quit college after five years, having earned only a year and a half of college credits. She moved to Harlem, determined to pursue a writing career. In New York, she was hired as a personal secretary by the novelist Fannie Hurst, who arranged a scholarship for her at Barnard College. There, she studied with the famous anthropologist Franz Boas and became interested in black folk traditions. She earned her degree from Barnard in 1927 and received a fellowship to study the oral traditions of her hometown. She wrote her first novel, *Jonah's Gourd Vine* (1934), while doing fieldwork in Eatonville. *Mules and Men* (1935), based on the material her fieldwork had produced, was attacked by African American intellectuals and writers for its refusal to acknowledge and confront racism. Nevertheless, Hurston was awarded a Guggenheim Fellowship to study voodoo in the Caribbean, which gave her the material for her second and most celebrated novel, *Their Eyes Were Watching God* (1937). During the last two decades of her life, she continued to write novels, plays, and an autobiography, *Dust Tracks on the Road* (1942), but drew increasing criticism from the African American press for her refusal to publicly condemn segregation. In 1950, she was the subject of a *Miami Herald* news story that carried the headline: "Famous Negro Author Working as a Maid Here 'Just to Live a Little.' " She claimed that she needed a break from writing and that she was busy making plans for writing projects and for a national magazine devoted to domestics. Her last years were troubled by poor health, emotional fatigue, and lack of money. She died of a stroke, penniless, in a welfare home in Fort Pierce, Florida.

Henrik Ibsen (1828–1906)   Ibsen was born in Skien, Norway (a seaport about a hundred miles south of Oslo), the son of a wealthy merchant. When Ibsen was eight, his father's business failed, and at fifteen he was apprenticed to an apothecary in the tiny town of Grimstad. He hated this profession. To solace himself, he read poetry and theology and began to write. When he was twenty-two, he became a student in Christiania (now Oslo) and published his first play. In 1851, his diligent, though unremarkable, writing earned him an appointment as theater-poet to a new theater in Bergen, where he remained until 1857, learning both the business and the art of drama. He wrote several plays based on Scandinavian folklore, held positions at two theaters in Christiania, and married. When he was thirty-six, he applied to the government for a poet's pension — a stipend that would have permitted him to devote himself to writing. The stipend was refused. Enraged, he left Norway and, though he was granted the stipend two years later, spent the next twenty-seven years in Italy and Germany, where he wrote the realistic social dramas that established his reputation as the founder of modern theater. Such plays as *Ghosts* (1881), *An Enemy of the People* (1882), and *A Doll's House* (1878) inevitably generated controversy as Ibsen explored venereal disease, the stupidity and greed of the "compact majority," and the position of women in society. In 1891, he returned to live in Christiania, where he was recognized and honored as one of Norway's (and Europe's) finest writers.

Major Jackson (b. 1968) Jackson was born and raised in Philadelphia. He earned a B.S. at Temple University and an M.F.A. at the University of Oregon. His book *Leaving Saturn* won the 2000 Cave Canem Poetry Prize. He has received awards and fellowships from the Bread Loaf Writers' Conference, MacDowell Artist Colony, Pew Fellowship in the Arts, and Provincetown Fine Arts Center. His poem "Duck Girl on the Occasion of Spring" was commissioned and performed by Philadelphia's Concerto Soloists. His poetry has been published in numerous journals, among them *American Poetry Review, Boulevard, Callaloo, Crab Orchard Review,* and the *New Yorker.* His work has been anthologized in several collections, among them *Beacon's Best of 1999: Creative Writing by Men and Women of All Colors, Spirit and Flame: An Anthology of Contemporary African American Poetry,* and *Xconnect: Writers of the Information Age.* He is a member of the Dark Room Collective and, from 1992 to 1999, served as literary arts curator of the Painted Bride Art Center in Philadelphia. Currently, he is an assistant professor in the English department at Xavier University of Louisiana, and lives in New Orleans with his son and his partner, Kristen Johanson.

Shirley Jackson (1919–1965) Born in San Francisco, Jackson moved with her family to Rochester, New York, in her teens. An episode of severe depression (a recurrent problem during her life) forced her out of the University of Rochester, but she later graduated from Syracuse University. She married the eminent critic Stanley Edgar Hyman, had four children, and kept to a rigid writing schedule. Although her major work tends toward the ominous, she contributed humorous pieces on the problems of housekeeping and raising children to popular magazines. These were collected in *Life among the Savages* (1953) and *Raising Demons* (1957). She wrote four novels, and her short stories are collected in three volumes: *The Lottery* (1949), *The Magic of Shirley Jackson* (1966), and *Come Along with Me* (1968).

Thomas Jefferson (1743–1826) The third president of the United States (1801–1809), Jefferson was born in Virginia and educated privately until he was seventeen, when he was sent to William and Mary College. After graduation, he studied law, and in 1769 he was elected to the Virginia colonial legislature, the House of Burgesses. He served as a member of the Continental Congress (1775–1776), governor of Virginia (1779–1781), American minister to France (1784–1789), secretary of state (1790–1793), and vice president (1797–1801). Jefferson's influence on the creation and history of the United States of America has been profound and enduring. He was the principal author of the Declaration of Independence. Fearful that the new country might move in the direction of a powerful centralized form of government, he opposed the adoption of the new Constitution until the Bill of Rights was added. As president, he supported the Louisiana Purchase (1803), which doubled the size of the United States. One of the paradoxes of this great champion of individualism and democratic rights is that he was a slaveowner himself who fathered at least one child by his black slave mistress Sally Hemings. While Jefferson did not write books in the usual sense, his political writings and his extraordinary letters rank among the great heritages of the nation's founding fathers. In 1809, Jefferson retired to Monticello, the home he had designed himself, and devoted the rest of his years principally to the University of Virginia (1819), whose buildings he also designed and whose first rector he became. Jefferson's lifelong commitment to the principle that an enlightened people could and should govern themselves through representative institutions is embodied in the inscription he ordered for his tombstone: "Author of the Declaration of American Independence, of the Statute of Virginia for religious freedom, and Father of the University of Virginia." In April 1962, at a White House dinner honoring Nobel Prize winners of the Western Hemisphere, President John Fitzgerald Kennedy observed: "I think this is the most extraordinary collection of talent, of human knowledge, that has ever been gathered together at the White House, with the possible exception of when Thomas Jefferson dined alone."

Ben Jonson (1572–1637)   Jonson was born in Westminster, England, and, after leaving school, began earning his living (in the manner of his stepfather) as a bricklayer. Though he never attended college, he taught himself enough to be considered learned. He soon abandoned construction work and earned his reputation as one of the preeminent playwrights of his period. A contemporary of Shakespeare, he also wrote poetry and translations of classical Roman authors for his English Renaissance audience.

June Jordan (b. 1936)   Jordan was born in Harlem, New York, and attended Barnard College (1953–1955) and the University of Chicago (1955–1956). A poet, novelist, and writer of children's books, she has taught widely at university campuses, including the City College of the City University of New York (1966–1968) and Connecticut College (1969–1974), where she both taught English and served as director of Search for Education, Elevation and Knowledge (SEEK). She is currently professor of English at the State University of New York, Stony Brook. In addition to many appointments as visiting professor, she has served as chancellor's distinguished lecturer, University of California at Berkeley (1986). Her numerous honors include the Prix de Rome in Environmental Design (1970–1971), the Nancy Bloch Award (1971) for her reader *The Voice of the Children,* and the achievement award from the National Association of Black Journalists (1984). Her many books include *His Own Where* (1971), *Dry Victories* (1972), and *Kimako's Story* (1981), all for juvenile and young-adult readers. Her collections of poetry include *Things That I Do in the Dark* (1977), *Living Room: New Poems, 1980–1984* (1985), *Naming Our Destiny: New and Selected Poems* (1989), *Poetic Justice* (1991), *Haruko: Love Poems* (1994), and *Kissing God Goodbye: Poems 1991–1997* (1997). Jordan is also the author of *Technical Difficulties: African-American Notes on the State of the Union* (1992) and *Affirmative Acts: Political Essays* (1998).

Jenny Joseph (b. 1932)   Born in Birmingham, England, Joseph graduated from Oxford University with honors (1953). She worked for a number of provincial English newspapers before moving to South Africa in 1957. There she worked for a publisher, and taught at the Central Indian High School in Johannesburg. She returned to England and, with her husband, managed a pub in London between 1969 and 1972. She began teaching English as a second language at West London College in 1972, and served for several years as an adult-education instructor. Between 1966 and 1968, she co-authored several children's books. Her more recent volumes of verse include *Ghosts and Other Company* (1997) and *Extended Similes* (1997). Among her several awards are a Society of Authors traveling scholarship (1995) and the Forward

Poetry Prize (1995). One critic noted that when compared to her earliest work, her later work shows "more warmth, more empathy, . . . she is concerned with human characters rather than archetypes." The same critic praises Joseph's ability to create dramatic monologues based on vernacular speech.

James Joyce (1882–1941)   Though educated in Jesuit schools, Joyce came to reject Catholicism; and though an expatriate living in Paris, Trieste, and Zurich for most of his adult life, he wrote almost exclusively about his native Dublin. Joyce's rebelliousness, which surfaced during his university career, generated a revolution in modern literature. His novels *Ulysses* (1922) and *Finnegan's Wake* (1939) introduced radically new narrative techniques. "Araby" — from his first collection of short stories, *Dubliners* (1914) — is one of a series of sharply realized vignettes based on Joyce's experiences in Ireland, the homeland he later characterized as "a sow that eats its own farrow." Joyce lived precariously on earnings as a language teacher and modest contributions from wealthy patrons. That support Joyce justified: he is one of the most influential novelists of the twentieth century. Because *Ulysses* dealt frankly with sexuality and used coarse language, the U.S. Post Office charged that the novel was obscene and forbade its importation. A celebrated 1933 court decision lifted the ban in the United States.

Franz Kafka (1883–1924)   Born into a middle-class, German-speaking Jewish family in Prague, Kafka earned a law degree in 1906 and worked as a claims investigator for an insurance company for most of his adult life. He remained in constant conflict with his domineering father, who belittled his literary aims. He became engaged to a woman in 1912 but broke with her after five years. In 1917, he contracted the tuberculosis that was to kill him at forty-one. Despite the deadening monotony of his job and his personal anguish, he created a remarkable and original body of work during his short life, including the masterful novels *The Trial* (1925) and *The Castle* (1926). His starkly realistic stories and novels take place in nightmarish dream worlds where stifling bureaucracy chokes his protagonists and diminishes their dignity and their lives. A fierce perfectionist, Kafka published little during his life and left written instructions to his friend and executor, Max Brod, to destroy his unpublished manuscripts. Fortunately, Brod could not bring himself to comply.

Mary Karr (b. 1954)   Mary Karr is best known for her 1995 memoir, *The Liar's Club,* about growing up in an East Texas industrial city. Karr chose not to disclose the real name of her hometown but gives it the fictional name of Leechfield. In language praised for its command of colloquialisms and poetic beauty, she describes a childhood marked by violence, neglect, and substance abuse. At seventeen she traveled to California, then on to Macalaster College in Minnesota, dropping out after two years. Later, she studied writing at Goddard College in Vermont. Karr has written for many periodicals, including *Poetry, Ploughhshares, Granta,* and *Vogue.* She is a two-time winner of the Pushcart Prize. Her first two books were volumes of poetry, *Abacus* (1997) and *The Devil's Tour* (1993). Following *The Liar's Club,* she published a third volume of poetry, *Viper Rum* (1998). Her most recent book, *Cherry* (2000), a memoir of her teen years, is again set in her hometown.

John Keats (1795–1821)   Keats was born in London, the eldest son of a stablekeeper who died in an accident in 1804. His mother died of tuberculosis shortly after remarrying, and the grandmother who raised Keats and his siblings died in 1814. At eighteen, Keats wrote his first poem, "Imitation of Spenser," inspired by Edmund Spenser's long narrative poem *The Faerie Queene.* The thirty-three poems he wrote while training to be a surgeon were published in a collection in 1817, and Keats then gave up medicine for writing. After more traumatic losses in 1818, including the departure of one brother for America and the death of his other brother of tuberculosis, Keats wrote his second collection, *Lamia, Isabella, The Eve of St. Agnes, and Other Poems* (1820). Ill with tuberculosis himself, Keats was sent to Rome to recover. He died at twenty-six, but despite his short career, he is a major figure of the romantic period.

Jamaica Kincaid (b. 1949)   Kincaid was born Elaine Potter Richardson in St. Johns, Antigua, in the West Indies, then a British colony. At age seventeen, she left home to become an au pair in New York. Determined to make something of her life, Kincaid took night classes and ultimately earned a high school diploma. She went on to take classes at the New School for Social Research in New York, and attended college in New Hampshire on a scholarship. When she returned to New York, she changed her name to Jamaica Kincaid and began writing. Of her life up to this point, Kincaid told a reporter: "Everyone thought I had a way with words, but it came out as a sharp tongue. No one expected anything from me at all. Had I just sunk in the cracks it would not have been noted. I would have been lucky to be a secretary somewhere." Her first publication, a collection of short stories titled *At the Bottom of the River* (1983), earned her wide critical praise and recognition as a new voice in American fiction. That was followed by three novels, including *The Autobiography of My Mother* (1995). The recipient of many literary honors, Kincaid served as a staff writer for the *New Yorker* (1976–1995) and visiting professor at Harvard University.

Martin Luther King Jr. (1929–1968)   King was born in Atlanta, Georgia, where his father was pastor of the Ebenezer Baptist Church. He attended public schools (skipping the ninth and twelfth grades) and entered Morehouse College in Atlanta. He was ordained as a Baptist minister just before his graduation in 1948. He then enrolled in Crozer Theological Seminary in Pennsylvania and after earning a divinity degree there, attended graduate school at Boston University, where he earned a Ph.D. in theology in 1955. At Boston University, he met Coretta Scott; they were married in 1953. King's rise to national and international prominence began in Montgomery, Alabama, in 1955. In that year, Rosa Parks, an African American woman, was arrested for refusing to obey a city ordinance that required African Americans to sit or stand at the back of municipal buses. The African American citizens of the city (one of the most thoroughly segregated in the South) organized a bus boycott in protest and asked King to serve as their leader. Thousands boycotted the buses for more than a year, and despite segregationist violence against them, King grounded their protests on his deeply held belief in nonviolence. In 1956, the U.S. Supreme Court ordered Montgomery to provide integrated seating on public buses. In the following year, King and other African American ministers founded the Southern Christian Leadership Conference (SCLC) to carry forward the nonviolent struggle against segregation and legal discrimination. As protests grew, so did the unhappiness of King and his associates with the unwillingness of the president and Congress to support civil rights. The SCLC, therefore, organized massive demonstrations in Montgomery (King wrote "Letter from Birmingham Jail" during these demonstrations). With the civil rights movement now in the headlines almost every day, President Kennedy proposed to Congress a far-reaching civil rights bill. On August 28, 1963, over 200,000 blacks and whites gathered at the Lincoln Memorial in Washington, D.C., where King delivered his now famous speech, "I Have a Dream." In the following year, Congress passed the Civil Rights Act of 1964, prohibiting racial discrimination in public places and calling for equal opportunity in education and employment. In that year, King received the Nobel Prize for peace. In 1965, King and others organized a march to protest the blatant denial of African Americans' voting rights in Selma, Alabama, where the march began. Before the protesters were able to reach Birmingham, the state capital, they were attacked by police with tear gas and clubs. This outrage, viewed live on national television, led President Johnson to ask Congress for a bill that would eliminate all barriers to voting rights. Congress responded by passing the landmark Voting Rights Act of 1965. King remained committed to nonviolence, but his conviction that economic inequality — not just race — was one of the root causes of injustice led him to begin organizing a Poor People's Campaign that would unite all poor people in the struggle for justice. These views also led him to criticize the role played by the United States in the Vietnam War. The Poor People's Campaign took King to Memphis, Tennessee, to support a strike of African American sanitation workers, where on April 4, 1968, he was shot and killed while standing on the balcony of his hotel room. Riots immediately erupted in scores of cities across the nation. A few months later, Congress enacted the Civil Rights Act of 1968, banning discrimination in the sale and rental of housing. King is the author of *Stride toward Freedom* (1958), dealing with the

Montgomery bus boycott; *Strength to Love* (1953), a collection of sermons; and *Why We Can't Wait* (1964), a discussion of his general views on civil rights.

Maxine Hong Kingston (b. 1940) Kingston was born in Stockton, California. She earned a bachelor's degree from the University of California, Berkeley (1962), and a teaching certificate (1965). After teaching English and mathematics at a California high school, she moved to Hawaii and taught language arts and English as a second language at a number of schools. She became a visiting associate professor of English at the University of Hawaii after winning the National Book Critics Circle Award for *The Woman Warrior: Memoirs of a Girlhood among Ghosts* (1976). In that volume, she fashioned a new sort of genre — essays with substantial fictive elements. Her next book, *China Men* (1980), further developed that form. Her latest work, *Hawaii One Summer* (1998), examines the social life and customs of the region. An early critic characterized Kingston's work as the blending of "myth, legend, history, and autobiography into a genre of her own invention." Another argued that though Kingston's works are classified as nonfiction, "in a deeper sense, they are fiction at its best — novels, fairytales, epic poems."

Carolyn Kizer (b. 1925) Kizer was born in Spokane, Washington. Her father was a lawyer, her mother a biologist and professor. After graduating from Sarah Lawrence College in 1945, Kizer pursued graduate study at Columbia University and the University of Washington. From 1959 to 1965, she was editor of *Poetry Northwest* (which she founded in 1959 in Seattle), and spent 1964 and 1965 as a State Department specialist in Pakistan, where she taught at a women's college and translated poems from Urdu into English. She chose to leave early after the U.S. decision to bomb North Vietnam in 1965. Later, she joined archaeological tours in Afghanistan and Iran. She has worked as director of literary programs for the National Endowment for the Arts in Washington, D.C.; has taught at several universities; and was poet-in-residence at the University of North Carolina and Ohio University. Her volumes of poetry include *Yin* (1984), which won a Pulitzer Prize the following year; *Mermaids in the Basement: Poems for Women* (1984); *The Nearness of You* (1986); *Harping On: Poems 1985–1995* (1996); and *Cool Calm & Collected* (2000). She has also published two collections of essays — *Proses: On Poems and Poets* (1993) and *Picking and Choosing: Essays on Prose* (1995) — and edited *100 Great Poems by Women: A Golden Ecco Anthology* (1995).

Etheridge Knight (1933–1991) Knight was born in Corinth, Mississippi, attended two years of public high school in Kentucky, and served in the U.S. Army from 1948 to 1951. After being convicted on a robbery charge and sentenced in 1960 to twenty years in Indiana State Prison, he discovered poetry;

his first collection is entitled *Poems from Prison* (1968). Knight was paroled after eight years. From 1968 to 1971 he was poet-in-residence at several universities. An important African American voice in the 1960s and 1970s, Knight rejected the American and European aesthetic tradition, arguing that "the red of this esthetic rose got its color from the blood of black slaves, exterminated Indians, napalmed Vietnamese children." His collection *Belly Song and Other Poems* was nominated for the National Book Award and the Pulitzer Prize in 1973. His awards include National Endowment for the Arts and Guggenheim grants, and the 1987 American Book Award for *The Essential Etheridge Knight* (1986).

Steve Kowit (b. 1938)　Steve Kowit (pronounced COW-it) was born in New York City and educated at San Francisco State University in California (M.A., 1968) and at Warren Wilson College in North Carolina (M.F. A., 1992). Kowit received a National Endowment for the Arts Fellowship as well as the *Atlanta Review*'s Paumanok Prize for poetry (1996). Since 1990, he has held the position of professor of English at Southwestern College in Chula Vista, California. His poems have been published in *Poetry Now, Wormwood Review, New York Review,* and *Beloit Poetry Journal,* among others. The title poem of his first collection, *Lurid Confessions* (1983), is reprinted in the anthology *Stand Up Poetry: The Poetry of Los Angeles and Beyond* (1990). In a note to the poem, the editor describes Kowit and the other poets included in the anthology as not so much favoring performance over print as moving "away from the dour and ponderous, toward creativity, spontaneity, and childlike (not childish) joy." His most recent collection of poems is *The Dumbbell Nebula* (2000).

Maxine Kumin (b. 1925)　Born Maxine Winokur, Kumin attended Radcliffe College (B.A., 1946; M.A., 1948) and has lectured at many universities, including Princeton, Tufts, and Brandeis. She is the author of several collections of poetry, including *Up Country* (1972), for which she won a Pulitzer Prize, and, most recently, *Nurture* (1989), *Looking for Luck: Poems* (1992), and *Connecting the Dots: Poems* (1996). She has also published several novels, collections of essays and short stories, and more than twenty children's books — several of them in collaboration with the poet Anne Sexton.

Philip Larkin (1922–1985)　Born in Coventry, Larkin attended St. John's College, Oxford University (B.A., 1943; M.A., 1947). He was appointed librarian at the University of Hull in 1955, wrote jazz feature articles for the London *Daily Telegraph* from 1961 to 1971, and won numerous poetry awards, including the Queens Gold Medal (1965) and the Benson Medal (1975). His first collection, *The North Ship* (1945), was not well received, but he gained recognition after publication of *The Less Deceived* (1960). Larkin once said, "Form holds little interest for me. Content is everything."

D. H. Lawrence (1885–1930)   David Herbert Lawrence grew up amid the strife between his genteel and educated mother and his coarse miner father. As a youth in the Nottinghamshire mining village of Eastwood, Lawrence resented the rough ways of his drunken father and adopted his mother's refined values as his own. Diligence brought him a scholarship to the local high school. On graduation, he worked as a clerk and as an elementary school teacher and, in 1908, earned a teaching certificate from Nottingham University. He published a group of poems in 1909 and *The White Peacock*, his first novel, in 1911. He resigned his teaching position to devote himself to writing in 1912. That same year he ran away with Frieda von Richthofen Weekley (the sister of the World War I German ace fighter pilot), who left behind a husband and three children. They were married following her divorce in 1914. In 1915, his novel *The Rainbow* was declared indecent and suppressed in England. Angered by this event and by continual harassment for his outspoken opposition to World War I and his marriage to a prominent German, the Lawrences left England after the war. They traveled widely — in Europe, Australia, Mexico, and the American Southwest — seeking a community receptive to Lawrence's ideas and a climate to restore his failing health. His output was prodigious and included novels, short stories, poems, nonfiction, travel books, and letters. As a mature writer, Lawrence rejected the gentility his mother represented and began to see his father's earthiness as a virtue. He died of tuberculosis in the south of France.

Ursula K. Le Guin (b. 1929)   The daughter of distinguished University of California at Berkeley anthropologists, Le Guin graduated from Radcliffe College and earned an M.A. from Columbia University. She enjoyed early success writing for science-fiction and fantasy magazines (a genre often stigmatized as subliterary popular fiction), but she quickly established a reputation that places her in the tradition of earlier writers who used fantastic circumstances to shape their understanding of the human condition, such as Jonathan Swift, Edgar Allan Poe, and H. G. Wells. A prolific writer of fantasy fiction, Le Guin's recent work, *Four Ways to Forgiveness* (1995), is a speculation on the future of humankind in space. *Wonderful Alexander and the Catwings* (1994) is the third in the Catwings series, which features flying cats. She is also the author of five collections of poems, including *Sixty Odd* (1999). Other recent volumes are *Unlocking the Air and Other Stories* (1996) and *Steering the Craft: Exercises and Discussions on Story Writing for the Lone Navigator or the Mutinous Crew* (1998).

Denise Levertov (1923–1997)   Born in Ilford, England, Levertov was raised in a literary household (her father was an Anglican priest) and educated privately. She was a nurse at a British hospital in Paris during World War II; after the war, she worked in an antique store and bookstore in London. Married to an American writer, she came to the United States in 1948, became a naturalized citizen in 1956, and taught at several universities, including the Massachusetts Institute of Technology and Tufts University. Levertov began as what she called a "British romantic with almost Victorian background" and became more politically active and feminist with time. She protested U.S. involvement in the Vietnam War and was involved in the antinuclear movement. Regarding angst-filled confessional poetry, Levertov once said, "I do not believe that a violent imitation of the horrors of our times is the concern of poetry. . . . I long for poems of an inner harmony in utter contrast to the chaos in which they exist." Her works include *The Double Image* (1946), *Relearning the Alphabet* (1970), *A Door in the Hive* (1989), *Sands of the Well* (1996), *The Life Around Us: Selected Poems on Nature* (1997), and the posthumous *The Great Unknowing* (2000).

Philip Levine (b. 1928)   The son of Russian Jewish immigrants, Levine was born in Detroit, Michigan, into a household where debates and discussions about radical politics instilled in him a political sensibility and an abiding sympathy for the poor and the powerless. After receiving his B.A. from Wayne State University (1950), he returned to Detroit and worked at various industrial jobs in the auto industry before enrolling in the University of Iowa in 1955, where he received his M.F.A. (1957). He earned his living teaching poetry, primarily at California State University at Fresno and Tufts University in Maine, and is now retired. Since his first collection of poems, *On the Edge* (1961), Levine has published more than twenty volumes of poetry, many of them exhibiting his radical political consciousness. Among them are *They Feed They Lion* (1972); *Ashes* (1979); *What Work Is* (1991), which received the National Book Award; and *The Simple Truth* (1995), for which he received the Pulitzer Prize. His most recent volume of poetry is *The Mercy: Poems* (2000). In 1997, Levine was elected to the American Academy of Arts and Letters. He has summed up his aspirations as an artist with the remark, "My hope is to write poetry for people for whom there are no poems."

Barry Holstun Lopez (b. 1945)   Born in Port Chester, New York, Lopez graduated from the University of Notre Dame in 1966 and earned a graduate degree there in 1968. He went on to further graduate study at the University of Oregon (1969–1970). His earliest book, *Desert Notes: Reflections in the Eye of a Raven* (1976), was the first of a trilogy that includes *River Notes: The Dance of Herons* (1979) and *Field Notes: The Grace Note of the Canyon Wren* (1994). Keenly interested in the traditions of the Northwest Indians, as well as natural history, he published a collection of Native American legends, *Giving Birth to Thunder, Sleeping with His Daughter* (1977), and a nonfiction study, *Of Wolves and Men* (1978). A collection of short stories, *Winter Count* (1981), reveals how deeply Lopez feels about the Native American experience, as does his children's book based on Native American traditions, *Crow and Weasel* (1990). *Arctic Dreams: Imagination and Desire in a Northern*

Landscape appeared in 1986. Lopez's skill as a photographer is evident in the artwork included in several of his works. His essay collections include *The Rediscovery of North America* (1991) and *About This Life: Journeys on the Threshold of Memory* (1998).

Audre Lorde (1934–1992)   Born to middle-class West Indian immigrant parents in New York City, Lorde grew up in Harlem and attended the National University of Mexico (1954), Hunter College (B.A., 1959), and Columbia University (M.L.S., 1961). Her marriage in 1962, which produced two children, ended in divorce in 1970. During these early years, she worked as a librarian, but in 1968 her growing reputation as a writer led to her appointment as lecturer in creative writing at City College in New York and, in the following year, lecturer in the education department at Herbert H. Lehman College. In 1970 she joined the English department at John Jay College of Criminal Justice and in 1980 returned to Hunter College as professor of English. Besides teaching, Lorde combined raising a son and a daughter in an interracial lesbian relationship with political organizing of other black feminists and lesbians. In the early 1980s, Lorde helped to start Kitchen Table: Women of Color Press, and in 1991, she was named New York State Poet. Lorde is probably best known for her prose writings, among them two collections of essays, *Sister Outsider* (1984) and *Burst of Light* (1988), and the autobiographical *Zami: The Cancer Journals* (1980), a chronicle of her struggle with the breast cancer that ultimately claimed her life. Her poetry publications include *The First Cities* (1968), *The Black Unicorn* (1978), and *Undersong: Chosen Poems Old and New* (1993). Near the end of her life, Lorde made her home on St. Croix, U.S. Virgin Islands, and adopted the African name *Gamba Adisa* (Warrior — She Who Makes Her Meaning Known).

Amy Lowell (1874–1925)   Born to a prominent family in Brookline, Massachusetts, Lowell was privately educated. After the death of her parents, she inherited the family's ten-acre estate, including a staff of servants and a well-stocked library. Lowell wrote a great deal of undistinguished poetry that, unfortunately, prejudiced critics and readers against her better work. While traveling abroad, she became associated with the Imagists, a group of English and American poets in London who felt that sharply realized images gave poetry its power, and she gained recognition promoting their work in America after 1913. Her first collection of poems, *A Dome of Many-Coloured Glass,* appeared in 1912. Though her poetry never reached a wide audience, her criticism helped shape American poetic tastes of the time.

D. W. Lucas (1905–1985)   Lucas was born in London (his father was a school headmaster); earned an honors B.A. (1927) from King's College, Cambridge; and remained to become a fellow, lecturer, and director of studies in classics at his alma mater. He wrote two critical works — *The Greek Tragic Poets* (1950) and *A Commentary on Aristotle's "Poetics"* (1968). In addition, he translated the plays of Euripides between 1930 and 1951, and was a regular contributor to both the *Encyclopaedia Britannica* and the *Oxford Classical Dictionary* between 1953 and 1959.

Antonio Machado (1875–1939)   Born in Palacio de las Duenas, near Seville, Spain, the young Machado moved with his family to Madrid, where his father had obtained a professorship. When his father's sudden death in 1893 left the family without financial support, Machado and his brother turned to writing and acting to support themselves. In 1899, the brothers traveled to Paris, where they found work as translators. Around this time, Machado's growing reputation as a poet led to teaching posts in various cities in Spain. He also went on to resume the education his father's death had interrupted, obtaining a degree from the University of Madrid in 1918. During the last decade of his life, Machado once again became involved with the theater, collaborating with his brother on a number of successful plays. Among his volumes of poetry available in English translation are *Times, Alone: Selected Poems of Antonio Machado* (1983), *The Castillian Camp* (1982), and *Roads Dreamed Clear Afternoons: An Anthology of the Poetry of Antonio Machado* (1994). Machado remained in Madrid after the outbreak of civil war, committed to the Republican cause, but the violence finally forced him to flee. He died an exile in France.

Katharyn Howd Machan (b. 1952)   Machan grew up in Woodbury, Connecticut, and Pleasantville, New York. She studied creative writing and literature at the College of Saint Rose and at the University of Iowa, taught college for five years, then returned to graduate school for a Ph.D. in interpretation (performance studies) at Northwestern University. She is on the faculty of the Writing Program of Ithaca College, New York. For eight years she coordinated the Ithaca Community Poets and directed the national Feminist Women's Writing Workshops. Her poems have appeared in numerous magazines (such as *Yankee, Nimrod, South Coast Poetry Journal, Hollins Critic, Seneca Review,* and *Louisiana Literature*), in literature anthologies, and in numerous published collections, including *Belly Words* (1994).

Bernard Malamud (1914–1986)   Born in Brooklyn, New York, and educated at the City College of New York and Columbia University, Malamud is one of a number of post–World War II writers whose works drew heavily on their urban New York, Jewish backgrounds. Malamud's works often dramatize the tension arising out of the clash between Jewish conscience and American energy and materialism or the difficulty of keeping alive the Jewish sense of community and humanism in American society. *A New Life* (1961); *The Fixer* (1966), which won both a National Book Award and a Pulitzer Prize;

and *Pictures of Fidelman* (1969) all have protagonists who struggle with these problems. Some of his other novels are *The Natural* (1952), *The Assistant* (1957), *The Tenants* (1971), and *God's Grace* (1982). His short stories are collected in *The Magic Barrel* (1958), which won the National Book Award in 1959; *Idiots First* (1963); and *Rembrandt's Hat* (1973).

Aimee Mann (b. 1960)   Mann quit the Berklee School of Music in the early '80s and formed a punk band called The Young Snakes. When the group broke up, she joined with three others to form 'Til Tuesday. The band had considerable success, but Mann rejected attempts by other band members to shape her musical imagination. She launched a solo career, and soon came into conflict with her record label over her musical imagination. She actually bought back the rights to *Bachelor No. 2* from the publisher rather than agree to their request for more commercial material. Her struggles with record company executives became a cause célèbre, and her musical integrity was more than vindicated by the success of the film *Magnolia* (1999), which not only features her music but was actually created out of the musical material that sustains it. In 1998, she married the singer-songwriter Michael Penn, and continues to firmly control her own destiny as a composer and artist.

Christopher Marlowe (1564–1593)   Born in Canterbury, Marlowe was educated at Cambridge University, where he embarked on a career of writing and political activity, eventually giving up his original intention of entering the priesthood. He was arrested in 1593 on a charge of atheism, but before he could be brought to trial he was murdered in a brawl apparently involving a wealthy family that had reason to want him silenced. Marlowe's literary reputation rests primarily on his plays, powerful in their own right and the most significant precursors of Shakespeare's poetic dramas. The most important are *Tamburlaine, Parts I and II* (ca. 1587–1588; published 1590), *The Jew of Malta* (1589; published 1633), and *The Tragical History of the Life and Death of Dr. Faustus* (1592; published 1604).

Andrew Marvell (1621–1678)   Born in Yorkshire and educated at Cambridge University, Marvell received an inheritance on his father's death that allowed him to spend four years traveling the Continent. Though not a Puritan himself, Marvell supported the Puritans' cause during the civil war and held a number of posts during the Puritan regime, including that of assistant to the blind John Milton, Cromwell's Latin secretary. In 1659, a year before the Restoration, Marvell was elected to Parliament, where he served until his death. Soon after the Restoration, Marvell expressed strong disagreements with the government in a series of outspoken and anonymously printed satires. It was for these satires, rather than for his many love poems, that he was primarily known in his own day.

Katherine McAlpine (b. 1948) Katherine McAlpine grew up in western New Jersey. She studied voice with Leon Kurzer of the Vienna Opera and worked for a number of years as a singer and voice teacher. She now lives in Maine, where she works as a freelance writer. Her poetry has appeared in a wide variety of magazines and in several anthologies, and she is co-editor of *The Muse Strikes Back: A Poetic Response by Women to Men* (1997). She was a 1992 winner of the *Nation*'s Discovery Award and the Judith's Room Award for emerging women poets.

Claude McKay (1890–1948) Born in Sunny Ville, Jamaica, McKay had already completed two volumes of poetry before coming to the United States in 1912 at the age of twenty-three (the two volumes earned him awards, which paid his way). The racism he encountered as a black immigrant brought a militant tone to his writing. His popular poem "If We Must Die" (1919) helped to initiate the Harlem Renaissance of the 1920s. Between 1922 and 1934 he lived in Great Britain, Russia, Germany, France, Spain, and Morocco. His writings include four volumes of poems, many essays, an autobiography (*A Long Way from Home* [1937]), a novel (*Home to Harlem* [1928]), and a sociologial study of Harlem. His conversion to Roman Catholicism in the 1940s struck his audience as an ideological retreat. McKay wrote in a letter to a friend: "[T]o have a religion is very much like falling in love with a woman. You love her for her . . . beauty, which cannot be defined."

James Alan McPherson (b. 1943) McPherson was born in Savannah, Georgia, and attended Morgan State University (1963–1964), Morris Brown College (B.A., 1965), Harvard University (LL.B., 1968), and the University of Iowa, where he earned an M.F.A. (1969). Since 1981, he has been a professor of English at the University of Iowa. In 1965, he received first prize in the *Atlantic* short-story contest. In 1969, his first collection of short stories, *Hue and Cry,* appeared. His many honors include the literature award of the National Institute of Arts and Letters (1970), and a Guggenheim Fellowship (1972–1973). In 1978, he received a Pulitzer Prize for his second collection of short stories, *Elbow Room*. His writing achievements earned him a MacArthur Fellowship in 1981. McPherson has been widely praised for his incisive depictions of ordinary people, mostly black, who attempt to cope with the indignities and desperations of everyday life. His recent work includes *A Region Not Home: Reflections from Exile* (2000), a collection of essays.

Peter Meinke (b. 1932) Born in Brooklyn, New York, the son of a salesman, Meinke served in the U.S. Army from 1955 to 1957, attended Hamilton College (B.A., 1955) and the University of Michigan (M.A., 1961), and earned his Ph.D. at the University of Minnesota (1965). He taught English at a New Jersey high school, Hamline University, and Presbyterian College (now Eckerd College) in Florida, where he began directing the writing workshop in 1972. His reviews, poems, and stories have appeared in periodicals such as the *Atlantic,* the *New Yorker,* and the *New Republic.* The latest of his books in the Pitt Poetry Series are *Scars* (1996) and *Zinc Fingers: Poems A to Z* (2000). His collection of stories, *The Piano Tuner,* won the 1986 Flannery O'Connor Award. He has also been the recipient of a National Endowment for the Arts Fellowship in poetry.

Herman Melville (1819–1891)   The death of his merchant father when Melville was twelve shattered the economic security of his family. The financial panic of 1837 reduced the Melvilles to the edge of poverty, and at age nineteen, Melville went to sea. Economic conditions on his return were still grim, and after a frustrating stint as a country school teacher, he again went to sea — this time on a four-year whaling voyage. He deserted the whaler in the South Pacific, lived for some time with cannibals, made his way to Tahiti and Hawaii, and finally joined the navy for a return voyage. He mined his experiences for two successful South Sea adventure books, *Typee* (1846) and *Omoo* (1847). On the strength of these successes he married, but his next novel, *Mardi* (1849), was too heavy-handed an allegory to succeed. Driven by the obligation to support his growing family, Melville returned to sea-adventure stories, with moderate success. But neither his masterpiece, *Moby Dick* (1851), nor his subsequent short stories and novels found much of an audience, and in 1886, he accepted an appointment as customs inspector in Manhattan, a job he held until retirement. He continued to write, mostly poetry, and lived to see himself forgotten as an author. *Billy Budd,* found among his papers after his death and published in 1924, led to a revival of interest in Melville, now recognized as one of America's greatest writers.

Robert Mezey (b. 1935)   Born in Philadelphia, Mezey attended Kenyon College and served a troubled hitch in the U.S. Army before earning his B.A. from the University of Iowa in 1959. He worked as a probation officer, advertising copywriter, and social worker; did graduate study at Stanford University; and began teaching English at Case Western Reserve University in 1963. After a year as poet-in-residence at Franklin and Marshall College, he joined the English department of California State University at Fresno, spent three years at the University of Utah, and settled in 1976 at Pomona College in Claremont, California. Mezey won the Lamont Award for *The Lovemaker* in 1960, and has published many other poetry collections. In addition, he co-edited *Naked Poetry* (1969), and was one of several translators for *Poems from the Hebrew* (1973). His recent work includes *Collected Poems: 1952–1999* (2000).

Edna St. Vincent Millay (1892–1950)   Millay was born in Maine and educated at Vassar College. By the time she graduated in 1917, she had already achieved considerable fame as a poet; in the same year, she moved to Greenwich Village in New York and published her first volume of poetry, *Renascence and Other Poems*. In Greenwich Village, she established her reputation as a poet and became notorious for her bohemian life and passionate love affairs. In 1923 she received a Pulitzer Prize for a collection of sonnets, *The Harp-Weaver,* that dealt wittily and flippantly with love. Her later works exhibit a more subdued and contemplative tone as well as a growing preoccupation with social and political affairs. Nevertheless, her best and most memorable verse deals with the bittersweet emotions of love and the brevity of life.

Arthur Miller (b. 1915) Raised in New York City, the son of a school teacher and clothing manufacturer, Arthur Miller studied playwriting at the University of Michigan. Although he wrote radio scripts and plays, during World War II he made his living as a steam fitter. His first Broadway play in 1944 was a failure, but *All My Sons* (1947), about a corrupt defense contractor, was named best play of the year. The 1949 production of *Death of a Salesman* (which won the Pulitzer Prize) was an immense success and established Miller's reputation. The infamous loyalty hearings conducted by Senator Joseph McCarthy contributed to the substance of *The Crucible* (1953), an investigation into the Salem witchcraft trials. He was married to Marilyn Monroe from 1956 to 1961. In 1956, Miller was cited for contempt by the House Un-American Activities Committee when, after testifying fully about his own political activities, he refused to name others. His plays invariably turn on moral issues and continue to illustrate the comment he made to an interviewer after the success of *All My Sons:* "I don't see how you can write anything decent without using as your basis the question of right or wrong." His dedication to individual conscience and suspicion of government repression led him to adapt Ibsen's *An Enemy of the People* for the Broadway stage in 1951. His most recent play, *Broken Glass* (1994), focuses on the aftermath of Kristallnacht, the night in 1938 in Nazi Germany when thousands of Jewish shops and synagogues were destroyed. Miller is also the author of an autobiography, *Timebends* (1987), and a collection of stories, *Homely Girl, A Life: And Other Stories* (1995).

Jessica Mitford (1917–1996) One of six sisters, Mitford was born in Gloucestershire, England, into an aristocratic and rather eccentric family. She was educated at home and early on adopted political views that contrasted violently with those of her sister Diana, who married Sir Oswald Mosley, the pre–World War II leader of the British Fascist movement. Jessica, on the other hand, traveled to Loyalist Spain during its civil war, where she met her first husband. He was killed in action during World War II, and she later married a labor lawyer. They moved to California and joined the Communist Party. They left the party in 1958, and Jessica embarked on a successful career as a muckraking journalist and writer. Her first work, *Lifeitselfmanship,* was privately published in 1956, but her attack on the funeral industry in *The American Way of Death* (1963) established her reputation as an incisive and witty enemy of social and economic pretentiousness. Her many books include *Kind and Usual Punishment: The Prison Business* (1973); the autobiographical *A Fine Old Conflict* (1979); and a collection of articles, *Poison Penmanship: The Gentle Art of Muckraking* (1979).

Felix Mnthali (b. 1933)   Mnthali was born and grew up in Malawi in south central Africa. He was educated at Malawi University and Cambridge University in England. He returned to Malawi, and worked as an academic and on a radio program for young people, "Writer's Corner." After a long detention began in 1976, he left for a year as a visitor at the University of Ibadan in Nigeria in 1979, where he wrote and privately published *Echoes from Ibadan*. Back in his homeland he became the head of the department of English at Malawi University and in 1982 became a professor at the University of Botswana. His published works include *When Sunset Comes to Saptiwa* (1980), a collection of poetry, and his first novel, *Yoranivyoto* (1999).

Bharati Mukherjee (b. 1940)   Born in Calcutta, India, Mukherjee attended the University of Calcutta (B.A., 1959), the University of Baroda (M.A., 1961), and the University of Iowa, where she took an M.F.A. (1963) and a Ph.D. (1969). In 1963 she married Clark Blaise, a Canadian writer and professor, and joined the faculty at McGill University in Montreal. In 1973, Mukherjee and her husband visited India and kept separate diaries of the trip, published as *Days and Nights in Calcutta* (1977). The diaries reveal marked differences in their responses: Mukherjee found her home environs, especially the status of women, worse than she remembered, while Blaise, after an initial revulsion at the squalor and poverty, found India a fascinating and attractive culture compared to the West. Mukherjee "left Canada after fifteen years due to the persistent effects of racial prejudice against people of my national origin" and joined the faculty at Skidmore College in New York. Later she moved to Queens College of the City University of New York. Her fiction frequently explores the tensions inevitable in intercultural relationships. Her first novel, *The Tiger's Daughter* (1972), deals with the disappointment of an expatriate's return to India. In her second novel, *Wife* (1975), a psychologically abused woman finally kills her husband. Her recent works include *The Middleman and Other Stories* (1988), which won the National Book Critics' Award; *The Holder of the World* (1993); and *Leave It to Me* (1997).

Alice Munro (b. 1931)   Alice Munro grew up on a farm near Lake Huron, Ontario, Canada, where her father raised foxes and later — when that business failed — took up turkey farming. Looking back on that period of her life, Munro remembered that despite her parents' expectation that she would become a farmer's wife, she had always wanted to be a writer: "I never wanted to be anything else since about nine, ever since I stopped wanting to be a movie star." In 1949, she won a scholarship to the University of Western Ontario, choosing a journalism major "as a coverup" for her writing ambitions. She sold her first short story as an undergraduate, but after two years quit school, married, and became a mother. In 1968, she published her first collection of short stories, *Dance of the Happy Shades,* which won the Governor General's Literary Award — the most prestigious literary prize in Canada. Since then, she has published to great acclaim almost a dozen collections of short stories, among them: *Something I've Been Meaning to Tell You* (1974); *Who Do You Think You Are?* (1978), which also won a Governor General's Literary Award; *The Progress of Love* (1988); *Open Secrets: Stories* (1994); and *The Love of a Good Woman: Stories* (1999). She has received numerous awards for her fiction, including the 1995 W. H. Smith Award for the best book published in Britain the previous year. Commenting on her work habits, Munro told an interviewer, "I don't have sudden bursts of inspiration, I can only do two things at once. Since housework is eternal and writing is eternal, that's all I can do."

Susan Musgrave (b. 1951)   Musgrave draws on her experiences in public schools, psychiatric institutions, and maximum security penitentiaries across the country. She has published nineteen books; she is a poet, novelist, children's writer, essayist, book reviewer for the *Vancouver Sun,* and editor. She lives on Vancouver Island in British Columbia, Canada, with Stephen Reid and their two daughters. She travels widely, both in Canada and abroad, to give speeches, writing workshops, and poetry readings. Her recent books are a poetry collection, *Forcing the Narcissus* (1994), and a book of personal essays, *Musgrave Landing* (1994). She has won numerous awards for her writing, culminating in the Presidential Writer in Residence Fellowship at the University of Toronto (1995).

Taslima Nasrin (b. 1962)   Born and educated in Mymensingh, Bangladesh, Nasrin began writing poetry in her childhood, her earliest works appearing in a literary journal edited by her eldest brother. Following in the footsteps of her doctor-father, she earned a degree in medicine from Mymensingh Medical College and for a few years practiced as a government doctor. Her study of modern science, Nasrin has written, "made me a rationalist." While practicing medicine, she continued her writing, publishing poems and novels. These works, along with the essays she wrote as a syndicated columnist in Bangladesh, earned her a number of important literary prizes in 1992 and 1993. However, her rationalism and her feminism, as well as her 1993 novel *Shame,* enraged Muslim fundamentalists. Forced into hiding by death threats, Nasrin fled to Europe in 1994, where she now lives in exile. Her poetry has been published in English in *The Game in Reverse: Poems* (1995). In an essay titled "Women's Rights," Nasrin writes, "My poetry, my prose, my entire output expresses the deprivation of women who have been exploited for centuries. . . . My expression is loud and for that crime I am now out of my country. Though I have come to the West legally, with the government's permission, I do not know when I shall be able to return. . . . Even now the fundamentalists demand my death by hanging in public."

Pablo Neruda (1904–1973)   Neruda was born in Parral, Chile, the son of a railroad worker. Shortly after leaving college, he joined the Chilean foreign service to begin a distinguished career as consul and ambassador at a variety of posts around the world, including Burma, Ceylon, Indonesia, Siam, Cambodia, Spain, France, and Mexico. He was elected to the Chilean senate as a communist. But when he published letters attacking the policies of Videla, the president of Chile, he was forced into exile. He returned to Chile after the victory of anti-Videla forces and rejoined the foreign service. His vast literary output won many prizes and honors. And, although American readers found it difficult to separate his poetry from his politics, he was, at his prime, generally considered to be the greatest poet writing in Spanish. One critic pointed out that Neruda "never bothered his head about the state of poetry. He has just gone on exuding it as he draws breath." In an essay on impure poetry, Neruda wrote: "Let [this] be the poetry we search for: worn with the hand's obligations, as by acids, steeped in sweat and in smoke, smelling of lilies and urine, spattered diversely by the trades that we love by, inside the law or beyond it. A poetry impure as the clothing we wear, or our bodies, soup-stained, soiled with our shameful behavior, our wrinkles and vigils and dreams, observations and prophecies, declarations of loathing and love, idylls and beasts, the shocks of encounter, political loyalties, denials and doubts, affirmation and taxes." *Five Decades, a Selection: Poems, 1925–1970* appeared in 1974. He was awarded the Nobel Prize for literature in 1971.

Joyce Carol Oates (b. 1938)   Born in Lockport, New York, Oates majored in English at Syracuse University (B.A., 1960) as a scholarship student and earned an M.A. in English (1961) from the University of Wisconsin. While still an undergraduate, she won the *Mademoiselle* college fiction award (1959), beginning an enormously prolific career as a writer and editor. She publishes an average of two books a year, to date well over fifty volumes including novels, short-story collections, poetry, drama, and critical essays. Her numerous awards and honors include the 1970 fiction National Book Award for her novel *Them* (1969). She taught at the Universities of Detroit and Windsor (Canada) before joining the faculty at Princeton University, where she is the Roger S. Berlind Distinguished Professor. Her latest works are a novel, *The Barrens* (2001), and a volume of short stories, *Faithless: Tales of Transgression* (2001).

Tim O'Brien (b. 1946)   O'Brien was born in Austin, Minnesota; attended public schools; and received a B.A. summa cum laude from Macalester College. Immediately following graduation, he was drafted into the U.S. Army (1968–1970), earning a Purple Heart. On his return to civilian life, he pursued graduate work at Harvard University and worked as a national affairs reporter for the *Washington Post*. His first novel, *If I Die in a Combat Zone, Box Me Up and Ship Me Home* (1973), is a semi-fictionalized account of his own Vietnam experiences. Many of O'Brien's novels either are set in Vietnam or focus on characters haunted by the war: *Northern Lights* (1975); *Going after Cacciato* (1978), which won a National Book Award; *The Nuclear Age* (1985); *The Things They Carried* (1990); and *In the Lake of the Woods* (1994). In an interview, O'Brien explained that his preoccupation with the Vietnam War was part of his need to write with "passion." Writing "good" stories, he went on to say, "requires a sense of passion, and my passion as a human being and as a writer intersect in Vietnam, not in the physical stuff but in the issues of Vietnam — of courage, rectitude, enlightenment, holiness, trying to do the right thing in the world." With his recent comic novel, *Tomcat in Love* (1998), O'Brien writes in a new vein about a womanizing professor's midlife crisis.

Flannery O'Connor (1925–1964) Afflicted with lupus erythematosus, O'Connor spent most of her tragically short life in Milledgeville, Georgia. She began writing while a student at Georgia State College for Women in her hometown, and in 1947 earned an M.F.A. from the University of Iowa. Back in Milledgeville, she lived on a farm with her mother, raised peacocks, and endured the indignity of constant treatment for her progressive and incurable disease. She traveled and lectured when she could. She wrote two novels, *Wise Blood* (1952) and *The Violent Bear It Away* (1960), and two collections of stories, *A Good Man Is Hard to Find* (1955) and *Everything That Rises Must Converge* (1965). She was deeply religious, and wrote numerous book reviews for Catholic newspapers. Her southern gothic tales often force readers to confront physical deformity, spiritual depravity, and the violence they often engender.

Frank O'Connor (1903–1966) Born Michael O'Donovan in Cork, Ireland, O'Connor later adopted his pen name to separate his civil-service career from his writing career. His family's poverty forced him to leave school at age fourteen. During the Irish struggle for independence, O'Connor served in the Irish Republican Army; after the establishment of the Irish Free State, he worked as a librarian. Despite his lack of formal education, he became director of the Abbey Theatre in Dublin. He moved to America in the 1950s and taught at Harvard and Northwestern Universities. A storyteller in the great Gaelic oral tradition, he appeared for a time on Sunday-morning television. A perfectionist, O'Connor constantly polished and reworked his stories. He added to his stature with fine critical studies of the novel (*The Mirror in the Roadway* [1956]) and the short story (*The Lonely Voice* [1963]), and introduced Gaelic poetry to a wide audience through his English translations.

Sharon Olds (b. 1942)   Born in San Francisco, Olds attended Stanford University (B.A., 1964) and Columbia University (Ph.D., 1972). She joined the faculty of Theodor Herzl Institute in 1976 and has given readings at many colleges. She is currently teaching at the Graduate Creative Writing Program at New York University. She won the Madeline Sadin Award from the *New York Quarterly* in 1978 for "The Death of Marilyn Monroe." Often compared to confessional poets Sylvia Plath and Anne Sexton, Olds published her first collection, *Satan Says,* in 1980, and won both the National Book Critics' Circle Award and the Lamont Award for *The Dead and the Living* in 1983. *The Gold Cell* was published in 1987; *The Father* appeared in 1992; *The Wellspring* was published in 1996; and her most recent book of poems, *Blood, Tin, Straw,* appeared in 1999.

Mary Oliver (b. 1935)   Mary Oliver was born in Cleveland, Ohio. She spent one year at Ohio State University and a second year at Vassar. Her distinctive poetic talent led to an appointment as the chair of the writing department of the Fine Arts Workshop in Provincetown, Massachusetts (1972–1973). Though she never graduated from college, she was awarded the Mather Visiting Professorship at Case Western Reserve University for 1980 and 1982, and among her many awards and honors, she received a National Endowment for the Arts Fellowship (1972–1973) and a Guggenheim Fellowship (1980–1981). The first of her several volumes of poems, *No Voyage and Other Poems,* appeared in 1963. Other books include *New and Selected Poems* (1992); *A Poetry Handbook* (1995); and *Blue Pastures* (1995), a collection of prose nature writing. One critic, commenting on her work, asserts that "her vision of nature is celebratory and religious in the deepest sense."

George Orwell (1903–1950)   Born Eric Blair in India, the son of a minor British colonial officer, Orwell was raised in England. His education at good grammar schools, culminating with a stay at Eton College, introduced him to what he later called the snobbish world of England's middle and upper classes. Denied a university scholarship, he joined the Indian Imperial Police in 1922 and served in Burma until he resigned in 1927, disgusted with the injustice of British imperialism in India and Burma. He was determined to be a writer and, living at the edge of poverty, deliberately mingled with social outcasts and impoverished laborers. These experiences produced *Down and Out in Paris and London* (1933). Although he was a socialist, his experiences while fighting alongside the leftists during the Spanish Civil War disillusioned him, and he embodied his distaste for any totalitarian system in *Animal Farm* (1945) — a satirical attack on the leadership of the Soviet Union. In his pessimistic novel *1984* (1949), he imagined a social order shaped by a propagandistic perversion of language, in which the government, an extension of "Big Brother," uses two-way television to control the citizenry. Orwell succumbed to tuberculosis at the age of forty-seven, but not before he produced six novels, three documentary works, over seven hundred newspaper articles and reviews, and a volume of essays.

Alicia Suskin Ostriker (b. 1937)   Ostriker was born and grew up in New York City. Her Jewish grandparents came to America in the 1880s, and her college-educated, working-class parents instilled the values she lives by: work hard, love books, promote social justice. Ostriker's mother wrote poetry and read poetry to her daughter. As an English major at Brandeis University and a graduate student at the University of Wisconsin, Ostriker read and wrote poetry constantly. She has since published nine collections — most recently *The Crack in Everything* (1996) and *The Little Space: Poems Collected and New* (1998). Both collections were finalists for the National Book Award. Her critical studies include *Stealing the Language: The Emergence of Women's Poetry in America* (1986) and *Dancing at the Devil's Party: Essays on Poetry, Politics and the Erotic* (2000). Biblical study led her to write *The Nakedness of the Fathers: Biblical Visions and Revisions* (1994). Her many awards include recognition from the National Endowment for the Arts, the Rockefeller Foundation, and the Guggenheim Foundation. She lives in Princeton, New Jersey, with her husband, the astrophysicist Jeremiah Ostriker, and teaches English and creative writing at Rutgers University.

Wilfred Owen (1893–1918)   Born in the Shropshire countryside of England, Owen had begun writing verse before he matriculated at London University, where he was known as a quiet and contemplative student. After some years of teaching English in France, Owen returned to England and joined the army. He was wounded in 1917 and killed in action leading an attack a few days before the armistice was declared in 1918. Owen's poems, published only after his death, along with his letters from the front to his mother, are perhaps the most powerful and vivid accounts of the horror of war to emerge from World War I.

Dorothy Parker (1893–1967)   Parker was born in West End, New Jersey, to a Scottish Presbyterian mother and a Jewish father as "a late unexpected arrival in a loveless family." She was educated in private schools and moved in 1911 to New York, where she lived in a boarding house and earned her living by playing piano at a dancing school. In 1915, one of the verses she had been sending around was accepted by *Vogue* magazine, and the editor later hired her to write captions for fashion illustrations. Her native wit captivated the editor, and he persuaded her to join *Vanity Fair* as drama critic, although she was fired when she wrote unfavorable reviews of several plays. She became the first woman among the regulars of the Algonquin Round Table — a group of writers who met regularly at the Algonquin Hotel in New York City that included Alexander Woollcott, George S. Kaufman, Robert Benchley, and Edna Ferber (among others). A master of irony and scathing wit, Parker, despite a troubled personal life that led to suicide attempts, flourished as a humorist, poet, short-story writer, playwright, and screenwriter.

Paul (d. ca. A.D. 64)   Paul was born Saul in Tarsus of Cilicia (located near the Mediterranean Sea in south-central Turkey, near Syria). He was an important Jerusalem Pharisee who, according to accounts in Acts of the Apostles (Chapter 9), vigorously attacked (both intellectually and physically) those who proclaimed the deity of Jesus. The same source provides an account of Saul's conversion. Traveling to Damascus to arrest followers of Jesus, he experienced an intense light that blinded him and heard a voice that declared, "I am Jesus, whom you are persecuting." In Tarsus, his blindness was cured by Ananias, a follower of Jesus, and Paul became, arguably, the most important disciple of Jesus in the early Church: his letters (and those attributed to him) constitute a quarter of the New Testament. His attempts to preach the new Way in the synagogues of the region were rebuffed, sometimes violently, and Paul was frequently jailed. He became the apostle to the Gentiles, traveling throughout the Mediterranean region to establish churches. His epistles to those young and fragile congregations helped formulate the political, legal, and spiritual institutions of the early Church. His final arrest brought him to Rome to answer charges, and after two years of imprisonment, he died about A.D. 64.

Molly Peacock (b. 1947)   Born in Buffalo, New York, Peacock was educated at the State University of New York at Binghamton and at Johns Hopkins University, where she received an M.A. with honors in 1977. From 1970 to 1973, she was the director of academic advising at Binghamton. She was appointed honorary fellow at Johns Hopkins in 1977 and, in the following year, poet-in-residence at the Delaware State Arts Council in Wilmington. Since 1979, she has directed the Wilmington Writing Workshops. She has published in many magazines, including the *Southern Review,* the *Ohio Review,* and the *Massachusetts Review.* She has published four books of poems: *And Live Apart* (1980); *Raw Heaven* (1984); *Take Heart* (1989), which deals with her father's alcoholism and the mental and physical abuse she endured while growing up; and, most recently, *Original Love* (1995). She was also co-editor of *Poetry in Motion: 100 Poems from the Subways and Buses* (1996), a collection of the popular poems displayed on placards in New York City's subways and buses. Her most recent book, *Paradise, Piece by Piece* (1998), which she calls a "hybrid memoir," blends real and invented characters and explains why she decided not to have children.

Marge Piercy (b. 1936)   Born in Detroit, Marge Piercy was the first of her family to attend college. In 1957, she graduated from the University of Michigan (where she won prizes for poetry and fiction) and earned an M.A. from Northwestern University (1958). She was active in social and political causes and fought for equal treatment of women and minorities while opposing the

Vietnam War. She supported herself with odd jobs in Chicago as she pursued a writing career, but her first novel was not published until after her 1969 move to Wellfleet, Massachusetts (where she still lives). She is an extraordinarily prolific writer. Among her more than a dozen novels are *He, She and It* (1991), *The Longings of Women* (1994), and *City of Darkness, City of Lights* (1996). Her many volumes of poetry include *My Mother's Body* (1985), *Available Light* (1988), *The Earth Shines Secretly: A Book of Days* (1990), and *Mars and Her Children* (1992). She has also written plays and several volumes of nonfiction and has edited the anthology *Early Ripening: American Women's Poetry Now* (1987). Most recently, she has published two collections of poetry, *The Art of Blessing the Day: Poems with a Jewish Theme* (1999) and *Early Grrrl* (1999), and a novel, *Three Women* (1999). In the introduction to a volume of selected poems, *Circles on the Water* (1982), Piercy asserted that she wanted her poems to be "useful." "What I mean by useful is simply that readers will find poems that speak to and for them, will take those poems into their lives and say them to each other and put them up on the bathroom wall and remember bits and pieces of them in stressful or quiet moments. . . . To find ourselves spoken for in art gives dignity to our pain, our anger, our lust, our losses."

Robert Pinsky (b. 1940)   The son of an optician, Pinsky was born in Long Branch, New Jersey. He earned a B.A. (1962) from Rutgers University and a Ph.D. (1966) from Stanford University, after which he embarked on a distinguished academic career. He taught at the University of Chicago, Wellesley College, and the University of California at Berkeley, and is now a professor of English at Boston University. *Sadness and Happiness,* his first book of poems, appeared in 1975. His most recent collection, *Jersey Rain,* appeared in 2000. Along the way, he created a new and much acclaimed translation of Dante's *Inferno* (1994). He has won numerous awards, including an American Academy of Arts and Letters Award (1979). In 1995, he won a *Los Angeles Times Book Review* Award and the Landon Prize for translation, both for the Dante translation. In his critical essays, Pinsky reveals his respect for the literary tradition. He asserts that poets need to "find a language for presenting the role of a conscious soul in an unconscious world."

Sylvia Plath (1932–1963)   Plath was born in Boston, Massachusetts, where her parents taught at Boston University. She graduated summa cum laude in English from Smith College (1955); earned an M.A. as a Fulbright scholar at Newnham College, Cambridge (1955–1957); and married British poet Ted Hughes (1956). Plath's poetry reveals the anger and anxiety that would eventually lead to her suicide. Her view that all relationships were in some way destructive and predatory surely darkened her life. Yet in 1963, during the month between the publication of her only novel, *The Bell Jar* (about a suicidal college student), and her death, Plath was extraordinarily productive; she produced finished poems every day. One critic suggests that for her, suicide was a positive act, a "refusal to collaborate" in a world she could not accept. Her *Collected Poems* was published in 1981.

Edgar Allan Poe (1809–1849)   Poe, the son of traveling actors, was born in Boston, Massachusetts. Within a year, his alcoholic father deserted his mother and their three infant children. When his mother died of tuberculosis in Richmond, Virginia, three-year-old Edgar was adopted by John Allan and his wife. Allan, a prosperous businessman, spent time in England, where Poe began his education at private schools. Back in the United States, Allan forced Poe to leave the University of Virginia in 1826, when Poe incurred gambling debts he could not pay. He served in the U.S. Army from 1827 to 1829, eventually attaining the rank of sergeant major. Poe next attended West Point, hoping for further military advancement. Shortly thereafter, Mrs. Allan died of tuberculosis. Poe angrily confronted his foster father about his extramarital affairs; for this candor he was disowned. Believing that Allan would never reinstate him as heir, Poe deliberately violated rules to provoke his dismissal from the academy. In 1835, Poe began his career as editor, columnist, and reviewer, earning a living he could not make as a writer of stories and poems. He married his thirteen-year-old cousin, Virginia Clemm, in 1836, and lived with her and her mother during a period marked by illness and poverty. Virginia died of tuberculosis in 1847. Poe died, delirious, under mysterious circumstances, in 1849. He perfected the gothic horror story ("Fall of the House of Usher") and originated the modern detective story ("The Gold Bug," "The Murders in the Rue Morgue"). Poe's work fascinated the French poet Baudelaire, who translated it into French.

Deborah Pope (b. ?)   Born in Cincinnati, Ohio, Pope graduated from Denison University and then attended the University of Wisconsin, where she earned a Ph.D. At present, she teaches at Duke University, where she co-founded the Duke Writers Conference. Using her Ph.D. thesis as a basis, she published a study in criticism, *Separate Vision: Isolation in Contemporary Women's Poetry* (1984). In 1990, she co-edited *Ties That Bind: Essays on Mothering and Patriarchy.* Her first volume of poetry, *Frantic Heart* (1992), was followed by several others, of which the most recent is *Falling Out of the Sky* (1999). Doubtless, some of her poems are generated by the pain and joy of a home life that includes two young sons. In an interview, she summed up her enthusiasm for teaching: "There is nothing like the joy and exhilaration that comes to me . . . when [students] have been able to bring some kind of formless chaotic experience into a balance in language."

Katherine Anne Porter (1890–1980)   Born in Texas and educated mostly at small convent schools, Porter traveled widely in her early years, living for some time in Mexico and, more briefly, in Germany. She gained a reputation primarily as a writer of finely crafted stories, gathered in *The Collected Stories of Katherine Anne Porter* (1965). She published one novel, *Ship of Fools,* in

1962. Porter's output of fiction was small, and she earned her livelihood mostly as a reporter, lecturer, scriptwriter, speaker, and writer-in-residence. Her achievement in fiction was recognized by a National Book Award and Pulitzer Prize for fiction, both in 1966. Her final work, *The Never-Ending Wrong* (1977), is a memoir about her involvement in the celebrated Sacco-Vanzetti case.

Ezra Pound (1885–1972)   Pound was born in Hailey, Idaho, and, eighty-seven years later, died in Venice, Italy. He graduated from Hamilton College in 1905, and went on to the University of Pennsylvania, where he earned an M.A. in 1906. In his early adult years, he taught romance languages and literature in both the United States and England. But this expatriate threw himself into the European intellectual ferment of the times and became one of the most influential poets and critics of the modern period. Forward, a bit self-aggrandizing, and certainly brash, Pound sought out and allied himself with the best minds of his generation. He became an unofficial secretary to W. B. Yeats during World War II; he persuaded the American founder of *Poetry* magazine to appoint him European correspondent; he edited and frequently wrote for several literary magazines that represented the cutting edge of modern poetry. He is, perhaps, best known for his friendship with T. S. Eliot and edited Eliot's early masterpiece, *The Wasteland*. His anti-capitalist politics led him to an admiration of the national socialism that emerged under Hitler in Germany and Mussolini in Italy. His propagandistic radio broadcasts from Italy during World War II led to his arrest and trial for treason in 1945. But those who had admired his aesthetic sensibility and profited from his critical intelligence rallied to his defense. Consequently, he escaped jail, but was declared insane and confined in a hospital from 1945 to 1958. Upon his release, he returned to his beloved Italy where he lived his remaining years. A list of his editorial output and copious writings — poetry, literary criticism, economic theory, translations — occupies several pages. In an introduction to the *Literary Essays of Ezra Pound,* T. S. Eliot declared that Pound "is more responsible for the twentieth-century revolution in poetry than is any other individual."

Wyatt Prunty (b. 1947)   Prunty was born in Humboldt, Tennessee. After earning a B.A. from the University of the South in Sewanee, he went on to earn an M.A. from Johns Hopkins University and a Ph.D. (1979) from Louisiana State University. His poetry chapbook, *Domestic of the Outer Banks,* was published in 1980. Several volumes followed, among them *Since the Noon Mail Stopped* (1997) and *Unarmed and Dangerous* (2000). His poetry has been anthologized in *Anthology of Magazine Verse and Yearbook of American Poetry* for both 1979 and 1980. He was awarded a poetry prize by *Sewanee Review* (1969) and has been a fellow at the Bread Loaf Writers' Conference. He has taught in the graduate program of the Johns Hopkins Writing Seminars, where he was Elliott Coleman Professor of Poetry. Currently, he serves as Carlton Professor of English at the University of the South, where he teaches poetry, and where he founded and now directs the Sewanee Writers' Conference.

Sir Walter Raleigh (1554–1618)   Born in Devonshire, England, into the landed gentry, Raleigh attended Oxford University but dropped out after a year to fight for the Huguenot cause in France. He returned to England, began the study of law, but again was drawn to a life of adventure and exploration. Through the influence of friends he came to the attention of Queen Elizabeth, and thenceforth his career flourished: he was knighted, given a number of lucrative commercial monopolies, made a member of Parliament, and, in 1587, named captain of the Yeoman of the Guard. During these years, he invested in various colonies in North America, but all his settlements failed. He was briefly imprisoned in the Tower of London for offending the queen but was soon back in favor and in command of an unsuccessful expedition to Guiana (now Venezuela) in 1595. In 1603, he was again imprisoned in the tower, this time on a probably trumped-up charge of treason, where he remained until 1616, spending part of his time writing *A History of the World* (1614). After his release, he undertook yet another expedition to Guiana but again returned empty-handed. As a consequence of more political intrigue, James I ordered him executed. Although Raleigh epitomized the great merchant adventurers of Elizabethan England, he was also a gifted poet.

Dudley Randall (b. 1914)   Born in Washington, D.C., Randall worked during the Depression in the foundry of the Ford Motor Company in Dearborn, Michigan, and then as a carrier and clerk for the U.S. Post Office in Detroit. He served in the U.S. Army Signal Corps (1942–1946), and graduated from Wayne State University (B.A., 1949) and the University of Michigan (M.A.L.S., 1951). He was a librarian at several universities, and founded the Broadside Press in 1965 "so black people could speak to and for their people." Randall told *Negro Digest,* "Precision and accuracy are necessary for both white and black writers. . . . 'A black aesthetic' should not be an excuse for sloppy writing." He urges African American writers to reject what was false in white poetry but not to forsake universal concerns in favor of a racial agenda. His works include *On Getting a Natural* (1969) and *A Litany of Friends: New and Selected Poems* (1981). He edited *For Malcolm: Poems on the Life and Death of Malcolm X* (1969) and *The Black Poets* (1971), an extensive anthology of poetry, from slave songs to the present.

Henry Reed (1914–1986)   Reed was born in Birmingham, England; earned a B.A. from the University of Birmingham (1937); worked as a teacher and freelance writer (1937–1941); and served in the British Army (1941–1942). His early poetry dealt with political events before and during World War II. "Naming of Parts" was based on his frustrating experience in cadet training. His collection of poetry, *A Map of Verona* (1946), revealed a formal, reverent, but also humorous and ironic voice. Another collection of poetry, *Lessons of War,* was published in 1970. Reed began writing radio plays in 1947 and generated as many as four scripts a year. His best-known satirical work is the *Hilda Tablet* series, a 1960s BBC Radio production that parodied British society of the 1930s.

Adrienne Rich (b. 1929)   Born to a middle-class family, Rich was educated by her parents until she entered public school in the fourth grade. She graduated Phi Beta Kappa from Radcliffe College in 1951, the same year her first book of poems, *A Change of World,* appeared. That volume, chosen by W. H. Auden for the Yale Series of Younger Poets Award, and her next, *The Diamond Cutters and Other Poems* (1955), earned her a reputation as an elegant, controlled stylist. In the 1960s, however, Rich began a dramatic shift away from her earlier mode as she took up political and feminist themes and stylistic experimentation in such works as *Snapshots of a Daughter-in-Law* (1963), *The Necessities of Life* (1966), *Leaflets* (1969), and *The Will to Change* (1971). In *Diving into the Wreck* (1973) and *The Dream of a Common Language* (1978), she continued to experiment with form and to deal with the experiences and aspirations of women from a feminist perspective. In addition to her poetry, Rich has published many essays on poetry, feminism, motherhood, and lesbianism. Her recent collections include *Dark Fields of the Republic: Poems 1991–1995* (1995) and *Midnight Salvage: Poems, 1995–1998* (1999).

Edwin Arlington Robinson (1869–1935)   Robinson grew up in Gardiner, Maine; attended Harvard University; returned to Gardiner as a freelance writer; and then settled in New York City in 1896. His various odd jobs included a one-year stint as subway-construction inspector. President Theodore Roosevelt, a fan of his poetry, had him appointed to the United States Customs House in New York, where he worked from 1905 to 1909. Robinson wrote about people rather than nature, particularly New England characters remembered from his early years. Describing his first volume of poems, *The Torrent and the Night Before* (1896), he told a friend there was not "a single red-breasted robin in the whole collection." Popular throughout his career, Robinson won three Pulitzer Prizes (1921, 1924, and 1927).

Randall Robinson (b. 1941)   Robinson was born in Richmond, Virginia, and educated in its segregated schools. "They never let you forget that Richmond was the capital of the Confederacy," he told an interviewer. "I remember going with my mother to a department store, and she'd have to put on a little cap before they let her try on ladies' hats. I recall sitting at the back of the bus with lots of empty seats up front. I remember delivering groceries to a white home, and when I came into the kitchen and they were discussing something very personal, they never stopped talking. It was as if I wasn't there. I was invisible." He dropped out of college after three years, served in the army, returned to Richmond, and earned his B.A. at Virginia Union University (1967). He attended Harvard Law School, where for the first time he sat in integrated classrooms. After graduating in 1970 and going to Tanzania on a Ford Fellowship, Robinson returned to the United States to become an attorney for the Boston Legal Defense Fund, a job from which he was fired for insisting that an office serving the African American community should have an African American as its director. He went on to serve as an aide to two Congressmen. In 1977, Robinson was named executive director of TransAfrica, an organization that grew out of meetings of the Congressional Black Caucus. In that position, he now lobbies on U.S. foreign policy issues affecting Africa and the Caribbean. Robinson has also taken his political beliefs to the street. He was arrested in 1984 for taking part in a highly publicized anti-apartheid sit-in at the South African Embassy in Washington, D.C. In 1994, he went on a hunger strike to protest the treatment of Haitian refugees — a strike that ended twenty-seven days later when the U.S. government changed its policy. Robinson's recent works include the autobiography, *Defending the Spirit: A Black Life in America* (1998), and *The Debt* (2000), a book-length polemic arguing for reparations by the U.S. government to its African American citizens.

Theodore Roethke (1908–1963)   Born in Saginaw, Michigan, Roethke was the son of a greenhouse owner; greenhouses figure prominently in the imagery of his poems. He graduated magna cum laude from the University of Michigan in 1929, where he also earned an M.A. in 1936 after graduate study at Harvard University. He taught at several universities, coached two varsity tennis teams, and settled at the University of Washington in 1947. Intensely introspective and demanding of himself, Roethke was renowned as a great teacher, though sometimes incapacitated by an ongoing manic-depressive condition. His collection *The Waking: Poems 1933–1953* won the Pulitzer Prize in 1954. Other awards include Guggenheim Fellowships in 1945 and 1950, and a National Book Award and the Bollingen Prize in 1959 for *Words for the Wind* (1958).

Affonso Romano DeSant'Anna (b. 1937)   Sant'Anna was born in Belo Horizonte, Brazil, and became a journalist at the early age of seventeen. He earned a Ph.D. in literature (1969) from the Federal University, Minas Gerais, Brazil. He has taught at many universities, among them the Pontifical Catholic University of Rio. He has also been a visiting professor at UCLA, the University of Iowa, the University of Texas, and the Universities of Koln (Germany) and Aix-en-Provence (France). An essayist, fiction writer, and poet, Sant'Anna made a particular impression on his countrymen with a 1980 poem "Que país é este" (What Kind of Nation Is This?), published on the political page of a popular newspaper. The poem questioned dictatorial censorship and its effect on Brazilian identity. He pointed out in *Popular Music and Modern Brazilian Poetry* (1978) that the lyrics of popular music had replaced the political writings of the intellectuals who were forced into exile by the dictatorship and, further, had become the vehicle for social and aesthetic expression usually provided by poetry. *Loving Cannibalism* (1984) is a psychoanalytic reading of Western love poetry. His considerable publications include examinations of political culture and modern art, as well as modern literature.

Muriel Rukeyser (1913–1980) Born in New York City, Rukeyser attended Vassar College and Columbia University, then spent a short time at Roosevelt Aviation School, which no doubt helped shape her first published volume of poetry, *Theory of Flight* (1935). In the early 1930s, she joined Elizabeth Bishop, Mary McCarthy, and Eleanor Clark in founding a literary magazine that challenged the policies of the *Vassar Review*. (The two magazines later merged.) A social activist, Rukeyser witnessed the Scottsboro trials (where she was one of the reporters arrested by authorities) in 1933. She visited suffering tunnel workers in West Virginia (1936) and went to Hanoi to protest U.S. involvement in the Vietnam War. She gave poetry readings across the United States and received several awards, including a Guggenheim Fellowship and the Copernicus Award. *Waterlily Fire: Poems 1935–1962* appeared in 1962, and later work was collected in *Twenty-Nine Poems* (1970). *The Collected Poems of Muriel Rukeyser* appeared in 1978. Her only novel, *The Orgy,* appeared in 1965.

Sappho (ca. 610–ca. 580 B.C.) Almost nothing certain is known of the finest woman lyric poet of the ancient world. She was born to an aristocratic family and had three brothers, one of whom was a court cupbearer (a position limited to the sons of good families). She is associated with the island of Lesbos, set in the Aegean Sea. She married and had a daughter. Until recently, her reputation depended on fragments of her work quoted by other ancient authors. However, in the late nineteenth century a cache of papyrus and vellum codices (dating from the second to the sixth centuries A.D.) containing authentic transcriptions of a few of her lyrical poems was discovered in Egypt. Unlike other ancient Greek poets, she wrote in ordinary Greek rather than in an exalted literary dialect; her lyrics, despite their simple language, conveyed women's concerns with intense emotion.

May Sarton (1912–1995) Born in Belgium, Sarton was brought to the United States in 1916 and became a naturalized citizen in 1924. She was educated at various private schools, including the Cambridge High and Latin School. In 1929, the year her first poems were published, she turned down a scholarship to Vassar College to become an apprentice with Eva Le Gallienne's Civic Repertory Theatre in New York. In 1936, when the Associated Actors Theatre, which she directed, disbanded, Sarton began to devote herself to writing. Her prolific output of poetry, fiction, and nonfiction brought her many honors, including appointment as a Guggenheim Fellow in poetry

(1954–1955) and awards from the Poetry Society of America (1952), the Johns Hopkins University Poetry Festival (1961), the Before Columbus Foundation (1985), and the Women's Building/West Hollywood Conexxus Women's Crisis Center (1987). She has taught widely in American colleges and universities and is the recipient of numerous honorary doctorate degrees. She is the author of eighteen novels, among them *The Single Hound* (1938), *Mrs. Stevens Hears the Mermaids Singing* (1965), and *The Education of Harriet Hatfield* (1989). Her volumes of poetry include *Encounter in April* (1937), *Collected Poems: 1930–1973* (1974), *The Silence Now: New and Uncollected Earlier Poems* (1988), and *Coming into Eighty* (1994). In 1986, Sarton suffered a stroke. In describing her difficult recuperation, she remarked to an interviewer that since her illness, her poems explore "where I am now, as a woman . . . who has really faced growing old for the first time."

Anne Sexton (1928–1974)   Born in Newton, Massachusetts, Sexton attended Garland Junior College and Boston University, where she studied under Robert Lowell. She worked for a year as a fashion model in Boston and later wrote her first poetry collection, *To Bedlam and Part Way Back* (1960), while recovering from a nervous breakdown. Writing a poem almost every day was successful therapy for her. From 1961 to 1963, Sexton was a scholar at the Radcliffe Institute for Independent Study. A confessional poet, Sexton acknowledged her debt to W. D. Snodgrass, whose collection of poetry, *Heart's Needle* (1959), influenced her profoundly. Her second collection, *All My Pretty Ones* (1962), includes a quote from a letter by Franz Kafka that expresses her own literary philosophy: "A book should serve as the axe for the frozen sea within us." *Live or Die* (1967), her third collection of poems, won a Pulitzer Prize. She committed suicide in 1974.

William Shakespeare (1564–1616)   Shakespeare was born at Stratford-on-Avon in April 1564. His father became an important public figure, rising to the position of high bailiff (equivalent to mayor) of Stratford. Although we know practically nothing of Shakespeare's personal life, we may assume that he received a decent grammar school education in literature, logic, and Latin (though not in mathematics or natural science). When he was eighteen, he married Anne Hathaway, eight years his senior; six months later their son was born. Two years later, Anne bore twins. We do not know how the young Shakespeare supported his family, and we do not hear of him again until 1592, when a rival London playwright sarcastically refers to him as an "upstart crow." Shakespeare seems to have prospered in the London theater world. He probably began as an actor and earned enough as author and part owner of his company's theaters to acquire property. His sonnets, which were written during the 1590s, reveal rich and varied interests. Some are addressed to an attractive young man (whom the poet urges to marry); others to the mysterious dark lady; still others suggest a love triangle of two men and a woman.

His dramas include historical plays based on English dynastic struggles; comedies, both festive and dark; romances such as *Pericles* (1608) and *Cymbeline* (1611) that cover decades in the lives of their characters; and the great tragedies *Hamlet* (1602), *Othello* (1604), *King Lear* (1605), and *Macbeth* (1606). About 1611 (at age forty-seven), he retired to the second largest house in Stratford. He died in 1616, leaving behind a body of work that still stands as a pinnacle in world literature.

Irwin Shaw (1913–1984)   Born and educated in New York City, where he received a B.A. from Brooklyn College in 1934, Shaw began his career as a scriptwriter for popular radio programs of the 1930s and then went to Hollywood to write for the movies. Disillusioned with the film industry, Shaw returned to New York. His first piece of serious writing, an antiwar play entitled *Bury the Dead,* was produced on Broadway in 1936. About this time, Shaw began contributing short stories to such magazines as the *New Yorker* and *Esquire.* His first collection of stories, *Sailor off the Bremen and Other Stories* (1939), earned him an immediate and lasting reputation as a writer of fiction. While continuing to write plays and stories, Shaw turned to the novel and published in 1948 *The Young Lions,* which won high critical praise as one of the most important novels to come out of World War II. The commercial success of the book and the movie adaptation brought Shaw financial independence and allowed him to devote the rest of his career to writing novels, among them *The Troubled Air* (1951), *Lucy Crown* (1956), *Rich Man, Poor Man* (1970), and *Acceptable Losses* (1982). Shaw's stories are collected in *Short Stories: Five Decades* (1978).

Percy Bysshe Shelley (1792–1822)   Born near Horsham, England, Shelley was the son of a wealthy landowner who sat in Parliament. At University College, Oxford University, he befriended Thomas Jefferson Hogg. Both became interested in radical philosophy and quickly became inseparable. After one year at Oxford they were both expelled for writing and circulating a pamphlet entitled "The Necessity of Atheism." Shelley married Harriet Westbrook soon after leaving Oxford. Though they had two children, the marriage was unsuccessful, and in 1814, Shelley left Harriet for Mary Wollstonecraft Godwin (author of *Frankenstein* [1818]). After Harriet's death (an apparent suicide), Shelley and Godwin were married. Escaping legal problems in England, he settled in Pisa, Italy, in 1820, and died in a sailing accident before his thirtieth birthday. A playwright and essayist as well as a romantic poet, Shelley is admired for his dramatic poem "Prometheus Unbound" (1820).

Leslie Marmon Silko (b. 1948)   Born in Albuquerque, New Mexico, Silko grew up on the Laguna Pueblo Reservation. She was educated in Bureau of Indian Affairs schools and at the University of New Mexico, where she graduated with highest honors. After three semesters in the American Indian Law program, Silko decided to devote her talents to writing about Native Americans. Her short stories quickly earned her a reputation; in 1974, she published a volume of poems, *Laguna Woman*. Her novel *Ceremony* (1977) was widely acclaimed and revived interest in her earlier short stories. *Storyteller* (1981) is a semiautobiographical collection of stories and poems. In 1991 the novel *Almanac of the Dead* appeared, and a collection of essays on contemporary Native American life, *Yellow Woman and a Beauty of the Spirit,* followed in 1996. Silko has taught at the University of Arizona and the University of New Mexico, but with a large award from the prestigious MacArthur Foundation, she has been, in her words, "a little less beholden to the everyday world." Her recent work includes the novel *Gardens in the Dunes* (1999).

Paul Simon (b. 1941)   Simon was born in Newark, New Jersey. Both his parents were teachers, and his father was a musician as well. He earned a B.A. in literature from Queens College in New York City, and attended Brooklyn Law School. He teamed with Art Garfunkel in a high school duo, and later, from 1964 to 1971, the pair became enormously popular for the poetry and intelligence of their lyrics and music. The two high school friends parted in 1970 (though they did record together occasionally), and in 1982 they reunited to perform a free concert before a half million fans in New York's Central Park. But Simon's desire for personal freedom to pursue his own musical imagination prevailed, and each now leads an independent career.

Stevie Smith (1902–1971)   Born Florence Margaret Smith in Hull, England, Stevie Smith was a secretary at Newnes Publishing Company in London from 1923 to 1953, and occasionally worked as a writer and broadcaster for the BBC. Though she began publishing verse, which she often illustrated herself, in the 1930s, Smith did not reach a wide audience until 1962 — with the publication of *Selected Poems* and her appearance in the Penguin Modern Poets series. She is noted for her eccentricity and mischievous humor, often involving an acerbic twist on nursery rhymes, common songs, or hymns. Force-fed with what she considered lifeless language in the New English Bible, she often aimed satirical barbs at religion. Smith won the Queen's Gold Medal for poetry in 1969, two years before her death. She published three novels in addition to her eight volumes of poetry.

Sophocles (496?–406 B.C.)   Born into a wealthy family at Colonus, a village just outside Athens, Sophocles distinguished himself early in life as a performer, musician, and athlete. Our knowledge of him is based on a very few ancient laudatory notices, but he certainly had a brilliant career as one of the three great Greek classical tragedians (the other two are Aeschylus, an older contemporary, and Euripides, a younger contemporary). He won the drama competition associated with the Dionysian festival (entries consisted of a tragic trilogy and a farce) at least twenty times (far more often than his two principal rivals). However, *Oedipus Rex,* his most famous tragedy, and the three other plays it was grouped with, took second place (ca. 429 B.C.). He lived during the golden age of Athens, when architecture, philosophy, and the arts flourished under Pericles. In 440 B.C., Sophocles was elected as one of the ten *strategoi* (military commanders), an indication of his stature in Athens. But his long life ended in sadder times, when the Peloponnesian War (431–404 B.C.) — between the Athenian empire and an alliance led by Sparta — darkened the region. Though Sophocles wrote some 123 plays, only 7 have survived; nonetheless, these few works establish him as the greatest of the ancient Western tragedians.

Helen Sorrells (b. 1908)   Born in Stafford, Kansas, the daughter of farmers, Sorrells earned a B.S. from Kansas State University in 1931. She married a technical writer, had two children, and was approaching her seventh decade when she won the Borestone Award for her poem "Cry Summer." In 1968, she won the *Arizona Quarterly* Award for poetry, and in 1973, received a creative writing grant from the National Endowment for the Arts, as well as the Poetry Society of America's Cecil Hemley Award for the poem "Tunnels." She has contributed to *Esquire* and *Reporter,* among others, and published a collection of poems, *Seeds as They Fall* (1971).

Gary Soto (b. 1952)   Gary Soto was born in Fresno, California, to working-class Mexican American parents. He grew up in the San Joaquin Valley and worked as a migrant laborer in California's rich agricultural regions. Uncertain of his abilities, he began his academic career at Fresno City College, moving on to California State University at Fresno, and the University of California at Irvine, where he earned an M.F.A. degree (1976). In 1975, he married Carolyn Oda, a woman of Japanese ancestry. Although his work earned him recognition as early as 1975 (an Academy of American Poets Prize), his first book of poems — *The Elements of San Joaquin,* portraying grim pictures of Mexican American life in California's central valley — didn't appear until 1977. In 1985, he joined the faculty at the University of California at Berkeley, where he taught in both the English and Chicano studies departments. He stopped teaching in 1993 to become a full-time writer. His prolific output of poetry, memoirs, essays, and fiction continues unabated and has earned him numerous prizes, including an American Book Award from the Before Columbus Foundation for *Living up the Street* (1985). Soto's recent novel, *Buried Onions* (1999), deals with the struggle and discomfort of a teenage boy's life in Fresno, California. One critic points out that Soto has transcended the social commentary of his early work and shifted to "a more personal, less politically motivated poetry." Another argues that "Gary Soto has become not an important Chicano poet but an important American poet."

Wole Soyinka (b. 1934)   One of the most prolific and versatile writers of our time, and the first African to receive the Nobel Prize for literature (1968),

Soyinka was born in Akinwande, Nigeria, to Yoruba parents. After attending Nigerian schools, including the University of Obada, he moved to England, where he earned a B.A. (1958) in English literature. For the next few years, he worked at the Royal Court Theatre in London, where his first works were performed. He returned to Nigeria in 1960, teaching drama in several universities and working on the creation of a Nigerian national theater. Because of his political opposition to the governing military dictatorship during the Nigerian Civil War, he was twice arrested and jailed during the 1960s. Following his release almost two years after his second arrest, he went into voluntary exile in England, where he lectured and continued to write. This pattern of exile and return continued, depending on the political situation in his home country. He again went into exile in 1994, declaring, "Some people think the Nobel Prize makes you bulletproof. I never had that illusion." Following the death of the military dictator Sani Abacha in 1998, Soyinka returned to Nigeria, where he now lives and teaches. Among his many plays are *The Lion and Jewel* (1959), *The Strong Breed* (1963), *The Trials of Brother Jero* (1964), and *A Scourge of Hyacinths* (1992). *The Man Died* (1972) is an account of his first arrest and imprisonment. His volumes of poetry include *Mandela's Earth and Other Poems* (1988) and *Early Poems* (1997).

David St. John (b. 1949)   David St. John was born in Fresno, California, to parents who were both teachers. He earned a B.A. (1972) from California State University at Fresno and an M.F.A. (1974) from the University of Iowa. He has taught at Oberlin College and Johns Hopkins University, and is now professor of English at the University of Southern California. He has published seven collections of poetry, among them *Study for the World's Body* (1994), which was nominated for the National Book Award in poetry. A selection of essays, reviews, and interviews — *Where the Angels Come Toward Us* — appeared in 1994. His 1999 volume *The Red Leaves of Night* was nominated for the *Los Angeles Times* Book Prize in poetry. Among the many awards he has received are fellowships from the Guggenheim Foundation and the National Endowment for the Arts. From the American Academy of Arts and Letters, he received both a Rome Fellowship in Literature (1984) and an Academy Award in Literature (2000).

Wallace Stevens (1879–1955)   Born in Reading, Pennsylvania, Stevens graduated from Harvard University in 1900, worked for a year as a reporter for the New York *Herald Tribune,* graduated from New York University Law School in 1903, and practiced law in New York for twelve years. From 1916 to 1955, Stevens worked for the Hartford Accident and Indemnity Company, where he was appointed vice president in 1934. He was in his forties when he published his first book of poetry, *Harmonium, Ideas of Order* (1923). Stevens argued that poetry is a "supreme fiction" that shapes chaos and provides order to both nature and human relationships. He illuminates his philosophy in *Ideas of Order* (1935) and *Notes toward a Supreme Fiction* (1942).

His *Collected Poems* (1954) won the Pulitzer Prize and established him as a major American poet.

Sir John Suckling (1609–1642)   Born into a prominent family (his father was secretary of state to King James I), Suckling was educated at Trinity College of Cambridge University. He inherited his father's considerable estate when he was eighteen, and traveled much in France and Italy (1628). Knighted upon his return to England (1630), he spent some time soldiering. He became a prominent courtier, and was thought of as "the greatest gallant of his time, and the greatest gamester both for bowling and cards." He supported the ill-fated Charles I in the civil war between the forces of the king and the forces of Parliament, and was forced into exile, where, according to contemporary authorities, he committed suicide in Paris. His lighthearted lyrics establish his reputation, and justify the words of Millamant, a character in William Congreve's play *The Way of the World,* who refers to him as "natural, easy Suckling."

Jonathan Swift (1667–1745)   Born in Dublin, Ireland, of English parents, Swift moved to England following his graduation from Trinity College, Dublin. In 1695, he was ordained minister of the Anglican church of Ireland and five years later became a parish priest in Laracor, Ireland. The conduct of church business took Swift to England frequently, where his wit and skill in defense of Tory politics made him many influential friends. He was rewarded for his efforts in 1713, when Queen Anne appointed him dean of St. Patrick's Cathedral in Dublin. The accession of George I to the throne in the following year, followed by the Tory's loss of the government to Whig control, ended the political power of Swift and his friends. He spent the rest of his life as dean of St. Patrick's, writing during this period his most celebrated satirical narrative, *Gulliver's Travels* (1726), and his most savage essay, "A Modest Proposal" (1729). Among his many other works are *A Tale of a Tub* and *The Battle of the Books* (both 1704), and many poems.

Amy Tan (b. 1952)   Tan's parents immigrated to Oakland, California, two and a half years before she was born, and she grew up in a rather traditional Chinese household. She earned a B.A. (1973) and an M.A. (1974) from San Jose State University and spent an additional two years in postgraduate study at the University of California at Berkeley. Her shift from a premed program to English and linguistics caused a serious break with her mother (they didn't speak for two years). She was a writer from the outset and earned her living for several years as a medical and freelance technical writer. But her interest in fiction led her to the Squaw Valley Community of Writers, and shortly after returning from a trip to China, she published her first novel, *The Joy Luck Club* (1989), consisting of sixteen interwoven stories that reveal the struggles of four Chinese mothers with their sometimes rebellious daughters. Four more novels followed — *The Kitchen God's Wife* (1991), *The Hundred Secret*

Senses (1995), *The Year of No Flood* (1995), and *The Bonesetter's Daughter* (2001).

Alfred, Lord Tennyson (1809–1892)   Tennyson was born in Lincolnshire and attended Trinity College, Cambridge (1828–1831), where he won the Chancellor's Medal for poetry in 1829. His 1842 collection, *Poems,* was not well received, but he gained prominence and the queen's favor with the 1850 publication of *In Memoriam,* an elegy written over seventeen years and inspired by the untimely death of his friend Arthur Hallam in 1833. That same year he married Emily Sellwood, after what had been a fourteen-year engagement. In 1850, he was named poet laureate of England after Wordsworth's death. His works include *Maud and Other Poems* (1855) and *Idylls of the King* (1859), based on the legendary exploits of King Arthur and the knights of the Round Table.

Dylan Thomas (1914–1953)   Born in Swansea, Wales, Thomas decided to pursue a writing career directly after grammar school. At age twenty, he published his first collection, *Eighteen Poems* (1934), but his lack of a university degree deprived him of most opportunities to earn a living as a writer in England. Consequently, his early life (as well as the lives of his wife and children) was darkened by a poverty compounded by his free spending and heavy drinking. A self-proclaimed romanticist, Thomas called his poetry a "record of [his] struggle from darkness towards some measure of light." *The Map of Love* appeared in 1939 and *Deaths and Entrances* in 1946. Later, as a radio playwright and screenwriter, Thomas delighted in the sounds of words, sometimes at the expense of sense. *Under Milk Wood* (produced in 1953) is filled with his private, onomatopoetic language. He suffered from alcoholism and lung ailments, and died in a New York hospital in 1953. Earlier that year, he noted in his *Collected Poems:* "These poems, with all their crudities, doubts and confusions are written for the love of man and in Praise of God, and I'd be a damn fool if they weren't."

James Thurber (1894–1961)   Born in Columbus, Ohio, Thurber went through the local public schools and graduated from Ohio State University. He began his writing career as a reporter — first for an Ohio newspaper, and later in Paris and New York City — before he became a staff member of the *New Yorker.* There he wrote the humorous satirical essays and fables (often illustrated with his whimsical drawings of people and animals) on which his reputation rests — the most famous being "The Secret Life of Walter Mitty." In 1929, he and another *New Yorker* staffer, E. B. White, wrote *Is Sex Necessary? or, Why You Feel the Way You Do,* a spoof of the increasingly popular new psychological theories. In 1933, he published his humorous autobiography, *My Life and Hard Times.* With Elliott Nugent, he wrote *The Male Animal* (1940), a comic play that pleads for academic freedom, and in 1959, he memorialized his associates at the *New Yorker* in *The Years with Ross.*

Leo Tolstoy (1828–1910)   Born in Russia into a family of aristocratic landowners, Tolstoy cut short his university education and joined the army, serving among the primitive Cossacks, who became the subject of his first novel, *The Cossacks* (1863). Tolstoy left the army and traveled abroad, but was disappointed by Western materialism and returned home. After a brief period in St. Petersburg, he became bored with the life of literary celebrity and returned to his family estate. There he wrote his two greatest novels, *War and Peace* (1869) and *Anna Karenina* (1877). Around 1876, Tolstoy experienced a spiritual crisis that ultimately led him to reject his former beliefs, way of life, and literary works. Henceforth, he adopted the simple life of the Russian peasants, rejecting orthodoxy in favor of a rational Christianity that disavowed private property, class divisions, secular and institutional religious authority, as well as all art (including his own) that failed to teach the simple principles he espoused.

Mark Twain (1835–1910)   Born Samuel L. Clemens in Florida, Missouri, Twain grew up in Hannibal, Missouri, on the banks of the Mississippi River (*mark twain,* a phrase meaning "two fathoms deep," was used by Mississippi riverboat pilots in making soundings). Sometime after his father's death in 1847, Twain left school to become a printer's apprentice, worked as a journeyman printer and newspaper reporter in the East and Middle West, and became a steamboat pilot on the Mississippi River until the outbreak of the Civil War. In 1861, he departed for Nevada with his brother, spent a year prospecting for silver, then returned to newspaper work as a reporter. In 1867, a San Francisco newspaper sent him as correspondent on a cruise ship to Europe and the Holy Land. He used the dispatches he wrote about this voyage as the basis for his first, highly successful book, *The Innocents Abroad* (1869). His second book, *Roughing It* (1872), described his western years and added to his already considerable reputation as an irreverent humorist. No longer explicitly autobiographical but still drawing on his own life, Twain published his masterpieces, the novels *The Adventures of Tom Sawyer* (1876) and *The Adventures of Huckleberry Finn* (1884). Twain remained a prolific and important writer and by the time of his death had become something of a national institution, although he never again quite matched the achievements of these early works. Financial problems and personal tragedies contributed to his increasingly bleak view of the human condition, expressed most powerfully in such works as *A Connecticut Yankee in King Arthur's Court* (1889), *Pudd'nhead Wilson* (1894), *The Man That Corrupted Hadleyburg* (1900), and the posthumously published *The Mysterious Stranger* (1916).

Jill Tweedie (1936–1993)   A reviewer of Jill Tweedie's autobiography, *Eating Children: Young Dreams and Early Nightmares* (1993), reveals that she was born into an economically comfortable family of "impeccable rectitude," presided over by her father, "a Scottish patriarch pathologically incapable of affection." Tweedie was encouraged to become "feminine" and marriageable;

she was given ballet lessons and sent to a Swiss finishing school while her brother and only sibling was given an academic education. Her inevitable rebellion when she was eighteen years old precipitated a disastrous marriage (the first of three) to a jealous and abusive Hungarian count. After an acrimonious separation, she took her two children to a hippie commune in Wales, where she discovered that even there, women were burdened with "women's work" while the men, generally, did no work at all. She moved to London and lived in poverty while she struggled to support her household by writing — the only skill she commanded. Ultimately, she became the *Guardian's* regular columnist on feminist issues. She has written several volumes on feminist themes, among them, *Letters from a Faint-hearted Feminist* (1982). Shortly before her death, when asked about the changes feminism had generated, she replied: "Assumptions about women are what has changed most radically. And a woman's whole psychic energy isn't wrapped up in men or nurturing the male ego. Young women don't appreciate that vast liberation."

Melvin I. Urofsky (b. 1939) Melvin Urofsky was born and grew up in New York City, where he earned an A.B. (1961), M.A. (1962), and Ph.D. (1968) from Columbia University. He taught at Ohio State University and the State University of New York at Albany, and is chair of the history department at Virginia Commonwealth University. In 1984, he earned a law degree from the University of Virginia. He has written and edited more than fifteen books, including a four-volume edition of the letters of Supreme Court Justice Louis D. Brandeis (with David W. Levy, 1971–1978). Urofsky has written and edited several books on the American Jewish experience, and was chair of the Zionist Academic Council (1976–1979). In *Letting Go: Death, Dying, and the Law* (1993), he examines the vexing relationships among dying patients, their physicians, their families, medical ethics, and the law. His most recent works are *Affirmative Action on Trial: Sex Discrimination in Johnson v. Santa Clara* (1997), and *Lethal Judgements: Assisted Suicide and American Law* (2000).

Alice Walker (b. 1944) Born in Eatonton, Georgia, the eighth child of sharecroppers, Walker was educated at Spelman College and Sarah Lawrence College. She has been deeply involved in the civil rights movement, working to register voters in Georgia and on behalf of welfare rights and Head Start in Mississippi. She also worked for the Welfare Department of New York City. She has taught at Wellesley College and Yale University and been an editor of *Ms.* Her nonfiction works include a biography for children, *Langston Hughes: American Poet* (1973); numerous contributions to anthologies about African American writers; and a collection of essays, *In Search of Our Mothers' Gardens: Womanist Prose* (1983). Her novels, all dealing with the African American experience in America, include *The Third Life of Grange Copeland* (1973); *Meridian* (1976); *The Color Purple* (1982), which won both the Pulitzer Prize and the National Book Award; *The Temple of My Familiar* (1989); and *Possessing the Secret of Joy* (1992). Her short stories are collected in three volumes, *In Love and Trouble: Stories of Black Women* (1973), *You Can't Keep a Good Woman Down* (1981), and *The Way Forward Is with a Broken Heart* (2000).

Edmund Waller (1606–1687)   Born in Hertfordshire, England, Waller was privately instructed as a young child, then sent to Eton College and Cambridge University. He served for several years as a member of Parliament, first as an opponent of the crown and later as a Royalist. His advocacy of the Royalist cause and his attempts to moderate between the crown and the Puritans in an increasingly revolutionary period led to his imprisonment and exile. He made his peace with Cromwell and returned to England in 1651. When the monarchy was restored in 1660, Waller regained his seat in Parliament. Waller was one of the earliest poets to use the heroic couplet, a form that was to dominate English poetry for over a century.

Walt Whitman (1819–1892)   One of nine children, Whitman was born in Huntington, Long Island, in New York, and grew up in Brooklyn, where his father worked as a carpenter. At age eleven, after five years of public school, Whitman took a job as a printer's assistant. He learned the printing trade and, before his twentieth birthday, became editor of the *Long Islander,* a Huntington newspaper. He edited several newspapers in the New York area and one in New Orleans before leaving the newspaper business in 1848. He then lived with his parents, worked as a part-time carpenter, and began writing *Leaves of Grass,* which he first published at his own expense in 1855. After the Civil War (during which he was a devoted volunteer, ministering to the wounded), Whitman was fired from his job in the Department of the Interior by Secretary James Harlan, who considered *Leaves of Grass* obscene. Soon, however, he was rehired in the attorney general's office, where he remained until 1874. In 1881, after many editions, *Leaves of Grass* finally found a publisher willing to print it uncensored. Translations were enthusiastically received in Europe, but Whitman remained relatively unappreciated in America; not until after his death would a large audience come to admire his original and innovative expression of American individualism.

Richard Wilbur (b. 1921)   Son of a portrait artist, Wilbur was born in New York City, graduated from Amherst College in 1942, became staff sergeant in the U.S. Army during World War II, and then earned an M.A. from Harvard University in 1947. He taught English at Harvard, Wellesley College, and Wesleyan University and was named writer-in-residence at Smith College in 1977. Former poet laureate of the United States and winner of the Pulitzer Prize, National Book Award, and the Bollingen Translation Prize, Wilbur has distinguished himself in his several volumes of poetry by using established poetic forms and meters to mine new insights from common, tangible images. A translator of French plays by Molière and Racine, Wilbur was co-lyricist (with Lillian Hellman) of *Candide,* the 1957 Broadway musical based on Voltaire's satirical novel. *New and Collected Poems* appeared in 1988, *Runaway Opposites* in 1995, and, most recently, *Mayflies: New Poems and Translations* in 2000.

Oscar Williams (1900–1964) Williams was born in Brooklyn, New York, and worked at various advertising agencies between 1921 and 1937. His first book of poetry, *The Golden Darkness,* won the Yale Series of Younger Poets Award in 1921. Although his own poetic productivity was modest, he carved himself a special niche as an editor and anthologizer. Since his anthologies were frequently used as textbooks in university courses, he exercised significant influence on the mainstream of Western poetry from the 1940s until his death.

Tennessee Williams (1911–1983) Thomas Lanier Williams was born in Columbus, Mississippi, but grew up in St. Louis, Missouri. His "lonely and miserable" childhood, as he characterized it, was in large part due to an unsympathetic father and to schoolmates who often taunted him because of his small size and lack of physical prowess. A year before he was to graduate from the University of Missouri, his father removed him from college and got him a job with the International Shoe Company, where he worked by day and wrote by night. Three years later, he suffered a nervous breakdown and, while recovering at his grandparents' home in Memphis, Tennessee, wrote his first play. With his grandparents' financial help, he attended the University of Iowa and earned a B.A. in 1938. In 1939, on the basis of a compilation of four one-act plays called *American Blues* (published in 1948), Williams won a playwriting grant and recognition as a promising playwright. The promise was fulfilled in 1945 with *The Glass Menagerie.* This was followed two years later with the equally successful *A Streetcar Named Desire* (for which he won a Pulitzer Prize in 1948). From then until his death, Williams's reputation as a premier American dramatist grew with such plays as *Cat on a Hot Tin Roof* (1955), *Suddenly Last Summer* (1958), and *The Night of the Iguana* (1961). Williams also published six volumes of prose and three volumes of poetry.

August Wilson (b. 1945) Wilson was born in a Pittsburgh ghetto known as the Hill where he attended public schools. Disillusioned by the pervasive racism of several schools, he dropped out at age sixteen and worked at menial jobs. He nevertheless pursued a literary career, reading widely in the local library, where he discovered and was encouraged in his own literary aspirations by the writers of the Harlem Renaissance as well as other African American writers. Drawn to the theater and inspired by the civil rights movement, in 1968 Wilson founded the Black Horizons Theatre in St. Paul, Minnesota. Wilson's first two plays failed to gain much attention, but his third, *Ma Rainey's Black Bottom* (1982), about a group of black musicians discussing their experiences in racist America, won him wide recognition as an important new dramatist and interpreter of the African American experience. His subsequent plays have made him one of America's most celebrated dramatists and have earned him numerous prizes, among them the Tony Award (1985), the New York Drama Critics Circle Award (1985), and the Pulitzer Prize for drama (1990). His other plays include *Fences* (1985), *Joe Turner's Come and Gone* (1988), *The Piano Lesson* (1987), and *Two Trains Running* (1990).

Virginia Woolf (1882–1941)   Born in London, where she spent most of her life, Woolf, because of her frail health and her father's Victorian attitudes about the proper role of women, received little formal education (none at the university level). Nevertheless, the advantages of an upper-class family (her father, Sir Leslie Stephen, was a distinguished scholar and man of letters who hired tutors for her) and an extraordinarily powerful and inquiring mind allowed Woolf to educate herself. She began keeping a regular diary in her early teens. After moderate success with her first novels, the publication of *To the Lighthouse* (1927) and *Orlando* (1929) established her as a major novelist. While Woolf's reputation rests primarily on her novels, which helped revolutionize fictional technique, she was also a distinguished literary and social critic. A strong supporter of women's rights, she expressed her views on the subject in a series of lectures published as *A Room of One's Own* (1929) and in a collection of essays, *Three Guineas* (1938). Her reputation grew with the publication of her letters and diaries following her suicide by drowning.

William Wordsworth (1770–1850)   Born in Cockermouth in the Lake District of England, Wordsworth was educated at Cambridge University. During a summer tour in France in 1790, Wordsworth had an affair with Annette Vallon that resulted in the birth of a daughter. The tour also made of Wordsworth an ardent defender of the French Revolution of 1789 and kindled his sympathies for the plight of the common person. Wordsworth's acquaintance with Samuel Taylor Coleridge in 1795 began a close friendship that led to the collaborative publication of *Lyrical Ballads* in 1798. Wordsworth supplied a celebrated preface to the second edition in 1800, in which he announced himself a nature poet of pantheistic leanings, committed to democratic equality and the language of common people. He finished *The Prelude* in 1805, but it was not published until after his death. As he grew older, Wordsworth grew increasingly conservative, and though he continued to write prolifically, little that he wrote during the last decades of his life attained the heights of his earlier work. In 1843, he was appointed poet laureate.

Richard Wright (1908–1960)   Wright grew up in Memphis, Tennessee, where his sharecropper father moved the family after he was forced off the farm near Natchez, Mississippi, where Wright was born. When Wright was six, his father abandoned the family, leaving his mother to support Wright and his younger brother with whatever jobs she could find. While their mother worked, the boys shifted for themselves. When he was eight, Wright's mother enrolled him in grammar school, but she fell ill and was unable to work. Consequently Wright and his brother were placed in an orphanage; later, the family was reunited and lived with relatives, and Wright was able to resume his education, graduating from high school as valedictorian in 1925. Wright left the South for Chicago in 1927, hoping, as he said, that "gradually and slowly I might learn who I was, what I might be." After working at odd jobs, his efforts at writing paid off when he received a job as publicity agent for the Federal Negro Theater. Wright joined the Communist Party in 1932 and was a member of the Federal Writers' Project from 1935 to 1937. He published his first collection, *Uncle Tom's Children,* in 1938. About the same time, he began a novel about a poor and angry ghetto youth who accidentally kills the daughter of his white, millionaire employer. The novel, *Native Son* (1940), was published to much critical and popular acclaim and remains his best-known work. Unable to accept party discipline, Wright quit the Communist Party in 1944, and in the following year published *Black Boy,* an autobiography of his early years. Discouraged with the racism of America, Wright soon moved his family to France, where he spent the remainder of his life writing and supporting the cause of African independence. His later works include the novels *The Outsider* (1953) and *The Long Dream* (1958) and the nonfiction works *Black Power* (1954) and *White Man, Listen!* (1957).

William Butler Yeats (1865–1939)   Yeats was born in Ireland and educated in both Ireland and London. Much of his poetry and many of his plays reflect his fascination with the history of Ireland — particularly the myths and legends of its ancient, pagan past — as well as his interest in the occult. As Yeats matured, he turned increasingly to contemporary subjects, expressing his nationalism in poems about the Irish struggle for independence from England. In 1891, he became one of the founders of an Irish literary society in London (the Rhymers' Club) and of another in Dublin the following year. Already a recognized poet, Yeats helped to establish the Irish National Theater in 1899; its first production was his play *The Countess Cathleen* (written in 1892). His contribution to Irish cultural and political nationalism led to his appointment as a senator when the Irish Free State was formed in 1922. Yeats's preeminence as a poet was recognized in 1923, when he received the Nobel Prize for literature. Among his works are *The Wanderings of Oisin and Other Poems* (1889), *The Wind among the Reeds* (1899), *The Green Helmet and Other Poems* (1910), *Responsibilities: Poems and a Play* (1914), *The Tower* (1928), and *Last Poems and Two Plays* (1939).

Yevgeny Yevtushenko (b. 1933)   Son of two geologists, Yevtushenko was born in Siberia. He attended Gorky Literary Institute from 1951 to 1954 and worked on a geological expedition while establishing himself as an influential Soviet poet. During the 1950s, his books were published regularly, and he was allowed to travel abroad. In 1960, he gave readings in Europe and the United States but was criticized by Russians for linking them with anti-Semitism in his poem "Babi Yar," the name of a ravine near Kiev where

96,000 Jews were killed by Nazis during World War II. Although considering himself a "loyal revolutionary Soviet citizen," he elicited official disapproval by opposing the 1968 occupation of Czechoslovakia (a performance of his play *Bratsk Power Station* [1967] was cancelled as a result) and for sending a telegram to then-Premier Brezhnev expressing concern for Aleksandr Solzhenitsyn after his arrest in 1974. His works include *A Precocious Autobiography* (1963); *From Desire to Desire* (1976); *Fatal Half Measures: The Culture of Democracy in the Soviet Union* (1991), an analysis of recent Russian history; and *Don't Die Before You're Dead* (1995), an autobiographical novel.

Glossary of Literary Terms

Abstract language   Language that describes ideas, concepts, or qualities, rather than particular or specific persons, places, or things. *Beauty, courage, love* are abstract terms, as opposed to such concrete terms as *man, stone, woman.* George Washington, the Rosetta Stone, and Helen of Troy are particular concrete terms. Characteristically, literature uses *concrete* language to animate *abstract* ideas and principles. When Robert Frost, in "Provide, Provide" describes the pain of impoverished and lonely old age, he doesn't speak of an old, no longer beautiful female. He writes: "The witch that came (the withered hag) / To wash the steps with pail and rag, / Was once the beauty Abishag."

Alexandrine   In poetry, a line containing six iambic feet (iambic hexameter). Alexander Pope, in "An Essay on Criticism," reveals his distaste for the forms in a couplet: "A needless Alexandrine ends the song, / That, like a wounded snake, drags its slow length along." *See* Meter.

Allegory   A narrative in verse or prose, in which abstract qualities (*death, pride, greed,* for example) are personified as characters. In Nathaniel Hawthorne's story "Young Goodman Brown" (p. 80), Brown's wife personifies faith and the old man in the forest personifies Satan.

Alliteration   The repetition of the same consonant sounds, usually at the beginning of words in close proximity. The *w* sounds in these lines from Robert Frost's "Provide, Provide" alliterate: "The witch that came (the withered hag) / To wash the steps with pail and rag, / Was once the beauty Abishag."

Allusion   A reference in a literary work to something outside the work, usually to some famous person, place, thing, event, or other literary work.

Ambiguity   A phrase, statement, or situation that may be understood in two or more ways. In literature, ambiguity is used to enrich meaning or achieve irony by forcing readers to consider alternative possibilities. When the duke in Robert Browning's "My Last Duchess" (p. 151) says that he "gave commands; / Then all smiles stopped together. There she stands / As if alive," the reader cannot know exactly what those commands were or whether the last words refer to the commands (as a result of which she is no longer alive) or merely refer to the skill of the painter (the painting is extraordinarily lifelike).

Analogy   A comparison that uses a known thing or concept to explain something unfamiliar. *See* Metaphor; Simile.

Anapest   A three-syllable metrical foot consisting of two unaccented syllables followed by an accented syllable. *See* Meter.

Antagonist   A character in a story, play, or narrative poem who stands in opposition to the hero (*see* Protagonist). The conflict between antagonist and protagonist often generates the action or plot of the story.

Antistrophe   *See* Strophe.

Apostrophe   A direct address to a person who is absent or to an abstract or inanimate entity. In one of his sonnets (p. 1384), John Donne admonishes: "Death, be not proud!" And Wordsworth speaks to a river in Wales: "How oft, in spirit, have I turned to thee, / O sylvan Wye! thou wanderer through the woods" (p. 146).

Archaism   The literary use of obsolete language. When Keats, in "Ode on a Grecian Urn" (p. 1385), writes: "with brede / Of marble men and maidens overwrought," he uses an archaic word for *braid* and intends an obsolete definition, "worked all over" (that is, "ornamented"), for *overwrought.*

Archetype   Themes, images, and narrative patterns that are universal and thus embody some enduring aspects of human experience. Some of these themes are the death and rebirth of the hero, the underground journey, and the search for the father.

Assonance   The repetition of vowel sounds in a line, stanza, or sentence: *road nowhere.* By using assonance that occurs at the end of words — *my, pie* — or a combination of assonance and consonance (the repetition of final consonant sounds — *fish, wish*), poets create rhyme. Some poets use assonantial and consonantial off rhymes (*see* Near rhyme). W. H. Auden, in a celebrated verse from "Five Songs," writes: "That night when joy began / Our narrowest veins to flush, / We waited for the flash / Of morning's levelled gun." *Flush* and *gun* are assonantial, *flush* and *flash* are consonantial (and, of course, alliterative).

Atmosphere   The general feeling or mood created in the reader by a work. *See* Mood.

Aubade   A love song or lyric to be performed at sunrise. Philip Larkin's "Aubade" (p. 1413) uses the form ironically in a somber contemplation of mortality.

Ballad   A narrative poem, originally of folk origin, usually focusing on a climactic episode and told without comment. The most common ballad form consists of quatrains of alternating four- and three-stress iambic lines, with the second and fourth lines rhyming. Often, the ballad will employ a *refrain* — that is, the last line of each stanza will be identical or similar. "Bonny Barbara Allan" (p. 1083) is a traditional ballad. Dudley Randall's "Ballad of Birmingham" (p. 451) is a twentieth-century example of the ballad tradition.

Blank verse   Lines of unrhymed iambic pentameter. Shakespeare's dramatic poetry is written principally in blank verse. *See* Meter.

Cacophony   Language that sounds harsh and discordant, sometimes used to reinforce the sense of the words. Consider the plosive *b, p,* and *t* sounds in the following lines from Shakespeare's Sonnet 129 (p. 1098): "and till action, lust / Is perjured, murderous, bloody, full of blame, / Savage, extreme, rude, cruel, not to trust." *Compare* Euphony.

Caesura   A strong pause within a line of poetry. Note the caesuras indicated by a double vertical line (‖) in these lines from Robert Browning's "My Last Duchess" (p. 151): "That's my last Duchess painted on the wall, / Looking as if she were alive, ‖ I call / That piece a wonder, now: ‖ Frà Pandolf's hands / Worked busily a day, ‖ and there she stands."

Carpe diem   Latin, meaning "seize the day." A work, usually a lyric poem, in which the speaker calls the attention of the auditor (often a young woman) to the shortness of youth and life and then urges the auditor to enjoy life while there is time. Andrew Marvell's "To His Coy Mistress" (p. 1104) is among the best of the *carpe diem* tradition in English. The opening stanza of a famous Robert Herrick poem nicely illustrates *carpe diem* principles: "Gather ye rosebuds while ye may, / Old

Time is still a-flying / And this same flower that smiles today, / Tomorrow will be dying."

Catharsis   A key concept in the *Poetics* of Aristotle that attempts to explain why representations of suffering and death in drama paradoxically leave the audience feeling relieved rather than depressed. According to Aristotle, the fall of a tragic hero arouses in the viewer feelings of "pity" and "terror" — pity because the hero is an individual of great moral worth and terror because the viewer identifies with and, consequently, feels vulnerable to the hero's tragic fate. Ideally, the circumstances within the drama allow viewers to experience a catharsis that purges those feelings of pity and terror and leaves them emotionally purified.

Central intelligence   *See* Point of view.

Character   A person or figure in a literary work, sometimes classified as either *flat* (quickly describable) or *round* (more developed, complex). *See* Protagonist *and* Antagonist.

Characterization   The means of presenting and developing a character, shown through the author's description, the character's actions or thoughts, or other characters' actions or thoughts.

Chorus   Originally, a group of masked dancers who chanted lyric hymns at religious festivals in ancient Greece. In the plays of Sophocles, the chorus, while circling around the altar to Dionysius, chants the odes that separate the episodes. These odes, in some respects, represented an audience's reaction to, and comment on, the action in the episodes. In Elizabethan drama, and even, on occasion, in modern drama, the chorus appears, usually as a single person who comments on the action.

Comedy   In drama, the representation of situations that are designed to delight and amuse and that end happily. Comedy often deals with ordinary people in their human condition, while tragedy deals with the ideal and heroic and, until recently, embodied only the high born as tragic heroes. *Compare* Tragedy.

Conceit   A figure of speech that establishes an elaborate parallel between unlike things. The *Petrarchan conceit* (named for the fourteenth-century Italian writer of love lyrics) was often imitated by Elizabethan sonneteers until the device became so hackneyed that Shakespeare mocked the tendency in Sonnet 130 (p. 1098): "My mistress' eyes are nothing like the sun; / Coral is far more red than her lips' red; / If snow be white, why then her breasts are dun; / If hairs be wires, black wires grow on her head." The *metaphysical conceit* employs strange, even bizarre, comparisons to heighten the wit of the poem. Perhaps the most famous metaphysical conceit is John Donne's elaborate and extended parallel of a drawing compass to the souls of the couple in "A Valediction: Forbidding Mourning" (p. 1102).

Concrete language   *See* Abstract language.

Conflict   The struggle of a protagonist, or main character, with forces that threaten to destroy him or her. The struggle creates suspense and is usually resolved at the end of the narrative. The force opposing the main character may be another person — the antagonist (as in Frank O'Connor's "My Oedipus Complex," p. 109) — or society (as in Harlan Ellison's "'Repent, Harlequin!' Said the Ticktockman," p. 399), or natural forces (as in Katherine Anne Porter's "The Jilting of Granny Weatherall," p. 1340). A fourth type of conflict reflects the struggle of opposing tendencies within an individual (as in Tolstoy's "The Death of Iván Ilých," p. 1286).

Connotation   The associative and suggestive meanings of a word, in contrast to its literal or *denotative* meaning. One might speak of an *elected official,* a relatively neutral term without connotative implications. Others might call the same person a *politician,* a more negative term; still others might call him or her a *statesman,* a more laudatory term. *Compare* Denotation.

Consonance   Repetition of the final consonant sounds in stressed syllables. In the second poem of W. H. Auden's "Five Songs," lines one and four illustrate consonance, as do lines two and three. "That night when joy began / Our narrowest veins to flush, / We waited for the flash / Of morning's levelled gun."

Couplet   A pair of rhymed lines — for example, these from A. E. Housman's "Terence, This Is Stupid Stuff" (p. 156). "Why, if 'tis dancing you would be, / There's brisker pipes than poetry."

Dactyl   A three-syllable metrical foot consisting of an accented syllable followed by two unaccented syllables. *See* Meter.

Denotation   The literal dictionary definition of a word, without associative and suggestive meanings. *See* Connotation.

Denouement   The final revelations that occur after the main conflict is resolved; literally, the "untying" of the plot following the climax.

Deus ex machina   Latin for "god from a machine." Difficulties were sometimes resolved in ancient Greek and Roman plays by a god, who was lowered to the stage by means of machinery. The term is now used to indicate unconvincing or improbable coincidences that are used to advance or resolve a plot.

Dialect   A variety of a language distinguished by its pronunciation, vocabulary, rhetoric, and grammar. When used in dialogue, dialect reveals a character's membership in certain groups or communities.

Dialogue   The exchange of words between characters in a drama or narrative.

Diction   The choice of words in a work of literature and hence an element of style crucial to the work's effectiveness. The diction of a story told from the point of view of an inner-city child (as in Toni Cade Bambara's "The Lesson," p. 134) will differ markedly from a similar story told from the point of view of a mature and educated adult, like the narrator of Frank O'Connor's "My Oedipus Complex" (p. 109).

Didactic   A term applied to works with the primary and avowed purpose of persuading the reader that some philosophical, religious, or moral doctrine is true.

Dimeter   A line of poetry consisting of two metrical feet. *See* Meter.

Distance   The property that separates an author or a narrator from the actions of the characters he or she creates, thus allowing a disinterested, or aloof, narration of events. Similarly, distance allows the reader or audience to view the characters and events in a narrative dispassionately.

Dramatic irony   *See* Irony.

Dramatic monologue   A type of poem in which the speaker addresses another person (or persons) whose presence is known only from the speaker's words. During the course of the monologue, the speaker (often unintentionally) reveals his or her own character. Such poems are dramatic because the speaker interacts with another character at a specific time and place; they are monologues because the entire poem is uttered by the speaker. Robert Browning's "My Last Duchess" (p. 151), Matthew Arnold's "Dover Beach" (p. 1108), and T. S. Eliot's "The Love Song of J. Alfred Prufrock" (p. 766) are dramatic monologues.

Elegy   Usually, a poem that laments the death of a particular person. The term often is used to describe meditative poems on the subject of human mortality. A. E.

Housman's "To an Athlete Dying Young" (p. 1389) and Theodore Roethke's "Elegy for Jane" (p. 1411) are elegies.

End-rhyme   *See* Rhyme.

End-stopped line   A line of verse that embodies a complete logical and grammatical unit. A line of verse that does not constitute a complete syntactic unit is called *run-on*. For example, in the opening lines of Robert Browning's "My Last Duchess" (p. 151): "That's my last Duchess painted on the wall, / Looking as if she were alive. I call / That piece a wonder, now: . . . ," the opening line is end-stopped while the second line is run-on, because the direct object of *call* runs on to the third line.

English sonnet   Also called *Shakespearean sonnet. See* Sonnet.

Enjambment   The use of run-on lines. *See* End-stopped line.

Epigraph   In literature, a short quotation or observation related to the theme and placed at the head of the work. T. S. Eliot's "The Love Song of J. Alfred Prufrock" (p. 766) has an epigraph.

Epiphany   In literature, a showing forth, or sudden manifestation. James Joyce used the term to indicate a sudden illumination that enables a character (and, presumably, the reader) to understand his situation. The narrator of Joyce's "Araby" (p. 100) experiences an epiphany toward the end of the story, as does Iván Ilých (p. 1286).

Epode   *See* Strophe.

Euphony   Language embodying sounds pleasing to the ear. *Compare* Cacophony.

Exposition   Information supplied to readers and audiences that enables them to understand narrative action. Often, exposition establishes what has occurred before the narrative begins, or informs the audience about relationships among principal characters. The absence of exposition from some modern literature, particularly modern drama, contributes to the unsettling feelings sometimes experienced by the audience.

Farce   A type of comedy, usually satiric, that relies on exaggerated character types, ridiculous situations, and, often, horseplay.

Feminine rhyme   A two-syllable rhyme in which the second syllable is unstressed, as in the second and fourth lines of these verses from James Fenton's "God, A Poem" (p. 1421): "A nasty surprise in a sandwich, / A drawing-pin caught in your sock, / The limpest of shakes from a hand which / You'd thought would be firm as a rock."

Figurative language   A general term covering the many ways in which language is used nonliterally. *See* Hyperbole, Irony, Metaphor, Metonymy, Paradox, Simile, Symbol, Synecdoche, Understatement.

First-person narrator   *See* Point of view.

Foot   *See* Meter.

Free verse   Poetry, usually unrhymed, that does not adhere to the metrical regularity of traditional verse. Although free verse is not metrically regular, it is nonetheless clearly more rhythmic than prose and makes use of other aspects of poetic discourse to achieve its effects.

Heroic couplet   Iambic pentameter lines that rhyme *aa, bb, cc,* and so on. Usually, heroic couplets are *closed* — that is, the couplet's end coincides with a major syntactic unit so that the line is end-stopped. These lines from Alexander Pope's "Essay on Man" illustrate the form: "And, spite of pride, in erring reason's spite, / One truth is clear; Whatever IS, IS RIGHT."

Hexameter   A line of verse consisting of six metrical feet. *See* Meter.

Hubris   In Greek tragedy, arrogance resulting from excessive pride. Creon, in Sophocles's *Antigonê* (p. 467), is guilty of hubris.

Hyperbole   Figurative language that embodies overstatement or exaggeration. The boast of the speaker in Robert Burns's "A Red, Red Rose" (p. 1106) is hyperbolic: "And I will luve thee still, my dear, / Til a' the seas gang dry."

Iamb   A metrical foot consisting of an unstressed syllable followed by a stressed syllable. *See* Meter.

Imagery   Language that embodies an appeal to a physical sense, usually sight, although the words may invoke sound, smell, taste, and touch as well. The term is often applied to all figurative language. *Images* illustrate a concept, thing, or process by appealing to the senses.

Internal rhyme   *See* Rhyme.

Irony   Figurative language in which the intended meaning differs from the literal meaning. *Verbal irony* includes overstatement (hyperbole), understatement, and opposite statement. The following lines from Robert Burns's "A Red, Red Rose" (p. 1106) embody overstatement: "As fair art thou, my bonnie lass, / So deep in luve am I; / And I will luve thee still, my dear, / Til a' the seas gang dry." These lines from Andrew Marvell's "To His Coy Mistress" (p. 1104) understate: "The grave's a fine and private place, / But none, I think, do there embrace." W. H. Auden's ironic conclusion to "The Unknown Citizen" (p. 449) reveals opposite statement: "Was he free? Was he happy? The question is absurd: / Had anything been wrong, we should certainly have heard." *Dramatic irony* occurs when a reader or audience knows things a character does not and, consequently, hears things differently. For example, in Shakespeare's *Othello* (p. 1144), the audience knows that Iago is Othello's enemy, but Othello doesn't. Hence, the audience's understanding of Iago's speeches to Othello differs markedly from Othello's.

Italian sonnet   Also called *Petrarchan sonnet*. *See* Sonnet.

Lyric   Originally, a song accompanied by lyre music. Now, a relatively short poem expressing the thought or feeling of a single speaker. Almost all the nondramatic poetry in this anthology is lyric poetry.

Metaphor   A figurative expression consisting of two elements in which one element is provided with special attributes by being equated with a second, unlike element. In Theodore Roethke's "Elegy for Jane" (p. 1411), for example, the speaker addresses his dead student: "If only I could nudge you from this sleep, / My maimed darling, my skittery pigeon." Here, Jane is characterized metaphorically as a "skittery pigeon," and all the reader's experience of a nervous pigeon's movement becomes attached to Jane. *See* Simile.

Meter   Refers to recurrent patterns of accented and unaccented syllables in verse. A metrical unit is called a *foot,* and there are four basic accented patterns. An *iamb,* or *iambic foot,* consists of an unaccented syllable followed by an accented syllable (bĕfóre, tŏdáy). A *trochee,* or *trochaic foot,* consists of an accented syllable followed by an unaccented syllable (fúnnỹ, phántŏm). An *anapest,* or *anapestic* *foot,* consists of two unaccented syllables followed by an accented syllable (in the line "If év ‖ ery̆thĭng háp ‖ pĕns thăt cán't ‖ bĕ dóne," the second and third metrical feet are anapests). A *dactyl,* or *dactyllic foot,* consists of a stressed syllable followed by two unstressed syllables (sýllăblĕ, métrĭcăl). One common variant, consisting of two stressed syllables, is called a *spondee,* or *spondaic foot* (dáy-bréak, moónshíne).

Lines are classified according to the number of metrical feet they contain (an iambic hexameter line is an *Alexandrine*):

one foot	monometer
two feet	dimeter
three feet	trimeter
four feet	tetrameter
five feet	pentameter
six feet	hexameter

Here are some examples of various metrical patterns:

Tŏ eách ‖ hĭs sŭff ‖ erĭngs: áll ‖ are mén,	*iambic tetrameter*
Cŏndemnéd ‖ ălíké ‖ tŏ groán;	*iambic trimeter*
Ońce ŭp ‖ ón ă ‖ mídnĭght ‖ dréary̆, ‖ whíle Ĭ ‖	
pónderĕd ‖ wéak ănd ‖ wéary̆	*trochaic octameter*
Thĕ Ăssýr ‖ iăn cămе dówn ‖ likĕ ă wólf ‖ ŏn t̃hefóld	*anapestic tetrameter*
Iŝ thís ‖ thĕ rég ‖ iŏn, thís ‖ thĕ soíl, ‖ thĕ clíme,	*iambic pentameter*
Fóllŏw ĭt ‖ úttĕrly̆,	*dactyllic dimeter*
Hópe bĕ ‖ yónd hópe:	*dimeter line — trochee and spondee*

Metonymy A figure of speech in which a word stands for a closely related idea. In the expression "The pen is mightier than the sword," *pen* and *sword* are metonyms for written ideas and physical force.

Monologue A long, uninterrupted speech by a character.

Mood The atmosphere or general feeling of a work. *See* Atmosphere.

Muses The nine daughters of Zeus and Mnemosyne (memory) who preside over various humanities. Although there are some variations, generally they may be assigned as follows: Calliope, epic poetry; Clio, history; Erato, lyric poetry; Euterpe, music; Melpomene, tragedy; Polyhymnia, sacred poetry; Terpsichore, dance; Thalia, comedy; and Urania, astronomy.

Narrator The speaker of the story, not to be confused with the author. For kinds of narrators, *see* Point of view.

Near rhyme Also called *off rhyme, slant rhyme,* or *oblique rhyme.* Usually the occurrence of consonance where rhyme is expected, as in *pearl, alcohol,* or *heaven, given. See* Rhyme.

Octave An eight-line stanza. More often, the opening eight-line section of an Italian sonnet, rhymed *abbaabba,* followed by the sestet that concludes the poem. *See* Sonnet.

Ode Usually, a long, serious poem on exalted subjects, often in the form of an address. Keats's "Ode on a Grecian Urn" (p. 1385) is representative. In Greek dramatic poetry, odes consisting of three parts — the *strophe,* the *antistrophe,* and the *epode* — were sung by the chorus between the episodes of the play. *See* Strophe.

Off rhyme *See* Near rhyme.

Omniscient narrator *See* Point of view.

Onomatopoeia   Language that sounds like what it means. Words like *buzz, bark,* and *hiss* are onomatopoetic. Also, sound patterns that reinforce the meaning may be designated onomatopoetic. Alexander Pope illustrates such onomatopoeia in this passage from "An Essay on Criticism":

'Tis not enough no harshness gives offense,
The sound must seem an echo to the sense:
Soft is the strain when Zephyr gently blows,
And the smooth stream in smoother numbers flows;
But when loud surges lash the sounding shore,
The hoarse, rough verse should like the torrent roar:
When Ajax strives some rock's vast weight to throw,
The line too labors, and the words move slow;
Not so, when swift Camilla scours the plain,
Flies o'er the unbending corn, and skims along the main.

Opposite statement   *See* Irony.

Ottava rima   An eight-line, iambic pentameter stanza rhymed *abababcc.* Originating with the Italian poet Boccaccio, the form was made popular in English poetry by Milton, Keats, and Byron, among others.

Oxymoron   Literally, "acutely silly." A figure of speech in which contradictory ideas are combined to create a condensed paradox: *thunderous silence, sweet sorrow, wise fool.*

Paean   In classical Greek drama, a hymn of praise, usually honoring Apollo. Now, any lyric that joyously celebrates its subject.

Paradox   A statement that seems self-contradictory or absurd but is, somehow, valid. The conclusion of Donne's "Death, Be Not Proud" (p. 1384) illustrates: "One short sleep past, we wake eternally / And death shall be no more; Death, thou shalt die." In Holy Sonnet 14, Donne, speaking of his relationship with God, writes: "Take me to You, imprison me, for I, / Except You enthrall me, never shall be free, / Nor ever chaste, except You ravish me."

Parody   An imitation of a work using the original's form or content as a model, meant to criticize or create a humorous effect.

Pastoral   *Pastor* is Latin for "shepherd," and the pastoral is a poetic form invented by ancient Roman writers that deals with the complexities of the human condition as if they exist in a world peopled by idealized rustic shepherds. Pastoral poetry suggests that country life is superior to urban life. In the hands of such English poets as Marlowe and Milton, the pastoral embodies highly conventionalized and artificial language and situations. Christopher Marlowe's "The Passionate Shepherd to His Love" (p. 1086) is a famous example, as is Sir Walter Raleigh's mocking response, "The Nymph's Reply to the Shepherd" (p. 1087).

Pentameter   A line containing five metrical feet. *See* Meter.

Persona   Literally, "actor's mask." The term is applied to a first-person narrator in fiction or poetry. The persona's views may differ from the author's.

Personification   The attribution of human qualities to nonhuman things, such as animals, aspects of nature, or even ideas and processes. When Donne exclaims in "Death, Be Not Proud" (p. 1384), "Death, thou shalt die," he uses personification, as does Edmund Waller when the speaker of "Go, Lovely Rose!" (p. 1103) says: "Go, lovely rose! / Tell her that wastes her time and me / That now she knows, / When I resemble her to thee, / How sweet and fair she seems to be."

Petrarchan sonnet   Also called *Italian sonnet. See* Sonnet.

Plot   A series of events in a story or drama that bear a significant relationship to each other. E. M. Forster illuminates the definition: " 'The King died, and then the Queen died,' is a story. 'The King died, and then the Queen died of grief,' is a plot."

Poetic license   Variation from standard word order to satisfy the demands of rhyme and meter.

Point of view   The person or intelligence a writer of fiction creates to tell the story to the reader. The major techniques are: (1) *first person,* where the story is told by someone (who often, though not necessarily, is the principal character) who identifies himself or herself as "I," as in James Joyce's "Araby" (p. 100); (2) *third person,* where the story is told by someone (not identified as "I") who is not a participant in the action and who refers to the characters by name or as "he," "she," and "they," as in Harlan Ellison's " 'Repent, Harlequin!' Said the Ticktockman" (p. 399); (3) *omniscient,* a variation on the third person, where the narrator knows everything about the characters and events, can move about in time and place as well as from character to character at will, and can, whenever he or she wishes, enter the mind of any character, as in Tolstoy's "The Death of Iván Ilých" (p. 1286); (4) *central intelligence,* another variation on the third person, where narrative elements are limited to what a single character sees, thinks, and hears, as in Richard Wright's "The Man Who Was Almost a Man" (p. 376). *See also* Unreliable narrator.

Prose   Ordinary written or spoken expression, resembling everyday language or speech.

Prosody   The study of the elements of versification, such as *rhyme, meter, stanzaic patterns,* and so on.

Protagonist   Originally, the first actor in a Greek drama. In Greek, *agon* means "contest." Hence, the protagonist is the hero, the main character in a narrative, in conflict either with his or her situation or with another character. *See* Antagonist.

Quatrain   A four-line stanza.

Refrain   The repetition within a poem of a group of words, often at the end of ballad stanzas.

Rhyme   The repetition of the final stressed vowel sound and any sounds following (*cat, rat; debate, relate; pelican, belly can*) produces perfect rhyme. When the last stressed syllable rhymes, the rhyme is called masculine (*cat, rat*). Two-syllable rhymes with unstressed last syllables are called feminine (*ending, bending*). When rhyming words appear at the end of lines, the poem is *end-rhymed.* When rhyming words appear within one line, the line contains *internal rhyme.* When the correspondence in sounds is imperfect (*heaven, given; began, gun*), *off rhyme, slant rhyme,* or *near rhyme* is produced.

Rhythm   The quality created by the relationship between stressed and unstressed syllables. A regular pattern of alternation between stressed and unstressed syllables produces *meter.* Irregular alternation of stressed and unstressed syllables produces *free verse.* Compare the rhythm of the following verses from Robert Frost's "Stopping by Woods on a Snowy Evening" (p. 1395) and Walt Whitman's "Out of the Cradle Endlessly Rocking":

> Whose woods these are I think I know.
> His house is in the village though;

He will not see me stopping here
To watch his woods fill up with snow.

Out of the cradle endlessly rocking,
Out of the mocking-bird's throat, the musical shuttle,
Out of the Ninth-month midnight,
Over the sterile sands and the fields beyond, where the child leaving his bed
    wander'd alone, bareheaded, barefoot,
Down from the shower'd halo.

Run-on line   *See* End-stopped line.

Satire   Writing in a comic mode that holds a subject up to scorn and ridicule, often with the purpose of correcting human vice and folly. Harlan Ellison's "'Repent, Harlequin!' Said the Ticktockman" (p. 399) satirizes a society obsessed with time and order.

Scansion   The analysis of patterns of stressed and unstressed syllables to establish the metrical or rhythmical pattern of a poem.

Sestet   The six-line resolution of a Petrarchan sonnet. *See* Sonnet.

Setting   The place, time, and social context in which a work occurs. Often the setting contributes significantly to the story; for example, the tawdry gloom at the fair in James Joyce's "Araby" (p. 100) destroys the narrator's expectations.

Shakespearean sonnet   Also called *English sonnet. See* Sonnet.

Simile   Similar to metaphor, the simile is a comparison of unlike things introduced by the words *like* or *as.* For example, Robert Burns, in "A Red, Red Rose" (p. 1106), exclaims, "O My Luve's like a red, red rose," and Shakespeare mocks extravagant similes when he admits in Sonnet 130, "My mistress' eyes are nothing like the sun" (p. 1098).

Slant rhyme   *See* Rhyme.

Soliloquy   A dramatic convention in which an actor, alone on the stage, speaks his or her thoughts aloud. Iago's speech that closes Act I of Shakespeare's *Othello* (p. 1144) is a soliloquy, as is Othello's speech in Act III, Scene 3, lines 258–279.

Sonnet   A lyric poem of fourteen lines, usually of iambic pentameter. The two major types are the Petrarchan (or Italian) and Shakespearean (or English). The Petrarchan sonnet is divided into an octave (the first eight lines, rhymed *abbaabba*) and sestet (the final six lines, usually rhymed *cdecde* or *cdcdcd*). The Shakespearean sonnet consists of three quatrains and a concluding couplet, rhymed *abab cdcd efef gg.* In general, the sonnet establishes some issue in the octave or three quatrains and then resolves it in the sestet or final couplet. Robert Frost's "Design" (p. 1395) is a Petrarchan sonnet; several Shakespearean sonnets appear in the text.

Spondee   A metrical foot consisting of two stressed syllables, usually a variation within a metrical line. *See* Meter.

Stanza   The grouping of a fixed number of verse lines in a recurring metrical and rhyme pattern. Keats's "Ode on a Grecian Urn" (p. 1385), for example, employs ten-line stanzas rhymed *ababcdecde.*

Stream-of-consciousness technique   The narrative technique that attempts to reproduce the full and uninterrupted flow of a character's mental process, in which ideas, memories, and sense impressions may intermingle without logical transitions. Writers using this technique sometimes abandon conventional rules of syntax and punctuation.

Strophe   In Greek tragedy, the unit of verse the chorus chanted as it moved to the left in a dance rhythm. The chorus sang the *antistrophe* as it moved to the right and the *epode* while standing still.

Style   The way an author expresses his or her matter. Style embodies, and depends upon, all the choices an author makes — the diction, syntax, figurative language, and sound patterns of the piece.

Subplot   A second plot, usually involving minor characters. The subplot is subordinate to the principal plot but is often resolved by events that figure in the main plot. For example, Iago's manipulation of Roderigo in Shakespeare's *Othello* (p. 1144) is a subplot that enters the main plot and figures prominently in the play's climax.

Symbol   An object, an action, or a person that represents more than itself. In Stephen Crane's "The Bride Comes to Yellow Sky" (p. 91), Scratchy represents the old mythic West made obsolete by the encroachment of eastern values. The urn in Keats's "Ode on a Grecian Urn" (p. 1385) symbolizes the cold immortality of art. In both of these, the symbolism arises from the *context*. *Public* symbols, in contrast to these *contextual symbols,* are objects, actions, or persons that history, myth, or legend has invested with meaning — the cross, Helen of Troy, a national flag.

Synecdoche   A figure of speech in which a part is used to signify the whole. In "Elegy Written in a Country Churchyard," Thomas Gray writes of "Some heart once pregnant with celestial fire; / Hands that the rod of empire might have swayed." That heart, and those hands, of course, refer to whole persons who are figuratively represented by significant parts.

Synesthesia   An image that uses a second sensory impression to modify the primary sense impression. When one speaks of a "cool green," for example, the primary *visual* evocation of green is combined with the *tactile* sensation of coolness. Keats, in "Ode to a Nightingale," asks for a drink of wine "Tasting of Flora and the country green, / Dance, and Provençal song, and sunburnt mirth!" Here, the *taste* of wine is synesthetically extended to the sight of flowers and meadows, the movement of dance, the sound of song, and the heat of the sun.

Tetrameter   A verse line containing four metrical feet. *See* Meter.

Theme   The statement or underlying idea of a literary work, advanced through the concrete elements of character, action, and setting. The theme of Harlan Ellison's " 'Repent, Harlequin!' Said the Ticktockman" (p. 399), in which an ordinary person defies an oppressive system, might be that to struggle against dehumanizing authority is obligatory.

Third-person narrator   A voice telling a story who refers to characters by name or as "he," "she," or "they." *See* Point of view.

Tone   The attitude embodied in the language a writer chooses. The tone authors take in a work toward readers, the subject matter, or themselves might be sad, joyful, ironic, solemn, playful. Compare, for example, the somber tone of Matthew Arnold's "Dover Beach" (p. 1108) with the comic tone of Anthony Hecht's "The Dover Bitch" (p. 1118).

Tragedy   The dramatic representation of serious and important actions that culminate in catastrophe for the protagonist, or chief actor, in the play. Aristotle saw tragedy as the fall of a noble figure from a high position and happiness to defeat and misery as a result of *hamartia,* some misjudgment or frailty of character. *Compare* Comedy.

Trimeter   A verse line consisting of three metrical feet. *See* Meter.

Triplet   A sequence of three verse lines that rhyme.

Trochee   A metrical foot consisting of a stressed syllable followed by an unstressed syllable. *See* Meter.

Understatement   A figure of speech that represents something as less important than it really is, hence, a form of irony. When in Robert Browning's "My Last Duchess" (p. 151) the duke asserts "This grew; I gave commands; / Then all smiles stopped together," the words ironically understate what was likely an order for his wife's execution.

Unreliable narrator   The speaker or voice of a work who is not able to accurately or objectively report events, as in Charlotte Perkins Gilman's "The Yellow Wallpaper" (p. 1021).

Verse   A stanza of a poem. More generally, verse can be used interchangeably with the term *poetry.*

Villanelle   A French verse form of nineteen lines (of any length) divided into six stanzas — five tercets and a final quatrain — employing two rhymes and two refrains. The refrains consist of lines one (repeated as lines six, twelve, and eighteen) and three (repeated as lines nine, fifteen, and nineteen). Dylan Thomas's "Do Not Go Gentle into That Good Night" (p. 1412) and Catherine Davis's response "After a Time" (p. 1414) are villanelles.

Acknowledgments

Chinua Achebe. "Marriage Is a Private Affair." From *Girls at War and Other Stories* by Chinua Achebe. Copyright © 1972, 1973 by Chinua Achebe. Used by permission of Doubleday, a division of Random House, Inc.

Sherman Alexie. "This Is What It Means to Say Phoenix, Arizona." From *The Lone Ranger and Tonto Fistfight in Heaven* by Sherman Alexie. Copyright © 1993 by Sherman Alexie. Used by permission of Grove/Atlantic, Inc. Excerpt from *Smoke Signals*, scenes 37–42, 59. Copyright © 1998 by Sherman Alexie. Reprinted by permission of the author.

Woody Allen. *Death Knocks.* From *Getting Even* by Woody Allen. Copyright © 1968 by Woody Allen. Reprinted by permission of Random House, Inc.

Maya Angelou. "Graduation in Stamps." From *I Know Why the Caged Bird Sings* by Maya Angelou. Copyright © 1969 and renewed 1997 by Maya Angelou. Reprinted by permission of Random House, Inc.

Anonymous. "Edward." From *The Earliest English Poems* translated by Michael Alexander. Copyright © 1966, 1977 Michael Alexander. A Second Edition Penguin Classics. Reprinted by permission of Penguin Putnam Ltd.

Aristotle. Excerpt from *Poetics* by Aristotle, translated by James Hutton. Copyright © 1982 by W.W. Norton & Company, Inc. Used by permission of W.W. Norton & Company, Inc.

W. H. Auden. "Musée des Beaux Arts" and "The Unknown Citizen." From *The Earliest English Poems* by W. H. Auden. Edited by Edward Mendelson. Copyright © 1940, renewed 1968 by W. H. Auden. Reprinted by permission of Random House, Inc., and Faber & Faber Ltd.

James Baldwin. "Sonny's Blues." Originally published in *Partisan Review*. Collected in *Going to Meet the Man*. © 1965 by James Baldwin. Copyright renewed. Published by Vintage Books. Reprinted by arrangement with the James Baldwin Estate.

Toni Cade Bambara. "The Lesson." From *Gorilla, My Love* by Toni Cade Bambara. Copyright © 1972 by Toni Cade Bambara. Reprinted by permission of Random House, Inc.

Samuel Beckett. *Endgame.* © 1958 by Grove Press, Inc. Copyright renewed © 1986 by Samuel Beckett. Used by permission of Grove/Atlantic, Inc.

Bruce Bennett. "The True Story of Snow White." Copyright © by Bruce Bennett. From *Navigating the Distances: Poems New and Selected* by Bruce Bennett (Orchises, 1999). Reprinted by permission of the author.

Jill Bialosky. "The End of Desire." From *The End of Desire: Poems* by Jill Bialosky. Copyright © 1997 by Jill Bialosky. Used by permission of Alfred A. Knopf, a division of Random House, Inc.

Elizabeth Bishop. "One Art." From *The Complete Poems 1927–1979* by Elizabeth Bishop. Copyright © 1979, 1983 by Alice Helen Methfessel. Reprinted by permission of Farrar, Straus & Giroux, LLC. and Random House, Ltd. (UK).

Bertolt Brecht. "War Has Been Given a Bad Name." From *Bertolt Brecht: Poems 1913–1956* edited by John Willett and Ralph Manheim. © 1976, 1979 by Methuen London Ltd. Reprinted by permission of Routledge, Inc., part of The Taylor & Francis Group.

Edwin Brock. "Five Ways to Kill a Man." Copyright © Edwin Brock. Reprinted by permission of the author.

Raymond Carver. "What We Talk about When We Talk about Love." From *What We Talk About When We Talk About Love* by Raymond Carver. Copyright © 1981 by Raymond Carver. Reprinted by permission of Alfred A. Knopf, a division of Random House, Inc.

Kate Chopin. "The Storm." From *The Complete Works of Kate Chopin* edited by Per Seyersted. Copyright © 1969, 1997 by Louisiana State University Press. Reprinted by permission of Louisiana State University Press.

Sandra Cisneros. "The House on Mango Street." From *The House on Mango Street*. Copyright © 1984 by Sandra Cisneros. Published by Vintage Books, a division of Random House, Inc., New York, and in hardcover by Alfred A. Knopf in 1994. "My Wicked, Wicked Ways." From *My Wicked, Wicked Ways*. Copyright © 1987 by Sandra Cisneros. Published by Third Woman Press and in hardcover by Alfred A. Knopf. Reprinted by permission of Third Woman Press and Susan Bergholz Literary Services, New York. All rights reserved.

Lucille Clifton. "There Is a Girl Inside." Copyright © 1977, 1980 by Lucille Clifton. First appeared in *American Poetry Review* (1977). Now appears in *Good Woman: Poems and a Memoir 1969–1980*. Published by Boa Editions, Ltd. Reprinted by permission of Curtis Brown, Ltd.

Judith Ortiz Cofer. "Latin Women Pray." From *Reaching for the Mainland & Selected New Poems* by Judith Ortiz Cofer. Copyright © 1995 by Judith Ortiz Cofer. Reprinted by permission of Bilingual Press/Editorial Bilingue, Arizona State University, Tempe, AZ. "American History" from *The Latin Deli: Prose and Poetry* by Judith Ortiz Cofer. Copyright © 1993 by Judith Ortiz Cofer. Reprinted by permission of The University of Georgia Press.

Billy Collins. "Sonnet." From *Sailing Alone Around the Room* by Billy Collins. Copyright © 2001 by Billy Collins. Originally appeared in *Poetry*, February 1999. Reprinted by permission of the author.

Bernard Cooper. "A Clack of Tiny Sparks: Remembrances of a Gay Boyhood." Copyright © 1990 by *Harper's Magazine*. All rights reserved. Reproduced from the January 1991 issue by special permission.

E. E. Cummings. "The Cambridge ladies who live in furnished souls," "if everything happens that can't be done," "nobody loses all the time," "O sweet spontaneous," and "when serpents bargain for the right to squirm." From *Complete Poems 1904–1962* by E. E. Cummings. Edited by George J. Firmage. Copyright 1923, 1925, 1926, 1931, 1935, 1938, 1939, 1940, 1944, 1945, 1946, 1947, 1948, 1949, 1950, 1951, 1952, 1953, 1954, © 1955, 1956, 1957, 1958, 1959, 1960, 1961, 1962, 1963, 1966, 1967, 1968, 1972, 1973, 1974, 1975, 1976, 1977, 1978, 1979, 1980, 1981, 1982, 1983, 1984, 1985, 1986, 1987, 1988, 1989, 1990, 1991 by the Trustees for the E. E. Cummings Trust. Copyright © 1973, 1976, 1978, 1979, 1981, 1983, 1985, 1991 by George James Firmage. Used by permission of Liveright Publishing Corporation.

Catherine Davis. "After a Time." Reprinted by permission of the author.

C. Day-Lewis. "Song." From *Collected Poems* (1954). Copyright © C. Day-Lewis. Reprinted by permission on behalf of the Estate of C. Day-Lewis and Peters Fraser & Dunlop (Writers' Agent).

Emily Dickinson. "After great pain, a formal feeling comes," "Apparently with no surprise," "I felt a Funeral, in my Brain," "I heard a Fly buzz — when I died," "Mine Enemy is growing old," "Much Madness is divinest Sense," "She rose to His Requirement," "There is no Frigate like a Book — ," and "What Soft — Cherubic Creatures — ." Reprinted by permission of the publishers and the Trustees of Amherst College from *The Poems of Emily Dickinson*, Thomas H. Johnson, editor, Cambridge, Massachusetts: The Belknap Press of Harvard University Press. Copyright © 1951, 1955, 1979 by the President and Fellows of Harvard College.

Joan Didion. "On Morality." From *Slouching Towards Bethlehem* by Joan Didion. Copyright © 1966, 1968 by Joan Didion. Reprinted by permission of Farrar, Straus and Giroux, LLC.

Stephen Dunn. "Bourgeois." Published in *Riffs & Reciprocities* by Stephen Dunn. © 1998 by Stephen Dunn. Reprinted by permission of the author and W.W. Norton and Company, Inc.

Lars Eighner. "On Dumpster Diving." From *Travels with Lizbeth: Three Years on the Road and on the Street* by Lars Eighner. Copyright 1993 by Lars Eighner. Reprinted by permission of St. Martin's Press Incorporated.

T. S. Eliot. "The Love Song of J. Alfred Prufrock." From *Collected Poems 1909–1962* by T. S. Eliot. Copyright © 1936 by Harcourt Brace Jovanovich, Inc. Renewed © 1963, 1964 by T. S. Eliot. Reprinted with the permission of Harcourt, Inc., and Faber & Faber, Ltd.

Harlan Ellison. " 'Repent, Harlequin!' Said the Ticktockman" by Harlan Ellison. Copyright © 1965 by Harlan Ellison. Renewed, copyright © 1993 by Harlan Ellison. Reprinted by arrangement with, and permission of, the Author and the Author's agent, Richard Curtis Associates, Inc., New York, USA. All rights reserved.

Louise Erdrich. "The Red Convertible." From *Love Medicine: New and Expanded Version* by Louise Erdrich. Copyright © 1984, 1993 by Louise Erdrich. Reprinted by permission of Henry Holt & Company, LLC.

William Faulkner. "A Rose for Emily." From *Collected Stories of William Faulkner* by William Faulkner. Copyright © 1930, renewed 1958 by William Faulkner. Reprinted by permission of Random House, Inc.

James Fenton. "God, A Poem." From *Children in Exile: Poems 1968–1984* (1983). Copyright © James Fenton. Reprinted by permission of Sterling Lord Literistic, Inc.

Lawrence Ferlinghetti. "Constantly Risking Absurdity" and "In Goya's Greatest Scenes." From *A Coney Island of the Mind* by Lawrence Ferlinghetti. Copyright © 1958 by Lawrence Ferlinghetti. Reprinted by permission of New Directions Publishing Corp.

Harvey Fierstein. *On Tidy Endings.* From *Safe Sex* by Harvey Fierstein. Copyright © 1987 by Harvey Fierstein. Reprinted by permission.

Donald Finkel. "The Great Wave." From *Selected Shorter Poems* by Donald Finkel. Copyright © 1987 by Donald Finkel. Reprinted by permission of the author.

Nick Flynn. "Cartoon Physics." Copyright © Nick Flynn. From the book *Some Ether* by Nick Flynn. Graywolf Press, 2000. Reprinted by permission of the author.

Carolyn Forché. "The Colonel." From *The Country Between Us* by Carolyn Forche. Copyright © 1981 by Carolyn Forché. Originally appeared in *Women's International Resource Exchange*. Reprinted by permission of HarperCollins Publishers, Inc.

Erich Fromm. "Is Love an Art?" From *The Art of Loving* by Erich Fromm. Copyright © 1956 by Erich Fromm. Copyright renewed © 1984 by Annis Fromm. Reprinted by permission of Harper-Collins Publishers, Inc.

Robert Frost. "Departmental," "Design," "Fire and Ice," "Nothing Gold Can Stay," "The Road Not Taken," "A Semi-Revolution," "Stopping by Woods on a Snowy Evening." "From *The Poetry of Robert Frost* edited by Edward Connery Lathem. Copyright © 1969 by Henry Holt and Company; copyright 1936, 1942 by Robert Frost; copyright 1964, 1970 by Lesley Frost Ballantine. Reprinted by permission of Henry Holt and Company, LLC.

Athol Fugard. "*MASTER HAROLD*" . . . *and the Boys* by Athol Fugard. Copyright © 1982 by Athol Fugard. Reprinted by permission of Alfred A. Knopf, a division of Random House, Inc.

Nikki Giovanni. "Dreams." From *The Women and the Men* by Nikki Giovanni. Copyright © 1970, 1974, 1975 by Nikki Giovanni. Reprinted by permission of HarperCollins Publishers, Inc.

Kate Gleason. "After Fighting for Hours." First published in *Green Mountains Review*. Copyright © 1995 by Kate Gleason. Reprinted by permission of the author.

Robert Graves. "The Naked and the Nude." From *The Poems of Robert Graves* by Robert Graves. Reprinted by permission of Carcanet Press (UK). "Oedipus" from *The Greek Myths*, volume 2, by Robert Graves. Copyright © 1955 by Robert Graves. Reprinted by permission of Penguin Books Ltd.

Lorraine Hansberry. *A Raisin in the Sun.* Copyright © 1958 by Robert Nemiroff, as an unpublished work. Copyright © 1959, 1966, 1984 by Robert Nemiroff. Reprinted by permission of Random House, Inc.

Robert Hayden. "Those Winter Sundays." From *Angle of Ascent: New and Selected Poems* by Robert Hayden. Copyright © 1966 by Robert Hayden. Used by permission of Liveright Publishing Corporation.

Bessie Head. "Looking for a Rain God." From *Collector of Treasures* by Bessie Head. © 1977 by the Estate of Bessie Head. Reprinted by permission of John Johnson (Author's Agent) Limited and Heinemann Educational Publishers.

Seamus Heaney. "Mid-term Break" and "Valediction." From *Poems 1965–1975* by Seamus Heaney. Copyright © 1980 by Seamus Heaney. Reprinted by permission of Farrar, Straus & Giroux, LLC, and Faber & Faber Ltd.

Anthony Hecht. "Dover Bitch" and "More Light! More Light!" From *The Hard Hours* by Anthony Hecht. Copyright © 1990 by Anthony E. Hecht. Reprinted by permission of Alfred A. Knopf, a division of Random House, Inc.

Ernest Hemingway. "A Clean Well-Lighted Place." From *The Short Stories of Ernest Hemingway*. Copyright © 1933 by Charles Scribner's Sons. Copyright renewed © 1961 by Mary Hemingway. Reprinted with permission of Scribner, a Division of Simon & Schuster, Inc.

Tony Hoagland. "The Dog Years." First published in *Many Mountains Moving* (Summer 1998). Copyright © 1998 Tony Hoagland. Reprinted by permission of the author.

Linda Hogan. "First Light." From *Savings* by Linda Hogan. Copyright © 1985 by Linda Hogan. Reprinted by permission of Coffee House Press.

M. Carl Holman. "Mr. Z." Reprinted by permission of Mariella A. Holman.

A. E. Housman. "Terence, This Is Stupid Stuff," "To an Athlete Dying Young," and "When I Was One-and-Twenty." From *The Collected Poems of A. E. Housman* by A. E. Housman. Copyright © 1939, 1940, 1965 by Henry Holt and Company, Inc. Copyright © 1967 by Robert E. Symons. Reprinted by permission of Henry Holt and Company, LLC.

Pam Houston. "How to Talk to a Hunter." From *Cowboys Are My Weakness* by Pam Houston. Copyright © 1992 by Pam Houston. Used by permission of W.W. Norton & Company, Inc.

Langston Hughes. "Harlem." From *The Panther and the Lash* by Langston Hughes. Copyright © 1951 by Langston Hughes. "Dinner Guest: Me." From *The Collected Poems of Langston Hughes* by Langston Hughes. Copyright © 1994 by The Estate of Langston Hughes. Used by permission of Alfred A. Knopf, a division of Random House, Inc.

Major Jackson. "Euphoria." Originally published in the November 6, 2000, issue of *The New Yorker*. Reprinted by permission of the author.

Shirley Jackson. "The Lottery." From *The Lottery* by Shirley Jackson. Copyright © 1948, 1949 by

Shirley Jackson. Copyright © 1976, 1977 by Laurence Hyman, Barry Hyman, Mrs. Sarah Webster, and Mrs. Joanne Schnurer. Reprinted by permission of Farrar, Straus and Giroux, LLC.

June Jordan. "Memo." Copyright © 1983 by June Jordan. Reprinted by permission of the author.

Jenny Joseph. "Warning." From *Selected Poems* by Jenny Joseph. Copyright © 1992 Bloodaxe Books Ltd. Reprinted by permission of John Johnson (Author's Agent) Limited.

James Joyce. "Araby." From *Dubliners* by James Joyce. Copyright © 1916 by B.W. Heubach. Definitive text copyright © 1967 by the Estate of James Joyce. Used by permission of Viking Penguin, a division of Penguin Putnam, Inc.

Franz Kafka. "A Hunger Artist." From *Franz Kafka: The Complete Stories* by Franz Kafka, edited by Nathum M. Glazer. Copyright © 1946, 1947, 1948, 1949, 1954, 1958, 1971 by Schocken Books, Inc. Reprinted by permission of Schocken Books, distributed by Pantheon Books, a division of Random House, Inc.

Mary Karr. "Revenge of the Ex-Mistress." From *The New Yorker*, February 26–March 4, 1996. Reprinted by permission of the author.

Jamaica Kincaid. "Girl." From *At the Bottom of the River* by Jamaica Kincaid. Copyright © 1983 by Jamaica Kincaid. Reprinted by permission of Farrar, Straus and Giroux, LLC.

Martin Luther King Jr. "Letter from Birmingham Jail." From *Why We Can't Wait* by Martin Luther King Jr. Copyright © 1963 by Martin Luther King, Jr. Copyright renewed 1991 by Coretta Scott King. Reprinted by arrangement with The Heirs to the Estate of Martin Luther King, Jr., c/o Writers House, Inc., as agent for the proprietor.

Maxine Hong Kingston. "No Name Woman." From *The Woman Warrior* by Maxine Hong Kingston. Copyright © 1975, 1976 by Maxine Hong Kingston. Reprinted by permission of Alfred A. Knopf, a division of Random House, Inc.

Carolyn Kizer. "Bitch." From *Harping On*. Copyright © 1996 by Carolyn Kizer. Reprinted with the permission of Copper Canyon Press, P.O. Box 271, Port Townsend, WA 98368-0271.

Etheridge Knight. "Hard Rock Returns to Prison from the Hospital for the Criminal Insane." From *The Essential Etheridge Knight* by Etheridge Knight. © 1986. Reprinted by permission of the University of Pittsburgh Press.

Steve Kowit. "Lurid Confessions." From *Stand Up Poetry: The Poetry of Los Angeles and Beyond* by Steve Kowit. Copyright © 1983 by Steve Kowit. Reprinted by permission of the author.

Maxine Kumin. "Woodchucks." From *Selected Poems: 1960–1990* by Maxine Kumin. Copyright © 1972 by Maxine Kumin. Used by permission of W.W. Norton & Company, Inc.

Philip Larkin. "Aubade," "A Study of Reading Habits," and "This Be the Verse." From *Collected Poems* by Philip Larkin. Copyright © 1988, 1989 by the Estate of Philip Larkin. Reprinted by permission of Farrar, Straus and Giroux LLC and Faber & Faber Ltd.

Ursula K. Le Guin. "The Ones Who Walk Away from Omelas." Copyright © 1973 by Ursula K. Le Guin. First appeared in *New Dimensions* 3. From *The Wind's Twelve Quarters* by Ursula K. Le Guin. Reprinted by permission of the Virginia Kidd Agency, Inc., on behalf of the author.

Denise Levertov. "Protesters." From *Evening Train* by Denise Levertov. Copyright © 1992 by Denise Levertov. Reprinted by permission of New Directions Publishing Corp. "The Mutes." From *Poems 1960–1967* by Denise Levertov. Copyright © 1966 by Denise Levertov. Reprinted by permission of New Directions Publishing Corp.

Philip Levine. "A Theory of Prosody." From *A Walk with Tom Jefferson* by Philip Levine. Copyright © 1988 by Philip Levine. Used by permission of Alfred A. Knopf, a division of Random House, Inc.

Barry Holstun Lopez. "Winter Count 1973: Geese, They Flew over in a Storm." From *Winter Count* by Barry Holstun Lopez. Copyright © 1981 by Barry Holstun Lopez. Reprinted by permission of Sterling Lord Literistic, Inc.

Audre Lorde. "Power." From *The Black Unicorn* by Audre Lorde. Copyright © 1978 by Audre Lorde. Used by permission of W.W. Norton & Company, Inc.

D. W. Lucus. "The Drama of Oedipus." From *The Greek Tragic Poets* by D. W. Lucus. Copyright © 1950, Routledge and Kegan Paul, Ltd. Reprinted by permission of Routledge and Kegan Paul, Ltd., and Dufour Editions, Inc. All rights reserved.

Antonio Machado. "Lament of the Virtues and Verses on Account of the Death of Don Guido." From *Selected Poems* by Antonio Machado, translated by Charles Tomlinson. Copyright © 1978 by Charles Tomlinson. Reprinted by permission of Carcanet Press Ltd.

Katharyn Howd Machan. "Hazel Tells LaVerne." From *Light Years 1985*. Copyright © 1977 by Katharyn Howd Machan. Reprinted with permission of the author.

Bernard Malamud. "Idiots First." From *Idiots First* by Bernard Malamud. Copyright © 1963 by Bernard Malamud. Copyright renewed © 1991 by Ann Malamud. Reprinted by permission of Farrar, Straus and Giroux, LLC.

Aimee Mann. "Save Me" lyrics. Lyrics and music by Aimee Mann. Aimee Mann. ASCAP 1999. Reprinted by permission of Michael Hausman Artist Management.

Katherine McAlpine. "Plus C'est la Même Chose." First published in *The Nation*. Copyright © Katherine McAlpine. Reprinted by permission of the author.

James Alan McPherson. "A Loaf of Bread." From *Elbow Room* by James Alan McPherson. Copyright © 1977 by James Alan McPherson. Reprinted by permission of the Faith Childs Literary Agency, on behalf of the author.

Peter Meinke. "Advice to My Son." From *Trying to Surprise God* by Peter Meinke. © 1981. Reprinted by permission of the University of Pittsburgh Press.

Robert Mezay. "My Mother." From *The Door Standing Open* by Robert Mezey. Reprinted by permission of the author.

Edna St. Vincent Millay. "Love Is Not All." From *Collected Poems*. Copyright © 1931, 1956 by Edna St. Vincent Millay and Norma Miller Ellis. All rights reserved. Reprinted by permission of Elizabeth Barrett, literary executor.

Arthur Miller. *Death of a Salesman*. Copyright © 1949; renewed © 1977 by Arthur Miller. "Tragedy and the Common Man." From *The Theater Essays of Arthur Miller* by Arthur Miller, edited by Robert A. Martin. Copyright © 1949, renewed © 1977 by Arthur Miller. Used by permission of Viking Penguin, a division of Penguin Putnam, Inc.

Jessica Mitford. Excerpt from *The American Way of Death* by Jessica Mitford. Copyright © 1963, 1978 by Jessica Mitford. Reprinted by permission of Jessica Mitford. All rights reserved.

Felix Mnthali. "The Stranglehold of English Lit." From *Penguin Book of Modern African Poetry*, Third Edition. Copyright © Felix Mnthali. Reprinted by permission of Penguin Ltd. and the author.

Bharati Mukherjee. "Orbiting." From *The Middleman and Other Stories* by Bharati Mukherjee. Copyright © 1988 by Bharati Mukherjee. Reprinted by permission of Penguin Books Canada Limited.

Alice Munro. "How I Met My Husband." Originally published in *Something I've Been Meaning to Tell You* by Alice Munro. Copyright © 1974 by Alice Munro and published by McGraw Hill Ryerson. Reprinted by permission of the Virginia Barber Literary Agency. All rights reserved.

Susan Musgrave. "Right Through the Heart." From *Tarts and Muggers: Poems New and Selected* by Susan Musgrave. Copyright © 1982 by Susan Musgrave. Reprinted by permission of the author.

Taslima Nasrin. "Things Cheaply Had." Translated from the Bengali by Carolyne Wright with Mohammad Nurul Huda and the author. From *The New Yorker*, October 9, 1995. Copyright © 1995 by Carolyne Wright. Reprinted by permission of Carolyne Wright.

Pablo Neruda. "The Dead Woman." From *The Captain's Verses* by Pablo Neruda. Copyright © 1972 by Pablo Neruda and Donald D. Walsh. Reprinted by permission of New Directions Publishing Corp.

Joyce Carol Oates. "Where Are You Going, Where Have You Been." From *The Wheel of Love and Other Stories* by Joyce Carol Oates. Published by Ecco. Copyright © 1970 by Ontario Review Press, Inc. Reprinted by permission of John Hawkins & Associates, Inc.

Tim O'Brien. "The Things They Carried." From *The Things They Carried*. Copyright © 1990 by Tim O'Brien. Reprinted by permission of Houghton Mifflin Company/Seymour Lawrence. All rights reserved.

Flannery O'Connor. "Good Country People." From *A Good Man Is Hard to Find and Other Stories* by Flannery O'Connor. Copyright © 1955 by Flannery O'Connor and renewed © 1983 by Regina O'Connor. Reprinted by permission of Harcourt, Inc.

Frank O'Connor. "My Oedipus Complex." From *Collected Stories* by Frank O'Connor. Copyright © 1950 by Frank O'Connor. Reprinted by permission of Writers House, Inc., as agent for the proprietor.

Sharon Olds. "Sex without Love" and "The Victims." From *The Dead and the Living* by Sharon Olds. Copyright © 1983 by Sharon Olds. Reprinted by permission of Alfred A. Knopf, a division of Random House, Inc.

Mary Oliver. "When Death Comes." From *New and Selected Poems* by Mary Oliver. Copyright © 1992 by Mary Oliver. Reprinted by permission of Beacon Press, Boston.

George Orwell. "Shooting an Elephant." From *Shooting an Elephant and Other Stories* by George Orwell. Copyright © 1950 by Sonia Brownell Orwell and renewed 1978 by Sonia Pitts-Rivers. Reprinted by permission of Harcourt, Inc., and from *The Complete Orwell* (published in the UK, 1998, Seeker & Warburg). Copyright © 1936 George Orwell. Reprinted by permission of A.M. Heath & Company, Ltd. On behalf of Bill Hamilton as the Literary Executor of the Estate of the Late Sonia Brownell Orwell and Seeker & Warburg Ltd.

Alicia Ostriker. "Poem Beginning with a Line by Fitzgerald/Hemingway." From *The Little Space:*

Poems Selected and New 1968–1998 by Alicia Ostriker. © 1998. Reprinted by permission of the University of Pittsburgh Press.

Wilfred Owen. "Dulce et Decorum Est." From *The Collected Poems of Wilfred Owen* by Wilfred Owen. Copyright © 1963 by Chatto & Windos, Ltd. Reprinted by permission of New Directions Publishing Corp.

Dorothy Parker. "One Perfect Rose." From *Portable Dorothy Parker* by Dorothy Parker. Copyright © 1929; renewed © 1957 by Dorothy Parker. Introduction by Brendan Gill. Used by permission of Viking Penguin, a division of Penguin Putnam, Inc.

Molly Peacock. "Our Room." From *Raw Heaven* by Molly Peacock. Copyright © 1954 by Molly Peacock. "Say You Love Me" from *Take Heart* by Molly Peacock. Copyright © 1989 by Molly Peacock. Reprinted by permission of Random House, Inc.

Marge Piercy. "The market economy." From *Circles on the Water* by Marge Piercy. Copyright © 1982 by Marge Piercy. "The truth according to Ludd." From *Mars and Her Children* by Marge Piercy. Copyright © 1992 by Middlemarsh, Inc. Used by permission of Alfred A. Knopf, a division of Random House, Inc.

Robert Pinsky. "An Old Man." From *The Want Bone* by Robert Pinsky. Copyright © 1991 by Robert Pinsky. Reprinted by permission of HarperCollins Publishers, Inc.

Sylvia Plath. "Daddy." From *Ariel* by Sylvia Plath. Copyright © 1965 by Ted Hughes. Reprinted by permission of HarperCollins Publishers, Inc.

Deborah Pope. "Bad Child" and "The Last Lesson." From *Falling Out of the Sky* by Deborah Pope. Copyright © 1999 by Deborah Pope. "Getting Through." From *Mortal World* by Deborah Pope. Copyright © 1995 by Deborah Pope. Reprinted by permission of Louisiana State University Press.

Katherine Anne Porter. "The Jilting of Granny Weatherall." From *Flowering Judas and Other Stories*. Copyright © 1930 and renewed © 1958 by Katherine Anne Porter. Reprinted by permission of Harcourt, Inc.

Ezra Pound. "Portrait d'Une Femme." From *Personae* by Ezra Pound. Copyright © 1926 by Ezra Pound. Reprinted by permission of New Directions Publishing Corp.

Wyatt Prunty. "The Actuarial Wife" and "Learning the Bicycle." From *Unarmed and Dangerous: New and Selected Poems* by Wyatt Prunty. Copyright © 2000 The Johns Hopkins University Press. Reprinted by permission of the publisher.

Dudley Randall. "Ballad of Birmingham." Reprinted by permission of Broadside Press.

Henry Reed. "Naming of Parts." From *Henry Reed: Collected Poems* edited by Jon Stallworthy. 1991. Reprinted by permission of Oxford University Press.

Adrienne Rich. "Living in Sin." From *Collected Early Poems 1950–1970* by Adrienne Rich. Copyright © 1993, 1955 by Adrienne Rich. Reprinted by permission of the author and W.W. Norton & Company, Inc.

Randall Robinson. "Can a Black Family Be a Legal Nuisance?" Originally titled: "Winter 1967: Cambridge, Massachusetts." From *Defending the Spirit: A Black Life in America* by Randall Robinson. Copyright © 1998 by Randall Robinson. Used by permission of Dutton, a division of Penguin Putnam Inc.

Theodore Roethke. "Elgey for Jane." Copyright © 1950 by Theodore Roethke. "I Knew a Woman." Copyright © 1954 by Theodore Roethke. "My Papa's Waltz." Copyright © 1942 by Hearst Magazines, Inc. From *The Collected Poems of Theodore Roethke* by Theodore Roethke. Used by permission of Doubleday, a division of Random House, Inc.

Affonso Romano DeSant'Anna. "Letter to the Dead." From *The New Yorker*, October 9, 2000. Copyright © Affonso Romano DeSant'Anna. Reprinted by permission.

Muriel Rukeyser. "Myth." From *Breaking Open* by Muriel Rukeyser. Copyright by Muriel Rukeyser. Reprinted by permission of International Creative Management, Inc.

Sappho. "With His Venom." From *Sappho: A New Translation* by Mary Barnard. Copyright © 1958 by The Regents of the University of California. © renewed by Mary Barnard. Reprinted by permission of the publisher.

May Sarton. "Aids." From *Collected Poems 1930–1993* by May Sarton. Copyright © 1988 by May Sarton. Used by permission of W.W. Norton & Company, Inc.

Anne Sexton. "The Starry Night." From *All My Pretty Ones* by Anne Sexton. Copyright © 1962 by Anne Sexton. © renewed 1990 by Linda G. Sexton. "The Farmer's Wife" from *To Bedlam and Part Way Back*. Copyright © 1960 by Anne Sexton. © renewed 1988 by Linda G. Sexton. "Cinderella." From *Transformations*. Copyright © 1971 by Anne Sexton. Reprinted by permission of Houghton Mifflin Company. All rights reserved.

Irwin Shaw. "The Girls in Their Summer Dresses." Reprinted by permission of the Irwin Shaw Literary Estate.

Leslie Marmon Silko. "The Man to Send Rain Clouds" From *Storyteller* by Leslie Marmon Silko. Copyright © 1981 by Leslie Marmon Silko. Reprinted by permission of Arcade Publishing, Inc.

Paul Simon. "Scarborough Fair (Canticle)" lyrics. Copyright © 1966 Paul Simon. Used by permission of the Publisher, Paul Simon Music.

Stevie Smith. "Not Waving but Drowning" and "To Carry the Child." From *Collected Poems of Stevie Smith* by Stevie Smith. Copyright © 1972 by Stevie Smith. Reprinted by permission of New Directions Publishing Corp.

Sophocles. *Antigonê.* From *Sophocles, the Oedipus Cycle. An English Version* by Dudley Fitts and Robert Fitzgerald. Copyright © 1939 by Harcourt, Inc., and renewed © 1967 by Dudley Fitts and Robert Fitzgerald. Reprinted by permission of the publisher. *Oedipus Rex.* From *Sophocles, the Oedipus Cycle: An English Version* by Dudley Fitts and Robert Fitzgerald. Copyright © 1949 by Harcourt, Inc., and renewed © 1977 by Cornelia Fitts and Robert Fitzgerald. Reprinted by permission of Harcourt, Inc.

Helen Sorrells. "From a Correct Address in a Suburb of a Major City." From *Seeds as They Fall*. Copyright © 1971 by Helen Sorrells. Reprinted by permission.

Gary Soto. "Oranges." From *New and Selected Poems* by Gary Soto. Copyright © 1995 by Gary Soto. Reprinted by permission of Chronicle Books, San Francisco, and the author.

Wole Soyinka. "The Telephone Conversation." Copyright © 1960 by Wole Soyinka. Reprinted by permission.

David St. John. "My Friend." From *Study for the World's Body: Selected Poems* by David St. John. Copyright © 1994 by David St. John. Reprinted by permission of HarperCollins Publishers, Inc.

Wallace Stevens. "Sunday Morning." From *Collected Poems* by Wallace Stevens. Copyright © 1923 and renewed 1951 by Wallace Stevens. Reprinted by permission of Alfred A. Knopf, a division of Random House, Inc.

Amy Tan. "Two Kinds." From *The Joy Luck Club* by Amy Tan. Copyright © 1989 by Amy Tan. Reprinted by permission of Penguin Putnam Inc.

Dylan Thomas. "Do Not Go Gentle into That Good Night" and "Fern Hill." From *Collected Poems of Dylan Thomas* by Dylan Thomas. © 1952 by Dylan Thomas. Reprinted with permission of New Directions Publishing Corp. and David Higham Associates.

James Thurber. "The Little Girl and the Wolf," "The Owl Who Was God," "The Unicorn in the Garden," and "The Very Proper Gander." From *Fables for Our Time* by James Thurber. Copyright © 1940 by James Thurber. Copyright © renewed 1968 by Helen Thurber and Rosemary A. Thurber. "The Greatest Man in the World." From *The Middle-Aged Man on the Flying Trapeze* by James Thurber. Copyright © 1935 by James Thurber. Copyright © renewed 1963 by Helen Thurber and Rosemary A. Thurber. Reprinted by arrangement with Rosemary A. Thurber and the Barbara Hogenson Agency. All rights reserved.

Leo Tolstoy. "The Death of Iván Ilých." From *The Death of Ivan Ilych and Other Stories* by Leo Tolstoy. Translated by Louise and Aylmer Maude. Copyright © 1925. Used by permission of Oxford University Press, Inc.

Jill Tweedie. "The Experience." Copyright © 1979 by Jill Tweedie. Reprinted by permission of Curtis Brown, Ltd (UK).

Melvin Urofsky. "Two Scenes from a Hospital." Reprinted by permission of the author.

Alice Walker. "Everyday Use." From *In Love and Trouble: Stories of Black Women* by Alice Walker. Copyright © 1973 by Alice Walker. Reprinted by permission of Harcourt, Inc.

Richard Wilbur. "Museum Piece." From *Ceremony and Other Poems*. Copyright © 1950 and renewed 1978 by Richard Wilbur. Reprinted by permission of Harcourt, Inc.

Oscar Williams. "A Total Revolution" from *A Little Treasury of Modern Poetry* (the Little Treasury Series) edited by Oscar Williams. Copyright © 1950 by Oscar Williams. Reprinted with permission of Scribner, a division of Simon & Schuster, Inc.

Tennessee Williams. *The Glass Menagerie.* Copyright © 1945 by Tennessee Williams and Edwina D. Williams. Renewed 1973 by Tennessee Williams. Reprinted by permission of Random House, Inc.

August Wilson. *Fences* by August Wilson. Copyright © 1986 by August Wilson. Used by permission of Dutton Signet, a division of Penguin Putnam, Inc.

Virginia Woolf. "Shakespeare's Sister." From *A Room of One's Own* by Virginia Woolf. Copyright © 1929 by Harcourt, Inc., and renewed © 1957 by Leonard Woolf. Reprinted by permission of the publisher.

Richard Wright. "The Man Who Was Almost a Man." From *Eight Men* by Richard Wright. Copyright © 1940, 1961 by Richard Wright. Copyright renewed 1989 by Ellen Wright. Reprinted by permission of HarperCollins Publishers, Inc.

William Butler Yeats. "Leda and the Swan" and "Sailing to Byzantium." Copyright © 1928 by

Art Credits

Index of Authors and Titles